Governments of Greater European Powers

A man who hath not much meditated upon God, the human mind and the *summum bonum,* may possibly make a thriving earthworm, but will most indubitably make a sorry patriot and a sorry statesman.
—*Bishop Berkeley*

Governments of

Greater European Powers

A Comparative Study of the Governments
and Political Culture of *Great Britain,
France, Germany,* and the *Soviet Union*

HERMAN FINER

University of Chicago

HENRY HOLT AND COMPANY · New York

22826-0216

Printed in the United States of America

To CHERRY
the Vessel of my Hopes
Borne Forward on the Sails
of her own Fulfilment

Preface

This is an entirely new study of the government and political behavior of Britain, France, Germany, and the U.S.S.R. I touch on American practices and principles by way of clarifying comparison.

Now that the political leadership of a power-loaded but distracted world has settled on the shoulders of the United States, the contents of this book have become an indispensable part of our intellectual equipment. This world is only one world physically, through geographic shrinkage consequent on speed, but morally and politically it is sharply divided, with hostile coalitions of Powers, great and small, arrayed against each other and heavy with armaments.

Never was it so vital to understand our allies and our rivals. The Balance of Power is not merely a series of abstract circles and oblongs in white chalk on a flat blackboard. Two of the Powers listed above were allies of the United States in World War II, another was a bitter and cruel enemy, the fourth was a friend of convenience. One has remained staunch and may never change; another was weak and is weak; the enemy has been transformed into a friend; the friend has become the most malevolent and unsatiated foe. The first three are in the community of Western nations called NATO. What are these tough corporate personalities, these nations, that jostle each other for security, wealth, prestige, and the preservation and expansion of their way of life? Each, said Thomas Hobbes, is an "artificiall Man." How constant is he? How strong? Does he use his tongue and mind or his gun first, last, or never? Are his conscience and his family in order? Is he reliable as an ally, cunning and ruthless as an antagonist? To avoid errors in the deployment of force and persuasion, to learn the way of intelligent persuasion, to become abler to assess the amount and manner of technical and economic assistance, we are under duress to know the facts of political life of other nations.

Yet this is a realm of dire confusion, making success in "competitive co-existence"—tricky phrase of cold warfare—an uncertain venture. Our habits are so different from those of other lands, so far away. Even our journalists too often misguide us, lacking solidity in their acquaintance with the facts here and now and the data of history and culture. Ignorance can only burden our budgets, play havoc with our military service, spoil economic opportunity, betray the fortunes of democracy everywhere—and it is on desperate trial—and, it may well be, cost us our lives, wiped out by rockets and hydrogen bombs. The nations now live in each other's front gardens: it is urgent to open all doors and see what kind of people live inside the houses in the light thrown by their own kind of lamps on the dusky shapes.

For many years my professional colleagues have urged me to write a work of this kind, pleading that the available books have already made such handsome acknowledgment of my own various researches that it was a pity I did not do the job myself. In particular, they were very anxious to have a book that would, in a sense, lead on later to my *Theory and Practice of Modern Government*. My appreciation of their trust in me is answered here.

I have tried to express the material of this new work in a form suitable for the general reader and students in the political and social sciences who come to the subject for the first time. I have attempted, therefore, simplicity without surrendering the richness and diversity of puzzling reality, vividness without sacrifice of precision, theory as an identification of problems than as an indulgence, and that kind of organization which educatively conveys political and governmental complexities without textbook petrifaction.

Political science teachers posed certain questions, and I offer my answers to them gladly, since they themselves have helped to solve them by many discussions on teaching at the meetings of the American Political Science Association.

1. Should a work of so broad a scope and such detail be written by one person or should it be by a symposium? They argued cogently that the nature of the symposium itself makes it well-nigh impossible to produce a *comparative* study, if, indeed, that is sincerely desired. If political science by the comparative method is believed to be essential to explanation and understanding, then the parts, surely, ought to be evaluated by the same broad criteria. The symposium, even at its very best in authors and editors, is but juxta-position by mail among members of a loose and fugitive committee, not the consistent comparison of co-relevant political problems and the diverse nations' answers to them. The offsetting de-murrer that a multitude of authors encourages a look at "the same subject" from different points of view is just too facile. True comparison needs a framework of significance steadily applied to a scholar's possessed body of facts.

2. Can we avoid the cut-and-dried presenta-tion, the static impression, that matters political as they are in the snapshot of today were always such and always will be? Can one avoid putting a thick pin through the body of the butterfly and killing it down to the extinction of the last quiver? For politics, for government, the most living, quivering thing of all? The work should give a sense of the dynamic, that what is seen today was not quite there in that form or activity yes-terday, and is on the point of changing here and there, tomorrow and progressively afterward. This is a process, not a museum. But this treatment costs pages, for the crepitating factors must be exhibited, and to "What is" must be added "What is going on?". This treatment has a practical educational advantage, as truth to Nature always has, for it inculcates in the student (*a*) the im-portance of the active will, the mind, the con-science, and the personality and (*b*) the necessity of continual political invention.

3. Should a comparative government text be organized by countries or by institutions, analyti-cally, as in my *Theory and Practice of Modern Government?* I have done both. I am more than ever convinced that the latter is scientifically bet-ter. But, as teachers have recognized, the nation-by-nation method has some important pedagogic advantages for the undergraduate.

They are these: (*a*) Political institutions cling together in a national configuration, a national whole or coherence. That integrated interde-pendence must be demonstrated. (*b*) These na-tional systems have been developed in their form and manner of operation over many centuries of cultural evolution unique in time, place, personali-ties, and accident, this culture including all the many elements and nuances of their geography, history, anthropology, etc. The nation-by-nation method better enables these forces to be exposed and is helpful to prediction, because of their articulated effect. They are especially necessary in a land in which Man seems hardly to have been created, current attitudes often suggest, be-fore 1776. However, the present work does not dump the national culture in the first chapter and leave it there like junk. The facts are adverted to and used again and again as causative and ex-planatory factors when the institutions are exam-ined one by one. Moreover, cross-references are supplied throughout the entire work to link, com-pare, and contrast the vicissitudes of the nations in philosophy and behavior, and to show the dif-ferential influence of these in their governments. (*c*) It may be easier for the beginner to grasp the nation as an operative social unit, especially a foreign nation, than to plunge into the analysis of institutions each with a multinational com-parison.

4. How simple must the language be? Baby language? I have written as simply as possible, with abundant illustrations and cases, to exhibit the active operation of the political laws and cus-toms. I believe—and the vast majority of my colleagues agree with me—that sophomores ought to be encouraged to master their native living language and not fly from it to the comics. They will do so whenever their teachers encourage their pride rather than pander to their self-pity. We certainly owe them lucidity and system. My ambition has been to write so that, when stu-dents are at home or in the dormitories or libraries, studying privately, they will have the material that will explain simply and clearly the

problem before them as though they had the assistance of their own experienced teacher present with them.

I have offered illustrations, examples, charts, statistics, and cases to avoid mere abstraction or desiccated legality or clichés taken from constitutions, to help the reader to active-minded study. This has added to the spaciousness of this volume (though already reduced from its original of twice the size for his benefit!). I have always and everywhere found that readers will happily assimilate two pages rather than one, provided the data are presented interestingly and abundantly enough for them to make their own generalizations and use their own judgment, instead of being forced by dry pabulum to commit an outline to memory, without rhyme or reason, subject to complete forgetfulness, even of the author's name (I vouch for this!) the moment the grades have been handed in.

5. Footnotes? I deliberately decided to omit them, or else I should have cited authority for virtually every sentence. Those who know my hitherto published works will know that the present volume, like them and even more so (for the years accumulate), is based on: (*a*) the official documents, laws, debates, etc. (for Russia assisted by my native postgraduate students); (*b*) the classic works; (*c*) contemporary secondary works; (*d*) contemporary special studies; (*e*) firsthand experience and interviews with participants at various levels of government; (*f*) the periodicals.

6. What kind of bibliography will serve? I have not produced an all-inclusive one. I have confined mine to the basic works in which the student may find, in many cases, further bibliographies of a much more comprehensive kind. There is such a thing as the snobbery or "lifemanship" of bibliographies.

7. Should the international position of each nation be allotted a separate chapter? I preferred to put this aspect of government partly in the first chapter where the cultural-evolutionary factors are discussed, and then to share out various aspects among the political parties, each of which takes a different view of the role and methods of its nation in the world.

8. How is such a work to organize its material? Surely, to show the answers given to the most significant problems of political science in general. This is accomplished by the comparative method. The Index will facilitate identification of the problems and the well-known institutions and concepts, such as, for example, dictatorship, civic-mindedness, leadership, centralization, the various philosophies, the "representative" thinkers, and so forth.

9. What parts, if any, might be omitted by the teacher to fit the artificial, inexorable (?) periods of the academic year? The teacher, in his place and time, is the best judge. But, as is now frequent in courses on American Government, the administrative and local government chapters might be deferred. It is my obligation to teachers, students, and science to envisage and describe the body politic as a whole. If it is decided to defer the first, or cultural chapter, the loss will be a very grave one to students.

Political science without history has no roots;
History without political science has no fruits.

In fact, is political science anything but roots, growing roots?

All valuable knowledge issues from comparisons. In political science, comparison exhibits the institutions of each country as an articulated, interdependent system, peculiar to that special environment. This is of especial importance to students of international government.

We are not dealing with equal phantoms but with exceedingly tough, historic, narcissistic personalities, the nature of whose individual virility in the politics of nations we had better learn.

Comparison and contrast force back the reader's mind into asking why the similarities or differences exist. Back—into what? The factors of history, of geography, of economic processes, strength and producers' relationships; the development of the "public mind" or civic-mindedness; different religions; the family; social standards of honor and the good life; the class structure; the international location; the ethics, and even the metaphysics of private and public life.

Such interrogations offer us the criteria and hypotheses by which to appraise the significance of generalizations, such as the Separation of Powers, the conditions of Governmental Responsibility, the nature of Career Administrators, Leadership qualities, and so on.

It is urgent that the cultural development, historically considered, be thoroughly mastered and regarded as only the first step to a deeper and wider study of this aspect of government. Now, this seems to give an air of inevitability, of predetermination, to the working of the political institutions. But the student should reflect that some of the historical factors, for example, the character of creative men and women, the leaders and masses and the social groups, have suffered change and will change still. Even the environment changes; for example, the impact on all nations of the new proximity of the U.S.S.R., with absolute weapons carried over space shrunken by speeds faster by far than sound.

I have faith in, and I appeal directly to, the ability and diligence of the American student to read and think, when the material he needs is put before him methodically and limpidly, and when he himself is not written down as a mindless teen-ager. Ask of the student, and he will give! He is of the national ancestry of Abraham Lincoln. The future of his great Republic, "the last, best hope," is secreted in his brains, conscience, and will. No other students in the whole world possess his facilities, funds and libraries. Nothing to do each twenty-four hours but to study! I believe he does not want to be talked down to; that he wants sense talked to him. The U.S.S.R. is gradually but zealously catching up with the U.S.A. in economic productivity, science, technology, and general education, and it draws level in pulverizing weapons.

Survival depends on knowledge, hard thinking, and hard work: this is the Toynbean "challenge." Many peoples have perished under pagan assault, because they grew fat in mind and body. The world asks a response in the heroic exertions and magnanimous examples of Americans, for many hundreds of millions cry out for bread, respect, and liberty. In such a context, it is wrong to treat American undergraduates as babies. They are men and women who need to study public affairs in the language of adults. For when we were children, internationally speaking, we looked through a glass darkly and did childish things, but now "we see face to face."

ACKNOWLEDGMENTS

I warmly thank the officials of the Libraries at the University of Chicago for their patience with me, especially the Harper Reference unit with Miss Ver Nooy, Mr. Breed and Mr. Narkis, the Circulation Desk and Mrs. Foster, and the Periodical Room and Mrs. Pietsch. They helped me to much provender, ample and excellent; I hope they will not be disappointed by the use I have here made of it.

H. F.

Chicago, Illinois
February 1, 1956

Contents

The Government of Great Britain

The Government of France

The Government of Germany

The Government of the U.S.S.R.

The Government of
Great Britain

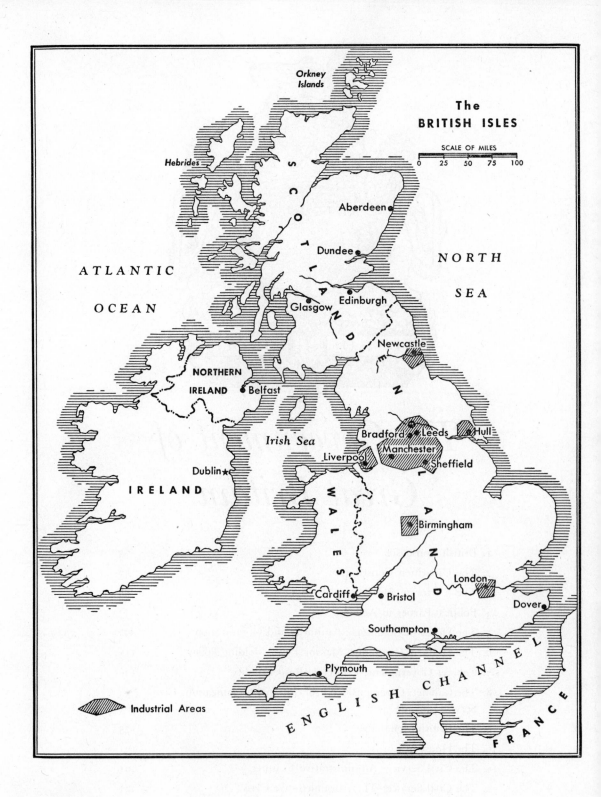

The
BRITISH ISLES

SCALE OF MILES

0   25   50   75   100

Orkney
Islands

Hebrides

SCOTLAND

Aberdeen

Dundee

NORTH

SEA

ATLANTIC

OCEAN

Glasgow   Edinburgh

Newcastle

NORTHERN
IRELAND   Belfast

Irish Sea

Bradford   Leeds   Hull

Liverpool   Manchester

Dublin ★   Sheffield

IRELAND

WALES

Birmingham

London

Cardiff   Bristol   Dover

Southampton

Plymouth

ENGLISH CHANNEL

FRANCE

///// Industrial Areas

British Consensus

Would twenty shillings have ruined Mr Hampden's fortune? No! but the payment of half twenty shillings, on the principle it was demanded, would have
made him a slave.

Magnanimity in politics is not seldom the truest wisdom; and a great empire
and little minds go ill together.

—Edmund Burke

In the modern world, political liberty and equality and social welfare, as the foundations of the
State, were invented in England and France and
developed in the United States. Neither Germany
nor Russia made any considerable contribution to
these gifts until the Soviet Union began to profess
a policy of social justice and Bismarck's Imperial
Germany established social insurance.

Combinations of these and their alternatives are
the diverse solutions offered to mankind's eternal
quest: through **government,** so to order the life of
great aggregations of human beings as to avoid
either of the two fatal extremes, Murder or Suicide—the former, man's rage for maximum satisfactions now, the latter, man's despair through
denial of his dearest minimum desires.

It has been no easy process, but wrought in labor, inventiveness, struggle, bloodshed. The different given environments of Nature have had much
to do with the results so far variously reached;
and, as the toilful centuries accumulated, to Nature was added the man-made Social Heritage,
"the cake of custom." Each nation is a unique answer. The British response may be expressed summarily as follows; and it has been much admired
and is widely copied.

Britain is a *unitary,* not a federal, State, consisting of the United Kingdom of England, Scotland,
Wales, and Northern Ireland. This is the heartland of the system of government that extends to
many Dominions and Colonies; it is the Motherland with which the latter are linked in various
degrees of association and dependency.

Its *constitution,* of great antiquity and never-
ending evolution, is unwritten. In it the powers
of government, especially Executive and Legislative, are not separated and Parliament is legally
and politically sovereign and master of the Executive—that is, Cabinet and Crown.

It is a soundly rooted, sincere, and sober democracy, with a high degree of liberty and equality, embodied in the *sovereignty of Parliament*
and founded on elections in which free political
parties responsibly guide the electorate in alternatives of policy (their firm commitments) and the
choice of representatives. This electorate is based
on universal franchise.

Her Majesty's Opposition is the fundamental
convention of the unwritten constitution and is
supported by parliamentary rules (the law and
custom of Parliament) and on the *mores* of democratic reciprocity. A House of Lords, the upper
(hereditary) House, forms with the House of
Commons, the popular assembly, a bicameral system; but the former has small power.

The Cabinet, an inner nucleus of Ministers

around the Prime Minister, has firm leadership of the Executive and Parliament, being itself composed of members of the latter and almost entirely from the House of Commons. In a broad sense it is a committee of the House of Commons, but a committee composed of the majority-party leaders. For continuance in office it is strictly dependent on the retention of the confidence of the House of Commons.

The Crown is titular, the dignified symbol of majesty, of sovereignty, and the unity of the national society, and has long since lost any personal political power.

The Civil Service is composed of career officials. They are appointed by Ministers but only via an open competitive examination conducted by the Civil Service Commission. They are obliged to render service to Ministers of whatever political party wins power, with constructive impartiality and personal anonymity. Local government is substantially decentralized, with popular self-government.

The Judiciary, appointed by the government (there are no elected judges), is provided with practical guarantees of independence of the government and of private interests, and stoutly exhibits this. It cannot, of course, invalidate laws or orders for constitutional invalidity because Parliament is sovereign. *Habeas Corpus* is *the* fundamental civil right (p. 261). It is an order made by the judges, based on statutes that *compel* them to act under penalty (the only threat to a judge in the whole system) by *immediately* ordering the release of any detained person so that he may appear in court at once and claim his liberty. This is the essential guarantee of free opposition to a Government—that is, of the minority to the majority. It is the basic protection of Her Majesty's Opposition. With the parliamentary immunity of members from arrest, it confirms the fundamental British constitutional convention of minority rights embodied in the "loyal" Opposition. Though there is no formal separation of powers, the judiciary is regarded as an independent authority to secure liberty and justice.

This is embodied in the classic *Rule of Law,* formulated by Dicey on the basis of observed British practice. It means that (1) regular law (as made by Parliament) has absolute supremacy against arbitrary power and wide discretionary power on the part of government; (2) equality before the law, and the equal subjection of all classes to the ordinary law of the land administered by the ordinary law courts; (3) the constitution is the consequence, not the source, of the rights of individuals, as defined and enforced by the courts. Officials are subject to the ordinary courts and the same procedure as ordinary citizens.

Finally, the government of Britain is *highly active and beneficent*. It is based on private property and private enterprise, but it regulates industry, commerce, and agriculture; it assists them to raise their standards of production; it supplies very substantial social services and social security; and it manages and owns, either centrally or locally, the coal, gas, electricity, railroad, communications industries and the civil air services, health services, and the Bank of England. It is at once a liberal democracy and a social welfare State.

Sociological Factors

The operation of a nation's government in spirit and institutions is conditioned by its sociological factors. The word *sociology* is used as a compendious word for geographical environment and habitat, economic activity and its modes, religious spirit, culture, the influence of greater men on lesser men in the interpersonal influences manifested at critical stages in meeting the challenge of historic social problems, art, and culture. The outstanding factors, touched on here regarding Britain, are these:

   I. It is an island:
      Its area is small;
      It enjoys dense and swift internal communications;
      It has an insular outlook.
  II. Its population is homogeneous and energetic and "cool."
 III. There are economic inequalities and diversities:
      There are educational inequalities;
      Its educational system is one of quality;

Its wealth is high but depends on acquired human skills.

IV. It has enjoyed long, unbroken parliamentary authority.

V. It has benefited from the notions of "the gentleman," trusteeship, primogeniture, and relatively loose family.

VI. Authority has gradually spread from aristocracy and *noblesse oblige* to mass democracy.

VII. Its characteristic political thinkers have been Liberal Utilitarians, not deep metaphysicians.

The observations that follow are an introduction to the same determining features in the other countries also treated of in this book.

I. A SMALL ISLAND: SIZE AND INSULARITY

Britain is an island, or, if it is necessary to be more precise, it is an island and the northern part of another, Ireland, some thirty miles distant at the nearest point. It is also very small in comparison with some other States. Less than 100,000 square miles in area (of which only some 50,000 are English), it is only about two fifths the size of France, one half the size of pre-World War II Germany, less than one thirtieth the size of the United States, and only about one thirtieth the size of the U.S.S.R. west of the Urals.[1]

Some deductive consequences may be drawn—best supported by historic events. First are those that follow from Britain's territorial smallness, especially England itself, as distinct from Wales, Scotland, and Ireland, since for centuries British life evolved there earliest.

Proximity of Government and People

Good government—that is, appropriate action as a solution of imposed problems—is assisted by the proximity of government to the complexities of the people and the subtleties of the natural facts that exact attention. The frontiers of Britain were never impossibly or insupportably distant for the

energy and speed available at the center—in London or (earlier) Winchester. The movement of men and material, by horse or rowing and sailing boats or human portage, was not defeated by distance—250 miles to the Scottish border, about the same to Land's End, much less right through Wales to the Irish Sea. Even at the farthest extremes and nearest to a foreign enemy, France, it is fifty miles from London to Dover. As communications improved, first with the building of roads (the model provided by the Roman occupiers) and then the first concern of the Kings, the King's Highway and the King's Peace became a basic instrument of government.

The area is more compassable than the size and kind of territory of other governments. But this takes us back to the human will to govern. Nothing but the demands of the human will require that the area of government shall be large. Yet, where no natural frontiers appear to stop potential enemies, it is a temptation for rulers and their people to march on and on until they do, indeed, reach a defensible condition. The defensible condition was given to England in either of two stages: either to stop at the mountain ranges of Wales and Scotland, or to go to the sea in all directions. The second finally occurred, including the whole of Ireland, to the Atlantic Ocean.

In the developing centuries the result was, and is today, a compassable, surveyable, and reachable unit. It takes only minutes to reach every British periphery by telephone, and almost instantaneously by radio and television; less than twelve hours by plane, train, or motor transport. It is possible in little time to obtain from the provinces a vivid picture of the situation on the spot, either by inquirers from London or by the deputations from the localities to London, whether it be Westminster, the seat of Parliament, or Whitehall, the offices of the Prime Minister, his Ministers, and the public services.

Communications must be speedy, vivid, and easily repetitive if a cumulative impact is to make an impression on the laws and if administrative regulations are to take effect. The central government's inspectors of the local authorities (see pp. 258–259), are the ears, eyes, arms, and the voice of the central authority.

---

[1] The other 5,000,000 square miles to the east may be disregarded in this context as not having been the subject of intense Russian governmental concern during the formative centuries.

A Comparison of Areas to Be Governed: Great Britain, France, Germany, the Soviet Union, and the United States

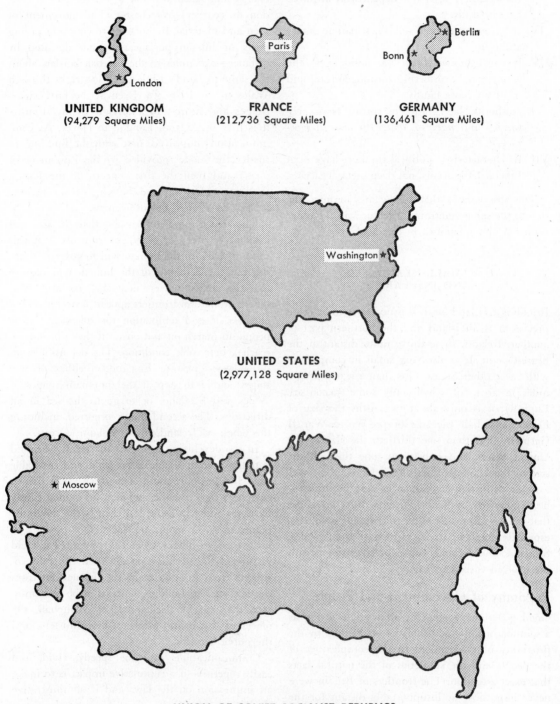

UNITED KINGDOM
(94,279 Square Miles)

FRANCE
(212,736 Square Miles)

GERMANY
(136,461 Square Miles)

UNITED STATES
(2,977,128 Square Miles)

UNION OF SOVIET SOCIALIST REPUBLICS
(8,570,600 Square Miles)

Dense Population

Some other factors must be added. Except for the outlying parts of Scotland (the Highlands and the islands) and large areas of Wales, the nation is densely populated. Comparatively speaking, it is practically a single urban society, one big city interspersed with only occasional grasslands and crop-bearing open land. Only a little over 1,000,000 of the population is occupied in agriculture—with families, say, 3,000,000 people—and 50,000,000 largely live in towns. These fall into the following groups:

Distribution of Urban Population, England and Wales, 1951

Population of Urban Areas		Number of Areas	Aggregate Population
Over 1,000,000		2*	4,460,676
500,000 and under 1,000,000		4	2,510,495
250,000 " " 500,000		8	2,449,841
150,000 " " 250,000		17	3,209,591
100,000 " " 150,000		35	4,181,858
75,000 " " 100,000		25	2,121,043
50,000 " " 75,000		65	4,041,234
40,000 " " 50,000		52	2,316,094
30,000 " " 40,000		69	2,373,463
20,000 " " 30,000		108	2,639,946
15,000 " " 20,000		95	1,670,100
10,000 " " 15,000		118	1,437,448
5,000 " " 10,000		185	1,329,771
4,000 " " 5,000		55	245,941
3,000 " " 4,000		49	170,956
2,000 " " 3,000		48	119,768
Under 2,000		30	43,869
Total		965	35,322,104

* London Administrative County is here reckoned as one area.

This leaves another 8,000,000 in localities classed as *rural,* defined as "under 1000 population."

This densely and cosily populated area allows of the swiftest dissemination of the facts of public life and their discussion and the formation of reacting and rebounding opinion. The physical situation allows of many local newspapers of substantial news service, of easily reached meeting places, of collective activity. The nation and its urban components are not places in which it is easy to hide—for example, by "lobbying"—anything that is of public importance. William the Conqueror was able to conduct a highly exact survey of all landholdings in England, recorded in the Domesday Book in the year 1086, 400 years before America was discovered!

In the twelfth century itinerant justices of the King's Council (who were also lawmakers and controllers of the execution of the law in the localities) began to circulate through England, commissioned to hear and determine cases—*oyer et terminer*—and instituted (confirmed by the Magna Carta) the Assizes, courts held in the counties. In the thirteenth century the magnates of the feudal regime who sat in the King's Council were joined by men summoned by the Crown from the shires and the boroughs throughout the country to a Parliament in London and sometimes in sessions held in the provinces. The communications ganglia were never cut, as, for example, in vast Russia (p. 734).

Direct Government

The rulers of a country may be resolved to govern or decide to abandon the attempt, and either of these choices admits of degree. If they decide to govern heavily, as the French Kings did (see p. 273ff.), as the Prussian Kings did (p. 540), as the dynasties of Kiev and Moscow in Russia did (p. 731ff.), they may attempt government either by devolving their authority in a kind of trust to great lords and captains or by acting by their own direct officialdom.

The English Kings proceeded first by feudal delegation of power to magnates or lords. No lord was so far away from their central might that they were unable to call him to account or unable to make visitation of his own manor. Nor in England was it territorially necessary, as it was in France, to permit the lords to stand between the King and the lords' own feudal tenants in their localities in the matter of police or the King's Peace.

The lords were unable to become separatists with their retainers loyal to themselves but disloyal to their King. All land, went the theory, belongs to the Crown: all holders of it owe him loyalty. All loyalty to fight is to fight in a *national* army, not for a local lord's own purpose. Furthermore, *all* take an oath of fealty to the Crown, not merely the lords. But in extensive lands, such as Russia and France, the devolution of authority turned out to be divisive, and William the Conqueror, who first demanded the oath, knew from his own Norman defiance of Paris what local rebellion could mean. To prevent divisiveness the would-be autocrats were obliged to send out governors or vice regents and officials. This either centralized the government rigidly, bureaucratized it, made it intimidatory and harsh, or, given the lack of skill and interest, useless.

British government was able to use feudal arrangements until their place was taken by civil local government through (1) the justices of the peace in the fourteenth century, who were local well-to-do men—gentry—not merely the high aristocracy, assisted by (2) parish-elected unpaid officers. This established a habit and tradition of local self-government that has lasted until the present day (Chapter 13).

It is, again, possible to abandon the attempt to govern firmly. It can be done in the form of federalism as it is established in the United States and Germany, among other countries. This alternative was not, and needed not to be, adopted in the British experience. Britain is a *unitary* state. But concessions of government had to be made by British government to the American colonies, then to the various self-governing Dominions, and also partially to the other colonies. Southern Ireland even became the Irish Free State in 1921, after 800 years of London's unsuccessful attempts to govern it often by force. Moreover, Scotland and Wales have been allowed substantial degree of local self-administration to satisfy firm nationalist feelings there.[2]

Area and Population

There are two aspects of size in government. One is the sheer range of territory, the other the magnitude of the population. So far our attention has been focused on the territorial order.

Attention should be concentrated on the effect of size of territory on British political parties. The more extensive the territory (and the diversity of interests within it, especially if these happen to coincide with a clear-cut area, such as the cotton land in the south of the U.S.A. or coal mining in South Wales or white-collar work in the home counties around London), the more difficult for the political parties to articulate it within a single polity. The spread-eagle nature of American political parties is one direct offspring of the enormous range of territory they cover and the coagulations of interests, regional and otherwise, therein. Even the Communist Party of the U.S.S.R. is baffled by Russia's great size, especially in the rural areas (see p. 867). British political parties are well knit because they have a small area to manage, and they knit together subareas, all of which have considerable diversification and mixture of interests. This, however, is to say that government is well integrated for the identical reason: political parties make the government.

The urbanization of Britain, the size of its population, the density of its 700 persons to the square mile (omitting the Scottish north), affects government simultaneously in two ways: The crowding together of people, even apart from the rivalry or complementary nature of their industrial occupations, forces problems on government. Since Englishmen are not identical in character or values, they come into conflict with each other and appeal to and create government to help their will prevail. But this is especially so where interests are diversified in an industrial and commercial civilization. An acute need for government arises. Yet, the crowding together of large numbers in a relatively small space makes easier the tasks of government for reasons already suggested, namely, the proximity of rulers and the people.

David Hume (p. 32) says that the moral virtues (including respect for government and justice) arise from the *sympathy* which people experience as they physically observe the pleasure or pain of others—for example, a smile or a grimace—reflecting their feelings of virtue and vice; hence such moral virtues will develop earliest and be more secure in a small than a large society. It depends on proximity, where the contacts are more frequent and more durable.

With many functions and a large area of government, the French State of pre-Revolutionary days died, very largely, of apoplexy at the center,

[2] Cf. *Report of Royal Commission on Scottish Nationalism,* London, 1954 for degree of self-administration.

and, as de Tocqueville added, of anemia at the extremities (see p. 280). The British system was less rigid, more flexible, and therefore lived without any violent explosion and was spared the dreadful aftereffects of civil war.

Two things must be added to this account of the possibilities latent in the factor of size. For about seven hundred years a central authority in the form of a Parliament has almost uninterruptedly debated the highest public policies. From the beginning the localities knew something of the issues before their representatives went to London, and they learned the story (as Cardinal Wolsey *complained!*) when these men returned. The country was small enough for this to be no merely formal representation—the House of Commons, that is, the House of the *communities*.

London was relatively so large in urban communities as to be an inescapable magnet; it contained the political capital, the splendid palaces, the "cloud-capped towers," it was the art and cultural center, with soon about one fifth the whole population!

The Press

Since the seventeenth century, the press [3] has been increasingly the medium of communication between the governors and the governed, a two-way process.

The first great blast of the trumpets against a fettered press was John Milton's, who wrote *Paradise Lost* and was state secretary to Oliver Cromwell. In his *Areopagitica . . . for the Liberty of Unlicensed Printing* in November 1644, he challenged not a King but Parliament itself (Star Chamber censorship had been abolished in 1641) for its ordinance requiring printed matter to be previously licensed. He gave censorship its spiritual death blow.

> Though all the winds of doctrine were let loose to play upon the earth, so Truth be in the field, we do injuriously by licensing and prohibiting to misdoubt her strength. Let her and falsehood grapple; who ever knew Truth put to the worse, in a free and open encounter?

Failure to renew the Licensing Act in 1695 left publication free of government license. The only restraints henceforth were in the law of libel, blasphemy, sedition, and obscenity. In Russia at this date hardly any printed material *at all* was even available!

A great popular press developed with the development of the mass electorate. In the eighteenth century taxes were levied on newspapers; in 1861 these "taxes on knowledge" were repealed. Today there are about 112 general daily newspapers and eighteen special dailies in London and the provinces. Their total circulation is nearly 30,000,000. In addition there are eleven Sunday newspapers whose circulation is also about 30,000,000. Besides this mass service of the people in the mornings, evenings, and weekends, there are numerous weekly periodicals, of which some thirty are of political orientation. Among the latter are six known throughout the world: *The Economist, New Statesman and Nation, The Spectator, Time and Tide, Tribune,* and *Truth.* They exhibit knowledge, probity, sober and responsible analytical thought on the problems of highest policy. The country is so small that politicians cannot say different things in different parts of it.

They and the rest of the newspapers are private property, even where, as in the case of *The Times* and the *Manchester Guardian,* they are organized as a trust that acts as a buffer between owners and editors. They rely substantially on advertising revenue to offset the immense cost of production and capital charges. They are private property exercising a public effect. Yet the Royal Commission on the Press (*Report*, June 1949, Cmd. 7700, His Majesty's Stationery Office) that was set up precisely to find fault with its public service gave it not only an almost flawless bill, but a distinctly affirmative answer to its own criteria. These were

> Democratic society, therefore, needs a clear and truthful account of events, of their background and their causes; a forum for discussion and informed criticism; and a means whereby individuals and groups can express a point of view or advocate a cause.

[3] The first English newspaper commenced publication in May 1622, London. It was a weekly called *The Weekly Newes from Italy, Germany, etc.* This had been preceded from the middle of the sixteenth century by privately supplied newsletters, circulated in manuscript form.

It also followed the criterion set out by the society of proprietors of the provincial newspapers:

> . . . to report fairly, accurately and objectively local and/or national and/or international news, according to its particular field; to provide, when necessary, fair, accurate and objective background information to enable the public to understand news items; to comment upon important subjects; to diagnose, express and lead public opinion and to give expression to this in the form of letters to the editor; and to further any political opinions it may hold.

The Royal Commission, after an extremely painstaking inquiry, concluded that the press was uncorrupt; that it gave a fair coverage of news; that all political views got reported well. It demurred somewhat to political bias [4] in news presentation, and sometimes a too-slanted editorial policy. But it recognized that the public was well served,

4   Circulation and Political Tendencies of Some of the Principal Newspapers, 1954

Title	Circulation Jan.–June Av.	General Political Tendency
"Quality" National Dailies (mornings)		
The Times	220,834	Independent
Daily Telegraph	1,041,613	Conservative
Manchester Guardian	146,242	Liberal
"Popular" National Dailies (mornings)		
Daily Express	4,069,211	Policy conservative, though not necessarily that of Conservative Party. Stresses importance of British Empire.
Daily Mail	2,127,227	Conservative
Daily Herald	1,810,911	Labour
News Chronicle	1,315,771	Liberal
Daily Worker	83,376	Communist
"Picture" National Dailies (mornings)		
Daily Mirror	4,664,919	Left-wing
Daily Graphic	825,829	Conservative
London (evenings)		
Evening News	1,430,862	As for Daily Mail *
Star	1,102,546	As for News Chronicle *
Evening Standard	761,292	As for Daily Express *
"Quality" National Sundays		
Observer	534,752	Independent
Sunday Times	577,869	Conservative
"Popular" National Sundays		
News of the World	8,134,826	Generally conservative
People	5,167,445	Independent
Sunday Express	3,243,489	As for Daily Express *
Sunday Dispatch	2,676,037	As for Daily Mail *
Reynolds News	627,834	Supports the Cooperative Movement and the Labour Party
Sunday Chronicle	863,462	As for Daily Graphic *
Sunday Empire News	1,961,230	As for Daily Graphic *
"Picture" National Sundays		
Sunday Pictorial	5,446,255	As for Daily Mirror *
Sunday Graphic	1,174,491	As for Daily Graphic
Periodicals (weeklies)		
Economist	50,640	Independent
New Statesman and Nation	70,598	Left-wing
Spectator	38,353	Independent
Time and Tide	About 40,000	Right-wing
Tribune	Not available	Left-wing Labour but strongly anti-Communist
Illustrated Weeklies		
Picture Post	999,959	Not given by source
Illustrated	1,020,963	Not given by source
John Bull	1,196,074	Not given by source

* Indicates same owner or controller.

because rival newspapers of a different persuasion were immediately available, whether they were provincial or from London. *The big nine London dailies circulate everywhere* and are in separate ownership, giving adequate and accessible diversity. For they are very cheap!

Political Bias. If the Conservative papers, *Daily Telegraph, Daily Express, Daily Mail,* and *Daily Graphic,* are grouped together, they reach (1955) over 8,000,000 circulation. The Liberal *News Chronicle* and *Manchester Guardian* nearly total 1,500,000. The Labour *Daily Herald* and *Daily Mirror* total over 6,500,000, to which ought to be added the *Sunday Pictorial,* nearly 5,500,000 on Sundays. There is a Conservative preponderance, but Labour is well represented. What they are every day and on Sundays, they are, of course, during elections.

The essential point still is that on the same day everywhere in town and countryside the London dailies are at the newspaper stands for all to read. Assuming, say, 17,000,000 families, there is a minimum of one London daily for each. There is a close common focus for all minds on the same subjects at the same time. It is a powerful integrating force, with news of parliamentary happenings quite well and continuously reported. There are high-quality papers like the world-renowned *The Times,* (220,834) and evening papers with circulations over a million.

The effect of size of country and influence of the center upon the whole national community may be represented by these figures: the average circulation of a British newspaper is 254,000 per day; in the United States it is less than 25,000 per day, —that is, less than one tenth, because so many small newspapers are published in the many localities far away from the center and from each other. These small newspapers do not contain an adequate coverage of national and international affairs.

It is an English maxim that publicity is the antiseptic of democracy.

In 1953 the publishers, editors, and journalists set up a Press Council, as an instrument of self-criticism made public. The British press avoided possible legal control by this voluntary act of self-discipline.

Broadcasting and Television

These important mass communication services belong to the government. They are administered by the Post Office; but actually they are managed in programs and personnel policy by a board of directors under a charter granted to the British Broadcasting Corporation for limited periods and then renewed and revised. It has nine governors appointed by the Crown, which means the Prime Minister, for periods of five years. They appoint a director-general as full-time administrator responsible to them. The B.B.C. is in monopolistic charge of all broadcasting and television. It is financed by annual license fees of £2 for one or all receiving sets in a household.

The great mark of the British Broadcasting Corporation is its independence of operation from government interference, yet its general responsibility to Parliament. This is not exercised in minute interferences. It is exacting in its self-control to eliminate partisan politics, treating the media as wonderful instruments of national education. There are several networks to allow of different grades of program. One of them is famous for its classic level of music, literature, plays, debates, criticism, poetry readings, uninterrupted (as are all the programs) by commercial matter; it is known as the Third Program. These miraculous inventions are not used as tools for drumming up trade.

Insularity

We turn to consider the results of insularity.

A small island leaves an indelibly sharp impression of oneness and definition—a brilliant consciousness of identity, "this precious little island set in the silver sea." This identity is easily visualized by all. It makes education in political affairs in the schools and through the political parties simpler than elsewhere. The coasts are undeniable facts; the unit is comprehensible and plain. The sense of separateness, marked by the surrounding sea, encourages oneness, selfhood and self-reliance. A sigh of relief could be heard all over England on the day that France capitulated to the Germans in June 1940, for people, being entirely alone, said "At least, we now know where we are and what we have to do!" The larger self is not too big a self to become one's own self. It engenders a loyalty to a "public interest" that counteracts "pressure groups."

Sea Power. All political loyalties must make terms with the ineluctable necessities of sea power. The conditions are conspicuous and undeniable. The lessons of the nation's history are brought to children in the schools in deep black and bright white from their earliest years. The simplicity of the conditions empower their teachability and their unforgetability. What is the meaning, and what does the far-off vague area on the German or the Russian or the French frontier mean to me?— the nationals of those countries have wondered. There is no wondering in England by any party that aspires to office about the meaning of England's being an island.

All have a standard fixed for them, are constrained to a sober acceptance of geography. They act under the same sedative against utopianism and extremism.

The island has, until very recently, been easily defensible, without large standing armies. Such armies were first maintained in Europe by France from the middle of the seventeenth century. By the seventeenth century Prussia was not a land with an army but an army with a land (p. 541). Louis XIV ate up the wealth and manhood of France through his armies and wars. The English were fortunate in having a less-immediate problem of invasion. They needed a navy. From Henry VIII's time the government created a navy, and by mercantilist and other policies of domestic encouragement (the linen manufacture for sails, the eating of fish as a support of naval reserve, and so on) provided for the island's defense by sea. Armies were not an English delight but a bugbear. The English fought the Kings over taxation, their right to billet troops, and forbade *standing armies in time of peace*. They won not only the specific argument but, in the process, reduced the royal prerogative (his unquestioned power to govern by his personal policy).

It was not necessary to conscript men or to regiment local government for economic-strength purposes or so severely to regulate trade and industry as in France and Prussia. They did not suffer from parasitic armies, nor was an officer class exalted as in Prussia (p. 548) or the nobles as in France. The English made do with a voluntary militia under the command of local gentry who were at the same time more or less directly connected with Parliament and local self-government by the justices of the peace.

Simplicity and Unanimity about Foreign Policy. Britain is a small and weak island. Geographically, it is not a "great" power. This may seem paradoxical to those accustomed to hear about Britain's Empire and might. But, basically, Britain is very vulnerable. She became more so in the nineteenth century as she became a predominantly industrial country with reliance for her food and raw materials on foreign supplies. Her life has become more precarious in the twentieth century, because her urbanized population is so dense, the perfect target for lethal missiles and atomic and hydrogen bombs from bases a few minutes away.

Britain has very small natural resources, chiefly grass and some coal. She has no oil, no cotton, no rubber, no aluminum, little iron, little hydraulic power, no natural gas, and only a short and wet growing season that gives little wheat and hardly any maize. If her population relied on home supplies it must dwindle from 50,000,000 to 12,000,000, or it would starve to death after a few months, for its population increased with the import of supplies from abroad in proportion as its skill in manufactures for sale abroad increased. Its wealth lies in brains, science, skill, thought, organization, and *esprit de corps*. Cut its naval or aerial lifelines and Britain will die.

All parties, all voters, know this dreadful, stark fact. It was brought home by the Kaiser's submarines in World War I, Hitler's submarines in World War II, and the *Luftwaffe* in the two wars, and rockets in 1944. The problem for any Government in England is survival. It means at least the balance of power on the Continent, to save the coasts of the "Narrow Seas," to have friends in Norway, in Denmark, in Holland and Belgium and France—and Ireland. The other problem is to have friends everywhere in the world where the smallest particle of trade can be won to give some more English workers employment. The latter can be achieved either by acquiring colonial possessions—pursued from the middle of the sixteenth century to recent years—or by treaty arrangements between free nations or emancipated colonies.[5] The Conservatives have been more inclined to the former solution, Liberal and Labour to the latter. The hope is that the growth of the Dominions (of English physical descent or culture)—Australia, Canada, New Zealand, the Malaya lands, even South Africa and native Africa —may develop in population, wealth, and defensive power in the next fifty years to re-create the international influence, standing, and might of the eighteenth and nineteenth centuries founded on Empire.

The Balance of Power. The European enemy was France, then the Netherlands, then Germany. Today the most powerful Continental and Asiatic force is the Soviet Union. The most powerful friend is the United States, whose own security interests are served by England's survival, fighting prowess, diplomatic skill, and geographic location as an aircraft base.

Sir Eyre Crowe, Permanent Secretary of the Foreign Office in the period of World War I, stated what had been a quite conscious policy since Henry VIII turned his mind to a navy:

The general character of England's foreign policy is determined by the immutable conditions of her geographical situation on the ocean flank of Europe as an island State with vast overseas colonies and dependencies, whose existence and survival as an independent community are inseparably bound up with the possession of preponderant sea power. . . .

History shows that the danger threatening the independence of this or that nation has generally arisen, at least in part, out of the momentary predominance of a neighbouring State at once militarily powerful, economically efficient, and ambitious to extend its frontiers or spread its influence, the danger being directly proportionate to the degree of its power and efficiency, and to the spontaneity or "inevitableness" of its ambitions. The only check on the abuse of political predominance derived from such a position has always consisted in the opposition of an equally formidable rival, or of a combination of several countries forming leagues of defence. The equilibrium established by such a

grouping of forces is technically known as the balance of power, and it had become almost a historical truism to identify England's secular policy with the maintenance of this balance by throwing her weight now in this scale and now in that, but ever on the side opposed to the political dictatorship of the strongest single State at a given time.

English expansionism, whether for religion or for military adventure or for wealth, was overseas. Any inefficiency, corruption, or cruelty took place out of domestic sight. This lightened the burden of coercion in government in the homeland. It also compelled all parties in England to face the problems of colonial government, its duties and responsibilities. Slavery was not permitted on English soil, and trading in slaves abroad was abolished in 1820, the government then buying out the trade.

II. HOMOGENEITY OF POPULATION

Britain's population does not include any large blocs of people with markedly different physical characteristics from the average diversities of the basic, general stock of well-mixed Teutonic and Mediterranean types with which it was chiefly peopled from before the Roman occupation to the Norman conquest. There are no large and localized groups of Negroes or Jews; there is nothing like the enormously diverse ethnic blocs of the Soviet Union. Nor has Britain any considerable groups of recent immigrants with foreign culture. Immigrants from Europe, of different language and culture, have preferred the opportunities of the New World. A trickle of immigrants has been easily assimilated.

British politics and society have been spared two disturbing and passionate causes of an angry conflict of wills: race discrimination and anti-Semitism. It appeases and reassures their unity.

A Christian People

It is a fact of supreme political meaning that the British people bow to the Christian ethic. The British combination of the Old and the New Testaments has deeply pervaded their private and

[5] See Herman Finer, *America's Destiny*, New York, 1947.

public behavior. The King James Version of the whole Bible was published in 1611. Its genius, a noble humanity acknowledging a heavenly Lord over man, is spoken in all the affairs of men where behavior may be influenced by speech, where the conscience may be turned by reflection, where man's arrogance would otherwise lead him to brutality and stupidity. This tremendous fact in British political life is so taken for granted that it must be especially redeemed from neglect and vagueness.

English civilization, and with it English government, began to be Christianized when the mission of Augustine from the Rome of Gregory I landed in Kent in the year 597. By the year 700 there was an English-born Archbishop of Canterbury, with the cure of all souls in England, uniting a people in one faith, teaching Kings to bow their heads to the Gospel of the King of Kings, and ministering through bishoprics and churches. Great churchmen, through doctrine, through learning and their schools for the clergy, through piety, and through administrative ability, influenced the people and the Court. Partly through native ability, partly through their Latin learning and as scribes and draftsmen, partly, again, through their feudal status as owners of substantial estates, they were members, often the *ruling* members, of the King's councils and were sometimes his chief Ministers—a Thomas à Becket, a Stephen Langton, a Cardinal Wolsey. Furthermore, embattled (as Church tradition required) against the domination of the Crown, the clergy were leaders of the ranks who fought for English liberty.

Before there was a firm English "State" there had come into existence a firm state of the Church, with its hierarchy and its elected councils. We must attempt to imagine the influence it had throughout the medieval period, when the local church was the only house of community meeting, of spiritual comfort, where births, deaths, marriages were endowed with sanctity, with enhanced grace, or with the ultimate consolations. Here were the centers of light and learning, of the picturesque, and of charity and sanctuary. The monasteries exemplified magnificence and a devout life. The ministered to the deepest yearning

(of vital political import) in men's souls—to know "What shall I do to be saved?"

Government is a grim business, for it attempts to accommodate the impingement of the raw nature of some men upon the raw nature of others. It is instituted to avert murder through social impatience at one extreme and suicide through social despair at the other. It could be, like Nature, red in tooth and claw, without inner restraint; but restraint, in the end, must rest on the conviction of right and wrong. Of this conviction, in the English people, the Christian religion is a powerful molder and humanizer.

The crudest comparison of all would be between the Christianized British community and the Soviet "materialist" rules and Communist Party. The former accepts such direct and controlling basic values as Charity, Mercy, the care of the individual soul, Truth, family affection, "Thou shalt not kill." Hence its *means* are disciplined in their unethicality by these ends. The rulers in Moscow despise this gospel; their ends justify all their means, however ignoble (pp. 928–929). Even if it is argued that such Christianity in Britain is rather vague, it is still nobly humane contrasted with the sharp executional and man-enslaving tenets of the Kremlin.

Yet religious differences were for centuries—at the minimum from the Reformation—a cause of savage conflict, of vehement debates and sweeping actions. The breach with Rome, the dissolution of the monasteries, and repression of those who dissented from the spiritual headship of the Crown and the attendant forms of ordained and enforced ritual and prayers, were backed by cruel force. People fought over the prayers to be said, whether worshipers ought to kneel or not, and about the robes the priest might wear![6] But the conflicts of Roman Catholics, the Anglican Churchmen, and the various Protestant sects, above all those with Puritan ascetic temper, finally found abatement, each going its own way in worship but participating in and contributing to national policy.

[6] Readers who might cynically respond that they were *really* fighting over economic goods know little indeed of the depths of human nature, as little as Karl Marx was prepared to admit openly for his purposes of incitement.

The Church of England is the established church, and its sacraments sanctify the new King or Queen in the most solemn rites of the coronation ceremony.[7] The two archbishops and twenty-four bishops sit as of right in the House of Lords. There has been tension within a lifetime among the religious groupings in matters of national policy—divorce, education, drink. But passion in the course of the everyday conduct of public affairs, in central and local government, and in voluntary social services is no longer acrimonious. No disabilities attend membership of the various denominations (see p. 70).

Scotland's and Ireland's religious faith could not be accommodated as the various faiths in England, which have been brought to live and work side by side. In Scotland the Presbyterian Church, the national church embodying a sinewy Calvinism, was preserved by a fundamental provision of the Act of Union of 1710. However, the long and bloody conflict between England and Ireland, England's fear of Ireland as a steppingstone for invasion (attempted several times from France), of its different religion owing allegiance to Rome, of English colonizing greed, and of Irish stubbornness, separatism, ethnic difference (Celtic), poverty and romantic mournfulness or vanity, could not be ended by anything but divorce. Southern Ireland in 1921 became a Free State beyond even an oath of allegiance.[8]

[7] On October 31, 1955, Princess Margaret, third in line in succession to the throne, decided not to marry a commoner whom she loved, and announced: "I have been aware that, subject to my renouncing my rights of succession, it might have been possible for me to contract a civil marriage. But, mindful of the Church's teachings that Christian marriage is indissoluble, and conscious of my duty to the Commonwealth, I have resolved to put these considerations before any others." The Church stood for duty and dignity.

[8] The available figures of membership of the various churches for 1954 are:

England, Wales, Scotland, and Northern Ireland

Church of England *	6,213,000
Roman Catholic	3,930,000
Presbyterian	1,753,000
Methodist	1,180,000
Baptist	335,000
Congregationalist	223,000
Calvinist	213,000
Jewish	400,000

* Nominal membership of the Church of England said to be 15,000,000.

Britain is not troubled by such impassioned crises as the Dreyfus case in France (p. 315), or a national capitulation, such as that of France to Hitler in 1940 partly caused by a split in loyalties founded on religious belief. Nor does England suffer from the religious cleavage among labor unions and political parties of social reform, as in France and Germany; nor the consequences of Russian Czarist connivance with the Orthodox Church (p. 743). England has had a Jew as Prime Minister, as Lord Chief Justice, as Viceroy of India; and, as Prime Ministers, members of the Church of England and Nonconformists, but never yet a Roman Catholic.

It may be mentioned that the Act of Settlement of 1701 laid down that only a Protestant could accede to the throne (see p. 175).

The various churches in Britain represent strong religious feeling of a Christian kind. Each in its time, and all at times, together, have given their strength, often initiative, to social and economic improvement. The Church of England fostered the people's education through day schools, Sunday schools, the Society for the Promotion of Christian Knowledge; secured the abolition of the slave trade; assisted prison reform, factory reform, and so on; and had its own Christian Socialist upsurge and workers' education movement (p. 61).

Religion and Political Liberty

The Reformation contributed to British political liberty.

Henry VIII's quarrel with Catholic spiritual supremacy, seated in Rome, did not begin as a theological dispute or one concerning either the political liberty of the Crown personally or representing England or the political liberties of the individuals who made up the nation. But since he could not get his own way in the divorce of Anne Boleyn, arguments and justifications began, to spin out over a hundred years. The spirit of freedom of religious worship and of a discipline autonomous to those who associated in non-Roman forms of worship and of doctrine had blazed with diverse flames since the fourteenth century, since John Wycliff, William Langland, John Ball, and the Lollards.

The whole problem of orthodoxy, of dissent, of the relationship between religious dissent and unified political authority, toleration, and freedom to worship, was made acute by Henry VIII's quarrel. It was aggravated by the clash between his successors, Edward VI, "bloody Queen Mary" ("bloody" from her persecutions and executions), between Elizabeth and Catholic Spain, and then between the Catholicizing James I and Charles I and the English gentry and yeomen and the population of the city of London. The Civil War was in large part (not altogether) a religious war, the Church of England and Romanizing tendencies on one side, and Puritans and Presbyterians on the other. This it was that gave birth to the majestic and noble doctrines of John Milton and John Locke concerning toleration and freedom of worship and, further, of freedom of opinion and a limited government based on the consent of the governed. The appeal to private conscience in matters of religious faith led to toleration doctrines and democratic government. As Neville Figgis put it: "Political liberty is the residuary legatee of ecclesiastical animosities"; for a man's personality is of one piece and the "religious" dominates it.

The demands of the private conscience are exacting in the government of England. One may not obtain forgiveness or mental ease or indulgence by Catholic confession. On the other hand, in Russia there was no Reformation, the individual conscience had no dignity; the conscience of the Czars was absolved. In France the Church triumphed; it produced orthodoxy that caused a reaction of skepticism and atheism. Had England not been an island, a pimple on the northwestern shoulder of Europe, the full, battering force of the Reformation—like that of Luther's blasts which bolstered the Prussian State by massacring the peasants to break their demand for liberty, or of Calvin whose Church became a persecutor—would have swept her also. She owed her temperateness, her blend of religious awe with liberty of conscience, to her distance from Europe's raging center.

The Reformation saved the West that pall of superstition and absolutism that enveloped Russian government—until the twentieth century, when the flood of godless Marxism swept away the Czar and Church together and set up Communism, Lenin, and Stalin. Britain retained the principle that means must be of a Christian nature when an end is pursued; the Communists fell to "the end justifies the means."

Language and Literature

What the everyday vision of a roadside Madonna and candles may mean in creating a society in some nations, the English language and literature mean to the British. They store the oneness of the ethical and political and aesthetic memories of a people. They are instinct with society and state, in subtle nuances.

In comparison are the bitterness and ungregariousness, even enmity, fortified by differences of language in such relationships as that of Great Russia to the Ukraine and other peoples in the Czarist dominions and the Soviet Union, their successors.

Margaret Mead has suggested—in my opinion rightly—that civic excitability is stirred up incessantly in a social environment where many differences of appearance, accent language, ethical standards, and religion prevail. British homogeneity may produce a more humdrum quality of public life, but it also leaves the people with a much more pronounced sense of security and quiet self-possession and so makes them steadier and more serene about their procedures and ability to solve their problems.

Climate

Finally, before the factors that breach homogeneity are reviewed, we may refer briefly to the *assimilating* effect of the climate. The climate is temperate, and, according to Professor Ellsworth Huntington, its range of 10° to around 55°F with some humidity,[9] is close to ideal for an active, vigorous life. It is the opposite of enervating. Its changeability is stimulating. Its lack of bright color tends, perhaps, to take men's spirits away from the carefree artistic exercise of the mind and imagination rather than to keep them spurred by

[9] See F. S. Markham, *Climate and the Energy of Nations*, London, 1939.

less-soaring motivation,[10] and send them to the cosy shelter of their homes rather than to tempt them to the Continental gregarious, conversational, and speculative life of the cafés, where they may split solid, consequential action-needs by chiseling words. "Life is real, life is earnest. . . ."

The great climatic diversity of the United States, that nevertheless lives under one government, has had a weighty effect on the industry, tempo, and outlook of the various regions. Indirectly it affected even the very fundamentals of the Constitution, as, for example, the equal representation of the states in the Senate where they seek to maintain their identity.

Ernest Crankshaw, a first-hand observer of Russia, has recently made a strong case (see p. 734) that Russian Czarist absolutism was historically inevitable because the climate destroyed communications for more than eight months in each year. No communications, no free government!

III. FACTORS PRODUCING DIVERSITY

The unifying, pacifying effect of the homogeneity of the British population on its government has been sketched. What of the factors that produce conflict and tension?

It is difficult to disentangle the unifying spiritual beliefs from economic interests. If we desired to be simpleminded or, in the technical language, "monistic," it could even be argued cogently that man is ruled by nothing except spiritual ends, that these determine how much attention and passion he will spend on economic satisfactions. Yet it is essential to realize the extent to which the functions of government and the spirit of its conduct in Britain have been molded by economic needs.

From the earliest times of which we have record in British society, men were not equal in the work they performed, the possessions they owned, their power to order others to labor, or their share in the

distribution of the product in relationship to their labor.

English history is, from one point of view, a seething panorama of conflicts arising from the everlasting struggle, paralleled everywhere, of men to reap where they have sown—and also to reap where they have not. Across a thousand years pass these scenes: feudal or manorial society with its serfs; the freeing of the latter through changes in production; a rise in prices and the tremendous toll of workers in the Black Death (1349); the readjustments of ownership and wages in the fifteenth century; the conflict of landlords and tenants; the impact of trade in wool on the nation's fortunes; wars for the protection of British wool trade and clashes with the interests that preferred that the wool be woven in the country rather than shipped abroad raw; municipal struggles about the regulation of trade and occupations by the guilds; the constitutional struggles of the seventeenth century, which were in part (but only in part) motivated by the desire to have trade free from authority, to have the State back overseas trade, by the older landlords to prevent the rise of new owners under conditions of easier purchase of lands; revolutionary inflation with the advent of gold from the New World in the sixteenth century, and treasure enabling the Stuart kings to live "off their own"; the struggle over the interests that enclosed the common land for pasture when the rich took the common from the poor man's goose and committed a crime more heinous than the poor man's taking the goose from the common; the treatment of the destitute, the workless, the widows and orphans, by aid, workhouse, apprenticeship, by imprisonment or transportation, the provision of work, the regulation of wages.

Capitalism or Free Enterprise

The nineteenth century saw the development of industry conducted outside the home, in large urban communities that had to be built fast, initiated by enterprising men with capital (though "capitalism" began earlier), and manned by a labor force that owned nothing except body and mind.

---

[10] When I say *soaring*, it is not in disparagement of the aesthetic subtleties. On the contrary. What kind of a life is it that is lived without suffusion in art? The reader may already have noticed the effect on the art of Van Gogh of his migration from the grim grayness of Holland to the sun and color of southern France. A visit to such areas, or to Florida from Maine, will reinforce the lesson.

The "capitalist" economy, and the political nation, came to be riven in three ways: (1) along class lines; (2) as between the occupations, vertically; and (3) between economically selfish individuals or groups and the common good. A brief glance at these three cleavages and their effect on government is advisable here, though the subject is taken up from another angle later in this chapter.

(1) Class Differences

Crudely this means the difference of interest of those who own the means of production and those who are possessionless. It includes, on the first side, the entrepreneur, the managers, the bosses and foreman; and, on the other side, the "workers," taking orders on what shall be produced, how production shall be technically undertaken

and under the discipline of the employers as to hours, effort, speed, and how the finished good should be sold.

The characterization of this cleavage owes most to the peculiar genius of Karl Marx, though indigenous English writers preceded him in recognition and analysis of its nature less ponderously, less methodically, less apocalyptically. Marx took the triad of factors of production revealed by Adam Smith (see p. 33ff.), Ricardo, and others of the classical school (land, labor, capital) and the division by three of the product (into rent, wages, and profits) and reduced them to a simple division by two: bourgeoisie (profits) and proletariat (wages). He rigidified and envenomed them by the animosities of the much more rigid and punitive class political and religious system of his native land—Germany (see p. 566). The British

Distribution of Incomes Before and After Income Tax, 1950–1951
(Year ending April 5)

Range of Incomes	Number of Incomes	Total Income before Tax	Tax	Net Income after Tax
	Thousands	Millions of £		
All incomes	20,200	8,750	1,107.0	7,643.0
Range of Total Income before Tax:				
Exceeding Not Exceeding				
£ £				
135 150	600.0	86.0	0.1	85.9
150 250	5,245.0	1,052.0	22.8	1,029.2
250 500	10,120.0	3,603.0	154.3	3,448.7
500 750	2,658.0	1,576.0	135.9	1,440.1
750 1,000	707.0	603.0	97.1	505.9
1,000 1,500	460.0	552.0	128.5	423.5
1,500 2,000	165.0	283.0	79.7	203.3
2,000 3,000	127.0	306.0	101.4	204.6
3,000 5,000	73.0	272.0	117.0	155.0
5,000 10,000	34.0	229.0	127.2	101.8
10,000 20,000	9.0	117.0	81.7	35.3
20,000 . . .	2.0	71.0	61.3	9.7
Range of Net Income after Tax:				
Exceeding Not Exceeding				
£ £				
135 150	652.0	93.3	0.1	93.2
150 250	5,668.0	1,167.1	30.5	1,136.6
250 500	10,320.0	3,840.9	188.8	3,652.1
500 1,000	3,045.0	2,228.0	289.5	1,938.5
1,000 2,000	419.7	802.3	238.9	563.4
2,000 4,000	89.9	494.1	258.5	235.6
4,000 6,000	5.3	114.4	91.3	23.1
6,000 . . .	0.06	9.9	9.4	0.5

Source: *Annual Abstract of Statistics*, Central Statistical Office (London, 1953), No. 90, p. 244.

people are more homogeneous and serene than Marx gave them credit for; they stuck to the Bible.

As for the inequality of property, the following figures are telling:

the relationship between the power of associated trade unions and the authority of the State.

Furthermore, inside and outside Parliament tension was incessant over the demand of the workers that the conduct of enterprises should

Prewar Distribution of Property in Private Hands in England and Wales
(Figures relate to persons 25 and over)

Property	Number of Persons		Amount of Property	
	Cumulative Number	Cumulative Percentage	Cumulative Amount	Cumulative Percentage
Total	25,201	100.0	15,853–17,548	100.0
More than £100	5,915–6,522	23.5–25.9	15,403–16,598	94.6–97.2
£1,000	1,727–1,874	6.8– 7.4	13,604–14,613	83.3–85.8
£5,000	465– 500	1.8– 2.0	10,695–11,458	65.3–67.5
£10,000	243– 261	1.0	8,983– 9,615	54.8–56.7
£25,000	87– 93	0.4	6,427– 6,859	39.1–40.5
£100,000	12– 13	0.05	2,975– 3,155	18.0–18.8

Source: H. Campion, *Public and Private Property in Great Britain,* Oxford University Press, 1939, p. 109.

Throughout the nineteenth century, Parliament and the judiciary were dominated by the employers' ability to sway the electorate (which was not based on universal franchise until the twentieth century). Yet the leaders of that class (and it cannot be called a monolithic and undivided class!) made considerable concessions to the demands of the workers by direct benefits and by successive extensions of the franchise. Finally, the right of the workers to organize and so to exert the pressure of strikes on employers was acknowledged. James McCulloch, one of the group known as the "classical economists," said as early as 1826:

Capacity to labour is to the poor man what stock is to the capitalist. But you would not prevent a hundred or a thousand capitalists from forming themselves into a company, or *combination* who should take all their measures in common, and dispose of their property as they might, in their collective capacity, judge most advantageous for their interests:—and why then should not a hundred or a thousand laborers be allowed to do the same by *their stock?*

It took many decades before this intelligent and unusual view was given the authority of law. The working-class power reached the point in the General Strike of 1926 that required a readjustment of

not remain vested in the owners or their agents alone. This led, in the end, to the nationalization of some industries and government regulation of others, as well as to certain mild forms of workers' participation.

Again, the workers chafed at the fact that as the means of production were in the hands of the employers, their own opportunities of advancement and the amount produced depended on the ability of the employers. The career was not open to the talents. In part, again, as a solution, the nationalization of industry was sought, and in some cases achieved.

The workers knew very realistically that men have unequal talents and that some are hardworking and some are lazy. But they resented the fact that they were doomed to poverty because opportunity for education and the higher posts (in industries, the Civil and Armed services, the judiciary) were not available to them. Some (perhaps the employers' relatives) were receiving higher salaries and other benefits than they would be entitled to by any comparisons of native ability. One of the solvents of this injustice was publicly financed education—and here again is one of the strong political drives in Britain in the nineteenth and twentieth centuries, stemming from the heterogeneity of interests. Indeed, in a famous political novel Benjamin Disraeli wrote of "the *Two* Nations." The educational theme needs a closer survey.

Education

The sorest blemish on English government in the nineteenth century was the *deliberate* repudiation of the governing class of the duty to provide the nation with free education. Free education did not come about in any massive way until 1870 for primary education; not till 1902 for secondary education; hardly yet at all for the universities. Yet there had been much private education at all levels: of the highest quality, provided by private means in private schools; and for substantial numbers of those who could not pay, by charitable endowments, by the Church of England since long before the Reformation, and by other denominations after it. The *quality* was always sober and high and demanded quite serious application by the pupils. From 1839 the Government began a policy of ever-increasing grants to schools maintained by the churches. Since 1870 and 1902 the schools provided and administered by the local government authorities with central government assistance of grants took over almost the entire field, although church schools still persisted with government grants, if they fulfilled its standards.

The Church of England had been most adamant against vesting education in the hand of the secular local-government-elected councils, fearing religious lost opportunities. Religion was provided for, however, in a daily session of "Bible teaching" first thing each morning at school by the ordinary teachers, except for pupils who conscientiously wish to be excused. It persists, to the nation's moral good.

By 1938 the Government was providing for 5,500,000 elementary pupils (to the age of 14), but only for 500,000 secondary schoolchildren. If in 1900 hardly 1 child in 70 could expect to enter a secondary school, in 1938, 1 in 7 did. It was a great improvement, but it fell vastly below American standards. This was a stark fact—even though the locally managed secondary schools were grant-assisted to provide as much as 25 percent of their places for free scholarship winners—because the fees were substantial and working men and clerks

needed their children's work to supplement the family income. Britain was plowing under her own brains and character.

The Education Act of 1944, a bipartisan measure stimulated by wartime appreciation of the valor of the British people, has introduced some substantial remedies. There have been established three stages of education: primary, secondary, and further.[11] The first goes from nursery school to the end of junior school at the age of 11. This is free and compulsory (not below the age of 5 is it compulsory).

Then follow the secondary schools—all children attend at least until the age of 15, and where, and as soon as, accommodation is available, to the age of 16, compulsorily and free. To satisfy the various aptitudes and later careers of the children these schools fall into three classes (often in the same school building): grammar, modern, and technical. The first cater for those going on to the universities and professions. The second cater for a good all-round education that might be terminal. The technical is obvious. The great present tribulations relate to the desire of many parents that their children be admitted to the grammar schools. For the decision is made by the school authorities on the basis of quite difficult examinations, and it is a matter of pride that the child should be admitted. Further, it is the path to scholarships and to the universities. They include many schools that were formerly on a private basis—even the great "public schools"; for the government pays them substantial grants on condition that they admit 25 percent of their pupils from the grant-aided primary schools. These schools must put a number of their places at the disposal of the local education authorities.

Universities. England and Wales have fourteen universities, Scotland four, Northern Ireland one. Most of them have claims to fame, especially Oxford, Cambridge (dating from the twelfth century—500 years before Russia had a single uni-

[11] Since the discussion will move on lines not integrating the "further education," it may be said at once that all education authorities must provide full-time and part-time education up to the age of 18, if not at full-time attendance at some school. Eventually all under the age of 18 will have to take part-time education. Further, of course, there are all manner of vocational schools.

versity!), London, Edinburgh, Glasgow, Manchester, and so on. They are not state-owned or administered, though the Government since 1919 assists them to the extent of about one third of their expenses, leaving them free, however, to say what they need the funds for and how they shall spend them. Until the beginning of the nineteenth century the universities were expensive places for the wealthier population (with the exception of some of the provincial universities and London) and they are residential. There were some scholarships. Since World War I the number of these, supplied partly by the Ministry of Education and by the local authorities, substantially increased; since World War II, even more so.

Still, in 1938–1939 there were only just over 50,000 university students in all the universities put together. If this number is multiplied by 4, to allow for the size of the population of the United States compared with that of Britain, then the "weighted" number would be only 200,000. But then the United States has some 1,500,000 in colleges and universities! The number of British university students has risen to over 85,000, and it is not expected that this will much increase. Of these, nearly three quarters now receive scholarships or other awards to enable them to attend. It is a remarkable achievement. Yet the total number is small, perhaps, compared with ability.

Quality Education. The British do not believe that everyone is entitled to an education of his own choosing at the public expense. They believe that only those should go to school who have abilities and potentialities, properly ascertained by skilled advisers. School is a very serious matter, partly because (with fewer opportunities of employment in desirable and well-paying jobs than in a land like the United States, for example) competition for the academic qualifications that entitle the holders to consideration for jobs is very severe. Also, the British believe their teachers know something about education and do not try to subvert their authority in order to reduce standards or promote the failures.

The result is a very high quality of education at all levels (especially among members of Parliament, p. 63) by devoted and well-trained teachers. The system is thorough and hardworking. It is

not exhibitionist in extracurricular activities, though sport plays a considerable part in it. The subjects are few and compulsory. From tender ages the pupils practice the writing of frequent themes and memorize the great passages of English literature, its poems, its Shakespearean and Dickensian heritage, and passages from the Bible. They are steeped in these—the object being to introduce them to great minds and characters, to exhibit the variety of values men may worship, and to inculcate habits of careful thought and *lucid* self-expression. Care is taken over the core subjects of English, mathematics, history, geography, science—no easy frills are available for soft option.

The whole of the education has a decided civic end; to produce ladies and gentlemen conscious of their community obligations and to be stout in assertion of individual values. Think! think! think! . . . is their motto. But this social outlook is not taught merely by courses of civics. Indeed, teachers are warned not to make deliberate attacks on this subject. Rather, the meaning of society is taught through illustrative inferences from English literature, history, geography, and in the Scripture lessons. These are made to precipitate the character of an active "gentleman," from Chaucer to Milton to Wordsworth to Tennyson and T. S. Eliot.

In the nineteenth century the feeling entertained by the underprivileged that they needed education caused a stimulus to workers' adult education that eventuated in the best mass adult-education system in the world: industrious, sober, aspiring. It was helped forward by the Christian Socialists and the university professors.

The *"Public" Schools* are "private" establishments, for "class" education. They were founded usually by charitable endowments for the "poor and needy" scholars: Winchester in 1382, Eaton in 1440 by Henry VI. Others with famous names, such as St. Paul's, Westminster (where John Locke studied), Christ's Hospital, were opened in the sixteenth century. The sons of rich men might enter also "if the gentleman's son be apt to learning," and in time the public schools were converted to the exclusive use of the wealthy. In the eighteenth century the wealthier rising middle class built more: for example, Harrow and Rugby. In the nineteenth century Samuel Butler at Shrewsbury and Thomas Arnold at Rugby encouraged a revival of good, "Christian" moral education by establishing prefectoral self-government and rule by the older boys and infusing contemporary and realistic meaning into their classical studies.

The public schools had become the preserve of the aristocratic and subaristocratic groups. Of course, their pupils monopolized the top of the military and civil services, the Church, the law, the Cabinet. They constituted the substantial majority of the Conservative Party and the Lords. The boarding system developed *esprit de corps,* patriotism and public spirit, *noblesse oblige* (in most), honesty and candor, authority and party loyalty, and (for many) good thinking habits. They mainly served a class; they often served the whole nation by self-sacrifice in "no surrender" on the battlefield.

Boys attended from thirteen and one half to nineteen. (Some girls' schools also flourished.) In 1942 the public *boarding* schools had some 36,000 students, taking 9000 per year. Not all schools were in the top twelve that gave rise to the symbolism of the "old-school-tie" caste. Some even were recipient of Government grants, if their standards were certified by its inspectors; some were day schools.

The Education Act of 1944, with Labour Party approval, offered not to abolish these schools but to share them. All schools that do not receive public money are known as "independent" schools. They are now inspected by the Ministry of Education for quality of premises and for efficient curriculum and methods. Those that fail will be closed. The local education authorities *must* provide boarding education for normal children who need it—in their own hostels or by agreement with independent schools that are prepared to receive their students. This makes it possible for the local authorities virtually to give scholarships to public schools to those who will benefit thereby; the general standards are set by the Ministry. The public schools clearly retain their freedom to contract on the principles and the price. As for the

lesser "grammar" schools, which used to receive grants direct from the Ministry of Education, they have been incorporated into the general secondary school system; they get grants if they provide 25 percent of places to nonfee-paying pupils who come from the primary schools. Many of these are famous for their quality, for example Manchester High School, the Perse School, St. Dunstan's, Exeter, etc.

Public school candidates still possess substantial advantages in the home, diplomatic, and colonial Civil Service and used to have it in the Indian Civil Service. But they are not lacking in brains and character. Mr. Baldwin and Mr. Churchill were both educated at Harrow, although the latter asserts he *avoided* being educated by getting lost in his big class.

(2) Economic Disharmonies

Another chief feature of the Industrial and Commercial Revolutions of the nineteenth century is the discordance of interests among the main branches of the economy—manufactures (small and large), commerce, agriculture, finance. Their common interest is prosperity, but under the capitalist system of *laissez faire,* or free enterprise, each firm in each branch pursues its own road to wealth. Their want of integrated effort—that is, integration by the pursuit of a plan agreed upon in common or enforced upon them—produced several serious crises in the nineteenth and twentieth centuries, involving widespread unemployment and misery. Employers were not as ready as workers to take the drastic steps necessary to avoid depressions and mass unemployment, because their freedom to do as they liked with their own plant, skill, money, or land was directly at stake, whereas for the worker already used to being bossed around by a stranger the sacrifices of government interferences were less. His only problem, at first sight,[12] was not his *freedom* from orders but who was to give them. The anticrisis, antidepression policies and the conflicts these involve are more particularly discussed presently. This conflict continues.

[12] *Cf.,* however, observations on the Soviet control of labor, p. 871.

(3) Individual vs. Community

Finally, the Industrial and Commercial Revolutions raised in a more acute and endemic form than before the relationship between the egoism of the individual and the whole community, whether that individual was property owner or a wage earner. Either could harm more than the other immediate party to the conflict; the national in general could be injured. If any withheld his inventions or his ability to innovate or used his plant to make noxious articles of consumption or destroyed the natural beauty of a large area for a short-run gain or polluted streams of water with poisonous chemicals and by-products of industrial or agricultural processes or built plants or houses that were liable to fall down or catch fire and endanger third parties or whole communities, the *community* was injured in its safety or its health or its standard of living. As the mechanical power and the property at the disposal of the people increased, their power to benefit or injure the community was magnified; the power that runs amuck calls for power that can tame it.

Essential Observations

Before leaving this mere suggestion of the "contradictions" inherent in the modern British economic system, some other observations are essential.

Professor D. V. Glass has provided us with a survey of class structure in Britain very different from the conventional one, and much more informative. This division of the adult male population is based on the ranking of occupations according to their social prestige. The population accordingly falls into these categories:

1. Professional and high administrative, 2.9 percent of all
2. Managerial and executive, 4.5 percent
3. Inspectional, supervisory, and other non-manual: higher grade, 9.8 percent
4. Inspectional, supervisory, and other non-manual: lower grade, 12.7 percent
5. Skilled manual and routine grades of non-manual, 41.2 percent
6. Semiskilled manual, 16.5 percent
7. Unskilled manual, 12.4 percent

In spite of the modern trend toward the modification of extreme inequalities to the benefit of the wage earner, much inequality still persists, as the figures at the bottom of the page show, and allowance is made for the size of the classes that share the amount of each category. These figures are before the deduction of taxes. But we know (p. 18) how substantial an equalizing measure taxes now are.

We have used the word *classes* in Karl Marx's sense. But we are not deceived by the simple division into two. For even the two, if found, are riven by differences. And there are at least three classes since the enlargement of the white-collar workers and the professions in the nineteenth and twentieth centuries. This complicates the pressure groups and the electoral conflict. The occupational groupings, the widespread holding of different kinds of property, and the unequal distribution of incomes indicate no simple twofold or threefold divergence.

Moreover, Karl Marx's strictures originated in the Prussia of his time, in which the German classes—noble, military, clergy, burger, professor, artisan, Lutheran, and Roman Catholic—were more inflexibly *hereditary* than in Britain. British

Division of the Home National Income at Current Prices, 1900–1950
(Millions of £)

	Profits	Wages	Salaries	Rent	Total
1900	494	674	297	192	1,657
1910	587	717	365	228	1,897
1920		Not Available			5,464
1930	876	1,489	931	337	3,633
1940	1,788	2,142	1,236	438	5,604
1950	3,129	4,510	2,480	442	10,561

Source: *The Economist* (Coronation Issue, May 30, 1953)

Distribution of British Manpower,
June 1954   *Thousands*

Total Working Population	23,531
Armed Forces	841
Total Civil Employment	22,466
Agriculture, Forests, Fishery	1,069
Mining and Quarrying	869
National Government Service	587 *
Local Government Service	725 *
Gas, Water, and Electricity	374
Transport and Communication	1,706
Manufacturing Industries	9,009
Building and Contracting	1,423
Distributive Trades	2,702
Professional, Financial, and Misc.	4,002

In addition some 230,000 registered unemployed.

* These figures do not square with those given in later chapters; the present figures are on a different basis, the later ones are valid for their purpose.

society was much more "open" and mobile up and down, and had been for many generations, than the German. But the flexibility of social classes (as the experience of America even more happily shows) permits an easier, less-violent process of government; its rigidity spurs on to a direct or indirect assault on the State. The hereditary privileges of the nobility and clergy in France before the Revolution and the abasement of the general population bloodily exacted a new constitution altogether. So also in Czarist Russia.

Acquisitiveness. To conclude this sociological factor of heterogeneity, brought about by the onset of the capitalist mode of production and distribution, one note ought to be added. In any system, the acquisitive passions—in other words, greed—may be more or less intense, or, to use the common term, the culture may be more or less "materialistic." The prevailing god of the nineteenth century became economic or materialistic, and god's name came to be spelled not GOD but GET, regardless of ethical scruples. British traders became more visibly acquisitive with the increasing opportunities of satisfying their desires, though they had been acquisitive enough—for example, the piracy and the wars with Spain and France over the riches of the New World in the sixteenth and seventeenth centuries—whenever they could lay their hands on wealth. Now the country grew rich. Per-capita wealth increased threefold be-

tween 1800 and 1954, while the population trebled. Current total income is £13,000,000,000 for the whole nation of 50,000,000 people.

When there is a larger total to be shared, if there is some sharing or the hope of it, conflicts die down. Abundance offers the opportunity of liberty, because the State does not have to be invoked to supply various social benefits, and the political fight is not so acute. It is hard to compare the natural or acquired cupidity of the various nations. Germany is more acquisitive than Britain, and she more than France. In the Soviet Union the people are forced into the economic program and obedience designed by their despotic rulers for the Communist Plans.

An Artificially Wealthy People. The island has few native resources. Grass and cattle and grains used to be the basis of existence before the Industrial Revolution of the early nineteenth century. What made the latter possible in England, first among nations, was inventiveness and deposits of coal and iron. Energy and the brains of the people did the rest.

Though the nineteenth-century and twentieth-century economy was and is precariously balanced, the nation is weathy. The comparison of incomes *per capita* is relevant. The table shows:

National and Per-capita Income, 1949

	Per-capita Income *	*Total National Income* †
United States	1,453	216,831
United Kingdom	773	38,922
Belgium	582	8,015
France	482	19,857
Germany (Western Zone)	329	15,300
U.S.S.R.	308	59,500

* In United States dollars, adjusted to 1949 dollar value in the United States.

Index number to up-date per-capita to 1953 with 1949 as 100: U.S.A., 115; U.K., 113; Belgium, 112; France, 138; Germany (W), 144; U.S.S.R., 165 (alleged). Index numbers deduced, roughly, from U.N. *Statistics of National Income, etc.,* 1955, H. 7.

† In millions of United States dollars, adjusted to 1949 dollar value in the United States.

Source: Adapted from publication of the Statistical Office of the United Nations (New York, 1950), Series E, No. 1.

Liberty a Function of Wealth. The comparative wealth is important, for the wealthier a people is, the more chance it has of settling its internal economic disputes in a regime of liberty and amicableness. This is especially so since the material standard of living almost everywhere became so emphatic a public craving from the middle of the nineteenth century.

The British have always to be on their toes to keep abreast of such economic rivals as Germany and the United States in high-grade manufactures for ever-varying markets, to maintain the standard of living of its very dense population. All British political parties agree on this basic need, though they may differ on the means and measures for the best results. The indisputable fact produces much basic homogeneity—but it did produce the most famous and intense political controversy of the nineteenth century: whether to let agriculture go as the nation's main way of earning a livelihood, or whether to choose free trade or protection to stimulate its commerce, manufactures, and its employment.

IV. LONG, UNBROKEN, GOVERNMENTAL EXPERIENCE

Counting from the Conquest, the spirit of government and the political institutions of Britain have been formed significantly in the unbroken course of 900 years into a single political system. This unitary structure was early centralized but not rigidified. A habit of responsibility was enforced upon its rulers by powerful subjects and influenced by men of the Church and by the "openness" of its central councils, via Parliament, to public view, to discussion, and finally to universal consent and participation.

No Public Schizophrenia

That rule was often challenged as to the dynasty or the extent of its authority, and armed rebellion was raised against it. Yet the links of past and present have not been severed completely, least of all in one combined guillotine dismemberment of religious, social, economic, and political habits and institutions, such as that of the Bolshevik Revolution of November 7, 1917, in Russia or in the subversion and transformation of France in 1789 or in the tragic disunity and "particularism"

of the Germanic states over the centuries, leading to the "blood and iron" federalism of a Bismarck and the lunatic *Volk* unity and expansionist bloodlust of a Hitler (p. 573 and p. 653).

The Civil War in England, from 1640 to the execution of Charles I in January 1649, and the subsequent Commonwealth and Restoration, followed by the public tensions leading to the Bloodless Revolution of 1688, the revolution settlement, and the reign of William of Orange, were neither bloodless nor without important changes in the philosophy of government, the liberalizing of the constitution, religious conflict and readjustment, and struggles of economic interest. But even this democratic ordeal was not provoked and suffered in the name of a radical and sudden departure in ideas about the basis of authority or for Utopia. Precedents and alleged precedents regarding the distribution of authority between King and Parliament were its basis. Appeal was always made by all parties to the legal continuity and validity of the charters and statutes from Magna Carta (p. 38).

It is true that some extreme thinkers and politicians, such as the clergy of Oxford and Cambridge, developed the principle of Divine Right on the one side, while the Puritans and various groups, such as the Levellers and Diggers, and men in the Cromwellian army set forth strong doctrines of equality, economic and political and popular sovereignty, and the independence of the churches. But the broad mass of the combatants and the nation were involved, in the main, in some practical answer to the practical questions raised in the Petition of Right of 1628 (see p. 40).

A parliamentary general called the Civil War "this war without an enemy." When the armies were English and Protestant the war was fought with humanity. The conflict cut through (not between) families, geographical territory, and social classes. Not that the social- and economic-class motive force was not present, for two thirds of the peers served the King, and some squires defended their lands as well as their parish church as established by the Act of Uniformity of 1559. But, again, almost *half the country gentry sided with Parliament,* and they were the political leaders of the time. They fought on the same side as some of the most pre-eminent and renowned of the peerage. On this side also, however, as has been suggested already, were democratically inspired Londoners (wealthy traders as well as apprentices) and smaller landowners and tenant farmers.

This was not massacre as was the Peasants' War of the central and south German princes against the peasants in 1522 (p. 529). It was not the shockingly ferocious war of minds and the decimation of the Thirty Years' War in Germany. Nor was it the French Revolution's hatred of the past and its possessors, or the unleashing of a Red Terror that was avenged by the White Terror of 1815, to be re-enacted in milder acts of force several times in the nineteenth century. The continuity and responsibility for an estate that could be improved but was not to be alienated, even though a little impaired, remained intact and was strengthened.

The British, in short, have never for centuries suffered the shock of the abrupt imposition of an altogether new set of social, economic, religious, and political principles. The past was not destroyed, nor was its long duration as a compeller of reverence and subordination in each individual.

Confidence and Compromise

The prevailing habit of mind is that there is no kind of political problem or conflict that ought to be approached in a mood of intransigence. If the majority of the claimants take this view, then a presumption of reciprocal appeasement and disposition to compromise peacefully prevails.

Furthermore, it is manifest to the close observer that the British exhibit an unwillingness to penetrate too deeply into the issues of principle, to go back to metaphysical absolutes in human values and will. Some theoretical reasons for this disposition are discussed later, especially Edmund Burke's political science (p. 35). For one thing, it is widely doubted whether anyone's unassisted ratiocination today can begin to match all the lessons of the long and legible, if puzzling, past.

The longevity of British governmental tradition, and the fact that substantial reforms have been made by the rulers (King or Parliament) by peaceful settlement, have precipitated the political lesson of what the Fabian Socialist Sidney Webb

called "the inevitability of gradualness." Now, it is true that many English people passionately hate gradualness, but they are in a decided minority and operate by pressing the "less sensitive" to a progress faster than "inevitable gradualness" would produce. The belief is that the principle of majority rule—since the Reform Act of 1832 (see p. 67)—will triumph, even if its force has to be exerted not at one election but at two or three, that the possessors of advantage in the *status quo* will yield peacefully, that they will not change the rules when they have to concede the game. There have been some who have distrusted this belief and so sought to teach the British the Marxist path. They were wrong.

The Parliamentary Method

What is of special influence in this tradition of reasonable transaction is the tremendously long habit of submission to procedures of a parliamentary kind. Since 1300, to take a round number, whoever was interested could participate intellectually in the proceedings of Parliament. Many thousands could share either actively as electors or as close spectators, giving political orders and hearing later how far they were carried out. It is true that even in 1832, just before the Reform Act was passed, there were only 400,000 parliamentary electors, and that these were unfairly grouped (see p. 66), and that many constituencies were not affected by the clash and life of election campaigns. Yet 400,000 in a population of 20,000,000 is no mean electorate. The country and the Commons were tied together; men went and came to it with local "instructions." They returned home to answer for what had been done. Here was a tradition—rich, interesting, vital to each one's fate—of Parliament: how to proceed by reasoning, by persuasion, by procedure, the limits to which one could go and the margins at which one must recede.

But, it might be asked, how is this lesson in comportment, in reciprocity, in decorous consideration for the weight of the evidence, transmitted to the present, even if it existed in the historic past? Simply, but not without effort. No generation entirely leaves the world without having taught the lesson it has learned to the young.

No new generation abruptly arises, or can possibly rise, to adulthood without being indelibly impressed by the practices of its elders, its family and its public men, and its formal education while it is still plastic and not yet in a position to understand complete and rival alternatives. As we suggested above, the British system of education places special weight on the formation of character, not to the neglect, however, of facts. It seeks the character of a "gentleman," and "individual," a "person," and a "decent" democratic citizen. The history of the British national culture and of its political struggles and creativeness—of the "Mother of Parliaments" [13]—reveals (and can be deliberately made to do so without strain) the picturesque crises of this evolution. Many of the classic figures of English literature were directly or closely involved or interested in political life: Chaucer, Spenser, Wycliff, Sir Thomas More, Milton, Clarendon, John Locke, Dryden, Addison, Defoe, Swift, Adam Smith, Hume, Burke, Shelley, Coleridge, Byron, Shaw, Wells.

The meaning of the actions and thoughts of the British past comes down to the British boys and girls, for every political party keeps it alive, even the most radical; but this excludes the Communists, who are neither a party nor radical.

The *example* of political dedication and honor is the supreme teacher.

V. PRIMOGENITURE AND THE FAMILY AND TRUST

The Norman Conquest established the principle of primogeniture, in order that the eldest son should undividedly bear the feudal duties of an undivided estate and fief. There must then be no mistake by the law as to responsibility. The consequence was that the younger sons of the family sank to the level of the general body of commoners. No blue-blood class, no *"sangre azul,"* severed from the rest of the nation the aristocracy that for centuries shared political power with the Crown. The Crown was the fountain of honor (see p. 184) and could ennoble commoners for service or favor and make them feudatories. The peerage

[13] This means the Mother of Parliaments in the Commonwealth and in foreign lands.

was a comparatively small group; some families died out, the House of Lords consists of quite modern creations of peerages (p. 192).

The number of "gentry," the next in the social scale, was very large in comparison and this, too, was open at the base for the rise of successful men. Social mobility was thus made possible and this has been conducive to social homogeneity. It has already been suggested that when Marx was attacking "class" he was incensed against the hereditary *Adel,* the nobles in the Germanic states. The French *noblesse* would equally have assisted his case, except that the latter were dealt a hard blow by the Revolution.

Primogeniture contributed toward two other sociological facts of importance in the conduct of government. The knights attended Parliament from the earliest meetings not as members of a noble class—this was reserved to the great magnates in the House of Lords—but as representatives of their communities as a unit as well as the commoners of their shires, and they sat, not in the Lords, but in the Commons, together with the men who represented the boroughs. The clergy were soon disqualified from seats in the Commons and were "represented" by the Spiritual Lords in the House of Lords. Thus only two Houses contained the "classes" of Britain, not three that ruined France (p. 281) or Germany (p. 562). No political barrier prevented the members of the House of Commons from mingling as commoners and, ultimately, from becoming the single mirror of the nation.

The Family

Different nations exhibit marked diversities in the internal loyalty and moral unitary strength of the family. This has a notable effect on the spirit and institutions of government, not yet given nearly enough scientific attention. F. C. Northrop has observed in his *Taming of the Nations* that the family in India (as well as some other places) is so deeply and instinctively a moral unit that the processes of law and order and government are obstructed by the conviction that it is right in "public" affairs to make exceptions in favor of the family at the cost of perverting policy and law. He has contrasted this with the Stoic-universalism of Western civilization that inspires the individual to submit himself to the rule of law that is as universal as the whole nation or even the whole world. The contrast is between the microcosmic family-favoritism and a cosmopolitan principle of accepted authority, even to the individual's pain, a submission to the rule of extensive law. The different consequences of these attitudes are of tremendous significance in the internal government of national communities and their international relations.

The English family is loosely bound, not emotionally merged. Parents are, as a general pattern compared with other countries, not oppressive to their members, not inhibitory, not patriarchally despotic. They do not demand an exclusive love or obedience or control. They are ready to see their children go to boarding school or be reared by nurses and governesses or be submitted to the authority of their public schoolteachers without their interference. English children, also, are not as filial as in some other countries; for example, France, Germany, or Russia (where the Mir, p. 738, was to blame). They are dissenters; they have learned to find their own way at school and in extracurricular educational and other activities independently of the wishes and guidance of their parents. Let it be remembered that the Boy Scout movement was invented and developed first in England. Both parents and children are *fondly detached* from each other. A very much longer urban, commercial, and industrial existence has marked England; the other lands, bound to the soil, were more bound to each other.

Now it is essential to emphasize the warning that these qualities are matters of degree and, even more, of degree that can be appreciated but not measured or concretely communicated to others. But the degree makes a serious difference to the policies of the French (p. 295), the Germans (p. 558), and the Russians (p. 738).

British family life, however, is not without affection and grace—but it is reasonable and silvery, not dark and hot. The example has in part been set by the younger sons who, having no inheritance, were forced to find a way of fortune for themselves. In France, on the other hand, the law of equal division reflected the sentiment of family solidarity and placed no great demands on individual enterprise to the extent observable in England. In the United States the family tie is very loose.

Trusteeship

Finally, in this sphere of ideas, we may draw attention to the exemplary influence of the law of trust. The reader has very probably already heard the phrases "the Empire in Trust," meaning that part of the British Empire that had no self-government but was dependent on the magnanimity of the British Government through the decent ministrations of its appointed officials. The word *trust* may be noted. He has probably also heard the phrase "Trusteeship Committee" of the United Nations, which designates the organ established by the Charter to take care that the nonself-governing countries shall be administered with charity by the ruling State. The idea of trust is suggested.

Now the English law of trust reaches back to the thirteenth century. It is part of private law, of equity. A person or persons, with little or no compensation, assumed responsibilities for the care of the property or, say, the education of minors at the request of another person, the trustor, for the benefit of the persons he names. The trustee obliges himself to undertake onerous obligations gratuitously. He cannot freely revoke his assumption of the obligation. He works for the benefit of another who has not the maturity or ability, by defect of age or other condition, to take care of himself. This law, and its multifarious practice over the centuries—nearly every adult is or knows a trustee—has permeated British public life. "Government is a trust."

John Locke's theory of political legitimacy was a more elaborated version of the principle of trusteeship (p. 32), connoting that there is a "public interest" beyond and above party or special interests that the statesman or lobbyist ought to respect when he has authority.

VI. FROM ARISTOCRACY—
NOBLESSE OBLIGE

The contemporary conduct of government in any nation is deeply under the influence of the historic succession of power and responsibility to it. The political morals of its predecessors, the ethics of its ancestors, who made the bequest or from whom it was wrested, go far to determine present-day morals.

In Britain the power to rule and the responsibility to govern descended to the present millions from royalty and aristocracy. It was not suddenly created for the first time as (almost) by Americans in the virgin wilderness or from an ancient system struck down, as in France or Russia, or mid-wived as in the passage from monarchy to democracy in 1919. In the nineteenth century there was transferred, *gradually* in time and in the step-by-step inclusion of more and more of the "lower" classes, the responsibilities that had been seized from the Crown and his adherents by the great Whig and Tory families in the Civil War of the seventeenth century. Tennyson said (in the middle of the nineteenth century):

A land of settled government,
A land of just and old renown,
Where Freedom slowly broadens down
From precedent to precedent.

But these great families, again, were not newcomers to the political arena. Their political ancestors crowded around the King at Runnymede in 1215 to enforce his signature of Magna Carta, which attested to a rule of obligation, of submission of sovereign power to decent limits. They created Parliament and the law courts. Their descendants, and new men (commoners or peers), through various assertions and revolts developed the rule of law. They were Christianized early, and the Church, after (as before) the Reformation, gave councilors and admonishers to Kings and lords at the highest levels of policy. The churchmen who wrote books and pamphlets and preached asserted the rights of the Crown but demanded equally that rulership be subject to Christian principle. But the Church could not, as in France until 1789, get a stranglehold on government, nor did it, as in Germany, weaken government by alliance with the Papacy or succumb to the State as in Lutheran Germany.

Education in public virtue—as well as in private virtue, of course—began in the hostels, schools, of the Church or in the private homes of the nobility and gentry, where the teachers were lay or ecclesiastical clergy—clerks—taught in the former. Oxford and Cambridge universities developed from the twelfth and thirteenth centuries, respectively, as the central seminaries of scholars and clerks (taking sides on "the divine right of Kings" controversies). It was there that students, poor scholars with conspicuous ability as well as the rich who were prepared for the Church's offices, were taught the code of the Christian "gentleman" to be applied in the public service for the benefit of the commonwealth.[14] From there, by the middle of the fourteenth century, radiated the light of learning and of piety to the hundreds of grammar schools, established by Church, guilds, merchant endowments, and the Crown. Chaucer's version of the virtues of a knight supplied the ideal.

At the end of the fourteenth century, Winchester School was founded by William of Wykeham to be a model of such "secondary" education (p. 21). More such schools were founded in the next centuries. Here were taught the gentry, the squires, and the yeomen (the rural freeholders) and the burghers, not infrequently joined by the upper gentry and even the sons of the nobility. G. M. Trevelyan has gone so far as to declare that the grammar schools were not, as used to be thought, the result of the English Reformation but were its cause! At any rate, by the sixteenth century the schools were to some degree blenders of the social classes, and to hunting, dancing, music, and high-spirited fun were added much book learning—and, for a motive—the proper exercise of public office.

The sons of the nobility and the gentry, from the sixteenth century on, attended such schools, or those like Winchester and Eton, and the universities and law schools (the Inns of Court) as part of a deliberately accepted curriculum of cultivation for the public service—in Parliament, as soldiers, as courtiers, or as the governing class in the counties. Indeed, a sense prevailed that this was not so much to strengthen the King as to make better the whole commonwealth. (John Locke attended Westminster School, provided in

[14] *Cf.* Fritz Caspari, *Humanism and the Social Order in Tudor England*, Chicago, 1954.

the seventeenth century for the lesser gentry, as had his father.)

Books were written or translated to form the mind of these classes, especially to transplant in an adapted form the ideal of Renaissance humanity, of the Renaissance gentleman. Plato's *Republic* and Plato's *Symposium* were studied. Castiglione's *Il Cortigiano* was put into English. In 1531 Sir Thomas Elyot's *Book of the Governor* was published, in 1570 Roger Ascham's *The Schoolmaster*. Both, but the former in particular, as well as other works and ideas much current, were concerned with the fitting of the gentleman by birth to be a scholar-gentleman-governor. They set their minds on the service of the "public weal," the concept of obligation, that character, not mere birth, made the "gentleman." One writer, whose work was not published until long after, chiefly aimed at the discovery of "civility," the nature of "the very and true civil life," and proposed a special school or schools where the nobility should learn "the discipline of the common weal." All, together, tended to the ideal of the magnanimous man, the mixture of strength, courtesy, grace, and obligation.[15]

We must leap into the eighteenth century, when government was in the hands of a landed gentry and rich mercantile oligarchy. The best case made for them is Edmund Burke's. He commends the value of "a natural aristocracy" to the government of his country, which ought, he declares, to be *used* in spite of the appeal of the majority principle. He is inclined, since he is the protégé and secretary of Whig aristocracy, greatly to exaggerate their virtues—but they *had* public virtues.

A true natural aristocracy is not a separate interest in the state or separable from it. It is an essential integrant part of any large body rightly constituted. It is formed out of a class of legitimate presumptions, which, taken as generalities, must be admitted for actual truths. To be bred in a place of estimation; to see nothing low and sordid from one's infancy; to be taught to respect one's self; to be habituated to the cen-

sorial inspection of the public eye; to look early to public opinion; to stand upon such elevated grounds as to be enabled to take a large view of the widespread and infinitely diversified combinations of men and affairs in a large society; to have leisure to read, to reflect, to converse; to be enabled to draw the court and attention of the wise and learned, wherever they are to be found [such as Burke himself!—*Author's comment*]; to be habituated in armies to command and to obey; to be taught to despise danger in the pursuit of honor and duty; to be formed to the greatest degree of vigilance, foresight, and circumspection, in a state of things in which no fault is committed with impunity and the slightest mistakes draw on the most ruinous consequences; these are the circumstances of men that form what I should call a *natural* aristocracy, without which there is no nation. . . .

Men, qualified in the manner I have just described, form in Nature as she operates in the common modification of society, the leading, guiding and governing part. It is the soul to the body, without which the man does not exist. . . .

The reader will have noted a most important phrase: *"To be habituated to the censorial inspection of the public eye."* The government of England was in the hands of an oligarchy, only a small portion of which was ready to transfer the final authority in government to the people. But this oligarchy was one of "gentlemen": by their classic and Christian schooling, at home, at school, in the universities, and on the Grand Tour by their accompanying tutors. They had many faults, chief of which was absence of social reforming zeal and an egoistic complacency.

Yet—they were not spoliators of the public. They neither took taxation exemptions against the rest of society (as the French nobility did) nor were they in a league with monarchy to keep it absolute and exclusive (as in Prussia and other Germanic states and in Czarist Russia). They had established a parliamentary system before, and especially through, the Bill of Rights that subjected them to the "censorial inspection of the public eye." There were lively and genuine rivalries in which the House of Commons' electors

---

[15] *The Schoolmaster*. Roger Ascham (1515–1568) was educated in the home of a patron who became Speaker of the House of Commons. He became Professor of Greek at St. John's in 1540. He was tutor to Princess Elizabeth, secretary to an embassy, and Latin secretary to Queen Mary.

were arbiters about the comparative merits of measures and men. The oligarchy was forced to be respondent to principle based on the public good.

The strength of the point is, of course, comparative.

Noblesse Oblige in the Masses

This sense of governmental decorum was transmitted to and taken over by the middle class that was brought into government on the passage of the Reform Bill of 1832. But it had been proceeded by a great movement of spirit almost throughout the eighteenth century: the awakening of a burningly intense sense of Christian duty through the evangelical movement,[16] more especially through the rise of John Wesley. It was nourished in the tremendous debate that raged from 1765 to 1782 over the War of Independence in America, where the fight against the system of George III and the corruption of office was an English fight for independence as well as an American one. It was carried forward by the indigenous movement for the widening of the popular franchise, and even the advent of an idea of popular sovereignty was carried on the gale of democracy that swept through England from the French Revolution, with its austere rage for the Rights of Man. Tom Paine was an Englishman, though he was a leader of the American War of Independence.

The sense of integrity, the obligation of public service, the consciousness of the prestige of political activity of the aristocracy mingled with that already possessed by the hitherto excluded groups, especially the upper and middle bourgeoisie who were then fast developing the Industrial and Commercial Revolution of Britain in the new towns that sprang almost overnight out of rural townships and hamlets. What they learned in their chapels as to duty and God, the Great Taskmaster, and the abstinence, the sobriety, the honesty, the rationality, their businesses required of them was what they expected to be the unrelaxing rule of government, and they contributed their resolution

16 Consult G. M. Young, *Victorian England*, New York, 1954.

to government. They were Utilitarians (see p. 34) of various castes of mind. Their elemental virtue was probity and an approximation to the activating principle, "the greatest happiness of the greatest number."

In the nineteenth century the broader masses received the conception of *noblesse oblige*. It came through their chapels, through the adult-education classes (first the Mechanics' Institutes and later the Oxford and Cambridge settlement houses and the Workers Education Association classes), through the linking of the new and old political class with the leaders of the industrial workers in their resolute fight to widen the franchise, to alleviate the evils of industrialism, and to get the right to trade unions. The extension of the cheap mass press and free and compulsory schooling further disseminated and fortified in the nation the principles of probity, integrity, and trusteeship.

VII. THE CHARACTERISTIC POLITICAL THINKERS

Every nation has a distinguishable characteristic line of political philosophers, even—if the paradox may be pardoned—when, like Russia (p. 750), it has no such line at all. It is no use believing that John Locke for Britain, Hegel and Karl Marx for Germany, Rousseau for France, Dostoevski for Russia, Hamilton and Jefferson for the United States essentially mean the same thing or are not at all representative of their particular communities. An author, like any artist, is a crystal of the past and a seed of the future in his community. He expresses its character in its literature; he is molded by it; and he influences political decision. In Britain it happened that the leading political philosophers *were also men of political action,* as the *Dictionary of National Biography* relates.

Six men stand out as representative and influential minds. They are John Locke (1632–1704); David Hume (1711–1776), a Scot; Adam Smith (1723–1790), a Scot; Edmund Burke (1729–1797), an Irishman, his father a Protestant and his mother a Catholic, of Dublin; Jeremy Bentham (1748–1832); and John Stuart Mill (1806–1873).

Locke

John Locke's contribution, chiefly in his *Treatise on Civil Government* (1690), summed up the liberal revolution against the pretensions of the Stuarts to absolute power, royal authority, divine right, and arbitrary action for *reason of state* decided by the King alone at his discretion. His doctrine was founded on the basis that government is a Trust to which governors are deputed and that the Trustee or Deputy owes an accounting for the welfare of millions. This led back to the Social Contract validation of the use of sovereign power. Men were originally in a state of nature, equally endowed at birth with reason and rights: life, liberty, and property (the last meaning *all* interests created by men's labor). But is was necessary to set up an authority that should be the arbiter of controversies, with sufficient power to get the judgment carried out. Thus, for this limited purpose, an Original Compact was made between men and government—voluntary, limited, and terminable. The basis of institutions to give the purpose of the contract effect was majority rule, the majority binding the whole, because it would be infeasible to wait until unanimity was secured. This would then be implemented by short terms of the legislature (to be supreme) and frequent elections and just representation in equal districts equally represented. The separation of the legislative, the judicial, and the executive powers must be established "because it may be too great a temptation to human frailty, apt to grasp at power, for the same persons who have the power of making laws, to have also in their hands the power to execute them whereby they exempt themselves from obedience to the laws they make, and suit the law . . . to their own private advantage."

There is little metaphysics in Locke. His reasoning is cool; it *limits* government, is not totalitarian. He represented the Whig and then the Liberal line of descent in British political parties, but he also influenced the Labour Party. The Civil War of the seventeenth century found in him the final exponent of the parliamentary (and, later, electoral) sovereignty side of the great debate between conscience-responsible monarchy and government responsible to the people. His theories are at the foundation of all the British communities at home and overseas and were written, sometimes verbatim, into the Declaration of Independence in 1776 by that other British community now the United States.

Hume

David Hume's contribution, through his essays, his *Treatise on Human Understanding,* and his *History of England,* was to introduce a cool and skeptical temper into the understanding of British political institutions. He thought that even John Locke had too much metaphysics in postulating an Original Compact, for Hume showed that historically such had never been the basis of government, hence the theory was metaphysics—that is, imaginary. He saw something worth while in both British parties and warned against excessive panegyrics and defamations of faction, because they damaged good sense and civil liberty.

Government was instituted piecemeal over the centuries to secure what men regarded as Justice. But what was Justice? Nor a single spirit immanent in man, of which his institutions and theories were an embodiment (this was the Hegelian's Reason, p. 554). Justice was a pattern of expectations that men developed regarding each other over centuries of living together in interpersonal relationships. This deposited an interrelationship of rights and duties, especially regarding one's property and family rights. Justice, over vast eras of developing society, was a reciprocity in practical matters, all going back to *self-interest* and *reason* (not something supernatural, as with Hegel), "nothing but a general calm determination of the passions founded on some distant view or reflection." Government was created in this way for a "more strict execution of justice" to "remedy inconveniences." Not to set a Master Race on high, or to make Reason's march in the world more manifest. These, to Hume, would have been the heresies of Nietzsche and Hegel and Treitschke (p. 607).

He still regards the consent of the people as "the best and most sacred of any" of the just foundations of government. He lauds civil liberties, especially the freedom of the press. He notes that the balance of property actually determines the balance of political power. He is the British Voltaire, who is skeptical, not cynical; satiric, not mordant. He represents a marked theme in Liberal as well as Conservative thinking, rather the latter since he was a Tory historian, yet both are blended.

His observation on knavery in politics represents rather felicitously the British governmental habit of removing temptation by the establishment of sober laws:

> Political writers have established it as a maxim, that in contriving any system of government, and fixing the several checks and controls of the constitution, every man ought to be supposed a *knave,* and to have no other end, in all his actions, than private interest. By this interest we must govern him, and, by means of it, make him, notwithstanding his insatiable avarice and ambition, cooperate to the public good. Without this, say they, we shall in vain boast of the advantages of any constitution, and shall find, in the end, that we have no security for our liberties or possessions, except in the goodwill of our rulers; that is, we shall have no security at all. (Essay, *The Independency of Parliament*)

Let that be contrasted with the nihilistic rejection of all government by such writers as Tolstoy and Dostoevski (their novels were political philosophy) or the myths of race and the German tribal community that gave Hitler *irresponsible* rights to create or annihilate the German people.

Smith

Adam Smith's *Wealth of Nations* appeared in the same year as the Declaration of Independence and Jeremy Bentham's *Fragment on Government*. His importance in the evolution of British government lies in his doctrine of what functions a government should undertake. Since he reasons for *laissez faire*—to leave things alone—this would mean a rather small and simple structure of government. Like Hume, Adam Smith started from "self-love" or "self-interest" as the natural propensity of man and argued that, since this was man's nature, so ought it be. Like other English thinkers, he did not delve into the nature of the universe or of God or Providence (as Continental thinkers do) to explain the actions of man and government, even in his *Theory of the Moral Sentiments*. He was interested in the experimental view of human nature as it operated in the English mercantile system, the government's traditional regulation of manufactures and commerce by tariffs, bounties, and monopolies.

Men would be wealthier if left to their "natural liberty" according to the "natural order." Let man's self-love decide how much help he needed from his brethren. He should place no faith in their benevolence, but in mutual advantage. "Give me that which I want, and you shall have this which you want. . . . We address ourselves not to their humanity but to self-love, and never talk to them of our own necessities but of their advantages."

This is the typical English prosaic and mundane, temperate, transactional bargaining in the process of government. Let the consumer's interest be paramount. Give no class of producers any advantage by law, for merchants and master manufacturers had an interest to deceive and even oppress the public. Let producer and consumer freely bargain with each other, and the wealth of the whole nation would be increased as they tried to increase their own individual wealth.

> He [the individual] generally, indeed, neither intends to promote the public interest, nor knows he is promoting it. By preferring the support of domestic to that of foreign industry, he intends only his own security; and by directing that industry, in such manner as its produce may be of greatest value, he intends only his own gain, and he is in this led by an invisible hand to promote an end which was no part of his intention.

The theory assumes that men know what is good for them better than others may know it (a government, for example), and that by an open-market process of bargaining, each man's good is promotable only by giving profit to other men. "What is prudence in the conduct of every private family can scarce be folly in that of a great kingdom." This is, of course, a *non sequiter.* The whole doctrine depends on a belief in the harmony of human wants and talents. It believes that the energies of a people would surge up tremendously if government took away its heavy and stupid hands.

Smith is shrewd enough to see that there are

works that no one will risk undertaking, "public works," such as roads, bridges, navigable canals, harbors, etc., that self-interest will not find profitable enough. Government must undertake this for the common benefit. We may comment that society may change in such wise as to baffle the knowledge of the individual or of joint-stock companies and so allow them to damage others while seeking their own good. It may change also in that some works must be added to the partial list given by Adam Smith.

He proposes that the government shall provide education, even make it compulsory. First, the "labouring people" employed in simple and mechanical operations will otherwise become ignorant and stupid, incapable of judging the interests of their country and even private affairs. Second, it is necessary to make the "inferior ranks of people" less liable to "the delusions of enthusiasm and superstition." (The German nationalist and *Volk* theories and Hitler above all [p. 552] looked to education precisely to *provide* those delusions.) Property required the establishment of civil government, subordination, and institutions of justice.

Adam Smith wrote when England was an agricultural-village economy. He ignored the effect of hereditary class inequalities. His standard of *laissez faire* was adopted by the Whigs and Liberals and the Radicals. Within fifty years industrial, commercial, and population changes required its substantial governmental modification. In the twentieth century it remained an important part of the Conservative doctrine of free enterprise against the Labour Party's principles of state intervention. It always raised the question of whether the wealth of a nation is to be regarded as the sum of the individuals' incomes freely produced or a recipe of the public good centrally conceived and then with economic activities planned accordingly. If the latter, it still did not mean that a mixed system was impossible or impractical or that it must be dictatorial.

Bentham

No jurist-political scientist of any time or any place has, singlehanded, even approached the practical, reformative influence that Jeremy Bentham had, not only on English government but all over the world. He was the governmental gadget inventor unparalleled, the inventor *in excelsis* in a nation of legislative and executive inventors. He was the chief originator of the Utilitarian doctrine that Happiness is the end and aim of the legislator, and that it is the lawmakers' business to determine what is the good of the community and use the art to realize it. "Utility" could replace "Happiness" as being more precise for governmental use. Happiness, be it remarked, not Virtue as Nietzsche (and his like) preached (p. 608).

Thus Bentham introduced what he called "moral arithmetic" or the "felicific calculus." The statesman must add up all the pleasures on one side and the displeasures on the other and try to make a balance of them before knowing whether to act at all or how to act in the event the answer was positive.

> Nature has placed mankind under the governance of two sovereign masters, *Pain* and *Pleasure*. It is for them alone to point out what we ought to do, as well as to determine what we shall do. . . . The *principle of utility* recognises this subjection, and assumes it for the foundation of that system, the object of which is to rear the fabric of felicity by the hands of reason and of law.

When he uses the terms *just, unjust, moral, immoral, good, bad,* they are, he says, merely other terms for certain pains and pleasures. He avoided any deep psychology of the Freudian, Adlerian, or Jungian type—they had not been invented—and he avoided other probings of the human sentiments, and, also, the contributions of religious experience. He stayed on the surface of his pleasure and pain, though as his *Table of the Springs of Human Action* shows, he was a shrewd thinker and offered the statesman acute guides to calculating the felicific balance. The whole system is quantitative—Bentham uses the word *quantum*—and he hoped for the day when law and political science could be put and communicated precisely in mathematical symbols. He ignored the *quality* of satisfactions among different people; he did not think of mystical Germans or soul-torn Russians or impassioned Frenchmen, just prosaic English men and women. Nietzsche, the immoralist, detested him (p. 608).

In his *Constitutional Code,* in his *Official Aptitude Maximised, Expense Minimised,* and in *Theory of Morals and Legislation,* he invented principles and gadgets galore: professional police, career civil service, modernized decentralization, parliamentary procedure, rational colonial administration, the theory of punishment, a registry of vital statistics, a code of public health. His purpose was to make in the moral world those reformations that he saw had come with so much potency in the material world in his time through scientific discoveries and inventions.

At first his principle of utility seared away the medieval abuses that still cluttered English government and legal institutions. Hence he was, at first, even more *laissez faire* than Adam Smith. "Get out of my light!" was his injunction to the State in matters economic. But later in the nineteenth and still more in the twentieth century, the greatest happiness of the greatest number became not merely a disencumbering instrument but one making for the welfare state, with excellent administrative and control devices. Bentham was first the philosopher of the Liberal Party, and John Stuart Mill was his theoretical successor; but later his ideas and inventions assisted the Labour movement. Tories never found him useful.

Burke

Edmund Burke soars higher and plunges deeper in human nature in government than his predecessors. He writes with more passion and color, more philosophically. He almost equates the State with the whole of society. This has duration: the individual was made by society; he owes a debt to society and its future; hence his own claims cannot be accepted as unqualified rights. Indeed, there is something immortal and religious about society; it is not a matter of today's utility alone. Hence the individual has duties; and government must require these, as well as provide him with happiness. Religion consecrates the State, so that they who govern shall weigh the material advantage of the moment, in exercising their sacred trust, against permanent fame and glory and their hope of immortality. Above all does democracy—the masses—need qualification by a sense of trusteeship accountable to the one great Master. For who

can punish *them?* "A perfect democracy is therefore the most shameless thing on earth." They must not be allowed to think their *will* is the standard of right and wrong.

He warned against probing too deeply by reason into the sources of authority—for human nature raw was so dreadful to look on that it might cause the overturn of institutions, unless we remained tolerably content with our "prescriptive" —that is, our custom-grown—constitution. We need to reform; but we also need to revere, and not overturn and so lose continuity, stability, property, function, education, and honor.

He would not argue from "natural rights" but rather from the inheritance of our ancestors. For metaphysics was dangerous because it was *unquantitative,* and "the lines of morality are not like ideal lines of mathematics. . . . Political reason is a computing principle; adding, subtracting, multiplying, and dividing morally, and not metaphysically or mathematically, true moral dimensions."

The balance of power in English government exemplified this: a balance between King, Commons, and Lords, as had been established by the Glorious Revolution of 1689. Should it ever be reformed? Yes, for a constitution without the means of improvement was one without the means of preservation. But slowly and reverently ("as tending the wounds of a father"). Why?

> It is one of the excellencies of a method in which time is amongst the assistants, that its operation is slow and in some cases almost imperceptible. If circumspection and caution are a part of wisdom, when we work only upon inanimate matter, surely they become a part of duty too, when the subject of our demolition and construction is not brick and timber, but sentient beings, by the sudden alteration of whose state, condition, and habits, multitudes may be rendered miserable. . . . The true lawgiver ought to have a heart full of sensibilities. He ought to love and respect his kind, and fear himself.

Why? Because the knowledge and reason of a part of one generation is insufficient—it must be, given our individual brains and limited imaginations—to comprehend society in all its aspects.

"The species is wise"; the individual is foolish; the multitude without deliberation is foolish. This is the parent of truth!

Hence Burke held that the legislature need not be completely and directly representative of the people; the national interest could be fulfilled with less. All agencies of government are trustees for the people—but the statesman must exhibit a judgment over and above that obtained from the expressed instructions of the electors. They may have the last word; but the representative's judgment must be obstinately obtruded and exerted for the *whole* country, above interests, passions, prejudices, and cabals. He believed in party government, because party made principle and disciplined the irresponsible (like George III and his Ministers) thereby.

He promoted justice, freedom, truth, tolerance, moderation, equity, mercy, family, property, peace, religious freedom, limits to power, the inequalities that derive from talent, hatred of cruelty. He venerated the Crown and religion, and both human and governmental dignity. He detested metaphysical systems, such as those then being erected by the followers of Rousseau in the French Revolution, and correctly predicted the disastrous results to social consensus (p. 291 and p. 295).

Almost every Englishman has a large dose of Burke in his political composition. He gave Whig principles—that is, principles of moderate liberalism—to the Whigs and in his later years provided the body of theory that informed the Tory Party of the nineteenth and twentieth centuries. It is not without its welfare aspect, embodied in the duty of a trustee to his trust. Burke was the great vindicator of the rights of the American colonies, not because of natural-rights doctrines but because Americans were entitled to the rights of British citizens even as were those who happened to reside in England.

The peculiar bent of Burke, which distinguishes his bequest to the English people from that of Locke, Hume, Adam Smith, Bentham, and Mill, is his appreciation of the corporate nature of the national community. It almost makes him say that the State and society are one and the same thing, in tremendous contrast to these men. The passage is of the utmost importance, since its wild exaggeration by German tribal thinkers wrought horrors in that country, and the development of State activity since Burke's time has much emphasized such truth as it expresses.

Society is indeed a contract. Subordinate contracts for objects of mere occasional interest may be dissolved at pleasure—but the state ought not to be considered as nothing better than a partnership agreement in a trade of pepper and coffee, calico or tobacco, or some other such low concern, to be taken up for a little temporary interest, and to be dissolved by the fancy of the parties. It is to be looked on with other reverence; because it is not a partnership in things subservient only to the gross animal existence of a temporary and perishable nature. It is a partnership in all science; a partnership in all art; a partnership in every virtue, and in all perfection. As the ends of such a partnership cannot be obtained in many generations, it becomes a partnership not only between those who are living, but between those who are living, those who are dead and those who are to be born. Each contract as each particular state [Note transition from *society* to *state. Author's comment*] is but a clause in the great primeval contract of eternal society, linking the lower with the higher natures, connecting the visible with the invisible world, according to a fixed compact sanctioned by the individual oath which holds all physical and moral natures, each in their appointed place. This law is not subject to the will of those, who by an obligation above them, and infinitely superior, are bound to submit their will to that law.

This spirit, incidentally, explains the spiritual significance of the British monarchy (p. 177). It contradicts the Rousseau-ite atomization of the State, the too-logical ruin of France. The Germans exaggerated the nationalism, and societalism, of Burke, and distorted his view of trusteeship into authoritarian rulership.

Mill

John Stuart Mill was the son of James Mill, a close friend of Bentham, and he himself edited a newspaper founded by Bentham to propagate his circle's idea of good government. He is the John Locke of the nineteenth and twentieth centuries. He was a Benthamite Utilitarian, but with the reservations that some account must be taken of the *quality* of pleasures and pains and that a more complex and subtle view of human motivation must replace that of mere self-interest.

In his *System of Logic,* he developed a logic of the social sciences. He demonstrated that it is not a science of positive prediction but only proximately so. For use in actual government, these predictions, founded on hypothesis, research, verification, still needed great caution and adaptation. He was a *laissez-faire* economist but supported trade-union bargaining, consumers' cooperatives, copartnerships. He championed the rights of women. His *Liberty* is one of the noblest and most persuasive of nineteenth-century arguments for trust in the discovery and revivification of truth by open and unlimited argument. For this would produce the most fruitful and beneficial variety of talents for mankind's delight. "Self-regarding" activities should be left untouched by the State; it would regulate only "other-regarding" actions. Bentham had made a similar (not by any means identical) differentiation between the Non-agenda and Agenda of the State.

In *Representative Government,* Mill made it clear that democratic government would work only where people were not cowards, had public spirit, and could not be deluded from its operation or defense by cheats, by panic, or by enthusiastic surrender of their liberties to a spellbinder. He tried to discover some standard by which to give the "wiser" extra votes—but unsuccessfully. (Who could succeed?) He was a pioneer of proportional representation in order to do justice to minorities. He opposed the secret ballot on the ground that the vote was a trust that could be misused if cast by the voter in secret—where he might cherish the same feelings on a humbler scale as a despot and oppressor.

He was *the* philosopher of the Liberal Party in the second half of the nineteenth century. He influenced the Labour Party to be liberal in its pursuit of social justice. His aspirations for a better future for the working class, through education and the institutions we have named, were ingredients also of the Labour movement.

British Political Philosophy Is "Flat"

The philosophies we have so briefly reviewed are not total metaphysical systems. They take men much as they find them. They are mundane. They are replete with common sense. The "felicific calculus" is uppermost, and it does not rise to God or Providence or Reason or delve into the Unconscious. It is not concerned to prove the need of a Super-Man. It says "Live and let live." For this reason it was detested by German political philosophers (p. 608) and despised by deep-thinking Russians. Yet the British have freedom and decency in their lives, and they are self-governing.

VIII. BRITAIN'S LIBERAL GOVERNMENT

Modern British political thought, then, took its rise in the seventeenth century (and Hobbes and Hooker could have been adduced with the others). It took its rise when British commerce and overseas enterprise (with the sight of plural cultures abroad) had impressed the public mind with a spirit of pragmatism and what may be called transactionalism. Religious dissent blended with this sometimes independently, sometimes as cause-and-effect. But this also was the age of the rise of natural science, when, in such bodies as the Royal Society (chartered 1662), experimental science and conscious invention based on its findings entered to challenge the reign of Greek myths and the Bible's and the Catholic Church's revelation and absolutism of ethics based thereon and on miracles and a nonscientific view of the universe. This entrance of experimental doubt and demonstrated partial verities in the material world assisted the development of the idea of searching for truth through doubt and argument in place of conviction of truth handed down by religious and royal authority. It led to democracy as the way of life of those who believed that the only demonstrable Truth is that there is no objective demonstration of Truth, and that all, therefore, had better be tolerant to hear and compete by votes for its proximate and reversible statement by free voting.

A Line Of Above-average Men

In the development of British liberal government there are few geniuses ("charismatic", see p. 559) of the order of Napoleon, Bismarck or Hitler, Lenin or Stalin. There was, of course, Cromwell, who fought for liberty; all the rest are men of subgenius but of very high talent, active, and steadily brave with civic courage. The barons of Magna Carta, Langton, deMontfort, Wolsey, Henry VIII and Elizabeth, their House of Commons men, Sir Thomas More, the Speakers of the House of Commons since the fourteenth century—Darnell, Eliot, Sir Edward Coke, Pym, Hampden, Cromwell, Walpole, Pitt, Charles James Fox and so on, down through our time to Gladstone, Disraeli, Asquith, Lloyd George, and Sir Winston Churchill—were men of courage, not dictators, actively able in parliamentary government and the skills of cooperation, and men who believed that men could and ought to govern themselves. They were very different from the forebears of the states of modern France, Germany, and the U.S.S.R.

A Constitutional Chronology

William the Conqueror introduced a firm central authority, blessed by the Pope, crowned by the Archbishop of York on Christmas Day 1066, and elected by the Witan. Here were consecration and symbols. He ruled by the feudal obligation of his tenants, which included the officers of the Church. Vassals, as well as magnates, took oaths of allegiance to him.

The magnates were restive and self-confident. They, the barons, forced rights of cooperation in government from the successive Kings by guile, ability, and civil war. The King challenged them with his system of law courts sent on circuit and organized through his developing Great Council, the *Magnum Consilium*. They made periodical inquests into the way the royal sheriffs exercised their local government, and at the center evolved a system of administration with the Exchequer, the Justiciar, and then the Chancellor, as the pivot.

Magna Carta. In 1215 the vicious and bloodstained King John was constrained to grant Magna Carta, when barons and people (which meant the cities that had bought charters of self-government) united against his treachery and avarice. They were led by the Archbishop of Canterbury. It is interesting to notice the continuous influence of the Church on English political destinies; the clergy were the technically competent men as well as the spiritual force.

The essentials of the Charter were the restriction of the authority of the Crown to raise money; the requirement that there should be a common council of the tenants in chief and the principal clergy; the institution of "due process"—that is, no imprisonment or outlawry or exile or harassment or expropriation "unless by the lawful judgment of his peers, or by the law of the land." Some living intellect some day had to invent these devices and their phrasing; probably Archbishop Langton composed them. It will be noticed that the barons had hit on the device of yoking the royal power by their power over the grant of taxes. This was the device that finally won parliamentary supremacy after struggles, always resumed until the Bill of Rights of 1689, the lineal successor of the Charter and its many subsequent confirmations. For the Kings always tried to escape control. Though the rights were obtained by determined barons, they were rights that then accrued to the man in the cities and the fields. They were remembered as being not creations but, in some obscure way, restatements of law from time immemorial. It was the establishment of *lex* over *rex*. It even contained the stipulation that the barons were to elect twenty-five of their number to invigilate the fulfillment of its terms, with power to demand redress if the King or his Justiciar or other servants violated them. Failing peaceful correction, they could require their peers to make war on the King or exert other sanctions.

Until 1295 the master developments of the constitution lay in the evolution of the King's Council, the *Curia Regis,* inside the Great Council. The bigger one was composed of the bishops and abbots and more considerable tenants, as chosen by the King, the *major* barons. (These subsequently became the House of Lords.) Inside the bigger council, the *Curia* contained some of the members of the former plus the King's learned officers for treasury, military, household, and judicial purposes, continually evolving into separate functionaries in separate offices or courts, but with the King personally at the head of all. The nation was linked to this through the itinerant judges and the sheriffs, the King's local officers in the shires, later called counties (Chapter 13).

In the localities, the jury system was established

by the middle of the fourteenth century, and a legal profession developed to deal in open procedure. This latter profession became a strong supporter of the Rule of Law; it had both a spiritual and professional interest therein and was one of the great champions of justice and later of Parliament, in a substantial way not equaled in Continental government, where the judges and lawyers were subordinated to the Executive.

A Parliament, 1265–1295. By the middle of the thirteenth century "lawful and discreet knights" had been brought in by writ to meetings of the Great Council on several occasions. Such mixed meetings gained the name of *parliamentum generalissimum*. Money was the spur. It was even announced in another charter that there ought to be three meetings a year! The Kings continued to break their promises when they thought they had enough barons on their side. In 1265 a baronial champion, Simon de Montfort, having overthrown the King in war, called a Parliament. Writs went out not only to the lay and spiritual barons but also to two knights from each shire—and two burgesses from each city and borough. By 1295 the Parliament summoned included some 71 lords spiritual, 63 *major* barons (earls and barons), 39 members of the royal council and officials, 2 knights from each shire, 2 citizens from each city, 2 burgesses from each borough. The lesser baronage, unlike their counterparts on the Continent, were merged with the shire and town representatives. The purpose was "common council"; the incentive, the acknowledgment of rising political strength.

A two-chamber system developed, whereas the Continent had either three estates or even more than three (p. 281). By the middle of the fourteenth century the House of Lords contained only the major barons; the House of Commons, the shire and town representatives; while the mass of the lower clergy absented themselves. The Houses sat separately. Parliament began as a petitioner for local and individual rights, for specific bills of justice in local cases, and to vote taxation. It became a general deliberative assembly, and exactor of general laws touching the whole kingdom, and the controller of the Executive because it had the pursestrings. Through five centuries, by continual insistence on its dignity and authority, by displays of self-confidence and by brave individual and collective sacrifices of life and liberty, it opposed the arbitrary pretensions of the Crown. It developed and arrogated its custom, procedure, many privileges, and its officer, the Speaker, to demand and maintain them: freedom of speech, freedom from arrest, freedom from royal and ministerial intervention, power over money bills, frequency of sessions, the institution of *habeas corpus*.

It required the Revolution of 1640 to 1689, under Cromwell until 1660 (allowing the interval when his son governed), to establish parliamentary sovereignty. This was created not by the mere advent of a single revolutionist, a man, say, of the caliber of Luther or Frederick the Great or Robespierre or Bismarck or Lenin or Hitler, but by a steady succession of near-great men, of the style of Archbishop Langton, Simon de Montfort, leaders of the Commons, Sir Thomas More, Sir Edward Coke, Pym, Hampden, Cromwell, and such like, men of middle estate of the country and of the cities, supported by a few thousand men determined on self-government and the security of their possessions and the exercise of their religion, "which was death to hide." They united against the royal (Stuart) attempts to impose the Roman Catholic religion on England; they rose against the attempt to use the royal prerogative to establish customs duties, other taxes, and forced loans without parliamentary grant. They rebelled against the royal (Stuart) attempts to keep the judges subservient in the King's Bench to the royal will. They made war against the special courts, the Star Chamber, and the Ecclesiastical Commission, which were not the ordinary courts of the land and which used secret and perverted procedure to further the royal will, economic, despotic, and clerical, often by producing "self-incrimination." [17]

These ordinary men of the gentry and sub-gentry rejected in 1627 Charles I's plea, about 240 years later, almost identical with that put forward *successfully* by Bismarck to destroy Prussian and German parliamentarism (p. 572):

---

[17] The Parliament's protest against *this* is the parent of the phrase in U.S. Constitution, Amendment V.

If you should not do your duties in contributing what the state at this time needs, I must, in discharge of my conscience, use other means, which God hath put into my hands, to save that which the follies of particular men may otherwise hazard to lose.

They fought him, and exacted the Petition of Right under the leadership of Chief Justice Coke, who had been dismissed because he would not bend judgment to the King's will. This was Coke's plea. He urged a Petition of Right. The Lords amended the draft, saving the "sovereign power wherewith your Majesty is trusted." The Commons rejected this. "What is *sovereign* power?" a member asked. Somebody mentioned the French jurist Bodin's name (see p. 287). Pym, the parliamentary hero, claimed "All our petition is *for the laws of England.*" Coke added:

I know that prerogative is part of the law, but sovereign power is no parliamentary word. In my opinion it weakens Magna Carta, and all our statutes; and they are absolute, without any saving of sovereign power. Take heed what we yield unto: Magna Carta is such a fellow that he will have no sovereign. I wonder this sovereign was not in Magna Carta, or in confirmations of it. If we grant this, by implication we give a sovereign power above all these laws. Power, in law, is taken for a power with force; the sheriff shall take the power of the county; what it means here, God only knows. It is repugnant to our petition; that is a petition of right, grounded in acts of Parliament.

Prerogative is the ancient word for the supreme sovereign power of the Crown (or other institution) unregulated by statute or judicial limit. Such a power exists in all governments where the statutes have not filled every gap of political action, especially in case of assaults from within or without on the very existence of the State.

The Stuarts made even metaphysical demands for their full prerogative in an age when British gentry, yeomen, and trade apprentices were imbued with the new spirit of experimental science and when they had the self-confidence of Protestantism, and even the firmer form of Puritanism, and when they were wealthy men of affairs. The final long stage of war against the Crown's pre- tensions (*not* a class war) came when the Crown attempted to raise money for building ships (ostensibly) from men such as John Hampden who lived *inland*.

The Bill of Rights. The upshot of the long wars was the Bill of Rights of 1689, which a victorious and incomplete Parliament (the Tories, who were Jacobite, were absent) passed to establish an alien King, William of Orange; to exclude any but Protestants from the throne; to recapitulate the ancient liberties; to strip the King of any power of making, suspending, or dispensing with the laws; to outlaw special courts; to fortify parliamentary privileges; to have frequent Parliaments and free elections; to purify jury composition of despotic influence—and to return again to the secular insistence against a standing army in time of peace. For this last had been a fundamental of British liberty and parliamentary supremacy. The governments of Europe failed in the latter respect (e.g., p. 273); the British succeeded by taking up arms.

Thenceforward, the Royal Ministers came more and more under the controlling and disciplinary influence of the House of Commons. The Great Council and the Curia had narrowed down to the King's Privy Council, since Parliament supplanted the Great Council. Out of the Privy Council stemmed the Cabinet since 1660; with parliamentary supremacy, the latter developed toward dependence on party support. A Prime Ministership began to evolve under Sir Robert Walpole from 1721 to 1739 onward, at first suspected by Parliament as usurpation. The Kings began to stay away from the Cabinet meetings under George I (1714–1721). George III (1760–1820) himself directed the Government of Britain (save for periods of clear madness) but not as president of the official Ministry, rather through the "King's friends." After 1782 the movement toward a "Prime Minister" at the head of a Cabinet more firmly independent of the royal will was fast. In 1803 Pitt was able to explain the position in these terms:

. . . with regard to the absolute necessity there is in the conduct of the affairs of this country, that there should be an avowed and real minister, possessing the chief weight in council, and the principal place in the confidence of the king. In that respect there can be no rivalry or division of power. The power must rest in the person generally called the prime minister, and that minister ought, he thinks, to be the person at the head of the finances. He knows, to his own comfortable experience, that notwithstanding the abstract truth of that general proposition, it is no ways incompatible with the most cordial concert and mutual exchange of advice and intercourse amongst the different branches of executive departments; but still, if it should come unfortunately to such radical difference of opinion that no spirit of conciliation or concession can reconcile, the sentiments of the minister must be allowed and understood to prevail, leaving the other members of administration to act as they may conceive themselves conscientiously called upon to act under the circumstances.

The age of parliamentary reform completed the process of the transformation of the prerogative of the Crown into the privileges of the people. Introducing the mass electorate in an age when industrial and social reforms were compelling, the Whigs and the Tories, emergent in the struggle between Parliament and Charles II and James II, became broader parties of national policy, needing mass organization. They needed to gather together their supporters by organization. This produced firm dependence of the Ministers on the majority party in *the* House and the establishment of a *regular* Opposition, which politicians in the eighteenth century had been reluctant to accept as their duty, being afraid of "faction."

The eye of the people is the eye of God. From the last decades of the eighteenth century, it had hardly been possible for the House of Commons to prevent the reporting of parliamentary proceedings by surreptitious note-takers. Even Cardinal Wolsey had complained about this two centuries before! By 1840 privileged publication was established by Parliament; by 1868 newspapers were made immune from suit if faithful reports were printed by them; by 1857 division lists were published daily. In Sir Erskine May's words: "The people are taken into counsel by Parliament."

Conclusion

What is the upshot of these considerations? The British people never started government with an absolute and rational assertion of natural rights to sovereignty as happened in other countries. In the nineteenth and twentieth centuries they inherited a system of government that did not flatly assert any such rights. It was already an ancient combination of duty with rights. They have no official declaration so unlimited (for good or ill) as the declaration "that all men are created equal, that they are endowed by their Creator with certain unalienable Rights: that among these are Life, Liberty and the pursuit of Happiness . . . ," in spite of the fact that John Locke, from whom these phrases were borrowed, and Tom Paine who pushed them to the extremity of reason in *The Rights of Man,* were Englishmen. The code of fair play, honor, and philanthropy that inspires almost all participants in British government in varying degrees, admits of such "natural rights." But it proceeds with a feeling that matters are not so simple in a world of men. Remember Hume's "knaves"! It may seem paradoxical but, because of this very actual moderation about rights and democracy, British government is very democratic. Countries (such as France) that have proceeded *ab initio* from rights and revolution tend to destroy a sense of the wholeness of the national community.

Men are governable in one of two ways. They may build or have built into themselves a principle of self-control that teaches them not to make extravagant demands on other people. Then life can be orderly and graceful. Or, failing this, a written or an unwritten constitution may permit and even encourage them to discover what is right by extreme demands on each other, backed up by a subwar within the nation, in which violent, foul, and even vile tactics are employed to dominate opponents and seize the spoils of society. The British have, on the whole, chosen the former. To some, they therefore seem tame; but they come out to vote 80 percent.

The Unwritten Constitution

Time whereof the memory of man runneth not to the contrary.
—William Blackstone

Every state has a constitution: the system of fundamental political institutions having supreme authority in its territories.

The British constitution is (1) unwritten; (2) extremely flexible, compared with the rigidity of others; (3) not, as elsewhere, safeguarded by a special body, such as the law courts, but left to the free mercy of the legislature.

"File me a copy of the British constitution!" This is said to have been the command given by a U.S. Senator during the Senate Judiciary Committee's hearings in 1937 on the bill to reform the Supreme Court. The embarrassed witness (a professor) may well have remembered the oft-quoted saying of de Tocqueville, "The English constitution does not exist." The Senator and witness meant the same thing: a written constitution, briefly phrased in a document composed and established by a special constituent assembly, such as the Constitutional Convention of Philadelphia of 1787, and perhaps ratified by popular vote, as in France in 1946. But Britain does not possess the former and never experienced the latter, though she had her revolution. The consequences are that no special *amending* procedure is provided for, and no authority above Parliament can declare an act of government unconstitutional. American students feel queasy about this apparent falling of the bottom out of the State. But they intelligently ask: "If the authority of government is not limited by the courts, and the British do not have their rights safeguarded as we do, what alternative security have they?"

The Ingredients of the Unwritten Constitution

What passes for a constitution in Britain is the harmonized materials of:

    I. Statutes passed by Parliament
    II. The customs of Parliament
    III. Judicial decisions
    IV. The Conventions of the Constitution.
Some authorities add (V) Advisory opinions.

I. STATUTES PASSED BY PARLIAMENT

Scores of laws passed by Parliament grant authority, establish institutions, limit office. They would be designated "constitutional" in lands with a written constitution. Merely by way of sample illustration we classify some of these.

Concerning the Territorial Order:

    1707   Act of Union with Scotland
    1801   Union with Ireland
    1902   Commonwealth of Australia Act
    1922   Irish Free State Agreement
    1931   Statute of Westminster (declaring Parliament's authority in the Dominions)

Concerning the Crown, or the "Executive":

    1628   Petition of Right, stripping Crown of lawmaking powers and fiscal and administrative authority without parliamentary authorization
    1641–47   Various statutes and resolutions,

some unsigned by the Crown, taking away powers exercised by the Crown in the name of the ancient "prerogative"

1689 Bill of Rights: the accession of William of Orange, the status of Parliament, denial of lawmaking powers of the Crown, etc., fixing annual revenue of the Crown, a "civil list" in place of private personal revenues

1701 Act of Settlement: succession to the throne, religious affiliation of monarch

1937 Regency Act, stipulating who reigns during the minority of the royal heir; many similar acts over the centuries dealt also with royal absence abroad and incapacity

1937 Ministers of the Crown Act, classifying Cabinet and non-Cabinet Ministries; mentioning for first time in statutes the office of Prime Minister, and listing salaries for Ministers and Leader of the Opposition

Concerning Parliament:

1215 Magna Carta and over 30 confirmations and extensions thereof, limiting the power of the Crown, and impliedly or explicitly establishing that of the Commons and Lords. Charter vested controls in 25 barons

1689 Bill of Rights. Then the annual Army Act consciously made subject to annual renewal from 1689 to compel the Executive to call Parliament at least yearly to vote funds and authority for the conduct of the Army

1694 Triennial Act, making 3 years the maximum duration of Parliament

1716 Septennial Act, making maximum duration of Parliament 7 years

1911 ⎱ The Parliament Acts reducing the
1949 ⎰ powers of the House of Lords, and the former reducing the duration of Parliaments to 5 years

1949 Representation of the People Act, latest of a series starting in 1832, conferring the right to vote. (*Yet,* there is no statement that all men are equal, or that the vote follows from the sovereignty of the people.)

Concerning Civil Liberties:

Habeas Corpus Acts, 1679, 1816, 1862
British Nationality and Status of Aliens
Defense of the Realm Acts, since 1914
Libel Acts; Abolition of Slavery; Juries; Criminal Libel

Concerning the Judiciary:

1701 Act of Settlement, on the irremovability of judges; and 1873, 1875, etc., the Judicature Acts

The tedious parade has been deliberate. For (1) it is noticeable that the constitution-making process has taken over seven hundred years, counting only from Magna Carta. We could go back to the Conqueror and even to his claim of family relationship with the Anglo-Saxon Kings. A thousand years is the duration of the assembly that created the British constitution. (2) The inventions of institutions made in seven centuries of bitter conflict by the British have been heavily drawn on by the democratic constitutions of the world. There is *no universal specification* of what should be included in a written constitution. Some constitutions (see Appendixes) even include clauses on education, the economy, labor unions. For England, the Trades Disputes Acts of 1927 and 1946 might well be included insofar as they regulate the right to strike where it would coerce the Government, etc.

The principles of the British constitution must be digested from the mass of such statutes. Even so, statutes do not contain the *crucial* elements, the rules that make British government democratic and responsible. They do not tell who calls, adjourns, and dissolves Parliament; its scope of power; its supremacy; the responsibility of the Executive. This gap is filled by judicial precedents and the conventions.

Made in Battles. The vital statutes, such as Magna Carta and the laws and resolutions and remonstrances of the English Civil War culminating in the Bill of Rights, were not passed in normal times. Nor were the occasions that gave birth to the constitutions of Canada, South Africa, Ireland, and India normal. The Civil War legislation was enacted by war or approach to war, and, in 1689 especially, some members of Parliament were absent or expelled. When scholars assert that a change can be made in the constitution by the legislative procedure used for "ordinary" (even trivial) laws, we must ask, "Under what tensions?" For the forms may be "normal," but the forces, passions, and behavior beneath them may have been indeed volcanic. Nearly a thousand years of conflict made the constitution.

II. THE CUSTOMS OF PARLIAMENT

Sir Henry Maine said in the nineteenth century: "Liberty is secreted in the interstices of procedure." The meaning of the pregnant oracle is plain: men who want to keep their liberty must enforce practical safeguards on the procedure of those in authority. The procedure of Parliament is a mighty and illustrious fulfillment of this canon. It is designed to get business done; but it includes protection of the freedom of minorities to enforce their will by amendments to bills and criticism of the Executive. This procedure is of vital significance to citizens; and since Parliament's authority includes foreign policy and economic and military determination, to other nations.

The procedure of Parliament is hardly contained in any statute; it exists chiefly by custom. It is called *lex et consuetudo Parliamenti* (the law and custom of Parliament) or, to use the title of the ruling treatise by Sir Thomas Erskine May, "the law, privileges, proceedings and usage of Parliament." To characterize his material that author quotes the poet:

> The clear and written law,—the deep-trod foot-
> marks
> Of ancient custom.

We shall see what it consists of when we discuss Parliament (Chapter 5). Merely as a temporary illustration we may point to: stages in the enactment of bills; special rules for financial legislation; the status of the Speaker of the Commons; questions by members to Ministers; protection of the rights of the minority; the allocation of time for parliamentary business by Government *and* Opposition in joint counsel.

In some countries of written constitution, some of the rules on subjects mentioned above are stated in their constitution. We may again quote Sir Thomas May:

> This law of Parliament is admitted to be part of the unwritten law of the land, and as such is only to be collected, according to the words of Sir Edward Coke, "out of the rolls of Parliament and other records, and by precedents and continued experience"; to which it is added that "whatever matter arises concerning either house of Parliament, ought to be discussed and adjudged in that house to which it relates, and not elsewhere.[1]

III. JUDICIAL DECISIONS

A very long line of common-law cases decided in the superior courts have furnished another most important ingredient of the constitution, for from the decisions general rules of law have been deduced. Thus, a part of the constitution consists of special portions of the common law and sometimes of its criminal-law branch.

(1) Parliament Is Sovereign

The courts have acknowledged the sovereignty of Parliament. It was at least conceivable that the courts (as in America) would not accept the sovereignty of Parliament. When Sir Edward Coke in the seventeenth century assailed the pretensions of the Crown, he was prepared to set limits to Parliament's authority, at least on one occasion. In *Bonham's Case,* he asserted

> And it appears in our books, that in many cases, the common law will control Acts of Parliament, and sometimes adjudge them to be utterly void: for when an Act of Parliament is against common right and reason, or repugnant, or impossible to be performed, the common law will control it, and adjudge such Act to be void.[2]

It was through Civil War that Parliament triumphed not only over the Crown but over any claims by the judges. The courts accept their subordinacy in two respects.

(*a*) The courts interpret the statutes that come

[1] May, 13th ed., p. 73.
[2] *Bonham's Case* (1610), 8 Co. Dep. 118a.

before them, and do not attempt to invalidate them (and this applies to Executive action also) on the grounds that they are "unconstitutional." Parliament's words are law. The only trouble occurs where those words are unclear or leave gaps. Then the courts interpret. The further meaning of this must be discussed later (see pp. 55–56).

(*b*) The courts are bound to yield their own interpretation of the statutes, as well as any rules they themselves developed in the past in the absence of statute, as soon as Parliament writes a statute on that subject. For instance, the right to freedom of speech is deemed by the courts to be inherent in all persons and to be limited only by court decision and by statute. *This, broadly, holds good for the other civil liberties also.* Until a statute is passed (for example, making seditious talk a crime) the common law of the matter prevails. It holds good, also, for many other parts of the law that contribute to the law of the constitution; for example, bribery (a crime) and various frauds at elections (a crime) that were later superseded by the Corrupt and Illegal Practices Act. We have already shown that the writ of Habeas Corpus was created by the courts at their own discretion but later regulated by statute.

Yet there is still a judicial interpretation to follow once a statute has been made. In the event there is obscurity in the words, the judges are bound to interpret, and, in doing so, they use, where relevant, certain common-law and equity principles to fill in the lacunae.

Parliament, with its statutes, is on top, in the sense thus implied, and the courts acknowledge its supremacy.

(2) Judicial Control of Officials

The courts have created some of the most powerful remedies for the citizen against illegal acts by public officials, sometimes as principles, sometimes procedures. One of the outstanding principles is that corporations, including local government authorities, are liable for damage done by their officials, a master–servant relationship being imputed. Among the procedures are the "court orders," formerly known as "the prerogative writs." The orders issued by the courts prohibit

(*prohibition*) courts and officials from taking action or demand to know on what grounds actions are taken (*certiorari*) or command (*mandamus*) public officials to do their duty. Habeas Corpus has already been referred to (p. 4 and see p. 261). The Administrative Justice Act of 1938 simplified procedure by writ.

(3) Shaping of Liberties

Assuming that at the beginning all British liberties existed in unlimited form, the courts progressively fashioned their concrete shape by limitations or affirmations in each case. Thus, freedom of speech was sculptured and buttressed by the law of libel and slander, judicial definition of sedition, treason, blasphemy, etc.

(4) Limiting of the Prerogative

The original unbounded authority of the Crown was steadily limited by judicial decisions. They developed the meaning of *ultra vires,* where an official went beyond the authority of law. They defined the immunity of the Crown (or State) from suit for tort or breach of contract, signifying the liability of officials or government *per se* for breach of the laws. (Since 1947 this has been largely regulated by the Crown Proceedings Act.)

The courts began to make case law in the fourteenth century, when they were still a dependent offshoot of the King's Court, the Curia Regis, and of the various councils that specialized in judicial work. They claimed authority to state the law in the ages when parliamentary sessions were infrequent and short and so not effective in legislating. They extended their independent role as time went on. The Crown personally resisted this and often tried to coerce the courts to its bidding. But the judges stated the law as it was in the authoritative books. If nothing was there, they used "custom" or "good sense and equity," often inventing these. In the end Parliament assumed the responsibility for making law. In doing so, especially from the first quarter of the nineteenth century and with the constantly expanding volumes of detailed "statutory instruments" (rules and orders), it reduced the judiciary's law-originating function, which is not the judiciary's function.

IV. THE CONVENTIONS OF
THE CONSTITUTION

A French student might ask, knowing that his written constitution calls for the resignation of the Council of Ministers (the Cabinet) when it has lost the confidence of the National Assembly, "How long can a British Cabinet last?" A German student, knowing that the Weimar Constitution and the Bonn Constitution (*Appendix*) both declared that sovereignty lies in the people and is exercised through the *Bundestag* (the representative assembly), might ask, "What is the equivalent rule in the British system of government?" A Soviet student of law or government might ask, knowing that the Russian Communist Party is the maker and sustainer of the Supreme Soviet, "What part does the political party [but he would be too sophisticated and sarcastic to use the singular, as he is forced to do in Russia] play in creating, stimulating, and controlling Parliament and the Executive?"

The answers to such questions as these are not to be found in the three parts of the constitution so far dealt with. They are to be found in the *conventions* of the constitution.

Conventions are rules of political behavior not established in statutes, judicial decision, or parliamentary custom but created outside these, supplementing them, in order to achieve objects they have not yet embodied. These objects, in the British constitution, can be summed up thus: to make the Executive and the Legislature *responsible* to the will of the people. To add concreteness we could use the terms *Crown, Government,* or *Cabinet* in place of *Executive* and *Parliament,* meaning the House of Commons (especially) and the House of Lords, in place of *Legislature.*

The principal statute—the Bill of Rights of 1689—certainly raises high the status of Parliament: the Parliament made a King, and it settled the succession. The Bill strips the Crown of many rights it had claimed and had, in fact, exercised over a period of 700 years. Previous statutes had stated the power of Parliament to legislate, to appropriate money for government and allow the raising of taxes. But none positively enumerated the consequently remaining powers of the Crown, saying how they should be exercised, what duration of authority the Crown's servants should have, whether the King could exercise these powers according to his personal discretion or must work through otherwise-determined channels. And the judicially made law extends only to the actions of officials and not to the policy-making and administrative-directing authority of the Crown. In the general perspective of government, it is but piecemeal and limited.

The law, customs, and privileges of Parliament relate to the internal activity of the two Houses, though they also open up the Parliament to the public view and impose limits on its own disposition to arbitrary behavior. But the customs have been molded to admit the role of a "responsible" Government, to allow it its due place, as for example in the Standing Order that prohibits the supply of money except at the request of the Crown, which means the request of the Government.

A. V. Dicey's view is that the conventions contrive that the prerogatives of the Crown shall be converted into the privileges of the people. "Our modern code of constitutional morality secures, though in a roundabout way, what is called abroad the 'sovereignty of the people.'"[3]

The conventions of the constitution may be thus summarized:

1. Parliament is the sovereign authority.
2. H. M. Opposition has a rightful status, to be upheld as representative of the largest minority in the nation by parliamentary procedure and mores against the gagging of dissent or majority imposition of steamrollered legislation.
3. A Government outvoted in the House of Commons is normally bound to resign.
4. A Government that cannot carry the House with it on vital issues may dissolve the House and appeal to the electorate.
5. If the electorate returns a majority against the Government, it must resign. It could not stay in office and dissolve the incoming Parliament.
6. The Cabinet is *collectively* responsible to the

[3] *Law of the Constitution,* p. 431.

Parliament for general policy and the conduct of the administration of each department.

7. The majority party in the Commons has a right to have its leader called as Prime Minister and entrusted by the Crown with the formation of a Government.

8. The Prime Minister has a formal primacy of influence in his Government; on his resignation the Government is dissolved, and he advises the Crown who should be his successor.

9. Treaties are made by the Crown, which means the Government, and not by Parliament; but the latter ought not to make treaties that cannot, on submission to the Commons, obtain its approval.

10. Foreign policy, the declaration of war and peace are vested in the Crown—that is, the Government—but must be sustained by the Commons and certainly not conducted against the Commons' will.

11. There ought to be at least one session of Parliament a year.

Parliament Is Sovereign and Omnipotent

The various statutes do not add up to this, though they are both numerous and sweeping. Continual and even forcible assertion in the course of centuries was needed to produce this. The result might have been otherwise, for the British form of government might have taken the way of the American. A written constitution might have been established, and Parliament, like the U.S. Congress, might have been fabricated as a subordinate creature and agent, with limited functions.

For a short time, it seemed as though this might happen in Britain. In 1649 Oliver Cromwell, Lord Protector, anxious to re-establish stability of government after the bloodshed and turmoil of some ten years of civil war and still assailed by the constitutional uncertainty engendered by the execution of Charles I and the doubtful authority of Parliament, gathered a Council that wrote the *Instrument of Government*. This Instrument shared supreme legislative power between the Parliament and the Protector. It might

have listed the subjects of Parliament's authority, as the U.S. Constitution does. In any case, it did not survive Cromwell's death.

The Restoration in 1660 under Charles II brought back all the dispute between Parliament and the Crown regarding the division of sovereignty between them—who was to have the more or the less. The Bill of Rights seems to have settled this in favor of Parliament. But throughout the eighteenth century Parliament was mightily challenged by the Kings, according to their personal character and political occasion. There occurred the gradual removal of the Crown from the scene of political decision. Ministers assumed the conduct of policy and administration freed from the King's interference and upon their own responsibility. The franchise was extended, making possible the manipulation of elections by the King and his friends as practiced to nearly 1800. Thus the phrase "sovereignty and omnipotence of Parliament" was given political substance.

What used to be said of the Crown—that "the King can do no wrong"—and all those impossible actions that Bagehot attributed to the Crown, like shooting the Prime Minister and going unpunished, is true. What has been said by Blackstone, quoting the Frenchman De Lolme, that "Parliament can do everything but make a woman a man, and a man a woman"—to symbolize its absoluteness of authority—is also true. All is true—*except* that, in fact, there are limitations in practice to the authority of Parliament, limitations that are embodied in the authority of the electorate, mediated or not through the political parties. The sovereignty of Parliament is limited by the power of the people—but by no other instrument.

Yet—what is Parliament? It is not merely the House of Commons, though it is almost predominately the House of Commons. It is the House of Commons as influenced by the House of Lords. But there is another factor, the Crown. Where the sovereignty actually lies, then, depends on the political forces. Their crystallization in the conventions settles the balance of actual authority among these three partners, who are mentioned in the formula that appears at the head of each statute—the so-called enacting clause:

Be it enacted by the Queen's most excellent Majesty, by and with the advice and consent of the Lords Spiritual and Temporal, and Commons, in this present Parliament assembled, and by the authority of the same. . . .

The respective authority of each of these three powers is chiefly settled by the logic of universal franchise and the conception of democratic responsibility in accompanying conventions, which mainly regulate the "Cabinet system." These are listed and fully discussed in Chapter 7 and Chapter 8.

The Character of the Conventions

The conventions may be regarded from two aspects: (1) their authority and (2) their utility.

(1) **Authority of the Conventions.** John Stuart Mill, in *Representative Government,* 1865, called the conventions the "unwritten maxims of the constitution." He said that in the British system there were three "co-ordinate" members of the sovereignty (Crown, Lords, Commons), each of which, if it went to the limit of its powers, could stop the machinery of government. What prevents aggressive action?

> The unwritten maxims of the Constitution—in other words, the positive political morality of the country: and this positive political morality is what we must look to, if we would know in whom the really supreme power in the Constitution resides.

(The reader may compare this observation with the present author's on the use by Bismarck of guileful language in Prussia in 1862, p. 572, and the use by President Hindenberg of emergency powers that ruined the Weimar Republic, p. 663. There the political morality *was lacking!*)

Mill explains that the Crown could appoint any Minister it personally chose against the objections of Parliament, "But the constitutional morality of the country nullifies these powers. . . ." He then explains that such rules are effectual only and can continue to exist only "on condition of harmonizing with the actual distribution of real political strength. . . . Constitutional maxims are adhered to, and are practically operative, so long as they give predominance in the Constitution to that one of the powers which has the preponderance of

active powers out of doors. This, in England, is the popular power."

(Of Germany, at about this time, Ferdinand Lassalle, was saying that the basic constitution was the King, his army, its cannon, the great landowners, the bankers who provided credits, the big industrialists: "The factual relationships of power written down on a sheet of paper . . . and turned into law, violations of which are punished." Above all, he added, it was cannon, for these belonged to the "organised, mobilised, disciplined and always-on-the-spot force.")

Mill's exposition leads us toward a sound answer to the vexed but supremely important and much-debated problem, What is the *authority* of the conventions? Dicey's answer was that the sanction of a convention (its authority) arose from the fact that sooner or later a violator of a convention would find himself breaking the law. For example, there is a convention that Parliament shall be called annually; no statute stipulates this. But, if Parliament did not meet, the Army and Air Force Act, which is an *annual* act (Observe the cleverness of those in 1689 who so contrived the Army Act), would not be passed, and the Standing Army and Air Force would be illegal. Furthermore, the financial legislation would not be passed: certain expenditures and taxes would be illegal. Again, if the Government refused to resign when it lost its Commons' majority and could not win one from the electorate, the statutes would catch them up. The law courts would declare illegal the actions of any officials maintaining an army or trying to collect taxes or spend moneys without statutory sanction.

Yet the nemesis of illegality does not follow all the conventions, and it is not that nemesis that regulates the legality of governments. For the Government could ignore H. M. Opposition, instead of acknowledging its approximate equality of status with itself. Before 1931 the Mother Country could have made customs treaties with, say, France, binding the Dominions. The convention of *collective* responsibility *was* violated in 1931 (p. 152), and the Commons did nothing to punish the Liberal, Labour, and Conservative Ministers who had made an "agreement to differ" in a coalition Cabinet. Then, Mr. Baldwin had argued that circumstances alter conventions.

What is a convention? It is a rule of political behavior, first established to cope with a specific problem (for example, how to overcome the deadlock power of the Lords), a precedent, perhaps, of intelligent practice. It commends itself to the actual holders of power in the nation at the moment of its establishment by its answering of their problem. It continues its authority as legitimate practice insofar as it seems just and reasonable to succeeding holders of power when applied to evolving circumstances that require a fresh look at the use of the rule. To stand, its justice must pass the test of new time and circumstances.

Have such rules any stability? Yes: when people, after the conventions have been first formulated, can continue to think they are *right*. If a convention embodies a principle of right because it fits developing values and environmental problems, then such development is molded by conventions, some being inhibited as others are encouraged.

How reliable are these conventions as constitutional rules? As reliable as the sense of trust and sober responsibility felt by and expected of each other in the several thousands of active political persons in Britain, and the many more thousands who closely follow their behavior with exacting vigilance.

Where are we to turn for a record of these conventions, since their expression must be learned by those who succeed to a trusteeship of their use in everyday politics? (1) To the gist of the historic development, the events and speeches and documents amply on record. (2) To the statements, in advocacy of or defense of the conventions in parliamentary debate. (3) To the record of the use of such conventions in the speeches and memoranda of parliamentary leaders with immediate responsibility, the challenge of the Opposition party or parties and the King's or Queen's correspondence with leading Ministers and Opposition and learned advisers. (4) Much of (1), (2), and (3) get set down in the autobiographies and biographies of the persons involved, and (5) in the treatises of learned scholars, such as Blackstone, Austin, Dicey, May, Anson, Keith, Jennings, and D. L. Keir, who amass and collate the above-mentioned sources and analyze and draw systematizing inferences from the "cases," injecting usually something of a value-tinctured interpretation of where sovereign authority ought to lie.

How clear are the conventions? The conventions are as compelling in authority and unmistakable in their terms as the clauses of the written constitutions of France and Germany. They are as clear as those of the United States regarding the powers of Congress and the authority of the Chief Executive—perhaps more definite and lucid in their terms. They are far more open and true to fact than the Soviet Constitution of 1936 about the political authority of the Supreme Soviet and the Presidium (p. 801). The Central Committee of the Communist Party, barely mentioned in the Constitution, is sovereign *in fact*. In British government, the "unwritten" conventions make the constitution; in Soviet dictatorship the "conventions" of omnipotence of the Communist Party annul the written constitution of the state.

Why not in writing? The conventions of the British constitution might well have been set down in writing. Why were they not? The reader can predict what would happen if it were tried. Each unwritten rule would at once become the object of intricate exercises by ingenious cogitators who would imaginatively anticipate in precious and volatile detail all kinds of contingencies to which human nature in the politics of the future might give birth. They would fly from brevity and simplicity into the hundreds of tentacles of elaborate formulas, from flexibility to rigidity, from comparative freedom and creativeness to formalistic confinement.

(2) Utility of the Conventions. Something more is served: no written constitution, any more than the ordinary law, can express the fullness of life's meaning and demands, because the human imagination, even at its most talented, falls far short of reality. Furthermore, compromise among the parties making the constitution (tending to hide some of the obstinately dynamic factors involved) is imperative, and brevity is desirable. Hence, from the moment the constitution is written it is, in a sense, out of date, to some extent: it does not correspond to the fullness of the realities of living political power and social values. To make it work, *it must be immediately supplemented* by practices.

Then, time passing, new needs demand amendment of the constitution. Formal amendment is usually a laborious process—the U.S. Constitution conspicuously demonstrates this. It has as few as 4000 words, and has needed as many as 40,000 law cases to interpret them. Even this tremendous plastic operation of lifting its face has been insufficient. For example, the President has been developed by convention into a "general political leader" of the party that nominated him from the mere status of "Chief Executive." The party system and the congressional committee system, with almost unlimited investigatory functions, have been developed by conventions and not in the written part of the Constitution.

In converting a monarchical into a democratic constitution, and in passing from the seventeenth to the twentieth century, the British eschewed writing the new articles: they preferred to rely on the growth and inheritance of customs—that is, the conventions.

One example may be given, by a quotation from Lord Grey, who was arguing in the Lords in 1832 that the King *must* make a sufficient number of peers to give the Government a majority for the Great Reform Bill, passed by the House of Commons but rejected by the House of Lords. Notice his argument and the *implied* imputation of legitimate political authority to the people (omitting the question of how wide the franchise ought to be):

We were under the necessity of offering advice to create as many new peers as would carry the measure of Reform through this House unmutilated in any of its essential provisions, or resign our offices. Now I say that, under these circumstances, the advice to create new peers was required. The noble and learned Lord says that it was not constitutional; But I say that it was constitutional, and I can refer him to books of authority on that subject . . . if a majority of this House is to have the power, whenever they please, of opposing the declared and decided wishes both of the Crown and *the people,*

without any means of modifying that power, then this country is placed entirely under the influence of an uncontrollable *oligarchy.*[4]

He did not argue that it ought to be a democracy, excepting that he was advocating a fundamentally reformed franchise. But he denied legitimacy to an oligarchy. It *must* give way to the House of Commons, after all the agitation and support in the country for the Reform Bill.

On these grounds we tendered that advice to His Majesty which we were well justified, by the spirit and letter of the Constitution, in tendering; nay, more—which, under the circumstances, it was our imperative duty to tender, considering the consequences that were likely to result from the failure of the measure.

This truth was well expressed by the Conference of Dominions on the Operation of Dominion Legislation in 1929, which was seeking to modernize the relationship of the legislative authority of the British Parliament to that of the Parliaments of the various Dominions, a subject that was then the uncertain blend of statutes and conventions regarding the force and finality of such statutes.

The association of constitutional conventions with law has long been familiar in the history of the British Commonwealth. . . . It has provided a means of harmonising relations where a purely legal solution of practical problems was impossible, would have impaired free development or would have failed to catch the spirit which gives life to institutions. Such conventions take their place among the constitutional principles and doctrines which are in practice regarded as binding and sacred whatever the powers of Parliaments may in theory be.

V. ADVISORY OPINIONS

We are now in a favorable position to understand the significance of advisory opinions on constitutionality. The phrase merely means that experts are resorted to for analysis of the facts and systematic interpretation, because the constitution

[4] *House of Lords Debates,* May 17, 1832, p. 1004.

is a welter of ingredients all of which are complicated in their historic evolution. The present discussion, whether well or ill accomplished, has actually been engaged in such advisory function. We have already referred to the many eminent scholars, whose works are resorted to by students and politicians and the private secretaries of the sovereign when knotty problems arise. (An example is the problem of dissolution by a Prime Minister, as in 1931, who has no majority in the Commons, and no party has a majority either, p. 141 and p. 152.) The value of the treatises is their help to clarity of intellect—though our "oughts" may remain our own. Their authority depends on the sagacity and its blendability with the values of those who are under the stress of applying the constitution.

VI. THE GOVERNMENTAL VALUE OF THE BRITISH CONSTITUTION

How does the British constitution, as we have presented its character, fulfill the purposes for which constitutions are established and written?

Certainty

The promise of a constitution is *certainty* about rights and duties. Men and women cannot work, live, make plans, unless they have some peace of mind. Life is lived in the future. If they do not reduce to some principle their method of settling disputes about what is just and good and what is right and wrong and abide by it, they fall prey to anxiety and fear. The area of the political is the area of most of life—and the political is uncertain. One will seeks to dominate another and its values for many reasons, which vary over time. Law came into existence in large part to satisfy the need people have for reliance on each other.

A constitution is a special form of law: it seeks to be the law of laws—the law of legitimate authority itself! A constitution is necessary because it grants and distributes the right to make and execute the laws—and even establishes who is authorized to change these fundamental rules of authority.

It was to secure a certainty about the nature and location of this high authority—of sovereignty—

that the political thinkers and statesmen of the eighteenth century in America and France advocated written constitutions. Once they had burnt their bridges, they were forced to build something new on the razed sites.

This is true of the making of the U.S. Constitution of 1787: it was composed, voted, and ratified by the barest majorities. It has lived by interpretation—artificial respiration, as it were. Once, in the Civil War, four years of bloodshed became irresistible because some of the Constitution's problems at the foundation were not, and perhaps could not, be faced.

It is true of the French Constitutions from 1789 onward—all with aspirations to be *immutable*—but the fourteen succumbed, and during their currency suffered modification or made people suffer.

Difficulty of Writing Constitutions. Writing a constitution is far from an easy enterprise. It is extremely difficult to get, by persuasion, a substantial satisfied acceptance of a new constitution by a majority of the people sufficient in size to establish, once and forever, all the principles needed in a good governmental system and to reduce minority dissent to a degree that the feeling of lurking injustice is tolerable. The French Constitution of 1946 was not accepted by a majority of the electorate (p. 326). In Russia the Communist Party made a Constitution by systematic and ruthless murder of all opposed.

The possibility is that if France and the other countries that sought for written constitutions in the eighteenth century had been nations with a large body of statutes—like Magna Carta, the Petition of Right, the Bill of Rights, and so on—and, above all, with the kind of Parliament that the English had had about four hundred years, with its presumed authority (giving rise to what the history books therefore call a "presumptive" constitution), they would have had no need for the quest of a concisely written constitution.

Instead of producing a short concise document, the British produced hundreds of decisions in cases before the courts, hundreds of statutes and declarations in Parliament, scores of usages in Parliament, and several conventions regarding the Executive branch (and the Dominions). These for the most part are in much detail. They are written somewhere—either in the rolls of Parliament or in its proceedings or in the reports of the courts of record and the conventions in the documents of the Cabinet, the Crown, the learned experts, and in reported events.

As Burke said, the Englishman did not have the "natural rights of Man," but the *specific* rights of Englishmen. The United States starts with an epitome and inflates; Britain starts with detail and complexity and epitomizes. But—is not detail the essence?

No Englishman feels any more uneasy about his rights than a sophisticated American does. He knows the courts will take care of him; he knows his party will take care of him; he knows the House of Commons will be passionate for justice to him; he knows the Cabinet will not overstep what it can get the House of Commons to accept; he knows the Crown has acknowledged powers to see that a Cabinet does not abuse its powers of resignation and dissolution. The statutes are law, and no one can transgress them without challenge and punishment. The courts are there; they cannot be flouted: fines and jail will catch up with the culprit. The conventions are respected as are the statutes and judicial decisions. As a biographer of George V put it: "In Great Britain, the balance between the rights of the Sovereign and the rights of Ministers, rests upon congenial experience, acquired tradition, instinctive feeling, frequent personal contact and unreserved mutual confidence." [5]

At the base, and rooted in the mass of the people, are the political parties—the true contemporary repositories of the principle of responsible government, and these make and unmake Parliaments and Governments.

Does a written constitution give more certainty? Most emphatically they do not. The powers of the U.S. President, of Congress, the meaning of the Bill of Rights, have been and are subject to the most bitter disputes as to meaning. Hardly a word of the Constitution is indisputable as to interpretation; hardly one exists that has not been variously interpreted by individuals, parties, and the courts.

[5] Harold Nickolson, *George V,* London, 1953, p. 475.

Amendment

Written constitutions contain an amending article or clause. This imposes conditions of procedure making it more difficult to enact a change in the constitution than does a statute that does not change the constitution. Such amending clauses may be very *rigid;* some are less so. Constitutions, then, exhibit varying degrees of rigidity or flexibility according to whether it is easy or difficult to amend them in respect of the formal procedure. They are sometimes classified into rigid and flexible constitutions. The U.S. Constitution is an example of a rather rigid kind.

There is no amending clause in the British constitution, since a written constitution does not exist. The British is the most flexible constitution among free states. The Soviet Constitution may be said to be flexible from the standpoint of the Russian Communist Party, but it is rigid unto death for any citizen who should seriously, or even as a joke, propose an amendment whatever. It is usually said that the British constitution may be changed as easily as any other law by the same procedure as any statute is passed through Parliament. This is true.

It applies, however, only to the *formal* aspects of passing a law. The difference is in the attitude of people, parties, leaders, the Parliament as a whole, the Government as a distinct and responsible element, and the Crown. It could not be expected, given the background of the British people as we have sketched it, that they should be anything but cautious about those statutes, cases, customs, and conventions that embody what other nations have in their written constitutions. The British need certainty and deliberation as much as any other nation. Change could be secured the way it is in other constitutions. It may be secured in another way: by the assumption of an attitude of mind, sober, careful with a sense of trusteeship. This is the British way. But this requires a procedure. And, indeed, the practice of the constitution exhibits a more rigid attitude to "constitutional" laws than to ordinary statutes.

(1) Long Deliberation before Action. No reform in the "constitutional" field has occurred without a very thorough airing of the matter in public many years before it is actually attempted and, above all, without the seeking of a "mandate" in an election prior to the proposal. The best example is the reform of the House of Lords (see Chapter 10) in 1911.[6] This was preceded by two elections: one in January 1910 to assist the Government to secure a popular majority in its fight against the House of Lords, which had refused to pass its Budget; and one in December 1910 practically on the specific issue to "mend or end" the House of Lords. The election was bound up with the unwillingness of the Crown (George V) to promise the Prime Minister to swamp the House of Lords by the creation of new peers until there had been such an election. The important point was the submission of the main issue to the people *before action*. The Prime Minister, Mr. Asquith, had a substantial majority (with the Irish and the Labour members), and he need not have dissolved. But the issue was so important—that is, fundamental or organic—that he felt he must first obtain authority from the people.

Another instance is the dissolution of Parliament in 1923. Mr. Baldwin, the Prime Minister, was at the head of a large Conservative majority, following Mr. Bonar Law, who had died in office. At the previous election, 1922, the former Prime Minister had pledged himself not to undertake any "fundamental changes in the fiscal arrangements of the country"—meaning a change from free trade to protectionist tariffs—in the life of that Parliament. Mr. Baldwin decided there should be a consultation of the electorate, though many of his colleagues advised against it. Mr. Baldwin lost the election.

In 1949, when the Labour Party introduced the Parliament Act, which further curtailed the power of the House of Lords, the Conservative Opposition accused the Labour Government of not having put the issue squarely before the electorate in the election of 1945. It was certainly not put as the *one* outstanding issue. Yet this was no original frontal assault on the House of Lords: that had been successfully undertaken in 1910–1911. This was merely a reduction of an already reduced power.

(2) All-party Agreements. In "constitutional" mat-

6 *Ibid.,* p. 379.

ters, the Governments are ready to attempt an all-party settlement before making a change. This was the case with the House of Lords reform. This has been the case with the changes in the franchise since 1918—they have been preceded by an all-party conference under the chairmanship of the Speaker of the House of Commons, not only an impartial official of the House but one representative of the House as a whole, the House as representative of "the nation," one and indivisible. Similarly, with the Home Rule Bill of 1912 and the 1936 Joint Commission on Indian Government Reforms and the reform of the House of Lords in 1949 (Chapter 10).

(3) Conscientious Expert Inquiries. Generally speaking, all important legislation since 1832, whether concerned with the functions of government or with the institutions of authority, have been first thoroughly investigated and reported upon by Royal Commissions of Inquiry—whose membership is not parliamentary but usually non-parliamentary and even of nonpolitical experts. The attempt is made to clarify the groundwork of fact and interests and values before the final political element of decision backed up by numbers is called in.

In 1946 Standing Order No. 46 of the Rules of the House of Commons was amended to provide that bills of "constitutional importance" should be dealt with in Committee of the Whole, not by standing committees.

Care, then, is fundamental—not writing, nor a difficult amending process—in giving fundamentality to a constitution.

British politicians and people are as careful about "ordinary" as they are about "constitutional" enactments. This makes the unwritten more dependable, not less. The spirit of the people is the salt in a constitution. Men can be reckless with a written constitution—for example, in the United States abusing the significance of the "Fifth Amendment" protection against self-incrimination or using violent methods to get an amendment passed, as in Germany. Hitler destroyed the Weimar Constitution with that same constitution's provisions for amendment (p. 663)!

(4) Judicial Guarantees. No country so carefully guarantees the supremacy of the constitution as does the United States, and that through that unique institution in the constitutional systems of the whole world, the Supreme Court.

Nothing in the British system compares at all with the role of the U.S. Supreme Court. No British politician has to fear, nor need he hope, that if he gets a law passed it will be invalidated by the courts. The supremacy of Parliament is the utter, inescapable, the peremptory and condign responsibility of the political parties: the one means the other. For no one can take a grievance about a statute or an action by any official to the law courts on the grounds that it is unconstitutional.

Unconstitutionality is no ground for the entertainment of a suit. If a suit is entertained by the courts on other grounds, they will not invalidate on the grounds of unconstitutionality. Parliament cannot be unconstitutional. The acts of public officials can only be *ultra vires* a statute or unsupported by such prerogative powers as remain to the Crown—and they are small, indeed—but they cannot be unconstitutional.

The Courts in the British System. In 1871 Justice Willes said, and the decision is decisive on the relationship of the courts to statutes,

> I would observe, as to these Acts of Parliament, that they are the law of this land; and we do not sit here as a court of appeal from Parliament. It was once said—I think in Hobart—that, if an Act of Parliament were to create a man a judge in his own case, the Court might disregard it. That dictum, however, stands as a warning, rather than an authority to be followed. We sit here as servants of the Queen and the legislature. Are we to act as regents over what is done by Parliament with the consent of the Queen, Lords and Commons? *I deny that such authority exists.* If an Act of Parliament has been obtained improperly, it is for the legislature to correct it by repealing it: but, so long as it exists as law, the Courts are bound to obey it. The proceedings here are judicial, not autocratic, which they would be if we could make laws instead of administering them.

How different this is from American doctrine and practice!

It will be immediately asked, What if the words are not precise and unambiguous? Then there are loopholes. How will the judges, when applying the act to specific cases, fill up the gaps? The history of judicial interpretation shows that the courts will so interpret as to keep the common-law rights of the subject and the powers of the Crown intact: they will only be deemed to have been limited if the intention is unmistakable. Otherwise the courts presume:

1. The Crown is not bound by Act of Parliament, unless expressly stated or necessarily implied. (*Crown* means *Government*.)
2. Private property will not be taken away without compensation.
3. A statute limiting personal freedom will be construed strictly.
4. A subject will not be deprived of his access to the courts or protection by them in respect of his common-law rights. (They *might* be deprived by "administrative" law [pp. 213–216].)
5. Penal statutes will be strictly construed— that is, if Parliament wants to impose penalties, they must be indisputably stated.
6. Statutes have no retrospective effects.
7. The general structure of government cannot be altered by an unintentional and an indirect phrase in an unrelated statute—they will not acknowledge "a constitutional change . . . momentous and far-reaching by so furtive a process," and "subject-matter and fundamental constitutional law [are] never to be neglected in favour of verbal possibilities."
8. In wartime the courts will incline to favor the Executive as compared with the liberty of the subject.

Let it once again be emphasized: these rules of construction come into play only when Parliament does not make its intention unmistakably clear that it wants, or clearly implies that it wants, things otherwise. It can always restate its will if it is dissatisfied with the courts' decisions, and prevail. *The issue is one of intelligent legislative draftsmanship, Parliament's responsibility.* Given parliamentary sovereignty, the road is perfectly clear for the majority to damage or benefit the nation, and everyone has unhampered visibility. Debate concentrates not on "constitutionality" but on the substantive merits. The responsibility here and now on today's electorate is plenary.

It feels perfectly solid, but full of personal responsibility, when a majority in the House of Commons can do what it likes with the constitution. Then it is incumbent on all men to ascertain that what a majority *likes* is wise and to strive to return only that majority which is likely to be wise. One thing no Parliament can do: it cannot bind its successors. Therefore, if a majority were to attempt to change any constitutional institutions, it could succeed only so long as successive majorities of the electorate were prepared to vote for this. The full responsibility for the constitution today is focused on the electorate and its leaders. When, in 1953, some delegates to the Labour Party Annual Conference proposed that the Conservative law denationalizing transport should be fought by strikes, the chairman, Arthur Deakin, quelled the impulse by stating the constitutional position: with a majority in the future this could be reversed in Parliament. *Memento:* Go out and persuade the people.

A Built-in Constitution

The experience of constitutional limitations as well as permissions is *within* the citizen; he has a built-in constitution. Does this, unexceptionally, safeguard basic rights and fairness? There are strains. It was possible to reform the House of Lords—but only after two elections. It was possible for an irate Conservative majority in 1927, after a great general strike, to legislate that trade unions could use only funds out of dues for political purposes, provided each dues-payer positively contracted-*in* to do so; whereas the law before had been that he could ask to be left out. This was a purposeful blow at Labour Party funds by a rich party. It was not until 1946 that the Labour Party was in office with sufficient power to reverse this injustice. Yet the party could reverse it with the formal ease of its original enactment. Again, the Labour Party, having obtained a substantial majority at the election of 1945, enacted a very considerable change in the economic institutions of the nation, introducing nationalization of several industries (of course, with fair compensation and through parliamentary proce-

dure), a fiscal system, and national welfare and social security systems, producing a marked egalitarian effect on the distribution of the nation's income and property. This can be reversed by a succeeding Parliament; it will be a laborious and temporarily unsettling process, but it can be done if people want it done. In fact, the leader of the Conservative Party not only disclaimed any intention of considerable reversal but claimed credit for his party's having participated in the preparation of at least the social security portion of the reforms.

Thus, though the Opposition might have been reluctant to carry out the changes the Labour Government had done, and though intense passions were aroused, no large proportion thought that the Labour Party had been "unconstitutional." For the principle of majority rule was accepted— and the long years of education and electoral persuasion that had been needed to bring about the victory of the Labour Party evidently convinced the major part of the Conservatives that the former's actions were not unfair, at any rate not "unconstitutional." Yet the possibility always remains that an agitated, impassioned majority might act to change the constitution—and do it— *easily.* There are far more fears about this outside England than in it. The English are a deliberate, self-confident, and sober people.

All the cardinal issues of the 1875–1950's in the modern State, have, in England, been solved by Parliament and the electorate without help or hindrance from the nation's judges. These have been (1) the entrance of the State into the regulation, control, management of economic activity; (2) the development of the central–local governmental problem; (3) the transfer of a certain degree of discretion of a legislative nature by the Legislature to the administrative authorities; (4) the enhancement of the powers of the Executive and the devising of the means of controlling it.

On all these issues, in the United States, the last word has not been said by Congress or the President or the electorate: it has been said by the Supreme Court—because the evolution of the American polity and economy are gripped in the framework of the Constitution, and that is what the judges say it is.

The British system stimulates the people to constant and sensitive vigilance. They are their *own* supreme court. The question is whether it would be workable as beneficially if the country were larger in size than it is, and without the benefit of tradition and age-long usage.

These considerations lead us on to two tasks that must be accomplished in order that the British government may be fully understood.

(1) One way to secure that no group within a system of government shall act "unconstitutionally" is to divide up the powers of government among several agencies, so that they check and balance each other. How far is this device accepted in principle and how far is it practiced in Britain? This question concludes the present chapter.

(2) If it is true that the constituent assembly or the constitution-making convention of Britain has been in session for a thousand years, then what were the creative stages and the decisive turning points in its development of the rules of the game? The answer was briefly sketched earlier (pp. 38–41) and is touched on repeatedly.

VII. THE SEPARATION OF POWERS

The U.S. Constitution assigns to one agency—Congress—*legislative* powers; to another—the President—the powers of the *executive;* and to a third—the courts—the *judicial* power. Its main scheme is this dissection of powers.

The statesmen of the American colonies certainly had bitter experience of the power of the British King and the unwise Ministers he was able to induce to carry out his policy, and of a House of Commons he and they were able to dominate by the "influence" of money and hereditary privilege over a small and venal electorate. George III mingled, fused, the "powers" in British Government and gave them all the imprint of the conceited monarch—himself. Instead of admitting *L'État c'est trois,* he came closest since James I to claiming Louis XIV's status, *L'État c'est moi!* This pun merely means that the British constitution of his time was supposed to be a balance of *three* powers—King, Lords, and Commons—not

"the State is me," but "the State is three," so acclaimed by Burke, Hume, and Blackstone.

The Durability of Democracy

The founders of the U.S. Constitution wanted a government based on the consent of the governed, not headed by a King. But they feared that though they could set up a "republic," meaning a popular government, something close to a democracy, they could not attain a *durable* republic. History, they feared, taught that republics, though happy, were not lasting. The trouble that destroyed republics was "faction"—that is, a fanatical will of a minority or *even a majority.* As *The Federalist* said, "All powers were drawn into the legislative vortex"; with attendant tyranny—to creditors and bondholders, and fears among those who held property—in the state legislatures.

Who was to bring the legislature to reason? It could only be the Executive or the Judiciary or both together. The lawyers of the colonies had been brought up on Coke—that is, Sir Edward—and on Blackstone's *Commentaries,* where the position of the courts as defenders of civil liberties of Englishmen and checks upon the prerogative shone out in all their strength and splendor. The founders of the U.S. Constitution deliberately therefore threw a monkey wrench into the machinery of government. The Physiocrats had said: "Let government cease to act!" Bentham (pp. 34–35) had said, "Be quiet!" But the American constitution-makers, children of this same generation, said, "Go slow!"

Montesquieu, whose theory they followed, was not excessively wrong about the British constitution in his time. There was no written constitution to make the separation. But King, Lords and Commons, and courts of law *did* constitute separate authorities.

In Blackstone's *Commentaries* (I, 154-5) we read:

And herein indeed consists the true excellence of the English government, that all the parts of it form a mutual check upon each other. In the Legislature, the people are a check upon the nobility, and the nobility a check upon the people; by the mutual privilege of rejecting what the other has resolved: while the king is a check upon both, which preserves the executive power from encroachments. And this very executive power is again checked and kept within due bounds by the two houses, through the privilege they have of inquiring into, impeaching, and punishing the conduct (not indeed of the kind, which would destroy his constitutional independence; but, which is more beneficial to the public) of his evil and pernicious counsellors. . . . Like three distinct powers in mechanics, they jointly impel the machine of government in a direction different from what either, acting by itself, would have done; but at the same time in a direction partaking of each, and formed out of all; a direction which constitutes the true line of the liberty and happiness of the community.

But even as it reached this high plateau of the eighteenth century, the separation of powers began to yield to their blending. The authority of the King became the authority of his Cabinet, the authority of the Cabinet came to be based on the confidence of Parliament, and this was converted into a House of Commons at the mercy of a wide electorate. As Lord Robert Cecil observed in 1911: "The real principle of our constitution now is purely plebiscitical"—that is, a creature of the people by the process of election.

Does this mean that the British government has descended to the arbitrary and capricious? Far from it. It is held stable by statutes; by judicial decisions; by political conventions of leadership and the responsibility of parties. The separation of powers is not formalized; there is flexibility in the ebb and flow of actual authority day by day between the one and the other agency of government in detail.

The chief balance wheel of the British constitution today is the sovereignty of Parliament and the organization and sobriety of the electorate. The tensions of the constitution, designed to keep people true to their trust, are resident *within* the agencies of government, *among* them and *outside* them in the electorate, if we care to consider the electorate as an external rather than an internal factor. My inclination is to put the electorate in the former category, since it is so continuously and intimately intertwined with the everyday operations of British government.

As we shall see, some governments, like the Soviet, have denounced the separation of powers as an obstacle to "progress." Revolutionary and dictatorial governments take this stand. Others that have begun with the idea of the separation of powers, such as the French government, have abandoned it, except for some vestiges that are still of some importance.

The Electorate and Political Parties

Taught Power's due use to People and to Kings,
Taught nor to slack, nor strain its tender strings,
The less, or greater, set so justly true,
That touching one must strike the other too;
'Til jarring in'trests of themselves create
Th'according music of a well-mixed State.
　　　　　　　　　　—Alexander Pope

We that had loved him so, followed him, honoured him,
Lived in his mild and magnificent eye,
Learned his great language, caught his clear accents,
Made him our pattern to live and to die!
　　　　　　　　　　—Robert Browning

Parliament is the sovereign political authority in Britain; and it is omnicompetent. The House of Commons[1] possesses the ultimate and decisive authority, because it emerges from election by the people. Since this is only convention, the vital problem, then, is its composition, the terms of its authority, how it comes into being and is extinguished, and, between these two terminals, how far it is dominated by the public.

The conventions of the British constitution, we have said, are rooted in the political parties. Hence the self-government of each of the parties, and the checks and balances they exert on each other, are of vital significance to the whole system of government. If the secret of the quality of the constitution is lodged in the parties, then their secret, again, is inherent in the ethics of the behavior of the men and women who constitute their leaders and membership.

Popular Sovereignty

No constitution or statute directly provides that Britain is democratic or that political sovereignty belongs to the people. Yet Britain is profoundly and extensively democratic, more so, it may be remembered, than lands that have their legislatures limited by judicial review. This democratic character results from the combination of two facts. (1) Parliament, sovereign and able legally to do anything it likes, has a statutory maximum duration of five years. (2) Its 630 members[2] are elected by universal suffrage (or franchise) of all British citizens, men and women alike, who have attained their twenty-first birthday.

Though history offers us no statutory or judicial provision that sovereignty lies in the people (as the present Constitutions of France [p. *xviii*] and Germany [p. *xxix*] declare), the sovereignty of the British people is implicit or explicit in the principles of the extension of the franchise. It is

---

[1] The House of Commons has, since 1955, 630 members (till then, 625); and its maximum legal duration is, since 1911, five years. The constituencies were reconstructed in 1955, adding 5.

[2] England, 511; Wales, 36; Scotland, 71; Northern Ireland, 12.

tersely but fully stated in a Labour Party pamphlet circulated in the election of 1945:

> It really does rest with YOU. You may complain about statesmen and politicians. You may criticize Parliament. But YOU give statesmen power. YOU elect politicians to Parliament. YOU determine the membership and thereby the policy of the House of Commons.
> Polling Day is YOUR Day.

YOU and *YOUR* meant the voters.

The Problems

Now the problems are these. Since the House of Commons consists of 630 members, and the nation, or public, has some 50,000,000 people and some 35½ million electors, what is the bond between the latter and the former? On what principles is it fashioned, and by what process is it fulfilled? Bagehot is famous for the observation that the Cabinet is "the buckle that fastens, the hyphen that binds" the Executive to the Legislature. We may paraphrase this by saying that *Political Parties* are the hyphens that fasten, the buckles that bind, the 50,000,000 people and the 35½ million electorate in the nation to the 630 who, in Parliament, exercise the highest political power in the land. Even more, British political parties choose and control, simultaneously, two bodies: the Commons and a Cabinet of twenty men—a Legislature and an Executive—though, formally, they choose only members of Parliament.

The current British definition of political party —highly accurate in its descriptive quality—is Edmund Burke's, phrased in a day when political parties were rather to be desired than already existent.

> Party is a body of men united for promoting by their joint endeavours the national interest upon some particular principle in which they are all agreed . . . every honorable connexion will avow it is their first purpose, to pursue every just method to put the men who hold their opinions into such a condition as may enable them to carry their common plans into execution, with all the power and authority of the State.[3]

[3] *Thoughts on the Present Discontents*, II, 82, Oxford.

Representative government becomes party government as soon as men and women begin to understand that, over the whole territory of the nation, many have much in common with so many others and therefore seek an organized connection. Representative government is party government, and responsible government is also party government, if it is admitted (as it is in Britain) that the actions of the Government as well as Parliament must be founded on the consent and confidence of the public.

The political-party questions that arise and are answered in the British governmental system may be thus listed:

> I. What are the main features of British political parties?
> II. Who may sit and vote?
> III. How did the parties arise structurally?
> IV. What are their functions?
> V. What is their authority?

Only Questions I and II will be answered in this chapter, the remainder in the chapter that follows.

I. THE MAIN FEATURES OF BRITISH PARTIES

(1) A Two-party System

From the first days of party alignment, long before the maturer organization of the nineteenth century, the British system has been a two-party system: first Whigs and Tories; next Liberals and Conservatives; then (after a brief period lasting from 1918 to 1950 of Liberal, Labour, and Conservative) Labour and Conservative. At first these parties were loose and merely nascent. Then in the nineteenth century they became more firm and set, but there were substantial internal divisions and minorities. In the twentieth century, since the formation of the Labour Party, a three-party system operated, with the Labour Party as an infant working with the Liberals, and then, after World War I, the Liberal Party dwindling, like Shakespeare's man in his sixth age. Two parties hold the field, most of the formerly Liberal voters having gone over to one or the other, Labour or Conservative. The utilitarian common sense of the

A Comparison of British and U.S. Government

Direct Authority-Responsibility in British Type Government

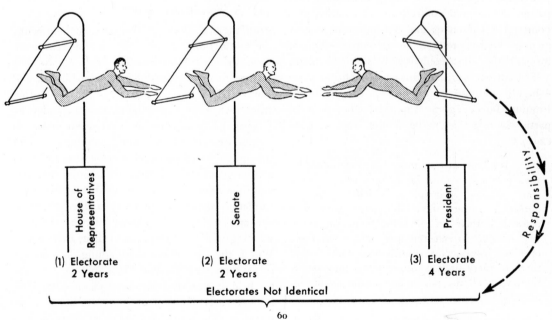

Prime Minister

CABINET

Responsibility   Responsibility

H. M. Opposition

Commons

Party   Party

Authority   Authority

One Electorate at One Time

Separated Authority-Responsibility in U.S. Constitutional System

THE PARTY TRAPEZE

House of Representatives

Senate

President

(1) Electorate 2 Years

(2) Electorate 2 Years

(3) Electorate 4 Years

Responsibility

Electorates Not Identical

electorate and its leaders has consciously steered away from measures and voting habits that might have multiplied parties. The single-member constituency assists this purpose.

British cabinet government acquired firmness in the early nineteenth century only when political parties had sorted themselves out, and on the basis of a wide electorate, and, under its impetus, began to form broad legislative programs and policies. The truth is *not* the reverse as so many people have suggested: that *because* the British have the cabinet system, they have the two-party system.

Yet there were not always only two parties. This is the most convenient point at which to refer to the characteristic outlook of the political parties, Labour, Conservative, Liberal, and Communist.

Labour Party. The Labour Party as such, was set up in 1906, the immediate offspring of a Labour Representation Committee. The latter had been established in 1900 to unite the efforts of socialist societies and trade unions and the cooperative movement in running Labour candidates and aiding the election of those of other parties who had Labour sympathies. This committee itself was the offspring of endeavors in the 1870's by trade unionists and middle-class sympathizers to elect representatives of the working class. And this again had been stimulated by the subordinated condition of the working classes in a still subaristocratic and capitalist nation. The ancestry of socialism went back far to the times of Wycliffe (p. 15), came up through the Levellers and Diggers of Cromwell's armies, was inspired by the French Revolution, and animated by the hardships of the Industrial Revolution. The French socialists of the early nineteenth century and the philanthropy of Robert Owen pressed forward the passion of the workers for social justice and decent treatment in industry, and the Chartist movement of the 1840's was a potent expression of the political demands leading to social and economic reform, of which another was the foundation of the Consumers' Cooperative Movement of 1844. Steadily, the trade unions built their membership, their strength, and their demands—against bitter opposition by the governing class, and against judgments handed down by the courts hampering the use of their associated power.

In 1901 the latest of a series of legal decisions (the Taff Vale strike decision) made unions liable for the damages caused by strikes. Labour saw that it must dare to be *itself* and no longer look to candidates of other parties to fight its battles. The Fabian Society, led by Sidney and Beatrice Webb (upper middle class) and Bernard Shaw, had, since 1883, begun its indoctrination of socialism by gradual and persuasive stages. The Fabian Society; the Independent Labour Party, non-Marxian, founded in Scotland in 1893 by Keir Hardie, a miner; and trade union groups flowed into the representation committee and then the party. In 1906 it won 29 seats. In World War I it rose to high office: the sinews of the workers made the arms and built the ships. Thenceforward, it began to supplant the Liberal Party. It is, virtually, the direct offspring of the trade unions, and the relationship of general members and trade-union members is a matter of peculiar interest and is treated later (pp. 76–78). The party stands for the social welfare state and national minima of services to the underprivileged. It carried through substantial nationalization of industry in its period of office, 1945 to 1951, and fiscal reforms of an equalitarian nature. Its general program and outlook may be seen in such policies as these and further extensions. It is sincerely, genuinely, and deeply liberal and democratic, and it is anti-Marxian, being inspired by the Bible rather than *Das Kapital*. It is pacific.

Conservative Party. The Conservative Party stems from the Tories and right-wing Whigs of the eighteenth and nineteenth centuries. It is the party of the possessing and patriotic and traditional governing class, of the wealthy, the aristocratic and subaristocratic, the gentry, the upper and middlemiddle class, as well as working-class patriots, disgruntled workers, and high-skilled workers whose pride aligns them with the party that preaches the rewards and opportunities of free enterprise. The name began to be used deliberately in 1831 as more reputable than "Tory." Its basic philosophy is that of Burke (p. 35), Hume (p. 32), and Adam Smith (p. 33). It is the party of King, Church, nation, hierarchy, and property. It was the bitter opponent and suffocator of political rights, economic fair shares, and education of the lower middle and the working classes throughout the nineteenth century. More recently it has reluctantly become reconciled to substantial social services and nationalized industries. In the nineteenth century some of its members, affected by notions of Christian Socialism and the patrician view of the obligations of nobility, fostered factory legislation and charitable works; generally, they were known as Tory Democrats. They have strongly nationalistic sentiments and were the party of imperialism and colonialism, British style, which means moderate and Burkian. Disraeli and Churchill are their bright stars. They are today's apostles of free enterprise—except for the accumulated results of governmental controls and regulation, of nationalization, and social equalization developed by Labour. They deploy the *motif* of free opportunity and rewards to the ambitious and able.

Liberal Party. The Liberal Party was born of the mentality and interests of John Locke (p. 32) and the liberal Whig elements. It was the chief medium of the French Revolution in British setting, the hero of that time being Charles James Fox. Though it represented a great class of propertyowners, and then of the new men of commerce and manufactures, such as Cobden, Bright, and Gladstone, it widened the parliamentary franchise, cut down the power of the House of Lords and the monarchy, removed religious disabilities, freed the press, instituted free trade, established free and compulsory education, established the social security and employment services (1906 to 1914), introduced egalitarian income taxes and death duties, gave trade unions guarantees in the law of fair collective operation, and tried betimes to give Ireland home rule.

World War I mortally wounded the Liberal Party, because it was already running out of equalitarian policies and because Lloyd George, the World War I Prime Minister, took it into necessary coalition with the Conservatives. Emerging from the coalition it became entangled in doctrinal and organizational and personal battles just when the Labour Party was growing fast,

having amassed the heritage of liberalism and moderate socialism. It dwindled: 1906, 397 seats; 1923, 158; 1929, 59; 1931, 37; 1935, 21; 1945, 12; and for the rest of the story, see pp. 71 ff. The great figures of the party were: Fox, Grey, Lord John Russell, Palmerston, Gladstone, Asquith, Lloyd George—leaders of a magnanimous and beneficent tradition and works.

The two older parties, Conservative and Liberal, had some likeness; the Labour Party was markedly different from both.

Communist Party. The Communist Party was founded in 1920, when Leninist Russia took command of the left-wing labor movements of the world. The peak of its British membership was 60,000 at the invasion of Russia by Hitler; today it is believed to have 40,000. Its membership first rose after the General Strike of 1926. Parliament has had in all only four Communist members. Only two ever served at any one time, 1945 to 1950, since when its candidates cannot get enough votes for election. In 1950 all the Communist candidates together mustered only just over 90,000 in a total vote of 29,000,000.

Its policy is roughly the same as that of the French Communist Party; Marx is its mentor and the Kremlin its master. It has tried to infiltrate the trade unions, with some small success; it has been rebuffed by the Labour Party on every one of the many occasions when it has sought to join that party. It has not had the opportunity to pursue the disruptive tactics open to the French Communists, because the House of Commons has not been its arena. For Communists in a democratic parliament one has to study France (pp. 349–351), and Italy.

Party Composition. Today there is a correlation between social and economic class and political party, but it is far from clear cut, and very distant from Karl Marx's simple division by two, a bourgeoisie and proletariat. Many in the "middle" class are Labour. Yet, if the Conservative Party could not persuade working-class men and women, they could never attain a majority of the voters. For the "working class" comprises about three quarters of the electorate, yet it divides its votes, as polls show, about 5 to 3 among Labour and Conservative, not 100 percent to Labour.

Some figures for Derby, a place of heavy Labour majorities, gathered by polls in 1953 show how substantial is this cross-class voting:

Occupation	Labour Percent	Conservative Percent
Nonmanual	41	59
Skilled manual	75	25
Semi- and unskilled manual	68	32
Not in paid employment	54	46

Put in another form, 26 percent of the "middle class" voted Labour and 74 percent Conservative, and the "working class" voted 71 percent for Labour and went 29 percent for Conservative.

Today it appears [4] that older voters, between fifty-five and sixty-nine years of age, vote more heavily Conservative than younger workers do. And there is observed, also, a difference between the loyalty of voters to general programs, such as "socialism" (or "full employment") or "private enterprise" and attitudes toward the immediate means thereto. They have been found to disapprove of the *means* (nationalization, state trading, closed shop, etc.) proposed to attain their principles in polls which, if effective in votes, would have unseated the candidate, yet the polled people still voted for the *general* end. *That* was to their taste. Others again, were not afraid of "private enterprise," even if this was not a future promise of *their* welfare, but preferred the immediate release from various controls and restrictions, and for example, that the working class should pay part of the cost of eyeglasses, dentures, and drugs provided by the National Health Service and so relieve the middle classes and, perhaps, better off skilled workers of the burden of taxation.

The main determinant of voting behavior is one's conception of the social class to which one belongs. This is adamant to appeals for change. But there is an ample number of votes that are prepared to "float" on nonclass appeals: imperial, foreign, immediate taxation advantages, a sense of justice or freedom in general, a mood of depression or exaltation. Hence party managers' anxieties about the "right time" for an election. In the

[4] See also R. S. Milne and H. C. Mackenzie, *Straight Fight,* for Bristol, 1951, London, 1954.

election of May 1955 nearly 1,500,000 Labour voters stayed at home, dismayed by quarrels among the leaders, being thus without clear guidance.

The occupational composition of the parties in Parliament is helpful to a further understanding of their outlook and policy.

Of the Conservative members, some 150 hold company directorships.

It is important to remember that in something over 120 years since the Reform Act of 1832, the clash of parties has, through mutual influence, much modified their original sharpness. For votes, the parties must move into middle positions, since there are but two parties. Their clienteles have made great concessions to each other's demands. They are now so evenly balanced that the Commons is the scene of an equipoise of popular votes. For the very *big* problems are largely solved; and there is a notable degree of social consensus, even of conscience, though still abundant militancy.

It is worthy of note that the Liberal Party was generally more rent with internal tension than the Conservative, for it was the party of advance and change. Like the Liberal Party, the Labour Party in our own time is the forward, reforming movement, the more democratic one, and therefore it too exhibits frequent internal disputes, for the ideas of what constitutes progress and the pace of action are very various. The Conservatives, on the whole, need only to stand pat and move only when they are driven by their opponents' impetus and policy. Conservative unity is also the product of upper class education, particularly at the public schools, where class solidarity is fostered simply because they are exclusive to the possessing and ruling class. In 1935 no less than 80 percent of the Conservative M.P.'s came from such schools; in 1955 still 75 percent (Labour, 25 and 22 percent respectively). It might be added that in 1951 about one fourth of the Labour members were products of the adult-education movement. Twenty-three percent of Conservative M.P.'s come from Eton!

Soviet spokesmen make a tremendous fuss about the rising level of education of their legislative and administrative and judicial personnel; they need to, the level is still shockingly low (p.

Candidates and Members, House of Commons, General Election, May 1955 *

Occupation	Conservative		Labour	
	Candidates	Elected	Candidates	Elected
Professions:				
Barrister	107	66	48	21
Solicitor	30	11	23	14
Doctor	6	2	12	4
Architect, civil engineer	11	6	1	1
Chartered secy. or accountant	22	11	5	3
Civil servant or local government	16	12	17	8
Armed Services	65	47	5	2
University teaching	9	2	25	15
Adult teaching	0	0	21	17
School teaching	15	2	84	59
Minister of religion	0	0	5	2
Total	281	159	246	146
Business:				
"Small Business"	19	0	16	7
Company director	86	62	3	1
Company manager	32	16	8	4
Commerce: manager	37	16	13	7
Commerce: clerical	26	7	46	32
Total	200	101	86	52
Miscellaneous:				
"White collar"	12	4	22	17
Private means	11	11	0	0
Politician, and political organizer	17	17	8	1
Journalists, etc.	33	19	57	30
Farmer	43	31	14	9
Housewife	1	1	7	5
Student	4	0	5	5
Total	123	83	113	67
Workers:				
Railway clerks	0	0	22	12
Miners	4	0	43	10
Skilled workers	13	1	74	45
Semiskilled, unskilled	2	0	36	11
Total	19	1	175	78
Total	623	344	620	343

* After D. E. Butler, *The British General Election of 1955*, London, 1955, with thanks for early communication.

866). But British political parties have for centuries enjoyed the preponderant membership of very good education. In the Commons of 1955, 221 Conservatives and 113 Labour M.P.'s had attended universities; only 44 Labour and 5 Conservatives had attended elementary school and no more. Above this level, almost all had gone through secondary school or public school, the quality of which we have indicated (p. 21).

Twenty-nine percent of Conservative M.P.'s had local government service; 56 percent of Labour M.P.'s.

(2) No Spoils, No Patronage

The victorious party at a British election has no jobs, contracts, national resources—spoils or patronage or graft—to give to its workers and friends and members of Parliament. It will have only blood, sweat, and tears to give them in the service of the nation. The laws relating to the

Civil Service at the center and in the cities, counties, boroughs, and so forth are unmistakable and stern, and their actual execution is honorable and strict. Contracts are let according to the laws, strictly administered. The virtue of men is not assumed to be unassailable, and so the laws are made to bolster the individual character.

What prevents a majority when it is returned to Parliament from contaminating the Civil Service and contract laws? Two things: the integrity of the public and *all* the political leaders. The public, led by its conscious and public-spirited men and women, would not allow the destruction of so valuable an element in the life of the nation— of value to *all*. They recognize the value of the technological and expert skills of an impartial and anonymous Civil Service in a democracy. Furthermore, there are nearly nonindustrial 700,- 000 Civil Service jobs at the center and about 1,000,000 in the local government services; these are employment opportunities, especially for the middle class and working classes. They do not intend to see them debauched.

What, then, impels the British to undergo the hardships of the electoral and representative struggle? Nothing but a desire to carry out certain ideals, to realize felt human values, to promote and safeguard certain interests. If it were suggested that this is *selfish,* it would still leave the question open, What is it that men define as their pleasure? Is it, following Mill, to be Socrates discontented or a fool contented, a man dissatisfied or a pig satisfied?

(3) Continuity of Operations

The parties do not slumber or even doze between elections. They maintain a continuous operation of "education" at a high intensity; they research, issue literature, hold meetings, conduct week-end and summer schools, organize local (district and ward) effort, participate in local government elections and membership, and, above all, keep everyday contact with the members of the Commons and directly with the Cabinet. The effort is not so intense as during the three weeks of election campaigns, but it is incessant. British parties are always present, everywhere present, and vocally present.

The universal and continuous operation of parties is fostered, among other factors, by two: (*a*) *the life of a government is not fixed,* as is that of the U.S. Congress and President; and (*b*) by-elections, when members vacate their seats, are extremely important in the tension of Government and Opposition. The election machinery does not operate solely for a certain day in November in the even years of the calendar. The parties in Britain are more nervous, for any day may be election day—within limits. A three-week election campaign is feasible because, so to speak, the campaign has been going on all the time since the last election.

(4) High Centralization and Deep Roots

A party is a kind of fellowship: it is an association of like-minded individuals and groups and, as such, it has procedures, institutions, conventions, and practices. Among these is a settled relationship between its headquarters and the mass of members. The British party system has evolved a high degree of leadership and the readiness of the spread-out mass of members to follow a comparatively few leaders in policy, tactics, the choice of representatives and Ministers. But there is no gulf between the former and the latter: there *are* levels of leadership, subleadership, intermediate leadership, and critical followers.

This is the direct chain of connection of the people to the Cabinet and the Prime Minister, which is the group of leaders of the majority party and leaders and organizers of the work of Parliament. These are M.P.'s like the rank and file and fighting for election as such. The connection is firm, vigilant, vigorous, and disciplinary over the Government. On the other hand, this same leadership (if it were not for aristocratic and priggish overtones and psychoanalytic undertones, we could say *élite*) is tethered deep down in the inward vitals of the whole country, to the constituencies, to the labor unions, the employers' associations, the churches, and all the individuals who belong to them.

Once again the small size of the country, the length of political practice and developed habits, the self-respect of each citizen, the educational system, and the press and radio assists this umbilical connection. A current of feeling and ideas and will power rises every minute from the roots toward the center of decision. And a current of explanation, responsible advocacy, appeals for further confidence, flows from the center of decision to the members (we cannot truly say just "rank and file," as in the military metaphor) whence cometh their help.

(5) The Fellowship of Party and Identifiable Personality

Party membership is voluntary. Beginning with local associations, the British political parties are still formally federations of the local and regional groupings in a "national" association in each case. It has taken about 125 years—if we merely count from the Great Reform Act of 1832—to nurture a kind of party conscience in each case. This means a policy, a design of ideals, programs, a kind of self-consciousness and collective self-respect and sense of duty, each with a general world outlook. Each party has a long history, philosophers, brilliant and evocative leaders, symbols; some have *martyrs,* heroes, times of trouble, and resounding successes in the creation of one more atom of humanity in the standards of right and wrong by which the national community and the world outside are governed.

A strong sense of fellowship prevails. The party constitution is accepted by its members; they may be ejected by certain rules if they violate it. *There is a rule of law within the parties.* They come before the public at elections and in between, as recognizable, identifiable entities. They possess a core of character that will determine broadly how they will handle emergent problems, over and above the several particular men who are now at the helm and the specific political, social, and economic riddles they now declare they are prepared to solve. This party fellowship and character bind the members of it. There will be no party cross-voting in the Commons, no voices raised against the leaders except after notice and caucus attempts at reconciliation.

(6) Sober and Christian Spirit

In the election of 1951, under the influence of Christian societies, the leaders of the major parties with wives and colleagues attended St. Paul's Cathedral at a service of "prayer and dedication" before the general election. Similar services were held outside London. The Archbishop of Canterbury preached:

> It is the proper business of politicians in a general election to urge their views upon the people with confidence, with vigor, even with passion, out of the sincerity of their own honest thinking and convictions, and yet never to forget that God is greater than us in all truth, in righteousness, in purpose and in love. Parties should be ready to learn from each other even in opposing one another.

II. "ONE MAN, ONE VOTE: ONE VOTE, ONE VALUE"

Who May Vote?

Some 35½ million men and women are enfranchised. This is the result of universal franchise—that is, the right to vote vested in all men and women who have attained their twenty-first birthday by the time the register of electors is compiled.

It took nearly two hundred years of incessant struggle on the part of the unenfranchised and their champions to induce the more privileged part of the nation to yield this right—little by little, and grudgingly on the part of many of them.

The main steps may be barely stated. The Puritan middle and poorer rank and file of the English Civil War vehemently demanded the rights of man, for equality of political power, shown by voting and the proportionate distribution of seats throughout the country, and for frequent Parliaments. John Locke urged this. Even James I advocated disfranchising decayed boroughs and enfranchising new ones: it was an implied admission of representativeness, if not of popular authority. Again and again, through 1689 and subsequent Parliaments, the matter was pressed by one or the other group, vainly, for an oligarchy was in the saddle.

However, from various boroughs came "instructions" to their members, pressing measures and implying external control over the House of Commons. Pitt the Elder agitated the people in seeking for the means to carry on the Seven Years' War (1756–1763). The press developed in quantity, vivacity, and circulation. In 1768 a tremendous outburst of popular feeling on issues of representation arose when "that devil, John Wilkes," returning from the exile into which he had been forced after his open vilification of George III, was elected to Parliament in the London area under the cry of "Wilkes and Liberty!" The Commons expelled him, just the kind of action to raise the question of popular sovereignty versus Parliament. From all over the country petitions poured in. Great political public meetings were held, the earliest regular political meetings. The Society of the Supporters of the Bill of Rights was started to support Wilkes, the redistribution of seats, annual Parliaments, the exclusion of placemen from the House of Commons, and the subordination of members to the instructions of their constituents.

There later followed the powerful advocacy of Pitt the Younger and his great liberal rival, Charles James Fox, for parliamentary reform. The former in 1782 introduced the subject into the House of Commons, and next year a bill for reform. A Society for Constitutional Information was established to propagandize reform and secure mass support—of country middle gentry, professional people, artisans. The reforms were damped down by the complacent Commons. It was satisfied with the kinds of argument brought forward so eloquently by Edmund Burke. He held that (1) the people should be led in government by those who know better, are wiser, are more elevated; and (2) majority rule and the acknowledgment of the doctrine of individual rights were not essential for good government and liberty, because the House of Commons *virtually* represented everybody in the nation, even though every part of the nation had no *direct* voice in it. Hence, the terms *virtual* and *direct* representation in contrast with each other, in political science terminology.

The French Revolution, another surge of human passion, entered the political ocean, not to be denied force until in 1832 it achieved its object. In 1792 middle- and upper-class reformers established the Society of the Friends of the People: they taught the doctrines of fully responsible and representative government. The London Corresponding Society, of radical working-class supporters, joined them. The whole country formed a network of such groups (the British equivalent of the American "Minute Men"). The Government suppressed them: Burke's cries of horror are to be read in the opening passages on his *Reflections on the French Revolution* over the claim of these societies to "choose our own governors; cashier them for misconduct; frame a government for ourselves."

But the tempest outside Parliament could not be stilled. The reformers were joined by some of the Whig leaders (Lord Grey, of the Reform Bill), by Bentham and the Benthamites (p. 32). "Hampden" Clubs of artisans (the nation was in the full tide of the Industrial Revolution), such men as Francis Place, the tailor of Charing Cross, rationalists and nonconformists, bandied "reform" in the streets. William Cobbett, a Tory democrat, and popular writer, agitated the masses by his cheap publication, the *Parliamentary Register,* hammering home the theme of the relationship between a reform of Parliament and a cure of the poverty of the people. Between 1793 and 1826 a dozen measures for reform were introduced into Parliament. Finally, a Whig Government under Lord Grey, taking office in 1830, pledged drastic reform.

Representation of the People. It is most important to notice that the title of Lord Grey's bill introduced statutorily a new principle of representation. It was "An Act to amend the *representation of the people.*" Our sketch of the rise of Parliament (pp. 39–41) made it manifest that the Commons consisted of communities, *communautés*—shires, boroughs. These were not represented by the *numbers* of population or electors —they were all of the most diverse sizes and characters. Henceforth representation was of *individuals.*

The Reform Bill was carried only after the most intense resistance by the opposition in the Commons, and a last-ditch defense of privilege by the House of Lords, led by the victor of Napoleon at Waterloo, the Duke of Wellington. Indeed, the nation was close to revolution in the weeks before the Lords surrendered. And surrender, too, was brought about only because the King had been induced by his Ministers to promise to make enough peers to swamp the Lords opposed to the bill.

Though the Act did not enfranchise all men over the age of twenty-one or explicitly admit the principle of fully representative and responsible government, it did two things: (1) it corrected the old abuses; and (2), by breaking with the past and by extending the suffrage, it admitted a reasoned argument. A new class of voters arose and aroused emulation among the still disfranchised. Within a little over fifty years it produced practically universal male suffrage and within another forty, universal suffrage of men and women. Furthermore, henceforth the House of Lords existed on sufferance, even though it exerted its powers drastically until 1911.

The Act took representation away wholly or in part from eighty-six boroughs and gave their seats to larger towns and more industrial counties. In the boroughs it enfranchised all householders owning or renting real estate of a certain but no great value a year; in the counties it enfranchised tenants, freeholders, and leaseholders of land, again, of moderate value. *It brought in the middle-class vote*—not the masses of workers or women. The number of votes had been 400,000; it rose only to 600,000. But these were different people, dwelling in different parts of the country; and the principle was different.

The rest of the nineteenth century was occupied in a retreating action by aristocracy and the upper and middle classes, which made reluctant concessions to the masses in 1867 and again in 1884. Conservative reformers were always afraid of "a leap in the dark."

In 1918 women over the age of thirty were admitted to the vote; in 1928, having behaved themselves adequately to satisfy the primmer Conservatives and the House of Lords, women were admitted on practically the same terms as men, on their own rights or as wives of male voters at the age of twenty-one. The Representation of the People Act, 1949, completed the process of enfranchisement.

But the liberalization of the right to vote occurred only under the impulse of popular deter-

mination. This was shown drastically in the vast popular association known as the Chartist movement (1838–1848), which, among other parts of its program, demanded equal electoral districts, *universal suffrage,* payment of M.P.'s, vote by ballot (*until 1867 there was open voting at the hustings*), and annual Parliaments. Indeed, there were revolutionists among its members—its following was divided into "moral force men" and "physical force men." Monster meetings and monster petitions to Parliament were among its methods of forcing action. The Continental revolutions of 1848 further produced efforts for change. Liberals as well as Conservatives were afraid of "a convulsion," but the parties in Parliament found it impossible in the end to do otherwise than compete for the authority that was lodged in the masses.

The number of voters (in round numbers) increased as follows by successive extensions of the franchise and in proportion to population over the age of twenty:

1832	from 510,000	from 5.0%
	to 721,000	to 7.1%
1867	to 2,231,000	to 16.4%
1884	to 5,000,000	to 28.5%
1918	to 20,000,000	to 74.0%
1928	to 29,200,000	to 96.9%
1948	to 34,900,000	to 96.7%

The Vote. By the Representation of the People Act of 1948, persons entitled to vote are those who are resident in a constituency on the qualifying date, who are then of full age (21), and who are British subjects or citizens of the Republic of Ireland. To this there are some exceptions to be noted presently.

The qualifying date is fixed by two points in the year in spring and autumn, because the electoral registers are made up twice a year: March 15 and October 1.

Members of the Armed Services have the vote. They are put on a special register, as are public officials and their wives serving outside the United Kingdom.

The register is made up by the returning officers for the various constituencies, being the county clerk in the counties and the town clerk in boroughs and cities. These are local government officials but have this duty of attending to the election machinery. They prepare the registers by house-to-house canvass twice a year through their officials. Instructions on these matters are given by the Home Secretary, empowered thereto by the Act. The register must be published, and free copies must be given to the parliamentary and local government candidates—their agents are avid for them.

A list also has to be made and published of "absent" voters—that is, chiefly, Armed Service voters or people with some special occupation or anyone who "by reason of blindness or any other physical incapacity to go to the poll unaided or if he cannot vote unaided." For these a postal vote is allowable: it came into operation in the 1950 election.[5]

The Disqualified. The disqualified voters are peers (this is a common-law prohibition); persons of unsound mind (again common law); persons convicted of treason or felony, until they have suffered the punishment to which sentenced or are pardoned; persons convicted of corrupt practices for five years after conviction (these practices are enumerated below, pp. 84–86); similarly, with illegal practices enumerated below at the same place.

Plural Voting. The ethos of democratic government is summed up in the British slogan: one man, one vote. But the statutes of the nineteenth century were so drafted in their residential and property and rental qualifications that some voters had several votes; many had two. In addition, a graduate of certain universities had a vote for a member of Parliament for the university. Again and again the Liberal Party in the early twentieth century introduced legislation to abolish plural voting. The Conservatives, with or without the timely support of the House of Lords, defeated the measures. Then, in 1918, the statute forbad more than two votes per person, which meant even including the university vote—a choice had to be made.

The Act of 1948 dealt drastically with this: it

[5] To the great advantage of the Conservative Party, since it is able seemingly to get wind of the sick people from sources that were of Conservative disposition.

abolished the university members of Parliament; it abolished the so-called "business premises" vote. The university seats had originally been established by the philosopher-king, James I, in 1603 (just after he had had a thief executed out of hand without trial!) as they were seats of religious orthodoxy and divine right. The number then, only two, was increased in the nineteenth century, being twelve before their abolition. They were advocated on the grounds that in an age when men were given over to partisanship, university members were "independent." But in 1945 five were then "independent," five Conservative, one Liberal, and one "national." Their prevailing vote was anti-Labour. The argument that they were "intellectual," put forward by their Conservative supporters, was not a cogent one to a modern electorate. Mr. Churchill promised during the election of 1950, if returned, to restore them. Afterward he abandoned the intention.

The business-premises votes numbered about 700,000. In an electorate of $35\frac{1}{2}$ million, it is small. But it was dominant in the City of London and made a difference in some big cities. It offended the major principle. It is gone.

Who May Sit in the Commons?

A property qualification for membership of the House of Commons was first established by a statute of 1445, which, by the way, even went so far as to try to restrict the membership to "gentlemen born." Then, in 1710 a statute was passed (designed to correct corruption of electorates by rich businessmen seeking election who had no local connections), allowing only landholders in the Commons, a high property qualification from estates being fixed. In 1838 the real estate was amended to personal estate; in 1858 the property qualification was abolished altogether. It had been systematically evaded in any case.

Today the disqualifications for M.P. are of aliens; infants; peers; bankrupts; lunatics; idiots; the clergy of the Church of England, of the Church of Scotland, of the Roman Catholic Church; those convicted of corrupt and illegal practices at elections, parliamentary and local; petitioners of the Crown, except for civil, military, and diplomatic service; and holders and undertakers of contracts or commissions for or on account of public services. The penalty for illegal sitting is exceedingly stiff, £500 per day!

Officeholders Cannot Be M.P.'s. There is another general class of disqualified for sitting in the House of Commons: officeholders under the Government. The Act of Settlement, 1701, laid it down that "no person who has an office or a place of profit under the Crown or who receives a pension from the Crown shall be capable of serving as a member of the House of Commons."

The prohibition is sweeping. The purpose is comprehensible: to oust from the internal affairs of the Commons those who had previously debauched it for the benefit of the Kings, especially the Stuarts. But the evil went back long before that. Yet the exclusion of "placemen" was found to be excessively sweeping, for it thereby ousted *Ministers*. On second thoughts, the anti-administration zeal was seen to deprive the Commons of the very benefits they were seeking—control of the Government. It was, after all, better to have Ministers *in the Commons where they can be seen* than outside, whence they might manipulate their managers within. Hence, in the Regency Act of 1706 a list of offices excluded specifically, instead of generally, certain officers, and also new places that should come into being. This opened the way for the *development of a Cabinet in and responsible to the House* (see further Chapter 7).

The U.S. Constitution adopted the overzealous clause of the Act of Settlement and, banished placeholders altogether from Congress, froze hard the separation of powers (see further pp. 56–57), and put the length of Pennsylvania Avenue between President and Congressmen.

Parliament thereafter proceeded, by various statutes, to exclude and except officeholders. The upshot is that Ministers and Junior Ministers, to a certain number, are qualified, even required (by convention), to sit in the Commons. But civil servants and all the Armed Forces that are active are not qualified. Regarding these public officials, especially the Civil Service, more is to be said later (pp. 210ff.). This differs from French, German, and Russian practice.

Various other forms of disqualification have passed away with the development of the idea that "a man's a man for all that," with modern rationalism and humanity. As Jews could not take the parliamentary oath "on the true faith of a Christian," they could not take a seat. An Act of 1868 altered the oath. Until 1829 Roman Catholics could not sit, because they were required to make a declaration against transubstantiation, a relic of the Reformation and the Revolution Settlement. The Relief Act of 1829 prescribed an oath making it possible for them to sit. Atheists could not sit, because they could not take the oath in the original form. The determined fight of the elected atheist Charles Bradlaugh in 1881 (supported by John Stuart Mill), who made shocking scenes in the House (he brought legal action and was also sued by the Crown), resulted eventually in the Oaths Act of 1888, which opened Parliament to atheists also. It should be noticed that Jews, who had been banished from the kingdom between Edward I's and Cromwell's time, could neither sit nor vote, because they were not allowed naturalization. In 1753 an act to liberalize this situation died in one year, so intolerant was the outcry in the streets. In the Parliament of 1955 there are 11 Roman Catholics in the Conservative and Labour ranks; 1 Jew and 16 Jews, respectively. Labour is largely nonconformist, Conservatives, Church of England.

One Vote, One Value: Equal Districts. When representation of communities gave way to the representation of individuals, the principle of "equal" size, long advocated, triumphed. It was difficult to break with the old principle, because counties, and more so boroughs, were historic social entities; it offended the sense of locality to disintegrate them. By 1884, however, single-member constituencies cut into them, but some boroughs got a single member while their area, with a larger than proportional population, was kept. Both political parties have always cooperated to avoid "gerrymandering."

The Reform Act of 1918 established election commissioners to redistribute parliamentary seats with the basis of 70,000 people per seat. These officers then and now act under the chairmanship of the Speaker of the House of Commons, whose impartiality is exemplary (pp. 107–108). Since the Acts (Redistribution of Seats) of 1949, the commissioners are called the Boundary Commission. Their basic formula is the population divided by the number of seats, allowing a plus or minus margin of 25 percent. The margin has been abolished in order to avoid disintegrating local government and historic areas. In 1955 substantial inequalities persisted, though since 1949, 400 constituencies suffered changes. The average county constituency is about 52,500, the boroughs, 56,500. Sixty-five are less than 45,000, and only twenty-eight are over 70,000, of which two are just over 80,000.

Bias in Election Results. The law does not require, as usually in Continental government, an absolute majority to win a seat, but a relative one or plurality. Two evils result from this. With more than two candidates for one seat, the winner may get in on a minority vote—40:30:30. A minority Government may be returned for this reason, as that of the Conservatives in 1951. In addition, there is a bias of the densities or sparsities of votes each party happens to have in its safest areas.

Minority opinions cannot get representation unless their votes, scattered over larger areas, can be collected. Therefore, since John Stuart Mill's *Representative Government* (depending on the system advocated by Thomas Hare) in the 1860's, proportional representation (henceforth referred to as P.R.) has been advocated by various societies, in Parliament, and particularly by the declining Liberal Party. For minority representation bigger constituencies are necessary, returning *several* members. There are several different systems in use, and many more conceived by mathematical wizards. The French and German systems are instructive (p. 368 and p. 702).

The tables presented below indicate that La-

bour, when in office four times since 1922 to 1955, in ten general elections did not have of its own separate strength higher than 47.8 percent of the total vote. The Conservatives have held office six times since 1922, and their highest vote was in 1935, being 53.6 percent when the National Coalition was less massive than in 1931. Otherwise the votes are less than 50 percent of the voters. The table tells the story.

Had representation been *proportional* to votes, then the seats would have been distributed thus:

Year	Cons.	Lib.	Labour	Other
1922	235	179	181	20
1923	234	182	188	11
1924	298	108	202	7
1929	235	143	228	9
1931	—413—		189	13
1935	330	41	232	12
1945	254	58	306	22
1950	272	57	288	8
1951	300	16	304	5
1955	313	17	292	8

The Labour Party needs something more than 2 percent more in popular votes to win as many seats as the Conservatives, owing to the size of their constituencies and majorities being heaped in certain places. Before 1950 Labour had the corresponding bias in its favor. Labour itself introduced the bill of 1948 that corrected the bias in its favor to one that is noticeably against it.

Yet, excepting the Liberal Party, the main weight of English opinion is hostile to P.R., or even a second ballot system with absolute majorities. They argue: (1) Larger constituencies would weaken the close attention of candidates to local views. (2) Even if they were subdivided for electioneering purposes, candidates on the same

Results of General Elections, 1922–1951

Year	Total	Seats				Percent of Votes				Govt.
		Cons.	Lib.	Labour	Other	Cons.	Lib.	Labour	Other	
1922	615	346	115	142	12	38.2	29.1	29.5	3.2	Cons.
1923	615	258	159	191	7	38.1	29.6	30.5	1.8	Labour
1924	615	419	40	151	5	48.3	17.6	33.0	1.1	Cons.
1929	615	260	59	288	8	38.2	23.4	37.0	1.4	Labour
1931	615	521	37	52	5	—67.1—		30.7	2.2	Coalition
1935	615	431	21	154	9	53.6	6.6	37.8	2.0	Cons.
1945	640	212	12	394	22	39.8	9.0	47.8	3.4	Labour
1950	625	298	9	315	3	43.5	9.1	46.1	1.3	Labour
1951	625	321	6	295	3	48.0	2.6	48.8	0.6	Cons.
1955	630	345	6	277	2	49.7	2.7	46.4	1.2	Cons.

party list would have to say identically the same things, thus giving the central headquarters even more dominance over personal originality than prevails. (3) The proprietary intimacy of member and constituents would be weakened. But, above all, (4) the major parties want no system that keeps the weakest parties alive or encourages small minorities to create political parties. The example of France, just across the Channel, with its coalition and weak Cabinets, horrifies them. They do not want small survivors who could upset the balance between the two big parties and spoil stable government or confuse electoral identification of political responsibility.

P.R. has been vilified as an "intellectual monstrosity," which prefers minute accuracy to the direct decision of the electorate on who is to form the Government and who is to be relegated to the Opposition.

Close Balance. The near equality of popular votes of the two parties is remarkable. Hence, an additional stimulus to win over the few that may make all the difference in gaining office. In 1951 no less than forty seats were won by majorities of less than 1000. A 500-vote turnover is a bait to the ambitious and a stern warning to the sitting M.P. and his canvassers. In 1955 the figure was the same; in addition, nineteen Conservative and nine Labour seats were won on a minority vote.

No Residential Qualifications for Members. In 1413 a statute had provided that both electors and elected should be resident in the county. The rule was evaded. Professor J. E. Neale, England's famous authority on Elizabethan government, shows how this evasion was practiced. More important, he observes its political effect. We quote:

The very name "carpet-bagger," that we have imported from America and given to intruding outsiders, is a term of obloquy; and yet we have

reason to thank God that things have turned out so. For how else could the House of Commons have greatly surpassed the average ability of the community; how else have provided room for the nation's best available skill and leadership; how else have secured that Parliament should have been nationally rather than locally minded? [6]

This was due to the way that society was constructed—the high gentry had estates in *many* parts of England, and so ambition and influence widely spread. The restrictions were repealed in 1774 by statute.

It is estimated that in the election of 1950 more than one half of the Labour candidates were locally resident; one fourth *not;* and one seventh lived adjacently; and almost exactly so for the Conservatives. There is ample latitude for people with ideas and loyalty to national political principle and fresh energies to move about from one place to another, and so assist in the producing of a nationwide community of understanding. Such people as Mr. Churchill,[7] Mr. Eden, Ernest Bevin, Mr. Attlee, Ramsay Macdonald, and other great figures have found several constituencies other than their places of residence.

In the United States, when such a man as Henry Cabot Lodge loses an election in his own state and district, where is he to go? Perhaps the *larger* the country the *more,* not less, necessary is the abolition of residential restrictions on representatives. It is good to integrate the community economically and socially, all, of course, up to a point.

[6] *The Elizabethan House of Commons,* London, 1949, p. 16.

[7] Mr. Churchill has sat for four different places; Mr. Gladstone also for four. Mr. Dalton, former Chancellor of the Exchequer, tried three different places and failed, then won at a fourth place, left it for a fifth (where he failed), and went on to a sixth for a lasting connection.

Political Parties in Action

I cannot praise a fugitive and cloistered virtue, unexercised and unbreathed that never sallies out and sees her adversary, but slinks out of the race, where that immortal garland is to be run for, not without dust and heat.

—John Milton

In Chapter 3 we offered answers to two questions about British political parties and elections—that is, concerning (I) the general features of the parties and (II) who may vote and sit in the Commons. This leaves for answer in this chapter questions involved in (III) the structure of parties, (IV) the functions of the parties, and (V) the authority of the parties.

III. THE STRUCTURAL GROWTH OF BRITISH PARTIES

Britain is the residence of 50 million people and 35½ million electors. The problem facing Parliament has been to find a size for the House of Commons that, when divided into the above figures, would give (1) an assembly not too small to be "representative" and to man its various committees, and (2) not so large as to be unwieldy for debate, so vast as to degenerate into an unorganizable shouting arena.

The size of the constituencies (p. 71) is large enough to pose the problem of linking up with your friends and getting to know your political rivals, assuming that force is excluded and persuasion is strongly desired. There is then a twofold linkage: within each constituency, in the form of an "association" or "club"; regionally and nationally through nationwide linkage by counties. In the last fifty years London headquarters have more strongly devised unity of policy, integration

by institutions, and strategy. The smallness of the entire nation has permitted a nonoppressive centralization, one that is organic and desired—*shared*.

Central–Local Structure

Structure is necessary, and it assumes creative loyalty and, reciprocally, promotes operational loyalty.

Up to 1832 the nation was a mosaic of almost independent constituencies, linked mainly by the influence of the Whig and Tory high leadership and the patronage of the King and Treasury. Later, the Conservatives' Carlton Club and the Liberals' Reform Club assumed a loose leadership. It was the increase of the electorate that made concerted action essential, at the minimum to see that one's friends registered for their vote. Hence, local "registration" societies developed, canvassing to get people to claim their votes.

The activity was given decisive momentum by Sir Robert Peel, the Conservative leader, one of the new manufacturing class to enter politics. In 1838, he wrote to a friend:

There is a perfectly new element of political power—namely, the registration of voters, a more powerful one than either the Sovereign or the House of Commons. That party is the strongest in point of fact which has the existing registration in its favor. . . .

In 1841 he urged his supporters to "Register, register, register!" His was the first modern election address: a potential Prime Minister appealing directly to the voters. Conservatives and Whigs, Liberals and Radicals proceeded to organize. At first oligarchic, they were in the 1860's forced to open their doors to the masses. Cities, such as Liverpool, Manchester, Birmingham, and Leeds, had three members at large, voters not being allowed to vote for more than two. "Vote as you are told," became the organizers' formula for beating this attempt at minority representation. In Birmingham, under Joseph Chamberlain, father of Neville (later Prime Minister) and Austen (later Foreign Secretary) and his manager Schnadhorst, remarkable feats of organization gave a stimulus thereto everywhere.

Party Organization

In 1867 the Conservatives linked their local associations into the National Union of Conservative and Constitutional Associations. In 1878 the Liberal Party established the National Liberal Foundation—its purpose, in Chamberlain's words (he was its elected president), was to have "a really Liberal Parliament, outside the imperial legislature, and, unlike it, elected by universal suffrage and with some regard for a fair distribution of political power." This idea of a "Parliament outside Parliament"—of what has come to be called the "mass party" as distinct from the old-style "collections of notables," aroused many protests from the latter. When the Liberal Prime Minister stumped the country, he was reproached with conducting "pilgrimages of passion." It was but a portent.

Conservative Party. The Conservative national organization is the National Union of Conservative and Unionist Associations, or N.U.C.U.A. It is a *federation* of constituency and central associations. Its purposes are officially stated as: to promote party associations everywhere; to foster thinking and effort to further the principles and aims of the party; to be a center of united action and a link between *the leader* and all party organizations; to maintain close relationship with the Conservative and Unionist Central Office. Its Central Council is composed of fifteen categories of members, such as constituency associations, central associations, provincial areas, university graduates, etc. Members and peers and prospective candidates are also entitled to membership. Party officials and Central Office agents in the provinces are entitled to attend. At its annual meeting it selects a president, a chairman, and three vice chairmen. It also then chooses an executive committee, composed of the *leader of the party* (pp. 92–94), various party officials, and some from the categories above-mentioned. It will be noticed that the leader is chosen elsewhere.

The Central Council organizes the party's annual conference. This numbers over 5500 people, of whom about 3500 actually attend. It is composed of all the Central Council, plus seven representatives from each constituency association, the latter's chairman, treasurer, Young Conservative committee chairman plus one other Young Conservative, the chairman of the labor advisory committee, one lady, and one more lady or gentleman. The M.P. or prospective candidate and the certificated organizer may also attend. The conservative annual conference was the first to permit TV of itself in 1954.

The various associations may submit resolutions. Divisions are rare; if so, each delegate has one vote. (Labour conferences use the "bloc vote" method, p. 76). Labour conferences have more authority over policies; the Conservative conference is rather one of advice, not orders, to its leader. Policy-making is rather more in the hands of the leader, the social auxiliaries and clubs, and the members of Parliament. A Conservative Party committee that recommended reforms of the party's organization in 1948 defined the National Union's purpose as, "an educative political force and a machine for winning elections." But it is more than this: it carries the word of the leader everywhere and it presses him to heed the mind of the Conservatives everywhere as to policy and leadership.

The Conservative Central Office is markedly in contrast to Labour Party organization, for Labour has a single national executive committee, which is elected annually by the annual conference; from the members upward. But the Conservative Party has *two lines* of authority. One is the *National*

British Political Party Organization

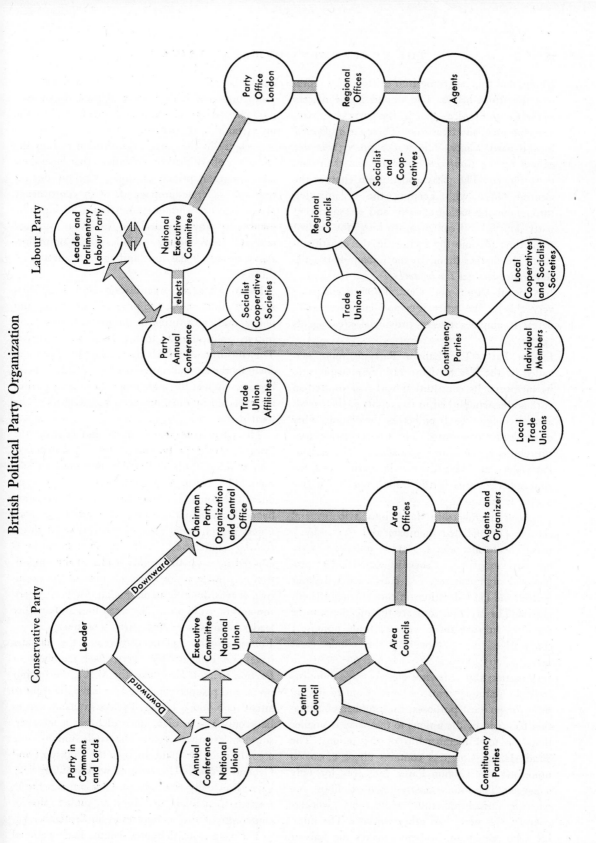

Conservative Party

Labour Party

Union, and this has come into existence by representation from below. The second is the officers of *the Central Office*—that is, the party chairman, vice chairmen, and treasurers. These are *appointed* by the party *leader.* The leader (p. 93) *is not chosen by the Conference* nor are the chairmen, treasurer, etc. The party constitution charges the Central Office with keeping the organization throughout the nation efficient and disseminating party policy, "and conveying to him (the *leader*) from time to time the feeling in the constituencies." He charges them! In the Labour Party, the conference charges *the leader!*

National Union and Central Office cooperate very closely; the latter lists and endorses candidates. It employs twelve provincial area agents (p. 79).

Labour Party. The Labour Party is more pervaded by the idea of democratic responsibility to its members. Its constitution was first drafted in 1918 and is republished in the report of the party's annual conferences. It embodies the responsibility of the leader downward. The Conservatives' constitution is vague as to responsibility. The Labour Party does not formally nor in spirit admit the stratospheric status of the leader, nor has it two bodies at the top.

Labour membership falls into two general classes: (1) affiliated members and (2) individuals. The former are: (*a*) trade unions, (*b*) cooperative societies, (*c*) socialist societies, (*d*) professional organizations, (*e*) constituency Labour parties, and (*f*) federations of constituency Labour parties. The organizations are the members, to be pedantic. In 1955 there were 84 trade unions; 1 cooperative society (covering the whole great membership); 4 socialist societies; 667 constituency parties; and 23 federations. As trade unionists have the statutory right to contract out of paying dues for political purposes, the number of affiliation fees paid by the unions to the party is smaller than the total membership of the unions. The Trade Union Congress contains about 8,900,000 unionists; the Labour Party gets fees for only 5,000,000. The miners are represented almost 100 percent; agricultural and "white-collar" workers contract out more than other workers. The number who remain in, however, makes the Labour

Party the offspring of the unions, and yet pervades unionists with a sense of state responsibility. The reciprocal effect is fundamental to the understanding of Britain.

A clause in the party's constitution forbids the affiliation of political organizations that have their own program, principles, and policy for distinctive and separate propaganda with constituency promotion of candidates, or those "owing allegiance to any political organization situated abroad." This sternly excludes the Communist Party, though it has time and again attempted infiltration.

Every affiliated organization and individual member must accept the program, principles and policy, and constitution of the party. It must submit its political rules to the National Executive. The constituency parties must adopt the rules laid down by the annual conference. If individual members are eligible for trade-union membership, they are expected to join; they must be members of the local party.

The party conference directs and controls the "work" of the party, subject to the constitution and standing orders. Regular meetings are annual. The National Executive may call special ones. The conference may amend the constitution by ordinary majority but only every third year, unless the National Executive specially advises a coming conference. Such an amendment was effected in 1953: the deputy leader of the Opposition was made an *ex officio* member of the executive. It was done to accommodate Herbert Morrison and to avoid a clash between him and another leader who was elected party treasurer.

Voting Rights. At the conference, the affiliates have one delegate for every 5000 members or fraction thereof. *Ex officio,* the M.P.'s, the Labour peers, and prospective candidates have the right to attend (no vote). Hence, the constituency parties have only 1 vote each, since each has a membership of less than 5000. The trade unions vote according to dues paid. In 1950 the Transport and General Workers Union could have sent 167 delegates; it actually sent only 40. (Reason: expense in relation to political usefulness to junket-value of conference at the seaside resort in September.)

The votes, not delegates, count. Each national

and constituency organization has 1 vote for each 1000 members with fees paid up. There is 1 voting card for each unit of 1000 votes. Voting is by these cards; hence the jargon, a "card vote." Each delegation leader casts x or y thousand to which his organization is entitled.

The Executive's Composition. On all matters, except the executive, no distinction is made between the kind of votes cast. The executive numbers 28. Representation on it is by compartments: 12 nominated and voted for by the trade unions; 1 by socialist, the professional and cooperative delegations together; 7 by the constituency organization; 5 women nominated by any organization and elected by the conference as a whole. Thus the trade unions, as such, must leave a substantial place for the "highbrows" of the party. To the 25 mentioned, must be added 2 *ex officio* members: the leader of the party and the deputy leader. Finally, the treasurer is elected by the conference at large. Usually a single nomination is uncontested (p. 76). Until 1937 the constituency members of the executive were voted for by the whole conference. Ernest Bevin persuaded his fellow unionists to make the change, as the conference felt unfairly swamped.

The party-organization chairman is elected annually at the conference. By custom he or she is the person longest on the executive.

Is the Party Merely the Trade Unions? At the conference of 1955 voting power was distributed thus: trade unions, 5,529,760; socialist societies, 9000; cooperative societies, 28,000; Labour parties, 933,657; federations, 19,000. Figures rounded, the unions have 5 votes in every 6. In 1955 the unions sponsored 128 candidates for election of whom 96 were successful, and another 15 members of trade unions were unsponsored M.P.'s. In 1954 the unions provided £139,000 of the party's annual ordinary income of about £200,000 or 70 percent.

This means that the Labour Party is a trade-union party—but *only* broadly speaking. The party was founded largely by the unions because they were more than merely economic organizations: they were *civic* groups. From the beginning the English trade unions were pervaded by a philosophy of the State, that of democratic social-

ism, the former meaning liberty, the latter meaning equality of opportunity and social welfare. This implied a sense of obligation to a nation; not merely a contest for more wages, less work, and less hours for organized labor obtainable by sheer strength. The trade-unions leaders sought industrial justice through Parliament. But, also, the Socialist societies (such as the Fabian Society) and the individual members—more consciously the thinkers of a just and humane State—have nurtured the Labour Party's sense of State.

When, then, the unions vote, they are already political, not industrial leaders only. They must be convinced by argument. In the 1930's it was necessary for Ernest Bevin, a powerful labor leader, to crush George Lansbury, the party leader, for his feeble utopianism in wooing Hitler and Mussolini to pacifism. Bevin also obstructed Sir Stafford Cripps who was trying to lead the party into a Popular Front with the Communists (who were meanwhile disrupting the unions), preaching nationalization *without* compensation and making untimely threats against the monarchy, the Lords. The unions strongly protested the party's pacifism as soon as they saw what Nazis and Fascists did to union funds and activities. But they showed remarkable discipline under the Labour Government's stable-wage policy in the reconstruction period after World War II. In 1954 and 1955 they preferred the leadership of Hugh Gaitskell to that of Aneurin Bevan, especially against the latter's pro-Soviet policy. Voting alignment at the conferences is not usually the unions *versus* the constituency parties, but mainly a majority of the unions plus the constituency parties *versus* a minority of the latter plus one or two Left-wing unions.

The reliance on the mass of trade unionists to pay dues and vote for the party makes it a "mass" party in modern terminology. The Conservatives are bitterly jealous of this following. They seek in vain for trade-union members. They are joyous when occasionally a trade-union leader suggests that unionists *might* have to reconsider whether unions *should* be permanently attached to one party! On the other hand, some Labour members deplore the fact that union strength decides policy, especially when the "bloc" vote obscures the divided situation in the unions themselves. It is voluntary on the part of the unions to use the "bloc" vote; they could decide on split votes.

The Work of the National Executive

It is entrusted with two duties: to ensure the establishment of and keep in active operation a party in every constituency; and enforce the constitution, standing orders, and rules of the party, by any action it deems necessary for this, *including disaffiliation of local party (an active power!) organizations* or expulsion of individuals. Its headquarters are at Transport House, a building near Parliament, shared with the Trades Union Congress. Its chief official is the "secretary of the Labour Party," selected by the National Executive Committee with the approval of the conference. This may be contrasted with the Conservative chief official who is appointed by the leader of the party.

The party owes very much to the secretary, who is a career political man, not an appointee for one campaign only. He is head of a large staff. Since he organizes and puts the drive into the regional organizations and agents, into the research departments and the production of literature, much, indeed, depends on him. He can help or hinder candidates to get constituencies. Moreover, depending on the personality, he may take very seriously the duty of keeping in touch with the Labour and Socialist parties of the rest of the world, attending meetings, being leader or choosing delegates, and so amass an understanding of foreign affairs that may be of substantial use to his political leaders.

The Conservative Party has twelve provincial regions (London being one), each with an area council on which the constituencies in the area are represented. For their party, they raise money and raise Cain. The Central Office has an office in each region or area and staffs it with its area agent. He is the Central Office's servant for the purposes of the party. But, at the constituency level, the agent is the servant of regional body, though some of his payment may be out of a grant by the Central Office. The Conservatives have a separately organized party for Scotland.

The Labour Party covers the whole of Britain with one organization. Like the Conservatives, it has its regional organization—eleven regions, each with an agent of the Executive. For both parties, coming up from the grass roots, there are federations of counties; but in the Conservative Party only one, in Labour twenty-five. The democratic character makes the difference.

Here then is the spiritual weft of the central headquarters, stretched through the whole body politic of Britain, giving aid, comfort—and hell—to the local constituency parties and receiving from these the sap of life and the kick of constructive and critical political will. From the localities come the votes, with the original meaning of voice and wishes; from the center, the added inspiration, the comprehensiveness of vision, the constancy of resolution to win everywhere, the attendant universal stimulation, the central skills and finance.

Professional Election Agents

The agent in the constituency corresponds roughly to the American "campaign manager." Candidates have used agents, in this connotation, since the beginning of parliamentary elections, but sporadically and with every local personal idiosyncrasy. Since 1885, when election expenditures were regulated by statute, each candidate has been *obliged* to have an agent, for the law requires that election expenditures shall be disbursed by him alone and accounted for to the central government, the Home Office, within a certain term after the election. Yet the political behavior and value of the agent are the consequence of the need for a professional manager of election campaigns, and, if it can be afforded by the candidate or the local constituency party or wholly or partly by party headquarters in London, between campaigns also.

The statutory requirement is: "A person shall be named by or on behalf of each candidate as the candidate's election agent . . . and *one* election agent shall be appointed for each." The Representation of the People Act then places on him certain obligations, especially in relationship to expenditures. Along with these obligations, penalties are enacted for some illegalities, involving loss of a seat won and banning from candidacy in the future. The purpose of the requirement was made plain by the Committee on Electoral Reform that examined the election laws prior to the passing of the Act. It said: "The object of the requirement is that there shall be an experienced person responsible to the candidate and to the public for the proper management of the candidature and in particular for the control of expenditure."

Many cases have come before the law courts in the past involving the behavior of candidates during election campaigns, in which persons claiming to act on their behalf—as it were, as master and servant—have been charged with violating the law purposely or by accident and thereby involving the candidate in great trouble. Furthermore, since the candidates have always been able and still may appoint *themselves* or their wives as agents under the statute, they have run the risk, through ignorance or inexperience, of violating the law. The law courts have drawn the responsibility of the candidate for the action of the agent with extreme stringency: "The affairs of the election should be carried on in the light of day and a respectable and responsible man responsible to the candidate and to the public should be there to do all that is necessary." [1] The agent manages a campaign—that is, he must do all those things that are necessary to amass the maximum votes for his side and diminish the votes his opponents are trying to collect. He must know the election laws thoroughly—but he can get sage advice from the legal counsel at the disposition of Central Headquarters. He, unassisted, must know his local constituency with detailed, vivid thoroughness. Since he is responsible legally, and he has both paid assistant agents (depending on circumstances) and many other workers, he must be a capable manager of human beings. When the money is available, the chief agent has deputies and specialized organizers of publicity, youth, women, education, public speaking (reciting party stereotypes!).

The Labour Party, being poorer, has only about half as many full-time agents. To compensate, it disposes these in *marginal* constituencies, nearly one half being so located. All appointments of agents require the approval of the National Executive. The scales of pay are about one third to one fourth less than the Conservatives'. Labour headquarters supplements salaries and pensions. It is at a disadvantage, however, in spite of zeal. Also, the local trade unions give steady help in organizing the campaigns, in strategy, getting out the vote, and secretarial help.

Here then is the grass-roots organization around the candidates, and the intimate nucleus closely connected with headquarters in London, for drawing together the voters and maintaining and recreating an organic and united fellowship of like-minded followers over the whole nation.

This organization the Conservatives reformed from 1948 onward, following their defeat in 1945; in 1955, Labour suffered the first shock of winning fewer votes at an election than at a previous one. It, too, turned to repair of its machinery.[2]

[1] Justice Field, *Barrow-in Furness Case,* 1886. See A. N. Schofield, *Parliamentary Elections,* London, 1950 and 1951, p. 190 and pages following for many other judicial decisions. The judges indicate the common-law master–servant relationship rules rather than principal–agency status. An excellent example of the relationship between statute law and law as developed by judicial decisions.

[2] On October 5, 1955, the Labour Party published the *Interim Report* of its committee on *The General Organization of the Party.* The Committee had pursued its inquiries over the previous few months. Its chairman was Harold Wilson, M. P., member of the National Executive (top of the list of "constituency" members) and former Minister (Board of Trade), by profession an Oxford don.

It reported itself "shocked at the state of the party organization in many parts of the country." It quoted the remark of one M. P.: "When the tide is with us our bad organization, relatively to the Tories', doesn't matter; when the tide is against us our bad organization is fatal."

Their findings may be thus summarized. Voluntary workers were fewer and less enthusiastic than in the past. Party workers were of the older generation and their organization "rusty and deteriorating with age." In some places no canvassing at all had been undertaken. Agents were lacking; the postal vote had not been organized, and cars had not been mobilized. The National Agent had had too little authority and staff, being overlapped by the General Secretary; there was insufficient drive, therefore, from this position. The relation between the national headquarters staff and the regions was too bureaucratized, for the latter supplied 7000 written reports to the former per year, but the amount of personal consultation was too scanty. The local machines spent too much time on trying to convert others to Labour voting and far too little time to identifying Labour certainties and bringing them to the polling booth. Indeed, so slack was this latter function that the committee estimated that *47 seats were lost through this cause!* Insufficient help had been given by the safe constituencies to the fighters in the marginal ones. Much more attention must be paid to organization, then; more

IV. THE FUNCTIONS OF
BRITISH PARTIES

When the behavior of British political parties in actual operation is analyzed and classified, six main functions emerge. We list them. It will be appreciated that these activities are intimately related to the structure of parties, as ends are to means.

The six functions are: (1) Parties bridge distance between electors—this has already been related to the development of the nationwide network of individual constituencies and headquarters in London (pp. 73–74). (2) They recruit members,[3] combat apathy, and (3) they educate—these are implemented through the local constituency parties assisted and coordinated by the center through a variety of techniques of communication with the voters, such as meetings, literature, speeches by candidates and national leaders and organizers, by radio and TV, etc. (4) They define policy and set time priorities—that is, establish programs through national conferences and official research organizations. (5) They select spokesmen, leaders, and rank-and-file candidates by means of regularized process of local nomination and headquarters' endorsements and selection, with disciplinary machinery to secure loyalty to program and leaders. (6) They assume political responsibility—through adequate, reputable, and permanently operative party institutions, the party's constitution and the obligations it requires, and interlaced connections with the leadership of the House of Commons and the Lords, they make electoral promises into serious political commit-

money was needed, to the extent of another £60,000 per year, to come substantially from the local constituencies; for more full-time agents were needed, together with a national team of agents to be sent into strategic areas. However, though more money and professional organizers were needed, special emphasis was paid on zealous party volunteers. "Compared with our opponents [the Conservatives]" we are still at the penny-farthing stage in a jet-propelled era. . . ." "Penny-farthing" is the adjective which idiomatically signifies the cheapest and poorest quality purchase.

[3] With its trade-union affiliates, the Labour Party has (1956) a little over 6,000,000 members and 667 local parties. The Conservative Party has some 542 local associations and about 2,805,000 members.

ments to enact the relevant laws and guide administrative and foreign policy.

The ensuing discussion bears these functions and their structural counterparts in mind, but it does not deal with them seriatim in this exact order.

The Election Campaign

A political meeting may arouse zeal, but it also has an intellectual content. A party badge or button may appeal to emotions that bring voters to the polling booths, but the symbols evoke the program that has been reiterated for years with something of the intellectual appeal of a printed page. Passion and facts are mixed in the electoral process. The three weeks of the campaign are only highly intensified versions of what goes on as a fairly substantial endeavor all year round. Here, we consider the activities of parties to mobilize party spirit and educate during the campaign.

The period available is some three weeks; latterly, it has been rather more, because the Prime Ministers in 1945, 1950, and 1951 and 1955 gave considerably earlier notice of the dissolution of Parliament and the date of the election. If an election is imminent, the leaders do not like it to be deferred, since the House may lose its sobriety.

The high campaign period is the time that stretches between (1) the date of the dissolution of Parliament and (2) Polling Day: the time between the first and second is twenty days or practically three weeks; thus, in 1955, the former occurred on May 7, when writs were issued to the returning officers in the constituencies, and May 27, Polling Day. Three days after the dissolution, nominations of candidates to the returning officers began, and they closed on the 17th—that is, one week after. The "clear twenty days" at the minimum was laid down in the Representation of the People Act of 1918 (Sec. 21:3). The Crown's proclamation at once dissolves and summons the next Parliament, stating the two terminal dates.

The campaign is strongly in the hands of party headquarters. The leaders on all sides have concentrated on the problems of victory almost constantly. The momentary Prime Minister and Ministers, and the Leader of the Opposition and the Opposition Bench, and their confidants and top managers and agents decide the lines, though they themselves, of course, are asking for their personal election merely as members of the Commons like any ordinary M.P. Policy is decided here at the top level, not in the constituencies. It is expressed in the Election Manifesto. These fairly brief documents state the chief issues and the party answers. Each is taken by its opponents *as a commitment,* on which *a mandate* has been asked from the electorate. Voters know that the local variations of the Manifestoes will not commit the leaders; also that the leaders will be expected to fulfill their promises. This is no *"platform from which to depart,"* in the American quip.

The Prime Minister and Leader of the Opposition tour the nation; so do the other party leaders. They cross-examine the speeches of the principal opponents. Their impact in the localities far outdoes that of the local candidate.

Normally there are two candidates for each seat (thus in 1955 Labour and Conservatives had 617 and 624 respective); and in some constituencies, in addition Liberals (110 in 1955) or Communists (17 in 1955) and a few Independents. It is good political education where the issues are presented by two rivals, and everywhere, as in Britain. It moderates exaggeration and distortion, blandishments, and illegalities. Systems that have more than two rivals (Continental) are prone to confuse the electorate. The British system tends to reduce the number of potential candidates by requiring, since 1918, the deposit of £150 by the candidate with the Returning Officer. The candidate loses this unless he polls at least one eighth of the votes cast at the election. It is quite a deterrent.[4] The British elections settle which party shall be the Government. This is different from the systems with many parties, where a coalition is formed *after* the particles have been elected. The

Soviet Union's Communist Party tells only one side of the story to the voters.

Intensity of the Fight. The electoral fight in Britain is extremely intense, though sober, because who will win depends on who gets the major part of about 3 percent of the voters, those who are not so precommitted as to be absolutely in each party's bag. Each vote may be the decisive one.

Moreover, the number of seats in the Commons will decide the magnitude of a Government's authority, legislative *and executive,* both domestic and foreign, and what strength is vested in the Leader of the Opposition. It is now well known that if votes are divided between the main two parties in the ratio $A : B$, seats will be shared $A^3 : B^3$. This cubic proportion multiplies the importance of getting the votes.

Supposing it is true, as a Gallup Poll of 1949 showed, that 84 percent of the electorate had already made up their minds, that the mood of the election was set? Still, 16 percent going one way or the other can give sovereign power for five years. The parties must at least make sure their own voters do not stay at home. The heavy Labour defeat of 1955 was caused by the very large number of deliberate stay-at-home voters. Many of these might have been brought to the polls; that was the lesson for the party. We have noted the marginal seats (p. 72); with a little more effort, people said, 47 could have been won (p. 79, *fn.*). Some candidates will win national spurs by getting results better than the average.

There is a general tendency for the pendulum of votes to swing against the Government in office. Its promises were a little exaggerated; the reality is not so nice; the taxes are usually heavier than predicted. Then, of course, there are serious issues that surge up for national solution, and changes occur in class composition and interests.

"Literature." The outstanding campaign literature is the candidates' election address. It runs about 1500 words. Since the Representation of the People Act, 1918, the law allows the candidate to send free of postal charge one communication to each elector containing election material, weighing not over two ounces. This is the candidate's personal composition, apologia, testament, and appeal. In

4

	1945		1950		1951		1955	
	Stood For-		*Stood For-*		*Stood For-*		*Stood For-*	
		feits		*feits*		*feits*		*feits*
Liberals	307	64	475	319	109	66	110	61
Communists	21	12	100	97	10	10	17	15
Conservatives	573	5	620	5	617	3	624	3
Labour	604	2	617	0	620	1	617	1
Independents (and some Welsh, Irish & Scotch Nationalists)	178	80	56	39	20	16	36	21

The Swing of the Pendulum

Government Majorities since 1832

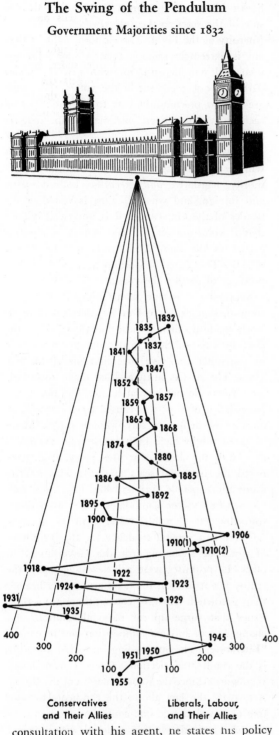

400　300　200　100　0　100　200　300　400

Conservatives and Their Allies | **Liberals, Labour, and Their Allies**

a photo of himself and wife and children with, perhaps, a picture of the party leader. There are some local diversities—housing, unemployment, etc. There is personal "kick" in these addresses, important in the central-local organism of the party. But they follow closely the Manifestoes and the regular party literature, which is plentiful. These are adopted not as copying, obsequious followers of the leaders but as voluntary communicants in the same church. The Labour Party, formally, does not permit its candidates to depart from the party Manifesto. But, in practice, candidates have the same prayerbook as their leaders because they have the same religion.

Although the local fight is between local candidates, *the* battle is between two teams of men and women, alternative Prime Ministers and Cabinets. The local base and victories decide the governmental apex. As Lord Robert Cecil declared, the British constitution is "plebiscitary": the people choose the Government. This is of tremendous significance, for the will to obey the Government later when it makes laws and asks for taxes and performance is conveyed simultaneously with the power. The voters vote only for M.P.'s, not for Prime Minister and Ministers, but their votes when added up will tell which party shall have the right to designate a government.

Other "Educational" Material. Each party headquarters issues, at cost to the candidates, various kinds of leaflets, placards, "election news," some on special topics—such as education, "war and peace," "the housewife and prices," etc. Slogans are invented for posters or window cards or mobile loud-speakers, such as "Fair shares for all"; "Whose finger is on the trigger?"; "Make Britain strong and free!"

The newspapers (pp. 9–11) participate heavily on party lines, though the major speeches and tactics of all parties are reported. Some papers enter the arena strongly: the *Daily Express* and the *Evening News* and *Evening Standard* on the Conservative side, and the *Daily Herald,* the property of the Labour Party, and the *Daily Mirror,* strongly Labour, so impassioned as to bring on itself a libel action by Mr. Churchill.

Each candidate addresses about 100 meetings, consultation with his agent, he states his policy and personal career, slaps his opponents, produces

all very small except two or three, in the course of twenty days. These take place outside factory gates, or for women in the afternoons. There are hardly any great, rowdy rallies, or actors and actresses, singers and bands as in American election tactics. Indeed, British law prohibits expenditure on bands.

The candidate is the most dramatic expression of the party cause to the ordinary voter. Yet less than 10 percent of the voters ever go to meetings. The candidate seeks face-to-face meetings by personal canvassing.

Heckling is an old-established custom: the short-raking question during the candidate's speech. It is designed to test his humor and resourcefulness. Perhaps in ten of 630 constituencies it is used by young enthusiasts to break up an opponent's meeting. This the law now forbids. A tame listening to a candidate is regarded as feeble-mindedness.

Canvassing. Personal house-to-house visiting by party workers is the most effective as it is the most fatiguing educational and vote-getting tactic in British elections. The canvasser is armed with his party's *Speaker's Handbook,* its *Campaign Guides,* "Shot and Shell," containing the party's record in and out of Parliament, its cross-examination of the rival party's record, quotations to prove its veracity. The ideal motto of the canvasser on Polling Day is to have all the workers and cars on the doorstep of the last, least-willing voter of his own party at the last moments of the poll. Till then, he seeks to persuade and to check off the friends, enemies, and neutrals on the electoral list.

Pledges. Central headquarters advise their candidates not to answer the demand for pledges made by pressure groups except in line with party statements. However, local situations may still be troublesome to candidates. Both parties may agree to say No! as in one place where Roman Catholics asked for legal changes to favor their own schools. It has occasionally happened that a candidate's answer has decided a local election.

Radio and Television. These are not privately owned in Britain (p. 11). Their value for education and culture is so highly assessed that immense care is taken by the B.B.C. to maintain political neutrality even in ordinary talks and even at all times *between* elections. During and before the campaigns the facilities are available to the parties on an agreed basis. No individual candidate can buy time for himself, however rich or eminent. In 1955 the number of party broadcasts was five each for the two major parties at the best evening period, after the 9 P.M. news bulletins. Repetition on different networks gave wider coverage. The Liberals obtained three much shorter periods. The Communists were given nothing, the parties having decided that parties with less than fifty candidates should not broadcast. The major parties had two TV appearances each in 1955. The parties choose the leader and his close associates to appear or, occasionally, a striking radio personality in the party; they sometimes use films of their record; they sometimes enact a dialogue. So far, British parties have not indulged in exhibitions of stagecraft, with candidates giving answers to questions by allegedly "representative" citizens from scripts written by other people and legible to them alone at six feet distance; nor have they paraded candidates' families, prowess, stooges, alleged photostatic copies of documents, etc.

Never have so many people been reached by voice or vision in previous elections. The B.B.C. estimates that in 1955 only about 12 to 20 percent of the adult population heard each individual speaker (in 1951, about 20 to 40 percent). About 16 percent of the population watched TV. Is it good? There is an increased overshadowing of the individual candidate. Local meetings appear to have shrunk, eliminating questions to the candidates. The plebiscitary nature of elections has been further emphasized, as also the nationwide communion of each party. Party commitments are more manifest and inescapable, for all who listen or look can hear each party call the other to account. It is a pity that the electorate cannot yet talk back.

On the whole, the wide publicity emphasizes the high degree of veracity in British elections. It assists what this author believes to be of supreme value: the clarification of political issues by analysis of the natural and social data that enter into a decision, without interest-begotten misrepresentation. Election campaigns in England have for long had a kind of sober, adult-education spirit about them. The speeches, etc., have been a responsibly-advanced pattern of party commitments, a kind of blueprint of law and policy, with quite elaborate exposition of administrative and financial consequences. The new media do not detract from this.

What Did the Voters Decide? The contemporary situation is bound to be uppermost in the mind of all concerned. Points are overstated. The pleasure of a policy is overemphasized, the attendant sacrifices underrated. The "mandate" cannot be argued closely enough, as across the table. Priorities and timing cannot be meticulous. Even in this very small land, modern communications, though excellent, still do not allow of subtlety of detail. *Yet*—the *general character* of each party has been amply paraded: its achievements, acumen, trustworthiness to keep promises, sincerity, the intellectual capacity of its members, followers, and leaders alike. It is *the team,* broadly but solidly pictured, that is voted for. Mavericks are amusing, but in the British system they cannot deliver. Divided, the followers of any party can only bawl; united, the party can and must deliver. The party as an entity will have to be trusted, once in office, to meet emergent situations according to its general character. Labour always is wary of Tory "stunts," as that in 1924, when the Communist Zinovieff's letter was used by the Conservatives, or in 1931, when a renegade Labour leader frightened the public with the statement that Post Office savings would be wiped out if Labour were returned. This wariness keeps the bogeys down.

Voting Participation. American journalists can never understand how it is that although the voters in Britain are quiet (*the journalists* call it "apathetic!"), they surpass most free nations (except where there is the compulsory vote) in voting. Since 1906 the lowest vote ever was in 1918, when it was 57.6 percent, owing to the bad registers after World War I. In fourteen elections to 1951 voting never fell below 71.2 percent. On five occasions it was well over 80 percent. In 1950 it was 84; in 1951, 82.6 percent. When, in 1955, it fell to 76.8, the explanation lay in the Labour follow-ing's discontent with its own leaders' dissension, the split between Aneurin Bevan and Mr. Attlee. This falling-off was generally deplored.

By-elections: Their Political Importance

When an M.P. dies or retires between general elections, a prompt election for replacement occurs in the constituency. Such by-elections are of exceptional importance. The voting is regarded by Government and Opposition as an indication of the strength of popular support, and particularly as an indication whether their more recent activities satisfy the electorate.

Most of the seats that are fought for in by-elections go to the party that won them in the previous election. The number of seat changes is negligible. But what is counted with avaricious sharpness is the *number of votes* cast this way or that, measured against the ratio at the general election. The decimal-point swing is the thing: up and down, and pendulum wise. If it happens that a *series* of by-elections occurs in the course of a few months, the swing may be especially significant. The result causes the Government and Opposition to veer and tack according to the electoral wind.[5] Since a changeover of about 3 percent of the electorate will cause a change of party strength in the Commons, it is this kind of figure that is looked for, plus anything that is the special character of the specific constituency. The by-election is a confirmer or modifier of the general mandate. If the constituency is important, the party headquarters may be particularly pressing to supply it with an important candidate. In countries where, like the United States, there are no by-elections, or in those where proportional representation does not allow for them or makes the result fuzzy, an important political value is lost.

The "Purity" and "Freedom" of Elections

The terms *pure* and *free* are taken from a famous case of bribery in 1869. From early times the Commons kept watch over the purity of elections, especially as regards bribery, and this not by force

---

[5] Prime Minister Baldwin *claimed* in 1936 that a lost by-election had caused him to change to a pacific policy regarding the dictators.

of statute law. In 1571 occurred *Long's Case,* in which the House fined the borough of Westbury for receiving a bribe from the member returned, Thomas Long.

Corrupt Practices. The law relating to corruption was codified in 1883, and amalgamated with various other stipulations regarding illegal activities in elections, to make the Corrupt and Illegal Practices Act. This is now incorporated in the Representation of the People Act of 1948. What is the general effect? Corrupt practices are those designed to influence the election by the practices enumerated: it is not the morality or immorality of the actor that is in question: the problem of immorality is already taken care of in the very embodiment of the practice deemed wrong in the statute.

Thus we have under *corrupt* practices the following: (1) *Bribery* to vote or abstain from voting —loans, gifts, promises of money; offers of employment to a voter or someone connected with him; payments for loss of time, wages, or travel expenses to vote, and so on—whether the bribery occurs before, during, or after an election. (2) *Treating*—providing or paying for meat, drink, especially drink, entertainment or provision to voters, relatives of voters, and so forth. (3) *Undue influence*—force or threat of force, violence or restraint, temporal or spiritual injury, or by duress or fraud impeding the free exercise of the franchise by another man. (4) *Personation*—applying for a ballot paper in the name of another person, whether alive or dead; voting twice at the same election; aiding or abetting personation; forging or counterfeiting a ballot paper. (5) *Unauthorized expenditure*—expenditure that is not authorized by the election agent in writing.

In all these cases a corrupt intention must be proved.

Illegal Practices. These include acts which are simply made so by statute, the intention having no bearing on guilt. This falls into four classes. (1) *Illegal payments.* You must not pay for bands of music, torches, flags or banners—but you may pay for cockades, ribbons, or marks of distinction. The Committee on Electoral Law Reform of 1945 (Cmd. 7286) had proposed to allow the now-disallowed objects, saying that so long as the total

expenditure per candidate were limited, he might be allowed to spend this as he wanted. But the Commons decided against bands, torches, flags, and banners—as excessively distracting from the issues. Nor can payments be made to convey electors to the poll. (In the interests of equality, the Act makes special provision for the conveying of voters to the poll [6] and penalizes the use of more cars than so permitted.) Payments may not be made to voters for exhibiting bills or poster. But those who are *not* voters may pay for exhibitions. You may not provide money to make the foregoing illegal payments. (2) *Illegal employment.* Canvassers may not be employed for pay. (3) *Conveyances may not be let or hired* to take voters to and from the poll where the conveyances are kept or used for hire. You must not hire or use premises as election committee rooms where intoxicating liquor or food is sold for consumption. (4) *False statements of fact concerning candidates are illegal*—unless reasonable grounds for believing they were true exist. In addition, false statements that a candidate has withdrawn and money inducements to a candidate to withdraw are also illegal. So are endeavors to break up public meetings.

The subject of corrupt and illegal practices is important from four aspects. First, what is regarded as making an election neither free nor pure? This is in the interests of candor and rationality of choice. The details are to be found in the cases that have arisen out of such practices, manifestly too voluminous even to be summarized here.[7] Second, it is interesting to see that the penalties are severe. Third, who decides cases where elections are contested on these grounds? Fourth, how many cases of corruption are there?

The penalties for forbidden election practices are severe, being fines, imprisonment, and dis-

---

[6] The Representation of the People Act, 1949, allows not more than one motor vehicle for every 1500 county electors or for every 2500 in boroughs for conveying voters to the poll. Labour had been the objector to the privilege other parties had. An extreme statement in 1938 in the Commons by a very respectable M.P. asserted that he had only forty cars (lent to him) while the Conservatives had 200. If each car took twenty-four voters to the poll, the latter took 4800 to his 960. It did make a difference.

[7] See A. N. Schofield, *Parliamentary Elections,* London, 1950 and 1951.

qualification from voting or standing as a candidate for a period of years. The ordinary courts will take care of the persons so charged. But what is of more importance is that from as early as 1384—over 100 years before America was even discovered!—the Commons called on the Crown to decide elections that were contested by an objector. Later, until 1868, it assumed that authority itself. Since that date such contests are decided by two judges of the King's Bench Division seated in special session called an Election Court.

The petition may be presented by voters, a person claiming he had a right to be elected or returned at the election, a person alleging he was a candidate at the election.

The penalty for a substantial illegality or a corrupt practice so extensive that it affected the result may be the loss of the seat to the next candidate in order of votes. This is a frightful penalty—one to deter any would-be corrupt practitioner, or his agent, and to enforce a clear-eyed scrutiny of the law and the punctilious practice by all concerned in the campaign. A partisan decision will not be given by a law court, but it might be given by the Commons or the U.S. Congress and is given in France.

In a whole generation only five cases of corrupt and illegal practices have been brought to court—they were on technical trivialities only. This cleanness is not due to chickenheartedness of candidates and supporters. For between 1837 and 1852 twenty-three seats were declared void for corruption. An act of 1854 commended legislation against corrupt practices and did much good. Public opinion, further laws, the remission of cases *to the courts,* the secrecy of the ballot (1868), and the more systematic organization of political parties purified elections.

Campaign and Other Expenses

The problem is to permit enough and to prohibit too much. The job of publicity and incitement must be done; but a proper equality between the richer and the poorer candidates and parties must be established, since democracy seeks to rule itself by the merits of the case.

Soviet law allows no private expenditure by candidates for election: all the expenses are paid by the State. Soviet lawgivers sneer at democratic practice wherein the State provides only a small proportion of the expense, leaving the election expenses otherwise, they say, to the commercial domination of the wealthy, of "Wall Street" (p. 813). But the Soviet system allows the submission of the Communist Party's candidates only! The democratic State tries to steer between freedom and overregimentation of candidature.

Tremendous sums, ruinous sums (compensated for by government jobs!) used to be spent by the county gentry before the Reform Act of 1832 to get their nominees elected, either in bribes or in dissuading rivals from contesting seats—the latter was by far the cheaper. Not until 1854, however, did a statute deal with election campaign expenses, and then only not by limiting the amount but by requiring that the expense accounts of the candidates should be submitted to auditors appointed by the returning officers, abstracts to be published and bills to be paid through the auditors only. The system failed: for there was no upper limit, and the auditors did not take their duties seriously. Treating on an immense scale was carried on. People sold their votes for such a mess of potage. It is, indeed, surprising how long the monied and social influence of the upper classes lasted in the nineteenth century! No wonder Bagehot in 1867 still claimed that the British masses were "deferrent" to the aristocratic governing class.

The Act of 1883 limited the amount of per-capita expenses per elector, generally defined expenses, and required submission of accounts to the Home Office. The law was further developed. The Labor Party often pressed for large reductions in the maximum permitted expenses. The Act of 1949 sets the amounts permitted. It is noteworthy that they were jointly agreed on by the national agents of the Conservative, Labour, and Liberal parties. A basic figure of £450 per constituency is allowed, plus 2 pence per elector on the register in the counties (normally more extensive areas) and 1½ pence in the boroughs.

All that now needs to be done is merely to compare the old figures (at the maximum) for 1945 with those of 1949 and then to indicate the items on which the money is spent. In county constituencies with an electorate of 70,000, a candidate could spend up to £1835 in 1945; in 1949 and since, £1033 plus. In a borough of 70,000 electorate in the former year, he could spend £1508 plus, against £887 plus in the latter year.

In 1955,[8] of a total of just under £905,000 for all candidates, the proportions were, roughly, for agents, 8.7 percent; for clerks, etc., 5.7 percent; for printing, stationery, etc., 61.9 percent; for committee rooms, 4.6 percent; miscellaneous, 9.4 percent; meetings, 4.1 percent; and personal expenses of candidates, 5.7 percent.

Conservative candidates spent 93 percent of their permitted maxima; Labour only 83 percent; Liberals, 55 percent (from him that hath not is taken away what he hath); and Communists, 31 percent. Where the issue was most in doubt, both big parties spent most heavily. The seats that can be won (the seats that were in fact won) caused the two parties to put their hands deepest into their pockets—they were miserly to the seats they lost.

Unpublished Headquarters Funds. The political party headquarters run propaganda mills all the year round, supply the local candidates with literature at cheap rates, and send in speakers. Money for these is not accounted for by law. Only one party tells openly where it gets such funds and for what it uses them: the Labour Party. The other parties have refused to follow the Labour Party's lead or join with it in its proposals that party accounts should be publishable by law.

"Pressure-group" Propaganda. One other kind of electoral propaganda is in use and ought to be mentioned—that is, the general but deliberate publicity of industrial and commercial firms designed to secure the victory, if not of specific candidates, then of one political party rather than the other.

The matter was raised just before the election of 1950 by the Labour Party, who felt the cause of nationalization was being prejudiced by the incursion of Big Business into propaganda on a bigger scale than ever before. The Attorney General (Labour) threatened to challenge seats that had been won by such help. This might have meant that perhaps half the seats in the House would be contested in the courts! The Act of 1948, following earlier acts, did forbid expenses

for promoting or procuring "the election of a candidate" being incurred by persons other than the candidate's agent—for meetings, public displays, advertisements, circulars or publications, or otherwise presenting the candidate or his views or his backing or disparaging another candidate. But these limitations had never been applied. Headquarters and their industrial friends had been careful. The Conservatives threatened to take up the question of trade-union political assistance should they themselves be challenged. This gave the Labour Government some pause. However, in the 1950 election a great sugar company took *down* its posters against the nationalization of the sugar industry. But in 1951, perhaps deliberately, a tin corporation advertised its hatred of the welfare state and limitations of dividends by government. The Labour Government prosecuted. The law courts in February 1952 held that the advertisement was not directed to the election of any *particular candidate,* therefore it was not illegal. It was held that the law placed no prohibition on expenditure for general political propaganda, even though it *incidentally* assisted a particular candidate against others. This might prove a serious disadvantage to the Labour movement—if its opponents are willing to spend without limitation, and *if* such expenditure did not, electorally, lay them open to the attack: "Whose cause are *they* serving?"

How Much? It has been estimated that each party for all purposes needs in all about £1,000,000 per year. This sum is obtained by Conservatives by subscriptions from the candidates, from private subscribers, by the constituency parties; and in the Labour case, by contributions by the candidates, the local parties, private subscriptions, and by the trade unions—the latter being by far the largest share. Thus, in 1955, of Labour's total annual income of about £600,000 (includes members' dues), trade-union affiliation fees amounted to nearly one quarter. In addition to this the unions make special donations for elections and special propaganda efforts or for the development of particular branches of the party's work, such as the professional career agents.

It is generally estimated that it costs each constituency organization £1000 a year for its regular party work; which means for two parties

[8] *Election Expenses,* H.M.S.O., *House of Commons,* Dec. 8, 1955, No. 141, p. 86.

£2000, which adds up to £1,250,000 roughly for the country as a whole, to be added to headquarters expenses. Conservatives narrowly analyze the other side's finances; they observe that, other than their affiliation fees, the trade unions collect well over £300,000 a year for political purposes; that the Cooperative Union conducts political education that is Labour-spirited to the tune of another £100,000 a year; and that the local cooperative societies spend annually nearly £400,000 on education. Conservative organizers have appealed for a "fighting fund" of £1,000,000, though not necessarily for one year's expenditure.

In the localities the constituencies find the money; the trade unions locally (which raises one kind of problem), and other moneys come forward from other dues from members (at least 6 shillings a year in the Labour Party) and various activities, but the better-off candidates supply some funds. But the Wilson Report (p. 79, *fn.*) says the average dues paid by members of the Labour Party is rather nearer 3 shillings than 6 shillings. It recommends raising it to 9 shillings.

In the Conservative Party, quite a crisis occurred a few years ago, when it was alleged that the younger and less-wealthy men desirous of being candidates were rejected by the local organizations because they could not promise to subscribe enough to run the part steadily. Headquarters was forced to require that the entire expenses of fighting an election shall be met by the local organization; that the candidate shall make no contribution toward the allowable election expenses; and that the selection committee must not mention an annual subscription *before the candidate has been selected.*

The Labour Party requires that the constituency parties be responsible for election expenses, but the candidate or a sponsoring organization may contribute up to 80 percent of these, yet other stipulated conditions actually reduce the contribution to about 50 percent. Nor may contributions from individuals or organizations for regular annual party work be more than £200 in a borough and £250 in a county. The Wilson Report recommended candidates make *no* contribution of this sort.

In spite of the limits, candidates bear a sub-

stantial burden. Their parliamentary salary is small, being £1000 per year, taxed except for proven expenses.[9] Because their duties are heavy, they have little opportunity of outside earnings—for example, in running law firms that are really lobbyists, as in Washington, D.C. (p. 120). In the Labour Party the trade unionists have the advantage, having organization support; in the Conservative, the middle-aged wealthy.

V. THE AUTHORITY OF THE PARTIES

Parties make policy—that is, they construct a firm order of selection for the nation as a whole from the competing values and demands of various social groups, the order in time for their satisfaction, and they produce some consistent accommodation among them. Party leaders devote themselves to such definition of order and priority. Groups and individuals do not see or want to or care about seeing the consequences to others in the pressing of their own egoistic claims, though British groups spontaneously moderate their desired claims, owing to "national" nurturing—the "built-in" constitution (p. 55). A broad philosophy of life, a nexus of principles, must be the criterion to set values and interests in subordination. The political parties are the instruments *par excellence* in fashioning this criterion.

The top leaders, arrived there *after some twenty years of parliamentary drudgery,*[10] become leaders in their highest party committees and among their parliamentary followers. Both of these fashion

[9] Payment of members was introduced in 1911, after many forecasts of the sinister effect it would have on the character of the people it would tempt to stand. It had been an ancient practice, from the Middle Ages, for the boroughs and counties themselves to support their representatives. Without public payment, the workingmen's representatives were handicapped. By 1949 the annual payment had risen to £1000; of which only £500 is taxed, as the rest is calculated to be toward necessary expenses. Members have free travel between their constituency and the House but no car allowance or free postal, telegraph, or secretarial services. The payment is not enough, according to a House report in 1954. But the House would not vote itself more, because it was conscience-stricken about the fate of pensioners who were suffering from the rise in prices.

[10] The seven Conservative leaders preceding and including Churchill served in Parliament an average of twenty-four years, and were acknowledged leaders of the Party for an average of nine and one-half, two dying in that office.

policy—not the "platform committees" suddenly called together as in American presidential conventions, then to disperse.

At the Labour Party's annual conference, the National Executive Committee (p. 76) presents resolutions of policy. The various membership bodies may submit resolutions to the National Executive and offer amendments to those of the Executive. The personal liaison between the National Executive and the parliamentary leaders approaches the likeness of Tweedledum and Tweedledee.[11] The Labour leader has usually had enough of his colleagues of the Parliamentary Labour members on the N.E.C. to make a majority. The conference debates the resolutions. It is very rare that the Executive's resolutions are rejected or amended. But it happens. Sometimes the members' resolutions are adopted. The Executive trims its sails to the expected storm.[12] The pattern and blueprint is well cogitated by high and lower levels. The public looks on via the press. All contenders have had their say. A majority vote commits all the party.

What Authority?

This policy constitutes the commitments of the party. But it is held by all parties (except the Communists) that the policy is not authoritatively imposable on the parliamentary leaders of the party except as these can accept it on *their responsibility as members of Parliament,* as Her Majesty's Government or Opposition. The principle of parliamentary privilege prevails: what is done in Parliament must not fall under the coercion of bodies outside it. This has been so even in the Labour Party, where democratic ideas of "delegated" leadership have been stricter than with the Conservatives, and where a minority has tried to impose conference and N.E.C. views on the leader and Parliamentary Party.

While this principle does not fully correspond

to the highly popular nature of the British form of government today, it is nevertheless maintained, so that the leaders in Parliament may be able (1) to act according to the emergent contingencies of time, place, circumstances, and the strength of their opponents and (2) to take a view that is national rather than bound to delegate-type instructions.

From the relationship of the individual member of Parliament to his constituents to the relationship between the leaders of the parties and their following has been instructively transferred the principle of representation rather than delegation enunciated almost two hundred years ago by Edmund Burke[13] and enshrined in the notion of Parliamentary privilege.

> Their [his constituents'] wishes ought to have great weight with him; their opinion high respect; their business unremitted attention. It is his duty to sacrifice his repose, his pleasures, his satisfaction, to theirs; and above all, ever, and in all cases, to prefer their interest to his own. But, his unbiased opinion, his mature judgment, his enlightened conscience, he ought not to sacrifice to you, to any man, or to any set of men living. These he does not derive from your pleasure; no, nor from the law and the Constitution. They are a trust from Providence, for the abuse of which he is deeply answerable. Your representative owes you, not his industry only, but his judgment; and he betrays, instead of serving you, if he sacrifices it to your opinion . . . if government were a matter of will upon my side, yours, without question, ought to be superior. But government and legislation are matters of reason and judgment, and not of inclination; and what sort of reason is that, in which the determination precedes the discussion; in which one set of men deliberate, and another decide; and where those who form the conclusion are perhaps three hundred miles distant from those who hear the arguments? . . .
>
> Parliament is not a congress of ambassadors from different and hostile interests; which interests each must maintain, as an agent, and advocate, against other agents and advocates; but Parliament is a deliberative assembly of one nation, with one interest, that of the whole;

11 They may *not* be the same. In 1953, the Executive included seven constituency members who (except Bevan) were all back benchers. None of the trade unionists or women was an M.P. Four were front benchers.

12 In 1954 the Executive avoided a defeat on German rearmament by rewording its resolution, yet retaining its freedom to act. Even so, it won by only 3,270,000 votes to 3,022,000.

13 *Speech to the Sheriffs of Bristol,* 1774, *Works,* Oxford, Vol. II.

where, not local purposes, not local prejudices, ought to guide, but the general good, resulting from the general reason of the whole. You choose a member indeed: but when you have chosen him, he is not a member of Bristol, but he is a member of Parliament. If the local constituent should have an interest, or should form a hasty opinion, evidently opposite to the real good of the rest of the community, the member for that place ought to be as far as any other from any endeavor to give it effect.

The Conservative Party's conference is a much larger body than Labour's. It, too, entertains resolutions from the local associations. Its members are much less contentious and far readier to follow the leader with warmhearted cheers. Whereas the leader of the Labour Party sits through the Labour conference, participating fully in its deliberations, the Conservative leader enters at the end, when business is over.

In both parties, day-by-day policy is made, with long-term significance, by the party caucus—that is, all the members of Parliament of each party, especially those of the House of Commons. They modify the resolutions of their party conferences by the needs of the political battle's front line. It is hardly possible to separate the leaders of the party from the leaders of Parliament. The Labour Party is led by the leadership-in-the-conference; the Conservative by the leadership-with-the-conference. The former is the more "democratic." Neither leaders can move far except consonance with the rank and file, and the latter allow some looseness of rein to the leaders.

The Party and Parliamentary Authority

The problem whether the authority of the party organization over the parliamentary leaders is compulsory was raised in instructive form in 1945. The Labour leader, Mr. Attlee, then in the Cabinet, the wartime coalition, was to accompany Prime Minister Churchill to the projected Potsdam Conference in July 1945. Before it met and on the eve of the June election campaign, the then chairman of the Labour National Executive, Harold Laski, issued a statement declaring that the Labour Party could not be committed to decisions "which have not been debated either in the Party Executive or at meetings of the Parliamentary Labour Party." The mention of *Party Executive* raised a *constitutional* issue. Mr. Churchill at once publicly asked what right had a body outside Parliament (the Labour Executive Committee) to subject Ministers to its will. Were secrets of government known only to Privy Councilors (meaning here Cabinet Ministers) to be divulged to the Labour Party Executive's twenty-seven members who were not Councilors (therefore not bound to secrecy)? Other Conservatives charged a dictatorship of the Party Executive over Parliament. The fundamental question involved of the identification of responsibility in democratic government, is no idle one. Mr. Attlee answered:

> At no time and in no circumstances has the National Executive Committee ever sought to give instructions to the Parliamentary Labour party arising out of the consultation. Indeed, as will be seen from the clause, it has no power to do so.[14] The chairman has not the power to give me instructions, nor do his remarks to a press correspondent constitute the official "authoritative and reiterated instructions" of the Executive Committee of the Labour party.

> With regard to continuity in foreign policy, it is obvious that a Labour Government will follow a policy in accordance with the principles in which it believes and on which its members in the House of Commons have been elected. This is sound constitutional doctrine. Presumably a Conservative Government would do the same.

Mr. Churchill persisted: "What is the real interpretation of these provisions?"

> By way of illustration, the constitution would apparently enable the Executive Committee to call upon a Labour Prime Minister to appear before them and criticise his conduct of the peace negotiations. How he could defend his actions without the disclosure of confidential information I fail to see.

Conservatives suffer no such pangs of conscience. Their leaders seek guidance from outside

---

[14] To confer with the Parliamentary Labour Party at the opening of each Parliamentary session and at any other time when it or the Parliamentary party may desire a conference on any matters relating to the work and the progress of the party.

social and economic groups, and have sometimes been hardly distinguishable from the Carlton Club,[15] the club of their élite.

The Leader's Responsibility. Leaders cannot lead in a vacuum. Their status has been attained by mounting as M.P.'s in the ranks of the party *outside* the Commons as well as inside it. They need its continual support. They cannot, in this democracy, totally sever themselves from the policies sued for by their supporters in the nation, whose votes, and therefore whose ends and interests, are the basis of their authority.

The Conservative Party leaders have, since the end of the nineteenth century, descended from an aristocratic idea of their leader's independence of the mass of the party to acknowledgment, though reluctant and hedged, of their need to respond closely to their rank and file; while the Labour Party leaders have ascended from the pristine conception of delegated authority to a recognition of the proper freedom for the leader: the two parties have met almost at the center. The Conservatives adapted their doctrine under the impulse of electoral defeats—that is, by being forced to pay closer attention to gathering votes; the Labour Party changed its demeanor on recognition of the responsibilities of actual government. Both had to draw logical conclusions from (1) the principle of cabinet government and (2) popular responsibility, while in competition with each other. Hence the formal statements in their constitutions or other organizational documents and leaders' speeches may indicate wide differences on the subject; the practice is almost the same.

Yet—it is urgent that the leadership observe a *constitutional detachment,* as expressed in Burke's principles (p. 89). Prime Ministers, Leaders of the Opposition, M.P.'s, need a marked zone of free choice of policy to satisfy the circumstances of the hour, without previous commitment, upon their own conscience, if that is in their judgment necessary, subject to future parliamentary and electoral repudiation. They will do something very possibly irrevocable, be it wrong or right. The discretion required is measured by the gap in immediate communion between leader and elec-

toral machine, and by that ignorance which is found in most men before they have actually come in touch with manifold and harsh reality in the seat of decision-making power. The Labour Party's conference resolution for an Israeli Palestine could not be carried out by a Labour Foreign Secretary, Mr. Bevin.

The "historic" character of the party as a whole is the best guarantee of the kind of man who may sometimes have to be trusted to take representative decisions without counsel of anybody yet committing everybody, the highest act of authority yet the lowest momentary mandate.

The theme is reminiscent of the theory of Robert Michels,[16] that however democratic a political system may be, only a few actually govern, an oligarchy *necessarily* grows inside the masses and governs them. True, and true everywhere; indeed, a truism. But the real point is to what extent these few are *held* to responsibility to the masses and by them, and what influences are brought to bear on the "oligarchy" by their followers, even, as in the British case, to making them highly subservient to the masses. The party organizations exact the responsibility.

Two observations on this problem, from very contrasting sources, are of exceptional interest for their basic agreement. One is from Aneurin Bevan, made at the Labour Conference of 1948 when he tried to defeat, for the Executive Committee, a floor resolution that the Government (Labour) should by law end the power of the landlords to tie their laborers in landlords' cottages. In fact, the floor resolution was one of those rare cases when the Executive was overcome. Bevan (he was Minister of Health) argued:

> It is quite impossible for a conference of 1100 people, even if it were constitutionally proper, to determine the order in which the Parliamentary Labour Party and the Government introduces legislation in the House of Commons. It is for the conference to lay down the policies of the parliamentary party, and for the parliamentary party to interpret those policies in the light of the parliamentary system. Any other procedure would merely confuse the whole situation.

---

[15] Cf. the entertaining history, by Sir Charles Petrie, of *The Carlton Club*, London, 1955.

[16] *Political Parties*, London, 1916.

Mr. Churchill, speaking to his constituents late in March 1955, said:

The first duty of a member of Parliament is to do what, in his faithful and disinterested judgment, he believes is right and necessary for the honor and safety of our beloved country. His second duty is towards his constituents, of whom he is the representative and not the delegate. It is only in the third place that a man's duty lies to the party organization or program. The further to the left parties go, the more rigid their discipline becomes until finally the personalities and convictions of individuals are ground up, as we see them in the Communist Party, with the power and rigor of the machine.

He added that members of any party should be given latitude and tolerance by their leaders and fellow members, demanding that the former prove their capacity to cope with personal opponents whatever the latter's ambitions and errors.

The Parties Select Leaders, etc.

In the seventeenth century, such men as Pym, Hampden, Cromwell, Laud, Strafford, the Stuart Kings, Clarendon, Ashley, Danby, and so on, holding values and ready to chance their lives for them, formed parties. They were self-chosen. Even the eighteenth-century leaders were largely self-chosen, as Whigs and Tories as parties were still embryonic. "Faction" was frowned on.

In the contemporary nationwide organizations, one enters the ladder that leads to the highest posts through Parliament on the lowest rung: as a candidate for the Commons. Ten or fifteen years of election campaigning, work as a delegate to the annual party conferences and to regional conferences, and of parliamentary experience will winnow the grain from the chaff. Men who have brains, character, charm, political skill, and some luck must demonstrate their active possession in one of the severest schools of government in the world known to history. This is the House of Commons, where all members have reason to believe in their own individual ability and not to be overly indulgent in assessing that of their potential rivals as high as these themselves evaluate it. Many, are called, but few, indeed, are chosen. Mere seniority will not help.

Moreover, they will not be free, or unassisted, during the period of Parliament, in deciding what they must do and the order in which to undertake affairs. The party organization is not disbanded—far from it. And the Opposition, as a concerted "Shadow" Cabinet, confronts the Cabinet in the House of Commons itself, to remind it of election commitments or to vary them as the mood and the needs of the nation evolves. The local agents, the deputations, unofficial and official, of publicly known groups, forcefully keep members of Parliament sensitively aware of their mandate.

This is the process of natural selection of leaders, up to the Prime Minister and the Leader of the Opposition, which may lead to the former. Those who thus come to the top are experienced electorally and parliamentary. Since the House of Commons is sovereign and is in control of administration, directing and controlling its functions, as well as law-making, their experience of business touches the broadest and highest aspects of government.

The Nexus of Extraparty and Intraparty Leadership Organization. For Britain above all, it is not only essential but especially fascinating to observe how the arteries of party are knit together in (almost) seamless unity. Thereby one may glimpse how the people outside Parliament stretch their minds and wills into the Commons, and how the leaders inside the Commons extend theirs beyond the walls to meet them and receive their support or to persuade them to restraining balance.

Inside the Commons each British party conducts parliamentary affairs by an assembly of the M.P.'s and party members of the House of Lords. It is the party meeting, and is occasionally (less so than in the U.S.A.) called the party caucus. But in the Conservative Party, the members of the Commons and the members of the Lords meet separately. The functions of the former are defined in the party's Standing Orders whose fundamental purpose is to secure that members of Parliament conform to the discipline of the party. Similarly, with the Conservative and Unionist Members' Committee, sometimes known as the "1922" Committee, named for the meeting at the Carlton Club in 1922 when the Lloyd George Coalition Government was brought to an end.

The conditions of discipline and the relations between rank-and-file committees of members of

Parliament in the two parties, with the Leader of the Opposition on one side and their own Prime Minister on the other, is not a point that is relevant to discuss here and now. But it is necessary that it be mentioned, and that we know that here is a liaison between the Cabinet and its parliamentary followers, and the Opposition and its parliamentary rank-and-file, and between all these and the party organizations outside. The particulars are properly analyzed in the chapters on Parliament and the Cabinet.

Choice of the Party Leader. One matter is, however, of outstanding importance at this point—the choice of the parliamentary and party leader. For this supplies cohesion and leadership to the party within and without Westminster; while once the party has chosen its leader, he will be the man for whom the Crown will send to form a Government on the appropriate occasions (pp. 139–140).

The *Conservative* leader in the House of Commons has, since 1922 (when Bonar Law was so elected), been chosen by a meeting of the Conservative members of the House of Commons, the Conservative peers, and the party's prospective candidates. In 1923, when Bonar Law retired from the Prime Ministership through fatal illness, the new Prime Minister was Mr. Baldwin, who was shortly after elected to be the leader of the party in an assembly like that which raised Bonar Law to the leadership. Then, in 1937, to this assembly also came the executive committee of the party's representative committee, the Executive Committee of the N.U.C.U.A. Neville Chamberlain was chosen as the leader in succession to Stanley Baldwin, retired. In 1940 an assembly so constituted chose Mr. Churchill to follow Mr. Chamberlain, when the latter died. On this occasion Mr. Churchill was already Prime Minister, which normally means that the party assembly makes the Prime Minister its leader at once. But Mr. Chamberlain had given way to Mr. Churchill as Prime Minister, yet still as leader of the party retained an office in the Cabinet until he retired to die. Once chosen, the leader is not required to resubmit himself to annual election like his counterpart of the Labour Party, though the annual re-election of the latter since 1922 became a steady certainty. Of the seven leaders of the Conservatives since Disraeli, Lord Balfour, Austen Chamberlain, and

Neville Chamberlain were ejected by their party.

In April 1955 Mr. Churchill, who had been leader of the party, retired as Prime Minister, and the Queen, on his advice, made Sir Anthony Eden Prime Minister. Eden was unanimously (note difference from Labour leader Mr. Gaitskell's election [below]) elected leader of the Conservative Party on April 21 at a meeting of the party of over 1000 members, being the Conservative and National Liberal members of both Houses of Parliament, the candidates of these parties, and the members of the Executive Committee of the National Union of Conservative and Unionist Associations. Sir Anthony appeared and spoke briefly *afterward*.

The leader of the Labour Party is elected by the M.P.'s and Lords meeting already referred to and needs re-election year by year, and normally goes on for life or resignation. Mr. Attlee had been elected deputy leader in 1931 to Mr. George Lansbury, leader.[17] The latter retired, disappointed in his quest of peace and hurt by the derision heaped on him by Ernest Bevin on behalf of the trade-unionist sections of the party in 1935. Mr. Attlee was elected to succeed him. Then, later in the year, a new Parliament met. The leadership was contested by Mr. Herbert Morrison and Mr. Arthur Greenwood. Mr. Attlee won against the former, a more vigorous and just as intelligent man, and the latter, an intelligent and highly popular man but less substantial. Mr. Attlee remained leader in spite of some opposition. The Labour movement does not care to remove a man unnecessarily from a job he holds. Later, he made a not unsatisfactory Prime Minister. Challenged by the dynamic and extremist Aneurin Bevan and with the 1955 election lost through defection of Labour voters, alienated by party dissensions, he suggested he vacate the leadership. In June 1955, when the parliamentary Labour Party met, it re-elected him unanimously. Following ill health, he resigned, December 7, 1955. On December 14, the Labour Party M.P.'s by secret ballot chose Hugh Gaitskell[18] as leader with 157 votes; Aneurin

[17] See his *Life* by Edgar Lansbury, London, 1937.
[18] Mr. Gaitskell, son of a colonial official in Burma, became by profession an academic economist, a colleague of the present author's in the University of London. He was educated at Winchester and Oxford, like Mr. Attlee. Strange confutation of Karl Marx's class doctrines!

Bevan received 70 votes, and Herbert Morrison, Deputy Leader until then, only 40. The Bevanites complained about trade-union domination!

The leaders of both parties do not occupy positions of easy tenure. Their followers in Parliament are restive men. Ramsay Macdonald was continually harried and, in a sense driven out; Mr. Attlee had to meet frequent revolts; Mr. Lansbury was forced out, largely by trade-union vigor. In the Conservative Party Mr. Balfour was toppled in 1906; Austen Chamberlain never became Prime Minister because he was held to have sinned in advocating continued coalition with the Liberals in 1922; his brother Neville Chamberlain was harassed for years (Mr. Churchill assisting) until he was contemptuously overthrown in May 1940 by leading members of his own party. Baldwin was driven from pillar to post by his own "friends" as he used to call them, and sometimes contemplated escape by resignation. The status of all leaders is on daily sufferance.

The executive officials at the top of the Labour Party organization are *selected* by the Executive Committee. In the Conservative Party, the chairman (director of organization) and other chief officials are *appointed by the party leader.*

Selection of Candidates

Britain has no primaries as America has, nor has their enactment ever been suggested. The political habits of the local constituency parties have been more responsible than those of American bosses. The process of selecting candidates is unregulated by statute. The desirous candidate approaches or is approached by the local party organizations. These make the choice. The function is important, for it can determine the amount of vigor and brains and conscience in the party, and also the quality of the party as a national political fellowship. In the largest number of cases, there are local men able and willing to stand; or men and women from some other part of Britain who are invited by the locality to stand, whatever their residence may be. The local parties choose according to their preferences of person, character, eloquence, brain, or obligation to trade unions, cooperatives, big employers or landed gentry, and so on. There are usually scores of people outside as well as inside the constituency, the county, or the borough, anxious to stand—even for hopeless seats!

Party Regulation of Candidatures. The Labour Party—not the Conservative or the Liberal Party —has a routine generally stipulated by the party (Constitution, Clause IX) for the process of local selection of candidates. On a vacancy, the constituency organization in the field sends a circular of invitation (formulated by the National Executive Committee) to affiliated and party organizations to appoint delegates to its general committee. Each of these organizations may nominate an individual member of the party or a member of an affiliated organization—excepting certain persons so defined as to exclude Communists. If a person so nominated is on the panel of available parliamentary candidates of an affiliated organization, his executive committee's written consent is necessary, as well as his own. If this consent is obtained, it will carry with it (say from the trade union concerned) financial contributions toward his candidacy and the general funds of the constituency.

In addition to this way of securing nominations, the National Executive Committee may, and does, send out the names of several persons. All the latter are interviewed by the general committee, and those left, plus the local names, are together considered by it. The delegates vote after having heard the interviewed make rival speeches. The trade-union members may have a substantial pull in the choice of candidates, because the number of delegates to the nominating session depends on the numerical dues-paying size of their organization. A series of successive ballots eliminates those at the bottom of the list successively. A clear majority finally is cast for one nominee, and then the delegates make it unanimous.

It is important to appreciate that the local constituencies of both parties are quite independent-minded. The final meeting of a Labour Party nominating session is attended by an official of the National Executive Committee. But the local parties are highly sensitive. Local trade-union officials are often named (p. 64 for figures), not for outstanding ability comparatively considered but out of fraternal gratitude and the fact that the organization is powerful and will find money only for *safe* seats. Similarly with Conservatives, where society motives prevail—rich men had the decided advantage until 1945, as we saw, when a revolt of younger men enforced the rule that the local party was to find most of the electoral expenses! Nor is the situation still much changed.

Central Endorsement. Yet in both major parties the central headquarters requires that a candidate will not be considered as the *party* candidate unless he has received *its* endorsement. It thus makes sure that the rules regarding his party membership, his acceptance of the constitution, and the program of the party are in order. It has an instrument by which it may request the weeding out of men who have a flaw in their character likely to embarrass the party.

Both parties have a register of men and women who are anxious to get into Parliament and have no easy convenient access to a vacancy in their own constituency or residence. For various reasons—local dissension or no one of good-enough quality or only very reluctant possibilities—quite a number of constituencies are glad to have names submitted to them. They do usually want good candidates, to make sure of winning, and to have someone to be proud of. The central office and the local constituencies try to accommodate each other. The Central Office of the Conservative Party sends down one or two names also. It has happened that sometimes the headquarters attempts to oust former members who have not been as compliant as they would like. It is then a tug of will between headquarters and local constituency.

Each party needs thirty or forty pretty certain seats for its leading members, because each party must look to a competent Ministry or Opposition. Or it may want to see a useful but unseated member back again. High-caliber intellectual equipment, debating ability, dignity, creativeness in policy-making and in counsel are urgent. Hence, headquarters negotiates with local party executives to find such a place for these men; and they are often welcome. It confers a distinction on the local party, while the latter are rendering their party a service, as well as forwarding their own interests, nationally elevated.

Endorsement and Party Discipline. Now endorsement is a powerful instrument in the hands of the leadership of the party to secure a loyal, at any rate, an obedient, following. For if a member of the House of Commons proves refractory, throws over the party platform, disobeys the by-laws which set down parliamentary and public discipline in the party, he may be denied the continuation of a political career *on this side* of the House. It is unlikely that the other side will want him—in a safe seat. The refusal of endorsement is rare. But its anticipation sets limits to local and personal license in policy and loyalty to leaders. A wild guess is that perhaps one fifth of the candidates might be improved on if the local hacks were rejected in favor of men and women from elsewhere. Those chosen are still good.

British parties are highly conscious of their moral leadership and the decency of the candidates and M.P.'s. It would be altogether unlikely for a demagogue like Senator Joseph R. McCarthy to get nominated.

Legal Requirements for Candidature. For nomination, according to electoral laws, all that a candidate needs is two electors as proposer and seconder and eight other electors as assentors to his nomination—electors, that is, of that constituency. In addition, £150 deposit must be made. Actually many candidates get hundreds, sometimes even thousands, of assentors—they make the handing of the papers, with press photographers, into an electoral demonstration. (For lost deposits, see p. 81 *fn*).

Clearly there are causes that seek the most dramatic and vivid of incarnations in the personality of an actual candidate.

Independent Candidatures

The maximum numbers of independent candidatures in elections since 1918, omitting Communists, were in 1931, when twenty-two New Party Candidates stood, and 1945, when twenty-three Commonwealth Party candidates stood—the former being a break-away from Labour and led by the later leader of the British Union of Fascists, the latter a kind of dissentient, new-humane-liberal-socialist deal created during World War II. They got nowhere.

Authority of the Parties—Summary

To be voluntary is the mark of political parties in democratic as contrasted with dictatorial states. No statute specifies the authority or status of British parties. What is their authority? It is measured by the *number of seats* in the Commons, whatever their popular vote. The members of Parliament possess an authority superior to and independent of their extraparliamentary party machine. However, both Government and Opposition are highly sensitive when a Government has only an electoral minority. Thus, immediately after the 1950 election, Mr. Churchill, Leader of the Opposition, argued that the Labour Government, having 1,750,000 votes less than the combination of other parties against it, "the Government have no mandate, as is recognised in the Gracious Speech, to proceed in this Parliament with their main policy." This happened to be the nationalization of the steel industry (Commons, March 7, 1950). In fact, after a few months the Labour Government did proceed to a *mild* measure of nationalization. Their other policies were of a deliberately less-controversial nature than they would have introduced. But, then, their majority in seats (over Conservative and Liberals alike) was only 5.

Conservatives are very severe about the constitutional proprieties—whenever Labour is in office. In 1949 Mr. Churchill argued that after the lapse of about one half the life of a Parliament, the Labour Government had no authority, no mandate, to undertake legislation of high controversial importance. However, in the Parliament that was elected in 1951, in which the Conservative Government, headed by Mr. Churchill, had a majority of seats of only 17 over the rest of the House (Labour, Liberals, and others) but *less popular votes* than Labour (48.0 percent compared with 48.8 percent), the Prime Minister pushed straight ahead with Conservative policy at home and abroad, acting as though he had a substantial majority in the nation. However, the majority of *seats* was greater than that of the Labour Government's in 1950. There is little doubt about the authority of the Conservative Government elected May 27, 1955 (p. 64).

The House of Commons seats are decisive; but some attention must be paid by a government to a marked smallness of its majority of seats and a popular minority *together*.

Comparison of British and American Parties

If a comparison is made between British and American political parties in this function of creating policy and program (or "platform"), these are conspicuous differences.

(1) British programs are made by the leaders who will have to carry them at elections and then fulfill them, without alibi, in Parliament.

(2) American programs are made by a body hastily assembled at nomination convention headquarters without previous bricks and straw, and either simultaneously with or after the choice of candidate. For the British, the platform is a previous commitment; for the American President and Congress, it is rather a set of election slogans, often abandoned in the election and demanding no special allegiance once the election is over.

(3) The British programs have quite firm roots in a general philosophy of life differentiating the parties markedly: it is not merely economic or social class that differentiates them, as will later be demonstrated. American platforms "straddle" —it is even an entertaining exercise by newspapers to show how closely they are the same, and often "the same" means words designed not to commit firmly. The British program is a pledge; the American a hedge.

This is due largely to the fact that British leaders are usually in politics for life as members of Parliament, while in the United States presidential candidates are personalities fresh from fields other than government or from levels of government that have not compelled them to think about or committed them to national policy and obligations. In Britain election campaigns are party campaigns; in America, to a large extent, personal campaigns, sometimes by men who are profoundly and candidly innocent of governmental knowledge. In the United States we have seen presidential candidates publicly and sincerely reviled by at least one half their party, and the same man invited to be a candidate by a large proportion of the leaders of *both* parties. In the United States the complaint of the opposition is that the victorious party does not keep its election promises, except occasionally; in Britain, it is the reverse—that the Government keeps its promises, with occasional exceptions.

Four C's of Responsibility

The qualities of responsibility assumed by British political parties may be compressed into four words beginning with C. They are (1) Clarity of Consciousness, (2) Comprehensiveness, (3) Constancy, (4) Conscientiousness.

Consciousness means that they have a sharper, more-informed knowledge of the facts, the pattern of values, the aims and ends of their society—they stand at the top—they have vision. *Comprehensiveness* means that the parties have the broad and interrelated view, not merely the close and sectional view. *Constancy* means that they function more steadily, and feel their responsibility and duty to take the initiative, and to organize it so that their sense of trust is perpetuated in a continuously operating vehicle. *Conscientiousness* means that they have their trust deeply set in the conscience—as an over-riding obligation. The point is that no other individual or group or organization provides the *four* qualities in combination in the same degree of political serviceability.

The House of Commons:
Authority and Organization

England is the Mother of Parliaments.

—John Bright

England is not governed by logic, but by Parliament.

—Benjamin Disraeli

It is essential to repeat: Parliament is sovereign and omnicompetent. It can do everything that law can do, and no law in Britain is higher. Almost all this authority is in the House of Commons; the House of Lords is but a feeble delayer. The Cabinet dominates the business order and decisions of the Commons, *if* it can persuade the House to let it do so.

The classic passage from Blackstone's Commentaries (1, 160–161) must be quoted in full:

The power and jurisdiction of Parliament, says Sir Edward Coke, is so transcendent and absolute, that it can not be confined, either for causes, or persons, within any bounds. . . . It hath sovereign and uncontrollable authority in the making, confirming, enlarging, restraining, abrogating, repealing, reviving and expounding of laws, concerning matters of all possible denominations, ecclesiastical or temporal, civil, military, maritime, or criminal, this being the place where that absolute despotic power, which must in all governments reside somewhere, is intrusted by the Constitution of these kingdoms. All mischiefs and grievances, operations and remedies, that transcended the ordinary course of the laws, are within the reach of this extraordinary tribunal. It can regulate or new-model the succession to the crown, as was done in the reign of Henry VIII and William III. It can alter the established religion of the land, as was done in a variety of instances in

the reigns of Henry VIII and his three children. It can change and create afresh even the Constitution of the kingdom, and of Parliaments themselves, as was done by the Act of Union, and the several statutes for triennial and septennial elections. It can, in short, do everything that is not naturally impossible, and therefore some have not scrupled to call its power . . . the omnipotence of Parliament.

True it is, that what the Parliament doth no authority upon earth can undo; so that it is matter most essential to the liberties of this kingdom, that such members be delegated to this important trust as are most eminent for their probity, their fortitude, and their knowledge; for it was a known apothegm of the great Lord-Treasurer Burleigh "that England could never be ruined but by a Parliament"; and, as Sir Matthew Hale observes, this being the highest and the greatest court, over which none other can have jurisdiction in the kingdom, if by any means a misgovernment should any way fall upon it, the subjects of this kingdom are left without all manner of remedy.

And of this high court, he adds, it may be truly said, *"si antiquitatem spectes, est vetustissima; si dignitatem, est honoratissima; si jurisdictionem, est capacissima."*

The Palace of Westminster, situated on the Thames, close by Westminster Abbey where Kings and Queens are crowned, raises its solemn gray dignity in Gothic stone, and the deep tones of

Big Ben in the famous tower are relayed by the BBC to strike the hour of its regular news bulletins, reinforcing visual memories or photographs of this first offspring of the Mother of Parliaments.

Here is the physical focus that human minds need to foster their oneness, to stimulate their communion, to draw all consciences to a more central and elevated point of interpersonal appraisal. It happens to be a wide, open forum of interesting debate, kept so by a rejection of the idea, elsewhere practiced, of disintegrating the legislature into many small committees.

Moreover, it is in the center of London, the capital city, the political, administrative, economic, and cultural center, concentrated in one mighty and vibrating organism, not scattered as, for example, between New York and Washington, D.C.

The chief functions of the Commons are (1) to make laws; (2) to vote money; (3) to control the work of the Executive and the administrative officials. These functions involve (4) to undertake investigations and (5) to inform and educate the public. We now consider the following subjects:

I. The place of Commons in the chain of democratic authority
II. The rules and officers of the House
III. The functions—as set out above and in Chapter 6.

I. THE STATUS OF THE COMMONS

This involves:

(1) Relationship to party and Cabinet
(2) Internal organization
(3) The duration and frequency of Parliaments
(4) Physical facts of the Commons
(5) The spirit of parliamentarism

(1) Electorate to Cabinet

The House of Commons is not something apart from Cabinet or political parties. It has a certain independence of mind and responsibility in the continuum of political will but it is of the same body politic, organic, unsevered, and untruncated. Party has made the Commons; party continues to propel, inform, and guide it; party is busy inside it for these purposes; the holding of the loyalty of party and the winning of more friends gives the members of the Commons aims and zest. And

back to and through it surges the life-force from the Cabinet and executive understanding to the parties and the people.

(2) Internal Organization

The House is an oblong; to the right of the Speaker's Chair sit the ministerial followers and Ministers; to the left, the Opposition, all on benches in rows. Rank and file sit in the respective Back Benches, on the Front Benches are the leaders, chosen by the parties (pp. 92–94). They are nothing but the men who a little while ago were the leading figures in the general election, and who, soon, will be leading their forces in another campaign, each side intent on increasing its strength over the other. Below the gangway that cuts the House at right angles to the seven rows of seats on each side of the Chair, on the Opposition side, a few seats are still held by the remnants of the Liberal Party. Sometimes an "independent" member or two sits here also. Surveying them on a raised chair is the presiding officer, the Speaker; and immediately before him are large tables where sit the clerks of Parliament. (See figure, p. 100.)

Parliamentary Committee of the Labour Party. The Labour Party, when it is in Opposition, has a leading body in the House, called the Parliamentary Committee of the Labour Party. It is composed of (a) the officers of the party, (b) the chairman (or in his absence, the deputy chairman) and the Chief Whip of the Peers' Labour group, and (c) twelve members of the party having seats in the House of Commons and one member of the party having a seat in the House of Lords. The chairman and deputy chairman and the Chief Whip are elected by the Labour members of the House of Commons without definite term—the chairman is the leader of the party, and has been otherwise designated as explained. The twelve members of the Parliamentary Committee (except the peer) are elected *each session* by the Labour members in the Commons, by ballot, the top twelve winning the places. Casual vacancies are filled by taking the next successful candidate. The peer is elected by the Labour peers.

This is the governing leadership of the Labour Party when it is in Opposition. When Labour is in office another type of organization is put into effect. This will be discussed presently. The func-

Floor Plan of the House of Commons

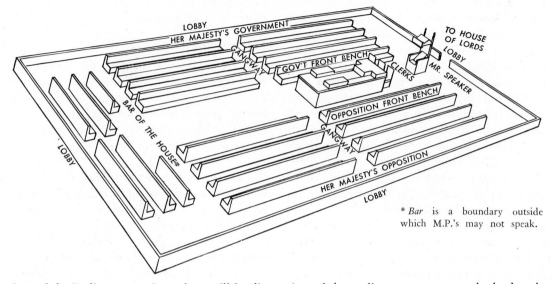

Bar is a boundary outside which M.P.'s may not speak.

tions of the Parliamentary Committee will be discussed as soon as the Conservative Party's parliamentary leadership has been sketched.

The Conservative "Shadow" Cabinet. We have already explained how the leader of the Conservative Party is chosen by his parliamentary followers. He has authority *over* the parliamentary party to the extent of himself *selecting* his "Shadow" Cabinet and the party Whips.

The contrast must be noticed; this so-called "Shadow" Cabinet is, in the Labour Party, elected; in the Conservative it is appointed by the leader.

If the Conservative Party's highest knot of parliamentary leaders are not elected by the rank and file, there is still a liaison with them. For the parliamentary party, which in America would be called the "caucus," meets weekly under the name of the "Conservative and Unionist Members' Committee" or "The 1922 Committee" (see pp. 92–93). When the Conservative Party is in Opposition, the leader attends these meetings for he is, after all, also only a Member of Parliament elected in the same way as they are.

The Conservative parliamentary party elects an executive committee of rank-and-file members. The rank and file in the British Parliament are generally called "Back Benchers" because they do not sit on the Front Benches in the House; these are reserved for Ministers and Junior Ministers. This executive committee transmits the point of

view of the parliamentary party to the leader, the Chief Whip, the Chairman of the party, and such others in the leadership as the nature of the business demands. When the party is in office, the leader (now the Prime Minister), *does not attend* its meetings. This tends to preserve his independence, "the prerogative of the Leader".[1]

When the Labour Party is in office, so that its leader is Prime Minister, this leader *does still attend* parliamentary party meetings whenever business allows. If he stays away, it is not on principle or in accord with usage.

The Labour Party prefers to have the party act as one, blending Ministers, Prime Minister, and Back Benchers. It has more of the spirit of equal and democratic fellowship.

The Conservative Party maintains a distance between the leader and the Back Benchers. *Their* committee stands a little aloof from him, as he does from them. They have their own chairman elected each session, two vice chairmen, a treasurer, and two secretaries, and twelve members who, with the officers, make up the executive committee of the parliamentary party. But the opinion of the meeting naturally weighs with the Conservative Prime Minister.

When Labour was in power, from 1945 to 1951, its now so-called Parliamentary Committee was replaced by a so-called "Liaison Committee." It

[1] *Report on Party Organization,* Conservative Party, p. 36.

consisted of the chairman and vice chairman of the parliamentary party (in 1950 an additional vice chairman was chosen), a high Minister, the Chief Whip, a representative of the Labour peers, and the secretary of the parliamentary party (the last named being a salaried official). This group kept a steady connection between their leaders in the Government and the Labour Back Benchers.

Labour Caucus. Decisions on policy taken in the parliamentary Labour Party meetings are *binding* on all members. This is the force of the party's parliamentary standing orders. Leaders had better be there. Their status is always one that must be justified. What might have happened in the period of office 1945–1951 under this rule cannot be known, because the standing orders were suspended. For the rules were framed some years past in order to maintain a discipline against "bolting" groups such as the I.L.P.[2]

The Labour Party's then enormous majority made such disciplinary rules unnecessary. This gave Back Benchers their freedom not to follow. It also gave the Government its freedom to lead. It may be confidently ventured that *if* the rule had remained in being, the members would not have framed policy pronouncements so as to bind the Government tightly. When Labour achieves office again, *members* will be bound to party loyalty but not the Government. It is hardly right to adduce cases during World War II, when Labour leaders were in the National Government, but on three occasions (the Beveridge Plan, Greece, and compensation for land-values development) the Ministers would not be bound by the party meeting's views and voted one way while some Back Benchers voted another. This is extremely rare.

In neither of the parties does the rank-and-file attempt to name the Ministers a Prime Minister shall choose or to get removed Ministers who are disliked. The latter occurs through less formal groupings and maneuvers. The former is not attempted because all are rivals for office some day in the future, and it is better not to antagonize the leader or split the party into contesting blocs.

Both parties have special groups for study and pressure on Ministers or the Leader of the Op-

position. They cover the various sectors of politics, for example, foreign affairs, defense, education, etc. These "functional" groups are composed of their M.P.'s. They are to some extent nurturing grounds for future leaders.

Party Whips. The Labour Party is served in the House of Commons by a Chief Whip, a Deputy Chief, and ten Whips. The Conservative Government of 1951 onward is served by a Chief Whip, two Joint Deputy Chief Whips, and ten Whips. The role of these officials—all Members of Parliament, of course—comes out clearly in a phrase of the Labour Party's standing orders: "2. The Parliamentary Party have the right to withdraw the Whip on account of things said or done by Members of the Party in the House." The Whip, in this sense, is the summons to take part in party affairs and to attend sessions *on behalf of the aims of the party*. It is a hunting term of the eighteenth century when a rural oligarchy, much accustomed to blood sports, dominated the House of Commons. The "whipper-in" was the huntsman's assistant responsible for driving back into the pack of hunting dogs any who had wandered, and he did it with a whip. The Whips, derivatively, are the party officials whose first business is to whip up the attendance of the maximum of their supporters in the House and at voting divisions and to find out why they may have strayed.

In the Labour Party the Chief Whip is elected by the party. He then appoints his assistants. In the Conservative Party the *leader* chooses the Chief Whip, who then chooses his colleagues. When the party is in Opposition, the Whips are unpaid. When the party is in office, the Whips are paid because they are given office; the Chief Whip is then appointed Parliamentary Secretary to the Treasury, sometimes known as the Patronage Secretary. The former term does not imply any Treasury duties whatsoever; it is a sinecure; the latter title comes from the age (1714) when, as we have seen, the Crown and/or the Government "managed" elections by the gift of offices and honors. In this latter sense the Chief Whip has some relic of bygone significance, because, since he has intimate contact with the members of his party and knows their standing with their party and with the House, since he is appointed for this and develops it, the Prime Minister must rely on

[2] The Independent Labour Party, the remnant of the Democratic Socialist left wing, had originally built the political side of the Labour Party.

him for counsel regarding promotions to Ministries and various honors, such as knighthoods and peerages. This patronage counseling endows the Whip with influence over members additional to personal force and the party's policy.

The other Whips of the party in office are five Lords Commissioners of the Treasury, and three ministers of Her Majesty's Household, with some minor household duties. The others, assistants, are unpaid.

The Chief Whip on both sides of the House is a key figure in the relationship of the members of the party to the leader; of members to each other; of all to the party's morale and tactics. When his party is in office, the Chief Whip sits not far from the Prime Minister's place on the Front (that is, the Treasury) Bench, ready to advise his leader on the feeling of the House or strategy, the points at which to yield or be firm, the time when to wind up debate. He rarely participates in debate. But he has a status of Cabinet level, though he is not a Cabinet member. He is one of the essential, sensitive officers vital to the leader's understanding of House of Commons opinion and—this is crucial to parliamentary and cabinet government—to the faithfulness of the party followers to him, and so he is consulted on policy.

The Whips want an accounting from each member for any default in voting; but they must often wink an eye at members of sharp conscience. Cross-voting is almost nonexistent.

If then a member wishes to challenge the party, it cannot be in a vote in the House. He can only take it to the party meeting. Hence these are extremely tense and exciting. In any case, he must not vote against the party. The maximum allowed him is to *abstain* from voting.

Party Discipline. The Labour Party practice is due to the strong democratic factor in its spirit and practice. The standing orders of the party (March 1952) require, and have long required, substantially complete obedience to a party vote on policy, with a reservation for "conscience."

1. The privilege of membership of the Parliamentary Labour Party involves the acceptance of the decisions of the Party Meeting. The Party recognizes the right of individual Members to abstain from voting on matters of deeply held personal conscientious conviction.

2. The Parliamentary Party have the right to withdraw the Whip on account of things said or done by Members of the Party in the House. The Member or Members concerned shall have the right to be heard at the Party Meeting before the Whip is withdrawn.

3. The National Executive Committee shall be informed of any decision to withdraw the Whip.

4. It is the duty of the Parliamentary Committee to bring before the Party Meeting cases of serious or persistent breaches of Party discipline, and in appropriate cases to recommend to the Party Meeting that the Member or Members concerned shall be reported to the National Executive Committee. The Member or Members concerned shall have the right to be heard by the Parliamentary Committee and the Parliamentary Party.

5. For the purpose of securing concerted action in the House, Members' shall consult the Officers of the Parliamentary Party before tabling any motion, amendment or prayer, or other proposal which may involve party policies or decisions.

These Standing Orders may be amended, rescinded, altered, added to, suspended or reinstated for such period and under such conditions as may be determined, after due notice, by a duly constituted meeting of the Parliamentary Labour Party.

The standing orders on party discipline were reimposed (though with revisions) in 1952 when Mr. Bevan and some friends, challenging Mr. Attlee's leadership, took fifty-seven Labour members with them into a division on rearmament *against* Mr. Attlee's lead. Contumacy may lead to withdrawal of endorsement of future candidacy!

Occasionally a plucky and able member of the party can get it to come round to his own view. Thus, in 1938, Hugh Dalton, later Chancellor of the Exchequer, took his objection to the party's voting against the estimates for the Armed Services from the committee to the whole party meeting, and won. But it is a rare member on a rare occasion who can achieve this.

The Bevan revolt referred to did not cease but increased in virulence. Bevan persuaded fifty-seven Labour members to abstain in a motion of censure on the Conservative's policy of making the hydrogen bomb, set forth by the Prime Minister on March 9, 1955, so that the Government won by 303 to 196. Mr. Bevan also attacked and taunted his leader's views in the debate. This open defiance, especially at a time when a general election was imminent, caused Mr. Attlee to lay the matter before the parliamentary party. The members of the "Shadow Cabinet" decided to require the withdrawal of the party Whip at once from Bevan, as a prelude to expulsion from the party itself. In his defense, Bevan accused the trade unions of keeping Attlee and the party from vigorous, progressive courses (more socialism and rapprochement with Russia and detachment from the U.S.A.). He was expelled from the parliamentary group (no discipline, no comradeship or authority) by 141 to 112 of the Labour M.P.'s. The next stage was to have the National Executive Committee discipline him. It was proposed that he be expelled from the party altogether. But Bevan has considerable popular support. Outright expulsion would have risked a splintering of the party. Bevan promised he would not form a "splinter party" whatever happened. Moderating counsels prevailed. The presentation of a united front against the Conservatives at the coming election was a powerful appeasing influence. The Executive voted 14 to 13 *not* to expel Bevan; Mr. Attlee's casting vote, as Chairman, saved Bevan from expulsion, Bevan giving acceptable promise of good behavior! When Parliament met after the election of May 1955 Bevan was one of those who voted Attlee into the leadership again, and Bevan was elected to the Parliamentary Committee.

Earlier in the year seven Labour members had been denied the Whip, because, following Aneurin Bevan's hostility to Attlee's policies, six had voted against a Government motion approving the Paris Pacts and one voted favorably, though the party had instructed abstention. The Whip was restored later when the culprits promised not to disregard the future Whips. Between 1945 and 1954 there were twelve occasions when rank-and-file members opposed the leader's policy in House of Commons' voting, the lowest number of rebels being 21, the highest 73. Fewer rebels came from the trade unionists; more from new members, "pacifists," and nonworking-class M.P.'s.

Commons' Agenda and "Usual Channels." Since the minority has its rights in democracy, the timetable is made through the "usual channels"— that is, the Whips of both sides. They are then a kind of committee for the allocation of time.

Each Thursday in the parliamentary session, next week's business is announced by the leader of the House (the Prime Minister or his deputy). A message is sent by the Whips to their members, underlining the items of important business and the expected times of divisions. These "whips" go out weekly to each member. There may be others on special occasions. The "whips" are one-lined, two-lined, or three-lined—that is, the items of business are underscored with one, two, or three lines according to gravity. Here is what a two-line "whip" looks like.

On Friday, 27th April, the House will meet
at 11 A.M.
Income Tax Bill; Committee.
Divisions may take place and your attendance
at 11 o'clock and throughout the Sitting
is particularly requested.
Motion to approve the Purchase Tax Order relating to Aluminum Domestic Hollow-ware
(Signature)

The lines are the temperature indications of importance and a kind of graduated direction to be present, the linear equivalent of shouts of varying shrillness. Woe betide a member who has no satisfactory explanation for ignoring a three-line whip! Sickness may be an excuse. Or he may be "paired" with a member of the other party—that is, with one of the Opposition who also cannot be present while, if both were present, their votes would cancel out. Pairing is not an easygoing procedure; the Whips do not like it. They want you there. It was particularly severe after February 1950 when the Labour Party had only five seats more than the Conservative and Liberal parties together and when even very sick members had to be helped to the House to vote. The Conservative Party did then cooperate with pairs.

It may be said at once that between the announcement of a division in the House and the closing of the division lobbies, Aye and No, four minutes elapses. In this time bells ring all over the House. Also, some members outside the House have bells set in office or home and get to the House in time. The Whips telephone to such places as are accessible and timely.

The receipt of the "whip" is the equivalent of a membership certificate in good standing in the party that sends it. Its withdrawal is equivalent to excommunication. Its refusal is equivalent to defiance. The defaulter is still a "Member of Parliament"; but, as it is the political parties that win elections, his shift as a member is probably short.

Thus, through the appointment of leader, of leading committee, of liaison between Back Benchers and Front Opposition and Government Bench, and the various special groups and the Whips, each party has concentrated its strength and put coherence into its mind and will. The House of Commons is the better will-organization; it is also a high-class thought-organization. For better work as the latter, it needs other instruments, to be considered later.

(3) The Duration and Frequency of Parliaments

To maintain popular control, Parliaments must be frequent; to serve the Commons' control over the Executive, sessions need to be continual and long.

The life of a Parliament is, by law, a maximum of five years. Dissolution can come at any time when the Prime Minister has good reason to want it. The duration of Parliament has long been laid down by statutes. In 1641 a statute laid down that a Parliament was to be called at least once in three years. Many violations by the Stuarts occurred. Even William of Orange would not at first subscribe to such frequency. But the Triennial Act of 1694 re-enacted this and added something more: that no Parliament would sit for *more* than three years. In 1716 the Septennial Act provided that a Parliament could sit for the maximum of seven years—the Whigs had been scared by the Rebellion of 1715 and wanted to avoid any disturbance of the new Hanoverian succession. (The Parliament that passed this act received the benefit of it—thus Parliament is so authoritative that it may extend its own life!) The Tories, who detested this measure (it kept them out of office), cursed the "standing" Parliament as being as dangerous as a "standing army." They argued that parlia-

mentary sovereignty could defeat natural right! The Whigs kept power for fifty years. Attempts to shorten the duration failed. The law remained in force until the Parliament Act of 1911, when the duration of Parliament was changed to five years.

Actually no Parliament in the nineteenth century lasted the full seven years except the one of 1867–1873. The duration on the average was about four years. The calling of Parliament each year, as already observed (p. 48 and see also below, p. 128) is made certain by the need of the Executive for money and disciplining power over the Armed Services. Nor could the other services of government go on without the votes of money.

Two Parliaments in the twentieth century have lasted more than five years: that of 1910–1918 and that of 1935–1945. In both cases war was the cause. It was undesirable—and in the latter case through bombing, almost impossible—to hold an election in wartime.

The fact that there is no absolutely certain fixed term of office keeps members and leaders very sensitive to the electorate, and makes the Back Benchers especially attentive to their leaders because the decision of the latter to dissolve may force them into fighting an election before the lapse of five years.

Modern government activities so affect the life of individuals that Parliament and Cabinet ought, perhaps, to be more tugged-at through the tensing effect of a shorter term, say four years. But the short term of the U.S. House of Representatives subverts leadership and independence of mind that ought to be out in front of the mass by some distance.

Long Sessions. The sessions have lengthened with the growth of parliamentary business. No statute regulates this; nor does statute regulate (as the U.S. Constitution does) when a session shall begin. Both are matters for the Government, which, in this respect, exercises the Crown's prerogative to call Parliament. Hence, the start and length of sessions is directed by the work that has to be done, the nation that has to be satisfied, the parties that will insist on their demands.

Until a few years ago the session began in February and ended in July or August. The session now begins in October or November, has an interval between the end of December and late January or early February, and then sits on until the next October or November with intervals at Easter, Whitsuntide, and a much longer interval in summer.

It may be conveniently stated here that the Cabinet and other Ministers are happy when the adjournments come, for then they and their officials can concentrate more on arrears of administrative work.

The figures of the number of sitting days indicate how vastly the business of the House must have increased.

	Days	Hours
1808	111	829
1865–1874	115	897
1895–1904	127	1099
1925–1934	149	1156
1935–1944	144	1050

More recently for the year ending November 30, 1954, the days had increased to 172 and the hours to 1425.

The House sits every day of the week, except Saturday and Sunday. On sitting days (except Friday) it meets at 2:30 P.M. and sits until 10:30 P.M. normally. On Friday the hours of sitting are 11 A.M. until 4:30 P.M. During World War II the Parliament sat in the daylight hours, slightly varied according to the habits of German bombing planes. In addition, Standing Committees meet in the morning, break between 1 P.M. and 3:30 P.M., and may sit again. It is a long day, and the 10:30 rule is often suspended, and sometimes there are all-night sessions. Thus the nation is alerted to its politics by the hum of continual business for 150 days of the year almost all day.

(4) Physical Facts of Commons

You would be forcibly struck with the smallness of the main debating chamber of the House of Commons. It measures 68 feet by 15 feet at ground level; hardly twice the size of a large drawing-room. It can hold only 346 members, though Parliament consists of 630. After the destruction of the House by German bombers on May 10, 1941, it could have been rebuilt larger. Its small

size was set in 1852 when it was reconstructed after the fire of 1834. It was then rebuilt to resemble St. Stephen's Chapel of the fourteenth century, the original home of the Commons. Thus its shape is a matter of chance; the chapel was rectangular. Where the altar was, a place was made for the Speaker.

Here it is possible to speak quietly, without ranting; to hear the other man's arguments and point out his errors and strengths; to catch nuances in the voice; *to talk to each other;* and, above all, to see each other's faces and the tell-tale eyes. Close physical proximity is a factor in spiritual and intellectual understanding and community; not many grounds for mistaken intention or facts are left. The other man can be seen as a human being. Even Members of Parliament on the other side who have ranted in the election campaign and are thought to be devils incarnate are seen to be scratching their noses and apparently suffering from age and perhaps stomach-ache. It is all appeasing.

In other assemblies—European and American, for example—the seats are in a very wide semi-circle, facing the Speaker's tribune. The members do not face each other. They cannot face the other *side* as a phalanx. In the Continental legislatures the members speak, if they wish, from the President's rostrum, down and outward to the whole assembly; not side against side, but one speaker in face of all.

The hands of the leader of the Opposition in the House of Commons and the Prime Minister can almost touch as they use gestures with which to reinforce their sentiments. (I have seen a Minister cowed by the continued glance of a member on the Front Opposition Bench or the banging of the Treasury boxes that lie on the Clerk's table near the Mace.)

Mr. Churchill thus commended the shape and smallness of the Commons:

I am a convinced supporter of the party system in preference to the group system. I have seen many earnest and ardent parliaments destroyed by the group system. The party system is much favored by the oblong form of the chamber. It is easy for an individual to move through those insensible gradations from Left to Right, but the act of crossing the floor is one which requires serious consideration. I am well informed on this matter, for I have accomplished that difficult process, not only once, but twice. Logic is a poor guide compared with custom. . . .

As to the smallness of the assembly, Mr. Churchill said:

The conversational style requires a fairly small space, and there should be on great occasions a sense of crowd and urgency. There should be a sense of the importance of much that is said, and a sense that great matters are being decided, there and then, by the House.[3]

He preferred this to harangues from the rostrum, for here quick, informal interruptions and exchanges are possible.

The force of these observations will become even stronger when we presently describe the control by the House over Ministers, through debate and questions. It might be conveniently said here that Members of Parliament have no fixed places on the benches, but may acquire them by habit. They have no desks on and in which to fidget or on which to lean.

(5) The Spirit of Parliamentarism

When the parties meet in Parliament, some very important political influences begin to operate. Men, rather than ideas, confront each other. They are, as we have seen, in close proximity to each other and will be for some years most days of the week and for many hours of the day. They would be inhuman if they did not listen more carefully to each other's reasoning and make concessions to each other as a result. There are feelings regarding values and interests not expressible in statistical terms, that are not to be learnt about others except by parliamentary intercourse with them. A fiery politician is witness:

The atmosphere of Parliament, its physical arrangements, its procedure, its semi-ecclesiastical ritual, are therefore worth careful study. They are all profoundly intimidating for the products of a board school system who are the bearers of a fiery message from the great industrial constituencies. . . . To preserve the keen edge of his critical judgment he will find that he must

[3] House of Commons, *Debates*, October 28, 1943.

adopt an attitude of scepticism amounting almost to cynicism, for Parliamentary procedure neglects nothing which might soften the acerbities of his class feelings. In one sense the House of Commons is the most unrepresentative of representative assemblies. It is an elaborate conspiracy to prevent the real clash of opinion which exists outside from finding an appropriate echo within its walls. It is a social shock absorber placed between privilege and the pressure of popular discontent.[4]

What happens when the new member speaks "with great force and considerable provocativeness"?

The stone he thought he had thrown turns out to be a sponge. . . . The classic Parliamentary style of speech is understatement. It is a style unsuited to the representative of working people because it slurs and mutes the deep antagonism which exists in society.

But—the alternative of muting is physical force?

Independence of Mind. Parliament developed "privilege" by centuries of self-sacrifice, to assure the M.P. of independence of mind and will; freedom of speech, from arrest during sessions, freedom from impeachment or questioning in any court or place outside Parliament. This is even summed up in a clause of the Bill of Rights, 1689 (see *Appendix*).

But the party, local and central, can question him. If he wants freedom he will have to fight for it *within his party caucus*. Political freedom is rather more the whole party's, to decide what it wants to do, independently of the electorate's momentary will. Without this freedom, a parliament would lose the power to render important political services. These are (1) to guide affairs on the basis of *feeling* displayed by the minority as well as the majority; (2) to seek a *peaceful* solution in the *long run* rather than act coercively. All that a constituency can do is to ask a member to resign; it cannot enforce its demand.

II. RULES AND OFFICERS

To preserve itself from chaos and blameworthy impotence, the House has developed Standing

[4] A. Bevan, *In Place of Fear*, London, 1951, pp. 5-7.

Orders to govern procedure on public business and on legislation requested by individuals and corporations (called Private or Local Legislation), and it varies these by amendment or the addition of Sessional Orders, which are applicable for a limited time. But within and outside these rules, there is a tremendous body of law—that is, more rules—the accretion of centuries, the Law and Privileges of Parliament.

These are to be found today in the first place in the great digest by Sir Thomas Erskine May, which runs to nearly 1000 pages. At any moment the Speaker and other presiding officers of the House, and any members who questioned their decisions, may need to refer to earlier treatises, such as that of Hatsell, and beyond that to the decisions that were explicit or implicit in proceedings which are recorded in the parliamentary debates and journals of the House. These systematized precedents are the accepted law of behavior in the making of law and the control of the Executive to which all members, Government no less than Back Benchers, are subject.

The Speaker of the House of Commons

The endeavor of the last 150 years has been to make the Speaker the objective embodiment of the rules and law of the Commons, purgating from him the last milligram of partisanship. He is the impartial presiding officer of the House, with the weighty functions of seeing that debate is orderly, that the authority of the House is respected, that the procedure for the making of law and control of policy is maintained, and he must keep speech free with special concern for the minorities in the House. He is as far as is humanly possible *not* a partisan. The Speaker of the U.S. House of Representatives *is* and necessarily must be, for there the Executive is not a part of the House and leading organizer of its business as the British Cabinet is.

How is this impartiality and effectiveness of the Speaker achieved?

(1) He is elected for a whole Parliament. In France the Speaker is chosen only for a session, so renewing disputes about his merits.

(2) If he is willing, he will (by a habit begun in 1722) be re-elected as long as he wishes. Speakers have sat for long periods. Since 1727, when the famous Speaker Onslow began a tenure of thirty-four years, periods of over ten years and over fifteen have been common. Such long tenure puts the Speaker in an authoritative position compared with most members.

(3) The House may propose rival candidates for the speakership, but, since 1839 it has become the custom for the leaders of the principal parties to fix upon a member who will secure unanimous and uncontested election. For this purpose, they will avoid choosing a member who has been a violent partisan, or, say, has been a member of a Government. The purpose is to secure general respect and no violent animosity.

(4) His constituency is not contested by the opposition party when a general election comes— this was the practice from 1895 to 1935, but in the latter year the Labour Party ill advisedly did so, and, fortunately for the habit, was defeated.[5] (Between 1895 and 1935 there were eleven general elections. Between 1714 and the present day only four times has the Speaker's seat been contested.)

(5) On election to the speakership, the member severs his connection with political parties and clubs.

(6) He has a casting vote, but its use, which in British party government can hardly be called for, is regulated by the convention that the Speaker uses it only to produce no change in the *status quo,* so that the House's will may be made up on further and later deliberation.

(7) He does not take part in debate.

(8) His constituency's chores are taken care of by his neighbor.

All these practices are designed to insulate the Speaker from politics, in order that he may better serve the whole House, and so the nation's march of government.

The Speaker's Authority. His powers stem from the position the House has thus given him and from the rules he has to apply, which are the rules made by the House. His authority is something higher. It stems from several factors. First, the Commons positively *wants* authority for proper business and fair play. (The maintenance of the conventions of an unwritten constitution

---

[5] It claimed that its local party organization needed a fight to keep on its toes.

depends on the ethics and the self-government of political parties.)

Second, the speakership is of great antiquity and dignity. It evolved coevally with Parliament itself. The Speaker is today's symbol of the conquest of sovereignty by Parliament from the Kings. Until the late eighteenth century, all through the many years, the Speaker was the spokesman of the Commons, summing up their deliberations and carrying messages to the Kings and Queens and transmitting their will to the Commons. The glorious and tragic events of British history were witnessed by them; they themselves made some: Sir Thomas More, the martyr's stand against Henry VIII; the holding down of a Speaker in his chair in 1629 because he had orders from the King to stop debate; the refusal by another to tell where the Five Members had fled at the King's pursuit in 1641. This long line of lawyers, royal officials, and high gentry stood between the two crushing masters as their go-between, their first duty to demand of the Crown the preservation of the privileges of the Commons. These dramatic and creative happenings are not forgotten. From being a kind of royal supervisor over the Commons, most insisted on by the imperious Queen Elizabeth I, the Speaker gradually became the incarnation of the independence of the Commons. Furthermore, after finding the speakership a steppingstone to high administrative or judicial office, to Ministries, and even in the eighteenth century to "prime" ministership, it became an office in and for itself.

Third, the Speaker has a large salary, £10,000 a year, untaxed. He has a residence in the Palace of Westminster itself. He will be raised to the peerage after his career is over, if he so desires. He is robed in gown and heavy wig, sits on a canopied chair, behind the Mace, and enjoys precedence in formal procession and official functions —before the Prime Minister and just after the Archbishop of Canterbury.

All has been arranged to secure him reverence; the members bow to him on coming in and leaving the assembly. They will sit down as soon as he orders them to do so—unless they are so irate that they disregard this and are "named" and ejected from the sitting by him. He has the power of asking the House to suspend such members from attendance. If the member becomes dis-

orderly, his punishment may extend to suspension for a number of days on a vote by the House on the Speaker's motion; if the Speaker must call the Sergeant at Arms to put him out, this may cost the member suspension for the rest of the session. **The Speaker's Chief Functions.** The Speaker presides over the House and applies the rules of debate and settles questions of order. (But he does not preside over committees or Committees of the Whole.) If he insists, his interpretation of the rules, though questioned, then and there prevails in that situation. It can be amended as a result of a formal motion in the House. Later a Committee of the House will meet with the Speaker, and the question (usually a subtle and novel one) may be reconsidered.[6] Each decision of his ranks as a precedent, to be heeded like the judgment of a law court on the next occasion.

The Speaker regulates the order of speech. Now the House of Commons has no set order of speech or time limit on speeches. The Government and the Opposition leaders have a conventional priority. But the Speaker will endeavor to see that both sides are heard in fair succession and that members of minority parties, like the Communists in time past or "independents" more recently, get an opportunity to inform the House. The choice of speakers is supposed to be spontaneous—he who catches the Speaker's eye. But, in fact, though it has often been strenuously denied, the Speaker scribbles a list (at the request of the would-be orators themselves at his chair or at the request of the Whips). He preserves his freedom to depart from this list, an essential attitude for the sake of the more independent members. It is heartbreaking for many with vital messages, but no time.

There is no set limit to speeches. But any member, other than the leaders of the House, who speaks for longer than fifteen minutes or thereabouts, must have something very informative to say to the House if he is to avoid being deserted or put out of countenance by the snorts of boredom. The House likes information but hates preachers or ranters or bores, and it has no desks on which to lean and rest.

The Speaker keeps order—that is to say, he

[6] See p. 164 below on the new problem presented by parliamentary questions about the administration of the nationalized industries.

represses unparliamentary language and conduct. Members are tempted, in the course of heated debate, to wander, to become frivolous, to use (in Elizabethan House of Commons phrases) "nipping" words. His power to stop "irrelevance and tedious repetition" kills "filibustering," though it is not tried. At the cry "Withdraw! Withdraw!", when a member has directly or too inferrably stigmatized another as a liar, a coward, dishonest, insincere, moved by desire for office instead of the national good, the Speaker imposes correction. Honesty and sincerity are taken for granted—thinking can be counterthought.[7]

There is a high level of decorum in debate, yet passions boil over. The Speaker cools them down. Members have thrown order papers at each other; a member has slapped another's face for a disparaging remark about his race. Sometimes the Speaker does not see or hear. Often ironic cries of "Hear! Hear!", a form of approval, may interrupt debate; cries of "Shame!" can only be tolerated to a degree. In gravest cases, without withdrawal and apology, the words may be recorded and appropriate action taken afterward.

Weighty Powers. The Speaker has other functions, some of crucial importance. He can prevent the putting of the question in debate to a vote, when moved by a member (usually by a member of the majority and usually a Government Whip) until he, personally, is satisfied that the minority has had adequate opportunity to debate its views, for closure constitutes "an infringement of the rights of the minority."

He has the power of decision on the admissibility of questions (see pp. 161–164). He may select amendments (this is more the power of the chairman of committees, since this is where amendments are moved [see p. 114]).

He may, on his own personal judgment, decide whether a matter is of definite public and urgent importance and so to be put on the immediate agenda for debate (see p. 161). He is vested with the authority by the Parliament Act of 1911 to certify that a bill is a Money Bill, whereupon the House of Lords cannot obstruct its passage to the monarch for signature. He draws up a panel of committee chairman. He decides *prima facie* what constitutes a breach of privilege, so that it may go to committee.

These are enormous powers to put into the hands of one man. They are predicated on his judgment and faithfulness and on the shared assumption that there is a "national" or public interest above a party vote—in which the majority is limited. Is it not a remarkable social phenomenon to find 630 men of opinionated character subordinating themselves to long-run rules to prevent any one of them from becoming a temporary rebel or tyrant?

The Speaker has a Deputy, also appointed like him by the House, for a whole Parliament. The House, in addition, elects a Deputy Chairman who may take the place of both the others. It is a convention that Deputy Speaker and Deputy Chairman be of *opposite* parties! They lean over backward *against* their own party.

Privileges

The House needs to safeguard its authority and its dignity. For the sake of the work of the House as a collective body each member has duties and privileges; the House will safeguard the latter for *its* sake. For this, it has the power to punish anyone for "contempt" of its rulings, a member or anyone else interfering with him. The punishment can extend to imprisonment (it has happened) or exclusion of the member from the House.

The privileges of especial importance are these. It is corrupt for members to accept bribes to influence them in their conduct as members, bribes being fees, compensation, or rewards to promote or oppose a bill, resolution, matter, or thing before or to go before the House. Nor may they accept fees for professional counsel about matters before the House. It is breach of privilege to initiate, promote, or advocate in the House proceedings or measures in which they may have acted or been concerned for money fee or reward. It is a high crime and misdemeanor to offer a bribe to members to influence them in their conduct on bills or resolutions and so on, or to offer fees or rewards to members for drafting or advising on matters to go to the House. Outsiders may not intimidate members by threats of any kind of retaliation, except the general electoral opposition and com-

---

[7] Motives must not be impugned. This custom is actually written into the Standing Orders of *local* government authorities.

plaint, for actions in the House—for example, threatening them with physical attack, sending insulting letters, interfering with their livelihood, or libeling them.

This has immediate regulating power over "pressure groups" and lobbies (p. 120). Furthermore, the rules require members who have an "interest" in a matter under debate *to disclose it.* If they disobey, they will be punished.

The subject of "pressure groups" will be resumed in the proper place, later.

Freedom from Libel Actions

Speeches in Parliament are not actionable at law. Neither individuals nor corporations can prosecute for anything said by a member in debate, however offensive it may be to feelings or injurious to the character of individuals. No action is possible for libel. So the courts have accepted the Commons' claim. *But*—if a member publishes *his own part* of a debate, separately, outside the House, he is actionable for libel and also for defamation. Not so if he publishes a fair account of the whole debate. So also with any other publishers—if unmalicious and fair and accurate and for public benefit, it is privileged.

Persons who print and publish papers by order of Parliament are protected from civil and criminal proceedings. This is settled by a statute of 1840, because two years earlier the publishers of the parliamentary debates, then the private firm of Hansard, were successfully sued by one Stockdale for libel.

In order to avoid here the parliamentary breach of order known as "tedious repetition" let it be said at once that the House of Lords has an almost identical law of privilege to the House of Commons.

Jealous of Rivals

A very instructive debate took place in the House of Commons on November 30, 1955. It was a battle over the rivalry of the BBC and the Television Authority over political discussion. The Commons voted for a Select Committee to study whether these should continue to be forbidden to allow statements or discussions in anticipation of matters to be debated in Parliament. Such a rule—with a fourteen-day period of limitation—had been established by the BBC in 1944 at its own discretion, then continued at the request of leaders of the Government and Opposition, and, finally, was imposed by the Government in July 1954.

The attitude of the Government and Opposition leaders was that Parliament must be preserved as "the only grand forum of the nation"; that there ought not to be another simultaneous debating arena; that in Parliament the minority, or dissentients, could be heard, and speeches were made in the presence of apt critics; that if M.P.'s wanted to build public reputations, they should do this in the service of the House; that it was in the House that they must speak with responsibility, whereas if they broadcast no one knew who chose them; that broadcasters were not chosen for their special authority or knowledge on the topic, but for reasons of histrionic talent, and that the public was not in a position to answer them; and that the logical conclusion to such a process would be for Prime Ministers to fill the Cabinet with actors rather than men of governmental ability and responsibility.

Against these views were pressed the values of freedom of speech, with analogies to the freedom of the press; the need to enlighten democracy; and the theory that party leaders were anxious to keep their rank and file under strong discipline.

The House of Commons: Making Laws, Molding Policy

A great and open council of considerable men cannot be placed in the middle
of society without altering that society. It ought to alter it for the better.
—Walter Bagehot

The questions to be dealt with in this chapter are
these:

I. Who organizes the time of the Commons?

II. What are the stages of legislation and the
role of Committees?

III. How is knowledge gathered for lawmaking,
and what is the role of "pressure
groups"?

IV. What particular procedure is used for financial legislation, the Budget?

V. How does the House control the Executive?

I. ORGANIZING THE COMMONS' TIME

The Cabinet governs the use of the Commons'
time—as an instrument of the House. The function of leading in a numerous assembly of legally
equal numbers is variously undertaken in different
countries, according to their constitutional arrangements and the habits of political parties.

In Britain, the Cabinet takes the lead. The
Standing Orders of the House of Commons divide
up time, not quantitatively but according to the
various months and parts of the session. They
allow time for individual members to introduce
motions for bills or of subjects of debate without
the force of an enactment. These will be noticed
as the process of lawmaking is described. The net
effect, however, is to give to the Government

(Cabinet) control over the work of the House.
This it can secure because it represents the majority. As such, it could crush the minority altogether. It does not do so, partly because *it has a
sense of fair play* (fairness to the Opposition is a
fundamental convention). It thinks that in the
long run majority intolerance would not be good
for the whole of the nation. Some day, also, when
it is in the Opposition, it would like to be decently
treated likewise.

About 80 percent of the time of the House is
reserved to the Government's use and 20 percent
to private members. Consequently, it has been
alleged that the latter are only "rubber stamps"
of the Government or top Opposition group's
ideas. Yet the members can and do *kick in their
party caucuses which make policy:* those are the
places for their freedom of dissent and stubbornness.

Members vote according to party, with rare
abstentions; cross-voting is almost unknown.
Within the Government's 80 percent of the time,
the Opposition is closely consulted and substantially heeded as to priority, time allotted, amendments to be debated, and so on. But the fact that
the Government is firmly in the saddle (so is
the Opposition for its side) gives a most desirable
and serenely predictable steadiness to business. In
1929–1931, when a minority Labour Government

had to rely on Liberal votes, it fumbled and stumbled, just as the French Cabinet (a loose coalition of minorities) always does (p. 408).

How the Government Takes the Lead

Let us draw together the several steps in a Government's management of the enactment of a law. (1) An election, say, was fought in 1945. During this, Labour Party candidates strongly promised substantial fiscal and social welfare reforms and the nationalization of coal, banking, communications, the utilities, etc. Among these latter were the coal mines. The promise could not be put in the scores of detailed articles of a completed law but the main principles were clearly advanced. These themselves had emerged from official (Royal Commission, p. 124) and unofficial studies made at least since 1919, while in 1936 the owners' royalties had been bought out by the Government. The arguments of Conservative candidates violently opposing nationalization added to the clarity of the main issues.

(2) The Labour Party obtained a big majority and a mandate. Its leaders became Prime Minister, Cabinet and nonCabinet Ministers. In office the Cabinet, through one committee of itself composed of Ministers, prepared a draft of a coal-industry nationalization law (while other committees drafted other laws); and another committee (p. 164) planned the way to use the time of the House of Commons over two or three years, to debate and pass these various bills in due order. Each bill went back to the whole Cabinet for final discussion and sanction of its draft.

(3) Treasury expert draftsmen (p. 119) helped the Cabinet committee and the officials of the Ministry of Fuel and Power to shape the bill exactly for printing and introduction into the House. The whole process was well known to the press and public, and drew the responses of the politicians and pressure organizations.

(4) The Government, especially through its Legislation Committee (p. 164), planned more minutely the timetable for the coming sessions of the House, allowing so much time for each bill and consulting with the Opposition on this matter in order to please them as much as possible. This timetable the Government was in an unassailable

position to impose and maintain, since it had a big majority and its own followers are loyal to the party as a whole and its leaders.

(5) The Minister then introduced the bill to nationalize the coal industry by the printing of the bill and the submission of it to the Speaker of the House. Thereafter, the bill went to debate on Second Reading and the usual stages as explained in the following pages. The Minister of Fuel and Power and his ministerial colleagues, especially the Deputy Leader of the House (deputy to the Prime Minister), and the Back Benchers of the party gave steady, sober, improving and unanimous support of the bill. At all stages the Government was in command of the House, because it was the acknowledged and traditional leader of its party.

The various steps traced above, and the internal operation of the Cabinet, are discussed more amply in the pages and chapters that follow.

Typical Organization

It was estimated (1951) by the Clerk of the House that the House spends its time roughly as follows: legislation, nearly 50 percent, of which 47 percent is on public bills; 1.6 percent on private bills; and 1.1 percent on delegated legislation. Then on control of finance, which is financial legislation, 10.3 percent; and on control and formulation of policy, about 40 percent. This is the time of the House as *spent in the main assembly itself.* There are, in addition, committee proceedings.

As we have noted, the House meets Monday, Tuesday, Wednesday, and Thursday at 2:30 P.M. and normally adjourns at 10:30 P.M. This time of meeting developed from the need to allow lawyers and businessmen to do their work in the morning. On Friday the sitting is from 11 A.M. to 4:30 P.M., and this peculiarity arises from the desire of members to have a long week end for recreation or to visit their constituencies.

On the first four days of the week the Speaker enters at 2:30 P.M. in procession, the Chief Badge Messenger going before him and the Sergeant at Arms bearing the Mace. Prayers are read by the Chaplain. Then until roughly 3:45 the time is spent on questions to Ministers. The Speaker then calls on the Clerk to read the Orders of the Day (roughly equivalent to "agenda"). From just after 3:45, then, the House is busy with this agenda until the end of the sitting. This is 10 P.M. formally for the "interruption of business," at which time a member may raise a debate, for half an hour, on the adjournment of the House until the next sitting.

Now, to go back, between 2:30 and 3:45 when questions start, some formal motions are taken, petitions may be presented, and so on, or the moving of new writ for an election.

Just after questions, and before getting to the main business, the order of business is special questions (called Private Notice Questions) outside the usual; statement of business for the coming week, and similar matters; introduction of new members; motions to adjourn the House to debate an urgent matter (see p. 162); ballot for notices of motions; then ministerial statements and obituary speeches; personal explanations; and the raising of a matter of privilege. Not all these will occur every day. A bill may be presented—a formal and almost voiceless procedure (p. 115 below).

From 3:45 to 10 P.M. the regular agenda will be in discussion: it may be a bill or the House sitting in Committee of Supply or Ways and Means for financial matters or a motion by the Government. It is always possible, but it occurs only two or three times a year, that this arranged business may be interrupted by 7 P.M., if the Speaker has allowed that a matter of urgent and public importance has arisen which must be debated that day.

There is a kind of interval around 7:30 or 8 P.M. when the Speaker will go to dinner and other members will follow suit. There is no formal hour now as in the nineteenth century (known as the "Speaker's chop") or, more formally, as in 1902 when 7:30 to 9 P.M. was a dinner interval.

On Fridays there are no oral questions, but as soon as miscellaneous business is over the time is spent on Government business, but, for twenty Fridays on private members' bills or motions. Private members used to have all Fridays for bills and all Wednesdays for motions, from the beginning of the session in November to Whitsuntide, sometime in May. This was too complicated. Therefore, since World War II, private members get ten days for bills and ten days for motions alternately in the first twenty Fridays of the session. This is rather less than private members used to have, because the Government has such a press of business. Members ballot for the few chances of introducing bills and initiating motions for debate on subjects they believe the nation ought to worry about.

The quorum of the House is 40; and a count will adjourn the House until the members have been whipped up. The House is spotty in attendance: during question time and on some debates it is very full. Hence, it has been feasible to provide seats for only 346; when there is a crowd some crush in, others stand, and some sit in the upstairs galleries.

There is a little more flexibility in the timetable than this account suggests.

The Closure of Debate

A time must come when debate ceases and action is taken. This is, alas, a law of life itself. Even down to the 1880's procedure was designed to obstruct and prolong rather than produce laws or oversee administration. The Commons was defensive against the Crown. Then, by a campaign of ingenious use of ancient procedures of obstruction and by disorder, the Irish members determined to stop the House from governing. The sitting of the House, which began at 4 o'clock on Monday, January 24, 1881, ended only at 9:30 A.M. on the following Wednesday. Speaker Brand took it upon himself to stop this destructiveness. He said:

> The dignity, the credit, and the authority of this House are seriously threatened, and it is necessary that they should be vindicated. Under the operation of the accustomed rules and methods of procedure the legislative powers of the House are paralyzed. A new and exceptional course is imperatively demanded.

He declined to call on any more members to speak, put the question, and asked that the House change its rules or give the Speaker more authority.

In the course of the next few years, and with the passage of time, more elaborately, the House did both. Its net effect today is as follows.

(1) **Simple Closure.** After a debate has pro-

ceeded for some time, any member may claim to move that the question be now put. The Speaker must appraise whether the Opposition has had sufficient say. It is his onus to accept or refuse the motion; this is a delicate judgment. If he accepts the motion, the question is put at once, without amendment or debate. If it is negatived, the debate is resumed. Should the motion be carried, and if 100 members at least vote in its favor, the question on the motion before the House when the closure was moved must be put at once, and this ends the debate.

This procedure makes the Government, if it is despotically minded, the master of debate, except that the Speaker can stem its will. The Government can get the motion to put the questions moved, can get it accepted, can get its followers in the number of 100 to stand up for it, and then close the debate by the weight of its numbers.

(2) Closure by Compartments. Closure by compartments or the "guillotine," has been developed in order to deal with long and obstinate opposition, and in order to give the Opposition some measure of choice as to how the time allotted by the Government (in its program) shall be used on allotted subjects for allotted times. The closure by compartments is introduced in a resolution before the House, planning the various stages, and provides that at the end of each, at a set time, the Speaker or his deputy shall put the question without further debate.

Even the debates on these closure-regulating resolutions last for days and are full of true or false resentment. The cry of "gag" is often heard in the land, though more frequently years ago when the procedure was novel than now when both sides have perceived in practice the inexorability of its application. The morality of the "guillotine" is the morality of the Government's committed and popularly supported policy.

Since 1946, Standing Committees use the "guillotine" also.

(3) The Kangaroo Closure. This power was vested *in the Speaker* in 1909, and extends to the chairmen of Standing Committees also. Its peculiar nickname comes from the fact that the Speaker has the power to jump over amendments, in his own discretion, when several have been submitted to the same clause. This is a substantial power to give to an impartial officer of the House; and it could only be given to an impartial one. It saves much time. The principle on which the Speaker or his deputies work is to choose those amendments that raise the most important points of principles and concern the most important sections of opinion, and the most effectively worded in this sense.

II. LEGISLATIVE PROCEDURE

There are two kinds of statutes: (1) public and (2) private. Our main attention is given to public bills.

Public Bills

These are either introduced by the Government or by private members. They run between 90 to 150 per year as finally enacted laws, of which a very small number indeed are consummated by private members. If they are introduced by private members, they are known as Private Members' Bills—not to be confused with Private Bills as above explained—for they are still public bills. These are bills for public purposes introduced by men who are not members of the Government—and the Orders of the House of Commons allow a time for their introduction—on ten alternate Fridays during the first part of the session.

To prevent confusion, let it be said at once that *Private Bills* are those brought forward by local authorities or private corporations or individuals for some privilege that is individual or local, for example, the right to control advertisements or barber-shop hygiene, or to run a utility (a gas company, before nationalization). Most come from local government authorities (see p. 243).

Any M.P. can introduce a bill (except one that recommends expenditure—that is the Government's sole prerogative). But only the majority—that is, the Government—will find the time to carry it through all its stages. Anyone can introduce a bill at any sitting—simply by submitting it to the Speaker to be printed: and that is its First Reading, *without debate*.

There is a second way: to move for leave to introduce, with the right of ten minutes for the proposer to speak on it before the House. This gives publicity; but—even if one member opposes it, there will be no further chance to push it along. Therefore, one must look to the ten Fridays. If the Government is heavily pressed for its own program, it may ask the House to relinquish these Fridays. Such happened during part of the Labour Government of 1945–1950. Otherwise the Private Members' Bills make their way along, with precedence to those that have made most progress. Since there are so few Fridays and so many bills by lawmaking enthusiasts, they ballot for the time. Members associate, according to their interests, to back a particular bill in the ballot. The private members' pregnancy with a law is sometimes induced by a "pressure group," for example, societies for the prevention of cruelty to animals, temperance societies, and, recently, the journalists' union (a bill to control the press).

Unless the Government is willing to find time for it, even a good and generally accepted Private Bill has little chance of the time it needs for passage, for some fifty or sixty per session have been introduced.[1] It, too, has to go to the House of Lords, and may be returned amended—and so time and arrangement are necessary. If the Government does take an interest in such a bill, it may get the benefit of draftsmanship by its special draftsmen, the Parliamentary Counsel to the Treasury (to be discussed shortly). In a good year, some eight or nine of such bills are passed. For example, in 1950–1951, thirty-two were introduced, and nine became law.

Some quite important bills have been passed as the result of private members' efforts: regarding divorce, the safety of ships; expenses of attending county councils; sale of methylated spirits to prevent conversion into drinkable alcohol. It might be noticed that in 1953 a bill was introduced to set up a Press Council (representative of the profession and owners of newspapers, etc.) to regulate the ethics of the press—it had little chance of passing, but the threat accelerated the profession's self-organization (p. 11). Some of these bills were actually prompted by the Government—it is the Whip's Office that gave the stimulus, or some administrative department.

[1] The highest was 226 in 1908.

Five Stages

Public Bills are then chiefly introduced and managed through the Commons and the Lords by the Government. The stages are *five*—not three as in the olden days when the routine of Three Readings was invented. They are First Reading; Second Reading; Committee Stage; Report Stage; and Third Reading. We must pay some attention to these.

The First Reading. This may occur in one or other of three ways already mentioned: by motion or written notice. The latter is now the most usual: all that happens is that there is no actual *reading*, but at a point in the procedure of the day the Minister in whose name the bill stands will respond at the request of the Speaker to a reading out of the title of the bill to the House, and then name a day for the Second Reading. The public has been served notice that legislation is intended. It gives all interest groups the opportunity to make themselves heard in their clamant and contending ways. If the former procedure is adopted, there is a short debate and sometimes a division—it is a more spectacular way of awakening the interest of the public.

The Second Reading. At this stage the procedure of the House of Commons very sharply diverges from that of the U.S. and European legislatures: *there* the bills go first to committee before a general debate occurs in the House at large. Not so in the British system. The Commons has stoutly preserved the principle that the *full House in open debate is master of the general principles of the bill.* The Second Reading follows the first *before* the committee stage.

This is an extremely important governmental truth. The Commons has not that dim period in the murk of the committee, which, however seriously publicized, cannot possibly begin to match the fierce light of deliberation in open assembly. For it is that open assembly that seizes all the attention of the press and the public for concentration on the main points. By this time, there is little more that can be said except to repeat the main principles.

Publicity is the antiseptic of democracy. Too many committees and too small ones shut out the cleansing light. Responsibility in government requires simplicity in locating the agents. Too many committees deceive the people's eye.

In the meanwhile, of course, the pressure groups are at work, on members and on Ministers. We shall pay attention to them presently.

On second reading there is a very full debate, with the Government and the Opposition leaders taking the principal part. The Minister may wind up, being allowed on such occasions to speak *twice* on the same subject (nobody else has this right) or have one of his colleagues wind up. The House goes at it hammer and tongs. The Government will win, for it has the votes. But the points made by the Opposition, and the intensity of the feeling behind its points, not to speak of the objections tendered by the Government's own Back Benchers, affects the subsequent shape of the bill and the concessions the Government will be prepared to make to the dissentients by way of alterations in committee. It is rare for the Government to allow more than three days for this stage: it is more usual to have one or two days only. The Government will move the closure of debate after that.

No amendments are moved at this stage. The only one amendment—that this bill be read a second time in six months—is designed to throw out the bill altogether. If carried, the bill would be dead—resurrectible only in a later session. There have been cases where the resentment of the Commons has caused the withdrawal of a bill —so with the Coal Mines Bill of 1936; again in May 1937, when Prime Minister Neville Chamberlain was forced to withdraw a part of the Finance Bill imposing an excess profits tax on industry, a retreat under pressure of Big Business.

It must be appreciated that the Government is fully on trial in second reading. A reverse would be tantamount to a vote of no confidence, and the Government would have to resign. But, short of this, it is influenced.

The Committee Stage. The committee stage has existed for centuries, since the Commons often wanted to discuss affairs without the presence of the Speaker, who was once a servant of the King and an office-seeking spy. The House also needs to be able to dispense with the rule that members speak once only on the same subject. But the recent evolution of committees derives from the increase of legislation in the nineteenth and twentieth centuries. To conduct committee proceedings on the floor of the House, with the bulging mandate of a modern government, would need more time than God has given man. The modern committee system was established in 1882. It was one answer (the other was closure) to the congestion of the House with business, aggravated at that time by the ingenious obstructive tactics of the members from Ireland, who had made up their minds that if Ireland were not to be freed to govern herself, they would not let England govern herself (p. 113). The main purpose was decongestion, to save the time of the Commons by having business devolved to other bodies and times.

Committees are utterly subordinate to the whole House in their status and role. They do not possess the power of life and death over bills such as is enjoyed by the committees of the U.S. Congress or even of Continental legislatures. They are lowly handmaidens to help clean up amendments, and their work is sandwiched in between Second Reading of an *already formulated* bill and Report (to the House) and Third Reading, when their work will be reviewed.

Now there are several types of committees and their character must be made clear here. There are (1) Committees of the Whole House; (2) Standing Committees; (3) Select Committees; (4) Private Bill Committees, and (5) Joint Committees. The Private Bill Committees are for the discussion of private and local legislation (p. 243). We now pass them by. The Joint Committees of Commons and House of Lords are Select Committees formed of an equal number of members from each House to consider bills or other matters in which both Houses are interested. We pass them by. The Select Committees will be discussed in their turn. *Committee of the Whole.* First in importance, in the present context, are the Committee of the Whole and the Standing Committees. The Committee of the Whole is the whole House sitting with the Chairman of Committees as presiding officer instead of the Speaker, so that it may conduct debate in a slightly less formal manner than ordinarily: no seconders are required, and members have the right to speak more than once, where advisable and permitted by the chairman. The committee stage of a bill is one in which every clause must be put separately and accepted, rejected or amended, with debate or without.

The House goes into Committee of the Whole always when the appropriations (that winds up as the Finance Act) are under discussion, and whenever, again, the House resolves that any ordinary bill shall go before Committee of the Whole rather than to a Standing or Select Committee. The procedure of the House in respect of finance bills must be reserved for later treatment.

Standing Committees. Every bill goes from Second Reading to Committee. Automatically, a bill (excepting money bills) [2] goes to one of the Standing Committees, unless the House resolves that the bill go either to the Whole or to a Select Committee. Why should a Bill go to the Whole? Because the House may think it is so important, of a "constitutional" nature, that it prefers to deal with it directly rather than in the miniature of itself. Or to a Select Committee when examination of expert evidence is necessary to carry the legislation on a stage further and with technical efficiency. We return to the latter case later.

Most bills, by far, go to Standing Committees. These committees are *not* named as in other legislatures by subject matter—for example, Armed Services, Education, etc.—but simply A, B, C, D, which makes four. If necessary another may be added, but five is the maximum allowed by the Standing Orders. Furthermore, there is always in being the Standing Committee on Scottish Bills.

The alphabet committees are composed of between twenty and fifty members of the House. Twenty of these are the nucleus. When a bill is referred to a committee, according to its substance, another twenty (and not more than thirty) members, especially interested, especially expert, are added. Since committees are manned according to the relative strength of parties in the House, it may happen that the committees will not take

all the specialist members available, because this would unbalance the proportionality of parties. When the committees were set up in the 1880's, they were over twice as large as today. Parliament was reluctant to make them small, as they are representative microcosms of the House. They are still larger than U.S. Congressional committees.

The Standing Committees are appointed by the Committee on Selection. This is a panel set up each session by the Speaker from among the most experienced members, some from the Opposition as well as Government. The chairman of the Ways and Means and the deputy chairman are *ex officio* members of this committee. It chooses the chairmen of the Standing Committees and their members. The Whips are interested in the panel.

Now the committees meet in the mornings from 10:30 A.M. but recess between 1 P.M. and 3:30 P.M., the latter to give a full House at question time, and may continue afterward. It was a great feat to get the House to admit that committees might sit while it was in session. But the desperate pressure of business forced its hand. The Commons does not like any extension of the malady known to all parliaments of members, "absentees," coming into vote without having heard the debates. Something of this is, however, everywhere inevitable—therefore the more need for reliance on political party guidance and trust and responsibility.

Service on the committees is very onerous; it is not much relished; there is nothing but hard work to be obtained from it—certainly no publicity of an electoral value. Members like to change from the more boring ones to the more interesting. There is a scramble among the experts to get on those of interest to them. This gives the Committee of Selection a hard task.

Besides the "alphabet" committees, there is the Scottish Committee. Its composition is peculiar. It is a concession to the nationalist feeling of the Scottish people: it is composed of all seventy-one members from Scotland, whatever their party. All bills that refer exclusively to Scotland go to this on committee stage. But to these are added expert members also from other parts of Britain.

When the parties are almost evenly matched in the House, the proportionality of the membership

[2] Imposing taxes; the Consolidated Fund Bills, in which more permanent charges are voted than the annually reconsidered ones; and Provisional Order Bills, which are bills embodying a number of powers conferrable on local authorities by the Minister after parliamentary approval.

of committees becomes a sharp embarrassment. For the Government cannot risk a defeat by the movement of one or two members away from it on some particular clause. The Committee on Selection is then forced slightly to violate the proportionality principle, in spite of protests.

It should be emphasized that these committees are composed of members of Parliament. They do not bring witnesses before them. They do not have hearings or take evidence as the committees of other legislatures may do and actually do. They are legislative, not investigative. Information is supplied to them, when it is necessary, by those in charge of getting the bill through—the Minister and his friends—and contrary information is supplied by the Opposition members and their party and extraparty sources. Pressure-group representatives keep close watch on the committee proceedings.

The chairman (sometimes a member of the Opposition) is in charge of procedure; the Minister and his parliamentary colleagues handle the progress of the bill. It is a laborious process: long hours, discussion concentrated. Some bills have lasted several weeks, verging on three months even. Many members absent themselves. Sometimes it is difficult to get a quorum. It has even been known for members to stay away in order to impede the progress of a bill. The "guillotine" form of closure has more recently become applicable to Standing Committees. The Government may also use its power to move the closure on each amendment.

The chairman has roughly the same authority over the committee proceedings as the Speaker has over the Commons. He sits with Parliamentary Counsel (the professional draftsmen) and departmental experts.

H. A. L. Fisher, historian and Master of New College, Oxford, when Minister for Education and steering the Education Bill of 1918 through committee, found the proceedings inordinately long. A former Minister, looking in, said, "What, not finished yet? The trouble with you is that you make the business *too interesting!*" For members may speak as often as they wish, and amendments can be moved on each clause and divisions can be forced on each of these.

In committee, the Government is prepared to do business—that is, to accept amendments in order to produce a better bill: that is, technically better, to wipe out a flaw, and better in that it satisfies the bigger number as being in the general interest. There is a Government Whip on hand to see that the bill gets proper support by Government followers.

It was the original intention in the 1880's to have the committees not concern themselves with anything but verbal and noncontentious issues. This is impossible. A word is an idea: an idea is an arena of contention. Hence committee proceedings have become more contentious than expected, and therefore more important. But proceedings are of an informal and ratiocinative type rather than public oratory. Governments have suffered defeats on phases of a bill, owing to this nonparty state of mind.

Furthermore the Minister asks advice of pressure groups *after* the Second Reading, and these submit lists of amendments. Time has elapsed and public opinion has now been better assessed. The results are dealt with consequentially and thoroughly. The bill is substantially altered as a result.

Sooner or later, at a time that has been planned by the Government and enforced by the "guillotine," the Committee reports the bill back to the House.

The Report Stage. The bill is reported back to the House by the Committee. If the Committee was of the Whole, the process is formal, a mere change from chairman to Speaker, and if there have been no amendments, the stage itself is formal. Amendments may be moved on Report. The House has the opportunity of seeing what the committee has done with its authority, and of changing the product if it wishes. There is always a tendency for Report to lengthen out: the tendency of a parent body to reconsider the discretion it gave its offspring. To save the time of the House of Commons it is esssential to withstand this. The Government does this by closure, and the Speaker assists by keeping the debate to the clauses rather than generalities.

It would be possible for the Government votes to discard a time interval between the various readings. Actually the Standing Orders do not prescribe intervals. When it is necessary, as in war-time and other mortal emergencies, the Government can put through the three readings and the committee stage in one day, as quickly as it takes men to read and talk and vote. But, in normal times, it is unthinkable to British political parties to abuse their power by annulling due deliberation.

The Third Reading. The Third Reading is like the Second: a political debate on the whole bill. No amendments are in order, except for purposes of drafting statutes. It is a vote for or against the whole bill. If carried—and, of course, it is carried —the bill is ready for the House of Lords. The Third Reading is a political mustering: the Government expresses its thankfulness that it has been able to do the country some good, in spite of the Opposition; and the Opposition replies by claiming that it has made a bad bill better than the Government first presented it, and that, even so, it has doubts for the future of the country's prosperity.

III. WHO INJECTS AND PRESSES "FACTS" INTO THE SUBSTANCE OF THE LAWS?

Drafting Laws

Great technical expertness is required in the drafting of statutes. (1) The mind of Parliament needs to be stated as unmistakably as humanly possible, to avert the need for appeal to the law courts for discovery of its intention (pp. 54–55). (2) Statutes are the authority for action by all government officials responsible for enforcement. Blurring, inconsistency, vagueness will either seem to give them undue power over people or subject them to judicial penalty. The area of inference must be minimized. (3) Most words have already been interpreted by courts and officials; is the new one an exception? (4) How does the new law fit into the existent body of common and statute law; is it meant to embody some by "reference" or to override some? To be clear to the courts and the administrators, "plain and simple" language must be replaced by the sophisticated and complex, the technically exact way of defining situations.[3] Else,

lawsuits will blossom! (5) The financial consequences of the laws must be watched for consistency and consequences.

In 1869 the Office of Parliamentary Counsel to the Treasury was established to be the legislative drafting office. Its personnel is sometimes referred to as Government Draftsmen. They are career officials; lawyers of some years' standing, specially skilled in drafting. There are seven counselors and eight assistants.

The department sponsoring the bill has gone ahead with its sketches, once the Cabinet has decided that the electoral mandate must be fulfilled. The Cabinet will then be consulted on the first draft. The Ministry concerned will have it back, with perhaps changes in principle, and its permanent officials work it up further. At a certain point, Parliamentary Counsel are called on for close drafting. They consult the Lord Chancellor (p. 137), the Law Officers of the Government (p. 138), and all the other Departments. The resultant draft goes to a Cabinet committee, then to the Cabinet. The draft is then printed, when care is taken to consult all possibly interested bodies of citizens, according to subject matter. The bill may need several redraftings. The Cabinet will give final approval, and its Legislative Committee, under the impulse of the Whips, will urge it on with a careful eye to the Government's timetable.

Parliamentary Counsel watch amendments moved in the Houses and committees, to warn Ministers of their effect on other parts of the bill. They regard themselves as servants of Parliament, with the ethic of helping Ministers objectively (not conniving in drafts so as to circumvent debate) and to make ideas workable.

In other countries drafting is more departmentalized (p. 433 and p. 592ff.). In the United States, Congress adopted the British system deliberately in 1913; but it was faulty until the Legislative Reform Act of 1946.

M.P.'s have much knowledge themselves valuable as ingredients of law. Yet it pales beside that possessed by the officials and the "pressure groups" and the academic and private experts.

---

[3] The reader is advised to study Professor Edward Levi's *Introduction to Legal Reasoning*, Chicago, 1951, a brilliant exposition of what happens to the law when it comes before the judges.

The Civil Service Writes the Law

The civil servants, who have made themselves experts by life-long devotion to a special segment of the natural or social sciences, of which the active government has vital need if it is to try validly to remedy social ills, take first responsibility. It is the Government which initiates legislation (p. 114).

Interest Groups; Lobbies and Lobbyists

Parliament is based on *territorial* representation—that is, representation by localities. It is not quite proportional. Not all interests are represented by their numerical magnitude in the Commons. The M.P.'s are rather amateurs, *more properly concerned with values* than detailed facts. Some do have special knowledge; some, indeed, are supported in the House by interests. But there are gaps. Hence, for decades territorial representation has been criticized and substitutes or supplements to it have been proposed. The main classes are "corporative" or "guild" representation (called "guild socialism" or "vocational representation").[4] All are varieties of the main idea: to represent the interest groups *directly* and not via their scattered votes in the territorial constituencies. Mussolini's Italy had twenty-two such "interest-corporate-parties" as it were! What a parlous action, however, when a country has once been unified, to divide it again into twenty-two segments of the economy! Failing this radical solution, the democracies have allowed informal lobbies to operate, and then have regulated them. Or, as in France and Weimar Germany, they added an Economic and Social Council to advise their Parliament (p. 453 and p. 626).

In Britain, Parliament is assisted by (1) M.P.'s who are special friends of certain interests, (2) pressure groups, and (3) official investigatory bodies.

First, a number of M.P.'s are honorary officers of various interest groups, for example, the National Farmer's Union or the British Medical Association or the various trade unions. They are fully imbued with the values and needs and, though without payment, are strong advocates. Others are,

[4] Cf. Herman Finer, *Mussolini's Italy*, New York, 1935.

in a sense, actually "retained" by such associations. They are paid a salary to take care of their interests when these arise in Parliament, and/or their election expenses are subsidized in whole or in part by their clientele. Still others are assisted in their election expenses only by groups whose views on certain matters coincide with theirs, as for random example, the National Union of Teachers or the National Association of Local Government Officials. The exact numbers of these cannot be discovered, because the source of income and the amount is usually private.

The facts are known; the facts are not deplored in themselves. Many among the company directors and the lawyers and businessmen and "organizing secretaries of the Conservative Party" and the union officials, journalists, secretaries, and so forth of the Labour Party are financially helped by business, professional, and employees' groups for service in Parliament on the rare occasions, after all, when some direct question will arise in which the interest is involved as such.

It is a breach of parliamentary privilege if members are subjected to bribery, threats of violence, abuse, loss of occupation or emoluments, or withdrawal of various social privileges (like membership of a club). This takes care of lobbyists who might seek to exert an influence on members: the House would secure their punishment. Furthermore, it is a rule of the House that when a member has a private interest, he will admit it in the House and, in some cases, refrain from voting. Disobedience of this rule might result in expulsion from membership. The misdemeanor is to speak without disclosure, not of an interest which is shared by the population generally or a general group, say, farmers, but where it is direct and personal and not shared by in common with the rest of Her Majesty's subjects. It is left to other members of the House to challenge an interested member's speaking and vote, when the Speaker takes action. Such an issue was raised, but not finally pressed, in 1953, when certain members who had interests in advertising firms were advocating the introduction of sponsored television in Britain.

Second, the associations, organizations, and so forth act directly on Parliament at critical times, and fairly regularly on the administrative departments. When a bill is going through Parliament of interest to any special group, its paid representatives outside Parliament—its secretary and some colleagues of its executive council or a member of its "Law and Parliamentary" committee—keep contact with M.P.'s, especially the leading members, and more particularly usually with the "special" members of the Standing Committee to which the bill is committed. Their business is to influence the legislation in the way *they* think best, and they will invariably claim it to be in "the national interest." It is vain to make a list of these interventions with the names of the outside bodies that lobby: it would be necessary to enumerate every bill and the hundreds of organizations. Their methods are much the same: buttonholing, letters, mimeographed information, sometimes the organization of letters and telegrams to the members, and constant dogging of the actions of members.

Third, some of the pressure that might be applied to Parliament itself is considerably relieved by the regular and acknowledged practice by Ministers and their permanent Civil Service of consulting the interest groups at considerable length when a bill is being prepared for drafting and submission to Parliament. Ministers and civil servants are fully conscious that they do not know enough about the inwardness of the subject and the conditions of securing a ready obedience to the law once it is made, and that they can be much helped by consultation with the vested interests. A Committee on Intermediaries (between Government and business) said:

> . . . the organizations have intimate and continuing knowledge of policy. Collectively one of these organizations knows far more of Government policy over a wide field than any individual can hope to attain to. . . . Secondly there exists between these bodies and the Government Departments with which they principally deal, close and friendly personal contacts at all levels. The members and officers of the organizations, senior and junior, know their opposite numbers in the Departments and have ready access to them. This truly facilitates the dispatch of business. Finally, there is continuity on both sides. When a civil servant who has been dealing with his opposite number in an organization on a particular matter moves to other work, his successor will, as a matter of course inherit the contact with the organization and vice versa.[5]

The organizations are not shown an actual draft of the bill, it has been said. That little matters to the process. They know the drift of the law; they may have suggested it and supported it with their information. The Minister will be *anxious* to have their views. When, as in the case of the establishment of the National Health Service, the question of payment or compensation arises, a long process (two years) of business negotiation occurs. The Government is anxious to be fair, for fairness' sake, but also because such fairness produces good morale and civic obedience. Also it must not be generous to the interests at the taxpayers' expense.

What has been said of consultation about statutes holds good also of the rules and orders made by the departments to carry them into effect. While the rules lie before the House, the organizations can lobby for their amendment. The Government prefers persuasion to coercion; for it must make the laws work.

Ought the Government and members of Parliament welcome or permit such a relationship? The answer is Yes, of course. These organizations represent the nation's wealth, interests, and culture. There is even the right to petition Parliament, of which very much less use is now made than in olden times, but it is still an acknowledgment of the proper accessibility of the seats of decision to the interests of the nation. It cannot be expected that all the multifarious and subtle diversity of national value-and-interest groups can be represented by 630 members elected every five years in single-member constituencies.

The next question is then, can any one of these organizations do damage to the rest of the nation by undue influence? On the whole the answer is No. First, there is no single overwhelming private organization without rivals or opposition, providing the departments and Parliament hear them all—and they do. Second, the problem is the strength of any of these groups relative to the

5 Cmd. 79044, March 1950, pp. 44–45, par. 121.

political parties. But the political parties are pretty firm entities of principle, with a quite clear responsibility for what they do and the need to answer for any mistake directly to the electorate. The smallness of Britain's area and the ubiquity of the London press, always alert for the smell of scandal or "stunt" or "ramp" or "vested interests," projects a light that is not only illuminating but searing on lobby activities. No special interest could get away with anything disreputable. The strength, the dignity, and the answerability of the parties in a two-party system strictly linked to the whole nation is the main factor of safeguard.

Again, is the situation open and acknowledged? It is. Thus Mr. Churchill, in the course of proceedings on a charge that a member of the House had been interfered with by an outside organization that was paying his salary, said:

> Everybody here has private interests, some are directors of companies, some own property which may be affected by legislation which is passing and so forth. It is always the understood thing in the House that everybody makes himself perfectly safe by declaring any special interest he has in any matter about which he speaks. A member says, "I have a special interest in this," and thereafter the House makes any discount they think right from what he says. Then there are those people who come to represent particular bodies, particular groups of a nonpolitical character in the general sense, and there again we must recognize that as one of the conditions of our varied life. . . . We are not supposed to be an assembly of gentlemen who have not interests of any kind and no associations of any kind. That is ridiculous. That might apply in Heaven, but not, happily here.[6]

But, as has been suggested and as may be inferred, there is no legislative regulation of the pressure groups or the lobby as in the U.S. Act of 1946. The reason is clear. The party system is too strong. Moreover, British pressure groups align themselves with either party; each *in turn* gets influence.[7] The committee system is subordinate, not on top of the House. The civil servants are permanent and have self- and national respect. Therefore, the groups are *domesticated;* their

values are used in the making of law; their disvalues are moderated or canceled. A great reliance then is placed on members and on civil servants. Regarding the latter's ethics, which are very high, we have more to say in a later chapter (pp. 214–217). All the combative interests are tamed by social nurture to put some patriotic moderation on their own impulsive egoism. They do not become altruists, but they are restrained by their socially structured, "built-in" sense of decency (p. 236).

Some members, but very few and very rarely, forget themselves. When this happens the House and *their own party above all* is swift and terrible in its judgment. For anything serious, they are expelled, or they would be if they themselves did not admit their disgrace and resign, never to be trusted again. As the result of one such case in 1947, the Select Committee on Privileges of the Commons having reported, the House resolved:

> That this House agrees with the Report of the Committee of Privileges, and in particular declares that it is inconsistent with the dignity of the House, with the duty of a Member to his constituents, and with the maintenance of the privilege of freedom of speech, for any Member of this House to enter into any contractual agreement with an outside body, controlling or limiting the Member's complete independence and freedom of action in Parliament or stipulating that he shall act in any way as the representative of such outside body in regard to any matters to be transacted in Parliament; the duty of a Member being to his constituents and to the country as a whole, rather than to any particular section thereof.[8]

Such attempts to influence M.P.'s go to the Select Committee on Privilege, composed of the senior and most honored members. Even the offer of two hundred and fifty dollars for "expenses" to an M.P. has been most severely condemned.

Fact Finding

Where the House of Commons desires to inform itself more particularly on the subject matter of a bill or to investigate some branch of adminis-

---

[6] *Select Committee of Privileges,* 1947, Question 83.

[7] House of Commons Debates, July 15, 1947.

[8] For example, regarding transport legislation. On the Tory side there will be the National Union of Manufacturers, the Chambers of Commerce, the British Road Federation, the Road Haulage Associations. With Labour, the transport and railway labor unions.

tration not covered by the constant committees, and where it needs information to make up its mind—distinguishing the situation from the handling of a bill before the Standing Committees—the House of Commons may establish a Select Committee.

Select Committees. The scope of the Select Committees, is, of course, the whole scope of parliamentary interests. The more frequent use of Royal Commissions and other types of departmental inquiry has brought about the reduction of Select Committees to some four or five a year.

Select Committees are most usually limited to fifteen members. They are nominated by the Government; but any member could so move. The members are exclusively M.P.'s. A member does not participate in an inquiry when the affairs of any body in which he has a personal interest are under investigation. If the Commons finds it needful, Select Committees may sit outside its precincts.

The witnesses who appear before Select Committees may be Ministers, departmental officials, or, as occasion demands, members of the public. Witnesses may appear voluntarily, and the committee has the power to call for persons, papers, and records under sanction of a power to punish for contempt. The House of Commons may give the committee the power—and it is plenary—to require evidence on oath, and the Select Committee enjoys the power of the House of Commons to compel attendance by the sanction of commitment, reprimand, admonition, a fine, or, if the House of Commons would wish it, the request to the Attorney General to prosecute offenders.

A witness cannot excuse himself from answering on the grounds that he may thereby subject himself to a civil action or because he has taken an oath not to disclose the matter or because the matter was a privileged communication to him. Nor can a witness refuse to produce documents. The parties may examine witnesses either by themselves or through their counsel. Members of the committee, of course, may and plentifully do participate in the examination. Perjury is punishable under the Perjury Act of 1911, though where evidence is not given upon oath its falsity is punishable only as a contempt.

The committee cannot require an official to produce any paper which, according to the practice of the Commons itself, is not usually laid before itself. In these limits, the Cabinet will supply papers the House demands. The minutes of evidence ("hearings" and memoranda) are made public by the Select Committee as a whole, *not by any individual member,* chairman or not—it is a serious offense to break confidence thus. The public may attend during the examination of witnesses, but it can be excluded. The power of investigation is conducted in such wise as to lighten to the maximum the pressure and damage to public servants or private citizens who must appear.

The conclusions of the majority are those of the whole committee. There is no place for a minority report, but the minority, even of one, can state its dissent for public notice in an alternative draft report. The House may ask the committee to expedite its work. Ultimately, the House will express its opinion in a debate on the report.

These committees are penetrative in their pursuit of the facts and the identification of responsibility. They impose practical remedies on Ministers through the merit of their recommendations so far as they are acceptable by the House. They are penetrating but not persecuting, severe but not sadistic, determined but not damning, magnanimous and not malicious, guided by the public welfare and not indulgent in personal spite, and anxious to preserve the rule that men are innocent until proven guilty.

Select Committees sit for a parliamentary session. There is need for other types of inquiry of longer duration and bringing in other citizens, expert or interested, not borne down by parliamentary duties. Such are the Royal Commissions, the Departmental and Treasury Committees, and the Tribunals of Inquiry.

Royal Commissions. Since the early part of the nineteenth century hardly a social, economic, or political statute of any importance has been drafted and introduced into Parliament otherwise than as the result of recommendations of a Royal Commission of Inquiry. This is the form of inquiry used in Great Britain to investigate facts and explore policy in political problems of first-class importance.

They have had that effect on the quality of law which the use of the microscope has had on health: they have discovered the minute relationship between cause and effect in society, even as the high-powered lens has identified the bacteria of disease. They are the social microscope.

A Royal Commission of Inquiry is usually set up when parliamentary or public opinion or the convictions of the Government or of any single department of the Government within whose purview the subject falls, have matured to the point where more information and guidance of an immediate sort upon policy are regarded as essential and no longer postponable, where a blueprint of legislation or administrative policy requires a deep and extensive inquiry into the facts and the contending opinions on action.

A Royal Commission is, in legal form, a command by the Crown, on the initiative and responsibility of Ministers or a Minister, requiring that certain persons named shall examine into a subject of inquiry, which is then stated in what are called the Terms of Reference. Thus, in its legal form the Royal Commission is an executive instrument that establishes, through the Executive, a body of men and women who are to make an inquiry into a subject whose bounds and scope are stated in the Commission. It is understood that since all parties desire that a Royal Commission shall render an impartial report, Parliament itself ought to remain impartial in its choice, leaving to the Government the responsibility of objectivity and competence. It is rare that any of the parties to such an understanding are disappointed in their hopes.

Royal Commissions of Inquiry are manned by people who are *not* members (save exceptionally) of Parliament. Parliament rarely intervenes in the process of the establishment of a Royal Commission excepting to make rather humble suggestions that different regions of the country should be represented, that women as well as men shall be appointed. Royal Commissions last as long as necessary to investigate and report; some for months, others for years.[9]

Commissions may be divided into the three main groupings of representative, expert, and general civic. In the first category are those Royal Commissions that are faced with a problem which must be settled fairly immediately and where great existing and traditional interests are in conflict—for example, reform of local government or reform of liquor licensing. In the second category are those whose problems are a little more remote, which do not call for immediate legislation, and where the issues of fact are more important than the discovery of a practical compromise that may be implemented in government policy or through a statute, and where expert knowledge is needed in the conduct of what is virtually a social-scientific research. The Royal Commission on Population is an example. In the third group, all the qualities of truth-discovery are needed, but general civic ability and culture are required—as, for example, on the Royal Commission on the Press.[10]

Usually the chairman calls together his commissioners. He is assisted by a secretary with assistants provided by one of the departments of the Civil Service. The chairman and the members of the Commission draw up the lines of the inquiry and consider and decide on the persons and bodies who ought to be questioned by them. At this stage the secretary (usually one of the more promising of the Administrative Class in the Civil Service) is of great value, since he has presumably been allocated to the Commission because of a special interest and special knowledge. The Commission invites the submission of memoranda from interested persons and civic organizations. Some Commissions inform themselves by questionnaires. Such documents focus the minds of witnesses and stimulate and guide the commissioners. In some cases research workers are employed to do field or documentary investigation.

Fact, opinions, and recommendations of policy are elicited in public hearings. The Royal Commissions sometimes have closed sessions, but very rarely. Before them appear those they find useful: government officials, academic experts, private ex-

---

[9] Thus the Royal Commission on Honors of 1922 lasted three months. The investigation begun in 1923 by the Royal Commission on Local Government continued for more than six years, and issued an enormous body of minutes of evidence and no less than three reports. The Royal Commission on Population was appointed in March 1944 and finally reported in June 1949.

[10] Cmd. 7700 (1949).

perts, spokesmen of the "lobbies." What is missing is cross-examination of witnesses *by each other*. The Commissions are not provided with the legal counsel or the publicly paid investigator who asks questions in cross-examination of the witnesses as though he were a prosecuting or defending attorney. The process of questioning and hearing is extremely quiet, sober, and decorous—and truth-finding.

Witnesses who appear before the Royal Commissions are volunteers. Their own material interests, their political interests, their fads, may be very much involved. A Royal Commission may obtain power to compel witnesses to come forward and give evidence on oath, but this is extremely rare. Nothing so severe as the laws of evidence of the law courts is applied to the examination of witnesses in Royal Commission procedure. It is out of place. It is not necessary. In fact, the far more desirable course is to put the witness at his ease and to get from him the maximum facts and reflections upon the facts by reasonable persuasion and colloquy.

A subordinate but not unimportant question is the evidence tendered by civil servants and Ministers. It is the convention that where questions of *policy* are investigated—that is, within the framework of the terms—that Ministers rather than civil servants are questioned, for the latter find it awkward to discuss questions of *policy*. They are usually the finest experts on their subject, but they try to confine themselves to factual analysis of alternative lines of policy submitted to them.

The net results of a Royal Commission consist of its Minutes of Evidence, the verbatim transcript of the hearings and the memoranda, which this author regards as the most valuable contribution, because, as it were, they are life without theory, and they offer any reader material for his own judgment.

The second result is the Report. The Report may be unanimous; there may be a majority and minority reports; or the Report may be split even more ways than two, the several minorities offering notes, addenda, and reservations. At any rate, most of the facts are there. The Report, majority or minority, presents a reasoned and sober statement of the truths, issues, problems, and perplexities; evaluates them; and makes recommendations regarding the practical policy that might be adopted in view of the various ends to be secured.

Commissioners are not paid, though expenses of travel and attendance may be met on an extremely modest scale. To serve upon a Royal Commission is not only regarded as a public duty and responsibility but is also sought by many people as an opportunity of making a contribution to the welfare and progress of their nation.

Shall the Commissions be representative or expert? The answer depends on the nature of the problem. If a problem in practical policy is posed in a field where organized groups, whether employers, trade unionists, local authorities, and so forth are well established with acquired interests, and if the administration of any solution is to depend on their cooperation and good will, then, to reduce the area of coercion, it is desirable to have a representative commission.

Ought the Commission to aim at a unanimous report? It has been highly recommended by a Commission on Commissions! It argued that unanimity was convincing to political leadership and to the public, and that action was all the more liable to follow. A divided report, on the other hand, would be inconclusive as to action. But, is not the question thus posed, nonsense? If there is no spontaneous consensus emergent from the enlightened good will of public-spirited men and women, is it worth having an artificially induced one? After all, the ultimate unifier is government, Parliament, and the public.

Tribunals of Inquiry. There may be situations in the conduct of government where considerable doubt prevails about the guilt of persons suspected. A charge cannot be exactly formulated or pressed with a proof of criminal intent, having regard to the severity with which the law courts require proof up to the hilt before fastening a conviction on a man. There may still be proof of harm done, short of crime and criminal intent.

The Tribunal of Inquiry in British law and practice is an attempt to find a procedure that fits such situations—removing a quasi-political misdemeanor from the political arena because the proof should be quasi-judicial but not taking the case to a law court because the problem is quasi-political. Hence, a "political" charge is submitted to the procedure of what is almost a court of law.

During the debate in 1921 on the Tribunals of Inquiry (Evidence) Act which set up a court of the kind we have delineated, it was argued that an investigatory body was needed which would give: (*a*) public satisfaction, (*b*) judicial proceedings, (*c*) public proceedings, and (*d*) evidence on oath. In the debate on the Report of the Budget Disclosure Inquiry of 1936, it was suggested to the satisfaction of the House that the inquiry ought to rest on five principles: speed of getting to work, impartiality, thorough and skillful investigation, full publicity, and absence of temptation to make political capital.

When both Houses of Parliament have resolved that it is expedient that a tribunal be established for inquiring into a definite matter described by the resolution as of urgent public importance, such a tribunal will be appointed by Her Majesty or a Secretary of State, and it will have the powers, rights, and privileges of the High Court concerning the enforcement of the attendance of witnesses, the taking of evidence on oath, and compulsion of the production of documents. Its scope is stated in the resolution. Its proceedings are public, except for the periods when the tribunal considers it expedient in the public interest to keep the public out. It is the tribunal that allows the right of representation of witnesses and other persons interested by counsel or solicitor. Those who are contumacious in nonattendance, or refuse to testify or produce documents, are citable to the High Court for the offense.

During the passage of the bill, Parliament struck out a clause *giving the Government* the right to decide on the establishment of a tribunal. Furthermore, at the cry of "Star Chamber!", the Government withdrew a clause that would have given tribunals the right to punish for contempt by three-month imprisonment.

It is left to the Cabinet to appoint the commissioners. It must satisfy Parliament that they are just and good men, or it will suffer political and public discredit. Once only has a member of Parliament been a member of a tribunal. Tribunals vary from case to case in number and composition. Prevailingly, judges and famous counsel have sat.

We sketch the main cases, of which there have been about a dozen.

In 1928 it was disclosed that Scotland Yard officers had given rough treatment to an arrested girl. The whole organization and procedure of police activities in relation to individual liberty was examined, resulting in important reforms later.

In 1933 administrative corruption in Glasgow city government was investigated. The tribunal made no recommendations to Parliament, but its report analyzed and assessed the allegations. The tribunal warned the press that current editorial comment would be punishable until the publication of the report.

An allegation that disclosures had been made of budget proposals in the Cabinet in 1936 was the subject of the Budget Disclosure Inquiry of that year. If such allegations were not grave, they would be ignored; if they were more specific, the law officers and the law courts would be called in. This tribunal pressed its inquiries far and wide, even into the means for the preservation of Cabinet secrets. It called witnesses from the press and the stock exchange. The Minister accused and the recipient of his tip-offs were found guilty; both forthwith resigned from the Commons.

The latest and most celebrated case occurred in 1948. The issue was political dynamite:

> . . . whether there was any justification for allegations that payments, rewards or other considerations had been sought, offered, promised, made or received by or to Ministers of the Crown or other public servants in connection with licenses or permissions required under any enactment, regulation or order or in connection with the withdrawal of any prosecution and, if so, under what circumstances the transactions took place, and what persons were involved therein.[11]

Some of the law officers of the Treasury and police officers made preliminary interviews. The material was placed before the tribunal, which directed further inquiries and eventually decided which witnesses should be called before them to give evidence. The witnesses were called, and where they appeared to have an interest justifying

[11] *Report*, Cmd. 7616 (1949).

representation by counsel or solicitor, this was permitted. The Attorney General opened the facts; counsel appeared; witnesses were examined and cross-examined. In any event, a final examination of witnesses was undertaken by counsel for the tribunal.

Dignified, upright, sober, sensitive in the extreme to the right of a man to protection from anonymous fiends and publicity- and spite-seeking men and women, the tribunal took over a million words of testimony and examination. Its report is a fair, discriminating, and clean-cut achievement. Two Ministers resigned. The Labour Party was satisfied that its honor had been cleared and the unworthy men in its own ranks purged.

There were still some sticklers for either criminal action or no action at all. There were complaints of the sensational behavior of some sections of the press. (Indeed, one editor received a sentence for contempt of court arising out of sensational comments.) A Conservative member, a lawyer who "detested the politics of the Attorney General [Labour] like poison," said in the Commons debate on the Report:

I think it was an Inquiry carried out without reproach, with great latitude by the Tribunal itself and with moderation by those appearing for the Crown. I do not regret it in any shape or form. It has not thrown a shadow across the fairness of the British and has done nothing but good, although with a great deal of pain, of course, to certain persons.

Defamation of character was not permitted. Indeed, considering the training of English lawyers and the self-respect of citizens, attempts were not made. All this, though the issues were passionately political.

Conclusions. First, the House is amply supplied with facts needed to exert its judgment in legislation and administration, especially since the parties also have research departments that clip and collate such information and make it available in convenient forms together with party appraisal. There is much common ground, then, between the parties, on the one hand, and Parliament and the Civil Service experts.

Second, the bodies of inquiry, whether special or parliamentary, are most sensitively regardful

of their trust, a power entrusted to them for the public good and not for their personal lusts. Parliament insists that:

The evidence taken by any select committee of this House, and the documents presented to such committee, and *which have not been reported to the House* [italics added], ought not to be published by any member of such committee or by any other person. *Resolution of the House, April 21, 1837.*

Such publication would be a breach of privilege of the House, and punishable. Moreover, it might well open the informer to an action for libel, since it could hardly be covered by parliamentary immunity in view of the resolution above quoted.

Thus the gross and vulgar investigatory cruelties of a Senator Joseph McCarthy are not possible under the British system of government. This is indeed ironic: for the American Congress is subordinate to the rule of a written and limiting constitution, while the British Parliament is a law unto itself! None of the forementioned sensitiveness is needed or used in the U.S.S.R. In France and Germany such work is done in the parliamentary commissions (p. 390 and p. 695).

IV. FINANCIAL LEGISLATION: A CABINET BUDGETARY SYSTEM

An Executive Budget

The legislation to provide the Government with right to spend money and to raise taxation is prepared by the Cabinet, and by the Chancellor of the Exchequer in particular, and is debated and voted by Parliament.

The first part of the process—that is, preparation of the estimates of expenditure and proposals for the raising of money by taxes and otherwise— is an Executive one. It is in the hands of the Government. This stage involves a long and careful procedure of consultation between the various so-called "spending" departments and the Treasury, which is equivalent to the Ministry of Finance in Continental countries and to some extent to the Treasury Department and the Bureau of the Budget in the United States. This side of the financial legislation is dealt with in the chapter on the Cabinet (pp. 168–171). The legislative aspect of it must be sketched here.

Once the Cabinet has made its decisions on both spending and tax-raising sides of the budget, Parliament has little it can do except to follow suit. For what is the Cabinet but the leading group of the majority party in the House of Commons? The *main* lines of the budget, then, are decided by the main lines of political party policy, settled, that is to say, in the parliamentary party meetings and the extraparliamentary advisory organizations of the two parties. The *narrow* lines, in between the main lines, are written, with Cabinet control and approval, by the technically expert officials of the Treasury assisted by the departments which have submitted estimates of the expenditure they deem it necessary to undertake.

The Main Financial Rules

The House has evolved rules to do its share of the financial lawmaking. They amount to this:

(1) No one except the Ministers may originate a new tax or increase an existing one—"this House will receive no petition for any sum relating to public service, or proceed upon any motion for a grant or charge upon the public revenue, . . . unless recommended from the Crown" (*Standing Order 63*).

(2) The House will not grant any financial demands unless they are initiated in Committee of the Whole House.

(3) Debates on the regular annual financial legislation take place over a space of time in the session allocated broadly but definitely as a timetable by the Standing Order.

(4) Parliamentary appropriations of money are assigned specifically to stipulated objects and time within which the money is to be spent.

The Estimates

The House has *never used Standing Committees for financial legislation* except for one year. After the Queen's speech has been debated, the estimates therein mentioned go to the Committee of Supply and the tax proposals to the Committee on Ways and Means, and both of these are *Committees of the Whole*. This is in strongest contrast to all non-British legislatures. The first business in the session beginning in November is with supplementary estimates to correct errors in past estimating. Later in the year the regular estimates for the future financial year are brought in and will take until the July of the coming year to be debated and voted.

Now come the peculiarities of the British method. Votes on Account are first made, to tide over for several months until the whole sums needed are granted. The Services estimates come first, then the Civil Service estimates.

Grievances before Supply. The request for this partial provision of money is the signal for the first of the parliamentary challenges to the Government. Pursuant to the ancient practice that the remedy of grievances comes before the grant of money (see pp. 38ff.), the House (except for Votes on Account, see *below*) resolves itself into Committee of Supply, with the motion that the "Speaker do now leave the Chair."

Amendments to this motion are moved by M.P.'s who have obtained the right by ballot taken each session—that is, neither necessarily a member of the Government nor Opposition leadership. The amendments are not designed to raise or lower the sum put forward in the estimates: they are designed to ventilate some matter of policy or administration connected with the service in question, for example, the problems of defense, the methods of organizations of the Armed Forces, their composition, equipment, morale and so on. Since it is not possible to propose a money charge, the amendment must be in the form of moving for *a reduction* of the forces, even when the intention is to debate the desirability of their increase!

The amendments are disposed of; and the Speaker is out of the Chair. Then comes the main committee debates on the estimates themselves. A rather similar process goes on to get them discussed—by moves for a reduction of money. Again, the debate is not one of economy in detail, but some matter of general policy and administration. The House supports the vote, since the Government has assured strength. The next stage is Report—formal because the House as a Com-

Budget—Great Britain, 1955–1956 *

Expenditure		Thousands
Interest and Management of National Debt, etc.		£689,000
Other Consolidated Fund Services		10,000
		699,000
Supply Services:		
Army Votes	£484,000	
Navy Votes	347,000	
Air Votes	540,000	
Ministry of Supply (Defense)	147,500	
Ministry of Defense	18,300	
Less American Aid	43,000	1,494,200
Civil:		
I. Central Government and Finance	21,344	
II. Commonwealth and Foreign	97,319	
III. Home Department, Law and Justice	81,741	
IV. Education and Broadcasting	372,360	
V. Health, Housing, and Local Government	638,731	
VI. Trade, Labor, and Supply	78,852	
VII. Common Services (Works, Stationery, etc.)	65,302	
VIII. Agriculture and Food	385,625	
IX. Transport, Fuel, Power, and Industrial Research	136,751	
X. Pensions, National Insurance and Assistance	437,254	2,315,279
Post Office (excess over revenue)	4,345	4,345
Tax collection (customs, excise, and inland revenue)	49,051	49,051
Total Expenditure		4,561,875
Surplus		148,275
		£4,710,150

Revenue		
Inland Revenue		
Income tax	£1,877,400	
Surtax	136,000	
Death duties	185,000	
Stamps	74,000	
Profits tax and Excess Profits tax	180,000	
Excess Profits levy	25,000	
Other inland revenue	1,000	2,478,400
Customs and Excise		
Customs	1,131,700	
Excise	796,050	1,927,750
Motor Vehicle duties		80,000
		4,486,150
Broadcasting Licenses		25,000
Sundry Loans		24,000
Miscellaneous		175,000
Total Revenue		£4,710,150

* Estimates. *Financial Statement, House of Commons,* April 1955. In round numbers.

mittee of the Whole has just changed back to itself with the Speaker sitting.

For these various debates normally seven days are allowed—not consecutive, but as the business timetable allows. At the end of the seven days (and *more* may be allowed) the "guillotine" closure is moved. On the eighth day, Report stage is taken and finished by the "guillotine." All this is over by March 31, the end of the British government's financial year.

In one day, the committee votes and reports the supplementary estimates; and the votes on account for civil departments; and the first parts of the service estimates; and excess votes to cover money spent on misestimates or surprise items of long ago just turned up. This is summed up in Consolidated Fund Bill (No. 1), an act of Parliament, allowing the expenditure and authorizing the Treasury to spend the money and borrow for the purpose, if necessary. Here debate is again on policy—and not much time is allowed for it—it is not on economic detail.

The Budget

Some time toward the middle or end of April, the Budget speech is made. The House is in Committee of Ways and Means.

This is a most important item in the life of the nation, historically, for it will be compared with other days and other eras and contemporaneously —for the great sheet anchor of modern finance, the income tax, will be reviewed, and almost certainly varied in its weight and particulars, and the economic health of the nation will be assayed. Other taxes may be amended, such as those on tobacco, tea, and so on. But the income tax and surtax, which bring in nearly 50 percent of the annual total revenue, is the great maneuvering ground. Here is a weighty electoral factor for Government and Opposition, especially in election years! [12] The speech commends the financial resolutions embodying the detail which the Chancellor has brought forward. Some need immediate effect as they concern excises on tobacco or beer or tea and so on. Cornering of supplies while as yet unsubject to higher taxes must be prevented. Hence *immediate* resolutions are passed where necessary, to be reauthorized when the annual Finance Act is finally passed later on.

There then follow several days of general debate on the Budget—not with specific amendments, a kind of second type of reading debate. The budget resolutions then go to the Report

stage, when amendments are in order. On the ending of this stage, the Finance Bill, embodying these and various particulars regarding tax laws, is brought in and goes to its Second Reading. Long days until the end of the session are then spent debating them, and debates may last very late of nights, because financial business is *exempted* from the Commons rule that its business ends at 10 P.M. or a half hour later, unless the House makes an exception.

Meanwhile, on other days, the House in Committee of Ways and Means debates the regular annual estimates. The total expenditure is about £4,000,000,000; there are nearly forty departments. These are analyzed and grouped in five divisions: Army, Navy, Air, Civil, and Revenue Department's estimates respectively. The civil estimates undergo a further subdivision into Votes, each of which is one of the ministerial departments. Each Vote is subdivided into items. The resultant volumes of estimates are tremendous. They contain last year's estimate in a comparative column. *Standing Orders permit only twenty-six days for the discussion of the estimates.* Those still undebated on the last of these so-called "allotted" days are voted for as they stand at 9:30 P.M. on day 26.

Fairness to the Opposition. What deserves applause is the fact that, since the estimates to be debated have to be chosen from so many that will never be reached, *the choice is left to the Opposition:* this, by agreement since 1902. Four of the days are assigned to debates on subjects raised by private members by balloting. This assures that the time shall be used for purposes regarded as most critical of the Government by those who have the best reason for criticizing. Sometimes, according to the mood of the country and the domestic and foreign troubles, one department of policy—for example, foreign affairs or colonial affairs or unemployment—will get several days' attention.

The Appropriation Act sums up these debates and voting: states the amounts and objects of expenditure; authorizes Treasury loans for its purposes; and allows the Service departments to make some switches from money from one Vote to another (called, technically, *virement,* French

---

[12] In 1955 the Conservative Government made welcome tax reductions in April and dissolved for elections for May 27. Everybody got something—the Government an increased majority. As predicted by the Opposition, the Government was forced to take back in Autumn what it had promised in Spring—more or less—in a second Budget!

for veering), while other civil departments are allowed a narrower right of virement *within* each Vote only.

Evaluation. The chief merit of this financial procedure is the reliance on the Treasury preparation, which is excellent. The chief demerit is that debate is on policy rather than on expenditure or economy. Can the latter be provided for, apart from the committee organization of the type used in the U.S. Congress, with all the subcommittees, and the hearings and the expert staffs, clerks, and examiners and so on? The answer is No. This is the way it has to be done if it is important and possible that it be done at all. Congress is forced to use this way because it distrusts the Executive and the Bureau of the Budget and the U.S. Treasury.

The Commons virtually put their trust in their one big quasi-committee, the Cabinet, to do the examination for them, with the cooperation of the Treasury. And twenty-six days for all the estimates make it inevitable that the House cannot possibly be a true and inward examiner of the relationship between policy and administration and the appropriateness of the amount provided therefor. It cannot raise the amount; the Orders will not let it. It cannot lower the amount; the Government will not let it. It cannot specifically question the amounts; its ignorance of internal detail will not let it. For policy it must rely on the Government; for detail it must trust in the Treasury. Therefore the estimates are rather general debates on governmental policy regarding the subject matter. It trusts in Treasury officials rather than in its own member-colleagues sitting with expert help on committees.

Select Committee on Estimates

British parliamentarians accept this, so far. But they are restive under the threatened escape of expenditure from detailed control. To secure some control, the Commons has set up (since 1920) from among its own members a continuing Select Committee on National Expenditure. This is a *developing* part of the constitution.

This Select Committee consists of twenty-eight members of the Commons, and it may work through subcommittees, to examine any of the estimates presented to the House and to "report economies consistent with the policy implied in those estimates." The form of words evidently reserves to the Government mastery over the "policy implied in those estimates." It is, in fact, to exercise a microscopic, not a macroscopic, view, to see if it can get "better value for money." It has the assistance of two Treasury officials.

It is impossible to examine more than one or two sets of estimates (or parts of a department) per year. It cannot be done in time to affect this year's debates. But the reports do make the departments and Treasury more money-value conscious, and offer to the House of Commons ideas of policy for future years. The Government in 1953, for example, was forced to answer the Select Committee's allegations that it had not spent economically on school buildings, and it furnished a good defense.

During World War II, the counterpart of this Committee was especially valuable, because the House as a whole was kept in the dark about details of wartime expenditures—of course. But the Select Committee spent an inordinate amount of time on the work—and, also, reported privately to the Government on many administrative—that is, war-production contracts—subjects that could be improved on the basis of its findings.

Operation through subcommittees, recently innovated, has given the committee a closer grip over departmental policies and enhanced the value of the committee.

Comptroller and Auditor General and Public Accounts Committee

We may merely add a note on the position of the Comptroller and Auditor General. This office was set up in 1866 by statute. His functions are two: he controls the payment of money from the Consolidated Fund, and he audits government accounts. As for the former, the Comptroller checks the request for money against the statutory authorizations and then the Paymaster General lets the money flow out.

As for the audit function, he audits the accounts annually, certifies the accounts, *and reports his findings to Parliament.* He checks the legality of the expenditures. But, by conventional interpretation of his duties, supported by parliamentary welcome, he reports on the "wisdom and economy" of the expenditure, on loss or waste. He is regarded as an officer of the House of Commons, though appointed (for the Crown) by the Government, whose officials and Ministers the Comptroller may restrain or criticize. His salary is charged to the Consolidated Fund, like that of judges, and he can only be removed on a joint address by both Houses of Parliament.

His reports are, as will be inferred, retrospective. They may call for a repayment by officials for misspending; they may even call for an act of indemnity by Parliament to void such surcharges in case of bona fide error. They will certainly teach the Treasury a lesson that it passes on to other departments in the form of Treasury Minutes—that is, administrative regulations to be observed in the future.

However, the Comptroller in the "findings" stage of his office does not work alone. The House of Commons has a permanent Select Committee, called the Committee on Public Accounts, set up every session since 1861. Consisting of fifteen members, *the chairman is a member of the Opposition,* always a well-known member of the House with a reputation for financial understanding and strict fairness. The Comptroller is its official adviser. It examines his report, and calls official evidence to help it. It finally reports to Parliament. It is on the basis of its reports that punitive or remedial measures are taken.

It is clear that some two years must elapse before the accounts have gone through this process. Even so, the admonitory and remedial effect is extremely valuable. Fear of the future keeps officials in the path of rectitude, said one committee chairman.

In 1946 proposals were circulated for the amalgamation of the Estimates Committee and the Public Accounts Committee, with an enlargement of the body and expert staffing, subcommittees, and the rest. The proposal was rejected by a Commons Committee on Procedure in that year (Third Report Committee on Procedure, 1946, Nos. 189–91), especially under Government objections. Herbert Morrison, then deputy leader of the House of Commons under Prime Minister Attlee,

objected on the grounds that such a committee would tend to interfere with the everyday working of the departments and would make the civil servants nervous. He objected to the potential interference with the Government's responsibility for current administration.

I say it is the Government that is responsible. It is responsible to Parliament, but if Parliament is going to set up another duplicating set of administrative experts to take an interest in current administration, there is going to be a clash between Parliament and Government which I think would be bad. . . . Parliament's business is to check the Government, throw it out if it wants to, go for it, attack it, criticise it by all means, but Parliament is not a body organised for current administration—not in this country. They have had a go of it in France, and the United States, and I do not think too much of it.[13]

V. THE COMMONS' CONTROL OF EXECUTIVE POLICY

Such control is even more urgent today, for the functions of the government are so much more extensive and deep-reaching into individual lives. The government departments are virtually forty great monopolies; they need a strong force outside them to shake them up. The practice of policy debates and questions, the devices for this purpose are considered in the next chapter on the Cabinet, the responsible Executive.

Statutory Instruments or "Subordinate" or Delegated or Departmental Legislation

We have seen that for the government of Britain, Parliament passes some 90 to 150 laws a year. It is a large number—yet it is not enough.

For Parliament has not (1) the time or (2) the inclination or (3) the special knowledge needed

---

[13] There are experts who insist that the position of the Commons as "the grand inquest of the nation" on the day-by-day activities of the Executive, is more important than the legislative function. It is an idle comparison: both are vital to the good of the nation. From its first years, nearly seven hundred years ago, the Commons, and along with it the then-powerful barons, demanded a control over policy and even over the appointment and dismissal of the Crown's councilors and household officers.

to pass these laws in the detail that is technically necessary. Not that it must be assumed that Parliament passes only the main principles or enacts only "skeleton legislation." In any case, what is main would need to be defined. Indeed, the laws show great prolixity and complexity; the draftsmen try to provide for all contingencies. But there is a limit to the detail to which the principles shall be taken.

Inevitably, for the reasons implied above, Parliament must delegate through its statutes power to Ministers and their administrative assistants—the power, that is, the discretion to make orders: that is, Statutory Instruments, to apply the statute's clauses to the situation they are intended to regulate. This workable-making power has been called "quasi-legislative"; and the product is often referred to as "subordinate legislation" or "delegated legislation." It is a large power in quantity: in 1890, 168 of such instruments (till 1945 called Rules and Orders) were issued; in 1913, 444; in 1937, 1500; and never less until, in 1945, it rose to 1706; it then fell from 1166 in 1951 to 706 in 1954.

Now some of these orders are nothing but forms and plans of safety devices or lists of drugs or specifications for certain plant or processes, or rules of the questionnaire type to secure statistical information for the Government. But even these can be important in their principle and in the job they put on, say, a factory owner or a merchant or a builder. Some are of more importance by far than this—the use of a new device in factories, safety regulations for mines and ships, and so on.

The British way is to delegate with a certain amplitude, for the constitution does not forbid, as the U.S. Constitution forbids Congress, a delegated agency to delegate any further on. Parliament delegates in its own discretion, and the law courts cannot say it Nay!

Safeguards

What safeguard is there, then, for the individual or the corporation over the authority to issue Statutory Instruments that may take away individual liberties of person and property out of parliamentary control? There are two safeguards.

There is an action in the law courts. This cannot be on *constitutional* grounds. It is on the plea that the instruments are, in fact, not warranted by the language of the *statute*—that is, they are *ultra vires*. This is a most important safeguard. The fact that there are special draftsmen for these instruments is an important technical safeguard.

The other control is the necessity, set down by the master statutes, that the instruments made under them need parliamentary approval before they have legal validity. Some must go to Parliament (both Houses) for an affirmative resolution. Others are submissible and are subject to a nullifying prayer against them by Parliament within a certain number of days. Others, again, are submissible to Parliament for a number of days, but require no action by Parliament. Others, again, do not have to be submitted. The categories rank according to their importance for their effect on liberty of person, property, thought, and so on. Examples are slum demolition, a right to search, denial of licenses in business operations. The time of submission is forty sitting days.

The development of the planned economic state, of regulation of social services and controls, necessarily is accompanied with the addition of such powers to the Ministers. It is a power that can be benign; it is a power that can hurt. It needs surveillance.

Acutest care is taken to consult representative interest groups on the drafting of the instruments. This is considerable protection against arbitrariness. At the parliamentary stage of sanction, the interests have an opportunity to deal with objectionable features. Hence, to make sure that some opportunity of challenge is formally available to the interest no less than members of Parliament, the House has set up a regular sessional Select Committee on Statutory Rules and Orders. Its terms of reference are to consider every statutory rule and order and draw the attention of the House to provisions that (1) impose a charge on the public revenues; (2) are made under an enactment which excludes challenge in the law courts; (3) appear to make some unusual or unexpected use of the powers conferred by statute; (4) have been withheld from publication by unjustifiable delay; (5) call for elucidation of their form or substance.

The Committee spends much time sifting those

that ought to be brought to the attention of the House. (The Lords have a similar committee, started in 1924.) Counsel and Speaker of the Commons assist it with advice. Civil servants are called to explain what it cannot otherwise understand. It reports to the House in batches within the time limits for action.

From 1944 to the end of 1952, 19,400 instruments were made. Of these some 10,250 were *public*—that is, the kind that had to come before Parliament. The Committee scrutinized 7000, and drew the attention of the House to 93 of them. In other words, over eight years, about 1300 *public* instruments per year were made; about 900 a year were scrutinized; and an average of 11 per year were brought to the attention of the House.[14]

It is the responsibility of the House to move against the instruments it dislikes. This occurs by a "prayer" against the instrument at the end of any day's business, and could go on all night. Indeed, in the early part of the 1950 Parliament, the Conservatives decided to wear down the physique of the Labour Government, with its very small majority and many elderly and frail persons, by so keeping the House up all night and many nights. This calculated cruelty was unusual in the British Parliament. It is curious that Tories should think this physical rack within parliamentary propriety. Labour members might be otherwise unfair, but it is very unlikely that they could regard this austerity as "fair play." In the session of 1951–1952, fifty-three affirmative motions occupied nearly fifteen hours of the Commons' time and thirty-six negative "prayers" took twenty-five hours.

The Select Committee on Statutory Rules and Orders makes special reports on the procedure on rules and orders, since it learns a good deal by this continued scrutiny, and about their drafting, and better criteria to discriminate between those which should be affirmed or not negatived, and so on.

The issues are involved in deep dispute, for they raise the issues of governmental responsibility and the general values of planning *versus* free enterprise. Some people will say that the delegated legislation is a violation of the Rule of Law, since it gives appointed officials a discretion. Others demand that the committee should have the power to challenge for issues of "policy." But then it would trench on the legislative authority of the House already committed in the master statute, and waste its time again.

The experts believe that there will be need of *more*, not less, delegation; and that it is inconceivable to allow the interest groups the right of a formal challenge to the validity of the instruments by direct appeal to the committee. For thousands of complaints would be made. Others, again, stigmatize Parliament as having "passed away," because it cannot legislate without vesting in the administration such substantial powers. This is wild exaggeration.

VI. PARLIAMENT IN PERSPECTIVE

Even the average member finds the part he has to play a laborious one—even if he falls to the minimum of duty exacted by his Whips. Those who take their work seriously lead very hard lives. On the whole, it is accomplished faithfully in public-spiritedness.

The Member of Parliament must, as his confrères in other lands do, take some care of his constituents' interests so far as these are affected by administrative action, by seeing officials or writing to them. But the M.P. is not snowed under as the U.S. Congressman is; for, on the average, he has only about one quarter of the number of voters, and it is publicly well known that he will not be able to do much, owing to the strictness of the laws and administrative practice. There are no jobs that he can get for constituents on the American scale. Nor is he regarded as a lawmaker for his own district alone: it is well known that the party has a policy and that he must conduct himself within that.

His foot and errand work is therefore lighter. But his correspondence is still heavy enough to require a secretary. Yet the law does not provide him with the pay for one. Nor has he separate office room. He must do his chores out of his parliamentary salary. This is ludicrously small

[14] In the session, December 6, 1954 to May 3, 1955, 257 instruments were reviewed, and only one reported to the Commons; ministerial explanations were asked of three.

compared with the sum paid to a U.S. Congressman, being £1000, on which he must pay income tax like anyone else. As for travel, he has simply a voucher for railroad travel between London and his constituency.

No spoils; no salary; no secretarial expenses—no chance of kickbacks! Some Labour members have lived very penuriously, sharing meager apartments.

Yet Parliament is the pride of Britain, even if its proceedings offer occasion for humorous gripes from time to time. It is the forum of high debate and a point of political, economic, and social enlightenment to the whole nation.

As Edward R. Murrow said in a broadcast in February 1946:

I doubt that the most important thing was Dunkirk or the Battle of Britain, El Alamein or Stalingrad. Not even the landings in Normandy or the great blows struck by British and American bombers. Historians may decide that any one of these events was decisive, but I am persuaded that the most important thing that happened in Britain was that this nation chose to win or lose this war under the established rules of parliamentary procedure. It feared Nazism, but did not choose to imitate it. The government was given dictatorial power, but it was used with restraint, and the House of Commons was ever vigilant. Do you remember that while London was being bombed in the daylight, the House devoted two days to discussing conditions under which enemy aliens were detained on the Isle of Man? Though Britain fell, there were to be no concentration camps here.

7

Cabinet Government:
Collective Responsibility

The Cabinet is a great education. . . . To listen to Cabinet debates, to watch
policy in the making, to be introduced to the vast miscellany of important business which comes before the supreme council of an Empire, and to enjoy the
treatment of it by the best political minds in the country is an experience which
ripens the judgment as the autumn sun ripens the corn.

H. A. L. Fisher (*An Unfinished Autobiography*, p. 138)

The Cabinet is the British government's "executive" branch. It is sometimes called by the more
inclusive name of *Government* or, sometimes, *the
Ministry* or *Executive*.

Without its peculiar connection with Parliament, the Cabinet would have no more life in it
than the head of a decapitated chicken. And Parliament, without the Cabinet, would hardly have
more sense of direction than a decapitated chick-
en's body.

The Apex of Leadership

To place the Cabinet in the system of government
as a whole, one observes a progress in definition
and tightening of political decision and responsibility as he rises step by step from the people in
their spontaneous associations. The political parties
are a more astringent stage. An even more intellectually and emotionally disciplined institution is
Parliament. And now, at the apex—but a living
and quivering apex—the Cabinet functions.

This is the highest focus of comprehensive
view, the agency vested with continuous responsibility for initiative, vigilance, the consummation
of law and of commands to administration. It is

the body to which is imputed incessant leadership and conscientiousness. It is, in fact, the group
of men and women (one!) informally deputed by
the Commons—almost a kind of great committee
of itself—to initiate legislation, to manage the
time of the Commons, to lead in the parliamentary
fulfillment of the promises made to the country,
to cope with all legislative and administrative
contingencies. On the other hand, it controls,
directs, instructs, and propels all the administrative officials in carrying out the will of Parliament.

The Cabinet simultaneously sits in the leadership of Parliament itself and at the managerial
head of the administrative offices of the government. It is the product of the political party its
members lead and cultivate. It is the thread that
simultaneously binds these offices to the Commons
and the people.

To understand the Cabinet system we must, in
this and the following chapter, provide the answers to twelve problems:

    I. What is the status of the Cabinet?
   II. What is the relationship of Cabinet and
       Ministry?

III. What is the status and role of the Prime Minister?

IV. How is a Government formed and its members selected?

V. What is the position of the Prime Minister in the Cabinet in operation?

VI. What are the ingredients of the convention of "collective responsibility"?

VII. What is the pyschological drive impelling to seek office?

VIII. What is the loyalty of the Army to civilian control?

IX. What is the role and status of the Opposition and the House of Commons in relationship to the Cabinet and its efficiency?

X. What is the Commons' control of the Cabinet?

XI. How does the Cabinet organize for efficiency?

XII. What is the special role of the Treasury in Cabinet Government?

XIII. What are the links between Civil Service departments and the Cabinet?

I. ORIGIN AND STATUS OF THE CABINET

The status of the Cabinet is conventional. It is the heir to and the dispenser of the ancient full prerogative of government. It replaces the Crown, as limited by the statutes and the statute-making power of Parliament, with the exception of the Crown's "dignified"—that is, picturesque-symbolic —role, and even this it has partly taken to itself. Whereas the textbooks continue to talk of the "King-in-Parliament" as the sovereign governing body, it would be better to substitute "Cabinet-in-Parliament." Even then, we would still have to remember that there are peculiar and not-too-common circumstances in which the Crown may have some slight personal power (see p. 154).

The Cabinet is roughly equivalent to the Chief Executive in the U.S. Constitution, except that (1) the powers of that Executive are enumerated and assigned to it, whereas the Cabinet is rather a residuary heir of the powers peeled from the Crown. What Parliament has not arrogated it has.

(2) The U.S. Executive has a fixed term of life independent of Congress, but the British Cabinet is dependent for its very existence on the continual confidence of the Commons. (3) The Cabinet is a collective body, not a single person.

II. MINISTRY AND CABINET

Her Majesty's Servants

There are twenty-three departments [1] and departmental Ministers and five additional Ministers occupying certain other offices: the Lord Chancellor, the Lord Privy Seal, the Lord President of the Council, the Chancellor of the Duchy of Lancaster, and the Prime Minister.[2] The latter are like those in Europe known as "Minister without Portfolio"—that is, without departmental duties. When it is necessary to relieve a Minister of a heavy burden, there is appointed under him a "Minister of State." It is an undersecretaryship with a more exalted title, and perhaps more responsibility and dignity. Thus in the first Eden Cabinet, June 1955, there were such in Foreign Affairs, Colonial Affairs, the Scottish Office. There was also one Minister without Portfolio, in the Lords, useful for business there.

The total, not counting Undersecretaries, was,

---

[1] Admiralty; Agriculture and Fisheries and Food; Air; Colonies; Commonwealth Relations; Defense; Education; Foreign Affairs; Fuel and Power; Health; Home Department and Welsh Affairs; Housing and Local Government; Labor and National Service; Paymaster-General; Pensions and National Insurance; Post Office; Scotland; Supply; Trade (Board of); Transport and Civil Aviation; Treasury; War; Works.

[2] The *Lord Privy Seal* is an office going back to the early fourteenth century. Its ancient duties of affixing the seal on issues of money from the Exchequer and certain other duties were abolished in 1884. The office is given to Ministers whom it is desired to have as general and not departmental counselors in the Cabinet. *Lord President of the Council* since 1679 is the presiding officer over the Privy Council. But the duties of the latter have dried up with the rise of the great departments and of the Cabinet. The Council rarely meets; its transactions require some two hours a week of the Lord President. Hence, the office is ideal for men who are needed for general counciliar duties in the Cabinet. *The Chancellor of the Duchy of Lancaster* represents the Crown in the management of the royal lands in Lancaster and elsewhere. It is, however, a sinecure, except for some formal transaction. The office then is given to a Minister whom it is desired to relieve of departmental duties.

in June 1955, thirty-eight with Law Officers [3] and Prime Minister.

The Cabinet

The Cabinet is a much smaller body than the Ministry. Its size varies. In the 1951 Government of Mr. Churchill it was sixteen; in June 1955 it was eighteen.[4] In the 1850's it was nine, ten, or eleven, and in the interwar years it ranged between twenty and twenty-two.

It consists of the principal Ministers, which only means those whose business is of especial importance to the welfare of the country. Another way of putting this is, perhaps, those whose offices have a *traditional* distinction and high modern utility, for the former were naturally given the distinction precisely because they governed an important part of the whole range of government, such as Foreign Affairs or the Chancellorship of the Exchequer.

However, the Prime Minister is at liberty to elevate departmentally less-important Ministers to be members of the Cabinet, if he feels that it is

---

[3] *Law Officers of the Crown.* These are the Attorney General and the Solicitor General and the Lord Advocate for Scotland, who are the legal advisers of the Government, as well as the prosecutors of the law in the courts, where, sometimes, private prosecution is not undertaken, or is inadequate to the task. The Attorney General is now, since 1912, usually in the Cabinet. They are, of course, men of marked legal professional distinction.

[4] The Cabinet in June 1955 consisted of eighteen members:
   The Prime Minister and First Lord of the Treasury;
   Secretary of State for Foreign Affairs;
   Lord President of the Council and Leader of the House Lords;
   Lord Privy Seal and Leader of the House of Commons;
   Lord Chancellor;
   Secretary of State for the Home Department and Minister for Welsh Affairs;
   Chancellor of the Exchequer;
   Minister of Defense;
   Secretary of State for Commonwealth Relations;
   Secretary of State for the Colonies;
   Secretary of State for Scotland;
   Minister of Labor and National Service;
   President of the Board of Trade;
   Chancellor of the Duchy of Lancaster and Minister of Materials;
   Minister of Agriculture and Fisheries and Minister of Food;
   Minister of Education;
   Minister of Pensions and National Insurance.

politically useful. For example, sometimes the Postmaster General, the Minister of Education, the Paymaster General, the Minister of Transport (in their time, though some titles have changed) have been included and sometimes not.

The Prime Minister may have to reward a political colleague, to take account of his following in the party, to train the novices, or he may need general support and counsel though not in an important Ministry. Mr. Churchill included the Paymaster General in his Cabinet, being Lord Cherwell, a long-time friend, an Oxford University professor of physics, in whose scientific knowledge he had trusted (justifiably) before and especially during World War II.

Until 1937 there was no statutory distinction between a Cabinet and a non-Cabinet Minister, because no statute dealt with the Cabinet. But the Ministers of the Crown Act, 1937, regulated the salaries of Ministers and needed to distinguish between the two classes for this purpose. Hence, it laid it down that "Cabinet" Ministers are those who are publicly stated to be such in the *London Gazette,* the daily official journal of the British government. That is all. But it says nothing about how many there ought to be or the principles of their selection. This, as always hitherto, is entirely in the realm of convention and expediency as determined by the Prime Minister.

Size of Cabinet. The size of the Cabinet depends on two chief considerations. One is to satisfy the diverse personalities and their following in the party: it tends to make the Cabinet large. The other is more technical: to keep it small enough as a wieldy, thinking, planning, and deliberating body, and yet not *too* few, for the so-called "span of control" of business of which any one man is capable, is limited.[5]

The experience of World Wars I and II showed

---

[5] "Span of control" means the number of subordinates, men and phases of business, a person can himself sufficiently know, sufficiently support with his memory, insight, strength of directing character, to secure their satisfaction of the demands of top policy he demands of them. It varies with the abilities of the man and width and complexity and newness of the up-surging problems, and the technical and personal reliability of those who have to be directed and coordinated. See Schuyler Wallace, *Federal Departmentalization,* New York, 1937; and Herman Finer, *Administration and the Nursing Service,* New York, 1952.

the need for an even tighter nucleus in the top council. Prime Ministers found it necessary to reduce their "War" Cabinet to only about eight or ten members, though, of course, maintaining a well-meshed connection with other Cabinet and non-Cabinet Ministers.

All this internal arrangement and choice, it must be noticed, is a call on the governmental wisdom of the Prime Minister: this is very much his business.

Cabinet Ministers Are Privy Councilors. Cabinet Ministers have this distinction compared with non-Cabinet Ministers: they are sworn of the Privy Council. The Privy Council today consists of three classes of persons. (1) Members of the Cabinet and normally Dominion Prime Ministers —for they are confidential advisers of the Crown. *The oath of secrecy, candor, and fidelity is taken by them.* (2) The highest judicial offices and the Archbishops are made Privy Councilors. (3) Distinguished people in politics, the public service, science, and literature are given the rank of Privy Councilor as a public compliment. Once a Privy Councilor always a Privy Councilor, except for some most unusual circumstance when the status is revocable. The Council is more a ceremonial body than an efficient, political-decision-making body. It meets to make Orders in Council, but they have been drafted by the Cabinet or under its authority; or to admit Ministers to their offices; or on high royal occasions, as at royal births and deaths and marriages, to put the seal of formal certification of events it has not decided.

III. THE STATUS AND ROLE OF THE PRIME MINISTER

We have already sketched the rise of the "Prime" Ministership from the days of its first maker, Sir Robert Walpole (p. 40). He was overthrown in 1739, in part because the Commons regarded the title (as well as the office) as an usurpation. The title had come from France under the absolutist Louis XIV where a *premier ministre* served the King, particularly in Walpole's time. "First minister" was, indeed, the more usual term in England. For decades the term was used in derision or resentment and was in eclipse under George III. It

rose to accepted status in the nineteenth century.

In 1878 the title was used officially when in the Treaty of Berlin Disraeli was described as Prime Minister. A Royal Warrant of 1905 gave the holder of the office of "prime minister" precedence next after the Archbishop of Canterbury, though it was held with some other office. The salary was still not attached to the prime ministership, but to the office always held by the Prime Minister, the First Lord of the Treasury. In 1937 the Ministers of the Crown Act said: "There shall be paid to the person who is Prime Minister and First Lord of the Treasury an annual salary of ten thousand pounds." Even now there is no clear-cut detachment of the prime ministership from the Treasury, the reason for which is discussed below (p. 168 and p. 208). But it has acquired statutory recognition.

However, the role and status of the office are entirely conventional—that is, they are political, and molded by the needs of responsible government in a nation in which Parliament has sovereign power and is composed by elections under universal franchise. He gets decisions made by his conventional headship of the Cabinet: but to transmute them into lawful actions it is the Ministers or the Privy Council or the Queen's various instruments that are legal effectuators. They follow his lead, not because it is statutory but because he is their party leader.

Ministers in the Government are appointed by the Crown on the nomination of the Prime Minister. They lose office collectively consequent on his resignation; or he can get rid of each one by offering him the choice between resignation and dismissal by the Crown at his instance.

IV. HOW IS A GOVERNMENT FORMED?

Choice of a Prime Minister

The rise of party government has set the convention for the formation of a Government: the Crown must choose as Prime Minister the man who is indubitably leader of the party indubitably able to carry on the government of the House of Commons. The latitude available to the Crown during the larger part of the eighteenth century is gone, because Parliament is no longer controlled by weak and loose "connections" of members with floating loyalties to rival leaders of the groups of Whigs and Tories or men of no "connection" at all. Even in the nineteenth century there were occasions when the two or three leading men of the Liberal Party and the Conservative Party were so placed by rivalry on policy or alleged intention to retire or divisions in the party or age and sickness that there was doubt about who ought to be regarded as *the* leader of the party. But, in the main, it was clear.

Certainly the twentieth-century organization of parties has imposed a clear unmistakable person to be called by the Crown. The process of selecting their leader has already been described in the chapter on political parties (pp. 92–94). It should be added that the outgoing Prime Minister, by convention, advises the Crown for whom to send as Prime Minister. He, being a Parliament man, knows who is the leader of the Opposition, now victorious in a recent election, which is the index.

The Prime Minister Must Be a Member of the Commons. Like all Ministers, the Prime Minister must, by convention, be a member of Parliament. For only in this way can the modern principle of political—that is, party and popular—responsibility be sanctioned. Every Prime Minister since Sir Robert Walpole has been a member of one or the other House.

But must a Prime Minister be a member of the Commons? The answer is Yes. There are two reasons as experience, the potent molder of convention, has manifested. First, if a Prime Minister is a peer, and therefore does not sit in the Commons, he must find someone to lead the House of Commons. This occurred in six cases between 1837 and 1902. In every case grave difficulties arose in the coordination of policy, of speeches, and the conduct of legislative business. One hand too frequently was called on by parliamentary circumstances to write clauses or amendments to law and policy without the other hand having the opportunity to cooperate—and the Commons was the sterner task-master. So with the Lord Melbourne-John Russell combination; Lord Derby-Benjamin Disraeli; Lord Aberdeen-Lord John Russell; less so with Lord Beaconsfield (Disraeli

ennobled)-Sir Stafford Northcote; and Salisbury-Northcote; and Lord Roseberry-Sir William Harcourt.[6]

The question, owing to the clarity of party selection of its leaders between 1902 and 1923, did not arise again until 1923. Then it arose because of the sudden resignation of Bonar Law, Conservative Prime Minister, through mortal sickness. Party predetermination had been a little confused, because the most eminent of Conservatives was Lord Curzon, while Stanley Baldwin had only just emerged to prominence through his leadership in breaking up the coalition of Conservatives with the wartime Government of Lloyd George. (This in October 1922). While Bonar Law was on leave trying to regain his health, Lord Curzon was Deputy Prime Minister and Mr. Baldwin, leader of the House of Commons.

A curious predicament arose. The acknowledged leader—Bonar Law—was too ill to advise the King. No clear succession had been established by the party. It was divided between Curzon and Baldwin. The King (it is of importance to notice as constitutional practice) took counsel with various Privy Councilors (all Conservative). Only one of these (a peer, Lord Salisbury) recommended Curzon, another peer. But the rest recommended Baldwin.

The deciding issue on the face of things was that as the Opposition in the House of Commons was the Labour Party—which had *no* representation in the Lords—the Prime Minister ought to be a member of that House. The deeper issue was the nonrepresentative character of the House of Lords, for the political center of gravity was in the Commons.[7]

The essence of a convention is revealed in this incident: it is not the mere event that counts, but the correspondence of the principle of decision to the political forces of the era. The Prime Minister

[6] Since 1902 no peer has been chosen Prime Minister. It is surprising that the occasional practice could have survived until then. It could not persist after the reform of the Lords in 1911, the knell of aristocracy.

[7] Poor Curzon not only had to hear the sad news from the King's secretary—whose summons he thought had been to make him Prime Minister—but thereafter to propose Mr. Baldwin for the leadership of the party and then welcome him—having been deputy Prime Minister—to the Cabinet room!

is head of the party organization that connects the Parliament to the nation; and that party organization has its leading intellects and characters in the House of Commons, not the Lords.

Where a Prime Minister dies in office, or retires from it, the successor is usually clearly designated by his position in the party and the Cabinet. Thus, in 1908 Mr. Asquith, deputy during Prime Minister Campbell-Bannerman's illness; thus, Neville Chamberlain, the Chancellor of the Exchequer in Mr. Baldwin's Government, on the retirement of the latter. But the case was a little different when Mr. Chamberlain was severely rebuffed by a vote in Parliament in May 1940. He resigned. But the Labour Party were unwilling to join any further Government headed by him; they were needed for a wartime coalition; they would consent to serve only with Mr. Churchill. This guided the King's hand, and also satisfied the Conservative Party.

While the Liberal Party still had enough strength to make a House of Commons in which neither the Conservative nor the Labour Party had an absolute majority of seats, some confusion was introduced into the problem of the Crown's choice of Prime Minister. In 1929 there were 287 Labour members, 256 Conservatives, and 59 Liberals. The largest party, though without an absolute majority, was called on—it being the one the more likely to get along with Liberal votes. If a choice had to be made between the two big parties, then the basic rule of popular support indicated that 287 is preferable to 256. What is of greater importance, however, is that, since the crystallization of the official position of leader of the Opposition, the defeat or resignation of the Government will automatically bring on the summons of the leader of the Opposition. It gives the Crown an automatically switched duty, and so keeps the Crown's neutrality intact.

The Crisis of 1931. Great controversies have centered around the behavior of Ramsay Macdonald in 1931. He was Labour Prime Minister over the Cabinet formed on the basis of the figures cited above. Then, in 1931, the Cabinet being split into a majority against his policies for dealing with an unbalanced budget, a drain on the unemployment payment funds, and whether to relieve the situation by tariffs and a surrender of the gold stand-

ard, Ramsay Macdonald resigned. He thus terminated his Labour Cabinet and advised the King to construct a coalition of Liberals, Conservatives, and his own few followers under his prime ministership. This was satisfactory to the King. The King had the alternative of accepting Macdonald's resignation and then calling on the Conservatives, who might have formed a Government and advised a dissolution. Or Macdonald could have advised a dissolution, and in all probability would have obtained it, as the convention is to make the dissolution automatically available to the Prime Minister. But this he did not advise.

Evidence now available shows that Macdonald was resolved to remain Prime Minister, and that he had formed this desire months before the crisis. That the King was pleased with his advice to make a "national" Government does not mean that the King could engineer the events, or that he moved out of the path of impersonal neutrality to one of personally deciding what ought to be done. The responsibility was Macdonald's.

How the Prime Minister Makes a Cabinet

The responsibility for the formation of the Government, and the designation of those who are to be in the Cabinet, is the Prime Minister's. What considerations move him? They are not statutory, no law lays down the qualifications; they are *political*. If we should wish to take a partisan note out of that word, we might substitute the word *governmental*—that is, an amalgam of technical considerations of fitness for political office and party power relationships. Some further analysis of this must be made. Space forbids that the discussion should be historical with personal instances taken from various Governments.

(1) Loyal Friends. First, the Prime Minister needs a few men on whose steady loyalty he can rely, men rather of the nature of warm confidential friends with whom he can be on constant and easy terms of frankness without their being too hard on his own faults. They are, of course, men at the head of the party. There will be only two or three such men—politics at the top is such a harsh and competitive sphere of human existence—like Asquith and Grey or Lloyd George and

Bonar Law and, perhaps, Baldwin and Chamberlain. "There is no generosity at the top," said Lloyd George. Naturally, these are of different degrees of warmth and trust. Such a group, with one or two others just on the inner-outer edge, make that entirely informal, yet exceedingly important "inner Cabinet" within the Cabinet itself. American students are especially aware of such relationships in their knowledge of such as the Roosevelt-Hopkins-Harriman connection.

(2) **Wings within the Party.** Second, there are various groupings within the party. In Labour, one will find a more or a less pacifist, a more or a less colonial, a more or a less ardent socialist, and so on. The men representing these groups (we observed one of them, the Bevanites, see pp. 102–103) must be conciliated, for the party must be kept together in Parliament and within the electorate. The trade-union element and the co-operative movement must be given places. The Conservative Party Prime Minister similarly must allow for those who represent a younger and more flexible social-welfare policy as against the strong Tories, almost the "die-hards," or the span between retreat from Empire and those with old-colonial views. The representatives of agriculture, the nobility—Stanleys, Cecils, Cavendishes—and the sympathizers with the working class in the Tory Democracy wing must come in. These men, after all, have followings, parliamentary and popular. Even when they are personally troublesome to the Prime Minister he must include them—it is his trust, and he cannot get along without unpleasantness in the Commons otherwise. The first Labour Prime Minister, Ramsay Macdonald, detested his left-wing colleagues, some of them trade unionists, some of them zealots for speedy social change. He was forced by sheer parliamentary expediency to include them. He managed to exclude one or two men of great nobility of character, fearing they would outshine him. In the main, the Prime Minister is compelled to act according to the dictates of party composition and strength.

(3) **Competence in Office.** Third, given the preceding considerations, the Prime Minister must find about thirty-five men at the top and another thirty-five as Junior Ministers, who possess outstanding abilities for government. This means skilled parliamentary resources for debate, for legislative tactics. It means ability to run a department, within the formula we deal with later in discussing the relationship between Ministers and civil servants. It means ability to make general policy and to counsel the Cabinet, its committees, and interministerial conferences.

Ministers Are Amateurs. Now most of the British Ministers are amateurs. They are Members of Parliament, not career departmental experts. They are not to be fitted into the various Ministries according to the special knowledge they have of the internal administration of those departments. But most of them will have developed an interest in one great branch of government: for example, a Phillip Noel Baker in foreign affairs; a Philip Snowden in finance; a Hugh Dalton in finance; Mr. Eden in foreign affairs; Mr. Butler in finance; others in education; and so on. They tend to establish a claim in the mind of the party and the party leader that such and such a department is theirs, for the technical good of the party.

Yet, as one looks at the formation of Cabinets, a remarkable latitude is observable in the choice of men for the various Ministries. Thus, Ernest Bevin was made Foreign Secretary as a tribute to his own personal magnitude, not his special knowledge that fitted him rather for the Ministry of Labor he had conducted during World War II. Or, in 1951, Harold Macmillan was made Minister of Local Government and Housing. He was formerly in the Grenadier Guards and a director of the famous publishing house. He is an admirable man, but not a housing expert. In June 1955 Eden made him Foreign Secretary; in December, Chancellor of the Exchequer. The examples are random and truly representative.

(4) **Training the Young.** Fourth, most Prime Ministers have special regard for the younger men in the party. They must provide for the next generation by arranging a progress through a junior ministership. The Prime Minister is constantly obliged to resist the arguments of the older men, who say, with tears in their eyes: "This is my last chance, but *they've* got plenty of time!"

Sometimes a Prime Minister must rely on many untried men (from the standpoint of office) and even of Parliament. For circumstances, such as a war, or the youth of the Labour Party in the 1920's, may force his hand. Some members of the Conservative Government of 1951 were quite untried men, for the six years of World War II (for Britain) had produced a sharp change in the age composition of the party.

Long Apprenticeship Is the Rule. Usually the entrant in a Government (especially the senior hosts) has had at least ten or fifteen years' service in Parliament and the party. This is the avenue to office and the time it takes normally to race beyond one's parliamentary and party colleagues. The House of Commons is the forum in which all the other several-hundred runners are assessing each other day by day as they get to the winning post. The House is a most exacting judge, especially as it consists of rivals with ambitions. The ordeal is a test of character as well as of intellectual ability and interpersonal skills. As we have already observed, members of the Government must by convention be members of Parliament— this is the one road to office. (There are very very unusual exceptions—for example, Ernest Bevin, in World War II, who was needed to be Minister of Labor and National Service in Mr. Churchill's war Government. Hence he was appointed, and *then* fought a by-election to enter Parliament. But he was well known parliamentarily and had been a labor leader in the party.)

Thus, the standards of the Commons measure the merit of Ministers. They are very high. Having won the regard of their parliamentary colleagues, Ministers are presumed to be able to cooperate when they have reached office. Both sides know how far they can go in influencing, pressing, and suffering the other.

(5) Duos and Trios and Undersecretaries. Occasionally parliamentary friends who have become "ministrable" try to influence the Prime Minister to take them as a duo or trio, each helping on the other's ambitions. Some are strong enough to prevail in this and the decision on how to fill the other offices. Of this, there is at least one good case study.[8]

The Prime Minister has more latitude in the minor than the major offices. He will normally follow the Minister's preference for his Under-

secretaries. But the balance of considerations is so complicated that he may have to refuse. He needs strength and diversity.

Ministers in the Lords. So long as the House of Lords remains part of the constitution, the Prime Minister must make provision for governmental leadership in that House. Complicated statutes had set certain minimum numbers to be in the Lords, but the number is now conventional or expedient. It will *not* be the chief Ministers. It will be the Lord Chancellor, its presiding officer, member of its Lords of Appeal (p. 265), the Government's highest legal adviser. He has held high judicial office, and if a commoner, has been raised to the peerage on becoming Lord Chancellor. In the Government of June 1955, the following offices were held by Lords: Lord President of the Council (Marquess of Salisbury, a historical pillar of Toryism); Lord Chancellor; the Colonies; Air; Paymaster-General; Minister without Portfolio; Minister of State for Foreign Affairs. Only the first four were in the Cabinet. In the Labour Government of 1950, only three Cabinet Ministers were in the Lords; two were outside. Then five Undersecretaries served in the Lords: Agriculture, Commonwealth, Foreign Office, Transport, Public Works.

No Smooth Process. In the 1890's the then Marquess of Salisbury, making a Cabinet said: "It is like the Zoo at feeding time!" Whatever the party, the humanity of the suppliants for office is an ingredient of the Cabinet once it is formed. They crowd for appointment and thereafter for their values over those of other men. Mr. Baldwin did not like Mr. Churchill and Lord Birkenhead; nor did Neville Chamberlain. They were too talented and of powerful personality. They were kept out of the Cabinet. Ramsay Macdonald, Prime Minister in 1929, speaking to Mr. Dalton (called to be offered the undersecretaryship for Foreign Affairs) said to him: "Yes . . . it's been terrible. I have had people in here weeping and fainting."[9] For men want office *now*; if they miss this turn of the carousel, they may be too old or elbowed out by the younger when it comes round again. It has an important bearing on the sense of responsibility (p. 153ff.).

[8] Hugh Dalton, *Memoirs: Call Back Yesterday*, London, 1953.

[9] Hugh Dalton, *op. cit.*

V. THE POSITION OF THE PRIME MINISTER IN THE OPERATING CABINET

What power has the Prime Minister by office; what role has he by governmental need and by the nature of his personality? These are at once separate and interconnected questions. His powers stem from two sources: the law, even if it be conventional, and his position as leader of the victorious party. His personality, however weak, is fortified as Prime Minister by his powers; but these may virtually be abdicated by his pusillanimity and fecklessness.

Powers of the Prime Minister

(1) Dispenser of Offices. The Prime Minister has been asked by the King to form a Government and the King will take his recommendations and no one else's. Office is therefore in his gift. If he resigns, then the Government has dissolved.

A most remarkable phenomenon, observable when any Ministry is being formed, is the recognition by those aspiring to be Ministers of the Prime Minister's independence and official detachment from them. This, in spite of what we have asserted about his dependence on his party's collaboration. As soon as he is named Prime Minister an official gulf seems to yawn, not impassably but perceptibly and sufficiently, between him and them. Perhaps it might be better said he is raised on a pedestal above them. No statute dictates this—it is a recognition that he has the disposition of offices. Even if one is certain that he can get some office, he has no certainty whatever that he can get the office he would like.

But above all, the Government of Britain has been entrusted in the first place to this one man and no other. His responsibility is recognized; the functional demands involved in his assumption of the trust placed in him are discerned. Clear inferences about the technical political conditions of success in the fulfillment of this trust follow. The net result of each man recognizing the conditions of merit that every other one ought to fulfill is to produce a general frame of mind favorable to the Prime Minister's official detachment and objectivity. The others recognize, in other words, the principle of official independence, which is that a

man entrusted with office ought to be as independent as possible to make appointments and take decisions on the basis of efficiency and not out of friendship or other sentiments. Most Prime Ministers have said: "It is very lonely at the top!" It is also hot.

This is the first power of the Prime Minister. He has to make the Cabinet work; it is his; he must give it cohesion; he must arbitrate differences of view and personality; he must fit all the necessary talents together into a reputable team.

(2) Party Leader. The second is the position of the Prime Minister as leader of his party—a victorious party with a majority in the House of Commons. For the sake of the party's principles and national reputation, he must be followed. He can only be displaced from the prime ministership if he is displaced from the leadership of the party. But in many years he has, in part, created his own following by his ideas and character. To repudiate a party leader is damaging to the electoral prospects of the party. While he is leader then, his prime ministership is unassailable. As Aneurin Bevan and his friends have found out in regard to Mr. Attlee, and as the group of men around Mr. Churchill in the late 1930's found out in their contests with Neville Chamberlain, it is hardly possible to dislodge the Prime Minister through the party machinery or to dislodge the leader of the Opposition, especially if he has once been Prime Minister. Party prestige with the electorate may not be thrown away.

(3) Leader of the Commons. Again, it has been made plain repeatedly that the Prime Minister is the leader of the House of Commons, even though he may depute one of his more trusted colleagues to relieve him of much House of Commons routine duty.[10] This places him in a continuously

10 Normally the Prime Minister is leader of the House of Commons. When he has been a peer, he has needed a member of the House as his leader there. But the heavy weight of affairs has led in the recent past to repeated suggestions that the Prime Minister should depute this function to a trusted colleague. This has actually occurred in three cases of Churchill, 1942–1945; Attlee, 1945–1951; and Churchill again, 1951–1955. In the first case the Prime Minister was assisted by Sir Stafford Cripps (for about ten months) and then Mr. Eden, Foreign Secretary; in the second, Herbert Morrison, Lord President of the Council; in the third, Mr. Eden, Foreign Secretary, was named Deputy Prime Minister and Leader of the House of Commons.

leading position—and, at that, against the other side. He makes the principal announcement of Government policy, answers questions on super-departmental lines. He can immediately correct errors made in deliberation by his Ministers, and he has the right to rebuke and reprimand.

(4) Link between Crown and Cabinet. The Prime Minister is the chief channel of communication between Cabinet and the Crown regarding public affairs. It is not conventional for the King or Queen to confer with Ministers behind the Prime Minister's back—his account of Cabinet meetings and the parliamentary situation, uncorrected by his colleagues, is the only one. It is he who has the audiences on the historic occasions of the formation (or the fall) of Governments and in crises, such as the abdication of Edward VIII.

(5) International Representative. The Prime Minister takes the lead, even in person, at critical international conferences and celebrations and in discussions with the Dominions on matters of Commonwealth and international concern. Indeed, so important is the field of international affairs that the Prime Minister often virtually assumes a close surveillance of his Foreign Minister—thus, Chamberlain and Eden, Chamberlain and Halifax, Macdonald and Henderson, Churchill and Eden.

(6) Emergency Powers. Finally, if time does not permit of consultation before action, the Prime Minister may give immediate authority to a Minister and commend acceptance to the Cabinet later—Disraeli bought the Suez Canal shares and consulted the Cabinet afterward.

Prime Ministers endowed with these formal supports of status may play a most potent, even a reckless role, as may be noticed later in the cases of Baldwin and Chamberlain in the 1930's, with irrevocable results, alas.

Personal Qualities of the Prime Minister

Endowed with these formal positions of strength, the position of the Prime Minister in the momentum of the Cabinet's operation depends on his personal qualities. He is firmly in the saddle, but whether he is a good rider or a stumbler, more

worthy of a hack than a charger or a racehorse, depends on him.

It is the business of a Prime Minister to take the lead. In this urgent function, his supreme qualities must be imminent alertness to all dangers, not a drifter; a wide-ranging knowledgeability, not overspecialization or ignorance; and capacity for immediate and lasting anxiety, nerve, not inertia.

First among Equals. He has been called *primus inter pares*, first or foremost among equals, and *inter stellas luna minores*, a planet among the stars. These phrases say only that he is bigger than they, and that all are at work in an articulate system of operation which in total is greater than any.

The remarkable fact about the Cabinet is that it is a looser organization than the word conveys. It is not something square, firm, ready-made and wooden, and destined to remain always the same to the end of its office. It is not that, it is a group of opinionated men, and yet it has coherence of principle, loyalty among its members, a unity of administrative drive and national purpose. It is, in truth, only a collection of about twenty men or less, each of high individuality and idiosyncrasy. Their party has given them a common direction, but the business of government is vast and various and contingent on emergencies, and so their oneness is always under strain. There is a remarkable sense of collective and reciprocal trusteeship about them.

Responding as they must do collectively, they must nevertheless construct the specific collectivity for this occasion—and they exert their individual ideas and values in formulating the collective answer. This may be seen in (1) the Baldwin Cabinet's reaction in 1922 to his proposal to dissolve Parliament and put his tariff-reform ideas to the country—there was much difference here; (2) the Macdonald Cabinet's reaction to the problem of solving the unemployment and depression crisis of 1931; (3) the Baldwin Cabinet's reaction to Mussolini's Abyssinian adventure, and, again (4) the Chamberlain Cabinet's reaction before and after the Munich Agreement with Hitler; and (5) the split in the Labour Cabinet of 1950, when Bevan and others could not condone armament expenditures at the expense of cuts in social services.

Hence, a British Prime Minister is not a grand vizier ruling over a set of slaves, or an automaton occupying the chair while his party defines policies on all points. Every Cabinet has at least two wings. It is the business of the Prime Minister either to subordinate them to a common policy that is his own or to handle deliberation in such a way that some other combined decision arises, which, if not the most satisfactory to all the members, is the one that is least unsatisfactory to most of them.

Every Prime Minister is *sui generis,* and so is the group of men he has with him. Consequently the qualities of every Prime Minister vary and the relationship that is governmentally beneficial vary. Some Prime Ministers run a good government by modest but irreversible intensity and tenacity of selfless purpose—thus Mr. Attlee, a reconciler, a chairman, a high-minded winner-over to a common view. Some are possessed by a kind of fury, a Pitt, a Palmerston, a Gladstone, a Lloyd George, a Churchill—a fury that is a moral and igniting potency, that wraps itself around the other score and draws them along with it, Hegel's "passion, without which no great deeds are accomplished."

Others, again, possess a knowledge of business and a narrow stubbornness that wins its way because not enough of the Cabinet members are prepared to oppose an equal and opposite force of purpose—such was Neville Chamberlain. More capable and broader minded and urbane was the first of the modern Prime Ministers, Sir Robert Peel, the man who first sat up to his administrative work "with mathematical attention," a man of first-class capacity and second-class ideas, and an interest in every department, possible more in Victoria's days than Elizabeth II's. But first-class ideas, unusual ideas, disturb other men; and neither genius nor originality is essential.

Others, again, such as Stanley Baldwin, are easygoing but possess an intense understanding of the country's mood and also that of the House of Commons. They become reconciling and emolient —though here, the Cabinet is not brought up to the height of its more difficult tasks, as in Baldwin's failure to rearm in the face of Hitler's threat.

Prime Ministers must be good debaters, or impressers; today, they must be men who can in one way or another win mass popularity.

Candor of Criticism. What is of especial importance is that members of the Cabinet should feel that though a deference is owed to the Prime Minister, it is their duty to speak their minds, taking their careers into their hands. Some Prime Ministers do not evoke this challenge. A former Prime Minister has told the present author: "There are not enough men in Winston Churchill's Cabinet [meaning that of 1951–1955] who will talk back to him!" I asked why this was necessary. The answer was the simple human one: "Because he has a lot of ideas—some of them are good, but some of them are not so good. He must be challenged on his bad ideas!" This throws a light on the rather average kind of committee the Cabinet is. A Minister's duty is constructive candor.

It is the business of the Prime Minister to know enough about each department and about each Minister so that he may keep generally *au fait* with his work, enough, at any rate, for the Minister to know he may soon have to ask explanations.

In the Cabinet the Prime Minister rarely calls for a vote. Decisions are taken by a developing consensus. When the discussion has proceeded long enough, the Cabinet knows it, and agreement has been reached. An obstinate Prime Minister who can carry with him, say, the Chancellor of the Exchequer and the Foreign Minister, is in a fair way to deciding the issue of the day as he would like it.

The Prime Minister, in prestige, authority, ideas, and character, is always on strict trial. He is badgered by the Opposition; he is harried by the dissatisfied segment of his own party. He is constantly under reappraisal by his own Cabinet colleagues, for his closest rivals nag him and contrast their qualities with his while the younger members assess him anxiously, if only to preserve the credit of their common party and to protect their own political future. These forces press incessantly on the Prime Minister's mind and constantly affect his policy and actions. One aspect of this is expressed in graphic metaphor by an M.P., Kenneth Pickthorn, who is also professor of political science:

The essential function of this House is that it should be the market on which the stock of the prime minister is made. . . . If we take the normal peace-time price of a good, decent, working prime minister's stock at 100, then I think we might say that it ought to fluctuate slightly—like Consols did in the old days, down to 99, 98½, up to 101—but one does not want it bobbing up and down with great leaps, least of all in war-time. We are blessed by our destiny in that we have a prime minister whose stock, I hardly think it an exaggeration to say, is now something like 1,000 on the basis I have just mentioned, that is, taking the peace-time norm at 100. But even so, it would be a most dangerous thing for the country and—if it is not impertinent to say so—for him, that his stock should be pegged at that value. It ought to be able to go up and down. . . . (House of Commons, Feb. 27, 1941)

To this observation from Cambridge, Mr. Churchill, the Prime Minister in question, made the partly debating answer:

I deprecate this squalid language of the bucket shop as applied to the serious, responsible functions of the State, and I think it would be lamentable if the youth of a great center of learning should be tempted to accept such slipshod and questionable guidance.

For Professor Pickthorn had argued that the Commons was only a subordinate factor in legislating and controlling finance and that its main function was assessing the value of the Prime Minister.

VI. COLLECTIVE RESPONSIBILITY

The Cabinet is a collective executive. It is the executive in commission. It is not an executive of the single-headed or single-person type. Ministers are, of course, individually responsible for their department; but the Cabinet, and in a derived sense, the whole of the Ministry, is responsible collectively.

This means that if a Prime Minister believes that the Cabinet is no longer united enough to be viable or that it has been repudiated by public opinion or that it cannot carry the confidence of the Commons any longer (in relation to what he believes to be *vital* in his policy), the whole Cabinet assumes responsibility for the overt occasion of failure. This may be a vote of censure, the refusal to vote a law or finance, or a vote of no confidence in a Minister for some special error. All go out together. There is no division of responsibility, or piecemeal resignations with others staying in office.

The doctrine has been thus stated:

The Cabinet, as a whole, is responsible for the acts of its members; but if this responsibility is to be real, the Cabinet must be a definite body of persons, every one of whom is informed, or can obtain information, as to any measure of importance contemplated or taken by the entire Cabinet, or by any individual member.

This is a twofold doctrine: of solidarity, and of responsibility.

Sir William Anson, the author of the above-quoted definition, shows that such solidarity and responsibility was not present in the eighteenth century. The cause is suggested: party coherence and organization had not yet matured, wide and firm.

Anson then summarizes the results of his analysis:

At the present time we are more ready to fear that ministers will mismanage our affairs than that they will break the law; they act under close and constant criticism, and, since loss of office and of public esteem are the only penalties which ministers pay for political failure, we can insist that the action of the Cabinet is the action of each member, and that for the action of each member the Cabinet is responsible as a whole. But a member may save his colleagues by resignation of office.[11]

This last, and wise, proviso might be noticed, for we revert to it later.

Let us now take a statement of the doctrine—central to the whole of the contemporary system of British government—by a renowned Prime Minister, Lord Salisbury (Prime Minister, 1886–1892). He said:

For all that passes in the Cabinet each member of it who does not resign is absolutely and irre-

[11] Sir William Anson, *The Law of the Constitution*, Part II, Vol. 1, p. 118.

trievably responsible, and has no right afterwards to say that he agreed in one case to a compromise, while in another he was persuaded by his colleagues. . . . It is only on the principle that absolute responsibility is undertaken by every member of the Cabinet who, after a decision is arrived at, remains a member of it, that the joint responsibility of Ministers to Parliament can be upheld, and one of the most essential principles of parliamentary responsibility established.[12]

The quotations from authorities were necessary, because no statute states this most fundamental of all conventions. It must be added that Cabinet responsibility carries with it in all its meaning *the whole Ministry,* because the Cabinet governs the business of *all* Ministers, whether in the Cabinet or not. It will be responsible for their conduct in office, and be praised or damned politically though theirs be not the actual hands that did the deeds, and so vice versa.

Significance of "Collective"

A multiheaded executive is vested with the executive authority that in the United States is concentrated in one head (it has even more power than he). For the moment, as the Cabinet faces the nation, *it is one,* with no external distinction in degrees of responsibility—formally. It is one for all and all for one.

The British Cabinet is not a single man but it is a single body. It is plural in personnel, but works in oneness of authority and responsibility. This double quality, of oneness of authority and a multitude of counselors, has important consequences for governmental efficiency, consequences which the growth of the Cabinet system was gradually but consciously developed to produce. These are (1) the securing of responsibility, and (2) the securing of efficiency as a high advisory and executive directorate.

(1) Unity Assists Responsibility. It is not easy for nearly 50,000,000 people and some 35,000,000 voters to know who is responsible for all that occurs in their Government. Some cynics might say, "We do not care if they cannot: they are fools just the same!" This is not the democratic

way of thinking, which is that, for peaceful evolution of justice and welfare in the long run, it is necessary that the maximum number of citizens who can and desire to check and balance the actions of their Government should have the opportunity to do so. But this role requires knowledge of the responsible agents. This again, derivatively, requires that there should be the maximum simplification of the processes of government, consistent with their actual nature.

Simplicity of identification, singularity and no confusion of indices, clarity of the causal agent—these things are altogether indispensable. The party system is one of the sorting out, responsibility-fixing agencies. The collective responsibility of the Cabinet, making of several one, gives this concentration, this focus. All will be blamed or praised for any one. There can be no mistake about that—though there may be broken hearts in the Cabinet for those who see their good advice rejected for something else that brings pain to all.

The most cogent case ever made for the collective nature of the British Cabinet system was made by Alexander Hamilton in *The Federalist,* when he advocated the singleness of the American presidency. He did it because he and his colleagues needed to avoid the confusions, backbiting, and inefficiency of British government under George III—as beautifully described in *Thoughts on the Present Discontents*—before the collective system had crystallized! His essential point was that wherever there is a number of agents and not simply *one,* we suffer "the difficulty of detection." Hence the British have institutionalized oneness—that is, collective responsibility and its attendant solidarity. Whereas the U.S. presidency is solitary, the British executive achieved solidarity.

(2) Unity Makes for Efficiency in Business. What is it that is required at the summit of a political system—that is, in the Cabinet? First, its members are vested with the final, surveying, comprehensive, and sweeping determination of policy—all departments, all activities, in the present, and predictive for the future, in the maximum attainable harmony and proportion. Secondly, they give drive to the joint and steady conduct of the various departments in the same direction, averting inner clash and inconsistency and minimizing wasteful and fatiguing jealousy and friction.

---

[12] Gwendolen Cecil, *Marquis of Salisbury,* II, pp. 219–220.

Experience shows this: the psychological and moral burden of government is borne not merely by the Prime Minister but equally by every participant in Cabinet deliberations and decisions. Each can fortify and encourage the other, and each knows tnat his brothers must carry a responsibility for any initiative that *he* takes. No one of them can disavow his own initiative, or his assumption of that of his colleagues, in adversity. The sharing of both authority and responsibility occurs corporately; it is not doled out separately and unequally by one chief executive to sixteen or seventeen individuals, as in the U.S. "Cabinet." The power is shared, and the whole body, as one, participates in the distribution of it. Hence, there is tolerable certainty and definition in who may do what. It is not necessary for any one person among them to amass power, but rather to spread it among trusted colleagues.

Every member of the Cabinet is expected to know what every other one is doing. He is expected to have an opinion on the work of his colleagues; he is expected to state and argue it; he is expected to be tenacious about it; he is expected to ask questions. He has a *right* to do these things. "A Cabinet Minister cannot escape his share of collective responsibility, and is steadily fed—often overfed—with information, oral and written, of the joys and sorrows of his colleagues." [13] He is a bad colleague if he stops matters from coming before the Cabinet, and when "They do not talk back!" They are expected to talk back to the Prime Minister and to talk back at their colleagues. [14]

We may consult Alexander Hamilton:

Energy in the executive is a leading character in the definition of good government. . . . The ingredients which constitute energy in the executive are, unity: duration; and adequate provision for its support; competent powers. . . . That unity is conducive to energy will not be disputed. Decision, activity, secrecy, and dispatch, will generally characterise the proceedings of one man, in a much more eminent degree than the proceedings of the greater number; and in proportion as the number is increased, these qualities will be diminished.

The result in the United States was a single, or solitary executive. But it did not attain the qualities that Hamilton anticipated. For the business of American government grew far too large for any one man to assume the constitutional authority and responsibility for it. You can endow one man with so much authority that it kills his physique, even as it confuses and paralyzes his ability to do anything but delegate. Hence, the vigor and despatch *and the responsibility* are lost. We have only to remember the destruction wrought on a man of conscience, Franklin D. Roosevelt; the moral and physical pressure on Harry S. Truman; and the distracted if agonizingly conscientious counsels of the subsequent Administration.

Maintenance of Solidarity

The British system went its own way. It aspires to the benefits of a multiple executive—which allows of division of labor, and the easing of excessive personal responsibility to the degree each man can tolerate; and also, to the benefits of oneness. Of course, the secret is the political luck of party organization, which makes each Cabinet the product not only of one party but of a coherent and self-disciplined party. Party unanimity is the essence of the collective oneness of the British cabinet system. The many human tensions and conflict in the Cabinet are restrained by a loyalty to its principles, program, and tradition, by a care for its future success, and by an ever-present recognition of the brutal fact that an Opposition is waiting to tell the nation that the Cabinet is in upheaval. Of this unanimity, obeisant to the health and victory of the party, the Prime Minister is the special guardian and embodiment.

By what means is this solidarity maintained, and how is it exhibited?

Saying the Same Thing. (1) A Minister will always be expected to vote for his party unless paired. This is his minimum obligation. (2) He cannot make a speech or other expression of opinion that contradicts that of the Government. As

[13] Dalton, *Memoirs, op. cit.,* p. 259.
[14] All our abundant information about the U.S. Cabinet is to the effect that members are more inclined to evade any collective questioning of their departmental bailiwicks and are not interested in their colleagues. Cf. Finer, *Theory and Practice of Modern Government,* New York, 1949, Chapter 26 and such works as Harold E. Ickes, *Diaries,* New York, 1953 onward.

Lord Palmerston said in mild admonition to Mr. Gladstone (a Prime Minister in his turn):

A member of the Government, when he takes office, necessarily divests himself of that perfect freedom of individual action which belongs to a private and independent member of Parliament, and the reason is this, that what a member says and does of the Government upon public matters must to a certain degree commit his colleagues, and the body to which he belongs if they by their silence appear to acquiesce; and if any of them follow his example and express as publicly opposition opinions, which in particular cases they might feel obliged to do, differences of opinion between members of the same Government are necessarily brought out into prominence and the strength of the Government is thereby impaired.[15]

The reader will notice the phrase *commit his colleagues* and the term *body*. It is by such turns of phrase that the nature of an institution is exposed, whether it be in unwritten or written law.

The Prime Minister, however, possesses more freedom to *lead,* by announcing an advance on hitherto accepted collective policy. He will not go too far in this path without previous consultation; but, like Mr. Chamberlain in his conversations with Hitler, the pressure of circumstances may compel it. All the more reason to be careful who gets to the top as Prime Minister in those apprenticeship years in the Commons and the party.

May a Minister Dissent? On some special matters, the pangs of conscience trouble members of the Government. Expedients have had to be adopted from time to time to meet them. Then a careful statement is made by the member or a leading Minister to separate these most unusual divergencies. Thus, a Labour Home Secretary in 1931 voted for a bill, which he had introduced, to allow certain types of theatrical performances on Sundays; some voted for and some against. Again, the Labour Party suffers a perennial and divisive gnawing at its conscience on the problem of capital punishment. When, in 1948, the Government proposed the suspension of capital punishment for five years, the Home Secretary was opposed to

[15] Philip Guedalla, *Gladstone and Palmerston,* London, 1928, p. 228.

it, as were his colleagues. But the rank and file were largely in favor. At a caucus meeting the Government allowed the rank and file a free vote. But it resisted the attempt of the rank and file to make the vote free among Ministers also: they were merely excused from voting at all, by collective decision.

Unity under Strain. Collectiveness of the Cabinet may now be seen from the reverse side: What happens when conscience or interests are strained beyond the possibility of agreement? For some things must be yielded to gain others, in the government of millions.

An attempt is made by the dissentient to get his point of view over by the cogency of argument. He will almost simultaneously seek for allies in the Government, as Aneurin Bevan sought for (and found) Harold Wilson and George Strauss (or they him) in the Labour Cabinet of 1950. He will press his argument in the Cabinet to the suggestion of resignation. It may be an error to go too far unless he means to resign—because a Prime Minister may welcome this, having a substitute ready. This happened in one of the most famous cases of all in 1886, when Mr. Churchill's renowned father, Lord Randolph Churchill, overvalued his own indispensability in the Cabinet of Lord Salisbury, as Chancellor of the Exchequer. Mr. Goschen was promptly put in his place.

A stage is reached, however, when the dissentient Minister resigns, as in the Aneurin Bevan case, then to take his fight to the party members; or, as in Ramsay Macdonald's case in 1931, the Prime Minister abandons the Cabinet if the dissentients are so many that he cannot cope with them. In the case of Mr. Eden's resignation in 1937 against Mr. Chamberlain's policy of friendship with Mussolini, Mr. Chamberlain let the Cabinet know that their choice was Eden or himself.

The British practice may be contrasted with American and with French Cabinet and parliamentary mores, where leakages to the press of differences among Ministers are common, not surprising when it is known that Cabinets are not founded on the unanimity of one party, but are transient alliances. In the U.S.S.R. the problem was solved by Stalin's murders; since his death the issue is perhaps open.

Individual Responsibility

It is not possible to operate collective responsibility without a safety valve: individual scapegoats.

(1) There are more departmental policies of high significance than a Prime Minister and a Cabinet, however well organized, can properly know and control and therefore be responsible for. It becomes unreal to impute responsibility to *all* of them jointly. But the general fiction that there *is* knowledge has to be maintained, while some relief from its dire effects must be devised.

(2) If a Cabinet could be overthrown every time that some individual Minister was in error and unsatisfactory to Parliament, then we should have far too many reorganizations of the Cabinet. It could not be tolerated in the British economic and social system, where a high degree of stability and continuity of policy is essential to the standard of living and the peace of mind of the population. **Discard Weak Ministers.** Hence, it has always happened that individual Ministers who have exhibited a weakness, either before Parliament or discovered by the Cabinet or Prime Minister earlier than public disclosure, are sacrificed. They are told to resign, and so save the whole Cabinet from sharing their fate. Such expulsions are fairly numerous—and they indicate, among other things, that even the long apprenticeship which Ministers serve in politics before they attain high office is not completely sufficient to reveal their shortcomings until they are tried and tested in the actual conduct of office. Mr. Churchill reconstructed his Ministry *substantially* three times between 1951 and 1955. In December 1955 Sir Anthony Eden carried through a massive reconstruction of his Government, but six months old, to correct demonstrated misfits. His Chancellor of the Exchequer, R. A. Butler, became Leader of the House, to plan and steer legislation and Parliamentary business, and simultaneously responsible for policy direction of the Conservative Central Office for the Leader.

On occasion, it will not be a Minister of moderate importance who has to leave, such as a Lord Macmillan, Minister of Information during part of World War II (an otherwise most admirable man), but one of the principal Ministers. The most celebrated recent example of this is Sir

Samuel Hoare's resignation in 1935 from the office of Foreign Secretary. Mr. Baldwin was Prime Minister, and his Cabinet was seeking a way to avoid the imposition of economic sanctions, which might in the long run lead to war—against Mussolini over the latter's aggression in Abyssinia. Sir Samuel Hoare, in Paris, tried to reach an agreement with French Prime Minister Pierre Laval (after World War II, executed by the French Government as a pro-Vichyite subverter of his nation). Without authorization, the agreement was made public. Its obsequience to Mussolini aroused a tempest of antigovernmental passion in Britain. The Prime Minister bowed before this storm: he forced Sir Samuel Hoare to resign. Otherwise, had Mr. Baldwin stood by him, it *might* have meant the overthrow of the Government (he had given the Foreign Secretary too much freedom to negotiate!) *The resignation was a safety valve* for the principle of *collective* responsibility, because the Prime Minister feared defeat in the Commons, or in an election, if dissolution should come.

That safety valve will have to be used more and more as a Government is well settled in office on the basis of its party majority, if the efficiency and the responsibility of the Government are to be dynamically maintained.[16]

It is part of the convention of collective responsibility that the resignation of a Minister gives him the privilege of explaining his resignation in Parliament. This privilege is not his outright: by convention the deliberations of the Cabinet are secret, and as a Privy councilor he has taken a special oath of secrecy; explanation requires the royal permission, which means the Prime Minister's permission. In other words, the explanations are permitted by the very person against whom they may be directed. They naturally take on a tone that is partly the product of the clash between personalities. The best recent example of this is probably the resignation of Mr. Duff Cooper in 1938 over the Munich Agreement made by Neville Chamberlain. Whatever the occasion of resignation, the resigned man, whether in Parliament or elsewhere, is bound to observe the obligation of *secrecy* of

---

[16] The subject is thoroughly treated, with a full review of precedents, in Professor S. E. Finer's two articles in *Political Studies* (London) 1955 and 1956.

Cabinet proceedings (see pp. 152–153), and this tends to put him at a disadvantage in his defense of himself.

The Coalition Cabinet of 1931. The Cabinet experience of 1931 showed in high relief two things about collective responsibility: (1) the value of solidarity of the Cabinet on the basis of one party, if it can be obtained, and (2) the nature of the convention of collectivity. Each of these facts must be briefly explained.

A coalition of Conservatives, some Liberals, and some Labour leaders was made in September 1931 to meet an economic crisis. Having abandoned the gold standard, it then dissolved Parliament to get a new mandate, feeling itself indispensable. As the parties in the coalition were so utterly divergent in outlook, they agreed on seeking "a doctor's mandate," to take all measures (not disclosed in detail) for the nation's good. All went forward as "National" Government candidates, with the agreement not to stress their differences, a matter of serious embarrassment to all of them and their supporters in the electorate. Conservatives extolled tariffs; Liberals, free trade! One Labour leader, Snowden, panicked the country with the menace that if the regular Labour Party were returned their post-office savings would be lost. A tremendous majority was secured, substantially Conservative.

Almost at once the coalition was in internal Cabinet trouble on the main question: the restoration of prosperity by means of protection—or some alternative. A public dispute then arose. A Cabinet committee in January 1932 recommended a general tariff: the Liberals and Mr. Snowden dissented. They should have resigned, according to the principle of collective responsibility. Instead, there was hatched a formula: an "agreement to differ." Because national unity was so necessary.

It has accordingly determined that some modification of usual ministerial practice is required, and has decided that ministers who find themselves unable to support the conclusions arrived at by the majority of their colleagues on the subject of import duties and cognate matters are to be at liberty to express their view by speech and vote. The Cabinet being essentially united on all other matters of policy believes

that by this special provision it is best interpreting the will of the nation and the needs of the time.[17]

The Labour Opposition challenged this departure from "convention." Mr. Baldwin answered with the curious but highly revealing argument:

Is our action constitutional? Who can say what is constitutional in the conduct of a *National* Government [italics supplied]? It is a precedent, an experiment, a new practice, to meet a new emergency, a new condition of things, and we have collective action. . . . It is approved by the broad common sense of the man in the street.

The need of the man in the street for clarity of leadership soon settled the issue, for the Liberal leader involved, Sir Herbert Samuel, soon found himself obliged to tell his Liberal followers in the country that the tariff proposals were vicious. The Conservatives resented this, and so did *their* men in the street. Lord Snowden, now a peer, told *all* men in the street of the malevolence of the tariffs and the Conservative Party. The Liberal Party Conference damned the proposals and denounced the position of their leaders in the Cabinet—*their* men in the street could not understand the party's confused involvement. In July 1933 the Conservative element of the Cabinet carried through their tariff proposals (the Ottawa Agreements). In September the free-traders Samuel (Liberal) and Snowden (Labour) resigned. The Liberals declared:

It is plain that the difference is so fundamental upon matters of such high importance that it is impossible for us to remain members of a Government which is bent upon giving to those agreements the force of law.

Thus was restored internal solidarity to the Cabinet: by the purgation of some members and the acquiescence of others, like Ramsay Macdonald, in the rest of the Cabinet's policy.

Secrecy and Party Solidarity

Somewhere in every form of government there must be a forum in which absolute frankness is

17 Herman Finer, *Future of Government*, London, 1946, Note 17, chapter on Britain.

possible. No fear of adverse consequences must be permitted to inhibit even brutal candor. This is in the interests not of the Ministers but of the solution of diplomatic and domestic governmental problems according to their technical nature and not obsequiously to popular pleasure, though this also is an ingredient in the solution. It is often necessary to be cruel to be kind: to take disagreeable economic or war measures today for the sake of the long-run good. (This is why trustworthy, disciplined political parties, based on principle, are desirable.)

This is recognized in the oath of the Privy Councilor which is taken by Cabinet Ministers. Its main terms deserve notice:

> You shall swear to be a true and faithful servant unto the Queen's Majesty, as one of Her Majesty's Privy Council. . . . You shall, in all things to be moved, treated and debated in Council, faithfully and truly declare your Mind and Opinion according to your Heart and Conscience; and shall keep secret all Matters committed and revealed unto you or that shall be treated of secretly in Council. And if any of the said Treaties or Councils shall touch any of the Counsellors, you shall not reveal it unto him, but shall keep the same until such time as, by Consent of Her Majesty, or the Council, Publication shall be made thereof. . . .

Two things are enjoined here: secrecy—but also frankness *within* the special forum.

In addition to the obligation of this oath, the Official Secrets Act of 1920 forbids the communication to unauthorized persons of official documents and information, under heavy penalty.

A famous Prime Minister, Lord Salisbury, said that privacy of discussion "could only be made completely effective if the flow of suggestions which accompanied it attained the freedom and fullness which belonged to private conversations—members must feel themselves untrammelled by any consideration of consistency with the past or self-justification in the future." He pleaded for "irresponsible licence in discussion." The Opposition, of course, cannot be let in, to brew mutual recrimination among Ministers. A Lord Chancellor, Viscount Hailsham, reaffirmed (House of Lords, December 21, 1932) the need to be able

"explicitly to rely" on their colleagues, without "any haunting fear that what happens may hereafter by publication create difficulties for themselves or, what is far more grave, may create complications for the King and country that they are trying to serve."

Party Solidarity Assists Secrecy. Manifestly, the danger of disclosure is great where a Cabinet is not founded on a single party. If British Cabinets were like those in France—ephemeral coalitions of parties—enemies yesterday, friends for a few hours, enemies again tomorrow, the possibilities of instant disclosure, of leakage, would be so great as to defeat frankness except of an insincere and misleading kind. (The Soviet dictatorship does not have such problems.)

Occasionally secrecy is violated. In 1934, in a biography of George Lansbury, his son Edgar divulged some facts of 1931. The author was compelled to expurgate the work. In February 1952 Mr. Churchill gave the House information regarding the military commitments made by Mr. Attlee and Mr. Morrison to the U.S. Government, if forces in Korea were attacked by air from Chinese bases. The information was evidently gleaned from Cabinet documents. He sailed very close to the wind of unconstitutionality, indeed, denying that he was "quoting."

On the whole, secrecy is well maintained, until such time as it is harmless to the men and policies involved; then such history becomes the very meat of political science.

The Nature of Responsibility

Responsibility is accepted for everything in the administration of policy so far as the Ministers have responsibility for it by law or custom. Responsibility is *political,* not legal as in the older practice of impeachment, though a wrongful act of a Minister directly performed against person or property must carry with it a personal liability to the ordinary civil and criminal law.

Impeachment was last used in 1805 against Lord Melville, several times a Cabinet Minister, for financial misdemeanors when Treasurer of the Admiralty. It was used before *political* ministerial responsibility was properly developed; it is too drastic an instrument to use where honest error is so possible and yet so easily subject to denunciation as transgression or sabotage.

To Whom Is Responsibility Owed? If a Government cannot persuade a majority of the House of Commons to accept its policies (legislative and in the conduct of the departments foreign and domestic) or its personnel, it must resign, if it regards the policies that are repudiated by the Commons as matters of principle. There may be small matters that on occasion are rejected by a snap vote. Or, when parties are closely balanced as in the Parliament of 1950, a Labour Government may regard it as not vital to yield on an occasional rebuff, as the last election is not distant while a new immediate election is not likely to resolve the close balance of seats. But, excepting for such contingencies, what a Government proposes is so well planned and weighed as being of governmental and popular importance that a repudiation by the Commons is a defeat on which the Government must resign.

How can a vote defeat a Government when the Government has been built on the majority? With the two-party system the Cabinet has stout and loyal phalanx of support. If any break away, they will, at maximum, abstain from voting, but they will not vote against. If, however, a Government is so internally divided (as the Balfour Government when tariff reform began to be agitated in its bosom and in the nation by Joseph Chamberlain and some adherents) or has some internal divisions and only a bare majority in the House of Commons, it will soon resign, even without being overthrown in the Commons. Human nature in the Cabinet could not stand the strain of keeping its followers together or the feeling that it has no substantial authority. In 1951 the Labour Government dissolved, having but a trifling majority and being internally riven.

The Disciplinary Power of Dissolution. The majority is kept intact by the strategy of the Whips, and the knowledge on the part of members that their own political careers may be ended if their flouting of the party leaders causes them to see that they will no longer receive the endorsement of the organization at the next election. The Government can bring this home at a time of revolt by the threat to resign and ask for a dissolution. This means that the members must fight another

election without certainty that they will be elected. Members do not need to be told this; they know it. A three-line Whip will reinforce it. A whisper from the Government will bring them to heel. (French Ministers shout, but their power of dissolution being hollow (p. 418), Deputies ignore them.

However, as is shown in Chapter 8, the monitory power of the Commons is *still* the first instance in the fixing of responsibility on a Government. The second instance is the next election and the electorate. This is the true meaning of the phrase already repeated: "The constitution is no longer Parliamentary; it is plebiscitary."

Dissolution is the prerogative of the Crown, but it cannot be exercised unless the Cabinet wills it. The Ministers must acquiesce—if not, where can the Crown find other Ministers who command the Commons? The Lord President must summon the Privy Council to make the Order of Dissolution—he is responsible, and could say No. The Lord Chancellor takes responsibility for the Proclamation and writ of summons of a new Parliament: he could say No. Failing advice that there should be a dissolution, all that the Crown can do is to dismiss Ministers; but this would produce not only a political but a *constitutional* crisis!

Before 1918 the Cabinet decided on dissolution; since then, the Prime Minister has reserved this right to himself. This enhances the Prime Minister's authority.

For over a hundred years the sovereign has never refused a dissolution when asked for by the Prime Minister. Yet there is a persistent rumor or sentiment that the Crown might do so in "certain circumstances." What are they? Nobody knows. The sentiment has been sustained over the years by Conservatives who think of the Crown as an arbiter—in "certain circumstances"—between "radical" or left-wing politicians and the Conservative Party before the people. Or there is the feeling that shortly after an election a Government ought not to seek a way out of its tie position or minority position in the House by a "diet of dissolutions." But this may be the only way for the country to recover its electoral health —by dissolution and an electoral attempt to resolve the balance of power.

There are times when the House of Commons,

in spite of the well-rooted majority of a Government, overthrows it. They are rare, but they happen. The most noted example of recent times is the overthrow of, perhaps, the most obstinate Prime Minister in the whole of British history, obstinate because narrow-minded: Neville Chamberlain, the sessions of May 7–10, 1940. The Labour Party turned a mere debate on war policy into one of No Confidence in his Government. Some severe critics in Mr. Chamberlain's own party, of the highest party and parliamentary prestige, joined in. Though Mr. Chamberlain had a majority of 81 at the end of the debate, no less than 50 Conservatives had voted with the Opposition! His authority was at an end. He resigned, and a new Government was soon formed with Mr. Churchill as Prime Minister. Shame and discouragement in the House can do what votes will not add up to: to be red in the face can be as effective as being in the red with votes. This will become more appreciated presently.

Responsibility to the Electorate via the Commons. Responsibility is then to the country through the medium of the House of Commons and, in part, simultaneously, directly, and collaterally to the people.

If responsibility means that the Cabinet experiences a persistent obligation to respond to the criticism and the admonitions of the House, to yield here and there on policy and personnel, to change its course, to accept amendments to laws which imply eventually a change in its tax and appropriations plans, if not now, then in the not-too-distant future, responsibility *potently* works. It exists in this sense to the House directly. The House has not the direst immediate sanction available—ejection from office—but it has the means of heaping up a public exposure of governmental incompetence that will bring the wrath of the electorate upon its head at the approaching election—it may be, in a by-election to be held soon.

Never a day passes without the fierce light and sting of the Opposition's challenge to the Cabinet's policy and methods. Both sides of the House know very well that the whole nation is listening; or, suppose we say that 1,000,000 out of 35,500,000 voters are listening intently and critically? Day after day, without intermission, the next election

is in the making. It is never out of mind. There is an umbilical connection between the Government and the nation through the parties' physiology. Voting figures in the House are secondary to that anxiety over the floating or stay-at-home vote and to the total cumulative effect of the record of both sides in action, argument, and mutual opposition. If a vote of censure in the Commons is merely the formal way of opening a debate against the Government, all the debates and questions form a developing vote of censure to be given voting strength and force in the nation at the next election. The Government must remember that almost one half of the voters in the nation did not vote for it: and sometimes that the Opposition already has more votes than it itself possesses. Public-opinion polls add to the influential sensitiveness of fluid opinion.

The Government is *forced* by the thought of the long-run accounting, as well as the incessant, direct, face-to-face possibility of being shamed among its fellow members, to offer serious, solid justification, capable of standing up as not nonsense. This is responsibility. Hence the democratic value of keeping all important decisions before the full, open House, and not consigning to the twilight of committees with executive sessions as in the U.S. Congress.

"The Sense of the House." Furthermore, members of the Cabinet are members of the Commons. They have been elected in the same way; fought the same kind of campaigns; suffered the slings and arrows of electioneering and of frank, rough handling in debate in the House. They are the flesh of the Commons' flesh. Tomorrow they may be not in the Government but in the Opposition. They might even not be re-elected. They know the electorate and have a respect for it, grounded in the recognition of its sovereign power to destroy or create. A seamless web holds together in one body the members of the Commons who happen to be in the Government and all the other members who happen to be their masters, mentors, and critics.

Sharp examples may be seen. In August 1947 the Labour Government was forced by Opposition argument to arrange to promote Sir Stafford Cripps to chief of economic policy planning and to subordinate to him, relatively, the two Ministers till then in charge of this: the Chancellor of the Exchequer and the Lord President of the Council, Herbert Morrison.[18] In July 1954 a very eminent Conservative Minister of Agriculture, Sir Thomas Dugdale, was made to resign by being badgered into taking responsibility for some errors of administration made by his civil servants (see p. 173, *fn.*). These merely exemplify a head of pressure that never relaxes.

If this analysis is not acknowledged as true to life, then the British Cabinet system is incomprehensible, and the student (or the journalist reporting events from London) will be misled. He will be one more of those who continually recite the clichés that Parliament is "the rubber stamp of the Cabinet" or "the registrar of the edicts of the Cabinet." He will have failed to appreciate the fear in the heart of Ministers; he will have missed their patriotic anxiety to do well as a team in the Commons.

VII. THE PSYCHOLOGICAL DRIVE TO SEEK OFFICE

The responsibility is no longer penal, as in the middle of the seventeenth century, when the Commons would impeach and the Lords conduct the trial and when punishment might be execution, imprisonment, or exile. Then the discipline of party and Commons over Ministers had not yet developed. Furthermore, Government was more concerned with the very crude questions of affirming its authority altogether, or preserving the nation, than fulfilling a large and compendious pattern of legislative reforms. But, now, supposing a Minister were liable to death if his policy of monetary deflation caused distress? Or if unemployment insurance caused a drain on the nation's budget? Or a scheme for getting cheaper edible fats by a governmental ground-nuts enterprise in Africa failed? Who would enter politics, except dictators or rogues?

Responsibility is political today—and it has been for nearly three hundred years. It connotes the loss of political reputation and the loss of office. The loss of office means the loss of a salary, but it is not so great a salary as to be the decisive factor. Almost every Minister could earn as much, perhaps more, certainly not much less, in alternative employment.

The psychological force in the loss of office arises from the passion for certain personal and social values and interests which possession of office gives to the holder of it. Office is the magnification of power of one man by his endowment for the time being with all the authority of nearly 50,000,000 people. Alternatively, it is the reinforced power to obstruct others who would gain supreme and unqualified power to do as they liked, if he were not there to say No.

The psychology is explained in a statement of Gladstone's:

> The desire for office is the desire of ardent minds for a larger space and scope within which to serve the country, and for access to the command of that powerful machinery for information and practice which the public departments supply. He must be a very bad minister indeed who when in office does not do ten times the good to the country that he would do when out of office, because he has helps and opportunities which multiply twenty-fold, as by a system of wheels and pulleys, his power for doing it.

Or, as Neville Chamberlain put it:

> There are very few and brief moments when I feel I can't bear to talk or think of the politics that have become my main purpose in life.[19]

The Cabinet in Britain is not limited to mere execution of the laws: it is master (yet serving the Commons) of *all* the sovereign power—foreign, domestic, administrative, and legislative—of the British nation. Its power is unlimited. What a prize to men who have an impulse of duty to society, an itch to give the lead to other people, a hunger for power and prestige, the enjoyment of business, a desire for fame, and who worship political heroes in their nation's history!

The Prime Minister and the Cabinet

This ambition—the ambition of service—finds its acutest expression in the prime ministership.

[18] Cf. H. Finer, "Central Planning Machinery in Britain," *Public Administration Review*, Autumn 1948.

[19] Keith Feiling, *Neville Chamberlain*, London, 1946, p. 287.

Furthermore, given the large size of the Cabinet, it puts the Prime Minister in a certain position of unifying aloofness, even a separation from his colleagues, varying from Prime Minister to Prime Minister.

Mr. Churchill says about his accession to the prime ministership in World War II:

In any sphere of action there can be no comparison between the positions of number one and number two, three, or four. The duties and problems of all persons other than number one are quite different and in many ways more difficult. It is always a misfortune when number two or three has to initiate a dominant plan or policy. He has to consider not only the merits of the policy, but the mind of his chief; not only what to advise, but what it is proper for him in his station to advise; not only what to do, but how to get it agreed, and how to get it done. Moreover, number two or three, will have to reckon with numbers four, five, and six, or maybe some bright outsider, number twenty. Ambition, not so much for vulgar ends, but for fame, glints in every mind. There are always several points of view which may be right, and many which are plausible.

At the top there are great simplifications. An accepted leader has only to be sure of what it is best to do, or at least to have made up his mind about it. *The loyalties which centre about number one are enormous.* [Italics supplied.] If he trips, he must be sustained. If he makes mistakes, they must be covered. If he sleeps, he must not be wantonly disturbed. If he is no good, he must be poleaxed. But this last extreme process cannot be carried out every day; and certainly not in the days just after he has been chosen.[20]

This position of primacy, the need for prompt action, the distraction of other Ministers by their own heterogeneous departmental responsibilities, can put a Prime Minister in a momentarily despotic position. It can happen. The comment of Mr. Churchill on his predecessor Neville Chamberlain is good doctrine, and we ought to notice that the tendency is rather in the spirit of Conservative than Liberal or Labour Prime Ministers:

Everyone must recognize that the Prime Minister is pursuing a policy of a most decided charac-

ter and of capital importance. He has his own strong view about what to do, and about what is going to happen. He has his own standard of values; he has his own angle of vision. He believes that he can make a good settlement for Europe and for the British Empire by coming to terms with Herr Hitler and Signor Mussolini. No one impugns his motives. No one doubts his conviction or his courage. Besides all this, he has the power to do what he thinks best. . . . He is willing to take the responsibility; he has the right to take the responsibility; and we are going to learn, in a comparatively short time, what he proposes should happen to us.[21]

This was written in November 1938. Mr. Chamberlain far exceeded the normal exploitation of the Prime Minister's status. He was able to do so because his Cabinet was weak, hand picked by himself, it was of *mixed* political origin (for example, Sir John Simon was a former Liberal). The Conservative Party overwhelmingly supported his policy, which had caused him to keep Mr. Churchill from the Government and to shed such men as Mr. Eden and Mr. Duff Cooper. His friends in *The Times* even wrote editorials extolling his behavior as showing Hitler that Britain could enact the *Führerprinzip* too![22]

In Wartime. Two world wars, with imminent extinction just averted, have shown it is possible to adapt the cabinet system of peacetime to one capable of meeting the exigencies of total war. Lloyd George limited the number of his War Cabinet to five or six members, freed from departmental duties, to act as the highest directorate. Dominion Prime Ministers who visited England were invited to take part in these meetings. He invented and developed the Secretariat.

In 1940–1945 Mr. Churchill's war administration, the personal, political and administrative genius of the man, instructed by the experience of World War I, was better conducted. His War Cabinet was smaller than the ordinary Cabinet: between five and eight, some of them, as time went on, with direct departmental duties, because he found and insisted that meshing in with the day-by-day operations of the departments was

[20] *Their Finest Hour*, p. 15.

[21] *The Gathering Storm*, p. 333.
[22] Finer, *Future of Government*, London, 1946, Chapter V.

needed. But, effectively, Mr. Churchill assumed highest direction of the war, becoming also Minister of Defense, thus presiding over the service departments and the joint chiefs of staffs' sessions. The other sections of the war effort were coordinated by other War Cabinet members, particularly through the Lord President's Committee (Sir John Anderson, formerly a noted civil servant being chairman). This took the war administration, so far as supply and civilian effort and existence in matters of executive detail were concerned, off Mr. Churchill's shoulders. Then, in addition, the many other departments (some outside the Lord President's ministerial committee) were coordinated for the settlement of common problems by Ministers assigned as chairmen of other committees.

Both War Cabinets remained responsible to Parliament, and both were subjected to steady and always heavy criticism by the Commons.

It will be seen, then, that the essence of wartime Governments in Britain is eminence and drive by one outstanding man; a small nucleus of top Ministers, with him to perfect the highest strategy and decision; coordination and the drive of a stream of tendency through the departments from the resolute and energetic top.

VIII. LOYALTY OF THE ARMY TO CABINET ORDERS

The loyalty of the Armed Services to the orders of civilian chiefs is in the same general category as the loyalty of civil servants (pp. 210–213). But clearly it is of mortal importance, and so deserves immediate treatment.

The control of the Army involves the very existence of democracy. Those who have arms and disciplined fighting methods can destroy majority rule, and also dictatorships (see for Czarism, pp. 764–766). The problem is focused in the career officers rather than in the drafted soldiers. (Army terms are used; but reference is also to the Navy and Air Force—the latter may well be the decisive one.)

Our sketch of English constitutional history (pp. 39–41) makes it clear how frightened were the antagonists of royal despotism to allow standing armies or the billeting of soldiers. For a cen-

tury after Cromwell had ruled the nation with his major generals, English politicians were nervous of the political power of a professional army. They could not have been reassured by the Duke of Wellington's masterful way with Parliament during the days when he stood out against passage of the Reform Bill of 1832. The military and bloody suppression of the people's political meetings of 1818 was satisfactory to the upper classes; the Army was neither democratically composed nor democratically devoted.

However, it was assumed that the Army would obey Ministers when they gave commands and not plan to obstruct the policies of the Government. This may still be assumed. The tying of the Army to the service of the symbol of the monarchy is a very important psychological factor in military subservience to the civil power. The monarchy represents the nation to the officers and men: they swear loyalty to the King or Queen; they are not distracted by the thought that the orders come from a political party they hate or men and women of a class they despise. This is today the situation.[23] With the peaceful advent of a Labour Government in 1945, the Armed Forces lost any reason to change their dedication to "national" service.

Yet military loyalty is always contingent on men's consciences not being overstrained by policy. When a civil servant resigns rather than carry out a Minister's policy (rare, almost to nonoccurrence, in Britain), the world does not come to an end; but if military men should do this, the world might well come to an end; and if they should have a hostile policy, that world might go up in flames.

Such a situation occurred in Britain when the Liberal Government in 1913 intended to enforce its Home Rule Bill (for Ireland), by repression of the opposition to it in Protestant Ulster. The act had been passed after several debates and wide-

[23] An illustration is furnished by a speech of Princess Margaret, Oct. 19, 1955, in presenting colors to a Scottish regiment of which she is colonel. This was *prior* to her renunciation (p. 176). "Today we are, thank God, at peace but it is a peace full of unrest and uncertainty. At no time, I am sure, has there been greater need for resolute and unwavering service. So it is appropriate to recall today the loyalty which these colors symbolize. It is threefold: Loyalty to your queen, loyalty to your country, and loyalty to your regiment."

spread public agitation since the 1880's, and after a very patient attention to the Conservative majority in the House of Commons. When the Ulster minority openly armed themselves for resistance, the leaders of the Conservative Party, indeed, the leader of H.M. Loyal Opposition Mr. Bonar Law, threatened revolution. Others organized a conspiracy with the Army officers at the Curragh camp not to march into Ulster. The Government, under Mr. Asquith, negotiated with the Army. Its Secretary for War and various military advisers had to resign as a result of failure to satisfy the Cabinet with their proposals. The Army killed the Home Rule Bill by its move—because before the problem could otherwise be resolved, World War I had broken out. Yet this same Army fought, to be wiped out in France and Flanders in complete self-sacrifice.

There is more security where the officers are drawn from the broadest representative mass of the people; where class distinctions are by all diverse means modified and diluted; by the constant preachment of democratic values. If the monarchy is continued, the Kings or Queens must be persuaded that they must not hesitate to support the orders that the Ministers, based on the Commons' majority, think it responsibly right to give. Above all, dreadful dangers are courted when such men as the Conservative leaders of 1913 (see p. 182) even argue that the royal power of veto is not dead, that the Crown can, say, refuse assent to a bill that would, as in lawfully coerced Ulster, "drive loyal men out of our community." The detachment of the Army from sole loyalty to the Ministers of the day, and their attachment to the Crown, "on Her Majesty's Service," is an excellent expedient (even if an accidentally discovered one)—provided the Crown stands above partisanship.

IX. THE ROLE AND STATUS OF THE OPPOSITION AND OF THE HOUSE OF COMMONS

Her Majesty's Loyal Opposition

The phrase "the Opposition" originated in the early nineteenth century, the adjective *loyal* being of later addition. On April 10, 1826, an Opposition member was criticizing an increase in the salary of a Minister proposed by the Government. When the critic used the phrase, the Prime Minister, George Canning, echoed it sarcastically and raised a laugh. Mr. Tierney retorted, "My honourable friend could not have invented a better phrase to designate us . . . for we are certainly to all intents and purposes, a branch of His Majesty's Government." Canning's proposal was abandoned because his majority was too slim. Whereupon, Mr. Tierney assured "His Majesty's Government that they had, by this act, justly earned the approbation of 'His Majesty's Opposition.' "

The idea and something approaching the term had been current for some eighty years or more, but not as one to be put into effect. The idea of a "formed general opposition" was regarded by George III's politicians as something immoral and unpatriotic, as factious. It was thought that just as Ministries should be formed of such groups in Parliament as could be brought together only for the occasion, so to speak, as servants of the Crown, so ought there be no consistent and permanent ready-made Opposition. What created the Cabinet as a unit, created the Opposition as a regular and continuous counter unit—that is, party commitments of policy made to the nation at elections. There are still political systems—for example, the U.S.S.R.—in which toleration and poise have not yet reached this level of admitting that men can be loyal to the constitution though they oppose a government on policy. Extremists in the United States even have assailed another party for "twenty years of treason."

Without a concerted Opposition, the collectively responsible Cabinet would not be spurred on to its highest merits; it would be fumbling and weak. Around the Opposition there is a nucleus of a dozen or so men, who sit on the Front Opposition Bench with the leader. They are virtually the alternative Government. Indeed, the Conservatives, echoing the Liberal Party as far back as 1876, refer to the group, slang-wise, as the "shadow" Cabinet, a term found along with "ex-Cabinet." **An Alternative Government.** The Opposition regards itself as the alternative Government, out of office today but to be in on some near tomorrow. The party that returns a minority from the electoral campaign does not disperse as individuals,

Their solidarity protects them from losing morale and a sense of responsibility.

Briefly, then, since 1937, by the Ministers of the Crown Act, the Leader of the Opposition receives an annual salary of £2000 from the State, to enable him to carry on his vitally important functions without worry for his living by other activities. This arrangement follows the practice, until that time, of the Canadian Government.

The tight organization of the Opposition confronts the Government with a planned, continuous, and inescapable set of critics, who have assumed the responsibility for opposition in two senses. (1) They will shadow the Cabinet wherever it goes and challenge it at every turn; (2) they feel committed to fulfill (when their turn comes) the principles on which they have charged that the Government was in error, and to implement the practical policies they have proposed as beneficial alternatives. They have the zest of the first kind of responsibility, and the sense of proportion of the second.

Indeed, the responsibility is so "governmental," as it were, that rebellions sometimes occur within the Opposition among individuals who want to be more castigatory. It was Lord Randolph Churchill who suggested that the business of an Opposition is to oppose. This is an advance on the earlier formula of Tierney, that the duty of an Opposition is to propose nothing, to oppose everything, and to turn out the Government. If this latter recipe is amended by "propose alternatives" in place of "propose nothing," one gets close to the role of the Opposition today. It is to put the Government under the searchlight of a rival and constructive set of principles and proposals, to expose the demerits of the Government's, and expound the superior merit of its own. Making the contrast compact, it invites the public to continuous comparative appraisal. Thus it puts the Government on its mettle.

The Opposition is therefore (1) a parliamentary tactic-planning and general staff; it divides time among its appropriate debaters; (2) it tracks down the Government; (3) it has its party research and reform committee organization to equip it with the ammunition with which to rake the Government; (4) it appeals to the electorate.

It takes part, as we have seen, in the allocation of parliamentary time together with the Government Whips. Its leader, sometimes accompanied by lieutenants, takes counsel with the Prime Minister and his lieutenants, "behind the Speaker's chair," to settle matters of policy or the business of the House. The Prime Minister will from time to time inform the leader of the Opposition of vital facts about foreign policy, defense, and the economic situation that he needs to know in order to enable him and his colleagues to conduct their rightful opposition without the danger of an ignorant plunge into delicate situations. This latter feature is very important. The Opposition is regularly consulted by the Government regarding the manning of various inquiry commissions and participation in national ceremonial functions. The Opposition Bench, of course, works in close connection with its caucus of members in the Commons.

More voltage is attributable to the Opposition when contrasted with the French Parliament. There the many groups outside the Cabinet form the Opposition; and each group is itself split. Hence Opposition is not articulated; it feels no mature responsibility; it falls to pieces. In the Soviet Union, the Opposition consists of the living dead or the dead. The American nation is seriously the loser for want of a coherent Opposition in Congress.

When the salary was established in 1937, it was decried by some as being an enfeeblement of the leader of the Opposition's independence of mind. All subsequent proceedings prove that the Opposition is at least as alive, and perhaps more so. In December 1937, when Mr. Attlee, then leader of the Opposition, visited Spain and made a speech favoring the Spanish Republicans, a vote of censure was moved by a Conservative member. Mr. Attlee strongly repudiated any responsibility except to his constituents.

The Opposition may never forget that while it puts the Government on trial, it itself is simultaneously on trial.

The Cabinet: Commons' Control;
Internal Organization; Civil Service
Linkage

It has been said that England invented the phrase, "Her Majesty's Opposition";
that it was the first government which made a criticism of administration as
much a part of the polity as administration itself. This critical opposition is the
consequence of cabinet government.

—Walter Bagehot

X. THE COMMONS' CONTROL OF
THE CABINET

The Commons, spearheaded by the Opposition, possesses substantial opportunities for control of the Government. The Queen's speech that opens the session is actually a statement of the Government's legislative and administrative policy. It is delivered from the throne in the House of Lords, where the Peers are seated as usual and the Commons, behind their Speaker, stand behind the Bar of the House—as in ancient days. (This gave birth to the U.S. President's Message on the State of the Union.)

In the Commons a debate follows *lasting six days;* it is in the form of an address of thanks to the Crown but is a wide-ranging debate on policy. Then there are thirty-two days or more applied to the estimates and getting the Speaker out of the Chair. Again, on two or more occasions in a session, debates spring up suddenly on "a definite matter of urgent public importance." The Government concedes time for debates to the Opposition, sometimes focused in a vote of censure,

amounting to twelve days or more. Private members have ten Fridays for their chosen motions. In addition, there are those last half-hours between 10 P.M. and 10:30 P.M. when private members can move resolutions for debate of all sorts of bees in their bonnets. Also, there are two days' debate each on the adjournment for the Christmas, Easter, and Whitsuntide vacations. This makes some seventy-three days of the year or, in terms of hours, almost half the time of the House of Commons.

Anyone who knows the inside track of a Cabinet's mind and of a Minister's mind will know that hearing and answering debate in the House is an anxious ordeal. Six hundred pairs of disbelieving eyes *may* look on. Some two or three hundred are sure to be present for anything serious. Six hundred and twenty-nine will soon know all about his discomfiture. General policy and administrative detail are blended. No item of policy or action, however minute, is free from the roving, self-righteous minds of those who calculatingly invigilate. This ordeal occurs in the open assembly of the House—not in the dimness of committees. A weakness discovered after an answer on a veteran's pension, the failure to certify a nurse, a rise in the price of cocoa, a lack of cigarette supply, slowness of action by the Ministry of Agriculture on a farmer's grievance, the leakage of official information (rare!) may produce a sharper debate, may produce a committee of inquiry. Here is where political reputations are made or marred, where men swing high or fall with a crash in the scale of the ministrable men in the future. It is, indeed, a formidable method of control.

Urgent Matters of Public Importance

Motions for adjournment—that is, to depart from the set order of the agenda—may be made after questions each day.

The motion for "the adjournment of the House on a matter of definite and urgent public importance," based upon Standing Order Number 9, permits debate that very day, if a member of the House, supported by forty others, moves the adjournment of the House on a matter of definite and urgent public importance and if the Speaker of the House of Commons accepts the motion.

This procedure places a very important responsibility upon the Speaker, because the decision whether the matter is definite and urgent and public is his. The Speaker has the power to decide whether the regular agenda of the House of Commons shall that very day be suspended in order that at 7 P.M. a debate may occur on a fresh emergency matter put before the House. The Savidge case has already been mentioned (p. 126). Other cases illustrate this power of parliamentary investigation: on May 7, 1946, when Mr. Bevin announced that the Government proposed to evacuate Egypt, the Speaker accepted Mr. Churchill's motion to adjourn the House. In July 1946, when the British Government arrested some members of the Jewish Agency, a member moved the adjournment of the House and Mr. Speaker accepted the motion. On the latter occasion the member who moved the adjournment was a member of the majority party in the House of Commons. In February 1947, during the great fuel crisis, once again a member of the Labour Party raised a question on supplies of coal not available

for a great motor-manufacturing works; a debate on the adjournment occurred on that same day. The Government was compelled to prove its case with satisfactory evidence.

Such motions are accepted roughly only twice a year. Yet the possibility of instantaneous arraignment keeps the Government alive to opinion in the House of Commons and efficient and lawful relationships with the millions who are under its democratic power. This kind of discussion in the House of Commons, like questions, also aborts the necessity of something more pretentious, rigid, and formal in its procedure, and also more ponderous. It is not always the number of times the instrument is used by the contingency that it may be used that exerts effective control over the minds and actions of Ministers.

Questions to Ministers

This is the fundamentally characteristic British way of keeping the Cabinet painfully sensitive to public opinion.

On Mondays, Tuesdays, Wednesdays, and Thursdays throughout the parliamentary session, Members of Parliament have the right to ask questions of Ministers between 2:45 and 3:45 P.M. Since these days account for 120 days of the session, a vast field of critical operations is open.

Questions may be oral or written. For either, twenty-four-hour notice must be given the Government through the Clerks of the House.

Questions that relate to specific departments are answered by their Ministers. More general policy questions are answered by the Prime Minister or his deputy who leads the House of Commons. Each member has the right to ask as many as three questions for oral answer ("starred"); as many as he likes for written answer ("unstarred"). The former are usually those with a political sting; the latter are used where a longer account of fact, especially statistical, is appropriate. For ministerial and members' convenience, there is some departmental grouping of questions and answers on stated days, but each day has a mixed bag. The answers to all questions are printed in the *Debates*.

An average of 70 to 100 oral questions are asked every day. The asking member may at once ask *supplementary* questions arising out of the answer given him. Anyone can ask a supplementary in a free-for-all, though the asking member has priority. If the right to ask supplementaries were abused, the later questions could not be reached in time. Therefore the sense of the House keeps them limited to three at the very maximum. Their purpose is evident. The Minister is ready with his first answer—his career officials have helped him to prepare it. It is on his file in front of him. The supplementary question is designed to get under the Minister's guard—either to reveal what he would rather not have exposed or to make him feel the power of the House.

The Effect of Questions

Now, to appreciate the effectiveness of this method of probing the Government, one will observe that questions are asked (except for the week end) on consecutive days, putting the Ministers under continual surveillance. It is an exquisite, never-flagging, sharp, short probe. Official incompetence may be revealed. There is a strain on the Ministers' readiness of mind and desire to be thought well of by the House and the public. Only to a limited extent can a Minister hide by a prepared and evasive answer, even a precalculated answer to a predicted supplementary question. His career official, a yard or two away by the Speaker's Chair, may offer him a whispered life-belt. But, if the members smell a rat, a debate, even a tribunal of inquiry, may be the consequence later in the session.

Fifty or sixty leading members of the House manage to ask most of the questions—several outside the official groups of both Opposition and Government. It is a great opportunity for the Back Benchers. The Opposition concerts its questions strategically, because the seeming trivial matter may entail high principle.

At question hour the House is most crowded, for this is the dramatic focus of everyday operation; the grand inquest of the nation is a tense and brooding menace to reputations. The underlying purpose is to make the Ministers nervous, to expose their faults of operation today and reveal their ideas for government tomorrow. Members seek to peer into the vast labyrinth of 700,000

career officials, Ministers, and Cabinet. All the limelight is on the Minister, for he is solely responsible; the officials are anonymous (p. 171). The questions, however innocent-seeming, are couched to suggest blame, so that the Minister is not simply supplying information but answering insinuated condemnation. As members gang up with a series of integrated questions and supplementaries, he cannot for long escape with murder. Moreover, his tell-tale face is only a few yards from the questioners' ringside seats. Day after day he is under ordeal before the Opposition, his own party Back Benchers, and the country via the press. His civil servants suffer an equal ordeal; woe betide them if they did not support the Minister's standing, by almost faultless administration! Here is a long-drawn-out X-ray treatment, with no lead casing for ministerial protection.[1]

Preventive and Coordinative. As questions are put day after day, they tend to prevent maladministration from reaching the magnitude of scandal, and so achieve correction before large-scale investigations are needed. Major surgery becomes less necessary. The Minister's burden is lightened when he knows the House now shares it, after he has answered. Also, administrative coordination is assisted when overlapping or confusion are exposed.

Should the Opposition or the Government wish

[1] For illustration here is a summary of oral questions asked on April 28, 1955. The total answered was 61, and these brought on 63 supplementaries: status of British men and women marrying foreigners; illegal signposts in a London street; passport situation in cross-Channel trips to France; elections to the Church of Scotland; official psychiatric report on a murderer in jail; adoption of children; homosexual offenses; employment in Northern Ireland; rebuilding of a magistrate's court; atomic exercises in Nevada; educational facilities for Servicemen's children; leaving age at grammar schools; condition and building of schools; size of classes; number of grammar-school places in certain areas compared with the average; offer of cheap price for purchase of a church hall; state scholarships; policy to assist Lancashire textile industry; freedom to purchase Calcutta jute at world prices; newsprint supply; restrictions on hire-purchase of furniture; income tax; carrying of U.S. oranges to Britain in U.S. ships; coracle fishing in Wales; horticultural research; safety of agricultural machinery; the Four Power Talks; relations between Britain and China; disarmament; unemployment in Lancashire; support of French North African policy; pedestrian casualties; salaries of East Nigerian officials; return of King Kabaka to Uganda; reduction of certain veterans' widows' pensions.

a question to be raised suddenly, then "behind the Chair" and with the Speaker's agreement, a "private notice" question is put on the agenda.

One problem not yet fully answered regarding questions is how far they may be carried into the operations of the nationalized industries. Members are keen not to be limited at all. The Labour Government set the precedent in 1947 that Ministers would not answer questions about the internal administration of the corporations, on the ground this would inhibit business risk and initiative.[2] Furthermore, Ministers may plead at their risk—and only up to a certain point—no answer in the "public interest." The House is master of this latitude—a latitude it must allow. Even a recommendation by a Select Committee in 1953 that a special committee of the House be established to supervise the industries has not settled the problem.

XI. INTERNAL ORGANIZATION OF THE CABINET

The Cabinet meets, by convention, once a week at No. 10 Downing Street, London, the official residence of the Prime Minister. It is in a street off Whitehall, in which most of the Government departments are located. At No. 11 resides the Chancellor of the Exchequer. A corridor connects the two houses. Across the narrow road is the Foreign Office. At need the Cabinet meets more frequently, sometimes in the Prime Minister's room at the House of Commons. Present are the Cabinet Ministers and, at the right hand of the Prime Minister's chair, the Secretary of the Cabinet, a career official. Non-Cabinet Ministers are called in for specific matters. Anyone may take the initiative in asking for a Cabinet meeting, having decided that it warrants the Cabinet's time by its public necessity, its newness, the burden and perhaps dissension it may bring, and the receptivity or hostility of the other departments.

Committees

The Cabinet needs help: its burden is Titanic. It is assisted by committees of itself and its secretariat.

[2] Cf. Report, *Select Committee on Nationalised Industries,* October 1952, H. M. Stationery Office, London. This is now the classic discussion.

The Cabinet committees are *deliberative* or *action-integrative,* sometimes both. The Cabinet, especially the Prime Minister, decides, expediently, their number, composition, and authority. Names of the committee members are kept private in order to avert public guessing as to who may be the leader in a given policy, because it is desired to maintain intact the idea of *collective* responsibility. The composition will, of course, reflect the various views held on the issue and satisfy rival ambitions. The chairman will be the Minister most especially interested. Law officers and top officials (less usually) are asked to attend; but ministerial decisions are taken in their absence. They study and propose a solution to the problem the Cabinet has devolved to them. They thereby save the time of the Cabinet by supplying a semimanufactured or polished policy and, incidentally, iron out interdepartmental difficulties.

Some committees are for a single time-limited matter (*ad hoc*); some are continuous. Of the former, these are examples: creation of national health service; housing problem; manpower; fuel and power; atomic energy. There might be as many as twenty at one time, varying with needs; they deliberate, report, and disband.

The Standing Committees. In 1951 there were five standing committees; and something like this continues.

(*1*) *The Legislation Committee,* once known as the Home Affairs Committee. It is presided over by the Minister most closely entrusted with the business of the House of Commons, under the Prime Minister. It reviews all legislation issuing from individual Ministers, proposes priorities, sets their timetable and parliamentary tactics. It gives special attention to statutory instruments (p. 132). Its members include the leaders of the two Houses, the Chief Whip, the Lord Chancellor, the Law Officers, and a few departmental Ministers. Ministers whose bills are being processed attend. All the departments are informed of the committee's activities, so that their Ministers may attend at request. In case of disagreements in the committee, appeal is to the Cabinet. Under the Labour Government, 1945–1951, an even smaller committee, the Future Legislation Committee, cogitated the future.

The British Cabinet

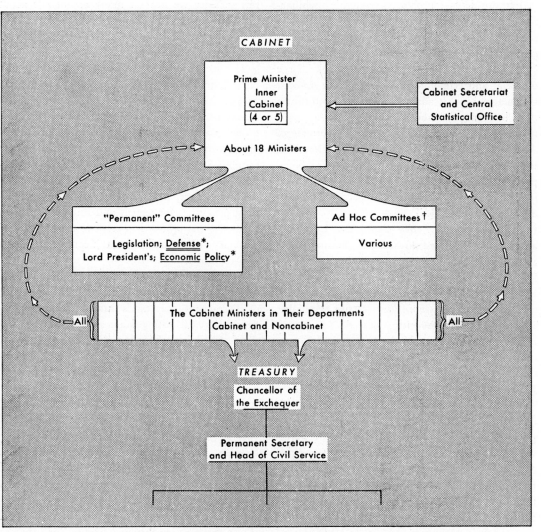

*Prime Minister is chairman of Defense Committee and also of Economic Policy Committee.
†Prime Minister is sometimes chairman of important *ad hoc* committees.

(2) *The Defense Committee* was first set up in World War II to replace the Committee of Imperial Defense. The latter had existed since 1902, *outside* the Cabinet, with the Prime Minister as chairman and diverse Ministers, defense experts, and imperial representatives.[3] It fell into abeyance when in 1939 the War Cabinet set up its own internal Defense Committee. Its chairman is the Prime Minister but his deputy, the Minister of

[3] For an account of it, see H. Finer, "Cabinet and Commons under the Impact of War," *Political Science Quarterly*, September 1941.

Defense, usually presides. This Ministry was put in the Cabinet just after World War II, having been set up over the three Armed Service departments who have their own Ministers but are not in the Cabinet. Its membership consists of the Armed Service Ministers, the Lord President, the Foreign Secretary, the Chancellor of the Exchequer, the Minister of Labor and National Service, and the Minister of Supply—most are in the Cabinet. The Prime Minister's chairmanship embodies the committee's role as something more than merely military, when total mobilization might be its subject. It is concerned with present and future defense problems, economic mobilization, transition from peace to war and thence to peace. It has a strong understructure of joint committees of career planners from the services.

(3) *The Lord President's Committee* took charge of social and economic planning for the Labour Cabinet in 1945. It adapted a wartime committee that had planned the coordinated interdepartmental action required by the various campaigns. The War Cabinet gave it its general directives; the Lord President, a member of the Cabinet, presides. It became, then, a kind of sub-Cabinet in civil policy, composed of all departments except defense and overseas.

(4) *The Economic Policy Committee* later took away from the Lord President's Committee its *economic* agenda, leaving it with the social services. It itself ranges over economic affairs, with the Prime Minister as chairman. It worked alongside the (5) *Production Committee* (set up September 1947) to command the entire domestic- and export-manufactures program of the Government in the critical postwar years. Its head was Sir Stafford Cripps, then combining the Chancellorship of the Exchequer and Ministry for Economic Affairs.

These committees combine two functions: coordinating the departments and decentralizing the preparation of policy. Both assist the Cabinet, which has prime responsibility for these functions. Ministers who are still disgruntled can appeal to the Cabinet. The committees function through their own subcommittees and with groupings of the appropriate civil servants. The Secretariat integrates their progress.

The Secretariat

Until 1916 the British Cabinet had neither secretariat nor carefully prepared agenda. From time to time, since 1689, separate Ministers or the "first" or Prime Minister might take notes, and even send minutes to the King, especially under George III. The convention of secrecy of proceedings (see pp. 152–153) and the interfactional disputes, with impeachment looming in the distance, with suspicion and hatred among the factions, and the much smaller extent of business at that time, accounted for the lack of business procedure.

It is remarkable that the Secretariat did not come earlier, since we hear of many complaints about the formlessness of proceedings; Ministers disputed alleged decisions and there were accusations of haziness of memory.

The advent of total war—that is, war demanding the mobilization of all the resources of the nation—in 1914, spurred on the development of a secretariat. Mr. Lloyd George, the great wartime leader, had such a secretariat instituted in 1916. It has gone through an interesting evolution, which cannot be traced here. But the main features are the enlargement of the staff; the improvement of methods of preparing and recording the proceedings; provisions for secrecy and impartiality, since a *non-Cabinet official* is present to take notes (the Secretary of the Cabinet); and a certain specialization of function.

Composition and Work. The secretariat is composed of career officials. It has a Secretary, who is of Permanent Secretary's rank, and a Deputy Secretary, each with private secretaries; two Undersecretaries; the Director of the Central Statistical Office; three Assistant Secretaries; a Chief Clerk and Establishment Officer; and a subordinate staff. It performs strictly secretarial functions. It circulates the memoranda and other documents necessary for the work of the Cabinet and its various committees; marshals the agenda for each Cabinet meeting under the direction of the Prime Minister; performs the same service for the Cabinet committees under directions of the respective chairmen; circulates the notices of meetings; records and distributes to those who are concerned the Cabinet's conclusions; draws up the reports of Cabinet committees; and keeps the papers and conclusions of the Cabinet subject to the Cabinet's directions. It is an accepted rule that Cabinet papers reach Ministers at least two days before a Cabinet meeting, for they are very busy men.

This means that the work of the Cabinet and its committees is carefully prepared for before the meetings. The general arguments, but not the record of the opinions of identified individuals, are set down together with a conclusion, except for the Prime Minister and the Chief Minister reporting. The Secretary sometimes insists on getting a formula for record where otherwise none is offered or where the discussion is inconclusive. It has been suggested that he sometimes needs to show "no little ingenuity and even inventiveness" in drafting it.[4] When the conclusions are reached, the secretariat sees that each Minister involved in the conclusions gets his appropriate part, when it is for him to convert the decision into administrative action.

Only the Secretary is present at Cabinet meetings. He sits on the righthand side of the Prime Minister and personally takes the record of the meeting. Naturally, the preservation of neutrality and anonymity, the two stoical characteristics of the British Civil Service, find their apotheosis in him—beyond the suggestion of even a wintry smile, it is said.

It should be emphasized that the secretariat is not advisory to the Cabinet or its committees: *it is solely secretarial.* For advisory functions there has been established another part of the apparatus, to which we now turn.

Economic Section of the Secretariat

From 1941 to late 1953 the secretariat included an economic section—that is, a corps of professional economists. It was needed urgently in World War II as a superdepartmental group of intellects who saw and advised on the economic implications of all aspects of the war effort. These men received Cabinet and committee documents and prepared commentaries; they were asked to solve problems; and they suggested problems that needed to be solved, for the use of the highest level of decision.

The after-war economic and social planning required their services also, and they served the Central Planning Staff as requested. One of the regular and conspicuous services of each year was the preparation of the annual *Economic Surveys*—"economic budgets"—of the nation's resources, targets, and the planning for production and capital investment.

In 1953 the unit was transferred to the Treasury, as an integral part of its general financial, economic, and administrative leadership, because

[4] Cf. L. S. Amery, *Thoughts on the Constitution,* Oxford, 1947.

it was felt that its memoranda were not necessarily the Prime Minister's business (to whom it reported) but were definitely the Chancellor of the Exchequer's.

The Central Statistical Office. This was set up in 1941 (wartime) to produce *supra*departmental comprehensive statistics of economic and social trends. Later, social and economic postwar planning had as much need of statistical answers to the Cabinet's problems. Its regular production is the *Monthly Digest of Statistics,* the compass of the highly planned State.

The work of the Economic Section and the C.S.O., combined, resembles that of the Council of Economic Advisers to the U.S. President. Both emerged from the new permanent policies of full employment, and temporary war mobilization and demobilization.

The Central Planning Staff. This was set up in 1947 to integrate still further the branches of the economy to meet postwar scarcities and assist physical reconstruction of a devastated land, and to repair Britain's life-line, exports and manufactures for them. It is interdepartmental, composed of the whole-time planning officers from the various departments, rather like the military joint planning staff. It has a Chief Planning Officer. It first served the Prime Minister through the secretariat, later through the Ministry of Economic Affairs. It is now lodged in the Treasury, working in partnership with the Economic Section.

Thus, the Treasury has achieved a remarkably wide integrating role (pp. 168–171).

Summary

Thus, the Cabinet is surrounded by expert help [5] channeled to it or its committees or to individual Ministers, marshaled as and when the Cabinet

[5] When Mr. Churchill became Prime Minister again, in 1951, he continued much the same arrangement of Cabinet committees. But he added a series of "co-ordinating" Ministers, to integrate the work of several departments or sectors of Government. These were the Lord President of the Council, to coordinate food, agriculture and fisheries (Lord Woolton); Secretary of State for the Co-ordination of Transport, Fuel and Power (Lord Leathers); and the Paymaster General, Lord Cherwell, to coordinate scientific research and development, including atomic energy. All were lords, hence in the House of Lords, and all were commoners originally, raised to the peerage for services to nation and party. Churchill's idea was to solve the problem

needs it to be used as its wisdom requires. Going up to the Cabinet are sifted facts and sifted evaluations and ideas. From it, outward and downward to the departmental officials flow will, policies, and desires asking guidance, counsel, facts.

This is the British answer to the problem of modern States: that the men at the top need expertness. They themselves, directly, are aided by the inquiries by Royal Commissions and departmental committees, as are their career advisers also. The British have preferred this method to the French and German partial alternatives of special economic and social councils, or plans for an "economic general staff" outside the day-by-day activity of the departments and the Cabinet. The latter suggestion, attractive at first sight, suffers from the tendency to ungeared theorizing that afflicts those who are not actually involved in the detail of current business and under the spur of inventing concrete answers to tangible problems needing immediate attention.

The drive that centers on the bodies we have been describing comes from the will of the Cabinet that has made commitments to the nation, and from the House of Commons also powerfully moved by commitments to constituents and party.

of Cabinet unwieldiness, and get a grip on various Ministries' fields of action.

The system ran into strong criticism. First, the Ministers were nicknamed "overlords"—because they were in the House of Lords and not available for questioning by the Commons, yet, presumably, vested with important functions. The problem of responsibility for the administration of the coordinated departments was involved. Who would answer questions in the House of Commons? It was argued that the administrative process was confused. The Opposition warned that delays might occur while Ministers waited for the green light from their overlords. It was argued that coordination of any of the fields in question needed an even broader basis of integration. Would the coordinators speak only to the Ministers or to the career chiefs in their respective departments? They suggested the usual method of Cabinet committees was enough. If coordinators were named in public, it tended to reduce the responsibility of Ministers they coordinated.

The Churchillian defense was not sharply sound: that there was value in coordination, but that if the several Ministers disagreed they could appeal to the Cabinet. In September 1953, the overlords were abolished. It had been, as the Opposition suggested, a personal device of the Prime Minister to restore something of his own wartime organization, using men with whom he had worked for many years. Mr. Churchill then increased the number of people in the Cabinet to nineteen—and critics criticized this as "too sprawling."

We see a kind of pyramidal system in the Cabinet. The Prime Minister is at the apex, and acts through the Cabinet as a whole and as chairman of the Defense Committee and the Economic Policy Committee. At his side, and nearly on his level, are the Chancellor of the Exchequer, the Lord President of the Council, and the Foreign Minister. Each of these marshals the activity and thinking of Cabinet and non-Cabinet Ministers, through two kinds of committee: ministerial and administrative. Work is thus devolved and thought, deliberation, and objective-seeking are integrated.

XII. THE TREASURY

The role of the British Treasury [6] is far more coordinating and commanding in the design of administrative organization and activity and in the financial harmonization of the Government's many services than in any other country in the world. Elsewhere, for example the United States, the Treasury does only a part of the work of the British Treasury, some being done by the Bureau of the Budget, the Civil Service Commission, and other agencies. In France the Ministry of Finance's scope is smaller, and also its political authority is far inferior to that of the British. It is not for nothing that the Prime Minister is, first, First Lord of the Treasury. In the eighteenth century this gave him immediate direction of patronage so that he might be able to win majorities for his Administration.[7] Today there is no patronage, but the majesty of the position of Prime Minister is reinforced by the practical eminence that the Treasury has acquired, while the traditional primacy of the Treasury is enhanced by its official (though sinecure) blending with the Prime Minister.

This eminence is exercised through four channels: (1) power in relationship to the Civil Service; (2) economic coordination; (3) an oversight over the general financial problems of the nationalized industries; and (4) the preparation of the Budget.

[6] See the able article by Professor Sam Beer, *American Political Science Review*, March 1955.

[7] This was the often-used term for Government or Cabinet in the eighteenth century; hence the American *current* usage.

(1) Head of the Civil Service

The title of the Permanent Secretary of the Treasury—that is, the highest career civil servant in the Treasury—is Permanent Secretary and Head of the Civil Service. This title was created in 1867. On July 15, 1937, Neville Chamberlain (Prime Minister) said in the House of Commons:

> Experience has shown that it is a convenient and businesslike arrangement, and one which—under ministerial control and particularly under the control of the Prime Minister as First Lord of the Treasury—forms an essential link in providing the requisite means of ensuring the efficient administration of public business.

Substantially, this means that the official representative of the nation and the Government as employer of nearly 700,000 central-government officials is the Treasury. The Establishments Branch of this mighty department settles the numbers, categories, conditions of appointment, retirement, dismissal, resignation, pay, promotion, working conditions, and so on of these civil servants (see p. 208).

Since 1920 appointments to the position of Permanent Secretary, the highest Civil Service career position in each department, and of their deputies, the principal departmental financial officers, and the establishment officers are made by the Prime Minister on advice submitted to him and the departmental Minister by the head of the Civil Service. This raises the authority of the Treasury over the departments. "They [Treasury and departments] are jointly trustees for the efficient and economical administration of the service," said the Committee on Public Expenditure of 1931.

(2) Economic Coordination

Economic coordination by the Treasury has already been sketched sufficiently. At the top of the Treasury is the Permanent Secretary, and just below him is one deputy and three "second" secretaries: Finance, Supply and Machinery of Government, Economic Planning. Each of these reaches down into its section of Treasury officialdom. This last-named coordinates economic planning in the Treasury and other Ministries of economic importance throughout the Government.

The Chief Planning Officer has access to the Chancellor, who is the political head of the Treasury and a power in the Cabinet second only to the Prime Minister. The Treasury organization under the Chief Planning Officer, composed of officials, enters the committees on N.A.T.O. and the Organization for European Economic Cooperation, and the various interdepartmental committees that have any economic functions. It now has the direct assistance (since October 1953) of the Economic Secretariat in the undertaking of various special economic studies—for example, coal and electricity production and use or a new turn in the problem of the balance of payments. It prepares the *Economic Survey* of the nation, providing the basic economic (not merely fiscal) facts on which the Budget is prepared annually.

"Economic" Budgets. The economic surveys are important new functions in government as far as their comprehensiveness and thoroughness are concerned. The old-fashioned *fiscal* budget has, rather since the depression of 1929 and the total planning of World War II and postwar reorganization, come to be accompanied by an *economic budget*. It is a necessity in an age of social services and full-employment policy. The *Survey* is given two or three days' discussion in Parliament. There is far more consciousness about the economic system since World War II—governmental consciousness is deeper and more compulsive—than ever before it, and this, in all nations.

(3) The Nationalized Industries

The nationalized industries—that is, coal, communications, transport, electricity, gas, and the Bank of England—are not directly administered by the Government departments. But a general surveillance is laid down in the relevant statutes. With the exception of the Bank of England, the other industries require Treasury permission for capital investment. This, at the minimum, draws the Treasury into an appraisal of their progress. Since capital resources are limited, the Treasury must decide the relative measure in which the industries shall be financed. It is a considerable power.

The British Treasury

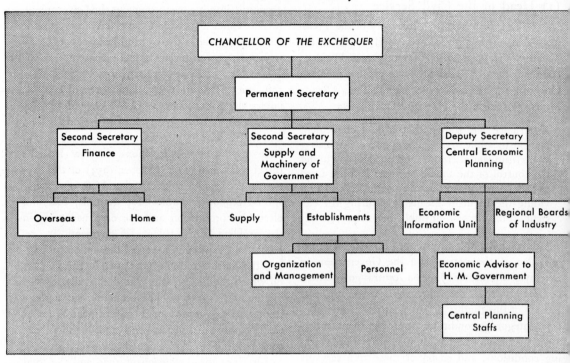

(4) The Budget

As we have seen (p. 127ff.), the budget is voted by Parliament, but it is a Cabinet budget. The executive process is of high importance politically and administratively.

The Treasury takes the permanent lead in the preparation of the budget. This is under the authority of the Chancellor of the Exchequer. Each October the Treasury sends the departments three documents: the warning that the estimates of last year are not to be taken as an undebatable base; an estimate form containing last year's figures in one column and its blank partner; and a form of explanation to be used in justifying any changes they may propose.

The departments send their estimates to the Financial Division of the Treasury. This compares the Treasury sanctions for the exit of money for each department made during the last year, so that the effect of the spending department's demands (staying as voted or needing timely variation) may be noted. The Financial Division is staffed with specialists in the needs of each spending department. They have a penetrating knowledge of these, acquired from long cooperation, from watching the course of expenditure during the year, and sometimes they have actually served in them. The Treasury and the departments engage in a process of justification, cross-examination, and counterjustification. A departmental budget is finally acceptable to the Treasury. If, after this process of extremely careful probing, the Treasury and the departments cannot agree—at this level of the Permanent Secretaries of the Treasury and of the departments—then the dispute goes to the Chancellor of the Exchequer and the Minister of the department. If they cannot agree, then the matter is taken up in the Cabinet: this decides who shall prevail, Chancellor or Minister.

"Treasury Control." The Treasury is responsible for two things: the grueling appraisal of the spending department's demands, and a general weighing of the several departmental budgets against each other and their combined amount against the total sum it is obliged to raise in taxation. It is responsibility for taxation that makes the

Treasury stiff in its disciplinary criteria. Hence the so-called "Treasury attitude"—that of a skinflint. Within reason, it is sound practice: it exerts severe onus on the spenders to justify their demands. Hence, the cardinal importance of the Chancellor of the Exchequer.

Treasury control, as it is called, is subject to the limits of respective ministerial strengths in the Cabinet. The Prime Minister may help decisively by siding with the one side or the other—more so than any ordinary Minister's influence, of course. For the substantial amount to be spent depends on policy, not on minor economies. The decision to pass a law is the decision to spend money on the service so established. The Treasury cannot change the statute book; though, in times of crisis, the law may be changed by the Cabinet and Parliament to suit the financial situation of the country. For example, the decision in 1950 to require that people who needed spectacles and dentures should pay part or all of the cost of them, whereas earlier they had been given them free by the National Health Service.

The Treasury will not tell the departments how to spend their money on their services: for the departments are responsible for efficiency in detail. That would be hardly possible in practice, and hardly acceptable in the acknowledgment of the principle of ministerial responsibility. Hence, Treasury control is a stiff challenge, calling for extremes of justification on the part of spenders.

The estimates so accepted by the Cabinet go to Parliament for the discussions and enactment according to the procedure we have already described. So careful a job has been done on the tooth-combing of the estimates, that matters of economy and efficiency, as distinct from policy, have been taken care of in a way that spares Parliament serious anxiety. Yet even the Treasury may be baffled by such conundrums as the estimating of the National Health Service; in 1948–1950 the Ministry of Health passed on to it *underestimates* of £50,000,000 per year. It was, of course, an entirely new branch of the public service.

The power of the British Treasury is thus conspicuously important in the constellation of forces of the administration and the Cabinet. It is greater than any of its counterparts bearing that name or synonym in any government in the world. "The power over a man's income is the power over a man's will."

XIII. THE CIVIL SERVICE AS AUXILIARY TO THE CABINET

Without the Civil Service—that is, some 700,000 officials (p. 202), departmentally and territorially distributed—the Cabinet would behave with the confusion of passengers in an airplane at high altitude, the engines of which had failed and the floor of which had dropped out.

To be its cogent, initiating, directing self, it needs the knowledge, advice, and executive aid of the Civil Service. The composition and functioning of this is the proper material for a later chapter. But here principles of liaison at the very pyramid of each department between career chief and ministerial chief must be adumbrated.

The principles of impartiality and anonymity rule this liaison. Cabinet Ministers are amateurs in the work of the departments they head. They are not deliberately assigned there as experts. Each department is the repository of a vast knowledge, compounded of all the natural sciences and the social sciences. Without the use of these government would be not merely ignorant and inefficient, it would be impossible. Often the justification of a Government's undertaking an activity (for example, control of credit in the economy) is the argument that it can employ skills and has authority to obtain information superior to those obtainable by a private authority however large and wise and rich.

The Cabinet must rely on men who have given their whole lives to the mastery of one particular skill by the usual process of subdivision of labor and specialization. The Ministers are there to harness these hundreds of different skills to the policies based on the values they and their followers hold. They could not possibly provide the knowledge. The instrument of this knowledge, both substantive and procedural and financial— they all weave in together in almost every atom of policy—is the Civil Service.

At the top of the pyramid of each department is the Minister and one or two political Undersecretaries. These are the political direction-givers

and exacters of obedience from the staffs in executing policy. Just below them is the Permanent
Secretary of the department. The relationship between political chief and permanent chief is regulated by the twin principles of *impartiality,* sometimes called *neutrality,* and *anonymity.*

Impartiality signifies the rendering of service
with equal faithfulness to any political chief of
whatever political party who has been designated
as the head under the principle of Cabinet government. It demands that the civil servant supply his
talent and intellectual capacities to the full in the
service of his Minister's needs, and that he appeal
with the utmost of his character to the Minister
to use all this in the determination of the exact-
ness of the political destination he heads toward.
He is not to use a brow-beating force, but he is
to be resolute to help his Ministers to avoid error.
To this service he leads a staff of thousands of
skilled men and women. Such services are to be
rendered without reservation of mind, imagination, or energy, whatever the political party of the
Minister. It is rare, indeed, that this convention
has not been followed in the letter and the spirit.
It survived what some skeptics thought it could
not, the advent of a Labour Government.

The Minister must listen to his Civil Service
advisers, by force only of the consideration that,
if he does not, he will surely bring his department
to grief. He has the alternative either of trusting
his advisers or bringing in his own "policy-making" experts, as they are called in the United
States. The latter alternative is not a trustworthy
one from the point of view of technical and
objective expertness. It always leaves a dirty taste
in the mouth, as the public finds it difficult to
distinguish between "spoils" and a faithful change
of public servants. The first alternative, if it is
obtainable, is indisputably the better. It allows a
man to devote himself all his life to the mastery
of the social or natural science the modern state
requires.

In the British system, for nearly a hundred
years, the principle of impartiality has prevailed.
Advantage has been taken of the excellent education and ethics of the Civil Service as aids to the
Ministers and, in total, to the Cabinet. Lord
Hankey (formerly Sir Maurice), the great artificer
of the Cabinet secretariat, the prince of committees, has said:

> The permanent head of a great department of
> state is on almost the same footing of intimacy
> with his political chiefs as they are with one
> another. Ministers talk before them with the
> same freedom as they do with their colleagues.
> These men would sell their souls before they
> would sell their chiefs.[8]

All this does not mean that the civil servants,
especially those at the top, are not up to their
necks in "party" politics; they serve a Government, but that Government consists of a party.
They are expected to supply the facts and ideas
that best defend its policy, to undertake the administrative activities that best further this; to
draft answers to questions that protect the vulnerability of their Ministers; to rescue them from
difficulties, even, as the alleged bribery case (p.
ooo) showed, personal ones; to provide the most
plausible answers to Opposition criticism. They
can do this effectively and not unhappily for either
party, turn and turn about, if the rival parties are
not so hostile to each other's political aims that the
Civil Service advisers of the gladiators would commit atrocity on their own consciences, by being
made to feel indecent, frustrated, dishonest, or be-
trayers of their own party and the national welfare.

Anonymity of these men and their subordinates
is necessary for two things. If the Opposition knew
what the Civil Service had advised their Ministers,
it would be tempted to blame them (mostly) or
but mildly praise them. Controversies might arise
about the activities of these advisers. Their names
would be bandied about in public, and they would
come to be distrusted. Then, the incoming party
would wish to purge the Service of those it had
come to dislike, or civil servants who had been
insulted in political dispute might not wish to
serve their insulters. The inestimable advantage
of a permanent and impartial career service would
be jeopardized.

Secondly, if the Civil Service advisers were
known by their advice, the principle of ministerial responsibility would be infringed and weakened. The power of the House of Commons over

---

[8] *Diplomacy by Conference,* London, 1946, p. 16.

a Minister is its total concentration of duty on him and him alone. There must be no confusion in the thought that the Minister meant well, but his civil servant frustrated or deceived him.[9] Thus, British political parties do not wish to know who

[9] On July 20, 1954, the Minister of Agriculture, Sir Thomas Dugdale, resigned, having been put in a predicament because some of his civil servants (p. 238) had not properly served him. In the debate in the Commons on that day, brilliant in its contribution to the problem of ministerial-official relationships, the observations of the resigned Minister and the Attorney General, speaking for the Government, are so instructive as to merit quotation.

Sir Thomas Dugdale: "I am quite clear that it would be deplorable if there were to be any departure from the recognised constitutional position. I, as Minister, must accept full responsibility to Parliament for any mistakes and inefficiency of officials in my Department, just as, when my officials bring off any successes on my behalf, I take full credit for them. Any departure from the long established rule is bound to bring the Civil Service right into the political arena, and that we should all, on both sides of the House, deprecate most vigorously. . . . It should not be thought that I am bound to indorse the actions of officials, whatever they may be, or that I or any other Minister must shield those who make errors against proper consequences."

(The Minister's error, it was charged, had been that he had not taken disciplinary action himself against the offenders in good time.)

The Home-Secretary: "In the case where there is an explicit order by a Minister, the Minister must protect the civil servant who has carried out the order. Equally, where the civil servant acts properly in accordance with the policy laid down by the Minister, the Minister must protect and defend him. I come to a third category. . . . Where an official makes a mistake or causes some delay, but not on an important issue of policy and not where a claim to individual rights is seriously involved, the Minister acknowledges the mistake and he accepts the responsibility, although he personally is not involved. He states that he will take corrective action in the department . . . he would not in those circumstances expose the official to public criticism. . . . But when one comes to the fourth category, where action has been taken by a civil servant of which the Minister disapproves and has no prior knowledge, then there is no obligation on the part of the Minister to indorse what he believes to be wrong, or to defend what are clearly shown to be errors of his officers. The Minister is not bound to approve of action of which he did not know, or of which he disapproves. But, of course, he remains constitutionally responsible to Parliament for the fact that something has gone wrong, and he alone can tell Parliament what has occurred and render an account of his stewardship.

"The fact that a Minister has to do that does not affect his power to control and discipline his staff. One could sum it up by saying that it is part of a Minister's responsibility to Parliament to take necessary action to ensure efficiency and the proper discharge of the duties of the department. On that, only the Minister can decide what it is right and just to do, and he alone can hear all sides, including the defence. . . . He can lay down standing instructions to

is in the official background: they will shoot at the Minister. It is for him, if he feels let down, to turn back on his servants and order them to behave better. And, if he cannot do it, the Prime Minister may get rid of him; and, if the Prime Minister does not quite see who is to blame, there will be other members of the Cabinet ready to explain to him that his trust is being abused.[10]

Here then are two intertwined strong cords that link the Cabinet to the great administrative engine of the modern State. The simile is not too good, any more than any simile is satisfactory that attempts to represent the truth about interpersonal living behavior. But, with its limitations, it must serve.

There is a jolly proverb that for six months the Civil Service alone could run the government better than the Cabinet, but at the end there would not be enough lampposts on which to hang them! There is another (Sir William Harcourt's): "Ministers exist to tell the civil service what the public will not stand!" A cautionary example is given later (pp. 238–9).

XIV. APPRAISAL AND DIFFICULTIES

Within the limitations of all human institutions, the British Cabinet is well conceived, well organized, and functions efficiently and beneficially. It is taut, knowledgeable, sensitive, and responsible. It is speedily adaptable to emergencies, such as war or economic crisis.

It labors under certain strains. Do not all governments labor under these strains?

Heaviness of Burden

The modern State has assumed a tremendous burden of activity, as already indicated (Chapter 1). A Cabinet Minister must apply himself to speaking at political meetings from time to time;

see that his policy is carried out. He can lay down rules by which it is ensured that matters of importance, of difficulty or of political danger are brought to his attention. Thirdly, there is the control of this House, and it is one of the duties of this House to see that control put into effect."

[10] An excellent account of the relationship of civil servants to Ministers emerges from Lord Beveridge's *Power and Influence*, London, 1953.

speaking on radio and television occasionally; being present to participate in Commons debates and certainly to vote; and to sit in the House sufficiently to get saturated with the sense of what it will or will not tolerate. He must answer questions. Furthermore, he must attend party caucuses; sometimes, as in the Labour Party, for strong interrogations by the committees that make liaison between the leaders and the Back Benchers. He must manage his department, certainly with much expert help; but it is a heavy job. He must be present at Cabinet meetings or meetings of the "inner Cabinet" or of the twos and threes that talk matters over. He must take part in Cabinet committees and subcommittees. He may be steering a complicated bill through the House of Commons and preparing far-reaching reforms. It is a tremendous burden. It can be believed that some of the work of some of the Ministers is slipshod—saved by the grace of the Civil Service.

Even the Civil Service chiefs are subject to a like pressure. The highest one of all has told this author of his serious anxiety: that too much still must come on his desk for his decision, even in the last resort, after all the most careful centralization of responsibility—too much for the health of the forty Permanent Secretaries; too much for their last ten or fifteen years when they have reached the top. The problem then is one of personnel. Can they be found to equal the strain?

Ministerial Age

The age of Ministers is normally high. To take three random Cabinets—of 1935, 1945, and 1953—we see their average ages are in the fifties and sixties. This is the age of wisdom, experience, and judgment. But it is not usually the age of vigorous enterprise.

No Policy Creation

No policy creation is possible in the Cabinet, it has been alleged.[11] For it is argued, and by men who have been Ministers, that the Cabinet has so much to improvise day by day that it cannot think ahead. This is not a valid criticism. For it ignores a fact as plain as a pikestaff: it is the political parties that make policy, who think ahead, who do their thinking continually and particularly *between* the periods of office. The harvest is garnered while they are in office; the seed is sewn in the seasons out of office. It ignores the research and cogitation of the Royal Commissions of Inquiry, of the party research departments, of the Civil Service departments, the multitude of interest and social reform organizations in society, and of the universities. The criticism rests on a false idea of what the Cabinet is: for it is not only an organizing or philosophical body, but a *will-directing* agency that chooses between the kind and degrees of alternatives already presented to it by other bodies, though, of course, it is not without ideas of its own, as it faces the heat of the day. Furthermore, it does create the policies of the day and year—that is a great deal.

Unwieldiness

There is still a struggle with the unwieldiness of the Cabinet. Its numbers tend to creep up.

The strains in the Cabinet must always give pause to those who are unmeasured in their demands of what the British Government shall undertake. A point could be reached where the men at the top would collapse or government get out of control. The choice will be somewhere between less welfare because affairs are left free outside governmental authority or less welfare because its assumption causes government to be so large of scale as to produce breakdown. Cautious experiment will prove the degree of tolerance permissible in the State's structure.

[11] L. S. Amery, *Thoughts on the Constitution*, Oxford, 1947.

The British Monarchy

He wrote that monarchs were divine,
And left a son who—proved they weren't!
—Rudyard Kipling's *James I*

God save our gracious Queen,
Long live our noble Queen
God save our Queen!
Send her victorious
Happy and glorious
Long to reign over us,
God save our Queen!
—*National Anthem*

On January 5, 1744, Lord Chancellor Hardwicke (virtually Prime Minister) had a very frank conversation with his King, George II. He was trying to persuade the King that the Government he was putting together, though it contained men who had been in opposition to the King, was strong and serviceable to him.

He then said: "Your Ministers, Sir, are only your instruments of Government."

The King, smiling, answered: "Ministers are the Kings in this country!"

A Powerless Crown

Yet it took nearly one hundred years of striving on the part of people and Ministers to raise themselves from the status of His Majesty's servants to become His Majesty's masters. The stubborn, head-strong, and mentally unbalanced George III even carried his insistence on being his own Prime Minister to the minutest point of administrative detail, and in policy, to disaster in the American Colonies and relations with India and Ireland. Such interference was over by the beginning of the reign of Queen Victoria in 1837.

Yet the Crown is still (and, under *her* in particular, was) both a cog in the machinery of government and an emolient in the conduct of party government.

It is a soaringly resplendent personification of man's government, of the abstraction known as *sovereignty;* it is the essence of a unity known as *the nation;* it makes concrete the dignity and authority known as *majesty;* it exemplifies the practice of civic virtue known as *society;* it is the shining countenance of the glorious aspirations felt as *empire.*

I. STATUS OF THE SOVEREIGN

The monarchy is hereditary. Its title is in the Act of Settlement, 1701. The descent follows the English law of primogeniture (as in property law) with priority for males over females. Roman Catholics and those who marry Roman Catholics are disqualified, and the sovereign must belong to the Church of England. The descent is hereditary. Yet Parliament may alter and has altered the succession: William of Orange, then (1701) to the

Electress of Hanover, James I's granddaughter. It is idle to ask whether a monarch would or would not use the old prerogative of veto against a bill changing the succession as he or she disliked. The circumstances of a change that raised such a question must surely be those in which the monarch would have no choice, either through disturbances leading to flight, as with James II in 1688, or those in which acquiescence was assured.

In 1936 King Edward VIII was forced to abdicate on, virtually, the refusal of the Archbishop of Canterbury to crown him with the usual holy ceremonies, causing the Prime Minister Stanley Baldwin to become prime mover, followed by a majority of Parliament, in the process. For they suspected him of unconventional relations with a doubly divorced woman, while he insisted on marrying her. His brother George, next in succession, ascended the throne, by Act of Parliament (His Majesty's Declaration of Abdication Act, 1936). By the same act, the heirs and descendants of Edward VIII were excluded thenceforward from the succession. The daughter of George VI, Elizabeth II, succeeded him on his death in 1952; she was crowned in June 1953, since George VI had no sons. The next in succession is Elizabeth's son, Prince Charles. A statute (1953) has provided for a regency during the prince's minority.

The sovereign comes of age at eighteen. The Royal Marriages Act of 1772 lays it down that until the age of twenty-five, the consent of the King (or Queen) is necessary to a marriage that might affect the succession to the throne—this is to avert undesirable marriages. After twenty-five, no consent is required, but only a year's notice to the Privy Council; but Parliament may disapprove. The issue arose with respect to the possibility of a marriage between Princess Margaret, sister of Queen Elizabeth, and a commoner who had honorably divorced his wife. The Archbishop of Canterbury expressed the Church's doctrine of indissoluble marriage, and therefore his inability to marry the couple. The Princess, warned perhaps by the hollow fate of her uncle, decided to give up the idea of the marriage (see p. 158).

The Value of Heredity

It must be acknowledged that the hereditary claim to succession is politically a most useful one. It leaves little dispute about the succession. In spite of so much reason against heredity as a claim to an office, it finds a chord of acquiescence in a large proportion of mankind—there is some kind of *right* in it—Fate, Destiny. At any rate, there is no vulgar election debate about the respective merit of rivals for the throne.

It has its *disvalue*. If the office requires a definite talent, there is no security at all that the posterity of capable sovereigns will be capable. Some pretty bad sovereigns have disgraced the British throne—among them George III, George IV, and William IV—madmen or drunkards or profligates and roués, the two last mentioned spat at in the streets. It may be necessary—as in the case of Edward VIII—to breed out certain qualities.

Providing this can be done, a hereditary monarch spares Britain all the difficulties found in other democratic countries in the attempt to secure a symbolic central figure to personify the State. France is involved in a double Executive—the President of the Republic and the Prime Minister and his Cabinet. The former is a rather weak, pathetic and *incredible* figurehead. In the Germany of the Weimar Period the attempt to make the President stronger by popular election produced a split Executive between the President and the Chancellor (the responsible Executive) and contributed to the downfall of the republic (see p. 624).

A recent gifted writer thus paints the role of the President of the United States:

The institutional side of the presidency, with its accompanying color and pageantry, is not unlike the role the Crown plays in a constitutional monarchy. Yet there is a difference of a marked sort, beyond the fact that the American President is elected to dignity while the Crown comes to it through birth. . . . The main duty of this one man, like that of his royal counterpart, is to foster a pious attitude toward the nation as a whole, and a will to sacrifice for it. But it is at that point that the difference sets in.

The American President not only reigns. He also rules. He *is,* and he *does.* Here is a basic cause of tension. He combines the sentimental aura of the Crown with the workaday labors of a unitary prime ministership.[1]

[1] Sidney Hyman, *The American President,* New York, 1954, p. 13.

The combination is difficult to make understandable to the people—or, rather, the separation between the two functions is hard to make quite clear. People constantly find themselves restrained from uninhibitive criticism of the prime ministerial qualities of the President, because they feel the inner need for his sentimental role—the father of his country. In the British system the monarch *is;* but he or she *does* not.

The British monarch personifies the oneness and durability of the nation, beyond successive Governments; he personifies sovereignty—that is, the necessary authority and consensus in a society. He is the exemplar of British morality.

The Monarch Reigns But Does Not Govern

The Crown can do nothing except on the advice of Ministers, and they advise on their judgment of what is politically desirable. This leads back to the state of political strength as measured by electoral and parliamentary votes. Therefore an enumeration of all the powers that the Crown once exercised that have been taken away by Parliament and the courts and Ministers who are popularly responsible is tedious, because hollow. It is a vast, sky-filling figure of splendor with a political power vacuum inside.

The Crown has the following sphere of duties, some of which permit of *personal* will while others do not. The spheres are (1) lawmaking; (2) execution of the law and the formulation and execution of policy; (3) justice; (4) social-dignifying and honors; (5) imperial unifying role and status. We shall return to these shortly.

Something needs a prior explanation. Why is there a monarchy at all? Why has the King or Queen any position whatever?

A Prior Question: Why Is Britain a Monarchy If It Is a Democracy?

If a person has a place in the machinery of government, if a live being has a title, he cannot be without attributes of authority. If he has *some* force of character and personality, he cannot fail to try to exert these on other people.

If the authority of Parliament and the Cabinet and the courts of law have been gradually peeled off from the original total power of the King to govern—that is to say, from the original prerogative—then why were not so many more peeled off that the Crown was wiped away altogether? Why, let us imagine, was not an elective President established as titular chief of the Executive, as in France or Germany and so many other countries? Why were not even the last substantial remnant of the personal powers of the Crown—namely, the dignified, glamorizing attributes, garments, jewels and gestures—taken away and given to some other institution?

There never was a time in English history (with the possible exception of the Cromwellian Interregnum) when the basic and radical choice between a republic and a monarchy was faced; and never by anything like the *whole* people or any but a minority of the leaders. Britain was monarchical; the onus of proof was on those who proposed a republic.

Though some citizens hated and despised particular Kings, the monarchy was bound up from before the year A.D. 1000 with the notion of religion in a vaster, more mysterious, and soul-captivating sense than the Church. It was inextricably bound up with the social order, as something more comprehensively embodying man's standards of right and wrong, virtue and vice, than political institutions more narrowly considered. For a large part of the population, monarchy represented aristocratic virtues and nobility, and an authoritarian, duty-advocating attitude to existence, alternative to, and corrective of, government by the people which they disliked. Among royalists of this sort, were, and still are, a large part of the population.

For all politics, in the end, is poetry. Our political values stem from the same depths of being as the magic lines of *Hamlet* and *Faust*. One of mankind's myths (a "representation" of ultimate mystic values) is the State. The student will not forget the classic line. "Poets are the unacknowledged legislators of mankind." Some people will rather do without bread than without glamorous propriety. They have the instinctive make-up that life must be lived in a gracious style or is not worth living. A King may exemplify and assist in giving all society this style. He paints their pictures for them, and they are willing to pay for the living myth as others will pay for saints in ceramics.

Further, they see that a Commonwealth spread over the entire world may be kept spiritually together by the right kind of single Crown. They appreciate that the idea of sovereignty—that is, of ultimate coercive power in a nation based on a principle of right and wrong and obedience—is for the multitude best brought home in a tangible form of a *person* rather than a thin theory in a book. They see that men will render services to society, with less regard of material reward and with heightened devotion, if someone, representing the nation, as our mundane existence, but also as the representative of virtue on earth,[2] gives them an honor, some recognition that they have merited well of the nation, that they have done their duty and become more humane.

In the words of Edmund Burke (*Reflections on the Revolution in France*), it is man's nature that his government be consecrated, and this by the established Church.

> This consecration is made, that all who administer in the government of men, in which they stand in the person of God Himself, should have high and worthy notions of their function and destination; that their hope should have been full of immortality; that they should not look to the paltry pelf of the moment, nor to the temporary and transient praise of the vulgar, but to a solid, permanent exercise, in the permanent part of their nature, and to a permanent fame and glory, in the example they leave as a rich inheritance to the world.

II. THE SOVEREIGN

The Name

The sovereign's personal name is a hybrid of family remembrance and public need as a promoter of unity in diversity. Thus Edward VIII was christened Edward Albert Christian George Andrew Patrick David: in the last four names England, Scotland, Ireland, and Wales are symbolized, and in an age of nationalism all communities excited by their individual history are flattered. The spiritual power and psychological grandeur of the name Elizabeth needs no empha-

sis, while her other names Alexandra and Mary recall two exquisitely dignified figures. Queen Elizabeth's consort was made Philip of Edinburgh —the Scottish appeal is manifest. The heir to the throne, Prince Charles, was christened Charles Philip Arthur George: Charles takes the world back to the "martyred" Stuart King and the Restoration. It also conciliates some Scottish nationalists, reminiscent of Charles Edward, the Young Pretender, who, in 1745, kept the field against England for a whole year with but a few thousand Highlanders, harrying England as far as the midlands. The plaintive melody of Bonnie Prince Charlie is still a popular song:

> My Bonnie lies over the ocean,
> My Bonnie lies over the sea,
> My Bonnie lies over the ocean,
> Oh, bring back my Bonnie to me!

The Title

The royal title has followed, first, the expanding unity of the realm, and more latterly the process of imperial decentralization or diversification. Queen Victoria began, "Victoria, by the Grace of God, of the United Kingdom of Great Britain and Ireland, Queen, Defender of the Faith," to which was added in 1876, "Empress of India." To Edward VII's title was added, after the word Ireland, "and of the British Dominions beyond the Seas. . . ." In 1927, after the secession as a Dominion of southern Ireland and the Imperial Conference of 1926, Parliament changed the title (Parliament had changed the others also) to "George V, by the Grace of God, of Great Britain, Ireland and the British Dominions beyond the Seas, King, Defender of the Faith, Emperor of India." George V fussed dreadfully over the change—insisting that the word *British* remain, and that *King* come before, not after, *Seas*.

The Commonwealth and Empire spreads and loosens and attains another kind of integration— a determined oneness in diversity—a community of friends who will help each other by common policies in war, by association in economic development, and by maintaining a standard of English social morality and humaneness.

The titles follow the flags and standards and the diversity.

---

[2] Eric Voeglin, *The New Science of Politics*, Chicago, 1951.

Queen Elizabeth's title *in the United Kingdom* is "Elizabeth the Second by the Grace of God of the United Kingdom of Great Britain and Northern Ireland [see how the Irish Free State has shorn itself of the Commonwealth and so been shorn from it in the title!] and of her other Realms and Territories Queen, Head of the Commonwealth, Defender of the Faith."

Territories is new, and the word implies no regime; *head* of the Commonwealth is new and implies neither queenship nor republic, and *head* is vaguer than previous titles. Then, in accordance with the decision taken at the Commonwealth Conference of 1952, each member uses for its own purpose "a form of Title which suits its particular circumstances but retains a substantial element which is common to all." Here is the metaphysics of unity.[3]

The process of suggestion and identification in the state of becoming can be discerned in the following quotation from a leading article in *The Times* (February 15, 1954), as Queen Elizabeth was about to visit Australia. (*He* refers to the Australian citizen.)

. . . behind his weatherbeaten mask he hides a strong vein of romanticism. He is romantic about his country, especially about her future; his pulse is thrilled by the faith of the most famous Australian poet:—

Love-lit, her Chaos shall become Creation:
And dewed with cream, her silence flower
    in song.

So, too, he is romantic about his Queen. As has been shown by the tumultuous welcome given her in every Australian town and village she

has yet visited, he will lavish spontaneously upon her a devotion and a respect that he would indignantly deny to any other person upon earth.

The Civil List

The sovereign is paid, and members of the royal family receive annual allowances, all being regulated by a statute that regulates the Civil List, meaning the annual income granted the sovereign.

Before William III the sovereign's finances and the public moneys were mixed together. The Civil List then meant not only the revenues the Crown obtained from its own estates but the budget of the year for nonmilitary public purposes. George III gave up his rights to the revenues arising out of Crown lands, the excise, and the post office in exchange for a fixed sum per year—then £800,000. The sovereign still retained some lesser revenues from property. Parliament proceeded to regulate the sovereign's income more specifically to meet his personal expenses. By the beginning of the reign of Queen Victoria, the lesser personal revenues had been surrendered. These accrue to the State, and very much exceed the income granted to the sovereign by Parliament.

Parliament grants the Civil List to the monarch from time to time, beginning with the accession and varying it as necessary; and grants are likewise made to the various members of the royal family. Today (by statute of 1953) the Civil List is thus constituted:

1. The Privy Purse	£ 60,000
2. Salaries of Household	185,000
3. Expenses of Household	121,800
4. Royal Bounty and Alms	13,200
5. Supplementary Provisions	95,000

making a total of £475,000. There are separate grants of annuities of £70,000 to the Queen Mother; £40,000 to the Duke of Edinburgh; £35,000 to the Duke of Gloucester; £6000 to Princess Margaret; and £6000 to Princess Mary.

It is a negligible sum in the total public expenditure in comparison with the services rendered to good government. The salary of other chiefs of state is not very much less,[4] and in relation to their

[3] Consequently Canada uses the title ". . . by the Grace of God of the United Kingdom, Canada and her other Realms and Territories . . .", and so to the end as the United Kingdom original. Australia does the same, with "Australia" in place of "Canada"; New Zealand, the same, with "New Zealand" after United Kingdom; Pakistan, the same, but not including the word "Pakistan"; Southern Rhodesia follows the original exactly without addition or omission; South Africa simply has "Elizabeth the Second, Queen of South Africa and of her other Realms and Territories, Head of the Commonwealth." Ceylon follows the South African formula except that "Queen of Ceylon" replaces "Queen of South Africa." India is a special case: India is a republic and therefore does not have a royal title, but India, the republic, recognizes the Queen as "Head of the Commonwealth." Indeed, it was for India's sake that the word "Head" was introduced.

[4] It appears from *U. S. News & World Report*, July 22, 1955, that omitting the annual rent and hire of the White

services might even be considered uneconomical. It will be realized that, as stated above, the Crown has surrendered private revenues of far larger amount and that some of the total granted is spent, compulsorily, in ways which the Treasury would otherwise have to meet—as, for example, hospitality and alms and pensions. Parliament's committee combs the request for the Civil List very rigorously.

Infancy and Incapacity

Many regency acts punctuate British history; provision had to be made for a representation of the royal authority and status during incapacity, absences, infancy. Today the situation is regulated by the Regency Acts of 1937, 1943, and 1953. The sovereign reaches his majority at the age of eighteen. Until that time—for instance, in the case of Prince Charles if something should happen to Queen Elizabeth II—a Regent will exercise the authority during his minority or total incapacity of the sovereign. The Regent is the next person in line of succession, who is a British subject of full age—that is, twenty-one—and domiciled in the United Kingdom, and who satisfies the Act of Settlement regarding religion.

This was the position until 1953, when Princess Margaret was the next in succession after Queen Elizabeth her sister—while Prince Charles is a minor. But, as is the way of Conservatives with the monarchy, the Government in 1953, foreseeing the departure of the Queen and her consort for a prolonged tour of the Empire and Commonwealth, and no doubt alarmed by the animation and love of pleasant company of the as-yet unmarried Princess, excluded her from the regency by statute, replacing her by Prince Charles' father, Philip, Duke of Edinburgh, the consort.

On the succession of a minor, regency is automatic. In the case, however, of total incapacity, the wife or husband of the sovereign, together with the Lord Chancellor, the Speaker, the Lord Chief Justice, and the Master of the Rolls, or any three of them, must make a declaration to the Privy Council that evidence (including that of physi-

cians) satisfies them that the sovereign, by reason of being infirm of mind and body, is incapable of performing the royal functions or that for a definite cause he is not available to perform them. The declaration must be communicated, also, to the Governments of the Dominions. A similar declaration may terminate a regency. The only thing a Regent may not do of all the things the sovereign may is to assent to a bill to change the order of succession to the Crown or alter the Act of Anne's Reign establishing the Presbyterian Church in Scotland.

Each Dominion makes the Regency Act applicable to itself by its own legislation.

Illness or temporary absence from the kingdom is met by the appointment of Counselors of State. The sovereign makes the appointment, conferring the various functions designed to be discharged, by letters patent. These devolved powers may not include power to dissolve Parliament unless on the express instructions of the sovereign—conveyable by telegraph—or to grant a peerage of any kind. The Counselors must be the sovereign's wife or husband and the four persons next in the line of succession to the Crown—excluding persons disqualified from being Regent or absent or intending to be absent from the United Kingdom for the time in question. The heir may be a Counselor of State if not under eighteen years of age, though he cannot be Regent until of full age.

When the sovereign is absent from the United Kingdom, he or she, and *not* the Counselors, exercises the functions of the Crown in relation to the Dominions, from whatever spot he may be in.

In 1954, for the first time in history, a Privy Council meeting was held in New Zealand by Queen Elizabeth on her State visit; the Privy Councilors (who were New Zealanders) attended the meeting, and the Queen there signed various State documents, to the immense delight of the New Zealanders.

Until 1867 (Reform Act) the death of the sovereign carried with it the dissolution of Parliament, and until 1901, when the Demise of the Crown Act was passed, the termination of all offices under the Crown. The principle formerly prevailing was that all offices are held at the royal will and pleasure and that Parliament is met on

---

House, planes, cars, and cabin cruisers, the President's pay and "fringes" amount to $2,138,000 per year. The British equivalent for the Royal Family is less than $1,700,000.

the personal summons of the Crown. This vestige of royal authority has passed away.

It may be noticed that *demise* may imply death but is not a synonym for it; it means *put on* or *conveyed on*—and embodies the idea that the Crown or kingship does not die: "The King is dead—long live the King!" At the abdication in 1936, there was a demise of the Crown though the abdicant did not vacate the throne through death—the demise occurred on receiving the abdicant's royal assent. The Dominions passed their consequent legislation, making the statute applicable to them. The purpose of continuity, and some mystery, may be discerned in these practices.

III. THE ROLE OF THE SOVEREIGN

The monarch has not been entirely bereft of rights. George V was taught his, for example, by Professor J. R. Tanner, and the King made, with some satisfaction, apparently, a résumé of Walter Bagehot's account of the status and role of the Crown.

Bagehot said that the personal discretion of the Crown in modern British government consisted of, "*first* the right to be consulted, *second* the right to encourage and *third* the right to warn. And these rights may lead to a very important influence on the course of politics, especially as under a system of party government, the Monarch alone possesses a *continuous political experience.*" This passage King George V (then Duke of York) did not summarize but copied out in full. The records show that he exercised a right of remonstrance, of deprecation, of various actions or aims, of grumbling, of a steady course of immixture in State affairs. In the main, he was defeated either by the refusal, almost always but not entirely tactful, of his Ministers to heed his opinions or by political-party activity, which was acting parallel to his apparent initiatives and ideas or took a course different from what he would have liked.

The whole of the Government of Britain, Her Majesty's Law Courts, Her Majesty's Ministers, the Queen in Parliament, can be represented as "in the name of the Crown." But "in the name of the Crown" does not mean by the will of the sovereign. The ancient legal label does not fill the bottle with power and authority. The royal ingredient is exceedingly small, faint in political decision-making. The sovereign is practically nothing but a purple rubber stamp. Let us examine the various provinces of power.

(1) Making Law

The sovereign opens and dissolves Parliament. The term of Parliament is set by statute. Opening, proroguing, dissolving, the length of the sessions, are decided by the Cabinet and the parties in Parliament. The sovereign has no discretion in the matter.

The sovereign addresses Parliament at the opening of the session—in the Queen's Speech. The speech is the product of the Cabinet and contains its general program for the session.

The Crown alone asks for money and to the Crown alone are revenues granted. The Crown means the Ministers: the purpose of the fiction is to deny an initiative in spending and raising taxes to private members of Parliament and to concentrate it in the Government. The order of the Commons on this subject could be changed any day at the decision of the majority party.

The rules of procedure forbid the use of the name of the sovereign to be used in debate, lest this influence votes. Such a mention recently was challenged in the House of Commons.

The days when George III could threaten successfully that he would deny his company to Lords who should vote in favor of a bill he opposed are far distant. But when in 1783 he did intervene in this way, the House of Commons retorted with the famous resolution that "to report any opinion, or pretended opinion, of his Majesty, upon any bill or other proceeding, depending in either House of Parliament, with a view to influence the votes of the members, is a high crime and misdemeanor, derogatory to the honour of the Crown, a breach of the fundamental privileges of Parliament, and subversive of the constitution." And three years before it had passed Dunning's resolution, "that the influence of the Crown has increased, is increasing, and ought to be diminished."

Yet, if the Crown does not interfere directly, the sovereign does from time to time make observations to Ministers on legislation that is in issue.

The sovereign certainly has an opinion, almost always more consonant with that of the Conservative Party. But the remonstrance or grumble does not necessarily come directly, but rather as defending some better established "right." For example, the royal reluctance to make peers for the passage of the Reform Bill in 1832; Queen Victoria's obstructing Gladstone's Home Rule Bill plans (1886) by granting a dissolution he asked for, believing he would lose the election; George V's involvement in the Home Rule Bill of 1912, since it brought the Armed Forces in Ireland into a state of insurrection; or the same sovereign's dislike of the House of Lords reform of 1910, when the issue of a dissolution and the swamping of the Lords with enough peers to pass the law were raised. George V also voiced his concern over unemployment during the depression, and sounded a faint warning against class warfare in politics more addressed to right-wing Conservatives.

Yet the legislation, though affronting the sovereign's idea of what was proper, was passed, or dealt with by the clash of party forces. In no way was its character influenced by the royal ideas.

The Veto Power. The veto power of the Crown stems from the still acknowledged requirement that when a bill has been passed by both Houses of Parliament the Crown's assent is necessary to make it valid law. The formal phrasing is *Le Roi le veut,* to signify assent; or, if assent is refused—that is, the bill is vetoed—the formula would be *Le Roi s'avisera* (the King will consider the matter). There is not, as in the United States, a "pocket veto." Can the Crown refuse its assent? It has not been refused since 1707. It is a settled convention that the Crown cannot veto a bill.

Yet the Conservative Party and some Conservative constitutional theorists (Anson, Keith, Halsbury) impute an active veto to the Crown. Some of the former asserted the claim in 1913–1914 (over the Home Rule Bill) that the Crown was "the guardian of the constitution," particularly since the "veto" power of the Lords to call in the people to give a clear indication of will on the law had been weakened deliberately. *Clear* meant, it must be supposed, something more than one half the electorate. The King did not like this attitude. It is recorded that he was "properly disturbed" by this throwing of the onus of deciding to withhold assent on his personal initiative. The leader of the Conservative Opposition, Mr. Bonar Law, even caused the King to turn red (in the old-fashioned sense) by almost browbeating him to veto the law.[5]

In times of acute constitutional conflict, someone will invoke the authority for the good of his party. The chances are that in the future it will be less invoked than it has been in the still-rare cases of the past.

(2) The Executive Power [6]

The sovereign's discretion is limited, as we have seen, in the appointment of Prime Minister and thence in the appointment of Ministers (Chapter 7). Queen Victoria and Edward VII intervened in some appointments of Ministers—less so the latter than the former—and the former behaved with extreme virulence and rudeness, especially to Liberals and Radicals, but with extremely small effect.

The cases of royal intervention in the time of George V related to a kind of burdensome but patriotic and dutiful welcome to the first Labour Government, and two occasions when the King tried to dissuade lesser appointees from resignation. The more important of the latter was Lord Hardinge, formerly Viceroy of India, then Permanent Secretary at the Foreign Office. He was under attack for defeats in the Mesopotamian campaigns of 1916–1917. Lloyd George reacted with extreme sharpness against the sovereign's intervention. The King retracted. The Foreign Secretary Lord Balfour (this was a wartime coalition Government) kept Hardinge in office. Query: Could this have happened under a normal one-party Cabinet? In 1929 Lord Burnham, a member of the commission studying Indian constitutional reforms, wished to resign. Sir John

[5] Cf. Harold Nicolson, *George V,* London, 1953, pp 199–201.

[6] The various forms in which royal consent is given to official acts are very complicated, both as to the diverse purposes for which each is used, and as to the official responsible for custody and authorizing the use of various seals, etc. Also, they differ regarding the necessity for actual signature by the sovereign. For this subject, see Sir William R. Anson, *Law and Custom of the Constitution,* Cambridge, 1935, Part II, Vol. 1, pp. 62ff.

Simon, the chairman, much distressed, asked the King to persuade Burnham not to resign. The King's private secretary would not let the King "too much into the controversy," but wrote on his own responsibility, using the King's name. Burnham stayed.

Two other examples were not happy. The King suggested Lord Haig, a brave but not-too-talented general, for the Viceroyalty of India, in 1926. An Army officer was hardly appropriate in that year. Edward Wood, afterward Lord Irwin, then Minister of Agriculture, received the appointment. He was the son of the then Lord Halifax. The King suggested this name also. Where he got it from, we are not told. But Irwin-Halifax made a good Viceroy. Then, in 1930, George V attempted to abort the appointment of Sir Isaac Isaacs (Chief Justice of Australia) to be Governor General of Australia. The nominee was an Australian and proposed by the Australian Prime Minister. The King held that he must act on his own initiative, because the Imperial Conference of 1926 had prohibited United Kingdom Ministers from advising him in such imperial appointments! The law and the resolutions were in a state of inextricable confusion. The King was very obstinate—arguing that it was better to have a political neutral from outside than a party-nominated man from inside Australia, and thus the King's representative "would be able to stand aloof from all politics as much as the Sovereign does at home." [7] The Imperial Conference of 1930 sided with the Australian Prime Minister as to the locus of royal advice—the Dominions. The Australian Prime Minister had his own way, after a quite candid and obstinate audience on both sides.

As to the exercise of executive power, royal interventions are frequent. One noted case is in the assuagement of the police and military measures against the Irish Republicans in Ireland just after World War I. George V did constantly bring to bear a moderating, pacifying influence on the Government of the day, headed by Lloyd George. He was used by the Government to visit Ireland and made a speech of pacification. There are, again, the incidents of deploring unemployment and poverty. There is the incident of preferring a National Government to a dissolution in 1931. There is the successful attempt of George VI to prohibit Mr. Churchill from joining the D-Day invasion of France in 1944.

Foreign Affairs. Much has been made of the sovereign's position in foreign affairs. He is represented as being in touch with "foreign potentates" —that is, the rulers—and as having a longer view of international relations as, normally, his reign is so much longer than the period of office of any one Cabinet or Foreign Secretary. Queen Victoria and Edward VII intervened often.

What did George V know, or what could he do, that his Ministers did not know and were more competent to do? An alleged observation of his to the younger brother of the Kaiser is alleged to have caused a serious misunderstanding that weakened the German view that Britain would fight if France were attacked.

However, George V did not wish to receive his cousin the Russian Emperor for asylum in Britain in the 1917 Russian Revolution, whereas the Government had originally made such an offer. He saw the difficulties among the left-wingers in Britain. But he had earlier compromised himself by sending a telegram of sympathy to the Russian royal family, just when the Cabinet was applauding the Russian people's progress toward responsible government.

Hence, though today there is a lingering tincture of prerogative about the Crown and foreign affairs, diplomatic relationships, ambassadorships, the Foreign Office, the making of treaties, war and peace are far, far beyond the personal influence of the sovereign. There ought to be no confusion about it,[8] even if royal visits abroad win friendship.

(3) The Administration of Justice

The courts of justice are Her Majesty's Courts, the judges, Her Majesty's judges. Yet, in practice, in no detail whatever does or can the Queen interfere in the course of justice, from arrest to execution. The sovereign neither appoints nor dismisses the judges. The sovereign cannot sus-

[7] Nicolson, *George V*, p. 479.

[8] This is one place in which Sir Ivor Jennings' *Cabinet Government*, Cambridge, 1949, p. 311, gives a wrong impression.

pend a law or dispense with the application of a law. Prosecutions in the form of *Rex* (*or Regina*) *v. John Doe* are the equivalent of *United States v. John Doe* or the *People v. John Doe*.

The prerogative of mercy is the right to pardon those who have been tried and sentenced. The prerogative is exercised by the Home Secretary, a Cabinet Minister. This responsibility in capital cases was transferred to the Home Secretary by an act of 1837, relieving the sovereign of it. By convention, the sovereign is informed of the Home Office's decision, which will need her signature.

(4) Titles, Honors, and Appointments

Rewards that call out life-long self-sacrifice are not necessarily of a coarse or material kind. Of public distinctions, in the form of titles and honors, there are very many in Britain, a land with a long history, where the order of nobility that played such an honorable part, on the whole, in the development of a decent polity was never abolished.

"The King is the fountain of Honor." This is one of the most ancient of attributes of the monarchy. All grants are made by him. But, here again, he must act on the advice of his Ministers. The Prime Minister is the adviser, with some less important exceptions wherein the individual Minister is in charge. The Royal Victorian Order is the one and only order bestowed by the sovereign alone (and, since 1946, the Orders of the Garter and the Thistle). Even where the sovereign might wish to bestow an order or a peerage on one of his own household, the Prime Minister must recommend. Hence, though the King is the fountain of honor, the stream flows through the Prime Minister's political grace and needs. Even the Order of Merit, established in Edward VII's time to be awarded by the King personally, has come to be awarded on the recommendation of the Prime Minister. It should be remembered that Prime Ministers are usually very distinguished and cultured men.

The development of political parties, and the decline of spoils and patronage, brought about the seeking of funds by the parties for election purposes. Hence, honors began to be given, here and there, for "political services"—meaning a contri-

bution to the party chests. In World War I the alleged practices of a regular tariff for various honors, used in order to fill the party coffers of Lloyd George's section of the Liberal Party (especially for war profiteers), caused an open scandal, and a Royal Commission on Honors was set up in 1922 to inquire into the whole matter.

The King had for some years past made sharp protests against several nominations and asked for some procedure to protect the Crown *and the Government* from the possibility of similar painful, if not humiliating, incidents—*"an evil, dangerous to the social and political well being of the State."*

It was now revealed how the suggestions for honors went through the Patronage Secretary of the party in power, who was sometimes the head of the party organization. Names also got to the Prime Minister by circuitous routes. Prime Ministers were sometimes misinformed or kept in ignorance of the personal character of the men who were to be honored. Naturally, the House of Lords took, and had for some time past taken, a peculiar interest in repressing any unworthy bestowal of honors.

The Royal Commission on Honors therefore recommended that a committee of the Privy Council of not more than three members, but not being members of the Government, should be set up for the duration of each Government. This committee was to be informed of recommendations before submission to the sovereign. The statement must contain a description of the service to be honored and a declaration by the Patronage Secretary or party manager that no payment was involved, and the name of the person who originally suggested the recipient of honors. Then the committee was to report to the Prime Minister whether the persons involved are fit and proper. If there was an adverse report, and the Prime Minister persisted, then the sovereign was to be informed of the committee's report.

These recommendations have been carried out. The present (1956) Political Honors Scrutiny Committee is composed of Lord Asquith of Bishopstone (chairman), a son of the late Liberal Prime Minister, Asquith; Lord Pethwick Law rence, former Labour Cabinet Minister; and Viscount Templewood (Sir Samuel Hoare), formerly Conservative Foreign Minister. These are impeccable.

The Royal Commission on Honors further proposed that a penalty be imposed on those who promised to secure an honor for pecuniary payment or other valuable consideration, and upon persons promising such payments for an honor. The Honors (Prevention of Abuses) Act, 1923, takes care of this.

Normally, then, twice a year, at New Year's and on the sovereign's birthday, lists of honors are announced. At a Coronation or a Jubilee, special lists are published. On these special occasions, the Prime Minister customarily asks the leader of the Opposition to make some nominations.

Raising the Standard of Public Service. Thus the sovereign does not personally choose who shall be honored. This choice is in the authority of the responsible Government of the country. But the fact that the sovereign's name and dignity are coupled with the bestowal of the *distinction* prevents the giving of honors except for meritorious service, of military or civil service, or social, economic, political, literary, scientific, artistic, or athletic achievement. The merit is measured on a national criterion of honorable worthiness; it elevates an ideal standard of virtue by which to value imperfect human beings. The newspapers bring to all homes the photographs and careers and service of those so honored.

The effect on British life (and citizens of the Dominions and the colonies are honored in the same way, also) is quite remarkable. It has its source in the deep yearning of men and women to have their personal qualities recognized by mankind. As Bagehot once said about the House of Lords, in paraphrase: it represents distinction and virtue; if mankind casts this kind of distinction, this valuation, away, then the only other distinction is Money.

Any person who has witnessed the joy experienced by a British official on receiving even the first rank in the high ladder of honors, and the congratulations upon this of his colleagues, the celebration dinner, lunch, or receptions, will know what a power for good, for style, for prob-

ity, honors are. The prestige of "the public interest" is enhanced.

Patronage. It may be said, in gross, that for administrative and judicial appointments and promotions, the royal power is sterile. There are in the Church of England, deaneries, and particularly the deanery of Windsor, the royal residence, canonries, bishoprics, and so forth in which the influence of Queen Victoria was very marked, she being guided by a favorite ecclesiastical adviser. But since her time, the Prime Minister is master of the situation and relies heavily for advice on the Archbishop of Canterbury.

The last facet of the role of the monarch, (5) imperial unifying role and status, will comprise the concluding section of this chapter.

Some Influence but No Power

The sovereign can act only upon the advice of Ministers. His power is small indeed. Since the early 1840's Ministers have dealt with the Crown on the principle that the sovereign is to be kept out of politics, that the Crown's very existence needs their safeguard by always putting it into a neutral position, to save it from the resentment of, say, one half the nation, on occasions of political controversy. Gladstone said:

> The association of the ministers, with parliament, and through the House of Commons with the people, is the counterpart of their associations as ministers with the crown and the prerogative. The decisions that they take are taken under the competing pressure of a bias this way and a bias that way, and strictly represent what is termed in mechanics the composition of forces. In the face of the country the sovereign and the ministers are an absolute unity. The one may concede to the other; but the limit of concession by the sovereign is at the point where he becomes willing to try the experiment of changing his government; and the limit of concession by the ministers is at the point where they become unwilling to bear, what in all circumstances they must bear while they remain ministers, the undivided responsibility of all that is done in the crown's name.[9]

[9] "Kin Beyond the Sea," *North American Review,* September 1878; also in *Gleanings,* Vol. I, pp. 225–244.

The volume and diversity of domestic and foreign affairs swamps the King or Queen.

Information for the Crown. The sovereign obtains information from three sources: (1) the Prime Minister, (2) the Cabinet Secretariat, and (3) newspapers, her secretary, and friends.

Until the beginning of the reign of George V, the Prime Minister used to send to the sovereign two letters: a daily one during the session of Parliament and an occasional one regarding Cabinet proceedings. The former was a résumé of and commentary on parliamentary events; the latter was an account of decisions taken. In addition to this last, there were such Cabinet memoranda or ministerial memoranda as casually happened to be drawn up. The former was discontinued by George V—after all, the *Parliamentary Debates* are promptly available. The latter still continues, though probably in a shorter form than before the institution of the Cabinet Secretariat. In addition, the Prime Minister has audience with the sovereign from time to time. (During World War II, Mr. Churchill made it a practice to lunch with the King once a week.)

As regards the proceedings of the Cabinet, it is usually considered conventional for the Prime Minister to be the sole channel of communication, and it is for him, so far as he wishes, to disclose differences in the Cabinet. He might do the latter if he thought it would get the sovereign's encouragement on his side; he might not disclose, out of prudence or shame. Prime Ministers have varied very much in their practice. Disclosure could mean a wedge for the sovereign into using dissension as a means of influence. Today, however, the issue is settled in favor of disclosure because the sovereign receives Cabinet minutes. If so—what can she do with the knowledge she gleans? The machine is too big for her.

The sovereign sees all Cabinet papers; they come to her through the Cabinet Office or the departments. She sees Cabinet agenda; departmental memoranda; the daily print of Foreign Office telegrams; the reports of the Defense Committee; subcommittee reports; the summary of the Commonwealth press; and letters from Governors of Dominions and Colonies and British Ambassadors. Any one of these documents can be made

the occasion for the request of more information.

There are writers who suggest the impression that this amassment of information is a measure of monarchial influence over political decision. Jennings even goes to the extent of saying, "Thus the King may be said to almost be a member of the Cabinet, and the only non-party member. He is, too, the best-informed member and the only one who cannot be forced to keep silent." [10] Surely this goes too far!

The secretaries mark the newspapers for the sovereign. We have no knowledge of which newspapers the sovereign prefers. There are evidences in the existing biographies that the Conservative Party type are preferred. The news in the press may suggest royal inquiries of the Cabinet before its action has become irrevocable.

Education and Character. This brings the subject back to three things: royal education and friends, royal character, and royal attitudes.

It has always and everywhere been difficult to know how to educate a young person to be the sovereign.

It is thought desirable by the parents and their tutorial advisers that the heir shall mix with his subjects—and yet *not* mix with them. He cannot go to every kind of school (he starts with private tutors) or to *all* the universities (though Edward VIII was given a try at Oxford). He has little stimulus to undertake years of hard study through his first twenty years or so, like middle- and working-class men and women who must earn their living. The naval education of George V and George VI (and Edward VIII) was good as naval education, and assisted in the knowledge of human nature. Nicolson's biography, sympathetic as it is, demonstrates that they simply did not know what the poorer of their subjects felt, and so does the Duke of Windsor's *A King's Story*. It is hard to believe that the heirs get anything better than a British country-gentleman or aristocratic secondary-school range of knowledge, philosophy, history, and social sciences. Queen Victoria was not merely Conservative, she was a Tory; she was not only Tory, she was reactionary. Edward VII's education was poor; so was Edward VIII's.

[10] *Cabinet Government, op. cit.,* p. 327.

Their friends from childhood are not the middle classes or working classes. Their private secretaries—Ponsonby (Henry and Frederick), Knollys, Stamfordham, Hardinge, Wigram, Lascelles (all very admirable men, more usually than not the souls of constitutional discretion)—were never known to *democratize* the royal sympathies or understanding, nor did the entourage of the sovereign.

The royal character is a determinant. All are "governing class," but each has a different way of making a contribution. George V, it is now recorded, demonstrated he was a man of peace; he was conservative; he was unimaginative; he had the gift of common sense; he was on the whole a gentle person and a conciliator, immensely dutiful, not self-assertive like his grandmother, very honest, orderly, and industrious. His son Edward VIII did not have these qualities, and the son violently and disastrously revolted from him because of the difference. The former could be "constitutional"; the latter utterly abhorred the thought of the propriety, the stiffness, the "receiving of homage" as though he personally deserved it; the immense amount of paper work; the sobriety.

The character and the circumstances produce an attitude. Thus George V showed special interest in the "empire" and social unity.

This was the time when the Dominions needed to be linked together by a figurehead, "the golden link of empire," to use the well-worn cliché. It suited his training (travel in the Navy) and sporting-squire temperament. He could be a moderator of extreme partisanship; a patriotic figurehead in an era of war; a sweetener of class jealousies; a promoter of harmony; a practitioner of "fair play" for a Labour Government, though "they [sic] have different idea to ours"; a man who was deeply acquiescent in the religious-political outlook of the Archbishop of Canterbury; and worried about the economic health of his country in crisis.

Thus, though there are many examples of royal usefulness, by way of warning, encouragement, questions, remonstrance, and moderating counsel, they were small indeed, in the effect on the mass political will.

IV. WHAT THE BRITISH SENSE IN A MONARCHY

The nature of the Coronation is one way of appreciating the political value of the monarchy to the British; the state of the public mind at the abdication of Edward VIII (an accidental occurrence that gave something of the data of a controlled experiment in social science!) was another.

The Coronation

The sovereign is proclaimed at once on the death of the preceding monarch, by the Lords Spiritual and Temporal and various leading personages of the City of London, reminiscent of the raucous assemblies of magnates in ancient days that elected and raised up their King. The first meeting of the Privy Council approves.

The Coronation is planned for good weather ("King's weather"), with due notice to overseas dignitaries. But God disposes.

The ceremony at Westminster Abbey, presided over most particularly by the Primate, the Archbishop of Canterbury, whose venerable office reaches back more than a thousand years, falls into three parts. (1) The people accept their sovereign, and the sovereign takes the oath of royal duties. (2) A religious ceremony introduces a more deeply spiritual note, and includes anointing and crowning. (3) The Lords Spiritual and Temporal render homage in person.

Let us merely emphasize some of the aspects of the Coronation.

The oath answers this formula:

Will you solemnly promise and swear to govern the Peoples of the United Kingdom of Great Britain and Northern Ireland, Canada, Australia, New Zealand, the Union of South Africa, Pakistan and Ceylon, and of your possessions and other Territories to any of them belonging or pertaining, according to their respective laws and customs?

Here is the contractual nature of the monarchy; and the limitation of absolute sovereignty; and the notion of government under laws imposed from the outside.

The religious ceremony is the part of the Coronation most fraught with meaning; and the anointing more than the crowning, though the latter may be the more dramatic. The monarch is hallowed, made holy, with holy oil and so "blessed, consecrated Queen over the peoples to whom the Lord God hath given her to rule and govern."

Symbolic vestments and accoutrements, closed canopies, spurs and rings, in gold and jewels, add solemnity and mystery; emblems of power, emblems of justice and mercy, all are employed in the "Name and by the authority of Almighty God." Queen Elizabeth was presented with the Holy Bible, the usual procedure, but now presented by a Moderator of the General Assembly of the Church of Scotland.

It is a powerful and most moving ceremony. Of the coronation service, Archbishop Lang said of George VI's ceremony:

> [It] is from beginning to end a most solemn religious act. It may truly be said that the service is throughout sacramental in its character, not only because all the rites take place within the Order of the Sacrament of Holy Communion, but because each of them is regarded as an outward and visible sign of an inward and spiritual grace sought from God and, as we may humbly believe, given by him.

The whole nation is religiously affected; a degree of abnegation is inspired.

They must be hard of heart, who, knowing the sorrows into which every life must at some time be plunged, will not be softened and themselves consecrated, who hearing or reading these words, will not be moved:

> The Archbishop, standing before the Altar, shall take the Crown into his hands, and laying it again before him upon the Altar, he shall say:
>
> "O God the Crown of the faithful: Bless we beseech thee this Crown, and so sanctify thy servant Elizabeth upon whose head this day thou dost place it for a sign of royal majesty, that she may be filled by thine abundant grace with all princely virtues: through the King Eternal Jesus Christ our Lord. Amen."

The onlookers see the Golden Coach, preceded and followed by 30,000 soldiers, in every uniform of the Empire and several other great nations, with forty-seven bands of heartening music. Prime Ministers, sultans, generals, admirals, the Lord Mayor and his retinue, add their brilliance, and the suggestion of their bravery and preparedness to sacrifice their lives to save the Queen's, and, at her command, the nation.

They must surely remember the hymn all have sung or heard from infancy:

> There is a happy land, far, far away,
> Where saints in glory stand, far, far, away!

On one side of their coins they will see the right profile of the Queen; and on the reverse side the figure of Britannia, that emblem of the nation's history on the waves, that matches the other personification of the nation—stout John Bull, with the Union Jack as his waistcoat.

The only exceptions to the universal wish for monarchy, regardless of class, are the Communists and a handful of republicans, the latter more noticable in the 1870's (rationalists and secularists) than today.

For the rest of British mankind, the sentiment appreciates the political utility and the sublimation of their drabber selves, in the monarchy. They worship their *better* selves, represented in the King or Queen.

Glamor

Romance accompanies the presence of the Queen at social-service activities (opening hospitals or meeting foreign dignitaries) and nationally interesting athletic events. The royal personages, well-groomed and immaculately spoken, are beautiful apparitions of public virtue and prowess: racing is the "king of sports." When men and women are honored, the former knighted with sword and accolade, the whole public can sense the brilliance of men at their maximum distinction. A Prime Minister would be only one half of such halo, for the other half might actually have the duty to sneer. Not so with King or Queen.

Hierarchy

The British acknowledge hierarchy: a graduated design of what is owed as respect and honor to others and themselves on a scale of public virtue that is stable, secure, and serene. The Crown personifies this, and helps to make a man or woman *somebody* in a spiritual scale. The people want the consecration of their standards of virtue and good behavior. It helps parents and schools in inculcating service and probity in their young. The mere living existence of the sovereign imposes an obligation on a Minister not to "let the monarchy down" by shady transactions; he would be ashamed to demean Queen Elizabeth.

Religion

We have seen in the Coronation the intertwining of the sovereign with the religion of the nation, more especially the Church of England. The Church, whether Thomas à Becket fighting Henry II or Sir Thomas More wrestling with Henry VIII, has claimed to be the King's conscience. The vast majority of the people has an interest in propriety, puritanism, and respectability even if but precisely sensed. Edward VIII lacked the quality to give them this.

> O! When degree is shak'd,
> Which is the ladder to all high designs,
> The enterprise is sick. How could communities,
> Degrees in schools, and brotherhoods in cities,
> Peaceful commerce from dividable shores,
> The primogenitive and due of birth,
> Prerogative of age, crowns, sceptres, laurels,
> But by degree, stand in authentic place?
> Take but degree away, untune that spring,
> And, hark! what discord follows; . . .
>
> .   .   .   .
> Force should be right . . .
>
> .   .   .   .
> Then every thing includes itself in power,
> Power into will, will into appetite;
>
> (*Troilus and Cressida*).

Shakespeare and royalty come hand in hand in the schools. The image of Henry V shimmers bright.

The Dominions

Mr. Baldwin, the Prime Minister, solicitously gathered the views of the Dominions leading up to Edward VIII's abdication. Those in far-away lands, still seeking for the oneness and security of institutions, are more sensitive to propriety than even the metropolis. They want to *look up* to the sovereign. There are many military and geographical factors and economic ones, tending to pull their loyalty away from the Mother Country to other neighbors (for example, the United States); the sentimental bond has become all the more important as a counterforce. They will give up other advantages for dignity and grace. Mr. Churchill played on this theme masterfully as Queen Elizabeth set off on her tour of 1953. He said (House of Commons, November 19):

> This will be the first time in history that a British sovereign has circumnavigated the globe. Her Majesty and the Duke will set foot in many lands owning allegiance to the Crown and will no doubt arouse the keenest signs of loyal devotion. We have no doubt of the cheerful welcome the Queen and the Duke will receive wherever they go. Her Majesty's ship *Gothic* is more spacious and travels faster than the Golden Hind, but it may well be that the journey the Queen is about to take will be no less auspicious and the treasure she brings back no less bright than when Drake first sailed an English ship round the world. We wish her Majesty and the Duke Godspeed and our fervent prayers accompany her toils and duties.

As a sovereign, then, the person of King and Queen, must offer an acceptable symbolic and credible personification, of these needs and services. They must be such as not to bring dissension in the moral unity of the nation. The sovereign must be the exemplar of civil service, evoking the instincts of human solidarity and sympathy among men.

Lord Ponsonby, of a family which gave two private secretaries to the Crown during the past century, said after the abdication of Edward VIII, "The rivets of the Halo have loosened the Crown. If we want to keep the Crown, let us finally dispense with the halo." But the Crown is halo, or nothing. To it is assigned the absolute minimum of personal political power that can possibly be associated with a live being in return for the maximum of grace. It is no accident that the monarchy has become the more popular concomitantly with the universalizing of the right to vote and the abolition of privilege. Among the masses, the proportion of stoics is quite small.

As a father-image, or an impersonation of the

romantic, says the psychoanalyst, king or queen stands scatheless, the noble father or mother, while the politicians may be vilified and scourged. This duality is politically comfortable. On the one hand, politics might be red in tooth and claw; on the other, royalty reminds the nation of its brotherhood amid their conflicts. The silk gloves are something to be thankful for. The French nation, above others, was silent with awe when the films of the Coronation showed them what they had destroyed in 1789. The accession of a young and pretty woman has stirred enterprise, adventure and quasi-romantic desires to excel in the hearts of almost every man in England. All peoples everywhere crave the deification of something; it is well if they deify their best selves in the image of their nation. It is not too good when they deify a Hitler, a Mussolini, or a Stalin, or a man who happens to have been chosen President by election, for that dazzles them to political blindness. In Britain it is accomplished by the convention that the Crown reigns but does not govern.

10

The House of Lords

The order of nobility is of great use, too, . . . in what it prevents. It prevents the rule of wealth—the religion of gold. This is the obvious and natural idol of the Anglo Saxon. He is always trying to make money; he reckons everything in coin; he bows down before a great heap and sneers as he passes a little heap. . . . From this our aristocracy preserves us. . . . Money is kept down, and, so to say, cowed by the predominant authority of a different power.

—Walter Bagehot in the 1860's

I. PAST AND PRESENT

Britain has the oldest bicameral Parliament of all nations. It consists of the House of Commons and the House of Lords, the former emanating from universal suffrage, with the Executive responsible to it; the latter not elected, but entirely hereditary. The House of Lords, descending directly from the medieval Magnum Consilium, is older than the Commons (p. 38).

Easily equal in power with the lower chamber until the beginning of the nineteenth century, the House of Lords lost authority steadily during that century, especially when the Commons' franchise was reformed in 1832, and when, in 1911 and 1949, its powers as a legislative body were seriously reduced by the Parliament Acts of those dates.

The House of Lords still has important legislative authority, but this is distinctly inferior to that of the Commons. Yet it still retains some, far from negligible. Beyond this, it remains one of the most distinguished forums of public debate in the world, for it has the right to discuss any phase of legislation, policy, and administration; and, as will be seen, a substantial part of its membership is of exceptional distinction in intellect and political, social, and business experience. These consti-

tute a body of public-spirited experts, able to talk with great intelligence and knowledge, and ready to do so with an aloofness from immediate partisan politics because they are not dependent for their status on appeals for popular election, and with abundant time to deliberate, as the Lords are far less pressed with decisive business than the Commons. This candid expertise has influence with the public, the Government, and the Civil Service.

Until 1832 the House of Lords politically topped the House of Commons, the latter being truly the lower house. The Houses often disagreed, because personal and party forces in the two chambers were at odds or social and political ambitions clashed at the royal court. Hence, conflicts on legislation, finance, the power of the Crown, and foreign and imperial policy. But the aristocracy of the eighteenth century owned much of the land in all quarters of the nation, and this gave it the power of local political bosses, not only in the counties but also in the boroughs, so that it could manipulate elections to the Commons. There was also the force of family relationship of the membership of the two houses. Far into the nineteenth century the Lords' prestige of wealth and ancient standing insured its leadership and influence.

In 1832 the House of Lords fought a last-ditch

fight against the Reform Act (p. 67), but it ended with its abject defeat, when the adoption of the representative electoral principle for the Commons laid the basis for extension of the franchise to the masses. The forces of the new age no longer "pitied the plumage and forgot the dying bird." The foundations of authority had shifted: the House of Lords, based on heredity, must wilt into a conscious excrescence since it lacked roots in popular election. Ultimately it must become close to powerless.

Present Composition

At present (1956) the House of Lords is composed of four classes of members: (1) hereditary peers by right, about 811;[1] (2) Scottish representative peers (elected for each Parliament), 16, and Irish representative peers (elected for life), 5; (3) archbishops and bishops, 26; and (4) Law Lords, or Lords of Appeal in Ordinary, appointed for life (no succession of title), 9. These were first established in 1876.

Class (4) is discussed in Chapter 14 (pp. 265–266). Class (3) become legislators simply by virtue of vocational eminence in the Church of England. They are not excluded from the functions of the House except religious affairs, yet vast numbers of religious persons outside this church have no representation as such. Class (2), the Scottish and Irish peers, are elected by their fellows; the Scottish are elected by their 40 colleagues, as arranged in the Act of Union, 1707; the Irish are the survivors of those 28 formerly elected for life, according to the Act of Union, 1800, until the Irish Free State Act of 1922 abolished the mechanism of election.

Class (1), the hereditary peers,[2] consists of two groups which may be distinguished: the "accidents of an accident," as Bagehot has called them, and those honored for proven or presumed virtue. The first group forms the great bulk of the House of Lords.[3] Their rank and title to sit and exercise power arises from the fact that they are the eldest sons of their fathers and mothers. All may, and some do, have ability, but the modern world has rejected the principle that ability may rule unless it is representative of the interests of those expected to obey the law. With the exception of about a score, these hereditary legislators are usually absent from the proceedings of the House of Lords, whose benches are conspicuous by their red-plush vacancy. However, the right to attend, speak, and vote exists; and it is used by large numbers when the interests of the country, in the estimation of the party managers, are in danger. We return to this presently.

The second group, quite large in recent years, is, in the generation that is first raised to the peerage, composed of commoners ennobled for political and social services. These services are, broadly, of three kinds: (1) contributing to the welfare of the nation by political office—as in the cases of Wellington, Disraeli, Asquith, Baldwin, Curzon, Balfour, Ullswater (former Commons' Speaker), Beveridge (civil servant and socioeconomic adviser)—or other kinds of service—as Admiral Nelson, Field Marshal Montgomery, or Citrine, trade-union leader; (2) those immediately serving a party, its organization or finances, as Lord Woolton, Conservative Party organizer, Earl Attlee, on resignation from leadership; (3) public charitable workers or men of eminence in science, education, art—as Lister or Cherwell, Lord Lindsay, formerly Master of Balliol, Bryce, John Maynard Keynes. Perhaps there should be added to this class those men of talent and loyalty who are raised to the peerage because the Government of the day needs spokesmen in the Lords or must fill Royal Household appointments—for example, Lord Passfield, formerly Sidney Webb, in the first Labour Government, and over a score of others since 1945–1946. Some, in these three subclasses have the qualities of two or more of

---

[1] Cf. Debrett's *Peerage,* etc., London, editions from time to time.

[2] Four peers of the Blood Royal; 21 dukes; 27 marquesses; 133 earls; 101 viscounts; 523 barons.

The bulk of the peerage is of recent origin. Thus: thirteenth century, 3 barons; fourteenth, 7 barons; fifteenth, 1 duke, 2 earls, 3 barons; sixteenth, 1 duke, 7 marquesses, 28 earls, 6 viscounts, 38 barons; nineteenth, 4 dukes, 12 marquesses, 58 earls, 17 viscounts, barons, 174; twentieth, 1 duke, 7 marquesses, 26 earls, 69 viscounts, 285 barons. In the twentieth century altogether, 388 peerages, or nearly one half of the total.

[3] Lest American students be mystified that Sir Winston Churchill and Sir Anthony Eden are still members of the House of Commons—as some students have been—their titles are those of *knights,* not peers, the lowest order of which is a baron. Knights, *per se,* are still commoners.

them. Among them is the Lord Chancellor (p. 137) who presides over the House, sitting on the Woolsack, symbolic of England's wealth by wool in the Middle Ages.

We have already discussed the process by which the Crown bestows honors on commoners (p. 184).

The members of the House of Lords are disqualified for election to the House of Commons. They cannot divest themselves of their titles or refuse to inherit them when their elders die. Consequently, it is a matter of much tribulation when the heir who has made a career for himself in the Commons and Ministry must leave the excitement of these centers of government with the prospects of high office, even the prime ministership, to go to the House of Lords. Three good recent examples of this are Quintin Hogg, son of Lord Hailsham, once a commoner who became Lord Chancellor. The younger man became an eminent lawyer, rose in the esteem of the Commons, wrote *The Case for Conservatism*. He bitterly suffered his "promotion," begging that legislation should give him the right to refuse it, in vain. The other is now the Marquess of Salisbury, but was Viscount Cranborne, a close associate of Mr. Eden in foreign policy, the two resigning against the policy that led to Munich in 1938. Mr. Churchill was willing to be knighted, but firmly refused the peerage ardently offered by Queen Elizabeth, for he rejoiced in remaining a "House of Commons man."

The membership of the Lords is entirely male. Although there are some twenty peeresses in their own right, holding titles by virtue of descent from male ancestors, they are not admitted to the Lords by the lords. They cannot even seek election to the Commons. But the wives of peers may sit in the Commons, and one, the Virginia-born Lady Astor did so for many years, poetically enough, for the borough of Plymouth.

Peers cannot vote for the House of Commons, but may vote in municipal elections. They are unpaid.

Powers

The House of Lords had until the Parliament Act of 1911 four branches of power: judicial, legislative, financial, and executive.

Judicial Power. The judicial nature of the House

is treated later (pp. 265–266). The House is the supreme court of appeal in civil cases for Great Britain and Northern Ireland, and in this function the Lords of Appeal and the Lord Chancellor alone participate. That work continues, untouched by the Act of 1911.

Legislative Power. As regards ordinary legislation, public and private, the House of Lords was coordinate with the Commons and had as full a right of initiative and amendment and rejection. In fact, however, few bills were introduced in the Lords, since the political center of gravity had shifted to the Cabinet rooted in the Commons. No arrangement existed to break deadlocks. The important question is: How did the House of Lords use its legislative power, and upon what theories did it proceed? The Act of 1911 curtailed this power.

Financial Power. As regards the financial power, by 1614 the Lords had admitted the exclusive right of the Commons to *initiate* money bills. In 1671 the Commons successfully challenged and denied the right of the Lords to reduce taxes. The convention that the Crown asks for supplies came to mean that the Cabinet alone, and not ordinary members, could increase expenditures or taxation. The general convention that money bills could not be amended by the Lords, but only be accepted or rejected "without diminution or alteration," was obeyed until the budget of 1909 (as will be seen later) though with some slight deviations regarding customs duties, upon which occasions the Commons saved their privilege by introducing a new bill incorporating the Lords' amendment.

The power to *reject* a money bill was used once, in 1860. The Paper Duties Bill repealed the relevant tax in order to make newspapers more cheaply available to the public. The Lords threw it out, after having enacted a property tax and stamp duties to provide the lost revenues. The majority of the Commons was furious, contending that the Lords ought not to use a power of rejection, thought to have been lost by desuetude, in a democratic age.

The Act of 1911 virtually abolished the power of the Lords either to amend or reject a money bill.

Executive Power. The Lords had and still has the

power to ask questions of the Government and a full right to debate its policies. It had and still has an equal power with the Commons to approve or disapprove of statutory instruments and in addresses to remove judges.

In the course of the nineteenth century the Lords lost actual power to control the Executive, but it contributed and still contributes some members to the Cabinet, especially in Conservative Governments (p. 143).

The Spirit of the House of Lords

No elective principle, popular or occupational, characterizes the composition of the House of Lords. Of those whose party membership is admitted, some 475 members belong to the Conservative Party, 60 are Liberals, and about 60 Labour. Beneath their robes of red and ermine, the peers are predominantly an economic interest; about a third are directors (some multiple) of the great industrial firms; a third own very large estates. Many are related by family and business to Conservative M.P.'s.

In earliest centuries, the peers sat in an order of individual precedence; they came to sit according to party, as Government and Opposition.

As Lord Acton said in 1881, writing to Gladstone's daughter, when the Lords opposed the Irish Land Bill (to make tenure less unjust to the tenants):

> But a corporation according to a profound saying has neither body to kick nor soul to save. The principle of self-interest is sure to tell upon it. The House of Lords feels a stronger duty towards its eldest sons than towards the masses of ignorant, vulgar, and greedy people. Therefore, except under very perceptible pressure, it always resists measures aimed at doing good to the poor. It has almost always been in the wrong —sometimes from prejudice and fear and miscalculation, still oftener from instinct and self-preservation.

II. THE HANDWRITING ON THE WALL

In the nineteenth and twentieth centuries the House of Lords knew increasingly that it lived on sufferance. But it claimed to save the people from their own elected parliamentary representatives, by revising, amending, and rejecting bills sent up by the Commons, until time had made clear that the people really desired the laws. It claimed it had forced the representative Commons to be really representative. The Lords conceded its eighteenth-century superiority. Some did so out of regard for the public welfare; others out of the last cry of reason; others sought to justify, and maintain, a remnant of power but were compelled to use the representative argument ultimately quite fatal to it.

During the nineteenth century the House of Lords had a large reserve of strength founded upon its social position and upon the widespread popular belief that there was something really virtuous in hereditary aristocracy and titles. "We need a highly refined reason to regard as an ordinary man the Grand Turk, in his superb seraglio, surrounded with forty thousand Janissaries," says Pascal. Estates, money, society, intimacy with the Court, commissions in the Army and the Navy, conspicuous and brilliant position at home and abroad, fine clothes, beautiful women and thoroughbred horses, the consciousness of ancient authority, the conceit of family and a strong, if narrow, love of "country"—all these contributed to strength of purpose and safety from a direct and doctrinaire assault by Commons and people. Moreover, mass democracy was young.

Almost every Liberal measure was amended or rejected, while Conservative measures that most accorded with its interest-begotten prejudices received usually a safe passage. The landlords' position in regard to tenants' improvements was defended; religious and political equality was denied; the universities were kept closed to Dissenters; Army privileges were maintained; counsel for poor prisoners was refused; Ireland was maltreated; municipal improvement was thwarted; parliamentary reform (bribery and ballot laws) were rejected or mutilated; humane measures (such as the Deceased Wife's Sister Bill) were held up for years; the first Employer's Liability Bill was decisively rejected. The House of Lords bolstered the Church of England at the expense of Nonconformist ratepayers, and then in the years 1906 to 1914, it well nigh stultified the great

Liberal Party majority by defeating the Education Bill and the Licensing Bill, the Scottish Land Bill, and the Plural Voting Bill of 1912. The methods adopted were ingenious: principles were destroyed individually, without disclosure of the true motives that caused their destruction. It was pretended that bills had come up to the Lords too late in the session for due deliberation. So many impossible amendments were moved that the purpose and efficacy of legislation were frustrated (forcing a compromise).

Nineteenth-century Attempts at Reform

The leaders of the House of Lords, however, had already seen by the middle of the nineteenth century that such tactics must end in self-destruction unless the Lords could improve the justification of its claims. Proposals for reform began to be made by the Lords themselves, tending to deny the sole claim of inheritance to govern and admitting the validity of the representative principle.

The first of these came in 1869, when Lord Russell's Bill provided that the Crown should be authorized to create peers for life only, but with the maximum total of twenty-eight and not more than four in any one year, and that these life peers be taken from any of six given categories, namely: (1) Scotch and Irish nonrepresentative peers; (2) persons who had been members of the House of Commons for ten years; (3) officers in the Army and Navy; (4) judges of England, Scotland, or Ireland, and certain other high legal officials; (5) men distinguished in literature, science, and art; and (6) persons who had served the Crown with distinction for not less than five years. This timid proposition was defeated because of its revolutionary implications of principle, 106 to 76.

Several other attempts at reform were made by Earl Roseberry and Lord Salisbury between 1874 and 1888, and another was attempted in 1907, a year after the advent of a very strong Liberal Government that put the writing on the wall for the Lords.

The Struggle of 1910

Only under the pressure of attack or imminent threat did the peers propose their own reform. Too late! For they attempted in the twentieth century of mass democracy to use their power of forcing a Government to take its measures to the country, especially the Finance Act of 1909. The situation is highly instructive. A Liberal Government had been returned in a landslide election in 1906, after twenty years of mainly Conservative Governments. The election returned 397 Liberals, 57 Labour, 83 Irish Nationalists (bent on Home Rule), and only 157 Conservatives. The changes in social and class relationships of the two Houses is especially well demonstrated by the Labour membership, the first spurt of the newly formed Labour Party (p. 61). They and the Irish were anxious to vote with the Liberals each for their causes, as well as liberal measures. Social reforms were overdue, and the Conservatives were swamped by the people's votes. Among the many important reforms introduced were old-age pensions, increased provision for the schools, an employment service system; other social pensions and a national health insurance system and further regulation of the liquor traffic were prepared. This required financing. The budget of 1909, sloganized as the "People's Budget," was designed to raise the money and to reduce the crass economic inequalities by fiscal means. It accentuated the difference of tax on earned as against unearned income, very steeply graduated the tax on the higher incomes, increased steeply the tax on inheritances, established a tax on mineral royalties, and laid a tax on the unearned increment of land establishing a national valuation of land for this purpose. The Lords were provoked in defense of estates and fortunes. By a vote of 350 to 75, it rejected the bill. This was a very large proportion of its then total membership of 554—usually absent, and therefore called "backwoodsmen." Thereby it employed a power that had never been used since the modern budget system had developed: a direct challenge to the authority of the Cabinet.

In the midst of universal political passions not experienced for decades, the Commons dissolved and a general election took place in January 1910, the Government returning with a big majority, though a depleted one. The bill was reintroduced and the Lords yielded to the popular mandate.

The Commons proceeded to the next logical step: the Parliament Bill of 1910. All-party conferences attempted to produce an agreed scheme. It was impossible.[4] The Government dissolved, and a fresh election took place in December 1910, the main issue being reform of the House of Lords. The balance of power in the Commons was unchanged. The intentions of the Government were carried, but accepted by the Lords only after the declaration that the King had consented to the creation of sufficient peers to overcome obstruction (p. 50 and p. 53). Various maneuvers followed, resulting in some queer cross-voting, but by 131 to 114 the Parliament Bill was passed.

The Parliament Act of 1911 and Its Effects

The Act [5] was declared to be only a stage toward a more fundamental reform and confined itself to immediate tasks. (1) It took away financial powers from the Lords, by providing that money bills, after passage by the House, must be sent up to the Lords at least one month before the end of the session, and if not passed without amendment within the month shall become an Act of Parliament with the royal assent and without the consent of the Lords. Money bills are defined, but not in such detail as to avoid conceivable conflict, and the Speaker of the Commons is the ultimate authority for the certification that a public bill is a money bill.[6] Broadly, the Lords had lost all powers over taxation and appropriations for expenditure.

(2) As regards other public bills, the absolute veto power of the Lords was converted into a suspensive veto of the uttermost limit of two years: a bill passed three times in three successive sessions, two years having elapsed between the Second Reading on the first occasion and the Third Reading of the last occasion, passes for the royal assent without acceptance by the Lords. This was the extreme power of the Lords—to hold up a

---

[4] The Constitutional Conference of 1910 numbered eight members including the Prime Minister (Asquith). It broke up without reaching an agreement.

[5] Parliament Act of 1911, 1 and 2 Geo. V. Ch. 13.

[6] The definition focuses on the hitherto normal budgetary provision—the expenditure and ways and means. A serious situation would arise if an attempt were made to enact socialist measures via the form of money bills.

bill for such a time. Within this time, it could amend as it liked—with the possible pain of having amendments rejected if the Commons could hold out for the two years and find the time for repassage as required by the Act.

Consequences 1911–1949. Whenever Conservatives were in office, the Lords merely amended details, except when electoral forces compelled those same Governments to undertake social reforms. With Liberal or Labour Governments, the Lords used their power above merely verbal amendments, so that these Governments were forced into the impossible task of finding time to go through the legislative mills thrice over. Hence, the Lords exacted concessions whenever the Government could not wait two years and more. The Lords were virtually supporters of the Conservative Opposition and worked hand in glove with it; and as Lloyd George declared: "The Lords would not be the watchdog of the constitution but the Conservative leader's poodle."

Only the Home Rule Bill of 1912 was forced through by the procedure under the Parliament Act. From 1919 to 1949 the House of Lords continued to show kindness to its favorite social groups of the nineteenth century and, in addition, fought increases in taxation generally, supported ordinary against administrative jurisdiction, preferred individual to governmental or municipal enterprise. It obstructed State economic activity, public libraries, housing, public education, and allotment-holding, the trade unions, and improvement of the condition of agricultural laborers. In 1931 it rejected the raising of the age of free education, killing in four hours the bill that had taken three months' work in the Commons. In 1933, against a Conservative Government, it reinserted whipping of juvenile delinquents that had been abolished by a bill. In 1930 it once again killed a bill against plural voting (p. 69) and rejected official restriction of the use of motor cars on election day (p. 85).

III. THE REFORM OF 1949

Moral Position and the Future

Normally, only eighty or ninety peers participate in divisions of the House of Lords, which are rarer than divisions in the Commons. But when the defeat of a progressive measure is desired, the Lords can bring up the big battalions ("the Back-woodsmen").

Then why does the House of Lords still exist? For several reasons. (1) A second chamber, any second chamber, has some utility where legislation is complicated and time and many minds are needed to secure the soundness of its substance and the excellence of its drafting. (2) Next, the House of Lords is still a forum of debate on the administrative activity of the Government, and lack of time in the Commons gives the other House some opportunity of useful service. (3) Again, the House of Lords contains a number of able legislators and administrators whose ability serves to weaken the full force of arguments against its existence. They are helpful in the passage of private bills. (4) Further, no non-Conservative government has yet come into existence with a strong-enough majority to abolish the House of Lords (including the Labour Government of 1945). (5) Finally, though the House of Lords does not issue from election, its opinion nevertheless coincides with that of some millions of Conservative people. It defends what they are glad to see defended. Yet there are Conservatives who see the need for reform. Some demand the strengthening of the power of the House of Lords, but that would certainly invite its abolition. Others seek to alter its composition, so that in the future it will be able to justify its power by popular elements. It is this House by sheer inertia, or none at all by abolition, because every one of fourteen plans suggested since 1911 is impracticable.

The Bryce Conference on the Reform of the Second Chamber in 1918 undertook a most careful, scientific inquiry. It proposed powers of revision of some substance for the second chamber. They were too substantial for the political liberals and too flimsy for conservatives. The method of composition was to be by indirect election through newly created regional colleges for this special purpose. The Lords would be composed of 327 members only, serving twelve-year terms. Of these, 81 were to be selected from the hereditary peers by a committee of both Houses of Parliament, and the remaining 246 were to be elected by thirteen regional bodies composed of the M.P.'s from these regions. This was very cumbersome; and too unrepresentative for progressive politicians and not aristocratic enough for conservatives.

But no Conservative Government seriously attempted reform of the Lords: for who knows where rebuilding once begun will end?

Reform by the Labour Government

In 1934 the Labour Party, having suffered badly at the hands of the Lords when it was a minority Government in 1929–1931, adopted the following resolution:

> A Labour Government meeting with sabotage from the House of Lords would take immediate steps to overcome it, and will in any event, take steps during its term of office to pass legislation abolishing the House of Lords as a legislative chamber.
>
> If the Party obtained a mandate from the people in support of its policy, the Labour Government would regard it as its duty to carry that policy through by necessary legislation and administrative action. The Party will therefore at the next General Election, make it clear to the country that in placing its policy before the people, it was also asking for a mandate to deal forthwith with any attempt by the House of Lords to defeat the will of the people by rejecting, mutilating or delaying measures which formed an essential part of a program approved by the electorate.

The Labour Party obtained its majority in 1945. So long as the Lords were not obstructive, the Labour Government, with a full program of social security and socialization measures and only five years to carry through the immensely elaborate legislation, did not intend to waste its time on a frontal constitutional battle against the Lords. Should a conflict on policy stir the people, and the government be obstructed, then it would be twice-armed.

The Iron and Steel Bill. The Labour Government's program called for an Iron and Steel Bill, nationalizing the industry. Its introduction raised the question of the powers of the Lords in a crucial form, for the Cabinet realized that the amendments the Lords would move would force it to suffer the two-year delay and the three submissions to the Commons required by the Parliament Act. The Government had several choices. It could use up the time of an already-overcrowded House and reread the bill, destroying its chance of passing other social-welfare laws. The Iron and Steel Bill and other bills ran into scores of complicated clauses, all open to amendment. Or it could take a different course. It could go to the King for appointment of enough peers to outvote the 600 or more potential last-ditchers in the Lords. Precedent would seem to require that the King not make these peers, unless after a general election in which the Government was returned with a clear mandate. But this would have blocked the party's program for a time. Or the Government could dissolve Parliament on the very issue of the abolition of the House of Lords—and again be frustrated in its immediate program until after the election.

It is much wiser to accept some amendments. But this means also that the House of Lords runs risks. The House of Lords dares not offer any amendment that is too clearly the object of its own special interests; such would lead to its mending or ending. Indeed, as we shall see immediately, this sequence occurred in 1947.

In August 1947 the Commons gave the Government strong powers to deal with the economic crisis. The Commons adjourned for the summer, and thus the opportunity of immediate debate on the Government's rules and orders regarding the crisis was postponed. But the House of Lords decided (most unusually!) that it would sit in September, by itself if necessary, to debate the Government's measures. It could, using its own intact rights, have actually vetoed the rules and orders. This raised important constitutional issues and was a direct challenge to the Government. It may have been in the party interests of the Conservatives. The Government was incensed.

Hence, on November 10, 1947, after a rather abrupt announcement in the King's Speech in October, the Labour Government introduced the Parliament Bill of 1947 to amend the Act of 1911. It left the statute intact, with one exception: in future, ordinary legislation would go through the procedure prescribed by it, but instead of a bill to which the House of Lords objected having to pass the Commons in each of three successive sessions, *only two* would be necessary; and instead of a two-year span between the Second Reading in the first of such sessions and the final passage of the bill, *only one year* would need to elapse. In other words the suspensive veto of the House of Lords was reduced to one year, while the House of Commons' stage was made easier.

The project caused the fiercest storm in British political life for many years—and indeed it seemed to come out of the blue.

All that the Labour Party had said in its election platform of 1945, *Let's Face the Future,* was, "We give clear warning that we will tolerate no obstructionism to the people's will by the House of Lords."

The Labour spokesmen supported their policy of reducing the veto power of the Lords by strong arguments. The will of the people, as expressed in the general election must prevail, especially as the Government had a mandate for its economic reforms and even for overcoming the House of Lords. The Government could not tolerate a delay or a disruption of its program as its various measures of economic and social planning required orderly sequence and contributed to each other's effectiveness. Delay was dangerous. Democracy ought not to tolerate a second chamber that steadily favored only one party, the Conservative. British government even looked as though it were unicameral whenever the Conservatives were in office because of the Lords' support. It was monstrous that a body not responsible to the electorate should have substantial power. Progressive governments were doomed to an effective life of only three years, so to speak, through the suspensory veto, while Conservatives could count on five years of uninhibited power. If a revising chamber was valuable, and, indeed, necessary, it still could not be entrusted to a body of hereditary legislators. All democratic countries that had bicameral systems did not compose their upper chamber on the basis of heredity. In any case, a twelve-month delay was ample time for revision and amendment.

The Conservatives argued that the Lords had done valuable revising work. If a Government complained about the loss of time by delay, this could be answered by the fact that the Parliament Act already allowed a Government to resume the attained stages of a bill, if it was returned by the election following the end of a Parliament or dissolution. If the voters wanted it, that Government would lose no time. Some check on Government and Commons was necessary to make sure that the "real," "permanent," "persistent" will of the nation supported the legislation, which might be introduced by a very small majority, or even a Government with less than 50 percent of the electorate.

The Conservatives particularly stressed the point that the power of contemporary government is so pervasive of all phases of social life that checks, delay, revision, ought to be interposed before such power is utilized—another facet of the arguments in favor of the separation of powers (p. 56). It was necessary to set up a check upon a government that might be overdominated by pressure groups inside or outside it, in the interests of the majority. Mr. Churchill heavily emphasized that, in the last two years of a Government's term, the authority of the mandate to it peters out, whatever the will 'of the electorate at its beginning. Some body ought to have the power to challenge a Government and compel it to seek a reconsidered mandate in an election. For such purposes a mere twelve-month delaying power was insufficient.

It was agreed on all sides that the Lords, or rather a second chamber, could substantially assist the governing of the nation. (1) It could revise, and offer second thoughts, in the sense already explained. (2) It could accelerate business since the Government could introduce bills of secondary importance there and so debate and amend them as to save the time of the Commons when they passed to that House. (3) It could be a national forum of debate by "elder" statesmen, giving public attention to issues that the Commons was too busy to consider at leisure. (4) It even offered the Government the opportunity of proposing amendments after long debate had convinced them of their value.

These arguments clashed *a propos* of the new Parliament Bill. Labour's resentment at the way the hereditary principle had been utilized was put by Mr. Attlee, Prime Minister, at the end of the Second Reading debate: "[Mr. Churchill] regarded that brake [on the engine of the popular will] as essential, and the engine had to go to be repaired every five years for a Conservative Government and every two years when a Labour Government was in power."

In this *impasse,* the Conservative and Liberal Parties pleaded that a "constitutional" change ought to go to an all-party round-table negotiation, as customary (p. 53). The Labour Government, *of course,* was responsive. An interparty conference, under the chairmanship of the Prime Minister (Mr. Attlee), was convened early in 1948 to consider the relationship of the composition of a second chamber to its powers. Though in good faith, inventive, and arduous, the discussions were in vain. The Conservatives wanted an eighteen-month delaying period, the Labour spokesmen, only twelve months. The Conference proposed the following general principles:

The Second Chamber should be complementary to and not a rival to the Lower House, and reform should be based on a modification of the House of Lords' existing constitution as opposed to establishment of a Second Chamber of a completely new type based on some system of election.

The revised constitution should secure that a permanent majority is not assured for any one party.

The present right to attend and vote based solely on heredity should not by itself constitute a qualification for admission.

Members should be styled "Lords of Parliament" and would be appointed on grounds of personal distinction or public service. They might be drawn either from hereditary peers or from commoners who would be created life peers.

Women should be capable of being appointed Lords of Parliament in the same way as men.

But this was dependent, still, on agreement as to powers—which was not attained! There was a Conservative suggestion that a twelve-month delay after the last passage of the bill in the Commons would be acceptable; but Labour held out for only nine months.

The Conference failed. The Government proceeded with its bill of reform, against the will of the Lords. On June 9, 1948, the Lords rejected the bill by 177 to 81. It was introduced for the second time on September 20, 1948, and was carried through under the Parliament Act of 1911.[7]

It is, indeed, difficult to redevise a second chamber in a unitary State, like Great Britain, where a federal-cum-state representation does not require it. Heredity in a democratic age is hardly tenable. Most peers still insist that heredity gives them at least the right to elect any newly devised second chamber from among the whole body of hereditary peers. If, on the other hand, the *elective* principle alone is substituted, it raises the fear that a body with authority (like the French Senate) will rival that of the popular chamber, confuse the electorate as to who is responsible for results, and disrupt the legislative programs and deflect the day-by-day conduct of government. If, on the other hand, the Government of the day were allowed to

---

[7] This was the third time the provisions of the Act of 1911 had been used. Previously, the Act of 1914 to grant Home Rule to Ireland and the act to disestablish the Church in Wales had been so enacted. They were suspended by Parliament when World War I started. But, also, a bill on temperance (liquor) in Scotland was carried, when the Lords and Commons arrived at a compromise under threat of the use of the Parliament Act; and the advent of World War I caused the Liberal Government to abandon its bill on Plural Voting (see p. 197).

appoint life peers, then, in the long run, the second chamber would be biased to the advantage of one party or the other. During 1953 a Labour Party caucus refused to discuss the future of the House of Lords with the Conservative leadership, afraid to condone any attempt to increase the powers of the Lords. Earlier, Viscount Simon (formerly Sir John, Home Secretary, Chancellor of the Exchequer, and Lord Chancellor) had revived the idea of creating an annual contingent of ten life peers. Others had proposed to penalize peers who failed to attend sessions regularly.

It still ambles along in its dignified, almost academic pace, for two or three hours a day, compared with Commons' eight; using its Committee of the Whole, rather than Standing Committees, supplemented by its sessional or select committees, and giving attention to textual revision through a Standing Committee for this purpose.

The question still perplexes: British political parties, mores, public opinion, and parliamentary procedure and manners are beautifully designed in combination to make policy cautiously, to protect the minority, yet in an age of vast legislative and administrative State activity, error is possible —what powers should a second chamber have, how should it be composed? Given the difficulty of finding an answer, is not the present House of Lords, with its powers reduced as in 1949, destined to survive for many decades?

The Civil Service: Administrative Features

I will not cease from Mental Fight,
Nor shall my Sword sleep in my hand,
Till we have built Jerusalem,
In England's green and pleasant Land.
—William Blake on *Milton*

Service of Administrators in Modern Government

Government is the process by which the interests and ideals, the values and impulses, of some people get transformed into the authorized and enforceable behavior of others. The process falls, conceptually, into two phases, the first being politics and the second, administration. The political phase, which we have fully described in previous chapters, is concerned with mobilizing the good will and loyalty of the people, in order that it may be possible to win legislative power and make statutes. These statutes embody the ideals and interests in an authoritative set of commands. Some of these commands are coercive, such as raising taxes. Others are benevolent: they give benefits to stated individuals or groups in the community, for example, pensions or hydroelectric rights. Whether of the former or of the latter kind, they find themselves embodied in legislation. A statute is a stage between the wish and vote to have things done and their being done. It is a blueprint of authority.

In order to come to life in the enforceable behavior of the community, the second phase of government must be instituted, namely, administration. Administrators concern themselves with the enforcement of orders or the provision of benefits,

taking the blueprint of the statute as their plan of action, the permission or command to them to act, the range of discretion allowed them by the law.

It would be possible for legislators, in our imagination at least, to administer or execute the law as well as to make it. But, considering the range of functions adopted by the modern State, their number would have to be increased by hundreds of thousands, even millions. Nor would it satisfy the technical conditions of good administration to have all the persons who are to perform executive duties elected. For what is needed in this subservient status is a corps of men and women educated and selected on the basis of their technical ability to perform the specific task in question, serving under conditions of independence and impartiality and, usually, in a career for life.

Administrators serve modern government in several ways. (1) They interpret the statutes and other expressions of the legislatures' will, for example, the continuing criticism and policy-molding process that goes on. (2) They set down the interpretations in clear and formal rules and regulations. (3) They appoint the diverse types of officials, each equipped with the technical education to perform the foregoing task and to use the various instruments of administration: apparatus, territorial organization, equipment, procedures, rewards and punishments of many different kinds to get the rules carried out. (4) They give advice to their political superiors, who are engaged in the further creation or amendment of policy, and they report on the course, strengths, and weaknesses of their administration of the law in past periods.

The politician may be temporary. Also, his pre-occupation with winning authority from those who have it in their power to give it—the elec-torate and his colleagues and rivals—sets the state of mind in which he approaches the problem of government. From the standpoint of any of the thousands of special abilities needed in the public service, the politician is an amateur. He has to learn enough about those jobs that most interest him, to get a control over them. He is not to perform them himself, but so inspire enough fear and encouragement to get them done by others.

From this order of ideas flows the merit of the professional or career official. It is devotion to success in a technical nature. The timing, the duration of his planning, the technical nature of his considerations are first. For the politician, the first concern is to get his principles and values accepted by the public.

If the politician is the bearer of the final law of numbers, of the majority, to decide what shall be done, then the career administrator is the bearer of the law of science and reflection as an ingredient of the final will. The problem is to inject into the sovereign power of numbers that other kind of sovereignty—what nature has made of things and men. The two should meld, values being modi-fied by science, and science being the servant of values.

In all this, staffing or personnel is crucial. Abil-ity and character determine all the nonhuman elements that enter into administration; how to departmentalize; how to classify; what apparatus and equipment must be used; what kinds of offi-cials are needed; what procedures and the purpose requires and what forms and rules will satisfy them; how to divide out the central and local re-sponsibilities territorially and how to solve the problem of the area of operations involved in every administrative decision.

The character, ability, spiritual standards, and ethical principles of the career officials is vital to the conduct of the administration and therefore the government in the widest sense of the modern State.

I. THE BRITISH CIVIL SERVICE

This constitutes the professional, career personnel of British Government. It is outstandingly excel-lent in quality, lauded as a model in all the demo-cratic countries of the world, and copied in some or other particular by them. Graham Wallas [1] somewhere called it "Britain's real Second Cham-ber"!

The term includes all the central government staffs of the Government but does not include, as in Europe, teachers in the public educational sys-tem or police or the judges and officials of the law courts. Furthermore, the term *Civil Service* was first introduced in modern statecraft by the British. It derived from the eighteenth-century East India Company, which distinguished between its *mili-tary* and *civil* service. The term corresponds to what in the United States is the *career* or *merit* service, which is rather wider than *Civil Service* in the U.S. terminology, which is used to denote the career servants who are classified under Civil Service rules.

The Numbers and Importance of The Civil Service

The size of the British Civil Service has increased with the expansion of the activities of the State. Without offering any special explanation of the forces requiring more civil servants, we enumerate them in a table at various dates.

1797	16,267
1821	27,000
1851	39,147
1891	79,241
1911	72,352
1922	317,721
1926	296,398*
1936	350,293
1947	717,000
1955 (April 1st)	635,663†

* Irish servants excluded.
† In 1955 their salaries amounted to some £350,000,000

It began with mainly customs and post office workers, and now covers practically every human

[1] Author of the famous work, *Human Nature in Politics*

Growth of the British Civil Service *
Persons Employed in Ministries and Departments

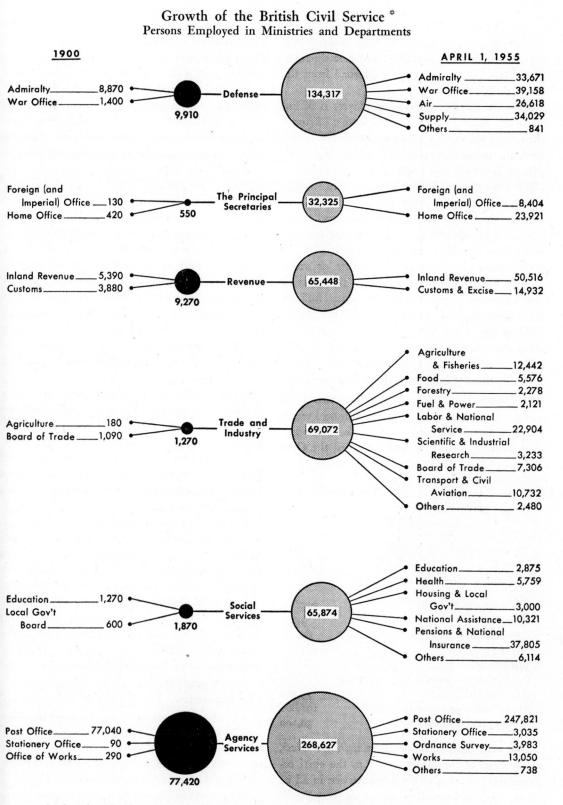

1900

APRIL 1, 1955

Admiralty _____ 8,870
War Office _____ 1,400

9,910

Defense

134,317

Admiralty _____ 33,671
War Office _____ 39,158
Air _____ 26,618
Supply _____ 34,029
Others _____ 841

Foreign (and
Imperial) Office ___ 130
Home Office _____ 420

550

The Principal
Secretaries

32,325

Foreign (and
Imperial) Office ___ 8,404
Home Office _____ 23,921

Inland Revenue _____ 5,390
Customs _____ 3,880

9,270

Revenue

65,448

Inland Revenue _____ 50,516
Customs & Excise _____ 14,932

Agriculture _____ 180
Board of Trade _____ 1,090

1,270

Trade and
Industry

69,072

Agriculture
& Fisheries _____ 12,442
Food _____ 5,576
Forestry _____ 2,278
Fuel & Power _____ 2,121
Labor & National
Service _____ 22,904
Scientific & Industrial
Research _____ 3,233
Board of Trade _____ 7,306
Transport & Civil
Aviation _____ 10,732
Others _____ 2,480

Education _____ 1,270
Local Gov't
Board _____ 600

1,870

Social
Services

65,874

Education _____ 2,875
Health _____ 5,759
Housing & Local
Gov't _____ 3,000
National Assistance _____ 10,321
Pensions & National
Insurance _____ 37,805
Others _____ 6,114

Post Office _____ 77,040
Stationery Office _____ 90
Office of Works _____ 290

77,420

Agency
Services

268,627

Post Office _____ 247,821
Stationery Office _____ 3,035
Ordnance Survey _____ 3,983
Works _____ 13,050
Others _____ 738

* Adapted, with acknowledgment, from *The Economist,* London, May 30, 1953.
† Stationery Office is the Government printing and publications office.

activity in some regard and to some much differentiated degree. The expansion and diversification of the last half-century may be gleaned from the figure on p. 203.

First, the mere numbers of employees is of importance: their budget is considerable. Second, their total number expresses a proportion of the working population who are withdrawn from private enterprise and who work under the peculiar conditions of State activity, to which reference will be made presently.

More significant, they direct, command, regulate, enforce other people's activities *at strategic and urgent points,* those regarded as so crucial that they have become governed by statutes, so much anxiety have they given to society. The titles of the Government departments at once indicate these areas of social concern. Hence, the watchdogs of the public have been invested with specially important duties, on this criterion.

The Various Classes of the Civil Service

The British Civil Service falls into two large groups: the industrial and the nonindustrial workers. It is intended only to analyze the nonindustrial workers, what may well be called the Civil Service proper. The numbers (1955) are:

Industrial	635,000
Nonindustrial	435,000
Total	1,070,000

The nonindustrial Civil Service workers (April 1954) fall into the following Treasury classifications (with a then total of 635,600):

Administrative	595,800
Executive	3,500
Clerical and subclerical	69,300
Typing	194,300
Inspectorate	28,100
Professional, scientific, and technical	3,000
Ancillary technical	75,700
Minor and manipulative	191,800
Messengers, porters, etc.	30,100

Our main interest is the *Administrative Class,* at the head of the career service as the chief organizer of the work of the whole service in all its classes, and the immediate adviser of the political heads of the departments.

Departmental Pyramid. Each department of the Government may be represented as a pyramid. At the very apex is the Minister and his Junior Minister, the political Undersecretary, or the Minister of State, and sometimes more than one of the Juniors. This is the political apex. On the average in numbers it is almost infinitesimal. For if there are, let us say, thirty departments and 630,000 officials, then each has on the average some 21,000 employees. (The figure [p. 203] shows the varying numbers per department.) The rest of the pyramid is composed of all the career officials, from the highest of all, the Permanent Secretary of the Department, down through the various grades of the classes we have mentioned, to the messengers, porters, and charwomen. The percentage present of the Administrative Class varies from department to department. Thus, of Assistant Secretaries and above, there were in 1950 in the Treasury 8 percent of all such officials; in the Ministry of Labor, 9.6 percent; in the Customs and Excise, the smallest percentage, 1.4.

Yet the pyramid is not the simple one of a descending hierarchy through the classes we have mentioned, because the classification puts the Inspectorate, the Professional, Scientific, and Technical, the Auxiliary Technical, and the Minor and Manipulative at the bottom. Even the last group (mainly post office workers) does not justify this treatment, if their position is to be understood.

The other groups, the Inspectorate and the Professional, etc., occupy a different position in the hierarchy of the departments than the classes under the Administrative. Their functions are far different in nature, for example, from clerical or typing; their whole purpose is different; and their education and selection and authority are different. Therefore the pyramid needs to be split under the Administrative Class, into two columns, as roughly represented in an "average" department. (See figure top of next page.)

The Inspectorate. The services of inspection are of tremendous importance in all modern states that have a large area, important local authorities services, and the need to connect the two by personal representatives, for communication and exact knowledge of what is going on.

The inspectors are special to each of some thirty departments (excluding income tax inspectors who

Civil Service Hierarchy of a Department

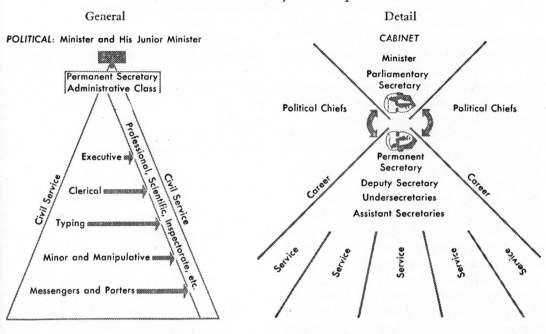

General   Detail

POLITICAL: Minister and His Junior Minister

Permanent Secretary
Administrative Class

Executive

Clerical

Typing

Minor and Manipulative

Messengers and Porters

Professional, Scientific, Inspectorate, etc.

Civil Service   *Civil Service*

CABINET

Minister

Parliamentary Secretary

Political Chiefs   Political Chiefs

Permanent Secretary

Deputy Secretary

Undersecretaries

Assistant Secretaries

Career   *Career*

Service   *Service*   *Service*   *Service*   *Service*

are in the Executive Class of the Civil Service). Their duty is to inspect and report to the department, not to execute the work inspected. Some inspect apparatus, for example, gas meters; some, factories, dockyards, explosives plant, and so on. Some inspect accidents and aeronautical establishments and aeroplanes. They clearly differ in their function from the other general classes of officials we have mentioned.

The inspectors employed by the Ministry of Education, Ministry of Health, Planning Ministry of Town and Country, Ministry of Transport, and the Home Office are of peculiar importance.

Numbering over 700 in a total of about 3000 inspectors, they are the personal links between the central government at Whitehall and the local governing authorities. They inspect the schools, the local government services in general, the roads administration of the local authorities, and the police services. Planning and principles and orders come from Whitehall, backed by substantial grants-in-aid; the former are the will of Parliament, the latter the assistance it provides to get its will carried out. A lesser self-government and local discretion and execution resides in the local authorities. This matter is pursued further in Chapter 13.

The Professional, Scientific and Technical Officials and Their Auxiliary Groups. These number about 115,000, of which about 75,000 are in the higher, thinking and planning group, and the rest in the more order-executing group. They comprise many professions—medicine, law, the various special fields in the natural sciences (for example, experts on poisons, entomologists, soil chemists), engineering, accountancy, economics, architecture, statistics, etc. The Administrative Class increased from 2100 in 1939 to 3500 in 1955 (of which 200 are women);[2] but the Professional, etc., class, with its auxiliaries, increased from roughly 37,000 in 1939 to the number already cited: a fourfold increase compared with the less than twofold one of the Administrative Class. This attests (1) the multifariousness of the British government's close administration of society and (2) the underproportionate increase of "overhead" to executants of policy.

The Professional, etc., groups have highly technical professional qualifications and are recruited by tests set up and administered by the Civil Service Commission. There is hardly a step the Government wishes to take in formulating law or carrying out the details of policy, which does not

[2] Its historic peak was in 1945 at World War II's highest point, 4900.

entail entire dependence on the advice of a scientific expert.

Relationship to the Administrative Class. The important problem is to get scientific and professional advice through to the Minister at the crucial stages of making and administering the law. The United States organizes its departments so that the chief sections of the departments are headed by the so-called "bureau chiefs" or men of equivalent position. These men are the top scientific and professional experts in the department. They *administer* their bureau and are direct advisers of the political head of the department. In the British system, the advice and comments of this group goes to the Minister *indirectly*, because it is first sifted through the Administrative Class, who are its recipients and processors. The British system is founded on the idea that the Minister needs counsel on policy —what to do. Now, since this has as its ingredients the raw professional data of many technical experts, somebody is needed to bring the material together with the focus of the policy problem and present it to the "amateur" Minister. The latter could only be confused by direct technical information from the expert. He has not the time or the education or the state of mind (preoccupied with the pressure of parliamentary duties) to weigh and assimilate the many facts in their raw state. To believe otherwise is to invite chaos and the collapse of the Minister.

Therefore the Administrative Class is on top. Of course, this imposes a severe responsibility on it. It must see that the best experts are chosen; respect their expertness; to be thoroughly briefed by them; leave to them the judgment on strictly technical issues; and consult them when the raw material has been gathered and put into shape in alternative policies for presentation to Ministers. This the Administrative Class understands and seeks to do.

The Professional and Scientific service, however, is restive under this system. They would like to speak directly to the ultimate decider of policy —that is, the Minister. They even propose that the Minister be advised by a mixed board of technicians and administrators and that the Minister make no technical mistake. They are afraid that the Administrative Class official who deals with them may be obtuse or dogmatically blind.

However, their claim cannot be conceded. It can only be grounds for looking rigorously at the education of the Administrative Class and its mores of consultation. For, if this class cannot do the job of assimilation, of integrating scientific advice from various sources, then *a fortiori,* the Minister, an amateur and a bird of passage, could never do it.

Another part of their anxiety is that they are not in the normal hierarchy for advancement to the highest levels of administrative appointment even if they possess high administrative qualities. This legitimate complaint has been given some redress in the recent arrangements made by a Treasury committee which recommended that these men and women be given full consideration when vacancies to be filled by promotion occur.

II. CHIEF CHARACTERISTICS OF THE CIVIL SERVICE

These features characterize the British Civil Service of today, but not all of them can be expatiated on in the following pages.

1. It is without spoils or patronage; recruitment is on proof of competence.
2. Open competition is the general principle of recruitment.
3. The system of recruitment is intermeshed with the general public educational system.
4. There are low age limits to recruitment, as the general rule.
5. Examinations for vacancies are assembled annually.
6. An independent Civil Service Commission defines the qualifications and administers the examinations.
7. The Administrative Class is recruited from the university level of the educational system (Chapter 12).
8. A progressive building of the *esprit de corps* of the Civil Service as a whole is having success.
9. Devices have been established to solve the problems of the subordinate classes of the

service; promotion, and reports on efficiency.

10. Joint and equal staff representative bodies— the Whitley Councils—exist to find answers to general and departmental problems of working conditions and improve efficiency and morale.

11. The problem of political rights of Civil Service and their relationship to Parliament has been given an ingenious, discriminating solution.

12. In recent years special attention has been directed *to training* recruits to the Service.

13. The general character of the Service is marked by honesty, integrity, and devotion to the public service and responsiveness to the will of Parliament and the needs and demands of the Ministers at the head of each department.

14. The political neutrality and anonymity that is essential to its serviceability in a democratic system is highly respected, and has been dealt with already (pp. 171–2).

Assembled Examinations

Examinations for the various vacant posts are assembled for all the vacancies in the various classes: those for the Administrative Class annually, for the other classes, annually or twice a year. The purpose is to assemble all the competitors at one time, for all the jobs to be filled a real competition of some magnitude is offered. The schools keep their eyes emulatingly on the dates; it is an annual event, and so has its own advertising effect.

The Civil Service Commission

The executive authority that establishes the rules of entry into the Civil Service (remembering that it is the Minister in each department who makes the actual appointment, for the preservation of hierarchical discipline) is the Civil Service Commission. Originally their number was three; but the immense increase of its work has raised it to six. They hold office during the pleasure of Her Majesty; are not subordinate or answerable to any Minister; and address their reports to the Queen. They have a kind of quasi-judicial status that gives them freedom from political pressure.

The Commissioners are career administrators and technical experts, not politicians or political appointees. They are appointed by the Prime Minister, advised by the head of the Civil Service— that is, the Permanent Secretary of the Treasury. Their independence is complete because they cannot be removed except by addresses of both Houses of Parliament, and even more by the universal understanding that the public service is not a mass of jobs to benefit political and private friendship but an institution for impartial national service of the highest technical competence.

The powers of the Civil Service Commission are laid down in their most recent form in the Order in Council of 1920:

> (2) The qualifications of all persons proposed to be appointed, whether permanently or temporarily, to any situation or employment in any of Her Majesty's Civil Establishments shall be approved by the Commissioners, and no person shall be so appointed until a certificate of his qualifications has been issued by the Commissioners.

This is linked with the Treasury, which is the supreme authority in Civil Service matters (except examination and certification), thus:

> (5) The Commissioners may, *subject to the approval of the Treasury,* make regulations prescribing the manner in which persons are to be admitted to Her Majesty's Civil Establishments or to any situation or class of situations therein, and the conditions in which the Commissioners may issue certificates of qualifications for the purpose of this order.

The Commission certifies promotions, though it does not set down or administer the principles of promotion, these being within the authority of the departmental Minister as regulated by the Treasury and the recommendations of the Civil Service Whitley Councils (see p. 210).

In respect to its decisions regarding the ascertainment of age, health, character, and ability of candidates, the Commission is subject to judicial appeal on the grounds of the "reasonable" and *bona fide* nature of its actions.

The Commission bears a tremendous burden. From June 1, 1945, to March 1950, it examined 300,000 candidates and certified as successful for posts some 84,000. In addition, it examined 30,000 other candidates for special positions, such as accountants, statisticians, and so on; and furthermore, 16,000 applicants for the scientific Civil Service, with 4000 successful candidates. In the year 1953–54, it examined over 38,000 in open competitions, certifying nearly 6500 for appointment; 11,000 in limited competitions, certifying, 3000; and dealt with nearly 41,000 ordinary and 460 special nominations.

The staff of the Civil Service Commission is about 1000, plus some 700 people on a fee basis who act as examiners and interviewers.

The Treasury

The Treasury (see p. 168) is in the position of master-employe relationship to the Civil Service. Its powers are thus built up. The various statutes that establish the different Ministries permit the Minister to employ such servants as he may determine—with the consent of the Treasury. The budget powers of the Treasury add to its power of establishments.

To implement its responsibilities, the Treasury has had since 1919 an Establishments Branch. It has added functions, since then, of education and training of civil servants. In addition, it set up in 1947 the Organization and Methods Division. Under a Government Organization Committee, with the Permanent Secretary of the Treasury as its chairman and consisting of the Permanent Secretaries of a number of departments, the Treasury guides the work of its own Organization and Methods service and numerous officials throughout the departments, in investigation of departmental organization and methods of work. Its officials keep contact with local government and with business and industry; bring them in as advisers, in order to keep the Government services abreast of the latest developments in the use of machines, rational organization, and better procedures. It will be remembered, also, that the appointment of the head of a department is made by the Prime Minister on the advice of the Permanent Secretary of the Treasury, who has the title of Head of the Civil Service. With all these means, the Treasury has a very pervasive influence throughout every office.

After-entry Training

After thorough examination (Treasury Committee of 1944) of the problem of fitting the entrants to the subordinate classes of the Service, the Treasury set up a scheme of training to be administered by a Director of Education and Training. It is conducted by the training officers appointed in each department. They collaborate with the Whitley Councils. Entrants are inducted into the department's place, its service relationships, its meaning to the community. They are instructed in organization and methods, the problems of confidential relationships, and the discipline, duties, and ethics of the service. Then follows actual training in the job. Those with supervisory abilities are given special training. There is further encouragement for vocational and liberal education outside office hours, and sometimes with leave and the payment of fees. The departments have a program of conferences, lectures, and so on.

The purposes are: to produce more clarity in business; to attune the official to a changing world; to counter routinization, especially the effect of working with machines; to develop for future and more important responsibilities; then to freshen up morale.

Payment

The Treasury uses the principle of "fair relativity" to the nearest comparable outside work. It sometimes advances the principle that it is a model employer. To carry out the principles there are occasional overhauls of the entire system, by means of Royal Commission of Inquiry. One, set up in 1953, reported in November 1955.[3]

[3] See *Report*, Cmd. 9613, 1955, Her Majesty's Stationery Office, London.

The Commission's terms of reference were confined to the desirability of changes in the principles and present rates of pay, hours, overtime, annual leave, and superannuation.

It posited that civil servants should be paid according to the principle of fair comparison with outside work of comparable nature, taking account of differences in other conditions of service. It did not want to take too much of the cream of talent from other professions and enterprises, but it wanted enough. It counseled against the idea that the public service should be in advance of the market, as this would tend to introduce politics into the determination of the rates as well as to skim off too much of the better talents. With this as the primary principle, the next, to

For day-by-day adjustments recourse is had to the Civil Service Arbitration Board. This, in 1936, replaced a similar arrangement started in 1917, when the board was a part of the Industrial Court. It is now autonomous. Cases are dealt with by a tribunal of a chairman appointed by the Minister of Labor, in consultation with the National Whitley Council, and one member each from a panel for the staff side and the Chancellor of the Exchequer. The salaries of classes up to the middle grades of the Service are referrable to the tribunal by either side, Treasury or "groups," not individuals. The procedure has proved on the whole very satisfactory. The interpretation of the awards lies with the Treasury.

Normal retirement is between the ages of sixty and sixty-five; it may be required by the head of the department at sixty, when the efficiency of all officers is reviewed. In "suitable" cases, officers may continue to be employed beyond sixty-five.[4]

---

supplement it, was "internal relativities" of the classes in the Service. This involved difficult problems of fact finding, and the Commission proposed that this should be undertaken by a branch of the Service not connected with the Treasury divisions that are responsible for pay and conditions—then the Whitley Council and other negotiating machinery could act with the facts in mind. For the Higher Civil Service, hitherto not catered to by the Civil Service Arbitration Tribunal, a committee of five persons representing informed opinion ought to exercise a general oversight over its remuneration, to be appointed by the Prime Minister after consultation with that staff.

The Commission recommended a raising of salaries. They may be thus summarized, representatively (compare with present rates in next column):

Administrative Class	
Permanent Secretary	£6,000
Deputy Secretary	4,250
Undersecretary	3,250
Assistant Secretary	2,000–2,600
Principal	1,300–1,850
Senior Executive Officer	1,220–1,450
Executive Officer	340– 950
Clerical Officer	225– 650
Principal Scientific Officer	1,300–1,850
Scientific Officer	575–1,000

These are London rates. In all cases, the staff associations of the various classes (excepting Permanent Secretaries) had asked for rather higher scales than those awarded, though the Commission's recommendations gave substantial increases.

[4] Before April 1952 the general age of retirement was sixty; then the Treasury changed the rules to those stated above. The aim was to "make the best use of manpower," especially in view of the changed age structure of the population.

Pensions are payable at retirement after a certain number of years of service. Pensions are not contributory. The purpose is to support the power of the Treasury to deny pensions for disciplinary purposes. No appeal to the courts is allowed on this.

Some Annual Salaries, November 1, 1954, on London Scale *

Administrative Class

Permanent Secretary (or Undersecretary)	£4,500
Deputy Secretary (or Deputy)	3,250
Undersecretary (or Assistant)	2,600
Assistant Secretary	1,700–2,000
Principal	1,185–1,570
Assistant Principal	492– 885

Executive

Controlling Executive Post	Up to £2,850
Principal Executive Officer	1,700–2,100
Executive Officer	302– 830

Clerical and Clerical Assistant Classes

Higher Clerical Officer	£680– 830
Clerical Officer	192– 595
Clerical Assistant	177– 459

Foreign Service Branch (Branch A)

Ambassadors Grade 3 to Grade 1	£2,850–4,500
Grade 6 Counselor	1,700–2,200
Grade 7 First Secretary	1,185–1,570
Grade 9 Third Secretary	492– 665

Scientific

Controlling Post	Up to £3,250
Chief Scientific Officer	2,500
Principal Scientific Officer (middle rank)	1,185–1,570
Scientific Officer (beginner)	492– 885

* These were the salaries (women received some 20 percent less) that prevailed shortly after the Royal Commission on Salaries began its deliberations in 1953. No account can be taken of various small changes made since then. But in 1955 the classes below the top received a 5-percent increase. Equal pay for women was established in January 1955, to be implemented in seven yearly steps, and affects about 160,000 officials. This consummates a struggle of at least thirty-five years.

Promotions

The promotion of the classes from Executive downward is an important matter in administrative efficiency and in human morale and justice. Since 1920 promotion has been dealt with by a proper system of annual reports by supervising officers and promotion boards headed by the departmental establishment officer. Reports are appealable to the joint representative councils— Whitley Councils they are called—in case of injustice. The attempt is made to get objective evaluation of job elements. The promotion opportunities are published. The National Whitley Council participated in the devising of the system.

Joint Representative Councils

In 1921 the Government established a National Civil Service Whitley Council and Departmental Whitley Councils. They deal with problems of civil servants of the classes and grades up to a salary of £1000. This excludes the Administrative Class. The councils have an equal representation of official and staff sides. The National Council includes three M.P.'s. Its chairman is the Controller of Establishments branch of the Treasury. The staff representatives are appointed by Civil Service representative unions.

The Whitley Councils have these functions: (1) to provide the best means for the utilization of the ideas and experience of the staff; (2) to secure to the staff a greater share in determining and observing their working conditions and the general provisions regarding recruitment, hours, tenure, pay; (3) to encourage further education and training of civil servants; (4) to improve office machinery and organization and to provide opportunities for full consideration of staff suggestions regarding this; (5) consideration and proposal of legislation on the Civil Service, especially in regard to terms of employment.

The authority of the Whitley Councils is advisory but also "operative" upon report to the Cabinet. The Cabinet can—of course—reject the agreements. This gives the official side a strong power, since it has access to the Cabinet by its status. But the Treasury representatives are unlikely to make an agreement that they do not know beforehand will be actually implemented.

The system has been of immense value to the Government and the civil servants. It has assisted in solving practically all the problems of the Civil Service that have arisen since 1920—reclassification; salaries; political rights; further education and training; reconstruction of war and postwar purposes; promotion; discipline; inventions; general morale; in the departments, the vindication of the promotions procedure and fairness in disciplinary cases.

Civil Service Unions, the Right to Strike

The various classes of the Civil Service have their associations—or trade unions—if the word is not shied at. They are necessary, for Parliament is not an overgenerous master, being responsible for economy. The constant existence and pressure of the unions are necessary to get fair play in comparison with all the other organized pressures.

Until 1927 Civil Service unions could affiliate with unions in private enterprise; and those below the Administrative Class were linked with the Trade Union Congress. In that year the Trades Disputes Act, following the general strike of the year before, forbad affiliation, though not the unions themselves. In 1946 the Labour Government secured a law restoring freedom to affiliate, and the unions rejoined. They are more restrained in their attitude than, say, the coal miners or transport and dockworkers, but still participate in the fashioning of the nation's economic and social policy. They say that if the State's principle of pay is that of "fair relationship" to that of the general body of workers and taxpayers, they ought to cooperate in the workers' struggles for better conditions.

The Conservative Party, which is the main opponent of affiliation and friend of nationalism, strongly expressed the fear that at some national crisis the Civil Service unions might be bound to come out on strike in sympathy with the rest. It might weaken national defense; it might reduce the nation's productivity, from which the civil servants derive their "sheltered" and career living. State services need continuity for the maximization of the nation's standard of living.

The right to strike has never been officially forbidden. If a civil servant strikes, however, he has thereby refused to perform his duties. For this the punishments rise from reprimand to dismissal with loss of pension.

The problem of the right to strike by the Civil Service has moved close to that of workers in a highly planned economy in any occupation and especially to that of the workers in nationalized industries. The right is acknowledged for ordinary workers in the highly planned British economy;

workers and their leaders and the statesmen of the trade unions are free to decide how much pressure they can exert for better conditions short of striking, or whether to jeopardize the nicely balanced economy for more pay.

Political Rights

Civil servants have the right to vote in parliamentary and local elections. Their neutrality is safeguarded by the secret ballot. Their influence is not undue, because their number is not overly significant compared with the 35,000,000 actual voters.

However, in the interests of neutrality, the Treasury and the various departments developed rules requiring in political activity a quiet demeanor, forbidding such activity while in official uniform (if any) or during office hours, and prohibiting officials from becoming secretaries of political clubs or associations (which means local party organizations). The student will not forget the statutory limitations, commencing with the Act of Settlement, 1701, prohibiting membership of the Parliament to those holding a place of profit under the Crown—civil servants, in other words.

Civil servants of the lower levels of the Service demand the right of candidature in Parliament and local government. The administrative and technical and professional servants of other types are on the whole so satisfied with their own position in the State and the Service as not to demand the right of parliamentary candidature.

A Treasury committee (with a representation of non-Civil Service and parliamentary citizens) reported in 1925 *against* allowing candidatures for Parliament. If a civil servant wished the latter, then he must resign from the Service. Departments were to continue to use their discretion in permitting candidatures for local government offices that are filled by election; where they involved no crass public damage to the reputation of the Service for impartiality they were allowed. Industrial staffs of the arsenals and dockyards were free to act as they wanted. These recommendations were embodied in an Order in Council of July 1927. Departments having local offices and service connections with local government authorities prohibited their officials from standing as councilors.

The Committee of 1925 made an excellent point:

The constantly extending disposition of Parliament to entrust the exercise of quasi-judicial duties to executive departments without providing any of the established safeguards operative against judicial excess—such as publicity, right of audience to persons affected, statement of reasons for judgment, right of appeal and the like—as well as the sharper alignment of political parties in these days, unite to make the high reputation for impartiality hitherto enjoyed by the public service a more valuable national possession than ever before.

It was not ready to risk the loss of this "existing ethic."

Many civil servants and some political theorists were still dissatisfied. In 1949 the Labour Government submitted the problem of political candidatures to a Treasury committee, once again broadly representative of public personages. It found itself trying to find a compromise between the two conflicting principles.

In a democratic society it is desirable for all citizens to have a voice in the affairs of the State and for as many as possible to play an active part in public life.

The public interest demands the maintenance of political impartiality in the Civil Service and of confidence in that impartiality as an essential part of the structure of Government in this country.

It veered toward the latter principle: "It must be maintained even at the cost of some loss of political liberty by certain of those who elect to enter the Service."

It proposed to draw a line *below* the Administrative, the Professional, Scientific and Technical, the Executive, the Clerical and the Typing grades and, with small exceptions, *above* the Minor and Manipulative, and Industrial Grades (see p. 204). The majority thought that the Post Office *supervisory* minor and manipulative grades should also be above the line; the minority, not.

All *below* the line could stand for Parliament, with one month's special leave for candidature—

without resignation unless elected. If elected, then they should be entitled to reinstatement if they ceased to be members after an absence not exceeding five years, and if they had been civil servants for not less than ten years before their election. Sympathetic treatment should be given to other requests for reinstatement.

Above the line, no parliamentary candidature. *Below the line,* there should be free participation in political activity, though not in office hours or in official premises and limited by the Official Secrets Act. *Above the line,* "reserve" must be maintained in matters political. Participation in local government elections and candidatures is liberalized.

The report calculated that the right to stand for election to Parliament was extended to 666,000 nonindustrial civil servants as compared with some 200,000 to that time—that is, to this number complete political freedom is available, though some require specific permission. The 430,000 industrial staffs had long been politically free.

It is to be noticed, however, that the Administrative, the Professional, the Executive, and the Clerical bulk of the service is restricted in its right of candidature. All have some limitation on their political activities.

These rules were put into operation, with freedom for *all* those below the line, though about one out of ten still needed special permission.

Officials may be members of the House of Lords; if so, the Treasury rule is that they may attend sittings when their duties permit but may not take part in debates or voting until they retire or resign.

The restrictions are a price the British think it wise to pay for the anonymity and impartiality that are vital to the serviceability of officials to any party that, by winning an election, comes into possession of the sovereignty of the State. Indeed, so liberal a newspaper as the *Manchester Guardian* thought the nation dangerously touched the point where political neutrality was jeopardized.

Loyalty

Until the post-World War II period, the problem of the loyalty of civil servants in Britain was couched in terms of whether a presumed conservatively biased Civil Service would faithfully assist or sabotage a Labour Government. Since that time the world has learned that the problem is whether men and women with Communist sympathies, or private ideas of how the world should be governed, will sabotage the efforts, economic and defensive, of any "bourgeois" government, Labour, Liberal, or Conservative. The disclosures of the Royal Commission (Canada) investigating the Soviet Government's espionage network in Canada in 1947, especially relating to the atomic bomb, prompted the British Government to take action. Intemperate accusations against some civil servants by an M.P. were disproved, and the Commons resented the slander, taking always a very, very strong view defensive of civil liberties, continued robustly to the present time.

The Government's knowledge of Communist treachery impelled Secret Service investigations. Some scientists were dismissed. The National Whitley Council in March 1947 took up the issue in a grave spirit. It required that officials not be dismissed just because they belonged to a suspected political party, and required disclosure to the accused of an adverse judgment. The Government (Labour) would not deny out-and-out its right to dismiss because of party association, but it did accept the request for disclosure and promise a proper procedure. The House of Commons *insisted* on fair procedure and was also adverse to dismissal merely for party membership. It demanded that a particular dangerous linkage and activity in that membership must be shown to affect the State's *security* and to be specifically demonstrated. The Government had views of this kind also and organized its protective system accordingly. It refused, however, to accept the Civil Service unions' and general trade unions' demands that one of their representatives should be a member of the advisory board to the Government that was to be established.

It is not "loyalty" in general but specific *security* that is the criterion of action by the Government. Positions "vital to the security of the state" is the phrasing that controls the decision of the Minister and the advice of the advisory board. The board is appointed by the Government; it consists of three persons, former civil servants. On being charged, the civil servant is suspended; he may appeal to the board, in writing or personal presence. He can bring character witnesses but no counsel. The board reports its finding of facts to the Minister in whose department the official is employed. It is the Minister who has responsibility for evaluating the facts. The accused person may then appeal to the Minister by letter. The board has evidence gathered by MI-5, the Secret Service, some members of whom have already been officially admonished for overzealous and unwise procedure. Parliament is on the watch against the Government. Under the influence of the staff side of the Whitley Council, suspended officials have been awarded full pay until the final determination of their case.

The Government then tries to find other non-vulnerable work for those found untrustworthy in specific jobs. If possible, they are given transfers. If none can be found for specialist qualifications, the official may choose to resign or may be dismissed.

The Government is especially on the alert about suspects in the headquarters staffs of the Armed Service departments and the Ministry of Supply.

It is tragic that men must lose their jobs, or be transferred from those to which they are used, to others they may not like. But in the age of the Hydrogen Bomb in a densely crowded island, whose vulnerability to attack has been boasted about by the Soviet Foreign Secretary, Mr. Molotov, a defense is necessary against the insidious and incessant operations of Communist and Fascist agents. The British have not thrown a miasma of suspicion over the loyalty of the whole of its body of officials, as in the United States, or made political football out of the menace to the nation or the individual fate of officials, but they have limited the instrument of action to the precise trouble to be eradicated—and *they* are far nearer to the line of atomic fire.

From February 1948 to March 1954 the Government has been compelled to dismiss twenty-four and transfer seventy-two; of the former, seventeen were industrial staffs; of the latter, eighteen were nonindustrial. The National Whitley Council has kept watch over fair procedures, and the Civil Service unions have assisted the accused during the period between accusation and through the advisory board. Since the revelations of the escape of Maclean and Burgess, Foreign office officials in May 1951, to the U.S.S.R. for whom they spied, all Foreign Service officials and recruits are carefully screened and techniques of vigilance are being reviewed.

III. ADMINISTRATIVE LAW AND ADJUDICATION

As we now undertake discussion of the general status and quality of the nearly two thirds of a million civil servants, and later (Chapter 13) of the greater number of local government officials and locally elected councils, this is an appropriate point at which to describe the problem that has come to be known as "administrative law" or the "judicial functions" of administrative departments. It can be coupled with the problem of redress of the public against officials who act illegally in the course of their duties.

Quasi-judicial Powers

Since about 1900 (in some cases earlier) the various Government departments have come to be vested with final judgment of disputes about the application of the law committed to their charge. Persons and local authorities and corporations who claim that the law is wrongly interpreted, or that improper and legally impermissible procedures have been used to carry out the purposes of the law, may appeal to the Minister. In the nineteenth century such disagreements would be carried by the aggrieved person or authority to the ordinary law courts. This ability to go to the ordinary courts and get judgment is part of what Dicey summed up as the Rule of Law, namely, that officials were liable to action before the ordinary courts of the land (p. 4 and p. 260).

Yet an enormous amount of legislation has been passed. It needs interpretation and execution. The departmental officials are experts and must make workable administration. The tendency has been to give them the final say in interpretation, because they have such a skilled knowledge of the issues involved and are concerned every day with the practical problems of the relationship between the State and the persons and companies (commerce, industry) and local authorities to be regulated.

Thus the Minister of Health, the Ministry of Housing and Local Government, the National Health Insurance Commissioner, the Ministries of Education and Trade and Transport, and the Railway Rates Tribunal (that sets freight and passenger rates and conditions of service, etc.), and other administrative departments are quasi-administrative, quasi-judicial authorities. Their power is especially conspicuous, say, if as, in the case of landlord and the community and the department there may be in dispute a departmental order for the demolition of slum property or one on freight rates, and so on. The issues are fought between the nation and the person or locality; or between local authorities; or between bodies of consumers or producers and the former. They affect the person and property of the subject. The fact that an appeal is allowed from the department's first decision makes the departmental procedure look like a judicial event.

Very strong criticism has been made of this procedure, especially by eminent lawyers; one Lord Chief Justice Hewart having entitled his work on the subject, *The New Despotism* (1929).

What Are the Issues Involved? If the ordinary courts were seized with these issues there would have to be very many more of them, and valuable time would be lost, because there are so many of such decisions to be taken day after day. On the other hand, the administrative departments are expertly aware of the issues of fact involved, and it is difficult for the ordinary judges trained in the ordinary ways of the law to acquire such knowledge by the method of a legal contest between the parties before them in court.

In a famous case (*Arlidge v. Local Government Board*) it was declared by a Lord Chancellor (Haldane) that all that the courts ought to do was to secure that the department should act "judicially"—that is, without bias—and give the parties adequate opportunity of presenting the case. He said hearings were not necessary, and that the Minister had the right to act through his officials.

This is the crux of the matter. The ordinary judges, by their legal training, and their experience

as contending lawyers while they are with the Bar, and then on the Bench, are imbued with the idea of impartiality as between the contenders. They have no personal interest in the result, such as that of more pay or promotion if they award the result one way or the other. The problem is for the departments actually to set up procedure and to choose such persons for these quasi-judicial functions as will produce independent judicial-mindedness. Yet the function is not *legal*.

The criticisms of on-going development became so severe that there was set up in 1932 a Committee on Minister's Powers to weigh the gravity of the charges and to propose remedial procedures.[5]

The Committee (with eminent practicing lawyers among its members) rejected the charge of *despotism*. But it did believe that the interest of a Minister in getting things done successfully and fairly quickly required safeguards on ordinary administrative decisions. These should be of two kinds: a proper procedure in the departments, and the reversal of the trend of some of the statutes denying a right of final appeal to the ordinary courts, especially as final word, the High Court. As for procedure, it is not well enough known to potential clients, and cross-examination is not allowed in many such tribunals.

The observation of the Committee on the subject of a Minister's interest, and therefore, by implication, of a civil servant's interest, in success, prestige, rewards, and promotion, perhaps regardless of the punctilios of just procedures, may be quoted and pondered:

> The minister should be regarded as having an interest in the cause. . . . It is unfair to impose on a practical administrator the duty of adjudication in any matter in which it could fairly be argued that his impartiality would be inverse ration to his strength and ability as a minister. An easy-going and cynical minister sceptical of the value of his department, would find it rather easier to apply a judicial mind to purely judicial problems connected with a departments administration than a minister whose head and heart were in his work.

[5] On this subject, see W. A. Robson, C. K. Allen, Keir and Lawson, and Schwartz for cases.

The Committee therefore proposed that quasi-judicial powers be assigned to departments only as an exception. If they were assigned, they ought to go to a ministerial tribunal rather than a single Minister. They proposed that the last word on *the law* should, so far as possible, be left to appeal to the High Court.

Yet perhaps the judiciary could learn to adjudicate such issues, especially with some technical expert assistance.

The British fear of this so-called "administrative law" was fanned by Dicey in his classic *The Law of the Constitution.* He mistook the special administrative law courts of France and Germany of his time (the 1870's) as bodies applying arbitrary and despotic law that safeguarded the officials at the expense of liberty and property of the individuals. Dicey was gravely mistaken (see pp. 518–520 and p. 629). Administrative law can mean a body of law created by the officials as they interpret the statutes committed to their administration by Parliament (pp. 132–134). It may mean, as Dicey meant, the law courts dealing with cases between State authorities or the State and the person.

In Britain the former exists, subject as we have seen to scrutiny by Parliament and to challenge in the courts on the grounds that it may be *ultra vires* (beyond the power) of the enabling statute.

The latter kind of administrative law (adjudication) has been growing, because the courts are overcrowded and administratively unskilled. So long as the departments are careful to choose good administrators of judicial temperament for the quasi-judicial positions in the department, and to institute procedures of due notice, local inquiry, the right of the aggrieved person to a knowledge of the inspector's or inquiring official's report, and to represent his side of the case, much will have been done to give peace of mind against the possibility of arbitrary administration. This has to a considerable extent been done. (It has a serious relationship to the kind of education and recruitment of the Administrative Class [Chapter 12].)

If then, in grave cases, an appeal lies to the High Court, on the interpretation of the law, then the fact that the statute has said that the Minister's decision has the force ascribed to it as though it had actually been enacted in the statute, is no unreasonable deprivation of liberty unless it is meant that Parliament's use of its authority is unreasonable at all times.

Claims against the Crown

Since 1947, by the Crown Proceedings Act, the Government as such may be sued for a tort committed by an official. Until that time the King "could not be sued in the King's court"—from time immemorial. Until 1947 an official wrong, like a tort or breach of contract, could only be remedied by a claim against the official *personally* or by petition of right and an act of grace on the part of the Attorney General. As for the first remedy, it hardly met the case if the damage was large; officials are not wealthy. As for the second, it allowed the public authorities the advantage.

To overcome this unfairness, in an age when the State was increasing its economic functions, some departments (for example, the Post Office and the Office of Works) and some government corporations were by statute expressly made liable to suit and damages for breach of contract.

The argument for the general immunity of the Crown from suit was that officials ought not to be impeded in their actions for the public weal under their statutory or prerogative responsibilities. It was also urged that the *personal* liability of officials kept them to a stringent responsibility.

The Government did, in fact, do its best to stand behind the official and give relief to the subject. It is, however, better to have a remedy by law than by good grace. In France and Germany, the lands of "administrative law," the Government has long been suable. The United States followed British practice until 1946, then made a change similar to that of 1947 in Britain.

It should be remembered that the central departments, the Ministers, and the local authorities (*created legal corporations*) did take liability on a master-servant relationship for the acts of their officials. They were liable to court actions to order them to act or desist (p. 45).

In 1947 the new statute, engendered and passed by a Labour Government, laid down the rules thus. The citizen may bring actions in the courts against the Crown in the same way as against a fellow citizen. This is to enforce claims in matter of tort and contract. The State will admit liability for the wrong committed by its servants as any citizen or corporation does. It answers for negligence, wrongful acts, default of action by its servants or agents, for breaches of the common law or statutory duties—for example, under the factory acts—by those it employs, and for breaches of duty arising from the occupation of premises or land. There are some minor exceptions.

The major exception applies to time of war. The prerogative to administer the Armed Forces (in time of peace as well as war), to administer aliens, harbors, patents, to suppress disorder and maintain peace—these remain not liable to suit. Nor is the State bound to produce documents that it believes the interests of the public require it to keep secret. The responsibility for this decision is the parliamentary one.

The Attorney General said of this legislation in the House of Commons:

> It will very greatly fortify that principle of equality for all before the law which all of us are agreed is a fundamental part of the British way of life, and not the less so when we are progressing toward the socialist state. . . .

IV. NO SPOILS, NO PATRONAGE

The British Civil Service is marked by a high degree of honesty and integrity. The number of those who are compelled to leave the service for dishonorable reasons is negligible, not because the supervisors are lax but (available figures show a dismissal for inefficiency and misconduct of one per 800) because the officials are people of good character. The checks and balances of the administrative apparatus serve to inhibit the propensities of those who are evilly inclined. The Treasury issues regulations regarding such matters as money-lending, backing horses, and so on that might get people into trouble.

There is no graft in the political system; there can be no favoritism in the Civil Service itself and its relationship with the community. Once in a blue moon some minor scandal occurs; it is condignly dealt with at once, without political parti-

san motives or investigations, and the example is set.

On one such occasion in the interwar years, when three misdemeanors known to this writer were austerely judged and long careers at once ended, a Civil Service Board of Inquiry[6] laid down the following rule for civil servants (circulated to all servants by the Treasury):

> The first duty of a civil servant is to give all his undivided allegiance to the state at all times and on all occasions when the state has a claim upon his services. With his private activities the state is in general not concerned, so long as his conduct therein is not such as to bring discredit upon the service of which he is a member. But to say that he is not to subordinate his duty to his private interests, nor to make use of his official position to further those interests, is to say no more than that he must behave with common honesty. The service exacts from itself a higher standard, because it recognises that the state is entitled to demand that its servants shall not only be honest in fact, but beyond the reach of suspicion of dishonesty. It was laid down by one of His Majesty's Judges in a case some few years ago that it was not merely of some importance but of fundamental importance that in a Court of Law justice should not only be done but should manifestly and undoubtedly be seen to be done; which we take to mean that public confidence in the administration of justice would be shaken if the least suspicion, however ill-founded, were allowed to arise that the course of legal proceedings could in any way be influenced by improper motives. We apply without hesitation an analogous rule to other branches of the public service. A civil servant is not to subordinate his duty to his private interests; but neither is he to put himself in a position where his duty and his interests conflict. He is not to make use of his official position to further those interests; but neither is he so to order his private affairs as to allow the suspicion to arise that a trust has been abused or a confidence betrayed. These obligations are, we do not doubt, universally recognised throughout the whole of the service; if it were otherwise, its public credit would be diminished and its usefulness to the state impaired. . . .

We content ourselves with laying down these

[6] Cmd. 3037, 1928, p. 21.

general principles, which we do not seek to elaborate into any detailed code, if only for the reason that their application must necessarily vary according to the position, the Department and the work of the civil servant concerned. Practical rules for the guidance of social conduct depend also as much upon the instinct and perception of the individual as upon cast-iron formulae; and the surest guide will, we hope, always be found in the nice and jealous honour of civil servants themselves. The public expects from them a standard of integrity and conduct not only inflexible but fastidious, and has not been disappointed in the past. We are confident that we are expressing the view of the Service when we say that the public have a right to expect that standard, and that it is the duty of the Service to see that the expectation is fulfilled.

All the central government jobs are covered by the Civil Service; no jobs of a civil service nature are outside it. No appointments can be made without previous certification by the commission. The status of *civil servant* is governed by the Superannuation Act of 1867, which laid it down that unless an official were certificated by the Commission, he was not entitled to a pension on retirement.

The statement that there are no spoils or patronage applies equally to the subordinate jobs, as well as what the U.S. public service calls "policy-making" positions—that is, the highest jobs of all in the departmental career hierarchy. This was not always so.

The Transition from Patronage to Open Competition

In the period 1789–1828, the American federal public service was more competent, more economical, more service-virtuous than the British public service of that time, arousing the envious admiration of British liberal and radical observers. For the British system cost much more in proportion to population and work done. It was encrusted by medieval "Gothic" [7] structures and methods of work. It was subject entirely to patronage, the procurement and gift of governmental adminis-

[7] See S. E. Finer, *Public Administration*, London, Spring 1953.

trative and clerical posts. It was still regarded by the eighteenth-century-minded politicians as the reward for the large amounts of money that it cost them personally to buy themselves votes to get into Parliament. Family relationship was the principal qualification for appointment; political association close to it. Indolence, profligacy, incompetence were not regarded, normally, as disqualifications. The aristocracy then rendered an important ultimate service to the affairs of the State (incomparably more so than the French or the Russian nobility, and more humanely and democratically than the public-spirited Prussian nobility), yet their morals were sensuous and lax compared with the republican dignity and fastidiousness of Washington, Jefferson, and John Quincy Adams.

The various Ministries were regarded almost as private, not public, establishments, because it was a current notion that the King lived off "his own income," and many of the functions performed by the public officials were paid for not by salaries but by fees. The administration was sacrificed to politics.

Whereas the American public service reached its zenith of competence and integrity about the year 1800, to decline then rapidly under the pressure of partisan politics (Andrew Jackson) not to arise again to general decency until the 1880's and beyond (by the example of Britain!), the British system was in the years of American decline raised to the beginnings of its present high quality in the years 1780–1830, and above all in the period of 1848–1852. For in those earlier years, British officialdom came under the pruning knife of the House of Commons, especially urged on by Edmund Burke in his battle for "economical reform" of the Service. It was his purpose mainly to cut down the number of officeholders in order to hamstring the hold of George III over Parliament by taking away the vote-getting power of his Ministers, who used the promise of jobs and sinecures to win elections or to avoid contests. The fewer the jobs, the weaker the King, and the stronger the House of Commons. The bill and the speech on Economical Reform of Burke in 1780 marks an epoch.

Furthermore, *under the influence of Adam Smith and of Bentham's utilitarianism* (pp. 32ff.), sharp and logical like Nicolai Lenin's (p. 000) though in a democratic cause, the Treasury was modernized and departments given one-man management (a single Minister) in place of the old-fashioned multiple boards. The surveying and regulating power of the Treasury was by 1828 well established as the result of several innovations. The Treasury acquired control over the estimates of the other departments of the Government, because the many new items of expenditure in a new age were not any longer masked under the Civil List of the King but appeared on the open, public items of the Consolidated Fund or the annual estimates.

Ministerial government gave way to party government and a deep connection with the classes and masses. No longer could it be held that, as in the eighteenth century, offices were freeholds, private property, and so undisturbable. The notion was founded that life-careerdom contributed to sound, rationally determined administrative efficiency. The older notion of private property in offices had prevented the full force of rotation of office from occurring; this down to the 1830's and the beginning of Civil Service reform. The new notion was yet to be worked out.

The new industrial and commercial upper middle classes were prone, by their aspirations for social recognition in a landed, aristocratic society and their rational attention to business and accountancy, to fight for practical improvement of the nation's working institutions. Let into British politics by the Reform Bill of 1832, their puritanical tradition (by severe and honest works, by the successful practice of a calling to get to the Kingdom of Heaven) leavened administrative reform.

The spirit of progress and utilitarianism was applied to the older universities, which were reawakened in the 1830's and 1840's, including the provision of scholarships *to be competed for by examination*. Thomas Babington Macaulay, the historian, and one of the three progenitors of the reform of the Civil Service in the next decade, was a Fellow of Trinity, Oxford, by such a competitive examination.

Machine and engineering triumphs were in men's minds: if renovation could come in industry by rational methods, why not civil government? Colonial administration was being reformed after the scandals in India and the loss of American Colonies and the revolts in Canada in 1839. In 1835 English municipal government and the Poor Law administration were radically reformed on principles of utility. Bentham's chief disciple, Edwin Chadwick, was the animator of these reforms.[8] Police administration in London, and then in Ireland and in the rest of England, came about by 1839.

Though the dates are later than the events just mentioned, the year 1848 and 1851–1854 were of forcing and causative importance in the Civil Service reform that came subsequently. As for 1848, there was no revolution in England for democratic constitutional reforms as on the Continent in that year (p. 306), but in the Chartist Movement (p. 61 and p. 68) there was a strong political mass movement for further democratization. And surges of excitement caused by events in Europe quickened the feeling in the British upper class that something must be done to make government better respond to popular aspirations.

Some improvements had been proposed and carried through on a minor scale in the Treasury beginning in 1840 through the influence and efforts of Charles E. Trevelyan. He entered the Treasury at the age of thirty-three as Assistant Secretary to the Treasury—not as a politician but as a career administrator. He himself had been educated at Haileybury and then had served in the East India Company's Bengal civil service, rising rapidly to high administrative posts, especially in finance and public education. He had exposed bribery and corruption, when only twenty-one years of age, in the Indian civil service and in the highest places! Gifted with a remarkable analytical and severe intellect and insistence on good works, he made perfect administration his single-minded purpose. His connection with Indian administration is important, for Parliament began competitive examinations for its Indian civil service in 1813, extended it in 1833. In 1834 Trevelyan married Macaulay's sister; the two men were already connected by an interest in Indian affairs.

---

[8] On this, see the magnificent history and biography by S. E. Finer, *Edwin Chadwick*, London, 1952.

As for 1851–1854, the full shame of administrative incompetence demonstrated in the Crimean War shocked *all* England, since thousands of common soldiers suffered and died and starved and froze as a consequence. The story of Florence Nightingale [9] was not one of reform in nursing alone: it involved the War Office—and more. (See p. 739 for the effect of Crimean defeat on Czarist reforms!)

The Treasury undertook an extensive inquiry into its own establishments following November 1848. The inquiry was conducted by Trevelyan and Sir Stafford Northcote, a Whig statesman, then thirty years of age but already having served as private secretary to W. E. Gladstone, later Prime Minister, and as legal assistant to the Board of Trade (equivalent to the U.S. Department of Commerce). The reforms were pressed by the more liberal and radical elements among the Whigs, men like Gladstone; but poo-poohed by the Palmerston type.

Their inquiry concerned the establishments and business of the Treasury "in order that such changes may be made as may be required to secure the highest practicable degree of efficiency, combined with careful attention to economy, etc." The report was published in November 1853 after long investigations into the various departments. Opinions and comments by some forty distinguished persons in public life and education (among them Jowett, Master of Balliol, Oxford; John Stuart Mill; Edwin Chadwick) were appended. Mill called the recommendations "one of the greatest improvements in public affairs ever proposed by a government."

On May 21, 1855, an Order in Council (an *Executive* act) began the application of the method of competition proposed (but still limited, as explained, p. 220) with the establishment of the Civil Service Commission, "to conduct examinations of young men proposed to be appointed to any of the junior situations in the Civil Establishments." It would certify their ability and charac-

ter; then the Minister of each department would appoint.

The reform was long scorned by the Tory and high Whig class. But it fairly soon took root, and more and more of the "junior" positions were scheduled for the Civil Service Commission's action. In 1870 an Order in Council completed the work of 1855, instituting "open" competition. The Superannuation Act of 1859 supplied a sanction to the Order in Council of 1855 by denying a pension to any who had not been certified into the Civil Service by the Commission.

To Serve a Changing Cabinet

It was realized that under the cabinet system there would be (there was) a fairly rapid rotation of Cabinets—that is, a mobile and changing Executive. All the more reason, therefore, for instituting a *permanent* career service. Indeed, it was in this connection that the term *Civil Service* became transformed into the *permanent Civil Service*. The senior civil servant of the time said:

> Their [the civil servants] humble and useful duty . . . is by becoming depositaries of departmental traditions . . . to keep the current business in due course, to warn Ministers of the consequences of irregular proceedings into which they might inadvertently fall; to aid in preparing subjects for legislation; and possibly to assist by their suggestions the development of a course of reform.

Almost the opening words of the Northcote-Trevelyan report were these:

> The great and increasing accumulation of public business, and the consequent pressure upon the Government, need only be alluded to; and the inconveniences which are inseparable from the frequent changes which take place in the responsible administration are matter of sufficient notoriety. It may safely be asserted that, as matters now stand, the Government of the country could not be carried on without the aid of an efficient body of permanent officers, occupying a position duly subordinate to that of the Ministers who are directly responsible to the Crown and to Parliament, yet possessing sufficient independence, character, ability, and experience to be able to advise, assist, and to

[9] The student is warmly recommended the biography by C. Woodham-Smith, *Florence Nightingale*, London, 1951. It is beautifully written, and reveals the men and methods then in operation in British administration. See also her *The Reason Why*, London, 1953, on the War Office during the Crimean War.

some extent, influence, those who are from time to time set over them.

By 1848 almost all the departments, and especially the larger ones, had already set up some rules for determining the comparative ability of the candidates recommended to them by politicians and friends. But the reformers had a high standard, indeed, and were looking to the needs of the future. Further, the aristocratic and near-aristocratic Ministers could not forget that, though patronage prevailed, the interests of *their nation* must be set on high and not be debauched by incompetent and slothful sons and relations, especially, let us say, in the Foreign Office.

Patronage was a serious trouble to politicians. This was a more serious complaint of Ministers and of Prime Ministers, who, being First Lord of the Treasury, had to be bothered for hours each day by patronage questions. They were glad to be rid of it.

Some argued that "open competition" would open the public service to "low people" and "clever scamps." They argued that the public service required men of high character and cultivation, not least to assure confidence in the keeping of secrets. This, of course, can be a merely aristocratic and class argument. Yet there is merit in it, generally. The problem of character, emerging in part from a good family upbringing, is of vital interest to the conduct of public affairs.

On the other hand, there were people who rejoiced at the idea of open competition. It was frankly argued by some that this would give the decided advantage to the *upper* classes! Lord John Russell, under whose prime ministership the immediate reform movement had been put under way, said:

I have a strong impression that the aristocracy of this country are even superior in natural gifts, on the average to the mass: but it is plain that with their acquired advantages, their *insensible* education, irrespective of book-learning, they have an immense superiority.

The *democratization* of the service was a less explicit force than this.

Value to Education. This introduces one other theme: the educational leaders at Oxford and Cambridge and some of the great public schools welcomed the reforms as offering an honorable object of ambition to the younger generation in the service of its country's affairs, a profession to be entered by way of the universities. Indeed, the argument was so strongly stressed as to dismay some politicians, whose first purpose was the Service, not the interests of schoolmasters. In the long run it did lead to the universities being democratized.

The method of the Order in Council was used to introduce the reforms in order to maintain the royal prerogative in the Executive branch of the Government and to retain its effect on morale. It was pointed out that constant opportunities for debate would in any case arise on the annual estimates for the new office of Civil Service commissioners.

Limited, not open, competition began in 1855. The Civil Service either (1) applied merely qualifying standards, unless the departments applied for competition; or (2) arranged a competition with at least three candidates per job. Few requested this; the Treasury did. It was an improvement. The Civil Service Commission itself introduced open competition for its own staff.

Yet a decisive breach had been made with the old patronage system. Queen Victoria was not pleased. She feared the Civil Service would be filled by "low people without breeding or the feelings of the gentlemen."

An exception was allowed (and it has its administrative importance) for professional officers of mature age.

The Order in Council of 1870 completed the arrangements of 1855.

1870: Open Competition

(1) *The test of open competition* was made obligatory throughout the Service, with small exceptions. (2) In the case of professional officials, the Commission could dispense with the examination at its discretion but had to be satisfied about the nature of the qualifications. (3) The Treasury was given special authority over departmental organization. Above all, it had the power of approval of the rules for testing of candidates as proposed by the Commission and the departments,

the times at which examinations should be held, the number of vacancies, and the grouping of situations to be competed for.

Since 1870 Royal Commissions of Inquiry have reviewed the work of the Civil Service and made further recommendations about its numbers, classification, education, salaries, morale, and other matters concerning its serviceability and the duties of the State toward it as master to worker. These occurred in 1875, 1884–1890, 1910–1914, 1918, 1929, and another is in progress.[10]

Thus, patronage and spoils have been swept away in the British Civil Service, from top to bottom, for the junior positions are obtained by open competitive examination while the senior ones are arrived at by promotion.

Brains and Character

The eternal problem was faced: What qualities ought a high official to have, what is the best education for these, general or specialist?

The reformers desired not to unhinge the university student from his normal course of general education. They would examine him in that, and on the principle that it was the best test of the mind that he should be examined not in *many* subjects, let alone administratively slanted ones, but in the *depth* of knowledge and critical grip over it, *Non multa, sed multum.*

The combination of intellectual with character testing can be seen from the arguments advanced by Macaulay in debates in the House of Commons on Indian civil service reform. On June 23, 1853, he had said:

It seems to me that there never was a fact proved by a larger mass of evidence, or more unvaried experience than this: that men who distinguish themselves in their youth above their contemporaries almost always keep to the end of their lives the start which they have gained.

He did not very much care what studies they undertook—the Cherokee or Iroquois languages no less than the European classics—so long as the studies were deep.

10 *Royal Commission on the Civil Service,* established 1953; already published is *Introductory Factual Memorandum* on the Civil Service, 1954, Her Majesty's Stationery Office, 1954. It is chiefly concerned with salaries.

The competition was among people of roughly the same age, for this would reveal strength of *mind, thinking capacity.* For the reformers looked not for the special service that a new entrant could render in his department the day after he joined it; they tried to choose minds that would develop with increasing and varied responsibilities as they remained in the Service, leading in time to the highest responsibilities, unforeseeable at the beginning of the career. Yet it surely was predictable that eventually they would not need the technical knowledge the official might possess when he first entered.

The question of *promotion* was thus indirectly involved; and the reformers emphasized the importance of proper attention to this in the departments.

Macaulay led the reformers in a further development of his educational theme: the connection between intellectual prowess and character.

Men who have been engaged, up to one and two and twenty, in studies which have no immediate connection with the business of any profession, and the effect of which is merely to open, to invigorate, and to enrich the mind, will generally be found, in the business of every profession, superior to men who have, at eighteen or nineteen, devoted themselves to the special studies of their calling. Indeed, early superiority in literature and science generally indicates the existence of some qualities which are securities against vice—industry, self-denial, a taste for pleasures not sensual, a laudable desire to obtain the approbation of friends and relations. We, therefore, think that the intellectual test about to be established will be found in practice to be also the best moral test that can be devised.

This passage is a most incisive expression of the English character in the public service and of its educational ideals. It also raises, but does not dispose altogether of, the problem of moral character, efficiency-character, in the public service, and the devices by which it may be discovered before the entrant has been inducted into office.

It would have been possible to operate on the rule that all candidates receiving a certain number of marks are qualified to enter the Service. The British method is the alternative, the competitive method. Those who head the list receive the appointments. This is an automatic safeguard, as Macaulay pointed out, against claims made by disgruntled candidates that they are good enough to be admitted. It can be shown by the lists that they may be good but that others are better. Furthermore, the competitive system is a spur to doing better than others.

As the Civil Service has developed in numbers and the intricacy of its operations, it has become more complexly classified, as the groupings given on an earlier page (p. 202) indicate. There has always been a conscious endeavor to fit the entrance stages to the products of the educational system at some point natural to the system itself. Then there is the least strain on the schools to warp their teaching curriculum to the special needs of the Service. There is the least incentive to "cramming" or "coaching" schools outside the normal public educational facilities. Some cramming occurs but the British arrangement has minimized their need.

The ages of entry then are as follows:

The Administrative Class: between the ages of $20\frac{1}{2}$ and 24 for the lowest—that is, the "assistant principal" grade; or, for those already in the Service in any level, between the ages of 21 and 28.

The Executive Class: ages $17\frac{1}{2}$ to 19, at the academic level of the general certificate of education; or among university graduates of $20\frac{1}{2}$ to 24; or among those who have recently completed their national service or come from the regular Armed Forces; or competitions limited to the clerical grades of service at the age limits of 21 to 28; or promotion by departmental selection from among clerical class civil servants over the age of 28. The percentage contribution of the various ways of selection in 1952 was this: young people, 16.1; university graduates, 1.1; ex-national servicemen, 2.3; ex-regulars, 3.5; limited competition, 11.5; promotion, 65.5.

Clerical Class: This falls into clerical and sub-clerical officers. Their methods of entry and the percentage that each method contributes to the whole is: *open competition:* young people, 16 to 18, 37.5; ex-national servicemen, 4.5; ex-regulars, 6.4; limited competition among the Minor and Manipulative grades already employed (25 to 35), 58.8; promotion, 35.8.

The Ministry of Education cares primarily that the mind of the student is cultivated first and foremost according to educational science itself.

Why Get Them Young?

The age limits are low. The deliberate intention is to recruit young people and to obtain older entrants only by way of exception and where some special need arises for an expert experienced outside the service. In the first place, if reliance is placed on competition, then it must be between competitors of roughly the same age. It is also desired to receive them from the schools. But here is a principle of even greater importance. The Civil Service needs to get young men when they can be educated in the principles that the State must employ in carrying out its peculiar functions. Its ethic is different from business. It *must* be scrupulously honest; it must treat its clients equally, without discrimination; it must follow the letter and the spirit of the law; it must keep official secrecy; and, in certain functions, it must maintain a highly judicial attitude to the parties before it, where administrative decisions partake of the judicial process. It must preserve the conventions of impartial and zealous service to whatever political party fills the public offices and to accept the principle of anonymity.

The British Civil Service may perhaps lose something by the exclusion of people from outside professions and experiences as compared with the United States, which takes many people from outside occupations, but it gains other qualities of great value.

The Civil Service: The Administrative Class

Government is the masterful administration of the unforeseen.
—Robert Bridges, Poet Laureate, father of
Sir Edward Bridges, Permanent Secretary
to the Treasury.

The vices of authority are chiefly four: delays, corruption, roughness, and facility.
—Francis Bacon, *Of Great Place*

Because the highest administrative-political functions are performed by the Administrative Class of the British Civil Service, and its morale and dignity and probity are the acme of the whole Service, attention can be focused, with such spaciousness as the context allows, on this class, except that very cursory observations will be made on the Foreign Service.[1]

The "Brain Trust"

On January 1, 1955, the Administrative Class numbered 3300, of which 3103 were men and 197 women. (The competition was not opened to women until after World War I.)

This is the pivotal and directing group of the whole Civil Service. This is the "brains trust" of British government, directly connected with and auxiliary to the British cabinet system, in the form of advisers and assistants to each Minister, and going down from the Permanent Secretary of each department to the Assistant Principals who are the lowest group of new entrants into the Administrative Class.

Each member of it supplies to the Minister, according to the place he occupies in the departmental level and the specific work he has been given, some part of the ingredients of supreme policy, not merely information. At the head of the department, on the permanent career side, two or three men just in the vicinity of the Minister—the Permanent Secretary, a Deputy Secretary, an Undersecretary—will be practically the political Minister's other and permanent and continuous self. They make the department do the work for which it has been set up and empowered, through to every local, foreign, and colonial nook and cranny. But infinitely more important is that they collect, elaborate, filter, improve, continue, and transmit to Minister after Minister the comprehension of the function of the department in relationship with that of all the other departments in the family of British Government. They are the permanent wise men of the department.

In 1929, when the Civil Service was undergoing reorganization, the representatives of the Administrative Class thus characterized their own role,

[1] Nor can the Colonial Service recruitment be described; nor now, the Indian Civil Service, which rendered such a generous and creative service to the Indian people and trained Indians themselves to take over their nation's responsibilities with competence and honesty.

and the quotation is an instructive expression of the nature of "administration." It said:

> The volume of official work which calls for decisions affecting the public is nowadays such that it is physically impossible for the Minister himself to give the decision except in the most important cases. And further, even when the issue is one which can and must be submitted for the Minister's personal decision, it has to be fairly and fully presented to him so that the material facts and considerations are before him. The need for services of this kind is present in every department which has political head.

There is another common feature of all work which is strictly administrative in character. It is usually described—for instance, by the Reorganization Committee of 1920—by the somewhat general expression "the formation of policy." What is meant is, we think, this. The business of government, if it is to be well done, calls for the steady application of long and wide views to complex problems: for the pursuit, as regards each and every subject-matter, of definite lines of action, mutually consistent, conformed to public opinion and capable of being followed continuously while conditions so permit, and of being readily adjusted when they do not. Almost any administrative decision may be expected to have consequences which will endure or emerge long after the period of office of the Government by which or under whose authority it is taken. It is the peculiar function of the Civil Service, and the special duty of the Administrative Class of that Service, in their day-to-day work to set these wider and more enduring considerations against the exigencies of the moment, in order that the Parliamentary convenience of to-day may not become the Parliamentary embarrassment of to-morrow. This is the primary justification of a permanent administrative service. Vacillation, uncertainty and inconsistency are conspicuous symptoms of bad administration. The formation of policy in this limited sense—subject always to the control of the Minister and to the supreme authority of Parliament—is typical of administrative work in all departments and in relation to all subject-matters whether of greater or of lesser importance.

All administrative work is carried out under statutory authority or, in certain fields, under the prerogative powers of the Crown. To a large extent it consists in the application to particular circumstances of general principles laid down in the statutes, or the administration of financial provision made by Parliament, in pursuance of the powers vested in the Department in that behalf. It involves necessarily the preparation or study of proposals for the alteration of the existing law in the light of changed circumstances, new policies or experience. It is indeed true that proposals for amending legislation within the administrative sphere do, to a large extent, and perhaps mainly, emanate from Departments.

In the course of its attempt to fix fairer rates of pay for the Civil Service, the Royal Commission on the Civil Service, 1953–1955, was faced with the question of the comparability of the work done by the Higher Civil Service and other outside occupations. In its *Report* (Cmd. 9613), the Commission very nicely stated the nature of their work. It said:

> 413. . . . We are mainly concerned, however, to draw attention to a difference between the Civil Service and the outside world, namely that the most significant function, and one mainly confined to the administrative class, has no direct counterpart outside. It is the part the class has to play in the formation and execution of policy on national issues, subject to Ministerial control and direction. The members of the class must be able to work from a very broad Government aim, first to thinking out a policy for the execution of that aim and satisfying Ministers that it correctly interprets the aim, secondly to putting that policy into legislative form and thirdly to its translation into action, frequently on a national basis. The effective discharge of this function requires a distinctive organization and the deployment of officials with qualifications and experience for which no direct comparison can be found outside. These duties have to be carried out in ways compatible with Ministerial control, the accountability of Ministers to Parliament and their accountability, in a less direct but very real sense, to public opinion. The civil service administrator must have a general ability to understand and allow for the interaction of these three elements in the formulation of new Government policy and the execution of established policy. This cannot be de-

veloped without a long period of working closely with and directly for Ministers, who bring to the work their special knowledge of the political side of government. Again the civil service administrator must have the ability to acquire a clear, extensive and detailed knowledge of the government machine and how it works. The machine is unavoidably complex and it must be thoroughly understood if it is to be operated to best advantage. It is mainly in the grades of principal and assistant secretary that opportunities are provided for members of the class to acquire the necessary knowledge and experience. In these grades, and increasingly so in the higher grades responsibility is taken for preparing briefs for Ministers and papers for the Cabinet and for seeing Bills through Parliament. These tasks demand an ability to master and apply complicated techniques and to produce results which in appearance are often deceptively simple. Frequently, the more important the issue, the shorter the notice and the greater the atmosphere of stress and strain under which the work must be carried out.

414. The work of the administrator, therefore, taken as a whole, requires in an unusual degree a capacity to master and to marshal detail in many different fields at different times, to interpret effectively the ideas and policies of others, and to operate a complex administrative machine. It is rare to find these qualities in balanced proportion in one individual but the Civil Service can never afford to be short of them and must therefore provide in its arrangements adequate opportunities for recruiting, training, developing and retaining enough of the exceptional talent required to man effectively its highest ranks. It is, of course, true that not all members of the class carry out the most significant duties of the class all the time. Much of the day-to-day work conveniently falling to it, particularly in the grades of assistant secretary and principal, would probably in the outside world be styled as executive. But this kind of limiting qualification is also found in the work of any group of broadly similar staff even in a finely graded service. It does not detract from the importance of the work of the class as a whole or from the need to ensure an adequate supply of persons capable at any time of discharging the characteristic duties of the class.

1. THE ADMINISTRATIVE CAREER

The general career in each department goes something like this, as described by the Royal Commission on the Civil Service of 1953.

> The permanent secretary is the official head of the department and is responsible to the Minister for all activities of his Department. He will be assisted by 1 or 2 deputy secretaries. Below this there will be from 4 to 12 undersecretaries carrying responsibility for advising Ministers either directly or through their supervisors, on major questions of policy and, as a rule, coordinating very large blocks of administrative work. Each undersecretary will be assisted by a varying number of assistant secretaries in operational control of divisions and carrying responsibility for all day-to-day work done in the division. It is only questions of major policy that should normally be referred above this level. Each assistant secretary is supported by from 2 to 5 or 6 principals or senior executive staff, each of whom will be in charge of a branch of section of a division. He will in his turn be supported by a varying number of executive and clerical staff. *Assistant principals form a training grade.*
>
> In addition to normal administrative work it is from the administrative class that Ministers and senior officials draw their private secretaries, usually of the rank of principal or assistant principal. . . .

It may be added that the assistant principals soon are drawn into active work. The business of the department normally goes down to them, or to a point a little above them, so that they may write minutes in the files sent to them, which then go upward carrying the information or suggestions at each level to the point in the department where the decision is finally made.

Clearly the method of recruitment is of the utmost importance, for twenty years from his entrance the recruit may be exercising advisory functions of epoch-making importance, though the decision is with the Minister and the Cabinet and is corrigible by Parliament.

Until World War I the principal method of recruitment was by examination under open competition. The claims and pressure of the already-established civil servants in the lower classes for an outlet in promotion into the Administrative Class became too strong and justified to resist. Hence opportunities were opened for them for about one fifth of the total (see p. 232); if promotions to higher posts in this class are added, the proportion filled by promotion is now about 1 in 3.[2]

The Administrative Class examination was before World War II uniform for all entrants by examination but since its close is recruited by two methods: Method I and Method II. Full attention is given to the details and principles of Method I in the account that follows, it being the traditional method and applicable to 75 percent of the places.

Method II is disposed of at once. The candidate must have obtained at least second-class honors for a degree at a recognized university. He enters a written examination in English; general and contemporary knowledge of important matters; a second general paper to test reasoning-power intelligence, and capacity to perceive implications and to distinguish between the important and the less important. Those qualifying in this examination go forward to the Civil Service Selection Board for an appraisal of their personal qualities. This stage is undertaken at a two-day session with other young men and women (as described on p. 229) under the watchful eye of experts. It used to be undertaken at a country house over a week end. But, since 1950, only 25 percent of the total entrants by examination (those under Method II) go through this stage. The 75 percent of the entrants by Method I no longer do so. Then, after the Selection Board, a Final Selection Board interviews the candidate on the same basis as for Method I candidates (p. 229). This Final Selection Board lists the competitors in order of merit. The candidate has not been required to take the long and arduous examination in many subjects set for Method I candidates.

2 In February 1952, the Treasury required the establishment in each department of a promotions committee of high members of the department, supplemented by a Civil Service Commissioner's representative (Commissioners or retired or active officials), the latter in order to ensure some uniformity of standards throughout the Service in such promotions and transfers, and to assist in maintaining the standards of quality of this Service-wide class, who may be moved from one department and duty to another.

The Civil Service Commission is watching the Selection Board Method-II entrants for a ten-year experimental period, in order to evaluate the comparative selective value of the two methods.

The quality of the entrant, so far as it is testable by examination, depends upon the education that examination presupposes. Both the subject matter and the character of the educational process are important.

The Subject Matter of Examinations

In the middle of the nineteenth century the examination subjects were in the major fields of study at the older universities: classics, mathematics, moral philosophy, history, and law. This continued for fifty years or more, while classics (Greek and Latin literature, language, philosophy, and history) played the largest part because those who advised the Civil Service Commission had themselves been classical scholars. These subjects are not so remote from administrative affairs as one might misimagine. *Properly taught,* they are not only humane studies but human views of social and political science. Then the history schools bulked large in the actual examinations; and this was an introduction to the evolution of political society and diplomatic activity.

However, new subjects taught at the universities, and the establishment of new universities, caused expansion of the syllabus of the Commission. There are over eighty-four subjects in today's examination list. Each subject carries so many marks: 100 or 200 or 300 or 400. Criticism in recent years has complained of the larger number of marks accorded to classics and history than political science and economics. The Commission is catching up.

Statistics show that from 1925 to 1935 classics supplied 35 per 100 entrants, modern languages, 8; economics and politics, 7; mathematics, 6; and mixed history, languages, and literature, 7. From 1945 to the present no appreciable change was shown. Classics and history together *still* supply well over 50 percent of the Administrative open-competition entrants. We must remember that history as taught in England is heavily fraught with "government"; it involves the whole tradition and ethic of British political evolution, including the character of the leading creative men of state. It is the genetic way of looking at government, culture, and the economy.

Two things might be added to clear up the position of classics studies as the approach to entrance into the Civil Service. The curriculum at the older universities is concerned with two years of the literary side of the Greek and Latin texts. It cannot ignore the philosophies of the great figures of Plato and Aristotle, the Stoics, the Ciceronian outlook. This is one branch of classics. The other two years are spent on Greats, which concentrate on highly modern philosophers, logicians, and so on, a lesser concentration on Aristotle and Plato, and much ancient history.

These subjects are favored by the older public school classes, which produce a very high proportion of candidates. Their traditional study is Classics in the above-mentioned sense. They are taught them very competently. Their examination successes most probably surpass their native wits in comparison with the products of the grant-aided schools.

The balance of marks has recently been redressed, and more entrants come from the more "modern" studies of political science, economics, and sociology, and so on, and also, from the younger universities offering these subjects. It must be remembered that it was at Oxford that "Modern" Greats—that is, a curriculum of politics, philosophy, and economics—was started. The change is of some value, for the mind is being trained and formed by reflection on phenomena within the authority of the state's administration. But the British method has, rightly, chosen general studies rather than the special facts of a department's responsibilities, during the educational stage. And *the method of study and learning is of far superior moment to the subject of information in the selection of administrative personnel.*

The Method of Study

The examination is pitched at an intellectual level attainable only (rare by exception) by those who have graduated high in the honor lists of the universities. The university stage is therefore decisive, especially as university professors set the examinations and mark them, as employees of the Commission.

The newer, so-called "red brick" universities, employ the method of lecturing more than do the older universities; but they use the tutorial method and seminars. The older universities are less addicted to courses of lectures, and teach mainly by the tutorial method. They have sent most of the entrants into the Service, and therefore in this analysis most attention is given to their method.

But this one feature is common to all education in England and Scotland and Wales especially at the university level: it is deeper, more thoughtful, more thorough, and more critical and thought-provoking than generally and normally in the university *formal* teaching in any other country. This does not mean that there are no failures or faults in the British system.

The Tutorial Method. The tutorial method consists, roughly, of the assignment of one or a few students to a tutor, especially in residential colleges, for the common development of the subject in which the tutor is a master and the students interested apprentices. He assigns them themes for writing, to be delivered to him. He may outline the nature of the problem he has asked them to solve, suggest books, give some clues. He is like an elder fellow student who has been along the road rather earlier and has reconnoitred. He is ready, first, to impart hints about what might be discovered on further exploration; and, second, when the essay is brought in by the younger man, he will put him through a Platonic cross-examination, until the contents of the younger man's mind are spilled out in front of both of them, but especially for the latter to see and appraise. It is an exceedingly intensive tilling of the mind, and a process of preparation not merely in assimilating facts but in evaluating them as an answer to a problem.

There are critics who believe that the tutorial method places an excessive emphasis on critical exercise, on negating other people's constructions, rather than building answers to situations of conflict between human beings or applying science to progress. I doubt this valuation, except that no system of education that ends at between twenty and twenty-four years of age can do very much more.

It is a tremendous service to have produced critical awareness, suppleness of thought, precision of phrase (which is precision of *thought*)—plus the grasp of the facts embraced by the student's sector of science. Above all, it must be stressed that it is a training in thought, in *thinking,* in using the mind for all it is worth; on circumspect, quiet, strenuous, steady, analytical thinking. This is a special mark of the British way in politics—it is Benthamic. The politicians and social philosophers and missionaries are already eager and fertile for action or inaction. The Civil Service is much needed to serve as their critical assessor—not their obstructor—to be, as Graham Wallas once observed, the true "Second Chamber" in the British system. We have already explained the Benthamic way of thinking (p. 32).

It must not be thought that the civil servants thus educated are not *constructive.* They are; but it is the Ministers and the Cabinet who have the role and responsibility of the higher political creativeness.

This education is more full of life's sap than the juridical training that was the feature of the German and Prussian Civil Service until almost our own day. It is broader and more cultural than the French training, which was in law and in specialized social sciences, until the reforms of 1946 (p. 480). (These have followed the British route.) It is deeper and more thoughtful and more humane than the usual American zeal for the special sciences, the lack of classical background, and excessive disregard for the history of mankind. It contrasts diametrically with the Soviet public-service education in its humanity and freedom of thought (as do the educational systems of the other Western nations just listed), which even Lenin's denounced as "uncultured" (p. 826).

The British system provides excellent semi-finished products; the rest is the work of practical administration, and any deliberate training it believes to be needed as a supplement.

British success in this respect has caused some to believe it is owed to a general éducation rather than specialization of studies. This is important, but it is not the real point. The tutorial method,

its enticement and mental penetration, *hard thinking* and close concentration—*that* is fundamental in the quality of the education.

Furthermore, political, social, and debating activities sound in the colleges. They nurture ready and broader minds and help to achievement in the oral part of the examination.

The theory then is that a student so distinguished in competition with his peers will readily learn the techniques of the department into which he goes on appointment.

Sir James Stephen, Undersecretary of State for the Colonies for nearly thirty years and then Professor of Modern History at Cambridge, described the qualities of the best of the Administrative Class vividly, when he commented on the Northcote-Trevelyan Report in 1854. He said: that the Civil Service as a whole could be distinguished into three classes, but that *"all* had the education, the manners, the feelings, and the characteristic principles of gentlemen." Let the word *gentlemen* be noted. He continued:

> In the narrow circle of the first class were to be found, large capacity of mind, literary powers of rare excellence, sound scholarship, indomitable energy, mature experience in public affairs and an absolute self-devotion to the Public Service.

The Mechanics of the Competition and the Viva Voce Test

In the ordinary examination known as Method I, the competition is by a short preliminary interview, an academic examination, and a final interview, the result being determined by the aggregate of marks obtained. The total of marks for the written part of the examination is 1000. Of this total, 700 marks are made up by the candidate's choice of four (usually closely related) subjects he has studied from the Commission's list of about eighty, while the other 300 marks of this 1000 are for *three compulsory subjects* that everyone takes: English, an essay, and matters of general interest at the present day.

It should be noticed that, with the present variety of subjects, the original idea of Macaulay's that candidates would be comparable meets difficulties. They can be as diverse as botany and jurisprudence or Greek language and geography. The really comparable subjects are the compulsory ones, those that carry but 30 percent of the total marks.

The Viva Voce Examination. It is clearly necessary that an intending employer *see* and *hear* the employee in person. Personability with colleagues and the public is a most important, and might be a vital quality for the success of a specific job.

From the beginning of Civil Service reform, the makers of the modern Civil Service insisted on the need for viva voce examination. The proportion of marks assigned is quite high: 300 out of 1300, or 300: the 1000 for the written examination. It has to be remembered that the candidates are very close to each other in ability—at least those that have any chance at all of getting into the few places annually available. Hence a few marks in the interview can have a decisive influence on success or failure. Further, it is unlikely because of the age limits that a candidate will have more than *two* attempts, so that the interview may be decisive for one's whole life.

The Civil Service Commission sets up selection boards to conduct the interviews. Their size varies from five to eleven members. They include two drawn from a panel of retired civil servants, plus a varying number of members from the higher Civil Service itself, businessmen, trade unionists, and university teachers. Usually two university teachers are present. These members are also drawn from panels already made up and changed from time to time.

This is quite a change, and from the standpoint of social representativeness, an improvement on the boards that acted before World War II, when they consisted *only* of university teachers.

When the candidate appears before the board, they have his examination results and testimonials from his teachers before them. The interview lasts from 45 to 60 minutes. It ranges over his interests, his hobbies, his ambitions, over public affairs, it may be some problem that he wrote about in his examination. The purpose is not to investigate the candidate's pregnancy with facts, full as he may be; it is to cause him to display himself or herself rather as a human being, to reveal character or exhibit personality.

It is not a long acquaintance the interviewers have with the candidate. Before 1945 the interview was even shorter and sometimes took place before the examination. The dispersion of judgment, summed up in the marks awarded, was often quite remarkable, reflecting rather the personal affinity of the men on the board for some human types rather than others, highly subjective. It tended to make the result of the interview a game of chance. Sometimes it excluded from the Service extremely able candidates who had written superior examination. It was also alleged that the type of interview and the kind of interviewer gave a premium to certain upper-class social manners and speaking accent. There was something in the criticism.

The new method has much to commend it: it is longer; the board is more representative; and the Commission has paid careful attention to the problem of the method of interviewing.

Shortly after the World War II there was adapted from the method of "live" testing of Army officer candidates, what may be called the "live and long" personal test. The candidates before their final viva voce interview were housed for a week end in a country mansion managed by the Commission. For two and a half days—Friday afternoon until Monday morning—the candidates, in groups of up to twenty-four, were in each other's company and under the friendly hospitality and supervision of interviewers. They were led in groups of eight by the Commission's staff: each group by three of the staff: a retired civil servant, a professional psychologist, and a young civil servant as the eyes and the ears of the future employer group.

The tests were written and oral: reports written on the basis of a file of papers concerning an immediate governmental problem to be solved; spontaneous and competitive discussions on subjects suddenly presented; the conduct of a meeting of other candidates. Each member was given a separate half-hour interview by each of the three members directing his group. The various written tests were quite tricky: of the intelligence test order not informational.

The system came under strong attack from the public and Labour Party critics. They believed it was once again an attempt to introduce into the factors of selection some social favoritism which the establishment of written examinations had tended to eradicate. Technical criticism were made also, regarding the weight given to personal pleasingness over, perhaps, the solid qualities of intellect demonstrated in written examinations based on years of university study. The Select Committee on Estimates (1948) thoroughly discussed the problem and was disturbed by the "highly subjective nature of the impressions reported." It thought that the tests favored candidates who were quick at intelligence tests but who might lack "some of the qualities especially valuable to the Government service." They recommended that no rejecting for "failure" be any longer permitted.

The general idea of the "live and long" interview was sound. The service of the State needs men of character as well as of intellect. Business takes chances and is fairly resolute in the early weeding out of failures or weaklings (generally speaking, so long as they are not family relations). The Civil Service offers an attraction to ability by the offer of a life career. The nemesis of this is that it brings in people when they are young and inexperienced, and is ethically tender with them when they demonstrate that they are not too potent administratively. Hence, the attempt to find out before admission whether they have character, which is the power to choose and act, to be original and dependable.

The program still continues, for one in four of the candidates; but the period of attendance is abbreviated, and the locale is no longer a country house, but London.

The ordinary *viva* then is conducted as indicated, with the interviewers in possession of the examination marks, tutors' reports, and a report from the "country house."

From Examination to Appointment

The total marks determine the candidate's place on the list of successes. A few more are kept on the list than are immediately required for the vacancies, lest in the interval between the examination and the appointments some may have fallen out for personal reasons—for example, have changed their minds about their profession.

Successful candidates are allowed the right to choose the department they would like to enter, according to their place on the lists. Until three years ago, however, and since 1920 no candidate was allowed at once to enter the Treasury. This was reserved for admissions after the entrants had had some experience of other departments—the departments that spend—a rule that had much to commend it. This is no longer the case: a small number may go directly into the Treasury, *if* their examination results warrant their choice.

All those who come into working contact with the members of the Administrative Class pay it the highest tributes. They are devoted, honest, industrious beyond evaluation, with a full identification of their personalities with the service of the State. They very rarely leave the Service until the natural age of retirement, sixty-five. They are not tempted by the higher salaries and chances of fortune in business to which their talents might arouse legitimate expectations. They are persons, men and women, of the highest intellectual qualities, and sensitive in personality as managers, associates, and cooperators with other departments.

Induction into the Job

Their induction into their work, until 1945 and beyond, was left to their own presumed ability to learn while doing from the moment they entered on their duties. The assumption was that their education enabled them to grasp the new experiences and problems swiftly. All they needed was the guidance for a little time of their immediate superiors who stood in the relationship of tutor—master-apprentice. In most departments some officer was given charge of the new Assistant Principals, and the latter were sometimes called "Administrative Cadets"—that is, young learners. The grade they enter is recognized as a "training" grade; they are not at once brought fully into the organization of the departmental division of labor.

The system of jumping into the water in order to learn how to swim was a brilliant success in most cases. Yet critics urged that the process could be accelerated by more deliberate arrangements to receive and train the entrants in their first few months, especially in administration. A Treasury Committee on the Training of Civil Servants reported in May 1944 on the problem of training in the Civil Service generally. It paid due attention to the problem presented by the Administrative Class. It rejected the idea that they should be enrolled in a staff college (attempting analogy with military officers' staff colleges), especially if it should be one in which high executives from business were included. (There is such a staff college for business executives.) The reluctance was due to the belief (which is correct) that the motives, ambitions, and standards of private and public business are of a different kind, though the rejection of the idea was grounded on differences of specialized business practice.

Instead, the Treasury Establishments Division concerned with training has made arrangements for the Assistant Principal roughly as follows. In his first three months at work, he spends something like two days a week in lectures (by university and other intra-Civil Service or retired Civil Service personnel), reading, discussion, on the departmental functions, their financial routines; the connections with Parliament; managerial problems and techniques; problems of cooperating with the public; statistical resources and methods. He is sent to branch offices to work; visits the various departments.

Post-entry Development Training. The civil servant enters a great monopolistic undertaking. He may suffer routinization and hopelessness. Against routinization, for people who give promise "of eventual promotion to high administrative work," a sabbatical leave has been put in operation. It is expedient that they might refresh themselves by observation of subjects of professional interest to them, especially abroad.

For they may come to suffer from "stoical realism." The phrase *stoical realism* was supplied by Sir Henry Dale, for many years Permanent Secretary of the Ministry of Agriculture, to express the state of mind that developed in civil servants with the passage of the years.[3] Summarized it

[3] *The Higher Civil Service of Great Britain*, London, 1941, pp. 92–93.

says: (1) pure reason is not an important factor in human affairs. (2) Even there, there is much to be said for both sides in a complicated and hotly debated question. (3) Great social economic and political changes cannot be made in a vast and highly organized society quickly without causing undeserved suffering. (4) A minority that feels strongly and shouts loudly will often prevail against both the majority and the merits, unless the majority feels strongly. (5) Any great measure is sure to have results, often grave, not foreseen— "in other words, the strongest intellect and the keenest insight cannot predict anything like the full consequences of important decisions." He adds that it may be possible to be enthusiastic for moderation and prudence. The chiefs of the Civil Service possess this attitude of mind. He asks, "Will any sensible man call it cynicism?"

Even supposing it were not "cynicism"—something, in addition to parliamentary questions and debate, is needed to replace the gad-fly effect of consumers' control over the private entrepreneur, dependent for his success on paying customers.

II. THE PROBLEM OF NATIONAL REPRESENTATIVENESS

Should the Civil Service in a democratic state be "representative" of the variegated group and class nature of the whole public? The question is raised acutely in Britain (as in prewar and postwar France and Germany) because the class structure, based largely on inequalities of inherited wealth, gives to the few, advantages in education and ability to wait until the right time for appointments that are denied to the many. The figures to be cited on the education of the Administrative Class entrants demonstrates that it is staffed by the wealthy out of proportion to population. We must beware, however, of crude inferences from the superficiality of the figures.

Class Bias

First, it is true that until the middle 1930's there was a heavy predominance of entrance from the older universities and from the public schools which led to them. Thus:

Period	Total	*Percentage from Public Schools*	*Number from Grant-aided Schools*	*Number from Scottish Day*	*Number from Miscellaneous*
1905–14	283	74	27	18	28
1919–25	197	63.5	43	18	11
1925–37	263	61.8	21	41	15

The grant-aided schools are those administered by the cities and counties; the public schools are private schools to which entrance is obtained by the payment of substantial fees. In the period 1925–1937 nearly 34 percent of the total coming from public schools came from the boarding schools alone in contrast to the public day schools. There is a social difference; and they come from a minute segment of the population compared with the numbers in grant-aided schools. A considerable proportion of the entrants who are educated at the public schools come from families who have themselves served in the Civil or military or Colonial or Foreign Service of the nation or are of professional origin.

Recently, the proportion of those coming from the grant-aided schools has substantially increased. In 1950–51, this author computed that entrants by Method I came to the extent of 50 percent from the grant-aided schools (23 out of 46); by Method II, 12 out of 18—that is, 67 percent; in 1951–52, by Method I, 27 out of 42 entrants—that is, more than 50 percent; and by Method II, 6 out of 18—33 percent.

It should be added that the number of the major public schools has much shrunk as a source of the Administrative Class, except for the Foreign Service, to which some observations will be addressed presently (p. 235). It might be added at this point that in the years mentioned, respectively, the university origin of the entrants was: 1950–51, Method I, 14 Oxford; 11 Cambridge; 21 other universities, scattered; Method II, 8 Oxford; 4 Cambridge; 6 others; 1953–54, Method I, 17 Oxford; 8 Cambridge; 8 others; Method II, 9 Oxford; 6 Cambridge; 2 others.[4] A large number of the Oxford and Cambridge graduates had attained university education by scholarships.

It cannot be denied that a quite substantial proportion of the Administrative Class entrants

are from the poorer sections of the population. It must further be remembered, if representativeness is the quest, that a large proportion of the whole of the Administrative Class is being drawn from the subordinate ranks of the Civil Service by promotion. Moreover, during World War II many of the Executive Class were promoted. Indeed, the progress of scholarships and the practice of open competition gave some way to solving the problem of representativeness. However, their class outlook must have been much modified by their education. It can be expected that the leveling tendencies will progress.[5]

[5] It is useful to summarize the data supplied by a recent study of the "higher" or "Senior" Civil Service—that is, from Assistant Secretary upward. It is by R. K. Kellsall (London, 1955). One half of the Higher Civil Service comes from Oxford and Cambridge, and 16 precent come from other universities. Some 33 percent did not attend universities, and this number includes two fifths of the Assistant Secretaries and one fifth of the Permanent Secretaries and Deputy Secretaries.

Less than 50 percent studied at public schools in the widest sense of the word; less than 25 percent were at boarding schools; only 5.5 percent were at Winchester, Rugby, or Eton, compared with 14 percent in 1929. In the period 1949–1952 only 3.5 percent of the competitors came from these three schools, whereas in the years 1909–1914 that proportion reached 16.5 percent.

One out of four of the higher civil servants studied at local authorities' secondary schools, and 1 in 5 more came from day schools like these though directly run by local authorities. For the Higher Civil Service as a whole 25 percent were educated at day schools as just described in the year 1929; in the year 1950, 40 percent; but of these senior civil servants who entered through open competition, only 25 percent had attended such schools, while over 33 percent had been at public boarding schools, and another 33 percent had been at other public schools, chiefly day.

Most of the Senior Civil Service are sons of professional, administrative, and managerial families, but only 1 in 10 is the son of a civil servant. But the percentage issuing from the upper section of such occupations fell from 40 percent in 1929 to 33 percent in 1950. Those in the lower section of these groups formed 25 percent of the Senior Civil Service at both dates. In 1929, 20 percent of these civil servants were the sons of small employers, shopkeepers, and employees; today these groups account for 25 percent. In the former year 80 percent of this group came from employers; now 50 percent are children of employees. Only 1 in 9 of the Higher Civil Service is the son of a skilled manual worker;

[4] For the Senior Branch of the Foreign Office, the figures were: 12 Oxford, 5 Cambridge, 0 others.

Persistent but Declining Bias

Yet, still nearly 50 percent of the entrants came from a very small proportion of the top of British society. The issue need not have been raised except for two things. In a class-affected society (providing it is ready for reforms and the governing groups accept the democratic principle), administration and legislative advice ought to be fructified by intimate knowledge, in addition to that provided by the parliamentary representatives. It is well supplied; it is being better supplied. Yet representativeness ought not to be made a fetish, for at the administrative level the work is of a scientific and objective nature; it is the Ministers in office who supply the "class" trends. "Representativeness" might cause a clash between a Minister "representing" one way and an official "representing" another.

The issue was, of course, presented strongly by the Labour Party and the Left wing in particular on one side and certain reactionary Conservatives on the other, who thought that the upper classes have "special claims." Yet Civil Service served Labour faithfully and creatively. For the Service was true to its professional upbringing and believes in democracy more than enough to serve the Government of its choice. Further, the civil servant could not jump the hurdles to commit a class-biased act. The opinion of his fellow civil servants in his own and other departments, the Cabinet criticism of the decisions of each department, the examination by Cabinet subcommittees of such decisions, and Parliamentary questions stand in the way.

A Case of Professional Bias. We have already referred (p. 173) to a case in 1954 concerning the blinding zeal of certain civil servants for Government management of a model farm, and the consequent ignoring of alternatives. The result was not the perfect candor the Minister of Agriculture had the right to expect. The culpable civil servants were almost immediately transferred to other duties from the posts held in which the inefficiency had occurred, except for some who were already in other positions. This occurred after another inquiry into the Civil Service aspect of the problem by three eminent men, two of them former permanent secretaries.

As a result of their inquiry, and using their words almost verbatim, the Treasury in 1954 added another to its circulated minutes on Civil Service ethics. It said:

> In present times the interests of the private citizen are affected to a great extent by the actions of Civil servants. It is the more necessary that the Civil servant should bear constantly in mind that the citizen has a right to expect, not only that his affairs will be dealt with effectively and expeditiously, but also that his personal feelings, no less than his rights as an individual, will be sympathetically and fairly considered. We think that the admitted shortcomings in this respect are the present case.

Speaking in the debate in the House of Commons (July 20, 1954) on the resignation of the Minister as a result of this case, Herbert Morrison said:

> But the faults and errors provided no case for the wholesale and general attacks which had been made on the Civil Service. There was a class of politician and a class of newspaper who, whenever there was the smallest mistake in the Civil Service, engaged in sweeping, wholesale denunciations of the service. [*Opposition cheers*] Any Government, the House of Commons, and the British people owed it a deep debt of gratitude for its ability, capacity, integrity, public spirit, incorruptibility, and willingness to be as loyal to one Government as to another.

---

this is twice as many as in 1929, and the proportion is being maintained. Of the senior promoted from the executive grades, 1 in 12 is the son of an unskilled or semiskilled worker, their total representation.

Limiting examination to the six Permanent Secretaries: the Treasury, Admiralty, War Office, Colonial Office, Home Office, and Board of Trade, the following facts emerge. In 1888 they all issued from the gentry and older professions and were educated at Eton, Rugby, or Charterhouse or by private tutors. In 1912 and 1929 they came from lesser families, including commerce and industry, their schools being in the lower ranks of the very good schools. In 1950 two were sons of manual workers with no university education.

In 1929 and 1939 about 33 percent of higher civil servants entered by promotion or from outside without competition. In 1950, 50 percent entered in these ways, while the number of the higher civil servants had grown from 473 to 1045. More than 33 percent have advanced by merit from the lower ranks, nine tenths of them without university education; in 1929 the figure was about 16 percent.

Civil Service is something of a fellowship, united by strong bonds of service ethics and professional uprightness.

The close similarity of attitude and sense of state and democratic progress and ethics of the high Civil Service and the members of Parliament and Ministers has been a very significant feature in their cooperation. With the solution of the more considerable social conflicts, they are likely to be more in harmony than before.

III. THE HIGHER SERVICE

The Assistant Principal proceeds by promotion up the ladder toward Permanent Secretary. The latest figures (1950) of the age distribution [6] from which one can infer the time it takes to arrive at certain high positions follow:

The age grouping, in general of the Administrative Class, including Branch A (see p. 236) of the Foreign Service, was in January 1955, as follows:

	Men	Women
20–24	69	23
25–29	282	25
30–34	383	37
35–39	558	24
40–44	507	26
45–49	376	21
50–54	290	8
55–59	438	1
60 and over	200	1

The numbers over 60 have increased since the change in retirement policy in February 1952, in the direction of keeping efficient officials at work to 65 and even beyond where the individually considered cases warrant it.[7]

Age Structure of Assistant Secretaries, etc. Upward

	A.S.	S. and D.S.	P.S.A. and U.S.	All above A.S.
60 and over	9.7	19.8	17.4	18.1
55–59	25.4	37.5	33.9	34.9
50–54	13.3	14.6	14.4	14.5
45–49	10.4	17.7	13.6	14.8
40–44	19.1	10.4	14.4	13.2
35–39	19.9	—	6.3	4.5
34 and under	2.2	—		

A.S. = Assistant Secretary; S. and D.S. = Secretaries and Deputy Secretaries; P.A.S. and U.S. = Principal Assistant Secretaries and Undersecretaries.

The opportunity to rise to the positions of higher responsibility and wider effective view is an important ingredient in the animation of morale that may counteract "stoical realism." Up to the year 1934 only one third of those who entered were at the age of 34 in the position of Principal; one third, Assistant Secretary at the age of 45; one fifth, Principal Assistant Secretary; one seventh, Deputy Secretary, and one seventh, Deputy Secretary to Secretary at about the age of 48. Civil servants have recommended that reorganization should be undertaken on the principle that the Assistant Secretary level should be reached at 32–40; Undersecretary at 35–49; Deputy Secretary or Secretary of department at 40–52.

The Severity of Competition for the Civil Service Positions

The figures refer to the entrants by normal processes, omitting the special "reconstruction" examinees, who were admitted by a different competitive process after World War II. In the five years, June 1945 to March 1950, the number of eligible and examined candidates for the Administrative Class was 2267; the number successful, 267; for the Foreign Service, 286, the successful, 63—that is, 9 to 1 in the first case; and nearly 5 to 1 in the second. In 1954 there were 50 vacancies; 655 applied; 53 were declared successful.

In the years 1949–1952—that is, three years—

[6] Adapted from R. K. Kelsall, *Higher Civil Servants of Great Britain*, London, 1955.

[7] In the "established" Civil Service of 489,689 officials, 34,577 are over 60.

in the Administrative Class competitions for 180 positions to be filled in all, 1615 candidates were examined and/or interviewed; a relationship of 9 to 1. The candidates were university *honor* graduates. We add the figures for the Executive Class, to save repetition at a later place: 12,178 examined against 2481 successful: 5 to 1.

Clearly the younger generation strongly desires to enter the Civil Service. The increase in numbers of applicants is partly accounted for by the increase of university students (and scholarships). But the Civil Service Commissioners are getting very anxious over *a clearly apparent decline in quality* of applicants compared with its criteria for the top men. Since 1951 the number of successful candidates has dropped steadily. In 1955, indeed, only 31 of that year's 474 competitors were successful, whereas there were 50 vacancies to be filled—the rest were not acceptable! The causes—given the increased numbers competing and the constancy of testing methods—are thought to be the increased prestige now attached to university graduates by private enterprise and expanded opportunities in university teaching. For example, of 32 candidates successful in recent years who decided *not* to accept Civil Service positions, 20 took university appointments. A veritable hue-and-cry has been raised in governmental circles and openly in the press over this predicament, and a search is on foot to make the Civil Service more attractive to good brains and character.

The Foreign and Diplomatic Service

Until 1880 the Diplomatic Service was recruited merely by a "qualifying test," with limited competition. Candidates were allowed to sit for the examination only if they were known to the Secretary of State or "recommended to him by men of standing and position on whose judgment he could rely and who themselves knew the candidate personally." A Board of Selection of the Foreign Office then looked over the candidates and decided who should be admitted to the examination. The candidate could not be nominated unless he possessed a private income of £400 a year at least: a handsome sum, worth about £1200 today, and equal to about $5000 at 1956 purchasing power in Britain.

The Service was thus the preserve of the aristocracy and the upper gentry, deliberately. Yet the Diplomatic Service did not serve the nation badly; for the governing class identified the honor and power of England with their own character, and therefore would not appoint oafs or profligates.

Until the advent of the Labour Government in 1931, Foreign Service appointments were made thus. The candidates were recommended to the Foreign Office and went before the Board of Selection, composed of Foreign Office officials, a representative of the Civil Service Commission, and one of the Defense Services, or members of Parliament. This Board excluded those it did not like. Those accepted took an examination between the ages of 21 and 25. The subjects were almost identical with those of the Home Administrative Class, but especially high marks were given for French, German, and Russian languages. The candidates were compelled to take modern European history at an especially high level of competence, and either general economics or elementary economics, and French and German. From 1851 to 1929, 53 percent of those in the Service belonged to the aristocracy or the gentry; 22 percent were the sons of professional people; 4 percent came from business families; 17 percent were sons of men already in the Civil Service, Foreign or Home. *All* came from the greater or lesser public schools; over one half from the eleven most exclusive, one third of all from Eton; 90 percent of those with a higher education went to Oxford or Cambridge. But only about 50 percent of all the entrants had any university education at all, because, as languages gave such a large total marks, the well-off went to foreign *pensions* and for the other subjects to crammers. Changes in the examination in 1919 drastically changed the education of the candidates: most, with practically no exceptions, have been educated at universities and, without exception worth mention, at Oxford and Cambridge.

In 1931, the Labour Government abolished the "limited" nature of the competition.

In 1943, as part of a drastic overhaul of all things British, a very new model was instituted. The Foreign Office and Diplomatic Service and the Commercial and Consular Diplomatic Services were amalgamated into one service: the Foreign

Service. It included also the foreign services of the Ministry of Information when that ceased to exist in April 1946. The purpose was to have a larger aggregate of officials, in order that business might be better distributed, to meet modern complexities in international relations.

The Foreign Service falls into two branches: *Branch A* or *Senior or Political Branch A* is the first. This consists of the Ambassadors, Ministers, Counselors, and Secretaries of diplomatic missions abroad, commercial counselors and secretaries thereto; Consuls General, Consuls and Vice Consuls at consular posts, information officers there, the higher officials of the Foreign Office, and the bulk of its political departments. Up to 1939, these numbered in total about 600; today they number some 750.

Entry into this, the Senior Branch, is by open-competition examination of men and women between the ages of 20½ and 24. The examination is still of the "reconstruction" type used since 1945 to fill the vacancies created by the suspension of recruitment between 1939–1945. The candidates take a test in ability to learn foreign languages, personality tests, a short written examination, and then are interviewed by the Selection Board, if they have at least a second-class honors degree at a university. If not, they must take a more elaborate written examination, in place of the short one. Ex-regular members of the Armed Forces obtain some age concessions; and two candidates a year, not over the age of 41 and especially qualified, are admissible. Branch B—Executive, clerical, etc.—is not considered for lack of space.

The successful candidates are then sent abroad at the Government's expense to study languages and national culture. On return they are examined in their studies, and, if they pass, they become members of the Foreign Service. They then have to pass through a probationary period. They are trained in European languages, inducted into the work of the Foreign Office and the various posts in foreign countries. They have something of the training of the Home Civil Service in economic, social, and commercial affairs and administrative science. Later there are refresher courses in England; and a rotation of officials among the gov-ernment departments, in the Dominion and Colonies, and so on.

The Social Composition of the Foreign Service's Senior Branch. In 1950–1951, of 21 entrants, 15 came from Oxford, 4 from Cambridge, and 2 from other universities. As for their earlier education, 18 came from public schools. In 1951–52, 8 were from Oxford, 8 from Cambridge, and 1 from elsewhere; 12 of the 17 came from public schools. (For 1954, see p. 232.) In both years the famous public schools, Eton, Harrow, Winchester, Marlborough, supplied a large proportion of those that came from the public schools: in 1954, fewer originated in the former. Evidently, young people who wish to enter the public service, if they have been educated at grant-aided schools, have a very much better chance of entering if they try for the home Civil Service than the Foreign Service.

Almost invariably the highest official advisers to Her Majesty's Government are drawn from these entrants by promotion. The highest diplomats sent abroad, as Ambassadors and Ministers, are drawn from the regular career Service. The selection of the entrants into the Senior Branch must take account of considerations such as uncouthness, clumsiness, coarseness, and personal ugliness.

They cannot be overweighed against acumen and resourcefulness, but they are important, other qualities being equal or nearly equal. Entertainment and social graces are not ignorable in the diplomatic connections.

All the entrants to the Foreign Service still take the intelligence and psychological testing week end described earlier, but now limited to only a small percentage of the home Civil Service.

Value of the Administrative Class

The Administrative Class develops a departmental point of view, a slant of mind, that derives from decades of immersion and thoughtful appraisal of the business of the department and its relationship to the other sectors of the Government and of British society. This constitutes considerable deposit of tested wisdom, of what is and what is not practicable. It is also a resource for future policy, perhaps more extensive and solid in its prevision and foreplanning than political electoral ties allow Ministers' to cultivate. They can face their

Ministers with decades of experience to advise them what not to do, what will not work. If Ministers persist, they can advise them on the best way to reduce the amount of damage by proposing the least costly means to the end.

The Minister cannot possibly know the intricacies of the thousands of facts that are the ingredients of his policy or the factors to make them workable. This gives the permanent Service a critical instrument of tremendous social importance; in colonial and foreign affairs the career officials, reporting on distant and alien events and complicated conflicts of cultures, have a special influence.

The conventions require that the official *must* offer his advice. He *must* press it against the Minister's initial unwillingness to consider. He can hardly browbeat the Minister. He must not be too easily parried and put off. He ought not to think of resigning because his advice is not taken; but he must carry out the policy the Minister finally decides on. If he cannot prevail, he must honestly and zealously fulfill the Minister's wishes. If he does not wish to do this, he must resign.

It is clear that he has a delicate duty to perform. No wonder then that the educational preparation and the mode of entry into the Service at the highest level are so important. It would not be helped forward merely by a specialized expert: something of an auxiliary statesman is needed.

This, of course, is only possible where the Ministers are sure of the impartiality of the civil servant. If they were not, then they would try to bring in their own "experts"; they would, as has happened in the United States, eject a physics and chemistry expert from the Bureau of Standards or an experienced and gifted chairman from the directorship of the Tennessee Valley Authority, or question the appointment of a Mr. Lilienthal to the chairmanship of the Atomic Energy Commission, and so on. They would be tempted beyond resistance, to bring in "Left" scientists or "Right" scientists and abjure knowledge for wishful thinking.

Independence of Mind. In 1915 Admiral Fisher (no relation to Sir Warren) accepted Mr. Churchill's policy of attacking the Dardanelles to get convoy passage to Czarist Russia. The expedition was a failure. At some point the Admiral, who was in the position of technical adviser (or civil servant), had not firmly pressed his objections, though he had objections. A committee of inquiry into the disaster said:

> It is the duty of the official not to resign but to state fully to the head of the Department, and should any proper occasion arise, to other members of the Ministry, what is the nature of his views. Then, if after due consideration, those views are overruled, he should do his best to carry out the policy of the Government, even although he may not be in personal agreement with it. . . . Undue loyalty would tend to cripple independence of thought, and would leave the parliamentary heads of the various Departments without the healthy assistance which they have a right to expect, and which is at times much more likely to be rendered by reasonable and deferential opposition than by mere agreement resting wholly on the ties of discipline.

Attention is drawn to the intention and the need to foster "independence of thought" or expressed differently, independence of mind. Without this, the civil servant is not worth his salt.

A direct inference is possible. If independence of mind is needed—and it sorely is—then the principle of *anonymity* is required also. If the name of the civil servant is known who gave certain advice—if the nature of the advice is divulged —it becomes the sport of political arena, and the possibility of neutrality or impartiality is undermined.

It might be remembered that the *Report* of the President's Committee of Administrative Management (U.S.A.), 1936, recommended the employment as White House assistants of six men "with a passion for anonymity." The phrase was borrowed from British Civil Service practice by Thomas Jones, creator of the Cabinet Secretariat.[8]

Minister's Duty to Civil Servant. If the civil servant owes these duties to the Minister in order that democracy may work at its highest degree of quality, then there is a code of duty owed by the Minister to the Civil Servant, that of the good superior to his executive assistant. This is not often formulated. But in the debate on the affair

[8] See Thomas Jones, *Diaries and Letters*, London, 1955.

of Crichel Down it was well stated by R. T. Paget, M.P., self-described as a high Tory. He said (Column 1260, Commons, July 20, 1954):

> Ministerial responsibility is a two-way traffic. It involves two profoundly important principles. First, the civil servant must be able to trust his Minister. He must be put in a position where he knows that his Minister will protect him or punish him, but that nobody else except the Minister will punish him. If he is to serve properly, the civil servant must know that he has only one man to fear—not all Parliament together, not the Press, not the yells of the crowd, not the 1922 Committee [see p. 92 and p. 100 for this committee of Conservative rank-and-file M.P.'s] —but one man, one man alone, the Minister. He must also know that if he does wrong the Minister will be ruthless in punishing him. Ministerial responsibility has this other function: the public must know that the Minister will be ruthless with his servants if they go wrong.

In the debate in question, it was generally deplored that the Minister's procrastination had resulted in the publicity and stigmatizing of the civil servants who had been in error, with the result that the Civil Service in general had been vilified most unjustly by those political groups who were so biased against State enterprise and the welfare State that they were prepared to undermine a great body of officials in the course of their other resentments. An M.P. of long and distinguished service, once a Minister in a Conservative Government, described the position in very instructive terms (Column 1251):

> This rough, raw and odious debate has had to be held. From time to time there has been a note of almost hysterical laughter in the House. I know when the House is not happy in its conscience, when it is not at ease; there is then a note of almost hysteria which enters from time to time.
>
> We are here analysing something that ought no more to be analysed in public than ought the relations between a man and his wife. This is the question of the relations between a Minister and civil servants—the closest, the most intimate and, if possible, the easiest of all relations. They must always remain so; but from time to time something like this arises and we have to ex-

amine these relations. It is the divorce court procedure. . . . It is an unsavoury proceeding, as divorce court proceedings are unsavoury, but if we do not have a safety valve the thing blows up, and if we had not had this safety valve [the House of Commons], this thing would have blown up.

It is far less difficult in Britain than in the United States or even on the Continent to dismiss an inefficient or irresponsive civil servant. There is no complicated administrative procedure of suspension, charges, and appeal to the Civil Service Commission, as in the U.S.A., or an appeal to courts, disciplinary and administrative, as in European countries. The power to dismiss is untrammeled, without appeal to the law courts, and the Civil Service Commission has no jurisdiction in dismissals and retirements. The Minister and the Treasury are fully masters of the situation. Since pensions are payable on retirement after ten years of service, economic hardship does not stand in the way of dismissal. But, of course, the Minister does not act arbitrarily but on the report of a board or committee of higher officials, with fair procedure for the representation of the civil servant's case, if he wishes this. Few people are ejected from the Service, largely because the quality is good. Nothing approaching the turn-over in the U.S. Civil Service is even conceivable.

Can the Service Accomplish the Modern Tasks?

In contemporary Britain, with vast economic and social-planning functions, it is now demanded that the civil servants "require knowledge of the world as well as highly specialised training"; for there must be, in planning, "extrapolation from the present," to reach out accurately into the future.[9] The trends must be known in the factors which enter into the business decisions of businessmen.

It is not to be expected that this can be taught to young men and women in a university, more realistically than it now is. It is difficult, also, to bring in more of the Administrative Class from the outside: it would disturb the attraction value

[9] Sir Oliver Franks, *Central Planning and Control in War and Peace*, London, 1947. An Oxford Moral philosopher in wartime administration, later Ambassador to the United States.

to the best minds at the universities. The outsiders can hardly have learned more than *one* class of business. What is needed is more careful attention to postentry training and to leave for observation and report. Nor can the anxiety of the Treasury and Civil Service Commission about sustaining the quality of applicants be ignored. Apparently, perhaps only momentarily, the professions and business are offering more rivalry for recruits. **Are the Burdens Too Heavy?** There is a point in the taking over of social and economic functions by the State that overburdens both Ministers and civil servants. Perhaps Britain now approaches it. If the State went much further, it might not be able to get resilient and unbureaucratic men hitherto obtained or, having them, would ruin them with intolerable duties. Indeed, it was told the present author by the highest civil servant, who at present is the best witness to the matter, that the burden is crushing. It is not that one could divide up the duties among eighty instead of forty Permanent Secretaries: the problem is not a function of numbers and devolution of authority. For there is a point where the decisions *must* come across the table of *one* man for final settlement. The witness intimated that one can hardly expect such burdens to be borne by any but the highest quality intellects and physiques, and, at

that, hardly for more than ten years or so. It pays to leave some things to private effort, even with more errors than one likes to envisage, than to threaten the great machine of the State with apoplexy.

Influence of the Administrative Class

The spirit that we have observed at work in the British Civil Service at its Administrative Class level is diffused all through it. This is furthered in thought and effort by the example of the Administrative Class. Its more distinguished men and women win titles of knighthood and others. It gives them *éclat* and a sense that not all rewards need to be in money or kind. Indeed, the Service has been honored by a succession of really great talents. Some of the names may be known: Trevelyan, Morant, Eyre Crowe, Sir John Anderson, Lord Beveridge, Harold Nicolson, Oliver Franks, Vansittart. They have been referred to by Graham Wallas as "administrative saints," or "secular saints." The ideas of service, trusteeship, probity have been handed down to them by their families —and class—and religiously applied to their work —that is, the fulfillment of self in the establishment by the community of more justice, more charity, more abundance, less pain, a fuller consciousness of truth.

13

Local Government

It is therefore our business carefully to cultivate our minds, to rear to the most perfect vigour and maturity, every sort of generous and honest feeling, that belongs to our nature. To bring the dispositions that are lovely in private life into the service and conduct of the commonwealth; so to be patriots, as not to forget we are gentlemen. To cultivate friendships and incur enmities. To have both strong, but both selected; in the one, to be placable; in the other immovable. To model our principles to our duties and situation. To be fully persuaded that all virtue which is impracticable is spurious; and rather to run the risk of falling into faults in a course which leads us to act with effect and energy, than to loiter out our days without blame and without use. Public life is a situation of power and energy; he trespasses against his duty who sleeps upon his watch, as well as he that goes over to the enemy.

—Edmund Burke

We describe only the system in England and Wales; Scotland has its own arrangements.

Decentralization in Unitary Government

Britain is not a federal State; authority is centralized. Yet over the centuries a sense of original and immemorial local rights, as well as individual rights, has remained strongly rooted among the people of the counties and the towns, the boroughs and the cities, and the parishes. It was for the gentry and the burghers a counterbalance to royal pretensions.

It was convenient for the central authority to make use of local territorial groupings of citizens as "units of local obligation"—to maintain law and order, to make roads and bridges, to keep places clean, to drain the land, to bank up unruly rivers and coastal areas, to police the villages and towns and take care of the destitute, and to raise money for these objects. Hence, the development of services in these local areas, and with it local civic pride and determination to keep as much control over local affairs as was possible.

Today, in spite of the rapid centralization of various local social and utility services, which has moved apace in the last quarter of a century and especially since the end of World War II, local self-government is still a very strong and highly prized feature of British government. It still retains much of the freedom and vigor that in its heyday, say 1825 to 1875, brought many Continental scholars to admire and recommend it to their French, German, and Russian countrymen.

The Table of Functions (pp. 244–245) attests the importance of the local authorities in British government. It deserves careful scrutiny. The local authorities spend £1,256,000,000 per annum, which is one fifth of the total annual expenditure of the British Government; and of this they raise £291,000,000 by local taxation, known as *rates*, the rest of their revenue coming from grants made to them by the central government, trading services, housing rents, etc. They employ staffs to the number of about 1,000,000.

Altogether there are 12,600 local government

authorities [1] (omitting London and various joint boards, etc.) classified as follows:

County councils 62
County borough councils 83
Noncounty borough councils 309
Urban district councils 571
Rural district councils 475
Parish councils 7300
Parish meetings 3800

Deconcentration and Decentralization. It used to be possible to speak of the local government system of "decentralisation." This meant that the local authorities obtained their powers by statute, including the power to raise money, and that the exercise of these powers was then in their hands, with free discretion to take the actions decided on only by the local councilors who are elected by the local voters. This admitted a right to self-government and imposed few limits to its local exercise. There was an implied admission that government in Britain *was not centralized,* an acknowledgment of independent authority away from London, in the local areas themselves. It was boasted that the system was not merely a "deconcentrated" one as in France or Germany, where the State was highly centralized and close to despotic, while the local areas were merely allowed some powers for the administrative convenience of the central government. Simply central power was deconcentrated, and the localities were regarded and treated as agents of Paris or Berlin or St. Petersburg and Moscow. A regime of *tutelage* (see pp. 500–502) was there manifested by a high degree of financial control, sometimes by centrally appointed officials, over the local governing authorities, whose decisions required central sanction.

The British system still retains the spirit of decentralization, but some of the motives and procedures of contemporary central-local relationships must be acknowledged to be rather of a nature of deconcentration. We shall appreciate why this change has come about, shortly.

History

Though of the most significant social and political importance, the evolution of English local government cannot even be sketched here. Only the briefest observations are possible. From the earliest times, the counties or shires were the widest territory of local government, acting at first through the royal sheriffs. The towns developed considerable self-government through royal charters and usage and the self-confidence of their guilds and wealth. Within them and in the rural areas, parish units of government—the villagers around

[1] These for such functions as burials, harbors, water, sewerage, land drainage, lighting, fisheries, markets, bridges, etc. number some 1200.

British Local Government System

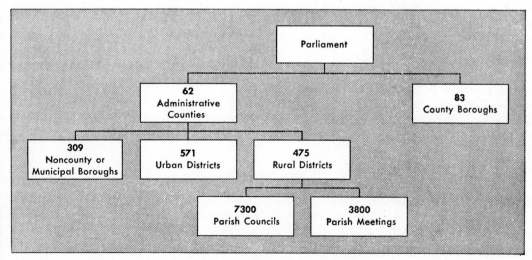

the church—were given important obligations: care of the poor, the roads, local policing, local health duties, especially from the time of the dissolution of the monasteries. They raised rates and elected their officers to unpaid duty year by year.

The counties were governed by Justices of the Peace in single or petty or quarterly sessions (the whole number of Justices for the county). These men were wealthy and (finally) Church of England; they were local residents, and they were appointed by the Crown. They regulated the work of the parishes and towns and their own members by haling the lax and law violators before them for judgment, fine, and perhaps, imprisonment. The general system took on a powerful character of self-government, as the Privy Council or Cabinet did not interfere with its operation. The ultimate check was the judiciary, who, indeed, on circuit, reviewed the judgments (which were of administrative regulatory kind) of the Justices, the local gentry. The Civil War forestalled an intention on the part of the Stuart Ministers to tighten up work of the Justices, the parish officers, and the corporations in the towns. Thereafter, with parliamentary supremacy, the gentry were largely left alone, save for judicial control.

The towns became for the most part close corporations, corrupt and inefficient. The new duties required in industrializing and urban conditions in the nineteenth century could no longer be entrusted to a nonrepresentative and technically inefficient council. Similarly, in the county, public health, new model policing, new model poor relief, the utilities, and so on could not be fostered by amateurs, merely men of property, with review *after* the local units had made some error: the risks of epidemics and swift-moving criminals on the better roads or in the denser populations were too great. They needed *anticipatory* administration, representative councils, career officials, central supervision, and more money.

The Development of Central Control

The rise of the new authorities, or the reconstruction of the ancient ones and their democratization, was accompanied by the institution of substantial central control over the activities, the administrative organization, the procedure, and the financing of the local authorities. Broadly speaking, until the Poor Law Act of 1834 and the Municipal Reform Act of 1835, the central government had relied on the Justices of the Peace to keep the lower local authorities within lawful and active. Then the Justices were themselves liable to control by the central courts of justice.

Out of their judgments and the higher courts' decisions emerged a kind of code of local government law and practice, sometimes couched in detailed administrative terms. But the control was judicial, not administrative and preventive of error. This latter type of central control developed from 1834 onward: it is a nineteenth-century creation. Its features will be presented later in this chapter.

The Main Features of Contemporary Local Government

The important questions that must be answered are these:

  I. What is the source of the authority of the local government bodies?
 II. What is the distinctive feature of the various areas and council?
III. What is the nature of their constitution and general mode of operation?
 IV. What officials do they employ; how do they recruit them?
  V. How do they finance their activities?
 VI. What are the principles and methods of central government control?

I. SOURCE OF POWER OF LOCAL AUTHORITIES

British local authorities have no inherent power to do as they like, such as ordering citizens, disposing of property, restraining persons, raising money. They are artificial persons—corporations created by the Crown or statute, with defined duties and powers. Power is restricted by the terms of statutes. They are subordinate legislative and executive institutions. To German and French local bodies the legislative body gives a general enabling power—over "the affairs of the municipality." Britain gives its powers only *specifically*—only this power and no more. (Even the Continental systems limit the *general* power of their municipalities by judicial interpretation, see France, p. 490). The British system does not know the more general form of municipal power in the American form of municipal home rule, either.

Powers are given (1) by general statutes made by Parliament and (2) by statutes called local or private acts. In the former, Parliament passes legislation applying generally to all local authorities of a given class or classes: for example, giving powers in secondary education to all counties and county boroughs.

Local Acts

The Local or Private Act is initiated by a particular local authority requesting some power beyond that given by general legislation for its own area. They are permissive, whereas the general laws may be either *compulsory* or permissive, and are rather more the first than the second. The local acts are the offspring of the progressive civic spirit of places that wish to do new things. They are the source of diversity among local authorities of the same classification. They are expensive; and they involve a town's meeting and possible referendum, with specially convened and advertised council meetings and an absolute majority approval by all the members of the council. Then, the authority may proceed to Parliament. Many have urged publicly that since the councils themselves are elected at intervals of only three years, the special meetings and referenda should be abolished. The rest of the procedure would remain. This is sensible.

General Permission

Some critics, usually on the liberal and left wings of politics, urge that local authorities should in some way be free to assume whatever powers they like. But this could not be permitted. First, the local authorities are very unequal in their competence, and it is better that the democracy of the whole nation have the last word on the power to act and tax and restrict individual liberty in the local democracies. Second, so many local authorities have nowhere nearly carried out the permissive powers already in their possession and are even slack about their compulsory obligations.

Third, in a national economy, which is fairly tightly planned, the adventurism of some hundreds of authorities would be awkward. The great cities lose little by the method of parliamentary grant.

Furthermore, when several authorities have experimented with certain powers by means of private acts, the Minister in charge of local government, every few years, consolidates the new powers into a single act and makes them available to all of certain categories of authorities.

Frequently, the idea of a new function or change in the organization or financial powers of the local authorities is initiated by the latter themselves. Many members of Parliament are or were local government councilors (see p. 64). The various categories of local authorities have representative associations that are very powerful, for local government has great prestige, and Parliament and the Cabinet must be able to rely on the local government councilors to make the statutes work.

Local authorities have to be most careful not to act *ultra vires:* for they are liable to action and damages before the ordinary courts of the land if they overstep the limits, permissive and mandatory, specified by Parliament.

Just before World War II the local authorities had attained the peak of their authority. Since then, as a result of wartime experience and the centralization of some services for financial or planning reasons, there has been a change touching each category rather differently. There is no space to reproduce the relevant tables from the present author's *English Local Government,* pp. 35–39. But this would be gleaned.

Recent Changes in Powers

Those country districts having them lost their education functions to the county councils in 1944, their remaining police powers in 1946, personal health services, 1946, the fire service, 1947, and town and country planning, 1947. They acquired more housing powers.

The county councils and the county borough councils lost to the central government public assistance (Poor Law) and hospital provision. The county boroughs lost their gas and electricity undertakings. (So did the noncounty boroughs and various district councils.) The county had never had these, but the boroughs had developed them; the new nationalized industries' authorities took them over.

All that was left to the counties and county boroughs of public relief by some changes (National Assistance Act) of their many centuries-old poor relief is accommodation of old people and relief in emergency cases. Here, the burden of treating the victims of mass unemployment, ill health, maternity, and so on had to be taken over by stronger shoulders.

All the hospitals that local authorities had acquired and managed as Poor Law infirmaries, then developed into general hospitals, and the special ones for infectious diseases, tuberculosis, and maternity cases were transferred to the Ministry of Health when (1946) the National Health Service was started; they are under the regional boards of the Ministry.

On the other hand added responsibilities have come to the local councils: civil defense; expanded fire protection; expanded education (see pp. 21–22), and the universalization of school milk and meals services; more services to young mothers and children, more health visitors and home nurses, and extended care for the tubercular, the aged, and blind. A revolution has occurred in town and country planning, by the acts of 1945–1947. Services "of convenience" have expanded; civic restaurants and civic theatres and housing.

Since, as indicated later, each class of authorities contains units which vary very widely in population and ratable value, there is a wide disparity in the actual exercise of the functions they must or may perform.

Table of Functions *

The Main Services	County Councils	County Boroughs	Borough Councils	Councils	Rural District Councils	London County Council	Metropolitan Borough Councils
Police and Protective:							
1. Police Force [a]	Yes	Yes	Some	—	—	—	—
2. Approved schools	Yes	Yes	—	—	—	Yes	—
3. Remand homes	Yes	Yes	—	—	—	Yes	—
4. Admin. arrangements for protection, certification, etc., of lunatics and mental defectives	Yes	Yes	—	—	—	—	—
5. Fire services	Yes	Yes	—	—	—	Yes	—
6. Weights and measures (verification and enforcement) [b]	Yes	Yes	Some	—	—	Yes	—
7. Enforcement of Shops Acts	Yes	Yes	Yes	Yes	Yes	—	Yes
8. Food and drugs:							
(i) Function of "Food and Drugs Authority"	Yes	Yes	Some	Some	—	—	Yes
(ii) Other functions, e.g., offenses relating to sale of unsound food	—	Yes	Yes	Yes	Yes	—	Yes
9. Control of nuisances under Public Health Act	—	Yes	Yes	Yes	Yes	—	Yes
10. Port Health Service	—	Some	Some	Some	Some	—	—
11. Receipt and enforcement of notification of disease, arrangements for disinfection, etc.	—	Yes	Yes	Yes	Yes	—	Yes
12. Civil Defense [c]	Yes	Yes	—	—	—	Yes	—
13. Coast protection	—	Some	Some	Some	Some	—	—

* Often county council powers are delegated to the noncounty boroughs and the districts or are committees and boards. County councils can act in allotments, sewerage, and rural housing, where the minor authorities default.

[a] Two noncounty boroughs are police authorities also.   [c] Also six noncounty boroughs.

[b] A few noncounty boroughs have their power.

The Main Services	County Councils	County Boroughs	Borough Councils	Councils	Rural District Councils	London County Council	Metropolitan Borough Councils
Communal:							
1. Town and country planning	Yes	Yes	—	—	—	—	—
2. National Parks and Access to Countryside Act	Yes	—	—	—	—	—	—
3. Building regulation	—	Yes	Yes	Yes	Yes	Yes	—
4. Highways and bridges (other than Trunk Roads):							
(i) Main, classified, and special roads d	Yes	Yes	—	—	—	—	Yes
(ii) Other roads	Yes	Yes	Yes	Yes	—	Yes	Yes
(iii) Cattle grids	Yes	Yes	Yes	Yes	—	—	—
5. Enforcement of private street works	Yes	Yes	Yes	Yes	—	—	Yes
6. *Public Health—Environmental Services*							
Sewerage and sewage disposal	—	Yes	Yes	Yes	Yes	Yes	Yes
Refuse removal and disposal	—	Yes	Yes	Yes	Yes	—	Yes
Baths, washhouses, etc.	—	Yes	Yes	Yes	—	—	Yes
Parks, pleasure grounds, etc.	Yes	Yes	Yes	Yes	Yes	Yes	—
Allotments and small holdings	Yes	—	Yes	Yes	—	—	Yes
Public lighting	—	Yes	Yes	Yes	Yes	—	Yes
Street cleansing	—	Yes	Yes	Yes	Yes	—	Yes
Burial grounds and cemeteries	—	Yes	Yes	Yes	Yes	—	Yes
Prevention of damage by pests	—	Yes	Yes	Yes	Yes	—	Yes
7. *Education*							
Primary, secondary, and further	Yes	Yes	Some	—	—	Yes	—
Agricultural	Yes	—	—	—	—	—	—
Public libraries	Yes	Yes	Some	Some	—	—	Yes
8. War Damaged Sites Acts, 1949	Yes	Yes	Yes	Yes	Yes	Yes	Yes
Social:							
1. *Local Authority Personal Health Services*							
Provision of health centers, care of mothers and children, supervision and provision of midwifery, health visiting, home nursing, arrangements for vaccination and immunization, ambulance services, care and after-care in illness, domestic help during illness	Yes	Yes	—	—	—	Yes	—
2. "Social Welfare" Services under the National Assistance Act, 1948	Yes	Yes	—	—	—	Yes	—
3. Care of children under the Children Act, 1948	Yes	Yes	—	—	—	Yes	—
4. Housing	Yes	Yes	Yes	Yes	Yes	Yes	Yes
Trading:							
1. Water Supply	—	Yes	Yes	Yes	Yes	—	—
2. Road passenger transport	—	Yes	Some	Some	—	—	—
3. Markets	—	Yes	Some	Some	Some	—	Some
4. Ferries and river tunnels	—	Some	—	—	—	—	—
Miscellaneous and ancillary:							
1. Small dwellings acquisition (loans)	Yes	Yes	Yes	Yes	Yes	Yes	Yes
2. Rating (levying and collection)	—	Yes	Yes	Yes	Yes	—	Yes
3. Civil aviation—aerodromes	Yes	Yes	Yes	Yes	Yes	Yes	Yes

d Noncounty boroughs and urban districts with over 20,000 population may claim right to maintain and repair "classified" roads.

II. THE VARIOUS AUTHORITIES

The Counties

Of these there are 62. It is territorially the largest area (normally) of local government. It originated in its modern form and boundaries in 1888, by force of the local government (county councils and county boroughs). Up to that time there had been 52 ancient counties or shires. The division of some of these into two or three areas (for example, the three "ridings" of Yorkshire) produced the present number. This number includes London, which is an exception in various particulars.

The county is a mixed urban and rural area. Its authority does not extend to the county boroughs within it: they are independent bodies. Its powers do extend to the other people within it, regardless of the fact that they live in the municipal boroughs or the urban or the rural districts.

The County Boroughs

These were created from among the municipal boroughs with at least 50,000 population (with a few exceptions of such historic cities as Canterbury) and places almost of that minimum population. In 1888 there were 61 such county boroughs; by a process of creation, as various other boroughs increased in population, they are now 83.

As already indicated, they are self-contained areas of local government for all purposes, enjoying the functions of the county and of an urban area. The largest, Birmingham, has a population of 1,118,500; the smallest (maintained for historical reasons) is Canterbury, 28,000.

The county borough is the busiest and most effective unit of British local government: urbanized, civic-conscious, with local pride; small enough to be watched and democratically managed and large enough to be able to afford efficient personnel and administrative techniques. Its density of population and its possession of one or more local newspapers give the proximity and means of communication that makes government economical and progressive.

More County Boroughs? It was and is possible for a municipal borough to become a county borough, and so acquire the fullness of powers possessed by the latter, and to be free of the services of highways, education, poor relief, police, administered by the county council in their area (except for some larger municipal boroughs in respect of education and police). Moreover, county boroughs may have their own boundaries extended on the accretion of population on their existing borders. These changes may be achieved by applying to the Minister of Health (in charge of local government), who could make an order, confirmable by Parliament, or they may be achieved by private legislation. The increase in the number of the county boroughs already signaled was accomplished in these ways.

The county administration is unhappy about such developments: they take wealthy areas away from the administration and taxable base of the county and often leave jagged areas of administration. The areas are extremely jealous of their powers.

Within the range of the county boroughs, it is not possible to determine precisely and *scientifically* that a larger or smaller size of population is more preferable for efficiency of large-scale government. The issue depends on values and who shall rule, in the main.

Long disputes between the various bodies of local authorities before Royal Commissions of Inquiry produced a new law. The Ministry of Health's power to make orders to be later confirmed by Parliament was diminished, therefore forcing the would-be county boroughs to proceed by private bill. Extensions were subjected to rather stiffer procedures giving the objectors better ground. But, above all, no proposal for the constitution of a county borough was even entertainable if the borough requesting it had less than 75,000 inhabitants. The raising of the limit of the population was designed to put off eleven municipal boroughs with over 50,000 but under 75,000 population which were prepared to graduate.

No new county boroughs have been created since the 1920's. The strength of the county representatives in the House of Lords, and their power to obstruct other private bills desired by the county boroughs, and the fact that a technical issue of public administration with much to be said for and against was involved, produced a stalemate. Very comprehensive proposals for boundary changes and a more logical order of local government authorities were made in January 1945 by the Government in a policy paper on the reconstruction of local government after World War II. It established a Boundary Commission—which, after interesting deliberations and proposals ran into the age-long hornet's nest of local governing authorities' mutual animosities. It was abolished in June 1949. Its proposals are of great theoretical interest.[2]

The Municipal Boroughs

The municipal boroughs vary greatly in size and wealth, some as we have suggested, the largest being 188,000, the smallest 912.

They differ from the urban and rural districts, the former of which are also urban areas of local government, by the fact that they may make orders and bylaws for the good rule and government of their area, a power flowing from their status, whereas the districts have such bylaw-making power only in pursuance of specific statutes.

The boroughs have a mayor as their residing officer and symbolic representative, whereas the districts have but a chairman.

The municipal boroughs were strong in the field of the utilities: gas, water, electricity, and bus and tram services, until the changes already mentioned.

The Districts

The urban and rural districts (often called indifferently county districts) are chiefly public health, lesser roads, and housing authorities. Some are very populous. Harrow has 220,000; the smallest is 786. Their presiding officer is a chairman. They exercise various powers in addition to those mentioned, by delegation from or permission of, the county in which they are situated. The largest rural district has 82,154, the smallest not quite 2000.

[2] See Herman Finer, *English Local Government* (4th edition), London, 1950, pp. 83–86.

The Problem of Areas

It is a nightmare to attempt to steer clearly enough through the tangle of historical illogicalities of the areas. Briefly, let it be said that these questions are involved in the problem: Ought the urban districts be assimilated to the municipal boroughs? Ought the county to have the power over higher education throughout the area, with the exception of the county boroughs? Ought the county to have the power over elementary education everywhere, with the exception of the county boroughs? Ought the local police forces of areas other than the county borough be extinguished and transferred to the county? Ought the county to have *complete* control over main and minor roads, excepting in the county borough?

The questions raise two issues: (1) The urban areas, first, regard themselves as more progressive with social and civic services than the country representatives, who are bound to a large extent to be people of rural inclination and usually conservative gentry. Second, They do not wish to pay rates to the *county* funds. They would prefer to spend even rather more per head on the units administered (schoolchildren, etc.) and be in direct control of their own services, for efficiency and pride's sake. (Local people like to become local personages and to merit honors.) Third, they put up the democratic argument that they prefer to have a sufficient agglomeration of substantial services to attract people to stand for election and take an interest in the government of their neighborhood.

On the other hand, (2) the county areas are badly torn (it varies from county to county) by the ragged and diversely sized and shaped boroughs, districts, and so on, several of which may lie contiguous to each other forming unequal enclaves of functions within the county and giving it awkward problems of location of its services, for example, police and schools and roads.

There is strong argument for the placing of the more personal services, such as education, in the hands of the boroughs and urban districts, since the authorities who manage such services ought to be within calling distance of the consumers of such services and, in the case of education, of the pupils' parents.

Problems of Wider Area

Local authorities have substantial powers to create joint plans of administration, with joint authorities, and committees and joint boards. Thus there are many such for burials, harbors, hospitals, water, sewerage, land drainage, river conservation.

Some areas are so placed, with a prevailing urban population extending over many square miles and under ten or more neighboring local governing authorities of varying status (as for example, in the West Riding of Yorkshire; in the Manchester area, in the Newcastle on Tyne area) that experts have proposed their unification in a single region. It is difficult to get more than occasional and incomplete joint schemes, since the councilors and the inhabitants of the areas value their "independence." So long as this does not throw them and the rest of the nation into ruinous expenditure or gravely bad services, they may as well continue the limited autonomy that is a spur to them to participate in local self-government.

In the case of the roads and police and education, the trend has been to the county borough and the county, coupled with increased central power of direction. Such utilities as gas and electricity have been nationalized; in water and transport, the central authority promoted regional administration.

The part played by local councils in the National Health Service is this. They send representatives to the regional hospital boards for each of the fourteen hospital regions of the nation and to the local hospital management committees. They closely cooperate through their own individual and public health services with the work of the National Health Service as coordinated by the Minister of Health. Their individual health services include maternity and child welfare, day nurseries, vaccination and immunization, health visitors, home nursing, ambulance service, health centers to house practitioners, specialists, clinic services, and education facilities.

Nonhierarchical and *noncompendious* are the marks of the local government authorities. By compendious is meant that each local authority has several functions: it is not merely a single-function authority, like, for example, the various boards of education or water boards in parts of the United States; or as one should say in England, an *ad hoc* authority. That mainly went out by 1898. The purpose was deliberate: to reduce the number of separate authorities, with separate councils and sources of taxation; and to accumulate in each class of council enough functions to be attractive to local civic interest.

Furthermore, the units are not in a hierarchical relationship to each other. The county council does not exercise control and tutelage over the boroughs and the districts. There were suggestions to this effect in 1888 when the county councils were established; but it petered out into merely a power of the county council to inform of reported neglect to the central authority, when it might be asked to take over the service in question, usually health services.

Each local authority, then, exercises its powers as specified in the law on its own responsibility while, as far as external control and responsibility go, each authority has its direct relationship to the Ministry of Health in London.

III. THE CONSTITUTION AND INTERNAL OPERATION OF THE LOCAL UNITS

Democratic Authorities

Local authorities are directly elected by the local population. The franchise is practically as wide as that for the House of Commons; it is based on residence. But *non*residents occupying ratable land or property of the value of not less than £10 per year may vote. No one can cast *two* votes in the same election. County councils are elected triennially; so are the rural district councils; so also the twenty-eight metropolitan boroughs within London. In the boroughs, county boroughs, and urban districts the councilors are elected for three years, but one third the councilors vacate their seats each year.

In the boroughs (both kinds) and county councils the direct vote of the electorate elects three quarters of the council; the other quarter are *aldermen,* indirectly elected. They hold office for six years; every third year one half of them vacate their places. The county council, on its own election, votes for aldermen to fill the vacant seats. In the boroughs, aldermen are elected every three years, since the councilors are elected, one third, annually. Qualified for election to alderman are councilors or anyone qualified to be elected as a councilor. The election of aldermen follows different ideas in different places. If party issues are serious, then the party in power elects its friends; or the leading parties may agree on an equitable sharing to correspond with the party strength of the councilors. If party organization and feeling is weak, the senior councilors have the tolerated authority to decide, though any councilor may offer opposition by a rival nomination, whereon the issue is settled by majority vote. The usual practice is to elect aldermen from among the councilors who have served long and well. In the counties such personages as peers are sometimes chosen, though without local government service—it gives *éclat* and maintains the idea of looking upward to "our betters."

Co-option. It may at once be added that all local authorities have the right, for certain of their services, to co-opt—that is, to appoint members of the public as members of their internal administrative committees. Expert and interested members of the public, who do not want or cannot for business or other reasons be councilors by election, can be utilized for the benefit of local administration. It allows for a link between the councils and the voluntary social agencies. But it may introduce representatives of clientèle groups, for example, allotment holders or teachers, who are blinkered in their interests.

The Mayor. In the boroughs the council elects a mayor for a year (re-eligible); where the city is of historic importance, he may be called the Lord Mayor (for example, Manchester). He is elected from within or outside the council. In the districts and the counties, he is merely a chairman. The mayor is paid a salary; the chairmen of the other authorities "a reasonable allowance" or "remuneration." The mayor has a busy life beyond the normal work of the various chairmen: a city demands a great deal of time for the chairmanship

of the council and the representative duties of the mayor.

The chairman or mayor of an English local authority is very different from the mayor of an American city that has a "strong-mayor" system or a commission type of government. He has no special executive powers not possessed by the other councilors, except what may come from his chairmanship of the council and his personality. There is no division of authority between him and the council. The authority belongs to the whole council. He is not, like the German *bürgermeister,* an official ratified by the central government with certain supervisory and tutelary power over the council (p. 632). He is not like the French *maire,* even though elected locally, vested with certain powers of tutelage, responsibility for which he owes to Paris; and certainly he is unlike the *préfet* of the French *département,* appointed mainly as the officer of the Ministry of the Interior.

Self-government. Whereas the number of voters who turn out for national elections is almost 80 percent of the electorate (uncoerced, not the 99.999999 percent of the USSR, where the electors are five centuries behind the English in their political and administrative literacy), the voters in local government elections show an average of some 45 percent in all authorities except the county councils, and there it is about 35 percent. The fact is that the voters are intelligent enough to appreciate that Parliament *is* more important to them than their local councils.

The present position of strength of the parties is as follows at the end of 1955:

Labour had majorities on

County councils	0
County boroughs	50
Noncounty boroughs	62
Metropolitan boroughs	19
Urban districts	168
Rural districts	25

The majority were held by conservatives, but some were controlled by Independents and even by Liberals.

A recent survey has offered a kind of profile of local government councilors: (1) directors of companies, manufacturers, lawyers (solicitors), an occasional medical practitioner, an architect; (2) farmers and "gentlemen" (in the county councils); business managers, lesser industrialists, company secretaries, civil engineers; (3) small tradesmen (meatmongers, fishmongers, grocers), the trade-union organizer and secretary; (4) commercial travelers ("traveling salesmen" in the United States), agents, clerks; (5) skilled workers, foremen, machinists, engineers, postmen; (6) railwaymen, miners, other semiskilled or unskilled manual workers; (7) housewives.

It must be remembered, however, that the composition of the councils is extraordinary in its diversity.

The total number of councilors in the 1500 major councils (omitting parishes) for all England and Wales is in the neighborhood of 40,000. For some of these places, especially in the counties, there is no contest. But it is not too unfair to double the total number of councilors in order to say that 80,000 men and women have an active interest in local government services, enough to do its drudgery and keep alive the right to local self-government. The parish councils have about 60,000 members.

The value of the whole process lies in (1) the practice men and women get in organizing, deciding, directing, and financing the services to be performed; (2) in meeting the arguments, complaints, and wishes of their constituents; (3) in standing up to the central authorities, whether at Westminster or in Whitehall, for local rights and local initiative. From this process an important ingredient of enduring democracy is distilled: *self-confidence* in the claim to be self-governing centrally as well as locally, and centrally because locally.

Internal Organization

The Committee System. English local authorities are known for their committee organization of business. Briefly, for each service the council establishes (some by statutory obligation) a committee consisting of councilors and aldermen in proportion to the party or group strength produced by the recent elections, with due allowance for those who are independent members. Each committee then is vested with responsibility for the *adminis-*

tration of that service or department, subject to the submission of its reports and recommendations to the full council for approval before action can be taken.

The committee, and especially its chairman and vice chairman, will be in continual touch with the career official in charge of that department: the director of education, the chief constable, the medical officer of health, the finance officer or treasurer, the head of the water department, the engineer, the superintendent of tramways and busses, and so on.

In local government the direct leadership, control, and guidance of the executive departments, including the making of appointments, are not vested in a simulacrum of the Cabinet but in a collegial body with its apex in the chairman, not a single Minister. It is educative, and viable for a well-knit local body with subordinate functions, as compared with the national Government. The chairmen of the various committees form something of a Cabinet for policy, tactics, and coordination.

Committees: Authority and Size. The council sets bounds to the authority of the committees. First, it may not give a committee the power to levy a rate or raise a loan. Therefore, the committees are beholden to the council for the authorization of the expenditures its policy entails. But, the council authorizes a budget per committee or department, which allows the committees or departments wide latitude of spending within the estimates. A committee cannot sell or buy property or make a formal contract; these require the corporate seal affixable only by express approval of the council. Committees must keep minutes and report proceedings at frequent intervals to the council. These constitute checks on the caprice of committees.

There is variation in the number and size of committees.

The committees are served by officers of the department they are concerned with. Minutes are taken by the town clerk's or county clerk's officials. The finance officer may have representatives present. One or another of these officials will be alert to warn a member whenever he has an "interest" in the matter being discussed, so that he may declare it openly.

The council passes the budget for the year. It does this on the basis of the estimates presented by its finance committee. This, in turn, has been assisted by the various committees, who have been instructed and coached by the officials at the head of the respective departments. When the budget has been accepted by the council, it decides on the amount of rates to be levied. *On this local taxation, there is no legal limit as to amount or freedom to levy.* (Compare France, p. 491).

The council keeps continuous track of and vigilance over the work of the committees.

IV. LOCAL OFFICIALS

There are, broadly speaking, two kinds of local officials: those that the central authority requires the local authorities to appoint; all the rest are at the discretion and financial willingness of the council.

Officials whose appointment is compulsory are: a clerk (town clerk or county clerk); a treasurer; and a medical officer of health—each of whom must be a different person. Rural districts must, in addition, appoint a sanitary inspector; boroughs and urban districts this, and a surveyor also. In addition, counties and county boroughs must appoint a chief education officer, a children's officer, and a chief constable.

Outside these officials, the local authority may appoint as many as it wants, on the qualifications it thinks proper, and dismiss them on the terms it believes good for the locality. But this warning is necessary: it is not entirely free to do as it likes. For the authorities that are subject, as we show presently, to the audit powers of the Ministry of Health may be restrained by the law courts from spending local funds in an "unreasonable" way.

General Officials

The general body of administrative, clerical, and secretarial officials of the local authorities were until recently in rather a different position from (1) the skilled technicians and the teachers, and (2) the manual workers and others in the utilities, the sewerage, lighting, cleaning, and other services. As for the skilled technicians, they have

their publicly known and approved qualifications, set down by the professional bodies that guide their education and interests. The teachers not only had such qualifications, but, since the Ministry of Education inspects the local authority's schools and makes a grant in aid of educational expenditure, its standards were effective. The manual workers were organized in various trade unions, and these had general principles of pay and stood out for fair treatment to their members. Thus, in these cases the local authorities were guided by certain external standards.

The great diversity of wealth and services of the 1500 major local authorities made uniformity of service conditions difficult to attain for the general body of their staffs. It conduced to some unfairness and here and there favoritism, though the existence of the National Association of Local Government Officials and the general probity and democratic control of the councils limited incompetence quite strictly.

In 1946 (following ten years of study and proposals), however, the staff unions made an agreement with the associations of local government authorities, to be operated through a national joint council and fifteen provincial Whitley Councils. Though it is not compulsory, all but fifty councils have entered it.

It applies to all officials who earn less than £1000 annually, excluding the clerks, accountants, treasurers, engineers, surveyors, chief education officers, and architects. It sets a minimum age of sixteen for recruitment; a period of probation; requires the passage of a test given at that age in the schools and a competitive examination and interview—set by the local authority. It classified the service into General, Clerical, Higher Clerical, and Administrative-Professional-Technical. For these there are pay grades. An annual report system is set up to govern promotions; and movement from the lower classes into the upper is dependent on the passage of examinations.

This is a tremendous advance on previous practice. The smaller authorities are plagued by the lack of entrants, as the pay they can offer is not competitive with other occupations. Since 1937 there is also a *compulsory* superannuation arrangement for the staffs.

The Town Clerk (or Clerk of the County or Council)

His employment is compulsory. This is because he has certain duties to perform as official in charge of elections to Parliament (he is the Returning Officer). Further, Parliament felt that there should be a responsible, *legally educated* person as the chief administrative servant and adviser of the elected councils, since the local authorities are operative inside a highly complicated web of specific powers, duties, and limitations, which, violated, may bring actions for damages against them.

He is usually a solicitor (a lawyer) of some years' standing. This is not required by the law, but results from the highly complicated legal basis of the council's rights and duties. It then depends on his personality and the organization of the work and departments and committees of the council (which he may influence) how much governmental influence he wields. He has legal duties: he is the legal adviser and protector of the council; he sets in motion legal action where citizens are remiss in their obligations to the various departments; he attends to parliamentary and Ministry's representation and deputations; he furthermore organizes the agenda for council and committees, summons the councilors to attendance, and sees that the minutes are properly kept.

Apart from the chief financial officer—that is, the treasurer, or such other title—he is the one man who has a purview of all the operations of the whole council. It has, therefore, been suggested by many observers that he *could* perform a function rather like that of the city manager in American cities or the *Bürgermeister* in German cities—that is, as a general coordinating, leading, and animating administrative nature. In some cases he already does—dependent on personal qualities. The suggestion that he shall occupy such a status, then draws with it the idea that he shall be recruited differently from heretofore, namely, from among the legally trained, while the strictly legal duties are performed—as already in some large authorities—by a solicitor to the council. Councilors fear that their authority will be encroached upon and also cannot afford the division of the services among two men.

It should be noted that many local councils are served by some part-time officers: where the authority is small and not wealthy and has not enough work for full-time officials.

V. LOCAL GOVERNMENT FINANCING

Local government authorities spend money on current operations, and on capital account. Further, to make another classification, they manage utilities that are liable to profit and loss. Let us, because of brevity of space, dispense with a discussion of the utilities, simply saying that the policy of the authorities is to charge such fees (tramway fares) which will pay all the costs of production; they aim at a small profit, which will then be turned over to the general revenue of the local government.[3]

Loans

We turn to expenditure on current and capital account. Again, let us eliminate the latter with a brief explanation. The capital owned by the local authorities, in land, real estate, various public works, houses, equipment, and so on, is considerable. It runs at about 25 percent of the total capital investment of the nation as a whole!

No expenditure on development that involves an expenditure greater than the amount that ought to be raised from two or more years of rates may be undertaken without a loan—that is, on capital account. No loan may be raised except either (1) by a local act of Parliament, or (2) by permission of a central department, acting under some specific act of Parliament, for example, for schools, for hospitals, for roads, and so on.

The central sanctioning authority for loans is the Ministry of Health, though the general superintendence and the recommendation comes from the Ministry of Education, the Ministry of Transport, the Home Office (police buildings), and so on. This allows for coordination and timing of the local council's demands. Most of the borrow-

[3] See Herman Finer, *Municipal Trading*, London, 1941, for a complete analysis of municipal utilities, structure, functioning, financing, etc.

ing is done not by private act of Parliament but through general act with central approval. Until 1945, once the power to borrow had been given, the local authority was free to go on to the money market; since then, planning having come to stay, the Local Authorities Loans Act requires they borrow from the Public Works Loans Board, a governmental body. It lends money, provided by Parliament, at rates that have been steadily less than the commercial market terms.

Local Rates and Government Grants

Roughly speaking, then, from the utilities and property (such as parks, rowboats, seaside amenities, meeting halls, etc.) and from loans, the local authorities obtained about one half of the total they spend. The other half, some £600 million, comes from local taxation—that is, rates—and from grants given by the central government. If we add to the revenue from the utility-cum-borrowing sources the amount from grants (about £300 million), then only some 23 percent has been recently raised out of rates of the total expended annually.

The Principles of Local Taxation, Known as Rates

The customary and legal term *rates* supplies the clue to what might be a confusing system. Rates comes from *ratio;* a local rate is the share each contributor pays to the revenue of the council in proportion to the *real estate,* known in Britain as fixed property, he occupies. If he is the owner and occupies, he is still rated as the occupier. Furthermore, the rate is levied on the land or house or other building *only when it is in occupation;* and further, the *contents* of the house or building are *not assessed* for rating purposes.

How is the value of the property assessed for its proportionate share in the tax contribution? The value is based on the rent at which the property might reasonably be expected to rent from year to year.

There are some exceptions to this principle. Agricultural land and buildings (like barns—*not* farmhouses, these are liable) do not pay rates. This is the result of evolution since 1896 when partial relief was given to such property. Mines,

Local Authorities Expenditure, England and Wales, 1951–52

Total on current account:	£987,679,000
Total on capital account:	£426,165,000

Current Account Expenditures

	Thousands
Education	£316,174
Libraries and museums	10,042
Individual health	38,455
Public health	75,870
Housing	104,173
National assistance	17,369
Child welfare protection	14,307
Town and county planning	5,573
Roads and bridges	69,991
Private street works	3,928
Street lighting	9,966
Fire service	16,500
Administration of justice	5,538
Land drainage	6,690
Small holdings and allotments	2,916
Civil defense	2,881
Other emergency services	16,425
Trading services:	
Cemeteries	4,513
Water supply	36,411
Passenger transport	56,676
Harbors, docks, and canals	29,754
Other works and purposes	22,360
Miscellaneous, unallotted	36,385

Receipts

Current Account Items

Rates	£318,087
In lieu (government property)	13,770
Grants from government	349,914
Private improvements	3,979
Housing (rents, etc.)	67,669
Town and country planning	1,119
Small holdings and allotments	1,608
Trading	
Cemeteries	2,395
Water supply	35,971
Passenger transport	55,375
Harbors, docks, piers, etc.	29,762
Other	18,878
Miscellaneous	103,907
Total	£1,002,434

Capital Receipts

Loans	£397,942
Grants	8,685
Repayments	4,930
Sales, etc.	7,853
Total	£419,410

factories, workshops, and other industrial premises are assessed at only one quarter their value; so also transport premises. The idea was to take the burden off "productive" property.

The principle is simple; the application is difficult. The application causes more grief as *between* local authorities than within them (though here there are inequities to some extent) because the most highly rated authorities get a grant from the central government that deducts allowances from the places with a lower incidence of rating. Until recently, valuation was in the hands of the local authorities; henceforth it will be undertaken by the central government, through the Inland Revenue Department. This will produce a more uniform valuation—which began in 1955, and thenceforward there are to be quinquennial revaluations. The ancient publication of the valuation lists and appeals to the courts will continue.

The rate is stated as so many pennies in the pound of ratable value: for example, 16 shillings and 4 pence in the pound. The ratepayer pays, then, this amount multiplied by the number of pounds at which his premises have been assessed. Thus, in 1953–54 the total ratable value for the whole of England and Wales was £347,278,000; the rates totaled £377,234,000; the "poundage" or average rate was 21 shillings 9 pence in the pound. In cases of low-rental tenements and cottages, the occupiers may pay their rates in a compounded form, within the rent. Then the landlord pays the rates and is allowed a commission by the local authority for his virtual assumption of the responsibility of collection.

This system of rates has been handed down to our own time from the era of Queen Elizabeth I. Ability to pay had to be tested by local unpaid, unskilled, and willing overseers. They took the obvious criterion: the one that could not run away or hide (as personal property can)—namely, real property in occupation. It is rather crude but effective, especially when it is compared with the awkwardness and inefficiencies of the American "property" tax.

Yet, since the nineteenth century, the flexible and accurate method of income taxation has been developed, with its allowances and deductions for family commitments. The rental value of a house is a *degressive* item of taxation. But the income tax is hardly applicable to the local authorities, for there would be disputes between them as to the location of the origin of the income; and the collection of the central tax, from which millions of the poor are exempted, is already a heavy administrative burden. The rating system therefore will stay—*relieved by central grants*.

Grants-in-aid

The chief services specifically subsidized by the central government's grants-in-aid are: education, police, roads, housing, development areas, health, and town and country planning. In addition, a general grant is made for equalization. Here, it is possible only to describe the general principles involved.

History of Grants-in-aid. In 1835, when the municipal boroughs were reformed, there were no grants-in-aid at all. Today (1951–52) their amount is a very substantial £350,000,000. The first grants were those given to the counties and boroughs for the costs of prosecution and for the removal of prisoners to the place of trial. It was the recognition of an obligation of the *nation* for a national service administered locally. The nascent education system, as maintained by the Government through the religious bodies, next called for grants-in-aid. Then, in 1839 it was recommended that the cost of the police forces of the counties should be subsidized, but the county authorities were unwilling to sell their liberties for a *quarter* of the cost. In 1856 they accepted *half* the cost of the police forces, subject, like the schools, to inspection by the central government's inspectors.

We need not pursue the matter of history further; it is wrapped up in the nature of the grants and the services as they newly arose.

The Various Kinds of Grants; Rationale. Parliament has recognized that some services, such as the police and education, are truly of national importance; hence it is equitable that some of the expense shall be borne by the Exchequer. It recognizes that there ought to be a national minimum quality of local services; it must sustain the poorer authorities at least. Further, it not only needs a national minimum, but the grants ought to be organized to stimulate authorities that want to spend beyond the minimum to do so; they deserve encouragement as pioneers and models. Finally, many authorities are very poor in ratable value, and the grants are measured according to *need,* a specially heavy grant being made to the poorer units.

Local authorities can spend as much out of the rates as they think it wise to levy: there is no legal limit to the rates they may raise. But there is a natural reluctance on the part of local councilors to increase expenditures and raise rates. That is unpopular, and they themselves pay rates also. The central authority is even impelled to force many local authorities to meet certain minima owing to their civic lukewarmness or apathy.

On the other hand the central authority has the advantage of two things: (1) local knowledge and interest in local administration, and this relieves it of a great strain, and (2) *a financial sanction for its powers to inspect and regulate and improve* the work of the authorities that fall below a tolerable standard.

The Types of Grants. Three kinds of grants cover practically the whole field: (1) *percentage* grants; (2) *unit* grants; and (3) *formula* grants.

The Percentage Grants. Such grants are typified by the payment of a percentage of the cost of certain services. For example, police: one half of the approved expenditure incurred by the local authorities; the approval means that the Inspectors of Constabulary of the Home Office are satisfied. So also, the fire service—one quarter the approved expenditure; so also for construction and maintenance of the roads, at a varying amount. These are on a *lump-sum* principle—no items of the expenditures (for example, salaries, clothing, boots, cars, etc., are not subsidized separately) carry specific amounts of grant. The percentage grant is simple to administer; it is encouraging of expenditure, for somebody else pays one half of any increase the local authority may decide to spend. It has the disadvantage of its advantage: encouragement for a local authority to call the tune for the central authority. It tempts the central government into setting "standards" of what may be approved expenditure, and hence interference in local discretion.

The Unit Grants. This limits the central gov-

ernment's commitment, and puts the onus of being extravagant or parsimonious on the local authority: the government pays a standard amount in aid of a service, for example, *x* pounds per year for so many years in aid of houses built by local authorities. This takes no heed of the amount the authority wishes to spend per house, or of the authorities' relative inability to pay. Nor does the percentage grant.

The Formula Grants. These combine the types of grant we have mentioned and, in addition, make allowances in subsidies for the poverty of the poorer units. For example, the outstanding case is the education grants. The central government gives special grants for school meals and milk. Then for the Main Education Grant, it has the formula of: (1) 120 shillings per child (capitation grant) in full-time attendance in the primary and secondary schools, as discerned from the school authorities' registers; and (2) 60 percent (a percentage) of the expenditures on teachers, equipment, etc., as recognized by the Minister, *less* (3) the product of a rate of 2 shillings and 6 pence in the pound in the area of the authority. The effect of this provision is to take away more from the places of high ratable value than of low.

Another kind of formula grant—and it accounts contemporaneously for one sixth of the total of all the grants put together—is the Equalization Grant. It is not appropriated to any specific service of the local authorities. It may be expended in their discretion. The areas vary so greatly by reason of (1) their population and (2) the per-capita wealth of their population that enormous disparities exist in ability to finance services. It is an intricate formula but the basic principles are simple. One element is the extent to which the ratable value of an area is higher or falls short of the average ratable value for all authorities in the country; all get some grant, but the poorer ones get more in proportion as they fall below the average figure. Second, a *weight* is allowed for the numbers of *children of school age* in the area; they are costly in the social services. Third, there is a weight for sparsity of populations in the counties; it costs more per head to administer a unit whose population is spread out than a crowded one—the principle works on the basis of number of people per mile of roads. The population of the areas, so doubleweighted, give a set of figures for counties and county boroughs: the first division of the total grant donatable by the Government is made by the ratios thus supplied. The county boroughs keep their amount and spend it themselves. The county's amount has to be shared between it and the various boroughs and districts. These lesser authorities receive an amount from the county for the boroughs and urban districts share on a formula set down by the Government—a sum per head of population based on the amount of the equalization grant received per head by the counties, and one half of this sum for the rural districts.

There are periodical recalculations of the grant every few years.

The history of experiments with different grants-in-aid in Britain, over a period of over one hundred years, is full of lessons on the problems of central assistance and control.[4]

VI. PRINCIPLES AND METHODS OF CENTRAL CONTROL

The principal departments in Whitehall having direct control powers over the local authorities are the Ministry of Housing and Local Government, the Ministry of Education, the Ministry of Health, the Ministry of Transport, and the Home Office. The names of the Ministries immediately denote their range of interest in local government services.

The Reasons for Central Control

There are good reasons for more or less central control. The knowledge possessed by a local unit is narrow. Powerful interests in the local area that have to be controlled may be in a position to interfere with the official independence of the officials, for example, butchers and the sanitary inspectors, landlords and the surveyor, taverns and the police. The local authority may make mistakes; the central authority prefers to anticipate and prevent these, though this seems (and is) a qualified distrust of local democracy. Thus, the audit of

[4] Most recently studied in John Harris, *Inspection of Local Government in England*, New York, 1956.

accounts by the Ministry of Housing and Local Government is an example of such watchfulness. Parliament, composed of much the same people (sometimes the same people) as the local councilors, has believed that it is better not to put an excessive strain on the conscience of average men in local government.

Furthermore, as we have already intimated, some local authorities do not see the distant danger of neglect. The neglect by some authorities may jeopardize the health and safety of their neighbors—fire prevention, police protection, the isolation of people with contagious diseases, the pollution of rivers are illustrations. The central authority seeks a national minimum, is prepared to pay toward getting it, wishes to control the quality of the service bought.

Two factors stand in the way of excessive central control: (1) a respect for local independence, sincere and deep. And (2) the local authorities are so diverse in wealth, size, and needs that the center is timid of trying to exact a clear-cut logical uniformity.

Further, the large authorities are considerable bodies, wealthy, with a substantial sense of their civic importance and dignity, with officials who are highly skilled and match the famous experts in the employ of the central government, and a sense that if they raise local taxes, the money is theirs with which to do what they like. Larger authorities are freer.

Long ago, in 1630, the Privy Council even established Commissioners of the Poor from among its members, as a controlling authority, circulating a Book of Orders to secure administrative control. The system failed, for the Civil War disrupted the connection between the center and the localities, even confusing the authority of the center itself.

The Contemporary Means of Central Control

These are:
  1. General tutelary and advisory;
  2. Application of the law through rules, orders, and regulations;
  3. Participation in the grant of powers to local authorities;

4. Powers of approval in certain fields;

5. Prescription of qualifications and tenure of some officials;

6. Power of action in default and invocation of judicial control;

7. Authorization of loans;

8. Certain administrative appeals;

9. Power of inquiry and demand for reports;

10. The audit of local accounts;

11. The power of inspection, usually coupled with its grant-in-aid power;

12. The grant-in-aid power already discussed, and given no further treatment: it is a help, and encouragement and a sanction.

We now explain each of these, compelled to keep some of the comments to hardly more than a sentence or two.

1. General Tutelary and Advisory. The central departments have each a responsibility for promoting or improving the services vested in them. In pursuance of this responsibility, they keep a general watch and ward over the local services within their field, conduct inquiries, public notes of impending legislation, statistics, skilled advice, call conferences. They maintain consultative councils, as for example, in education, public health, or water supply, made up of experts and representatives of the local government associations, for the discussion and recommendation of various advances in science and technology, of an invaluable type.

2. Application of the Law. The central authorities are vested with the carrying out of various local government service statutes. An immense body of such rules and orders regulate the administrative practice of the local authorities (for example, road building, training of police, building regulations) —they carry them out, and there is *still* room for local diversity of judgment. The departments formulate the rules with the assistance of experts and the local authorities' associations.

3. Grant of Powers. Where the local council wishes to acquire additional powers, the central department concerned has a powerful say in Parliament on the wisdom and feasibility and financial correctitude of the request.

4. Power to Sanction. (1) *Bylaws:* local authorities need and have a large power of making bylaws,

in order to implement their powers, to make rules and set down penalties, enforceable in the courts and appellable to the courts. For example, advertising through billboards, enforcement of attendance at school, not making disturbing noises by singing or loitering in the streets or using profane language or spitting in detriment of health. The bylaws need the approval of the department concerned. This is in order to secure some national uniformity and to help the local authorities to avoid being so "unreasonable" as to provoke action in the law courts. To help this forward, the central authorities have for many years past published model bylaws that local authorities may follow. *But* the approval of the central department does not preclude the local council from action by a citizen for unreasonableness of fine or language or other infringement on the rights of the citizens.

(2) *Administrative Schemes.* For many powers they exercise, the local authorities are required by the statute of permission, to produce a scheme of what they intend to do. For example, "It shall be the duty of the council of every county and county borough . . . to contribute to the establishment of a national system of public education . . . and shall when required by the Board [now Ministry] of Education, submit to the Board schemes showing the mode in which their duties and powers . . . are to be performed and exercised. . . ." The central department gives these schemes a very thorough going over from the technological, administrative structure, and financial point of view.

(3) *Sanction of Fees and Tolls.* The prices charged by the local authorities for certain services they perform—burials, markets, slaughterhouses, water, etc.—need the authorization of the Ministry concerned.

5. Officials. For medical officers of health, sanitary inspectors, health visitors, inspectors of weights and measures, poor law officers, teachers, chief constables, the respective central department has set down certain basic qualifications and procedures of appointment. All these are specially skilled officials in areas of social importance or urgency to the community.

In the case of the medical officers, they are not removable by the local council without approval of the Ministry of Health, lest local interests should interfere with the due exercise of the officer's enforcement powers.

6. Action in Default. If a local government authority neglects its public-health duties, the Ministry of Health can appoint persons to carry out the work by default and to charge the rate fund of the authority with the expenses. It is very rarely used; but it is a final shaming device that keeps the local councils to an acceptable minimum. The law courts can be invoked by the Ministry for a *mandamus* order to compel performance. This is even more rare. It has sometimes been necessary for Parliament to pass a special law to allow a central Ministry to act in default of a refractory or wayward local council.

7. Authorization of Loans. This is discussed on page 252.

8. Appeals. There are a number of situations in which the central departments are appeal authorities: disputes among local authorities over certain matters; among officials and councils other than their own over information they must supply. There is a last appeal on law to the courts, if desired; but the administrative procedure is expeditious and skilled, and the local authorities are not averse to it.

9. Inquiries and Reports. The statutes give the central departments powers to call for information, statistics (for example, of diseases), and enables and sometimes requires them to make local inquiries, as for example, for private act purposes or for the alteration of boundaries.

10. Audit. The accounts of all counties, urban and rural districts, and parishes are audited annually by the district auditors, who are central officials, formerly of the Ministry of Health, now of the Ministry of Housing and Local Government. As for county and noncounty boroughs, their general accounts are not so auditable; but various statutes have subjected specific accounts of theirs to audit: education, housing, public assistance, public health, and fire services. These local councils may submit voluntarily to general audit. It has its advantages for the locality. About one half of the noncounty boroughs have done so; but only one in nine of the county boroughs. If a council gets into fi-

nancial difficulties, it may be maneuvered into asking for voluntary audit. The boroughs are exempt only because in 1835 it was then believed that the control of the councils by the electoral process would be adequate to secure purity of administration—and the exemption stuck.

The powers of the auditors are these: to audit the accounts, and then to *disallow* any item contrary to the law and to *surcharge* the person authorizing or making the illegal payment—that is, to charge against the person or persons spending illegally the payment of the amount in question.

It is possible to appeal to the courts against a surcharge, for there may be an error of legality by the auditor—for example, over the words *negligence* or *misconduct* that appear in the statute.

The power of control by audit is very potent: the misdemeanant may have to pay out of his own pocket for his errors.

In most cases, the issues are clear. It is in the power of the central department to quash a surcharge—since too many small errors are *bona fide* or are accountancy errors. Embezzlements are few—restitution is made. The average of all surcharges per annum is of the order of £50,000 as against audited expenditure of about £500,000,000 or more.

The courts have held—for the surcharged councilors have appealed—that a local authority holds a position of trust to the local community. The language that permits it to spend may be wide, but it must be regarded as limited by the principle that the local councilors *cannot* do altogether as they like; they must not spend *excessive* amounts of money for a legitimate purpose when a lesser sum could have done the job. Thus, the issue that arises is what is *excessive* in a specific case. On this there can be tension between auditor and local council: there is some. Then town clerk and financial officer know the cases and can advise the council when they are becoming so excessively excessive as to bring trouble on themselves.

The district auditors number about ninety, of various grades. They may hear ratepayers' objections to certain expenditures. Their knowledge must embrace the law and accountancy and local government practice. In addition, they need sound managerial and interpersonal principles. The Civil Service Commission has devised an appropriate examination for their recruitment.

11. **Inspection.** The principle of inspectability was formulated first by Jeremy Bentham (see p. 32). The purpose is to bring about a direct personal contact between the central authorities in London and the 12,600 local authorities and their many thousands of institutions, such as schools, police stations, roads divisions, and so on. Writing between the center and the localities, even telephoning, lacks the intimate and minute qualities of the operation of the five senses on the spot. The central authorities consequently have inspectorates, men and women, who are its personal links, its personal servants, to be its eyes and ears, and not infrequently, its voice. The grants-in-aid it pays, or arranged to be paid, are dependent on either a certificate of approval of the local services or its not denying approval to the local services and councils. There is no hierarchical arrangement of inspection: the inspectors are *direct* contacts between center and each local unit, whether county borough or rural district.

It will be remembered that among the grants is one dependent on a formula for equalization (p. 255). The Ministry of Health may reduce this grant by any amount for failure of the local council to maintain a reasonable standard of efficiency and progress in any of its health services—it is a formidable instrument to back up the Ministry's inspectorial duties.

It is impossible to enter into an analysis of the various inspectorates: for public assistance, public health, roads, education, and police. Each is specialized; each is appointed by methods of recruitment devised and administered by the Civil Service Commission.

The inspectors acquire the ability and influence to secure the improvement of local services, without coercion or sanction. They have initial skill—the education inspectors have had experience in the schools, for example—they accumulate considerable knowledge of comparative practice and standards as they make their itineraries among a great diversity of local authorities (the diversity is important in their learning process); they are neutral outsiders. All this gives weight to their mere counsel. This is a most important sphere of his duties.

To avoid delay and misunderstandings as to the central authority's standards and wishes on many matters of control and obligation, the central authorities have given an informal but effective amount of decision to be made on the spot.

VII. SUMMARY

A vast amount of decentralization in the social and protective services is prevalent in the British system of government. It is incomparably freer than the vaunted freedom and power of the local Soviets in the U.S.S.R.; it is much freer than the local government systems of the Continent. It is democratic, being democratically elected; and the powers of control of the central departments are established by a Parliament responsive to the good sense of the electorate. The freedom is implemented by the fact that a considerable amount of the funds is raised by local rates and local utilities; the control is exerted through inspection sanctioned by grant-in-aid, for these maintain standards. If the center has of recent years (since 1900) increased its authority, it still has left a wide sphere of day-by-day discretion to the locally elected councilors, enough to secure a still robust interest in local affairs. Its powers of control are exerted by and with the advice of the local councils in question and, at another level, by and with the advice of the associations of County Councils, County Boroughs, Municipal Corporations, Urban Districts, Rural Districts, and Parishes—powerful associations, by reason of their personnel, their legal advice, and the crude fact that, if the Ministries wish to get the law carried out, they can hardly do it in the British atmosphere by coercion, but only with the good will of the councilors.

14

Civil Rights and the Judiciary

We will deny justice to none, nor delay it.
—*Magna Carta,* 1215

A judge ought to prepare his way to a just sentence, as God useth to prepare His way, by raising valleys and taking down hills: so when there appeareth on either side a high hand, violent prosecution, cunning advantages taken, a combination, power, great counsel, then is the virtue of a judge seen to make inequality equal; that he may plant his judgment as upon an even ground.
—Francis Bacon, *Of Judicature*

The Rule of Law. It has already been pointed out that the basic convention concerning civil rights is the Rule of Law (see p. 4). Further, it has been made clear that there is no constitution to write out a list of personal rights in general and abstract terms (Chapter 2). Finally, it has been noticed that (as part of the Rule of Law) all judicial controversies, crimes, and torts come before the ordinary courts of the land, whether the inculpated be a private person or an official, for there are no administrative tribunals as in France (see pp. 518–524) or in Germany or "Special" military and other courts outside the general judiciary, which abound in the U.S.S.R.

I. CIVIL RIGHTS

Now the question is, What is the nature of civil rights in Britain and how are they guaranteed?

Civil rights are not stated in a written constitution. Freedom of person, freedom of speech and print, freedom of association and assembly were the *ancient liberties* to which reference was always being made in the course of English constitutional struggles from Magna Carta onward, congruously with technical and social changes. When the

King's appointed judges liked, the rights were allowed in specific cases; when not, they did not exist. The development of the common-law courts and the legal profession from the fourteenth century was favorable to liberty. As for freedom of religion, given the control of the Church over worship down to the sixteenth century, there was none. The taking over of the discipline and headship of the Church by Henry VIII and his successors ushered in a period of religious unfreedom lasting until the late eighteenth century and the nineteenth—we return to this presently.

The civil rights, then, are today the net result of a long series of judicial decisions in specific cases stating what limits are applicable to the specific liberty sought—for example, the home is inviolable by search, unless there is a specific search warrant allowed to the police by a law court, or that sedition or blasphemy or libel are limits to the freedom of speech. There are other limits in the various statutes that will be mentioned presently, for Parliament has taken a hand by such laws as the Incitement to Disaffection Act, 1934 (subverting the Armed Forces), and the Emergency Powers Acts to deal with interferences with the national self-preservation in wartime.

These limitations depend on the willingness of the majority and the Opposition to impose them—that is, on their acceptability to the majority, with a minority representation on guard lest the essential liberties needed for the functioning of democracy be violated. The law courts enter again at a later stage and interpret the laws thus made; but their interpretation, we have seen, is considerably more terminological and logical than substantial. Whether the judiciary hands down a decision on common law (where the statutes have not yet been made) or on the interpretation of a statute, a precedent is set; and the accumulated precedents secrete the prevailing law. It is very difficult to find an argument to upset the precedents.

It must always be remembered that the protection of the individual is, in the end, based on *habeas corpus,* the laws, and procedure; and the final fact is that the only wrong for which a judge may be punished is the fine imposed upon him for not being available to issue this writ on application.

The right to personal liberty, unless a man is charged with or convicted of crime or civil debt, was a common-law right even before Magna Carta. Writs were available from the King's Bench to command release of prisoners to a court, where the judge might decide that imprisonment was legal or admit bail or discharge them. In the fifteenth century the writ was used by the central law courts to supervise imprisonments by local and feudal courts. In the sixteenth century the writ challenged the power of the prerogative and admiralty courts successfully. *Darnell's Case* (1627) showed that the King intended to be above the writ (see p. 39). But Parliament passed the law of 1640 expressly subjecting to the writ even the King's own "special command" to imprison.

Royal despotism aided by arbitrary Ministers still (under Charles II) tried defiance of the writ. Hence, in 1679 the House of Commons (after attempts aborted by the House of Lords) achieved the passage of the Habeas Corpus Act, "An act for the better securing of the liberty of the subject, and for the prevention of imprisonments beyond the seas."

The statute requires *immediate* obedience to the writ. The writ *must* be awarded by the Lord Chancellor or any of the judges of the superior courts in *vacation* or in term. (The judges must make arrangements to be available.) Obedience means production of the prisoner before a judge, who disposes of the issue—return to prison, bail, or discharge. The law provided for very heavy penalties on the detainers and the judges who do not do the duty prescribed.

The law had some defects. It fixed no limit to the bail. The Bill of Rights, 1689, remedied this. It applied only to imprisonments for criminal charges. The Act of 1816 abolished the limits—for debt, for instance. The judges also then obtained the right to examine the truth of the warrant of arrest—that is, to go deeper into the warrant than before.

Freedom of Person

Arrest is illegal without a lawful basis, in statute or common law. The arrester is punishable at law (even if he be a policeman) for assault, for wrongful arrest. A general warrant for an unnamed person will not entitle to arrest. Yet in suspected treason or felony or dangerous wounding, private persons as well as police may arrest without warrant: *habeas corpus* will take care of a fault. Papers cannot be seized unless there is a specific search warrant; but in the course of searching for them others of *any* crime by *any* person may be seized (so said the court in 1934 when a lawful arrest was in progress). The search warrants may be issued in pursuance of some statute: the Official Secrets Acts, the Incitement to Disaffection Act (here a High Court judge's warrant is necessary). About seventy statutes allow search, for example, for firearms, forged documents, etc. Case law allows search for suspected stolen goods.

Otherwise you are free.

Freedom of Property

Judicial precedents (Magna Carta helped) and such laws as the Town and Country Planning Acts, the Acquisition of Property Acts, etc., jointly prescribe freedom of private property and a fair procedure to determine fair compensation for that needed by the community. The nationalization acts were a remarkable example of justice to the dispossessed owners.

Freedom of Speech

You may say what you like, but libel and slander are limits. It is not legal to make untrue statements about others that will hurt their interests, character, or reputation. If the statements are *true,* and of provable public benefit, speech and printing are free. The courts are very strict about these matters, to save the persons injured. They require responsible expression of opinion, inferentially.

The Blasphemous and Seditious Libel Act of 1819 still survives. Passed in the near-revolutionary climate just after the Napoleonic Wars, this Act makes it a misdemeanor to bring the Government, the monarch, the Houses of Parliament, the administration of justice, and the constitution into hatred, contempt, or disaffection; to wound the feelings of mankind; or to excite contempt for God, Christ, the Book of Common Prayer, or to excite ill feeling among the various classes of the community. Where is the liberty?

But the courts—and the juries find on *fact*—are lenient regarding the expression of antireligious views, demanding, however, restraint of obscenity and profanity. Even the vaporings of crackpots, as at Hyde Park, will demonstrate the almost boundless horizon of liberty in practice. As for sedition, judges and juries of today set hardly a limit, except incitement to violence. Fifty years, almost, have passed since the latest case.

As we have seen (p. 9), the press needs no previous licensing; it is not subject to censorship, except in wartime, and then by special legislation, such as the Emergency Powers (Defense Act, 1939). There, in Regulation 39b, it was laid down that it was an offense to make any statement, report, or circulate a document prejudicial to the defense of the realm and the prosecution of the war. The Government used its powers (it was in the hands of Herbert Morrison, Labour Home Secretary for a long time) not to prevent criticism—far from it—but it did prosecute the Communist *Daily Worker* for bitter provocation after much forbearance and, in 1941, suspended it.

In normal times the press, relieved from the strict law of libel by two statutes (1843 and 1881),

may plead error of printing, give proof of no malice or negligence, offering an immediate printed apology. It is also helped by the requirement of the approval of the Attorney General by those who wish to undertake suits against newspapers for libel. The intention of the last is to get a settlement in a judge's chamber first.

Freedom of Assembly and Meeting

This comes up against the need for the maintenance of public order and passageway for pedestrians and vehicles. The police have authority granted to them by statute (Public Order Act, 1936, brought about largely by the Fascist tactics of the British Union of Fascists under Sir Oswald Mosely in the middle 1930's) to prohibit processions and parades in various places where there is a clear danger to the public peace. Meetings within private homes or halls, etc., are free. But if they turn out to be criminal in purpose, they may afterward be punished. Meetings in public places can be held more safely if the police officer is asked for permission beforehand. This will insure against interference, unless the peace is actually disturbed—that is, on the approach of violence. If permission is not previously obtained, interference may be encountered if the highway is blocked or other people are otherwise inconvenienced, by noise, for example. The widespread public meetings, especially at election times, indicate that the freedom is highly honored. The police authorities have wide authority in this respect. The danger of their politicization arose in the 1930's, owing to the Fascists' tactic of pretending that they were attacked and their posing as the defenders of public order.

Freedom of Religion

For nearly two centuries—let us say from 1550 to 1750—the succeeding Kings and Governments treated vast numbers of their people as heretics and traitors, especially the Roman Catholics who were tied in loyalty to the Pope. The Church of England, as by law established with the Crown at its head, persecuted both the Roman Catholics and the Protestant Dissenters. The Test and Corporation Act excluded from office, and from teach ing, those who would not take the oath of supremacy and subscribe to the Thirty-nine Articles of the Church of England. In the nineteenth century, as we have indicated (p. 69), the disabilities were abolished. All religions are tolerated; no one is excluded from office because of religious faith; a liberal interpretation of blasphemy allows not only dissent but antireligious propaganda.

Restriction in Emergency

Since World War I national emergencies, usually associated with war, have come to be dealt with by Emergency Powers Acts, which define the situations to be met and the corresponding procedure and penalties. In World War I the statute was called the Defense of the Realm Act (D.O.R.A.). Such statutes give enormous powers over persons, property, contracts, civil conscription, and so on. If these powers were not enough for the circumstances, and before they were put in statutory form, the Government had at its disposal *the prerogative powers of the Crown,* the so-far statutory unregulated original powers of the Crown to govern in matters of foreign policy, aliens, the preservation of the nation and the peace. "Force can be met by force." Martial law could be declared in areas where the ordinary law courts could not function.

What was the remedy, and the anticipatory deterrent to arbitrary behavior? The officials or soldiers or private persons or Ministers giving and carrying out the orders could later be personally sued in the courts, even tried for murder. The judges in such cases would have respect for the paramount public need at the time but would carefully scrutinize the circumstances and judge whether the amount and kind of force used was truly necessary. Famous cases have established that there is no impunity in such wrongful behavior, even in a patriotic mood and a dangerous situation. Finally, if the courts should be too strict, it is open to the Parliament to pass a statute of amnesty, absolving the inculpated from punishment and damages. This brings political circumstances before a parliamentary deliberation.

In minor emergencies, such as riotous assemblies, the local magistrates may call on them to disperse and, after due warning, act against them with force—the procedure is regulated by the Riot Act, 1714.

It is clear, then, that the judge and jury are fundamentally the guardians of civil rights. And who are their final guardians? Parliament and the rival and free political parties!

II. THE COURTS AND THE JUDGES

The present system of law courts, and the principles of judicial appointment, flow from the Judicature Acts of 1873, as amended by the Act of 1925, and procedure is based on the Rules of Court made by virtue of these acts. But we know that the courts have had a history since their specialized emergence in the Middle Ages from the Kings Council (see p. 38), and that they have established themselves *as a political "estate of the realm"—that is, with acknowledged independence of authority.* The statutes referred to systematized and reorganized and made more rational what the growth of centuries had deposited.

The Courts

There are two hierarchies of courts: criminal and civil. (There is no special hierarchy of administrative courts, see p. 4).

Civil Courts. The lowest civil courts are county courts, numbering 450 in England and Wales. They function in circuits, and justice is administered in them by sixty-two county court judges. The Crown appoints the latter, the minimum qualification being seven years' experience *as a barrister.* There is a relatively low limit to the property value in issue or damages sued for. If the amount disputed is over £5 and a party requests it, there may be a jury of eight. Procedure is simple; many cases are settled out of court.

The next tier above the county courts is the Supreme Court of Judicature. It is divided into the High Court of Justice and the Court of Appeal. The former has original jurisdiction over civil disputes of any amount or kind; very grave actions will be taken to it; the others keep to the county courts. It falls into three divisions. The

Queen's Bench is the present name for King's Bench, whose medieval origins we have noticed. Chancery, as indicated, is the court of equity. Probate, Divorce, and Admiralty indicate their own jurisdiction.

In each of these divisions judgment is administered by a bench of judges, sometimes singly, sometimes in trios. The Queen's Bench is presided over by the Lord Chief Justice of England and contains twenty other judges. The Chancery is under the nominal presidency of the Lord High Chancellor and is served by five other judges. The Probate, Divorce, and Admiralty division is headed by a President and is served by seven other judges. Any of these judges may sit in any other division, and all may apply the common law or equity, in spite of their usual specialization.

From the county courts and the High Court appeals on *law* (sometimes on *fact*) may go to the Court of Appeal. From this again appeal is possible, by permission of the House of Lords, to *it,* only on legal points. Thus a county court litigant *may appeal three times.*

The Court of Appeal is composed of the Master of the Rolls and eight judges. For appealed cases, the court sits in trios.

We have already foreshadowed the supreme appellate position of the House of Lords, the relic of its transformation from the Magnum Consilium of the Crown in the thirteenth century (p. 67). Only the Law Lords and the Lord Chancellor, by convention, discharge the law business of this House. The procedure is, of course, judicial. The Law Lords are appointed for life, being given peerages for life, for the purpose; they are drawn from men who have distinguished themselves in other benches.

Criminal Courts. The lowest run of these courts is the Justices of the Peace. We have already noticed their origin and development (p. 242). They are (and always were since the middle of the fourteenth century) commissioned to serve the King's peace. In the eighteenth and nineteenth centuries they were also the regulators of local self-government. This power was finally taken away in 1888 (see p. 247), since when they have been exclusively judicial. Furthermore, until 1888, statutes required that they be chosen only from those with a high property qualification and attachment to the Church of England. It was the preserve of the country gentry. The commissions are issued by the Lord Chancellor on nominations by the county Lord Lieutenants, but the latter gets to know who are worthy to be appointed by recommendations from the local political parties. There are now some 13,100 men and 3700 women who are active J.P.'s, as they are called. They are "the great unpaid"; they are unskilled in the law. It is a public distinction to be a J.P. They administer justice in petty larceny, minor assaults, and violations of the bylaws and ordinances made by the local self-governing authorities.

A Justice of the Peace may sit alone for petty cases up to £5 or fourteen days in jail. Two or more may make a petty sessions court in a division of the county, when their penalty powers are rather higher. In certain big towns J.P.'s have given way to paid magistrates, known as Stipendiary Magistrates in the provinces and Metropolitan Magistrates in London. They are now appointed by the Crown on advice of the Lord Chancellor from barristers or solicitors of seven-year standing. From 1835 to 1949 boroughs could have such stipendiaries by petition to the Crown; the Justices of the Peace Act of that year allows counties also to petition, alone or jointly with boroughs.

Above the single and petty sessions is the Quarter Sessions. Four times a year all the J.P.'s of the county, county borough (and some non-county boroughs) meet in a single court. The scope of their jurisdiction is as with the single or petty sessions, but the violation is graver and the penalties higher; it also hears appeals from single justices. The collection of all or nearly all of the J.P.'s makes them no more skilled in the law. They are assisted in the law by a Clerk of the Court whom they appoint. He is a barrister, local and part-time. Some boroughs have replaced this system by a barrister, known as Recorder, to preside over their court; he is appointed by the Home Secretary.

There is not complete satisfaction with the J.P.'s. They grow old, and not always in wisdom. The local barrister who serves them is not always as well versed in the law as he should be. Yet, vexing a problem as this level has been, Parliament has been reluctant to replace the J.P.'s by professional judges, because it feels it is desirable to keep the lay element. The Justices of the Peace Act, 1949, required retirement at the age of seventy-five—for some of the J.P.'s had acted though doddering—and tightened up the rules on the appointment of the Clerks and Stipendiary Magistrates. There are rights to jury trial here; before individual J.P.'s it is at the defendant's option.

In the tier above the J.P.'s are the Assize Courts, courts of criminal jurisdiction, of great antiquity, the twelfth century. Each is presided over by a *single judge* from the Queen's Bench division of the High Court. His progress to the court in the provincial cities is highly picturesque in ceremony. The scope of the Assizes embraces all the grave crimes—for example, arson, armed robbery, embezzlement, kidnaping, murder. The grand jury of other days that used to weigh the bill of indictment and bring in or throw out a "true bill" has been abolished. Indictment comes after preliminary examination by the J.P.'s or by the Public Prosecutor. (This is rather like the French system of *juge d'instruction* and the *parquet* (p. 512). The jury of twelve persons is part of the procedure of these courts. They settle issues of fact; the judge sums up the facts and the law for them.

Appeal from conviction at Assizes may go to the Court of Criminal Appeal. It is composed of three judges at the minimum drawn from the Queen's Bench division. Appeal may be on law, and on a question of fact if the Assize judge agrees or the Court itself does. It may sustain or quash the Assize verdict; it may modify the sentence—upward, also! Here there is no jury.

An appeal lies to the House of Lords if the Attorney General certifies that an important legal issue is involved. Here there is no jury.

The Appointment and Status of Judges

Judges are appointed for life. Removal is by an address by both Houses of Parliament. Those of the superior courts cannot be sued for any judicial act on any plea. There is no way at all of getting rid of a bad judge, or a good judge either, except Parliamentary resolution.

The Prime Minister nominates the Law Lord,

the Lords Justices of Appeal, the Lord Chief Justice, the Master of the Rolls, and the President of the Probate, etc., Division. He does so, it is known, with the advice of the Lord Chancellor. The ordinary judges of the High Court, often called "puisne judges", are nominated by the Lord Chancellor. A puisne judge must be a barrister of at least ten years' standing; for Lord Justice of Appeal or a High Court judge it is necessary to have a minimum of fifteen years' standing as barrister. For Lord Chief Justice, Master of the Rolls, President of the Probate, etc., Division, one must be qualified to be Lord Justice of Appeal (Court of Appeal). The Law Lords (otherwise known as Lords of Appeal in Ordinary) must have fifteen years' standing as barristers or have held judgeships in the High Court or Court of Appeal for two years. The judges of inferior courts (not the J.P.'s) are appointed by the Lord Chancellor on seven years' barrister's standing, and he can remove them for inability or misbehavior. They retire at seventy-two with maximum extension to seventy-five.

It is clear from the above description that there are not very many paid judgeships. Omitting J.P.'s, and including Stipendiary Magistrates, the total numbers just over 150. They can therefore be well paid, and they are.[1] For England is a well-off land compared with France (which has many times more judges, p. 512), and it is considered that high salaries will be proof against the temptation of favoritism (an unnecessary thought for other protections are available). But, above all, the judges are chosen from among distinguished practicing barristers who make exceedingly substantial fees—some have risen to nearly £100,000 a year. The salaries are on the Consolidated Fund Bill (see p. 130), which removes them from annual parliamentary debate.

---

[1]

	Salary	Pension
1. Lord Chancellor	£10,000	£5,000
2. Lord Chief Justice	£8,000	£4,000
3. Lords of Appeal and Master of Rolls	£6,000	£3,750
4. Lords Justices of Appeal and other Superior judges	£5,000	£3,500
5. Attorney General	£10,000	None

Compare Prime Minister and First Lord of the Treasury, £7,000; Foreign Secretary, £4,000; Permanent Secretary in Civil Service department, see p. 209.

No Promotion. One other thing is clear. There is no career of judge the top of which is reached by promotion, except perhaps the Lord Chief Justice. The number at the top is too small. The barristers are appointed judges at such an age as to make it most unlikely that they may hope to step into higher shoes with any assurance at the death or retirement of their brethren above. This is a most important fact; they have nothing to hope from their decisions by way of promotion as their French and German counterparts may have, where the judicial career is a separate profession with grades ascended by promotion (see p. 45 and p. 46). They are well paid; they are honored; they must be content with the distinction of their judgments to satisfy their pride.

The Barristers. The judges come from the ranks of barristers. This, also, is an important fact. The mentality of the judges is molded out of the material of the mentality of the lawyer. The profession began to grow, as we said earlier, when the courts began to admit evidence of fact before juries. This led to the establishment of law schools and a corporate professional ethic and interests. Maitland said:

> What is distinctive of medieval England is not Parliament, for we may everywhere see in Europe assemblies of estates, nor trial by jury, for this was slowly suppressed in France; but the Inns of Court, and the Year Books [that is, the medieval law reports] that were read therein, and we shall hardly find their like elsewhere.

Those Inns of Court still exist; they are the law-teaching bodies for the Bar examinations. The "eating of dinners" by the scholar is simply the admission of men and women into a company of professional colleagues who are interested in the dignity, probity, and good character of their recruits. Lincoln's Inn, Inner Temple, Middle Temple, Gray's Inn are masters of the rules for admission to the Bar and conduct the examinations. They continue to act as a club for all scholars and "Benchers" (their judges) and for some as offices (chambers). Lincoln's Inn goes back to 1422 at least. One must be a robust scoundrel, indeed, to violate the traditional standards thus represented.

The lawyers in their inns successfully resisted

the incursion of Roman law into Britain. They were the support of the common law. They were not something separate from the judges but led into the Bench. Moreover, they practiced for clients, in charge or defense, and this inclined them to the protection of the individual rather than the "State," as Roman law inclines its professional justices. The judge interprets the law and facts as presented in a contest before him between two parties; he is not a quasi-prosecuting magistrate in the European or Roman sense, not, as it were, to conduct the trial of the inculpated.

Figures we have cited show that there is still a marked upper-class domination of the judiciary. Is the judiciary therefore class-biased? Eldon was a Tory; Campbell a Benthamite. There is a bias of the time and a bias of the class. They have far less scope or weight in the British system than the American, because judges are not called on to interpret the general rights and duties written in a constitution (see p. 54). They interpret the statutes in view of opposing interpretations between the parties (see p. 54). Yet in some cases a bias appeared in the past, notably against the trade unions (see p. 61). Otherwise the bias appears in favor of the individual. For it has been well said that there is something like an "ideal constitution" in the minds of the judges (p. 54).

There is a marked professional antibias to the class bias, if any. It is provided by the fact that the judges are the heads of the legal profession. They aim at logic and symmetry and consistency. They aim at certainty rather than originality. They respect precedents. Their notion of justice for their client, learned in their years as barristers, make a powerful structure by which to straighten bias.

The Solicitors. There is one other branch of the legal profession by the side of the barristers, solicitors. The client goes through the solicitor to a barrister, briefed by the former. The solicitor also transact much miscellaneous legal business such as the drawing of trusts, contracts, wills, and they prepare the arguments and get witnesses to go before the court with the barrister. They are like the barristers, of high professional conscience and their own Law Society keeps watch and ward

2 Pages 20–21.

over their fees, their training, and their professional conduct. For both barristers and solicitors the discipline is strict in principle and condign in practice.

The combined efforts of the judges, the Bar, and the solicitors and their professional societies, and the absence of pressure by the Government or members of Parliament give the British a decorous administration of justice with a protection of the community against malefactors and fairness of verdict and sentence to the individual.

III. EXPERT AND EXPENSIVE JUSTICE

There is very much more praise than criticism of the judiciary in Britain. It is comparatively very prompt in business and expeditious in procedure.

British court procedure is expensive because the British law on most matters is not codified, as on the Continent. It has to be deduced from masses of past cases and precedents in the judicial opinions. It is also expensive because several appeals are allowed—in Europe, practically only one, except on points of law.

Often a court (Assizes) consists, it will be noticed, in only one judge. The bias may be corrected by the fact that a jury is almost always involved.

The nation is fortunate in having no elective judges or elective court officials, and a complete severance of the judiciary from politics, once appointed, with the explicable exception of the Lord Chancellor (see p. 137). Also, the rules of procedure are not made by Parliament but by the Rules Committee, composed of judges and barristers. The judges are sharp with barristers who should attempt finagling delays of procedure; the preliminary tussles over the composition of the jury are limited very strictly by technical rules; the bullying of witnesses is not permitted, though persistent questioning is. Newspaper comments on cases *sub judice* are very strictly punished as contempt of court. Criminals cannot take advantage of legal procedural complexities to delay justice. As former barristers, the judges know all the tricks of the trade and will not let them defeat speedy justice, which is the surest deterrent of potential criminals poised between decent and evil behavior.

The concentration of the appeal courts in London and of some of the courts of first instance makes justice costly, since witnesses and principals must go there. Conservative and Labour Governments have sought to ease the burden on poor persons. This is done, partly by a taxing of costs of counsel, solicitors, etc., and partly by providing free legal aid at the expense of the public.

It will now have been appreciated how important are the courts in the preservation of British civil liberties. They must be stout and independent, and they are.

The Judicial Committee of the Privy Council

We may conclude by mentioning one other court: the Judicial Committee of the Privy Council. Formally, it is an administrative body to advise the Crown on the use of its prerogative regarding appeals from the courts of the colonies and the Commonwealth. It inherits its authority from the right of British subjects abroad to appeal to the King in Council to disallow the decisions of the supreme courts in the colonies. This was a common-law right of ancient origin. In 1833 such cases were vested in the Judicial Committee, now composed of the Lord Chancellor, the Law Lords, and some high judges of the Dominions and Colonies and of India made Privy Councilors. Its docket is multifarious almost beyond imagination; it recently heard a case involving the ritual murder of an African prince, the problem being whether the ritual, allowed by native law, was murder. It has, on almost jungle law, had to decide on the right of succession to distant native thrones, and so forth. It surveys mankind in all its systems of law, from Ceylon, from Pakistan, from Fiji, from Nigeria. One year it was interpreting the Cambodian constitution; earlier, in 1928, it allowed the appeal of a native chief in Nigeria to the effect that a person might ask for a writ of *habeas corpus* successively to judges of the same court. This helps the freedom of the person everywhere.

Until recently constitutional cases in Canada were appealed to it: and still, *if the High Court in Australia assents,* such cases may go to it from that country. In 1949 the Dominion of Canada abolished by statute all such appeals.

No Ministry of Justice

Britain has no Ministry of Justice to administer the high supervision and reforms needed from time to time by the judicial system. European countries do have such Ministries at the apex of the hierarchy of the magistrature (see p. 515 and p. 597). In England such responsibility is shared between the Home Secretary (police, magistrates, local courts, prisons, reprieves, pardons, probation, remedial measures, treatment of prisoners, etc.,) and the Lord Chancellor, responsible for the composition of the courts, parts of criminal procedure, and the administration of the civil law. The Lord Chancellor has a Permanent Secretary and staff in his department. But he is tremendously overburdened, for he is a judge, an appointing officer, the presiding officer of the House of Lords (legislative) and a part of that House's judicial body, and an important member of the Cabinet.

It is hard for either the Home Office or the Lord Chancellor to initiate codification or even lesser systemization of the accumulating precedents and pruning of anachronisms, even though they have several expert committees to help them. Many attempts have been made to establish a Ministry of Justice, perhaps by the reorganization of the Home Office. But there is a widespread prejudice against this alien kind of Ministry; it sounds like a sinister attempt to control justice by the Executive. Instead, the Lord Chancellor's office has been enlarged, and added sense of responsibility for judicial improvement is manifest. The political headship of the Lord Chancellor has been stoutly defended as a link between Government and the judiciary that ought not drift apart, the former being advised by a distinguished lawyer (the Lord Chancellor) and the judiciary being surveyed by a distinguished statesman, the Lord Chancellor.

The Government of
France

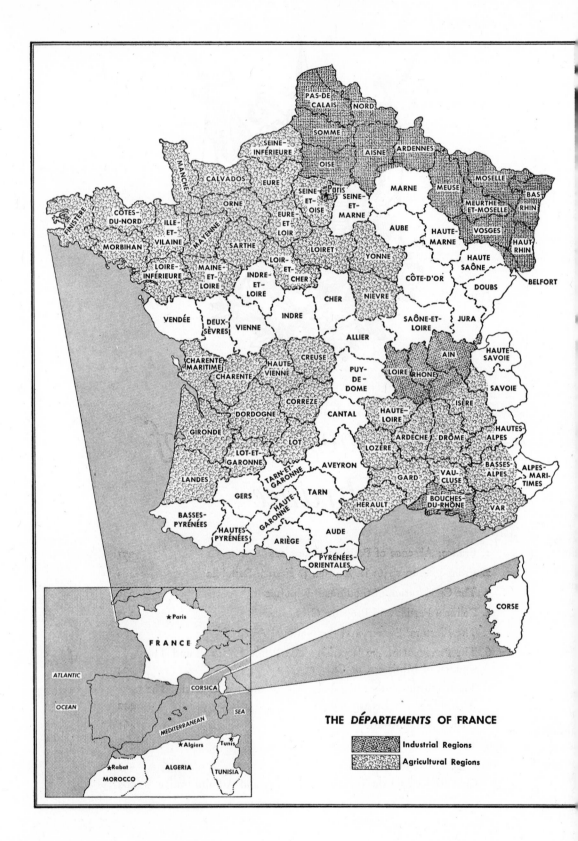

THE *DÉPARTEMENTS* OF FRANCE

Industrial Regions

Agricultural Regions

1

France: Absence of Political Consensus

Allons, enfants de la patrie,
Le jour de gloire est arrivé!
Contre nous de la tyrannie,
L'étendard sanglant est levé,
L'étendard sanglant est levé!
Entendez-vous dans les campagnes
Mugir ces feroces soldats?
Ils viennent jusque dans nos bras
Égorger nos fils et nos compagnons!
Aux armes, citoyens!
Formez vos bataillons!
Marchons, marchons!
Qu'un sang impur
Abreuve nos sillons!

—*Marseillaise*

Culture and Polity

A nation may contribute to the clarity, decency, and grace of the whole world, and yet have a present system of government that is sick. Another nation may possess a vigorous and well-ordered government today, yet its culture may be crude, vulgar, and even corrupt, "a city of swine" in Plato's phrase. The French fall into the former class. In contemplating the disorders of French government, we must not forget for a single instant world civilization's tremendous debt to France—her literature, her theater and dramatists, her painting, her music, her sculpture, her architecture (Nôtre Dame and Chartres), her science, her philosophers, her novelists and poets, her grace and manners, her cuisine and dress, and her wine. How poor are these few words even to draw the attention to her radiant and massive benefaction!

France is a democracy, with a parliamentary system, rather more like that of Britain than the United States and in diametrical contrast to the Soviet Union's dictatorship. But her multiplicity of parties, her judiciary, her centralized administration, her written constitution, her administrative courts, now embodied in *the Fourth Republic*, represent governmental practices different from Britain's. The drastic difference is the instability of her Cabinets (twenty-three Prime Ministers from 1945 to 1956!), the overweening strength of the National Assembly, and the central grip on local government.

With the nation so different from Britain, the government cannot fail to be different. The French nation is internally divided in religion, attachment to historic ideals, economic interests, and visions of humanity. A bent toward a steady majority of its voters in one main political direction cannot be obtained, yet it is a system founded on the right of the majority to rule. The want of a majority in the Assembly and the Cabinet stems from the absence of *social* consensus; social dissensus produces the amazing instability of the Executive.

French Government—the Fourth Republic. The present Constitution of France is written: it is the Fourth Republic, whose Constitution was ratified by the electorate on October 13, 1946. Only just over 53 percent of the votes cast approved the Constitution; nearly 47 percent disapproved; 31.3 percent of the voters abstained from voting; 9¼ million voters said Yes; 8 million, No; and 8½ million did not even vote—in spite of (or, cynically, because of?) a whole year of debate and discussion by the Constituent Assembly. One abortive draft was rejected some months earlier.

Thirteen Constitutions. Until 1789, the year of the Revolution, France had a prescriptive, or customary, Constitution—an absolutism. If we do not count this, then including the present Constitution, France has had *twelve* constitutions in just over 150 years. Some were written with the idea that they would be *immutable,* lasting; but the affirmation and hope and boast were unfulfilled. Even the Constitutions that were thus made were not established in serene circumstances by sober processes. The versions that failed had almost as much claim to succeed as the ones that triumphed for their short lives. Each time a Constitution was made, large elements of the nation were resolved never to make it work, or to work within it, but to destroy and replace it by another that must equally outrage rival millions of the population. **The Succession of Regimes and Constitutions.** They may be thus listed:

> To 1789: *Ancien Régime*—From Charlemagne, Christmas Day, A.D. 800, let us say, to 1789
> 1789–1804: *The First Republic,* thus classified—
>> 1789–1792 Constituent Assembly and Legislative Assembly (1791)
>> 1792–1795: Convention
>> 1795–1799: Directory
>> 1799–1804: Consulate
> 1804–1815: *The First Empire*—Napoleon Bonaparte

The Instability of the French Governmental Edifice

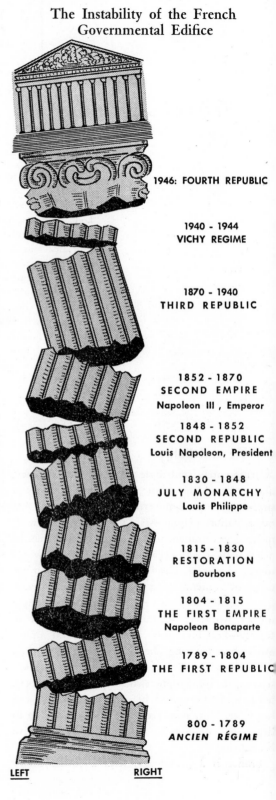

1946: FOURTH REPUBLIC

1940 - 1944
VICHY REGIME

1870 - 1940
THIRD REPUBLIC

1852 - 1870
SECOND EMPIRE
Napoleon III , Emperor

1848 - 1852
SECOND REPUBLIC
Louis Napoleon, President

1830 - 1848
JULY MONARCHY
Louis Philippe

1815 - 1830
RESTORATION
Bourbons

1804 - 1815
THE FIRST EMPIRE
Napoleon Bonaparte

1789 - 1804
THE FIRST REPUBLIC

800 - 1789
ANCIEN RÉGIME

LEFT   RIGHT

1815–1830: *The Restoration*—Louis XVIII (to 1824), then Charles X

1830–1848: *Monarchy, July*—King Louis Philippe

1848–1852: *Second Republic*—Napoleon III as President

1852–1870: *Second Empire*—Napoleon III as Emperor

1870–1940: *Third Republic*—the longest lasting regime since 1789—70 years!

1940–1944: *The Vichy Regime*—Marshal Pétain, President

1946 onward: *The Fourth Republic*—a constitution in that year, but in provisional authority since 1944.

I. SOME FUNDAMENTAL SOURCES OF DISSENSUS AND HETEROGENEITY

Some political scientists lead this heterogeneity back, to the French Revolution of 1789. This does not go far enough back for the appreciation of the causes to the dissensus of the whole of the nineteenth and twentieth centuries. The Revolution shattered French society and drenched it with blood and forced French minds back to first principles in government (dangerous, as Edmund Burke observed, p. 35), but it itself was produced by the *ancien régime*. The traumatic experience, as Freud would say, began long before 1789, and produced it. The results are still operative. It is useless to begin the study of a government as though it had no history. "Political science without history has no roots; history without political science has no fruits."

Heterogeneity in a large territory could be overcome by an enforced unity. This was the way of Germany and Russia, with dire consequences. Or the other way is patiently to await the growth of free mutual understanding and calculated compromise. The French abominated the first alternative; and their second, inaugurated in the Declaration of Rights and Revolution in 1789, is as yet far from complete. National consensus varies in degree; it is far more substantial in Britain than in France, and perhaps more substantial in France than in Germany, while in Russia we know of no consensus because the Communist Party's dictatorship of force does not allow the social groupings spontaneous expression.

Geographic Location

France is some three times the size of Britain, having 213,000 square miles to 90,000, but 43,-000,000 people against 50,000,000. The task of government is more difficult, to rule by common values (p. 5).

The French frontiers have led for 1100 years (from Charlemagne) to painful anxieties regarding the intentions of those who now people Germany, Belgium, Switzerland, Spain, and Italy. Each of these regions had tempting territories and booty; each was a menace. Moreover, the would-be governors were always racked with anxiety about how to extend the dominion of the Paris region—the *Île-de-France*—over the Gauls, the barbarians from the north and east, the Roman settlers and the Latins, who were on the outer marches. Even today the frontier at Alsace Lorraine—annexed by Louis XIV (1680–1697) as the "natural frontier" to the east, retaken by the Germans in 1870, recovered in 1919 by the French, overrun by the Nazis in 1940, restored in 1945—exhibits this tension. The Saarland, rich in iron, is in contemporary dispute.

The sea was a threat: from Britain, which held possessions in France down to 1558, Calais itself; from the Normans, who occupied Normandy, to be a deadly thorn in the side of the French monarchy for centuries; from the Mediterranean, leading to colonial pretensions in North Africa and adventures in the Near East.

The French have never been able to be as single-minded as the British about foreign policy. It has affected their government deeply to this day. Above all, from the seventeenth century, the French monarchy had established *a standing army* in time of peace, as Prussia had, just when the British fought their Kings to prevent this menace to civil liberty. In fact, a French regular army and taxes imposed for its support go back a century earlier. Hence, also, the centralization of government and the limitation of local self-government. A strongly unitary State, highly regimented, "the Republic, one and indivisible" (France invented

The Principal Regions and Cities of France

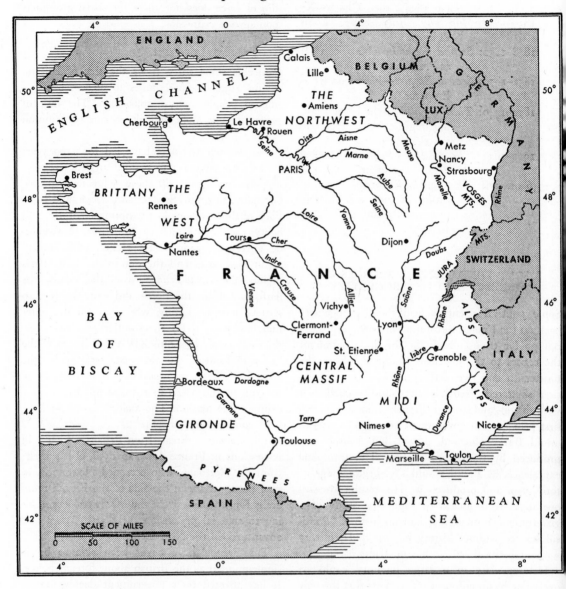

this current American slogan during her Revolution), is the result.

Population

The origin of the French population is very mixed: an almost equal contribution of Mediterranean (Latin), Alpine, and Nordic, respectively stemming from southern France, the Midi, central France, and northern France. The Latins are short, swarthy, long-headed, mentally agile, im- aginative, animated, romantic, rhetorical, artistic, and anarchic. The Alpines are short, sturdy, round-headed—the "peasant" type—patient, industrious, slow, conservative, avaricious for the soil, unadventurous. Savoy, Burgundy, and the central plateau are their habitat. The Nordic French are tall, fair, long-headed, blue-eyed, and vigorous; they are venturesome, constructive, prudent, capable organizers, intelligently responsive to collective effort.

These people have mixed and moved for many generations. It is difficult to sever location and occupation from the effect of biological origin. The north is industrial; the south, agricultural, the place of fisheries on the warm seacoast; the center is agricultural. Yet some of the contradictions of French life come, we may guess, from the personal encounter of the varieties of humanity and brains in the political forum. French scholars insist on this; they allege a consequent intellectual vivacity, independence, a propensity to twist the law in one's own favor, shabby cunning, and preference of profit for private affairs to the detriment of the collective good.

Immigration. In the 1880's, and still more after World War I, France received millions of immigrants. By 1939 these numbered some 5 million, or one eighth of the population, coming chiefly from Italy, Poland, Spain, and Belgium. They joined the urban centers and most became heavy industrial workers.

Proximity to Papal Rome

The Church lost the west and the north because it could not administratively master distance, especially in the absence of roads in the critical sixteenth century. France came under Catholic domination; massacred and exiled its Protestants; and became heir to the gravest intellectual, educational, industrial, and liberty-authority problems, still a plague in politics and government. Only a million Protestants live in France, and but few Jews. Dissent became atheistic, agnostic, or materialist, and certainly anticlerical, on a very large scale.

II. ECONOMIC DIVERSITY

French commentators are accustomed to talking of the French economy as a "balanced" one. But "balance" is a matter of planning and willing. The crude fact is *diversity*.

In 1955 the work force in France fell into the following occupations. (The figures in parentheses give the percentage of those working on their own account, the rest being workers or employees.)

Agriculture, forestry, fishing	31.5	(37.1)
Industry	34.9	(14.6)
Transport	5.1	(4.0)
Commerce	13.4	(43.7)
Administrative and professional	9.8	(9.7)
Domestic service	4.1	—
Not declared	1.2	—

The "Administrative and professional" figure includes the national and local government public service. The total work force is about 22,000,000, a very large proportion of the population because the peasant families of working age are included and because, in what till recently was a stationary population, the old members worked longer years than in richer countries.

Vertical Groupings. Four groups can be said to make massive interests: "industrial" (manufactures, etc.) workers and employers, agriculture, commerce, and the public service. The rest are also important as nucleated interests. This multiplicity of policy-building and party-forming groups (further containing internal contradictions, to be introduced later) is formidable compared with the British situation. For there, industry and commerce are dominant, and only one twentieth of the employed are agricultural, and so, subordinated.

France compares, awkwardly for government, with the diversification in the United States, where in 1953 only 9.6 percent of the occupied were in farming; where industry (in the sense we have used the term for France) includes some 44 percent (even when we exclude some among the professional and technical workers who ought to be included). In France, agriculture is a powerful element along with the other "pressure groups" of manufacturing and commercial interests in the tug-of-war of making decisions about the nature of the national economy and the distribution of the rewards of industry among the various classes.

Horizontal Cleavage. If, then, there is potential political trouble in the variety of *vertical* economic groupings (vertical includes the employees as well as employers in each occupation), there is further variegation. It represents, broadly speaking, the differences between employers and employed, between owners and the propertyless, in each of these groupings. They have interests in common against the other groups; but within each group there is a further conflict of interests.

The Agricultural Workers

The Communists estimate (*Cahiers du Communisme,* June 1949) that the farming population falls into these groups: 800,000 tenants, 200,000 sharecroppers, and 1,200,000 laborers. Of the tenants, same 100,000 farm on a very large scale and are regarded and stigmatized by the Communists as "capitalist" tenants. This means that, in total, about 2,250,000 persons on the land are *landless.* This is a little more than one half of all the peasantry: the rest—that is, some 2,250,000—are owners, most of them of small plots. Some of these holdings are very small. Moreover, in the last twenty years, there has been a very marked decrease in the number of small holdings. Indeed, the figure of 2,250,000 must be reduced to something like 1,600,000 for this reason! Ownership is extremely uneven: 10 percent of the owners hold 50 percent of the cultivated land.

The small peasant proprietors are to be found in the east where the Alpine type of Frenchman dwells, and in the south where both Alpine and Mediterranean (prevailingly) live. The great estates are in Normandy and Brittany, so developed because the Normans who settled and ruled the areas from the eighth century or thereabouts (in Brittany with a Celtic population) instituted feudal aristocratic rule, and this tended, through the laws of inheritance, to large estates. In Brittany, in particular, the French Revolution had only a moderate effect either economically or ecclesiastically—it remained, as did Normandy, strongly Catholic (see effects on today's political parties, p. 336).

Among the peasant farms (the 4,500,000), nearly one in three is managed by the family, without paid help. This produces a closed-in, self-centered, individualistic kind of man, not quick to change his family farming habits or give up anything to the State, but very ready to make demands on the State, which means on other people, for subsidies.

Acquisitiveness. Until World War I the French farmer was inclined to frugality. He envied richer peasants, but the standard of hope was still relatively moderate. But increasing urbanization brought sharp contrasts of wealth and poverty. Foreign influences, from Allied Armies and through the press and cinema, stimulated a greedy demand for a high standard of living. The peasantry, conservative *laissez-fairists* throughout the nineteenth century, now saw that gains might be had from the State's coffers. They are not prepared to render obligations to the nation, but those without land would like to possess it, the laborers would like higher wages, and all would like higher agricultural prices. Hence, they choose strangely different parties.

The Industrial Workers

Among the industrial groups are employers and wage earners and white-collar workers. In industry there is large and small industry. The latter predominates, with some 70 percent of the workers employed in firms of less than 100 employees. The U.S.A. has 25 percent only in units of under 100; and 50 percent in units of 500 and over and 20 percent in those of 2500 and over.

Of the occupied population, 7,000,000 are industrial workers. Today, with the nationalization of the railroads, the total of public employees is about 2,500,000. This means that altogether nearly one half of the entire work force is "proletariat." This number has increased remarkably since 1870 with the acceleration of the Industrial Revolution. Here is the horizontal grouping of proletariat-bourgeoisie, supervening, we shall show, on an already developed socialistic ideology and passion.

In 1890 the industrial workers amounted to some 15 percent of the labor force; by 1930, 30 percent, with population almost stationary. This rapid expansion put a severe strain on the nation's policy. The new masters of industry had no sense of obligation to their workers and were themselves, as yet, insecure. The transformation of the nation's occupations by industrialization, and also urbanization, was fairly abrupt. There is still no mass production in France on the scale of the United States or Britain or Germany. But the exigencies of national defense have thrust France in that direction against a millennial habit of fine, individual craftsmanship, so that, although there is still a very large proportion of workers in this category, the larger portion are now to be found in mining, metallurgy, vehicle production, construction, textiles, and so on.

This has brought about (1) a division of interests between the small craftsman and small workshop, individualist and prudent, and (2) the interests of the mass and assembly-line workers. For the latter it is, on the whole, indifferent whether they work in factories owned by the Government or by private employers, except that more benefits might be obtained from the former, under pressure of the political vote.

A trade-union (*syndicat*) movement resulted, powerful, vivacious, insurrectionary. Yet it came to be split into three major forces: the free, democratic Socialist trade unions; the Communist-organized unions (the majority); and the Catholic trade unions. Its political-party expression also came to be seriously divided: among the Socialist Party, the Communist Party, the *Mouvement Républicain Populaire* (or the Christian Democrats), the M.R.D.

Small Tradesmen

Commerce and domestic services account for nearly a quarter of the whole occupied population. In commerce alone, today, of over 3,000,000 nearly 1,400,000 are self-employed; in services, nearly 750,000. The number of small businesses and shopkeepers is vast in relationship to the total population and other occupations. Instead of department stores, drug stores, dime stores, supermarkets, amalgamating the sale of many articles, the French stick to the overplus of little special shops, the *boutiques,* each selling grocery or dairy products or meat or bread, separately, or only shirts or drinks, a few meals a day. This tenacious insistence on such independence is a powerful egoistic, even anarchic political force. The employees of such businesses look forward to their own independent shop and swell the "pressure group" of shopkeepers. They swell the violent Poujadist *Fronde* (p. 297 and p. 280).

The Distribution and Standard of Wealth

Using the best estimate so far made,[1] the following table indicates the inequality of incomes in France.

[1] Hubert Brochier, *Finances Publiques et Redistribution des Revenues,* Paris, 1950, p. 29.

We have deliberately taken the figures for 1938 in order to avoid the abnormalities of the period of World War II and its aftermath.

Income in Francs	Number of Taxpayers	Net Revenue: Millions of Francs
100 to 5000	1,361,670	3,402
5000 to 10,000	740,170	5,702
10,000 to 20,000	3,578,930	50,449
20,000 to 50,000	926,380	26,595
50,000 to 100,000	124,330	9,062
100,000 to 200,000	38,760	5,454
200,000 to 500,000	17,370	4,830
500,000 to 1,000,000	4,390	2,535
More than 1,000,000	2,130	7,148
	6,774,130	115,177

The indicated inequality is closely though not completely associated with "class" loyalties and demands that the State protect or redress it, by standing aloof or by action. The consequences in party affiliations and political pressures and alliances or hatreds are developed later (Chapters 4, 5, and 6). But here it has been necessary to point to the grounds of cleavage.

The Comparative Standard of Living. France is a fertile land of the most diverse agricultural products. Not possessing abundant iron and coal, her traditional industry has been craftsmanship rather than mass production. Nor does she need to export to live in the degree the English do. Her very bounty, indeed, has caused her farmers to be slow in introducing methods that could increase production by some 30 percent. The subdivision of peasant holdings, resulting from the law of divided inheritance, contributes to backwardness. The fertility of the soil caused Frenchmen not to be so colony-seeking as the English; they yielded Canada to the latter as a "few acres of snow."

The standard of living is a crucial factor in a nation's politics. If it is low, it produces a strain in the competition for a living through the medium of politics. Those who possess are tenacious; those who are poor are grasping. The State is the instrument of both. The French standard of living—by per-capita income—is low enough in comparison with that of the United States, Britain, and other democratic countries to stimulate her social groups into bitter political battles over a few francs more or less.

The total national income is also important, for it is the source of the tax fund for common purposes, such as defense or industrial investment.

Inequality and the Educational System. French education is thorough and of the highest intellectual quality. This aspect of it is discussed later in this chapter. Here one may merely dwell on its still-prevailing inequality of opportunity to the young. In 1952–1953 the total of children in nursery, elementary, and complementary schools of all kinds was about 6,250,000. The total in all secondary education was only 843,000. Clearly the vast proportion of those who finished elementary school did not proceed to secondary education. This is in part due to the high standards of admission into the latter, but largely to economic inequality. The universities and *grandes écoles* have all-in-all only 160,000 students (compare U.S.A. with over 3 million, even allowing for larger population). Once again the exacting standards are a factor; more so is economic inequality. This, then, is a factor in the political battle, and a task of government to extend opportunity and protect standards, as the French have so much respect for the intellect that they do not believe that everyone is entitled to an education merely because he was born.

III. UNFORTUNATE CONSEQUENCES OF LATE TERRITORIAL UNITY

The union of area is essential to that of values and interests. In France it came 400 years later than in England. The distances from the Paris-Orleans center—300 miles to Bordeaux, 280 to the Brittany coast, 340 to Nîmes in Languedoc, 230 to Belfort —baffled the feudal monarchs from the Merovingians (A.D. 511–752) onward. Charlemagne (768–814) extended the Frankish Empire from the Elbe to the Ebro and from the Eider to the Tiber. But the areas had to be held by the military retainers of the Kings. The land was divided among dukes, military commands; and divided again among the sons of the Kings; while the mayors of the palace (akin to the Justiciars, the chief administrative counselors of the King in Britain) usurped the areas entrusted to them and became enemies of their masters. The result was constantly fissiparous. The contenders inside France were assisted by allies from outside: Britain, Flanders, Spain, the Austrian Habsburgs who came via Spain, Italy, and the Netherlands. Britain was saved such depredations by her "defensive moat." Great provinces and dukedoms—Normandy, Champagne, Blois, Burgundy, Brittany, Gascony, Toulouse, Acquitaine, the Spanish Marches— were carved out and held by separatists.

Considerably different local customs and laws were developed. The reaction to this was, in the thirteenth century, a particular central insistence on the concepts of Roman law: "Law is what suits the interests of the prince"; and the strength of the State is superior to moral and religious considerations. Not so in England. It required constant wars to make the principle accepted; and it was denied by the counterwaves of the dukes, sometimes aided by the growing cities, bent on acquiring freedom for the burghers or *bourgeoisie*.

The Estates General (États Généraux

A kind of Parliament like that developing in England (the Model Parliament met in 1295), was first called in 1302 by Philip the Fair. This was an advance on the councils of the Kings called earlier (which included only barons and high clergy), for it included the *tiers état,* the third estate, the delegates of the towns. There was some prospect that they might develop into a united and powerful Parliament as in England, but as we show later they did not do so for various reasons. Instead, they were fairly powerless against the power of the Crown and *in 1614 sat for the last time until 1789,* when they met to develop the Revolution. In this long interval there also developed other deliberative bodies besides the Estates General for the nation as a whole, the Provincial Estates and the so-called *Parlements.* The Provincial Estates were local bodies composed of the three estates; the *Parlements* were not legislator-enacting bodies but judicial authorities with some power of authenticating decrees. Between the three kinds of authorities the connection was mainly that of the personal service on two or more of these bodies of the same men. But it is necessary to look at the reasons why a central Parliament did not materialize to represent the nation's legislative will. It is hardly possible to do this without criss-crossing it with the Kings' struggles against the separative will of feudal lords, religious factions, and foreign invasions.

The Estates sat as *three* separate orders, separately: clergy, nobles, and communes (or *bourgeoisie*). Each order was castelike. They could not reconcile their conflicting interests. The class of nobles did not dry up into a small number as in Britain; it remained swollen in numbers and in pride. The clergy was not reduced in power by the Crown and Parliament as in the dissolution of the monasteries in England in the sixteenth century. Hence, there were always three houses, not two as in England; and the classes did not mingle.

Furthermore, the land was in war crises from 1337 to 1453, in the Hundred Years' War with England (conducted on French soil, with the dukes taking different sides, for French Kings had been English Kings and family possessions in both countries were involved, and in the religious wars that blazed up from about 1540 with frightful ferocity for another hundred years. Hence, the Estates could not secure control over the royal revenues and legislative power, as Parliament had done. Nor could they meet always at one center, Paris; for the distances the deputies had to travel were too great; so the locations were varied. Hence, also, the hold of Paris on the nation was not allowed to crystallize. In the larger country with bad roads, Estates' delegates preferred to stay at home and develop Provincial Estates, and so try to bring the capital into provincial subordination. Another type of local jurisdiction arose: *Parlements,* composed of wealthy personages of town and country; they were not representative bodies, but lawyers, with judicial and decree-authenticating powers (p. 281). They arrested the national unification of justice. In the fifteenth century Paris was the scene of ferocious tumults, the tradesmen, butchers, students, artisans taking one side or the other for the Crown, the dukes, this religion or that, for the city council against the Crown.

In the fifteenth century, also, the feudal lords, led by Burgundy, fought Louis XI, vilifying him as the "universal spider." They resisted rule from Paris, with the dictum, "We will have six kings of France, not merely one!" Their method was to encircle and choke off Paris. Burgundy was overcome finally in 1477 by force, cunning, broken pledges, violated peace treaties, and foreign allies. It was not an end, for the Burgundian heiress married the Austrian Habsburg, thereby giving him the claim to Burgundian possessions in Spain and the Low Countries and producing an enemy to France who was an aggressor for the next 300 years!

The French feudal arrangements allowed the local vassals to swear loyalty to their lords but did not require a direct loyalty to the King. But even had the English principle of fealty of vassals to the King at the apex existed, the territorial distances would still have defeated the power of the Kings to make it good. Ferocity on both sides was endemic; the Kings had to make their state, but hardly a nation, by blood, terror, and the coarsest frauds.

Religious Wars

From the middle of the sixteenth century the wars between Catholics and Protestants began. A large part of the urban middle class were split thereby from their Catholic counterparts; the nobility was so divided; another division was between those who propounded a bireligious settlement and the extremists on both sides, but mainly the fanatical Catholics. The spiritual division coincided with a territorial decision, the Reformation's seed sprouting mainly in the cities. The leaders of the Protestants were some great nobles, such as General Condé and Admiral Coligny, and they were helped by armies supplied by Protestant foreign countries.

After the massacre of the Huguenots in March 1562, which started a train of blood-lusting cruelty, these people were conceded fortified cities —a state within a state. They were again massacred on St. Bartholomew's Day (August 21, 1572). A Holy League of the most bigoted middle classes and lesser nobility fought the expanded safeguards given the survivors, a charter of dissent embodied in the Edict of Nantes in 1598. Richelieu wiped out the Huguenots in 1629—by death or exile. The *Politiques,* a party of moderation, had failed against the Holy League's Catholic frenzy.

Centralization

Two devices aided the centralization of authority in the sixteenth century, torn by wars in Italy for the Popes' sake and wars with the Austrians operating from the Low Countries and Germany. The bourgeoisie, the wealthy townsmen, were partly seduced by the sale of government offices, which gave them office, titles, standing, a share in power, and tax exemptions (see below). The nobility remaining after the weeding out of the wars were gathered to Paris and Versailles by luxury, dignities, sensual gratifications, and the luxuries and graces suggested by the Renaissance spirit and literature emanating from Italy. But this gathering in the capital was not the grave gathering of Englishmen in their House of Commons, then in its Elizabethan florescence as the most potent agency of national policy, liberty, and community.

Richelieu's determined centralization through provincial governors—called *intendants* officially but "thirty tyrants" popularly—was finally triumphant when his successor Mazarin put down the *Fronde*, 1648–1653. *Fronde* means a game of sling-and-pellet played by children, mischievous, irresponsible, and infantile. An outburst of general peevishness against any authority, exertable by anyone else, caused insurrections and riots of the Parlement of Paris against the King's Minister (who wanted taxes); the Paris mob against the Minister; the princes and the nobles first with the Parlement and then against it; of generals' and lords' armies against each other for personal power; Mazarin and camarillas of the court against each other and with each other against still others. Spanish armies helped devastate France, amidst this purposeless madness, predecessor of French riots and malaise in the year 1934 (p. 316).

Richelieu and his successor had made a state, but not a national consensus. There was no community of all the French.

Autocracy

The French Estates, were unable to make use of the opportunities presented to them. In 1302, they had been called by Philip the Fair to support his authority against that of the interfering Popes. He needed money, since he and his feudal lords had been ruined by the Crusades, and so forbad the payment of tithes to the clergy. The Pope commanded the clergy not to pay taxes out of their enormous estates. The King banned the exit of gold to the Pope. He needed money so urgently that he called the *États Generaux*. The *Communes* Estate did not, as in England, include the counties.

Thenceforward the Estates General were called only *at very long intervals*. There were movements as in England for guarantees, such as Magna Carta, more especially demanded in France by the Third Estate, the communes; and under leadership of the burghers of Paris who from time to time challenged the authority of the Kings.

Estates' Dissension. The reason for the maintenance of absolutism until 1789 (whereas in England it had been curbed 400 years earlier) was the dissension among the three Estates. The clergy were close enough geographically to Rome to be kept together as a consolidated caste. The townsmen were separatist, since the law and the nobles' contempt kept them at arm's length. The nobility was a large caste, for it included *all* the children of noble parents—not merely the first son as in Britain—and so were too numerous to be pinched off. Only the great magnates were in England summoned to the House of Lords. In Henry VIII's reign the maximum number of lay peers was 51 the bishops 26; how could 77 stand against 340 in the Commons? Nor did the French nobility and bourgeoisie intermarry as did the English gentry and yeomen and bourgeoisie.

De Tocqueville says, in his *Ancien Régime:*

If we pursue the fate of the word *gentleman* through time and through space, the offspring of the French *gentilhomme,* we shall find its application extending in England in the same proportion in which the classes draw near one another and amalgamate. In each succeeding century it is applied to persons somewhat lower in the social scale. At length it travelled with the English to America, where it is used to designate every citizen indiscriminately. Its history is that of democracy itself. . . . In France the word *gentilhomme* has always been strictly lim ited to its original meaning. . . . The word which was used to designate the members of the caste was kept intact, because the caste itself was maintained as separate from all the rest as it had ever been.

Many French sources speak of the inordinate vanity of the French people. Did this issue from their enclosure in Estates; is it principally supplied by the Mediterranean section?

The Estates always scrambled to finish their sessions and get back home, for theirs was a very extensive country. De Lolme, in his *Constitution of England,* published 1784, adduces a very important fact about France:

> But being parcelled out into so many different States, they [the people] could never perfectly agree, either in the nature, or in the times, of their complaints. The insurrections which ought to have been general, were only successive and particular. In the meantime, the lords, ever uniting to avenge their common cause as masters, fell with irresistible advantage on men who were divided. . . .

The mutual hatred of the nobility and the Third Estate was unappeasable. The latter, remembering its serfdom and the nobles' contempt, was inclined to common cause with the Crown, and thereby lost its independence to it. The nobles were interested in war, national grandeur, and in the Estates fought the bourgeoisie's attempts to reduce feudal privileges, the nobility's tax exemptions, monopoly of high offices, military and civil. The Third Estate was placed in a position of inferiority because voting was not by heads or representative numbers but by an equal vote for each order as a whole: nobles, clergy, and Third Estate. Far outnumbering the other two Estates, the Third was habitually outvoted by the combined vote of these. For the clergy, partly through its landownership and partly through the creed of hierarchy, were allies, in the last resort, of the nobility, even if the lower clergy were hostile to their bishops. Hence, the courage and business capacity of the Third Estate was frustrated, and with it its nation-building ability.

That there was such popular capacity for government was seen in the *cahiers* which the

"orders" (or Estates) drafted, much like the petitions that were presented in the early English Parliaments as the basis of legislation. The local elections for the Estates in the municipalities and among the clergy were nation-building. Sometimes the three orders got together to protect provincial interests, as for example, in Brittany. The royal authority was not pleased with this and used its influence and threats to stop the practice or to subvert the local Estates.

Provincial Estates

These developed in the fourteenth century. They could have been intermediate bodies of opinion and authority, community-builders. Their sessions and procedure were ordained by the Crown; they could not meet for more than forty days a year; their decisions needed royal approval for validity; the local taxes, loans, and budget required royal assent. Yet they were forums of free discussion. They undertook important public works. They apportioned and levied the general and local taxes and were more careful and fair than in the provinces (known paradoxically as *pays d'élection*), where this was done by the royal officers. Such provinces as Languedoc showed the beneficial results. The "orders" deliberated together under the liberal and businesslike influence of the Third Estate.

The royal officers understood their potential power, and stifled them by centralizing direction and by making some members officeholders in the municipalities so that these ceased to be true representatives of their constituencies.

The Parlements

The Parlement of Paris developed from a medieval royal council of judges, vassals, and prelates summoned by the Capetian Kings. By 1300 this high *judicial* body had regular annual sessions fixed in Paris. It gathered independent judicial momentum. Such bodies arose, allowed by the Crown, in the provinces also, especially in a province that had been independent until conquered by the Crown. The Parlement of Paris and the *twelve provincial ones* were supreme courts of appeal in civil and criminal cases and courts of first instance for certain actions over which the Crown had special authority.

The acquisition of judicial offices by purchase made the seats hereditary; the Parlements were a class-owned institution. These men—called the *nobility of the robe*—claimed a certain political power. As guardians of the fundamental laws, they had the authority to register the laws made by the Crown, or approved by it; failing this registration, the laws were without legal effect. As a corollary of their duty to give counsel to the Crown, they exercised a power of remonstrance and refusal to register. This gave them some political leverage. But the King could overrule them by his presence or by *lettre de cachet*. The Parlements were sometimes vociferous, but had nothing resembling the power of the British Parliament.

The Parlement of Paris was the most demanding. From 1589 the Kings and their Ministers set out to tame it. In 1641 Louis XIII forbad it to interfere in administrative and state affairs. Louis XIV ignored it during his whole lifetime because it had had the temerity to register Louis XIII's edict. But on his deathbed Louis XIV did ask the Parlement to register the Papal Bull condemning the Jansenists as the heretics in their controversies with the Jesuits—it did so, though it hated the Jesuits, for the Parlement was made up of lawyerlike men of the world.

Inspired by eighteenth-century liberal philosophy, the Parlements became the more determined foe of absolutism that cost so much in taxes on their friends. In 1770 the Paris Parlement resigned in a body and refused a summons to return, because it had rejected an edict of Louis XV. He exiled its members and suppressed all the Parlements. To the people the Parlements were a group of privileged nobility; they did not go to their support. The Crown set up new tribunals, announcing that offices would not be sold and that justice would be cheap. On the accession of Louis XVI, the Parlements were restored. Revengeful, they impeded the levy of all new taxes, and claimed that these needed the assent of the Estates General. This led to the revolutionary meeting of 1789—to which the Parlements themselves fell victim. Within four months they were abolished

by the Constituent Assembly, in favor of popularly elected judges!

The Estates General had not been called since 1614. Louis XIV could say, after the conscious centralizing by his tyrants Richelieu and Mazarin, *L'Etat, c'est moi!* He was; and he emasculated the nobility by wars and the pleasures of his court, of which his own creation, Versailles, was the glamorous and sensual center.

The Peasantry

All French classes had betrayed their nationhood. The nobles were most blameworthy; the clergy closely followed; the bourgeoisie next. The peasants were hardly to blame any more than the Russian peasantry were for Stalin's dictatorship, unless we wish to impeach for ignorance. Derided by the upper classes as "Jacques Bonhomme" and bearing dreadful tax burdens, they had rebelled from time to time in ferocious massacres called *Jacqueries*. The Crown did not come to their aid. They also, then, had cause to hate the government. (Yet by 1789, about one half of the peasantry held their own free land; and feudal oppression was far milder than in eastern Germany or Czarist Russia.)

Paris

To the rest of France, Paris was a plague: to the Huguenots, a bigoted Catholic plague; to the provincial bigots among the seigneurs and peasants in the eighteenth century, an irreligious plague. The nobles were sucked away from their estates and duties to Paris, and society was immoralized by it. Later on the Revolutions welled out from Paris, disturbing provincial complacency. There had never been a real representative assembly in Paris, even in 1614, to attract national loyalties. And the taxes were drained away to the vicious city, which gave nothing back, save iridescent immorality.

Neither a great capital, then, nor a dutiful intermediate class of magnates were interwoven in a national community. By the reign of Louis XIV a wide gulf yawned between nobles and people, and between the centralized Crown and the localities.

IV. CLASS PRIVILEGES AND CENTRALIZATION

Nobility, Old and New

Toward 1789, 250,000 individuals ranked as nobility. (The House of Lords contained only 200 peers, omitting bishops, etc., at this time.) The French nobility consisted of a few of the old families, called the *noblesse d'épée*—the nobility of the sword—the dukes, the marquises, the counts, the viscounts, etc. A new nobility, the *noblesse de la robe* or *de la cloche,* had come up through service, the acquisition of commercial wealth, and the purchase of office, estates, and titles. Their offices in the judiciary, the treasury, the local government bodies, the central administration, they bought. Old and new nobility hated each other. Yet they had a common interest in their exemptions from taxation and exclusive hold over the judiciary, the day-by-day government, the Army, and the Church. Of the 139 bishoprics in 1789, almost all were held by nobles; and they disposed of nice posts and sinecures, again for the nobles.

The nobility were exempt from the direct tax known as the *taille* (a "cut," as in *tailor*), since it was, from 1439, for the support of a standing army, and the nobles were supposed to satisfy this by military duty. Royal officials were also exempt. The clergy paid a lump sum to the Crown *in lieu* of it, as did the burghers. The major part of the tax fell on the peasants. The poll tax was evaded by the nobility and bourgeoisie. An income tax (*vingtième* or "twentieth") was managed by the Parlements in favor of the nobility. The *corvée* was a tax in direct labor for the State, especially so many days on the roads: the peasants bore the duty.

France was internally divided into regions and subregions around the cities with customs barriers, or *octrois,* tax levies on goods going to and from the countryside. Such indirect taxes hit the poorer people most.

In England, such exemptions and evasions did not exist: nobility and gentry and city men bore their fair share of tax burdens.

The Intendants

The Crown smashed the provinces when it crushed and seduced the nobility. It sent out itinerant justices on circuit; then commissioners who stayed in the localities for longer terms to attend to the enforcement of the King's rule in military, financial, and administrative as well as judicial affairs.

There followed, about the end of the sixteenth century, under the great royal leader, Henry IV (1553–1610), a spreading of *"intendants* of justice, police, finance, victuals and of military authority," to be organizers and arbiters in the wake of royal subjugation. They had unlimited power. By the middle of the seventeenth century their military power was shed, but their civil power was all the more firmly fixed with the final victories of Paris. Such a class of central officials was threatened by Charles I and the Privy Council in England just before the Civil War (1640–1649). The victory of the gentry and Cromwell's armies ratified the power and obligations of the gentry in the English localities (pp. 39–40). There were no strong local assemblies or collection of families or towns and gentry, as in England, to challenge the *intendants:* there was appeal only to the Crown. Richelieu invigorated and electrified the office of intendant.

Henry IV had been served by the renowned Minister Sully. He had manifested the energy of an active State, perhaps as the beginner of French *étatisme*—that is, State authority in economic and social affairs. He had reduced the *taille;* freed trade in agricultural produce; established commercial companies for silk-weaving, glass-making, tapestry; roads, canals, land-drainage works were pressed forward. This was essential because the country was dying under the blows of the religious wars.

Yet, among measures taken by Sully to replenish the royal treasury was the sale of office, sometimes called venality of offices, or, in French, the *vénalité des charges.* We return to this disaster shortly.

Colbertism. Jean Baptiste Colbert, Comptroller of Finances under Louis XIV, has given us the word

Colbertism, the French equivalent of *mercantilism* in England and *cameralism* in Germany. In each case is meant, the planning by the State of economic welfare and national strength, from the government's point of view, imposed on the people by law, in the case of France by absolute decrees, backed by the force of royal officials. It is the early form economic planning.

Louis XIV himself received the name of *roi administrateur,* because of his own sedulous attention to the administrative detail of his centralized kingdom. Colbert's work was comprehensive and went into unbelievable minutiae. Every kind of public works was instituted, and if not manageable by the municipal authorities, then immediately transferred to the *intendants.* They constantly reported back to him. Industries of lace, silk, Venetian glass, war munitions, mining, forestry, horse-breeding were pressed on. The qualities of manufactures were regulated in detail; the prices set; inspectors appointed to see that the rules were fulfilled. The guilds were given powers to carry through the regulations and were themselves regulated. All the important agricultural products were fostered. Exports were encouraged; imports were obstructed by tariffs. A vast stream of instructions gushed from the center to the provinces; minute reports and requests for permission to proceed ascended from the provinces to Colbert.

By the time of the Revolution, the initiative of the nation itself had been hollowed out. All motor force came from the King's Council—his own selected officials, usually middle-class capable officers but not running counter to royal authority. The chief of the royal center was the Comptroller of Finances. The nobles would have felt insulted to be appointed *intendants* or really working officials: for they were *gentilhomme!*

Centralism

The administration of France, let us say, from the middle of the seventeenth century to 1789, appeared somewhat as follows. The largest area of local government was the *province* an anciently developed historic area, of which there were 30. These were governed by the Provincial Estates (p. 281), and their highest local judicial institution

was the *Parlement* (p. 281), while below the Parlement, for judicial purposes, were the various tribunals in the smaller areas, over 400 of them, called *baillages,* or as the Anglo-Saxon world knows them, *bailiwicks.* All these authorities were manned by an oligarchy of the nobility, clergy, and wealthier bourgeoisie and officeholders who had bought or inherited their offices. They themselves came under the tremendous and almost omnipotent authority of the royally appointed *intendants.* The *intendants* and their own subordinate officers, called *sub-délégués,* worked in areas within the provinces called *généralités* or synonymously *intendances,* the area of their office.

Within these areas were the ancient formations of the municipalities—that is, towns and villages and parishes. Growing freely for centuries, their government fell into the hands of various restricted oligarchies of the bourgeoisie, nobility, and clergy, as in England the municipal boroughs came under the rule of so-called "close" corporations because their ruling group was "closed" or restricted against the general body of inhabitants. An early royal ordinance of the seventeenth century required the officers to be elective. This rule fell into scornful abuse. A few selfish families shared out the offices among themselves—that is, of mayor, syndics (councilors and executive agents), treasurer, seal officers, etc. The rule varied from locality to locality. Occasionally the general meeting of inhabitants elected the officers and councilors; more often the "notables" among the nobility and clergy and the various craft, professional, and merchant guilds chose them; the slate was even more often prepared behind the scenes by their politicians. Sometimes the Crown interfered in the appointments, especially of the mayor, for the towns (sometimes called *communes*) were resisters of royal, central power. The result was mismanagement, the nature of which may be deduced from a royal edict of 1683, giving a sharp tutelary power to the *intendants* over these municipal authorities: the *intendants* were to authorize their expenditures, their sale and purchase of property, the loans they wished to raise, law suits they wished to press, the suitability of the officers. This resembled the central government controls set up in England in 1835, 150 years later!

Yet in 1692 the Crown made the offices *vendible!* This further removed local decision from the local citizens, and the offices were much multiplied, on the claim of more efficiency but with the purpose of simply raising revenue for the Crown. In 1764 royal edicts were issued for the various classes of local units, graded by number of inhabitants, establishing their officers and council; the mayor was made a royal appointee; the syndics and councilors who worked with him were made elective by the notables, as mentioned above. At the village level, there was no mayor, but only a syndic, who was the agent elected by the general meeting of inhabitants at the parish church, to take care of sales, purchases, repairs, law suits, nomination of schoolmasters, collectors of dues, etc. Here the local feudal lord, the *seigneur,* was an interfering and vetoing nuisance.

As the *intendants* acquired the whole range of royal authority to govern in every kind of governmental activity, financial and otherwise, initiatory, inspectorial, punitive, and investigative, local self-government was destroyed from outside; and from inside, the general body of Frenchmen were excluded from self-government and lost all the values of its training in public duty and self-confidence.

Ironically, the whole nation, owing to its uneven historical inclusion in the realm, was a patchwork of very diverse legal systems, called *coûtumes,* or customs, highly resistant to many attempts at unification. It required the power of the Revolution to overcome these.

Administrative Law. In this system began the famous French system of *administrative law*—that is, the transfer of all cases in which the public authority was concerned from the ordinary courts to special courts under the domination of the Crown. This was precisely the development, in the Star Chamber in England, that was resisted and helped to bring on the Civil War (p. 39). On the other hand, the *intendant* frequently interfered, successfully, in the conduct of criminal trials.

Sale of Governmental Offices

Now it is necessary to characterize the *venality of offices.* The offices of government may be filled by popular or semipopular election *or* by patronage and spoils, by favoritism and gift, *or* by sale. This last—sale—is a singular system, not practiced by either England or Prussia or other Germanic states, developed in France from the fifteenth century until it became a disastrous affliction. By the time of the Revolution some 300,000 offices had been invented, established, and were sold or salable. This included all officials, central and local; the judiciary; the financial, roads, forestry, postal, and customs officers; all the thousands of curiously classified government industrial and occupational inspectors—mayors, lieutenants of mayors, the police.

National Damage. What did the King's treasury gain from this arrangement? The first price of the office; then perhaps a tax on its bequest; then taxes on the income therefrom; then the trick of doubling or trebling of officials in the same category occasionally brought in more money. What did the purchaser get out of his office, and for his money? The right to charge fees for the service his office rendered. For example, a fee for the inspection of manufactured goods or the registration of some document or the entrance of pleadings at the law courts. He also obtained the monopoly of the office, and the right to resell it, and—a title, with exemptions of taxation, and the right to tax the lower classes. What did the nation get out of the system? Bad and expensive service —for against incompetence, and even malice, there was only a protracted and insecure appeal through the law courts, as hierarchical administrative control was practically nonexistent.

Perhaps the immense strength of the royal *intendants* had its source in the absence of ordinary hierarchical departmental controls over these officials, and the absence of popular redress of grievances through elected councils. For incompetence could in the end endanger the royal authority itself—as in the end even with the intendant system it did—to bring on the Revolution.

Moreover, the office buyers and holders developed into a caste. They could not be penetrated by the penniless. Within the caste itself there were quarrels about importance, precedence, and status. But the collective arrogance, aloofness, authoritarianism, and red tape was immense. France became the prey of administrative feebleness, the law's delay, official arrogance and vanity, and bureaucracy. *Paperasserie* is the French word for doing too little business on too much paper.

The State's Exactions and Belligerence

How could any class of those mentioned look upon the nation, as represented by the State, as anything but a tax-gatherer, a punisher, an inquisitor? It certainly was a newspaper censor and even started a newspaper of its own, the *Gazette de France,* to make quite sure that the information (all innocuous) was really gathered and published. The people, in their various classes, had no share in saying how the heavy taxes were to be spent, no practice in financial probity. It has been estimated that the farmer paid some 80 percent of his income in taxes and dues to the Church. Suppose it is only one half true: it is ruinous. Even the privileged Third Estate—the city folk— had cause to hate the State. Their taxes were still stinging, and the inequalities brought about by the unequal administration in different parts of France, ranging per capita from 14 livres in Strasbourg to 64 livres in Paris, for an average of 32, irked the higher taxpayers. Besides, the debasement of the currency, the prodigal loans from financiers, the suspension of national debt interest payments, the exorbitant commissions paid to the farmers [2] of the revenues, no less than the insane luxury of Versailles, produced a detestation of government.

V. DOMINATION OF THE
CATHOLIC CHURCH

As in medieval England, France, which had been Christianized, say, with the conversion of Clovis in A.D. 486, had a Church that possessed itself of broad lands, counseled the Kings, conspired with factions of the royal family. Many of its highest Ministers were wicked and cruel, in spite of Christ. French Kings had taken Popes captives and held them at Avignon. Rome was too close

[2] Persons who contracted to pay the government the total of the tax it levied, they then making the collection at a profit or harvest for themselves—or a loss!

for either not to fear or have need of the other. The Spanish Catholic Kings (of the Inquisition!) were on French borders; the Catholic Austrians were on the frontiers at Lorraine, the Netherlands, and Provence. In 1557 Philip of Spain's armies were victoriously marching on Paris from the northeast—boasting that they were only three days' march away!

Between 1562 and 1598 eight horrible wars rent France, ending only in the destruction of the *places de sûreté* of the Huguenots, who were Calvinists, and of their seaport, La Rochelle, the link to England and other Protestant allies.

The French were overwhelmingly Roman Catholic; the highest estimate of dissenters was 300,000. But the latter were wealthy and good soldiers, men of the upper bourgeoisie and some nobility. The war was between the King as head of the Gallican and Catholic Church and the dissenters. The Catholic bigots would overthrow him, perhaps assassinate him, unless he acted as bigotedly as they; their allies on the frontiers would invade France on a crusade against Paris.

The Gallican Church had been established in 1516, after centuries of tension between the Kings and Rome over the control of the clergy in France. The Concordat, obtained when the King was militarily feeble, allowed the King to nominate to high clerical office, taking this right away from the Church communities. Then the Pope would present the said prelates. Thus, the Pope got a hold on French policy, for the high Church officials were counselors of the Crown. The Parlement and University of Paris resisted this arrangement, but in vain. Only the lower clergy were elected by the local communities. In 1535 a French Inquisition, the *Chambre ardente,* began to burn heretics.

The Huguenots followed the Genevan tradition, the *Institutes of Christianity* written by John Calvin, a Frenchman born. Paris was the Catholic center; the Calvinists were located along the Rhône, the Bay of Biscay, Normandy, Brittany, and the Dauphiné.

The Catholics attacked. On St. Bartholomew's Day, 1000 Protestants were massacred in Paris, and between 10,000 and 20,000 in the provinces, on Sunday, a day of special worship when they could be conveniently caught in droves.

Political Theory

The Huguenot school of thought sometimes favored the King, hoping royal power would save them from Catholic destruction. But in Francis Hotman's *Franco-Gallia,* they developed a theory of limited monarchy supported by the history of the Parlements and Estates, and in Du Plesis-Mornay's *Defense of Liberty against Tyrants,* they argued on the basis of the social contract and the King's trust from God to support *true* religion, a right of resistance.

The ultra-Catholic Holy League, linking a network of local associations, were inspired by the Jesuits. In Juan de Mariana's *Kings and Royalty,* they asserted the inseparability of the spiritual from the secular power and supported tyrannicide to secure it. Henry III was accordingly killed by a mad friar. The general theory of papal authority over nationalistic and irreligious Kings was developed by Robert Bellarmine in his *Disputationes.* More moderate Catholics, known as the *Politiques,* organized to propose toleration and the enforcement of peace on all by the Crown. One of these was Jean Bodin, at any rate in spirit. In his *Six Livres de la République,* 1576, he urged politics above religion; peace, to end the religious wars; a State endowed with *sovereignty,* to keep the peace and assure free worship for all faiths. This was a tremendous advance on the universal intolerance of the sixteenth century.

Henry IV—the first Bourbon King—was a Protestant, but for policy's sake accepted the Catholic communion, with a policy of peace and tolerance. It was the policy of a famous political tract, the *Satyre Menipée* (1593), directed against the rending of France by Spaniards, papal legates, and Lorrainers for Spanish advantage. "We are Frenchmen, and we shall march like Frenchmen . . . to help our King, our good King, our true King. . . ."

He accepted papal absolution, and in the end he could not save the Protestants. For he needed papal help to block the routes into France from north, south, southeast. The Catholics could never be appeased, when they had power. They contrived the assassination of Henry IV. Richelieu finished the job of crushing the Huguenots.

Dissent Crushed

France was without dissent of a religious nature. It was a grave political tragedy, felt bitterly today and disruptively all through the intervening centuries. For the Church was never satiated. It became the accomplice and sometimes the master of the Kings, and its higher ministers were not friends of the people but of the nobility. It had no French ecclesiastical rivals and therefore was not forced to purify itself and offer social mercy to the poor. No corrective was left to temper its arrogance, enlighten its obscurantism, relieve its malice against the masses and the poorer clergy, stay its suppression of the *Encyclopedia* and the censorship of books and its blacking out of the Enlightenment, that glory of the French mind in the eighteenth century.

Before the Revolution, the Church was immensely powerful by function and property. It registered baptisms, marriages, and deaths; dispensed all charity and welfare. All levels of education were in its hands, from the parishes to the universities. It laid down the principles of book and press censorship; drew up rules against heretics and Protestants. It was, so to speak, an arm of the State, vested with the power of damnation and salvation.

It had considerable wealth from estates and from tithes, the one-tenth taxes. The highest ministers of the Church, secular or in the monastic orders, drew the largest part of this to themselves. The thousands of lower clergy were the Church proletariat. These, who not only attended the spiritual ministrations in village and parish but also undertook what otherwise would have had to be welfare functions of the State, were despised by the upper clergy, and were woefully underpaid.

The noble families, men and women, monopolized the wealth and power of the Church, most of them spending their time in irreligious pleasures in Paris salons. Some sustained the faith and charity; some promoted agricultural improvement. They detested the lower clergy who, usu-

ally unlettered and ignorant men, were nevertheless revered by the peasants for their spiritual,
educational, and social help. The aristocratic
bishops sensed that the lower clergy were essentially friends of the Third Estate and interested in
the Enlightenment.

The clergy was obscurantist and cunning. It
did not believe in the opening of any minds, least
of all its own. It used the doctrine of Original Sin
and the monopoly of the Sacraments and the
Confessional to enslave the French mind, especially that of the peasants. Essential in its social
gospel was the supremacy of revealed truth, anti-
equalitarianism, the exaltation of absolutism, the
denial of democracy.

This was no influence making for active social
consensus among free men, where people think
for themselves and must choose their own leaders
by their own judgment. They had no choice between being believers in *that* Church or being
infidels. If they became the latter, as millions did,
they were open in their politics to forget the
magnanimity implied in Christianity and to lose
sight of the brotherhood of man. If they remained
the former, then they would be enemies of democracy and the cooperation of political parties in secular tasks.

The Catholic orthodoxy that came to dominance,
and pursued it down to our own time, was met
by the dissent of the Radicals, Radical Socialists,
the Socialists, and, later still, the Communists.
The parties were sundered from those with whom
policies of social welfare and education might
have been carried; for the Catholic Church in
France has always been a political party as well as
spiritual ministry, as the pages on French political
parties will show (p. 336).

France has lacked the ever-reawakened political
conscience that is the effect of Protestantism in
Britain and the United States and other democratic countries. Though French Catholicism became so orthodox as to be merely conventional, it
did tend to be a soporific of the conscience, a drug
of social responsibility. Ernest Renan said of the
French Church, of which he was to be a minister,
"Indifference and orthodoxy are closely akin. We
cannot even produce a heresy."

The scrupulously honest mind of André Gide, a
French Protestant, entered in his *Journals* many
observations on the Catholicism of France, some
seventy years after Renan's appraisal:

> Nations, as much as individuals, grow stupid
> through laziness. There is no more harmful doc-
> trine than that of the least effort. That sort of
> ideal which invites things to come to us instead
> of our going to them disregards the *vires ac-
> quirit eundo* [from Virgil: "it gains strength in
> its course"]; and, in this regard at least, I be-
> lieve the rule of conduct of Protestant nations to
> be more virilizing than that of the Catholic na-
> tions, for it encourages effort more.[3]

He quotes from Jules Lemaître, the essayist, this
opinion: "The root of the evil in the French is
their lack of individual initiative, whereas among
the Anglo-Saxons each man counts on himself."
And he adds: "Yes, this is the result of their Protestant formation; and Jules Lemaître is here indicating not so much France as Catholicism. But
just try to say this today."[4] Today was in February 1943, the height of the Pétain-Vichy regime.

VI. FRENCH POLITICAL THOUGHT: METAPHYSICAL AND RATIONAL

The characteristic English political thinkers (pp.
31–37) are Utilitarian and *flat;* the French are
more metaphysical, comprehensive, logical, and
deep. We have in mind Voltaire (less characteristic in the before-mentioned respects), Montesquieu, the *Encyclopédists,* the Physiocrats, Rousseau, and the socialist thinkers of the early nineteenth century.

English thinkers were *skeptical* of metaphysics
also, unsure that from the world that *is* could be
deduced and proved the duties and rights men
ought to have. However, liberty was better served
by the French thinkers than the German metaphysical political philosophers of the same age
(pp. 31–37), because the French thought man to
be naturally noble and taught the need to *free* him
of political and economic misgovernment, while
the Germans taught submission to *external* authority and compensatory satisfaction in one's own
inner self as a *self*-approving moral man. The

[3] Vol. IV, p. 122. New York, 1951.
[4] *Ibid.,* p. 172.

German could identify his self with his group or tribe—the Frenchman never.

Voltaire

Voltaire established no theory of the State. His histories and belles-lettres were polemical, expressing cynical and hateful abhorrence of the Church and the monarchy. Though he came of a socially distinguished lawyer's family, his pleas for freedom of opinion (nourished by three years in England with men like Congreve and Pope), cost him imprisonment in the Bastille without judicial trial, and frequent exile. *Lettres de cachet,* writs issued by the Government to consign to prison without trial, went out against him. No writ of *habeas corpus* was here to secure his release, for there had been no Parliament as in England to insist on it.

The Church was his principal target; *Écrasez l'infâme,* "Crush infamy!", his doctrine. He personally saved the "heretics" Calas and Sirven from the vengeance of the Church. He practiced ridicule, satire, stabbing phrases without limit. It was a legacy he left to French politics. It helped to kill the Old Regime, without helping the construction of a more reasonable one. Politics ought to be taken with reverence as Burke said (p. 34). Voltaire taught men—so black was the Church—to deride authority, and prefer verbal quips to responsible self-commitment. They would wound the body politic in wounding each other.

The Encyclopédists

The Encyclopédists, led by Diderot and D'Alembert, began in 1750, to write the French encyclopedia. (It had been commenced in England by an Englishman.) Voltaire contributed many articles to it. It was suppressed by royal decree; obstructed by the Parlement of Paris; suppressed by the Jesuits. For the articles were theistic, but heretical, and anti-absolutist. Diderot said: "The edifice of mud ought to be toppled over."

Montesquieu

Montesquieu *Esprit des Lois* appeared in 1748. It investigated the remoter foundations of good government (geography, custom, etc.), not utilitarian reforms. It extolled certain political virtues and institutions by which the French monarchy might be judged wanting: a spirit of honor and emulation in the nobility; probity in the Parlements, a place in which Montesquieu had inherited from an uncle; the separation of powers—among king, the central and local estates, the judiciary—to secure escape from arbitrary government and civic tranquillity.

His doctrine of virtue as the basis of a republic prescribes what France still lacks.

> When virtue is banished, ambition invades the minds of those who are disposed to receive it, and avarice possesses the whole community. The objects of their desires are changed; what they were fond of before has become indifferent; they were free while under the restraint of laws, but they would fain now be free to act against law; and as each citizen is like a slave who has run away from his master, that which was a maxim of equity he calls rigour; that which was a rule of action he calls constraint; and to precaution he gives the name of fear. . . .
>
> It is in a republican government that the whole power of education is required. The fear of despotic governments naturally arises of itself amidst the threats and punishments; the honour of monarchies is favoured by the passions and favours them in its turn; *but virtue is a self-renunciation which is ever arduous and painful.*
>
> This virtue may be defined as the love of the laws and of our country. As such love requires a constant preference of public to private interest, it is the source of all private virtues; for they are nothing more than this very preference itself. This love is peculiar to democracies. In these alone the government is intrusted to private citizens. Now a government is like everything else: to preserve it, we must love it.

Perhaps the cruelty of the State and Church did not allow Montesquieu to be more specific; but certainly public virtue had not been taught by Church, King, nobility, Third Estate, or peasantry till that time. One could be specific about wrongs in England.

Doctrinairism of the Physiocrats

They were *political* economists, like Adam Smith (p. 33). They intended to expel Colbertism and install *laissez faire,* which phrase they coined. In their doctrine that all wealth came from the soil, that commerce was parasitic, that government should become do-nothing and let all men be free in their enterprise and markets, they were hopelessly doctrinaire in comparison with Adam Smith (p. 33) and David Hume (p. 32) who learned from them. For they believed in starting from Natural Rights—the "fundamental and invariable principles of the natural and essential order of societies." Nothing so simple! Dr. Quesnay wrote this motto for his fellow Physiocrat Du Pont de Nemours' book called *Physiocracy:*

> Out of nature: justice, order, and laws.
> Out of man: the arbitrary, government, coercion.

The English thinkers looked to human nature rather than human reason; the expedient, rather than the deep principles of the just.

Jean Jacques Rousseau (1702–1778)

"Man is born free, yet is everywhere in chains. . . . How did this change come about? I do not know. What can make it legitimate? That question I think I can answer." These lines open *The Social Contract*. Hume and the others in England were more interested in "How did this change come about?" Rousseau's untrue postulate that man is born free is an index of his metaphysical, or meta-historical absoluteness. And the chains are not all coercive; some are willed by man; some are hereditary; some are the price of the chains he fastens on his fellow men.

Rousseau began that long line of French romantic preachers of the natural goodness of man corrupted by social institutions.

> If man is good by nature as I am confident that I have proved him to be, it follows that he will continue so, as long as he is not perverted by alien influences. If, then, men are wicked, as I am so earnestly instructed that they are, it follows that this wickedness must come to them from without. Close, therefore, the door to vice, and the human heart will always be good.

Compassion, goodness, virtue will follow the making of new institutions. Here is the almost exact antithesis of the Church's teaching that man is originally sinful; and Hume's remark on *knaves* is relevant (p. 33). Rousseau demands a reliance on the spontaneous passions. This is his main innovation in his time, a return to the instincts of the state of nature. The stories brought back from China and the American backwoods had produced the image of the "noble savage"; and Rousseau proposed the world become savage in order to be noble again. Thence, with freedom, the road to human progress and constant perfectibility would be the remaking of institutions. But the remaking must be by the free will of the people, by the "general will" as established in periodical elections.

The present State is bad: it ought to be swept away. Yet—a State is necessary to prevent mutual destruction, to allow of reflection and long-run views. Then the legitimate State should be composed of the noble-savage-atoms. Rousseau atomized the State. He did not recognize what we have been observing (with Hume, Burke, Mill), the making of the State by a community that grows up slowly and painfully out of man's inherent sociality and unsociality from smaller communities to bigger. Rousseau, let it be repeated, pulverized the State; to start anew through the reasonable formation of a "general will." This, in three senses: one, in a contract that founds society; the second, in the giving of authority to institutions of government; and, third, the Will that must be formed continuously through elections to make the policy of every day. He atomized the State, by taking back sovereignty to its original fully empowered individuals. He reduced the State to fragments.

Like all those who do this (in fact, rather like the Physiocrats), he had to introduce a cohesive element to prevent the foundering of the State under the criticism of noble savages. The Physiocrats produced public education in the "principles of enlightened behavior," according to "the natural order" as they diagnosed it. Rousseau had to invent a "civil religion," a faith, that should be the minimum bond of union, and he was prepared to banish those who scouted it, civil heretics as they would be.

It is not intended to overlook the brilliance and ingenuity with which Rousseau wrote, or his stimulating ideas. But, he atomized the State. Jeremy Bentham said of Rousseau's reducing the foundations of government to "natural rights," simply to the rights of man in a state of nature carried into the making of his society today:

> What has been the object, the perpetual and palpable object, of this declaration of pretended rights? To add as much force as possible to those passions already but too strong,—to burst the cords that hold them in,—to say to the selfish passions, there—everywhere—is your prey!—to the angry passions, there—everywhere —is your enemy!

Rousseau left to the French (for example to Robespierre who instituted a Reign of Terror in order to kill off the opponents of his Republic of Virtue) an evil legacy in the doctrine that the first principles of virtue must be sought as the critical basis of the State, that the slate should be swept clean by a return to the Noble Savage's nobility, that one must start with the adding up of the theoretical human atoms. Burke detested him, arguing that Rousseau (the men had met) loved virtue so much that he would hate men, and that he was an exhibitionist and for this sake vitiated his political thought, teaching men to look for the "marvelous" instead of the more mundane.

Root-and-branch Thinkers

French monarchy and the Gallican Church had not left it open to political thinkers to deal in quantitative and reformative terms. They had to be as revolutionary as those were despotic. Early nineteenth-century thinkers had the same propensity to radical, remote and universal schemes, fascinating as speculation, and so most attractive to Frenchmen who have a passion for ideas, but little help to compromising sobriety in the conduct of government. The leading minds were Saint-Simon, Charles Fourier, Auguste Comte.

Saint-Simon. Claude Henri Saint-Simon was the founder of French socialism; he invented the word. Seeing that the Great Revolution had not produced Liberty, Equality, and Fraternity in fact, he jumped to the conclusion that man must go behind politics for his salvation. Man was inherently Noble; Humanity was Noble. The State perverted him. The nation was truly a "great industrial society," an economic grouping. To get more out of it and human nobility, man must know more. Suppose the universality of the Church's doctrines were supplanted by universal scientific laws? This would provide "positive" rules of statesmanship—drawn from man's history.

Then Society would be governed by Priests who would proclaim prophetically the supreme good and inspire men to seek it; the Savants would discover the scientific generalizations to support the prophecies, researching, teaching, synthesizing, and then linking the Industriels to the Priests to carry out their laws.

The Golden Rule, offspring of Saint-Simon's romantic and Rousseauite love of Humanity, would lead to raising the workers' standard of living and their moral elevation. The big community would give way to many small communities organized federal-wise under the central government. Statistics would guide the Industriels to know the needs of the consumers and the producers' services to the community and assist the planned economy to work when free enterprise was abolished.

These Priests, Savants, and Industriels were not to be elected; the people were to be commanded. Eventually men would be moralized, for the State and the Church had failed to do this.

Fourier. Charles Fourier was another Romantic, his *bête-noire* being free enterprise, for he had seen from his vantage point as a grocer's assistant that needy people had been unable to buy groceries at the price charged by his master, who allowed the goods to rot rather than not get the profits far in excess of what he paid to the original producers.

He, too, accused the Church as "a doctrine of inertia, and a denial of personality." State socialism might help. But better was a detour around the State and the present economic system. Little communities, called *Phalanstères,* phalanxes of autonomous cooperative groups, should replace the State. If they were small enough and united people of diverse talents and needs, their mutual dependence would spontaneously produce societies in which *coercion* (the mark of the big State) was replaced by mutual love. All property would be held in common. The small groups could *federate* where they were not self-sufficient.

He detested politicians as intriguers and parasites who fastened coercion on the good people. The discovery of what is right would render coercion unnecessary. Coercion shows something is wrong; and the capitalistic State is coercive. Hence, away with it; it is the instrument of the powerful employers. The vote is useless: for forms of government let only fools contest!

Comte and Positivism. August Comte gave the Saint-Simonian essays comprehensive and methodical perfection. Mankind had progressed through Fetishism, a Theological stage, a Metaphysical era; but now it was at the Scientific or Positivistic age.

> No more empiricism, no more *a priori* reasoning. In political philosophy there can be no order or agreement save by fastening social phenomena down to unchanging natural laws, the sumtotal of which traces for every epoch, free from any possible uncertainty, the essential limits and nature of political action.

He invented the term *sociology;* its laws would replace the infallible decrees of the Pope. He was enamored of *Du Pape,* Joseph de Maistre's reactionary absolutist medieval tract written to counsel the returned Bourbons how to govern post-Revolutionary France, for he despised the democratic idea and the "anarchy" of production and social activity. He believed science and history could give reliable, measured, and invariable knowledge. This would be so convincing as to be obeyed. Bankers, priests—even a kind of Order of Jesus—would impose these perfect tenets on the common man and release the goodness that was inherent in him. In the end he was forced to realize that knowledge alone is no animating force, but passion; and that passion must be love. His motto became: "Love as our principle, Order as our basis, Progress as our end." This, however, means that men and women have different kinds of love—hence, politics again, but this he would not acknowledge. His ideas led to a Positivistic Church and authoritarianism. On this, Mill (p. 36) withdrew his friendship.

What these men were teaching was "If we know, all must obey! And we can know social truth fully and exactly! The dissenter and disobedient are wicked because ignorant."

An Antigovernment Legacy

Thus the French thinkers reflected French society and government—it was so anti-authoritarian as to become absolute by reaction; it rejected tinkering with institutions; it was insolent with intellectual vanity. Therefore, it was a desertion of politics. The heritage is revolution, instead of the expedient second-best combination of Liberty-Order-Welfare. Hence, large sections of the French public were premanufactured, assimilators of Karl Marx's apocalyptic "closed" system, and of George Sorel's revolutionary syndicalism (p. 317) which equally abhorred parliamentary action, preferring a regime of strikes and the ownership and management of industries by the workers' unions.

What if the utilitarian and rather fuzzy principles of Anglo-Saxon democracy produce consensus, while sheer Descartesian reasoning applied to politics by the fallible-mind thinking of complicated Frenchmen does not? For the French love ideas. They are passionate to go to the logical extreme with ideas, and apply them in action, or abandon action for their enjoyment. André Gide discerningly says:

> Probably no country has offered a greater diversity of cultures, of aspirations, of tendencies, of manifestations, of creeds than ours. And this is indeed what constitutes her complex beauty. . . . Who would dare to say that our genius used itself up in forming a single one of them? More than any other country in Europe, our country had and cultivated a sense of *dialogue* [italics added] (conversation, discussion, controversy, debate). Most likely on the approach of a common danger she can and must unite her energies in unanimity, as we have seen that she can do. But never, save for a short time, and at her worst moments, has she listed altogether in a single direction.[5]

VII. THE EDUCATIONAL SYSTEM

The intellectual quality of French education is among the highest in the world, perhaps the highest. It stimulates the traditional propensity to

[5] Vol. IV, p. 94.

logical extremes and the mutual demands for *clarté*, light and clarity. It seems rather to aggravate extremeness and practical governmental unsociality, and seems to abate little, certainly not enough, of the *incivisme,* or uncivic-mindedness, discussed later (pp. 296–297).

Private schools are allowed, if parents want to pay for them; but degrees and entry to the professions depend on the passing of State examinations. The State is the main educational authority, enforcing attendance and providing the schools. Since 1949, to satisfy Catholic interests, some subsidies are paid to private schools. The State unification began with Napoleon, who established the "University" that includes all levels of education, though the French Revolutionists had moved toward this.

Free Education Is Recent and Incomplete

Free elementary education was established in 1881–1883. The schools became *laic*—that is, religious instruction in State schools was abolished—a great achievement of the young Third Republic against the power of the Church. Education is serious in the elements of algebra, geometry, French history and geography, civics, and ethics. French history includes the Revolution and July 14, when the Bastille fell. The egalitarian and individualistic outlook is, indeed, glorious—up to a point. Beyond it, it can be politically disruptive. The whole tradition of the overthrow of the *ancien régime* is taught, of Jacobin virtue and relentlessness, every date in the revolutionary and reactionary calendar, all the birthdays of blood, of glory, of oppression, and new births of liberty are recounted as though they were the struggles of today. There is no forgetting or appeasement. France remains divided as the Revolution divided her. The rhetorical cry of Georges Clemenceau, "The Revolution is one whole," is repeated, meaning that its spirit is alive and not to be qualified.

The educational system is extremely thorough. It is coeducational until the age of eight; thereafter it is separate until the university stage, thus saving French children from needless distractions and social breakdown.

Some leave school at the age of fourteen altogether, especially among the peasantry and urban workers. They will have taken advanced elementary education from their twelfth year. At twelve the rest choose between alternatives: a four-year course, leading to a teachers' college or the higher classes of the *lycée;* or, direct to a *lycée* at twelve (or to a technical school). Elementary schooling concludes with an examination for certification; another exam is required for passage to secondary school.

Lycée

The *lycée* is the heart and pride of French education and sets the tone for the French public services of all kinds (Chapter 9). It requires seven years of intense intellectual labor. It is concluded with two examinations for the *baccalauréat,* or, in slang, *bachot.* Only about one half the examinees pass the comprehensive tests, taken but once a year. If a student fails not too badly, he may retake the examination shortly afterward; if he fails badly, he returns to school for another year. Students cannot get by with an accumulation of miscellaneous credits without any limit of time and with a choice of soft subjects and soft teachers.

The curriculum is Latin, French, a modern foreign language, mathematics, Greek (or a second foreign language), physics and chemistry, history and geography, all for six years except four for Greek and two for the natural sciences. The seventh year is given to philosophy or mathematics (including logic and ethics), advanced French literature, a modern language, history, natural sciences. The bent is markedly philosophical; but the student is allowed some emphasis on the literary or scientific side, so that his *bachot* will be either *bachélier-és-sciences* or *és-lettres.*

This is the essential gateway to the university. Up to 1937 this avenue to the professions, a rigorous one, was open only to those who could afford the fees and other expenses of maintenance. In 1930 only one of each fifteen elementary pupils entered the *lycées.* In 1937 (under influence of the Blum Government, Socialist and liberal), fees were abolished. In 1953 one in five is the number entering.

Less than one third the *bachots* go to the universities, for their entrance examinations are highly competitive and selective. At the later stages of university education severe examinations (*concours*) take place for various professional positions: these are for doctorates, or *agrégé* to admit to being teacher in *lycées* and at the universities. We have said that admission to the university requires passage of an entrance examination; this necessitates an additional year at the *lycée*. In 1952, 2000 students out of 4500 candidates failed; they did not meet the high intellectual standards expected of entrants to a university.

Teachers in France are regarded as the salt of the earth. They would not cast pearls before swine. Their salaries are very low compared with those in the United States or Britain; but the French standard of living is generally low. But their authority is immense. The French believe in the power of the mind. In the villages the *instituteur,* the elementary schoolteacher, is the most influential person, having taken the place of the curé in the eighteenth and nineteenth centuries, *curé* and teacher—these men—being the living symbols of *ancien régime* and the Revolution.

At the summit are the universities and the *grandes écoles,* the "distinguished schools," such as the Polytechnique, the Normale Superieure, the College de France, the Conservatoire des Arts. These also come under the Ministry of Education. The École Normale Superieure takes only fifty students a year, twenty in science and thirty in letters. It prepares for the *licence,* a higher level degree, and for the faculties of the *lycées.* It is a nursery of famous men: Victor Cousin, Taine, Lavisse, Bergson, historians; Charles Péguy, Jules Romains, Jean Giraudoux, men of letters; Jean Jaurès, Herriot, Painlevé, Léon Blum, politicians of a higher order.

The observations we later make (Chapter 9) on the intelligent reforms in preparation of higher officials in France since World War II incline to the view that the severe intellectualism of French education may not be the best one for public life in general and that this is becoming recognized. But this is not to withdraw from the deepest admiration for French educational standards; they produce splendid minds all the way through society.

VIII. PASSIONATE POLITICAL FEROCITY

Other countries have had their civil wars, often bloody and barbaric; Germany's history is studded with blackest murder (pp. 529–533). From the first great Jacquerie in 1357, Kings, the court, the Church, the Parisian populace, and the peasants behaved from time to time mercilessly in the interests of their policies and egoism. Civil war burst out on a mighty scale in 1789. The red terror was followed by the white terror. In 1830, in 1848, in 1871, the mobs invaded the parliamentary assembly bent on murder. In the Commune of 1871, some 20,000 to 30,000 were killed in shocking carnage. The uproar seethed over again during the episode of Boulanger and the wicked Dreyfus case (p. 315). In 1934 the Chamber of Deputies was attacked. The ferocity of the Vichy regime, 1940–1944, is tragic and recent; the reprisals were exacting. The passion in politics is overwhelming; it is never absent from the press.

> Yet from this relaxed state of manners a Revolution of unexampled inhumanity was about to spring. . . . This contrast between the benignity of its theories and the violence of its actions . . . will surprise no one who has remarked that this Revolution had been prepared by the most civilized classes of the nation, and that it was accomplished by the most barbarous and most rude. . . . As they had borne almost alone for centuries all the burden of public wrongs—as they had lived apart, feeding in silence on their prejudices, their jealousies, and their hatreds, they are become hardened by the rigour of their destiny, and capable both of enduring and inflicting every evil.[6]

I believe that the passage of time is tending to mitigate the ferocity, though still to leave France much less cool-headed than British, American, and Scandinavian politicians.

The Revolutionary Heritage

The Revolution overturned not merely the mechanism of government but authority itself and social institutions, property, religion, the family, and the order of classes. The French were thereby forced—as the British never were, as the Amer-

---

[6] From Alexis de Tocqueville, *L'Ancien Régime.*

icans avoided (who merely transferred authority from London to Washington), as the Germans never dared, and as the Russians of Czardom were never permitted—to return to their origins again and again, forced into the quest for perfection, to regard society as a *tabula rasa* on which each might write his individual conviction about human nature and destiny. One formula of Noble Humanity was challenged by another, or by de Maistre's Original-Sin-in-Man—revolution and reaction followed each other. In 1940 Marshal Pétain replaced Liberty, Equality, Fraternity by Nation, Order, Family, Religion, and Authority—the Bourbon reaction of 1815 against the ideas of 1789. For the Great Revolution itself could not live by anarchy. Then *de novo* one inimitable Constitution follows Constitution. If one has been overturned for good reasons, why not others? The Declaration of Rights had to be rewritten again and again. But such writing demanded brevity; and brevity does not include all the degrees and qualifications of the practical application of a right, least of all which right is superior to other rights. This leads to constant reargument. Burke said the French had reduced the nation to "the *organic moleculae* of a disbanded people." The principles of the general will had to be found.

What was the consequence in governmental practice? Turbulence; insurrectionism; or the latter in its most extreme form, Jacobinism to institute Virtue (p. 299). Bentham correctly tells (*Anarchical Fallacies*) what the declaration of broad rights and faith in the nobility of human nature leads to: "the natural and imprescriptible rights of man," as the Declaration says (p. *ix*) of men being born free and equal, and of their liberty, property, safety, and resistance to oppression. "The more *abstract,* that is, the more *extensive,* the proposition, the more liable it is to involve a fallacy."

> By justifying it [the Revolution], they invite it: in justifying past insurrection, they plan and cultivate a propensity to perpetual insurrection in time future; they sow the seeds of anarchy broadcast . . . a shallow and reckless vanity.

The Guillotine and the Barricades were the fruits of absolutism, absolute revolts against absolutism, in the service of what William Pitt called "Armed opinions." When the blood of compatriots flows, it is hard ever again for a people to believe in each other's *peaceful* intentions. Many in each generation in the nineteenth century and the twentieth personally remembered the time, not many years back, when a larger or a smaller civil war caused Frenchmen to kill and wound other Frenchmen. We have to multiply for France by ten the disruptive effects of one civil war in 160 years in the United States. It produces permanent political mistrust. No one is so sure as in Britain of his property, economic prospects, social position, prestige, his own person, his place in that "ocean of being," the world, the respect he feels to be his due. How can he trust other political parties; how trust his *own* or let it be magnanimous? Education in his own history will teach the Frenchman the revolutionary pulsation of the *Marseillaise,* or the Jacobin Robespierre's perversion of Pascal on justice:

> The mainspring of popular government in a revolution is at once virtue and terror; virtue without which terror is baleful, terror without which virtue is powerless.

The political parties keep the memories and symbols alive, vividly, whether for revolution or reaction. (The Communists specialize in Jacobin virtue, for example.)

The discussion of political parties in Chapter 4 shows how, on this basis of ideological radicalism and social mistrust, the confusion of a multiplicity of parties supervene, since each party has its assortment of historic conditionings about religion, authority, foreign policy, and the economy.

Does it not take a long time, sensitive handling, many acts of magnanimity between social groups to nurture a nation with one vision, a consciousness of likeness, and faith in each other's mercies and use of power? Perhaps the spasms of violence in France, mental and physical, are decreasing in their extremism.

IX. THE FAMILY

The French family is extremely closely knit. Its sentiments and interests are centered in the *foyer,*[7] the family circle around the family hearth. Independence and exclusiveness of affection and mutual obligation are its strong marks. Father, mother, and children surrender their individuality to the organic cell of the family. This has its support in the law's protection of private property and the law of bequest and the family council to help minors. The children are under close parental control in their upbringing, the choice of a career, important social decisions, marriage. This nucleated family is rooted in the Catholic Church. "I would rather give to my family than to the government" is a typical phrase, denoting the frame of mind of peasantry and bourgeoisie. To the family they give probity, prudence, good sense, consecutiveness, gravity, and financial care—the qualities they do not lend to their government. They care less for other families than do the British or the Americans, in social welfare; they want to give less in taxation to the State.

One other matter may be mentioned. It is tenable that sex love has in the past—the time of Chivalry, the Troubadors, the influence of mistresses on the Kings and the court and nobility— and does now divert the energies, interests, and objective prudence of men and women from the tasks of government, more so in France than in the other democracies of the West. The ironic novels of Anatole France are not a complete caricature of love and French politics. A man's mind cannot be in two places at the same time. Ironically the last Cabinet of free France in 1940 under M. Reynaud was called the "Cabinet of Mistresses." Nor is it accidental that in his *Cult of Incompetence,* Emile Faguet, a Frenchman, coined the phrase "the average sensual man."

X. THE WANT OF NATIONAL SELF-RESPECT: OR INCIVISME

A long and painful history of absolutism, or exactions by government; of a Church allied with the privileged orders and obstructive of the march of intellectual light; bloodshed every generation; no apparent social and moral improvement from radical changes in governmental forms; economic divisions and inequalities; addiction to fierce and extreme logic and a passion for ideas of an inexpedient nature; delight in the pleasures of personal and family sentiment—these have denied to the French community a contemporary want of national self-respect. Not altogether, of course; for since 1870, there is evident a strong impulse toward mastery of the utilitarian art of government. Yet the factors we have named give to the Frenchman a personal and family self-satisfaction while allowing him to do in public affairs that of which other nations would be *ashamed.*

Elsewhere individual self-respect is regarded as incomplete without a substantial engagement of one's self to all other selves, the submission of one's self to something like the Golden Rule, the self-government of the libido by the super-ego. We sometimes call this "public spirit" or integrity or probity.

This blending of one's ego with the community's standard of right and wrong in the affairs of the community—the admission that a community has rights, also—where the absolute right of judgment does not lie with the individual or the family alone, is national self-respect as distinct from individual self-respect that may show itself, for instance, in love of one's own children or tenacity in one's own carefully thought-out convictions.

The French, as a whole, are wanting in such national self-respect, even to the point of occasionally being disgusted with themselves. They themselves, refer to this deficiency as *incivisme civisme* being the inner acknowledgment of civic duty. A Frenchman has defined *civisme* as "a fidelity without exaltation, an habitual devotion." Tristan Bernard has said, "Civic courage is that which is active when no danger threatens us: a virtue difficult for Frenchmen." *Incivisme* is acknowledged to be a fundamental datum of French national psychology. Observers of French behavior under attack in 1940 have insisted that a "national" revolution is needed to put France back on her feet and resume her place in world society, meaning that it is still necessary to create *a people.*

How strange that this should rightly need to be said of a people whose thinkers have been more

[7] See the intensely interesting study by Rhoda B. Métraux, *Themes in French Culture,* Stanford, 1953.

discerning and eloquent about *civic virtue* than any other! André Gide, shortly after Bastille Day in 1940 when Hitler's vandals had marched into Paris wrote in his *Journals:*

> Indulgences. Indulgences. . . . That sort of Puritan rigor by which the Protestants, those spoilsports, often made themselves so hateful, those scruples of conscience, that uncompromising integrity, that unshakable punctuality, these are the things we have most lacked. Softness, surrender, relaxation in grace and ease, so many charming qualities that were to lead us, blindfolded, to defeat.

Two features of indulgence that affect government, enfeebling its operation and calling for its functions, may be mentioned. France, a land of vineyards, is a land of alcoholism.[8] A large proportion of its people drinks two liters of wine a day; and there is an abnormal mortality and morbidity in men between thirty and sixty, due, it is claimed, to general intoxication. The 4,000,000 to 6,000,000 people estimated to be producers and sellers of alcohol make a most formidable pressure group (p. 341). For in 1922 the Government was forced by the Deputies representing the vineyard and beet-growing districts to establish the monopoly of purchases of wine alcohol and beet-distilled alcohol at State-set prices—subsidies, in short—in the interests of self-sufficiency in sugar. The surplus it either destroys outright or mixes with motor gasoline. The Deputies have not been able to resist the pressures, though the sugar supply has long since been in excess. It has been said that "The sugar-beet governs France!" The cost to the national economy, by subsidies and by diversion of

manpower, is claimed to be 400,000,000,000 francs (in prices of 1954) or a little over 3 percent of the nation's annual product. The cost of disease from alcohol, because of its plentifulness, is estimated at $420,000,000. The pressure to maintain overproduction has led to exports to the West and Central African colonies, where five times as much wine and ten times as much spirits find a market now as did in 1938. Indulgence, indeed, to maintain what the French static-minded farmer and bourgeois call *situations acquises,* or serene vested interests! At each annual budget a tremendous battle is engaged over the level and conditions of the subsidies—and local strikes and violence and road barricades are deployed by farmers to intimidate the Cabinet and the Budget Commission.

Further, in the nineteenth century, France suffered a declining population, even omitting her horrible losses in war. A decline of constructive hope and vigor was noticeable, a submission to the feeble politics of 1900 onward, merely punctuated by outbursts of vile temper, not reforming persistence. The tendency is strongly reversed since World War II.

Perhaps the coming decades may see the development of that patriotism which is public magnanimity, for lack of which republics become sick unto death: the rendering of duties to society without the exaction of equal compensation. Of this, the cessation of general tax evasion would be the best concrete evidence, as would also a universal French repudiation of such demagogues as M. Poujade, who, ex-Fascist and a small-town stationery-store owner, founder of the Union to Protect the Businessman and Artisan of France, made himself the demagogue of the roughly 2,000,000 little businessmen of France when he incited them successfully in 1955 to refuse to pay taxes unless the government withdrew its tax inspectors from their shops and cafés, a civic disgrace! (See further p. 401.)

---

[8] It is estimated by a United Nations' agency that of each $100 of national income, Frenchmen spend on alcohol per year $4.25; the British 70 cents; Americans 40 cents; the Swiss, $1.00; and that, per annum, a French adult consumes 28 quarts of alcohol; the British, 8.5; the American, 8.8; the German, 5.1. The safe maximum is 23.2 per annum.

From 1789 to 1946: Revolution to Fourth Republic

Liberty, equality, fraternity.
—Slogan of 1789

From the beginning of the French Revolution in May 1789 to October 1946 France had eleven regimes. The period of "democracy" in the Revolution lasted only from 1789 to 1797 when Napoleon took power. Thenceforward "democracy" was installed only in a very limited and truncated form for intervals in the period 1815–1848. Shortly after 1848 began Napoleon III's Empire, twenty years of cunning dictatorship—1851 to 1870. This was followed by the Third Republic that lasted to 1940, when the Vichy authoritarian interlude was the response to collapse in World War II. On France's liberation, the Fourth Republic was established, with a newly drafted Constitution.

Some account must be offered of French governmental experience and the development of tradition in the period 1789 to 1946.

I. THE FRENCH REVOLUTION

The Great Revolution broke out as a result of the combination of misery and grievances over absolutism, class privileges, and unfreedom and the gnawing of the theorists (as sketched in Chapter 1), and the example of the American War of Independence.

It was *not* a socialist revolution, though much later, in 1796, a "communist" insurrection was planned by "Gracchus" Babeuf and his "Conspiracy of the Equals." It was a bourgeois revolu-

tion; one for liberty first, then equality, the latter term meaning equality of rights and opportunities to participate in the government, to own property, and before the law courts. It was the city and middle classes with upper-class leaders who made it, joined by the peasants who seized the land of the nobility (who fled or were killed), the lower clergy, and the mobs of the towns, especially of Paris, where it was engendered and broke out.

This was the rise of the Third Estate to sovereignty, initiated when the Third Estate, assembling with the other two Estates in May 1789 by summons from Louis XVI, rejected the ancient method of voting by Estates in order not to be again, as in the distant past, outvoted by the two superior orders. It claimed more, even to be exclusively sovereign. In the words of its constitutional theorist, the Abbé Siéyès, in his classic pamphlet *Qu'est-ce que le Tiers État:*

1st What is the third estate? Everything.
2nd What has it been heretofore in the political order? Nothing.
3rd What does it demand? To become something therein.

Soon it claimed to be everything and the other two Estates nothing, proclaiming itself the representative of the nation and designating itself the National Assembly, the first time the term appears in French government. The lower clergy, then *al* he clergy, joined it; and together they swore the oath at the Tennis Court not to separate and to reassemble when necessary "until the constitution of the kingdom is established and consolidated on firm foundations."

The first intention, quite general, was to have only a constitutional monarchy. The resistance of the King and the Queen (Marie Antoinette) and the courtiers and the refugee nobles, and the Austrian and Prussian intention to crush the Revolution (acclaimed by all Europe and the Americas until it showed extreme and infectious tendencies) caused the execution of the King and later the Queen, and the establishment of the *Republic,* the first republican form of government in a really big European state.

The Revolution, having abolished ancient authority, was obliged to create new institutions and principles of action. It discarded traditional principles and had no experience of parliamentary democracy.

At once "parties" made their appearance or, as the eighteenth century expressed it, "factions" in the form of clubs. For with free opportunity came appetite for political, social, and economic change. The Revolution had been born out of the eighteenth-century gospel of Progress and the Perfectibility of Man (p. 291). The then National Assembly, followed by the Constituent Assembly, was an elected representative body.[1] Through the various regimes to Napoleon's usurpation of the Revolution, the franchise was reshuffled between a highly limited one (based on taxpaying levels and ability to work at an occupation) and universal male franchise (to suit the clienteles of the rival factions), while plebiscites (referendums) were used to ratify successive Constitutions. The Executive bodies rose out of the Assembly and were subject to its turbulent factionalism. The Declaration of Rights required the Separation of Powers as a democratic fundamental, but *the passion of revolution necessarily centralized all powers,* either in the hands of the legislature or the Executive, whichever happened to be actually stronger at any given moment. The regimes went always leftward, with more and more mutual virulence, under the influence of doctrinairism, foreign war, and economic distress, for currency inflation had been started as a fiscal expedient. Moreover a total mobilization for war in manpower—called the *levée en masse*—and in economic production, involved the nation in economic disorganization.

The extreme Left wing used the mob of Paris, which had gloriously stormed the Bastille on July 14, 1789 (establishing the Republic's national holiday), to support the authority of the municipality of Paris to overawe the duly elected but more moderate members of the Assembly. These were the Jacobins,[2] one of the factions, taking their

---

[1] French parliamentary assemblies underwent the following transformation in name as well as political significance: 1789, National Assembly almost directly into Constituent Assembly and then by the Constitution of 1791, National Assembly; 1793, the Legislative *Body* (*corps*) Assembly; this through various changes of constitution through the Napoleonic era to 1814, when, on the Restoration, it retained the same general name but divided into Chamber of Deputies and Chamber of Peers; so in the Constitution of 1830; the Republic of 1848 used the term National Assembly, a unicameral system; under Napoleon II, two bodies, the Legislative Body, being the popular chamber, and an appointed Senate; in 1871, a return to National Assembly, being the Chamber of Deputies and the Senate; under the Fourth Republic, a Parliament, in which the National Assembly is the popular chamber, the Council of the Republic the revising body. Note the use of National Assembly in the time of democratic or revolutionary swings.

[2] The two most famous of the clubs were the *Jacobins* and the *Girondins.* The Girondins moved away from their early friends of the Left when the Jacobins partly led and partly succumbed to the influence of the Paris mob to a translation of their democratic republican tenets taken from the *philosophes* (Rousseau *et al*) into ferocious action (*e.g.,* regicide) and ultimately the Reign of Terror. The Jacobins took their name from the Dominican refectory they rented, for the Dominicans in France followed *St. Jacques* (James). Their constitution had all the features of a modern political mass party: purpose and the organization of affiliated clubs all over France, although they had first congregated as Breton's deputies. Their upper-class membership seceded and formed a club of their own, the *Feuillant Club,* near-monarchist. The leaders of the Jacobins were such men as Marat, Danton, Robespierre, and the composer of the *Marseillaise,* Camille Desmoulins. At one stage Jacobin Terror saved the Revolution. They succeeded against their Girondin opponents by having in Paris a small organization of no great membership, but well knit, sure of itself, and on the active offensive. They came to represent the sentiments of the lower classes, especially urban and Parisian. Their *élan* carried the ideas of 1789 all over Europe in the victories of the Revolutionary armies. Because they came to occupy the highest seats in the Legislature on the left, a vantage point for extreme oratory, they were sometimes called the *Mountain.*

The *Girondins* were Left-wing deputies first from the

name from the club to which the leading members belonged, for the factions were located in the various clubhouses, lay or clerical mansions they had seized. Simultaneously terror increased, in the provinces as well as Paris, under the guidance of the Committee of Public Safety, an agency and then the principal and dominating institution of the Executive. From September 1793 to July 1794, 20,000 people were massacred (officially), the guillotine being the favorite official method of execution. This was countered, as soon as circumstances and public opinion allowed, by a White Terror in the south and west, *La Vendée*. For the revolutionary factions seemed to see no limit to what could or ought to be done with human nature; they were on a quest for Perfection, and so they were forced by their own ideas or their supporters to liquidate all who stood in the way of their "Republic of Virtue" and the worship of "the Supreme Being."

The bourgeoisie and the clergy and the peasants could not tolerate this forever. In July 1794 conservatism overtook revolutionary passion; the Constitution was amended by the middle- and upper-class representatives to one with indirect election, substantial property qualifications, and a bicameral system whereas hitherto the legislature had been unicameral. This change was known as the Thermidorean reaction, from the time—July (hot with therms) 1794—when Robespierre, the severest of the Jacobins in the terroristic quest for Perfection, was overcome, and he and his followers executed. The young aristocrats, known as the Gilded Youth, *Jeunesse d'Orée* (cf. p. 315 and p. 317), flushed with family- and clergy-inspired arrogance, formed punitive bands against the radicals.

The Gains of the Revolution

Above all, the Revolution—whatever the faults of its first years in violence, tumult, and injustice— had established popular sovereignty. Compared with the German people, the French had at least asserted the Rights of Man (see *Appendix*) so firmly that absolutism and abject obedience could never return. If they had not yet learned to govern themselves, they had asserted the right freely to try.

This was summed up in the Declaration of Rights. The crucial articles were: (1) Men are born and remain free and equal in rights. (2) The aim of every political association is the preservation of the natural and imprescriptible rights of man. These rights are liberty, property, security and resistance to oppression. (3) The source of all sovereignty is essentially the nation; nobody no individual, can exercise authority that does not proceed from it in plain terms.

Also, some truly fundamental social and economic changes had been effected. Feudal privileges and exemptions of the nobility and others were abolished; the land had been taken by the peasants or could be bought without subjection to a feudal lord. Church property was confiscated and made available for free purchase. The Church itself was given a civil constitution, the clergy to be elected by local chapters of the Church, to swear allegiance to the Republic, and to be paid salaries by the State; civil registration of births marriages, and deaths was instituted, and divorce was permitted through the civil courts. This Church reform provided immediately millions of peasant friends for the Republic, and other millions of peasants and upper classes who hated the Revolution for its sacrilege.

The titles of nobility were abolished; guilds and *compagnonages* (similar to trade unions) were abolished to make free trade for the bourgeoisie possible, even as private property had been guaranteed in the Declaration of Rights and enforced by the triumph of the conservatives at Thermidor.

Local government was reformed: the old provinces gave way to eighty-three *départements* of almost equal size, divided into *arrondissements* cantons, and communes. A kind of mathematical uniformity was to replace the old *coutûmes* of local customs. They were to be governed by elected councils, with a limited franchise, and to be subject to a hierarchy of protective controls through the various levels up to the national executive.

Gironde. Their inspiration came from the philosopher Condorcet; it was milder and more magnanimous than the Jacobin. As they fought the Jacobins for power, they became rather the representatives of the middle and upper bourgeoisie. Their strength was in the provinces. But they were far from being royalists. Their unwillingness to go to extremes brought on them Jacobin purges and fixed elections, and many were guillotined by the Robespierrists.

hat control being called *tutelle.* Justice was administered by courts elected by the local citizens—one of the alternatives to the administration of justice by the old *Parlements* (p. 281) and nobility-ridden courts. The Jacobins, entrenched in Paris, were centralizers; their opponents (the more-moderate) Girondins, were *"fédérés"* and sought, but vainly, to loosen the grip of Paris, to decentralize.

II. NAPOLEON, FIRST "MAN ON HORSEBACK"

The instrument of the conservatives, *including always the peasants,* was the brilliant young adventurer-general Napoleon Bonaparte, a Corsican. "I seek a sword!" the Abbé Siéyès, high in the Government, had cried, for the Revolution had to be saved from a return of the Bourbons. Bonaparte had helped put down a counterrevolutionary thrust in Paris, by his famous "whiff of grape-shot"—he needed the Revolution for his own sake. By a subsequent *coup d'état,* the exertion of force in the Assembly itself, he and his attendant brother and soldiers, in 1799 on the ninth of November—the "month of fogs" (hence the Eighteenth Brûmaire in the Revolutionary calendar)—changed the Constitution to one establishing a Consulate (the Executive) of three consuls, of which Napoleon was First Consul. This was the Constitution of the Year VIII (December 1799). It was ratified by a plebiscite, or referendum, by 3,000,000 to 1562 votes, by almost universal franchise. Then the Declaration of Rights was dispensed with; the electorate was limited to those qualified to practice a trade and to read and write, and the election of the various local councils and the Assembly subjected to *indirect* election of notables, more highly qualified men, at the various levels, a triple- or four-fold sieve, upward, who finally elected the Paris list for the legislature.

A *Sénat Conservateur* was given life tenure: 60 chosen by men named personally in the Constitution, and the other 20 chosen by these 60. Then the 80 members of this Senate appointed the 300 members of the legislative body (with annual renewal of one fifth) and the judiciary and the Executive. The 60 members of the Senate and the

20 they chose were all chosen out of the National List of notables produced by the successive elections at the lower levels from the original body of electors in the communes. The Senate also chose a kind of upper chamber within the legislative body, called the *Tribunal:* 100 members, annual renewals of one fifth. The Senate was the guardian of the Constitution.

The Consuls were elected by the Senate. These alone had the right to propose laws, which went first to the Tribunal. But amendments were not in order, only discussion and outright acceptance or rejection; whereupon the Consuls sent three orators to the legislative body, which *without discussion* would again accept or reject the law by secret ballot.

The First Consul had the widest power of appointment and dismissal of the Council of State (Chapter 11), Ministers, Ambassadors, all members of the local authorities (from the elected lists), all judges, government attorneys and executives in the law courts; power to make decrees; budgets; command of the Armed Forces; and diplomatic authority.

The above sketch has been introduced simply to convey the idea of absolutism and a most tortuous constitution written craftily to make possible the despotism of Napoleon. He had dominated the drafting; his slogan: "Constitutions must be brief!" He had said "I am the revolution!" and his friends had declared the French Revolution concluded. He proceeded, with the connivance of the Senate (he could always control a majority of its 80 members!) to make changes in the Constitution, referred to as the *Imperial Constitutions,* by acts called *Sénat-consults.* On August 2, 1802, Napoleon was elected First Consul for life by a plebiscite of 3,600,000 to 8365. On May 18, 1804, the Senate offered him the Emperorship: hereditary and in his line of descent. On November 6, 1804, 3,574,898 voted for this, and only 2569 against. The brevity of his Constitution was warrant for the longevity of his dictatorship.

It is idle henceforth to talk of constitutional detail. For foreign glory, for retention by the peasants of their lands, for bourgeois stability, the Revolution was surrendered to a dictator. The results have been powerful on the French governmental system, by admiration of or by aversion to the Man on Horseback, for Napoleon provided the first example of a brilliant one-man dictatorship that for a time gave military glory and welfare to the various classes, by means of a highly centralized administration. France, in a sense, had since 1789 taken unto herself two constitutions: a propensity to popular government with a sovereign Assembly, and an opposed centralized administrative system. The two clashed throughout the nineteenth and twentieth centuries. Some indication of the governmental bequest of this reintroduction of Caesarism into France is esssential.

Napoleon's Personal Qualities

Napoleon made France a strong hierarchical government, dependent from beginning to end on his personal powers, exercised in policy, appointments, discipline, and dismissals. He substituted his own genius for government in place of that of all Frenchmen. He was the modern Caesar: neither his administrative glory nor austerity is erased from the French mind. His body lies in the Pantheon in Paris; his spirit brings revulsion to many, producing a potent anti-State sentiment. To other men, Bonapartism, the glamor of one-man leadership, is a powerful temptation. His mind was encyclopedic in knowledge of humanity, the scientific and cultural potentialities of his time. He had a perfect comprehension of the cold-blooded means that could accomplish his ends. His "span of control" (p. 138) was extremely wide. He worked eighteen hours a day; while others needed sleep he reviewed the reports from his *préfets* (Chapter 10). One of his officials, Chaptal, declares in his *Memoires* that the natives did not know how "the Emperor exercised on his servants, however far away they were from him, the *miracle of the real presence;* I believed I saw him in front of me, when I was at work shut in my study." This answered the dictator's problem: to project his personality through distance and time, penetrating what we today call "informal groups." He established "the career open to the talents." He chose and directed the top 500 men, and through them managed various departments on his principles and invigilated them by informal and formal reports from the local and central officials.

Intellectual Repression. His police and spies pervaded all France. He held about 2500 people a political prisoners. The printers of Paris were limited to sixty and had to take an oath of obedience to the Government. Paris was reduced to four newspapers in 1810 (it had had seventy in 1800); they were governmental megaphones. Provincial papers were replaced by official gazettes. All plays, new or classic, were heavily censored. All works came under a board of censors, their approval being needed prior to publication.

Education. The revolutionists had abolished monastic and clergy-conducted schools and planned a new system of public education. Little was accomplished. But Napoleon rejected freedom of thought.

> The system we propose is not only moral; it is also a political system. Its purpose is to rally behind the government both the new and the old generations, the old through their children and the children through their parents, to establish a kind of public fatherhood.

The law of May 1, 1802, accomplished this. The communes were vested with the *permissive* power to establish elementary schools; hence there were few schools, for the poverty-stricken peasant did not build them. However, public communal and private secondary schools and *lycées* were opened. The Government appointed the *lycée* (p. 293) teachers, paid their salaries, prescribed their conduct, even their clothing, formulated the syllabus, and closely inspected the schools. These were militarized; the students were in uniform; each day began and ended with the roll of drums; all had military instruction. In 1808 the Imperial University was created, meaning the total system embracing all educational levels, elementary to the universities (Chapter 10). Napoleon declared:

> There will never be a fixed political state of things in this country, until we have a body of teachers instructed on established principles. So long as the people are not taught from their earliest years whether they ought to be republicans or royalists, Christians or infidels, the State cannot properly be called a nation.

Every school was politically controlled. All were compelled to inculcate the Catholic religion, fidel ity to the Emperor, to enforce obedience to teachers, to produce citizens "attached to their religion, to their prince, to their fatherland, and their family."

The Centralized Despotism. Napoleon purged the legislature of opposition. He replaced selection by the Senate of members of the legislature in place of renewal by lot of one fifth the membership each year—it meant that he nominated. In 1802 the Tribunal was reduced to fifty; in 1807, it was abolished. Through the Senate, he had power to dissolve the assemblies, suspend jury trials, and annual the law courts' judgments.

He thrust centralized despotism into the local authorities. He announced:

Since 1790, the 36,000 communes look like 36,000 orphan girls, neglected or pillaged for ten years by the municipal guardians of the Convention and the Directory. A change of mayors, adjuncts (*adjoints,* associate mayors), and communal counselors, has meant, as a rule, nothing but a change in the method of robbery; a robbery of the roads, robbery of the paths, robbery of the trees, robbery of the Church, robbery of the personal effects of the commune.

Now Napoleon proceeded to the arch robbery— if we mean that men's freedom to govern all these things, paid for out of their own pockets, was expropriated by him.

Centralized Administration. Each *département* was given a *prefet* (henceforward we shall call these prefects). Each *département* was divided into a number of *arrondissements,* over which a subprefect was placed, appointed by the Government. Each commune was given a mayor, appointed by the Government. Each of these authorities was flanked by a locally elected administrative council, elected on a high franchise, by indirect stages. The appointed officials saw that the councils did their duty. This was no system of local *self*-government. The appointed officials were there to see that the councils assessed the taxes, voted their budget, and advised on local needs and interests.

The Law Courts. The innovation by the first Constituent Assembly of trial by jury and popular election of judges, conceived in the most humane spirit, had fallen before the passions, factions, and terror of the Revolution.

Napoleon retained the local Justices of the Peace in the cantons—but appointed them from lists presented by the electors. He nominated all other judges, excepting the highest court of appeal, which was appointed by the Senate (see p. 281). Juries were kept for criminal cases but chosen from lists of the more educated citizen established by the prefects.

Napoleon by-passed the courts for sedition, treasonable activities, corruptors of the Army, threats to purchasers of national property (confiscations were sold, and the former owners tried to get restitution), robbery under arms, and crimes committed by vagabonds and convicts.

The Codes. Napoleon rejoiced in the idea of constructive legislator. In 1800 a committee of distinguished lawyers set about the task (started by the revolutionaries): within six months the first draft code was printed. The *Conseil d'État's* experts then examined it in detail, in Napoleon's presence and with his inspired analytical mind fully involved. It was not until 1804 that the Civil Code emerged from the legislature's deliberations.

The New Nobility. Napoleon created a new nobility from the princes around his throne—chiefly his brothers and his sisters' husbands and favorite generals and administrators—down through a well-conceived hierarchy of military, political, and household dignitaries. For the generality of the population—on condition of obedience and service —he instituted the Legion of Honor (1808).

The hereditary character of his titles aroused popular apprehension that he was returning to the privileges of the old regime. Napoleon plausibly answered that this was only another expression of his famous and genuine principle, *la carrière ouverte aux talents* (the career open to the talents), which was equality: for whoever showed eminence, all with equal opportunity to do so, could win titles. His institution of the Legion was also an expression of his cynical (or realistic) belief that men are led by baubles and trinkets. By the time of his fall Napoleon had created about 3000 titled nobility.

The Church. If Napoleon was so realistic about titles and honors, it could not be otherwise in religion. The control of religion must be vested in the sovereign; he said: "It is impossible to govern without it." If the State were confined only to the temporal power, he fulminated, then all that the priests left to the State was a carcass, while *they* kept the soul!

He restored the organization of the Church which the Revolution had dismantled, based on a Concordat with the Pope in 1801. The Pope caused all serving bishops to resign. Then new appointments were given to all priests, whether they had sworn to accept the Revolution's civil constitution of the clergy or not. This healed the cleavage between them, and a source of social disturbance was overcome. The Pope was conceded the right to institute the priests. In exchange, he condoned the sales of Church property during the Revolution, and acknowledged that the clergy were salaried officials of the State. Furthermore, no papal council might be held in France. Teachers in Catholic seminaries were to be State appointees. They accepted the Gallican declaration of 1682 that developed[3] the Concordat of 1516 (p. 287). No priest could be ordained unless he approved the Declaration.

As for Jews and Protestants, tolerated by the Revolution, Napoleon instituted their churches, nominated their clergy, and provided the Protestants with State salaries. From each other, they could dissent; to him, all must assent.

The sincere Catholic clergy were disgustedly constrained to look to *ultramontanism,* loyalty "beyond the mountains" to the Pope, for spiritual firmness of support. This drove deep into the spirit of France one more arrow of civic division.

The catechism officially enforced in the educational system of the country could not but make worse ultimately the sickness of the French civic spirit and consensus.

> *Question.* Are there not special motives which ought to attach us more strongly to Napoleon I, our Emperor?
>
> *Answer.* Yes. For it is he that God has raised up, in difficult circumstances, to re-establish

[3] This stipulated that royal and temporal sovereignty is independent of the Pope; that a general council is superior to the Pope; that the ancient liberties of the Gallican Church are sacrosanct; that the Church's infallibility inheres in the Pope and the bishops together.

the public observances of the holy religion of our fathers, and to be its protector. He has restored and preserved public order by his profound and active wisdom; he defends the State by his powerful arm; he has become the anointed of the Lord by the consecration he has received from the sovereign pontiff, head of the universal Church.

> *Question.* What ought to be thought of those who should fail in their duties towards our Emperor?
>
> *Answer.* According to the Apostle St. Paul, they would be resisting the order of God Himself and would render themselves worthy of eternal damnation.

Glory and Despotism

Napoleon had achieved power to create order out of revolutionary anarchy. The misfortune was that his personality was not content with order: it mounted to despotism. His pursuit of military glory, sometimes on the plea that he wished to unite Europe into one polity (and he was occasionally sincere in this vow), gave France a dazzling glamor in place of sober progress. In the end his frantic ambitions *for* France—a world empire —became ambitions *against* the French people. Two million died in his wars. He did not open the liberal way for the French to govern *themselves.* His glory, like that of Louis XIV, *le roi soleil,* was bought by the emasculation of self-government. The problem of democratic government for the French was still to be solved.

Napoleon's main positive and beneficial contribution to the future of the French was the definite rejection of privilege and favor for an equality based on service and social justice dispensed by the State. Clergy and nobles were unable to get back their feudal and ecclesiastical privileges. Furthermore, the idea of the career open to the talents was powerfully impressed on the populace long enough for it to be an irreducible, if heavily contested, possession.

Political Symbols. The tremendous upheaval of 1789–1815, not suffered by Britain or Germany or Russia, forced on Frenchmen the traumatic, inciting political symbols of the extreme Left of political virtue—the Jacobins—the now-worldwide distinction of Right, Center, and Left among political parties, the Jacobins being then seated on the extreme left benches of the Assembly. These symbols were: the Bastille; the Red and the White Terrors; the Commune of Paris; political "clubism," always tending, ideologically if not in practical duties, leftward, *toujours a gauche;* La Vendée, the reactionary insurrection and terror; the barricades; the Rights of Man; legislative turbulence; "immutable" written constitutions; the "Republic, one and indivisible"; *la patrie,* the absorption of the nation in each human atom, the individual units *en masse* of modern nationalism; and then Bonapartism—that is the glamorous Man on Horseback, operating above political parties.

III. THE BOURBON RESTORATION

The Bourbons returned in 1814. Louis XVIII's charter was one given, he said, by divine right. A Chamber of Peers and a Chamber of Deputies were instituted. The electorate, "the *pays* legal," numbered not the millions of the Revolution but 100,000 high propertyowners in a nation of 25,000,000 people. The peers were appointed by the King and included the returned nobility and the Napoleonic nobility. The imperial administrative and judicial system was kept intact, as were the Codes, the position of the Church, and educational centralization. Yet only the merest impression of what followed to 1871 can be offered here.

Political parties began to develop—from the extreme Right (Ultras) who, inspired by de Maistre's *Du Pape,* affected to bring back the kingship and social-class rule by divine right. Parties were hampered by the prohibition of associations, of meetings, and the censorship and suspension of the press. In fact, they were until 1871 illegal! The Church never ceased to press its claims over education, and to bring in its religious Orders to assert a monopoly over education, or to press the King toward a hierarchical and conservative social policy.

All elections were interfered with, by the Government's power to dismiss central and local officials and judges.

The King, of course, claimed to be master of his Ministers, in spite of the claims of the Chamber of Deputies, and to initiate the making of domestic and foreign policy.

A White Terror at the origin of the Restoration, of great murderousness, kept alive the fission in the body of the nation.

Toward the Revolution of 1830

Secret societies and open Left-wing parties (not yet socialist) fought the program of the Church and the absolutism. They deliberately took example from John Hampden (p. 39), refusing to pay taxes and agitating the public to this effect. Finally the revolutionary groups, the party of the Tricolor,[4] rose and overcame the Government's troops in three days of fighting in Paris in July 1830. Louis Philippe (of the Orleans branch of the royal family), a good bourgeois with cynical, agnostic leanings, was given the throne by the Chamber of Deputies. The regime became a little more liberal, for the liberal middle class came into power. The Chamber of Peers was purged. The taxpayers were formed into a National Guard, that of Paris being a powerful political force.

The censorship was eased. The right to vote was given to more people by the reduction of the tax qualification. Peerages were converted into life tenure only. Jury trial was established. The Catholic religion was set down as only the religion of the "majority of the French."

There was high tension between the conservative side of the Deputies and the more liberal: the "party of resistance" and the "party of movement." For only 200,000 people were enfranchised, and the officials planted in the Chamber numbered no less than one third of a Chamber of about 450. Under pressure, the monarchy gave the power of election to the municipal and departmental local authorities. Yet *tutelle* was strict. The "party of movement" asked for universal franchise; popular election of all administrative and judicial officers (!); abolition of the peerage (they attained this); perfect liberty of the press, religion, and education. The Church still gripped the educational system, its Orders always seeping in, whatever the law said.

Now the Saint-Simoniens and the nascent So-

---

[4] The flag of 1789 against the Bourbon white flag with its *fleur de lys.*

cialist movement began to cause a ferment among the urban workers and underprivileged against the complacent bourgeoisie. In February 1848 an insurrection occurred in Paris. The rest of France accepted it. The monarchy was overthrown. A Republic was declared by Lamartine, Ledru-Rollin (republicans), and by Louis Blanc and other Socialists, with violence in the Chamber.

But it was too early for the triumph of socialist ideas or a socialist republic. The social structure of the country was decisively against it. The only result of Louis Blanc's declaration of a socialistic system of "national workshops" was the payment by the Government of the National Guard in Paris—100,000 men, desperate because an industrial crisis afflicted the nation—of a per-diem allowance for some time. Terror presided over this system.

Now there was universal franchise: 8,000,000 cast their vote in April 1848. Four hundred of the 900 Deputies were monarchist, but not all intransigent. Another Louis Blanc insurrection occurred in May, with the cry "Bread or lead!". The Government won at the cost of 900 killed and 2000 wounded to itself. Blanc and many others were proscribed.

A single-chamber system was set up, of 750 members, directly elected for a three-year term. All males over twenty-five had the franchise— the most advanced in Europe. The President *was elected by the people*. Though he had no legislative power, the everyday Executive power was in his hands. The Ministers were supposed to depend, as in Britain, on the confidence of the House of Commons.

Election of the President by the people at large was a constitutional error, in French circumstances. Farsighted leaders warned against it. The result was that Louis Napoleon, nephew of Bonaparte and son of the former King of Holland, was elected President! He was a shrewd politician, even if generally a vain and ultimately a stupid man. He had been elected Deputy on returning from exile in America and England. He fancied himself as the true successor, in status and vision, of his great forebear. All the brave and liberal policies of the Chamber, being cogitated, were

overthrown by him. For, once he was President he turned the Republic into the Second Empire.

It was the peasants whose votes elected him. They were unused to universal suffrage. Napoleon meant to them the guarantee of their land, the protection against any return of feudalism, the rights of inheritance. He was imperial glamor. Napoleon's platform was "peace and prosperity," literally. He obtained 5,400,000 votes against two other candidates who divided 1,750,000 between them. He swore to defend the Constitution.

Assisted by the reactionary Chamber, he harassed, suspended, dispersed, and suppressed all means of public expression. The Church resumed its domination of education and the catechism was in all the schools. The franchise was restricted.

IV. THE SECOND EMPIRE

In December 1852 Napoleon made himself Emperor. He did this after a softening process, by dissolving the Assembly; re-establishing universal suffrage; conniving with the Army; arresting the leaders of the Assembly. A horrible massacre occurred. Twenty-seven thousand people were arrested; 6500 released; 500 put under police supervision; 15,000 transported to Algeria and other penal settlements or confined to specified French cities. Some Republican deputies were banished.

The terror was induced by the rising strength of the working class and the students, developing from the belated Industrial Revolution and incited by the spread of Karl Marx doctrines; *The Communist Manifesto* was published in 1848.

We need not follow the Empire in detail. Until the 1860's it was absolutist. Then it became liberalized. The Assembly was allowed to initiate laws and offer amendments to those put before it by Ministers, to question the latter, who were now made formally responsible to the Assembly. Social security reforms and public works were undertaken.

Yet Napoleon fought wars in Mexico, Italy, and the Crimea; he repressed parties, meetings, the press; and he faked the elections. The opposition became inflamed. Gambetta, the great lawyer and public tribune, incited the people to overturn the ystem. An attempt was made to assassinate the Emperor by throwing a bomb.

Karl Marx

The French workers were now inflamed by the diatribes of Karl Marx: [5] the workers were now the proletariat, a class made conscious of its status, its rights, and the Utopia that could be theirs, inevitably, as the economic relations of producers had changed. They were moved to violence now, on philosophic principles as well as resentment of social injustice. The First International was inaugurated in 1866 at Geneva—it became a center for the rallying and association of the workers, their hope, their flame. Waves of strikes swept France. The Government became terrified of this organized threat. It had done next to nothing for the workers; it had merely relieved them of their leaders and their free votes. They began to organize to vote *No!;* and that is why there were as many as 1,500,000 adverse votes in the May 1870 plebiscite.

The vain and stupid Emperor let himself be inveigled by Bismarck into a war with Prussia—the war that unified Germany against French disruptive policies going back two centuries. The French were beaten in seven weeks of war, July 15 to September 1, 1870.

V. THE THIRD REPUBLIC

The Making of the Constitution

The social bases of France that existed before the *débâcle* of Emperor Napoleon's armies before

[5] Karl Marx's pamphlets, *The 18th Brumaire of Louis Napoleon* and *The Class Struggles in France* are brilliant accounts of this era. Marx's view can be surmised from his passage: "It was not the French bourgeoisie that ruled under Louis Philippe, but a fraction of it, bankers, Stock Exchange kings, railways kings, owners of coal and iron works and forests, a section of the landed proprietors that allied round them—the so-called finance aristocracy. The real industrial bourgeoisie formed part of the official opposition. . . ." Then the power of the workers put the bourgeoisie into office in the Parisian insurrection of February 1848. He claims that in the June uprising 3000 working-class prisoners were massacred by the bourgeoisie through its National Guard. Napoleon, the President, he called "the adventurer who hides his trivially repulsive features under the iron death mask of Napoleon."

Bismarck's in 1870 existed after it for a number of years, until their respective strengths changed and their individual interests and values underwent alteration. They were, we may recall, a vast peasantry, recently called into political participation; a relatively small but growing and highly restive urban proletariat, republican, embittered, Jacobin, revolutionary, partly Marxian (if unread in Marxism) and partly Utopian and visionary (if unread in Saint-Simon, Fourier, and Proudhon), and even Bonapartist. The middle classes broke into the employers in commerce and small industry: they were liberal for democracy but afraid of the proletariat, anti socialist and anti social welfare even in a mild degree: some were monarchist, some Legitimist, some Orleanist, some Bonapartist, some devout in the bosom of the Church, some cynical as was Louis Philippe, their hero.

The upper-middle class, made up of larger owners, substantial landowners, bankers, rentiers, manufacturers, owners of mines, the press, and so on, looked to a conservative regime, unavoidably democratic, monarchist if possible (for they had not done badly under the last two regimes) but republican if necessary, yet with checks and balances on the surge of forces in the urban centers. The Church was, broadly speaking, divided among the liberal churchmen, asking for privileges for its teaching and influence, and others, desirous of restoring the full power of the Catholic Church in an anti-democratic way against the forces of change—of the working class and the developing white-collar groups inclined to atheism, anxious for education but not for a religion-dominated educational system. An aristocracy of landowners and of inherited wealth still existed, small in numbers compared with the groups we have mentioned. But it had been potent in politics and remained a power until the end of the 1870's when it was eclipsed (it was badly wounded in 1876 when Marshall Macmahon, first President of the Third Republic, was forced to resign) to find alternative authority in the Church, in social welfare, society, and the Army and civil administration.

One third of France was still occupied by Bismarck's armies when the election of the National Assembly was held on February 8, 1871. From this election the Imperialists stayed away. A "clodhoppers" legislature resulted. The peasants wanted peace and voted monarchist: two thirds of the Assembly of 750 consisted of Orleanists or Legitimists. Only the invaded *départements* and the southeast were substantially Gambettist Republicans. The method of election was by *departemental* units: *scrutin de liste,* party lists at large.

Thiers, conservative leader of the Left Center, who were constitutional monarchists, was voted "Chief of the Executive Power of the French Republic"—on the theory that the Assembly was a continuation of the Second Republic of 1848. He held this position from February 17, 1871, to May 1873. The Monarchists acquiesced, submitting to the argument that, without the Republic, horrible civil war would break out. This period of economic restoration, and the suppression of the Paris Commune,[6] gave time for a constitution to be developed. The Rivet Law of August 1871 made Thiers President of the *French Republic,* with responsibility to the Assembly and power to appoint and dismiss Ministers, also responsible. The Monarchists had acquiesced, anticipating that the presidential status could later be taken over by a King. They failed in this because they could not agree among themselves who should be King: the Comte de Chambord, grandson of Charles X,

Bourbon, or the Comte de Paris, grandson Louis Philippe, the one gravely reactionary, t latter mildly liberal. But the matter was settle when the former refused, even with papal plea to accept the tricolor flag and insisted on t white fleur-de-lys, for this was a symbol of h divine-right terms of acceptance, terms mediev in their authoritarian character.

Ever since 1872 by-elections had increased R publican strength, although Thiers restricted pu lic meetings and the freedom of the press. He w overthrown by the Republicans and the Rig Center on which he had relied, since he refuse to the latter more liberal press laws and educ tional liberalism as well as insufficient counte action of the Gambettist Radicals. The Rig Center agreed to a law banning him from t Assembly deliberations, and demanded he "resolutely conservative." He resigned, May 2 1873, and was replaced by Marshal Macmahon, candidate of the Orleanists, Legitimists, and Bon partists, a man "in place of a dynasty" to kee the throne warm.

The Government fell into the hands of duke career administrators, generals, and Bonapartist while the Left, now nearly one half of the A sembly, joined with the Left Center to give Ma mahon, the new President, a seven-years tern monarchists seeing in him, again, the *locum tene* of a monarchy, the Left Center, the avoidance a monarchy.

As far back as 1873 the Assembly had begun ponder on a constitution. Then in January 3 1875, an amendment to one of its drafts (Lef wing) put by a M. Wallon established that "T President of the Republic is elected [for seve years] by an absolute majority vote of the Sena and the Chamber of Deputies." This was t rock of the Republic, lasting till 1940. The seve year term had been obtained by the aforeme tioned temporizing of monarchists and republica by *a majority of 1 in 705 votes, when an u punctual Deputy had intended to produce deadlock by voting against!* Universal suffrage ha been established for the municipal councils; was now voted for the Assembly, for the co servatives believed the peasantry would vote, ever before, conservative, while Gambetta believe

[6] From March 3 to May 1871 Paris was held by the Commune, an insurrectionary movement. The *communards* (*not* Communists) were a miscellaneous grouping of radical and socialist workers and employees, of anarchist idealists, of Utopians, of practical Rousseauites, of some Marxists, of the hungry, the miserable, the disillusioned by the war, certainly of the lower-middle and working class. The leaders were inspired by Auguste Blanqui, the professional revolutionary leader of the socially submerged; by Saint-Simon and that line of theorists (pp. 291–292), by Proudhon's idea of a federation of municipalities (influential in various ways on Lenin, p. 817). The Commune established an autonomous government. What exactly it would have made of its Jacobin-Simonien-Marxist mixture of ideas and passions is not known, for the government of Thiers crushed the movement by bloody onslaught: the official number buried was 65000 (cf. p. 294); 7500 were deported to New Caledonia; 3000 were given prison terms; those who escaped were treated as fugitives from justice. Not till 1876 did military tribunals cease punishing the *communards.* Yet they had not even tried to establish a socialist State or seized the Bank of France. The violence exhibited by both Left and Right stressed the tradition of force.

he could enthuse them to modernized republicanism, seeing the already-strong surge of republicanism. In February 1875, by 435 to 234, a Senate
was voted, with a nine-year term, elected by
indirect elections, in which the rural areas were
given gross overrepresentation, and with a quarter
of the members chosen by the existing Assembly
to be life members. This was the Right's guarantee
of conservatism. Other particulars are given later
(pp. 313–314).

The law on the "organization of the public
authorities" was passed a day after that on the
Senate. The legislative power was placed in two
Chambers; the President endowed with powers;
the lines of ministerial responsibility laid down;
and passed by 425 to 254. In July the law on the
relationship between the authorities added detail
on sessions of the Chambers, their sessions, the
promulgation of laws by the President, war, impeachments, and so forth.

Achievement. According to Thiers, this was the
"republic that divides us the least." But it was not
one that united Frenchmen most. It was not a
single document; it lacked the Declaration of
Rights, which, however, was assumed by the judiciary (Chapter 11). It was accepted with the explicit or implicit reservations that it was about to
be revised. It was not a *strong* structure, either for
international survival or for solving internal social
contradictions. It lasted nearly seventy years, the
longest-lived single system of government known
in France since the *Ancien Régime*.

Operation of the Third Republic

Since the manners and governmental institutions
of the Third Republic are so like those of the
Fourth Republic, we here intend only to *indicate*,
and no more, their nature and effect.

The Legislature. This bicameral system was the
embodiment of popular sovereignty. The Senate
had equal powers with the Chamber of Deputies,
except that the latter had the sole right to *initiate*
financial legislation. The President had the right
to *dissolve* the Chamber with the consent of the
Senate. The Chamber, with some 600 members,
elected for a four-year term, became the predominant assembly, even the master of the Cabinet or Council of Ministers.

Laws were initiated by the Government or
Council of Ministers and by deputies and Senators,
the Government, in practice, being responsible
for some four times as many laws as the rest.
The Chambers elaborated the laws, after introduction, in Commissions,[7] of which there were
some twenty, broadly paralleling the government
departments, and each finally numbering forty-
four members. The most important was the Commission of the Budget. The Commissions were
elected by the party groups according to their
strength annually. They exerted a heavy strain
on the Governments because they played the part
of rivals to the Ministers, and had powers of
administrative control over them as well as responsibility for legislation. All bills went to the
Commissions, who then reported them back to
the whole house for debate. They could be dilatory; they were often of different party-coalition
composition from the Government, as Governments lasted from a few weeks to a few months
while the Commissions were of overlapping duration. The Presidents and the *rapporteurs,* who
headed the Commissions, challenged the Ministers,
being themselves former Ministers or desirous of
being future Ministers.

President Poincaré, several times Prime Minister, said the Government had to please forty-two
parliaments: the two Chambers, and the twenty
Commissions in each!

The Elections. Universal male suffrage was established in the Constitution itself, but special
laws changed the details. The Chambers could
not keep to the same rules for long, but changed
from *scrutin de liste* to *scrutin d'arrondissement*
(*uninominale*) as follows: respectively, the former
1871; the latter 1875; the former 1885; the latter,
1889; 1919, the former with P.R. (see Chapter 5);
the latter 1929; the former, with P.R., 1945. *Scrutin
de liste* means election in large constituencies,
normally the local government *département* for
all the members for the area; *arrondissement,* is a
smaller constituency, with a single member to be
chosen, and *uninominale* is another way of saying
district or single-member constituency. The alter-
nation came about according to any existing ma-

[7] Translate *commission* literally; not by the word *committee,* a semantic bad habit!

jority's hopes of perpetuating its strength and injuring its rivals' by a different method of election.

The single-member constituency favored the middle parties, above all the Radical Socialist, who were able, by their local *rapport* with their clientele of teachers, officials, small tradesmen, peasants, and employees, to insinuate their spread-eagle policies to each particular place. The great demerit, nationally considered, was the disintegration, thus, of the national consensus, or the prevention of its development. Such little constituencies were often called "stagnant swamps." The conservatives liked the system, also, for in the rural areas the gentry, the priests, and the *curés* long dominated the scene. The Socialists would have liked the wider constituency, for purposes of political education and agitation.

With the small constituencies, *the second-ballot* system operated. "Run-off" elections took place a week (earlier, two weeks) after the first election if that had not given any candidate an absolute majority of the votes cast. In this period, since all the candidates and even some new ones would run, bargaining over policy, administrative favors, and public jobs took place. This was no inducement to honesty or firmness. The parties lost definition and character. Small parties were encouraged since all might profit. A kind of Center "Moderate" was produced, which was nothing to all men, which could attract votes from the wings. Of some 600 Deputies, about one third required a second ballot at each election; from 1914 onward, the proportion was sometimes one half; twice it was two thirds!

The system was also seriously nonproportional. We take two figures only from the many produced by the assiduity of the most devoted student of this subject, M. Georges Lachapelle. In 1932, compared with full proportionality of the nationally totaled votes, the Radical Socialists would have had 42 seats less than they obtained; the Socialists, 4 less; the Right would have gained 23 more; and the Communists, 38 more. In 1936 the conservative Front Nationale would have won 37 more seats; the Radical Socialists, 20 less; the Socialists, 28 less; and the Communists, 21 more. No wonder the Radical Socialists were and are

warm friends of the single-member constituency no wonder also that a few seats more or less t this and that party can make such a difference t the stability of Cabinets.

Thirteen of the sixteen elections of the Thir Republic were held with this system: they mad for confusion and fluidity of French political an social values and will, a kind of quagmire of th center, or swamp in the terminology of 1789.

The Chamber of Deputies. The Deputy, stemmin from the Rousseauite atomization of the genera will (p. 291) and the French Revolutionary trad tion, claimed a heavy electoral sovereignty. Th sentiment of the *imperative mandate* (*mand imperatif*) or voting according to the district instructions, was strong in the French traditio not so in the British (p. 89), and the Deput converted this into his own individual sovereig status. Hence, his opposition to the authority o party; hence also the indiscipline of the Chambe Any Deputy could propose an increase of e penditure and taxation; the budget was neve voted in time, and the Commissions held th Ministers of Finance in the hollow of their hand The timetable could not be steady and well pr portioned, as it was not decided by the Gover ment but by the fortnightly conference of th Presidents and Vice Presidents of the Chamber and of the groups, and of the Presidents of th Commissions, and the Government—their resol tion then being overturnable by the Assembly.

The Executive. The Council of Ministers wa responsible to *both* chambers; the President powers covered all the Executive field, but r quired the countersignature of the Ministers, s relieving him of political responsibility and crea ing a parliamentary Executive.

"Le Seize Mai," 1877. The hopes of the monarc ists that the presidency would be taken over by King were soon dashed. On May 16, 1877, *seize Mai,* Marshall Macmahon dissolved th Chamber with the consent of the Senate for ne elections, according to his constitutional authorit His reason was that the Chamber, which und Gambetta's inspiration was strongly Republican 360 to 170—was urging a progressive progran which meant a cleansing of the central and loc

dministration of monarchists, aristocratic and onservative officeholders; the right of the smaller nunicipalities to elect their own mayors; complete reedom of the press and freedom to sell news-apers in public (suppressed under the Empire nd Thiers); and such other measures. It did not vant "the Republic without the Republicans," or he continuance of a "Republic of dukes." It would ot appropriate money for Army chaplains, as these vere Catholic propagandists—that is, monarchist nd reactionary—among the troops, especially the fficers. Then the Left denounced the Catholics' gitation for French help to the Pope to fight the Kingdom of Italy so that the Vatican might re-ossess itself of temporal power in Rome.

The royaloid and authoritarian President dis-olved, on the advice of his friends who led the Rightist parties. He dismissed a Left Center Min-stry under Jules Simon, adjourned the Chambers or a month, dissolved the Chamber, extended the eriod before the elections from two to five months y a legal twist of the Constitution, and proceeded o allow the Rightists to manage the elections in he time-honored way by suspending Republican nunicipal councils, dismissing officials, appointing liant ones, mobilizing the clergy. The Republi-ans of all persuasions fought back: they employed he Gambettist slogans: "Clericalism—there is the nemy!" and "When the nation has spoken, the 'resident must submit!" The Church used all its ower of damnation to win Macmahon votes. In he election of October 1877, the Left won by 330 o 210 Rightists; they quashed 50 seats captured nder pressure, won most of these seats, and ob-ained a total of 370 Deputies against 170. Mac-nahon would not yield; and tried to govern with onparliamentary experts. The Chamber would ot vote the budget. Some Conservatives were nxious to try to raise taxes directly and risk a *oup d'état.* In the 1878 partial renewal of the enate, Republican strength rose to 178 against 26. The Marshal was cornered. The Republican Ministers demanded that he sign decrees to cleanse he *Conseil d'État* and the judiciary. He resigned.

Weakening of Presidency and Dissolution. Two onventions of the Constitution were engendered y Macmahon's behavior. The presidency was never again entrusted to a really strong man, and no President or Cabinet ever again tried to use the power of dissolution. As for the presidency, as Georges Clemenceau, Radical Prime Minister and war leader of France in World War I, said, "I vote always for the most stupid!" The presi-dency became little more than a fairly picturesque figurehead.

The President of the Republic was Chairman of the Government in one kind of its ministerial meetings, the *conseil des ministres;* when Ministers sat as *conseil de cabinet,* he was not present. The distinction is explained later (p. 431). In the *conseil,* the various Presidents could exert influ-ence, according to experience and character; but the limit was what the Cabinet would defend in the Chambers, small, indeed.

The Executive had lost its power to discipline the Chamber, by dissolving and seeking a choice between the Cabinet's policy and that of the dis-tracted Chamber from the electorate. In Britain such a disciplinary instrument had had real power in forcing the M.P. to face his own passions of opposition, lust for power, and public responsibil-ity. In France, the power to implement consensus by pitting the policy of the Cabinet against the factions of 600 individualists did not exist. The Chamber fell into abject disarray; its habits ag-gravated the already-existent social dissensus.

Multiplicity of Parties and Short-lived Cabinets. The party system of France determined the mean-ing that collective responsibility of the Council of Ministers to the Chambers would bear. It was a multiple-party system and had been from the out-break of the Revolution in 1789. There was never a time in the seventy years of the Third Republic when any party or Chamber group came near to having a majority of Deputies. The parties are more conveniently described later (Chapters 4 to 6). The table of party distribution (p. 313) in the Chamber (followed more conservatively by the Senate) indicates the number of the major parties, about nine, and their creed-disposition, as well as their strength. The situation was worse than it looks, for parties apparently close to each other were on some grounds—say, religious—foes, while until 1936 the Socialist Party would

French Political Parties in the Chamber of Deputies at the Election of 1936 *

	Seats	Millions of Votes
Right		
Republican Independents	13	
Republican Federation	59	
Popular Independents	16	
Independent and Agricultural Republicans	40	
		2.25
Center		
Popular Democrats	13	
Left Republicans and Independent Radicals	44	
Democratic Left and Independent Radicals	38	
		1.94
Left		
Radicals and Radical Socialists	111	1.46
Socialists and Republican	29 ⎱	0.52
Independent Left	28 ⎰	
Socialists	149	1.92
Communists	72	1.50
Nonparty	6	
	618	

* The last election before World War II.

never *enter* a Cabinet, though it might give support.

Cabinets were difficult to form; the compromises on jobs and policy were fragile; they soon broke up. Thus:

Duration of Cabinets, 1873–1940

Duration	Number of Cabinets
Under six months	50
6–12 months	31
12–18 months	9
18–24 months	1
24 months and over	8

In 99 cabinets between 1873 and 1940, only eight lasted two years; only one between eighteen and twenty-four months. Even this is too good; for the fight against the Church at the turn of the century and the need for stability in World War I were required to produce long-lived Cabinets.

Ministerial Feebleness. The consequences, in detail, are left to the account of Cabinets in the Fourth Republic (Chapter 6), for they are identical. Summarily they were: disintegration of policy; no leadership; inadequate grip over the civil servants and the Army. It was no mitigation that Cabinets were sometimes merely reshuffled, retaining members of the outgoing Cabinet; for now they were in a new constellation of policy, if any. In Britain the Cabinet collectively makes the policy for the Ministers; in France the Ministers, as it were, made it for the Cabinet; they were not embedded in the policy of a strong unified party.

The President of the Republic sought out the Prime Minister, taking advice from the Presidents of the Chambers and from the leaders of the groups. He had considerable latitude and, therefore, some power, given the variety of groups, to choose where the gravity of the coalition should be: Left, Center, Right, and nuances in between. Some of the Ministers and even Prime Minister thus called on did not belong to a parliamentary group at all but were so-called *sauvages* (thus Briand, Millerand, Poincaré, and Laval at various periods), "mavericks." These *combinaisons* were even less stable than the size of the component groups would suggest, because they were *not internally stable*, for about 15 percent of their membership would not vote for their leader or colleagues in the Cabinet. They sought their own pure doctrine, down to three decimal points of disagreement, and their individual power to command Ministers and become *ministrable* themselves. The slang for the reshuffling of Ministers was a *dosing* (*dosage*); the "waltz of portfolios," "replastered cabinets" (*replâtrage*).

Between 1873 and 1937 thirty-eight differ-

men were Prime Minister, averaging eighteen months in office; from 1928 to 1940, fifteen, averaging ten months, and their service was *intermittent.* Thus:

Length of Service of Prime Ministers, 1873–1940

	Number of Cabinets	
Duration	1873–1928	1928–1940
Under 6 months	10	7
6–12 months	13	5
12–18 months	3	2
18–24 months	5	1
24–30 months	1	0
30–36 months	2	0
36–42 months	1	0
42–48 months	0	0
48 months and over	4	0

Number of Ministers, 1873–1940

Foreign Affairs	27	War	41
Interior	37	Navy	42
Finance	38	Justice	55
Agriculture	42	Commerce	52
Instruction	41	Works	55
Colonies	42	Labor *	40

* Since 1940.

Of course, in this system the Prime Minister could not possibly contribute the collectivizing, unifying, articulating services of a British Prime Minister; for the latter secured his status of *primus inter pares* from indubitable leadership of the majority party. The French Prime Minister was not even *pares inter pares,* for there were no *pares* but little but rivals of tomorrow if not today; men met together for a day but kept their own unequal opinions and status. French Governments could not exert that essential function of government, choice between alternatives, because they did not start with a consensus on criteria.

There is an enormous difference between two political parties in command of the electorate, each with free dissenters who merely have to be persuaded not to be excessive in their dissent and *who will not break away,* and some sixteen parties (in 1939), each with a big enough proportion of votes, even if it be absolutely small, to topple the small majority of a Government, for the sake of its own policy, will, and conceit.

During a decisively critical prewar period, Gen-

eral Charles de Gaulle (p. 320), from 1932 to 1937, not then of that high rank but still already distinguished, was detailed to the Secretariat General of National Defense. In that period he was involved in defense planning under no less than fourteen Governments. He says [8] it showed him the feebleness of the State.

For the disjointedness of government was rife all over the field. Not—certainly—that the men who figured there lacked intelligence or patriotism; on the contrary, I saw men of incontestable value and sometimes of great talent come to the head of ministries. But the political game consumed them and paralysed them. As a reserved but passionate witness of public affairs, I watched the constant repetition of the same scenario. Hardly had a Premier taken office when he was at grips with innumerable demands, criticisms, and bids for favour, which all his energy was absorbed in warding off without ever contriving to master them. Parliament, far from supporting him, offered him nothing but ambushes and desertions. His Ministers were his rivals. Opinion, the press, and sectional interests regarded him as the proper target for all complaints. Everyone, indeed—and he first of all—knew that he was there only for a short time; in fact, after a few months, he had to give place to another. As regards national defence, such conditions prevented those responsible from achieving that organic whole of continuous plans, matured decisions, and measures carried to a conclusion, which we call policy.

This passage deserves much meditation. It explains why, also, when de Gaulle later found his brilliant and correct military recommendations ignored and neglected by the French, but employed by the Germans to destroy his own country, he cried in his mortified desperation: "All I have managed to do since was resolved upon that day," which meant to "fight . . . until . . . the national stain [is] washed clean." [9]

The Senate. The Senate was elected by electoral colleges in each *département* made up of the departmental councilors, the departmental deputies, and the representatives of the municipal councils in the *département.* The delegates from

[8] General de Gaulle, *The Call to Honour,* New York, 1955, p. 6.
[9] *Ibid.,* p. 39.

these councils were allocated according to the size of the councils; but the numbers were deliberately rigged in order to give a most heavy bias to the smaller: the rural towns and villages. The main weight was in the local councils in communes of 4000 to 5000 inhabitants. This chiseled away the rule of universal suffrage with one man, one vote. For example, Lille, a very great industrial city for France, with 216,000 people sent twenty-four delegates to the electoral college of the Nord *département*, while twenty-four villages with a total of 4000 inhabitants, also sent twenty-four. The senatorial electors for all France numbered 75,000; in social composition, they were middle bourgeoisie, middle and higher officials, proprietors elected by their tenants and workers through the communal councils, tradesmen, manufacturers, and merchants.

Communes	No. of Municipal Councilors	Delegates
Below 500 population	10	1
500–1500	12	2
1500–2500	16	3
2500–3500	21	6
3500–10,000	23	9
10,000–30,000	27	12
30,000–40,000	30	15
40,000–50,000	32	18
50,000–60,000	34	21
60,000 and above	36	24
Paris	56	30

Broadly speaking, the Senate was steadily conservative in social and economic policy, nationalist, and tight-fisted compared with the Chamber. At any rate, it was different, a result of its higher age, at least forty by law, sixty in fact; by its long duration; by its composition, depending on councils that had themselves been elected some years ago. It blocked the Chamber's bills, particularly by amendments to financial bills, above all the budget. It also overthrew Ministers; it did this eight times between 1890 and 1938, by denying to the Government the financial or other support it needed for policy already voted by the Chamber.

The Governments were compelled to include Senators in their personnel. From 1873 to 1940, the Senate contributed twenty-two out of fifty-four Prime Ministers and over one third of all the Ministers. Hence the Senate was an attraction to

the Deputies; they had much power and no need for reelection every four years. Pierre Laval, hi nation's betrayer in 1940, was rejected by hi popular constituency, but worked his way into th Senate through its smaller constituencies an among its senile members.

It is worth adding that this system of depart mental electoral colleges did add another con nection to the administrative one of *tutelle* be tween local and central politics, for the municipa councils were potential vote-getters for the Senate

The Constitution. *The Constitution was flexible* for it could be amended by an absolute majorit of the total membership in a joint session of the Chambers, called when each had separately passe an amending resolution in identical terms b absolute majority of those voting. However, i the disarray of parties such conditions were har to fulfill. In 1879 Versailles ceased to be the sea of the Government, by amendment. In 188 amendments deconstitutionalized the compositio of the Senate; and the republican form of gover ment was put beyond the power of amendment and members of formerly reigning families (Bou bons, Orleanists, and Bonapartists) were made in eligible to be President.

No referendum of ratification was required i the Constitution.

The Administrative System. The centralized sys tem remained, but local government was slightl liberalized in 1874 and 1883 (Chapter 10). B 1900 the era of wild purification of the Civi Service had passed. Thenceforward, decrees an certain statutory provisions began to produc something like a fair career and merit system o appointment and promotion, and to mitigate th politicization of the Service. But this may b noticed that (1) the lower- and middle-grad officials were affected by revolutionary syndicalism (p. 292), were turbulent, and went on strike i 1906 and 1909; and (2) the higher officials in ke positions were antirepublican and antiparliamen tary, obstructing Left legislation and fulfillmen and siding with the Right in the political crises o Macmahon, Boulanger, Captain Dreyfus (p. 315) Church and school policy (p. 315), the Fasci tensions in the 1930's, the policy toward the Nazi and the support of the Vichy regime. Their edu ation was expensive and it was specialized; it reduced *general* wisdom and democratic service-bility (Chapter 9).

The Chamber was so divided by material and ideological egoisms that, to remedy the paralysis of will, Governments were entrusted with powers to settle financial problems and others by decree, with little parliamentary control. Too soon, the Government was overthrown (see p. 313)!

Fate of the Third Republic

Domestic and Colonial Developments. In spite of this ramshackle and emotionally unstable charac-ter, the Third Republic did some surprisingly good work—at any rate, much work. It saved France from subjugation in World War I. It de-veloped tariffs for industry and agriculture, public works, soil conservation, good agricultural prac-tices. It passed much good social legislation and promoted private thrift. It permitted the develop-ment of trade unions by the Laws of Associations in 1884 and 1901. It sponsored the growth of a colonial empire in Africa and the Middle East. It disciplined the administrators.

Church and State. In the face of the greatest op-position from the upper bourgeoisie and diverse element of the population, it, led by Émile Combes and the Radical coalition, separated Church and State by the law of 1905, after a long campaign, ending the Concordat (p. 304) and enforcing, against insurrection, the new nonhierarchical ad-ministration of Church affairs by local communi-ties, financed by their own contributions, thus withdrawing State payments. Similarly, led by Waldeck-Rousseau and a Left bloc, it forbad re-ligious associations to conduct educational activi-ties, on the principle that the "moral unity" (equals *consensus*) of the nation required a single system of education, not a divided one. It thus produced a state monopoly of education, and also made it secular, *laic,* and enforced the policy, often against rebellious local magistrates and mili-ary officers.

Defense against Subversion. These policies were, in part, forced on the statesmen of the Left and even the Right, by the arrogant interference of the high clergy and the Pope in French politics, always in a reactionary direction. This persistent attempt to turn the clock back to obscurantism and authoritarian government was especially no-ticeable in the nationalistic activities, ever more chauvinist, of monarchist circles. It was exhibited with particular poisonousness in the Dreyfus af-fair that shook the Republic to its very soul. There Captain Dreyfus, a Jew, the first ever to be ap-pointed to the General Staff, was falsely accused of selling secrets to Germany. The high officers and the Church (especially through its newspaper *La Croix*) knowingly sustained the forgeries and perjury and denial of justice involved in the charge, and produced a gale of antirepublicanism and anti-Semitism. They even incited to murder: the President, Felix Faure, was beaten by young Catholic and royalist toughs of the wealthy, even as the *Jeunesse d'Orée* had maltreated the liberals before Thermidor (p. 300), and as they were to do again to Léon Blum, Socialist Prime Minister in 1936, beating him almost to death. Eventually the iniquity of the Church and the aristocratic officers was defeated by the Left, led by Clemen-ceau of the Radical Party and Émile Zola, the novelist.

The Third Republic kept the Republic alive in spite of such insidious attacks. One other on-slaught was made by the reactionaries' use of General Boulanger—a Man on Horseback—a Minister of War. His megalomaniac ego was in-flamed by a Patriotic League, led by Paul Derou-lède. This was supported by some Radicals, and the monarchists and Bonapartists, to secure a revision of the Constitution and to fight Germany. The General was elected by several *départements,* so that it seemed he had enormous popular back-ing. Catholic politicians assisted him. By January 1889, when he was elected in Paris, an attack on the Elysée, the presidential palace, was plotted. He quailed; was impeached and convicted by the Senate, and fled to Belgium. The League was dispersed. To prevent such widespread elections, the Left enacted a change over to *scrutin d'ar-rondissement.*

The Constitution that "divides us least" kept the Republic alive—that is, democratic govern-ment—but only just. As since the break with the *ancien régime,* there were political parties—the royalists, extreme conservatives, and Catholic politicians on the Right and, from 1919, the Communist Party on the extreme Left (and before that some of the adherents of the Socialists Party)—anxious to overthrow the regime altogether, unreconciled to it, even though some Catholics had been induced by the 1890's to become *ralliés,* to rally to the Republic. The fissiparous tendency, the subversiveness was immanent and often manifested; it triumphed in 1940 under the tragic pressure of defeat by Hitler.

Scandals. There were many scandals in the Third Republic. Just as Boulanger had fled, some Deputies and Senators were involved in financial misdealings concerning the Panama Canal Company. It embittered parliamentary life and the public. A son-in-law of the President Grévy was caught selling titles in the Legion of Honor. In 1930 the Ostric financial scandal was reminiscent of the Panama affair. In 1934 financial manipulations of a network of people, in the center of which was one Stavisky, showed police and judicial connivance on a large scale and led to an attempted *coup d'état* by Fascist gangs and Communists.

The Press. The press was scandalous, in large part. Many newspapers wallowed in scurrility and slander, *knowingly,* in order to kill their political opponents, as one Minister, Roger Salengro, was foully driven to suicide by charges of cowardice in World War I. The *Action Française,* edited by Charles Maurras (a ferocious monarchist, an atheist supported by Catholic antirepublicans, a frenzied nationalist, an anti-Socialist, and anti-Semite), carried daily incentives to violence. Its editor ended as a pro-Nazi and pro-Vichyite; he was the instigator of the attack on Léon Blum.

The Communist *L'Humanité* was as iniquitous from the extreme Left. Several smaller papers run by political coteries, the so-called *journaux d'opinion,* specialized only in vilification, most being subsidized by private interests, some by foreign States, some even by the French Government itself out of secret funds. The libel laws were too politically interpreted to save private reputations or the public weal.

In the Parliament of 1924 there were 123 "gentlemen of the press" in the Deputies, and sixty-one in the Senate—that is, one fifth of the membership of the former and of the latter! In

1932 the number of journalists in the Deputies wa fifty-six. The government departments had secre funds with which to bribe journalists.

Thus the wells of truth, essential to the health o the Republic, were poisoned at the source. Ther were some newspapers with public probity, bu all had a distinct political bias (e.g., *Le Temps*) Politicians came to be afraid of the press; som arrived at high office by their dexterous use of th press, such as Clemenceau, Millerand, Caillaux Sarraut, Laval. An editor of *Le Matin,* very con servative, once said, "This seat is worth thre thrones."

The figures of the circulation of the chie Parisian dailies, though large, show that the could have reached hardly one third as man people in the provinces as are reached by Londo papers in Britain. The size of the country an the diversity of interests and regional tradition kept an independent field open for provincia papers, and these were the nuclei around whicl political parties and personages kept local powe and positions in the Chambers even against thei own parties, men like Laval buying up chains o provincial newspapers.

A sure way of killing the sovereign, as Hamle showed, is to pour poison into his ear while he i politically asleep.

Toward Defeat. The Chambers had a record o achievement. But it was not enough. They shoulc as Blum proposed in 1936, have made the pres more wholesome. They should, as they were re quested by Gaston Doumergue, Prime Ministe after the February 1934 riots had driven M Daladier out of office by the virulence of th streets, have reinforced the Government's powe (with the Senate's consent) of dissolution, bu their egoism would not give the Executive this in strument of discipline and stability (p. 314ff.).

They should have, above all, seen that socia justice was developed much further than they hac done. For instance, since 1870 the industrial work ing classes had grown in numbers and need, wit the progress of the Industrial Revolution. In th 1890's that class numbered something over 3,000. 000 or 15 percent of the labor force; by the 1930's increasing steadily, it had risen to about 30 per cent. Because it was still a minority, it could n get the welfare and social-security services in the measure the British or even the German workers (these latter by authoritarian socialism, p. 604) had obtained. Some alleviation of its lot had been provided, but too little and very late. At the same time, the taxation system pressed unduly hard upon this class. In the 1890's the urban and rural low-income groups paid 20 percent of their income in taxes, while the average tax burden was only 14 percent; and it was 20 percent on a much smaller income. Middle-income groups paid between 9 and 11.3 percent; high-income groups paid less than 12 percent. Half the taxes came from consumers' goods. In 1895 a Radical Cabinet asked for an income tax; the bills were repeatedly brought forward and defeated. Only in 1914, twenty years after legislation in Britain, was such a tax enacted—in July 1914. The Senate had helped in its earlier failure. The peasantry had many ways of evading payment of taxes; so had the small tradesmen and the big businessmen, and they used them.

Economic Distress and Privilege. The whole country, but especially the working class, suffered from the instability of the currency, the franc, owing partly to foreign trade difficulties but owing also to administrative waste, the lateness of the governmental budgets and their constant deficits, and the manipulations of the commercial and financial circles bent on exporting their fortunes. Prices and wages were constantly out of line. The big body of lower civil servants suffered especially, as the Government and the Chambers could suppress their demands. The workers and even the small tradesmen and craftsmen, the officials and the teachers, were alienated from the nation by the economic tactics of the high financiers, manufacturers, and the owners of the mines and metallurgical industries (largely votaries of the Church), closely knit in the *Comité des Forges,* around the Bank of France (owned by 200 shareholders—a strangleholder on Government financing and the destroyer of Left-wing Cabinets), called in slang the Monied Wall (*Mur d'argent*) and disposing of the power of the Press. These, especially through the Senate, cut down the benefits in wages, vacations, working conditions, shorter hours, and reduction of prices that had been

instituted by the Government of Léon Blum. This was a coalition of Socialists and Radical Socialists, supported by the votes of the Communists, that had come into existence in the Popular Front *bloc* formed to fight Fascism and upper-class egoism at the elections of 1936. (Such *blocs,* of Right or Left parties, had been tried several times before to mitigate the fissiparous membership of the parties and the Chambers, always to fall apart within a few months.)

The high capitalists were often Catholic devotees allied with Catholic politicians and various Fascist-type leagues, such as the *Camelots du Roi* and the *Croix du Feu,* punitive hunters of the working class and more congenial with Mussolini and Hitler than Frenchmen who were Socialist or Communist. They especially resented Léon Blum's reforms, particularly his democratizing of the governing board of the Bank. Nor could they forget he was a Jew. Like the Communist Party, they were anxious to destroy the Republic.

Communism. The Communist Party, founded in 1920 (p. 345), pursued its reckless, disruptive tactics of incitement without constructive responsibility. It found a welcome in the bosom of French trade unionism, for this was (1) lukewarm to reformist parliamentarism and so maintained its separateness from the Socialist Party, though its members individually voted heavily for it; and (2) it had been under the influence of Marx, Blanqui, and Georges Sorel, to become revolutionary syndicalists, meaning that violence was good if it could be surgical, *that the trade unions, even of public officials, should organize a State in which they would run the economy directly* (as Guild Socialists in England suggested), that the instrument of the general strike would be more efficacious than political tactics in securing concessions from the complacent bourgeoisie, with the parliamentary system finally overthrown.

Social Cleavage. The indicated social conflicts, and reckless class egoisms, were incarnated in the political parties. These could not find a satisfaction-giving majority. They could not be agreed about military service or armament or strategy, and were torn by the menace of Hitler and the blandishments of Moscow. The Church, the royalists, the Fascists were for Hitler, the Duce, and

Franco. The leaders of the various groups were all too small to give the leadership of mind and the inspiration of magnitude that might draw parties together, even for the final need to preserve the nation against foreign aggression. They condoned Hitler until the last moment—even beyond it.

The period of the Third Republic is studded with the names of good, republican politicians: in an earlier generation, Gambetta, Thiers, Jules Favre, Jules Ferry, Jules Simon, Waldeck-Rousseau and Émile Combes, and Clemenceau; in the younger one, Millerand, Jaurés, Briand, Barthou, Poincaré, Herriot, Daladier, Tardieu, Painlevé, Reynaud, Chautemps. Yet the conditions of French parliamentarism did not allow them to develop statesmanship but required of them, above all, partisan ingenuity, even personal ingenuity, to stay alive in the atmosphere of rancor, jealousy, separatism, and passion for office.

Robert de Jouvenel, a gifted journalist, said in his *République des Camarades* in 1914:

> Among the men charged in some way or another with controlling public affairs, an intimacy develops. It is not sympathy or esteem or confidence; it is actually *camaraderie* [pal-ship], something, in fact, midway between *esprit de corps* and complicity.

The nation had no stomach for war, remembering the 1,500,000 dead, the 750,000 mutilated, the 3,000,000 wounded, the 500,000 prisoners of World War I, and the shocking economic devastation. For whom should each class fight, for whose interests, for whose ideals? There was no consensus.

No Leader. A man may assist the weaving of consensus. Since Georges Clemenceau, of Jacobin energy, who was called to the leadership in World War I at the age of seventy-eight, there had been no such leader, conspicuous in mind, energy, policy, and spirit. This misfortune can happen to a people: that when a leader is needed, a hero, he is not born into its midst or the institutions militate against his assumption of authority—in spite of ridiculous theories to the effect that the sociological occasion always produces the man. What the spirit of a man can do is suggested by Freud:

> Since the process of recognizing a thing as a separate entity involves giving it a name of its own, I will henceforward call this function in the ego the super-ego. . . . The function which I am beginning to distinguish within the ego is the conscience. . . . I feel a temptation to do something which promises to bring me pleasure, but I refrain from doing it on the ground that "my conscience will not allow it." Or I allow myself to be persuaded by the greatness of the expectation of pleasure into doing something against which the voice of my conscience has protested, and after I have done it, my conscience punished me with painful reproaches and makes me feel remorse for it.
>
> Conscience is no doubt something within us, but it has not been there from the beginning . . . The role, which the super-ego undertakes later in life, is at first played by an external power, by parental authority. . . . We have allocated to it the activities of self-observation, conscience, and the holding up of ideals.
>
> For us the super-ego is the representative of all moral restrictions, the advocate of the impulse towards perfection, in short it is as much as we have been able to apprehend psychologically of what people call the "higher things of life." Since it itself can be traced back to the influence of parents, *teachers, and so on* [italics added] we shall learn of its significance if we turn our attention to these sources.[10]

The old men, Marshal Pétain, General Weygand, and the defeatists behind them (like Pierre Laval), Catholic or cynically pagan, preferred that France be a Nazi province than an equal partner of Britain in an international union. In forty-five days Hitler's *blitzkrieg* overthrew a well-equipped army by dynamic and novel tactics. On July 10, 1940, the French legislature, one third the Deputies being absent involuntarily, and on false representations by the new leaders, like Pétain and Laval, abandoned the Third Republic for the state of Vichy, from the city in which they met. It is not possible to say that the people in general continued to fight either the Nazis or the new regime: they were obedient.

VI. THE VICHY REGIME

Suppression of the Third Republic

The nationalists, the Catholic-ultras, the Fascist-corporationists, the antidemocrats, the antirepub-

---

[10] Sigmund Freud, *New Introductory Lectures on Psychoanalysis,* Lecture XXXI, New York, 1933.

licans, the Royalists, the provincial gentry, the Parisian cynics and neo-Fascists (*Cagoulards* [11] and *Croix de Feu* and *Camelots du Roi*) gripped the nation through Marshal Pétain (now eighty-four years old), and Pierre Laval, whom the Third Republic had neglected to expel from its politics. The Bourbon Restoration was back again—without the King; brought back, as the Bourbon oppositionists had cried, "in the baggage of the enemy," this time, Hitler. But if it was a Bourbon restoration, then it was a return to the *Ancien Régime:* the absolutism, feudalism, and the domination of the Church.

In the National Assembly held in Vichy, the capital of the part of France the Germans had agreed to allow free of occupation,[12] inspired by the diabolic tactics of Laval, the old Constitution was voted out of existence, July 10 and 11, 1940. Albert Lebrun, the feeble President of the Republic, countersigned the action and was soon dislodged from office.

Of 666 members present (out of a total, Chamber and Senate, of 900), 569 voted for the law and only 80 against. This was most ominous for the future of French politics. Even more ominous was the voting of two parties: out of 112 members of the Radical Socialist Party, 62 voted for, 13 against, 2 abstained, and 35 were absent; out of 152 Socialist Deputies, 83 voted for Pétain's law, 29 voted against, 62 abstained, and 34 were absent. The Socialist record was the better.

Of the 80 Deputies who voted against Pétain's law, most were Socialists and Radicals: only 7 were of the Center and the Right. Of the total of the Left forces no less than 277 voted for Pétain's law. It has been estimated that only 12 percent of the Left Deputies and Senators together voted *against* Pétain's regime.

All the Communist votes were absent: they had been expelled at the outbreak of war and were underground. These events could not but provoke

cynicism among the masses, who expect to be guided by those who are supposed to know better.

In November 1944 the Socialist Party, after careful investigation readmitted 65 of its errant members; the Radical Socialists excluded 34 of their culpable members.

Antidemocracy

How was Vichy France governed and what did it do? Briefly, in place of the Chamber and Senate a National Council was set up in January 1941, composed of 200 members nominated by the Government—that is, Pétain, President, and Laval, Prime Minister. The false promise of a new constitution was ignored. Political parties were suspended, except for a sponsored veteran's organization of a Hitler Storm-Trooper variety. A "corporative" employer-worker association system replaced the trade unions; and State-supervised peasant corporations took care of the farming population. A militia supplied the regime with force; it was the anti-Dreyfusards of the 1890's, now armed. Foreigners were harried; Jews were persecuted; deportations to Germany were carried out. The educational system was enfeebled, the Church schools subsidized, textbooks revised. The press was censored and ordered to obey the Government on pain of suspension and suppression. The slogan Liberty, Equality, and Fraternity was supplanted by the "moral order" of Work, Family, and Fatherland. In line with this, family allowances were extended; women were ousted from public life; divorce was attacked.

Gradually the Resistance outside and inside France was built up, fighting as much against mass popular lassitude as against the Nazi occupation and the Vichy officials, who included so many of the former higher civil servants (Chapter 9).

Many people, but especially the trade unionists, Catholic as well as "free"; the teachers, the backbone of the Socialist, Radical Socialists, and Communist parties; the younger Catholic and minor clerical leaders; the Socialist Party in the form of local groupings of partisans; fewer of the Radicals; hardly any of the Right; the Communist Party *after* Hitler's attack on Russia, but not before, when it had connived in the Occupation—fought against the regime and with the liberating foreign

[11] Meaning "Hooded" men, though the hoods were not K.K.K. style.
[12] Hitler occupied the northern and eastern provinces, including Paris, and in return for the capitulation and cooperation, allowed the rest to remain under Vichy rule. But, in November 1942, as a consequence of the Allied landing in North Africa and cooperation by some of the French authorities there, all France was occupied.

nations. The Communist Party was the most tight knit, intent on preserving its identity, on maximizing its public reputation, on serving Moscow and the Communist revolution; and it profited most by the partisan operations, for *all* anti-Pétainists were denounced as "Communists." It came to be known as the *parti des fusillés:* the party of the executed. It was the great beneficiary of the record and the legends of resistance, and it callously lied its way into the public mind as the *only* body of self-sacrificial anti-Nazis.

De Gaulle

General Charles de Gaulle was not a career politician but a schooled Army officer, the son of one of those French subaristocratic families who gave their young men to the civil, colonial, or military service of their nation. From youth he felt destined to lead France in days of fate. His book, *The Edge of the Sword,* 1930, (dedicated to Marshal Pétain!) revealed a nonpolitical, authoritarian mentality, though a devoted patriotic one, and a man of attack, of mechanized *blitzkrieg,* not of the prevailing Maginot-Line mentality. He divined that men had a completely instinctive passion to be led by the man of character and *charisma* (he did not use Max Weber's technical term), a man unimaginable without "a powerful element of egoism, pride, toughness, wile." He would be (deliberately) distant, laconic, sparing of gesture, and might appear rude and exigent; mystery would surround him.

Like his family and their like, he was an ardent Catholic, and an exceptionally sedulous student of history, philosophy, and the classics, indeed, a professor of history at St. Cyr, the nation's military academy.

A most gifted soldier, he bore himself with distinction in World War II, which he entered with the rank of colonel. He had been adviser to Paul Reynaud, conservative party leader, nationalist, Minister and later Prime Minister, especially in the last crisis of France in the spring and summer of 1940. But his ideas had been used by the Nazis, not by his own military superiors. Reynaud made de Gaulle Undersecretary of War in June 1940, far too late. He fled Hitler to London to build the Free French movement. He now became a politician (though, as he claimed, very different from the *party* politicians), stiff, arrogant, exasperatingly rude, yet as Mr. Churchill, who had to suffer these traits pleaded, still the spiritual descendant (de Gaulle claimed the *physical* descendant) of Joan of Arc.

A Bonapartist strain is evident in him.

A leader will have to arise whose judgment is independent, whose orders are irresistible, and who is well thought of by public opinion. He must be in the service of the State alone, free from prejudices, disdaining patronage.

In resisting Vichy, de Gaulle was breaking the French law of treason, and this was brave. Some of his aides in London and Algiers had been *Cagoulards;* he opposed suggestions that men, such as Herriot, Daladier, Blum, and Reynaud, Third Republic party leaders be rescued from the Nazi prisons. He was most highhanded in his control of the Resistance Council and the Provisional Government: a Man on Horseback?

VII. THE FOURTH REPUBLIC

Eventually, the Resistance groups accepted de Gaulle as the leader of Fighting France and the Provisional Government. From September 1943 until the liberation of Paris, these forces were mustered in the Provisional Government in Algiers in North Africa, with de Gaulle as its President; this was flanked by a Provisional Consultative Assembly, representing all the resistance movements. De Gaulle's associates manipulated the nominations to get men amenable to de Gaulle.[13] In August 1944 the Provisional Govern-

---

13   *The Provisional Consultative Assembly*

	Nov. 1943	Nov. 1944
Metropolitan Resistance *	40	149
External Resistance *	12	25
Reorganized political parties	(20)	(60)
Communist	3	7
Socialist	5	15
Radical Socialist	5	21
Rightist	7	17
Conseil Generaux †	12	12
Total	84	246

* About two thirds were of the Left, the rest Right or of indeterminate party.

† The local-government-elected assemblies in each *département.*

ment and Assembly moved into Paris, and the Assembly was expanded to include 300 members, adding to its membership members of the French home underground, the members of the legislature of the Third Republic, the foreign resistance. Later those released from German prisons were added.

De Gaulle's prestige and glamor were at their zenith. He might have attempted a Man-on-Horseback *coup d'état;* he chose free elections for a Constituent Assembly. While political parties were malleable, and still glowed with a unifying patriotism and disgust at the conservative parties and social groups, reforms were hurried that would otherwise have been impossible: wages were raised; social security was broadened; some industries, including coal, the railroads, big automobile works, and electricity, were nationalized (Chapter 8); and works councils were set up in large plants. Woman suffrage was established, overcoming the decades of opposition of the Right and the Catholic politicians (especially manifested in the old Senate), and Proportional Representation was introduced, to overcome the stagnation of small constituencies and personal politics in favor of large ideas largely represented.

The Making of the First Constitution

It is more economical of space to refer to the party attitudes on specific branches of the Constitution in the course of their analysis at a later stage. Here the bare details of the building of the Constitution are narrated. It has been implied already that the old parties had by now reassembled; less so those of the Right and Center, most responsible for the humiliation of defeat and the Vichy government. An election for the Constituent Assembly was organized, and constitutional drafts and suggestions in plenty had been discussed among the parties and in the press.

Three Questions. The election demanded of the electorate, on the ballot papers, answers to three questions:

(1) To cast their votes for the men on the various lists.

(2) "Do you wish the Assembly elected today to be a Constituent Assembly?"

(3) If the electorate shall have answered "Yes" to the first [that is, about the Constituent Assembly] question, do you approve, until the new constitution is put into effect, the organization of the public authorities in conformity with the bill, the test of which appears on the back of the ballot papers?

The "organization" was de Gaulle's provisional presidency, with his Ministers responsible to the Constituent Assembly. It was a complicated task for the voters!

The results of the election, for the questions asked, were these:

For the Assembly to be a Constituent Assembly:

		Percent
Affirmative	17,957,868	96.4
Negative	670,672	3.6
Total	18,628,540	100.0
Abstaining	4,968,578	20.2

For the "limited" organization of powers:

Affirmative	12,750,000
Negative	6,500,000

Clearly, in spite of de Gaulle's prestige and services, the Left had not roared out "No!" altogether in vain. He was on the way out.

It is a contribution to the understanding of French political parties to notice the appeal each made to the electorate to answer the ballot questions. Thus (simplified):

(a) YES-NO This was the Communist answer; *in favor* of a Constituent Assembly and *against* the restriction of its powers while the Constitution was being made. It was backed by the C.G.T. (see pp. 348–349).

(b) YES-YES The Socialists and the de Gaullists were *for* a Constituent Assembly and of the limitation of its powers over finance and the power to overthrow the Government in accordance with the draft bill that appeared on the other side of the ballot.

(c) NO-YES The Rightist parties maintained this combination. They hankered for the Third Republic, but, supposing the voters rejected the idea, they favored the restrictions on the Assembly's power. The Radicals advised this. They wanted to return to 1875, and were therefore opposed to a Constituent Assembly. If the voters, however, voted for one, then it advised *full* powers to the Assembly.

(d) NO-NO

French Elections for National Assembly, 1945, 1946

Party	Millions of Votes	Seats	Percentage of Voters	Percentage of Votes Not Rewarded Seats Gained in Proportion to Votes Received
October 21, 1945				
Communist and Resistance	} 5.024 {	151 8	} 26.52	
Socialist and U.D.S.R.	} 4.809 {	139 31	} 25.01	
M.R.P. and Jeune Republique	4.580	150	23.9	
Peasants	}	11	}	
Independent Republicans	3.012 {	14	15.7	
Entente Republicans	}	39	}	
Radicals	1.701	29	8.87	
Algerian Mussulmans		7		
Totals *	19.126	586	100.00	

(or *ca.* 78.5 percent of electorate)

June 2, 1946
Metropolitan France Election

Communist and affiliates	5.199	146	26.2	3.3
Socialist and affiliates	4.188	115	21.1	5.5
R.G.R. and affiliates	2.295	39	11.5	46.7
M.R.P. and affiliates	5.559	160	28.1	3.0
P.R.L. and Right	2.340	62	12.8	19.3
No party	.070	0	0.3	100.0

Overseas

Communist		7
Socialist		12
M.R.P.		9
R.G.R.		16
P.R.L.		8
Algerian parties		13
No group		5
Totals *	19.661	586

(or *ca.* 80.3 percent of electorate)

November 10, 1946
Metropolitan France

Communist and affiliates	5.489	166	28.6	1.9
Socialist and affiliates	3.432	90	17.9	10.7
R.G.R. and affiliates	2.381	55	12.4	27.2
Gaullist Union	.313	5	1.6	42.1
M.R.P. and affiliates	5.058	158	26.3	3.2
Peasants	.229	8	1.2	7.7
P.R.L. and Right	2.237	62	11.7	9.3
No name	.064	0	0.3	100.0

Party	Millions of Votes	Seats	Percentage of Voters	Percentage of Votes Not Rewarded Seats Gained in Proportion to Votes Received
		Overseas		
Communist		17		
Socialist		13		
R.G.R.		9		
Gaullist		1		
M.R.P.		8		
P.R.L.		1		
Indep. Repub.		4		
Algerian parties		13		
Malgache		3		
No name		5		
Cochinchina		1		
Totals *	19.203	586		

(or *ca.* 76.2 percent of electorate)

* Figures do not add to these correct totals because certain small groupings have been omitted.

M.R.P.—Mouvement Républicaine Populaire: P.R.L. *Parti Republicain de la Liberté* (later dissolved); R.G.R.—Rassemblement des Gauches Républicains; U.D.S.R.—Union of Democratic and Social Resistance.

The Table of seats and votes cast gives the resultant strength of the parties returned at the same electoral trial of strength, and in the two elections of the following year.

The main results, producing the first Constituent Assembly, that of 1945, were these: that the Communists had polled 5,000,000 votes; the Socialist and allies, over 4,560,000; the M.R.P., 4,781,000; the Radicals and related 2,131,000; the Right, 2,546,000; and there were 165,000 votes cast for other candidates. The three big parties of the far Left and moderate Center (the M.R.P.) had over 14,250,000 votes between them, compared with 4,600,000 on their right, of which only 2,546,000 were Rightists.[14]

In terms of seats, the situation was: Communists and affiliates, 159; Socialists, 146; M.R.P., 150, including the colonial territories. The difference between the numbers given, when added, and 586, is made up of various small groupings or individuals. That is, the three big parties had 455 members, or three quarters of the representation between them.

The Assembly almost immediately set to work

[14] The figures given here do not exactly match those in the preceding tables. This is because both of them were totaled by different official or unofficial authorities, and because the names of the party groups are in traditional confusion and fluidity. On electoral statistics, see p. 335.

to frame a constitution, remitting the preparation of a draft to the Committee of the Constitution, numbering forty-two, chosen by proportional representation of the groups in the Assembly, thus giving the Big Three the overwhelming predominance: Communists, 12; the M.R.P., 12; the Socialists, 11; and minor parties, 7.

No Consensus. Yet this produced no inward consensus. Far from it! What could be more different than the outlook of these three parties—most of all, the M.R.P. with its Catholic outlook and the Communist Party with its Bolshevik mentality (see p. 343)? The Socialist Party could share the social-welfare objectives of the M.R.P. but definitely not the dictatorial and totalitarian ethics of the Communist Party. Yet without their votes, neither of the other parties could obtain a majority; with it, a draft could be voted.

The Socialists were forced to lean toward the Communist Party, in part to counteract the imperious behavior of General de Gaulle, then provisional President. He wished to rule, somehow, *above* the political parties. He resigned, as will be explained later, in January 1946. The President of the Assembly, the Socialist Vincent Auriol, attempted conciliation, but the M.R.P. was ever more alienated from the two Left parties. François de Menthon, of the M.R.P., the General Reporter of the Constitution, resigned. His position was taken by Pierre Cot, a former Left-wing Radical deputy, but now highly inclined toward the Communists! The two parties of the Left stamped their strong impress to the Constitution.

Party Attitudes to the Constitution. The Assembly was trying to set down the basic rules of the political conflict for the future, to give authority to the laws of changing the social and economic nature of France and to forbid it to others. Like all constitutions, this was the law of laws. The constitution is the authoritative distribution of legitimate sovereign power. It is a grave decision to make that binds or licenses your authority, and does so with an amending clause and in a state of mind designed to have permanence.

The three parties agreed on two fundamental matters: a new constitution *was* necessary, and the United States type of presidential-congressional system would *not* satisfy the needs of France. (The latter with a seemingly strong Executive had appeared attractive when the war was going badly.)

The Communists. The principal determination of the Communist Party was to put the maximum power into the hands of the elected Assembly, unicameral. The President (the Executive power) would be responsible to that Assembly, with extremely limited power and certainly without authority to dissolve the Assembly—that is, would have no power to hit back. They scorned the referendum as a means of solving a deadlock between Assembly and President, for the memories of Louis Napoleon's plebiscites horrified them—so long as *they* were not in command of the management of the plebiscite.

The M.R.P. The M.R.P. aimed for the Third Republic institutions, generally speaking, but with a stronger Executive. This was to be achieved by the strengthening of the power of dissolution, and a *cooling-off period* between the debate and the vote in the Assembly on confidence or no confidence in the Government. It was inclined to judicial review as a safeguard of the constitution, generally as practiced in the United States.

The Socialist Party. The Socialists sided with the Communists to establish a unicameral system. This, as in Switzerland, would elect the Prime Minister. The Communists were favorable to this also. However, the Socialists did not like the absolute predominance of the Assembly proposed by the Communists. They proposed a power of dissolution—it would be automatic after a rejection of a Government by the Assembly, and after an interval between votes for cooling off or reflection. The Socialists, further, recommended the abolition of the presidency of the Republic as a valueless figure.

M.R.P. and Socialists. The M.R.P. and the Socialists agreed in recommending articles to regulate the status of political parties. For they recognized their fundamental significance in constitutional government. Therefore they proposed obligations for parties. The Communists detested the idea. For the rules would have regulated the parties' budgets and organization, excluded *foreign control and nonresponsible leadership.* Aimed primarily at Fascist parties, by that token it was too much of a strait-jacket for the Communists. Powerful, the Communist Party wanted the maximum freedom of maneuver; and by nature it is extremely hierarchical.

The Socialist Party and the M.R.P. cooperated to gain more power for the Assembly *and the electorate* than the Communist Party was at first willing to admit. They even proposed the remission of bills before the legislature to a juridical committee before its final voting for errors of form—a second chamber, without excessive power—and suggested other technical committees as revising bodies.

Amendments of the Constitution would need to be submitted for ratification to the people; and this referendal power would be invoked to declare a law unconstitutional. These internal and popular checks did not suit the Communist Party's philosophy of power.

Nor was this all. These parties demanded that Deputies should be compelled to follow the policy of the party within whose organization they had been elected or to resign from the legislature (discipline the vote). They wished that the old vice of popular abstention be dealt with by a fine. Campaign expenses were to be limited and propaganda media equalized, and the State was to contribute to campaign expenses, in the interests of electoral equality. This latter the Communists most fiercely resisted. For when they had been in a small minority, they had made lurid propaganda out of the capitalistic influences on the electorate. Now, in a position of relatively great electoral power, through dictatorial organization and unscrupulous agitatory tactics and foreign subventions, they did not intend to lose a single seat in the interests of fair play. During and after the Resistance they had acquired considerable wealth, purloining the property of "collaborators," and killing others.

M.R.P. and Socialists further looked to party subscription to a Declaration of Rights, publication of the source of party funds, and each party's repudiation of the monopoly-party state to achieve this. The Communist Party opposed these.

Communist Party and the Rest. In all this encounter of wills, it became clear that the Communists wished to have a constitution in which they could either have their own total way in their policy of social revolution, as in Russia, and France subjected to Moscow and the Cominform (though this organization was not formalized till 1947), or to be able to block any effective government at all. It was rule or ruin. But the M.R.P. and the Socialists, though in rather different ways, were interested in a constitution that preserved the full liberty of the electorate to decide from time to time on the desirability and expediency of policies.

The Declaration of Rights. The Big Three agreed on a very elaborate Declaration of Rights. But there was a strong difference between M.R.P. and the Communist Party on private property. The M.R.P. was willing, being Catholic, to ascribe communal limits to private property rights and power. It was thus at odds with the Radicals and the Right and even, as time showed, with many of crypto-conservatives who had swelled its own vote in the recent elections. The Communists were with the M.R.P. on the limitation of property rights—for complete national planning of industry and agriculture and the abolition of private enterprise and property. For the M.R.P. was, above all, interested in the preservation of the virtues of the family; but the Communist Party held no institution sacred between the millions of individ-

ually powerless persons and the omnipotent State. M.R.P. and the Socialists and other parties sought a "plural" society, the Communists, a "monistic" one, the former an "open" society, the Communists a "closed."

Communists and Socialists refused to guarantee freedom of education to the M.R.P., which was anxious to win back for the Church the right to educate.

Three Chambers? To accommodate the aspirations of the French colonies a new expression, albeit vague, "the French Union" was developed. To meet the demands for a revising body and technical advice on legislation, an Economic Council was devised. Thus, all parties finally agreed to the proposal of Vincent Auriol that there should be virtually three chambers: an Assembly, a Council of the French Union, and an Economic Council; while the M.R.P. lost its demand for a Senate.

Defeat of M.R.P.

The M.R.P. demand for the guarantees of a statute of parties, of a second chamber, of a referendum on constitutionality of the laws, of guarantees for private (that is, Church) schools was voted down.

On April 19, 1946, the whole of the draft constitution was approved by the Assembly, 309 to 249. The M.R.P. members voted against it, together with the Center and the Right.

Before we analyze the referendum campaign, the main political events between the end of 1945 and the voting of the constitutional draft must be sketched.

General de Gaulle's Course. General de Gaulle had been unanimously elected President of the Provisional Government on November 13, 1945. He took power under the provisions of the law on the organization of authority that had appeared on the referendal ballot of October 1945. It stipulated that he should be elected by the Assembly by open vote and a majority of all its members. Then he was to make a Government and present it for acceptance to the Assembly, whose approval was necessary to its existence.

The Communists demanded three key Ministries as their share of the Coalition Cabinet under de Gaulle. De Gaulle refused, and offered the

Assembly his office. The Communists, flushed with being the largest party in the Assembly, claimed that Maurice Thorez, recently returned from a long sojourn in Moscow, should be elevated to the presidency. The M.R.P. refused to be member of any Cabinet unless de Gaulle was its chief. A compromise was reached whereby the Communists were offered a Minister in the Ministry of National Defense by the division of that Ministry into two, the innocuous section only falling to the Communists. The Socialists had sided with the Communists rather than the M.R.P.

There was already high provocation to de Gaulle. Late in December 1945 the Socialists had decided on a 20-percent flat reduction of the military credits requested by de Gaulle for 1946. The debate involved the nature of the responsible Executive. Communists and Socialists insisted that the Assembly should not be grudged the right to overthrow the Cabinet, otherwise this would connote dictatorship—for de Gaulle was insisting that the credits he proposed be given, without amendment, or he would resign. A compromise was reached.

De Gaulle could not tolerate this play of party politics that put the main authority into the hands of the Communists. His hopes had been pinned to an integrated bloc of Center parties, no further Left than the Socialists. These events occurred by January 16, 1946. The disgust of the Third Republic's Executive impotence had come upon him again (p. 313). De Gaulle suddenly resigned.

The M.R.P. stayed in the Cabinet, on one indispensable condition: that the next President be no Communist. The Socialist President of the Constituent Assembly, Felix Gouin, was the compromise candidate. The Socialist Party, knowing their own man, was now less afraid of a strong Executive, and the M.R.P. was disarmed.

The referendum on the draft constitution—heavily Assembly-weighed—was proclaimed for May 5, 1946.

The political parties entered the arena. The M.R.P. (then heavily de Gaullist) called on the electorate to block the Communists, the one-party dictatorship. The Communists worked with the slogan "against reaction," political and clerical. The trade unions (C.G.T.) called on the workers to vote for the Constitution as a means of a better economic and social future.

The Communists committed a shocking fault of electoral strategy, being arrogant with the de Gaulle's humiliation. They shouted the slogan, *"Thorez au pouvoir!"—Thorez in office!*—to wit, for the presidency. They ran straight into the hands of their enemies who were warning the electorate of Bolshevik dictatorship.

The Draft Rejected. The electorate rejected the draft constitution. Never before had a French electorate voted negatively at a plebiscite or referendum. *For* approval, there were 9,109,771 votes, or 47 percent of those voting. *Against* were cast 10,272,586, or 53 percent. The number of *abstentions* was 4,767,717, or 19.3 percent of the total register.

This was, indeed, a bad augury for France's future stability and progress. A consensus was very far from achievement.

A Second Constituent Assembly

It was necessary to elect a new Constituent Assembly. The election took place on June 2, 1946. The results of the voting may be seen in the Table on page 322.[15] For our immediate purpose, the chief results were these. The Communists scored 153 seats against 159 in 1945; the Socialists, 129 compared with 139. These were slight losses but, when every seat is scanned for significance in hot issues, of importance. The M.R.P. scored a tremendous victory: it was now the largest party, with 161 seats as compared with 150. As for the popular vote, the Communists had 25.9 percent, the Socialist Party, 21.1 percent, and the M.R.P. 28.2 percent. The total votes for the Communist Party was about equal to that of 1945; that of the Socialists showed a loss of nearly 300,000; and the M.R.P. had added no less *than 1,000,000 votes* to its supporters.

The rest of the Assembly, rightward gained a little.

The draft constitution just rejected was taken as the basis for compromises on the most stubborn points of conflict between the parties. The balance between Right and Left, if the M.R.P. is included in the former, was sometimes held by

[15] Discrepancies explained in previous footnote, p. 323.

eleven Arab deputies from Algeria. Their vote made a difference to the Constitution! The Constitutional Committee was reconstituted much as before. The chairman was the Socialist André Philip, and a new member was the leader of the Algerian group, not strictly entitled, according to proportional representation, to this one seat. The Left needed him to have 22 votes out of the 40.

The M.R.P. leader, George Bidault, became President. The Assembly's powers had again been set as seven-month tenure. The Big Three once again formed a Cabinet, but the Socialists were weakened in the number of Ministries held. At this point, the Radical Socialists' seats had again become important enough for the M.R.P. to invite them to enter the Cabinet. They declined. But the maneuver was certainly a return to the mores of the Third Republic.

A decided trend was given to the Constituent Assembly by the speech made by General de Gaulle, in retirement but in ever-present, looming influence. At Bayeux, June 16, 1946, he announced his principles of constitutional government. He demanded a bicameral legislature, in which the upper chamber would represent territorial (local government), professional, and family associations. The French Union ought to be federal. Then he insisted on a strong Executive. His observations on this must be quoted:

It seems necessary to us that the Head of the State should be elected so as really to represent France and the French Union, that it should be his function to ensure the proper functioning of institutions above the parties and to make the permanent interests of the nation prevail in the midst of political contingencies. It seems to us necessary that Parliament should be one, that is to say, that it shall make laws and control the government, but should not itself govern either directly or through intermediaries. This is an essential point, and implies that the executive power must not proceed from the legislative power, even indirectly. . . . At a time when it is clear to all how the State is undermined by the impotence and division of the parties, is it good to ordain that these parties dispose at their will and without counterweight of all the powers of the Republic? When everybody observes the deplorable results of Ministers being dependent on their parties, is it good to arrange for this system to become definitive?

A President, above parties, would be chosen by indirect popular vote, and the Prime Minister he chose would have the power to dissolve the Assembly in order to call on the electorate to decide any conflict between Cabinet and Assembly.

Communists and Socialists vilified the proposal as *"The Program of Louis Napoleon"!* The Right sided with de Gaulle, and it was flanked by the Radical Socialists. The M.R.P. was close to de Gaulle's idea of a strong Executive, but could achieve nothing without Socialist votes. Fortunately, de Gaulle again withdrew from the scene.

Awkward Changes. The Assembly was in an awkward position regarding the redrafting of the Constitution. It had earlier exhausted all attempts at a better draft, after very long discussions. Over half the voters had voted against it. Twenty percent had abstained. But—what had the negators and the abstainers in mind?

The changes produced were these, as compared with the first text (p. *x*). Instead of a Declaration of Rights of immense breadth, a short Preamble was voted (p. *xvii*). The M.R.P.'s penchant for a bicameral system was gratified; but the second chamber was assigned a distinctly inferior position. Nor was the Council of Ministers (Cabinet) to be responsible to both Chambers—it would be rooted in the National Assembly only. The Council of the Republic (the second chamber) was given weak revising power only, but also the power to notify the President of the Republic of the unconstitutionality of the Assembly's laws. The President's range of powers was increased. The President of the Council of Ministers—that is, the Prime Minister—was to be nominated by the President of the Republic, as in the Third Republic. Appointment would follow only when the Prime Minister-designate had been invested by the Assembly by absolute majority. Revision of the Constitution was couched in a more difficult form than in the earlier draft.

The Communists were dissatisfied with the reintroduction of a bicameral system and the accentuation of the President's authority. The M.R.P. was not satisfied with the subordinate role of the Council of the Republic and the Assembly of the

French Union. But it had secured much in a second chamber, especially as it was, as in the Third Republic, a Senate to be founded on election by delegates of the local authorities. It won other victories also. The out-going Cabinet would, during the elections following on dissolution, remain the Caretaker Government until the results came in. A Prime Minister-designate would himself be approved by the Assembly, after which his Cabinet would be formed and presented to the Assembly for similar approval (the double investiture). M.R.P. was pleased with a Constitutional Committee to watch over the constitutionality for the laws. It compromised with the Socialists by withdrawing its proposal that the Prime Minister should have the power to dissolve the Assembly. It accepted the Socialist proposal, allowing for a longish interval between the election of an Assembly and the date when dissolutions could occur, after which dissolution would follow automatically on two votes of no confidence by the Assembly.

The Communists succeeded, with the help of the Socialists and the Algerian deputies, to "federalize" the French Union, even going to the Soviet Russian constitutional clause allowing for secession from the Union. Here, the centralizing ideas of the M.R.P. and the subordination of the colonial self-government to Paris were voted down. But—in the debate on the floor of the Assembly, the Left victory on the French Union was negatived.

The Communists had, with deep disgust, voted against the new draft in committee. They now went to the nation with the cry that the dictator's place had been made for de Gaulle. They tried to split the nation into "patriots" (who agreed with the Communist Party) and "the forces of reaction." They stayed in the Cabinet, but their members in the Assembly voted against the Government!

The M.R.P., supported by President Georges Bidault, demanded a reconsideration of the French Union articles, especially the clause allowing secession. White minorities in the colonies would obtain special representation. The Assembly in the future would decide how much self-government there would be. (The Communist Party of France would not have been so generous in subverting the Soviet "multi-national state"! (See Russia, p. 820.)

On September 29, 1946, the draft constitution was accepted by 440 to 106 votes: the Big Three against the rest.

It ought to be added that at the end of August 1946 de Gaulle had again emerged to declare himself dissatisfied with the draft, especially the weakness of the Executive. This hurt the M.R.P. badly, for their Right-wing followers began to steal away to a newly formed party—the Gaullist Union. It also hurt the Communist Party, because de Gaulle's intransigence showed that the Communist argument that the M.R.P. was wholly de Gaullist was false; thence they had to support the draft.

In the imbroglio that followed, the ramshackle compromise almost collapsed. It was the arduous work of the Socialist Party and, above all, of the President of the Assembly, Vincent Auriol (later to become the first President of the Fourth Republic under the new Constitution), that kept the compromise firm.

The Voters' Ratification. In *favor* of the Constitution 9,109,771 votes were cast, or 53.6 percent of the voters. *Against* it were cast 7,790,856 votes, or 46.4 percent of the voters. This made a total of 16,793,143 voters, out of a total electorate of nearly 24,500,000. Thus, 31.32 percent of the voters had *abstained* from voting.

The affirmative vote was only some 36 percent of the registered electorate. This was a rather sorry affirmation of the new law of laws. What was it? Ignorance? Disgust? Negligence? Or sophisticated, rational preference of some other constitution in the mind's eye? Ignorance-*cum*-fear of the unknown? A cosy dream that de Gaulle would save them some day, for, in the referendum campaign, his views were strongly represented that the draft was bad.

General elections took place under the new Constitution on November 10, 1946, for 618 members of the National Assembly; and the first Council of the Republic was elected on December 10, 1946. In both cases, the electoral law was not included in the Constitution, but special laws regulated the numbers, duration, and electoral method.

It is vital to imagine the deep and violent emotions of the time. The Resistance had expected and had even, vaguely and generally, looked for the reign of a superior justice and welfare in a future that would reward their faithful fight and their heavy losses. The humiliation of defeat was sublimated into the ardent aspirations, often utopian—for they were not statesmen, but only little men and women—of wealth, security, fraternity, and peace. They were hungry to wreak justice on the old betraying parties, on effete statesmen, on class rule, straining to purge by death, imprisonment, or banishment from public life the horde of collaborators. They believed that the Resistance, uniting so many divergent and hostile political groupings, once having liberated the land through their committees and their arms, would form a united party that would play the old parties off the field.

They were fairly soon disillusioned. The old parties reformed, or new ones, such as the M.R.P., were formed—without them and in spite of them. The Resistance was discarded—it was not a basis of organization that corresponded to the social, economic, and traditional family foundations of France. The Communists had too obviously appropriated it.

The vast majority of French people, who had been docile under the occupation and Vichy, were not interested deeply in constitutional niceties. They were led by the returned political parties, even if these had a large contingent of younger generation leaders and new names were in circulation. They even got bored with the purging of collaborators. For the days of shooting in hot blood were over. The question of guilt resolved itself so often into perplexing *degrees* of guilt, from which practically no one was immune, or action under unbearable duress. The problem of private vengeance and false witness complicated the achievement of clear evidence. Disgust developed at the Communists' murder of opponents under the guise of patriotic "justice." In their arrogance, they had even set up Soviet republics in Toulouse, Limoges, Montpellier, and Nice, in the usual Communist way!

Difficulty of Writing Constitutions

The social bases of France had hardly changed; then why should her politics and Constitution change? In an age of deep social cleavage, rigidified by "pressure" groups and party organization and tactics on a nationwide basis, and of unusually clear political consciousness shared by millions of voters, it is a marvel that any constitution, which is a nation's minimum political consensus, can emerge at all. Past ages were more propitious for the writing and adoption of constitutions. Much forgetting and forgiving are needed for social consensus.

The Constitution of the Fourth Republic

France has always plenty of men of talent, but it is always deficient in men
of action and high character.

—*Napoleon Bonaparte*

I. THE FORM OF THE CONSTITUTION

The Constitution is a "Bill to Establish the Constitution of the French Republic" and was approved November 10, 1946. It entered into force on December 24, 1946, on the first meeting of the Council of the Republic which had been elected on December 10, 1946. On January 16, 1947, Vincent Auriol was elected President of the Republic in joint session of the two Chambers. On January 21, 1947, under the Socialist M. Ramadier, the first Ministry of the new regime was confirmed by the Assembly after designation by the President of the Republic. Meanwhile the Chambers had chosen their presiding officer.

The Preamble is not numbered. The Constitution then falls into the following sections, called Titles:

Title

Preamble

The Preamble, containing the Declaration of Rights, is lengthy, as reference to the text in the Appendix will show. It is as ambitious a manifesto as the one that introduced the text of the draft constitution, which is also reproduced. Its constitutional value needs some comment. In greatest brevity, it combines the individual rights of 1789 with the recognition of social and economic needs and opportunities of the welfare and "pressure" State in the industrial era.

The Constitutional Committee evidently meant no more value to be attached to the Preamble than as a general written affirmation, a moral exhortation, of the rights Frenchmen were entitled to in the twentieth century. The rights are not numbered as they are in the U.S. Constitution as parts of the directly operative institutions of the State. One Deputy observed that in the absence of numbering there was a weakness: the rights did not connote articles of *the law*. Furthermore, the rights are not sculptured, in clean and proportioned out-lines, as a law must be—rights and duties being questions of degree and not absolutes. The Pre-amble does not include the implementing laws or articles; it does not state sanctions, enforcement rights and methods, and penalties for abuse of the rights.

Some constitutional jurists argue that where the laws are silent on subjects in the Preamble, the Preamble would prevail as positive law. For ex-ample, one court, in January 1947, nullified a bill of anti-Semitic character because the Preamble affirms sacred rights of every human being with-out distinction of race, religion, or belief. On the other hand, the *Conseil d'État* refused, in 1948, to commit itself on the legality of strikes in the pub-lic service, though the Preamble proclaimed the right to strike. For no law yet regulated strikes: the matter was political rather than juridical (see pp. 474–475).

Other jurists note that the Preamble *is* part of the Constitution and ask why, if the Committee spent almost a quarter of its time on its delibera-tion, it should mean nothing? The contents, espe-cially the freedom of education and the guarantee of private property and so on, were certainly heavily contested in the referendum campaign. Does this mean nothing? What of the compati-bility of decree laws, if not of general laws made by the Assembly, with the Preamble's princi-ples?

Yet, the phrases are very general, vague, ob-scure, open to a wide variety of interpretations. It was even more difficult for a consensus to be reached in 1946 on "rights" than on institutions, and the state of mind the Preamble embodies was a very confused one then. Yet, all in all, these phrases do represent a libertarian and anticollec-tivist spirit that may be a *generally* useful compass for a State unusually at the mercy of passionate social and economic cross-currents.

Guarantee of the Constitution

The issue is tied up with the problem of the guar-antee of the supremacy of the Constitution over the agencies it establishes, notably the Legislature and the Executive.

Since the Napoleon's Consulate, some Constitu-tions included an agency of government, usually the second chamber, with the power to challenge the constitutionality of the laws. Never, however, was there established in French practice the Amer-ican arrangement whereby the Supreme Court has jurisdiction over the constitutionality of laws and Executive actions: the French tradition of the sep-aration of powers forbad such power to the law courts. The Third Republic followed suit.

In the Constituent Assemblies some small Right-ist groups advocated judicial review "by independ-ent personalities." But American experience, which had been studied in France for several decades, was looked at askance: it was regarded as a "gov-ernment by judges," and so many federal and state laws had had their intention and spirit per-verted by the Supreme Court's subsequent inter-pretation. It was a democratic abdication.

Yet, with the exception of the Communist Party, unwilling to allow any external control over the Assembly (as in the Soviet of the U.S.S.R.), all the Deputies acknowledged the need of some out-side control. The Socialists and the M.R.P. had in mind some arrangement combined with a refer-endum. The Communists asked what better guar-antee of constitutionality could the people have than the Assembly, itself and alone?

The result was a highly complicated arrange-ment, in which a reference was possible. From this safeguard, the *Preamble is excluded*. The Bill of Rights, which is distinctively *included* in American judicial review, is excluded in France.

The arrangement may be consulted for its de-tails in the text. Here, briefly are its outlines. It includes Titles I to X, hence it also excludes the articles on the amendment of the Constitution.

II. AMENDMENT (REVISION) OF THE CONSTITUTION

The gist of the long Article 90 (see p. *xxiv*) amounts to the following:

1. The resolution for revision (synonymous with amendment) must pass in the Assembly, by an absolute majority, and on two occasions with an interval of three months between them at the minimum. This second reading may be omitted if the Council of the Republic has sometime after

the first reading accepted the resolution by an absolute majority.

2. Thereupon, a bill embodying the amendment must be passed by the normal legislative procedure—that is, by the Assembly, by a simple majority, if such is the case—*provided that* the Council of the Republic amends or rejects the bill by an absolute majority, when the Assembly needs an absolute majority to override the upper chamber.

3. A referendum follows—*but* it need *not* be undertaken if the bill is passed by either a three-fifths majority in both houses or a two-thirds majority in the Assembly, the majority in this case being of the numbers voting.

Thus, the Council of the Republic is subordinate in the matter of constitutional amendment, whereas in the Third Republic it was on an equal footing with the Chamber of Deputies (p. 315).

One of the phrases used in the article on amendment has given rise to difficulties. "This resolution shall stipulate the purpose of the amendment." Does this require the details of the amendment, or is it enough to say "Articles X, Y, and Z, are to be amended"? In the attempted revision of November 1950, the Commission on the Franchise of the Assembly accepted the latter interpretation and was sustained by the Assembly. But the Assembly was in the dark on the terms of the amendment excepting for the inferences it might make from the Commission's report. The Council of the Republic was perturbed, for it believed that the purpose of the amendment was to curtail certain powers it had been acquiring (p. 448). It put in a strong protest. In any case, the resolutions were allowed to lapse for nearly three years, as will be appreciated later.

Limitations on Amendment

There are some special limitations on amendment.

1. The Council of the Republic cannot be abolished by the Assembly even with a two-thirds majority. For this, either the Council must consent or a referendum is obligatory. The text of the proviso leaves open the question how far the powers of the Council can be *reduced,* for it merely runs "No constitutional amendment relative to the existence of the Council . . ." Does *existence* mean its composition, duration, general role, or does *existence* mean its powers, and all or any of its powers? Could it be left standing, but emasculated?

2. No amendment of the Constitution may be made or introduced while a foreign enemy is in occupation of part or all of France (Article 94). The stable door of the Third Republic is thus locked in the Fourth: Vichy let out the horses.

3. Article 95 repeats the Third Republic's ban on any revision that affects the republican form of government.

It only remains to add that the M.R.P. would have liked to give the Council of the Republic the more positive power that its consent to a constitutional amendment *should be required*. It was defeated by a tie vote—which in France entails the negative.

Under the abortive constitution, there was no Council of the Republic. This meant a single-chamber revising body, but *compulsorily* followed by a referendum. This was not pleasant to the M.R.P., to some Socialists, to the conservative parties; but it smelled sweeter to the Communists.

The Constitutional Committee, Guarantor

Supposing the Assembly ignores the special rules hedging the amendment to the Constitution? A watchdog is necessary. De Gaulle had even made the impossible suggestion that the President of the Republic be the Watchdog.

Articles 91 and 92 set out the guarantees. There is established a Constitutional Committee. It consists of thirteen members: the President of the Republic is chairman; the Presidents of the two Chambers are members *ex officio;* the other ten are appointed by the Chambers—seven by the Assembly and three by the Council of the Republic by proportional representation of the political parties. But these ten members must not be members of either Chamber. They have been chiefly professors of law; and the parties choose the lawyers whose bias harmonizes with their values.[1] One at least is well known: André Siegfried, a political scientist not a lawyer.

[1] At the end of 1955, besides the three ex-officio members, its membership was: 3 members of the *Conseil d'État,* the former President of the Paris Bar, 4 law professors, a professor of psychology, and a well-known political scientist, André Siegfried.

How contorted the mind of the intermingled constitution-makers was in their striving after their conflicting purposes will be gathered from the procedure.

The initiative can be taken only by the Council of the Republic, if it votes by absolute majority. It can get no further until the President of the Republic *and* the President of the Council of the Republic jointly refer the issue to the Committee. This reference must occur within ten days, unless urgency is claimed by the Council, when the period is cut down to five days. The Committee attempts to reconcile the text of the Assembly and the objections of the Council of the Republic. In case of failure, it decides within five days of being seized with the issue (two in urgency) whether the law is unconstitutional or not. If constitutional, the law is immediately promulgated. If it violates the Constitution, the bill goes back to the Assembly, and it can then only become law under the amendment procedure.

Only the institutions of government through Article 89 are thus safeguarded. The Socialists and M.R.P. did not relish external interference with the development of social progress by the elected assembly, hence the limitation to the institutions of government only. Their leader in constitution-making, Vincent Auriol, even went so far as to say that the main object was only to protect the Council of the Republic against the attacks of the Assembly.

The different political composition of the Council of the Republic insures that the power of complaint will be used. Nor can the Assembly be sure of having its own way, for its members are of different parties. They are not members of the Assembly, and if the Council of the Republic members can win over two of them, the latter's interpretation would prevail.

Cases. In fact, in June 1948, the Committee was appealed to. The Communists raised a demurrer to the use of the challenge procedure because the issue involved was the Assembly's own Standing Orders regarding urgency. They claimed the Committee's jurisdiction did not extend to this. The Council of the Republic nevertheless appealed to the Committee, which favored the appeal, and its decision was accepted by the Assembly. In this case, the President referred the bill back to the

Assembly, to facilitate conciliation. He has this power under Article 36 governing the legislative relationships between Assembly and Council.

In July 1949 the Council of the Republic objected to a bill passed by the Assembly limiting parliamentary immunity, directed against the Communists (p. 408). Its amendments were overridden by the Assembly—it is its right. As the Assembly had adjourned, the Council was also adjourned (Article 9). The term of ten days in which to cite the case had elapsed already. But the President of the Republic, under Article 36, sent the bill back to the Assembly rather than promulgate it.

One other case. The Constitution requires that the Bureau of the Assembly—that is, the group of presiding officers, at the head of which is the President of the Assembly, then followed by Vice President—be elected by proportional representation of the groups. But the President of the Assembly has a most important function to fulfill in the event of a dissolution, in the interval between this and the consummation of the elections. In early 1948 M. Herriot, President of the Assembly, disclosed very bad health. The Senior Vice President was Jacques Duclos, Communist leader of the then largest party in the Assembly. All the other parties were horrified to think that in the event of a dissolution *he* would be Prime Minister in the Caretaker Government (see p. 420). The Assembly moved him down to the Third Vice President. The Communists claimed that this was unconstitutional! They appealed to President Auriol to intervene. He refused. The Council of the Republic made no move.

It is difficult to get an absolute majority of the Council, the originator of a constitutional appeal. It would be forthcoming only to safeguard its own powers or to win a major political conflict. In August 1948 a full-power decree bill won by M. Reynaud was attacked by opponents as violative of Article 13 which prohibits such decree laws (this has been powerfully flouted since that time), but the Council sided with M. Reynaud. Necessity knows no constitution. In September 1951, when a law (introduced by Barangé) subsidizing Church schools had passed, the opposition (that is all the anticlerical members) tried to block it by citing it to the Constitutional Committee for violation of Article 1 of the Constitution, to the effect that "France is a Republic, indivisible, *secular,* democratic and social." The secular (laic) term was the grounds of objection. The Council voted against citing the objection—the clerical members predominated in its membership.

III. PROPOSALS FOR THE REFORM OF THE CONSTITUTION

As we shall see, the Constitution has been subject to wrenching strains in its first eight years. Comprehensive amendments have been proposed. One such set was introduced in November 14, 1950, and passed by the Assembly, November 30, 1950. The Council of the Republic passed it on January 25, 1951. It then took the Assembly's Commission of the Franchise (which has constitutional reforms within its jurisdiction) till June 2, 1953 to fashion in detail the eleven articles to be revised. The various Ministers called to make a Cabinet in the crisis of May–June 1953 told the Assembly they wanted power to complete the reform in short order. The Laniel Cabinet, with procedure of urgency, got the Assembly to pass the revisions on July 23, 1953; 468 Deputies voted in favor, and 127 against. No Deputy abstained. The Communist Party was in complete opposition, accounting for most of the negative votes. On November 30, 1954, some amendments were passed and promulgated, December 7, 1954 (see pp. *xxv–xxvi*).

This constitutional change was voted for by 412 against 141, with 58 abstentions. The groups voted thus:

Group	For	Against	Abstained
Communists	0	94	
Progressists	0	4	
Socialists	103	0	
Radicals	74	0	
De Gaullists	61	0	7
Independent Republicans	51	0	1
U.D.S.R.	23	0	
Peasants } Independent Peasants }	49	{ 0 { 0	
A.R.S.	33	0	
M.R.P.	10	21	50
Overseas Independents	2	13	
"Not in group"	6	0	
Others	0	9	
Total	412	141	58 *

* Nine Deputies were absent, including 4 M.R.P. and 2 Independent Republicans.

Since there was an absolute majority in favor, and also a two-thirds majority, this brought the amendments into immediate operation, without raising the question of sending the amendments for popular referendum.

This is not the place to discuss the particular amendments. Their purposes are mentioned at the places where the original text of the Constitution is discussed in its operation. But we draw attention to their effect. Even these amendments do not satisfy all Deputies. M. Reynaud in March 1955 proposed that the simpler amending clause of the Third Republic be reintroduced so that, among other changes, refractory Assemblies would be subject to almost automatic dissolution.

1. Lengthening of the session and restoration of a right of adjournment to the Government (p. 379).

2. No longer any proportional representation for election of the Chambers' secretariat (p. 380).

3. Increase of number of Deputies required to demand an extraordinary session from one third to one half of Assembly members (see p. 380).

4. Increase in legislative initiative of the Council of the Republic (p. 334).

5. Establishment of a procedure for producing compromises between the views of the Assembly and the Council of the Republic on bills when the latter disagrees with the former (p. 334).

6. Restoring the power to arrest members of the Chambers only when Parliament is not in session (p. 375).

7. Abolition of *absolute* majority for investiture of Prime Minister, and of requiring him to submit his Cabinet for confidence with himself (p. 411).

8. Spelling out the meaning of "one full day" as the interval before a vote of confidence in the Government is taken (p. 420).

9. Similarly with a vote of censure (p. 420).

10. Almost eliminating the "Caretaker" Government during an election after dissolution. Object—to keep the Communists out of such Government (p. 420).

Political Parties and Pressure Groups

With a few exceptions, where is the Deputy who thinks of anything but making and repairing his fortune, and selling the electors who, in turn, have sold the country to him? What is the Chamber? A great bazaar, where everyone barters his conscience, or what passes for his conscience, in exchange for a place or an office.

—Lamennais, 1841

I. THE GENERAL NATURE OF PARTIES

Democracy requires decisions by a majority. Political parties assist in gathering voters into a majority. Suppose, however, that the public mind is so divided as to fragment the parties, to disintegrate the integrator? Where, then, is a majority to be found? This is the predicament of France.

The prewar constellation of French political parties is represented in the table on page 314. We do not pay specific attention to their nature but, insofar as it is useful, merely allude to their relationship to the parties in the Fourth Republic, our principal concern. There is a substantial continuity in the parties of the Third and Fourth Republics.

It is intended to describe the parties, one by one, concentrating on these elements: history and general character, including strength at various dates; organization; clientele and pressure groups; policy and relationship to other parties and to the Government of the nation.

Some general observations on French political parties must be made first concerning (1) electoral maps; (2) electoral statistics; (3) multiplicity of parties; (4) Red and Black is too simple a division; (5) two parties are destructive of the regime itself; (6) distinction between groups and parties; (7) seating in the chambers; (8) pressure groups;

(9) backward *versus* progressive areas; (10) lack of inner party cohesion; (11) a "Christian" party; (12) P.R.; (13) small parties; (14) the Communists and poverty; and (15) duplication of office.

1. Maps of Electoral Geography

These have become very popular—the facts at a glance!—especially as a result of recent French detours from the traditional legalistic study of constitutions to the sociological appreciation of political pressures of will. This is all to the good. But too many maps can be confusing. Therefore, as a common-sense compromise, we print two maps only (p. 270 and p. 274). One is of the *départements,* with an indication of their rural or industrial character. The second shows the salient geographical features and indicates certain customary designations given to some of the regions— the Central Massif, the West, the Midi, and so on. These will enable the student to follow the references to party strength regionally and occupationally.

2. Variations in Statistics

It will be noticed that the analyses of the votes for various parties do not always add up to the same totals. This is for two reasons. Sometimes the data needed is available only for the Deputies for metropolitan France, sometimes for the overseas territories as well. But, much more important, no central office—let us say, the Bureau of the Census or the Ministry of the Interior—has a complete analysis of the election figures as sent into the Ministry by the mayors and prefects (p. 491 and p. 497). Collations have been made by famous students, such as Georges Lachappelle and, more recently, Raoul Husson, François Goguel, Maurice Duverger. Serious trouble arises from the confused names of parties in the election and the groups in the Assemblies to which the votes are ascribed. Since, however, our figures are not usually needed to prove a micrometric point, those we have chosen, with the warning given, will suffice, we hope, to support the observations made.

3. Multiplicity of Parties

In the Fourth (as in the Third) Republic, French government is bedeviled by the existence and passionateness of many parties. It is not a two-party system. After the general election of 1951, as the table shows, there were six major parties (including the Radical-Socialist clustering) and more smaller ones.

There were in all 802 lists; and these contained in all no less than 4182 candidates (1956 about 5000!). The latter figure may be compared with the, roughly, 1400 in British general elections and 900 in U.S. elections for the House. The greater number in France is a fomenter of electoral confusion.

The inability to secure a stable and inwardly unified majority remains. But this warning is necessary: though it has been possible to secure coalitions that possess a majority of the votes of the Assembly, this has been attended with difficulty. Sometimes, as with the six and a half weeks elapsed between the fall of the René Mayer Government in May 1953 and the acceptance of the Government of M. Laniel on June 26, 1953, all effort has been excruciating. Furthermore, the coalition formed, the dissensions outside have been merely transferred to the sessions of the Council of Ministers.

4. France Is Not Divided Merely between Red and Black

Some writers have at different times sought to reduce the confusion of French political will to a neat division into two. One of the most famous is that between the forces of anticlericalism (red, being atheist, Communist, Socialist, and so forth), and the other, clerical (black, the garb and obscurantism of the Church). It is insufficient. Another is that between Right and Left in general. It obscures the very different character of the parties of the Right and the differences between the Communist Party and the Socialists on the Left. Another division is between the forces of stability—the static forces, the forces of the present order—and the forces of movement, dynamic with reforms. Nor does this dichotomy—reminiscent of the "Party of Resistance" and the "Party of Movement" of 1830–1848—satisfy the variegated and complicated realities of the mixture of policies inside each party.

Whichever bisection of French political parties is taken, not one is simple. The confusion is symptomatic.

François Goguel has talked of "two adversary coalitions and *only two,*" indeed, "two temperaments." Paul Marabuto has talked of some principal formations—"great political families," sharply defined. He ranges the parties into *four* of such families: conservatism, progressism, reformism, and revolutionary innovation.

There are other party groupings. For instance, according to their outlook on (1) capitalism and private property *versus* anticapitalism and social ownership or heavy controls over private property; (2) democracy *versus* dictatorial rule, which puts the R.P.F. (de Gaullists) in an awkward category, because they claim that they are not dictators and not in favor of a one-party monopoly; (3) the welfare state *versus laissez faire* (which might as well be put as *laissez mourire*); (4) equality of man and equality of economic rewards *versus* a hierarchy of human beings according to merit and unequal fortunes; (5) religiously founded parties (for France, Catholicism) *versus* unbelief and anticlericalism; (6) nationalism *versus* pacifism and internationalism.

Any application of these distinctions soon finds a mixture of these, it would seem incongruously, in each of the six bigger and the several smaller political parties.

French Elections of June 17, 1951

		Percent
Registered	24,530,523	
Abstentions	4,859,655	19.81
Voting	19,670,638	80.19
Blank and spoiled	541,231	2.21
Valid	19,129,424	77.98

	List * of Party Candidates	Total Votes	Percentage of Valid Votes Cast
1	Communistes	4,910,747	25.67
2	Listes div. d'extrême-gauche	140,647	0.73
3	S.F.I.O.	2,661,686	13.91
4	S.F.I.O.-R.G.R.	132,363	0.69
5	S.F.I.O.-R.G.R.-M.R.P.	54,351	0.28
6	Listes div. de gauche	43,804	0.23
7	U.D.S.R.	40,266	0.21
8	Rad.-Soc.	293,053	1.53
9	R.G.R. (homogène)	227,946	1.19
10	Différents partis du R.G.R.	876,333	4.58
11	R.G.R.-M.R.P.-Modérés	118,439	0.62
12	R.G.R.-Modérés	651,416	3.41
13	R.G.R.I.F.	223,409	1.17
14	M.R.P. (ou Rép. Dém.)	2,110,424	11.03
15	M.R.P.-Modérés	403,516	2.11
16	U.I.P.R.N.	1,349,207	7.05
17	Listes div. Modérés	288,089	1.52
18	Groupement des Contribuables	90,899	0.48
19	Modérés-R.P.F.	276,893	1.45
20	R.P.F.	3,987,072	20.85
21	Divers	87,346	0.46
	Total	18,967,906	99.17

* "Lists" are lists of candidates put up for election by each party or other electoral grouping necessary in a multi-member constituency under systems of Proportional Representation, especially where *apparentés* (p. 369).

Key to Party Lists

1 Communists
2 Extreme Left
3 Socialists
4 Socialists-cum-Left Republicans
5 Socialists-cum-Left Republicans-cum-M.R.P.
6 Various lists of the Left
7 Union of Democratic and Socialist Resistants
8 Radical Socialists
9 Left Republicans Entirely
10 Various Parties of Left Republicans
11 Left Republicans-cum-M.R.P.-cum-Moderates
12 Left Republicans-cum-Moderates
13 Republicans and Independent French
14 M.R.P. (or Democratic Republicans)
15 M.R.P.-cum-Moderates
16 Peasants, Independents and National Republicans List
17 Diverse Moderates
18 Taxpayers Associations
19 Moderates-cum-R.P.F.
20 R.P.F. (de Gaullists)
21 Various

Distribution of French Parties, 1871–1956

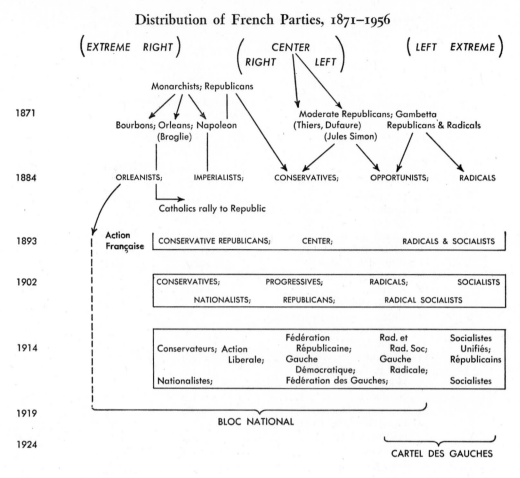

(EXTREME RIGHT) (CENTER RIGHT LEFT) (LEFT EXTREME)

Monarchists; Republicans

1871 → Bourbons; Orleans; Napoleon (Broglie) — Moderate Republicans; Gambetta (Thiers, Dufaure) (Jules Simon) — Republicans & Radicals

1884 ORLEANISTS; IMPERIALISTS; CONSERVATIVES; OPPORTUNISTS; RADICALS

Catholics rally to Republic

1893 Action Française | CONSERVATIVE REPUBLICANS; CENTER; RADICALS & SOCIALISTS

1902 CONSERVATIVES; PROGRESSIVES; RADICALS; SOCIALISTS
NATIONALISTS; REPUBLICANS; RADICAL SOCIALISTS

1914 Conservateurs; Action Liberale; Fédération Républicaine; Gauche Démocratique; Rad. et Rad. Soc; Gauche Radicale; Socialistes Unifiés; Républicains
Nationalistes; Fédération des Gauches; Socialistes

1919 BLOC NATIONAL

1924 CARTEL DES GAUCHES

1928

ELECTION ORGANIZATIONS:

Fed. Républ. Démocratique; Alliance Démocratique;	Gauche Républ. Démocratique;	Gauche Radicale;	Rad. et Rad. Soc;	Socialistes S.F.I.O.
Démocrates Populaires;	Parti Républicain Démocratique et Sociale;		Républicains Socialistes;	Communistes

GROUPS IN THE CHAMBER:

Union Républ. Démocratique; Démocrates Populaires; Action Démocratique et Sociale;	Gauche Sociale et Radicale; Républicains de Gauche;	Gauche Radicale;	Rad. et Rad. Soc; Républicains Socialistes; Independent Socialists;	Socialistes S.F.I.O.
Independent Conservatives;	Center Independents;		Left Independents;	Communistes

1956 Union of French Fraternity (Poujadists); National Rally; De Gaullists or Social Republicans; Independent Republicans; — M. R. P.; — Overseas Independents; U. D. S. R.; Radicals (Mendès-France); R.G.R. — Socialists; — Communists; Progressists;

5. Parties Destructive of the Regime

France has two political parties of substantial representation in the Assembly and the Council of the Republic, and of strength in the electorate, who are prepared to destroy the Fourth Republic altogether. They are, as oppositions, not "loyal." These are the Communist Party and General de Gaulle's *Ralliement du Peuple Français* (the Rally of the French People), abbreviated to R.P.F., the one on the Left, the latter on the Right. The former, in the Third Republic and, since May 1947, in the Fourth Republic, refuses to enter into any Government. It prefers the dictatorial regime of the U.S.S.R. to the democratic system of France, and it is in politics chiefly to ruin the Fourth Republic, and in the meanwhile to affect the actions of the Assembly in the interests of the U.S.S.R. The R.P.F. disbelieves in political authority based on free political parties, is intransigent, and only in recent years has entered into Governments and assumed a responsible though contorted attitude *within* the Republic.

6. Groups and Parties

An element that adds to confusion in the understanding of French political life is that in the Assembly the parties are not called parties but groups. A distinction is made between the party Deputies—the *group*—and the *militants*—that is, the *membership of the party* outside the Assembly. These ought to be fused, one instrument. In fact, there are great strains between the French *militants* and the *parliamentary group,* the Deputies. In some of the parties, especially of the Center and the Right, the group means more than the party, for the grass-roots *militants* are not a well-organized and geared-in mass.

The Socialists, the M.R.P., and the Communists are well organized, and so the grouping of their members in the Assembly corresponds to the party in the electorate. But the other groups in the Assembly, such as the U.D.S.R. (p. 366), or the *Rassemblement des Partis du Gauche*, likewise, are groupings of members who have been elected by an organization bearing a different name and with electoral loyalties different from their parliamen-

tary. The footnote at bottom of this page shows the electoral parties and the Assembly groups.[1]

7. Right and Left Seating and the Groups and Parties

As the illustration shows, the chamber of the Assembly (also the Council of the Republic) is semicircular. It is a notable difference from the British practice of a rectangular chamber (see p. 105). The general description of the groups in the Assembly follows the distinction between Right and Left, now a worldwide political terminology, first made in the French Revolution's Assembly.

The distinction is demonstrated by the seating arrangements of the chamber. The "progressive" and liberal forces, the men who wish for a change in the *status quo,* have been seated on the *left hand* of the presiding officer as he looks down at the hemicycle of benches; the battalions of stability and order, on his right.

These general dichotomies do violence to the mind and spirit of the groups. For example, the Communists are socially progressive—that is, they wish to bring about a more egalitarian society, to add opportunities of free development of talents and ambitions, and they hate the de Gaullists; for these, they will overthrow the present order, by revolution if the chance comes their way. They may be classified as Left. But what of the ulterior and instrumental policy, the abolition of free association and voting, and the establishment of the monopoly of a totalitarian and dictatorial party? This is reaction—and it is analogous to the intentions of the Rightist parties of monarchists and Church-dominated politicians, who hanker after hierarchy and authoritarian government by divine right. What of the M.R.P.? It is Catholic-pervaded in spirit—that is, authoritarian —yet pursues a warmhearted and sincere policy of social welfare and of working-class cooperation in

---

[1] The names of the parties are given in the tables of elections and need not be repeated. The *groups* were: Communists; Union of Progressive Republicans; African Democratic Rally; Socialists, with affiliates; M.R.P. and affiliates, plus Overseas Independents affiliated with M.R.P.; Radical Socialists; the Union of Democratic and Social Resistance (the U.D.S.R.); the Independent Republicans, Independent Peasants and Social Action, and French Independents, and affiliates; the Rally of the French People, and affiliates; a group of unaffiliated members.

This was at the beginning of the 1951 Assembly; many changes later occurred.

Floor Plan of the French National Assembly

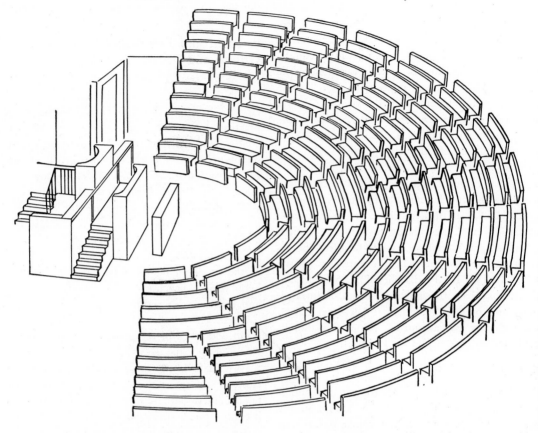

the management of industry. Right or Left, Conservative or Liberal? Or, again, the R.P.F., the curiously composed party of General de Gaulle? This is bitterly nationalistic (which used to be a sign of the Right-wing groups); it is authoritarian in its constitutional theory and party practice and organization to the point that has brought the stigma "Fascist" upon it, and it hates the other dictatorial group, the Communists. Yet it has a sincere doctrine of promoting the social services and workers' participation in management, giving it a distinctly Left flavor, to the point of winning it perhaps a million *working-class* votes.

These difficulties of classification cropped up in the seating of the Radicals, the M.R.P. and the R.P.F. The others were not dissatisfied with their location. The groups mentioned did not want the electorate to think that they were conservative, unliberal, unprogressive. The M.R.P. claimed to be Leftish enough to be seated to the left of the Radicals, and this was allowed by the Assembly's vote. The Radicals were pushed rightward. The R.P.F. demanded to be exempt from the stigma of conservatism. But the Assembly consigned them to the extreme Right, the rival parties enjoying the process of pinning a visible label on what they believed to be an undesirable commodity. The R.P.F. Deputies made a good point, in one sense, in arguing that the Radicals were conservative and should go to *their* Right. In the Council of the Republic, since it has so much less political power, the R.P.F. was treated more magnanimously and allowed to sit at the back of the chamber, high up, an excellent position for debating conspicuousness.

8. Pressure Groups, or Interest Groups, and Parties

France, like all other democracies permitting voluntary association and acknowledging that politcal authority is representative and responsible, has a large number of economic, social, and intellecualizing groups that press the legislators for atention to their demands. These are known to us n the graphic language of American politicians s "pressure groups" or the "lobbies." Even the lictatorial Soviet Union has "pressure groups," ncongruous with the spirit and stern rules of the Communist Party (see p. 343).

It is, perhaps now an axiom of political science hat, where political parties are weak in principle nd organization, the pressure groups will floursh; where pressure groups are strong, political arties will be feeble; and where political parties re strong, pressure groups will be curbed.

René Mayer, sometime Radical Prime Minister, xpressed at a Radical Congress his disgust with he pressure groups that frustrated his budgetary ustice and economy. These groups were currently eceiving much alarmed attention in the press see, for example, *Esprit,* June 1953), as "states vithin a state," "neo-feudal lords," and even "economic congregations," reminding Frenchmen of he sinister power of the illegal religious congreations, especially of the Jesuits and the ChurchState conflict. Echoing these phrases, Mayer (a big usinessman with Algerian interests) declared that the Radical Party is no class party" or such a ongregation, and concluded: [2]

A formula of the type CNPF *plus* CGA *plus* CGV *plus* PME cannot supply a basis for a decision of a political kind, any more than the formula FO *plus* CFTC *plus* CGC *minus* CGT. All those entities, all those associations have the right to be heard, to be listened to, but political decision belongs to the Government.

The reader will follow these initials in the oranizations referred to below. Thus: the *Confédération Nationale du Patronat Français* for arge business; the *Petites et Moyennes Entreprises,* or small and medium firms; the *Confédération Générale des Viniculteurs,* the wine and alcohol istillers group, and the *Confédération Générale e l'Agriculture.* These are on the employers' and roprietors' side. Then are arrayed the *Force*

Ouvrière, the liberal-socialist trade unions, the *Confédération des Travailleurs Chrétiens,* Catholic-oriented trade unions, and the *Confédération Générale du Travail,* dominated by the Communist Party. There are many other groups, within some of those mentioned, and outside them, organized by product made or by manufacture, finance, commerce. Some trade unions maintain independent organizations, as the C.G.C. or *Confédération Générale des Cadres,* unions of foremen and technicians.

The chief pressure groups are shown at work in the discussion of the political parties.

9. Tension between the Backward and the Progressive Areas

There is parliamentary tension between the highly productive *départements* and the less productive in France—it tears at the vitals of the parties. They have very different needs and therefore policies. Over one half the national income is lodged in nine *départements* centering on Paris— that is in one tenth of the nation.

26 Highly Productive Départements

	Thousands of Votes	*Percent* *
Electorate	11,137	100.0
Abstained	2,015	18.0
Communist Party	2,498	22.4
R.P.F.	2,159	19.3
Moderates	881	7.9
R.G.R.	611	5.4
M.R.P.	1,153	10.3
Socialist Party	1,316	11.8
Diverse	179	1.6

64 Less Productive Départements

Electorate	13,385	100.0 *
Abstained	2,847	21.2
Communist Party	2,437	18.2
R.P.F.	2,107	15.7
Moderates	1,414	10.5
R.G.R.	1,369	10.2
M.R.P.	1,301	9.7
Socialist Party	1,467	10.9
Diverse	60	0.4

* The percentages do not add to 100 owing to faults in the figures attributing votes to the various parties. The argument is unaffected.

[2] *Le Monde,* Paris, Jan. 2, 1953; recalled when he was (in ain) trying to form a new Ministry.

The disparity between the parties, internally, as between the various areas, and the parties among each other, is only too evident. It casts a wrench into the conflict between a "national vision" of policy and the centrifugal, fissiparous egoisms.

10. Lack of Inner Party Cohesion

The only French party that has anything like the inner cohesion of the British Labour or Conservative parties is the Communist Party! This it has by its faith, the chicanery of its own leaders, and the impulsion from Russia. The next parties with inner loyalty and discipline are the Socialist Party and the M.R.P., the former highly democratic and rather loose in party structure, the latter rather more hierarchical. Neither can always rely on the votes of its parliamentary Deputies, especially when most needed, on the truly significant issues. Again and again French parties are split right down the middle in their voting, except when they are split four ways (p. 421; p. 429). The de Gaullist Party, though intensely hierarchical, suffers the same frequent fission in voting and (like the others) in readiness to support members of its own group for inclusion in a coalition and the policy that coalition tries to carry through.

In this fissiparousness, French parties are rather like American political parties. But they are like the British, and unlike the American, in that their policy is formulated in annual congresses where the influence of the party membership, the *militants,* is brought to bear on the parliamentary politicians. The other French parties are not so well knit organizationally as those mentioned, some being hardly more than a congeries of local personages. They, too, exhibit advanced inner disunity.

11. A "Christian" Party in the Political Arena

The M.R.P. seeks to gather the masses on the basis of Christian Catholic ethics. Can it remain (if it ever could become) homogeneous when confronted with the concrete rivalry of other political parties? A church, as a religion only, offers rewards in eternity; parties must deliver in the brevity of *time;* a church seeks to persuade, with all eternity in which to try, but parties are compelled by the clienteles to use *force* and guile in material battle. This connotes the difference between a religion and a policy. Is it not impossible for the M.R.P. to jilt the religion in order to be successful in the policy? Or must it lose votes because it remains religious, and become divided because there are many subtle but obstinate differentiae even among different versions of Catholic Christianity?

12. Proportional Representation

Proportional representation has, on the whole, strengthened the disciplinary power of the *département* and national nominators of candidates, or in other words, has tended to reduce the insubordination of the Deputies.

13. Importance of Small Parties

The reader must notice from various tables of votes in the Assembly how important are the votes of the groups, and the dissentient votes within the groups in the formation of Governments and policy. This is especially so when the Communists (always) and the R.P.F. (till 1952) refused to take office and were in permanent negation for when their extremist votes (numbering 160 omitting the dissident de Gaullists) were subtracted, the middle parties now numbered but 484. The number of combinations which could give a steady majority of 313 in an Assembly of 624 with the bludgeon of 160 votes is extremely limited, as the middle parties have so much that divides them. Hence the importance of the individual Deputy; hence his vanity and recklessness, not what might be expected, his sobriety.

14. The Communists and Poverty

The low per-capita income in France relative to that of other democracies has been noted. Also it had been observed that the political conflict over increments or losses of wealth is likely to be the more intense where the standard is already so low. The low average means that millions of white collar workers, industrial workers, civil servants and peasants are miserably poor. This widespread and desperate poverty in an age of potential abundance, visible in such lands as the United States and Britain, is the breeding ground of the Communist Party.

The peculiar spectrum of political parties in France reinforces the fact that Marx's simple division of society by two is too simple for civilized Europe, was too complicated for the barbarian Stalin, and is too lacking in incentive for the Soviet intelligentsia.

15. Duplication of Elected Office

The law permits Deputies or Senators to hold simultaneously the elected offices of mayor or councilor of the *département* or municipality. Many do (Chapter 10). The practice started with the July Monarchy. It enables Deputies, etc., to obtain a so-called "fief" locally, to give him stability; it links central and local authorities and enables the regimented local councils to penetrate into the Ministries for favors. But it confuses the powers; it diverts the attention of the Deputy to affairs of importance less than the nation's; it cuts across the making of bigger and more coherent parties by entrenching members locally. It is bound up with the fact that the areas of local government and those of electoral districts are identical. Edgar Faure, Prime Minister in 1955, was for years re-elected *départemental* councilor and mayor of his commune; he was challenged there by the antitax lobby of M. Poujade!

Is it not interesting that the French should have resuscitated the feudal term *fief*, seeing for how long the feudal lords defied the creation of the kingdom?

II. THE CHARACTER AND CLIENTELE OF THE PARTIES

We analyze the political parties, starting with the extreme Left and proceeding to the moderates and the Right.

The Communist Party

Member of the Comintern. The Communist Party is here given more space than the rest, for it is interesting to understand the role and tactics of a dictatorial party inside a democracy.

The party is a section of the Third International, or the Comintern (now Cominform), founded by Lenin in Moscow in March 1919. It is Bolshevized in spirit, principle, and organization. Its position in a parliamentary government is defined for it by the Twenty-one Conditions of Admission into the International, written in August 1920. It is revolutionary, underground, and faithful only to the gospel of Moscow. Thus:

9. Every party that desires to belong to the Communist International must carry on systematic and persistent Communist work in the trade unions, in workers' and industrial councils, in the cooperative societies, and in other mass organizations. Within these organizations it is necessary to create Communist groups, which by means of practical and stubborn work must win over the trade unions, etc., for the cause of Communism. These cells should constantly denounce the treachery of the social-patriots and the vacillations of the "Center," at every step. These Communist groups should be completely subordinate to the Party as a whole.

11. The parties desiring to belong to the Third International must overhaul the membership of their parliamentary fractions,[3] eliminate all unreliable elements from them, to control these fractions, not only verbally but in reality, to subordinate them to the Central Committee of the Party, and demand from every Communist member of parliament that he devote his entire activity to the interest of really revolutionary propaganda and agitation.

3. The class struggle in almost all the countries of Europe and America is entering the phase of civil war. Under such conditions the Communists can have no confidence in bourgeois law. They must *everywhere* create a parallel legal apparatus which at the decisive moment could assist the Party in performing its duty to the revolution. In all countries where, in consequence of martial law or exceptional laws, the Communists are unable to carry on all their work legally, a combination of legal and illegal work is absolutely necessary.

The rules of the International require, not cold, but hot war, and so the character-assassinating

[3] *Fraction*, in Russian political terminology and in that of other parliamentary systems of the Continent, including France, is synonymous with the "group in parliament," with its own policy and independent organization. It is an object of hatred inside the Soviet system (see p. 854); but loved by it where it is disruptive of the political stability of democracies.

Party Distribution in the Chamber of Deputies and the National Assembly, 1914–1955

CHAMBER OF DEPUTIES

1914
202 Radical Socialists
33 Rep. Soc.
103 United Soc.
52 Rad. Ind.
73 Rep. Left.
69 Progressives
64 Cons. + Act. Lib.

1919
209 Rep. Left. + Left. Rep. + Act. Rep.
40 Rep. Soc.
55 S.F.I.O. (Socialist)
14 Communists
127 Rep.-Dem. Entente
30 Right.

1924
138 Rad. Soc.
42 Rep. Soc.
101 S.F.I.O.
23 Communists
49 Rad. Ind.
87 Rep. Left.
14 Dem. Pop.
108 U.R.D.
15 Right.

1928
123 Rad. Soc.
47 Rep. Soc.
101 S.F.I.O.
16 Communists
55 Rad. Ind.
106 Rep. Left.
17 Dem. Pop.
131 U.R.D.
15 Right.

1932 – AFTER ELECTION
159 Rad. Soc.
37 Rep. Soc.
136 S.F.I.O.
23 Communists
69 Rad. Ind.
79 Rep. Left.
16 Dem. Pop.
76 U.R.D.
35 Right.

1932 – AT END OF TERM
17 Left. Ind.
17 Ind.
18 Un. Soc) + Rep. Soc.}
159 Rad. Soc.
101 S.F.I.O.
20 Communists
74 Rad. Ind. + Left. Ind.
77 Rep. Left. + Center Rep.
16 Dem. Pop.
66 U.R.D.
12 Right.

1936
26 Union Soc. + Soc. Ind.
116 Radical Socialists
146 S.F.I.O. (Socialists)
10 Pup.
72 Communists
99 Left. Rep.
23 Dem. Pop.
88 U.R.D. (Several Republican Groups)
11 Right.

NATIONAL ASSEMBLY

CONSTITUENT ASSEMBLY: ELECTED OCTOBER 21, 1945
139 Socialists
150 M.R.P.
159 Communists
14 Misc.
60 R.G.R.
64 I.P.R.N.

NOVEMBER 10, 1946
101 Socialists
164 M.R.P.
190 Communists
10 Misc.
69 R.G.R.
74 Moderates
10 R.P.F.

AT FALL OF MENDÈS-FRANCE FEBRUARY 1955
Total 627
23 U.D.S.R.
16 Overseas Independents
74 Radicals
84 M.R.P.
105 Socialists
98 Communists
72 R.P.F. De Gaullists
55 Independent Republicans (Conservatives)
32 A.R.S. Dissident Gaullists
28 Independent Peasants
22 Peasants
10 No Group

344

actics of the party in the Assemblies and the press
nd public meetings reinforce the rancorous pas-
ions of so many Frenchmen already inflamed by
he tradition of extremism.

The French Communist Party was formed in
December 1920, breaking away from the Socialist
Party. It entered the parliamentary arena not to
vork faithfully but to destroy it, meanwhile using
t as a sounding board for subversive propaganda.
Many of its original adherents left it, when the
rue nature of the Leninist-Stalinist dictatorship
became plain. Its membership numbered 120,000
n 1922; by 1929 it was only 25,000. Foreign
ascism made it grow to 50,000 in 1934; and when
t joined with Léon Blum and the Radicals in
he Popular Front, giving it the appearance of a
national party, it rose to 350,000. A great slump
came with the Hitler-Stalin pact—to 75,000. At
he outbreak of war, the party was legally pro-
cribed and went underground. The leaders asked
he Nazis to allow them to publish L'Humanité.
On the invasion of Russia by Hitler, they became
stout members of the Resistance and party membership rose by the middle of 1947 to 1,000,000.
Then it entered the political arena for Russia's
sake, constantly fomenting strikes and a general
disruptive uproar. Membership began to decrease:
by 1952, to 600,000; by 1955 (it is knowledgably
guessed), to 300,000 and declining somewhat. Up
to May 1947 the Communists and the Socialists
and the M.R.P. had cooperated in Cabinets, in this
period of tripartisme; [4] then the Communists were
expelled for disruption in the Cabinet and the
Assembly over wage policy. It will be noticed that
the party waxes and wanes as Moscow's interests
and French interests coincide. If the party had
not been banned in 1939, many members, even
Deputies, would have deserted it out of patriotism.

The party does not accept entrance into Governments, for it would then be inhibited in
its demagoguery and mischief-making. For its

strength lies in being unscrupulously the fomenter
of all kinds of discontent and distress, remediable
or not.

Year	Thousands	Percentage of Total Votes
1924	896	9.84
1928	1,063	11.37
1932	787	8.36
1936	1,487	15.57
1945 *	5,024	26.52
1946	5,489	28.6
1951	5,039	26.5

* Here woman suffrage swelled the electorate over 1936,
more than doubling it.

Organization. Like the Mother of Communist
Parties, the French party is dictatorial to its membership, and is organized on the basis of occupational cells, not territorially, as other French parties
and foreign democratic parties are. The party units
in the factory, mine, workshop, farm, etc.—cells—
tie the leaders into the very heart of the interests
(and grievances) of the workers. Where the factories, etc., are too small there is a territorial
linkage by city districts or across the countryside.
The organizers at the grass-roots level prefer
territorial grouping of members, as this facilitates
propaganda and election organization. But the
leaders prefer the cells in which deep penetration
is possible—and for an "underground" warlike
party, more desirable. Nevertheless, the local cells
have grown to be twice as numerous as the factory cells: in 1946, 15,860 as against 8363.

The cells are composed of from three to thirty
members in the same plant. Some are twice and
even thrice the preferred optimum of thirty. The
cells meet weekly at least; and the top few are
always face to face. This has great fanaticizing
value. The cells each elect a secretary and bureau,
or executive committee. But the elections are
manipulated by those who are about to be elected
and by planting by higher levels of the hierarchy,
which may deprive the lower officers of office.
Also, the officers are the executants of orders
from above. The higher level above the cell is a
territorial unit called the section, manned by
delegates from the cell secretaries and bureau and
not of the rank and file. Thus direct contact be-

[4] Tripartisme may be translated "three-party-ism" and
refers to the uneasy cooperation of the Communists, Socialists, and M.R.P. from shortly after the liberation of France
through the time of constitutional construction to May 7,
1947, when the Communist Ministers were dismissed from
the Cabinet, breaking the loose alliance (p. 410).

tween rank-and-file members of the cells is avoided, so that the top leadership has an exclusive line of command and pressure downward. Above the *sections* are *départementale fédérations,* again of delegates from the *sections.* The federation secretaries are chosen by the regular bureau selected by the sectional delegates, but only in *consultation with the national leadership,* and the latter has decisive power to expel and replace secretaries and departmental committeemen. A minimum of three years' membership is a necessary qualification for secretaryships.

The party's supreme authority is its National Congress, composed of delegates elected by the conferences in each department. Supposed to meet biennially, the Congress misses beats, as in Russia: it met in 1947, in 1950, in 1954. In between, if necessary in the opinion of the top leaders, delegates chosen by the committees in each *département* meet in national conference. A committee is elected by the party congress of sixty to eighty members. It rarely meets and is subordinate to the top leaders: the Political Bureau of fourteen, the Secretariat of four, the Control Committee of six. The Political Bureau, like the Soviet Politbureau (p. 876), is the iron hand of all the apparatus already sketched. The Secretariat was manned from 1932 to 1952 by Maurice Thorez, Jacques Duclos, André Marty. In 1952 they continued with a M. Lecoeur. While Thorez was in Moscow recuperating from a brain ailment, Étienne Fajon replaced him; since his return Thorez occupies his old post. In 1953 Marty was dropped for heresy; Francois Billoux replaced him. In 1954 Lecoeur was replaced by Marcel Severin. The former had been general secretary of the miners' federation, a notable inciter of strikes.

All these men are "elected" without debate and with no previous discussion of the list. Similarly with expulsions. The Control Committee is an inspectoral, detective, and policing body within the party. It invigilates for zeal, party honesty, militancy, and obedience. It weeds out the *cadres* —that is, the officer-type men and women—and discovers, trains, and plants leaders.

The principle of "democratic centralism" applies—that is, no subversion of the leaders—fanatical obedience (p. 866), and also the principle that "the Communist end justifies the means" with no ethic to impede it.

Members of the Assemblies. The International, having designated the "present epoch" as one of "acute civil war," all members of Parliament and municipalities are completely shackled by the party executive. The *discipline de vote* operates absolutely only in this party of all the parties in the French system. The Deputies have already given the party a written undertaking to resign when called on by its executive, though the practice is unconstitutional (Art. 21). Its disciplinary power is rigorous and unforgiving. The Communist *group* is dominated by the party executive, which attends all its meetings and exercises a veto. All speaking and introduction of bills, etc., are decided for the automatons by the executive. The members of the latter are given safe seats by the party so as to be on top among the parliamentarians.

The Militants. As already noted, the dues-paying members of all French political parties are known as *militants.* The more ardent and active members are meant. These zealots in all French parties are often at loggerheads with the parliamentary Deputies and even the party executive, since the latter has responsibility for measured action while the members are zealots of purpose and increased strength. In the Communist Party they are the conscious class-war party workers. Of the membership it is calculated that only something like a half or less are militants; they are referred to as "the gold reserve"; they thrive on the Marxist religion, and believe their leaders to be divinely inspired and sacred; they are a large proportion. They swear complete obedience to the party, will undertake almost any duty however menial or malign, and regard themselves as the elect of the French people, for whom in general they have the vanguard's contempt.

The Communist Party fuses the militants with the leaders, while the militants of the other parties, being democratic, give their leaders the trouble of free debate and free voting. The Communist militants are persuaded that they are a new and better kind of humanity, and their leaders confirm hem in this, if they obey. They have removed hemselves from the body of French society by a wall of hatred and contempt, and self-worship within that wall, the elect.

The Leadership. This is of working-class origin almost 100 percent and so differs enormously from he Socialist Party, its closest competitor. Thorez was a coal miner; Duclos, a pastry-maker; Marcel Cachin, a policeman's son; Marty, a sailor, son of a *communard*. All have had no career except to foster the party or reside in Moscow or foment and help insurrection at home or abroad.

They have refused to enter Governments, and therefore appear pure as regards careerism—though they have stayed out for the purpose of ruining the parliamentary system. The Socialists now have adopted the same nonacceptance of office, in order that the Communists should not have this monopoly of prestige with the working class. The Communist leaders lead fairly impecunious lives; and the Deputies surrender their parliamentary salary to the party, which then repays them the equivalent of a skilled Parisian worker, about one third of the amount surrendered. The Deputies (1951) are 33 manual [5] workers, 11 employees, 8 elementary schoolteachers, among its 91 members for metropolitan France. If this betokens inferior education, it is immaterial because the leaders dictate the policy and voting. In Russia, the party is now dominated by the "intelligentsia"; in France, it is the non-Communist parties that have the intelligentsia of the secondary and university levels.

The leaders can perpetuate their own power by the party's rule allowing co-option of colleagues at the central committee's discretion, as well as removals of the lower echelons of officers. Heresy and dissent are frustrated by the cell linkage that prevents the meeting of the rank and file in larger assemblies; hence opposition cannot run widespread across the party. "Freedom of discussion," according to Lenin is treasonable; factions or "fractions" (groups) are impermissible; the party is a monolith; those who disagree are "opportunists," to be expelled and disgraced.

Clientele. The basic strength of the party lies in

[5] Probably a fake definition.

the industrial and mining workers. Then follows the peasantry and some intellectuals.

The French equivalent of the Gallup Poll, called *Sondages*,[6] of March 1952, provides the following analysis of Communist voters:

Occupation	Party * Percentage	Population † Percentage
Workers—industrial	44	19
Workers—agricultural	10	3
Government officials	4	5
Employees	6	ca. 8
Employers and technicians	1	5
Merchants	3	6
Self-employed farmers	5	16
Professions—liberal	1	ca. 2
Rentiers and pensioners	3	6
Women, no occupation	22	30
	100	

* Round numbers cause total to be 99 not 100 percent.
† For purposes of comparison, the table may be used for the other parties also.

The "proletarians" number some 54 percent, plus the 22 percent of unoccupied women, their wives mainly.

The clientele is nationwide, with not less than 6 percent of the voters anywhere and nearly 25 percent in more districts than any other party. Its great strength is in the industrial regions and two agricultural areas, Ardèche and Corrèze; in the Nord; and in Pas-de-Calais (coal mines). In the northeast suburbs of Paris the party won nearly 40 percent of the vote. But the Socialists and the M.R.P. and even some young de Gaullists dispute the industrial vote with the party.

The party can win these votes, surely, only because the true knowledge of the Soviet Union's way with trade unions and the workers is hidden from them. It has its voters, 48 percent in towns of under 5000 population and 22 percent in towns above 100,000.

The Peasantry. One would not expect peasants to vote for Communists, seeing that the inward agricultural policy of the party is, as in Russia, collectivization and practical serfdom. An industrial worker might think it is just as well for him to work in a government factory as a privately owned

[6] Ensuing tables of this kind are from *Sondages*, Special Number, 1952, No. 3 Paris, 1952, and concern the electorate at 1951–1952.

one: he could not expect to own one himself. But a peasant and his family can manage his plot of land, and join free cooperative societies for greater income. John Locke has given classic expression to the idea of free peasant ownership:

> The labor of his body and the work of his hands, we may say are properly his. Whatsoever, then, he removes out of the state of nature that hath provided and left it in, *he hath mixed his labor with,* and joined it to something that is his own, and thereby makes it his property.

Why should French peasants, then, notoriously in love with the land, court becoming collectivized and suffer the fate of the *kulaks* (p. 780)? Yet the Communist Party gets 500,000 votes from the agricultural laborers, 250,000 from land owners, and 500,000 from the peasant women.

The reasons become plain. The laborers have nothing to lose by the claims made by the Communists: higher wages, overthrow of the capitalists and landlords, better housing, lower prices for manufactured goods; so also with the *métayers,* who share the produce with the owner of their rented farms. The free smallholders are hungry for more land—to be taken away from the larger owners. The Communists promise the confiscation of all land except that of the cultivators on a small, personal acreage, and without compensation except to the latter. They promise redistribution to all working peasants—but do not say in private ownership. They promise electrification, mechanization, and so on, cooperatives, and pensions for the old.

Furthermore, there are traditional propensities to vote extreme Left, for salvation by utopian measures. A French scholar has shown that the party's strength almost exactly coincides with the extreme Left votes of 1849, except for the more recently developed industrial areas! They are the Jacobin areas of the South, Languedoc, the Midi, the Central Massif. Republicans (Gambetta), Radicals, and Socialists have successively reaped this harvest. The Communists represent the extreme *feelings* better with their rule-or-ruin slogans and active irresponsibility. It brings well-to-do farmers, winegrowers, landowners into their net.

Therefore, they have the satisfaction of knock-ing over the bowling pins with a great clatter, but it is doubtful whether they would cast enough votes for the party to bring on themselves the positive fate of their Russian counterparts: there is a saturation point in the peasant vote.

The Communist Party, prompted by Leninist teaching, has ever since 1920 sedulously cultivated and organized the rural areas. It tried to "colonize" the peasant organizations, and even run its own. It runs a weekly paper, *La Terre,* in the countryside. This condones such peasant misdeeds as black-marketeering during the Occupation, incites peasants by claiming that farm prices are lowered by American surpluses. Its prestige grew so by such tactics and its Resistance activities that it even tried to capture the C.G.A. (p. 341). It was beaten by the owners, tenants, and *métayers;* and left with only the laborers and small farmers and *métayers.* It still has their sturdy support, for it is unscrupulous in its propaganda of greater welfare, though it will not meet the arguments that high farm prices will hurt the industrial workers, and better industrial wages will mean higher prices to the peasantry.

Labor Unions or Syndicats. The *Confédération Générale du Travail* is, since 1945, Communist-dominated. It was established in 1906 to group the trade unions; then and later it always rejected connection with any political party. This weakened the Socialist Party as compared with the British Labour Party (p. 77). But, individually, the majority of the workers voted for Socialists. The *Confédération* was always in a state of internal tension between the revolutionary syndicalists (p. 292), and the "reformists," those who sought working-class improvements by political party action as well as strikes, etc. It was difficult for their able leader Léon Jouhaux to keep an even keel, to win over the conservative politicians to working-class benefits and collective bargaining, social services, and so on. But this was achieved in large measure: labor was a power to be reckoned with, though a minority in the nation's labor force. After World War I the Communists began to bore from within, encouraged by the Red International of Labor Unions. A body split off to found the *Confédération Général du Travail Unitaire* (C.G.T.U.), connected with the

Communist Party, and took away one third of the C.G.T. members. The C.G.T. pursued its policy of detachment from political parties but pressed, successfully, for economic and social improvement and so won over the Civil Servant Federation.

Catholic Unions. Catholic politicians founded the *Confédération Française des Travailleurs Chrétiens*—reformist, nonrevolutionary, nonparty, and allowed to strike only *in extremis*. It grouped 25,000 members in 1936, when the C.G.T. had 775,000 members, and the C.G.T.U. about 230,000. Shortly after, during the Popular Front, the total trade-union membership multiplied by 4; only to run down very fast. The French worker is a mercurial "member" of labor unions, in and out with promise of advantage and passing winds of doctrine.

At the Liberation the C.G.T. had 5,000,000 members and the Christian Unions nearly 800,000. Had they stuck together, the sense that labor was on top of the world might have been translated into a better deal for workers and peasants. But they were divided, and the greatest divider was the Communist Party. It took over the key points in the C.G.T., locally and nationally, as Léon Jouhaux was still in a Nazi prison. It purged the trade unions as it did the press of all who did not follow its line and Moscow's. They captured all the big unions. Jouhaux returned to find his associates in a 4-to-1 minority. He was unwilling to split the C.G.T., which he had spent his life creating and leading, and his colleagues were of an older and less-militant and certainly less-unscrupulous generation. But in December 1947 secession was effected and the *Force Ouvrière,* the non-Communist labor federation, was established, officially known as the C.G.T.-F.O., taking then only 250,000 members with it.

The Communists unions, completely dominated by the party and its cells, pursued a completely reckless policy of sabotaging the French economy for the sake of the party's total program and the relative strengthening of Russia in the tension with the West, organizing revolutionary strikes to defeat the benefit sorely needed by devastated France from Marshall Plan Aid. They were finally defeated by strong police measures, when success at revolution seemed on the point of achievement,

and by the responsible bearing of the C.G.T.-F.O. and the Christian Unions, which are not less ardent for just claims for the workers than the C.G.T.

The Communist tactics are, as in all parts of the world, fathered by Lenin and fostered by Stalin: to be destructively extreme in every situation of workers' distress, and to throw scorn on every democratic accomplishment (such as, in France, the progress in social welfare and social security and wages and the nationalization of various industries) and to fulminate maliciously against parliamentarianism and free enterprise. The party has great advantages: extremism and no permission for open dissent; and the claim that France consists of the workers and the workers only.

On the best estimates made by the best scholar, the C.G.T. has about 1,500,000 members; the C.G.T.-F.O., 500,000, and the Christian Unions, 500,000. In November 1955 it lost substantially in representatives on the social security and family allowance administrative councils, the *Force Ouvrière* gaining.

French governments can only be formed from the Center and Right groups, as the Communists and Socialists will not join. This is bad for the C.G.T.-F.O. and the C.F.T.C., which cannot hope to wring concessions from the coalitions dominated by the shopkeepers, big business, and the wealthy farmers. But the Communist Party and the C.G.T., remain possessed of all the disruptive and agitatory possibilities. The party can always demand more from the public funds because it has no responsibility for the levying of taxes.

The Intellectuals and Youth. How can such men as the poet Louis Aragon, Langevin, Joliot-Curie —the flower of French intellect and art—be Communists, seeing the servility into which such people have been flung by Stalin and his successors? They are not good statesmen; they have no sense of the possible, only of what is, logically or aesthetically desirable. Only the Left extreme, therefore, always pleases their fancy. They continue the tradition of the French intelligentsia's total revolutionary love of Humanity and Utopia, intensely hungering for Justice, Freedom, and Progress. Some hate the complacency of the French bourgeois and his family *foyer,* Catholic orthodoxy and callousness, as the Russian Alexander Herzen did (p. 751) to his disillusionment. Some, like Dostoevski, are *nihilists*—that is, they deny the right of anybody at any time to govern, since there is Injustice everywhere—and they are fed by Communist hatred. They also have a passion for *ouvrièrisme,* idolatry of the manual worker, hatred of his poverty.

Youth gives the party exceptional *élan,* for the leaders profit by adolescent aspirationalism. The age composition of all electors in 1952 was: over 50, 37 percent; 35 to 49, 29 percent; 18 to 34, 34 percent; but the Communist voters showed only 23 percent in the over-50 group; 35 percent in the 35 to 49 group; and *42 percent* in the age group of 18 to 34. So with the average of Communist Deputies—40—as compared with other Deputies. (In 1952 one half of the Politbureau members were in their forties.) Two thirds of the delegates to the party conference of 1953 were between 25 and 35, and almost none was over 45.

The party has its organizations among students; its sports associations; its Brave Boys and Girls (*Komsomols* in Russian), and an organization against American comics; associations of tenant, French women, children's clubs. It runs libraries. It has its political schools, with thousands in earnest attendance.

Its principal newspaper is *L'Humanité* with a circulation of 200,000, having fallen from 460,000 in 1947. It has twenty provincial newspapers, whereas just after the Liberation and its seizing of abandoned presses, it had one in every *département.* Its weekly, *France Nouvelle,* circulates 90,-000; and *La Terre,* 200,000. *Ce Soir* used to circulate 200,000 in Paris each evening, but it ceased publication in 1955, an ominous sign of loss of party strength.

Finances. All Communist members of all French political assemblies, including the municipalities, pay over their official salaries to the party (p. 374). Then there are members' dues and extra contributions by the militants. It is most probable that the party is assisted by the Soviet Union and satellites.

Policy. The Communist Party maintains an isolation from other parties and from Government coalition, using its vote mainly to negate whatever is proposed, except when it suits the Soviet Union, as for example when it supported Mendès-France

who had promised to make peace in Indochina. I likes to be thought of as outside the pale of bour geois France. This brought on it the electoral law of 1951, which put it at a disadvantage in seat gained, since it would not "relate" with othe: parties in *apparentement* electoral lists (p. 369).

It is perfectly identified since May 1947 with th interests of the Soviet Union in all matters o foreign policy, meaning enmity to the rest of th world, including France. It is virulently anti American, denouncing France's servitude to Wal Street for Marshall Plan Aid, etc., and entranc into NATO and the Western Union Pacts. It ever obstructed physically the entrance of America arms' shipments from the United States.

At home, its policy has already been suggeste *passim.* But it may be mentioned that it has in cited to sabotage. It has been the beneficiary o parliamentary immunity from arrest, inciting t violence and sedition in the colonial areas (p. 375. and metropolitan France. In June 1952 even M Duclos was arrested during a riot in Paris, in th act of incitement, and with carrier pigeons in hi car alleged to have been used in its organization He was charged with conspiracy against th security of the State, as others were in 1953. The were not convicted, though their language an actions certainly reached the "clear and present danger, and as it was accepted that the pigeon were his lunch.

The Socialist Party (S.F.I.O.)

Closest on the Left to the Communist Party, bu worlds apart because it is soundly rooted in th principle of responsible democracy and civil rights is the Socialist Party. It is referred to officially b the initials S.F.I.O., meaning *Section Française d l'International Ouvrière,* the French section of th Second International, the democratic one.

When it was established in 1905, it represente a fusion of two separate and antagonistic groups the liberal, reforming one then led by Jean Jaurè comprising the majority, and the other, revolu tionary and syndical led by Jules Guesde. Th former believed in parliamentary action and c operation with the Radical Party, with gradualis policies tending to increased workers' welfare an freedom; the latter was revolutionary and Marxis

When the Socialist Party broke into two sections in 1920, 50,000 members were for the S.F.I.O.; and 150,000 went to the new Communist Party; parliamentary Deputies, for the Socialist, 53, and for the Communist Party, 13. Attention is drawn to the fact that the extremists took so much fewer parliamentarians and so many more members in the country.

Policy, 1920–1940. Between this time and 1940, the Socialist Party did not undistinguished work, given the domination of the French political electorate by the Center and Right conservative parties. It cooperated leftward with the Radicals and Radical Socialists. It did not participate in the Coalition Governments, partly because it was not wanted but also because the *militants* outside the Chamber of Deputies would not permit it. Some concessions to the working classes were obtained by a policy of parliamentary support of Governments without participating in Cabinets, and through such electoral coalitions as the *cartel des gauches* of 1924 and 1932. The Socialists, however, were never strong enough electorally to compel the Radicals to prefer a combination with them rather than the parties to their right.

The party lost virility through refusal of office. It suffered internal divisions, faced with the terrible social and economic demands of the era of Fascism, Nazism, and economic depression. Two leaders, Marcel Déat and Jean Marquet, broke away to form the Neo-Socialist Party—virtually a Nazi Labor Party—and to become Vichyite traitors later on. There was also a division between pacifists and defense-responsible groups.

Its policy of social services, welfare, nationalization, a reformed constitution, democratic freedom and civil rights unsullied by Marxist dictatorship and brutality, its humanism, and true internationalism, brought the S.F.I.O. the promise of a bright political future at the Liberation. But the evolution of political parties worked grindingly against Socialist strength.

The Socialist Party is wedded to the principle of majority rule, with tolerance of minorities, humanism, and it is antirevolutionary. To be gradualist in an era of widespread and deep economic distress among the millions is to lose effectiveness to the more extreme and irresponsible advocates

of drastic action. The Communists damaged the party on the Left (see p. 337). On the other hand, the M.R.P. took over the leadership and votes of a substantial working-class and peasant element, its Catholic social doctrine having an additional appeal for hundreds of thousands of Frenchmen.

The Socialists held office, as leaders in Governments that contained Communists, until May 1947, and as lesser partners until 1951. The maximum they could achieve, and it was considerable, was to prevent the nationalization and social reforms of the Provisional Government from being whittled away. But they could not make substantial gains beyond these, though they made Governments give something. They voted for Coalition Governments they did not like and their *militants* disliked even more.

Younger men, like Guy Mollet, the General Secretary, arrived in 1946, outvoting the older generation. After the elections of 1951 the party refused any longer to take office, since now there was no fear the R.P.F. (de Gaullist, p. 337) would take over the Government. It then ceased to suffer its former torments of *militant* accusations that the Deputies were betraying working-class interests, such as had been hurled ever since Millerand and Briand had started as Socialists and ended as middle-of-the-road parliamentarians. In November 1954, invited by Mendès-France to enter his Cabinet, it countered with a stiff Socialist program, and refused.

Organization. The Socialist Party is democratic, rising from its local *sections* in wards, cantons, and communes, as primary party organizations, to form *fédérations* in the *départements*. The *national party congress* is made up of all federations with at least five sections and at least 100 members. The federal and national congresses are formed by election, with P.R., each federation, however small, getting at least one vote. The congress is especially attentive to the smaller federations since they represent places where the party is weak. A federation can buy extra party cards and increase its votes.

The nationally known leaders take the initiative, centrally and locally, in formulating policy to be urged at the middle and lower levels, so that these may be mobilized at the approaching annual congresses where programs are adopted and executives chosen. This local debating is truly democratic, scorning the Communists' lack of faith in the masses. The executive committees at each level are elected by majority vote, not P.R.

The *National Council* and *Executive Commitee* act between the annual congresses. The National Council is composed of one delegate from each federation, voting as his federation instructs at its frequent meetings. It is the deliberative-executive body, with some 90 members. The slate for it is not planted, as in the Communist Party. The Committee and the party's Deputies may attend Council meetings, but they may not vote.

The Executive Committee is composed of thirty-one members, and is elected by the federations convened for the purpose, in a meeting at which each federation has two delegates plus one more for every additional 15 votes to which the size of its membership entitles it. In 1944 majority vote for the Committee replaced P.R. (which had had fissiparous effects) with lists *versus* lists. The smaller federations have the advantage. The rivalry is individual, the delegate votes unbound. Such regions as the Nord, Midi, and Paris bind the local sections together. The Executive Committee controls the party press, propaganda, the *militants*, the party's representatives on elected bodies, the fulfillment of the decisions of the Congress and the Committee, and is supreme in the decisions on party policy, tactics, and election strategy, such as ordering that local groups not affiliate in *apparentement* with Communists or de Gaullists, and requiring central endorsement of affiliations. The Committee can dissolve federations for insubordination; can discipline sections. The Congress elects conflicts committees for national and federal levels; the federations elect conflict committees for its own members.

It is the Executive Committee that brings to bear the voice of the *militants* on the parliamentary membership, for the former pay for and win elections, and the latter are inclined to politicking. This external control is rather sharper than that exerted by the British party executives over the parliamentary membership. Assembly Deputies are represented on the Executive Committee (since 1913), 10 out of 31. This is opposed to the feeling of the original near-Marxist founders of the party who wanted the *militants* independent. Deputies may also represent the federations or the National Council. A bridge, then, is built between electoral fighters and Deputies. The Executive Committee may exert the *discipline de vote,* with the sanctions of warning, censure, or suspension from party duties and spokesmanship (like British withdrawal of the Whip, p. 103). Expulsion is the extreme penalty. In August 195. the Committee required voting discipline for EDC. Yet Jules Moch, high in the party and chairman of the Assembly's Commission on Foreign Affairs, reported against EDC, spoke against it, and carried 50 Socialist Deputies with him against the treaty, and the 55 who voted as directed. The Executive Committee expelled four members from the party, including Jules Moch and Daniel Mayer then chairman of the Commission on Foreign Affairs. This they contested.

The party is regionalized in its appeal; nearly two thirds of the 36,000 communes of France have no Socialist sections. The sections and federations, not headquarters, fix the members' dues; they give the central office about one third to one half the amount. The scale is from a dime to 30 cents per month. The local caucuses are thus master of the center; and the Deputies are not forced to pay their salaries to the latter.

Thus the Socialist Party has the looseness of democratic organization.

Clientele. The peak of membership was in 1936 with 285,000; by 1939, it was down to less than 200,000; by 1946, it rose to 354,000; by December 1953, it had sunk to about 100,000. The party voters have been in continual decline: 1951, 1. percent of the voters against 23 percent in 1945. Its losses seem to be slackening.

The Socialist Party does not attract youth, because it requires five-years' membership of those who wish to be delegates to the Congress or members of the National Council or Executive Committee or an editor of a party newspaper or a candidate for the Assembly or Senate. The party is afraid of anti-Socialist intruders; the Communists welcome them for emasculation. Since World War II new members have been entering at the rate of less than 4 percent; before the war it was over 15 percent. Marxist controversies disturb its youth organizations; women seem to prefer the atheism of the Communists to that of the Socialists, and have small part in the organization, while the benevolent family associations of Communism and the Church attract them.

Its voters fall into the following social groups:

	Percentage *
Workers—industrial	25
Workers—agricultural	9
Government officials	9
Employees	4
Employers and technicians	4
Merchants	3
Self-employed farmers	9
Professions—liberal	1
Rentiers and pensioners	3
Women, no occupation	28

* Imprecision of percentages due to round numbers and borderline vagueness about data. Same for other tables of this kind.

The total number of Socialist votes is about one half that of the Communists. It is, thus, largely still a working-class party, but it is followed by a considerable proportion of civil servants, teachers, and peasant proprietors, and its local machines are manned by lesser percentage of manual workers than the voting strength of the latter. Its civil-service clientele is relatively double that of the Communists'. It is a provincial rather than a Parisian party, and its chief centers are in the principal towns of the *arrondissements* and cantons, only 25 percent of them with populations over 20,000.

It is still strong in the thirty-two highly or moderately industrialized *départements,* and one third of these are in the list of the party's twenty strongholds. It has peasant strength, but chiefly in only five of the forty-one heavily agricultural *départements,* winning votes here from the Radicals. In the industrial areas, it runs close to the Communists—south of the Loire, the Nord, and the Pas-de-Calais. Clearly there are substantial numbers of Frenchmen who prefer the reform of society by the democratic way rather than by Communist murderousness. But the Socialist Party cannot rally great mass meetings like the Communists.

Policy. S.F.I.O. is above all the defender of the democratic Republic, which is no mean achievement in France. It is the party of the Welfare State, planned economic investment, public housing, industrialization, educational opportunity, a more equal tax structure, more municipal liberty, and more local welfare services. Its demand for the pursuit of tax evaders is not liked by the peasantry, who can evade while the employees and workers cannot. The Socialists follow the Western foreign policy leading to the Brussels Treaty, NATO, the Schuman Plan, EDC (split), the Western Union Pact, the Council of Europe. They are disturbed by the excesses of American capitalism and American diplomacy. Some, like Jules Moch, would have preferred to find French security in the Franco-Soviet Treaty and the neutralization of Germany, remembering France's bitter suffering at the hands of Germany. The party, as a whole, however, is the foe of old-style authoritarian French colonialism and an advocate of extended self-government of the colonies, but not outright independence.

The Socialists have toed the humdrum path of evolutionary socialists, and participated in Third Force Governments [7]—that is, neither Communist nor Rightist. This is honorable, but debilitating. The millennium is called for quickly by the miserable. Even on more or less nationalization and free enterprise, the leaders and the *militants* are divided and hesitant; for they *think. Le Populaire,* the party daily, prints 15,000 copies, ten times less than in 1930! Yet one has a feeling that strength may flow to its humane pursuit of social justice. In 1955 it gained in the social security elections.

[7] When *tripartisme* broke down, and Communists, Socialists, and M.R.P. no longer made a stable governmental coalition (not that it ever was or could be truly stable or sincerely a coalition), some other grouping of parties had to be found to provide France with a majority in the Assembly. The "Third Force" was invented: an alliance of Socialists and M.R.P., joined by any Radicals, Moderates, and Conservatives but *not* de Gaullists, since these, like the Communists, were enemies of the regime itself. Hence, it means a middle grouping, that excludes the other two forces, Communists and de Gaullists. It worked fairly well until the Socialists also would not join in Governments; but they helped by voting for "middle-of-the-road" Cabinets though not entering them. "Third Force" was a term applied to international affairs by some people, meaning groups of countries who belonged neither to the American nor the Russian orbit.

The M.R.P.: The Mouvement Républicain Populaire

Origins. This is a post-World War II party and is assigned the position on the moderate Left that was before the war occupied by the Radical Socialists. It does, however, have roots in the late nineteenth-century rallying of more reasonable Catholic politicians to the Republic, lest the desperate needs of the poor be supplied by infidel labor unions and parties. The chief restorer of the "democratic" Catholic tradition was a Marc Sangnier, who followed the views of such social philosophers as Lamennais and Lacordaire against the black medievalism of de Maistre and de Bonald. He was condemned by Pope Pius X in 1910, the hand of the Catholic "eminent classes." Two currents battled each other among Catholics, those like Albert de Mun (a *rallié* leader in the Chamber) wanting social welfare given from above to the masses and those looking to authority stemming from those masses. Sangnier's *Sillon* (founded 1897) took the latter view, that the Declaration of Rights embodied the spirit of Christ in that it enacted "the acute sense of the infinite value of each single human soul." Two movements developed: the *Partie Democrate Populaire* and the *Jeune République* on the one hand, as political parties; the other movement was social, and found its expression in the Christian trade unions, the Young Christian Workers, and agricultural and youth organizations. Before the war the *Jeune République* gained two or three deputies in Catholic regions, helped by Left-wing Catholics. The Popular Democrats gained fifteen, by Right-wing assistance, in the Catholic strongholds of Brittany, Lorraine, and the Jura. Both parties moved in the line of anticapitalism, yet supported prewar conservative coalitions.

All the movements were drawn together about the newspaper *L'Aube* (*The Dawn*), founded in 1938 by Françisque Gay. In the Resistance the groups were valiant, and Georges Bidault rose to be second to de Gaulle in the National Resistance Council; his colleagues were Robert Schuman (of the Plan), Maurice Schumann, François de Menthon, Pierre-Henri Teitgen, professor of law.

Their religious outlook caused them to refuse the Socialist Party's offer of an alliance; the Socialist anticlericalism caused it also to retreat.

The new party was founded at Lyons by the youngish men we have named, as a "movement," not a party, an effort at Catholic democratic welfare rebirth. It was to be "socialist" and also a party of *"croyants,"* believers.

The new party aspired to be a monolith of the masses, like the Communists, but with a far different faith and a democratic constitution, resting on youth and its Catholic social organizations, Catholic unions, and the parish *curés,* the local equivalent of the elementary schoolteachers for the Socialists. The newness was a tremendous attraction. The French conservatives, guilty of Vichy flocked to its guiltlessness. The M.R.P. was swamped with unwanted reactionaries. In the election of October 1945 it polled 4,745,000 votes, second in the Assembly only to the Communists. In June 1946, when the draft of the constitution it disliked was rejected, it polled 5,589,000 votes— the first party in the Assembly by a substantial margin.

Then it was deserted in droves by the nesting de Gaullists, as the M.R.P. cooperated with the mediating Socialists in establishing the Fourth Republic's Constitution. When the de Gaullist R.P.F. was founded in 1947, the M.R.P. votes in the October municipal elections dropped from 28 to 10 percent of the total cast. In the elections of 1951, it polled but 12.4 percent of the total votes, almost exactly one half of the number it had won in June 1946; and was deflated to 94 seats or the fourth largest group in the Assembly, the R.P.F. being the largest.

A Christian Party. A party's ideology is not identical with its everyday policy, though ideology guides policy; for a party must compromise if it is democratic. It is "Christian" or "Catholic"; but what can this mean? Such a shattering question was long asked of the German Center Party (p. 613). The M.R.P. contains greatly discordant elements.

We may look at its basic faith, which derives from the Church through St. Thomas Aquinas. It is insistent that the duties of rulers and ruled are the only way to eternal salvation and that God

[8] Allowing for warning about electoral statistics.

he author of all being, has appointed these duties. This is derided by Marxist-Socialism, which cannot see either a God or eternal salvation. Rulers must be obeyed, and, according to the Church's ethics, a hierarchy of authority stretches *downward* from the infallible Church, to which truth is revealed, through the rulers, to citizens. For men were created with Original Sin, and they are ursed to be ruled for their good. This is what oseph de Maistre had taught in his *Du Pape* as he hope of the restored Bourbons (p. 305). Rulers must be just and paternal, but what kind of government is thereby warranted the Church is not sure. Yet it is unmistakably authoritarian and not individualistic, free, and popular. The rationalist social-contract theory of authority is rejected. But all men are equally and fraternally subordinate to God who commands that the State must irst seek the welfare of the people's soul by religious teaching and next physical welfare. For he end of man is eternal salvation of his soul, not material enjoyment. Hence the sanctity of marriage, the authority of the father, the cohesion and fundamentality of the family, parental obligation. Charity ought to be a family obligation; then follows voluntary Christian charity; only in he very last resort is the State to be asked to help, or otherwise the opportunity of salvation by charity is lost. Education by the State is sinful; he right belongs to the father.

This same solicitude for the family and for individual souls requires the guarantee to "private societies," for association is one more "natural ight" of man, deriving from the natural tendency o cooperate with his fellow men. These associations should be allowed the maximum internal elf-government. Clergy and State must act according to the Commandments, especially that against false witness, and to the end of producing a collaboration of social classes. Peace is the supreme decree; but wars are just when the Christian ethic must be defended against pagans. Revolt is awful against Governments that attack religious and civil liberty, though generally insurrection is impermissible, and the clergy may teach resistance o violation of Christian living. As for property, t is an instinct that, with bequest, links man to he future; but a man ought not to have too much,

and a course must be steered between "individualism" and "collectivism." Wages must be just, even with the State's intervention; and to secure and ascertain the economic feasibility of a demand, employers and workers should form unions based on Christian harmony.

The M.R.P. has moved along these lines, certainly in general opposition to that other faith-pervaded total doctrine of a "closed" and perfect society, the Communist. It is hostile to the atomistic Jacobin tradition also, looking to the social coherence offered by corporations. It wants capitalism modified, with worker joint management, social welfare, and more equality.

The practical consequences for the Constitution have been already noted (p. 324ff.). It is a believer in self-government. Hence doctrine and creed isolate the M.R.P. in important matters from both Left and Right.

Organization. M.R.P. is substantially organized by elections upward as the Socialist Party is, with *sections, fédérations, national center.* But two differences set it off from Socialists and Radical Socialists: it contrives to impose a degree of hierarchic control, and it has specialized "teams." In the first instance, while the federations nominate the party's candidates for all types of public office, an endorsement, or *investiture,* of the National Executive Committee is required (as in the Socialist Party). The weaker federations are deliberately overrepresented in the National Congress by the mandates or votes accorded them under the rules, and this aids the leaders, since the opposition to *them* comes rather from the *militants* of the stronger, not the weaker, federations. Also the party allows the national committeemen and the M.R.P. Deputies to vote in the Congress, thus blending *militants* and parliamentarians and taming the *militants.* The M.R.P. believes hierarchically, that the Deputies have a knowledge significant to weigh with the local rank and file—in this it takes Burke's view (p. 89). The Congress elects the president and the secretary general—such as the internationally well-known Georges Bidault or Maurice Schumann. They may serve no more than three successive terms. The secretariat reports to it; the Deputies' group lay its record before it. It decides on policy and tactics.

Top Leadership. The leadership principle is even more pronounced in the National Committee which has frequent meetings. For it is composed of the president and the secretary general plus present Ministers or five ex-Ministers (M.R.P.); delegates of the M.R.P. Deputies and Senators up to one third the membership of the Committee; the M.R.P. delegates in the French Union Assembly; federation representatives proportionate to their membership; 12 representatives of the specialized teams nominated by the National Committee that has named the teams; 2 representatives of the M.R.P. municipal and departmental councils named by the National Committee; and 10 *militants* named by the former National Committee for individual distinction. Thus, the *militants* make only one half the membership of the Committee; the parliamentary leaders are normally in control, as in British parties. And the Committee applies the Congress's resolutions on policy to the daily needs of practical politics. It is more authoritative than the Socialist Party's Executive Committee which has a great majority of *militants*. Furthermore, the federations may choose Deputies as their militant representatives on the National Council and Executive Committee, and some do this to save the expense of sending people to Paris.

Between the normal bimonthly meetings of the National Committee, there operates the Executive Committee of 50; the president, the general secretary, the treasurer, the M.R.P. Ministers, the presidents of the M.R.P. groups in the parliamentary bodies, who provide from 17 to 19 members. Then there are 12 Assembly Deputies; 2 French Union Councilors; 18 federation representatives; 5 *militants*. All these are chosen by the National Committee from its own membership. Thus, some 18 federation representatives confront 30 party leaders and distinguished officeholders. The parliamentary are on top by 2 to 1; in the Socialist Party the situation is reversed.

The general secretariat watches the federations' activities lest they deviate from the headquarters' general policy, and intensively cultivates them with literature as the seed to be planted by the *militants* in the voters. It is aided by the research sections, headed by Deputies or Senators.

Facts and Harmony. The specialized teams are study groups for special clienteles: industrial, agricultural, social welfare, and so on. The teams are *militants* from the "interests." Their reports go to the research sections at headquarters. Thus *before* the Congresses, the party attempts to meet the claims of the various clienteles, whereas the American platform-builders do this during the presidential nominating conventions. Sometimes these teams strongly turn the current of party policy. In 1953 the industrial teams defeated the party's resolutions on workers' cooperation in factory management. In 1954 the workers' team (unsuccessfully) fought the expulsion of a Left wing member for opposition to EDC by the National Council against the appeal of his federation. The attempt at study and harmony is worth while.

Thus, the feeling that it has a central faith is reflected in the oneness which the party constitution puts into the hands of the parliamentary leadership, though there is abundant personal dissenting energy in the movement.

Finance and Internal Discipline. The federations fix the subscriptions and meet the headquarters' claim for a share as affiliation fees, but partially and tardily. The Deputies, for the most part, contribute a part of their salary to the federations, though not compelled to do so. There are donations from wealthy members.

A committee of discipline and arbitration settles controversies over internal discipline. Its four members are elected by the National Council (two Deputies, two *militants*), and the general secretary is chairman. Where the Executive Committee is in conflict with the member's federation, the National Council deals with the dispute.

The Executive Committee may ordain the M.R.P. group to observe *discipline de vote*. The split vote on EDC resulted in the expulsion of one Senator and two Deputies who voted against the measure. The discipline committee decides on expulsion; and there is an appeal to the National Council. The disciplined structure of the M.R.P. has been made fairly rigid because the constitution of the party can be changed only by (1) a proposal of the National Council or Executive Committee, or one fourth of the federations, subject (2) to ratification by a two-third majority of the National Congress.

The Press. The M.R.P.'s M. Teitgen was Minister of Information at France's liberation, and the party was early in the field with presses and newsprint. But *L'Aube,* with a daily circulation of nearly 250,000 in June 1946, fell to 45,000 in 1951, and in 1952 no longer appeared. Parisian voters had almost deserted. The party has four substantial newspapers in the west, around St. Étienne, around Limoges, and in the nothern *départements.*

Clientèle. Its voters fall into the following groups:

	Percentage
Workers—industrial	15
Workers—agricultural	3
Government officials	3
Employees	11
Employers and technicians	3
Merchants	5
Self-employed farmers	20
Professions, liberal	2
Rentiers and retired	6
Women, no occupation	30

The *women* are especially notable; it was always argued that with the vote they would vote clerical-ward. The Catholic trade unions are strong (p. 349), especially in metals and textiles in Alsace, textiles in the north, silk about Lyons and St. Étienne, and among the white-collar workers in Paris. They give support to the M.R.P. since it is a party of social welfare participating in all Governments since 1944, excepting that of Mendès-France. But they have demanded more wages and lower prices against the party's policy from time to time. Of its voters, 53 percent live in towns under 5000 and 19 percent in towns of over 100,000 population.

Movement and Policy. M.R.P. still has some 80,000 members, with 20 percent of these *militants.* The latter comprise more civil servants and professional people than the proportion of its voters' occupations indicates. The party is rather *region-alized* and *clerical:* in the Brittany region, on the eastern border of Germany, the Alsace industrial area—strongholds of the Church—which account for 50 percent of its Deputies in metropolitan France. In the north and east, the most industrial-

ized areas, it won 41 percent of its total vote in 1951. Its ambition to be a nationwide party has not been fulfilled.

The M.R.P. has moved rightward. It is believed that the Catholic peasantry (self-employed farmers) take it this way, while the urban *militants* have provided the zeal for social reforms, but with growing disappointment. It is stronger in the areas of urban social problems and where the population is also Catholic. It is weakest where piety is weakest, in the Central Massif, and there the Communists are strongest. The figures given show that it has become a bourgeoise party, winning from the Right rather than the Radicals. It detests the Communists, but can work with the Socialists and the de Gaullists.

It is torn between the stand-patism of its Catholics, which pull it rightward, and its Left-wing urban social reformers, who sometimes make it more socialistic than the Socialists. It has pushed workers' cooperation in management, and nationalization, co-partnership, and profit-sharing (unsuccessfully). It has tried to liberalize the administration of the nationalized industries with the independent corporation device and workers' representation. It has been a strong supporter of the Monnet Plan (p. 462) for modernizing industry and agriculture. It has pressed forward more generous social welfare and family participation in management of the services. It secured subsidies for Catholic schools by the *loi Barangé* (p. 384).

It has sternly defended the rights of France in the colonies, though pressing for social welfare therein and the extension of self-government under France. It was more adamant about Indochina than were the Socialists or Radicals, desiring to maintain French spiritual responsibility and prestige.

In international relations it was the stepfather of EDC, believing that Franco-German reconciliation was essential for France and Europe, that modification of national sovereignty in the European Army was a noble and feasible means thereto. This, also, was its peculiar answer to France's problem of security—with the West, not with the U.S.S.R., France's other alternative. From December 1946 until June 1954 the Ministry of Foreign Affairs was held by the M.R.P., by

Georges Bidault or Robert Schuman. They had developed France's role in the UN, created the Schuman Coal and Steel Authority for Europe, led in the making of the Strasbourg Council of Europe, in Marshall Plan Aid, Mutual Security, and the NATO Pact. The leaders were drawn toward Germany, also, because it was now governed by Chancellor Adenauer and his Christian Democratic Party, akin to the M.R.P.

Squeezed by the Socialists on the Left and the Radicals on the Right, both of which are anticlerical, M.R.P. has pursued curious electoral alliances. Many were dissuaded only by the stern *croyant* Robert Schuman from affiliating with the de Gaullists; yet 25 percent of the Deputies in 1951 won seats by *apparentement* with the Right and the de Gaullists. The de Gaullists forced the M.R.P. away from the Socialists by appealing to the Catholic vote, the M.R.P.'s special clientele.

Its *militants* have an average age of thirty; they can be chosen for the party Congress after but one year of membership (Socialists, five!). Its service in Third Force Governments has compelled concessions to expediency that wrack its internal ease.

The Radical Party

Established in 1901, its official name is the ambiguous *Parti Radical et Radical Socialiste*. In the Third Republic it was said to resemble *un radis* (a radish): red outside and white inside—with "its heart on the Left and its pocketbook on the Right." *Socialist* is even a self-deception. It throve on the single-member constituencies and was the characteristic party of the Third Republic—all things to all men, nothing to anyone in particular, constantly in office, and steadily against any substantial welfare for the industrial workers. Its clientele became the oratory-loving shopkeepers, schoolteachers (being anticlerical), small farmers, rural doctors, and lawyers. Its flabbiness of policy and character, men and ideas, of influx of voters at the second ballot, helped the digging of the Third Republic's grave. It had a miserable record of connivance with the Vichy regime, although some members, such as Herriot and Daladier, were Nazi prisoners and some were executed.

By 1945 it was in national contempt, for it per-

sonified *French incivisme* its very self. It has no faith like the M.R.P. or Communists or Socialists. It is organized around local notables, committees, and provincial newspapers. Its formula was and is to get back to the Third Republic. It went rightward for allies; but in 1945 it had only 24 seats in the Assembly compared with 120 in 1936. It showed an inclination to ally with the de Gaullists, until Herriot for the 1951 elections secured a Congress resolution against "political bigamy." Hereupon the party resumed its traditional hatred of MacMahon and Boulanger and de Gaulle, the "men on horseback." In 1951, 58 of its Deputies won in *apparentement* with Socialists or M.R.P.; 3 with the de Gaullists; while 17 others *opposed these allies*, winning conservative or personal victories.

Its leaders are scattered over the whole political spectrum: Marie, Queuille, René Mayer, do-nothing or conservatives; Edgar Faure, center-liberal; the outworn Daladier, rightish-liberal; Mendès-France, vigorous Left-wing liberal. In February 1955, René Mayer of the Radical Socialist Party fiercely led the Assembly to overthrow the Government of Mendès-France, Radical Socialist, claiming the latter had no policy. In November 1955 Mayer, Mendès-France, and Faure, Prime Minister, openly fought each other over whether an election should be held earlier than June 1956 and on what electoral system.

Organization. The Radical Party is similar in form to the Socialist, moving up by free elections from the local *comité* to the next tier, the *cantonal* federation, to the *départementale* federation, to the capital. In some places there are *arrondissement* and regional levels in between. Though the headquarters in Paris gives its *investiture* of candidates, the *départementale* federations have a large independence in selecting candidates with great freedom of electoral strategy! The federations retain the bulk of the members' dues.

The party's National Congress is formed of delegates elected by the federations in the main— *but* the editors of pro-Radical newspapers are members, so also the members of the National Council. The newspaper editors retain this status because they were the historical nuclei of the party: Herriot with *Le Progrès* of Lyons; Sarraut with *La Depêche* of Toulouse. Laval bought Radical newspapers and so obtained the right to vote at Radical congresses! There are parallels in American politics.

Individuals may buy admission tickets to the Congress. They cannot vote, but wealthy men can so provide *claques*. This is the level at which policy is resolved on.

Between the congresses, the National Council functions as a formulator of policy, and it prepares the agenda for the next congress and appoints *rapporteurs* for the subjects to be discussed. The party leaders are *ex officio* members—that is, the president and general secretary of the federations, the ex-presidents and ex-general secretaries of the party, members of the party's Executive Committee, party men of public standing who are members of the *comités,* for example, the Deputies, the Senators, members of the advisory assemblies, the overseas assemblies, the councils of the *départements*. The federations send delegates proportional to their membership. The total size of the Council is 1200; the *militants* number only 300. As few can attend its quarterly meetings, the leaders in Paris take command, with a quorum of 150. The Council elects the committees on discipline, finance, and the Executive Committee.

The Executive Committee has 70 members, 40 of which are rank-and-file delegates who cannot be Deputies. They are elected for two-year term, 20 by the National Council, 20 by the Congress. Further, 10 are chosen by the Assembly Deputies, 10 by the Senators, 5 by the French Union Assembly. The rest are the top five officials of the party. It meets monthly; its official title is *commission executive*. In case of Cabinet crisis, decisions are taken by it and the Deputies in joint session, as though, in England, the Labour National Executive were to meet with the Parliamentary Labour Party.

All this apparatus is *ungeared* to the rank and file; there is a want of loyalty and self-subordination, of devoted membership. It is rather a congeries of local (*départementale*) groups voting for sometimes contradictory policies, but backing each other for election and office.

Clientele. Its voters fall into the following broad categories:

	Percentage
Workers—industrial	10
Workers—agricultural	5
Government officials	5
Employees	1
Employers and technicians	4
Merchants	7
Self-employed farmers	31
Professions—liberal	1
Rentiers and pensioners	14
Women, no occupation	19

Its total vote in 1951 was almost 2,000,000. It has the highest percentage (60) of voters of all parties in towns of under 5000 and 23 percent in over 100,000.

Cabinet Leaders. Since the Liberation France has moved rightward. In 1945 the Radicals, unaffiliated, had 24 Deputies; in 1951, the number had risen to 68. This is a very substantial number in a group system, especially when the Communists and the extreme Right will not enter Government coalitions but mischievously can vote them out of office. It is a most useful maneuverable number, especially as members are detachable for the purpose of the Left and the Right and the Center coalitions, or coalitions inclined in these directions. Hence, since August 1948, the Radical Party has supplied *no less than eleven Prime Ministers,* through Mendès-France and Edgar Faure (February 1955); three of the six key Ministries since 1947; and has won considerable strength locally and in the Council of the Republic for whose election P.R. is not used and where therefore the party's incongruous alliances favor it. It has been nicknamed the "Party of Presidencies." Right and Left are less afraid of it than of each other.

A new Mendès-France-Edgar Faure generation has entered the leadership—they are in their forties. The table of the composition of the Assembly (p. 376) shows that the party is the representative of the rural townsfolk, professions, farmers, shopkeepers, civil servants; that it is weak in the industrial areas. The Paris bourgeoisie votes Radical. Its favorite home is south of the Loire; with some strength in the east, the west and the Paris basin.

Policy. It is do-nothing liberalism and the defense of the Republic and the *status quo*. What has it voted *for*? The old Constitution; single-member districts; against wage-raises; government economy; amnesties to tax evaders; safeguards for the interests of farm lessors (it used to favor the tenants!). It has been deeply split on sliding scales for wages; welfare policies, 50-50; tax increases, similarly; the budget, similarly. It has, for two thirds of its membership, voted against, or abstained from supporting, subsidies to Church schools, one third thus breaking with the anticlerical past. This vote was calculated according to the local electoral prospects. It represents the areas most backward in ideas, ambitions, and productivity.

Anti-German and pro-West, it was the principal destroyer of the EDC Treaty, but the supporter of the Western European Alliance. It still feels attracted by the traditional policy of friendship with Russia pursued by its leaders since 1902, to face Germany with an eastern front as well as a Western.

Two of its leaders, Edgar Faure and Maurice Petsche, are big businessmen. Hence, in the lack of gearing of the parliamentary group with the local *militants,* the party is heedful of the *Patronat,* Big Business. It is exceptionally responsive to the *Petites et Moyennes Entreprises,* which, in 1951, organized the *Front Économique* to get pledges from candidates, and it put forward candidates under the title Taxpayers' Defense. The resistance to tax investigators, under M. Poujade a wild demagogue, found practical response in the party's policy. It would not support Mendès-France's antialcoholism policy: the growers and distillers are its clients. The self-employed farmers in the C.G.A. are close to it; the René Mayer Cabinet of May 1953 succumbed to the C.G.A.'s opposition to the lowering of agricultural prices.

In October 1955 Mendès-France won control of the party organization in a bitter struggle with such men as Faure, and then converted his *journal d'opinion* from a weekly to a daily, to be a means of converting Frenchmen to his policy of economic and social reconstruction based on the non-Communist Left.

The Conservative Parties: The Right

Omitting for the moment the R.P.F., the de Gaullists, dealt with later (p. 362), there are three conservative groups, very loosely organized representatives of the upper classes of business, finance, manufactures, and landowning. They are the *Independents Républicains,* the *Action Républicaine et social* (the A.R.S.) who broke away from the de Gaullists in 1952, and the *Paysans* (who fall into two groups).

In the Assembly, at the end of February 1955, these mustered together 137 members, distributed thus: Independents, 55; A.R.S., 33; Independent Peasants, 28; Peasants, 21. Together, they are a substantial proportion of the distracted Assembly. The first two are the descendants of the parties of the Right that bedeviled the Third Republic with unwillingness at first to accept its existence even, with Catholic antirepublicanism, with permanent malice toward the urban working class, with use of high finance to overthrow liberal Cabinets, with alliances with Fascist leagues, and finally with the overthrow of the Republic and the establishment of the Pétain regime and its nefarious works. They had all along looked for the occasion to "strangle the hag," *la gueuse,* the Republic. They masqueraded inside the M.R.P. after the Liberation and inside the de Gaullist ranks since then, for they had disgraced their country with homage to Hitler, Mussolini, and Franco—above all, Hitler.

They are of divided interests and outlook. Many prefer the R.P.F., but de Gaulle has rejected them. Others would ally with the Radicals to fight the extreme Left, to make a "Fourth Force," of the Center and moderate conservatives against the Third Force of Socialists, M.R.P., and Radicals, the First Force of the Communists, and the Second Force of the de Gaullists.

No Masses; No Discipline. The conservative groups are linked by a *Centre National,* a committee of twelve Deputies and Senators, and this is linked with centers in the *départements,* which are little but local personages, such as business leaders, activists in the agricultural associations, the wealthier municipal and *départementale* councilors. They have local personal influence, no common specific concerted policy yet have a common conservative outlook. The Peasant parties are developing federations in the *départements;* the one inclines toward the de Gaullists, the other toward the M.R.P. and the Radicals or moderate conservatives associated with the Radicals. There is no *discipline de vote* in these groups; the Peasant group has actually resolved *for* freedom of voting of its Deputies.

The electorate of the conservatives for 1951 was about 2,300,000, and it fell into the following proportions:

	Percentage
Workers—industrial	10
Workers—agricultural	4
Government officials	6
Employees	3
Employers and technicians	10
Merchants	7
Self-employed farmers	35
Professions—liberal	1
Rentiers and pensioners	8
Women unoccupied	15

Farmers, employers and managers, rentiers and civil servants (certainly of the higher classifications, Chapter 9), stand out as the clientele. Its strength lies 55 percent in towns of under 5000 and 29 percent in those over 100,000.

What is a curious phenomenon is that the conservatives even have something like 250,000 industrial workers. There are in all democratic countries industrial workers, more often skilled than not, who have an ideology not entirely stemming from their economic interest. They are nationalist or militarist or believe in authority and hierarchy or detest the parliamentary maneuvers of the Communists and the weakness of Socialists and Radicals. Some genuinely believe that the economic policy of the conservative financiers and budget planners benefits the long-run economic efficiency and wealth of the nation. Others oppose social-welfare legislation that takes from them in taxes to give to the unskilled workers whose foibles they happen to know from first-hand experience when at work. Others again have an intense dislike of governmental regulations and officials, and believe that the conservatives would curb these. Yet, withal, the conservatives are very weak in the industrial *départements*. The conservative Deputies include no workers, employees, or artisans.

They are parties of the high bourgeoisie whose Deputies are elderly lawyers, officials, businessmen, and farmers. Their regional strength lies in the Cévennes, less so in the west; they have strength in the east (where there is new industrialism, Catholicism, and anti-German memories), and in the Alpine *départements*. This can be broken down into the Peasant regions, which are in the Cévennes (strongly) and south of the Loire—rural areas, some quite benighted; and for the Independent conservatives, the east with modern industries.

The conservatives have had one Prime Minister since 1945—M. Antoine Pinay, who held office for nine months in 1952. He was noted for his consummate ability to avoid any decisions, and cursed by his successors for this success.

The conservatives were, of course, adamant against a Thorez prime ministership, and hardly less so to those of Blum and Ramadier, though they preferred the latter to the former. They have been friendly to M.R.P. Prime Ministers, and came to be reconciled to those of the Radicals, especially the tame ones, such as André Marie and Doctor Queuille. They have favored rearmament; NATO; Church schools (almost 100 percent); the Schuman Plan, with some dissentients; EDC by some two thirds of their Deputies; amnesty for tax frauds (100 percent); a Laniel Government (big businessman) and special powers to him to effect economies; ultimately, for sliding wage scales, as an alternative to governmental lowering of prices, but have been steadily against a policy of raised wages. They have opposed a levy on capital and the *lois des maximum* [9] and increases of taxes. Their foreign policy is a strong, rearmed France, alliance with the United States, an anti-Soviet policy, a tenacious hold on the colonies; they were split on the final EDC vote into Independents: 12 against and 36 for, and Peasants: 10 against and 9 for. They steadily support high tariffs and protection and subsidies for agriculture. Their most recent acts of significance were support of the Mendès-France and the Edgar Faure Cabinets.

In a sense the conservatives are almost two pressure groups in themselves: big business and their professional associates, especially the lawyers and

[9] Annual laws voting the Government the power to spend *up to* such a stated amount per government department, in advance of detailed discussion (see pp. 395–399).

high administrative officials, and the better off farmers.

As for the "peasantry," no less than 41 of the officials of agricultural associations (numbering in all 87) who won seats in the Assembly in 1951 were conservatives! The other officials were scattered in other parties thus: Communists, 7; Socialists, 6; M.R.P., 8; Radicals, 8; de Gaullists, 13. Two are unspecified.

"Farm Bloc." At this point it may be warned that the "peasantry" is not a homogeneous interest or class (see p. 278 figures of the groupings in agriculture). There is a "farm bloc" in the legislature —and the farm bloc is also split. Some of the matters on which the peasantry is a bloc are these. In 1950 almost as a whole, the Deputies and the associations attempted to get the proportion of investment through the national Monnet Plan made more generous to agricultural works (agriculture was receiving some 17 percent, compared with 37 percent for industry and commerce, and 70 percent in the nationalized industries). The effort was extremely vigorous but was repulsed by the votes of the Communists and Socialists and the urban votes of the M.R.P., while the rural votes of this same party collaborated with the conservatives.

The conservatives, along with the other parties with a substantial agricultural interest—for example the Communists!—combine in an intraparliamentary "study group" (see p. 342) for assisting the agrarian interests. (The study groups are rather like the "institutes" set up in the United States by various big industries, ostensibly and perhaps sincerely, for research but not without attention to "pressure" and "lobbying.") For example, the Study Group on Alcohol, numbering 100 Deputies from conservatives to Communists, have defended the alcohol interests from increased taxation since 1949. Its members hold the chairmanships of the parliamentary commissions on Finance, on Agriculture, on Industrial Production, and on Fermented Liquors. Since the estimates of the total of persons who live by producing or selling alcohol in one of its various forms vary between 4 and 6 millions, this is evidently a significant "lobby." It was able to force the Government in 1950 to decree that surplus alcohol should be used as motor fuel, as in the interwar years. This was the consequence of the "lobby" securing that the Government should not reduce its subsidies for the cultivation of beetroot, which had been commenced under the Monnet Plan to increase the sugar supply, although the cunning farmers used the beetroot to distill alcohol (more profitable and simpler than refining sugar!). The "peasants" and parliamentary friends would not permit the Government to reduce the subsidies, which bear wickedly on the national budget and encourage alcoholism (see p. 297). By January 1955 they had infiltrated the parties that had voted for decree powers to Mendès-France so potently as to negate his various decrees against alcoholism, making his downfall certain also!

The R.P.F. or the de Gaullists or the Rassemblement du Peuple Français

What began as the Gaullist Union in June 1946 and was reconstructed on a broader basis in April 1947 was first formed by René Capitant, one of the General's principal Resistance associates. The referendum on the first draft of the constitution showed that masses of conservatives and M.R.P. people were ready to follow de Gaulle in preference (p. 322). The Communists, ejected from the Socialist Cabinet in May 1947, carried on their ruinous tactics by wild political strikes. The result was the search for a "Man on Horseback": the *Rassemblement*, or Rally of the French People, (with conservative and Radical affiliates) won 6,000,000 votes at the municipal elections of October 1947, more than the total of Socialist and M.R.P. votes together. It claimed 1,000,000 members in December. The Rally's appeal was not without a Bonapartist (p. 301) appeal of proletarian welfare, attractive to industrial workers, especially veterans, and feeding the disgust with pusillanimous politicians.

The Two Characteristics of de Gaullism. It wants to "gather" the ill-assorted segments of French Society; it values "technocracy." The first may be appreciated from a speech by de Gaulle on January 1, 1946:

> . . . if you do not take into account the lessons of our political history of the past fifty years and, in particular of what happened in 1940, if you

do not take into account *the absolute necessity for governmental authority, dignity, and responsibility* [italics added], you will reach a situation such that sooner or later, I predict, you will bitterly regret having taken the road which you will have taken. . . .

Do we want a government which governs or do we want an omnipotent Assembly selecting a government to accomplish its will? This second solution means a regime which we ourselves have sometimes tried, and others also have done so.

Personally, I am convinced that it in no sense answers the necessities of the country in which we live, nor those of our era, in which *problems are so numerous, so complex, so rapid, so brutal* [italics added], that it appears impossible to solve them within any such constitutional framework. . . .

The formula which is forced upon us . . . is a government which has and which bears alone —I say, alone!—the entire responsibility for the executive power.

The "technocracy" theme has been supplied by his associates, who argue that so long as a return to *laissez faire* is impossible, then the pressure groups will disrupt the State that is now active in giving or withholding benefits and imposing duties. "The system will demand an executive to re-create the principle of unity." This will be planned and imposed by technicians (the Managerial Class), such as engineers, natural scientists, planners, productions managers, and civil administrators. Many of the original followers of de Gaulle in the Resistance were such men, especially higher civil servants (antiparliamentary, Chap. 9). René Cassin, actual head of the *Conseil d'État* was one of these variously trained intellectuals, who planned an American presidential system for renewed France, with a Cabinet of experts responsible only to the President with a fixed term.

A Party or Not? Political parties were and are despised by the inexperienced General; therefore the first idea was to form an intergroup, a rally, of all parties, except the Communists and Nazi collaborators. But the Socialists and M.R.P. rejected "political bigamy." The Gaullist Union collected many conservatives, while the Radicals and friends joined a rival rally, the *Rassemblement des Gauches Républicains*. The General wanted the 1946 Assembly to dissolve itself (by a two-thirds majority, it can) and give his following in the country the chance of overwhelming the Center and Left. The latter merely laughed and closed their ranks. Only eighty Deputies joined his intergroup, soon to be the R.P.F. The leadership ordained disciplined voting. The Deputies were Frenchmen and conservatives: they disobeyed and thirteen resigned when asked to oppose the budget of a good conservative, Paul Reynaud, in 1948. Then the General thought he had captured 150 out of 320 Senate seats. They had gulled him: ninety of the members had used his name in their campaigns, but as Radicals and conservatives they repudiated his leadership. The other fifty-eight were unreliable.

Into Politics: Exit de Gaulle. The nation entered smoother waters under Dr. Queuille, whose Radical Ministry lasted thirteen months; harvests were better; American aid improved the economy; prices fell; in 1949 the Government could raise a public loan. The *militants* in the R.P.F. began to fight inside the group; clericals and anticlericals; the Radicals defected; the conservatives left. The electoral law of 1951 was passed (p. 368) to hit the R.P.F.'s parliamentary representation as well as the Communist's, because in the General's stiffness of view the R.P.F. could not take advantage of *apparentement*. The R.P.F. won only 120 seats instead of the 200 it had expected, and instead of the 130 it would have had with strict proportional representation of its vote.

A tank battle in an open plain was tried by the General: to detach the M.R.P. from the Socialists by forcing the former to vote for the Church-school subsidies. The objective was the overthrow of Governments by a coalitions of Socialists, Communists, and R.P.F. until, out of desperation, the de Gaullists would be asked to form a Government. The Assembly is not an open plain, and its party groups travel more like crabs than tanks. The conservatives formed a Government, with Radicals and M.R.P., and even some conservative R.P.F. members. This in September 1951.

In the by-elections the R.P.F. lost heavily among its middle-class supporters. Its voting in the Assembly was divided among its conservatives and

Leftists. The General met this similarity to other political parties by the command in July 1952 for severe *discipline de vote*. The thirty most conservative immediately resigned and established the A.R.S., followed by other Deputies later. The remaining de Gaullists went Leftward to join a Radical Cabinet under Mayer and the M.R.P., with one ministerial place. Further losses were suffered in municipal elections. The General declared that *his* R.P.F. was withdrawn from the parliamentary and electoral seeking of votes. But the group continued to exist until the election of 1956 (p. 400).

R.P.F. Organization. The pyramidal organization by election is rather like that of the M.R.P., excepting that members are called *compagnons* (like "comrades" among the Communists) and the annual congresses, *assises nationales*. In addition to local area units, the R.P.F. has followed the Communists in setting up factory cells. These have prescribed for them an order of business reminiscent of the Saint-Simonian and Comtist Positivist Church (p. 292): ten minutes for current politics, twenty for de Gaulle's doctrines, twenty for the factory situation.

The party councils at the level of the *département* are elected half by the lower areal units, and a half by the occupational, professional, family, and veterans' associations, and the latter elect one third of the National Council and the National Congress.

De Gaulle and the Leadership. Statutes vest de Gaulle with the presidency and power to choose the secretariat and executive body. The former are his personal aides in constant council and operation in province or capital as directed by de Gaulle. In choosing the Executive, he is compelled to include the movement's eminent men, whatever his own dislikes. Starting with 12 members it rose to 29 toward the end of 1952; furthermore, the rule against Deputies as members had to be waived, so that at the end of 1952, it (was composed of 12 Deputies, 4 Senators, 3 from the French Union Assembly, 4 past Deputies, and the rest prominent Parisians and provincials. Until November 1952 these are entirely nominated by de Gaulle. This was high-handed centralization assisted by a general staff not to be called by the President when he was displeased. The recalcitrant were not summoned! Then the rules were amended: R.P.F. Deputies and Senators and the *militants* were given the right to name some of the executive.

The composition of the *assises nationales* has already been suggested; its numbers are decided annually by the secretariat and the Executive. There is little discussion in full session of policy resolutions; the creative work is done in committees. The reelection of the General is not debated. The *assises* elects a National Council of the component groups of *départementale* delegates, social groupings; some are added by the Executive. For example: 70 departmental delegates; 70 for the organizations (of which 26 for the working-class); 63 Deputies and Senators; 30 distinguished men of letters, churchmen, generals, ambassadors, mayors, actors, by the Executive. The latter, containing men like André Malraux and Raymond Aron, is de Gaulle's "Chamber of Peers." The Council formulates policy and meets two or three times a year.

An official of the central office makes the policy; the departmental councils, elected annually by the rank and file, are merely deliberative and formulative. The delegate sent from the central office and his assistant delegates operate at the grass roots to accept policy or reject it; to invigilate the operation of the party's services of the working class, propaganda, youth, families, veterans, etc., whose directors are appointed by the central office. This is rather like the Soviet Communist Party's hold over the primary party organs in the localities, especially the 22 "regional" delegates to supervise the departmental delegates.

This unusual centralization (except for the Communist Party) included the power of de Gaulle to make personal choice of the R.P.F. parliamentary candidates! The center also settled the propaganda and electoral tactics. However, the local associations have become increasingly evident.

Clientele. R.P.F. has a young membership; its Deputies are under fifty. Of its electorate of 4,250,000 voters in 1951, 55 percent were under fifty and 30 percent under thirty-five. The conservatives had 45 percent over fifty; the Radicals, 65 percent; M.R.P., only 34 percent; the Socialists, 37 percent; and the Communists, 23 percent.

The occupational grouping of the voters is:

	Percentage
Workers—industrial	18
Workers—agricultural	4
Government officials	2
Employees	7
Employers and technicians	7
Merchants	7
Self-employed farmers	18
Professions—liberal	1
Rentiers and pensioners	4
Women—no occupation	32

The striking figure is that of the women voters; the R.P.F. is the French mass party of women, and the word *mass* is even a pun. Women like shining generals, regardless of their capacity for statesmanship, especially if they are pious churchmen. Employers and technicians are a characteristic segment. In its National Council, one third of the 150 members are engineers, industrialists, and employers; the next largest segment are the civil servants. The industrial and white-collar workers make up 25 percent of the General's following; the little man who suffers the boredom and frustrations of office work as seen in Elmer Rice's *The Adding Machine*. The R.P.F. has a social-welfare and corporative appeal for some workers. It is strong in the rural areas, the habitat of the Right. Its middle-middle and upper-middle urban followers have departed, leaving the very wealthy, the very poor, the humdrum white-collarites, the smug farmers, and the glitter-loving Catholic women.

The R.P.F. is strong in the conservative west, the nationalist and Catholic east, and the Paris Basin. In the west it has inherited the prewar Rightist vote. It has strength in thirteen of the most industrialized and progressive *départements*. In the west it is Catholic and socially sedate; in the east it is zealous for and with social-welfare services, the gifts of the State to the poor. It is rather reminiscent of German National Socialism. It has roots to the extent of only 45 percent in towns under 5000 population and surpasses both Socialists and Communists with 22 percent of its votes in cities of over 100,000.

Policy. R.P.F. found the formula for helping the Catholic schools: educational allowances to the parents. Until 1951 the R.P.F. group in the Assembly voted against (or abstained) all Prime Ministers, Governments, and policies before the Assembly. It resisted the employers' confederation. Two thirds voted against amnesty for tax defrauders. Almost unanimously it voted with the Left for a sliding wage scale. It has favored more generous policies in housing, health, family allowances, allied here with the Left. It has viewed with suspicion the budgets designed to "effect economies" in the public service.

It has been violently nationalistic, bitterly French. It has voted against the Schuman Plan and solidly against EDC, and was troublesome on the Western Union pacts. In the name of French sovereignty and pride, it opposed the Marshall Plan and NATO. De Gaulle's animosity against Britain and the United States, born in World War II out of his irascibility and ingrown Frenchness, is almost as intense as that of the Communists omitting for them the French-ness. French independence seems to be sought by him at the expense of French survival. On the defeat of EDC, the R.P.F. sang the *Marseillaise* in accompaniment to the Communists' *Internationale*. It seems that the General would prefer a Germany federalized back to 1871 (pp. 576–577), and then allied with France, and the smaller European nations to be a bloc independent of the United States and the U.S.S.R. But in October 1954 the R.P.F. had come round to vote for the Western European pacts, though the General himself agitated for a previous *rapprochement* with Russia! It is imperialist-minded, sternly opposed to concessions to North Africa and Indochinese nationalism. In November 1955 it voted in favor of fresh elections in the morning and against them in the evening of the same day—pure mischief.

The A.R.S. (Gaullist Dissidents). The leader of this group is M. Barrachin, former general secretary of the Fascist Party, the *Parti Social Français,* an offshoot of the *Croix de Feu!* Another of its leaders was one of the fomenters of the Fascist riots against the Deputies in February 1934 (p. 316). They are inveterate nationalist conservatives.

Lesser Parties

Small as they are, the lesser parties help to make or mar Governments; every vote counts. We pass from Left to Right.

The Union Progressiste. The union is near-Communist. It is made up of secessionists from the Left Radicals (Pierre Cot); from the Socialists; from the Christian Democrats. It affiliates with the Communists at elections. It has fifteen members, and the votes usually join the Communists'; but some seek a middle way between the U.S.A. and the U.S.S.R. Their intra-Assembly group name is *Union des Républicains et Résistants,* or U.R.R.S. Even then there are three additional "splinter" groups near the Communists, of shades of intransigent differentiae.

The Union Democratique et Socialiste de la Résistance. The U.D.S.R. is democratic Socialist, and is the remnant of the Resistance grouping for national liberation after the Communists, the Socialists, and the Radicals had gone to their old homes. It has some organization in about half the *départements;* a central committee of electoral free lances linked in the Assembly, who have individual strength in the constituencies as local government councilors or journalists, etc. Its nine French Deputies and fourteen colonial Deputies are conglomerate, so that it sways to the Left or Center and even the Right with the issues and the places in the Cabinet. Twenty-three votes are important. René Pleven is its leader, originator of the EDC idea. He has twice been Prime Minister. It is especially friendly with the Socialists and Radicals, yet it voted for the Church-school subsidies.

The Rassemblement des Gauches Républicains. This is but a loose federation of the U.D.S.R., the Radicals, and a few other less-than-usually-determinate groups. Its bureau is composed of the parliamentary representatives of the allied groups. So far its elected congress has never been convened. The local organization is that of the allied groups, not its own. M. Daladier, the Radical leader of a past generation, was elected its president in May 1950. The term *R.G.R.* is used at elections; but each component group has its own way of life.

Others. There are conservative "splinter groups": the *Alliance Démocratique,* remnant of a prewar group of conservatives, with the notorious M. Flandin then as a leader, who went over to Vichy. One of the present membership, M. Pinay was Prime Minister for a time in 1952; and in February 1955 became Minister for Foreign Affairs under Edgar Faure. It has held other Ministries.

The Reconciliation Française is the wan descendant of the prewar *Parti social Français* (p. 365). The *Parti Socialist démocratique* is the remnant of the pacifist dissidents from the Socialist under Paul Faure. He went over to Pétain, after having been for years general secretary of the Socialist Party. It lives a precarious life in the southwest, glad to be put on the R.G.R. electoral lists.

Some other small conservative groups need mention. One is that of *Taxpayers' Defense,* the pressure group of small and middle-size business (p. 341). It won one seat in 1951, allying with any list except the Communists. Then there is the *Rally of French Republican and Independent Groups,* composed of Radicals, Socialists, and extreme Rightists at odds with their parties. They group together for electoral reasons (p. 369) in *apparentement.* The small groups were to have been wiped out by the rule that the benefits of *apparentement* cannot be claimed unless a group can put up lists in at least thirty *départements.* "Rallies" are a way of evading extinction. They are far from having a common policy. Five conservatives and one Socialist were successful. The *Union Nationale des Independants* is pro-Pétain. It fought alone, and won three seats, for friends of the Marshal's. They vote conservative and with the Peasants.

There are still Royalists, supporting the claims of the Comte de Paris, the pretender to the French throne, uniting the older and younger branches of the Bourbons. He believes in a British-type constitutional monarchy, in social welfare, and is opposed to the old-fashioned chauvinism of the *Action Française* (p. 316). He has eleven children, and fought bravely in the Foreign Legion. The law forbidding the pretenders and their eldest sons to reside in France (enacted 1886), was repealed in 1950 against the opposition of the Socialists and Communists. Prince Napoleon, descendant of the Bonapartes, is allowed to live in France also. He, too, fought well in the war.

Overseas Parties. The overseas territories send Deputies to the Assembly and elect Senators. This is in marked contrast to the British Commonwealth.

Some of the representation occurs through direct membership in the French parties we have dealt with. This includes most of the overseas Deputies, who are scattered among the M.R.P., the Radicals, the R.P.F., to represent the white colonists and native friends of the colonial power, while the native electorates have variously joined the Communist or Socialist parties or the M.R.P.

There are, then, the Algerian, Madagascar, and West African irreconcilable nationalists. There are no direct representatives of the Algerian movement (it would be better to say movements), because one group refused to take part in elections in protest against the new Constitution, while the more extreme one lost its seats at the election of 1951. These groups were called—we give the names in English—the *Democratic Union of the Algerian Manifesto* and the *Movement of the Triumph of Democratic Liberties*. The latter used to vote with the Communists.

There were three Deputies returned for Madagascar in 1946, extreme nationalists. In 1947 they were put in prison for inciting to rebellion. In the 1951 election three native moderate nationalists won seats.

The West African nationalists in the R.D.A., or Democratic Rally of Africa, first was associated with the *Progressistes* of the extreme Left (see p. 366). After a spell of internal dissension, its handful of members turned toward cooperation with the Third Force coalitions. It became an affiliate of the U.D.S.R. in 1952 (see p. 366).

Finally, there are moderate nationalists. These, of various tendencies, have moved toward the U.D.S.R. in a grouping of their own various tendencies in the Overseas Independents organization. By 1952 two thirds of the U.D.S.R.'s members of the Assembly were overseas Deputies, and these were chiefly of the *Overseas Independents* and chiefly natives.

The total number of Deputies from overseas (1951) for all the categories mentioned is eighty-three. Naturally, they do not all vote the same way, for the settlers who have joined the chief political parties and the native members have opposed interests. Hence, only about fifteen votes is the benefit accruing to a government-in-the-making or in stalling off defeat. This is still of some strategic importance. The native members induced a change in the electoral law, widening the franchise, for West Africa in May 1951.

In November 1951 the Government amended its North African policy under pressure from the settlers Deputies to militant resistance of native nationalist movements, but by 1955 was compelled to change its policy radically (p. 456).

Election of the thirty Deputies for Algeria was suspended on January 2, 1956, owing to the disturbed situation there.

5

The Electoral System and the National Assembly

Ignorant no doubt of natural phenomena, every man is none the less a just judge in all that concerns mankind. He is sovereign master by right. When he sits in his natural praetorium and judgment seat, in the square of the great city, or on the bench at the church door, or else on a stone at the cross-roads, under the judgment elm, he judges there without appeal. There is no gainsaying his sentence. Kings, queens and tribunes, Mirabeaus, Robespierres, appear humbly at his bar. The great Napoleon himself holds his hat in his hand, as Luther had done before him. . . . He judges; all is over; for you, historians, philosophers, critics, cavillers, to seek and find the "why." Seek, he is always just; and the injustice you discover, feeble and subtle that you are, is the defect of your own intelligence.

—Michelet, History of the Revolution

Four Chambers! The preciousness of the French political mind has saddled France with (1) the National Assembly, (2) the Council of the Republic, (3) the Economic Council, and (4) the Assembly of the French Union. The National Assembly is the sovereign body that makes law; the others are advisory, except the Council of the Republic, which now has some law-initiating powers in addition to its suspensory and revising powers.

I. THE ELECTORAL SYSTEM

Proportional Representation

Scrutin d'arrondissement was abandoned (p. 309) and proportional representation, or P.R., was required by the Constitution itself. The latest electoral law is that of May 7, 1951, which changed the details of P.R. in order to reduce the number of seats the Communists and de Gaullists might have won on the basis of the law as of October 5, 1946.

The law of October 1946 made the whole *départements* the electoral constituencies, except that the six largest were each divided into a number of more convenient-sized constituencies. Each party or other grouping put up a list containing the number of candidates equaling the number of seats for the constituency—that is, the whole *département*. The number of seats is settled by the law: the largest was ten for Finistère, with 483,000 registered voters; the smallest, the Basses Alpes, with two candidates and 56,000 electorate. Splitting the ticket was permitted. The candidates were put in order of the party's preference. No names could be written in by the voters. The voter could change the order of preference as established by the party by changing the number attached to each. The seats were distributed first to each list according to the number of votes the whole list obtained, divided by the average votes cast by the electorate per seat available. Then the seats in each list were divided among the men on the list according to the preferences expressed on the list against their names by the voters. No provision was made for remainders from each *dèpartement* to be gathered nationally and once again divided among the various parties proportional to their respective votes.

The French, on the whole, wanted to maintain the system for the future, because it did "justice" —that is, it gave proportionality of the representation to the strength in the nation. But the Radicals challenged this system, preferring to return to the old nonproportional system with run-off elections, because this had given them tremendous advantages and had kept other political parties weakly organized and disciplined, as each man, coming from his own single-member bailiwick, could cock a snook at his leader—and even the electors. They proposed far-reaching changes. Changes were made, but not to *their* advantage, for the purpose of the changes was to enable the middle parties, including the Socialists, to reduce the representation of the two destructive extremes, the de Gaullists and the Communists. The "justice" of representation was subordinated to the higher "justice" of making the democratic system enduringly operative. They would *not* go back to the system that pleased the Radicals; the latter had hardly a policy or many policies, making success at the maneuvers of the second ballot valuable for them, whereas the other parties were anxious to retain their firmness of policy, program, and strong, unified organization.

It was not easy to find a system or get a majority for one that would achieve just this object and no more. The major change agreed on was this: political parties could affiliate with each other to present single electoral lists, and then the list getting the majority of votes would capture *all* the seats.

1951 Modifications. This, then, was the system as it operated in the elections of June 1951 and Jan. 2, 1956 (pp. 371ff.). (1) There is only one election, no second ballot. (2) The basic electoral district is the *département,* with the very large ones broken into several. (3) Three days before the election, parties may declare to the district prefecture that they wish to be "coupled"—that is, *apparentement.*

But only those parties that are designated as "national" may list themselves as members of an *apparentement.* This significant term means that each one of them must have candidates running in at least thirty *départements.* The candidates must be ranked, and the voter has the freedom (rather theoretical, below) to substitute his own write-in choice over the official candidates. The voter may also take names from one list and put them in another: this splitting of the ticket is called *panachage* or *variegation.* This, too, is subject to a crippling proviso, mentioned below.

A party list that obtains *a majority of all votes cast is declared elected in its entirety,* while all the other competing lists get no seats at all. If no one list obtains a majority, then *apparentement* may begin to function. The votes of all the affiliated lists are added together, and if *their* total vote amounts to a majority, the *apparentement* is declared elected. All the seats available are then apportioned among the member parties according to proportional representation on the basis of the method of the "strongest average." In other words, the seats are apportioned according to the system of 1946, excepting that now only the votes of the *apparentés* lists are counted. *Apparentés* parties that obtain less than 5 percent of the total vote get no seats.

(4) Article 1 of the Law of May 9, 1951, defines the electoral system for France as "a majority-list system with the *département* as the electoral district, with one ballot, with provisions for the alliance (*apparentement*) of lists and the possibility of ticket-splitting and preferential voting." In ticket-splitting, the voter is given the opportunity to write the names of candidates of other lists on his ballot. In preferential voting he can list in his own order of preference the names of the candidates on the ballot. But the law also specifies that at least one half the ballots must be modified by the voters to have validity for ticket-splitting or preferences. If this proviso were not inserted, the legislators thought, the confusion and weakening of majorities would not be worth the freedom allowed by the elector.

(5) By-elections, not allowed in the Law of 1946, are held by utilizing the system of the Third

Parliamentary and Executive Structure of the Fourth Republic

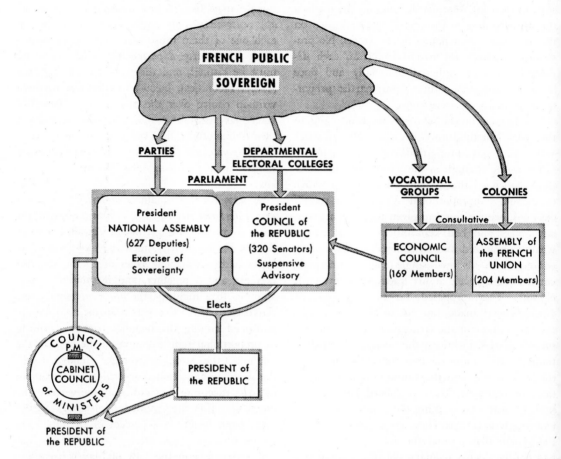

Republic: single-member districts, and run-off elections, with majority voting.

(6) The law does not apply identically to the *départements* of the Seine and Seine-et-Oise (comprising 8 constituencies and 75 seats), but P.R. prevails, not on the basis of the highest average, but on the "largest remainder," which favors the party lists with the fewest votes.

The tables of 1951 election results (p. 337 and p. 402) show that the object all sublime of the law was attained: (1) the Communists and R.P.F. received seats distinctly below their proportion of the total votes, for the Communists would not affiliate and the de Gaullists could or would not find allies; and (2) the Communists and new Rightists got the disproportionate advantage.

Altogether, *there were seventeen different combinations,* a drastic commentary on French political parties soon to be masters of the legislature

and the Executive. The Communists combined with none—how pure! The de Gaullists joined other parties in twelve constituencies; the Third Force in eighteen; in thirty-five, the Third Force (Socialists, M.R.P. *plus* Socialists *plus* Radicals) joined Right-wing Independents and Peasants; in thirteen, Radicals, conservatives, and progressive Catholics combined; in four, Socialists affiliated with the Radicals but not the M.R.P. The electors were confronted with no less than eleven national party lists.

The *apparentement* indicated that a majority had been attained but not for what that mixed bag stood for; party responsibility was confused at the very source. Some 9,000,000, or 48 percent of the electorate, voted for the Communists and the de Gaullists. All the middle parties lost votes, but wherever affiliation took place, the other parties gained seats and the Communists got none.

In thirty-seven *départements,* the affiliated parties obtained an absolute majority and divided all the seats among them. In fourteen *départements,* the Communist Party was the largest single party but obtained no seat.

Taking France as a whole, the Communist Party won one seat for every 52,000 votes; the R.P.F., one for every 40,000; the Socialists and the M.R.P., one for every 30,000; and the Radicals and the Right, one for every 28,000. Under the new law, the Communists won 106 members; under the old, they would have had 181. The Gaullists won 121 but would have had 155. Together they could have destroyed the democratic legislature. The M.R.P. should have had 63, not 84, by pure P.R.; the Socialists, 67 not 105.

P.R.'s Value and Disvalue. The large constituencies have made the personality of the candidate rather less important than the program; the party machine tends to control this and to consign candidates to places on its list *not* decided by the electors. Yet there are places where local nomination of the candidate is practiced among Socialists, Radicals, and Rightists challenging party domination. On the whole, parties have been given more backbone. If this goes too far, they will be even more intransigent in the Assembly than now. Parties unable to "affiliate" were reduced in size—a "political" good.

The results of *apparentements* are not altogether sound, on the criterion of securing clarity and responsibility of parties. For these were made not by the people but by the party machines. A voter might find he had helped to elect M.R.P. when he was Socialist or, what would be more painful, a Catholic might secure the election of a Socialist. This, again, might be an ultimate good, for it is based on the parties with the nearest affinities working with each other. Moreover, the electorate is forced into *big* choices between competing parties, if not the obtaining of a party that is sculptured minutely to his individual taste. In 1951 the choice was certainly between the middle-of-the-road parties that favored the democratic system and those that wished to overturn it for heaven knows what alternative.

We merely add a word on the system operating in the excepted areas of Seine and Seine-et-Oise. The method of the "highest remainder" is this:

The number of seats is divided into the total vote and a quotient is so obtained. If a party list attains the quotient, it gets a seat. For the remaining seats, it will make claims on whatever votes it has according to the *remainder* after its quotient has been subtracted from the votes it has polled. It was deliberately introduced into the statute for the areas in question to give added seats to the weaker parties. For the stronger ones (here the Communists and the R.P.F.) cannot obtain more seats than the number they are entitled to on the basis of the quotient plus one.

The War for the Elections of 1956

The pathological behavior of the political groups in the Assembly and Cabinet during 1951 to 1955 came to a head in October 1955, with the incoherence and recriminations over the North African policy in that month. The Assembly was a quagmire, the Cabinet a stricken field of battle from which the corpses were carried out (p. 429). Prime Minister Faure claimed that there could be no continuity of domestic recovery, colonial readjustment, and foreign relations unless a new Assembly was elected. His own bias was to benefit his Center-Right coalition and to thwart his rival Mendès-France of the Left wing of his own Radical Party.

On October 24, 1955, he introduced a bill for terminating the Assembly in December 1955 or January 1956, some six months before the legal date of termination, June 1956. He had had more than enough of "hairbreadths' escapes in the imminent deadly breach," by provoked votes of confidence. He proposed no change of the electoral system, as his Cabinet was divided on its nature!

At once the pathological obstructiveness of the Assembly sprung into action. Faure was accused of self-seeking, to maintain his Center-Right coalition by a popular appeal against an Assembly that was despised by the public. His chief enemies were two leaders of his own Radical Party, Mendès-France and Daladier. The former wished the postponement of elections for two reasons: to get a better grip on the party, whose organization he had captured in May, and to secure a return to the *scrutin d'arrondissement* method of voting (p. 310), without P.R., since this had been so disproportionately favorable to his party in the Third Republic and would enable him to form second-ballot alliances with the Socialists and the U.D.S.R. and various Left-moderates for a Left-wing program. We refer to this electoral system as the district system, for brevity.

Every trick in the parliamentary trade in France was now employed to defeat the proposal of prompt elections, for the Deputies had to give the impression of voting for it, as the public liked it, while the individual Deputies wanted to kill it in order to stay in office to the last syllable of legally recorded time. Furthermore, the Communists decided to throw their votes in favor of early elections, since on principle they had to show the "masses" that they believed in a popular mandate, while they could calculate that (1) they might gain power by alliances with the Socialists in the second ballot of the district system—between them, Maurice Thorez claimed, all the seats in twenty of the most populous *départements* of France!—or (2) do as well as before, which was perfectly adequate to disrupt the work of the Assembly, rule or ruin. The M.R.P. favored the present system. The de Gaullists did not want the district system since it might assist the Communists and Socialists. Thus, the issue of what electoral system should replace the one of 1951, if any, was thrust in as the delayer of the proposal for early elections.

The Commission of Universal Suffrage of the Assembly was plagued with some eleven rival proposals for electoral change as a prior consideration to early elections, on the grounds that it would be useless to have elections which might produce as incoherent an Assembly as the present one—as if any electoral system short of a dictatorial one could remove this incoherence! The rival proposals went all the way from pure P.R. to the district system. Voting on the main proposal was delayed by debates on the Government's general policy. Faure's demands for confidence were defeated by less than the constitutional absolute majority, and this ruined his proposals without his gaining the weapon of dissolution, available because Mendès-France's Cabinet had fallen less than eighteen months before (p. 428).

At one time the Commission on Universal Suffrage, by 22 to 19, voted for undiluted P.R., which would have given the Communists as many as forty additional seats. It even considered, but rejected, the old-fashioned *scrutin de liste* (p. 309).

The Assembly debated the district system of Mendès-France—this was given a smashing defeat. Each Deputy was considering only which system would bring him back to Paris. Day after day, vote after vote, the war proceeded. The Faure Government was sometimes saved narrowly by Communist votes, against its pleasure, and Thorez himself had returned to the Assemblies, scenting electoral carrion. The Radical Party Congress met (November 6, 1955) and, by supporting Mendès-France's leadership, backed his policy as that of the *militants* in passionate hostility to that of M. Faure, a leader of that same party, and many of the more conservatively inclined Radical Deputies.

Meanwhile, the Council of the Republic, being more Center and Right than the Assembly, sent back the bill with the district system as an amendment. How wise Mendès-France had been to carry through the constitutional amendment increasing the powers of the Council in November 30, 1954! The Assembly's bill for early elections went back to the Council. It reinserted the district-system amendment, and the bill came before the Assembly a third time, November 15. The Mendès-France delayers and others now secured a new delay by demanding that before the bill was proceeded with the Prime Minister should provide a new set of districts, 487 in 89 *départements*. There had been no such list since 1936, and great shifts of population had occurred. This entailed the possibility of 487 objections. The Ministry of the Interior and the prefects provided the schedule within about ten days. This proposal had been supported by 334 to 265 votes. The de Gaullists had voted one morning 52 in favor of consideration of this system, and then in the evening 64 in favor of demanding that redistricting be examined first by the Commission —that is, to delay the district system and the election.

Twenty-four days of debate had produced a futility. *Le Figaro* wrote, rightly, "The National Assembly has given us—after three weeks of insane discussion—the measure of its incoherence." During this time M. Faure had pushed his proposal through twice by calling for votes of confidence— that is, a threat to resign and perhaps dissolve the Assembly. By November 17 the Assembly had rejected the Council of the Republic's rider of the district system. The election would be in late January at best. If then, why not wait till June or, say, May?

On November 26, M. Faure called for a decisive vote of confidence. The debate lasted three days, and on November 29, he was defeated by 318 to 218. The opposition parties (no less than the Government parties) were so split internally, and so incoherent in their aggregate action, that they had committed suicide—for 318 votes is above the correct "dose" (slang) of 312 that make an absolute majority. Hence, Faure had the right to demand a dissolution of the Assembly as allowed by the Constitution, Article 51 (see p. 418). This had never been resorted to since May 16, 1877, the history of which we have narrated on page 310. The Deputies seem to have thought Faure would not have the courage to use his authority. He did, by the procedure and with the political consequences analyzed later, on page 420. An election followed on January 2, 1956, the electoral system used was the one used in 1951, because the already described filibustering and egocentric National Assembly had failed to vote a new one.

THE CAMPAIGN AND ELECTION RESULTS ARE PRESENTED ON PP. 399-403.

Conduct of Elections

French law does not limit election expenditures or regulate the receipt of donation of funds for political purposes. The laws (going back to 1914) prescribe an approach to equality of placarding, in order to prevent clashes between the parties for placard space, overpasting, and destruction and to reduce corruption by means of overpayments for billposters. The purpose was to give an equal opportunity to the poorer candidates. Special places are therefore provided by the municipality for placards, an equal surface for each list. No placarding elsewhere during an election is permissible; nor are advertisements that have the same purpose as open placarding. All get equality in equally frequented places.

The parties pay per list a bond of 20,000 francs per candidate. This entitles them to a full grant of paper from the election officials—enough for so many placards, so many notices of meetings, envelopes, ballots, and two circulars. The lists choose their own printers. The bills are affixed at State cost. The circulars are government-franked.

The State pays for the printing and bill-posting and for the gasoline the candidates use, scaled according to the size of the constituency. If a list of candidates gets less than 5 percent of the votes, its bond is forfeited. Those above 5 percent, get their bonds and bill-posting and gasoline reimbursed.

French parties are inclined to many more, but smaller, meetings than the parties of Britain and place more value on meetings, as the expenditure on placarding has been limited. The placards can be very vivid, for the French are artists.

In spite of P.R. and large constituencies, the Deputies and aspirants nurse their districts intimately and continuously. The larger the area, the more time they spend in it. The Deputy (or candidate) runs errands for the place in which he is known in the *département,* pushing the interests and grievances of his electorate in the various Ministries. Residence does not apply (as in the United States), but there is not so much wandering as in Britain by candidates on the search for a seat.

Parties are allowed each one radio program of ten minutes and one of five, and one five-minute TV program, at times settled by lot.

The parties that are near enough in outlook to each other to have a chance of winning away some of their neighbor's votes tend to be embittered beyond the passion of British parties, because a few votes to the neighbor on the Left or Right of one's own party may make all the difference. Nothing is expected to be given or taken from the extreme parties. Yet, it is the "neighbors," those with whom one would arrange an *apparentement,* that will need a spirit of cooperativeness later, when the groups meet each other in the Assembly.

The old criticism of the electioneering result, so far as a mandate to the Assembly is concerned, still holds good. The electorate is not voting for a Government, for it does not know which constellation of parties will get back to form what kind of coalition.

Corruption. The corruption of the elections by "repeater" votes, by bribery, by intimidation, by stuffing ballot boxes, by treats and widespread gifts that marked nineteenth-century and even twentieth-century elections (particularly in the conservative, rural, mountainous, backward areas) has greatly abated. The law has had its effect. Challenges of elections are made to the credentials bureaus of the Assembly (and the other bodies, also). The bureaus report to the Assembly. In the election of 1951 no question was raised about 341 Deputies (in 75 constituencies). In the case of 150 Deputies from 34 constituencies only trivial or unsubstantiated complaints were certified. No action was proposed to be taken against them. In 36 constituencies with 136 Deputies, the complaints were of sufficient gravity to be reported and so were debated by the Assembly. The largest part by far in this group were in French overseas territories (not the technical classification, merely a conventional one, see p. 455). In these places, backwardness, discontent, illiteracy, and intimidation caused the derelictions.

The faults of behavior in France itself were chiefly trivial legal irregularities. (We omit the unchallenged and unexamined allegations that the prefects had in some cases been the midwives of *apparentement* arrangements to satisfy the Government.)

One trick alleged was to claim a valid *apparentement,* with as many as thirty-six *départements* included, and then not to fight a genuine campaign except in ten of them! The Assembly let the challenge fall.

There were complaints about a lack of title to the party label; about literature distributed by organizations for the benefit of certain candidates, outside the arrangements allowed by the law as before described; occasionally, about treating and bribery (very rare, indeed).

The Assembly voted on these subjects by strict party alignments. We must conclude by asserting that the elections showed a high degree of purity.

The Deputies

Payment. French Deputies have been paid salaries ever since 1791, with intervals in 1815 to 1848 and for a short time during the empire of Napoleon III. The Constitution, Article 25, requires it. The amount is fixed according to the salary of a category of civil servant designated by the Assembly from time to time. It is now equated to that of a *conseiller d'état,* and is 2,000,000 francs a year. The other assemblies pay their members

also. The Senators are covered by the same article as the Deputies. We have made some observation on the practice of some political parties in demanding from their Deputies a regular contribution from their salary to the party funds (see p. 35 and p. 356. The salary is worth about $6000 per annum. About one half is not taxable, being regarded as expenses of office. In addition to this payment, there are other material compensations: lower rates for railway fares; franking of letters written in the assemblies themselves; free telephone privileges from the assemblies to people in Paris; a contributory pension scheme, with payments up to a maximum of 75 percent of the prevailing salary but the total amount dependent on the length of service.

Immunity. The Constitution says:

> ART. 21. No member of the Parliament may be prosecuted, sought by the police, arrested, detained or tried because of opinions expressed or votes cast by him in the exercise of his function

> ART. 22. No member of the Parliament may be prosecuted or arrested during his term of office for a criminal offense except with the authorization of the Chamber of which he is a member, or in the case of a major crime. The detention or prosecution of a member of the Parliament shall be suspended if the Chamber of which he is a member requests it.

Article 21 gives the members the freedom they need to carry out their function with candor and without fear. Article 22 is the sheet anchor of freedom from the menaces and revenge of the Executive whom the members of parliament are elected to control. We have noticed the rise of this privilege in the development of the British constitution (pp. 38–40).

In the Third Republic, the immunity in the latter case applied only when Parliament was actually in session. Its extension is the consequence of the experience of various countries that have lost their democracy partly by the Executive's exertion of the power of arrest. Of course, if caught in the act of committing a crime (in *flagrante delicto* the police would arrest, and the courts condemn, though the latter have shown leniency (for example, in regard to Communists arrested, see p

,50) in judgment. This is out of special respect or the sovereignty of the Assembly. The Communists have particularly benefited from the Assembly's complaisance and the courts' tolerance. The Government in 1949 had obtained from the Assembly the right to prosecute three violently expressive Malgasy Deputies; the charge was non-capital, as permitted by the Assembly's committee, but the Government then prosecuted for treason. This matter was regulated by a statute passed in 1953 after four years of wrangling between the Assembly and the Council of the Republic. Immunity was further protected by a law of 1951, which required newspapers edited by Deputies to name another person to be responsible at law, because the prosecutions of Deputies for libel in the newspapers they edited was a threat to immunity.

The amendment to the Constitution (December 954) annulled immunity outside the parliamentary sessions (see Appendix). The arrested Deputy keeps his vote by proxy.

The Chamber of the Assembly. The chamber is a hemicycle, and its diameter is not very big, only forty yards. In the center, facing the halfcircle of seats is a raised platform, mounted by steps. This is the *tribune* from which speeches may be delivered, and often are. In its middle is another platform, smaller and raised again. On this is the chair (*le fauteuil*) for the President, and in front of it is a great desk (*le bureau*). A little behind the President and on his right sits the Secretary General; on either side of the desk are the secretaries and officials who take the reports. At the *tribune,* in front of the President is a parapet, where the speakers stand or pace about when speaking from the *tribune.* At the foot of this speaking platform is space and desks for the official reporters of debate.

The Deputies' benches rise in ten tiers, facing the President. Nine stairways from top to bottom cut through them, with additional stairways for the five upper tiers. The rows contain desks, one for each Deputy, so numbered and appropriated (see p. 338 on seating).

The central portions of the two lowest benches are kept *for the Government* and are so marked in gold lettering. To the left of these Government seats—that is, the left hand of the Ministers —are benches reserved for the permanent Commissions, to seat their Presidents and *rapporteurs*. **Occupational Composition.** The occupational composition of the Assembly after the election of 1951 is not any more than any other assembly in the world a proportional representative mirror of the occupations in the nation. It hardly matters, for the lobbies and pressure groups as we have shown are very active among parties and are given special representation in the Economic Council.

Here is the occupational picture of the Assembly shortly after June 1951. For convenience it includes the figures relating to the Council of the Republic also.

II. THE ORGANIZATION OF NATIONAL ASSEMBLY

The legislative-governmental assemblies—the National Assembly and the Council of the Republic —are together called the Parliament of France (Constitution, Art. 5). National sovereignty is vested in the people in a "republic, indivisible, secularistic (laic), democratic and social." That sovereignty is exercisable through the Deputies of the National Assembly, except for possible referenda on constitutional amendments. Yet the Council of the Republic has powers of delay, and these, in practice, modify this formal vesting of sole sovereignty in the Assembly.

The Size of the Two Chambers. The Constitution does not state the size of the National Assembly, but it stipulates that the Council of the Republic shall not be less than 250 or more than 320. The size is settled in the electoral laws. These are separate and outside the Constitution, as we have seen.

Based on the electoral law for the National Assembly, this body since 1951 is composed of 627 seats.[1]

The Council of the Republic was composed of 315 councilors (the Third Republic Senate had 314 members) according to the law of October 27, 1946; the law of September 24, 1948, amended this (and other matters) to reach the maximum constitutionally permitted of 320.

[1] The preceding Assemblies were: October 1945, 586; June 1946, 586; November 1946, 618.

Occupations of Deputies in the National Assembly, 1951, and Council of Republic, 1954

OCCUPATIONS		Totals	Communists	Progressives	Socialists	Radicals	U.D.S.R.	M.R.P.	Independent Republicans	Peasants	French Independents	R.P.F.	No Group	Council of Republic
Agriculture		66	1	—	6	7	—	8	5	18	—	15	—	53
Seafaring		1	—	—	—	—	—	—	—	—	—	—	—	—
Commercial and Industrial	Employers, directors	30	—	—	—	7	—	2	7	2	—	10	2	25
	Company directors	5	—	—	—	—	—	1	—	1	·	3	—	3
	Merchants, businessmen	14	1	—	2	2	—	1	2	1	—	5	—	11
	Artisans	2	—	—	1	—	—	—	—	—	—	—	1	2
Salaried, private Business	Engineers	18	1	—	2	1	—	4	2	1	—	7	—	20
	Managers	22	4	—	3	1	—	4	2	1	1	5	1	4
	Employees	15	11	—	2	—	—	2	—	—	—	—	—	6
	Workers	42	33	—	3	—	—	4	—	—	—	2	—	7
Medical	Physicians, surgeons	22	—	—	8	5	1	1	1	—	—	6	—	16
	Pharmacists	7	—	—	2	1	1	2	—	—	—	1	—	5
	Veterinary	5	—	—	—	1	1	—	1	—	—	2	—	5
	Para-medical	4	2	—	1	—	—	—	—	—	—	1	—	1
Judicial and Liberal	Attorneys	67	1	—	10	17	—	9	10	4	1	13	2	47
	Notaries	6	—	—	—	2	—	—	1	3	—	—	—	8
	Solicitors	3	—	—	—	—	—	—	—	1	—	2	—	2
	Judicial officials	3	—	—	—	—	—	—	1	1	—	1	—	1
	Legal advisers	2	—	—	—	—	—	2	—	—	—	—	—	1
	Other liberal	5	—	—	—	—	—	1	3	—	—	1	—	11
	Clergy	2	—	—	—	—	—	1	1	—	—	—	—	0
	Journalists, editors	37	3	1	10	3	1	7	4	1	—	7	—	13
	Men of letters, artists	2	—	—	—	1	—	—	1	—	—	—	—	2
	Architects	3	1	—	—	—	—	—	—	—	—	2	—	1
Teachers	Full professors	14	—	1	2	2	—	6	1	—	—	2	—	5
	Professors second-rank	28	4	—	13	4	1	5	—	—	—	1	—	13
	Lower grades education	28	8	—	19	1	—	—	—	—	—	—	—	12
	Concerned with education	1	—	—	1	—	—	—	—	—	—	—	—	0
	Private schools	1	1	—	—	—	—	—	—	—	—	—	—	3
Government Officials, active or retired	Magistrates	2	—	—	—	1	—	—	—	—	—	1	—	0
	Higher Civil Service	18	—	—	1	3	1	4	1	—	—	8	—	16
	Ministerial Cabinets	4	—	—	—	3	—	—	—	—	—	1	—	0
	Higher and intermediate officials	14	2	1	3	3	—	4	—	—	—	1	—	17
Military, active or retired	Generals	6	—	—	—	—	—	—	—	—	—	6	—	1
	High officers and subalterns	1	—	—	—	—	—	—	—	—	—	—	1	2
State Railroads	Managerial	2	—	—	—	—	—	1	—	—	—	1	—	3
	Employees	3	1	—	—	—	—	2	—	—	—	—	—	0
	Workers	7	7	—	—	—	—	—	—	—	—	—	—	1
Posts, telegraphs, etc.		2	1	—	1	—	—	—	—	—	—	—	—	0
Directors of nonprofit organizations		3	—	—	—	—	1	2	—	—	—	—	—	2
No information		27	2	1	5	1	2	10	2	2	—	2	—	1
Totals		544*	91	4	95	66	9	83	45	36	2	106	7	320

* Most overseas Deputies and some others not canvassed. Hence this total and not 627.

Length of Office. The National Assembly is elected for five years—but it can be dissolved, on certain conditions (see p. 418) any time after its first eighteen months of office. The Council of the Republic, first elected in 1946, was given a term of two years only, by one of the transitional provisions of the Constitution. It was then, by the law mentioned above, endowed with *a term of six years.* Whereas the members of the National Assembly are all elected at one time, the Council of the Republic is elected one half each three years. The first renewal was in May 1952; the second in May 1955.

The National Assembly, as we have seen, is elected in equal electoral constituencies, by P.R. The Council of the Republic is elected indirectly, by electoral colleges in the *départements,* as explained later (Chapter 7). Its Deputies are eligible at twenty-five years of age, the Senators at thirty-five. Two corporate wills confront each other; they are *bound* by sheer separateness itself to be different.

The Powers of the National Assembly

It is useful to enumerate the powers of the National Assembly.

1. The Assembly's vote is necessary for a declaration of war—and needs concurrent opinion of Council of the Republic.

2. It "alone" enacts laws. It may not delegate this right. The purpose of the latter proviso is to make it illegal to pass laws endowing the Executive with special powers or *plein pouvoirs* or a limited blank check to make decrees, as happened in the Third Republic. The Fourth Republic has been obliged to ignore the proviso that was desired by the three big parties and some of the conservative-nationalists. The proviso was contained in the defeated draft constitution also.

3. It alone has the right of initiative in financial appropriations.

4. It audits the national accounts—assisted by the Court of Accounts.

5. No amnesty is grantable except by a law— hence this is in the hands of the National Assembly.

6. Its legislative act is required for the ratifica-

tion of international treaties, in the absence of which they are not valid.

7. The Assembly, in joint session with the Council of the Republic, elects the President of the Republic.

8. Its officers have duties, in some cases, to act in place of a President of the Republic, and to lead a Government during an election resulting from a dissolution.

9. It may indict the President of the Republic for high treason.

10. Its vote of confidence is needed for the appointment of the Prime Minister [2] and his Council of Ministers (Cabinet), after the former has been designated by the President of the Republic and the latter by the Prime Minister.

11. Its continued confidence is necessary to the holding of office by Ministers—shown in a vote of confidence demanded by the Prime Minister or by a vote of censure initiated in the National Assembly. This is the implementation of responsible cabinet government laid down and given detail in Articles 48 to 51.

    Its power to defeat a Government by vote of censure that automatically entails collective resignation of the Council of Ministers is absolute.

    The Council of the Republic is excluded from the authority to keep the Council of Ministers responsible.

12. It is the forum for the indictment of Ministers for crimes and misdemeanors in their functions—the High Court renders judgment, as in an indictment of the President of the Republic.

13. The High Court of Justice is elected by the National Assembly, legislative session by session.

14. It initiates, and is the major authority in, the amendment of the Constitution (pp. 331–332).

15. It elects a number of members to the Constitutional Committee, which is the watch-

[2] The official title is President of the Council of Ministers. We will, however, refer to him as Prime Minister rather than by the more customary term, *Premier.*

dog over the supremacy of the Constitution to the legislative power, and its presiding officer is *ex officio* a member of the Committee.

Hence, (1) the National Assembly is the chief legislative chamber; (2) it is the chief authority for the voting of the budget; (3) it is the creator, discipliner, invigilator, and cashierer of the Council of Ministers—that is, the responsible Executive —and a powerful master of the presidency of the Republic, the titular Executive and possessor of important personal powers; (4) it is potent in international commitments and war and peace; and (5) it is the initiator of judicial action against the Executive officers mentioned.

It is the center of gravity of French sovereign political life. Its character gives character to the Executive, and its character is largely that of the French political parties to which, therefore, we were obliged to give so much attention.

A Distracted Opposition

The efficiency of the British House of Commons is immensely raised by the existence of a coherent, concentrated, and continuous Opposition. It is founded on one party. The multiplicity of parties in France means that the Opposition is a fortuitous gathering of groups opposed to the Government and its timetable, each for different reasons on different bills, and this occasional constellation is transformed after any one deed of opposition is performed. This situation puts a premium on maneuvering for personal ambition, to help pressure groups, and on irresponsibility for principle. There are many oppositions; there is no one articulated Opposition. The consequences are seen in what follows, and in the feebleness of Cabinets (pp. 407–441).

The Procedure and Organization of the Assembly

In France, procedure had to be established *de novo* in 1789. There was no body of precedent as in Britain in 1789. French parliamentary procedure was then embodied in autonomously elaborated Standing Orders by the Revolutionary assemblies. But Napoleon I and the restored monarchy to 1871 interfered in the rules by which the assem-

blies made law and regulated other business, for a power over the procedure of a legislative body i a power over the freedom of its will.

The Third Republic's Chamber of Deputies adopted those of its predecessor, and then revised the Standing Orders, in its autonomy, from time to time; so did the assemblies that paved the way for the new Constitution. They were adopted in final shape in March 1947 (the Council of the Republic, June 1946). They are almost identical with those of the Third Republic, and these again drew very largely on the practices of the Second Republic. The Standing Orders, and much of their interpretation as cases have required, have then a substantial history of being tried and tested and made into habits.[3] The accounts and digests of precedents, which rule the rules, are in two large volumes by M. Eugene Pierre,[4] formerly secretary general of the Chamber of Deputies. They are the equivalent of Sir Erskine May's *Parliamentary Procedure* for the British Parliament and *Hind'. Precedents* for the U.S. Congress.

Duration. Nothing in the Constitution seems to prevent an Assembly from prolonging or reducing its own term by ordinary law. The Assembly of November 1946 enacted its own termination five months before the five-year limit, and a five-year term is settled for future assemblies, on May 31 The law had great majorities in its favor, but it was not a formal constitutional amendment. The future will decide. It is desirable that in time of war a Parliament may prolong its own life, as in Britain and France in World War II. Before such emergency, it is the more urgent that leaders and people make sure that their parties are composed of men of responsible probity.

Self-dissolution. The Assembly can use its power of amendment to dissolve itself. The Socialists, in the interests of popular control, injected this into the draft constitution, allowing self-dissolution by a two-thirds majority. The clause was dropped General de Gaulle, an innocent, tried to get the Assembly to commit hara-kiri (p. 363) so that he

[3] The history and text of the rules are in Roger Bonnard *Les Réglements des Assemblées Législatives . . . depui. 1789,* Paris, 1926.

[4] *Traité de droit politique, électoral et parlementaire* Paris, Vol. 1, 1902 (being the second edition), and Vol. II Supplement, 1924.

might take advantage of the wave of sentiment in his favor in 1948, vainly.

Sessions. Under the Third Republic, the Chambers met in ordinary session each year on the second Tuesday in January for a minimum length of five months. After this time the Government could close the session, and then could not call the Chambers again for the rest of the year. But, in fact, as the budget was never voted in the limits of the session, the Government always called the Chambers into session for longer.

During the session the Government had the right of adjourning the Chambers, and it used it to get a respite for itself as well as to provide the Deputies and Senators with vacations. This practice aroused the suspicions of the Chambers against a too-potent Executive.

Under the Fourth Republic, the rights of the Government in the matter of the Assembly's sessions have been abolished. Article 9 of the Constitution empowers the National Assembly to convene by right every year of the second Tuesday in January. It says nothing about adjournments by the Government. The total duration of interruptions of each session may not exceed four months, and adjournments of more than ten days must be considered as interruptions. This means an eight-month session. If the budget is not passed by December 31, the end of the financial year, the clocks are stopped (it happens almost every year) shortly before midnight (as happens in the United States Congress) until the business is concluded, though it may take a few days into the New Year.

The decision on adjournments—"interruptions" —is the Assembly's. It has therefore been chary of using it, being sensitive to the popular charge of lack of conscientiousness. Whereas the Chamber of Deputies sat for about 140 sittings a year, the present Assembly has never sat for less than 218 (in 1947) and in 1950 sat for 243, in 1953, 230; in 1954, 231. This is more than the House of Commons because the Assembly sits Saturdays and sometimes Sundays, though not on Mondays. Yet its total hours of session are less than one half the House of Commons'.

It must not be thought that the denial to the Cabinet of a right of adjournment is an unmixed political blessing. Ministers are the administrators of great departments of governmental affairs and the top managers of the activities of scores of thousands of public servants. The incessant occupation with parliamentary business, especially in so turbulent, volatile, and unstable an Assembly, is nervewracking and necessarily precludes the continuous and timely dispatch of business. This is proven true even in Britain, with a highly competent collaborating Civil Service. A breathing space is urgent in the omnicompetent State for the managers and staffs.

It was with no sinister purpose, then, that, as already mentioned (p. 334), the Assembly voted in July 1953 a proposal for constitutional revision to the effect that the Government have the right of adjournment—but not until the Assembly has sat for seven months, not counting interruptions of eight days or under. It would begin the ordinary session in October (much like the House of Commons), and so elect officers and committees and save much valuable time which, when so spent in January, was one of the impediments to the passing of the budget within the financial year and the ordinary session.

An Intersessional Watchdog Committee. Long recesses occasion anxiety in those who believe in popular and parliamentary control over the Executive. The Weimar Constitution was the first to establish an intersessional watchdog committee of the legislature. Article 12 of the French Constitution says:

> When the National Assembly is not sitting, its secretariat, exercising control over the actions of the Council of Ministers, may convoke the Parliament; it must do this upon the request of one third of the Deputies or of the President of the Council of Ministers.

The secretariat is the Bureau of the Assembly (p. 380); hence the importance of its method of composition and struggles to capture it.

Article 12 has been invoked twice. In September 1949, during the summer recess, the Government devalued the franc. The Communist Party, avid for agitation, demanded the recall of the Assembly. It expected the R.P.F., the other extreme, to join it, making over the one-third votes required. The de Gaullists refused. The Bureau itself rejected the demand, 15 to 6.

In July 1953 the Laniel Cabinet (p. 414) announced a policy of reducing civil service pay. Very damaging strikes broke out, owing to fear that a general onslaught on the workers' standard of living was intended. By letter and telegram, over a period of days, 211 requests for a convening of the Assembly accumulated. The Bureau declared four signatures to be false. The majority of the Assembly was averse to a recall, and the Bureau rejected it, 10 to 8. Another agitation for recall gained impetus. This time the Bureau, forced into action, used delaying tactics, taking three weeks, so that the recall became effective only one week before the Assembly would have met ordinarily.

The Socialists were angry at such tactics. They submitted a constitutional amendment to make recall require a *majority* but to be automatic and immediate; this is one of the amendments of December 1954. (Appendix.)

The President and Bureau of the National Assembly. The functions of presiding over the deliberations of the Assembly and organizing its staff and services is vested in a Bureau of twenty-four members. This is elected annually. It is one of the parts of the procedure of the Assembly that was in part regulated by the Constitution itself, though its practice is the delicate embodiment of hundreds of precedents reaching back to 1789.

Article 11 required that the Bureau be elected annually, when the session begins, and that such election be by proportional representation of the groups. This stipulation gave the groups a grip over the very vitals of the Assembly, and was particularly pressed by the Communist Party. The Bureau of twenty-four consists of the President, six Vice Presidents (who deputize for the former in taking the chair), fourteen secretaries, and three *questeurs*. The secretaries supervise the counting of the votes and the drafting of the minutes, and the attendance of some of them for this purpose is obligatory. The *questeurs* attend to the physical, administrative, and financial problems of the Assembly.

The "Speakership." The election of a presiding officer (and his adjutants) never was so smooth an affair as the modern election of his British counterpart, the Speaker of the House of Commons. For the presiding officer—the President of the Bureau—has never been taken out of political strife and neutralized the better to fulfill his function of interpreting the rules, as in Britain (pp. 107–108). Hence his election is always a time of tension and conflict. The Chamber of Deputies did not use proportional representation; and the introduction of it increased rather than calmed political passion and had to be abolished in December 1954.

The Bureau (and consequently its officers) is elected *only for a session,* whereas the Speaker of the House of Commons is elected for a whole Parliament. The first sitting at a new session of the Assembly is presided over by the oldest deputy—by age—and the six youngest members in the role of secretaries.

In the Assembly of 1946 to 1951 the oldest deputy was Marcel Cachin, a Communist Party leader of venerable vintage. He took the opportunity to enable the Communists to throw the election of the Bureau into a violent uproar, especially over the issue of the proportional election of the Bureau. Marcel Cachin refused to submit the list of the Bureau to the Assembly for its approval, which is necessary. For the Communists claimed that a fair *interpretation* of the Constitution required that they the largest ought, by proportional representation, get the post of First Vice President! He and his party were forced to leave the Assembly—and the second-oldest deputy took his place. The Communist Party appealed to the Constitutional Committee for a ruling—unsuccessfully (see p. 333).

The reason for the battle (even physical) lies in the functions assigned to the President, and therefore, his senior Vice President, in case a Caretaker Government is needed during elections brought on by dissolution of the Assembly. This is a ridiculous involvement, produced by the exaggerated *ingéniosité* of constitution-makers anxious to provide for every possible case conceivable. It would not matter if only presiding over debates were the question.

Hence the amendments of December 1954 substitute majority vote for P.R. in the election of the Assembly's Bureau.

The President's Status. The President of the Assembly is virtually the second most important political figure after the President of the Republic. The present Constitution itself gives him a more political partisan character than under the Third Republic. He substitutes for the President of the Republic when the office is vacant through death, resignation, or other circumstance or for reasons voted by Parliament, until the new President is elected. He promulgates the laws if the President of the Republic does not do so in the time set down in the Constitution. The Constitution refers to "customary consultations" which the President of the Republic undertakes, leading up to his designation of a Prime Minister: the President of the Assembly is a customary consultant, in the first degree. When the Assembly is dissolved, he could become Prime Minister in the interim Cabinet till December 1954; since then only if the Cabinet has been censured.

He does not, customarily, speak or vote. But this has happened exactly when, in a sense, it should not—on important and critical occasions. Thus, in July 1926, to refer to precedents, M. Herriot, President of the Chamber of Deputies, did not want the Briand Government to get the decree-legislation powers it asked for. He went down to his seat, and his speech overturned the Government. Herriot was then called on to head a new Ministry! In June 1935 Fernand Bouisson, Socialist, President of the Chamber since 1926, resigned to become Prime Minister. When he was overthrown in a few days, he came back to the chair! In December 1949 M. Herriot, once again President of the Assembly, decided that the Bidault Government might fall as a result of the opposition of some of the members of his own Radical Party to the budget—Herriot voted to uphold the Government, as an example to his party, which it followed.

Presidents of the Chamber stepped into the prime ministership at least eight times in the Third Republic. In that period also, three Presidents of the Chamber and five Presidents of the Senate became Presidents of the Republic itself—directly from one office to the other. Others were spoken of. In January 1946 Félix Gouin, President of the Constituent Assembly, replaced General de Gaulle as chief executive. Vincent Auriol, who then succeeded Gouin as President of the Assembly, became first President of the Republic.

The Assembly President in January 1954 was M. Le Troquer, a Socialist; elected by 300 votes of Socialists, Communists, Radicals and some Gaullists. He vowed to "preside as an impartial umpire, careful to respect the rights of all and to see that they are respected," and then reviewed France's political problems—quite contrary to British customs. He pleaded for the development of an *ésprit de corps* in the Assembly's representative function. He resumed the Third Republic's custom of wearing evening dress. In January 1955 he was dumped in favor of an M.R.P. nominee, since that party thereby wished to show Prime Minister Mendès-France, who relied on Socialist votes, which party was really master. This new President, M. Schneiter, was in December to advise the President of the Republic on dissolution that could favor his party coalition.

Though the President of the Assembly may not be as crudely partisan as the Speaker of the U.S. House of Representatives (because that Speaker is necessarily the leader of the majority in *driving* a program through the House), the foregoing customs and constitutional provisions, as well as the power of the President of the Assembly in the determination of the day-by-day agenda of the Assembly (see below, p. 382), gives him a party virility. This, necessarily, results in a diminution of his authority—for some will not recognize its fairness, its impartiality. The Assembly is by reason of French emotion and volubility an unusually temperamental forum; the position of the Chair does not tend to tame this, especially since the call to order is by the clanging of a bell. The tocsin in Revolutionary Paris was a daily alarm signal!

Sittings. The Standing Orders oblige the Assembly to meet on Tuesday, Thursday, and Friday of each week, in the afternoon. This leaves Wednesday, in principle, for committee work. The Assembly may meet on other days at its decision. It meets almost every day, excepting Saturday—but it has done this and has also met on Sundays when business has been pressing. It has sat not merely in the afternoons, but in the mornings. The afternoon sitting begins normally at 3 P.M. It often sits until midnight. The length of the sitting depends on the press of business and convenience.

III. LEGISLATIVE PROCEDURE

The parliamentary stages of a bill in the process of becoming a law are five. (1) It is introduced, without debate, into the Assembly by the Government or a Deputy. (2) It is examined and reported upon by the appropriate parliamentary committee. (3) It is debated clause by clause in the Assembly (if the Assembly decides that it is contentious). (4) It may be subjected to a second deliberation, as a whole, or in part. (5) It is then put to the vote as a complete text. When it has been voted, it goes to the Council of the Republic, and there it is given a similar treatment in the same stages.

Legislation raises a number of questions. They are:

(1) Who commands the timetable of the Assembly?

(2) Who introduces a bill?

(3) How is the debate on bills conducted?

(4) Is debate subject to obstruction and closure?

None of these problems is a problem in the U.S.-S.R.; the dictatorship commands all (see p. 796).

(1) Command of the Timetable

In sharpest contrast to the House of Commons (pp. 111ff.), the most significant facts about the timetable of the French Parliament are (1) the weakness of the Government in command of the time and agenda, (2) the substantial sharing of legislative initiative by the Deputies, and (3) the fact that the President and *rapporteur* and leading members of the relevant Commission rival the Ministers in conducting the debate on their bills.

The President's Conference. The agenda is fixed, not by the Government, but by a kind of committee of the Assembly. This is the President's Conference. It is composed of the President, the six Vice Presidents of the Assembly, the chairmen of the Commissions, numbering twenty, and the chairmen of all political groups containing at least fourteen members. This meant, say, on January 15, 1956, something like a body of 40 people,

to which the Government has the right to send one representative. A member of the Prime Minister's secretariat holds a watching brief (see p. 432) for comprehensive ministerial liaison. Originally this body was to meet weekly to draw up the agenda for the next two weeks. But this proved to be insufficient forward notice. In October 1950 the advance agenda was to be for three weeks. Some time later the Assembly went back to two weeks, as the forecasts of business were too committing for the Assembly's volatility.

The arrangement drawn up by the President's Conference goes to the Assembly for ratification. It is frequently amended, quite seriously. This may be due to some unforeseen sudden event, such as a demand by the Government for a vote of confidence, which requires a day's cooling-off period before vote. But the tentativeness of the Conference's recommendations is due to the contrast between the party composition of the Conference and the political balance of forces in the whole Assembly, which balance may change fast. The Government coalition may now be made up of groups different from the groups and the men of the various groups that command the chairmanships of the Commissions. The Government, because of the way in which the chairmanships (see p. 391ff.) go less to the Opposition parties, may be unfairly strong in the Conference in the opinion of the Assembly. Hence, the agenda is not an agenda until it has gone through the process of Assembly reconstruction.

Fluid Agendas. The Assembly is very restive about its authority. In 1952 the groups that had been in opposition to the Third Force Governments, made the demand that the Conference be constituted by proportional representation. This was rejected. It was advanced that, with P.R., its authority would preclude the Assembly from discarding the recommendations—but the Assembly ought to have precisely such freedom.

The Assembly spends much valuable time on arguing for and against the agenda proposals. By 1948 the Assembly was eager for a limit to this expenditure of time. It ruled that one member only of each party might speak on the subject, and this for five minutes only. It further ruled that once the Assembly had accepted the agenda, a proposal for its change could be submitted only by the Government, a Commission, or thirty members from *three different groups,* and that the proposal must be voted by absolute majority. The change was prompted in part because up to that time the proposal for a change could be made by any fifty Deputies, so that the Assembly was at the mercy of the obstructive tactics of the Communists whenever they chose. Later, changes were added, banning certain additions to the agenda by the Assembly—but they could not be enforced.

An excellent case in point is the debate on a vote of confidence November 25, 1955. Having been frustrated for a whole month in his bill to produce elections ahead of time (p. 372), Prime Minister Faure asked the President's Conference to put an urgent debate on the bill on the agenda. The Conference rejected the request, because the groups opposed to the Prime Minister, Communist (who had until then been voting *for* the Prime Minister's proposal!), the Socialists, Peasants, the U.R.D.S., and the Radical Party, too, combined 375 votes in the Assembly; and only the M.R.P. and the Independent Republicans and some smaller groups supported him, these controlling about 224 votes in the Assembly. The Conference put on the agenda, instead, a motion arraigning the Government in general. This would have delayed the matter of an early election. To counter this, M. Faure demanded a vote of confidence, which has priority. He was beaten by 318 to 218 after four days of debate.

An Ungovernable Assembly. The ungovernableness of the Assembly is evident from the foregoing. It is a product of the multiplicity of parties, and of the internal want of cohesion of the parties. It goes back to the Deputy's sense of his sovereign independence. It is further demonstrated in this, that even when the timetable has been thus set, the decorum during the individual sessions so allotted is time wasting. The President finds it hardly possible to stop what the British call "frivolous repetition." The Standing Orders require the member not "to wander from the subject"; and the President has ample authority to bring him back to the subject. He can forbid him even to speak on the subject for the rest of the sitting, if he can get Assembly sanction for this. Therefore,

to avoid the further loss of time, he lies low and says nothing.

This is not all, for, unfortunately, the seats of the Deputies have desks attached to them. This is an encouragement to shuffle papers, write letters, and bang the lids. This creates a storm when the Deputies wish to express violent disagreement. Hence, the debates are noisy and protracted.

The Deputies do not observe the marked respect that members of the House of Commons manifest toward their Speaker in demurring to a decision he may give, but continue long and loud protests, accompanied by impassioned hue and cry from their friends. Even when the Assembly itself had settled such disputed points of procedure, the settlements are not lasting, because the majority that voted them is ephemeral. For rules of order, above all, one needs a prior consensus on their substantial justice, as with the Constitution itself.

Penalties for Disorder. Deputies may be subject to an ascending degree of penalties for disorderly conduct: call to order; a call, recorded in the minutes; censure; and censure with temporary exclusion from the Assembly. The first two can be administered by the President—they are rebukes. (So what?) The censures need a vote by the Assembly, after a defense is put up by the Deputy. The censure with exclusion comes for persistent disorder that is censured several times and/or has involved calls to violence in the Assembly or outrageous behavior to the President or the Assembly or insults and threats to the Executive and the other assemblies.

(2) Introduction of Bills

In the House of Commons, the Government introduces about 85 percent of the bills, and private members 15 percent. Ninety-five percent of those passed are Government bills, and only 5 percent are private members' bills. The Government's bills were enacted in 98 percent of the cases; the private members' bills in only 30 percent.

The French Assembly presents a marked contrast following the Chamber of Deputies in this as in most other procedural malpractices (see p. 309). Of all bills introduced in recent years some 26 percent were sponsored by the Government, while 68 percent were introduced by Deputies, and 6 percent by Senators. Of the bills passed, 60 percent were Government bills, 40 percent were those of the Deputies and Senators. The Government saw 45 percent of its bills passed, private members only 10 percent of theirs.

British Governments may have their bills amended; French Governments clearly have their bills defeated by the rank and file of Deputies. The power of the French Deputy, being a power to kill, is also a power to compel the Government to withdraw its own proposals.

Much Legislation. The total number of bills proposed and passed in the French Parliament is tremendous compared with the British. The latter passes about 70 laws a year, with about 80 introduced. The French National Assembly (very much like the Chamber of Deputies) sees nearly 1400 bills introduced each year, and some 275 passed into law. The production is nearly four times that of the British Parliament; the seed sown—or rather, scattered—is nearly twenty times as much. What a cluttering up this means.

Why do so many bills come before the French Parliament? Because the large majority are not bills concerning the nation as a whole, but those which give rights and benefits to persons, localities, and economic groups. Furthermore, some matters settled by rules and orders in Britain require laws in France; more bills are required for the budgetary appropriations, etc., than in Britain. But also in Britain private members are strictly limited by the rules in their opportunities to introduce bills and, even more so, in getting the subsequent time for their passage. In spite of the rules of the Assembly, which are most categorical and clear in forbidding members to cater to special interests, the members do this. In 1952, for illustration, the satisfaction of such special interest groups took these forms: 2000 private bills were introduced; some were concerned to quash legal proceedings against Deputies, to protect local industries, to protect the wine industry, to compensate victims of floods, storms, to bring tax relief, to prevent closing of uneconomic railway lines. As for the local industries designed to be supported, they included canvas shoes, French olives, French oyster and mushroom growers, the iodine

and seaweed industry, the trade name of *vanilla*, the cauliflower that ought to be supported in commercial treaties. It was proposed that the wine ration to the Army be increased by another liter a day. The profession of druggist should be codified.

Sometimes, it should be noted, a Government will deliberately steer clear of a bill, and much prefer a private member to introduce it, though it would prefer it should not be introduced at all. For example, Deputy Barangé, a de Gaullist, pushed the bill to subsidize Church schools (see p. 357). The Minister of Justice in the Government of the day, Edgar Faure, neutral like the Cabinet, was constrained to say: "To govern and to legislate are two different tasks." No British Government would, or could, take this attitude: for to govern and to pass laws are to it a single and coherent act of responsible political will.

It should be added that of the 110 private members' bills passed annually by the Assembly, something like two thirds are not controversial. The Commissions do the work of sifting their individual justification. But the Assembly formally votes the clauses and then the whole bill.

Drafting the Laws. The French Government has no such arrangement for the expert drafting of laws such as is embodied in the Office of Parliamentary Counsel (pp. 119–120). Private members draft their own bills; the parliamentary Commissions take such care as they are able of the wording. They may ask the law officers of the Assembly, who serve the President, for help. Government bills are drafted by the civil servants, putting a premium therefore on law studies in their preparation. They may call, and almost always do, for help from the *Conseil d'État*. The Prime Minister's office watches the drafting and assists the departmental draftsmen. In May 1952 M. Pinay, then Prime Minister, pleaded that the departments be more precise and concise in their draftsmanship. The British Treasury Counsel supply these qualities better than the French system does.

(3) Debate on Legislation

On introduction, a bill is immediately assigned to a parliamentary Commission. This commission stage is vital to the bill, as will be seen later (p. 390). This is more like the American congressional status than that of the very subordinate one of British parliamentary committees (p. 117).

When the Commissions report back to the Assembly, the latter begins a debate (if any at all), called *discussion générale*. It ends with a vote for *passage aux articles*—that is, that the Assembly pass to the consideration of the clauses of the bill. The next stage, then, is the discussion of the clauses, when amendments may be moved and are debated and voted on, and the clauses are voted on. Finally, there is the stage of the vote on the bill as a whole, and this entails a limited debate of a general nature, in which speakers are allowed only five minutes each. The *discussion générale* is rather similar to the Second Reading of a bill in the British House of Commons, though it comes *after and not before* the commission stage.

"Restricted" Debate or No Debate. The report of the Commission may advise the Assembly to vote the bill without debate. A Deputy or the Government can oppose this, whereupon the bill goes back to the Commission; this will hear the objections and again report. If it repeats its proposal for vote without debate, the Government or fifty Deputies may oppose the proposal, and this time the bill returns to the Commission which then cannot again propose a vote without debate.

The Commission must then propose either ordinary precedure for opposed bills or a procedure, begun in March 1952, of restricted debate. Such a restricted debate cannot be used for important bills: it was designed to evade obstruction on unimportant bills, in order to save time. A "restricted" debate on a bill limits the right to speak to one representative each of the groups, of the Commissions and of the Government, and to sponsors of amendments that have been rejected by the Commission concerned. Nobody's speech may last for more than five minutes. The same speakers and time limit are admitted in a debate on whether to use the restricted procedure. The disciplinary withdrawal of a Deputy's right to speak in its name by his parliamentary group thus, in practice, loses him the right to speak!

Ordinary Debate. When the Commission does not propose a vote without debate or a restricted debate, the ordinary procedure comes into operation. The President's Conference puts the important bills on the agenda and distributes the period of debate among the Commissions, the groups, and the Government, having decided first on the total amount of time available for a bill. The timetable thus set up, we have already suggested, is a target rather than a strait-jacket. The President allows flexibility to the groups, to donations of time by one group to another, and so on. But, if not so rigid as the British allocation of time (see p. 114), it still introduces some order in the use of the Assembly's time. Furthermore, if it is a Government bill, the Government is very likely to have its own way as to the total time allocated to it, if it is strong enough to threaten resignation to get it. This is frequently attempted, and often successful.

In the actual debate, the leadership and steering is in the hands of the *rapporteur* of the relevant Commission and its chairman. They have seats together in the front center seats of the Assembly, the *bancs des commissions* being next to the *bancs des ministres*. This enables the Assembly to experience their guiding hand, and it stands in between them and the Government! The leading members of the Commission have almost unlimited rights of speaking and an accepted priority of intervention. They do not adjourn, normally, to deliberate in the Commission rooms on amendments, but confer around their appointed places and report verbally. They and their reports get to the Assembly before the Government does in debate; the Commissions have, maybe, condemned the Government before it has had a chance of even being heard. The bills also have usually not been read by the Assembly in general when they have been introduced by the Government: the Commission stands in between it and the Assembly! The Commissions are the masters of the debate. Hence, when the Commissions on Foreign Affairs, on National Defense, and Finances reported adversely to EDC, the jig was up.

Results of Weak Cabinet [5] Authority. It is not the Government, then, that steers the bills, Government-introduced, through the Assembly, but the President and *rapporteur,* and these may be seriously opposed to the Government. The Ministers

[5] We will use this term for members of the Council of the Republic (Chapter 7).

may intervene in debate when and for how long they like to support their requests and advocate what shall be done with amendments. The Assembly is not seldom pushed into the position of choosing between ministerial requests and the Commissions' recommendations. There may be complete conflict, say, when the Government demands that its original text be voted instead of the Commission's. The Government's last resort is its threat to resign or to ask for a vote of confidence, as for example, when, in February 1952, it did this no less than twenty times! The tension between Government and Commissions is therefore always acute, except when the Government can by wheedling, maneuvering, and importuning, get it party friends appointed Presidents or *rapporteurs*.

Yet, it must still be emphasized how *incoherent, distracted, and jagged* is this process of legislation as compared with that in the House of Commons, whose Committees are entirely subordinate to the House, while the Government is the sole advocating navigator for the bills which, to the amount of 95 percent, it gets passed, by direct and unhampered confrontation of the members in open assembly.

When the clauses have been debated and voted, it is in order for the Assembly to give the whole bill or parts of it a second discussion, called a *délibération,* or return it to the Commission for drafting revision and tying together. The motion for one of these courses may be offered by the Government or the Commission or any Deputy. The Assembly may vote for a second discussion, in which case the Commissions ought, according to the rules, subject the bill to an examination, but, in practice, they do not always do this. They may feel that the extent of revisions do not justify it or that speed is required.

The bill, after this new deliberation or on its being averted, is, as a whole and with its amendments, put to the vote.

Who May Speak? The President of the Assembly is the sole authority on the right to speak; his leave must be requested and obtained. He is asked: *Je demande la parole:* "I ask to be allowed to speak." He calls a speaker with the phrase: *La parole est à M. ABC:* "Mr. ABC has the right to speak (or

has the floor)." Those who speak otherwise than by permission are out of order.

Once the debate has started, various members will rise to ask for the right to speak, as they realize with excited joy and perhaps some colleaguely malice that the previous speaker is at long last coming to an end. This goes on to the end of the time allotted, unless the number of speakers and the kinds (Commission members, etc.) have been designated for specific bills.

To be sure of a chance of speaking, the Deputies apply to the President beforehand. These Deputies on the *ordre d'inscription* are called before others. Some rights of interchange of position between those on and those not on the order is allowed, unless the President's Conference has tightly organized debate.

Urgent Discussion. Urgent discussion may be voted for a bill regardless of the Order of the Day. For a Government bill, the Prime Minister, for a Deputy's bill, the Commission, may initiate the request, the latter by an absolute majority after its report has been out twenty-four hours. The private Deputy may force the Commission before its report is issued by a request notified to all the Assembly's authorities. Within three days, Prime Minister and Commission must declare whether urgency is desirable; if default, consent is assumed. For urgency, both must agree; if they disagree, the Assembly decides. The Deputy needs fifty signatures to speed up the Commission. When urgency is granted, no other business may interrupt debate. This procedure was so much abused, that competing urgencies got in each other's way.

Priority in Speaking. Ministers, the chairmen and *rapporteurs* of the Commissions must be allowed to speak whenever they ask to. The Deputy who has proposed a bill that has come up for debate has no special right to speak during the debate; the *rapporteur* of the relevant committee starts the debate. The proposer of an interpellation has the right of opening the debate. As a debate on an interpellation is most usually a debate on several which have been joined together, the team mates have the right one after the other to introduce the subject.

However, to safeguard the rights of the Assembly at large, whenever a privileged person, as above, has spoken, a rank-and-file Deputy has the right to speak.

When he moves an amendment which is opposed by a Minister or a member of the Commission, the Deputy has an extra right of reply. A right of reply is also accorded to the Minister or *rapporteur* who opened the debate. On some bills and procedural matters, the Assembly allows Deputies the extra right to explain why they voted the way they did; these are speeches of five minutes or less duration.

The Chamber of Deputies was rather more prone to the temptation that besets any parliamentary representative in any country once he has a captive audience in front of him: unending speech. In 1926, during another of the financial crises and nagging self-resentment, the Chamber set up a framework for the duration of speeches: no limit to Ministers; one hour to the leading members of committees, authors of interpellations, etc., half an hour for authors of amendments, etc.; fifteen minutes for speakers on chapters of the budget; ten minutes, and five minutes for other scheduled issues, etc. Some of these rules had already been a long practice: for example, the five minutes for explanation of one's vote, and the ministerial no-limit. Something of this order still exists for some matters. The intelligent practice of the National Assembly is allowed for, with something like the duration mentioned above, by the President's Conference.

The British House of Commons by habit leaves the duration of speeches to a fair latitude for Ministers, and for other members fifteen or twenty minutes or less, according to their acknowledged eminence and the desire of the rest of the members to hear them. It has a short and unnerving silence or ironic "Hear, hear!" or absenteeism for bores.

Commissaires du Gouvernement. Ever since the Consulate (p. 301), Ministers may be assisted by so-called "government commissioners" during the deliberations in the Assembly. These are civil servants, and are named by the relevant Minister's decree for the specific discussion. The President of the Assembly announces the names of the officials at the beginning of the discussion and they sit on the Ministers' benches. If advisable to the Minister, they may speak in order to explain technical points on which they are expert, not to debate policy. They rarely do this; but they are of great value to the Ministers, and thereby to the Assembly. It is a practice for civil servants in Britain to hover behind the Speaker's chair within whispering distance of the Government Bench, especially during the question hour. Deputies have the right to speak *à propos* the *commissaire's* speech.

(4) Obstruction and Closure

It is possible, given the almost universal unwillingness of the Deputies to be governed and self-governed, to frustrate the work of the Parliament by obstruction. The development of the rules of orderly debate and the allocation of time and systematic closure in Britain has been a direct function of a responsible cabinet based, normally, on a majority party. This gift the French chamber has not enjoyed, because it relishes individualism more. This is the atmosphere in which obstructionism can flourish. All the more so, when the Assembly includes at least two strong parties that seek the destruction of the parliamentary system (p. 338).

One way of obstruction is the making of long speeches—filibustering—by deliberate introduction of irrelevant matter. For example, in March 1950 a Communist Deputy spoke for nearly six hours, in the course of which he reviewed price statistics in the Soviet Union. Two years later another Communist Deputy held up the business of the Assembly (a change in the Standing Orders), by filibustering on a variety of irrelevant matters of extraordinary incongruity. The Communists in the first half-session of 1952 had, per Deputy, spoken 50 percent more in time than the members of other parties.

Closure. Now discussions must end some time, for obvious reasons. The Standing Orders allow for the immediate ending of a debate, one apart from the time limit allocated by the President's Conference and the Assembly on the agenda. It is called the *clôture,* or closure, and was practiced before the British House of Commons adopted it in the 1880's.

The closure can be asked for only after two

speakers at least have spoken in a debate, on opposite sides. Then, a Deputy may orally request the *clôture*. The speech in actual progress cannot be interrupted by the request. On the request, no debate is permitted—except when a bill is in the *discussion générale* stage, and then one Deputy only is allowed to speak *contra* for five minutes. The right is given either to an inscribed speaker who has not yet spoken or to the first Deputy who applies, if the former does not exercise his right. The President then puts the question of closure to a vote by raised hands. In cases of doubt, a vote is taken by sitting and standing. In case of further doubt, the closure is not allowed—the debate goes on. On the closure of a general discussion, the Deputies have their five-minute explanations of vote open to them; this, too, may be closured. The Supreme Soviet of the U.S.S.R. is not worried by such scruples: the Ministers speak. The others re-echo them and applaud.

Now, the merit of the closure in the British system is that it has behind it a majority of the Government and is managed by the Government in negotiation with, and respect for, an official leader of the Opposition with a sense of responsibility to the House as a whole and the nation as a whole. But in the National Assembly, the Council of Ministers has not the authority or prestige of the British Cabinet in the House or the nation. It is ephemeral and it is internally and externally weak. It would court defeat if it proposed to stop debate by the Assembly.

The *clôture* is the instrument of the majority of the Assembly that becomes convinced that a subject has been debated enough. But it is not a homogeneous or responsible majority: it is a majority that has to be found on the particular occasion for the specific debate. It is a poor curb on tedious repetition, waste of time, and maliciously designed obstruction.

No Selective Closure. The President of the Assembly has not been given the power that has been vested in the Speaker of the House of Commons, of the "Kangaroo Closure"—that is, the right to select amendments and to permit debate only on those he selects (see p. 114). Manifestly, the Assembly can hardly give its President—who has not been sculptured into an impartial officer as the Speaker has—such powers of life and death over amendments. Such a power has had to be taken, but rarely indeed, by the Government in grave circumstances, as in November 1947, when the Communist Party had produced a revolutionary strike situation, when it introduced a bill to maintain public order in view of existing and anticipated violence. Then it moved and obtained the rejection *in toto* of all amendments. On this occasion the Communists obstructed by debates on procedure and by defying the President—one member refused to leave the *tribune* all night, his friends draped around him, until the *Garde Républicaine,* unarmed, escorted him away at 6 A.M. The Communists have even provoked open violence: in March 1950, when the antisabotage law was up, they provoked fighting on the chamber floor.

The Assembly is not infrequently swept by moments of extreme turbulence; but it is not normally violent. It is always, however, on important issues, on the point of losing its temper.

The "restricted" debate procedure referred to earlier (p. 385) is one of the ways used by the Assembly to save its time—used here, however, only on the less-important bills. By *important* is meant bills on constitutional, electoral, financial, and some judicial matters, bills for amnesty, to ratify treaties, laws the President of the Republic or the Constitutional Committee sends back for reconsideration (see p. 333), proposals to revise the Standing Orders.

In spite of these devices and others, such as making it easier to count a quorum which is the absolute majority and abolishing the right to demand a vote by individual appearance at the *Tribune,* the Assembly is still rather chaotic in the way it organizes its timetable, its priorities, the amount of time to be spent on each item, the sudden changes of tack in the middle of debate, the irrelevance, and the obstructionism. It is a mercy, then, that the system of commissions has been organized, for this provides some coherence and order. This matter needs to be taken up again *via* a discussion of the commission system and of the voting of the budget (pp. 390–395, 395–398).

A few observations at this point on the mode of voting and the nature of French parliamentary oratory are apposite.

Voting Methods and Oratory

The quorum for a vote is the majority of the Deputies within the precincts of the Assembly. It is normally taken for granted. But the Bureau may be asked to discover whether there is a quorum. If a ballot is to be held at the *Tribune,* it *must;* if by ballot at the seats, it *may* be asked. If there is no quorum, the ballot is postponed. The quorum is very different from that of the British House of Commons where a "house" exists when forty members are present.

Raised Hands. There are three types of voting: raising of hands, sitting and standing, and open ballot. The first two are brief methods, and effective when the majority is clear and when the minority does not want to press its opposition further. The votes of hands are counted, first the yeses and then the noes, by the secretaries. If the secretaries disagree as to the numbers, then the President calls for standing votes—yeas, then noes.

Open Ballot. If there is a disagreement among the secretaries on the count, a vote is held by open ballot—or this method is used if, after a raised-hands vote, a single Deputy asks for this method. The open ballot is held at once, compulsorily, if asked for by the Government, the relevant Commission, the president of a group with not less than twenty-five members, or any twenty-five Deputies; and automatically for any vote on a bill that imposes or alters taxes. It is used customarily whenever it is desired that the members' votes be individually registered. It cannot be used on closure (it would waste time).

The votes are actually cast by means of colored cards—white, *pro;* blue, *contra.* Each Deputy has a supply of both kinds of cards with his name printed on them. Messengers go to the desks when a ballot starts, carrying blue metal urns, into which Deputies place their white or blue cards—unless the messengers throw them *en masse* into the urn by taking off the lid through the slit of which the card is supposed to go. (Saves time!)

The President calls that the ballot is closed, at a certain point. Until then any Deputy may decide to change his vote—he cancels by giving in a card of opposite number; he reverses by giving in two cards of opposite number! The secretaries sort and count the vote, and the President announces it. This takes about the same time—ten minutes—as a House of Commons' divisions. The President may wish to check the count—but this will take from thirty to forty minutes. In close votes (under twenty-five votes' difference between *pro* and *contra*) or if the number of votes cast appears to be greater than the total number who could have taken part, a check is compulsory. So also on a vote on a motion of confidence or censure, or when twenty-five Deputies or a group with not less than twenty-five demand it.

Proxy Voting. On July 26, 1955, the Assembly amended the rules to this effect: when votes of confidence or of censure are being voted on, Deputies must vote in person; so also on treaties if the Agenda Conference votes it and the Assembly endorses the recommendation. Only the Communists opposed this amendment. Otherwise proxy voting is allowed. A Deputy gives cards to another he trusts to put into the urn: the proxy man is nicknamed a *boitier* (postman or mail carrier). Even the cards of a whole group, in an envelope, can be thus cast by a party Deputy. This practice masks the fact that often the Assembly is badly attended. A vote cast by a Deputy personally is alone valid to cancel that cast for him by a proxy.

This system, unknown to the House of Commons or the U.S. Congress, is justified by the French constitutional authorities with the argument that the vote belongs to the Deputy's constituents, not to him personally—and yet he cannot be in the Assembly continuously, for he has much more work to do on their behalf. It is almost as good an argument as that presented to justify the sudden rush of members of the House to vote on matters they have not heard debated according to guidance of the Whips (see p. 103). The same French authorities smile at the British (and U.S.) practice of "pairing"—allowing men to vote before they have heard the debate. It is a curiously antiquated kind of argument: in the French case, it supports the blanket judgment of the party; and in the British, it denies it.

Roll-call Vote. There is another form of open ballot that is not a card vote. It admits of no proxies. It is a kind of roll-call vote. Each Deputy mounts the *tribune* at the call of his name in alphabetical order, and there gives his card to a secretary. The latter places the card in the urn and ticks the name of the Deputy on his list. The count must be checked. The ballot is open for an hour— a Deputy may come in any time during that span and get listed. For this type of ballot—called *scrutin public à la tribune*—a request by fifty Deputies is necessary; they must be present when the ballot is to start; the quorum must be available. Thus, the solemnity of the ballot is expressed, for solemnity is its purpose.

In total, with the roll call and the checking and the open hour, this *scrutin* lasts nearly two hours. Hence, a party with fifty Deputies can obstruct the work of the Assembly by asking for it. The Communist Party, true to its purpose of making democracy impossible, used this method of blocking the work of the Assembly during the votes referred to earlier on the bill for public order, November 29, 1947. The other parties voted that the Assembly turn from this business at once to the amending of the Standing Orders in order to stop the Communist tactics. It was then enacted that no group of fifty Deputies *of the same party* may present more than *one* request for *scrutin* during the same debate! It worked. Before it was passed, seven *scrutins* used up ten hours out of twenty-three of debate; after it, only two were held (that is, about three hours) in the next three days.

The votes—when by ballot—are published as *for, against, not voting, absent on leave. Voluntarily abstained* is a label for those who ask to be so designated.

Oratorical Influence. The fact that political parties (except the Communists) are, as we have amply shown, not perfectly disciplined, even when the *discipline de vote* is invoked, and that a few votes skimmed off from this group and that may easily change the majority for or against a measure or a Government, allows a greater potency for oratory than in the parliaments of Britain or the United States. Perhaps that element of character and spirit which produces French oratory and philosophical finesse also produces the *amour propre* of the individual Deputy and his unwillingness to be altogether subservient to party. Rhetorical abil-

ity is, therefore, a powerful element in the affairs of the Assembly. We have already quoted de Jouvenel, who said that the Deputies are more interested in the debate than in the resolution they are debating. For the rest we may cite the words of a great parliamentary orator, Louis Barthou: [6]

For a speech pronounced at the *Tribune* should be an act; when the discourse or the act has commenced, emotion has already taken another form. A battle is begun, one must win; one has thrown oneself into the water and one must swim towards the bank. Some go under beneath applause, others beneath sarcasm, but the success of an act is not a judgment of its value. The idea vanquished today will perhaps be triumphant tomorrow, and perhaps tomorrow's events may make the orator acclaimed yesterday pay dear for his passing triumph. . . .

The *Tribune* is a great peril, because it is a scene where one plays a part in a hall where the spectators take their part in the piece. Different from a play in this: all is unforeseen—one does not always know how it will open because the Government has the right of intervention at any moment, and may—by an initial declaration which may even bring about an adjournment or the closure—disturb the order of the spectacle; still less can one foresee how it will finish.

It may be added that, sometimes, after the votes are counted a few Deputies will announce that they had not intended to vote as they did—it is a deception of their constituents.

The Parliamentary Commissions

The general place of the *Commissions Générales* (*Parlementaires*) has been indicated; it is central and vital to the making of law. The Commissions also participate in the control of the Executive; they are part of the Assembly as the grand inquest of the nation on Ministers and administrative departments. At this point, it is only the first function that is discussed; the function of control is considered in the chapter on the Executive.

The Standing Orders regulate the number and

[6] *Le Politique*, Paris, 1926: he was first elected a Deputy in 1889; a Senator in 1922; many times a Minister; Prime Minister in 1913; a famous Foreign Minister between the wars.

composition of the Commissions. The Assembly has these nineteen:

1. Economic Affairs
2. Foreign Affairs
3. Agriculture
4. Fermented Liquors
5. Defense
6. Education
7. Family, Population, Health
8. Finance
9. Interior
10. Justice and Legislation
11. Merchant Shipping and Fisheries
12. Communications and Tourist Trade
13. Pensions
14. Press
15. Industrial Production
16. Franchise, Constitution, Standing Order, and Petitions
17. Overseas Territories
18. Labor and Social Security
19. Food Supply

In addition, there are two smaller Commissions, on Accounts and Parliamentary Immunity.

Their scope corresponds roughly to that of the various government departments. Some hold that an exact correspondence would be useful, defining thus the tie between the department to be controlled and the Commission. Others believe that the Commissions should be broader to get a comprehensive view of interdepartmental problems.

Size. The Commissions each have forty-four members. The multiple of eleven goes back to the pre-1910 days when the Chamber was divided into eleven *bureaus,* these being chosen by lot to cut across political groups, as the Deputies thought that there was something sinister in group or factional discipline damaging to the "general will."

Annual Appointment. The Commissions, though known as "permanent," are elected annually. At one time in the Third Republic they had been elected only or temporarily for each bill, except the *Commission des Finance.* Later the practice changed to the present method. This "permanence" was established so that the Assembly might get a grip on the "bureaucracy" and the work of legislation in face of so much Cabinet instability. The principle of P.R. in their com-

position was also developed as a convention. Conservatives were hostile to permanence and P.R., fearing that the Commissions would, as during the French Revolution, foment chaotic and demagogic opposition to the Executive.

The Standing Orders now require composition by P.R. based on the groups. The constitution of groups is therefore basic; no access to a Commission is open except through membership of a group.

The Groups. The Standing Orders (Chapter V. Article 12 ff.) say:

Deputies may organize themselves into groups according to their political affinities.

The groups are constituted after lodging with the Bureau of the Assembly a list of their members accompanied by a declaration, made public, common to all their members, signed by them and representing the program of political action.

No Deputy may appear on the list of more than one group.

The interior management of the groups containing at least 14 members required by Article 16 (on the composition of Commissions) may be discharged by an administrative secretariat whose rules, recruitment and means of payment are exclusively the business of the group itself.

The constitution within the Assembly of groups said to be "for the defense of special, local or professional interests" is forbidden.

Today the Commissions are of a size that requires mathematically that a group be at least of fourteen members to get a place on each Commission. Those that are less than this in size are allowed to "relate" themselves to a larger group. Thus, the *Progressistes* affiliate with the Communists. The same rule applies to the several Deputies who belong to no group, the *sauvages.* When a group falls below the required number—say, through defection or death or resignation followed by the loss of the seat to another party—it may be helped by the temporary adherence of some other obliging Deputy for the moment of the election of the groups at the beginning of a session, and then his resignation from it.

The groups work out the formula of distribution of seats; and some trading is done between them for seating in preferred Commissions. The groups are internally sovereign in their decisions about which of their members are to go on which Commissions. The groups then agree to the lists and the Assembly confirms them. A challenge may be made if fifty Deputies make it in the Assembly, and a contest will follow. The possibility is there; it has occurred once; the Assembly is the protector of an aggrieved member. No member may sit on more than two Commissions.

As parliamentarism has developed, French politicians have come to recognize the crucial value of their Commissions, though they looked at them askance down to 1910 at least. The Commissions are now even mentioned in the Constitution (Article 15) that requires the National Assembly to study the bills before it in its Committees, and endows it with the authority to decide their number, composition, and power. There was even a proposal (a Communist one, bent on sovietization but with much wider backing) in the Constituent Assembly's committee (on the first draft) that the Commissions should themselves be allowed to pass laws, the Assembly's role being called into play only if one third of the Commission called on it. The "restricted" procedure on the less important bills (p. 385) certainly assigns a considerable extra authority to the Commission.

Lidderdale [7] advances two interesting reasons why the Commissions are so much more essential a stage in legislation in France than are committees in Britain. First, the Assembly, like the Chamber of Deputies, permits private members' bills without limit. The Commissions save the Assembly from being swamped. Second, Cabinets are not in power long enough to prepare and revise the laws they introduce; hence, the Commissions see that the faults of hasty drafting are remedied and the bill given coherence and consistency.

Operation and Value of the Commissions. Like the U.S. Congressional committees, some Commissions are more important electorally, more significant politically, and carry more prestige than others. The most distinguished are Finance, Foreign Affairs, Defense, Interior, and Franchise. The Assembly is not wedded to the system of appoint-

ing members of the Commissions by the principle of seniority *per se;* it puts its best members forward on the Commissions, as a first principle. For the parties have more to gain by appointments on merit than is the situation in the American Congress; the Commissions have legislative power, but they also have administrative and governmental power, since France has a cabinet system and not the disintegrated arrangements of the separation of powers. Wise committee assignments might lead to ministerial office in the course of time. However, seniority does play a part, though here again the seniors have advanced largely by way of merit and not merely by arid years.

Thus, the members who get on to Commissions or are known for service on them are fairly steadily reelected. They become expert in the subject of their competence in a way that is not called for in the British system of Standing Committees. Furthermore, they acquire a group spirit, just as in the British system, and the absence of debating warfare produces a disposition to minimize party strife in committee. Hence, the Assembly is served by a comparatively valuable technical appraising agency, technically oriented. Since, however, the chairmen tend to hold their positions for years (we refer to the practice of the Chamber, continued now to the Assembly), they and their Commissions become strong rivals of the Ministers. The *rapporteurs* are stimulated by their status to hanker after a Minister's blood on the way to his job. These powerful leaders of little legislative guilds wielding such power are *en route,* very often, to becoming Ministers. From 1946–1951 five Commission chairmen became Ministers; from 1951–1953 (two years only) eight did, some directly, some indirectly; most going to the Ministry that paralleled the Commission they had headed. Prime Minister Mendès-France was Chairman of the Accounts Commission prior to his highest office.

At any given moment, Commissions may not correspond to the composition by groups of the Cabinet. They have been in session and will continue in session with the same membership for their annual term, though the Government majority has changed complexion, it may be seriously. Groups

[7] *The Parliament of France,* London, 1949.

choose members to represent them on Commissions often because these have gained distinction in this specific field, and this is rather more than less certain to cause them to vote against the proposals of their own fellow party members who are in the Government. They are more knowledgeable; they certainly have convictions. We have appreciated also that parties are riven by internal differences and voting discipline is weak. This is in spite of the fact that since 1952 the rules require that when a Deputy leaves a party he vacates the Commission seats it sent him to. Some Commission chairmen are actually from groups in violent opposition to the Government coalition. For example, two R.P.F. members held Commission chairmanships (Defense and Franchise) when in opposition and unwilling to enter Cabinets in 1952; and the Socialists held six (Foreign Affairs, Justice, and the Interior among them) in 1953, and these cannot see eye to eye with a right-inclined Government. Jules Moch, Socialist Chairman of the Foreign Affairs Commission in 1954, both led one half the Socialist Deputies against the party executive's directive on EDC and would have negated it against the Radical-led Cabinet in August 1954, even if the latter had not been merely neutral. A dissentient part of a group whose group's members are in the momentary Cabinet may join with hostile groups to get a presidency or rapporteurship of a Commission!

Regional and "Interest" Cliques. Other factors give a twist to the outlook of the Commissions to produce incongruity between them and the Assembly's state of mind and also the Government. Members may have special interests, even obsessions—such as anticlericalism or the defense of labor interests or housing or pensions—and in such cases they make their way to the relevant Commissions. Such special interests may be not merely personal enthusiasms but may connect with the "pressure groups" to which some attention has already been given (see pp. 340–341) and/or with regional objectives. The latter produces the over-manning of Commissions for reconstruction of the war-devastated areas by members from Normandy and Brittany, members from the seaports on the Merchant Shipping and Fisheries Commission, the industrial areas on the Economic Affairs and the Labor and Social Security Commissions. The Overseas Commission is especially stuffed with colonial members, in spite of the smallness of the group in proportion to the whole Assembly.

These pull against each other, particularly for appropriations for their respective purposes, more wages, more houses, high Civil Service salaries, increases in family allowances, student scholarships, against a Government almost invariably vowed to economies and no increase in taxes. This, however, already trenches on finances and on the relationship of the Commissions with the Government—and is resumed later.

Organization. Each Commission appoints its own *bureau*—that is, a president, two vice presidents, and two secretaries—from among its members. The president arranges and convenes the meetings. On receiving a bill, the Commission appoints a *rapporteur*. Each Commission has its special room, with other necessary offices and staff provided by the Assembly's permanent staff. It may be assisted at its wish by a civil servant; some Commissions have been thus helped by the same official for many years. They rely on him for information; he does not participate in the deliberations or the writing of the report. In this, he is rather in the position of the assistants to the committees of the U.S. Congress.

The Commissions have all day Wednesday for their activities, in principle, plus the mornings of other days. The heavy congestion of the Assembly has, however, compelled the Commissions to sit when the Assembly is in session. This is similar to the experience of the British House of Commons. All legislative assemblies are congested and have been since the latter part of the nineteenth century.

A member is obliged to attend, but practice allows for absenteeism. He may designate an alternate for any single meeting. After a number of consecutive absences, he may be deemed to have resigned. The rule is not applied, owing to the facts of life in the Assembly.

The rules of debate and balloting are relaxed, though they exist. To conduct an inquiry outside the Assembly itself, a Commission needs authority from the Assembly, when it may appoint up to seven of its members to undertake the inquiry.

This procedure occurs often. The examination of witnesses on oath is permitted only when the Assembly gives this power under authority of the law of March 1914 that provides for the punishment of persons who are recalcitrant or unwilling to take the oath or who are guilty of perjury or bribery of a committee witness.

Private Sessions. The meetings of the Commissions are private, the exclusion of the public being deliberately intended to preserve the conditions of frankness and businesslike attention to the issues before them. This is all the more important as civil servants attend to give information, some of which is in the high-secrecy category, and Ministers may attend at any time and speak, and be accompanied by experts if they so desire. The minutes are kept but not published, any more than British Cabinet minutes are published. There is, naturally, then, no verbatim record available for the public; and such is only taken when a Minister attends. The minutes are kept by the Commission and can be looked at by any Deputy. But a précis of Commission proceedings is published weekly, with records of votes. The Deputies are bound to subsequent reserve on these speeches during debate in the Assembly, and special care is taken to safeguard the confidences of Ministers who appear before them.

However, on occasion, a Minister and a Commission cooperate on the issuance of a fuller account of a Minister's speech—when it has very great public importance. An example is the Bidault speech on the Three Power talks at Washington in July 1953, when the Foreign Minister was anxious to let the public know what had transpired, since the session was drawing toward the vacation and the agenda of the Assembly had no place for a discussion of it.

Rapporteur and Report. The *rapporteur* is responsible for guiding the work of the Commission from the standpoint of legislative policy, while its president, participating in this also, is the guide of its proceedings and its link with the Assembly and the Government. The *rapporteur* concludes the work of the Commission on a bill by writing a report on it. The report consists normally of the original bill; the text now proposed by the Commission after examination, discussion, and the voting of its clauses; a history of the problem the bill seeks to solve, with a confrontation of the texts (their gist, it may be) of the previous bills on the subject. Included also is an appraisal of the social or economic or foreign policy problem that has called for the attention of the Government or a Deputy; a critical description of the original bill; a recommended course of action.

Most of these reports are usually extremely valuable foundations for the debates in the Assembly, enabling Deputies, if they wish it, to gain a substantial familiarity with the subject; and, if insufficient for a recasting of the bill, or policy, at least an excellent design of pegs whereon to hang questions and criticisms and demands for better alternatives. Not all the reports are of the highest quality. Many are overstuffed, in order to bring reputation for massiveness to a *rapporteur*.

The reports must be supplied within the period of three months after the assignment of the bill to the Commission. In practice, some latitude is permitted. The Government or fifty Deputies may move the discharge of a bill to the Assembly.

The Assembly can assign a bill to the Commission it thinks most appropriate if doubt should arise on this score; and to require two or more Commissions to deal with a measure that has a spread of substance.

When finance is involved, the Commission on Finance must send its *rapporteurs* to the Commission in charge of the bill, where they have a consultative part. Furthermore, since the institution of the Economic Council and the Assembly of the French Union, a Commission of the Assembly that is charged with a bill that has come before either of these bodies must allow their *rapporteurs* a hearing, and hear the minority as well as the majority views of those bodies if they have not been unanimous.

There is no special provision for minority reports. The minority may, however, make its points in the Assembly, since a spokesman is allowed the floor out of turn on the list. Deputies with an amendment may speak to it. The authors of the bills must be heard. A summarized view of the minority's opinions appears at the end of the *Journal Officiel's* report on the debate.

The Supreme Soviet of the U.S.S.R. has no

such democratic scruples in its procedure. The Executive produces the bills long *after* decreeing them for unanimous acclamation.

The Council of the Republic deals with legislation and the control of administration in much the same way as the Assembly, and its rules on the Commissions are almost identical. A major difference is that the Commissions in the Council of the Republic are not forty-four members in size, but thirty. The Council is only about half the size of the Assembly.

Considering the multiplicity of parties, the subtlety of the differences which separate the groups and wings of the groups, from each other, and considering the brevity of the life of Cabinets, the commission system is essential—yet it introduces its own troubles, especially visible in the conflicts with the Executive.

Financial Legislation

The Budget. The remarkable feature of the British budgetary system, as we have seen (pp. 127–131), is the lodgment in the Executive of the initiative in formulating the budget; and the cooperation of the party machinery in the Commons to discipline the rank and file of the members to accept the budget almost as it comes from the Chancellor of the Exchequer. The remarkable feature of the budgetary system of the U.S.S.R. is, as we show (p. 890) that it is *entirely* Executive, in the hands of the Council of Ministers with only a handclapping role assigned to the Supreme Soviet.

In France the budgetary system is a product of the insurgency of the individual Deputies, the strength of the Finance Commission of the Assembly, and the weakness of the Cabinet, including, of course, the weakness of the Minister of Finance.

Expenditure and taxes must be enacted annually by the legislature and are supposed to be contained in *one* financial bill. The fiscal year ends December 31, and the law should be voted by then. In the Third Republic this was rarely accomplished. The Assembly in the Fourth Republic is no better off.

The Constitution has not required the annuality that has just been mentioned: it is good parliamentary practice. But the Constitution has required that an organic law regulate the presentation of the budget. This law has not yet been enacted, approaching ten years' delay. Article 16 requires that the budget contain only strictly financial provisions. This is to avoid the trick—by Cabinet or the Assembly—of "riders" that are substantial legislation, to which the Third Republic was prone.

Appropriations en Bloc. There has never been a single year since 1946 when the budget has been voted on time; in 1947, the budget that should have been passed by December 31, 1946, was passed in August 1947; for 1947 the budget was passed in September 1948—the Assembly having covered its misbehavior by a bill at the end of 1947, saying in effect "You can spend the same in 1948 as you did in 1947."

Furthermore, the Assembly, to save time (and avoid correcting its anarchy) then allowed the voting of a maximum (*loi des maxima*) for each department for the year 1949 and onward, instead of voting the appropriations by chapters. This took away from the Assembly the power to criticize the appropriations in detail—except that later on, a change in procedure allowed a *post facto* review! It requires tremendous self-discipline to carry through a budget that contains, as the French budgets do, about 1500 chapters (more recently), let alone the 5000 of 1949. The Assembly has not the discipline, and yet the number of chapters is greater than that of the U.S. Congress (about 1000) and inordinately complicated as compared with Great Britain.

Unfortunate Consequences. One of the consequences of the method of voting bloc ministerial amounts was to incite the Assembly to challenge them the more: it resented the curtain effect. The result was the putting of very many votes of confidence by the Cabinet, to do by force what supple reasoning on accurately stated appropriations might have averted.

The lack of self-discipline in the Assembly, among the groups, and within the Cabinet forced the Government to proceed piecemeal with the financial law. The "provisional twelfths" required separate laws per monthly appropriation. The total appropriations were put into extraordinary as well as ordinary budget laws—that is, provision for special matters, such as reconstruction. They divided up civil and military expenditure, in order to be able to rush one and then the other to the Council of the Republic.

Experts and the Court of Accounts expressed their horror at the sight of ten or twelve separate bills per year carrying the pieces of one picture (as it should be) of the nation's public finances. Furthermore, a device was adopted in one year of getting the military expenditures only, and *all* the tax increases, voted first. It worked. But when, in a later year, all the appropriations were passed before the taxation to meet them was proposed, the Assembly overthrew the selfsame Cabinet (when it made its tax proposals) for reducing desired expenditures, and then overthrew a subsequent Cabinet that requested increases in taxation to meet the unreduced expenditures!

Another serious consequence of not passing the budget at the right time is loss of revenue, since there is no authorization for its collection. The result of the misbehavior indicated so far is to bring the Treasury into a deficit, therefore to force it to go to the Bank of France for loans, and therefore to give that bank and the financial powers in France something of the ability to influence the choice of Ministers of Finance and thereby the composition of the Cabinet.

A further result of the incontinence of the Deputies and the groups is to force Governments, responsible in their brief time for the continuous movement of the governmental machine, to ask for "special powers," such as we have already referred to as a defect of the Third Republic (p. 315), and to which further reference is made shortly (p. 398). Is it not a matter of dismay to those who are vindicators of democratic government that Prime Ministers have to be given authority to postpone or cancel the spending of appropriations already enacted, because the taxation to meet it will not be there?

The Financial Rights of the Deputies. In the House of Commons only the Government has a right to propose expenditures or the putting of charges on the nation. In the Third Republic individual Deputies had this right in plenitude, until some slight amendment was made, ineffectively.

The amounts that would have been necessary to satisfy the Deputies' avidity for expenditure would have amounted to several times the total of the actual budget for the year.

Of all the constitutional tragedies perpetrated by the Fourth Republic, Article 17 is the prime example. It runs:

> The deputies of the National Assembly shall have the right to initiate appropriations.
>
> However, no proposals which would tend to increase appropriations already decided upon or create new ones may be presented during the discussion of the budget and of prospective or supplementary appropriations.

The proviso allows the Deputies to play the fool eleven months out of twelve, in Paul Reynaud's words. Indeed, it allows them to play the fool for more months than twelve per budget, because the budget is not voted in the single year. A motion for "urgency," backed by fifty members, could, until 1948 get around the proviso, and was used for demagogic purposes by the Communist Party. It would get bills involving expenditures before the Assembly parallel with the budget debates until the procedure was changed (p. 386).

Attempts to Curb the Deputies. The rules of the Assembly seek to restrict the financial fertility of the Deputies. The Government, the Finance Commission, and other Commissions dealing with nonfinancial legislation may require the *disjonction* (disjunction) of amendments that increase expenditures or reduce revenues. This means that such amendments can only come before the Assembly in a separate bill. Since the Finance Commission is corporately proud of its authority, some check is placed on such proposals because the Commission can report adversely. The word of this commission is law on whether there is truly a rise in expenditure or fall in taxes involved.

Another device to check irresponsibility is one to which reference has already been made, namely, the setting of a maximum expenditure for each department, known as the *loi des maxima* (*des depenses*). These *lois* from 1949, when used, have contained a clause forbidding proposals for increased expenditures or decreased revenues. The clause has been of great pruning and disciplinary value. It met, when operative, with the furious opposition of the Communist Party. Whether that party or others were demagogic or not in their amendments (and some were sincere), the amenders were forced into the British procedural device for raising a debate on a proposal to *reduce* the expenditures.

When the Governments, on their knees before the Finance Commission, have not been able to check the Deputies and groups by these means, they have had to resort to the vote of confidence. In the years 1946 to 1951, the vote of confidence was put forty-six times. Of these, twenty-three were on the budget. In 1952–53 the vote of confidence was put thirty-five times, of which nineteen were on the budget. But a Government can be beaten on such demands: this happened in June 1950 to M. Bidault, when he attempted to challenge the Finance Commission to abandon a Socialist proposal to increase the salaries of civil servants by the technical trick of regrading them. Or the Government may get its way partly—as when it compromised on an increase of war pensions (April 1949) demanded by the Finance Commission, bringing the amount down from 16½ percent to 15.

The Finance Commission. This is the "Queen of Commissions," mistress of the budget, and, therefore, in a highly planned and subsidized economy, powerful over policy. Its members tend to become Ministers of Finance or other important Ministers; some have already held the former office. In the Third Republic, Ministers of Finance and even Prime Ministers became the vanquished in their incessant power struggles with the Commission, whose members were avid for the offices held by the former. As the Cabinet has skimmed the party groups of their best members, it is the *opposition* members of the Commission who are the most forceful. Much of the value of the brilliant officials in the French Ministry of Finance is lost in the parliamentary weakness of their Minister.

The Commission has a general *rapporteur* and Special *rapporteurs* for the Ministries. Members of the other Commissions attend the Finance Commission as consultants when their field is being discussed; the latter must invite them. The Finance Commission also sends its special reporters to the other Commissions to present its views on subjects they are submitting to the Assembly, and its views must be included in their reports. In its forums all appropriations and tax problems are minutely examined, with the help of departmental experts. Even the Western Defense Pacts, 1954, were examined by the Finance Commission—have they not a financial aspect?

Like the other Commissions, it steers bills in its field, through Assembly debates. In this, it may actually support the Government's budget proposals integrally.

Yet, again as a corporate body, it is a rival of the Government. M. Barangé had been general *rapporteur* from June 1946 to July 1953, covering twelve changes of office in the Ministry of Finance. Who knows more about the budget?

Again and again, it fights the Government's budgets, sometimes to a standstill, always to a substantial amendment and compromise. It frequently deletes important taxes, leaving the Government and the Assembly the business of their restoration or the discovery of an alternative or the reduction of expenditures to match the loss of expected revenue. We have indicated that the Government may be forced to ask for a vote of confidence from the Assembly to beat the efforts of the Commission. The appropriations and revenues are subject to a kind of tennis game, being shot over the net from Commission to Assembly, from Government to Commission, and so on. The Government exerts pressure on the members who are of its coalescing parties: sometimes successfully, sometimes not. The attacks by the Commission almost invariably weaken the Cabinets and soften them up for subsequent overthrow in the Assembly. In the debates in the Assembly, the members of the Commission split their votes, some for, some against, the Government.

An excellent case in point occurred on November 9, 1954. The Finance Commission refused to report the post office budget to the Assembly; it did this in order to force the Government to put in certain new appropriations demanded by some Deputies. The Deputies used this method of evading the rule that they may not propose new expenditures. Mendès-France declared this was unconstitutional, and demanded that the Commission and the Assembly study the chapters of the budget seriatim and listen to ministers' explanations of why the budget was set up as they had presented it. He made the issue one of principle, called for a vote of confidence on this, asserting that he would apply the rule, if he obtained his vote, on all other departmental budgets also. He won by 320 to 207 with 69 abstentions.

We give the figures of the voting so that they may be compared with the coalition that voted for his assumption of office in June 1954 (*italics*). They are:

Party	For		Against		Abstained	
Communists	0	*95*	95	*0*	0	*0*
Socialists	104	*104*	0	*0*	0	*0*
Radicals	70	*72*	0	*0*	5	*3*
M.R.P.	5	*10*	67	*1*	2	*74*
De Gaullists	55	*59*	0	*2*	12	*12*
Democratic Social Union	23	*19*	0	*0*	0	*3*
Overseas Independents	15	*15*	0	*0*	0	*0*
Independents	14	*12*	10	*14*	27	*25*
Independent Peasants	10	*4*	12	*15*	4	*7*
Peasants	9	*13*	9	*4*	2	*3*
Dissident Gaullists	8	*5*	8	*11*	17	*16*
Progressists	0	*4*	4	*0*	0	*0*
Not in a group	7	*7*	2	*0*		
Total	320	*419*	207	*47*	69	*143*

The Finance Commission assists in the supervision of expenditure and the public accounts. The special *rapporteurs* of the Commission visit the departments and keep constant liaison with the departmental representatives of the Ministry of Finance. Sometimes Parliament, bedeviled by its own lack of self-discipline, gives the Commission powers to further the operation of a financial measure. For example, the Government was given power to transfer some credits from one chapter to another (*virement,* or diversion), but only with the assent of the Finance Commission and the advice of the Council of the Republic's Commission.

We have already referred to the power of the Assembly, assisted by the Court of Accounts, an official and independent body, like the Comptroller and Auditor General in the British and American systems (see p. 131).

Finances and Special Powers to Govern by Decree.
We have noticed the origin of this device (p. 315);

it is a danger to democratic government, though grave emergencies and especially the exigencies of war justify it—when it is a matter of self-preservation.

The Fourth Republic's Constitution objected to the use of such powers, since the makers of it remembered the contemptible conditions that had given rise to it. But they abolished the effect without abolishing the cause. The Constitution says: "The National Assembly alone shall vote the laws. *It may not delegate this right.*" This is categorical enough; and the categorical intention was forcibly expressed in the constitutional committee. But the causes that demanded decree-laws have become more pronounced.

By July 1947 members of the Government were claiming they needed these powers. In August 1948 they were first granted to Paul Reynaud, who, it is interesting to notice, had been a minority of one in the Constituent Assembly to demand that such powers *be* permitted. The grant of such powers to the Government has been an almost annual event since then.

The main feature of them all is the stipulation of a time limit for which the powers may be used —so many months, a date being set; and then certain general permissions for the raising or lowering of taxes, the effectuation of economies in the appropriations, and various economic measures that may strengthen the economy and simultaneously make the budget sounder.

Governments have been allowed to reduce taxes; and, as we have seen, to *raise* taxation, provided the Finance Commission agreed. The powers granted Reynaud permitted him to reorganize the Civil Service, to reconstruct the nationalized industries, to reform the machinery of social security, and to make considerable changes in financial administration.

On August 10, 1954, the National Assembly granted special powers to the Mendès-France Government. It was, of course, in the form of a law. By 362 votes to 90, which meant that *close on 200 deputies did not vote,* the powers were granted until March 31, 1955. They covered all measures deemed necessary to bring about economic expansion, enlarging the national income, lowering production costs, increasing purchasing power, assuring full employment, developing foreign trade, raising the standard of living in the overseas territories, and developing financial and economic cooperation between France and her overseas territories. There were strict limitations on changes in the current budget. The grant followed a speech by and debate on the Prime Minister's economic and financial policy.

It is important to notice that such powers clearly do not have a merely temporary significance; they have a deep and long-term reach and effect. Sometimes a grant of power of this kind is continued in some of its specific aspects. For example, the powers given to Reynaud regarding the reform of the administrative departments were continued for M. Laniel in the special powers granted to him on July 10, 1953.

A former Prime Minister, René Mayer, Radical, urged that, since the Assembly had found it necessary for the fifth time since the war to give special powers, Article 13 of the Constitution be amended. There is, in fact, some dispute among constitutional lawyers in France, whether the power to make a "decree" is the delegation of the Assembly's powers *to make law*. To this author there is no doubt about it, especially considering the width of the powers granted and the fact that some of the decrees enter into force immediately. It is better to amend the Constitution in this case. The practice is a serious abdication of parliamentary self-discipline. It hits at the roots of democracy, for in the breadth of the language it does permit a government, quite honestly, to interpret the powers otherwise than as the mind of the Assembly allows. The consequences are twofold. Sometimes the Finance Commission has to protest because the use of the power granted is dubious. In October 1951 the Government chose to increase the petrol tax because projected economies had not been made. Or, when a Government begins to use its powers, there are strikes and parliamentary objections, to such an extent that the Government must reverse itself or compromise. Prime Minister Paul Reynaud's Cabinet was overthrown ten days after being granted special powers, because his use of them did not please the Assembly. Who was hum-bugging whom? Similarly with Mendès-France's decrees to reduce alcohol sale and consumption; his emergency powers lasted until March 1955; his Cabinet lasted only until early February! The grant of special powers takes on the appearance of a mere device of postponement of awkward problems the Assembly should, indeed, solve.

IV. THE ELECTION OF JANUARY 2, 1956

The election of January 2, 1956, produced a potentially more unworkable Assembly than the one that had overthrown eight Cabinets since June 1951, for the French social structure had undergone no substantial change and the electoral system was identical.

The election was for 594 seats, since the thirty Algerian seats were to remain unfilled by reason of civil war. Of these 594, fifty-three were in overseas areas.

Faure's objective (see pp. 371–373) depended on astute electoral alliances. Clever tactics in 1951 had cut down the Communist and de Gaullist seats far below their proportion of votes (p. 370). If the middle parties wished to benefit at the expense of the Right and Left extremes, they needed to unite in tactically useful alliances. But a fierce quarrel continued to rend them, especially violent and personal between the Mendès-France Radicals and the Faure Radicals, the M.R.P. siding with Faure and the Socialists with Mendès-France. Failing *apparentements* between these former allies, the Communists would gain, for the total seats for each constituency would often be divided among the parties in direct proportion to the votes each obtained separately; and wherever it got over 50 percent of the votes, it would get all the seats. The votes of each party falling short of the quota required to win a seat would be entirely wasted, for the French do not allow, as the Weimar P.R. did (p. 622), a credit in seats for the accumulated remnant votes all over the nation. Small parties were at a special disadvantage.

Many Parties

No less than twenty-seven "national" parties appeared, being political groupings with candidates in more than thirty *départements,* were entitled to make alliances. Of these, ten were the major ones listed in the voting figures given below, some adding "national" to their title; one was the *Jeune République* (p. 354). Three were Poujadists: the Union of French Fraternity, the Group for Defense of Agricultural and Winegrowers' Interests, and the Civic Action in Defense of Consumers and Family Interests. These created fake alliances in some forty constituencies, fake, since the law permitted them only between *independent* parties, while these were only Poujade's Union for the Defense of Commercial People and Artisans with other names.

Alliances

The Communists asked for *apparentement* with the Socialists; these refused firmly, fearing contamination. Two Socialists who disobeyed the ban were expelled. Guy Mollet hoped to win the workers, in time, to the Socialist Party he led. He made forty-seven alliances with Radical Socialists, and in nine of these were included the social-welfare-democratic members of the former de Gaullists (Social Republicans). These Radical Socialists were, of course, led by Mendès-France, not by Faure. The R.G.R., including the Faure Radicals, made sixty-seven alliances, including forty-seven with the Socialists (friends of their foe Mendès-France) and twenty with the M.R.P. and/or the "Moderates"—that is, "clerical" candidates who were foes of Mendès-France and the Socialists both over Church-school subsidies and social welfare. The M.R.P. made fifty-two alliances with the "Moderates," another name for very strong conservatives, such as Pinay, Laniel, Pleven, and Petsch, and various other alliances with Social Republicans (Right-wing de Gaullists) and conservatives in the R.G.R. The "Moderates," officially called Independents, allied with the M.R.P. and in five places with the Right-wing Social Republicans and Peasants and Independent Peasants. The stand-pat de Gaullists, Social Republicans, entered thirty-seven alliances, including twenty-eight with "Moderates" and/or the M.R.P.

No party had nationwide coverage; all had variable coverages; some parties were highly local or had ragged networks across the land. Moreover, France either had no leaders or too many. Mind did not meet mind on the same topics, but floundered in the localities, fixed often on petty issues and personalities. The eighteen bigger parties each had one ten-minute and one five-minute spot on the radio and one five-minute TV appearance, free of charge.

The Campaign

Space permits only a mention of the "Left"—that is, the Republican Front of Socialists and Mendès-France Radicals and the Poujadists. The parties of the Center and the Right took their traditional positions of financial stability, colonial conservatism, and free enterprise, and the Communists their well-known class-war ideas, as described in our earlier pages. The Republican Front fought strongly, and Mendès-France with violent passion, for change; their device was the French Revolutionary Phrygian bonnet. They put Algeria first on the agenda, to be pacified by liberalism, federalism, and self-government; they combated alcoholism, which cost 250 milliards a year to the national budget, the price of 150,000 houses; promised better housing at the rate of 300,000 units per year against the grudging 210,000 of the previous government; demanded *universal* coverage in the spotty social-security system; urged vast improvement in the too class-ridden educational opportunities; supported progress in industrialization; advocated the single-member electoral district. They were, of course, adamantly anticlerical. On foreign affairs they stood with the United States and Britain. Furthermore, they demanded the raising of the income and like taxes, and the reduction of direct taxes. For France still raises only 36 percent of her revenue by direct taxes, and at least 64 percent from indirect sources.[8]

But the Center and the Right had no intention of such democratic taxation. The M.R.P. and the Right stood firmly in favor of Church schools. François Mauriac, the novelist, joined Mendès-France in charging that the M.R.P. had become nothing more than a clerical party of the Right, under Georges Bidault. The *Jeune République,* liberal Catholics, fought against clerical conserva-

---

[8] British revenues come more than 50 percent from income and profits taxation; the United States raises only 22 percent by indirect taxation (though the situation is otherwise in the states); and West Germany raises about 66 percent by customs and excise, the rest by direct taxes.

tism. The Communists concentrated on pushing the Socialists program to impossible extremes, supporting Russia and denouncing the sending of reserves to Algeria—but they did this through intensive work in their cells rather than placards, etc.

Poujade himself (like the early Hitler) did not stand for election but managed the campaigns of his three groups. His movement (p. 297) had now expanded to include meanly disgruntled "little men" of several classes, peasants, Communist workers, some rich people. The originating grievance was the shopkeepers' and artisans' turnover taxes. These required complicated records of many trivial taxes on articles very similar, but taxed differently according to origin or quality. The Socialists had introduced a bill (voted down by 400 Deputies) for only one tax solely on manufacturers or wholesalers, so relieving nearly 1,500,-000 shopkeepers and artisans. To this grievance, the heterogeneous followers added a poisonous malevolence against parliamentarism and democracy, anti-Semitism, imperialism, anti-industrialization, hostility to the cities. It introduced unprecedented violence into the campaign, beating candidates, kidnaping opponents, breaking up meetings, throwing missiles. It practiced scandalous slanders, one of these by Poujade himself against M. Schneiter, previous President of the Assembly, that the latter had participated in an assassination in the post-Liberation period. Poujade was judicially convicted and fined.

Pierre Poujade is an unprincipled, illogical, and uneducated demagogue, a former member of a Fascist group of the 1930's, a boorish provincial from St. Céré in Lôt in central France. His father, an architect, dying young, Poujade became a casual laborer, a roustabout, a racing cyclist. In World War II he served with the British R.A.F. He was elected a municipal councilor in his native neighborhood and started a small bookshop. On the demand that he pay taxes, he founded his antitax movement.

In the election he counseled his followers *not* to discuss policy! He demands that small businessmen not be treated as poor relations by inferior provision of social security. If he has a program, it is thus concocted: compulsory voting; abolition of the Economic Council and Assembly of the French Union, and replacement by a Senate of "corporations"; a strong veto power lodged in the President (!) to strengthen the "Executive"; abolition of all price-fixing and supervision of the economy; reduction of public expenditure; economies in the nationalized industries; the holding down of Algeria, whatever the cost; no subordination to NATO; friendship with the United States, provided she does not meddle with the French colonies; anti-Communism; "France First." He demands, moreover, an "Estates General" (pp. 278–279) meeting of the "people" to consider grievances and remodel the constitution, but he does not say how. Here is another of those quasi-KKK groups, so often found in various forms on the French Right, denying that it is Fascist or anti-Semitic, but ready to overturn democracy. It gained some 2,500,000 voters! It is without the majesty of Charles de Gaulle.

The Election

A total of 5381 candidates stood on 955 lists for the 547 seats in metropolitan France. This average of over fifty candidates per *département* was bewildering indeed to the voters, if not to the candidates themselves. The champion *département,* Lozère, confronted its electors, looking painfully for guidance, with twelve lists containing twenty-four candidates fighting for two vacant seats: 1 Progressist (a Communist ally); 3 Poujadist; 5 affiliated lists of R.G.R., Peasants, Independents, Social Republicans, and M.R.P.; 1 Republican Front; 1 Independents of the Left; and 1 *Jeune République*. Friends and foes were mixed up. The electorate numbered 26,353,278, an increase of about 2,180,000 over 1951; 21,794,-974 actually voted, being 82.8 percent of the electorate as compared with 80.2 percent in 1951; 21,138,159 votes were cast validly.

We give the results in votes and seats (simplified and collated) for metropolitan France (less the Moselle, where seats were in dispute at the time of tabulation). Later, we present the groups as they formed in the new Assembly that met on January 19, 1956, and that contains all the metropolitan seats and overseas seats, except Algeria.

Parties *	Millions of Votes 1956	Millions of Votes 1951	Percent of Votes	Difference from 1951	1956 Seats	1951 Seats	1956 Seats if Fully Proportional
Communists and Progressists	5.42	5.01	25.6	−0.9	145	93	143
Socialists	3.17	2.72	15.0	+0.6	88	94	79
Radicals, Mendès-France					34		
Radicals, Faure, R.G.R.	2.92	2.09	13.6	+2.7	67 { 15 } 82		80
R.G.R. alone					18		
U.D.S.R. and "Left"	0.35	—	1.6	+1.3	8		9
M.R.P.	2.26	2.32	10.0	−2.2	70	85	63
Independents, A.R.S. and Peasants	3.00	2.33	14.1	+1.8	94	125	83
De Gaullists	0.89	3.98	4.2	−76.9	16	57	15
Poujadists	2.57		12.1	+11.1	51		78
New Right (National Rally)	0.34		1.5		3		

* The total of these seats is 591. The figures are approximate.

Interpretation. Only ten *apparentements* won an absolute majority in any constituency, so that, in the main the clumsy P.R. system operated. The Communists benefited, especially wherever their one list attained 50 percent of the votes. They increased their total votes by something less than 500,000 but fell in percentage, yet abundantly retrieved their loss of seats in 1951 suffered through tricks of the middle parties, to become by far the largest party in the Assembly. The Socialists gained nearly 500,000 votes, rose in percentage, but lost some seats. The de Gaullists were shattered in both respects. Constituency analyses show that their vote was taken over by the Poujadists, who gained their more than 2,500,000 votes mainly in the rural and small-town areas, and primarily south of the Loire (volatile, radical, vociferous), not in the progressive areas of industry. And only in thirty *départements* did they get seats. The grouped parties of the Right gained slightly in every respect. The sufferers were the Radical Socialists, split badly. Proportionately, they should have gathered 80 seats, but they won only 67. After the election, M. Faure was excluded from the pre-Assembly Party Conference.

The "Left," from Mendès-France and the U.D.S.R. leftward through the Socialists and the Communists, gained in votes, seats, and percentage. On this same basis, the Right-of-Center seats fell from 267 to 234, even including all the M.R.P. Deputies, some of whom must still be counted Leftish. The "Left" claimed a victory. Guy Mollet, Secretary of the Socialists, obtained first call

as Prime Minister designate. Mollet formed a Cabinet exclusively of Socialists and Mendès-Francites and U.D.S.R. with a combined democratic Radical and Socialist policy, giving no hostages even to the M.R.P. for the time being. Communists pressed for office, but Mollet firmly refused; they promised to vote for his Cabinet nevertheless—so long as it suited them.

The vote of confidence, 420 to 71, given M. Mollet by the Assembly on February 1, 1956, pictures the final state of parties and groups after the fifty-three Overseas Deputies (not Algeria) had been elected, with 594 Deputies altogether. But there is no official distinction in it between Mendès-Francite and Faurian Radicals, or the split in the U.D.S.R. Mendès-France leads thirty-four Radicals and Faure fifteen; who the rest, no one knows.

Never was it so clear that the French voters produce by their votes only a collection of variegated molecules, by an incoherent decision that allows them the choice of a piece of a jig-saw puzzle but gives them no comprehending part in the final shape of the coalition Cabinets which can alone be the product of a distracted Assembly. The next chapter shows the consequences in short-lived Cabinets, transient Ministers, and general debility and feebleness so dire that dissolution was undertaken in December 1955—only to produce the present result, all over again.

Immobilisme will again be the agenda of France! At once, M. Mollet advocated a strong Executive, supported by dissolution.

The Poujadists are utterly without political ex-

Group	For	Against	Abstained	Absent	Total	1955 [*]
Communists	147	0		3	150	98
Socialists	93	0		2	95	104
Radicals	57	0		1	58	76
U.D.S.R.	19	0			19	23
R.G.R.	12	0	1	1	14	
M.R.P.	64	0	9		73	87
Overseas Independents	10	0			10	16
Social Republicans	16	0		6	22	68
Independents	1	14	67	1	83	54
Peasants	0	6	5	1	12	21
Union of French Fraternity (Poujade)	0	49		3	52	
Noninscribed	1	2	1	2	6	15
Total	420	71	83	20	594	

[*] In the comparison with 1955, being the vote of no-confidence in the Faure Government on November 29, the R.G.R. an electoral organization had no place; today they are mainly Faurists, he being their president. By January 1956 the Independent Republicans, set down as Independents in table, included the remnants of the Independent Peasants—that is, wealthy farmers—and the A.R.S., the dissident or Right-wing de Gaullists.

perience.[9] Will they obey Poujade? Will not some be won over to constructive measures? To office? Twelve of their seats were challenged in the Credentials Commission (p. 374) for faked *apparentements*. There seems to be an unwillingness to apply the law to them, lest antiparliamentarism grow. But this would be to bow to Hitler's type of fake "legality" (p. 651). The Assembly has the right, further, to disqualify members for obe-

dience to an outside master (p. 374), for their oath to Poujade is a desperate one.

France is once more saddled with a distraught Assembly. The result may be normal dissolution by the Prime Minister within eighteen months, or the Assembly could dissolve itself at any time by an ordinary law, since its tenure is *not* established in the Constitution! This would require the Left and middle parties to agree on the law needed.

[9] They are 10 foodshop-keepers; 10 miscellaneous shop-keepers; 6 large shopkeepers, one chemist, 7 artisans, 3 engineers, 4 manufacturers, 2 building contractors, one farmer, one hotelkeeper, one printer, one school principal, 2 students of law, and one ex-police commissioner, Jean Dides, the dingy agent in defense secrets' peddling (p. 435).

Party Strength in the National Assembly, February 1956

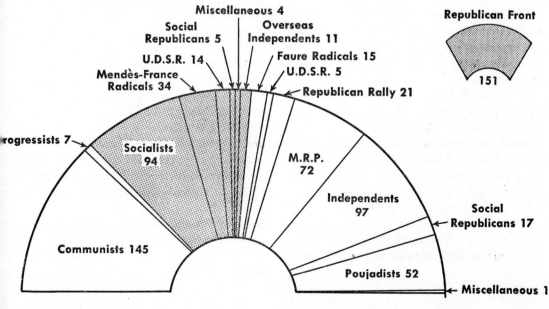

The President of the Republic;
The Prime Minister; and The Council
of Ministers, or Cabinet

In fine, all these differences contribute to render the Englishman more powerful and the Frenchman more happy. The costume of the former is more substantial; that of the latter more comfortable. The former has reason to let out the seams of his suit which is tight at the elbows; the latter would act wisely in avoiding those hasty movements which may tear his flimsy material. But it appears to me that each of them has the style of dress which he prefers.

—Hippolyte Taine, 1871

I. THE PRESIDENT OF THE REPUBLIC

The Presidents of the Third Republic, excepting MacMahon and Poincaré, were weak men (p. 311). The Fourth Republic reduced even the formal powers of the President; his chief strength derives from his right to designate Prime Ministers and appoint Ministers and, to some extent, from his chairmanship of the *Conseil des Ministres* (p. 431).

He is elected by the Parliament—that is, the Council of the Republic and the National Assembly in joint session. He is elected, as in the Third Republic, for seven years and is eligible for re-election but once. The Constitution says nothing about the manner of the conduct of the election. This was by design. The old custom of secret ballot was assumed. Nor is the majority required for election stated; the old rule of absolute majority was applied when the Assembly chose its first President of the Republic in 1947, M. Vincent Auriol.

Vincent Auriol served out the full seven years but was firm in his resolution not to serve again. A clue to his unwillingness may be found in some remarks of his on the burdensomeness of the office. For it is burdensome, with many chores yet without the zest and pleasure that enable the politician of the Assembly and the Government to bear these chores lightly. Perhaps the greatest strain for a formerly practicing politician and a man still in his vigor (when elected first) is to suppress his feelings when he strongly disagrees with the behavior of the parties he has been partly responsible for calling to office.

Election, 1947. Four candidates stood for election in January 1947: the oldest member of the *Conseil de la République* for the Radical-moderates; Michel Clemenceau, supported by his father's fame and the group (p. 318) he led; an M.R.P. candidate (its second choice to Robert Schuman, party leader, who refused to stand); and Vincent Auriol, the veteran Socialist. The Communists voted for Auriol and did not present a candidate of their own, vaunting that "the election should have a national and republican character." Auriol was elected on the first ballot: 452 votes out of 883; the closest to him was the M.R.P. candidate.

Election, December 1953. When, in December 1953, Auriol laid down his heavy and unusually well-performed charge, he was followed by René Coty (no relation to Coty the parfumier and former financier of Fascist groups). This time the election was more difficult. By the time the election day, December 13, had arrived, there were no fewer than eight candidates; each party had its favorite son. Included were one former Prime Minister and Foreign Secretary, Georges Bidault, and the then-serving Prime Minister, Joseph Laniel.

The de Gaullists tried to bargain their votes and the withdrawal of their nominee for the virtual abandonment of EDC. They could not get the assurances, and so left their members free to vote as they wanted. By the fourth ballot the battle was narrowed down to a fight between Laniel in the lead and Naegelen, the Socialist nominee. Laniel was almost sure of winning. But the Radicals disliked him. At the sixth ballot the Deputies became ashamed of the spectacle they were exhibiting to the whole world and tried to get Auriol to reenter, as a way of bringing down the curtain over the futility. By the ninth ballot, Laniel needed only twenty-two more votes to win. Then his votes fell off. When the tenth ballot produced no decision, Laniel was induced by the pressure of domestic and foreign opinion to withdraw for the sake of the reputation of France. René Coty, age seventy-two, was found and elected on the thirteenth ballot, the Radicals going over to him. The Socialist candidate was second to Coty; the latter 477 votes, the Socialist 329.

Vincent Auriol was sixty-two years old when elected in 1947, and had begun a Socialist Party political career over forty years before, being elected Deputy first in 1914. He had quite a distinguished service in the Chamber and as Minister. He voted No at Vichy. He took part in the Resistance; was imprisoned; escaped and joined de Gaulle's government in October 1943 (see p. 320). M. Coty was in 1953 a Senator, one of the Independent Republicans, a lawyer by career. Since

the age of twenty-five he had been elected to local government offices in his native district of Havre. He was elected to the Chamber in 1923, after a valiant career in World War I, with the Left Republicans—that is, conservatives. He entered the Senate in 1935. He was Minister of Reconstruction in three postwar Cabinets—not a fanatic; eloquent, with respect for others' opinions; human understanding. And old? It is extremely doubtful whether Coty will rise to his predecessor's attainments.[1]

The Powers of the President

We list the powers of the President elsewhere (see *Appendix*) and here briefly characterize M. Auriol's manner of employing them. The irony is that M. Auriol, as we have suggested (p. 324), was a leader of the party that had proposed abolition of the very office he was to hold!

Auriol's Use of the Powers. His general view of the presidency, which is not set down anywhere in the Constitution in so many terms, is given in a speech that he made to the foreign press at a dinner on November 16, 1951. He there defended speeches he had recently made on profiteering, tax frauds, the selfishness of the French community, and the grinding of the faces of the poor by the rich. Furthermore, he had vigorously denounced the undermining tactics of the Cominform, supported the NATO policy, rebuked the "iron curtain" of Russia, and proposed effective disarmament. The Communists did not find this at all to their taste. His was the doctrine of *"the moral magistracy"* of the President.

> To believe some people, I am supposed to have exceeded my powers. I regret to contradict those who would wish to make of the Presidency of the Republic a passive magistrate, silent, and merely a figurehead. But the Constitution has confided to me responsibilities which I intend to discharge scrupulously and completely. I have declared since I was installed that I would never

[1] During the summer of 1953 it was rumored that Marshal Alphonse Juin (see p. 438) would be put forward as a candidate for the presidency, one more attempt of the conservative-*cum*-military group to gain power. The General publicly stated that he would not stand, as the office was without power and merely a burden. As a rebuke, M. Auriol announced that the General would no longer be received at Elysée receptions.

be either a nonentity (a King Log), nor a personal president. Between being mute, *laissez-faire,* and do as you like, and decision, effective action reserved to the responsible government, there is a place for that *moral magistracy* about which people speak, for that power of counsel, of warning, of conciliation, which ought to be that of the chief of the State, sensitive and on the alert—above the currents of opinions, superficial and transient, and above the clashes of the parties—and the profound and permanent will of the nation. Impartiality is quite the contrary of indifference, and I shall neglect my duties of my charge if I do not try to express, to foreign lands as well as in our own, and in total accord with the government, that which ought to unite Frenchmen and all the free peoples. . . .

To defend the State, its institutions, its constitution, and in the same time the permanent interests of France that the State represents, that is my conception of my role.

Hence at Cabinet meetings, where he was Chairman, he had often spoken his mind forcefully. He put up an alternative candidate (from his own personal cabinet) for a high diplomatic position (head of cultural relations in the Foreign Ministry) against a candidate of Foreign Minister Robert Schuman in the midst of quite a press uproar. He pressed the Government to fight Communist sabotage of the Indochina effort and the French defense policy. He sought conciliation in French-Tunisian tensions in March 1952, drafting a letter to the Bey and pressing its delivery.

Such interventions were the outcome of his position as presiding officer of the Council of Ministers (Cabinet) and of the Defense Commission (which includes the military chiefs and the relevant Cabinet Ministers) and of the Council of National Defense, which meets from time to time. (Attention is drawn to the revelation of secrets of its proceedings, p. 435). As with the President in the Third Republic, having access to all diplomatic documents (for example, to jump some years, M. Mendès-France's disclosures to President Coty of negotiations for EDC and the Western Union Pacts while they were proceeding) gives the President great opportunities of early and effective intervention. If he is an intelligent man, practiced in politics, he has the great advantage of years in

office against Ministers who have only months in office; he has the advantage a permanent civil servant has over the amateur in the field in which he likes to specialize.

Again and again Auriol publicly challenged the disruptive tendencies of de Gaulle's peculiar policy and speeches, particularly the demand for new elections out of season.

The President of the Republic is President of the High Council of the Magistracy (Chapter 11). As such, Auriol prevented the Cabinet from traversing the judgments of the courts in favor of certain Communists, urging that this be left to the High Council. He personally urged the High Council to see to it that the judiciary more strictly applied the law against the speculation in food.

The President has the right of pardon—on the advice of the High Council. Auriol used the power to mitigate some of the unjust severities and iniquities of punishment of offenders during the Vichy period. In the case of the Malgasy Deputies (p. 375), he pardoned them for their part in the insurrection of 1947.

The President is chairman of the Constitutional Committee (see p. 332). Auriol used his power to refer back bills for another deliberation as follows. He refused a Communist request that he refer back a bill for the maintenance of public order. This was under the power in Article 36— a mild suspension power, involving not the immediate promulgation of the law but its reference back to the Assembly. The power was used eight times between 1946 and 1951. Once it was used at the request of the Constitutional Committee to settle a procedure conflict between the National Assembly and the Council of the Republic (see p. 448); once as an alternative to putting the dispute before the Constitutional Committee. The rest were to avoid unforeseen inconsistencies in parliamentary procedure. The presidential power in this respect needs countersignature; though it is a formality that must be discharged, the President's personal judgment in the matters referred to was free from ministerial pressure. It was especially important in the reference back of the intended law of the Assembly reducing parliamentary immunities (see p. 333), in which case the

President was taking a longer and more libertarian view than the irate Assembly.

French observers point especially to Auriol's
personal inauguration of the Assembly of the
French Union. The Presidency is one of the organs of the Union (see Chapter 7).

In general policy (apart from what is to be
gathered from the ensuing pages on the French
Cabinet) some typical interventions of the President were these. He supported the Minister of
Finance and the Minister of Justice in an attempt
in November 1951 to raise the compensation of
the magistracy; the Cabinet outvoted them for it
was afraid that teachers would then demand an
increase in their salaries. During the dissensions
in the Cabinet over the reform of the electoral law
in 1951, he worked for appeasement, and against
a ministerial crisis, on the ground that this would
not solve the differences, and that account must be
taken of the international situation of France that
could ill afford the fall of the Government by invoking a vote of confidence and that on this occasion it could lead to a dissolution (p. 419). During
the crisis in the Cabinet over the Moroccan policy
in October 1955, the R.P.F. or de Gaullists appealed to the President (Coty) to get rid of the
Faure Government and replace it by one of "national union," an appeal that was courteously rejected.

What the substantial power of the President
amounts to, then, depends even before the last
resort on the status and role of the Council of
Ministers or Cabinet, and to an account of this we
now turn.

We may, at this special point, add some agonized observations of President Coty on the instability of French Cabinets, seen from his vantage
point and made during the attacks on the Faure
Government's existence, concerning North African
policy, as he was endeavoring to rally opinion to
avoid the twenty-third overturn of a Government
since 1945. He said (October 14, 1955), a propos
of Cabinet instability:

> It is better for the fuses to blow, than for the
> house to burn down.

This is true, yet it is a tragic feebleness in government when the fuses are constantly blowing; a
house may be destroyed in the midst of such
changes of light and darkness. "Fickleness and
passion" were the causes of blowing fuses; the
phrase was General de Gaulle's, Coty repeated it.
Then he said:

> In the course of their [the Cabinets'] ephemeral
> existence, the successive chiefs of government
> have unceasingly, and for no reason, seen their
> confidence and authority questioned by those
> who vested them with office. Day after day,
> they are tormented and harassed until too often
> —the most gifted and the most robust do not
> escape it—they are morally and physically ex-
> hausted.

Article 51 of the Constitution calls for the President's signature of a decree dissolving the National
Assembly and the Prime Minister asks for it after
taking the decision in a *Conseil des Ministres*. At
such a *Conseil* the President of the Republic is in
the chair. Article 51 leaves him no discretion, it
would appear; and under the general theory of
ministerial responsibility, he would have none. He
had to be persuaded to accept such a decision, made
by nineteen Ministers against four at the request
of M. Faure on November 30, 1955, the first time a
dissolution had been sought since May 16, 1877.
He evidently accepted the position of the Crown in
Britain, one who reigns but does not govern. He
happened to be a former member of the Independent Republican Party which was represented
in the Cabinet, and that Party is favorable to the
Executive power of dissolution. Had he been able
to deny the decree, he would have had the impossible job of finding a new coalition for the last six
months of the legislature's legal term!

II. MAKING A GOVERNMENT: THE APPOINTMENT OF THE PRIME MINISTER AND THE CABINET

The Constitutional Provisions

Little practical change has occurred in the formation, role, and status of the Cabinet in the Fourth
Republic as compared with the Third Republic.
Some formal changes were made; then in December 1954 even some of these were amended.

The Constitution gives the power to actuate the
sovereignty of the French people to the National

Assembly; that sovereignty is not split into several branches, such as Legislative and Executive, as in the United States (p. 56).

The President of the Republic and the Council of Ministers are endowed with a series of powers and at the same time subjected to a responsibility, either political (that is, loss of office) or judicial, which in the end comes back to submission to the will of the National Assembly.

The text, in the *Appendix,* should be at once consulted, for Title VI, Articles 45 to 55.

The President designates the Prime Minister [2] —of course, dependent on his estimate of the strength of the parties in the Assembly. He formally appoints Prime Minister and Cabinet by a decree. In a Caretaker Government (p. 420), he appoints the President of the National Assembly to be Prime Minister for the time being. Article 32 gives him the duty of presiding over the *Conseil des Ministres,* which is different from the *Conseil de Cabinet,* but, most important (p. 431), it also requires him to order the recording of the minutes of *these* meetings and keep them in his possession.

These are powers of some personal, political weight.

The Designation of the Prime Minister

In order to keep our eyes straight on a complicated situation—the making of French Cabinets—let us state in briefest terms (1) what the practice of the Third Republic amounted to, for this is (2) what the Fourth Republic reverted to, informally some five years after it began to operate the letter of the new Constitution and formally when the amendments of December 1954 were passed. Summed up, (1) and (2) amounted and amount to this. The President of the Republic weighs the respective strengths and policies of the Assembly's groups. With some small latitude, he chooses a Prime Minister-designate who can combine those groups to make a majority that are rather more to his personal tastes than one or two alternative groupings. In this process he is helped by consultations with the Presidents of the two Chambers and the leaders of various groups, including

the outgoing Prime Minister. Then the Prime Minister-designate undertakes his closer negotiations with the groups and forms a combination. He goes to the Assembly for approval of himself and his Cabinet with his statement of policy.

The reader may mentally review this tedious, experimental, confused, and roundabout way of establishing a Government with the swift and solid transitions in the British cabinet system, where there is but *one* alternative party to that which has power; *one* alternative policy; *one* single and united Opposition, and *one* indubitable leader of the party already in office and the "Shadow Cabinet," which will take its place as soon as the Queen calls for a new Prime Minister as a result of the verdict of the House of Commons and the general election. The French Prime Minister-designate has to bargain with four or five groups over policy and ministries and undersecretaryships and minor appointments, and with dissentients within the groups, to persuade them to form a combination. Rebuffed by some groups, he must try an alternative combination of four or five groups. He must promise and trim. If all presidential candidates and platforms in the U.S.A. must "hedge" and straddle, then these tactics are brought to the *nth* degree in the making of a French Cabinet; the finesse is extraordinary, and the structure is flimsy in the same degree; no solid loyalty is produced, but the acme of self-seeking in jobs and individual preferences of policies.

The Role of the President. The part played by the President of the Republic in cabinet-making is a consequence of his own character and ability and ideas and the array of political hard facts before him. The latter include the pressure of the domestic and foreign necessities on France and the strengths, cooperativeness, and mutual aversions of the many political parties in the Assembly.

Cabinet-making in the Third Republic was not regulated at all by the Constitution; for that said no more than that the Cabinet was responsible to the Chambers and nominated by the President. A few gambits had been learned, invented, and practiced by the President, always confronted with a multiple-fractured Chamber and Senate. He might name men for Prime Minister distasteful to the Chambers so that they would be rejected in the

---

[2] The French title actually is *President of the Council of Ministers.* We shall, as noted earlier, use the term *Prime Minister* rather than the customary *Premier.*

early stages of party bargaining, in order to get smoother sailing for a preferred candidate when matters had become acutely intolerable in the absence of a Government. Apt maneuvers had kept out Gambetta (by Grèvy); and Poincaré had shelved Clemenceau. The Presidents were never too anxious to appoint a strong Prime Minister, as this overshadowed themselves. They succumbed when political circumstances were too strong for them. Clemenceau *had* to be appointed, lest World War I be lost. Albert Lebrun was compelled by conditions he had not the strength to cope with to appoint Marshal Pétain at the fall of France in June 1940.

The President consulted those most likely to know who could obtain the Chambers' support— that is, he went to the Presidents of the Chamber of Deputies and the Senate. These men were (1) immersed in the political currents that flowed in front of them day by day and (2) could *feel* these themselves since their own positions had been founded on a free vote by the various groups. As we have appreciated, these same men might themselves be candidates for the prime ministership or had been Prime Ministers, and so were acquainted with the various moves. These became the regular, conventional consultants of the President. In addition, there was no such constitutional convention as prevailed in Britain strictly to limit the other party's sources of advice. For such a convention is hard to develop where the parties are soft.

This process of inquiry and investigation was actually a threefold one. The President was interested in the strength of the leader he had in mind; he was concerned for his policy; and, simultaneously, he was anxious about what groups might be brought together for this specific occasion to make a coalition Cabinet, involving both posts and policy. The three matters formed one amalgam, and the maneuvers and negotiations went forward on a daily changing blend of the three. The history of the presidency of Raymond Poincaré and of the abortive one of Alexandre Millerand (1920–1924) shows this amalgam clearly.

When the Prime Minister was nominated, he then nominated his Cabinet. The President appointed them all together. They then went as a Cabinet-designate to the Chamber to get a vote of acceptance *en bloc,* with no differentiation between the Prime Minister and his Cabinet members.

Fourth Republic Cabinet-making. The Fourth Republic changed this informal system into a formal one. In addition, the Constitution laid down rules that interfered with the free process. It distinguished (as the text shows) between (1) the *designation* of the Prime Minister, which comes first and is then converted by the Assembly into an *appointment* as Prime Minister when he has, singly, appeared before it and submitted his policy; and (2) the approval of the Cabinet he *thereafter* assembles and brings to the Assembly for a second approval. What is the meaning and effect of this finesse?

The constitution-makers wanted a cabinet system both stronger and more responsible. The Socialist and Communist parties wanted the Provisional Government's practice continued: election of a Prime Minister-designate by the Assembly after the preliminary maneuvers, and then the submission of his Cabinet to a vote of confidence. They put this in the abortive draft, for they wanted the Executive dominated by the Assembly, fearing de Gaulle and hoping for increase of stability of the Cabinet if founded deeply in the Assembly. The M.R.P. and the Center and conservatives opposed this, arguing the infeasibility of choosing a Prime Minister by 600 Deputies. For what might happen when the wise assistance of Vincent Auriol, President of the Assembly, was lost? For Executive strength they preferred the designation of the Prime Minister from *outside the Assembly*—by a strongish President of the Republic.

The compromise is in Article 45. (1) The President designated the Prime Minister "after the customary consultations." [3] (2) This Prime Minister-designate submitted his program and his future Cabinet's policy (but *not* the Cabinet) to the Assembly. (3) The next clause needed interpretation. The Prime Minister and his Ministers might not be formally appointed until the Prime Minister secured a vote of confidence. Did this mean two *separate* votes, one first for the Prime Minister and then another for his Ministers? Two *"investitures"* or only one? Only one, where Prime Minister, pol-

[3] A convention legislated!

icy, and Ministers were all voted on together, as in the Third Republic?

Down to September 1948, an M.R.P.—Robert Schuman Cabinet, the Prime Ministers and political groups practiced the "double investiture." It was a period of strong Prime Ministers because these were the years of *tripartisme* and of Third Force Governments, when Socialists, M.R.P., and Radicals readily cooperated in coalitions. They got along well with the President of the Republic also. It almost seemed that the quasi-independent strength to lead of the British Prime Ministers had been attained. The hope was reinforced by two events. Prime Minister Ramadier asked the Communists to resign from the Cabinet in May 1947 for undermining it (p. 345). On their refusal, M. Auriol, the President of the Republic (attending the *Conseil des Ministres* and able to see for himself) signed a decree stating that their duties were terminated in consequence of an Assembly vote affirming confidence in the Prime Minister. The Government was repatched; but the reconstructed Cabinet was not submitted to the Assembly for approval; the Prime Minister's authority covered repatching.

Then, later that year, in October, M. Ramadier thoroughly reconstructed his Cabinet after having asked all Ministers to resign, but he did not resubmit himself or the Cabinet to the Assembly for investiture. Finally, when in February 1950 the Socialists quit the Bidault Cabinet, the Prime Minister repatched it and continued in office. On this occasion M. Blum declared that this was sound constitutional practice, as well as the proper duty of a Prime Minister intent on making the republican system of government work properly. M. Mendès-France followed this practice in September 1954, when some Ministers resigned over EDC and repeated the process later.

This is certainly the British practice—but it was not the theory or the practice (except for undersecretaries) in the Third Republic.

Fate of the "Double Investiture"

The Prime Ministers since the Schuman attempt in September 1948 varied in their attitude and fortune. Some went to the Assembly *with* their Ministers on an occasion after they had been personally confirmed as Prime Minister—and then met defeat because the Assembly did not like one or the other of the Ministers. For example, the Schuman Government above mentioned fell because it lost the conservative vote by the time it had found a Minister of Finance, for he was a Socialist. Some Prime Ministers have refused to bring their Cabinets in for a debate on both policy and the Ministers simultaneously—but they have been forced into it by the Assembly which put a question or interpellation. Some have been able to avoid the second investiture because the crisis of the finding of a potential Prime Minister has been so prolonged that public shame and anxiety have forced the Assembly to be satisfied (until it could hit back) with the Prime Minister's freedom to collect his Ministers later. Some have tried to postpone the second investiture, have been forced to face the Assembly for it, and have then been overthrown. This happened to Dr. Queuille in July 1950; the Socialists overthrew his Cabinet after having voted for *him*. Thenceforward to the amendment of 1954, the Prime Ministers, with one exception, asked and obtained from the Assembly the waiving of a vote on the Cabinet.

The decisive point that should not be forgotten, however, is that the politicians pretty well knew who exactly was going to be in the Cabinet: groups, wings, Ministers, and undersecretaries.

Hence, the cabinet-making process had come back very closely to the practice of the Third Republic.

The Prime Ministers would have been foolish men had they dared to neglect careful preliminary group soundings and seek firm promises; indeed, they would have been dead ducks. Some even published the news of their initiatives and the approaches of the parties to them. Two of them, Jules Moch and René Mayer, both in the space of eight days, played a noble, lone hand; each got his individual investiture of over half the Deputies—and then, as proud Prime Ministers, found that they could not get a Cabinet to join them!

The tide seemed to turn irresistibly at the attempt of Dr. Queuille to form a Government in July 1950. When his Cabinet was announced, the Socialists and the Left wing of the M.R.P. deserted him—they had previously supported him.

He had 365 votes to 208 for his own investiture; in two days his vote fell to 221 *versus* 334.

Henceforward the submerged prows of the political groups in the Assembly, visible from the surface of the political sea, jutted grimly above the surface. The parties publicly announced what they expected as policy, as Prime Ministers, as associated groups, as Cabinet posts, and who should be kept out of the Cabinet. Not always did they speak with a definiteness that would exclude negotiations or some loaves and fishes as a second best to their maximum claim, but their coyness could not be neglected by the Prime Ministers-designate or by the President of the Republic, who had to see that a Cabinet was formed and the government of the French Republic functioned.

This deviation of the practice from what the Constitution *may* have intended (for the clause .was fashioned out of competing drafts and amendments) was an apparent return to the well-worn ruts of the Third Republic. The change was summed up in one of the amendments to the Constitution adopted in 1954, making it formal.

This amendment was voted on December 7, 1954,[4] and replaces the second, third, and fourth paragraphs of Article 45:

> The latter [the Prime Minister] chooses the members of his Cabinet and makes the list known to the National Assembly, before which he presents himself in order to obtain its confidence on the program and policy that he intends to pursue, except in the case where force *majeure* prevents the meeting of the National Assembly.
>
> Voting takes place by roll call and simple majority.

The reduction of the necessary majority in this case from an *absolute* one to a relative one is also most worthy of note.

Operation of the Absolute-majority Clause. One of the greatest sins of the Third Republic was the extent to which members abstained from voting. Thus they avoided disclosing their opinions. They evaded subjecting themselves to public responsibility. They deprived Governments and colleagues of an insight into their intentions. This

was the reason for stipulation of the "absolute majority" as well as to avoid snap votes. But the awkward results of this rule *caused its abolition in the amendments of December 1954 (Appendix)*. For an absolute majority was very hard to get, given the fact that the Communists and R.P.F. are in permanent opposition,[5] and the middle parties so numerous.

The old habits of abstention returned, now made the more deadly because a fixed minimum number of votes had to be obtained, even if it seemed more gracious to abstain than openly vote against a Minister or his Government. For retaliation was possible if a group were forced into an openly hostile vote.

It was an awkward clause. To the end of *tripartisme,* it was a foregone conclusion that the Prime Minister would obtain not only an absolute majority but substantially more. Four out of five had 200 votes in excess or more. When the Communists went into permanent opposition in May 1947, the situation changed drastically. It became worse when, in 1951, the R.P.F. won so large a number of seats, for they also were in rancorous opposition. Between them, abstaining or opposing, these two parties mustered 227 out of 627 seats.

After the Communists left, and including the arrival of the Mendès-France Government in June 1954, there were sixteen Governments. Whereas the absolute majority was 314, seven had less than 50 votes above the constitutional minimum, seven between this number and 100, and two had over 100 majority. Of the two last mentioned, one was the Mendès-France Government of June 18, 1954. He obtained 419 against 47 votes, with 143 abstentions. He announced in his speech of self-commendation that he would not accept office if his absolute majority were dependent on the Communist votes. The Communists argued that such an attitude was unconstitutional. They had a political reason for taking this point of view, apart from the fact that the Prime Minister-designate's rebuff seemed to throw them outside the national community and invalidate them as bearers of French sovereignty, while they preferred to with-

---

[4] On insistence of Mendès-France, a *Radical Socialist* Prime Minister.

[5] But see p. 364, on the R.P.F.'s return to cooperation.

draw from it only at their own pleasure. They knew that he sooner or later would help to kill the European Defense Community. They came out of their permanent opposition—and voted for him nevertheless. He took office because he had *an absolute majority of 10 votes* even when their 95 were subtracted. His declaration stood him in good political stead for he preserved his independence as a representative of the interests of France, against a party that represents the interests of the Soviet Union, as required by the Twenty-one Points of the Third International.

Between November 1946 and June 1953 fifteen Governments enjoyed these votes of approval; eleven, an absolute majority; one was not voted on; two were beaten; one obtained a relative majority. All Cabinets but one were given fewer votes than their Prime Minister. Disappointments, malice, and honest disagreements account for the falling away of votes. The Edgar Faure Cabinet that took office February 24, 1955, after the fall of Mendès-France was voted in by 369 to 210, a clear-cut absolute majority, legally no longer needed.

Several quite possible Prime Ministers and Cabinets failed to get going because they had majorities, but not absolute majorities. Thus, eight Prime Ministers-designate before the Faure Cabinet won relative majorities—and so failed; one came down (Jules Moch) after having obtained an *absolute majority of 1,* the validity of which was questioned over the transatlantic telephone, since the proxy vote of a member on a mission to the U.N. was cast in favor, but challenged.

In the crisis, lasting from May 21 to June 26, 1953, when the nation had only a defeated Government in office, four out of the five unsuccessful Prime Ministers had majorities, two very substantial ones, while one (René Mayer) had no majority. Mr. Laniel was, at the sixth attempt, voted in by 398 votes to 206 after agonized efforts, as fully discussed presently. If the absolute majority rule had not existed, Mendès-France might well have begun his beneficent term a year earlier than he did.

Thus the attempt to strengthen the premiership fell foul of the fragmentation of political parties, for it cannot be appreciably stronger than the coalition of groups. Policy cannot be separately conceived and approved apart from the Ministers who may fulfill or spoil it.

The Crisis of 1953

The part of the President of the Republic in cabinet-making comes out well in the crisis just referred to; so does *the pathology* of group government and the feebleness of French Prime Ministers.

A Cabinet headed by René Mayer, Radical, had been in office since January 1953. It was quite conservative, with no Communists, no Socialists in it; with six M.R.P.'s, nine Radicals and allies, eight conservatives. M. Mayer had obtained 389 votes at his investiture, 75 above the absolute majority, and his Cabinet had been voted in by only five votes less than his own investiture. It was dedicated to stopping the franc from losing further value by inflation, to meeting working-class distress by a reduction of prices by government authority, and to reduction of the expenses of government. It was also lukewarm about EDC and was anxious to bring the Indochinese war to some kind of an end.

For four months the Government did very little except merely keep alive—the very first law of Prime Ministers. By May it had its program ready: to reduce payments to recipients of relief, to curb the payment of government employees and reduce the number of people on the public payroll, to raise fares on the railroads, government-owned. For this Mayer demanded decree powers (see p. 398). A sop was thrown to those who might not like this program by the Government's last-minute arrangement with Britain and the United States for peace talks with the U.S.S.R. then pushing one of its periodical peace drives. If this succeeded, then military expenditures could be reduced—and perhaps EDC would not be necessary.

The Socialist votes supported the Government. The R.P.F. wanted to get the Government overthrown and, reversing its previous policy, enter a new coalition. But the Socialists were opposed to the Mayer economies and favored an increase in wages rather than sole control of prices, which was ineffective. The R.P.F. accepted the economic program. It was willing to give decree-making authority but . . . not to this Government, for they were not in it. The R.P.F. drive was pushed by the A.R.S., the Rightist de Gaullists. The Mayer Government was overthrown by the withdrawal of the votes of these two groups. The figures in the table on page 415 show the heterogeneity of the opposition.

Efforts of President Auriol. The President of the Republic began his consultations through the "customary channels" the day after the fall; he consulted former party Prime Ministers and party leaders. The R.P.F. was keen on joining a Government, but it was bitterly hostile to EDC. It could not live happily with the Center groups, certainly not the M.R.P. whose fostering of EDC was more than parental.

Auriol tried hard to persuade the Socialist Party, his own, to abandon their permanent self-exclusion policy. They were reluctant. But by May 23 the President had persuaded Guy Mollet, secretary of the Socialist Party organization, to try to form a Government. The M.R.P. appealed to the Socialists to abandon the opposition. The Socialists declined. By-elections had been favorable to them, and they believed that the workers were supporting the party's attitude of steady opposition to Governments. Indeed, they had a real problem of competing with the Communist Party as the enduring and irreconcilable friend of the working class—they were competing for much the same clientele. They would not budge.

On May 25 the President invited one of the leaders of the R.P.F. to form a Government. He refused. This drove the President back to the Socialists. He berated them, balancing this rebuke with one to the R.P.F. for obstructionism. He turned to Paul Reynaud, member of no group but *lightly* affiliated with Independent Republicans, a former Prime Minister several times, now seventy-four years old.

At that age anyone would try. But Reynaud was in difficulties because the Socialists did not like his conservative finance—perhaps more austere even than that of Mayer. Some in the M.R.P. liked him because he was a leading supporter of EDC

(he had been Prime Minister when France fell in 1940 and had learned the lesson of allied solidarity), but others did not like his conservatism. The R.P.F. waited until he announced his policy before opening up.

Reynaud appeared before the Assembly on May 27. He insisted on constitutional revision to strengthen the Executive by firmer powers of dissolution, as a condition for taking office. He offered an austere and energetic policy of improving French production, wiping out governmental deficits, giving strength to the franc. He was harder than Mayer. He was defeated 276 for, 235 against—while 116 did not vote. The absolute-majority rule sent him packing. As for the R.P.F. that had started the crisis, 37 voted for Reynaud and 45 abstained from voting. The major parties were split on him; the Socialists and Communists were against; he got firm support from only four conservative groups.

The President then turned to Mendès-France, Radical—from a Rightward to a Leftward orientation. He was an advocate of winding up the Indochina war, European rearmament but not EDC, with funds saved from Indochina invested in economic reconstruction. He was not too conservative for the Socialists, perhaps, and not too Leftish for the conservatives. He had a gallant wartime record in the Free French Air Force. He went before the Assembly on this program, promising to get relief of the drain of Indochina on French welfare at the Bermuda Conference that was then in preparation, and thus avoid the need for taking the resources from the working classes and the government employees. He intended to bring a swift end to the Indochina war.

He missed office by 13 votes. The Socialists voted for him; the M.R.P. to the extent of 52 against 37; nearly all his own party (but not all!). The R.P.F. and the Right groups and the Communists opposed him. His doctrine to the Assembly, June 3, 1953, was exactly the one that is right and exactly that which the groups do not like to hear:

> I have already said that the fundamental cause of the ills which beset our country is the multiplicity and the weight of the tasks it tries to assume all at the same time: reconstruction,

modernization and equipment, development of the overseas territories, raising of the standard of living and social reforms, exports, war in Indochina, a big and powerful army in Europe. . . .

Now experience has confirmed what reflection permitted us to foresee: it is not possible to do everything at once.

To govern is to choose, no matter how difficult the choices are.

To choose does not mean forcibly to eliminate this or that, but to reduce here and sometimes to increase there; in other words, to fix the ranks of priority.[6]

Where was the President to look now? He had tried Left, Center, and Right. He tried André Marie, with a national Cabinet—that is, with members from *all* groups except the Communists. (This *might* have brought together a majority, but what kind of a policy could it have produced—a conspectus of an utterly incoherent and distracted Assembly?) Marie had held office as Prime Minister in 1948—for a month and three days—in a coalition that had included the Socialists.

This time the Socialists would not join him. He went to the Assembly on June 19, proposing reductions in military expenditures; that the *Assembly* find a way of raising substantial amounts of taxes; to borrow twice as much as the taxes proposed from the Bank of France. This amounted to hardly more than a come-and-get-me-and-we-will-see policy. Marie was overthrown by the heaviest opposition of all since the crisis had started.

An impasse had been reached. The Assembly could not agree on *any* Government!

A Desperate President and Nation. It must be noticed that during this period consultation among the groups, between the President and the various leaders, and among each new designated Prime Minister and those who had just failed were incessant and anxious. De Gaulle, whose party had brought on the crisis, declared to a national conference of his party on June 13, "I am certain that the present system, which has led to impotence, will bring the country to a shaking up.

[6] As shown later, Mendès-France was less in love with Executive strength when on December 1, 1955, his party rival, Faure, dissolved the Assembly!

We cannot go on indefinitely in this immobility."

The President was receiving a large mail from all over the nation expressing disgust with the National Assembly—with particular contempt for the practice of abstentions from voting. He was obliged to take drastic action. He contemplated a letter to the Assembly but felt that this would increase the moral and social crisis, causing the public to fear a tension between the presidency and Assembly that did not actually exist. He called to the Elysée all the Prime Ministers and Prime Ministers-designate since 1947 and the heads of all the political groups in the Assembly. He appealed to them to form "a government of national and republican safety, embracing the widest union possible." He described to them all the negotiations and the varied combinations of parties, policies, and personalities, tried and untried, that he had attempted. "Divergencies of opinion have been accentuated, and the clash of personalities has created a climate making any agreement difficult." He rebuked them with his insistence that he had no right to allow a situation to be prolonged that threatened to assail the Republic and weaken France and the French Union in the world.

He asked them to report to him within a week in order to form a Government.

Two days later the conference agreed on Antoine Pinay, a conservative. The Socialists had already demurred to a "national" Government that merely masked differences. Pinay took two days to explore the situation but gave up, as he expected to be voted down by the M.R.P. and the A.R.S.—the former because it thought his opposition to new taxes would damage its welfare program, and the latter because Pinay now favored EDC and West German rearmament. On announcing his failure, June 23, Mayer and Bidault, still heading the Government that had been voted out of office five weeks before, announced that unless the crisis was settled by July 8, when the Bermuda Conference was to start, they would not attend it, lacking authority to commit France.

Laniel Succeeds. Then the conservative parties and the Radicals, including the M.R.P. found a man on whom they could agree, Joseph Laniel. This

Votes for Prime Minister, May–June 1953 *

	Mayer			Reynaud			Mendès-France			Bidault			Marie			Laniel		
	PRO	CON	N.V.	PRO	CON	N.V.	PRO	CON	N.V.	PRO	CON	N.V.	PRO	CON	N.V.	PRO	CON	N.V.
Communists		96			96			96			96			96			96	
Socialists		105			105			105			105			105			104	1
M.R.P.	74	15	15	38	14	37	52	2	35	88	1		12		77	87		2
Radical Socs.	65	4	6	46	13	16	68		7	27	18	30	56		19	74		1
U.R.A.S.	6	71	6	37	1	44	25	2	54	64	1	16	42	1	37	62	1	17
Progressives		4			4			4			4			4			4	
U.D.S.R.	18		5	15	1	7	19		4	11		13	20		4	22		2
Ind. Rep.	44	5	6	52		3	5		50	41		14	54		1	55		
A.R.S.	14	13	5	31		1	1		31	29		3	33		1	34		
Peasants	22	17	8	41		6	10	14	23	37	3	7	43	2	2	47		
Overseas Indep.	1	12	1	13		1	14		1	14			10		5	15		
Indep.		1	3	3	1	1	2	1	3	2	1	2	2	1		2		1
Totals	244	328	55	276	235	116	301	119	207	313	228	86	272	209	146	398	206	23

Note: "Pro" indicates those voting for the candidate.
"Con" indicates those voting against the candidate.
"N.V." indicates those not voting for one reason or another.

* Compiled from reports in *Le Monde* and *Figaro*.

dark horse had served in minor positions in four Governments since 1945. Though a member of the Assembly since 1932, he was not one of the Assembly's men of distinction. He was a manufacturer of canvas at Lisieux, Normandy, with several hundred workmen, engaged also in the sale of agricultural machinery. He had an excellent World War I record and was a founder of the National Council of French Resistance.

The Socialists and the Communists opposed him; but he had considerable support elsewhere in the Assembly. Though he sat in the conservative benches, *he was not affiliated with any group* (notice this!). The President designated him on June 24; and on June 26 the Assembly gave him a 398 to 206 majority. He was not even called on to reply to the debate on his policy, which differed in hardly any particular from that of René Mayer, except perhaps that it was put forward in a speech which *The Times* described as "mineral water to champagne" compared with the speeches of those who had preceded him and failed. He put the heavier emphasis on the foreign aspect of France's troubles, especially the need to be united for Bermuda. He postponed the problem of internal economic policy by saying he would ask for special powers later, and these he did in fact later obtain. His Cabinet was almost identical with the one René Mayer had led, excepting that he included three de Gaullists, but in technical offices (post office, reconstruction, without portfolio) to keep them out of the foreign-policy conflicts on EDC that their party opposed.

The Laniel Government lasted nearly a year. It solved no basic problems, though the inflation was halted, French exports improved, the deficit was reduced, and something was taken out of the welfare of the poorer sections of the nation by a curbing of government pensions. But something was done for the poorer people by forced reductions of some prices. The new aid given by the United States toward the cost of the Indochinese war enabled Laniel's Government to survive several attempts at upsetting it. But it evaded the settlement of the Indochinese war, and it evaded fighting it with conscripts instead of merely the regular Army. It evaded bringing EDC to a vote, and also evaded the problems presented by the basic reconstruction of French industry. It fell on June 15, 1954, chiefly on the Indochina issue.

This case has been sketched, in order to give illustration to the intricate and dismaying process of making a government in a free country, and to indicate the responsibility of the President of the Republic to assure the nation of a viable government (even if it does nothing). It also demonstrates his necessary subjection to the fierce party forces that rule his will, whatever it might happen to be personally, in the effort to get some government into office that the Assembly will accept and not topple within a day or two—as one of those designated, André Marie, lamented might happen to him. We have also appreciated the subjugation of French foreign policy by the same forces of dissension.

Attention is called to the observations on North African policy (p. 429) and the dissolution of December 1955 (p. 420) as apt cases further revealing governmental sickness.

A Powerless Prime Minister and Minister of Finance

The cases examined throw a direct light on the weakness of the Prime Minister and of the Minister of Finance in a French Cabinet, two positions that in the British cabinet system (p. 145ff.) hold exceptional strength and are filled by men of character who are followed by the rank and file who put them there.

The desire to establish by constitutional fiat something like the authority and independence of the Prime Minister in relationship to the Assembly, to his Ministers, and to the President of the Republic failed. The tendency to seek a superior authority for the Prime Minister was rather similar to the establishment of the prime authority of the Chancellor in the Weimar cabinet system, who was given the right to compose his Ministry after he personally had been designated by the President of the Reich (p. 627). It also failed.

In the British Cabinet the Prime Minister sits solidly astride the saddle of a single political party that has a sound majority in the nation and the House; in France the Prime Minister has his legs on several wild horses, and to live must prance from one horse to another as the terrain demands and the jogging of his team of steeds dictates. In the British Cabinet a Prime Minister is supplied with a clear and almost blueprinted program by his colleagues and party organization; it is one and homogeneous. The French Prime Minister has the policy of his own party, which itself is invariably split, or like M. Laniel, he may even belong to *no* party, and he must try to weave a policy out of the insistencies of passionate rivals who have come together for a time and for a short time only; and these again have no steadiness, for their own parties are split and bear no steadfast allegiance to the Ministers of their own persuasion in the Cabinet. If the simile of horses be maintained, then the parties can sweep the ground from under the hoofs of their colleagues in the Cabinet, and the Assembly is the arena within which such tricks are consummated. A British Prime Minister has normally a life-expectancy of considerable certainty; for a French Prime Minister all his work is cut out merely to keep his Cabinet and himself from being overthrown; the British Prime Minister lives to consummate policy; the French Prime Minister lives in order merely not to die, qua minister. The British Prime Minister is *primus inter pares;* the French Prime Minister is a suppliant among men, some of whom are more potent than his peers; his limbs are tied to horses running in different directions as we have seen in the pictures of certain barbaric tortures; he is the prisoner of his Cabinet.

The Prime Minister's Powers. The constitutional document produced a substantial panoply of formal powers for the Prime Minister, although this term was never so much as mentioned in the constitutional laws of the Third Republic. He is now mentioned fourteen times, in Articles 14, 38, 40, 45 (twice) 46, 47 (three times), 49, 52 (twice), 54, and 55. The Constitution appears to make his Cabinet simply his personal creature, for he alone is required to be invested. Only he may ask a vote of confidence, whereas in the Third Republic any Minister could do this when his policy was challenged. And Ministers frequently did so, even on petty matters, so that sometimes (as in 1924) a Government might be overturned by the heedless votes of the Deputies, made lighthearted by such challenges. On the occasion mentioned, the Prime Minister was not even present—he came out of committee to find his Government had fallen.

The right of initiating bills is exclusively donated to the Prime Minister and the Deputies, not to the other Ministers (Article 14).

The countersignature clause, to take responsibility for the acts of the President of the Republic, is now placed in the hands of the Prime Minister and another Minister. Earlier it was consigned to any two Ministers.

Decrees. The Prime Minister is now made responsible (Article 47) for the execution of the laws. This has always implied a substantial power of making rules of public administration or decrees, even use of prerogative powers (see Chapter 8). Perhaps the actual change from the Third Republic is not so great as the formal one, for then the power was given to the President of the Republic and was exercisable over the countersignature of two Ministers, but formally it marks the desire of the constitution-makers to elevate the Prime Minister. It does, in practice, also; for he is not dependent on the consent of the President if he desires to make a decree—it rather depresses the President.

Appointments. The same article gives the Prime Minister the power to "appoint all civil and military officials" except some (Arts. 30, 46, and 84) reserved to the President. Both officials act through the Cabinet. The authority used to be lodged in the President. The change of its location was to enhance the prime ministership, and it does in regard to lesser appointments. Further, the Prime Minister "shall assume the direction of the armed forces and shall coordinate all measures necessary for national defense."

Can the Prime Minister Be Prime? All these powers, just mentioned, need to be countersigned by the Ministers in charge of the departments concerned. This diminishes the eminence of the Prime Minister. Yet—he has been vested with a superiority to the rest. Is this effective? It depends entirely on his character and political coalition. He has certainly been saddled with more constitutional *responsibility*. Whether this implies more power than any Prime Minister possessed in the Third Republic is entirely doubtful—we have seen the ephemeral and volatile conditions on which it depends. No Prime Minister has equaled Clemenceau. Furthermore, the important political issues, such as putting the vote of confidence or securing a dissolution of the Assembly, can only be decided in the meeting of the Council of Ministers at which the *President of the Republic* presides.

It is useless to beat about the bush. The Prime Minister in the Fourth Republic is at least as weak as was the Prime Minister in the Third. The tendency of the Assembly groups has been to entrust power to the weakest-policied and weakest-charactered man, men who have again and again postponed decisions or pursued sterility by a process of not resigning when outvoted and adopting compromises that kept them in office. Their gravest preoccupation has been to keep from defeat. Mendès-France even adopted (Machiavellian-wise in French style) a policy of neutrality on the vote on EDC, after having vowed his Cabinet to the same attitude and having stayed in office when some of his Ministers resigned prior to the vote, in order to live long enough to be able to effectuate his policy of economic salvation.

The tacticians of survival were much sought after by the President of the Republic to be Prime Ministers. They had usually been members of the just-fallen Cabinet.

III. THE FATE OF GOVERNMENTS: DISSOLUTION AND RESPONSIBILITY

Dissolution

It was widely believed that the lack of power to dissolve left the Third Republic Chamber omnipotent and the Government helpless, and that the strength of the Government in future must depend on the full use of dissolution. The fallacy lies in neglecting the effects of the multiplicity of parties. For this produces Governments that can hardly discipline the Deputies, for they are dependent on a similar constellation of groups which one day will become a Government. Dissolution could hardly change the nature of the group system; many successive dissolutions attempting this might provoke revolution.

The constitution-makers merely tried to make the overthrow of Governments a matter of cool deliberation and sober judgment. It was believed, it may be inferred, that the terrible instability of

Governments was due to sudden storms of passion that might be expressed on an interpellation or when the Government asked for a vote of confidence and was met with hostility.

In one respect the present constitution strengthened the Prime Minister's hand—**he no longer needed the consent of the Senate.**

Procedure. The devices embodied in the Articles are: (1) that the Prime Minister shall invoke a vote of confidence and that this shall be denied only by an absolute-majority vote; (2) that an interval of a day for cooling-off intervene between the placing of the vote on the agenda and the Assembly's action; (3) that the Assembly itself may offer a vote of censure, requiring the same vote, and also the cooling-off period.

This arrangement was solemnized by the connection with it of the Government's retaliatory right to dissolve the Assembly—after a certain interval and *two* adverse votes of confidence. These were largely wrought out of the proposals of two Socialists of long experience—Léon Blum and Vincent Auriol—who hankered after Cabinets of long life. The British experience was much admired, but wrongly interpreted. For it was believed that the British Cabinet could not demand a vote of confidence from the House, and so could be defeated on a measure and still remain in office. Where they obtained this notion is a mystery, for both ideas are false.

The practice of the Assembly and Government have defeated the Articles of the Constitution. For the Governments either used the vote of confidence as a threat *very frequently* and so defeated the independent will of the Assembly and the idea that the vote should be used only on serious occasions. Or they circulated the news that they were going to, when matters worked out without the cooling-off period being invoked. This was the same as its use in the Third Republic. The one-day cooling-off could not be afforded on the many votes that arose on the finance bills—for example, forty amendments to the Mayer budget in January 1948. The Assembly's procedure was changed to admit of the collection of the amendments into a few categories, and then merely one day's delay before all were voted on! Ways have been found of putting off in the beginning of the starting point of the one-day delay to save the

Government until some of the opposition it fears has cleared away. Or a short debate occurs on a confidence motion—and then the vote is put off for the day, allowing compromises in the interval.

Some Prime Ministers, then, have used the informal whispered warning in the Assembly; others, the official demand for confidence. The latter was used by Governments unafraid of arriving at the *two* votes of no confidence which would entitle them to a dissolution and its consequences. The Radical Prime Ministers were not in this position, as they feared the loss of strength to their party. The M.R.P. could use it against the Radicals but not the Radicals against the M.R.P. Mendès-France in November 1954 pressed through his will on the budget by daring the Assembly to deny him a vote of confidence (see p. 399)!

No Government defeated on a vote of confidence has stayed in office. Many Governments have been defeated on their proposals by ordinary and substantial majorities but have stayed in office, being themselves the judge of whether the defeat was serious enough to be met by resignation from office. The decision is a necessary consequence of the feeling that government must go on, and that if this one did not, the next alternative would hardly be any better.

Effect on the Cabinet. The groups within the Cabinet were put under tension with each other, in addition to their normal hostility, by the invocation of a vote of confidence, since the Prime Minister must consult the Cabinet before tabling a vote of confidence. In the olden days, he would make the decision singly and put the other parties not of his view in the dock. The new procedure brings the debate into the Cabinet. It also hampers the Prime Minister in immediate Assembly maneuvers. The parties fight in the Cabinet whether to authorize a vote of confidence appeal or not—in February 1951 the M.R.P. threatened resignation if M. Pleven went ahead with a reformed electoral bill they disliked; the Radicals made the threat if he did *not*. The Prime Minister resigned, and the Cabinet fell with him.

Vote of Censure. As for the vote-of-censure procedure, it has been invoked by the Communists six times; by the R.P.F. four times; and the Socialists once. It usually has been treated rather frivolously, its date being put off until impossible times; or the Government and its supporters have simply abstained from voting and so defeated an *absolute* majority.

The Collapse of Governments without Censure or Vote of Confidence. In the Third Republic the Chamber was not always called on to give the Cabinet the *coup de grace*. So in the Fourth Republic. Of ten cabinets in the first Assembly, 1946 to 1951, three broke up internally; one dissolved as the result of a vote on an issue on which the Government claimed neutrality. The first, the Blum Government, resigned when the President of the Republic was newly elected, as tradition required. Another resigned, as Article 45 of the Constitution required, directly after the election of 1951. Two were killed by the Assembly on first meeting it. And one, the Schuman Government of July 1948, fell on a relative majority defeat in the Assembly but was falling because the Socialist Party seceded during the debate itself. The only one of the ten to fall according to the constitutional formalities was that of Bidault in June 1950, the Socialists having joined the opposition after having merely abstained.

Then, the Socialists no longer being willing to participate in Governments, the ensuing Cabinets from early 1950 onward had a more precarious basis in the Assembly. They fell in that house; or they resigned to avoid the coming defeat. They avoided internal strife sufficiently to kill them before they came before the Assembly (one did this).

The President of the Republic intervened with Cabinets discouraged by the failure of their proposals before the Assembly to keep them from breaking up at once, and preferred to wait until the Assembly overthrew them. He failed twice or thrice; he succeeded the same number of times; and so gave the nation a little more stability.

How to Invoke Confidence. It is dangerous for a Government to invoke the vote of confidence—just as it is dangerous to bring a libel action, for it may be proved against you. Once the close period of eighteen months from the beginning of the legislature is over, when two votes of confidence have gone against a Government, the Prime Minister may dissolve the legislature. Then the Prime Minister must consult the Cabinet and the President of the National Assembly whether he should dissolve. If he dissolves after an adverse vote of confidence, the act of dispersing the Assembly also transforms the Government. For, in the period of the election, a Caretaker Government comes into office after the Prime Minister and Minister of the Interior have vacated their offices.

The Caretaker Government. This (Article 52) consisted until amendment in 1954 of the President of the Assembly, who would become Prime Minister *pro tem*. The other departments would remain manned by existing Ministers, and Ministers of State added from among *members of party groups not represented in the fallen Government*. These and the new Minister of the Interior would be appointed by the President of the Assembly, the latter with the approval of the *Bureau* of the National Assembly. They would act during the general election—that is, for a period of between twenty and thirty days. Thus the parliamentary rivals (including the Communists) of the Prime Minister could lord it during the election. (This caretaker arrangement only applies to general elections produced by dissolution, not to those by the lapse of the Assembly's legal term.) The amendment of December 1954 replaced these stipulations with the simple one that *only if a vote of censure* on the Cabinet has preceded the dissolution, the President of the Republic would appoint the President of the National Assembly as Prime Minister and the Minister of the Interior (who has control over the local machinery of elections) while the rest of the Cabinet would continue. Otherwise, the existing Cabinet would function intact.

Limitations on Dissolution. There are some limitations on the two-confidence-votes rule. The two crises must come within a period of eighteen months. They can be votes of censure, and presumably one of one sort and one of the other. The Government's defeat in this wise does not count for dissolution purposes if occurring in the first two weeks of its tenure. How reasonable! A closed session of eighteen months at the beginning of a Parliament, to save the Assembly from the trouble of re-election and the country from another expression of opinion so soon after the first, when its views may not have had reason to change. And, later, some little time for breath-taking by the new Government.

We shall see later that the Government of the U.S.S.R. is never plagued by these niceties of procedure or preciosity of reasoning.

The various rules—the time limits, the *double* defeat, the need for an absolute majority—stultified the dissolution possibilities. A definite feeling is evident that it is hardly cricket for a Prime Minister to threaten to call for a vote of confidence and hurt the Assembly by so bringing the threat of dissolution closer. Mendès-France was careful, or his parliamentary friends were careful, to let it be known that he would *not* use this power in order to dissolve the Assembly and get a new national vote on the issue of EDC, although it was widely claimed that the Assembly of 1951 did not represent the France of 1954. Perhaps he preferred the want of correspondence, for it helped him to defeat EDC.

The meaning of "one full day" as the cooling-off before a vote of confidence or of censure is taken was so inexact that amendment of December 7, 1954, substituted "twenty-four hours" (p. 334).

M. Reynaud, March 12, 1955, introduced a bill for amending the Constitution to make it more feasible than at present. It proposed that if, during the first two years of a legislature, a Cabinet loses a vote of confidence or receives a censure, the Prime Minister may ask the Assembly to confirm such a vote. If the second vote is again adverse to the Government, the Assembly would be automatically dissolved for new elections. Thus would merely personal ambitions of the Deputies be countered. It was opposed by M.R.P., Communists, and Socialists generally. It cannot be to the liking of the Radicals.

The First Dissolution in Seventy-eight Years!

Until December 1, 1955, though a dissolution could have been decreed fifteen times since the Assembly elected June 1951 had convened, Prime Ministers had not used it, for reasons already mentioned. M. Mendès-France had on one occasion actually declared that if a vote of confidence went against him on North African affairs he would not use dissolution, but would respect the Assembly's will.

But on December 1, 1955, prime ministerial impatience at last could not be contained. For the

Assembly persisted in its distracted *"immobilisme"* —that is, incoherent do-nothingness, milling about in a quagmire while throwing out every Government that attempted action. We have elsewhere explained (p. 371) the trials of M. Faure, who had been Minister of Finance during Mendès-France's prime ministership and for many months before that. He tried to find relief in early elections. The Deputies put him to the usual torture, so that he had to demand no less than four votes of confidence from October 18 to November 24, 1955, twice on North African policy and twice on his attempted solution, namely, to clear the air by an early appeal to the electorate. The latter two votes found him sustained by the votes of the Communist Party, which he did not welcome—on the last of these votes, only 191 non-Communist Deputies were for him and 247 were against. Then he was harassed by blame for the Saar voting which went against France's policy of internationalization (p. 720) and because he was calling up reservists for North Africa service. This was not his faulty doing; he inherited a nasty past. Finally, he challenged a fifth vote of confidence on his policy for earlier elections, after weeks of futile and often insincere debating and voting by the groups. The result of the vote against confidence in his Cabinet was as follows:

	For	Against	Abstaining	Not Voting	Absent
Socialists (104)	0	97	0	7	0
Communists and allies (98)	0	92	0	6	0
Popular Republicans (87)	75	1	4	5	1
Radicals (76)	31	34	3	5	3
Gaullists (68)	3	51	3	8	3
Independent Republicans (54)	34	12	4	2	2
Dissident Gaullists (32)	25	5	2	0	0
Independent Peasants (28)	21	4	0	2	1
Union of Democratic & Social Resistance (23)	6	8	2	7	0
Peasants (21)	10	7	2	1	1
Overseas Independents (16)	8	1	0	7	0
Unattached (15)	5	6	0	3	1
Total (622)	218	318	20	53	12

A most noteworthy feature of this table is the split in M. Faure's own party, the Radicals, almost exactly half and half—the kingpin party, the hinge, which Faure wished to use to bear to the Right of Center and Mendès-France to go to the Left of Center for future Cabinets.

At the declaration of the vote on November 29— with six votes over the absolute majority—the M.R.P. cried out "Dissolution!"; while the other Deputies, shocked at what their groups had done, put themselves in the hand of M. Faure. They had underrated the courage of the little Prime Minister. He had not obtruded the possibility of dissolution, and they had not taken it seriously, for it had not been used for seventy-eight years, and previous Prime Ministers had yielded to the will of the Assembly and bowed out. And now, no consent of the Senate was needed, either! (p. 418.)

The Ministers went in a body to the Elysée, the palace of the President of the Republic, M. Coty, and conferred with him until nearly dawn, for almost four hours. The next day M. Faure asked the President of the Assembly for his opinion on dissolution, as required by the Constitution (Art. 51). Pierre Schneiter, the officer in question, would not make public what he had said, but he probably advised dissolution, since he is a leading member of the M.R.P. whose Ministers in the Cabinet were numerous and very strong for it. This role of the President of the Assembly, highly political, is in strongest unfavorable contrast with the impartiality of the Speaker of the House of Commons. Next day M. Schneiter conferred with President Coty, just after M. Faure had conferred with M. Coty for nearly an hour. On December 1 a Council of Ministers was held, presided over by M. Coty, as is proper for this kind of Council. Nineteen Ministers were in favor of dissolution and six, Radicals, were opposed.

The objections advanced at this meeting, according to rumor, were these. The Assembly had evinced a desire for a different method of voting; this should be respected. The Council of the Republic's will was being ignored. There would not be enough time to organize the electoral campaign and get a true representation of the will of the people, because (1) the election must take place within twenty to thirty days of the dissolution and (2) three days before the formal opening of the election period, which is twenty days before the polling day, the groups must declare to the election authorities their *apparentements,* the affiliations of parties (p. 369) they make, if they are to be valid. A weightier argument, if sound, was that the use of Article 51 was within the letter of the Constitution but in violation of its spirit! How could this be? It was advanced that dissolution is a way of settling a conflict between Parliament and the Government —but here was the Government deciding in favor of itself. This is, indeed, a curious theory; for the right of dissolution was vested in the Prime Minister and Cabinet deliberately to give strength to the Executive. Who else was to use the power, if not the Government? The Assembly was never anxious to vote for its own dissolution. Those who favored dissolution observed that the Assembly had twice voted for it; and that the President of the Republic had neither political nor moral responsibility for dissolution; he simply signs the decree conformably with the decision of the Council of Ministers.

The President of the Republic signed the decree; few persons thought he had any discretion in the matter. The dissentient Radicals wrote a protest; M. Faure refused to accept this as resignation. An attempt seemed to be in the making in the Assembly to unseat M. Faure by a vote of censure, for this, if passed, would have ousted him from the Caretaker Cabinet. He countered this by a decree of dissolution at once, whereas he had intended to give the Assembly more time to prepare for the election. Since thirty days after December 1 fell on January 1, 1956, a national holiday and a Sunday, the *Conseil d'Etat* was consulted whether the date could be remanded until January 8. It was decided that it must be no later than January 2, decreed a public holiday.

The Radical Party leaders took action in retribution against their dynamic leader, M. Faure. The Party Executive Committee (p. 359) was summoned, where, under the powerful influence of Mendès-France, nineteen voted for Faure's expulsion from the party, six for censure, two for no action. As the Committee has seventy members, this meeting was only of those available in Paris. Against this M. Faure appealed. The views of the Mendès-France Radicals, the Socialists, and the

Communists crystallized. Faure was accused of a *coup de force*—that is, a blow without legality— with the argument that he had violated the spirit of the Constitution, which was centered in the will of the Assembly. As this will had expressed itself against M. Faure and against the system of P.R. which would now, by default, be used, it should have been accepted. Otherwise it was in Mendès-France's words:

> . . . a defiance of Republican principles, for the right of dissolution was never conceived to permit a discredited Government, after having sacrificed and betrayed for months all the national interests, after having sabotaged parliamentary life, after having scandalized all Frenchmen by its lack of authority and cohesion, to cast democracy into an adventure without issue.

This was a most unjust indictment; but the appeal to "Republican principles" takes one back to the Revolutionary Assemblies of 1789–1793 and the contemporary morass made by the Deputies.

The Radical Party belongs to the *Ralliement des Gauches Républicains,* the R.G.R. (p. 366), an electoral combination and parliamentary alliance. M. Faure was its President. The Radicals therein, assisted by the very old veteran, M. Herriot, and led by Mendès-France, then sought to oust Faure. But by twenty-six to nine he was sustained; the nine in opposition were of the U.D.S.R. whose leader François Mitterand is a close ally of Mendès-France. But the next day, M. Mitterand declared he was not opposed to the value of a dissolution, that a non-Communist Left alliance could still be formed and win a victory against Faure's Right-inclined friends. Furthermore, Mendès-France proposed at the R.G.R. meeting that no candidate appearing at the election as a member of the R.G.R. should be treated as one unless he had the investiture (endorsement) of the Radical Party first—that is, the Mendès-France-dominated party organization. The R.G.R. rejected the proposal. The R.G.R. would continue, not as merely an alliance, but as a party.

Significance of December 1, 1955

John Stuart Mill once observed that whether an action is a precedent does not depend on those who acted but on those who come later and decide whether to accept or ignore the example. What will French politicians make of dissolution now that the ice has been broken? It will be easier in future for any Prime Minister with even less courage than M. Faure to hold out its use as a warning for disciplinary purposes and to call out its power to break a parliamentary stalemate. Will French Deputies be more timorous to risk their seats in a conflict between their personal ambitions and the Government's appeal to the public interest? Will they, instead, be more careful to torture and topple a Prime Minister by "dosing" the votes against him to only one short of an absolute majority? Will they eliminate the power to dissolve from the Constitution, out of resentment and alleged "Republican" principles? These questions are answerable only in the future, as the French political mind is too fickle. I would guess that the second course will occur, with a noticeable influence of the first.

One can understand the resentment of Mendès-France at the dissolution, though he has expressed it not too well. In Britain the Prime Minister who advises a dissolution is founded on a single party (or nearly so), with duration, responsibility, a clear and concrete program. It seems to have a right to challenge its own dissentients and the solid Opposition, *which can form an alternative Government,* also responsible, coherent, steady, and well-founded in policy and popular following. But in France the Prime Minister has no substantial following, and in Faure's case articulated Cabinet policy, or even a party solid behind him though in a minority, for the Radicals with seventy-six Deputies were split in the middle for and against him. What kind of moral authority does this give to set in train so significant an event as a general election? For (1) the P.R. system must return the groups not very different from the Parliament of 1951 and (2) what kind of alternative Government and policy may one expect to emerge—surely nothing much different from what already exists, a "mixt-maxty, queer hotch-potch," in the absence of a radically different electoral system?

It certainly needed courage in M. Faure to undertake the dissolution. The passage quoted from Mendès-France at the end of this chapter in reality spiritually supports his action, though Mendès-France did not like this specific use of the

power, for his plans for a Left-wing campaign in June 1956 had been jumped.

Collective Responsibility

The Constitution (Art. 48) says:

> The Ministers shall be collectively responsible to the National Assembly for the general policy of the Cabinet and individually responsible for their personal actions.
>
> They shall not be responsible to the Council of the Republic.

The Cabinets of the Third Republic often resigned after an adverse vote in the Chamber. They almost as frequently foundered on the secession of one or more of the groups of which the coalition was composed. Sometimes they decomposed by the voluntary or enforced resignation of single Ministers whose incompetence had been demonstrated, thus saving the rest of the Cabinet.

This is not collective responsibility as the British constitution knows it. It could not be, because there was no true collective uniform party basis for the Cabinets. "Collectivity" was exactly what was missing—that is, consensus. Collectivity is also absent in the Fourth Republic, even if by reason of rather fewer parties and slightly better discipline among some than before. The responsibility for the break-up of Governments in one or the other fashion mentioned above is rather more visible. Yet the greater possibility of clarity has been a stimulus to deviousness and camouflage.

Some Ministers Leave, Others Remain. As the table will show, the Third Republic practice of *dosage* or *replâtrage* of Cabinets is still in robust use. A number of the previous Cabinet Ministers remain in the new Cabinet. This does not mean that the government of the country is better run than if the Cabinet went out as a whole, as in Britain, and an entirely new set of men came in. On the contrary, it confuses the issues and obscures responsibilities. For, though a Minister may hold onto a chieftainship of a department for a long period, longer (as the tables show) than the duration of successive Cabinets, he is surely subject to a generally new corporate set of values and priorities, or none! Especially is this true of the Minister of Finance.

Party Composition of Cabinet Posts

Cabinets	Same Party as in Previous Cabinet	Different Party than in Previous Cabinet
Pleven	9	11
Faure	21	2
Pinay	12	6
Mayer	13	5
Laniel	8	10
Mendès-France	4	11
Faure	6	13

Second, if there is some replastering, then there are new men. There is still what used to be called the *waltz of portfolios*. The successive Cabinets still have kaleidoscopic changes. They cannot settle down into a collectivity. If, as sometimes happens, a Minister of Education or a Minister in charge of housing or health ultimately produces a bill that his new colleagues will support, it is something of a wonder. The tables presented sug-

gest that if the person representing a specific party is not included in a new Ministry, that same office may now be given to one of his party colleagues, and the implied suggestion is that this mitigates the distractedness of the Cabinet and, specifically, of that Ministry. This is unrealistic. The too-frequent consequence of continuity is a hollowness of policy; Ministers stay on because they have nothing constructive to propose.

No Guidance to the Civil Servants. It is precisely in the administration of the departments that trouble occurs. It is not that brusque change will cause some agony to the officials and some pain of readjustment to the country; it is that the officials cannot predict accurately as they can in Britain (where a party program is known) what changes are now to be undertaken.

I personally vouch for the fact that top career officials worry (1) because they are trying hard

Membership of Fourth Republic Cabinets

Cabinet Formed by	Dates of Formation and Fall *	Members of Previous Cabinet In Same Posts	In New Posts	New Members	Total
De Gaulle †	11-19-45 to 1-22-46	8	5	9	22
Gouin	1-26-46 to 6-11-46	11	1	8	20
Bidault	6-23-46 to 11-28-46	16	1	7	24
Blum	12-16-46 to 1-16-47	6	—	12	18
Ramadier	1-21-47 to	9	1	16	26
"	5- 9-47 to 10-22-47	21	—	4	25
"	10-22-47 to 11-19-47	12	1	—	13
Schuman	11-24-47 to 7-19-48	7	1	7	15
Marie	7-26-48 to 8-28-48	7	4	8	19
Schuman	9- 5-48 to 9- 7-48	10	3	2	15
Queuille	9-11-48 to 10- 6-49	8	2	5	15
Bidault	10-29-49 to	9	1	8	18
"	2- 7-50 to 6-24-50	13	—	4	17
Queuille	7- 2-50 to 7- 4-50	10	3	8	21
Pleven	7-12-50 to 2-28-51	12	3	7	22
Queuille	3-10-51 to 7-10-51	20	1	1	22
Pleven	8-10-51 to 1- 7-52	6	9	9	24
Faure	1-20-52 to 2-29-52	17	4	5	26
Pinay	3- 8-52 to 12-23-52	11	4	2	17
Mayer	1- 8-53 to 5-21-53	9	2	12	23
Laniel	6-30-53 to 6- 8-54	7	3	12	22
Mendès-France	6-18-54 to 2- 5-55	3	1	12	16
Faure ‡	2-24-55 to	1	17	1	19

* The gap in date between resignation of a Ministry and formation of the next is the time taken in finding Prime Ministers-designate and their trying their luck before the Assembly.

† Members of previous Cabinet from Provisional Government.

‡ The difference between the figures of the Mendès-France Cabinet and the Faure Government is calculated from the former as it stood in September 1954, not at its inception. It is interesting to note that before it fell it underwent *four* "replasterings," this being the third. So much for the idea that French Cabinets are "much the same."

Party Affiliations of Cabinet Ministers †

Prime Minister	Party	Comm.	Soc.	M.R.P.	R.D.G.*	Ind.	U.D.S.R.	Rad.	Gaullist†	Others
De Gaulle	—	5	5	5	3	1	—	—	—	3
Gouin	Soc.	6	7	6	—	—	—	—	—	1
Bidault	M.R.P.	7	6	6	—	—	—	—	—	2
Blum	Soc.	—	18	—	—	—	—	—	—	—
Ramadier	Soc.	5	9	5	5	2	—	—	—	—
"	"	—	12	6	5	2	—	—	—	—
"	"	—	7	3	2	1	—	—	—	—
Schuman	M.R.P.	—	5	6	3	1	—	—	—	—
Marie	Rad.	—	6	6	5	2	—	—	—	—
Schuman	M.R.P.	—	4	6	4	1	—	—	—	—
Queuille	Rad.	—	5	5	4	—	—	—	—	1
Bidault	M.R.P.	—	5	6	5	1	—	—	—	1
"	"	—	—	8	6	2	—	—	—	1
Queuille	Rad.	—	—	9	9	2	—	—	—	1
Pleven	U.D.S.R.	—	5	6	8	2	—	—	—	1
Queuille	Rad.	—	5	7	8	2	—	—	—	—
Pleven	U.D.S.R.	—	—	7	1	7	2	6	—	1
Faure	Rad.	—	—	8	—	6	3	7	—	2
Pinay	Ind.	—	—	4	—	4	2	5	—	2
Mayer	Rad.	—	—	6	—	4	2	8	—	3
Laniel	Ind.	—	—	5	—	5	2	4	4	2
Mendès-France	Rad.	—	—	1	1	3	2	4	4	1
Faure	Rad.	—	—	4	—	3	1	4	5	2‡

* Includes Radicals.
† Includes Dissident Gaullists.
‡ Peasants.

to guess the mind of the Ministers who *may* become their chiefs—and they do not know what their party wing or personal views may be; and (2) they languish because they are not so much subject to instability, as to *getting no guidance at all!*

Party Claims to Certain Posts. In the Fourth Republic certain parties have seemingly claimed or been acknowledged to be more rightfully entitled than others to certain Cabinet posts. The M.R.P. has been in almost unbroken control of the Foreign Office; it has been M. Bidault or M. Schuman (with a short break for Léon Blum) until the Mendès-France Government of June 1954. The Ministry of Finance has been the preserve of the Socialists to 1946 when it went to the M.R.P. (spenders and taxers!), after which, in 1947, it became the appanage of the Radicals or conservatives (no spending; no taxing; sound!). The Ministry of the Interior has been kept from the clerical M.R.P. because it is the administrator of the Church relationship to the State; the Socialists held it until 1950 when they left office, and the Radicals followed them in monopoly. The Ministry of Justice has belonged to the M.R.P. and the Radicals followed them in 1947 and kept it throughout the period with small exception.

The Ministry of Defense was coveted by the Communists when they were willing to join Cabinets. But they were circumvented by the division of the Ministry into two halves, only the less important and innocuous going to the Communists. Since then the office has gone the rounds of the parties of the Third Force but not the Prime Minister's group.

The prime ministry was held by the Socialists until July 1948, with an interval of the M.R.P. Then it drifted Rightward to M.R.P. and Radicals, about equally, and since the 1951 elections such conservatives as Pleven, Pinay, and Laniel have held it.

The conservative groups are small, yet they have

supplied Prime Ministers in coalition with larger ones, such as the M.R.P., whose social and financial outlook is quite different from that of the conservative Prime Ministers. This phenomenon indicates several facts: (1) the cohesion of the Cabinet is too loose for a valid use of the term *collective* responsibility. (2) The Prime Minister can hardly be "prime"; the formal term "president" is more descriptive. (3) Is it possible for any Prime Minister, in the circumstances of a French Coalition, to be other than a cynic—made so, if not born so, by the nature of his colleagues and the false position he is placed in by the Constitution? The Faure Government of 1955 was distinctly Right-wing, but the Radical Prime Minister picked the more liberal members of the Rightest groups!

The Radical Party's spinelessness and formlessness qualifies it to be the leading contender for the prime ministership, but what does this indicate about that office?

Predilections for Ministries are evinced by the parties. The Socialist Party liked those of the Interior, Works and Transport, Labor, Production, Pensions, Health, covering the social services and pleasing to the Civil Service clientele. The M.R.P. has sought the Ministries of Production, Labor, and Health; the Radicals, Education, the Interior, and the Post Office. Agriculture, with its clientele of half the population, has been the object of rivalry—the Socialists, the M.R.P., conservatives, and the Peasant Party.

This kind of unofficial division of spheres of interest among parties who do not agree with each other on an integrated body of policy makes the idea of *collective* responsibility nonsense in the circumstances. The appraisal is emphasized when we take into account the hard bargaining for position, sometimes commanded by the aspirant's party, to take office or to stay away from it, sometimes sought by secession or threatened secession from the party.

Party in Cabinet *versus* **Party Deputies.** This division is further stressed when the manner of fall of some Cabinets is remembered. Sometimes the Ministers representing a party go along with the Cabinet, while their fellows in the Assembly abstain; or all the Ministers abstain; or a whole Cabinet may remain "neutral" while the rank and file of its constituent groups vote variously and individually, internally divided.

There are open agreements to differ; whereas when an agreement of this kind was made in 1931 by the Conservative, Liberal, and some Labour partners in a National Cabinet in Britain, the outcry against it was as against a grave sin (see p. 152). Ministers have sometimes voted against their Government or some have been permitted by their colleagues to abstain from voting on a tender issue, as for example when the Socialists in January 1951 were permitted by René Pleven to abstain if the Assembly challenged the dispatch of an ambassador to Franco Spain.

Hence, the Article on collective responsibility has no inward meaning for the dynamic cohesion of the Cabinet. Its only meaning is that, when a Government is refused a vote of confidence or is treated to a vote of censure or suffers serious setbacks through relative majorities against it, it must resign or is forced to resign.

The Instability of Cabinets

Thus the Fourth Republic has fallen into the old rut of unstable and short-lived Cabinets, weak while they are alive and staggering to an ignominious fall, to be replaced by others as weak and short-lived. The table tells the story.

Period	Cabinets in Office
Less than a week	2
One month	4
2 to 3 months	1
Over 3 to 4 months	2
Over 4 to 6 month	4
Over 6 to 8 months	5
Over 9 to 11 months	3
Over 12 and less than 13	1

For 21 Cabinets since November 19, 1945 to June 1954, including the fall of the last-mentioned in February 1955, the average span of life has been a little over 5 *months*.

The tortured distraction of the Cabinet, the Prime Minister, the Assembly, and the dazed public may be slightly surmised from some crucial votes of the Assembly. See also the vote of confidence, November 30, 1955 (p. 421).

Prime Ministers of the Fourth Republic of France, 1945–1956

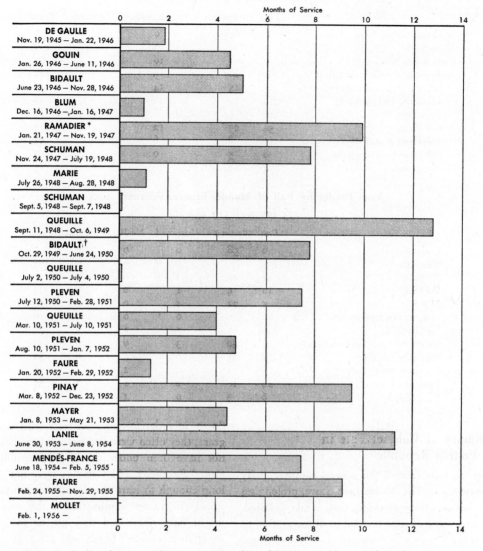

* Ramadier headed three successive Governments, formed January 21, May 9, and October 22, 1947, respectively.

† Bidault headed two successive Governments, the first formed October 10, 1949, and the second, February 7, 1950.

The Paris Pacts, December 24, 1954

	For	Against	Abstained	No Part	Total
Communists	0	94 plus 4	0		98
Socialists	83	21	1		105
M.R.P.	6	61	16	2	85
Radicals (with U.D.S.R.)	63	28	9		100
Independent (Conservatives)	23	15	14	3	55
Peasants, Independent	11	4	13		28
Peasants	10	8	1	3	22
Gaullists	34	25	12	1	72
Dissident Gaullists	17	8	8		33
Overseas Independents	8	5	0	3	16
No group	4	7	0	2	13

Vote Producing Fall of Mendès-France, February 1955
273 for and 319 against

	For	Against	Abstained	No Part	Absent	Total
Communists	0	98	0	0	0	98
Socialists	105	0	0	0	0	105
Radicals	52	20	2	0	1	75
U.D.S.R.	18	4	1	0	0	23
M.R.P.	5	73	4	0	2	84
Overseas Independents	16	0	0	0	0	16
De Gaullists	45	17	7	1	1	71
Independent (Conservatives)	12	40	3	0	0	55
Dissident Gaullists	5	27	0	0	0	32
Peasants, Independent	3	21	2	1	1	28
Peasants	10	16	2	1	1	30
No group	6	3	0	1	0	10

Summary of Cabinet Fate in the Fourth Republic

From the facts recited, the general summary may be drawn. (1) The double investiture, prolonging the crisis of cabinet-making, was, while it lasted, a serious waste of time and led to disintegration of government rather than to integration and prime ministerial leadership. (2) Although the eighteen-month delay was designed to prevent too-easy dissolution with a view to more stable government (in part), nevertheless many Governments fell in that period, as many as six at one stage. (3) Ways were found to circumvent the overthrow of a Government by an absolute majority needed for a vote of confidence: by beating it on measures, by seceding from the Cabinet, by withdrawing votes at interpellations. (4) Cabinets were usually afraid to use the vote-of-confidence-dissolution clauses against the Assembly, fearing the caretaker-government arrangement. (5) Yet when they tried to do so, in order to make progress with their program, they often were successful when they might not have been under the Third Republic's disarmed Executive. (6) Cabinets were not in office long enough to learn the departmental jobs; or to impel the career administrators the way policy might have demanded they go; or to make an integrated collective policy and get a grip on the helm of the State. They were too patched together to be genuinely frank with each other, though they might cynically bicker. The fact that occasionally some 50 percent of the former Ministers stayed on in the newly formed Cabinet was very little mitigation of the general incoherence and departmental feebleness. Nor did the fact that such ministries as Finance, the Foreign Office, Justice, the Interior, and Agriculture were held by the same persons for twice as long as the average life of Cabinets as a whole or the period of office of Prime Ministers act as palliation of the rudderlessness of French government. The shocking state of the public finances and the fumbling with the European and colonial problems are partial demonstrations of this.

A Case Study. An excellent case in point is the attack on the Edgar Faure Cabinet in October 1955. The Cabinet was built out of the Center and Right parties, supported by Socialist votes, though that party did not allow any of its members to join the Cabinet. It included a more than usually substantial number of Gaullists and Dissident Gaullists. The new Prime Minister knew, when he took office, that he would have to face a North African crisis in the near future, for Mendès-France has been ostensibly overthrown because of his policy on Tunis, and this moderate liberalism had been shared by Faure, who was then Finance Minister in the Cabinet. Yet the disarray of the Assembly left him little other choice. For he took office after three attempts to form a Cabinet had failed: one, under an Independent Republican (Pinay), had been rejected by the M.R.P., the Socialists, and the Gaullists; another, to be headed by M. Pfimlin, an M.R.P. leader, had been rebuffed by the Socialists, Gaullists, and Mendès-France Radicals; the third, under a Socialist, combining Radicals, M.R.P., Socialists, U.D.S.R., and Gaullists "technician ministers," was rejected by the Assembly. Faure believed that his coalition, starting with the M.R.P. and distinctly to the Right, might work. It contained five Gaullists and one Dissident Gaulist.

From the formation of the Faure Government in February 1955 until October the Gaullists conducted a passionate opposition to concessions of self-government for Tunis, Morocco, and Algeria. These became more urgent under pressure of imminent rebellion and strikes by the natives and the French colonists against the French authorties. M. Faure and the moderates developed a middle policy of less direct rule by the French yet with permanent inclusion of Morocco and Algeria in the French Union. During the most delicate negotiations for the abdication of a Sultan the French had substituted in 1953 for the true line of sultans and his replacement by a Council of Regency, on which war and peace hung, the Cabinet was rent several ways, and deeply, by its Gaullist members. The dissensions were made public—as always in

France. The Minister for Pensions was giving advice to the Resident General of Morocco behind the back of the Minister for Moroccan Affairs (a Dissident Gaullist); the Minister of Defense, General Koenig, a Gaullist, was advising a Moroccan general *not* to accept a seat in the Council of Regency when the rest of the Cabinet was begging him to accept.

Time, here of the essence, elapsed, while massacres were perpetrated by French and natives. Finally, the Gaullists took the offensive, when the National Council of the party demanded that Faure resign and that President Coty set up instead a "Government of National Union." Faure thereupon dismissed four of the Gaullist Ministers, the only one kept being his Minister of Public Works. The Gaullist Minister of Defense was replaced by General Billotte, a Dissident Gaullist. The Cabinet was in a dire position, for the Independent Republicans (strong conservatives) also wanted to withdraw their Minister, M. Pinay, Foreign Minister, from the Cabinet, but he would not go.

M. Faure then dared to accept interpellations on his policy and proposed solutions for Morocco. A three-day debate ended in a victory for him, by 477 votes to 140, in which the Socialists *and Communists* (!) and M.R.P. and Radicals were substantially in his favor, and the Gaullists and other conservative groups against.

	For	Against	Ab- stained	Not Voting	Ex- cused
Communists	94	—	—	—	—
Progressists	4	—	—	—	—
Socialists	103	—	—	—	—
Radicals	68	5	1	—	1
U.D.S.R.	21	—	2	—	1
M.R.P.	84	3	—	—	—
Overseas Independents	16	—	—	—	—
Independent Republicans	39	13	3	—	1
Gaullists (Republican Social)	4	55	2	6	2
Independent Peasants	4	22	—	—	—
Peasants	7	13	—	—	1
A.R.S. (Dissident Gaullists)	5	25	2	—	—
Not in groups	13	—	—	2	—

Two others excused from voting were the President and another official of the *Bureau*. Among the "nonvoters" were two of the Gaullists who had been ejected from the Cabinet. Among the M.R.P. who voted against the Government was Georges Bidault, leader of that party (!), against 84 of his own followers. The former members of the Mendès-France Cabinet were highly divided in their voting behavior. Two of those excused from voting were Pleven, former Prime Minister, of the U.D.S.R., and René Mayer, former Prime Minister, of the Radicals.

Within three days a debate was staged on Algeria, into the discussion of which the problem of Morocco was again injected, as though it had never been settled by the previous vote. The Deputies had put up six alternative proposals for action in Algeria (then under notice of the United Nations) and three of these resolutions were votes of censure. After three days of debate, the Prime Minister's proposal was not even reached. It included (1) neither assimilation nor separation of Algeria (see p. 456); (2) improved local government and reform of land use, separation of Islamic religion from the State, and more teaching of the Arab language; (3) more truly democratic elections for the Algerian Assembly as a step to legislation for improvements, political, economic, social, and administrative; and (4) measures to raise the standard of living.

Frustrated, M. Faure demanded a vote of confidence from the opinion- and emotion-wracked Assembly. The Gaullists and the Right were still determined to bring down the Government, but the Right and the Moderates were not so united as before, because the Prime Minister, the President of the Republic, and other French notables publicly expressed horror at the spectacle of one more government crisis, just before the Saar plebiscite and as France was about to enter the Big Four Geneva conference of November. Moreover, agonized appeals were made to national pride at such a political mess; and those who supported the Prime Minister—one being Mendès-France, who a week before had started a daily newspaper of his own group's opinion, *The Express*—urged that to support the Government was to support its walkout from the United Nations Assembly, which had voted to put Algerian policy on its agenda. The Communists had to support Russia, which had helped to lead the United Nations Assembly to this tactic, and therefore voted against the Government, which, a week before, they had supported, in order to make their party appear liberal for the elections in 1956. The Socialists, who had supported the Government the week before largely by conviction, now voted against it, having calculated that the Right and Moderates would sufficiently support the Government and not wishing, then, to leave the Communist Party with monopoly of colonial liberalism when the two Left parties should appeal to the workers at the election of 1956. The results of the vote of confidence were 308 *for* and 254 *against*.

This time (October 18, 1955), so soon after the Moroccan vote, the Assembly was differently split-minded. This illustrates the fortuitousness of the Opposition and its kaleidoscopic changes, matching that of the Cabinet. The student will notice that in many cases even the state of mind of Deputies is unfathomable by government, opposition, or public; for they chop and change, and they do not even vote. Thus:

	For	Against	Ab-stained	Not Voting	Ex-cuse
Communists	0	89	5	—	—
Progressists	0	2	1	1	—
Socialists	—	100	—	2	1
Radicals	71	2	—	1	1
U.D.S.R.	14	2	4	3	1
M.R.P.	85	1	—	1	1
Overseas Independents	14	—	—	2	—
Independent Republicans	43	6	—	2	4
Gaullist (Republic Social)	15	39	9	3	3
Independent Peasants	19	4	1	2	—
Peasants	14	4	—	1	2
A.R.S (Dissident Gaullists)	27	2	2	—	1
Not in groups	6	3	3	2	1
	308	254	25	20	16

Who, after this, could know what is the policy of "France" or its Government (for the time being) or its Assembly (for which time being?) on its colonies or anything else, for the vote o his was bound up with feelings about other policies?

IV. THE PRACTICE OF CABINETS AND THE SECRETARIAT: MEETINGS, MINUTES, AND SECRECY

Meetings

The French Council of Ministers has two kinds of meetings: the *Conseil des Ministres* and the *Conseil de Cabinet*. The former is presided over by the President of the Republic, the latter by the Prime Minister. The *Conseil des Ministres* is the smaller group: it consists of the President of the Republic, the Prime Minister, and all the Ministers—but none of the Secretaries of State, or the Undersecretaries, the two classes of political chiefs lowest in the hierarchy. The Secretary to the Cabinet attends, and the President of the Republic safeguards the minutes taken by the latter.

The *Conseil de Cabinet* consists of the Prime Minister and all the Ministers and Secretaries of State and usually the Undersecretaries—that is, all the Government. It is the more "political" or Assembly-conscious of the two meetings, while the *Conseil des Ministres* is the higher statesmen's group, the one in which the longer and broader view of national policy is deliberated and in which is settled whether a vote of confidence shall be called for. (In this latter, then, the President of the Republic is heard.)

Size of Cabinet. The *two* councils suggest a hierarchy among members of the Government. The Prime Minister has the authority to decide the size of the Cabinet; but its exercise depends on his bargaining power. The tendency is for it to grow larger. When the Communists were in the Government the number of Ministers was twenty-six. Afterward, for some time, there were fewer groups to satisfy. Until July 1950, the Socialists still participating, the Cabinet was under twenty, with one exception. From July 1950 it rose to twenty-two, reaching twenty-six under Edgar Faure (Radical) in January 1952, and with one exception has not been below twenty-two. The Mendès-France Government of June 1954 had seventeen Ministers, including the Prime Minister who was also Minister for Foreign Affairs, and thirteen Secretaries of

State,[7] and the Faure Government in February 1955, nineteen Ministers and only seven Secretaries of State.

Undersecretaries are never allowed to attend Cabinet meetings or sign decrees. The Secretaries of State do both but do not attend the presidential Cabinets. Their title goes back to the *ancien regime;* they are a response to the need, in part, for compensation prizes to the groups who get fewer ministerships than they wish.

The Secretaries of State are rather in the position of the Undersecretaries in the British departments, the close political collaborators of the Ministers. They are, normally, departmental political chiefs rather than men involved in the high collective policy of the Government. The tendency is, for obvious reasons, to increase the number of both categories; as hostages for on-coming group crises. *Ministers of State.* In nearly all French Governments there are two or three men designated as "Minister of State." These do not hold a departmental portfolio, in order that they concentrate

[7]

Minister	Party
Prime Minister	Radical
Foreign Affairs (Prime Minister)	Radical
National Defense	Gaullist
Justice	Radical
Interior	U.D.S.R.
Public Works	Gaullist
Overseas Territories	M.R.P.
National Education	R.G.R.
Commerce and Industry	Radical
Labor	U.D.S.R.
War Veterans	Ind. Rep.
Agriculture	Ind. Rep.
Reconstruction	Gaullist
Finance, Economic Affairs, and Planning	Radical
Associated States	Ind. Rep.
Moroccan and Tunisian Affairs	Gaullist
Public Health	Overseas Ind.

Secretaries of State	
President of the Council	Ind. Rep.
A Colleague	Radical
Armed Forces—War	Ind. Rep.
Air	Gaullist
Navy	M.R.P.
Scientific Research and Technical Progress	R.G.R.
Budget	Gaullist
Economic Affairs	Radical
Overseas Territories	U.D.S.R.
Foreign Affairs	Ind. Rep.
Communications	Gaullist
Agriculture	Peasants
Technical Education	U.D.S.R.

their attention on general policy (as happens in Britain, p. 137). They are invariably politicians of the first rank, perhaps former Prime Ministers or distinct leaders in their groups, such as Ramadier, Queuille, Gouin, Teitgen, Reynaud, Mollet, Laniel (!), Coste-Floret.

Vice Presidents. The Prime Minister may designate a Vice President. He will perhaps be a former Prime Minister, and almost certainly a man of eminence in the Assembly's feverish life, soon to be a Prime Minister himself.

The General Secretariat of the Government

No democratic parliamentary Executive more needs the structural buttress of a permanent secretariat than the French Cabinet. Yet the very nature of the sick Cabinet tends to evade its true remedy and, when the remedy was supplied, to deprive it of its potency.

The permanent secretaryship never existed before 1935, though since 1916 the Prime Ministers had had an undersecretaryship for departmental coordination. The device was used entirely at the Prime Minister's whim, and the criticisms of the jumbled departmentalism and want of continuity in Cabinet focus and policy continued to be bitterly leveled. Another attempt failed in 1924 under the guillotine of economy. After the riots of 1934 the Prime Minister sought "services of coordination," and in 1935 a budget appropriation enabled a decree to establish a small permanent staff of administrative and clerical officials, plus other men released from their departments, to serve successive Prime Ministers. One of these was appointed Secretary-General of the Administrative Services of the Prime Minister. The "floating" staff was established to allow the Prime Ministers to choose those in whom he could repose personal and political confidence. M. Blum appointed a university professor, two former Deputies, three journalists.

But a sick Cabinet made a sick Secretariat.

The Secretariat Today. General de Gaulle, located in London until 1943, learned the value of the British Offices of the Cabinet, and as a soldier he had mastered the importance of good staff work.

In Algiers, he established the General Secretariat of the Government.

The secretariat is not provided for in the Constitution itself, but the Articles devoted to the fortification of the prime ministership are held by French constitutional lawyers to verge, at any rate on constitutional authorization. This is further emphasized by the duty of the President of the Republic (Art. 33) to "order the minutes of their meetings to be recorded and [to] keep them in his possession."

The Prime Minister is given a permanent seat the Hôtel Matignon. This place was reserved for such a purpose as far back as 1934 but not used Now there is a regular set of offices and a meeting place for Ministers. A decree formulates the Secretariat services.

The Prime Minister's office consists of a number of responsibilities with authority and personnel to match. These are: the operation of the Cabinet, the organization of the Civil Service, the organization of national defense, and the supervision of national planning, and certain other services Thus the organizations and personnel within the authority of the Prime Minister, designed to enable him to keep *au fait* with happenings and to exercise a top managerial vigilance, are:

1. A general secretariat of the committee of national defense, which includes the Armed Services Cabinet Ministers and the chiefs of staff

2. A general commissariat of atomic energy

3. The general commissariat of the Plan (see pp. 460–462), consisting of about thirty high career officials who develop and supervise the execution of the Plan

4. The general secretariat of the Government thus organized:

   (a) Direction of the Civil Service (see p 472)

   (b) Direction of Documentation—a research and information service for the Ministers (in practice) as well as the Prime Minister, and (in practice) the various Chambers and the public

   (c) The *Journal Officiel*—the official re

port of the transactions of the Government and the Chambers

(d) The *Écôle national de l'Administration,* the official school for training and selecting the higher branches of the public service (see p. 480ff.)

5. The Direction of Radio and Television
6. The Posts, Telephones, and Telegraphs

Over the whole of this, staffed by permanent officials of the Civil Service, the Prime Minister appoints, from Cabinet to Cabinet, one or two Secretaries of State. They are not usually the first of the new Cabinet to be chosen—attesting to the subordinate importance they bear politically and even administratively to the other offices of the Ministry.

The Prime Minister is, then, at least in the organizational position to be the master of the highest plans of administration in the French Government. Whether he is entirely conditioned by the political circumstances we have already fully plumbed. It is parlous.

Work of the Secretariat. The Cabinet or the *Conseil* meets at least once a week, with smaller inner-Cabinet meetings in between, as exigencies demand. The General Secretariat prepares the agenda for these meetings, with the exception of the smaller and less formal gatherings, though even here it may be called on for assistance. It provides the secretaries necessary to service the meetings. Only the Secretary General attends the Cabinet. He takes the minutes; sends them to the Ministers, in part as reminders, in part as prime ministerial orders. He staffs a number of administrative interdepartmental commissions that are in the nature of the British-type career-servant planning and coordinating agencies, and similar to the committees of the British Cabinet. He then pursues the decisions taken with the top civil servants in the various departments, and the Ministers if results can be obtained only in this way.

Legislative Service. There is an attempt at centralizing the issue of drafts of laws and decrees from the various departments. The Legislative Service of the Secretariat is in charge of this, as well as the services already referred to. Its twelve members (slight variations in number from time to time) secure all texts of bills and decrees drafted by the departments for the Prime Minister's supervision. The Secretary General sees to it that all the Ministers are acquainted with these texts and agree with the substance, or offer their objections, when the Prime Minister will enter as the arbiter. Then, the texts are sent by the Secretariat to the *Conseil d'État* for legal study and advice. It is a process that includes the equivalent of the advice of the Bureau of the Budget and the Attorney General in the United States in addition to the advice of Parliamentary Counsel to the Treasury in the British Government (see p. 119). Then the texts are ready for the *Conseil des Ministres* and the National Assembly.

Some of these texts need to be submitted to the Economic Council and the French Union Assembly (see next chapter). If this is so, the Secretariat sees to it. Decrees come from the departments to the Prime Minister and then on to the President for approval and signature.

The Secretariat watches the publication of the finished decrees and laws in the *Journal Officiel* and keeps the originals.

The Secretariat is also engaged in research and studies, particularly in the Plan, and military policy (through the Secretary General of National Defense) and in legal studies.

Liaison with the Assemblies. It assists the centralized in-gathering of all parliamentary written questions and items concerning the agenda of Parliament. The Secretariat details a representative to attend the Presidents' Conference that makes up the agenda of the Assembly (p. 382); it follows the course of Government bills and the amendments to them in the Assembly and the Council of the Republic. This enables the Prime Minister and the Cabinet to know the parliamentary situation and to plan what they propose to do.

All this evidently enables the French Cabinet for the first time, in an organized way, to be linked to the legislature by administrative and continuously operating officials, with a representative *in* the agenda-making body of the former and a secretariat lodged contiguously to the Prime Minister. It provides also a conspectus of depart-

mental and parliamentary programs for the Prime
Minister and the Cabinet as a whole.

> The common characteristic of these services and
> organs is, in principle, neither management nor
> execution (excepting the administrative and
> financial division which takes care of the per-
> sonnel and materiel of the Presidency itself, the
> direction of the Official Journals which assure
> the publication of all the official texts, and in a
> certain measure the service of the Press), but
> solely thinking, study and synthesis, to see if
> they correspond or not to the legislative or con-
> stitutional obligations of the Prime Minister.
> Thanks to them, the Prime Minister is better
> informed, better armed for action, better able
> itself to impose its views on its colleagues when-
> ever the Government deliberates.[8]

Conditions of Operation. Students are now in possession of the best judgment on this system that
could be made, by a former chief of the Legislative
Service of the Secretariat, from whose brilliant
study the quotation given above is made!

The practice of fairly permanent cabinet committees as in Britain, and the institution there of
"overlords" (see p. 164ff.), is not easy in France. It
would fall foul of the idea of the equality of Ministers. (Hierarchy is possible among recognized
equals in a homogeneous cabinet: equality is more
insisted on where the group understructure is
heterogeneous.) The newly arrived Cabinet would
be at odds with the formerly established interministerial committee. France has to be content
therefore with *ad hoc* interministerial *conferences,*
which, having deliberated, then dissolve.

There is no doubt that M. Bertrand is concerned
over two characteristics of the French political
system we have already had occasion to assay. (1)
The Cabinets are always made up of Ministers belonging to different parties politically heterogeneous, and (2) they do not stay in office more than
a few months.

> These two characteristics cannot fail to weigh
> heavily on the conditions under which the work
> of government is carried on. The first makes it
> very difficult, in the bosom of any given govern-
> ment, to have a unity of views regarding po-

litical impulsion: programs and conceptions of
the various parties to which the ministers belong
conflict and very often tend to neutralize each
other (when *"immobilisme"* with which governments are almost invariably reproached)
The second, experience shows, spoils the continuity of governmental action. . . .

All the more urgent is it to have the Secretariat
with its legislative and administrative responsibilities. It does valiant work in frustrating circumstances; it palliates, but does not come near to
curing, the chronic defects of French politics.

How utterly difficult, and near to impossibility
it is in the French cabinet system to evaluate the
French Prime Minister's personal contribution to
particular policies, especially foreign policy as a
recent study has attempted to do![9]

Secrecy

Making Cabinets and Taking Spheres of Interest
The predilection of the different groups for favorite ministries has had some unfortunate effects
It has been very difficult since 1871 onward to
purify the Civil Service of political bias, in spite
of successive spasms of *épuration*. Not that grea
strides had not been made in the last three decades
of the Third Republic (Chapter 9). But politica
parties in France are so passionate in their ego
centric interpretation of the "good of the nation"
that the pressure is constant, as the postwar phrase
goes, to "colonize" various administrative depart
ments, or as the term is used elsewhere to "in
filtrate" them.

The onrush of the stronger groups at the Lib
eration into the departments, and the death, retire
ment, expulsion of Vichy collaborators, and so
forth, had left gaps in the higher and highest ranks
of the career positions. The recruits to be obtained
from the newly founded *École national d'Adminis
tration* could not yet be forthcoming.

The Communists were first and most ingeniou
in placing their *protégés* in strategic positions, espe
cially as they are sworn to the Third Internationa
to act as a secret conspiracy as well as an oper
political party. They infiltrated into the depart
ments dealing with social security, industrial pro

[8] André Bertrand, *Les Techniques du Travail Gouverne-
mental dans l'État Moderne,* Brussels, 1954.

[9] Edgar S. Furniss, *Office of the Prime Minister in Frenc
Foreign Policy,* Princeton, 1954.

duction, power and fuel, and military equipment (such as aircraft and atomic energy), and placed their friends on the boards of the nationalized industries. They were furthered by the multiplication of the various departmental subdivisions and the appointment of numerous new directors.

The Socialists and the M.R.P. followed suit, the former in the Ministry of the Interior, the latter in the Foreign Office and the important overseas residencies and departments.

It has to be remembered that France is a highly centralized administrative State. Important local government appointments, especially in the semi-police-semimilitary security ranks, are made by the prefects as agent of the Ministry of the Interior. The Communists took full advantage of the era of *tripartisme,* especially in the early part of it, to plant their members in places that endangered the State.

Two scandals exemplify the possible consequences: one "the affair of the generals" in 1950; the other, the scandal of the leakage of defense secrets from the veritable *sanctum sanctorum* of the Secretariat of the Presidency of the Republic, interconnected with the Secretariat of the Prime Minister, to which we have given attention (p. 432). These need brief observations.

The Disloyal Generals. In September 1949 it was accidentally discovered that a report of the Chief of the General Staff, Revers, had proposed the appointment of a friend, General Mast, to be High Commissioner in Indochina. The report had been given by the latter to an agent of Indochinese politicians, who claimed that the two generals had been given large sums of money for the report. The Prime Minister and the Ministers of Defense and the Interior decided not to let the affair leak out, for fear of scandal. The generals were allowed to resign, without being prosecuted. They admitted their friendship with the intermediary, but denied accepting money. Other Ministers in the quaky Cabinet were determined to take up the matter more thoroughly, especially as it was alleged that money had gone to the Socialist Party to replenish its funds. Jules Moch would not tolerate this.

The leakage occurred through a member of the *Cabinet* of M. Coste-Floret (Minister of Overseas France)—it is alleged. The fat was now in the fire. Revers withdrew his resignation; he was befriended by the deputy head of one of France's several secret-service agencies, anxious to hit at Jules Moch and Ramadier whom he accused to covering up spies. A de Gaullist paper now leaked information of a Revers statement known only to the latter, the go-between, and the secret police. A parliamentary committee of inquiry was set up.

It would want a long analysis [10] to carry one through this remarkable affair, involving many characters, Prime Ministers, Ministers, Deputies, Generals, and the "colonization" of various departments and security agencies by nominees of the parties who spied for party advantage. The Communist member of the inquiry committee (secret session had been decreed) passed out news to *L'Humanité.* The truth was never discovered for the members of the committee were designated by their groups. The Communists reaped the maximum political advantage.

The Disloyal Secretariat. The second affair was even more serious—it went to the very center of the Cabinet's secretariat. Here were leakages from the National Council of Defense to Communists about the situation in Indochina at a time (summer 1954) when this would weaken French resistance in the colony in war with Ho Chi Minh and China. The line of leakage was through a newspaper man and member of the Communist Party, one André Baranès, later alleged to be an informer for the Communist Party. He was able to pass out the authentic report of the meetings of the Defense Council on May 26 and July 1, 1954; and one again on September 10, concerning NATO strategy in Europe! The information was first discovered in the hands of Police Commissioner Jean Dides, who paid Baranès for spy reports. The leakage was traced to M. Mons, the Secretary General of the Defense Council. He, by sheer indiscretion, had let two of his assistants see these reports. These two men were notorious pro-Communists, bent on helping that party and stopping the Indochinese war. All three, Secretary General and assistants, had been fine Resistance fighters, and their Communist friends had levered them into sensitive places for future use. Jules

[10] See Philip Williams, article in *Cambridge Journal,* Cambridge, 1951, pp. 469ff.

Moch, a Socialist Minister, recognizing Mons' brilliance, had given him (*bona fide*) his promotion to the prefecture and then residency-general of Tunis.

In this case it was alleged also that the leakages went to various political parties, for their political advantage in opposition. The Communist leader Duclose amusedly boasted that he already had certain of the minutes in *extenso!* It is unlikely that the full truth will come out—once again because the political parties, or some of them, are determined to guard their sources of information.

Three Pressing Problems

Three matters emerge from these cases: the problem of official secrecy; that of the cabinets or secretaries that form the entourage of each minister; and the loyalty of the Army.

Official Secrecy. The Ministers in France are engaged to secrecy of official discussions by a rule contained in the regulations governing the procedure of the Cabinet. It runs: "Secrecy of the deliberations constitutes a State obligation which engages the honor of all present at meetings of the Council of Ministers." It engages the Secretariat present as well as Ministers.

Besides this obligation, it is a crime to harbor and impart to those who have not the right to receive the information in any professional relationship. The penal code further (Article 114 *et seq.*) punishes for arbitrary acts or conspiracies against the Constitution by officials (as well as against individual liberty and civil rights).

Furthermore, the penal code (dating from Napoleon's time), in Articles 75 to 294 covers every conceivable crime and misdemeanor against the security of the State. It includes the transmission to foreigners by any means of national defense secrets, action to demoralize the Army or national defense; the secrets of national defense are given wide interpretation, to include military, diplomatic, economic, and industrial information. Punishment of a dire kind is established for the passage of such information belonging to the Government, especially concerning the Armed Forces and services connected with them, to anybody without authorization (Decree law, March 1939).

We have already dilated on the importance of the maintaining of secrecy about matters governmental *a propos* the operation of the British Cabinet system. Some facts belong to the whole people and not to any particular group or individual who might draw a private and unauthorized advantage from knowing them. If secrecy is preserved, men are the more encouraged to speak their minds frankly about public policy.

In the British system, the keeping of confidential matters is much assisted by the political homogeneity of the Cabinet. Party fellowship encourages mutual confidence among the Ministers and militates against the seizure of political advantage by leakages of information adverse to others. But the French coalitions of rival groups rather encourage the divulging of secrets for party advantage and personal advantage. These groups were publicly hostile yesterday and may be so again in a month or two's time, perhaps even tomorrow. Such leakages of information have been deliberately sought by the rival parties, especially in the first four or five years after the shame of Vichy was ended by the Liberation. They relied on friends inside the departments to pass out information to a kind of intelligence service belonging to each party—especially the Communists and the de Gaullists. This is not an atmosphere in which men can afford to risk the punishment that may come before they have offered all the contents of their minds, their hopes and fears, in Cabinet council.

The Minister's Personal Cabinet. When a Minister takes office, he needs two kinds of assistance: that of the highest administrative career officials, and that of a few trusted *political* friends. He forms a personal cabinet in which for some purposes the two are mixed in membership: his *cabinet*. The political group, three or four or half a dozen friends help him in his political duties and administrative responsibilities. He devolves to them the watch over administrative action, relations with the press, and political duties—that is, relations with his group and the Assembly, and the political group organization. This they perform for him. Without this help, the Minister might be even more at the mercy of the career officials than the instability of Cabinets makes certain he will be, in any case.

Sometimes the political group, headed by a *che*

de cabinet, are efficient and honest; sometimes they lack these qualities in some degree. The trouble is that, representing the Minister, they may be in possession of the highest secrets; that they necessarily have an influence with the Minister, because he is dependent on them for information and some planning of action; and because they are in a position to dispense governmental favors (to do with jobs, contracts, and honors, and obstructions of judicial action) in the name of the Minister.

Sometimes the cabinet is better than the Minister—Pierre Laval is a case in point. The sparring partner is better than the champion. Often he has been let down. Thus, the Socialist leader Felix Gouin, who was Prime Minister in 1946, brought in some friends from his home town of Marseilles. They used his authority as a cloak for making profit out of imports of wine from Algeria. Their misdemeanor ruined his career.

In the Third Republic many scandals of this kind and many press intrigues and leakages occurred through these cabinets.

It is in the possibility of the loss of secrets, documentary and oral, that the cabinets are dangerous, even though they must be used by the Ministers. They may well form the first "contacts," as for example, in the 1951 affair of the betraying generals.

Loyalty of the Army to Cabinet Orders. France without a monarchy is in a worse position than the civilian government of Britain to rely on unconditional obedience of the Armed Forces to its normal government (pp. 158–159). Even in Britain a time of stress has shown that the loyalty of the regular officers to obedience can be shattered under the tension of their political views that may be fiercely in opposition to the Government of the day. Yet Britain has a two-party system, with great stability of government, and strict conventions of good ethics in the conflict of parties.

France has not these advantages. Under the Third Republic the relationship of Army and civilian government was for long very uneasy. The Commune was suppressed by the regular Army; generals were killed by the insurrectionists. Then, in 1879, following the Marshal MacMahon affair, the Army was purged of old and suspect officers,

in part because they were antirepublican. The Army became the last stronghold of the antirepublican and clerical forces. Boulanger (see p. 315) who, as Minister of War carried out some important technical and administrative reforms, then exhibited enmity to the regime of the Third Republic, almost leading up to a *coup d'état.*

This was followed by the dreadful behavior of the high officers in the Dreyfus case, when it was revealed how much of an antirepublican and antiliberal caste the Army was, with Jesuit confessors and Catholic politicians nurturing these destructive embitterments in it.

As a consequence of the need to get the Army under control, the Republican parties and Freemason organization, in the late 1880's, spied on officers and kept a list of those who would not be promoted on account of their mentality. Promotions had been taken out of the hands of the Army command, which could not be trusted, and lodged in the Ministry of War.

The Army was the more alienated when used to break strikes, as happened often. During the disorders over the subjection of the Church to State authority in 1902–1906, some officers resigned rather than carry out the Government's orders.

The last great defection occurred, when France surrendered to Hitler in 1940, under Marshal Pétain and General Weygand. The Army was put in an awkward position, because by now it had been indoctrinated with the idea of unconditional obedience to the civil government, and Marshal Pétain had obtained his authority according to the letter of the law of the Third Republic! Hence, those, like de Gaulle, who organized Free France or fought in the Resistance were the mutineers and rebels, not Pétain and those who obeyed him. It was, indeed, as Mr. Churchill has most graphically pointed out, hard to dissuade Army and Navy officers to come over to the Allies.

Once again, the Armed Forces were suspect, particularly the officers, the regular career men who had passed through St. Cyr and the naval academies, etc., for they were, indeed, concerned not for the Republic as it appeared but for "France" as it appeared to them, and the two images were very different. General Weygand's policy to capitulate in 1940 to thwart a mythical "communist" revolution is one illustration of it.

Hence, the fear of de Gaulle as the "man on horseback." Hence, also, the riddling of the various departments with the nominees of various parties, in order to spy on rival political parties and their Ministers, to divulge information about military activities, and the inmixture, as we have seen (p. 435), of generals in political affairs, in spying, intrigues, and divulgence of military secrets.

The most recent incident demonstrating the continued existence of military insubordination toward the civilian government and even the Republic occurred in March and April 1954. Then Marshal Alphonse Pierre Juin, valiant commander of the African Forces in 1941, Chief of Staff, 1944–1947, Resident General in Morocco, 1947–1951, France's chief representative on NATO, for which he is Commander in Chief in Central Europe and chief military adviser to the Government, made a speech at a meeting of military officers, seriously criticizing EDC at a moment of great anxiety for the Cabinet, leading to its possible downfall. He charged that in France there was "no longer a State but only an administration." The Prime Minister, M. Laniel, had called the Marshal in for a talk: he did not attend. He did not repent, but repeated his charges in similar surrounding: "an administration without ears or guts that will pursue its responsible duty." M. Laniel consulted the Cabinet on what to do. The Cabinet considered Juin's behavior as "a grave lack of military discipline." It withdrew certain of his military prerogatives. Could he be ousted from his NATO command? Juin was supported by de Gaullists, who hated EDC. He was criticized by the M.R.P. and the Radicals. Great passions had been stirred in the public, the press, and Assembly. The de Gaullists, who had members in the Cabinet, threatened to defeat the defense budget if the Government and the Assembly too rudely censured the Marshal. That budget was adopted 302 against 232, after bitter debate. In the *place* around the Arc de Triomphe riots occurred to the cry of *"Vive Juin!"* led by veterans and retired and reserve officers, countered by Left-wing rank and file. This same Juin had set Morocco in turmoil by his favoring the colonists and the Ber-

bers against the Arab sultanate and the Istiqlal, the nationalist movement, and by constant persecuting of the latter.

The regime of a multiplicity of parties and brief cabinets without authority or enduring prestige make it hard for an officer to know whom to obey

The loyalty of the Civil Service is similarly jeopardized (Chapter 9).

V. ADMINISTRATIVE CONTROL BY THE ASSEMBLIES

The Assemblies secure a day-to-day control over the Executive through three devices: the commissions, interpellations, and questions. This is over and above the control that derives from the pangs of cabinet-making and cabinet-breaking by the persistent drip-drip of personal influence in *les couloirs* and the blowing hot and cold of the groups in debate.

The *permanent Commissions* (pp. 390–392) have by eager custom the general control over the Executive, as well as over lawmaking. The Commissions prepare resolutions by which the Assembly will demand action. They invite a Minister to attend and answer criticism and give explanations He may bring government commissioners with him on these occasions (p. 387). This process is continuous. It is reinforced by the occasional statutory requirement that certain decrees receive the approval of the Commissions to be effective. The more important Deputies and Senators make *de marches* to the Ministers themselves for information and discussion of troublesome matters. The interfere deeply in administration and subject Ministers to harassing and time-consuming interrogations. But the Minister will rebuff them at his later peril, for they are all-potent in the raising of questions in the Assembly and especially in incubating interpellations.

However, this is one method of keeping a hand on the march of policy and administration. It is indispensable, in some form. The problem is to limit the Commissions to seeing that the job is done and to fend them off from trying to do the job themselves. The testimony is that they overstep the limits. As soon as an important affair looms before the Assembly's horizon, membership of the Commissions undergoes a change. The groups compel some of their members to resign to be replaced by others who are more reliable executants of the policy of the group's majority and the party executive's majority outside the Assembly. For example, leading up to the debates on the European Pacts in middle December 1954, the Finance Commission and the National Defense Commission chose *rapporteurs* hostile to the Pacts; de Gaullists had refused these posts (being in favor) at the direction of their group.

The members of the two chambers participate in various consultative councils that are attached, sometimes more than one, to each of the administrative departments (see Chapter 8).

Special Commissions of Inquiry

There are appointed from time to time by the chambers, special commissions of inquiry or control. For example, the commission to investigate the leakage of information about defense matters through certain accused generals in January 1950. It was composed of twelve Deputies, four named equally by the Commissions of Defense, Justice, and the Interior. Or there are established special permanent commissions, like that which represents the combined Finance, Production, and Economic Affairs Commissions to watch the administration of the nationalized industries.

The Commission on Finance supervises the legality and economy of the expenditure of national funds, and in the course of this its members keep a very close supervision over the process of expenditure, close in attention and in their presence in the Ministries.

The British House of Commons does not use the commission method of controlling administration. It has preferred to give latitude to the Government, and then challenge and guide it day by day through its question time, and through the method of Select Committees and Tribunals of Inquiry for special difficulties (see pp. 123–126). This is a supple system that leaves the Administration free to get on with its work, but not to get away with incompetence or dishonesty.

The French method is more interfering. Its commission method has been rejected in Britain, though several proposals have been made to use them.

Questions

French control over administration is aided further by questions and by interpellations.

Questions are quite subordinate in importance in contrast to British practice. The Standing Orders allow a short question period every Friday, and a whole sitting once per month. This is about one fiftieth the question time in the House of Commons (see p. 162). In the Assembly, a question is not answered unless it has been on the agenda for a week. The Minister answers, and the questioning Deputy or his substitute may reply— both have five minutes only—and no other Deputy may (as the Commons may) ask supplementaries or join in the colloquy. Questions may be asked for written reply. The General Secretariat of the Cabinet picks up these questions and brings them to the attention of the Prime Minister and thence the Cabinet, as part of the process of reply. The Prime Minister is enabled to take note of the delicate political problems posed by the answers his Ministers give, thus allowing a certain control.

In France some 70 oral questions are asked *per year,* whereas in the House of Commons some 13,000 are asked, and some 7000 answered orally, the rest in writing. In France, again, some 4000 written questions are submitted, almost all answered; in Britain, about 3000. It seems clear that the French Deputy has found an alternative way —the Commissions—to satisfy his thirst for information and an opportunity for pressure on Ministers. The R.P.F. tried in 1952 to get a regular question time instituted *in the Commissions.* It was rejected on the ground that the ministerial burden would be excessive and cause his absence from his post of administrative control.

The Council of the Republic also has the power to ask questions of Ministers: it asks some 80 questions a year, orally; and between 600 and 1200 written.

Interpellations

The interpellation is a question to which a reply is made by a Minister allowing a debate on the reply, the procedure ending with a resolution by the Assembly in favor of or adverse to the Government's attitude as expressed in reply and debate. It was the favorite weapon of the legislature for bringing the Ministers to heel, used in the Third Republic with lethal effects on the Government. Questions in the British House of Commons let a Government live, subject to correction; the interpellation was an instrument to kill.

Interpellations can be initiated only by a single Deputy; his job is to get it on the agenda. The Deputy informs the President of the Assembly summarily of its object. The Government is immediately notified by the latter, and the President of the Republic informs the Assembly the day after he has been approached. The problem then is to get a date for the interpellation. It is obtained by appeal to the Assembly on a Tuesday afternoon sitting, either on the recommendation of the Presidents' Conference or when the Government and the interpellator have agreed on the date.

Furthermore, at the written request of the interpellator, backed by fifty Deputies (counted by roll call), the Assembly itself may proceed forthwith to the fixing of a date, and this by a vote without discussion, immediately after the Government has been informed that an interpellation has been asked for. The Government must be heard before the date is fixed.

The people allowed to speak on the question of fixing the date are the interpellator, the presidents of the groups, and the Government—each for five minutes.

Unless the Assembly votes to the contrary, the discussion of interpellations has priority over the regular agenda already fixed by the Presidents' Conference.

It is a habit to join interpellations to each other, a number of dissatisfied groups thus combining in a collective interpellation on the identical theme or on themes sufficiently close to be grouped. This *jonction* may take place when the Assembly has decided to fix the date of discussion.

Once the interpellator has had his right of first reply to the Government, the discussion becomes general. Any Deputy may participate subject to the order and time of speech already described (pp. 386–387).

The debate ends with a simple passage to the regular business of the Assembly—"order of the day pure and simple." On this, there is a five-minute rule of speech.

But another outcome is possible. The order of the day may be *motivé*—that is, charged with an adverse judgment, or requiring that the Government take remedial action.

Sometimes interpellations are employed for minor matters indeed, rather like the discussions that occur almost daily at the end of business, on the adjournment in the House of Commons—merely ventilative. Others have the appearance of a House of Commons motion for the adjournment of the House on a matter of urgent and public importance (p. 162) or a vote of censure.

The interpellation, while remaining a powerful weapon, sometimes a veritable pole ax, has declined in importance since the 1930's. In 1947, 200 demands for interpellations were made; in 1951 and 1952 the number had risen to 248 annually and in 1953 to 350. Discussion on the actual fixing of a date occurred in 1952 on but 35 demands; these were grouped so that the discussions on the date were cut down to nine. Interpellation debates actually occurred *only three times:* for of the seventeen demands sanctioned, a grouping into three was made. In 1953, 248 interpellations were submitted; they embodied nearly 400 "demands"; only 24 were given a date; only 9 were debated.

Here are the two examples of interpellations debated in 1953. In October the Laniel Government was interpellated on the course of the war in Indochina. After the debate, the order of the day was *motivé,* and said, in brief, that it invited the Government to try by negotiation to bring about a general pacification in Asia; to see that there was a fair division of the burden among the nations interested in the parts of the world where they had a solidarity of interests; urged that the defense of Indochina take place within the French Union . . . and rejected any addition to this resolution.

The son of a former Communist Deputy and four other candidates with Communist "connections" were struck off the list of candidates at the examination for entry to the *École nationa. d'Administration*—the one route to the higher

Civil Service (Chapter 9). The explanation given in the Prime Minister's office (section on the public service) was that the Government must see to it that candidates have an absolute loyalty to republican institutions: it was normal to refuse entry to a person whose attachment to the Communist Party was known for a certainty. Five persons, it was then found, had been so rejected. A U.R.A.S. Deputy moved an interpellation; many parents of students and personages protested, it was reported, such an inadmissible manifestation of *"maccarthyisme."* The interpellation (in fact, several joined together) was embodied in an order of the day, by 355 to 214, put by a Communist Deputy, a famous trial lawyer, that the *Conseil d'État* should treat the case as one of excess of power (Chapter 11). In fact, the *Conseil* already had the case before it. It declared the refusal of candidacy illegal. But by that time the candidates' ages disqualified them.

The Council of the Republic has a similar procedure, called "oral question with debate." However, since the Government bears no responsibility to the Council, the order of the day does not openly avow confidence or the lack of it in the Government.

As a final safeguard, petitions from the citizens to either chamber are allowed. They are dealt with by the Commissions on the Franchise, Constitution, etc., and passed on to the appropriate Minister, who replies in print in the report of the debates. They are not debated, though they can be.

VI. A LAMENTABLY WEAK CABINET SYSTEM

The lament in June 1953 of Mendès-France, then experienced as a Deputy, President of the Accounts Committee, and Minister tells the story:

The Assembly is the judge without appeal of the action of the government. But a government cannot fulfill its mission if it is assailed every day in this body, if its members and its chief are obliged to consecrate their efforts and their time to innumerable discussions so often sterile.

Parliament legislates, it controls the execu-

tive. But the executive ought to be in a position to govern and to administer (*very good! very good! from the extreme Right benches*) to meet its responsibilities without any other preoccupation than to realize the program fixed in clear agreement with the National Assembly. It ought not to be arrested in its work by the constant fear of being overthrown. Parliament has the right to withdraw its confidence from the government at any instant; the government ought to be able, at every instant to act as though it were assured of existing for twenty years. (*Applause from various seats on the left, in the center and on the extreme right.*)

But the Parliament will not give the Government this administrative peace of mind. It is possible for freedom to be so avidly desired, that other goods, such as justice and welfare, are lost.

In the Soviet system of government, the worries expressed by Mendès-France, then aspirant Prime Minister, do not exist. The Presidium (presidency) and the Council of Ministers legislate and administer. They have the guarantee of much more than twenty years of peace of mind: fortified by machine guns, tanks, and strafing airplanes and the consignment of the voices of freedom, justice, and welfare to the dungeons, the prison camp, and the stillness of abrupt death.

For, as we have seen in the discussion of French political parties and the Assembly and the Cabinet, the characteristics of the Frenchman in politics is high individualism and almost petulant self-confidence and a kind of challenging querulousness toward government. But, as we show in regard to the people of the Soviet Union their characteristics are, above all, inertia, almost complete don't-careness about who rules or the objects of the rulers, coupled with and partly based on centuries of the deepest ignorance and servility. One culture produces a multiplicity of parties; the other what its rulers call a "monolithic" party—that is, a block of stone: one, that of France, a skidding *immobilisme* in which the government is trodden underfoot by the citizens; the other, Russia, where all movement comes from the active and crushing initiative of the government and the subjects are trodden down.

The Council of the Republic;
The Economic Council; The Assembly
of the French Union

It is a different conception of society, customs, life, and of the individual himself. It [public health administration, etc.] is hardly compatible with life in
France which is based on an entirely different set of principles, and especially on
another scale of values. The emphasis in the one case [France] is laid on the individual who thinks, and in the other [American] on the individual who lives.

—André Siegfried, 1930

I. THE COUNCIL OF THE REPUBLIC

For reasons already noted (p. 325), a kind of
second-chamber system was instituted by the
Fourth Republic. The Socialist Ramadier has en-
dearingly called it a "crippled bicameralism
strongly resembling a qualified monocameralism."
Those who would have it stronger have stigmatized it as "despotism [the Assembly] tempered
by a sham [the Council of the Republic]." It is a
legislature of one and a half chambers.

Original Composition

The powers of the Council of the Republic are
set out in the Constitution, Articles 7 to 24. These
were determined at once. The composition was
laid down in ordinary law, made reviewable in
two years after the coming into effect of the law.
But the Constitution did lay down certain basic
rules that must be the core of the Council's
structure. It was to be elected on a territorial basis.
This excluded the "corporate" or "professional"
representation desired in variant forms by the

M.R.P. and the de Gaullists. It was to be elected
by the communes and the *département* local authorities, and this by universal and indirect suffrage.

It was the stipulation of *indirect* suffrage that
pleased the M.R.P. and the Radicals—for this
could be used to offset the effect of mass voting
for the parties of the Left; by the same token, this
provision irked the Socialists and disgusted the
Communists. Then the Council was made renewable one half at a time. Its number was to range
between 250 and 320, neither less nor more. Of
these, the National Assembly might elect up to one
sixth of the membership, and by P.R.

The law of October 27, 1946, first provided
fully for the composition of the Council. It was
considerably amended by the law of September 24,
1948. The barest reference only is therefore made
to the original law. It provided for 315 councilors—henceforward called Senators (the reason
appears on page 446). Two hundred were elected
by the councils of the *départements* and their
Assembly Deputies, thus by indirect election; 50

442

were chosen by the National Assembly (5 for French residents in the colonies, and 3 for Frenchmen living there, and the rest by P.R. among the groups). Groups three (14 members) and four (51 members) were respectively chosen by Algerian local governing bodies and by the local governments in the French colonies.

By party, the first Senate was thus composed:

Groups	Number
Communist and affiliates	88
Socialist	64
M.R.P.	76
R.G.R.	42
P.R.L.	11
Ind. Rep.	16
Social and Peasant	5
Algerian Manifesto	4
Algerian Mussulman	4
No group	4
	314

The political spectrum was very closely proportionate to the political representation in the National Assembly.

Final Composition

Article 102, one of the transitional articles of the Constitution, required the Council to be reelected after the election of new local governing authorities—a classic connection with central politics—within two years. The climate of opinion was now tremendously altered. *Tripartisme* was over long since. The Communists had been revealed as destroyers of the Republic. The R.P.F. was in full spate. If proportional representation were continued, these two extremes would dominate the Council. The middle parties of the Assembly could not tolerate this. Hence, highly drastic changes were made in a new electoral law—September 24, 1948—all within the same broad skeleton of constitutional requirements.

The number of Senators was raised to 320. The term became the six years as in the Constitution, the halves to be reelected each three years, beginning May 1952; the first half to be renewed being settled by lot among 160 alphabetically arranged senatorial names, and the rest in a second list. The 320 are divided into 246 for metropolitan France and 74 overseas councilors. Of the 74 overseas representatives, the National Assembly does elect 7: 3 for Frenchmen living abroad, 8 for Frenchmen in Morocco, and 1 for such in Indochina.

The method of election was transformed. The National Assembly's one sixth of the membership was discontinued. The metropolitan seats were distributed to the *départements,* each of which was entitled to one seat for the first 154,000 inhabitants and additional ones for each 250,000 or fraction thereof, above this. The rules designed to secure P.R. on the nationwide electorate were abolished. **Electoral Colleges.** The electoral colleges system was maintained but their composition was changed profoundly. They still were to be composed of the local Deputies and the *départemental* councilors. But instead of the 85,000 delegates, or "grand electors," elected by the voters at large (which was on a proportional basis), representatives of the municipal councils became members of the colleges. The latter body numbered 100,000 and was made up of a number of municipal representatives according to the size of the various councils. But this was far from proportional representation: because the size of the councils does not rise by any means in proportion to population represented by the councils. Here, again, a complication was introduced. The 1312 communes with over 3500 inhabitants chose their delegates by proportional representation. Those with less—which means nearly 35,000—chose theirs by absolute majority, allowing three ballots to attain this.

When the colleges per *département* were thus chosen, they then proceeded to the choice of the Councilors of the Republic. In the eleven largest *départements,* each with a population of more than 654,000 and entitled therefore to four seats or more each, P.R. was introduced. These accounted for 72 members. The other 79 *départements* elected their total of 174 members by majority vote and the second-ballot system. Here election on the first ballot was valid if a candidate got an *absolute* majority, with a quarter of those on the register actually voting; while at the second ballot a *relative* majority was adequate.

The Fourth Republic had now come round to an electoral basis for its second chamber very similar to that of the former Senate. The smaller, the more backward, communities were favored, though it was not feasible with the change of political opinion since the fall of the Third Republic, to restore all the territorial conservatism and rural backwardness of the Senate by extreme overweighting of the latter.

Thus, Marseilles used to have 7 percent of the *département's* delegates; it now has 25 percent; still it is underrepresented, because it has 75 percent of the population. Paris used to have 14 percent of the Seine's delegates; it has 22½ percent; it ought to have 60 percent, by population. If the eleven towns next after these two are contemplated, containing together 2,500,000 people here almost two thirds of the municipal delegates come from communes of less than 1000 population, containing in all less than half the population of the *département!*

Thus, two aims were accomplished in this reform of the electoral basis of the Council of the Republic. It became again, in a sense, as Gambetta had called it, "the grand council of the communes of France," and it was solidly founded in the more conservative and religious clientele. It includes 107 mayors of municipalities of very different size and 124 members and chairmen of the general councils of the *départements* (p. 488).

Its members were thus distributed among the various groups:

Group	Numbers, August 1954	Election of June 1955 * Outgoing	Change
Communists	16	2	−1
Socialists	56	31	+2
M.R.P. and affiliated Republican Center (3)	27	6	+1
R.G.R.	70	32	+3
Overseas Independents	13		
Independent Republicans	61 ⎫		
Affiliated: A.R.S.	6 ⎬	44	−1
Peasants (for Rural and Social Action)	19 ⎭		
Social Republicans (U.R.A.S.)	39	13	−9
Affiliated—the Overseas Rally	9		
Unaffiliated	4		
	320		

* For the Overseas Territories, losses and gains were: Communists, 1 out, 1 loss; Socialists, 7 out, 2 losses; R.G.R., 3 out, 3 elected; M.R.P., 3 out, 1 loss; U.R.A.S., 5 out, 1 gain; Independents, 4 out, 1 loss; unaffiliated, 2 out, 3 gains.

out of a national total of 40,000,000, or something over 6 percent, then they used to have 264 delegates but now have 900. That is a rise from 0.33 percent to less than 1 percent—that is, 264 delegates out of about 71,000 (total electoral colleges after subtracting the Deputies and the *départemental* councilors) against 900 delegates out of 100,000.

The countryside is heavily favored. The population in communes of over 3500, statistically regarded as "urban," is one half of the nation; but it elects only one third of the delegates from the municipal councils. The very small communes, in the country, get the greatest weighting: in the *département* of Oise there are no big towns, and

The contrast with the Council of 1946 is tremendous: the Communists cut to one fifth; the Socialists losing 12 percent of their seats; the M.R.P. losing nearly two thirds; the Radicals on the way to being doubled; the conservatives, Peasants, and de Gaullists holding nearly one third of the Council, instead of about one tenth! A conservative sheet anchor! The design to make the Council a reflection of the strength of opinions in the Assembly, in order to make it but an echo, not an obstruction, of the latter, has been frustrated, for the strength of parties in the Council is highly conservative compared with the Assembly. Their percentage strengths (less the "noninscribed") may be roughly compared; thus:

Percent of Seats, December 31, 1952

Party	Assembly	Council of the Republic
Communists	15.3	5.0
Socialists	16.8	17.5
M.R.P.	14.0	8.5
Radicals	12.0 } R.G.R. } 22.9	
U.D.S.R.	3.7	
Conservatives	8.8	20.1
Peasants	7.5	5.9
R.P.F.	13.6	15.4
A.R.S.	5.1	—
Overseas Independents	2.4	3.8

The percentages remain much the same after the partial elections of June 1955.

The application of the majority principle in place of the proportional representation of the earlier electoral law hurt the Communists especially. The Socialists fought them at the first two turns of the ballot and, on the third, fought the Radicals and their friends. The urban electors of M.R.P. went elsewhere, over to the Right. The Radicals came back to their prewar heritage, because with the nonproportional system they profited heavily in the small municipalities, in the southwest, the south of the Paris Basin, and in some places in the southeast and center of France.

The difference between the Chambers was, therefore, marked, and interesting results were to be expected.

Powers of the Council

Relegating till later the effect of the constitutional amendments of December 1954, to strengthen the Council, we commence with an account of the powers of the Council of the Republic till then. War may not be declared without a vote of the National Assembly—and the concurrent opinion of the Council. It sits at the same time as the National Assembly: this, then, by its own arrangements for sitting, determines the sessions of the Council. It joins with the Assembly in the election of the President of the Republic.

The Council is given an indirect right of legislation by Article 14, which gives the true initiative to the National Assembly through the Prime Minister and the Deputies. The final authority, says the Article, is the National Assembly alone; it shall vote the laws. But the Article also says that proposed laws introduced by the Council shall be filed with its secretariat and sent without debate to the National Assembly's secretariat. "They may not be received if they would result in the reduction of revenues or the creation of new expenditures."

Thus, the Council is of little importance as an initiating assembly, since a legislative discussion of its own propositions of law are excluded; while the financial initiative is monopolized by the Assembly, both by the *exclusion* of the Council and the lodgment (Article 15) of the right over the budget in the National Assembly.

Hence, the Council is put into the position of a revising chamber—the classic role of a second chamber in democracies, whether unitary States or federal States that require a second chamber to maintain the identity of the States federated.

Revising Power. Article 20 lays down the terms of this revising function. The Council is to examine the bills voted by the National Assembly. The term *first reading* is used. This is not the same as *first reading* in English and American terminology. It does not mean the first reading in the usual three in the procedure of either chamber. It means the entire readings and passage of the bill in the National Assembly; and the second reading means the reconsideration of the bill when it has been to the Council and has been sent back to the Assembly for that consideration under the conditions now explained.

The Council receives and handles the bill that comes from the Assembly "in order to give its opinion thereon." This is a weak phrase: "to give its opinion." It was intentional. The Council was intended to be the agency of a pause and second thoughts for the Assembly, not an obstructive chamber like the old Senate, execrated by progressive minds.

It must give its opinion not more than two months after the National Assembly has sent it a measure. If the law in question is a budget law (the Constitution says *the* budget law, but we know that the Assembly cannot contain itself to make only *one* comprehensive law of the budget annually), then the time of the Council's handling of it may be reduced to the time taken by the National Assembly for consideration and vote. This takes care of any possible increase of the political power of the Council by bargaining based on *the power to delay*—it has not got it.

Whenever the National Assembly adopts a rule for emergency procedure (see p. 308), the Council's handling of the bill is limited to the time that the Assembly has allowed itself. Interruptions of a session do not count in the two-months' time limit; and the latter may be extended by the Assembly.

Thus, the Constitution has subordinated the Council so far as its power to delay is concerned. **The Two Chambers.** If the opinion of the Council of the Republic agrees with the National Assembly (or is not given in the time limits), the law is "promulgated as passed by the National Assembly." The Council cannot make changes that may have become desirable in the meanwhile, even down to punctuation—that is the Constitution.

If the Council's opinion disagrees with the Assembly's, then the Assembly *must* give the bill a second reading. Whatever the Assembly now decides—that is, to accept or reject the Council's alternatives—it decides finally and absolutely.

But—if the amendments are *rejected,* completely or partially, by the National Assembly, it must express its vote on the now revised law, by roll call and *by absolute majority* of its members, *if* the vote on the whole of the bill was taken by roll call and absolute majority in the Council of the Republic.

This last proviso has given the Council leverage over the Assembly, because as we have only too amply seen, the securing of an absolute majority of the votes on any measure (even the investiture of a Prime Minister and a Cabinet while the nation is waiting for a Government) is extremely difficult. Abstentions alone can prevent an absolute majority from being reached.

Senators All! Now whenever a body of men form a separate group, with powers and responsibilities entrusted to them and not to be ignored and are paid a stipend, their pride and self-approval are evoked, and they will attempt to make the most of, even extend, their authority. This was demonstrated in December 1948, when the members of

the newly elected Council of the Republic, no longer dominated by the Left-wing parties (who had not wanted it even to be conceived, let alone be born), voted that their title should henceforth be: "Senators, members of the Council of the Republic." They comport themselves as the Senators of the Third Republic.

Assembly Tactics. The Assembly subordinates the Council through the time-limit stipulations—usually inadvertently through its own lack of self-discipline in timing, but also as a deliberate tactic of sabotaging the powers of the Council. It sends batches of bills forward all together; and at the end of the session. It has used the "urgency" procedure, which demands from the Council an answer in a very brief time. Individual Deputies in the Assembly, anxious to be the lawgivers of their nation, not least when the bill is of a pork-barrel type and aiding the ends of regional or nationally organized pressure groups, have constantly invoked the urgency rule. The Government itself has rushed legislation, even madly.

Naturally, this gives scant time to the Commissions of the Council of the Republic to deliberate and write reports in the way that the Assembly's Commissions do. For the general organization and methods of discussion in the Council follow the Assembly's and roughly those of the Senate of the Third Republic.

A crisis occurred in the relations of the two Houses in June 1948. A bill to pay salaries *in arrears* (!) for the National Society of Studies and Construction of Airplane Motors had been treated under the urgency procedure of the Assembly and passed to the Council of the Republic with the demand that it be treated by the Council in the same brief period—that is, thirty-three hours, including two nights. The bill did need urgent treatment but also careful consideration, if the Council were not to be a nullity. Therefore the Council, with the exception of the Communist members, unanimously resolved to exceed the time limit. The Assembly, supported by every group, demanded the pound of flesh. The Council appealed to the Constitutional Committee (Chapter 3) against the Assembly's view of Article 20; and won the concession that it must be given a minimum of three days in which to give its opinion, including its Commission procedure. (The Assembly's urgent action requires the three days, but *not* including Commission time.) The Assembly itself has had to control its own urgency spasms, thus giving the Council more time to breathe also.

The deadlock between the Assembly and the Council cannot be eased by a compromise proposal of the Assembly; it is its bill or the Council's bill. This sometimes produced nightmare arguments on grammar and spelling as a way of finding a compromise that was *not* a change of text! This was a ridiculous situation; until remedied by the amendment of December 7, 1954 (below).

In financial legislation Senators may not offer amendments increasing expenditure above that proposed to the Assembly by the latter's Finance Commission. But they may *increase* revenues. This exactly reverses the situation in the Third Republic.

Growing Strength of the Council. It is difficult for the popular Assembly to ignore or excessively depreciate a second chamber that has been established, like it, by the Constitution; which has a popular representative foundation; that is endowed with powers of revision and delay; that is one of the two Houses entitled to elect the President, and enjoys its share of the prestige of being called "the Parliament of France." Moreover, the Council has an electorate, and its parties are almost the same parties as those in the Assembly. Are the Socialists and the M.R.P. to ignore the claims of their confreres in the Council?

As soon as the Communist Party, beginning in May 1947, entered into steady opposition, the Assembly found it politic to pay rather more attention to the Council's opinions than before, when it had been almost contemptuous of ideas that the Council had labored on, repudiating them without even the courtesy of the briefest debate.

Furthermore, the Council had improved its procedure of meeting the mind of the Assembly by explanations offered through its *rapporteurs* to those of the Assembly. It occasionally persuaded the Government to facilitate a rapprochement.

The drift of the Assembly Rightward assisted the Council's claims to consideration. These were enhanced by the cleavage between the Third Force, thus inclined, and the Communist Party,

determined to get in the streets what they could not achieve in the Cabinet or the Assembly—a ruined French economy or Communist dictatorship. The Communists obstructed bills sent up from the Assembly to give the Government powers to check violence and disorder in the Communist-fomented strikes.

The Council rallied to the help of one Government in December 1947 when it *increased* the taxes desired by René Mayer but denied by the Assembly. It came to the aid of the comprehensive bill for decree-making powers asked for by Paul Reynaud, already mentioned (p. 398), since the Assembly was unwilling to take the responsibility, for the first time after the Constitution had come into effect, of giving such broad powers. When the bill came back with the Council's amendments, the Assembly, feeling itself covered, accepted them.

Thus, in cases where the Council can offer intelligent assistance, and where the parties in the Assembly are not too deeply engaged by their passions and electoral commitments, the Council has had effect. Also, as the decree-making-bill case indicates, the Council may cover the Assembly's fear to take sole responsibility.

Limits to Its Powers. So far the Council has mounted in power. But there are limits the other way. It can hardly act so as to subvert the governmental coalition of the day. The Assembly enacted in September 1948 a law to postpone the elections for the general councils of the *département* local authorities. These are try-outs for general elections and affect the trend of national opinion and also the composition of the Council of the Republic. The Council was bold enough to reject this, the Communists making up the vast majority in a small house. This was a serious challenge to the Government's general policy and caused dissensions within its coalition. It was rejected with the maximum firmness.

When the Council was elected on the new basis in November 1948 and became heavily conservative (gaining members at by-elections also), a new era in the pretensions of the Senators began, carried along by the two devices of absolute majority votes and the attempt to restore the power of interpellation, though the Government is not, under the Constitution, responsible to the Council.

It attempted to secure the right to initiate laws. It could not openly debate these in full session, but it intended to have this done in Commission. The Assembly by a vote of 429 against 150 repudiated this device, the three Left parties in the majority; the Radicals, conservatives, and R.P.F. in the minority. The Council receded. But the constitutional amendments of December 1954 allow the claims of the Council except on bills to ratify treaties, financial bills, and bills resulting in the reduction of revenues on the creation of new expenditures.

The Council tried to convert its right to ask oral questions, with a debate to follow, into a full interpellation. As matters stood, no Senator alone (or a Deputy alone) could initiate this kind of questioning and ministerial answer; it required the president of a group, a committee, or thirty Senators. No vote ended the discussion, to put the Government in responsibility to the Council.

Right to Interpellations. The Council in June 1949 assimilated its question power into an interpellation, as in the Assembly. The Assembly reacted adversely and strongly. Its President (M. Herriot, of the party that favored a more powerful Council) called on the President of the Republic to have the Constitutional Committee rebuff the Council on the basis of Article 48, which denies governmental responsibility to the Council. M. Auriol regretfully (since he was a Socialist) answered that he could not do this, because the Committee was empowered to defend the Council, not the Assembly. The Council was on good ground, for after all, an interpellation does not *in the Council* lead to a vote of confidence that can bring the Government down, though adverse votes in an assembly founded on popular election, even if indirect, must bring annoyance and humiliation. The Council's claim prevailed, especially as it argued that the Constitution gives it powers to give an opinion whether on laws, on treaties, on a declaration of war.

Determined to obstruct the more Leftish Assembly, the Council embarked on a series of maneuvers whenever the Assembly's always fragile majority was faced with a particularly difficult partisan-political issue. It fomented Assembly dissension over gasoline rationing and pricing; it amended the Assembly electoral law of 1951 to include single-member constituencies, whereas the Assembly had reached an agonizing compromise on a new kind of proportional representation. It annually challenged the Assembly on the budget, precisely because the moderate and conservative groups there were solid with the Council in opposition to the raising of taxation.

This could be done because the Council could steadily *vote by an absolute majority* and so impose the same condition on the Assembly. The Assembly was forced into concessions. On the electoral bill, indeed, the Assembly needed 314 votes to reject the Council's audacious proposal, and obtained only 308. It was necessary to encourage the desperate Robert Schuman (M.R.P.) Cabinet not to resign, and to try again by sending the bill back to Commission, which found amendments that could muster an absolute majority against the Council! The supporters of the Government in the Council had to refrain from voting their favored bill in numbers sufficient to produce an absolute majority. For example, when the M.R.P. members in the Council abstained from voting on the bill that gave subsidies to Church schools, in order to stop the Council's amendments from getting an absolute majority, they very probably led to defeat in the Assembly where the same kind of majority could not be obtained.

Financial Legislation. The Council has indulged in contortionist maneuvers on financial legislation. Wishing to wound but not to kill (especially, perhaps, to commit suicide), some groups have abstained, to prevent an absolute majority from being obtained—these would be members of governmental parties. The de Gaullists and Communists have sometimes found common cause in embarrassing the Assembly and the Government. They have forced reconsiderations and compromises on the Government, especially as their amendment of one side of the balance—the reduction of appropriations (the *maxima*)—throws the taxation side out of symmetry. For the Council, as elected in 1948 is a conservative and Radical-minded body—middle class. Antitaxers, and unwilling to use its power to *increase* taxes, it acts by reducing government expenditures. It has opposed such measures as those that favored the labor unions in collective bargaining and the support of national rather than private enterprise by the Government's planned investment policy.

When the Assembly of 1951 was elected, though more conservative than the previous one, the Council was still more conservative. It still obstructed the Assembly's legislation that might favor the urban workers, as, for example, with the defeat of a sliding scale for wages in 1951.

Its history is one of illiberalism, and a penchant for the peasantry and the middle classes of the cities. Thus, it has opposed increases of taxes again and again on the ground that nationalization and the social-security services have burdened the budget. It has obstructed the measures for substantial liberalization of the franchise in the colonies. It was hostile to the grant of special powers to Mendès-France which the Assembly voted 3 to 1, only 146 being for it in the Council, with 41 against and 123 abstentions. It demanded a larger share of the Monnet investment funds for agriculture, to the detriment of industry and urban housing. It willingly voted for family allowances to peasants. It forced the prolongation of its delaying power in treating the Assembly's bills, in order to increase its influence in the constitutional revisions of 1954. On this occasion the de Gaullists were disconsolate at the loss of the "absolute majority" provision (below) in the Council's powers of "advice," which enabled the Council to put on the Assembly the onus of revoting its bills by an absolute majority, a difficult condition to meet.

. In November 1955 it supported the group in the Assembly (led by the Radicals under Mendès-France) that wished to avoid early elections and to return to the single-member-district of voting. Twice it inserted the latter as an amendment to M. Faure's bill. The majority was on November 11, 225 votes against 60, with 35 either abstaining or not voting. Thus, the whole Council was for thwarting the Assembly's bill, except the Communists, the M.R.P., the Overseas Independents, 8 Peasants, and a couple of others. Its action lengthened the debate finally ending in defeat of the Government and dissolution. Of all the subjects on which a second chamber should keep its hands off, the electoral method of the popular

Assembly would seem to be the one. But this one repeated the said obstruction.

Summary of Its Power. A general statement of a quantitative nature on the relations between the two chambers might be thus put. Up to March 1953 the Council had passed 168 dissentient opinions by absolute majority. The Assembly was able to find an absolute majority for all but six of these bills. Of all the bills sent to the Council by the Assembly, 60 percent have been unamended by the Council. Of the 40 percent to which amending opinions have been attached, about one third have been accepted by the Assembly with the amendments intact. In about half the cases the Assembly has accepted some Council amendments; and the rest have been completely rejected by it. Yet the figures do not tell all: for (1) the Assembly has accepted mainly the smaller drafting and technical amendments; (2) the Council cannot initiate; (3) the interpellations have no force; (4) the Council cannot kill Governments—usually or easily, for the Assembly's corporate spirit is roused; and (5) the Government cannot play off a powerful Council against a popular assembly whose behavior it does not like, for the Council has not the power. Yet the Council clearly has some power; it is embarrassing to the parties, each in their turn; and it constitutes one more distracting influence for both people and the harassed Governments.

In April 1955 so entrenched had the Council become that Prime Minister Edgar Faure, let it be understood that, unless the Council voted for the law passed by the Assembly ratifying the Western Union Pacts without need for a redeliberation in the Assembly, he would resign! This is reminiscent of the power of the Senate in the Third Republic to overthrow Governments.

By the constitutional amendments of December 7, 1954 (see *Appendix*), the powers and status of the Council are amended. It also can initiate bills, excepting those for treaties, the budget and financial enactments, the reduction of revenues, or creation of new expenditures. Of these exceptions, the prerogative belongs to the Assembly. The bills of each chamber go to the other on adoption, with the aim of securing the adoption of an identical text. The Council has two months in which to pronounce itself after receiving the Assembly's text. On budget and financial bills, however, the Council has no more than the time the Assembly took on its consideration and vote. If the Assembly adopts emergency procedure, the Council has *double* the time allowed by the Assembly for itself. If the Council does not pronounce itself in the two months or the emergency time limit, then the Assembly's text is due for promulgation as a law. If no agreement is reached, each chamber continues its examination of the bill. After two readings by the Council, each chamber shall be allotted a time limit equal to that taken by the other chamber for the previous readings, but the limit of time cannot be less than seven days nor more than 100 for ordinary legislation, for then the Assembly may readopt its latest text or modify it to accept one or more of the Council's proposed amendments. For financial legislation the delay is one month; for urgent matters, fifteen days. When the Assembly exceeds or extends its time limit for examination of a bill, the Council benefits from this time limit also. Time limits are broken by recesses of the session; they may be extended by the Assembly.

Thus the *navette*, the power to pass bills to and fro between the chambers, well-known practice in the Third Republic, has returned. *Plus ça change. . . .*

Miscellaneous

A few other points must be added. No Prime Minister has been a member of the Council of the Republic. Senators included in any Cabinets have been of recent date and very few—such as the Ministry of Posts, Telegraphs, Telephones. This is a striking contrast with the Third Republic. But some Secretaries of State are drawn from the Council of the Republic.

It may be well, by way of conclusion, merely to draw together the other powers of the Council besides participation in lawmaking. It participates in the election of the President of the Republic. It has members on the Constitutional Committee (p. 332). It nominates a third of the metropolitan members of the Assembly of the French Union (p. 459). It has no place on the High Court or the Superior Council of the Magistrature, whereas the Senate of the Third Republic was the highest

political court. Though it must be consulted on a declaration of war and the ratification of treaties, its consent is not needed for final action. It can obstruct a revision of the Constitution, providing that it is not approved by two thirds of the Assembly or a popular referendum—but it has no power to initiate a revision, as the Third Republic Senate had.

It will be remembered that the present constitution sheared away its former right to prior consent to the Government's dissolution of the Assembly.

II. THE ECONOMIC COUNCIL

The Fourth Republic Constitution establishes an Economic Council and states its powers and composition in Article 25. This follows and develops further, within the Constitution itself, the National Economic Council established by decree in 1925 and reconstructed in a law of March 19, 1936.

Theory of Interest Representation

This is the point at which some general observations on the idea of an economic council are especially relevant.

The Weimar Constitution first established an economic council to assist the sovereign *Reichstag*. It was one answer to worldwide anxiety about pressure groups and their relationship to the adequacy of territorial representation (p. 67). Its experience was used as a "model" elsewhere. It was founded on the representation of interest groups, and these had given rise to the following theories.

The "Interest" or Pressure Groups. The pressure groups were fully and fairly parts of the public entitled to a hearing in the making of law and its means of enforcement. They could not be suppressed even if that were desirable. They could not be ignored, for at the very least democratic constitutions admit a right of petition. Furthermore, since the modern State has entered on wide and deep economic regulation, the interests involved are affected, and they can offer to the Government and the legislators a wealth of internal facts enabling the laws to be more justly and intelligently drawn and more realistically applied. Moreover, they need to be propitiated if the laws and administration are to be made workable. For it is better to proceed by persuasion that produces citizen cooperation than coercion, which is unpleasant, costly, and often inefficient.

One other reason contributed to the movement toward "economic parliaments." Since the economy of each nation is broken up by associations of the types we have mentioned—Big Industry, Big Agriculture, Big Labor, and others, and within these many still large and powerful groupings—a problem of integration of their views and wills is urgent. Each can exert pressure on the nation, if it is master of an economic technique or commodity or service needed by the rest. It can lock out, go on strike, or featherbed its efforts—and make others pay. Monopolies they may be, and make other groups smart. They may exert their pressure without regard to other such groups, get a rise in wages, etc., or a larger share in the total product of industry, only to cause a rise in the cost of their service to the rest of the community, which, then, impels the injured groups to react by more unrest and conflict. If groups are not well organized and strong enough to retaliate, their clientele suffers the exactions of the well-organized. This is hardly fair. Out of this violent chaos, a way must be found. At least it ought to be a confrontation in a single forum of all the conflicting groups, where they may survey the economic and social state of the nation and be appraised of the effect of their respective demands on all the rest of the community.

Finally, groups of this kind feel that geographical representation through constituencies with mixed population does not give to each group the ability to represent its special point of view as forcefully (numerically) as its own "lobbyists" can. They also think that the contribution each makes to the national economic product should be the criterion of policy and not mere numbers.

Corporativism. Hence, the impulse to economic representative bodies to advise the popular representative bodies. Hence, also, in such dictatorships as Mussolini's Fascist Italy,[1] the actual institution of "corporativism"—that is, a sole parliament founded on the allied associations of employers and employed in the great branches of economic

[1] Cf. Herman Finer, *Mussolini's Italy*, New York, 1935.

effort, and their representation therein. In this system, the normal democratic parliament chosen by local electorates was discarded. It could work only when the dictator imposed his final will on the corporate parliament, since its position was to give representative expression of what ought to be done, while the dictator arrogated the reconciling of conflicting views and the final imposition of obedience on them, not their accepted harmony.

The French Experience

Largely through the pressure of the C.G.T., the Government organized a National Economic Council by decree, January 1925. This was an experiment. It was of a consultative nature, devoted to studies and research but possessing strength because it was representative. The Council consisted of forty-seven members, divided among the representatives appointed by labor, capital, and the consumers and a contingent of "experts" supposed to represent the "public interest."

The Council made some useful reports on housing, investment in productive capacity, antidepression measures, improved agricultural production, and progress in rivers and canal development.

Reforms of 1936. Critics wanted a broader representative base, the C.G.T. taking the initiative in 1934, at the height of the Great Depression, in a meeting, called the Estates General of Labor. The Council was recognized by a *law* of March 1936. It still remained only consultative. The Minister of the National Economy, a new apparition—was made president. The Council was now to advise not only the Government but Parliament also. A system of liaison was established between it and the parliamentary Commissions. The *rapporteurs* of the Council and its twenty occupational sections were high civil servants. The Chambers gave little attention to the Council's work in the grim years from 1936 to the outbreak of World War II. But some of the reports were of value to the Government—for example, on collective bargaining and the forty-hour week. There is even a connection between its reports on public investment and the Monnet Plan of post-World War II.

The Council of 1946. Vichy abolished the Council. But the idea lived on, especially in Socialist circles, and then in the principles of the M.R.P. and the de Gaullist movement. These wanted a second chamber, no less, based on occupational groups. Their purpose was, in part, an additional motivating force toward such representative bodies. Parties which have a hierarchical view of politics —that is, who place special emphasis on national *unity* or social *unity*—do so because they are afraid of the social and economic consequences of electoral democracy. They believe that the full theory of democracy tends to disintegrate society, to pulverize it, as Rousseau said, to take men back to a state of nature. Where, then, will one find the bond of society? One of them—perhaps the most powerful—is in the occupational organization, of men as producers. This stems from the *guild organization* of the Middle Ages, the ages of religion.

In fact, as we have noticed (p. 325), the rejected draft of the constitution provided only for a sovereign National Assembly and an Economic Council, not the kind of crippled Senate that finally emerged. This draft Economic Council was given advisory jurisdiction over laws, as sent to it by the Assembly. It was subject to giving its opinion thereon *within ten days,* even two days at the Assembly's demand, failing which it was dispensed with. The Government could consult it. It was bound to consult it for the establishment of a national economic plan. (See Chapter 8.)

The accepted Constitution contained a fairly strong Council of the Republic—and an Economic Council. Article 25 reads:

> An Economic Council whose statutes shall be determined by law, shall examine the bills and proposals within its purview in order to give its opinion thereon. The National Assembly shall send such bills to this Council before considering them.
>
> The Economic Council may also be consulted by the Council of Ministers. It must be consulted by that body concerning the establishment of a national economic plan for full employment and the rational utilization of our material resources.

This takes us to the statute. In the debates on this, two tendencies found an uneasy compromise. One was to make of the Council a really power-representative legislative body, with some 300 representatives. Some Deputies entertained the idea that the Council would take charge of the economy and so liberate the Assembly from political domination. This is a ridiculously impossible view, if the power of the political Assembly was not to be emasculated in favor of a kind of technocratic body of interests. The other view was to keep the Council as a technical advisory body; about 100 members, without a regional basis or a permanent committee to impinge on the everyday government. It would be a kind of panel of occupational experts called to advise in specialized sections.

The Law of October 1946. The Law of October 27, 1946, mixed the two conceptions, but as to *authority* accepted the technical, not the political, kind. It is an "interest" organization, or a "thought" organization, and not a "will" organization. The law says that the Council is competent to examine bills of an economic and social character—but excluding the budget (!) and international treaties of economic and financial character that require approval of the Assembly.

If the Council's role had had an obligatory authority, then, as the Socialist *rapporteur* warned, the agenda of the Assembly would have been put into subjection to the Council, for all laws have a more or less economic, social, and financial aspect.

Its Authority

The chief thing then is that the National Assembly and the Government, in the last resort, decide whether the Economic Council shall be consulted. It *may* be consulted when regulations and rules of public administration (see Chapter 8) concerning the national economy are being drafted by the departments. It *must* be consulted when rules of public administration are being drafted to apply the laws that have been previously submitted for its advice.

Thus, the hearing of the interests, when rules and directives for law enforcement are being drafted, which in other countries is accomplished sometimes by a free consultation of the interests by the departmental officials and sometimes by the consultation of bodies named in the laws, is here organized through the Council. But it would be a sorry mistake to believe that this puts an end to deputations from the interests direct to the Government or to pressure activities on the Assembly and through various political parties! (See pp. 340–341.)

The Economic Council *may*, at its own discretion, undertake the examination of economic, social, and financial questions and for this purpose conduct the necessary inquiries and then make recommendations.

It gives its counsel on the Plan (see p. 462) and on the bills and questions on which it is consulted by the Government; on bills submitted to it by the Assembly and its commissions; or on its own initiative. Its time for offering counsel is limited to twenty days, or the time set specifically by the body asking the counsel—more or less. Its opinion on the rules of public administration on which it *must* be consulted is to be given in thirty days. The last is a useful check on the quality and legality of administrative action, of the nonjudicial, and yet not the merely political kind.

The Economic Council's recommendations must be printed and circulated among the Deputies of the Assembly, and must be read out at the opening of a debate on the matter in the Assembly. If the appropriate Minister or Commission should so desire, the *rapporteur* of the Council may participate in the Assembly debates.

Finally, it can be seized with questions arising out of economic disputes at the request of the parties and Ministers, and may act as arbiter.

The Composition of the Council

It was difficult to achieve an acceptable composition. No one wanted a competitor to the Assembly. It was desirable to avoid a duplication of the numerous consultative councils that are attached to the government departments (Chapter 8). No one wanted merely a group of notables without roots in a clientele. A technically capable and closely articulated economic and social grouping was needed. We do not list its first composition, because it underwent a reform in March 1951, but give the Council as affected by this reform.

The amendment referred to excluded two of the "intellectual" group and replaced them by two representatives of the Middle Classes (a grouping of associations concerned with middle-class business, etc.), and added another five members for

various categories, such as the tourist industry. Moreover, each region was provided with corresponding members; the big interests were deprived of some of their strength in numbers; small employers were given their own representation apart from the big employers; the C.G.A.'s representation was reduced and its twenty-eight members were distributed among its constituent units; the C.G.T. representation was cut in half, the other labor organizations being endowed with the seats so economized.

Thus the composition of the Council at the end of 1955 was as follows:

Labor organizations:		45
Delegates of: Workers	39	
Independent engineers	1	
Intellectuals	1	
Technicians	4	
Nationalized enterprises		6
Private enterprises		14
Commercial enterprises		10
Artisans		10
Agricultural organizations:		35
Delegates of: General Confederation of Agriculture	28	
Chambers of Agriculture	3	
Mutual Benefit, cooperatives, proprietors, credit	4	
Cooperatives		9
French Union		15
French thought (intellectual workers)		8
Family associations		8
War-stricken		2
Savings institutions		2
Building activities		1
Tourist activities		1
Export interests		1
Middle classes		2
		169

The Effectiveness of the Council

The Council has had a chequered experience. It was a Cinderella to the Assembly for its first year or so—either being ignored or given small chores for which "urgency" had been declared. The Government cold-shouldered it regarding decrees and rules of public administration. It was not invited to be an arbiter of economic disputes. The Monnet Plan was developed without its cooperation being asked.

Its composition, personally, was not conducive to ready trust in its helpfulness. For, as so often happens in "interest representation," the representatives were not technicians but employers and employees. The voters came to the recommendations, or would have done so, by the taking of sides on an interest-conflict basis, not a technical one. This voting predetermination affected the conclusions of the committees, which, as intended, did the real close-to-the-facts work, rather than the full Council that, debating in public, might have become another partisan forum.

Yet it has been of some constructive value. From March 1947 to December 1949, a little over two years and a half, and with little concern for the body in the first year, some 180 questions were examined by the Economic Council. Of these, 70 had been submitted by the National Assembly or the Government. It had made an inquiry into wages and prices at the request of the Assembly's Commission on Economic Affairs. Of the 180 questions, the Council had reported on 126. Of these the Council believed that 53 had had an influence on the policy of Assembly or Cabinet, and that nearly 40 had been altogether or in part embodied in bills. The influence of the Economic Council is, perhaps naturally, more effectual when it responds to some task put up to it by the Cabinet or the Assembly than when it itself initiates a study.

However, some examples of its work, indicate that the least that it offers is the dragging into the light of day of the pressure groups, where they may be recognized for what they are. It has also been of value as a technically inspired supporter of economic and social thinking in the Assembly and of the public, even though it cannot but be, by nature, a political body. For it *cannot* divest itself of a will to particular pressures satisfying to its clients.

A report by André Philip, Socialist, a vigorous supporter of a united Europe, was influential in helping the Schuman Plan through the Assembly in December 1951. A unanimous report against compulsory arbitration and one on a special court

to discipline economic cartels were of assistance in impeding or defeating these by the Assembly. The Council helped on the acceptance of the Franco-Italian customs arrangement, though the representatives of labor and of agriculture were hostile. The small effectiveness of the customs treaty in practice is a tribute to the obstructionism of the agriculturists, whose representatives in the Economic Council could foresee in themselves whence the future obstruction would come.

In 1952 the Council reported 141 to 0 in favor of a law to prevent "snowballing" salesmanship. On a proposal to explore for petrol in Alsace, with a subsidy for the purpose (a self-given study), 31 were in favor, 106 against, 14 abstained. The C.G.T. and the Catholic unions (Alsace!) were in favor; all the other groups, including the *Force Ouvrière* unions were opposed; agriculture was split. In a study to bring agricultural wages up to a par with industrial wages, 67 were in favor, being all the agricultural organizations, the cooperatives, private enterprise, the veterans, a few of the French Union; against were 61, the artisans, the Thinkers, all the workers; while the engineers and middle class abstained, with some French Union delegates. The Council elaborated a law on the manufacture, sale, import, etc., of alcohol, taking the problem of alcoholism very seriously. The decrees of Mendès-France owed much to this comprehensive study, but were torpedoed by the Assembly.

We merely list some of its studies in 1952, self-undertaken: the vending of goods in the streets; unemployment assistance; foreign exchange problems; modernization of technical equipment; improvement of technical education in the Overseas Territories; reform of the Ministry of Economic Affairs; the development of the steel industry; studies of employment, production, prices, and wages; the effect of rearmament on the supply of raw materials and the standard of living.

Normally, the interests are at loggerheads with each other. Labor has spurred on reports on collective bargaining in a sense favorable to itself, and not desired by the Government. It was able to win over the whole Economic Council to a hostility to compulsory arbitration, which the Government wanted but which the employers also did not much want—and this bill was then defeated in the Assembly. Labor has been able, largely through the unwillingness of the other sectors of the Council, to get favorable reports against reduction of the government's investment program (which would have meant some unemployment) and for an increase in family allowances.

It is dismaying to find a tendency to abstention from voting by some interests, rather than the voting of a conviction when it happens to be opposed to that of some claim (as above-mentioned) made by their colleagues. It may well be that the vote was allowed (through abstention) to be favorable because the abstentionists knew that in any case the Assembly or Government would destroy the proposal, so that opposition would be merely academic—or academic in any case, because the Assembly is too busy or too committed to take notice of what the Council reports.

There are battles between the groups that cut across political parties, and so the allies and enemies vary from battle to battle. The labor unions fought the employers on collective bargaining— and won. Then the employers cooperated with one of the labor unions only, the C.G.T. (the Communists!), against profit sharing recommended by the other unions (especially the Catholic unions) and by the intellectuals on the Council. When the *Force Ouvrière* unions (like the British trade unions for many years) stood out against higher family allowances, believing that this would cut away the ground from under the feet of the unions in wage conflicts, the C.G.T. (Communist!) and the Catholic unions were on the other side; yet the *Force Ouvrière* abstained. The employers were opposed.

Yet, in 1953, when economic issues were raging, the Council's voice was still. *Inter arma, silent scientia.* It must always be in an uncomfortable role, like lobbyists, subject to suspicion and to being ignored. Its existence has not diminished the boring in of pressure groups—*they* impinge directly on Government and Assemblies! They may even feel that the Economic Council is too staid and wide visioned. It meets intermittently; there is considerable absenteeism. Why should one expect that industrial employers should have valid things to say about farming operations? Occasional

open debates (not expected) provoke passions that disturb factual thinking and lower its public dignity. The Communists, of course, have even walked out, ready to rule or else to destroy.

Perhaps the British method of Royal Commissions, etc. (p. 455ff.) is more expedient and simpler. In the Soviet Union's State-owned economy, interests are *officially* suppressed.

III. THE ASSEMBLY OF THE FRENCH UNION

The status of the French overseas territory,[2] whether regarded as an empire or as a congeries of colonial territories, cannot be analyzed here. Here a brief account is given of the Assembly of the French Union,[3] as founded in the Constitution. It

[2] I use the terms *overseas territories* and *colonies* in a colloquial sense.

[3] The French Union consists of (1) the French Republic, comprising metropolitan France and the Overseas *Départements* (Algeria, Martinique, Guadeloupe, Guiana, and Reunion); (2) the Overseas Territories (French West Africa, French Equatorial Africa, Madagascar, the Comoro Islands, French Somaliland, St. Pierre and Miquelon, the French settlements in India, New Caledonia, and the French settlements in Oceania); (3) the Trusteeship Territories (Togoland and the Cameroons); and (4) the Associated States (Cambodia, Laos, and Southern Vietnam).

The most important and controversial of these are the North African possessions, on which some all-too-brief observations may be made. It is not a simple issue of "colonialism" but a highly complex clash of rights.

Tunisia, Morocco, and Algeria stretch across the Mediterranean coast facing Spain and France. The former are Protectorates; the latter, a part of France, acquired as Texas was by the United States by conquest, except that whereas in Texas there was another claimant, Mexico, in Algeria there was never a unified sovereign authority but only rival and piratical local chieftains.

Tunisia has a present population of some 3,600,000; 90 percent are Arabs, the rest Italians and French. Arab and Berber rulers governed in ancient times; in the sixteenth century Tunisia was conquered by Turks, a native dynasty ruling under their suzerainty. The French, in rivalry with the Italians, occupied the land in 1881, establishing a Protectorate over the native ruler (called the Bey) by treaty. But what is the authority of a Protector State over the Protected? This has never been determined, nor the rights of the people against the Protector. Italian and French colonists arrived and developed the main economic resources, agriculture, and processing industries and commerce, in what was a Moslem, superstitious, and actually a pirate State, which had lived by pillaging ships in the Mediterranean.

In May 1943, after the war between the Anglo-American forces and the Nazis and Italians, de Gaulle took over the government and removed the pro-Nazi Bey, replacing him

was established largely to secure the dual purpose of some unity of design for democratic rule and social progress and to associate the aspirations to freedom of the territories with the Mother Country's continued family relationship with them.

The Socialist and Communist parties had long been advocates of more political and civil rights for the natives, and the Communists even proposed severance of the colonies from France—until, at any rate, there was a Communist Govern-

by a more friendly cousin. A native nationalist movement had developed and now assumed more strength under the *Destour,* the Tunisian nationalist party. As in the other areas mentioned above, the movement was supported and incited by the direct and indirect activities of the Arab League, with the reawakening of Arab and Mohammedan demands for national recognition (and even Moslem "holy war" pretensions against Christians) everywhere. Constant mutual irritation and French attempts to press direct rule very deep and to hold all the official and professional posts and clumsy military rule resulted in endemic civil war. Then the Mendès-France and Edgar Faure Cabinets pacified the country by giving a substantial right of cooperation to the native population through the Bey and his Cabinet's right to full power in domestic affairs.

Morocco, in its French section, has a population of some 8,500,000, of which 300,000 are French *colons* (colonists) while the natives are divided among 3,500,000 Berbers and 4,500,000 Arabs. Its strategic position opposite France and Spain made Morocco a military anxiety; its products a commercial opportunity. Moslem Sultans, absolute autocrats and religious leaders, negligent in economic and social progress, had ruled from ancient times. Between 1904 and 1906 the French and Spanish governments divided the original area into respective "spheres of influence" and then into separate Protectorates, acknowledged internationally to prevent German might from penetrating the region. General Hubert Lyautey was sent by France to govern French Morocco for thirteen years; he did this through the Sultan, with a show of force but also a steadfast devotion to public works, law, and order and the beginning of social service. He was a remarkable example of that French governing class which detests the Republic but is dedicated to the State (Chapter 8). Under Vichy during World War II the Pétainists, imperialist-minded, governed. In 1942 Morocco came under Allied control.

Here a nomadic, superstitious, illiterate, and disease-ridden people were introduced to modern education (but 1 in 10) and social services by the French government, the settlers, and Christian missions. Between 1912 and the present day the population tripled; since 1930 infant mortality had fallen from 32 to 19 per 1000. French investment, science, hard work, and thrift developed the neglected land and produced a flourishing Mediterranean agriculture, cattle industry, and small industry and opened up the phosphate, iron, lead, zinc, and manganese mines. But the *colons* lived apart from the natives as superiors. A nationalist movement developed, with a desire for a better standard of living. The French government exercised indirect rule through the Sultan and his native advisers. Frenchmen or favored natives occupied all official posts. To maintain this rule firmly, government and *colons* allied themselves with the Berber chiefs (and people, shepherds) of the Atlas Mountains and foothills and in the Riff, against the nationalist movement and Arab city dwellers and factory workers on the coast and against the Istiqlal Party, which organized and led the campaign for nationalism. To

this end the French government in August 1953 forcibly ousted the favorite of this movement, the reigning Sultan Ben Youssef (Commander of the Faithful or *Immam*) and replaced him by his uncle Ben Arafa, supported by the leader of the Berbers, the chieftain El Glaoui—"divide and rule," but *division* there was already. This inflamed the Istiqlal. Recent governments have sought to reacknowledge the former Sultan's rights, oust the uncle, yet have the government conducted by a Council of Three Regents; at the same time conceding more self-government and opening government jobs to the natives. Finally, in October 1955, *four* regents were appointed, on the whole inclined to moderate nationalism and attachment to France.

There is here, as in the other areas, a struggle between moderate and extreme nationalists, for some natives have become assimilated to the French way of life and more would like to be. Moslem religious orthodoxy *versus* emancipation plays a considerable part in the turmoil; it is not merely French "colonialism" against Moroccan "nationalism," for Moroccans are themselves of diverse degrees of nationalism and follow rival leaders.

Ben Youssef was reinstated, El Glaoui groveled at his feet for pardon, a representative Moroccan cabinet was appointed, and revolt flared anew with the Berbers now the aggressors. A new definition of interrelationship with France is being negotiated.

Algeria has a population of over 9,000,000, of which 1,000,000 are French, 8,000,000 a blend of native Arabs and Berbers, and the rest other Europeans. Its principal city is Algiers (320,000). It was never a united kingdom but a land of conflicting local chiefs, with Turkish occupation from 1518, the lair of the Barbary pirates. During one more "holy war" among the local claimants in 1847, the French, who had long had a trade interest in the area and a grudge against its pirates, took possession. This led to the area being united *for the first time* under one ruler, the French, who finally decided to give Algeria the status of a part of France itself, organized as three *départements* of France. But it has only fifteen Deputies in the National Assembly; and a special electorate; for if the 8,000,000 natives were numerically represented (which their leaders claim they should be), the Assembly would be swamped with aliens, although the French government has proclaimed a policy of assimilation. Its Governor General is responsible to the Ministry of the Interior and the Ministry of Overseas France, though much more to the former. In August 1947 an elected assembly was granted the Algerians and the colonists as a concession to nationalism; but the major share in rule lies with the Governor General. And as the *colons* were given a disproportionately large representation, the Nationalist Party withdrew and instigated a bloody insurrection.

The French colonists created the modern economy on the coastland, now rich in agriculture, small industries, and opened up the mines as in Morocco and, as everywhere hereabouts, developed the roads, water supply, railways, harbors, schools, hospitals, etc. Before this, the land was almost derelict.

ment in France. The experience of World War II had provided the British example of Commonwealth cooperation. On the other hand, the shame of French nationals (Vichy *versus* Free French) then warring against each other in all the colonial areas was painful. Furthermore, the restiveness of the natives and the whole world against authoritarian colonialism, of which France had remained a belated example, demanded a renovation and liberalization of ideals and institutions.

The British policy progressively to prepare the colonial peoples for self-government and for emancipation was a powerful leaven; but, for all parties except the Left in France, it was an anxiety rather than an ideal that they must realize. So much has been necessary to place the role of the Assembly of the French Union in its place, which is but a subordinate advisory one.

First Attempt

The first draft of the constitution provided for a Council of the French Union to be elected by the local government councils of continental France and the territorial assemblies of the Overseas Territories. It was to meet side by side with the National Assembly and examine, in advisory

capacity, the bills sent to it by the Cabinet or the National Assembly at its own request or their discretion. It was subject to a time limit. If this Council agreed with the Assembly, the matter was settled. If it disagreed, the Assembly must redebate the bill and decide in sovereignty what attention should be paid to the Council's demurrers.

The President of the Republic was brought into the imperial picture: Article 92 of this abortive constitution declared that "He represents the permanent interest of the French Union. . . ."

A constitution is a structure designed to serve an object. But the Constituent Assembly was both fiercely divided and hazy about the nature of the object to be served. The M.R.P. and the Rightists wanted a framework of Union within which, "in the course of time," the territories would develop their institutions, but maintaining now and later a "federal" relationship. Their experts led them to propose second-class citizenship of native populations, to be satisfied by their part in the composition of this advisory body. For if they had accepted the principle of undiscriminating citizenship ("integration") with a vote for the 60,000,000 natives, then the 40,000,000 Frenchmen would have been outvoted in the National Assembly itself.

The Council of the Union was a sidetrack, though it could fairly be described also as an interim advisory body leading to more substantial self-government in the course of time. The representation of the French settlers in the National Assembly itself was maintained simultaneously.

The Left would have started with the development of mildly empowered colonial assemblies and at some time later would have developed the central organs in Paris.

The M.R.P. and the Right-wing members were influenced by General de Gaulle's views (announced at the Brazzaville Conference in January 1944, a conference of French colonial officials) that autonomy could not even be considered, since France's civilizing work was not to be impeded, a famous imperialist view, not without sincerity, calling for France's *grandeur*.

The term *French Union* was a casual remark made by de Gaulle's Colonial Minister to describe some form of federalism. Its nature, however, was

---

The nationalist turmoil is envenomed by (1) religious differences, flowing from Moslem fanaticism and Arab modernism; (2) clashes between the government in Paris and the stubbornness of the French colonists, who have a powerful "lobby" and a strong local defense force; (3) the agitation aroused by Arab settlers in France, upper class and workers, especially in and around Paris; (4) class differences among the natives themselves, some of whom share in French-created prosperity and own some of the 30 percent of the estates that are richest and mainly French-owned. Then, (5) there are the differences among the political parties of France in the National Assembly. For as we have noticed in the chapter on political parties, the Gaullists and Right-wing parties and the representatives of the *colons* are imperialist, while no party except the Communists favors independence for the areas in question. The steering of a path among these forces is, then, a perplexity for any French Government, since every such Government is a coalition of heterogeneous groups, each with an intransigent colonial policy of its own. The parties Left of center have talked of "integration" of Algeria, but when this means making Algerian natives into full-fledged French citizens, it is nonsense or deception. Substantial domestic self-government is on the way.

In 1955 the flaring insurrections in North Africa necessitated the deployment of 300,000 French troops there. The burden in life and budget (half of the total military budget!) was another source of conflict in the National Assembly.

hazy, for the term has always bedeviled constitutional debates everywhere, and did so again in France; politicians have now to find a meaning for it. A Socialist Deputy seems to have been the first one to propose an advisory council of the French Union (André Philip). The M.R.P., anxious for a bicameral system, now secured that the Council of the French Union should play this part, including in the Council not merely representatives of the territories but of metropolitan France itself! With how little concerted *thought* was the Constitution fabricated!

The Final Outcome

When the second Constituent Assembly met, the debates over the French Union were actually the most conspicuous of all controversies. The native deputies were now insurgent over the insults offered to them, as "second-class" citizens, yet animated by promises of developing freedom made by the Socialist Prime Minister and by rising nationalism. In the Constituent Assembly's committee (see p. 327) the native colonial Deputies now held a knife-edge balance between the Right and the Left of the Assembly.

The M.R.P. had changed its views as a result of moving away from the imperial ideas of de Gaulle, who had repudiated the M.R.P.'s general attitude to the Constitution (see p. 327). They were rather more tolerant toward the Left-wing views, but still wanted a top colonial council structure, especially afraid that if this were not provided *before* the territories began to evolve separately, the empire would disintegrate. They aroused the resentment of the native Deputies by proposing that in the future these be excluded from the National Assembly and find representation *only* in the Assembly of the French Union, merely an advisory body with no compulsion to make the Assembly enact its advice!

The native Deputies swung over to the Left—to a very loose federal system, indeed, which included continued representation in the National Assembly. Even this was to come to pass only if and when each colony had freely decided to join the French Union!

The then President of France, the leading M.R.P. leader, M. Bidault, intervened. He brought back a new plan, the core of which was the M.R.P.'s plan, not allowing secession, keeping the native peoples as citizens of the "French Union," but not of France itself, promising developing local autonomy through the laws to be made by National Assembly later. He proposed setting up three organs of "federalism": the Assembly of the French Union, the President of the French Union, and a High Council of States. The Left accepted the plan, because Bidault threatened resignation and they could not face the prospect of a loss of the strength he had in the M.R.P. in view of the potential rival threat of de Gaullism. The native Deputies made scenes in the Assembly itself, but they were conciliated by Bidault and Auriol with concessions not concerning this federal structure (see p. 328).

What does it amount to?

Organization of the French Union

The President. The central organs of the French Union are the President, the High Council, and the Assembly. The President is the President of the French Republic: "He represents the permanent interests" of the Union.

The High Council. The High Council is composed of the President, a delegation of the French Government, and representatives from each associated state. It assists the Government in the general conduct of the affairs of the Union. The Council did not meet until November 20, 1951, as Tunis and Morocco refused to participate. In 1951, indeed, only the delegates from Indochina and the French Government attended. The law of October 24, 1949, regulating the composition until then, provided for seven French Cabinet Ministers and for the three states of Indochina. At the 1951 meeting the Council approved one annual meeting at the minimum. The President would convene it at his discretion or would do so if any single member state should request it. There were to be no public sessions. Decisions would be reached by a consensus rather than by a voting process. There were discussions of diplomatic, military, and economic problems over a period of two days. It is expected that its function, which is purely consultative, will embrace similar matters of this sort, intercolonial rather than the internal government of the various states.

The Assembly. This is composed now (1956) of 204 members who come from various categories. There is an equal division of the total number between representatives of metropolitan France and the various overseas territories. Its size may rise to a maximum of 240; it began with 150 when it first sat in November 1947. (It is located at Versailles.) The rise in the total number is explained by the progressive decision of the overseas areas to claim representation, which is open to them. Tunis and Morocco have stayed out.

The territorial representation is 75 for the Overseas *Départements* and Territories and the Trusteeship Territories, elected by their local assemblies. In Algeria 12 are designated by the *Conseils généraux* and 6 by the Algerian Assembly. The Associated States have 27 representatives and decide freely how they are to be appointed.

This leaves 104 members that "balance" the total —the French members. The metropolitan category is chosen by the French Parliament, two thirds by the metropolitan Deputies in the National Assembly, and one third by the metropolitan Senators— all by proportional representation of the political parties.

The members of the Assembly of the French Union organize in groups rather like the National Assembly and the Council of the Republic. There are the usual party groupings to be found in the latter bodies, naturally, because they have emanated from proportional representation. Then, in addition, there are groups of the overseas representatives. For instance, in the year 1953: *Rassemblement Démocratique Africain;* the *Indépendents d'Outre-Mer; Groupe du Vietnam;* and the *Groupe d'Union Française,* with 6, 12, 19, and 8 respectively in January 1953. Some of the overseas delegates join the other political party groups,[4] but none joins the Communists.

It will be observed, then, that the proposal in the abortive constitution to allow the French metropolitan Union Councilors to be elected by French local government councils was discarded

[4] See, in this connection, p. 367.

for election by the National Assembly; its domination of the Assembly of the Union was thus made firm.

The Assembly's powers are limited, but they are valuable to those interested in the fair progress of the colonies and the Union. The President convenes it; if half the members request it, he must convene it. It may sit when the National Assembly is in session, not otherwise.

The Assembly is purely consultative. It is obligatorily consultative on laws determining the status and internal organization of each overseas territory (Article 74) and after consultation with the respective territorial assembly. Consultation is also obligatory for laws modifying the respective status of the French Republic and the French Union and the status and progress of territories from one colonial category to another—that is, Associated Territories and States and Overseas *Départements* of France herself (Article 75). It is also obligatory (Article 72) for decrees that apply a metropolitan law to the French possessions or put into force special provisions of the laws in specified territories.

This is an immense climb-down from the almost bicameral status given to the Council of the French Union in the first draft of the constitution (pp. 324–325). There is still afloat an anticipation that the National Assembly and the Government ought to consult the French Union Assembly before passing a law that has significance for overseas lands. But they are not obliged to.

The Government of France, as well as of any of the Associated States, may introduce bills in the French Union Assembly, and the latter may send resolutions on its own initiative to the National Assembly, to the High Council of the French Union, or to the Government.

It continually presses forward with studies and reports and proposals for colonial improvement. In 1952, for example, it constantly agitated questions, asking the Ministry of Foreign Affairs and the Ministry of Overseas France about the financing of education in the Overseas Territories, the institution of educational standards for nurses and midwives, social assistants, the admission of foreigners, agricultural associations, etc. Its reports comprehend every imaginable phase of economic and social improvement of the colonies, especially the raising of productivity and the standard of living, and the whole range of the social services needed by backward, diseased, undernourished, uneducated, and seriously illiterate peoples. It hammers away at the establishment of cooperatives with their own native experts. It demanded representation on the *Conseil Superieur* of Civil Aviation, an important body for extensive colonial areas that need air transport. The Government has asked its advice on purity of elections and tariffs in various colonies.

The Assembly of the Union is far from enthusiastic about the role it has been allowed to play by the government and the National Assembly. It is consulted by them only on about one subject in seven before it, and less attention is paid by these authorities to the Assembly's initiatives than when its opinion is asked for. It has had to suffer the National Assembly's arrogance and to protest against the withholding of information it needs to carry out its function. It complained it had not even been invited officially to the ceremonies for the centenary of Savorgnan de Brazza. The National Assembly has even sent its own lame ducks to be members of the Union's Assembly. And in 1951 the National Assembly enacted that the French Union had *no power over Algerian affairs* (not being technically a colony, but France itself!). The truth is that the colonies can gain more through their direct representatives to the National Assembly (p. 367) than through the Union's technical studies.

In the election of 1956, so much violence and unrest beset Algeria that elections for its thirty Deputies to the National Assembly were suspended.

French Administration

The error of the administration is to think that administration marches by itself.
—*Napoleon Bonaparte*

France, like other modern States, relies heavily on a vast career service at the center to translate the will of its Parliament as enacted in the statutes and stated in the debates into the living rights and obligations of Frenchmen. It is for the Administration to make decrees and issue orders to enforce the citizens' contributions and to bestow the benefits established by the law. They operate through ministerial decrees, direct action, orders to local authorities, making use of career experts, administrators, and consultative councils. The local authorities have an assigned sphere of duties, administered by locally elected councils and the career officials in their employ or (like the prefects) appointed by the central ministries. The chief features of this apparatus are dealt with in this and the following two chapters.

Chief Features

The chief features of French administration are:

I. It is highly centralized, authoritarian, and routinized.

II. Its scope of activity is wide.

III. Its numbers of personnel are large.

IV. Its personnel has but recently been statutorily protected from political and personal favoritism.

V. Recent reforms have created a single career for the higher appointments, transcending departments, generalizing and energizing its outlook and giving access to wider circles of the population.

VI. Administrative as well as ordinary law courts control the administrative authorities, local and central, culminating in the *Conseil d'État*.

Only I through IV will be discussed here; expanded treatment of V and VI comprise the remaining chapters in this section of the book.

I. HIGH CENTRALIZATION

The *ancien régime* had been centralized (p. 283); Napoleon centralized government in Paris (p. 303), and the various revolutionary and reactionary regimes instituted centralization in pursuit of their own principles. What Daniel Halévy said in 1931 is still too true:

> Republican France has, in actual fact, two constitutions: one, that of 1875, is official, visible, and fills the Press, is parliamentary; the other is secret, silent, that of the Year VIII, the Napoleonic constitution which puts the direction of the country into the hands of the administrative corps.

The Vichy regime, the counteraction to it in the Liberation period, and the measures against the Communists' violence have retarded decentralization. The general flavor is still Napoleonic. Hence, the quality of the central career officials is all the more important as it is exerted throughout the 38,000 communes and 90 *départements*.

Moreover, central and local politics must affect administration, for local government elections supply the Senators, and the central Cabinets and officials can and must meddle with the local authorities. Of 627 Deputies in the National Assembly of 1951, 179 were mayors of communes (including M. Faure, Prime Minister in 1955); out of 320 Senators, 147 were mayors. Twenty-nine Deputies and nineteen Senators are presidents of *conseils généraux* (p. 488).

The law and the spirit of French local administration in this unitary State savors far more of *deconcentration* for more services and activities than of *decentralization*, when compared with English local government (pp. 240–241). Its peculiar methods of central control, known as *tutelle* —tutelage—are described later (pp. 500–502). Centralization is the more significant because the French State undertakes so many activities.

II. WIDESPREAD STATE ACTIVITY

France has almost never experienced a period of *laissez faire;* Colbertism (p. 283) developed into royal benevolent interference in the eighteenth century, after which modern State intervention was promoted. This is villified as *regimentation, dirigisme, étatisme,* variously. Against *laissez faire* the French, with more force and scope than in Britain or the United States, have always pitted the idea of "police" powers—meaning the right of the State to protect and improve the health, morals, and safety of the people and the State. France is interventionist to about the same degree as Germany, more so than Britain, far less so than the U.S.S.R., for she is still founded on private property.

We must pass by the history of the various activities and briefly say that today the State heavily intervenes in agricultural and industrial tariffs; that posts, telephones and telegraphs are State owned, and radio and television are partly State owned and heavily regulated by the government; that a national network of roads, bridges, and ports has been built and maintained; that the railroads, formerly subsidized and regulated, have been since 1946 State owned and managed, as is also civil aviation since that year. The full series of measures needed for good agriculture, such as conservation, drainage, forestry, credits, etc., as well as price supervision and subsidy, are deployed by

the government. All phases of the tobacco trade are government monopolies (begun in 1678): manufacture, sale, import; so also with matches; and since 1926 the import and sale of industrial alcohol, with subsidies to home production. Public reconstruction and investment in industrial plant have been on a very great scale since World War I, owing to the terrible devastations of that war and World War II and to the desire to re-equip France with modern industrial equipment. The latter includes remarkable hydroelectric works and power networks centering on the Rhône. Housing has been a special anxiety since so vast a proportion of dwellings has been destroyed in war and so large a proportion was built more than 100 years ago! This housing problem is one of the most tragic in France.

Monnet Plan

A great Plan for reconstruction and nationalization and housing has since 1945 been undertaken in a plan drawn by M. Jean Monnet, on the basis of recommendations made to the National Assembly (1946) by the Commissariat General of the Plan of Modernization and Equipment, with its 1000 experts. In April 1954 a second Plan was enacted by the Assembly.

In the first Plan, capital investment was provided to develop national production and foreign trade, to increase the output of labor, to guarantee full employment, and to raise the standard of living. Special emphasis was laid on developing power, steel, cement, fertilizers, and tractors. In the second Plan, the object has been to raise national income by 25 percent in four years through a 20-percent rise in agricultural production, 30-percent rise in industry, and 60-percent rise in construction. Here the expanded means include scientific research, modernization of production methods, specialization of firms, cost reduction (especially of distribution), and organization of agricultural markets. It owes much to Edgar Faure's tenure of the Ministry of Finance, especially after M. Monnet took service with the Coal and Steel Authority. M. Monnet is the wealthy owner of the Cognac firm who has devoted his life to the public service, especially of French modernization and the "European Idea."

The main principle of the first Plan was (1) to plan by cooperation between government and private industry and (2) to conduct operations not through direct State action and officials but by the government's investment policy and increased investments, the total needs being met by government subsidies, government loans, and matched contributions by private industry.

At the head of the planning organization is the Commissariat of the Plan, directly responsible for advising the Prime Minister's office of what must be done and the general means to this end. The Commissariat is staffed by career experts from the various Ministries. It is assisted by a general planning council of career officials and representatives of interests and outside experts (the latter largely on a nonpaid basis). It is further assisted by the reports of many officially appointed specialized committees, composed of experts (mainly unpaid) and the representatives of the various branches of business, labor, technicians, agriculture (also on a voluntary basis). These committees are interlocked with the Commissariat. The Plan is not organically geared into the Economic Council but benefits from its substantial researches and reports.

The Ministry of Finance has a special nurturing relationship to the fulfillment of the Plan. For the operation of the Plan has meant a battle for funds that must come from the budget; a fight among the various economic interests that contend for assistance; the government control of imports, exports, and prices; the drawing in of the local authorities to a part in sharing and facilitating local application; and a steady public propaganda in favor of modernization and mass production in a land of artisans. Though the results have fallen short in the time planned of targets, a truly remarkable work has been accomplished in the modern re-equipment of the French economy, and some of the benefit has already profited the mass of workers, though they claim it should have more.

Other State Activities

In addition to these various State activities, a highly developed system of social services and social security is in operation. It includes family allowances, old-age, sickness, maternity, disability,

and unemployment assistance. The Ministries of Finance and of Labor and Social Security set the standards and enforce them, but they are administered by institutions composed of employers *cum* employees and local authorities. Under the Ministries of Education and Health, social services of hospitals, school health, and feeding and municipal care are administered.

The result of these manifold and important activities is a large public budget and large Civil Service.

French National Budget, Year Ending December 1953

Total Expenditure: On current operations, 2,327,6 *milliards* of francs. (A milliard is 1 billion or 1000 million.) To which add: investments, 671,1 *milliards;* loans and guarantees, 755,4 *milliards. Total Budget:* 3,754,1 *milliards.*

Services	Milliards
Foreign Affairs	14,7
German and Austrian	2,4
Agriculture	25,4
Veterans and War Victims	86,2
Economic Affairs	76,1
Financial Administration	93,8
Education	230,1
Overseas France	7,9
Interior	85,8
Justice	17,9
The Saar	1,5
Prime Minister's Office	10,6
Associated States	7,2
Industry and Power	19,7
Reconstruction and Urbanism	13,3
Health and Population	58,4
Labor and Social Security	27,1
Public Works	211,7
Aviation, civil and commercial	14,9
Mercantile Marine	15,4
General charges	554,3
Total	2,327,6

Revenues	Milliards
Direct Taxes	954,2
Registration Taxes	122,8
Customs	247,7
Excise	58,9
Production Tax	870,1
Business Turnover Tax	214,7
Special (Wines, etc.)	90,9
Public Enterprise	31,5
State Domains	16,4
Various revenues	240,3
Exceptional revenues	190,1

Total National Net Product in 1952 was 12,010,000,-
000 francs. It was composed of the following items:

Salaries and wages	5,900,000,000
Agricultural income	1,130,000,000
Other individual enterprises	1,990,000,000
Property	350,000,000
Distributed by companies	160,000,000
Minus Public domain	(80,000,000)
Direct business taxes	660,000,000
Indirect taxes	2,120,000
Minus Subventions to business	(220,000,000)

Local Government Expenditure, in francs, 1952:

Départements, including Seine	248,676,000,000
Communes, including Paris	467,436,000,000

III. THE NUMBERS OF THE CIVIL SERVICE

The best figures available are those of Professor
Lucien March, made in 1913, and the budget reports since then. They give:

1839	130,000
1871	220,000
1911	350,000
1921	403,000
1927	400,000
1933	700,000

The figures exclude temporary and industrial
workers, and they exclude the railwaymen on the
State lines. The exclusions are made in order that
there may be at least some comparability with
other countries. But the figures include teachers
and judges.

If the officials of the various local authorities
were added, then France in the middle 1930's
would have added some 350,000 of these, bringing
the total public officials, the *fonctionnaires,* to
about 1,000,000—or nearly one civil servant in
every fifteen families.

Fonctionnaire is the French legal term for permanent civil servant. It excludes *temporary* and
industrial workers. It is not the equivalent of what
has become a scornful epithet among some enemies
of public activity—*functionary.* But some Frenchmen share the distaste of *étatisme;* their more
usual reproach is of *ronds de cuir,* people who sit
on leather seats, or *paperasserie,* people wrapped
in reams and reams of paper or "red tape."

Officials and Departmental Organization

The total staffs of civil and military employees
(*fonctionnaires et agents des services de l'état*)
on April 1, 1950,[1] was 1,203,170 for the central
government only. But this figure does include the
90 prefects, 300 to 400 subprefects, and the 90
chefs de cabinets of the prefects, in all some 550
appointed by the Ministry of the Interior to administer central tutelage.

Of the 1,203,170 officials, 241,600 are regular
military officers and men. This leaves just over
970,000 in civil positions.

Of the 970,000, three groups stand out for their
size: Ministry of Education, 253,000 plus; Posts,
Telegraphs, and Telephones, 194,000 plus; and the
Ministry of Public Works, 72,000 plus.

Curious Inclusions. British figures of the corresponding kind *do not include teachers.* But the
French Ministry of Education figure of 253,000 is
made up of teachers of all levels (indicating the
centralization of the educational system), their
laboratory assistants, their librarians, archivists,
and the corresponding administrative personnel.

Nor do British figures of civil servants include
nearly 17,000 officials, of which *all the judges* in
the regular judiciary are included! This contrasts
with the British (and American) practice of keeping the judicial tribunals independent of the hierarchy of the administrative services.

The Ministry of Public Works figure includes
the 35,000 engineers who maintain the road network.

The Ministry of the Interior has over 70,000
employees. Of these many are in the local government inspectorial service and the police, and the
prefectoral officials already mentioned. In the British figures *the police would be omitted.*

The National Defense (civil) figure of some
136,000 comprises the engineers and workers in
the arsenals. In the British figures of civil service
the latter would be omitted.

The Ministry of Finance has 120,000 officials,
mainly tax collectors and accountants of the public
finances and domains.

[1] We are compelled to use the government's own census
of officials taken for that year. More recent ones are only
estimates.

One other observation needs to be made. The 970,000 civil personnel fall into the categories:

Established career employees	622,725
Temporary auxiliaries	110,529
Contractual basis	46,273
Temporary basis	45,216
Established industrial workers	100,046
Temporary workers	35,499

We give the table of all the ministries but confine the figures only to the total of all categories.

Distribution of French Central Civil Service
April 1, 1950

Departments	Numbers
Foreign Affairs	2,035
German and Austrian Affairs	6,546
For the Saar	637
Agriculture	16,602
Veterans	10,408
Education	253,158
Finance	119,109
Economic Affairs	7,310
Overseas	1,883
Industry and Commerce	3,407
Interior	70,486
Justice	16,874
Posts, Telegraphs, and Telephones	194,399
Prime Minister's (see p. 432)	3,329
Radio and TV	4,365
Reconstruction and Urbanism	15,944
Public Health and Population	5,002
Labor and Social Security	9,286
Public Works	72,299
Aviation, civil and commercial	7,730
Merchant Marine	1,816
Special Accounts Treasury	2,526
Defense, Civil	136,425
Defense, Military	241,600
Total	1,203,170

Of which civil personnel: 971,576

Total Number of Government Employees

The total civil employees of the central government is about a million. The employees of local government amount to 370,000. This gives a total of local and central government direct employees of 1,370,000; or 1 in 30 of the entire population (42,000,000).

The employees and workers in the industries of the government—nationalized and monopolized—are of this order:

Railroads		446,000*
Coal		240,000
Electricity		25,000
Gas		34,000
Insurance	ca.	15,000
Automobiles		128,000
Radio diffusion	ca.	50,000
Total		938,000†

* Called S.N.C.F.—Société nationale des Chemins de Fer.
† Call it 1,000,000 with tobacco, etc., workers.

And if we now add to this the grand total of the local and central government—that is, 1,370,000—the final figure is 2,370,000, or 1 in every 17 of the population.

Significance. Here is an index of *étatisme:* the swelling of the responsibilities of the departments and their officials; the extent to which enterprise has been given over to official and political rather than private impetus. Further, so large an officialdom must surely escape control by the short-lived Cabinets. What authority have the departments and Ministers?

IV. ADMINISTRATIVE AUTHORITY AND DISCRETION

Owing to the larger part played by the State in France before and since 1789 than in Britain, French administrative discretion has always been wider and deeper than British, resembling other Continental nations. Indeed, in principle, much greater predominance has been allowed the pretensions of the State in France than in Britain altogether.

The Minister's authority issues from the regulatory power of the Prime Minister given to him by Article 47 of the Constitution.

Regulations and Decrees

Ministers, collectively and individually by delegation, and most usually by their departmental initiative, have a power of issuing regulations that have the force of law. These may be undertaken simply because the law cannot be executed unless it is spelled out in technical detail, which the

Assembly has not done. They may take the form of circulars, *arrêtés,* decrees.

The circulars are rather explanatory but have the force of law, since they are Executive instruments. They, as well as the other instruments, either derive from the direct permissive power given by a law, or are commands that a rule of public administration *shall* be made by the Minister. In the silence of the law on the means of execution, the Prime Minister's power and the power of the Ministers are still needed, applicable, and legal, unless there are laws that forbid the action.

(1) A Minister (and prefects) may issue *arrêtés.* They are usually applied to cases of individuals. Some of this class are *réglementaire,* when they apply to a general situation (let us say, all markets in a locality).

(2) These, it would seem, as well as the other types to be mentioned, all come under the general title of *decree.* They are administrative instruments. They are not regarded as *laws,* though they have the force of law. For it has been argued in the *Conseil d'État,* that if by any chance they were regarded as *laws,* then aggrieved citizens could not challenge them in the administrative law courts, since the Assembly has a sovereign power to make law and, by the French interpretation of the principle of the separation of powers, the judiciary cannot interfere with the legislator. We have seen (p. 377) that the Assembly may not delegate its powers. Though it does delegate discretion to the Ministers, nevertheless, this is not construed as a power to make *law.* Hence, the use of the power to utter decrees is subject to the control *by* the administration (through the *Conseil d'État*) of the decree-making activity of the departments. The fiction of the nonviolability of the separation of powers is maintained.

The decrees are divisible into these kinds: simple *réglements* (henceforward this word is translated by *rule*); rules made in *Conseil d'État;* and rules of public administration. The simple rules are made departmentally without any consultation of the *Conseil d'État.* It may be said that, because this throws a *legal* burden on the departmental officials, for the policy and draftsmanship may lead to an action against the legality of the decree,

there is a strong impetus to make sure that the education of officials includes a considerable measure of administrative and constitutional law.

The rules made in the *Conseil d'État* are those which are made in consultation with one or more of the special sections of that body (see p. 520). The rules of public administration are those which *must* be made after consultation with the General Assembly of the *Conseil d'État.* These last-mentioned are, normally, the most important and substantial of the decrees to execute the laws, required by the law enacted by the National Assembly for their validity.

The decrees are published in the *Journal Officiel.* They have the force of law at once, even though the parent law has required that they be subject to ratification by the Assembly.

Limits on Validity. There are limits, emanating from the Constitution, or from its customary interpretation (with the latter accumulated by the *Conseil d'État* for many, many decades), to the executory power of making decrees. Other laws cannot be abrogated; other laws may have expressly forbidden such action; the liberty of the citizen is not to be infringed (this means, "unduly") without legislative authority. These limits are enforceable by the right of appeal the citizen has to the administrative law courts, beginning with those in the local government departments and rising to the *Conseil d'État.* It is the latter body, then, that is put into a position faintly analogous to the U.S. Supreme Court, since the determination of such an appeal may well depend on interpreting the constitutional and customary laws and how the decrees in question are consistent therewith.

Legal Control. Such legal control over the decrees is the principle safeguard of the citizen in France. But the watchful eye of the parliamentary Commissions will not be forgotten (see p. 390). Yet the latter are so busy, so officious, and in such political disarray that one wonders whether the administration is properly invigilated. It will be remembered that the British Parliament has a quite steady procedure of invigilation (p. 161ff.).

In the Soviet regime the Government is uncontrolled master of laws, decrees, ordinances, and every other instrument of power.

V. DEPARTMENTAL ORGANIZATION

The Directors

A French ministry typically comprises a number of *directions,* each with a *Directeur* heading it, rather like an American department and its bureaus. This lack of a supreme departmental administrator, like the Permanent Secretary (p. 204) of British departments, has two consequences. (1) It is necessary to find a coordinating mechanism to help the disoriented, inexpert, and short-lived Minister. This is accomplished in some degree by the ministerial *cabinet* already sketched (p. 436). (2) It has called for the creation of a corps of high officials (pp. 475–478)—*grands corps de hauts fonctionnaires*—having a mission and loyalty that transcend single departments. The latter subject is treated a propos of the reform of the higher civil service since the Liberation.

As for the ministerial cabinet, it will be remembered that this is composed of political "buddies" and of permanent officials. It is hardly a good instrument for its purpose, because each such cabinet is the personal choice of the Minister and it ceases to be when he does. The career officials who are in these ministerial cabinets are not usually highly placed in the hierarchy and therefore do not always possess either the authority to get the Minister's will imposed on the Directors or the experience to advise him sensibly.[2]

Otherwise, each separate Director deals directly with the Minister. This must be more time-wasting and distracting for him than having it all sifted through the mind of the one man at the top, who, being a career man (like a British Permanent Secretary), has come into possession of the coordinated knowledge over the years. The Director helps him in Parliament, being his "commissioner" (p. 000) for explanations to the Assembly and the Commissions on technical matters.

[2] A former Minister has said: "The Cabinet, in fact, makes contact with the civil servants. It pushes a matter to signature, or keeps back the files. If the head of a service accepts the need of explaining a decision to his Minister, it is more disagreeable to him to use up some of his time explaining matters to a representative of the Cabinet who is only an intermediary—often considered—sometimes too lightly—as insufficiently informed." *Promotions,* Paris, 1954, No. 28, p. 17.

Status of Directors. The Directors evidently have something of a quasi-political importance. Their relationship with the Minister is one that mingles the political with the technical administrative. Hence, *they are outside the statutory rules of appointment.* They are appointed by the Cabinet, as a whole, with no conditions imposed, and they may be dismissed in the same way. Hence, persons who are not career officials may be so appointed; though, in fact, all of them are career officials before nomination to any of the "great bodies of the State" (*grands corps de l'État*). Yet, as Directors, they have no claim to their status. They can be fired at once or sent back to the ranks from which they came.

The only departments in which there are career officials superior to the Directors are the Ministry of Foreign Affairs and the Armed Forces, where there is a Secretary General. Wherever else the title of Secretary General appears, it is a chance designation given to a Director but carries no superior status.

French scholars say that the reason for not establishing the post of "permanent secretary" is the political fear that such would acquire great power in relationship to the responsible Ministers, since the latter are in office for so short a time. It goes back to the instability of Ministers. Furthermore, the Vichy Government installed such a system—and this stigmatizes it, though it is technically good.

Consultative Councils

Each department, with the exception of the Foreign Ministry, has as part of its regular organization one or more consultative councils to help it in the planning of legislation and major lines of administrative policy. Some originated a hundred years ago.

According to their scope, some departments have several such councils; the Ministry of Education has at least six: for public education in general; for higher, secondary, primary, and technical education, respectively; and for fine arts.

The councils are composed of two elements. One is purely expert; it may be of officials, retired or still in service, and members of learned and scientific institutes. The other is representative of related interests, plus (occasionally) some members

French Ministry of Work and of Social Security

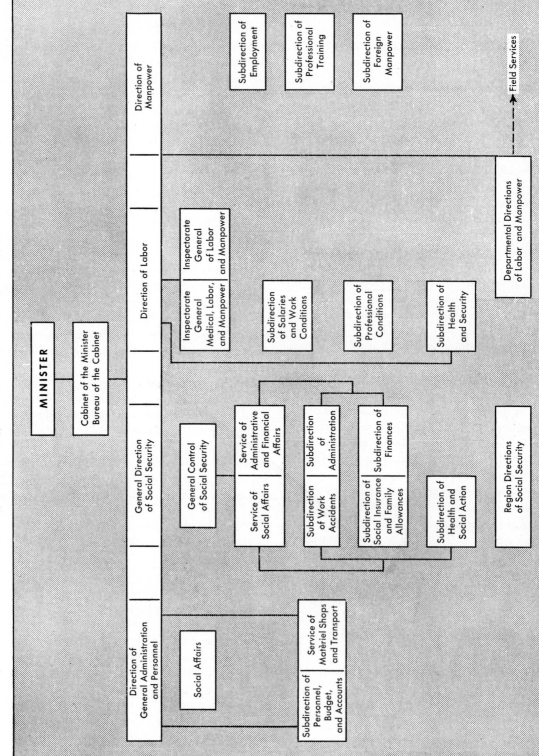

of the National Assembly. Those councils that serve the economic and social ministries have as leading members the trade unions, the peasant associations, the chambers of commerce. The French chambers of commerce and agriculture have for many decades played a larger and more official representative part in the conduct of public administration than their counterparts elsewhere, Germany excepted; they are consulted and have an official role in making demands of the public authorities.

Some councils are designated committees; they are composed as described. But, as in the case of the Ministry of Public Works and its Superior Council of Roads and Bridges, the Minister is not authorized to make certain decisions unless he has previously consulted the council. Also, the Superior Council of the Posts, Telegraphs and Tele-phones consists of representatives of the personnel, of consumers, and officials. It includes high officials of the Ministry of Finance and various ministries with economic and technical scope. The consumers' representatives are chosen from the chambers of commerce, agricultural associations, the cooperatives, and the cities. Its advice must be asked on all questions of organization of the services, programming of works, and postal, telegraphic and telephone rates, and budgetary changes.

The councils and committees meet periodically; some rarely, others once a month. The last stipulation holds good, for instance, of the post office councils. The Minister or his deputy presides. His officials keep the records and prepare the material and agenda. Of course, the members of these councils themselves initiate a good many topics.

9

The Civil Service

It was imperative then [after the Liberation] and, no matter what happens, it is essential now, that the French people reacquire the desire and taste for authority, an authority freely accepted. . . . We felt that our main task was to persuade Frenchmen gradually to resume the necessary practice of civic discipline.

—*Robert Schuman, 1948*

I. THE REFORM OF 1946

The shock of defeat in 1940, the shame of failure to stand the strain of war in better consonance with the inner strength of the nation, the spectacle of administrative probity and vigor in the nations in which the Free French found a base for rescue and revival combined to produce considerable reforms of the personnel of French public administration in 1946. This took two forms: one was the General Statute of Officials of October 19, 1946; the other was the establishment of the *École nationale de l'Administration,* founded also in that year, designed to recruit and train the higher Civil Service.

Nineteenth-century Conditions

After the Bourbon Restoration, 1815, the departments appointed officials by virtue of their administrative regulatory power. They obtained the funds from the parliamentary bodies on the annual budgets. But Parliament did not lay down the rules of appointment, qualification, test, discipline, and dismissal. Each department was almost entirely a law unto itself in these matters. Until 1946 France was not served by anything of the nature of a single Civil Service Commission like Britain or the United States, the one set up by Executive Order in Council, the other by the Pendleton Act

of 1883. Nor was the Ministry of Finance, as the Treasury in Britain, the "employer" of the civil servants in all departments. The years from 1815 down to the latter part of the nineteenth century saw then the departmentalization of the Civil Service at all levels and gross inequalities in classification, duties, qualifications, promotion, pay, and discipline.

Favoritism played a great part in recruitment, almost inevitably owing to the brevity of the various regimes. Neither time nor security were at hand to enable the fashioning of a Service with a "national" vision. The exceptions were made in the recruitment of technicians; they had to have technical diplomas. For even a favorite political ally may build a bridge that falls down. It was also attempted to get the very highest officials educated at a special school on the model of the engineers who were trained at the *Polytéchnique,* but without success. Purges continually took place to influence elections and to block the tide of liberalism and revolution.

The Constitution of the Third Republic was silent about the personnel of the Civil Service. It merely gave to the President of the Republic—on countersignature—the right to make appointments to all civil and military positions. Thereafter, on something like thirteen occasions, some parliamentarians attempted to secure the passage of a general statute of civil servants. They were defeated either by the brevity of the Cabinets that had sponsored them or through the inability of the groups to agree. These attempts were made under the impulse, as time went on, of the unions of civil servants that, especially in the postal and other services and then later among the state railwaymen and teachers, became exceedingly powerful by reason of the strategic social and economic services they performed. They were animated by the syndicalist doctrine of the general strike and direct action on the government. They had good cause to be aggrieved. For French law does not recognize that its employees have a contractual right like ordinary employees—that is, they cannot have a right to strike. Yet they lived in insecurity of tenure and had no guarantees against shockingly authoritarian treatment in the conditions of their work, their pay, their tenure and subjection to the indignities of discipline. Ministers still appointed officials under departmental rights to make executive decrees.

From 1882, however, a year in which the full force of liberal republicanism began to sweep into the old monarchical and imperial system, the Chambers began to build up Civil Service rules by law and permissive regulation based thereon. The statute of that year (Finance Act, December 1882) required that the organization of each ministry was to be regulated solely by rules of public administration. This limited the personal caprice of the Ministers. In 1900 a law required that the increase in the number of higher level posts could be accomplished only by a statute enacted by Parliament. (Hitherto, Ministers had been able to slip members of their personal cabinets—outsiders —into career posts, regardless of the claims of long-standing members of the Service.) But conditions of recruitment, salaries, and so on were subject still to departmental determination—by decree after consultation with the *Conseil d'État*. The *Conseil* could be ignored, after it had spoken. In 1920 new ministries and undersecretariats, the posts of Secretary General and Director, and transfers of functions were made subject to statute.

But Ministers often ignored the law. If an anticlerical Minister could put a fellow anticlerical and Freemason into the job of a Catholic, he found a way of interpreting or amending his department's rules of appointment to do so. The Deputies were constantly interfering in promotions—some of the Deputies were civil servants themselves, for the law allowed officials to stand for Parliament, then giving them leave of absence. The practice was damaging both ways. Some of the members of the Minister's personal cabinet found that positions were created for them (forbidden in a clause of the Finance Act of 1912). The coalition nature of Ministries encouraged the evasive interpretation of the rules—which could easily be modified by the Minister, since the *Conseil d'État's* advice *did not have to be followed*— since each group was anxious to have in the ministries trusted friends who could divulge secrets to them.

Early Improvement

Against these practices, the Civil Service unions exerted their strength. Incidentally they were serving the cause of efficiency, but only incidentally. They were interested foremost in having their own positions protected from arbitrary behavior. This conduced to routinism and a certain disregard for efficiency first.

Each department developed a *direction* dealing with personnel, to develop and administer recruitment through various types of examinations, promotions, records, and final appeals on discipline. These rules, it must be emphasized (after the year 1900 mainly), did begin to give the State competent personnel and the personnel fair guarantees of working conditions and just security. Under pressure, often, of the workers' syndicates, the departments set up decree-based rules. The first department was the Posts, Telegraphs, and Telephones in 1906. It and the other ministries came to be regulated by literally thousands of decrees, important and less important and unintegrated. The difficulty of improvement lay in the hold that the upper bourgeoisie and the aristocracy still had on the higher posts and in their feeling, shared by many political leaders, that the Executive must have free sway over its personnel. Nevertheless, it was impossible ultimately to obstruct the course of democratic sentiment and the feeling that the State needed technically competent personnel.

Once such rules were made, *any civil servant* had the right of appeal to the *Conseil d'État* (which is not an expensive process) that his interests had been injured by the ministerial ignoring of the rules. Upon this, the *Conseil* in the determination of the case might well lay down a principle of action "in the interest of the public service" or declare that such and such actions were "against the interest of the public service." This jurisprudence added to personnel security and the safeguard of technical competence.

The *Conseil d'État*, from 1903 on, served the cause of merit in allowing civil servants to bring actions to challenge wrongful promotions for others as well as themselves, with the sanction of damages. Civil Service unions could bring such actions and these were available concerning examinations and disciplinary action as discussed later. It was still an uphill battle, as the candidates for Parliament, especially between the two ballots, made their promises and later laid siege to the Minister to get their man appointed or promoted.

An exceedingly important law of which the *Conseil d'État* made a considerable system of guarantees was Article 65 of the Finance Act of 1905:

> Every civil and military official, every employee, every laborer in the public service has the right to demand the confidential communication of all papers and documents in his *dossier*, if he is threatened with a disciplinary penalty, a transfer against his will, or a postponement of his advancement by seniority.

The deterrent effect of this on unfair superiors may be judged; the effect of the implication that seniority has its rights, unless merit is advanced as a counter to it, may be imagined—and many other implications of the terms, when challenged by interested suitors and looked at by the *Conseillers* from the standpoint of justice and competent public service.

The Five Classes. By 1914 five classes were fairly clearly defined; each with an educational qualification:

1. *The higher administrative* in all departments, but departmentally selected; with a diploma of the university specialized for the department. This is dealt with more particularly presently.

2. *The executive-clerical* groups: requiring the *baccalauréat*, often the *licence* (see p. 293) and sometimes special technical training, as for example, for accountants.

3. *Subordinate clerical and manipulative:* postmen, typists, copyists, and so on: elementary education; the posts for exservice men to the majority; *baccalauréat* where special knowledge was required.

4. *Labor and custodial.* Tests of aptitude; or trial on the job.

5. *Technical:* the various special diplomas from the special schools: science; *Polytéchnique; École des Chartes,* etc.

The Statute of 1946

This has introduced the following principal features.

(1) The pattern of the Civil Service is unified by means of the centralization of its management in the Prime Minister's office and authority. The only approach to such before the war was the financial control exercised over the departments by the Ministry of Finance. The regulations of all kinds concerning officials need the signature of the Prime Minister.

For the exercise of this unifying management, the law created a Direction of the Public Service (*Fonction*) under the Prime Minister's authority, its mission being to "prepare the bases of an integrated policy for the public service, to establish, and to see to the establishment of, comprehensive documentation and statistics on the public service, to study all legislative proposals concerning the organization of the public services, to coordinate the particular statuses of the various categories of officials, to elaborate the principles of their payment and of the system of social security for such personnel."

The Ministry of Finance has an important role in the process of personnel administration for the whole Service, because there is assigned to it the right to sign or countersign all the texts relating to the public service where there is a financial aspect direct or indirect. This necessarily means practically everything. Hence, as in the relations between the British Civil Service Commission and the Treasury (though with different detail), the French Civil Service operates under the joint rulership of the Prime Minister's office for public service and the Budget Division of the Ministry of Finance.

In practice, the Prime Minister delegates his powers to a Minister, a Minister of State, or a Secretary of State in the Prime Minister's office. The separate departments are the direct employers and directors of their personnel: the Prime Minister's personnel office is concerned with the embracing rules.

(2) A four-fold classification has been adopted: 1. With functions of planning and direction; 2, with functions of application—needing administrative understanding, some initiative, and judgment; 3, specialized functions of execution—where technical competence is required; 4, nonspecialized functions, requiring elementary and simple professional ability.

The thousands of jobs have been classified into these categories, with grades and pay rates to correspond.

Security

The problems that especially worry the lower and middle ranks of the French Civil Service have been solved much as in Britain. Security has been attained by the judgments of the *Conseil d'État,* and the statute stipulates the continuance of salary even if the job is suppressed, for permanent officials, and gives compensation if it is abolished. Promotions follow the British method; the old-fashioned general appraisals have ended.

Official Secrecy and Confidential Documents. Confidential care of official secrets must be maintained. This follows directly from an article of the *statut;* but the Penal Code (Article 378) has already imposed a more general, but nevertheless rigorous, duty of keeping "professional" secrets, as for example, for doctors, lawyers, priests, etc. (p. 437).

We need only translate literally the text of the law on this subject, on which is founded the stability and security of States, especially democratic ones, in which the development of policy is consigned to free electoral and public battle between free political parties.

Independently of the rules laid down in the penal code regarding professional secrets, every official is bound by the obligation of professional discretion for all that concerns the facts and information of which he has knowledge in the exercise of or occasioned by the exercise of his functions.

Any diverting, any communication, contrary to the rules of material or documents belonging to the service to third parties are formally forbidden.

Excepting cases expressly provided for in the rules in force, the official cannot be relieved of this obligation of secrecy or relieved of the prohibition decreed in the previous paragraph except with the authorization of the Minister to whom he is answerable.

Of course, the temptation to violate the rules comes from highly politicized men and women who come into the possession of secrets useful to their party friends. Such cases have already been discussed (pp. 434–435). And in a time of violent transition of France and the world, and especially the ideologies of Europe, political parties will even encourage men to enter the administration in order to betray it. The history of France in the nineteenth century remains a bad example in this respect.

Loyalty to Chiefs

In France, the violent fall and rise of regimes for hundreds of years, even down to yesterday, has not been propitious to impartial loyalty. The breach of this convention so strongly obeyed in Britain has not seldom produced public battles over the actions of named civil servants. The French Governments, as we have noted, have been more concerned to make rules that protect the interests of the officials than to cultivate their sense of service. Nor is that all. The officials, central and local, especially the prefectoral corps, were used to put pressure on the public and on other officials to secure the return to power of particular parties and regimes. It was a virtue, and certainly a necessity, *not* to be impartial. The prefectoral officials, even, were in something of a policy-making, public-involved status: it could be argued that these and others like them *ought* to be political!

Now Article 3 of the *statut des fonctionnaires* actually makes it possible for successive Governments to use their own political discretion in top administrative appointments. The rules of public administration that are required by the statute to lay down the terms of recruitment and working conditions, etc., etc., may be framed, after consultation with the Superior Council of the Public Service, to leave to the discretion of the Government such and such posts. These men (like the *directeurs*) can be officials or nonofficials, and they are revocable by a new Government. Appointment to these posts does not give the status of "established" career official. Thus, whether a career official is chosen or an outsider brought in, there is a political interference with the principle of official independence. This affects the spirit of the whole department. It may have an unfair influence on promotions in the lower ranks, in spite of the new guarantees.

Political Activities

Political candidatures of officials have never been forbidden in France as in Britain. At the most, the candidate cannot stand for an area very close to the place of his official duties. The Government gives leave of absence, with full pay, during the electoral period. It is a relic of an undemocratic history. There were Governments that almost forced officials to stand for the Chambers in order to obtain an official phalanx unreservedly loyal. Some did their office jobs in the morning and sat in the Chamber in the afternoon! Then the Third Republic, in order to secure its own survival, allowed the same practices. The teachers (not regarded as civil servants in other countries) benefited numerously from this.

Until 1950 a Civil Service official who got into Parliament retained his seniority rights and could return to office when he lost his seat. Deputies were given jobs in the Service—and still sat in the Chambers. But though the latter rule (of "detachment" from the Service) is still contained in an article of the *statut*, the law of January 6, 1950 has forbidden continued membership of the National Assembly, the Council of the Republic, or the Assembly of the French Union from the moment the Deputy is appointed or promoted to a paid Civil Service job or to any service paid by the State directly. (From this prohibition, the Ministers are excluded, so also, professors with chairs and persons on temporary governmental missions.) This provides for the independence of Parliament, properly so. *Yet it is not universally respected!* The departments still appoint and promote Deputies, ignoring the clash between the new law and the statute that allows "detachment." The Government has not had time to resolve the contradiction. Furthermore, in the same law that prohibited further membership in the Assemblies to those taking paid office, it was stipulated that when the salary of an official who is elected to any of these Assemblies is greater than the pay of these members, then his department is to pay him the difference! As for this purpose the parliamentary pay is reduced by certain deductions, each department is made to pay a handsome sum to these officials-cum-Deputies. It is not good for Civil Service morale.

Civil Service Unions and the Right to Strike

Because civil servants were not secure in their positions or were unjustly treated in their pay and conditions of work by heedless parliamentary Deputies, they were restless and ill inclined to be loyal to the State. They formed unions—*syndicats*—and from time to time went on strike. The right to strike was forbidden them, on the argument that they were not ordinary contract workers in business with private employers, but in a status of service of the nation, the sovereign authority.

The present *statut* (Art. 5) settles the matter of the right to strike in a negative sense. For it says that the officials are vis-a-vis the administration in a situation that is "of status and subject to rule"— that is, they are not contractual and *must* obey orders. If this is violated, then the rules of dismissal apply.

The right to associate is recognized, with the right to bring actions against official behavior concerning the status of public personnel and against individual decisions that challenge the collective interests of officials.

Each official's service record is kept and registered. No mention may be made in this *dossier* of the interested person's political, philosophical, or religious opinions (Art. 16).

The *Conseil d'État* followed this point of view. Sometimes the right to associate was forbidden; sometimes permitted. A settled policy forbad nationwide unions and affiliation with nonservice unions. The latter was ignored by the unions. The present Constitution stipulates: "the right to strike may be exercised within the framework of the laws that regulate it." But such laws have not been enacted!

Some beginnings of collaboration of the employees with their chiefs in developing personnel administration, found particularly in the Posts, Telegraphs, and Telephones before the wars, have been developed and made general. In each department there is a joint council of equal numbers of employee representatives (selected by the unions) and the chiefs of the Service for advice on general questions of organization and the status of officials. For the whole Service there is a Superior Council of the Public Service (chairman, the Prime Minister or his deputy), composed of twelve representatives of the top administration (Councilors of State, director of the budget, directors of personnel in the most important departments), and twelve representatives of the Civil Service employee unions. This is consultative on the regulations applying the general statute.

Furthermore, there are in each department, joint committees of administration and representatives of the employees. But the latter are chosen not by the unions but by the employees directly. They are councils of discipline, advisers on proposals for promotions, and control the employee-evaluation process.

The employees still enjoy their power of appeal to the *Conseil d'État* and the beneficent protection it affords. It has its disadvantages, since, to make sure that it will not make a contestable promotion or discipline or dismiss, etc., a department is inclined to seek the opinion of the *Conseil* beforehand.

II. THE GRAND CORPS [1] OR HIGHER CIVIL SERVICE

Before World War I, in the Third Republic, the recruitment of the officials corresponding to the

[1] *Grand Corps:* the term of prestige applied to the *Conseil d'État,* Court of Accounts, Diplomatic Corps, Inspectorate of Finances, Prefectoral Corps, Civil Administrators, Administrators of Overseas France, Engineers of Bridges and Roads and Mines, etc.

British Administrative Class and the German Higher Civil Service was regulated by decrees (rules of public administration) for each department. All of them, with slight exceptions, applied open competition by written examination and oral examination for this, the so-called *rédacteur* class. In some departments members of the already-serving executive class, say, with two years' service were allowed to compete, as well as holders of certain designated qualifications of education. The latter, for instance, were past students of certain schools, such as the *École Normale Supérieure* or the *Polytéchnique,* or the *École Libre des Sciences Politiques;* and those who held the *licence en droit,* of *lettres* or *sciences;* or doctorates of specialized education (medicine, engineering, etc.); a diploma of the *École des Chartes,* and so on.

The age limits of entry were rather higher than in England—usually under thirty—say between twenty-one and twenty-eight or "up to twenty-six" variously in the departments.

We already know that French education, intellectually, was and is of remarkably high standard. Generally the candidate, having fulfilled conditions of nationality, army service, and medical examination, found no obstacles (social, etc.) to impede his entering the examination. The written tests were severe, consisting of reports of an essay type on general topics, and on special topics *concerning that department's possible field of problem.* A test in general knowledge, the language, and so on as in the British Civil Service examinations was not administered to the French. They probably needed no examination in their language considering the care of their secondary schools over this.

The oral test was more severe than the British—being addressed to the subjects included in the candidate's specific field of written examination and requiring both oral answers and the dictation of a five-minute letter on the subject. At this oral the examiners were the personnel director of the department, another of the *directeurs,* three principals (*rédacteurs*) in the upper reaches of the department, and a younger man as secretary. This body examined and rated the candidates.

The examination was thus specialized in two senses: in the scope of the knowledge to be demonstrated, and in the actual procedure of departmental selection among the candidates. For instance, the Foreign Ministry required diplomatic history, economic geography, and public international law. And *it* was preceded by a previous interview—which did introduce a social and character sieve. The *Conseil d'État* required constitutional, political and judicial law and organization, the various other branches of law, and economics. For the Ministry of Finance, another *élite* corps, mathematics, public finance (law and organization), and economics were required.

The *rédacteur,* appointed, then moved upward by promotion *in his own department* to *souschef, chef, directeur.*

Appraisal of the Higher Service

Let us now consider the elements making the quality of this Service of perhaps 700 or 800 men.
1. Intellectuality. It would have been difficult to find their equal anywhere in the world so far as the severity of their intellectual preparation and selection was concerned, excepting the German and, coming close, the British.

Yet the high intellectualization had its drawbacks as well as its eminent qualities of legislative and administrative serviceability. It was theoretical; synoptic; and technical; consisted of cut and dried formulas. It slowed them down in inventive enterprise. This was partly due to the same effect of blight that had afflicted the production of economic and political science and the sociology of law and so forth since the time of the great minds, such as St. Simon, Auguste Comte, in spite of such pioneers as Durckheim. The observer will look in vain for a Keynes, a Wesley Mitchell, an Alvin Hansen in the economics of the Third Republic. He will not find a Corwin, a G. D. H. Cole, a Sidney and Beatrice Webb, a Graham Wallas, a Walton Hamilton, a Lowell, a Jennings, a Laski. Nor will he come upon the work and findings of the great commissions of inquiry and congressional committee investigations of the Anglo-Saxon nations for a half-century and more past.

In other words, the education tended to produce a rather static body of officials; they were not trained to discover problems and offer creative solutions to them. Nor were their political chiefs, the Ministers, as we have seen, sure enough of their own dynamic and constructive policies or their tenure of office to give the impulses of movement that could affect official inertia. We have shown, indeed, how negative were the Chambers and French society.

What has been said is a matter of degree and varied from man to man in the departments. The appraisal is a general one, made by Frenchmen themselves. It can be argued, of course, that the function of the officials is to subject the Minister's creative proposals to thoughtful criticism (see pp. 236–238). This, however, for the last half-century is to misread why society needed civil servants.

2. A Disintegrated Service. The specialization of qualifications, of educational preparation, and the fact that recruitment was departmental, not servicewide as in Britain, promoted a want of coherence and articulation among the departments. No theory of departmentalization can surgically separate the fields of governmental activity without leaving some veins to bleed. The sutures of administration are to be found in a common education. What the departments put asunder, the unstable Cabinets could never join: a united mind *de res publicae.* Hence, an unintelligent departmental autonomy; obstructions beyond the point of noncooperation. They did not see national objectives steadily and whole to be pursued in willingly coordinated behavior.

3. Unevenness of Departmental Quality. Some departments, for example, the Foreign Service, the Ministry of Finance, the *Conseil d'État* (controlling, not an innovating agency), the Ministry of the Interior, attracted brilliant and ambitious men. Other departments, for example, Labor, Commerce, War (!), could not even fill their vacancies or recruited inferior men who hated to be assigned to less prestigeful and adventurous duties. Why should able young men enter departments from which transfer to more inspiring opportunities was not available? For, without a *single* Service, transfer was almost impossible. The migration of talent to its most useful post was obstructed. Impediments of this kind produce frustration and static-mindedness.

4. Confusion of Ranks. A confusion of ranks was caused by lack of a common classification for the whole Service. Each department found it convenient from time to time to confound the line that separated the *rédacteurs*—that is, the "administrative"—from its executive-clerical officials. A common class, with a common education and entry methods, is one of the indispensable ways to check such confusion. Furthermore, the law was stringent as to seniority in promotions—they obtained them, regardless of merit; and the deficiency was made up by the appointment by special decrees of the men who had the qualities that were required at the top, either on an established or an unestablished basis.

5. A Biased Social Outlook. Some would regard the alienation of the spirit of the higher Civil Service from French republic institutions and exacting social needs in the course of galloping development as the gravest deficiency of the prewar era. To this some attention must be given.

The higher Civil Service was recruited from a narrow social class—the upper bourgeoisie and a declining but still resistant aristocracy. The cost of tuition and maintenance in *lycées,* at colleges, and universities was a decisive restriction on entrance into the public service. It was then further weighted against the middle and working classes by promotions, which down to World War II were in the hands of the older men, less adapted even than the new generation to developing French society in its domestic change and international position.

The consequences were far more serious for France than for Britain (p. 233), for in Britain the Commons was clearly in control over policy, and the principle of Civil Service impartiality had been built by Ministers under the control of Parliament. But in France, the very regime was on trial frequently. The upper classes, loyal to the Right, monopolized the top official jobs. They were conservative, authoritarian; and if they were devoted to the State, it was not the State of the republican Ministers, whose parliamentary activities they despised.

Certain schools supplied the highest ranks of the Civil Service. The *Polytéchnique* supplied the Ministry of Public Works, the Armed Services departments, for example. But of far greater influence were the elite introduced from the *École Libre des Sciences Politiques*. A private foundation, this was established in 1871 by Émile Boutmy, a noted political scientist, to give France officials and statesmen capable of avoiding such disasters as that suffered at the hands of Prussia the year before. It was hoped that a realistic political science would supplant the legal-philosophical outlook.

Its supply of the highest *cadres* of the Service was extraordinary. In the twenty years up to 1925, the *École* supplied 153 of the 192 persons appointed to the vacant career diplomatic and consular posts; all except two of the *auditeurs* (the first rungs of the ladder) of the *Conseil d'État;* all, excepting only three, of the entrants into the *Inspecteurs* of the Ministry of Finance and into the *Cour des Comptes*. And its graduates were many in the other departments.

The school was not a school for the poor or the middle classes. It did not, as Boutmy had hoped, enrich France's knowledge of political reality; it did not want to, for knowledge may lead to unrest. Its teachings were highly formal—that is, doctrinaire—except that they had a technical antipolitical bias and antidemocratic scorn of the masses. The professorial faculty were contemptuous intellectuals; not the inmixtures of political and governmental life of Oxford and Cambridge, often deeply involved in social and economic movements and political parties at the finest level, and constantly the suppliers of active-minded graduates to the British Civil Service. It came to be blamed for its support of Pétain and Vichy.

The position is summed up by André Géraud, pseudonym *Pertinax,* in his *Gravediggers of France* (confirmed by the debates of June 21, 1945, in the Assembly). He says:

As I looked over the programs listing the various subjects taught in this institution, I was often amazed at the number of degree-spangled pedants who now replaced the founders. The majority of Treasury officials were recruited from this School. Vanity of examinations and competitions! These fellows were not chosen because of their intrinsic merit, the strength of their personality, or their fine character, but merely because of the supposed orthodoxy of their views, their powers of mimicry, their connections, and their position in Parisian Society among the two or three thousand people who held the big jobs, set the fashion, handed out favors and made the law. . . . Inspectors of Finance were one huge family, and that connection could not be healthy.

They became sympathizers of the Royalist enemies and Fascist-style leagues of rioters against the Republic in the critical 1930's. In the Vichy regime, the "corporative" State let their intellects loose from the interferences of democracy. The Service was purged of "foreign elements"—that is, Freemasons and Jews.

At the Liberation large numbers of these collaborators were purged, low as well as high officials. The doors were open to waves of appointees by de Gaulle and the Left-wing parties. Above all, de Gaullists and Communists "colonized" the important posts. They constituted party-biased administrators and spies while they held on. Some remain even now (p. 434).

On Liberation, the best of the younger generation were commissioned to fashion a higher Service worthy of the Resistance.

The Basic Reform: the École National d'Administration

A new system for the recruitment and career of the highest-level civil servants was commended with the publication of a decree of October 10, 1945. It resulted from the order given by General de Gaulle, head of the Provisional Government, to Michel Debré, *"master of requests"* in the *Conseil d'État,* to prepare a radical reform. (M. Debré was then a commissioner for the region of Augers, with France still on a war-footing administration.) The reform was prepared with the cooperation of the *Conseil d'État,* the Cabinet, and the Consultative Assembly of that period.

The *rédacteur* class (like the British Administrative Class in general) was abolished for the various departments and was replaced by two classes:

(1) the Civil Administrators.
(2) the Secretaries of Administration.

(*1*) *The Civil Administrators.* These are almost identical with the British Administrative Class. They were modeled on it, consciously. They form a single corps of servants, no matter in what department of the central government they serve or whether their service is in the local government areas or in France overseas or in the foreign service. They constitute a single career. Their hierarchy goes upward and is the same whatever department they may serve in at any time. They begin as Administrators-adjoint; then Administrative Class 3; upward to Administrative Class 2; then Class 1; and then Class *exceptional.*

All of them are recruited through the newly instituted school: the *École National d'Administration.* Their role has been thus described (by M. Debré):

To fit the conduct of administrative affairs to the general policy of the Government, to prepare drafts of laws and rules and ministerial decisions, to formulate the directives to their execution, and to coordinate the march of the public services.

(*2*) *The Secretaries of Administration.* These are rather like the Executive Class in the British system. Indeed, the short description of their role could have been taken directly out of the official descriptions of their British analogues:

Their task is to assure the works of execution, current operations, and certain specialized functions which require sound administrative knowledge and experience.

Debré described them as "the technicians of the administrative services," for they fall into a top managerial group and two special categories of accountants and translators. They are recruited by an examination open to officials aged thirty-five and over, with five years of public service, and also to young persons between eighteen and twenty-five, holding a diploma of higher (secondary) education or the equivalent—*which opens the Service to wider sections of the public* than ever before, for it does not specify the *lycées.*

The Civil Administrators. Let us first look at the prescription of what is required by the State, again from the report of M. Debré:

Certain services have a simple character of execution and those who carry them out have no part in the direction of the affairs of the State. Others, on the contrary, are at the very heart of the life of the nation, and their officers may be considered as *influential collaborators of the political authorities* [Italics added].

When we talk of a School of Administration and when one envisages the administrative reform bound up with its establishment, the word *administration* has a special sense. It means that combination of services of a civil character which constitute the superior structure of the State and whose members have as their principal task to prepare or study the decisions of Parliament and the Government and then to direct their execution. It is among these officials that the Government would naturally choose a number of its high officers, notably those who will occupy the situations which wield authority or of administration linked with policy.

Of the relevant services these principal ones come rapidly to mind: the central administrations of the ministries, the prefectoral and diplomatic services, the services of inspection, the administrative bodies involved in lawmaking and control [the *Conseil d'État* and the Court of Accounts]. There are others like these.

The prescription is much like Macaulay's for the Civil Service in Britain (pp. 219–221) and the description of its work is like that of the Administrative Class of the Civil Service more recently (pp. 224–225).

The Problem of a Special Civil Service School. The reformers rejected the idea of a *Polytéchnique* for Civil Service officials that would take candidates direct from secondary school and, after three years of training, put them in the Service. This was starting too young and too uneducated. This reverts to earlier efforts in the nineteenth century to solve this problem of the education of higher civil servants.

In 1830 administrative law teaching had been resumed, and in the more liberal atmosphere a *theory* of administration had been developed at the universities. This, too, was insufficiently alive and real. The law faculties defeated the alternative proposals of (1) the teaching of political science inside the law faculties; (2) the establishment of special faculties of political science and administration; and (3) the establishment of a separate School of Public Administration. The Revolution of 1848 aborted such proposals.

However, the thinking bore some fruit. For the Minister of Education in 1848, Hippolyte Carnot, son of the great administrator of the Revolution and father of a President of the Third Republic, set up a school of public administration—to be like the *École Polytéchnique* that produced engineers for the service of the State. The candidates were recruited by open competition. They lived in college, to develop an *ésprit de corps*. They took lectures at the *Collège de France* and their own special school. To finish their law education, they were allowed to enter law faculties. To give them practice before being appointed to permanent positions, they were apprenticed to high officials. Within a year and a half it was dead. Napoleon III's regime was not interested in it. Once again, in 1858, the practice of the First Empire to apprentice recruits for the *Conseil d'État* was resumed. The defeat of 1870 made it mere flotsam and jetsam.

Then came the foundation of the *École Libre des Sciences Politiques* to which we have referred. We may add that some great minds inspired its birth beside Boutmy: Renan, Albert Sorel, philosophers and historians. Its faculty included high administrators as well as professors. At its virtual breakdown in 1939, it had 1800 students, one fifth of whom were foreigners.

In 1936 Léon Blum's Popular Front Government attempted to convert and reorganize the *École* into a State-based school of public administration. The law faculties were hostile to a competitor. The high officials were opposed because it would challenge their separatist corporate departmental spirit. A more general enmity arose out of public fears that it might get a political twist. Though the law was enacted, the World War II came before it could be made effective.

Improved Political Science. Now, it was feared that candidates entering a special school of administration, and at that, when young, might lack breadth and humanity of education. Hence it was necessary to take care of a good general education and to take people at some maturity. Hence, side by side with the establishment of the *École National d'Administration,* then, a reform of university education in political science was essential. Therefore, to escape the steely mental grip of the law faculties, it was planned to have separate institutes of political science—for the early period at four centers: Paris, Strasbourg, Toulouse, and Lyons. Political science means also social sciences. These institutes develop and co-ordinate the work in their field of other faculties that teach economics, administration, social studies. Their plan is to educate students in the work methods and concrete problem-facing and problem-solving as seen in actual social life. In fact, there is an idea prior to this: it is once again to fertilize the scholars themselves.

The institutes have been established only after a careful scrutiny by the *Conseil d'État*. Entrance to them is by a diploma of advanced secondary education. The candidates who deserve and need it *are given state scholarships,* an approach to social breadth in selection of talent.

The State appoints some of the members (civil servants) of the board of management of the institutes, as also the director of each of these. The Prime Minister's approval of their curriculums and administration is required by law. His Civil Service Office is linked with the board.

In these institutes (corresponding to undergraduate education), the students in their first year take an almost identical common course. In the second and third years, some optional courses allow of adaptation to the natural interest and vocational outlook of the individual. But the purpose is as yet not specialization. On the contrary, a broad humane education is sought through the study of law, the humanities, and social sciences. It proceeds by lectures, discussions, practical tasks, and seminars; and is conducted by university professors and persons from the administration and outside social and business affairs.

At the end of the first year, a severe examination gets rid of those not competent. The three-year course is concluded with another severe examination and a diploma. The students have simultaneously been registered as students in the faculties of law or letters: and obtain a *licence* in this, as well as their Institute diploma.

This diploma is decisive for entrance into the public service: for it is the passport to admission into the *École National d'Administration.*

The National School of Administration

This school is housed in the former premises of the *École Libre des Sciences Politiques* and in the same building as the *Institut des Sciences Politiques* of Paris. Its director (the first) is a noted Resistance combatant, one of General de Gaulle's former administrators in Brittany during the Liberation, a person of high administrative morale, civic dedication, and unusual sagacity—Henri Bourdeau de Fontenay. The director of the *Institut* is M. Chapsal, again a man of the qualities notable in M. Fontenay, with a superb first-hand knowledge of the political science and administrative problems of foreign lands. These men are supported by some of the ablest of the younger French minds, men so able and devoted and intelligent as to arouse the hope that they will restore France to her civic vigor and glory.

The school serves several purposes in the formation of a cultured and thoughtful Civil Service. It replaces the seventy-five separate departmental entrance examinations by one single, assembled examination of a competitive kind. It also provides the financial means for the talented, by paying them a salary for the three years during which they will study. It receives annually about ninety students and has designed a mixture of the theoretical and practical, the general and the special in a most intelligent endeavor to produce active-minded and thinking officials with a knowledge of social realities and, moreover, of a democratic outlook.

Who Can Enter? The school is accessible to two streams of entrants: students, and officials already in the Service. The students are given a competitive entrance examination of a general cultural kind, to test their capacity for analysis and synthesis, based on the range and level of knowledge their diploma has given them, in political institutions and geography. They need one foreign language also.

Then the serving officials have their own examination: it is less scholarly. They are examined in order to demonstrate their qualities of method and precision within one of the four sections into which the school is divided: general administration, economic and financial administration, social administration, and foreign affairs. They take no language. They are asked to précis a text, once in 1000 words and a second time in 50. (Try it; and see what it proves!)

Both kinds of candidates are examined in one more general essay subject. For example:

> The evolution of the modern world is dominated by a tendency to the rationalization of all forms of human activity. In what measure does it seem to you this tendency is compatible with the conservation of the most precious values of our traditional type of civilization?

For this essay (and similar ones in other years) [2] six hours are allowed.

Then both kinds of candidates are given a twenty-minute conversation with an oral board, following on a ten-minute commentary on a general proposition.

Each kind of entrant takes an examination in one or other of the four fields of the school, in order to qualify for specialization in that field.

When it is remembered that there are some 1000 desiring to enter and only 100 are chosen, it may be accepted that the school is getting the cream of French intelligence (and physique, as we shall see) and character that desires to serve the State.

Once admitted, the students are under the disciplinary code of the Civil Service; they are paid a salary; they commit themselves to serve the State for a period of twelve years, failing which they must pay back the three years' salary at the school.

In each of the four sections of the school, as above mentioned, there is a mingling of the entrants from two doors of access—institute and office. They are on equal terms. It is difficult to devise a curriculum that suits the former and also the latter, who have experience but have not usually had a university education.

The Course of Studies. This falls into three years: the first is one of practical apprenticeship; the

[2] See a collection of examinations and *answers* in *Épreuves et Statistiques des Concours de 1952, École nationale d'Administration*, Paris, 1953.

second is a year of studies; the third is a year of practice in business enterprises, practice in government service and mingled studies. Let us look at these a little more closely.

First Year of Apprenticeship. The purpose is to take the recruits away from their former environment and studious atmosphere; to shake up their state of mind, let them look at the impetus of realities, and to get a sense of the general interest presented to them. It is designed also to confront them with their own selves. They are, therefore, sent away to work with the prefects or the civil administrators in Morocco rather than in the central ministries. They are placed as closely as possible to the official who will supervise them and the greatest possible distance away from their usual homes—never in Paris, and never at the prefecture of the *département* where they normally reside. Those from the south are sent north, and so on.

The supervising officials are asked to give the cadets (or probationers) a share in executive responsibilities. Sometimes such young persons have, by force of circumstances (say, the absence or sickness of their chief), been forced to take truly serious responsibilities that reveal and develop character. The supervisor can then attest whether they are brave or not; hesitant or alert, and so on. The school sends its faculty to see these youngsters during the year on the spot, and there is a dean especially charged with this phase of the school's formation of officials.

At the end of this first year, the student draws up a report on a subject suggested to them by his experience.

The Second Year. A year of studies at the school follows. It is one that puts a strain on the student, since he must turn from affairs, sometimes exacting and exciting, to very close paper work and lectures indoors. The candidates are distributed among the four specialties, but their studies are, in part, general. The common courses cover such areas as the public services at home and abroad; problems arising out of nationalization of industries; the technical facts of French industry and agriculture; the economic and financial problems of investment policy and French reconstruction (in 1950 given by Mendès-France, later Prime Minister!); labor problems, comparatively treated; the problems of defense; North Africa; South East Asia; Islam. The African problems are very intensively studied. In addition, there are the courses that fall in the special area of the four fields. They are conducted in seminars of fifteen or twenty students and are oriented to educating in methods of problem-solving, in expounding, in how to work with a team or the parliamentary commissions.

> Method, the ordering of one's thought and language, precision of expression, elegance and sobriety of style, confidence in speaking, that is what an official should possess.

For his knowledge and work have to be made useful to others.

The second year is concluded with a very stiff examination. It falls into two parts: (1) a paper taken in common "except those destined for the foreign service" on the same general but politico-administrative theme; (2) several weighty questions in the student's specialty. In addition, there are elaborate oral examinations in the specialties— but all have at least one question on North Africa. The written part includes a report or administrative memorandum.

The examination gives each candidate a comparative rating. Its components are: 50 percent of the marks for the examination; 25 percent for studies (essays, class work, etc.); 25 percent for the year of practical experience.

This list, in order or priority, enables the candidates to choose their government departments, central, local, overseas, and foreign service. The assignments to positions are notified in the *Journal Officiel*.

The Third Year. This is spent thus: one term in a private enterprise, whether industrial, financial, or commercial. This is by arrangement with various employers, who have given the arrangement a warm welcome. (It is hoped in the future to send them for a short time into mines, workshops, and factories.)

For the rest of the third year, the student is back at school. Here he is coached in practical exercises by officials of the department into which he has been placed, sometimes in the department itself, sometimes on missions or researches.

The director of the school says:

> Our hope is that in leaving us our students pass at once into the administrative service or special body (like the *Conseil d'État*) to which they belong and at once render to their departments the effective services which they have the right to expect of them and the School which they have attended.

Some Statistics. The school, said its director, has rounded the cape on which its predecessors foundered. Let us look at some of the points on its chart.

From March 1946 to September 1954 it graduated about 620 men and women into the higher Civil Service through the normal procedure we have described. In addition, it conducted special postwar examinations for some 165 in 1945, 1946, and 1947. This makes nearly 800 officials altogether that have satisfied its tests of what a good civil servant should be. It is already a substantial proportion of the higher Civil Service.

All of them had an excellent preeducation; many of them superb educational records, with the relevant diplomas, doctorates, and so on.

Including the special examinations of 1945–1947, the age of the students has been something over one half, from twenty-one to twenty-six; something over one fourth, from twenty-six to thirty; above thirty, nearly 12 percent; and less than twenty-one years old, 7.5 percent. (The figures here go only to 1951 inclusive.)

For all the entrants since 1945, the following (inclusive to 1951) were thus distributed by *social origin*:

Parents' Occupation	Percentage *
Government service	41.5
Commerce and industry	19.5
Liberal professions	11.1
Property owners—no profession	5.4
Agriculture	4.1
Artisans and small industry	3.9
Banks and insurances	3.9
Not known or no profession	10.6

* The loss of 3 percent is due to faults of decimal division.

In the figures for 1952 and 1953 these proportions are maintained, though the classification is slightly different. What is striking is the paucity of the children of the white-collar workers; and I see practically no working-class entrants at all.

Morale. The students must be good physical specimens and are compelled to be active in some sport. Their physical examination, with a standard that qualifies for entry, has shown that almost all need physical culture. The school had foreseen that if no care was given to this, the officials, however clever, might not be able to give the service needed of them, especially in the more active posts.

A weekly physical-culture session, therefore, is compulsory in the second year of studies, although it is a little strenuous for those candidates who, in their thirties, have come from administrative jobs. They play tennis, swim, do physical exercises, ride horses, practice fencing.

Thirty-five percent of the students, on entry, are married (10 percent of those from school and 60 percent of those who are already civil servants).

About 40 percent of the students are Parisians, but with recent provincial connections; and the rest of France is well represented in its breadth.

In order to inspire each class to maintain its *ésprit de corps* when it is scattered on service, the classes are given glorious names: Fighting France; the French Union; the Cross of Lorraine (Joan of Arc and de Gaulle); the United Nations; Jean Moulin (the heroic prefect of the Resistance); the 1848 (that is, the Second Republic); Europe; Jean Giraudoux (a playwright of genius); Paul Cambon, classic diplomatist; Felix Eboué, distinguished native Governor General of the Chad, who early joined de Gaulle's Free France.

The alumni have a Society of Former Students, quartered in the school; it publishes an annual volume and an excellent review called *Promotions,* meaning (roughly) "classes of . . ."; it has an annual ball; it has the privilege of annually rekindling the flame at the tomb of the Unknown Warrior. The alumni association takes a keen interest in the continuing problems of study at the school, and it is represented on the board of management and the committee of studies. Its

members lecture in the school and are sometimes members of the oral boards for its examinations.

The graduates of the school are spread throughout the French administration. They (omitting the *special* examinees) have entered the

	Percent
Conseil d' État	6.0
Court of Accounts	6.5
Moroccan civil government	7.0
Foreign Affairs Ministry	1.75
Education Ministry	2.75
General Inspectorate of Finances	10.0
Ministry of Finance, central department	16.0
Ministry of the Interior	8.0*
Ministry of Labor and Social Security	3.0
Economic expansion abroad	5.0

* Includes those who join prefectoral service (see p. 497).

while the rest are scattered in many departments.

Further Education. At the school, a Center of Advanced Studies has been instituted to reeducate and refresh officials of some years of service. It takes officials between the ages of thirty and forty-five, from the home, the foreign and the local services and offers a diploma for advanced studies in domestic, foreign, local, and imperial administrative problems. Persons may enter from private enterprise. Officials and professors teach; officials from different departments meet each other. The diploma does not entitle to promotion; but a good one would be helpful thereto.

Conclusion

One career has replaced twenty, the State in place of the departments. For the very institution of a single class of civil administrators was to facilitate transfer. It establishes the principle that any of its members, wherever they started, might, in the course of time, be moved to other responsibilities when the exigencies of government required it, without unwillingness on the part of the official to go elsewhere or a departmental *ésprit de corps* to keep him out.

The political importance of the reform is potentially tremendous. For no country needs a class of civil administrators to serve it so much as one that is governed by a disintegrated National Assembly and ramshackle Cabinets of mixed composition and short duration, and responsible to a people that, for reasons amply explained, tends to be uncivic and to suffer from a broken national vision. The Service has been chosen and educated to see in a national vision, but to be responsive to the Republic—and to avoid military and civic collapse as in 1940.

Perspective. However, there still remains the task of flushing the whole Service through with an active, enterprising, originating spirit. Though the figures are not available, the composition of the Service is known to have an undue proportion of old officials. The age of retirement is sixty-five generally, but in the *Conseil d'État,* seventy. In the British Civil Service (p. 234) officials retire at sixty-five, a substantial proportion at sixty. The French Civil Service needs to have washed out of it the slow red tape, defensive and authoritarian and frightened "written-on-official-paper" (*papier timbré*) habits induced by the practices of the past—especially the idea that the citizen is either a political buddy to be given favors or a subject to be given orders. This trenches on the overaddiction of the French to excessive legalism embodied in cocoons of legal codes. They overdo the law; and underlap on robust common sense and venture.

Local Government

The most highly developed sense in the French is probably their gift of sight. Physically and morally their most permanent attribute is clearsightedness, clarity, and lucidity of vision. To see "things as they are" is the great French preoccupation. . . . Their approach is naturally realistic.

—*Pierre Maillaud,* 1943

Deconcentrated Local Self-Government

There is greater centralization of authority in France than in England; the principle, as we have noted, is rather deconcentration than decentralization. Yet the latter is considerable, and France has substantial local *self*-government by her locally elected councils, which flourish in interest and activities. The contrast between this system, subject to some central *tutelle,* and centralization in the U.S.S.R. makes the former seem free as the wind.

The Laws of Local Government. We know by what means Napoleon I established centralization (p. 303). It persisted to the Third Republic, slightly modified in the Second Empire.

Then, in the laws of 1871 on the *conseils généraux* and the law of 1884 on the municipal councils, the modern basis of local election of these bodies was laid down, and the general grant of powers and obligations was made. Various laws since then have modified, extended, allowed of variations of power and territorial area, and amended the central and local relationships. But these two basic laws still regulate the essentials of the matter.

The Constitution of 1875 did not include stipulations on the subject of local government. Title X of the Constitution of the Fourth Republic (following the abortive draft) is "Local Administrative Units" (Articles 85 to 89). It is extremely general and even hollow. The main positive law contained in the articles is the rule that local administrative units "shall be governed freely by councils elected by universal suffrage," and that the *execution* of their decisions shall be insured by their mayor or president (Art. 87). Coordination and control and the representation of national interests are vested in the Cabinet of the Republic. Then there is a promise that "organic" laws will extend their liberties and provide for certain large cities different rules of operation from the small ones. These organic laws have not been passed.

The observations have been made in order to indicate how strongly the local authorities are imbedded in the national structure of law. The old congeries of diverse authorities—villages, towns, *provinces*—were swept away in the Revolution of 1789, and the communes, the *départements,* and the lesser subdivisions were set up to reduce the whole system to a new order and uniformity under the central government (p. 336). That is still the situation—as the Constitution of the Fourth Republic says, to keep France "one and indivisible." That Constitution calls them "local administrative units," finding no more free-sounding title for them.

The Areas

The Communes. The communes were created in 1789 to take the place of the diverse "natural" entities that had grown up over the centuries; the

80 to 90 *départements* were made out of the carving up of the "natural" provinces, which still keep their famous historic names and something of their millennial regional character. It was essential to root out the remnants of separatism that had made France very late in achieving its national unity. However, the communes remained a fundamental natural unit, the law being drawn in very general terms to enable administrative adaptation to the needs of the extremely variant habitations, from a hamlet to a great city. For on a legal basis, the general form and authority of the communes, as of the *départements,* are the same for all.

The communes are gathered into the *départements.* Both commune and *département* are corporate bodies.

Size of Communes, 1954

Inhabitants	No. of Communes	Population
Uninhabited	6	0
1–49	619	21,431
50–99	2,406	186,615
100–199	7,112	1,065,044
200–299	6,176	1,518,749
300–399	4,418	1,528,715
400–499	3,076	1,371,033
500–699	4,467	2,621,634
700–999	3,127	2,590,391
1,000–1,499	2,667	3,204,868
1,500–1,999	1,109	1,888,387
2,000–2,499	663	1,485,032
2,500–2,999	418	1,144,474
3,000–3,999	493	1,092,591
4,000–4,999	267	1,177,979
5,000–8,999	473	3,128,523
9,000–9,999	45	422,191
10,000–19,999	250	3,492,732
20,000–29,999	86	2,084,694
30,000–49,999	59	2,234,686
50,000–79,999	28	1,717,622
80,000–99,999	11	971,668
100,000 and over	24	7,205,186
	38,019	42,734,445

Of the 63 towns with population over 50,000, Paris has 2,850,189; 7 have over 200,000; 14 between 100,000 and 200,000, and 21 between 50,000 and 100,000.

The variation in the size of the communes is immense. Of the 37,983 we have mentioned in 1946, 22,665 had a population of under 500; some 16,000 had fewer than 200; nearly 600 had less than 50. On the other hand, there are many substantial towns and great cities. This means that,

in fact, there is great variation in the scope and importance of municipal services, the amounts spent, and their ability to resist the tutelary power of the prefect and the Ministry of the Interior.

Paris is the only big city that has a form of government special to itself (see p. 507). But otherwise the basic law equates all the communes from such immense places as Lille to hamlets in the Alps. This system avoids the legal complications of the British system with its various tiers of authorities, and the American. But it does not avoid the complication of tremendous variations in practice according to the urban, rural, industrial, agricultural, and topographical character of place.

The Départements. The 90 *départements* contain an average of about 425 communes; some contain twice as many (for example, Pas-de-Calais, the mining region on the Channel, has 900), while some have about 100.

The *départements* are, on the average, much larger than the biggest territorial unit in British local government: nearly 2400 square miles, as against 1107. Larger area makes a great difference in the conduct of local government. It should be remembered that the average is obtained in Britain by dividing by 60; in France by 90. France is a much bigger country territorially. The task of central control and of the control by the *département* over the communes is made the more difficult and, in the opinion of the latter, the more necessary if national unity is to be maintained and further developed.

Four Groups. The *départements* are classified according to their importance: they fall into four groups. Fifteen of them are "beyond classification" —they contain the chief cities of the nation. Then follow 19 first-class; 22 second-class; and 34 third-class *départements*—the dignity depends on their wealth, population, and political importance. The chief legal differences in the classification concern police powers. For in the 15 beyond class, the prefects have special police powers. In all, the hierarchy of the prefects, as an official career, has a system of career promotion from the lower to the higher categories.

Arrondissements. The *arrondissements* are subdivisions of the *département,* which contains three or four of these. This means that an *arrondissement* has about 100 to 150 communes within its area; or about 100,000 inhabitants. The capital of the *département* forms an *arrondissement,* with the suburbs around it.

The Nature of the Local Unit

The commune and the *département* are both simultaneously areas of local self-government and local units of national administration. Their local councils are in this dual position. But even more so is the mayor in the commune an officer of the central government as well as a servant of the municipal council. The prefect is even more strongly marked as an official of the Ministry of the Interior. The mayor is selected locally; the prefect is appointed and is totally under the disciplinary authority of the central government.

Differences between France and Britain. This duality of responsibility and duality of masters does not exist in the British system or the American system. The British system has considerable control over such services as police and education that are either legally or virtually compulsory, and control is exercised through standards of attainment and committee organization enforced by the withholding of grants-in-aid. The British began with unbelievable local liberties at the beginning of the nineteenth century and proceeded to organize the local authorities in a tight network of legislation and administrative control (pp. 241–243). The French began the nineteenth century with unbelievable central direction of even the most trivial affairs of the smallest communes; they have moved toward a loosening of the bonds. The two nations still do not quite meet in the mixture of local authority and central regimenting, but the difference is not so great as it was, say, in 1875. The British, however, is freer.

One substantial difference is, of course, the actual appointment of a central government official—the prefect—to operate in the *département* under the direction of the Ministry of the Interior to be the controller of the national interests as entrusted to the *département,* and even the local discretion entrusted to the *conseil général.* There is no such officer throughout present-day English local government. Napoleon, who invented the prefect, said: "I desire that Frenchmen shall date their happiness from the establishment of the Prefects." They were to the *départements* what he—the First Consul—was to all France: the Chief! Quite a number of first-level Ministers and even Prime Ministers of the Third Republic started in the prefectorate.

Second, the educational system of France is different, being a function of the central authority and under the authority of the Ministry of Education (see p. 302). This virtually removes education from the field of local self-government.

Third, in the British and American systems, the financial transactions of the local authorities are, at most, subject to examination when a scandal is reported or when a grant-in-aid is being appraised or when (in England) the district auditors make their examinations of accounts. In the *départements,* however, in the place of the treasurer, who is an officer of the local authorities in the British system, there is an official appointed by the Ministry of Finance, called a *trésorier payeur général.* He conducts the management of the revenue offices of the *département,* assisted by a number of subordinate officials, for the *arrondissement* and the communes (with over 10,000 population).

This again illustrates the difference between the British system of a post-hoc intervention *after* the local authorities have used their discretion in their own way and the French system, which has central officials on the spot entrusted with the actual current administration of functions.

Another central government influence of current administrative significance is the power of the centrally appointed roads and mining engineers (Ministry of Public Works), who supervise and direct all public works—which includes departmental roads and ports. Similarly with the police system (below).

I. COMMUNAL AND DEPARTMENTAL ADMINISTRATION

Conseil Municipal and Conseil Général

The Municipal Council. The local government authority is the *conseil municipal* or municipal council. It is elected for six years, by universal suffrage. All councils are elected on the same day in May. The number of councilors varies widely: the law relates this to population. The smallest has eleven members; those over 60,000 have thirty-seven. This is smaller than the numbers in English local government. The largest towns, and Paris, have larger numbers—though the proportionality decreases.

The central government officials and the paid officials of the commune are ineligible for election.

The method of election is varied according to the size of the commune. Those that have over 9000 population have a list proportional-representation system—with the whole area as one constituency. Those under 9000 use the method of competing the lists of candidates where the elector votes for a list, and the list that gets an absolute majority of the votes gets all the seats. In the event of no such majority being obtained, another ballot takes place a week later, and a relative majority will win all the seats for the party attaining it.

The Conseil Général. The *conseil général* of the *département* is a far more important body than the municipal council, even of the greatest cities which lie within their borders, as to powers and final authority over what it can do, and in "political" weight in the nation and prestige.

Many of the members of the National Assembly and the Council of the Republic are departmental councilors—between 200 and 300 (see p. 444). We know that election to these Chambers is based on the communes and departmental councils. Moreover, the political parties that have any strength have their local roots in their departmental conferences and executives. This is the basis of national electoral organization. Hence close relationships between the personalities that work in or strive for membership of both levels of representative bodies. The locally rooted parties pay a great attention to the *département* and the commune: to capture their authority and power over the services they dispense, to assist their prestige among their clientele, and to sway the local clientele toward them at the coming elections. There have been cases where the councilor of the *département*, perhaps its president, has been elected Deputy and then has become Minister of

the Interior—the latter exercising control over himself as the former!

The membership of the *conseil général* is settled in number by the number of cantons in each, for it consists of one member for each of these. The number of cantons varies in each *département*. This would raise no political concern were it not for the fact that the cantonal boundaries were marked out over a hundred years ago, which means that the rural areas have a very considerable advantage over the urban areas in representation. Once again the backward parts of France are in undue authority, as in the composition of the Council of the Republic. The numbers vary from 20 to 68 (the latter in the *Département* du Nord, "beyond class," of which Lille is the chief town.

The councilors are elected for six years, but half triennially. Elections were held in May 1949; October (the regular month) 1951; others were held in October 1954, and so on, triennially.

The qualification age for candidacy in the municipal councils is twenty-one; in the *conseil général,* twenty-five. Similar disqualifications regarding central and local officials to the municipal councils hold good. The elections are held per member per canton. Hence the system of ordinary ballot applies: by absolute majority. If this is not attained, there is a second ballot a week later. About one half of the seats to be filled in 1951 required a second ballot. As with the use of the *scrutin d'arrondissement* in the Third Republic for the Chamber, the interval of a week between ballots is used for maneuvers and promises of local services and influence. The arrangements are very frequently pure politics in a national sense—that is, anti-Communist or pro-Catholic or anticlerical, against the M.R.P. or the R.P.F. This has already been noted in the discussion of the national political parties and their regional strength and weakness.

We have the right impression, therefore, when we note the intermixture of general party alignments with local interests, especially in the big urban centers where the Big Four parties dominate. But far more frequently than in the national elections, local personalities are able to break through, even fend off, the intervention of party interests. For the two systems of government, though closely related, nevertheless pivot on different issues, and the state of the local services is the prevailing one with the electors; the parish pump, not the *Palais Bourbon*.

Range of Authority and the Mayor. The mayor is appointed by the elected council at its first meeting. With him one or more assistant mayors are chosen (*maires-adjoints*) according to the size of the commune. The choice of the mayor is political, not technical. But like the Prime Minister or the President of the Republic, his votes will not often be thrown by one majority party but will be composed of the contingents of a number of small parties. And, like the President of the National Assembly, the mayor may, therefore, be a man who is not of the party with the largest number of votes, but a compromise among the minorities.

The municipal councils meet at least four times a year, in sessions of two weeks each: in February, May, August, and September. The Mayor can convene extraordinary session for urgent business. One third the membership of the council can call for a special session, the Mayor notwithstanding. Special sessions may also be called by the prefect or subprefect. There are many such special sessions.

The Mayor is chairman at all sessions, except when he wishes his assistants to take his place. But he cannot be chairman when his annual accounts are discussed and voted, nor vote therein, though he may be present to answer questions.

The committee system that operates so characteristically in English local councils has its counterpart in the French, but with an important difference: The latter have no committees that are statutory—that is, imposed by law.

The municipal council in France is fully master over the committee structure it wants: general caretaker committees for the intervals when the council is not sitting, and others for special departments of its work. These are private. Some are set up for the subject—for example, a loan—and some are standing—for example, public assistance or the local parks. It does not, like the English committee, practically run the service, executively; it merely reports and recommends. For above all, whereas the power of execution in English local

government is vested in the council as a whole, in the French system *the executive power is vested in the mayor*. The latter is a system of separation of powers—whether in the commune or the *département*, whether for local or for state services! This theme will become more emphasized presently.

Powers of the Communes

The powers of the communes are set out, positively and negatively, in Article 61 and following of the law of April 5, 1884, Chapter III, on the attributions of the municipal councils. It is applicable to all the nearly 40,000 communes. Its most general statement is: "The municipal council rules the affairs of the commune." But what are they? Who is to define them? Can it do anything? No! Another article contains a general ban even on *deliberations* about objects "alien to its attributions."

In law and practice the powers have assumed the following form: Set down in the law are the *obligatory* duties the council has to perform and for which it will have to find the money. These are the official buildings, cemeteries, the pay of its officials, its debt service, public assistance, public education, communal roads, rural police, and fire brigades. These comprise a large proportion of the services that in England are left much to the discretion of the local authorities—though if they did not carry them it is to be surmised that some branch of English law could be invoked to force their performance. Some of these (police, for example) are obligatory in England also. Naturally, how substantial these shall be and what they will cost depend on the size and needs of the commune. It must undertake them; but how well and on what scale is very different for Marseilles than for Pau. But the law has taken a hand in the obligatory services: public health, sanitation, social welfare, education are required of them.

For these services the local council must raise the money. Since this is so, the interpretation of the obligation is a sensitive matter. If it ends in deadlock between the council and mayor, or the council and the prefect, then recourse is had to the *Conseil d'État* to make a legal determination.

Outside these obligatory services the municipal council has a *sovereignty of action* in communal affairs, at its initiative, if it is prepared to back this by raising the funds.

This raises the famous distinction between the English method of granting powers (see pp. 242–243) and the French. As we have shown, the English local authorities can undertake action only by specific grant, piece by piece, by Parliament to act. This tends to inhibit the progressiveness of progressive authorities. The French method leaves the route and rate of progress to the local authorities. It certainly allows for the variety that mirrors the diversity of the 37,983 communes.

Interpretation by Conseil d'État. Yet what does it mean? If the council or the mayor is challenged on interpretation of "communal affairs," the recourse is to the *Conseil d'État*. But what does it think? The *Conseil* has never produced an enumeration that is a certain guide to innovation. Its judgments are extremely complicated; and councils or mayors in trouble must put any innovation to this administrative judicial test.

The liberality or otherwise of the *Conseil d'État's* jurisprudence is the measure of the width of initiative open to the communes. It is best shown by its attitude to the public social services and utilities. To set up a new public utility, the *Conseil d'État* must be asked for permission by the commune. In England the issues used to be settled by Parliament; the permissions have not been generalized—indeed, most have been nationalized. It might not have been possible to proceed thus in a group-ridden Parliament like the French. But to leave it to a body of career servants? English local authorities would not have liked this.

The *Conseil d'État* says in effect: the commune may certainly have freedom for municipal activities (bounded by its limited area), provided that what it wants to do does not unduly reduce the opportunities of free enterprise to the citizens. Further, the financial soundness of the commune must not be jeopardized by the particular organization of the service projected. This is a limit on municipal activity that does not apply to the central government.

Even well beyond World War I the first criterion was applied quite rigidly to restricting local government services. The commune's lawyers had to prove alternatively that private enterprise had failed to provide the service; that if it had provided it, it was inefficient and inadequate; that the service run by the private entrepreneur was a monopoly; and that a monopolistic service was the only method of administration that would be successful.

In the last generation the *Conseil d'État* became more enterprising: It now merely asks is the service *adequate* and *efficient?* If either is lacking, the communal powers may go ahead. This means that the field of utilities has been thrown wide open, even including funeral service, low-price food canteens, low-cost housing, slaughterhouses, municipal baths, medical dispensaries, and educational movie theaters. This is in addition to the great utilities of transportation, gas, electricity, water, etc. Moreover, though there is a variety of possibilities in the administration of these—mixed enterprise or franchise to private enterprise—the communes mainly prefer the *direct* ownership and management.

Extent of the Council's Authority. In the British system, what the local councils have decided to do, for which they are willing to raise rates and loans, they may proceed to do, by a form of organization of committees and career officials they themselves judge proper.

In France, the decisions of the municipal council, once made, are divisible into those that are directly executable and those that need *prior sanction*. Until they get sanction from the tutelary authorities, the communes cannot proceed to act on the following subjects: communal property, its acquisition or sale; abolition, widening, or alignment of roads; street-name changes; the raising of loans; creation of markets; administration of industrial or commercial services; creation of new municipal monopolies—and the budget of the commune!

The tutelary authorities cannot force the communes to do anything—except the obligatory services. They cannot make them take the initiative and cannot initiate services themselves. They must wait on the willingness of the commune to act. Even in the case of the obligatory services, there must be a tension over the *amount* deemed appropriate to meet the obligation between council and prefect, etc. This gives the local council a great deal of power. The prefect can hardly be willing to act by coercion even in the field of control; and outside it, he is dependent for good communal services in *his département* on pleasant relationships with those who dispose of the public property and raise the local taxes.

It is important to stress, therefore, that though subject to *tutelle,* the French communes are not in swaddling clothes altogether. As for the bigger cities, they are given many liberties. Often a mayor or some powerful councilor is a member of Parliament and close to the Minister of the Interior, since he is a Deputy and the Minister is the employer of the prefects. M. Herriot, former Prime Minister and President of the Chamber of Deputies and of the National Assembly, Mayor of Lyons for years, can hardly be checked by the prefect of the *département* of the Rhône, when his council wants something badly, or does not want to do something which may be lawfully discretionary but is not to its taste.

The mayor immediately submits the council's decisions to the prefect or subprefect. These tutelary officers then decide whether their sanction is required or not. Those decisions that do not require it become effective after two weeks. There may, however, have been, or be, a challenge to them on legal grounds by persons and corporations who claim the decisions are illegal in some way, procedurally or substantially. The prefect will challenge them at once on such grounds.

If the decision is subject to prefectoral sanction, it may be given positively or become automatic in the case of silence for forty days. Most usually the positive approval is conveyed, and then the decision is executable within a week after that. If the power of sanction is higher up, by the Minister or the *Conseil d'État,* then approval may be assumed not to be denied after a lapse of three months; but, for public utilities, six months.

The Municipal Budget

The prefectoral power extends to the budget of the municipality. How different this is from the freedom of English local authorities! The French municipal budget is not valid until the prefect has approved it. He will see that it is balanced; that the obligatory expenses are met; that matters extraneous to the commune are not included. If dissatisfied on these counts, the budget is returned to the council with a request to repair the errors. The mayor must call a special meeting to attend to this and then send the amended budget back to the prefect. If the prefect is still dissatisfied, *he* can amend the budget appropriately. He may cancel appropriations or exclude services. He "inscribes" obligatory expenditure. He cannot levy new taxes or raise existing ones unless to meet obligatory expenditures.

The budget has been made by the municipal council on the sole proposition of its mayor. The members have no initiative in budgetary matters— they may reduce either side but not increase it. The power they have gives them, of course, the power to make informal suggestions that have great force. Since all budget-making is the epitome of the political function *par excellence,* the municipalities and the prefects have their hardest tussles, normally, in this field, especially as a great body of services (not obligatory) is nowadays necessary for city life, and the prefect could not happily see a council spite him by their reduction or abolition.

Appeal to Paris. The prefect is not the final authority over the councils or mayors. The council can appeal to the *Conseil d'État* where the interpretation of legal bounds and definitions is involved, and the prefect must justify his judgment. He is not dealt with tenderly in a conflict with the authority of an *elected* council.

The council has another appeal to the Minister where the prefect is legally impeccable. The Minister can overrule him in any way it wishes.

Mayor and Council

The mayor is the executive authority of the municipality. But he is like a coaxial cable: he has three strands of obligation. He executes the decisions of the council. He is, apart from this, statutorily responsible in his own person for the public security, morality, cleanliness of the commune. This is the restricted sense of the word *police* power: the power of public authority in basic matters. Finally, he is an agent of the State so far as making certain reports and maintaining various registers are concerned. As the municipal executive, he is subject to the council; as "police" authority and registrar, he is responsible to the prefect.

The mixture of the functions in one man exercisable all on the same day, turn by turn, gives the French mayor an awkward role. The mayor in British cities is more of a figurehead than an executive, for the executive is broken up into the committees and their chairmen. He owes no special duties to Whitehall or Parliament.

The French mayor alone may prepare the municipal budget. He is the administrator of its personnel of all kinds. He is responsible for the collection of municipal revenues. He is a responsible and powerful figure, for the spending of the money voted by the council is in his hands; and many matters of the rate, the amount, the timing, the variation of expenditure from appropriation to appropriation are at his discretion. He watches over the fulfillment of contracts that people have made with the council. He may be authorized to bring or defend actions. This allows of discretion in seeking advice, employing law firms, and seeing the case through as far as he deems wise. Very much then is left to his judgment. He may be a slow and cautious spender: the council's will may have been tempered by his own.

The council can sue the mayor before the *Conseil d'État* for malicious abuse of power. That is hard to distinguish from clever politics. The council can appeal to the prefect to order the mayor to stop plain obstruction. This, also, is hard to prove, and a mayor does not usually expose himself to such a charge when he may use more subtle means. The tutelary authorities can, of course, order him to act properly if such impropriety is proved. They can act in default if he continues contumacious. If the mayor exceeds his authority, the council may sue him upward, for annulment, or it may even surcharge him for expenses he has illegally allowed.

Most must depend on the political give-and-take of council and mayor. Party alignments and the strength of personalities, the local newspaper, and the assertion of the citizens are more at work than the ultimate hierarchical sanctions mentioned.

The Conseil Général and the Prefects

The council is in session ordinarily twice a year: in April, for two weeks; and between August and September, for up to a month. There are provisions for special sessions called by the prefect or at the request of two thirds of the councilors or the departmental standing committee, known as the *commission départementale*.

The sessions are public unless five councilors or the prefect or the president of the council ask for a secret session. A vote decides whether it shall be accorded.

The prefect is the executive officer of the *conseil général* and the high officer of the State tutelage. But he is not the president of the council. The council itself annually elects a presiding officer. As used to happen with the county councils in England, some notable (in England, a lord or a knight) is chosen, often a Deputy or Senator. The council also elects a secretary and several vice presidents.

The prefect and his secretary general (not to be confused with the secretary of the council) may enter any session they like. Actually when the council is in session the president is usually flanked by the prefect on the right and the secretary general on his left. It is essential, for the prefect (*not* the president) is the executive officer, and the secretary general is his immediate assistant. All of these, councilors and authorities, will have the benefit of the attendance of the departmental officials and the prefectoral staffs at their disposal to report and answer questions. The council's scope of discussion is unlimited, except if it trenches on "political resolutions." Then the prefect can outlaw the session by his personal decision. This is the result of bitter experience in the nineteenth century, when the departmental councils were used to give aid to, or to rouse revolution against, the government in Paris, not seldom under the agitation of the central government itself.

Powers of the Conseil Général. The powers of the *conseil général* fall roughly into three categories. (1) It has command of the development, financing, and supervision of the administration of departmental services, such as its property, the departmental highways, public assistance, welfare services. (2) It has a supervisory authority in some fields of communal activity—for example, social assistance (fixing hospital charges and allowances to the destitute). It divides the cost of works between cooperating municipalities in case of dispute. It may assist the poorer communes by grants from its equalization fund, raised by its general taxes. We know the influence of such grants: they become aids to policy suggestion. There are many intermunicipal arrangements, since so many are small and poor, and cooperation is necessary and economical; the *conseil général* lays down the appropriate policies. (3) As helpers of national administration or quasi-agents thereof, the councilors are required to provide some of the public buildings in which the regional services of the nation are housed—prefecture, subprefectures, educational headquarters, police barracks, the judicial courtrooms.

They administer State services: those of social assistance in its many branches, including the establishment of sanatoriums, the grouping of communes into hospital areas. Here they can be venturesome above the elementary demands the State makes.

There is a two-way communication between the council and Paris: it has access to Ministers; Ministers are expected to consult the council on matters that concern the *département,* which are substantial political units.

The Prefect and the Council's Authority. The prefect makes the budget; the council debates and amends it at its will, up or down. The accounts for the year are controlled by the council, which demands answers from the prefect on his financial management.

The respective political power of each of these parties rests on their respective abilities and moral strength in and around the budget. The permissions to spend must come from the council; but to spend and to answer for spending is the prefect's business.

Between the two, the prefect is not a legal despot; on the whole, the dominant power is the council's. The prefect has considerable standing, as he represents the Republic as a whole. He has the right to take the initiative in planning new

policies and to recommend the council to undertake new works. He is also the channel of advice to the various Ministers who are the guardians and helpers of the *département*. Yet it is important to appreciate that the power of tutelage over the *conseil général* is not exercised by the prefect as he is empowered to control the communes, because that tutelage for the *conseil général* is exercised by the Ministry of the Interior, the Ministry of Finance, and the *Conseil d'État*. The prefect is in this case not an authority but only a channel of communication.

The power he has in local affairs depends on the length of his tenure in that area—it is normally about five to seven years,[1] not a sufficient length of time to get a final grip—and on his own character and ability. He does have the advantage of knowing other situations.

The Commission Départementale. The *Commission Départementale* is a body of from four to seven councilors elected by the *conseil général* to hold a kind of administrative watching brief when the former is not in session. Its regular meetings are monthly. Its powers are given to it by the *conseil général,* though it is a body provided for in the law of 1871. It has some power regarding the expenditures of the budget not foreseen; it examines the prefect's accounts, controls the budget expenditures. It sees the budget for the ensuing year (sometime before the opening of the August session that usually attends to this business) and prepares a report for the *conseil* of its views on the prefect's draft supplied to it. It also reports on the agenda for the sessions. Here it works a little like the parliamentary Commissions for the aid of the Assembly.

The foregoing authority is derived from the statute of departmental local government. In addition, the *conseil général* may give the *commission* any other powers within its own competence it desires, except the budget, the authority to amend this, or the power it has of authorization of the prefect's accounts.

The prefect can appeal from the *commission's* point of view to the *conseil général.* This can

---

[1] He gets a subprefecture at about 30; a prefecture at 45–50; this leaves him about 20 years, spread among, say, three *départements*.

involve long delays on action. The prefect can also appeal to the *Conseil d'État* for legality of *commission* decisions; then the action is suspended. If the prefect wishes, he may call a special session of the *conseil général* to decide between him and the *commission*. This could end with the replacement of the members by others. These powers of suspension and challenge give the prefect a strong power position for several months in the year.

The *commission* acts rather like a single focusing of all the various standing committees of an English local government authority.

Central Control over the Département. The Ministry of the Interior must approve the departmental budget for its validity *in much the same way* as we see the prefect treats the municipal budgets. The way to change the Minister's mind is to appeal to the *Conseil d'État* on law and to the *département's* parliamentary representatives on the merits of the expenditures, etc. The issues are often susceptible to a meeting of minds somewhere between the original position of either party. Such a case would be the attempted considerable favoritism by a *département* in giving scholarships to Church schools for higher education as compared with the regular public schools. The Minister could moderate the favoritism, but not entirely eliminate it—for the *département* is in the west of France, a Catholic area. He could not avoid the assertion of the principle of assisting Catholic-maintained schools, but he could reduce its bias.

The *département* must supply obligatory services in the same way, in principle, as the communes must. The Ministry may inscribe these in the budget if provision is not made for them—to the extreme of levying taxation himself for this purpose. The Minister's consent is necessary for the raising of loans of large amounts or more than thirty years' amortization.

It must be noticed that, with the growth of modern local social and other services, the *obligatory* services of a *département* have been reduced to but a small proportion of a departmental budget. Hence an attenuation of the central government's powers. The Minister could hardly save his political life in Paris if he were to push the Ministry's career officials' demands for more or differently supplied obligatory expenditures in the face of a stubbornness in the *département* that could refuse to vote any appropriations at all for any of the other services, since it is mistress of its budget!

This puts the French power of central tutelage in a rather less sinister light than in the nineteenth century, especially in comparison with modern British methods of central sanction of administrative schemes, of loans, of grants-in-aid, etc. Moreover, when a decision has been taken by, say, the Minister for Local Government in Britain (within the terms of the last sentence) there is no recourse at all except parliamentary pressure. In France the tutelary authority knows that it must beware of a possible local appeal to the *Conseil d'État*, and questions of law are often mixed with questions of discretion.

The prefect, within this framework, has only the power to challenge the legality of the *conseil général's* policies. These must wait until ten days after the close of the session to become executable. In that period the prefect can bring the matter he objects to before the *Conseil d'État* for illegality. If the latter does not annul the *conseil général's* proposition within six weeks, it stands, however dissatisfied the prefect may be.

Yet the prefect *is* the departmental executive. It would be curious to see an English local authority presided over not merely by its mayor or chairman but, sitting next to him, the prefect and his secretary general—that is, some official appointed to a longish term of office by Whitehall to represent Whitehall. Or in an American city or county, to see the mayor at council meetings flanked by officials appointed by the governor and owing responsibility to the latter. Yet the prefect is mixed into local affairs in this way.

The central government has the last word; but it cannot be harsh with the departmental government authorities locally elected. They are too powerful politically. Hence, the *départements* are areas of very substantial self-government. They have the advantage (if, as it were, the minority status) of not being their own day-by-day masters of the administrative services—here the prefect holds sway.

II. LOCAL GOVERNMENT SERVICES

We list the services supplied by a commune; and then those supplied by a *département*. Their range, magnitude, and quality have marked variations. We make the lists in order that there may be a fairly concrete appreciation of what social and other services are provided in local government areas.

A Commune

Police services: buildings; fire services; laws regarding the conduct of business and the conduct of farming; conscription, civil defense, nationality.

Cultural services: education; regulation of Church affairs (see pp. 303–304); art; library; museums; theater; schools of music and arts.

Social services: social welfare (medical assistance, old-age assistance, family allowances, maternity assistance, welfare of the blind, child welfare of all kinds, free milk, tuberculosis service, etc.), public assistance, charitable assistance, aid to the unemployed.

Public health services: medical care for poor patients; public health; school health and dentistry; sanitary inspection; encouragement of sports.

Technical services: highways; land survey; car parking, parks, and open spaces.

Economic services: aid, encouragement, and regulation (devolved from the center) of industry, commerce, artisan workshops, agriculture, wine making, cattle breeding, fairs and markets, tourism.

Enterprise services: utilities; baths, slaughterhouses.

Property services: pawnbroking; municipal estates, land, forests.

A Département

Police services: law courts, penal law, supervision of aliens and foreign labor (see p. 275), nationality and naturalization.

Public-assistance services: of the kind mentioned in the work of the communes; social security; hospitals and medical service; charitable institutions.

Educational services: elementary, technical, physical, theaters, libraries, museums.

Public-works services: housing; town planning; building societies; highways, ports, bridges, airfields, canals, electricity supply.

Economic services: regulation of and assistance to business and industry, transport, tourism, agriculture, forest cultivation and conservation, hunting and fishing, livestock and breeding, rural police, prosecution of frauds, price control (the central government is not infrequently called in to enact laws and decrees on this, the *département* polices them); labor affairs, social security, mutual benefit societies.

Local Government Expenditures, 1952

Départements (including Seine)

Services	Millions of Francs
General and property administration	21,251
Justice	581
Roads and transport	45,255
Public assistance	119,685
Grants to local authorities and persons	5,393
Utilities, direct	4,019
Utilities, franchised	3,822
Various and contingent	5,720
Debt service	8,128
Acquisitions, works, and repairs	16,965
Special grants	10,728
Special and miscellaneous	7,129
Total	248,676

Communes (including Paris)

Services	Millions of Francs
General administration	58,069
Justice and police	32,984
Safety, health, morals	15,006
Roads, urban and rural	74,383
Slaughterhouses and markets	3,421
Utilities	22,512
Property	29,446
Education, physical education, sports	38,069
Public works and unemployment	1,064
Public assistance, family allowances	37,269
Various and contingent	23,825
Debt service	14,328
Acquisitions, new works, repairs	103,454
Special and various	13,606
Total	467,436

These lists of functions—carried out, of course, in ramifying detail—give support to the importance of the capture of the local councils by the centralized organized political parties. Once installed, they have much to give: the Communist Party has taken the maximum advantage of this largesse.

III. LOCAL GOVERNMENT OFFICIALS

Municipalities may employ such employees as they decide they need. In the smallest places a part-time secretary to the mayor is enough; usually the elementary teacher. Other places employ a large number, full time and part time, in all the categories. The compulsion to fulfill the obligatory services is a minimum limit on their numbers.

Since April 1952 the General Statute for the Personnel of Communes is applicable. It followed on earlier attempts to give officials security of tenure, promotion, discipline, etc., with model charters supplied by the *Conseil d'État.*

First, the law stipulates the general rules for all communal officials of salary, recruitment, conditions of employment, and discipline so far as all permanent officials are concerned. It is possible here only to refer to a few outstanding features of this innovation. Qualifications are laid down for the secretary general of a municipality where there are over 20,000 population—he requires a university degree and must be over thirty-five. If the municipal Civil Service is so big as to employ *chefs de bureau,* heads of departments, then these also must have degrees. For communes under 20,000 the secretary must have passed an examination administered by the Ministry of the Interior, a qualification for admission to which is the holding of a diploma of advanced secondary education or from the Paris School of Municipal Administration *or* three years' service and lower secondary education certificates.

Second, there are advisory councils and disciplinary councils rather similar in their mixed employer-employee composition to those in the national Civil Service, to advise the mayors on service matters and to watch over the fair application of the disciplinary sanctions exercisable by the mayor. In the latter case, a Justice of the Peace presides.

Third, communes which are so small as to employ less than forty permanent officials must join intercommunal associations (a joint board of several communes) to form the advisory council mentioned above. The advantage is obvious.

Fourth, promotions may be made between communes, and the joint communal areas facilitate this.

It must be remembered that the municipality, however small and however big, is free to employ and manage its officials only insofar as it meets the rules suggested above (and also the technical qualifications laid down for the technical officials).

Secretary General = Town Clerk = City Manager

The secretary general is appointed responsible head of all the administrative services and, under them, the technical ones in the commune. His full authority is derived from the mayor, the executive chief. The various bureau chiefs come under the executive authority of the secretary general and, thence, of the mayor. In Britain, the town clerk (p. 252) is a kind of coordinator of the various departments of his local authority; he has no hierarchical authority over them. The equivalent of the bureau chiefs of a French municipality report, not to the town clerk, but to their committees of the council, which has given the latter delegated executive authority over the service headed by the bureau chief. The French have no committees of the English type: the coordination and supervision is therefore drawn together in the hands of the secretary general. The city manager is closer to the secretary general than to the English town clerk: except that where there is a city manager, the fundamental authority he possesses has been delegated to him by the elected council and not the mayor, and the mayor is a figurehead compared with the French mayor, who has the executive authority that is administered day by day by the secretary general.

Officials of a Département

These comprise the body of men around and including the prefect, called the *corps préfectoral,* as well as the various officials of the departmental services.

We consider the latter first, remembering that they are centered in the prefecture, in the capital town of the *département,* a powerful and very distinguished, even awesome, point in the administration of the *département* down to the details of the administration of all its included communes.

These are regulated by a decree of July 4, 1949. They are classified into three senior grades: division chiefs, prefecture attachés, and administrative secretaries of the prefecture. The last-mentioned are the most numerous class of intermediate administrative-clerical officials, the others cluster at the top of the *départements,* as advisers and executants of the secretary general's orders.

The lowest of these groups is recruited by national examinations of junior-college level or from serving State officials over thirty-five of age with five years' service who take a special examination. The attachés are filled by promotion or another university-type national examination. The division chiefs are chosen by the Ministry of the Interior from the top class of attachés—they mount in four classes by promotion. These have access to the position of subprefect to be explained presently. There is the possibility and practice of movement from *département* to *département* and for transfers between local and national service.

Let it be noted, then, in comparison with both England and the United States, how the local-government-control authority at the center of the State has not only laid down rules of local service but *participates* in the actual process of appointment.

The Prefect. The prefect is the kingpin of the *département;* he is, above all, the presence of the State, one and indivisible, in the local scene.[2] He is the appointee and servant of the State, appointed by the Ministry of the Interior entirely at its discretion—and with no voice heard of the *conseil général.* No qualifications are laid down in the law or orders regarding the prefects. They were, in the agitated nineteenth century and even as late as the 1920's, political arms of the government in Paris. Though a tendency to professionalization developed, the Vichy experience caused a recurrence of the olden-time "massacres" of prefects—the purgations followed by new appointments. At the Liberation, once again the connivers were swept out. Hence, the present body is very mixed

but very substantially composed of younger men who constituted the most vigorous of defenders of France's existence against the Nazis; with these are the best of the older generation.

Prefectoral Status. Though the government is kindly toward those who are thrust out of the Armed Services or who retire—by a pension, or other appointments in administrative positions in the central departments, the financial services, in the *Conseil d'État,* and so on—it is strict in demanding the prefect's absolute obedience to its orders. The Minister of the Interior can reverse a prefect on any subject of departmental and communal administration and order him to do as the government wants.

This severity in centralization of appointment and direction is a direct consequence of the size of the country, the distances from Paris, and the hard job the political parties have to get a grip on the administrative structure in their brief spans in office.

The prefect has the extraordinary position of being not only head of the local government of the *département* but head of *all* the services of the State there localized: finance, education, civil engineering. These plan and recommend, but need the prefect's fiat for authority to execute.

From a local point of view the prefect has a "police" power like that of the mayor in the commune, in addition to the executive power to carry out the decisions of the *conseil général.* Whereas in the English system there is a by-law power vested in the council, the prefect has the similar power exercised by *arrêtés* (see p. 466). The main body of the police forces are central and regionalized, but the prefect commands their departmental activities. To safeguard the security of the State, he may arrest people without warrant and search and seize documents. He is the top director of all the State services, administrative and technical, with considerable powers of junior appointment and employee management. All state contracts for works in the *département* need his approval. He is the confidential informant of the central ministries on economic conditions, public opinion, industrial unrest, and political tensions in the *département.*

We have already sketched his status as the exerciser of tutelage over the municipalities.

---

[2] One prefect has listed 5000 functions imposed on prefects by the accumulated laws going back to Napoleon I.

Evidently, he must be à man of exceptional abilities and force of character and discretion.

The Rest of the Prefectoral Corps. We have observed that each prefect is flanked by subprefects, one for each *arrondissement* in the *département,* and by a *chef de cabinet.* Furthermore, the subprefect who is assigned to the *arrondissement* in which the chief town and prefecture are located is the secretary general of the *département.*

All these are appointed by the central government and are subject to retirement at the unfettered discretion of that government.

Many efforts to make a stabilized career of these important offices have culminated in the Decree of June 19, 1950, on the special statute of the *corps préféctoral.* According to this, the entering level of the *corps*—that is, the *chef de cabinets* of the prefect—must be 75 percent filled by persons who have passed through the *École National d'Administration.* This has already been described (pp. 475–483). The graduates are given the choice between the prefectures or the Ministry of the Interior. The prefect is consulted. It is possible for a graduate with an especially good record to start above a fourth-class prefecture. The prefect's wishes are canvassed, because the *chef de cabinet* is the immediate personal assistant of the prefect, a position of immense educational value to the entrant, the most confidential and sensitive spot in the whole *département,* since it includes the affairs of the State, its security, and its politics.

The way of the career is promotion to a subprefectoral position in a *département* of law category. Thence, after intervals of a few years, he moves to higher ones, and some day he will be eligible, by reason of experience and reputation, for a lower category prefecture of his own.

The subprefectoral experience is truly indispensable to a proper discharge of the multifarious responsibilities of prefect at a later stage. For the subprefect is practically the prefect's other self in the *arrondissement,* which is a substantial area of devolved prefectoral administration—it must be, because the area is a large one. He has a range of duties directly stemming from his subordinacy and responsibility to the prefect and only the prefect. He is the election officer; he is the channel of communication in all normal times between the municipalities and the prefecture, upward and downward, for information, authorizations, orders, official documents. His endorsement is needed for the appointment of the rural and municipal police. He exercises the power of the prefect of *tutelle* over the municipalities (some of which, it must be remembered, are very large towns), particularly as regards the budget and police rules, and more widely as devolved by the prefect. He executes the prefect's policy and the government's plans for his area and, like the prefect, is an adviser on the politics of his district —intensely so in the era of the single-member constituency (*arrondissement*) (p. 310). Political contacts and general conviviality offer problems; if he visits a socialist, an M.R.P. Minister may be on his track; if he goes to Mass, must he also attend a Laic Club?

Locally, he is deeply involved in the day-by-day administration of the municipalities, especially the smaller ones, where the personnel is neither plentiful nor well skilled and where, still, the legal complexities of the mayor's tasks are formidable cobwebs gathering food for the spiders in Paris. He may help in the formulation of their budgets and advise on the minutiae, legal and technical, of any one of the innumerable matters—contracts, public works, legal claims to public assistance, arrests of suspects and so forth—that arise in the detailed management of the lives of civic communities. In the small communes, distant from Paris, local affairs become the maelstrom of passionate battles among the citizens, to plague the life of the subprefect by their virulent concentration.

Some subprefects act as secretary general of a *département,* and as such are the right-hand men and deputies of the prefects. A subprefect is the chief administrative official at the head of all the services of all kinds of the *département* and is, therefore, head of personnel administration also. The recruits to the prefectoral service who have a bent for law and indoor administration tend to get themselves into the position of secretary general. It is a most important post, since the secretary general will be the representative of the prefect when the latter is absent or involved in other affairs.

Promotions. It will have been appreciated that the

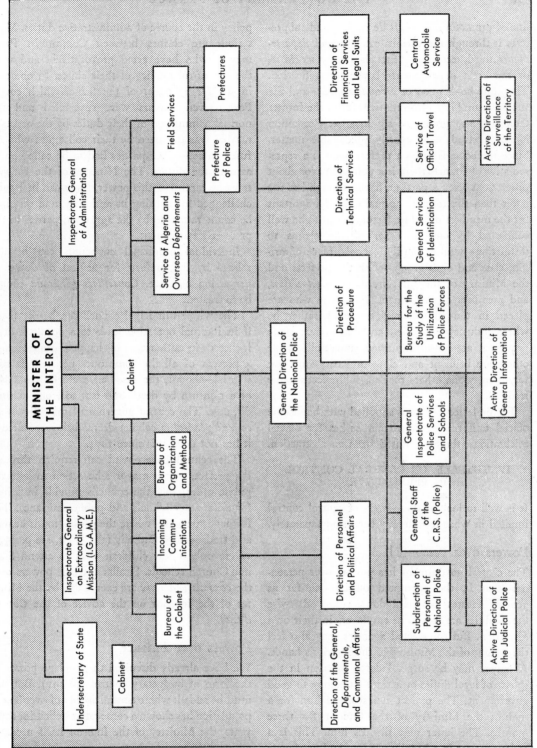

line of promotion for *chefs de cabinet* and subprefects is through the various categories of *départements,* third, second, and first class and *hors classe,* or the great *départements* beyond classification. The same holds good of *arrondissements* and the subprefectoral line of promotion, for in the former there are also grades of significance. Promotion is not a steady and exactly predictable matter. Since the acme is to be a prefect, who is a representative of France, there is a political flavor about promotions, even a partisan flavor, though less the latter than the former, normally. It is important for the members of the prefectoral *corps* to be well connected by one or other of the claims to distinction—wealth, family, schools, place of origin, class and class group—with the prefects and the Ministry of the Interior, the *Conseil d'État,* and members of Parliament. For some who are placed in the Riviera region would rather be where industry flourishes, and vice versa; some provinces are undistinguished and dull, while others are brilliant and close to Paris; some are forgotten, while others make a subprefect's name resound.

The prefectoral corps is supplied with handsome official uniforms with tricolor sashes for official celebrations: the State raised from an abstraction.

IV. TUTELLE, OR CENTRAL CONTROL IN PERSPECTIVE

It is well to look at the powers of central control implied in what has already been said separately.

Powers over Personnel

The central government has powers over personnel—that is, the appointed officials—so far as general statutes have laid down rules; otherwise the localities are free to be employers in their own discretion. But the elected agencies may also feel the weight of the Ministry of the Interior's hands. A mayor may be suspended for inaction in the sphere of legal duties or actions damaging to good government. The prefect can suspend him for a month; the Ministry of the Interior for three months. The latter may dismiss him. This is a serious matter in a heavily partisan and passionate country: men have been so treated for anticlerical behavior, for diatribes against government foreign

policy in the course of administrative duties. More serious are clashes between Communist Party mayors who have acted provocatively and with the rule-or-ruin policy of their chiefs. In one case in the *Département* of the Seine, which covers Paris, seven mayors were suspended and the normal assumption of their duties by the assistant mayors was thwarted by their colleagues who refused to act—other parties had to be called on to assume the duties. The Ministry of the Interior must be careful of this power, for *it* can be legally challenged for abusing its authority, and certainly be counterattacked by the aggrieved parties in the press and Parliament.

Individual municipal councilors can be dismissed by the prefects for neglect of duties or perversion of office. *Conseillers généraux* cannot be so treated.

The whole municipal council can be dismissed if its internal operation leads to a deadlock or if it exceeds its authority. This happens quite often—4 percent of all the communes per year is substantial—though the cases arise chiefly from loss of a quorum by death and less so from internal disputes. The central government may dissolve a *conseil général,* a cabinet decree being required—it has not done this since 1874.

The central government can require, through the prefect, that a mayor take action to preserve public order; that the councils provide buildings for elementary schools and public assistance. The former issue arises where the population is heavily and traditionally Catholic (the West, see p. 357) where only a few children wish to attend State non-Church schools. Similar tutelage powers over the *conseils généraux* are exercisable by the Minister of the Interior on the advice of the *Conseil d'État.*

Powers over Finance

We have already discussed the tutelage power in the form of budgetary control (p. 491). But this must be added: where a municipality of over 80,000 population has shown a consecutive deficit for three years, the Ministry of the Interior itself needs to approve the next budget.

The foregoing may be compared with the British system whereby the local authorities may be compelled to do their legal duty by the issue of an order from the law courts at the instance of an aggrieved person, or may be stopped from an action by a law court injunction where it is acting beyond its legal powers. There is no Minister's power to suspend or dismiss councilors, but in some cases (for instance, public health and assistance) there is a power to act in default and to charge the locality with the expense.

Besides these, as it were, external and catastrophic controls, there is a current control of the decisions reached by local councils. This comes in the form already mentioned of control of legality —and applies to everything the councils decide, whether the substance or the raising and spending of money. In the latter case, the council must beware of the intricate regulations of the Court of Accounts (*Cour des Comptes*), even as a British local council must beware of the court decisions in district auditors' cases. The former, like the latter, may find themselves personally liable to pay the financial burdens they have enacted. The prefect may not feel that he can give the local decision the benefit of the doubt, and so may prefer to raise a case.

Decisions involving the need to raise loans or acquire or alienate local property become valid only when the prefect has given assent, or, if they are unusually substantial, when the Minister has.

As for the kind of control of the efficiency or policy of a local authority's administration that may accompany the audit of its accounts, to the extent that it is combined in Britain with the control of legality, it seems in France to be as minimal as in Britain. But the control of legality is strict. The accounts are audited by no less than three agencies, whereas in Britain it is only one: the Ministry of Local Government through its district auditors. Three agencies of the central government verify the accounts of local authorities in France: the *trésorier payeur général,* the *inspection des finances,* and the *Cour des Comptes.* The first acts in the *département* for the Ministry of Finance; under his authority direct taxes are collected, local authorities' transfers and payments made, and local debts paid. The power over finance includes that of investigation and sanctions over financial officials.

There are some special powers of financial control in difficult circumstances. Thus, if a municipal budget shows a deficit of more than 10 percent in the previous year, the prefect will be joined by State financial administrative officials and the mayor and two of the municipal councilors, to work out the draft and refashion it in such a way as to avoid another deficit. If the local council will not accept the new draft, the prefect can decree it and also (with the persons above mentioned) take over the budget and financial powers of the locality to enforce the budget.

When the *trésorier* audits the prefect's accounts, he tends to assume the role of an administrative-policy arbiter.

The *inspecteurs des finances,* officials of the Ministry of Finance, move on circuits of audit, regular and extraordinary.

More generally, the last few years, they have shown a tendency to go the way of the central government in Britain over the past few decades, in the matter of demanding a previous sanction of the organization to be given to new local activities, such as the utilities. This is done by setting out standard forms of contracts, when, if followed, tutelage-consent is given more readily than otherwise. Also, the leasing of local government property and acquisitions voluntary and compulsory are subject to very exacting control by the prefect, the chief officers of the State services, and three *conseillers généraux* per *département.*

The local representative bodies are not happy in being subject to a multiple tutelage. They prefer the prefectoral line of supervision alone rather than to have it mixed with that of the Ministry of Finance, especially when the latter, through the *trésorier payeurs généraux,* is given a coordinate power with the prefect in sanctioning appointments of local officials in places over 20,000 population or in settling internal financial disputes among the authorities in the *départements.*

Central Inspection and Contacts

Inspection by the central authority is less necessary in the form in which it exists in Britain. There the method is not to set down permanent watchers of local government in the form of the prefectoral *corps* and inspectors of finance, and so forth, but to have visitations from London and regional headquarters. Yet high officials of the Ministry of the Interior make periodical visits to the prefectures in order to amplify for the Minister the reports which they continually receive from the prefects themselves.

There is an association that groups the prefects and subprefects, the civil administrators (see p. 475ff.) of the Ministry of the Interior, the councilors on the administrative tribunals of the *départements,* and the members of the *Inspection Générale* of the Ministry of the Interior. This last-mentioned body of officials is the supervisor of all the services of the Ministry, "interior" and "exterior" in French administrative language. There is thus an intermixture of the supervised and the supervisors. But we have already suggested that there is a substantial movement of employment between the *départements* and *arrondissements* and the Ministry of the Interior. Many of the *directeurs* and *directeurs généraux* at the head of divisions in the Ministry are former prefects. The association we have mentioned cultivates the relationships mentioned. They have an annual meeting at the Ministry of the Interior where for a day or two the anxious problems of local-central administration are discussed with some conviviality.

V. LOCAL SOURCES OF REVENUE

In 1952 local authorities in France drew their revenues from the following sources:

Source	Communes (percent)	Départements (percent)
Additional Centimes*	10.5	34
Various local taxes	46.0	14
Estates	3.5	0.3
Utilities	5.2	2.0
Grants	16.4	33.5†
Loans	10.4	5.6
Various and special	7.5	11.0
Total	*ca.* 100.0	*ca.* 100.0

* Explained below.
† Includes local levies.

The total for the communes was 485,543,000,000 francs; for the *départements,* including the Seine was 247,913,000,000 francs.

Ten years earlier, for the communes, the per-

centages were different to a considerable extent because the receipts from *octrois,* one of the most ancient of local taxes, were still being collected. In 1938 they contributed 8 percent of the total. We return to this in a moment.

The great merit of the British system of local rating to support local services (p. 253) is its stark simplicity of assessment and collection. Whatever injustices it possesses as between individual ratepayers and between localities is to a large extent offset by grants-in-aid from nationally raised taxation.

The French local revenues are both *complicated* and *unjust.* The local councils may raise their funds from a wide variety of sources.

Until 1948, stemming from the *ancien régime,* one such tax was the *octroi,* a local customs duty levied by the commune at its borders on all articles of consumption entering it. (This was one of the causes of the invention of the famous phrase *laissez aller, laissez faire* by the Physiocrats —see p. 289.) From the end of the nineteenth century, however, the Chambers had encouraged the abandonment of this stupid and unjust atavism by allowing the substitution of a variety of direct taxes: dogs, domestic servants, musical instruments, balconies, business transactions, horses, drains, etc.—that is, on visible evidences of wealth. We return to this shortly.

The Additional Centimes

The additional centimes are additions that the local authorities may add to certain taxes raised by the State. Up to 1918 the State actually raised taxes on property, real (land, built-on and not-built-on) and personal, and trading licenses. Then the State changed its sources of revenue, but the local authorities still continue to levy their additional centimes on the revenue that the State would have raised *if* it now actually raised it! The valuation of property that is not new, not demolished, or is (if land) put to other use. Hence a very substantial part of the valuations remain as before 1918.

The communes and *départements* are free to raise the sum of money they want by a process of calculating it by centimes on the basis of that valuation—that is, so many 1/100ths of that valuation. The main variation is in the valuation of the trading licenses—but even this has been stabilized as of 1948, owing to the protests of business that it was being disadvantaged as compared with property.

The communes and *départements* are unequal in the number of additional centimes they must levy to meet their needs, because, apart from the magnitude of these, the value of the land and personal property and trading licenses varies immensely from place to place. It should be added, also, that the value of the franc has changed drastically since 1918, and this makes the valuation doubly fictitious.

In 1913 the communes raised 66 additional centimes,[3] the *départements* 78, on the average; in 1938, 596 and 616; in 1949, 3860 and 6742.[4]

Until 1948 the right to levy these centimes was limited only as to the maximum, which was very high, while the specific purposes were also stated, and they were very various. Since then the levying is limited by categories of permission: for ordinary expenditure; for debt service; for extraordinary expenditures and by tutelage, which operates whenever a locality raises over 80 additional centimes for the three categories already mentioned. The averages mentioned imply, then, that all local budgets are under tutelage.

It is a most clumsy method of raising money, antiquated in valuation, cumbrous in computation.

Local Taxes

This is, as the table shows, the municipalities' main source; for the *départements,* rather subsidiary. There are about 200 local taxes! They fall into three general groupings of convenience. Some are added on to taxes the State itself raises. They are collected by the central government tax officials and the local authorities' share credited to them, less the State's charge for collection. The chief sources are: income from property, furnished dwellings, the rents of hunting, shooting, and fishing rights. Some are required of the com-

munes: a tax on dogs, and this is graduated to make lap dogs pay more than sheep dogs. Others are the entertainment tax, a tax on the sale of alcohol, and a stamp duty on property and financial deals. Finally, the local authorities have freedom to raise various taxes; we have given a list of these above, and to it may be added mechanical musical instruments, hucksters and street vendors, public meeting places. The *Conseil d'État* may give permission for the raising of the rates of these, since a limit is set by ordinance. There are others in this category that are in the nature of a price: for disposal of household refuse, paving of roads, street cleaning, etc.

The predominant character of French local finance as so far discussed is the intervention of the State by laws, ordinances, in the imposition of specific sources and the dictation of maxima. This contrasts with the great freedom of British local authorities to raise rates for the services they may or must perform, without any limitation of the size of the burden they may impose except the revolt of the local democracy. The latter is self-government.

Grants-in-aid

These began to develop early in the nineteenth century, since it was perceived (as in Britain earlier) that some local services are in the national interest and some local authorities are unable or unwilling to raise the sums needed for a proper quality and magnitude of the services. As in England, the idea of a "national minimum" took root. The local authorities are granted a percentage of their expenditure (obligatory) on building schools, air-raid shelters, etc., and public assistance. The percentage is varied according to population, needs, wealth, and density or sparsity of population. Further, until 1940 the Chamber of Deputies, from time to time, enacted various taxes for itself and for the local councils together, sharing the proceeds, say, of motor licenses or business taxes, between itself, the *départements,* and the municipalities, each in a different proportion and each by a different method of distribution.

A stimulus to the giving of such grants was the State's desire to encourage such objects as rural electrification and irrigation. It has come to be

---

[3] That is, 66/100ths of the value of the taxes specified for the State.

[4] So high because local expenses have increased and the valuations are fictitiously low.

extended to "modernization" of town planning, sanitoriums, important roads in the rural areas, forestry, the attack on cancer, consumption, venereal disease, to encourage physical education, to provide out-patient clinics.

There is not, as in Britain, a well-concerted, integrated plan of grants. Each central government department that masters a field of local government endeavor—public health, agriculture, education, the Ministry of the Interior for utilities, and the Ministry of Public Works—disposes of funds within its own department. The grant is given in accordance with the central department's allowance of costs for the works in question; this and the grant vary with the size, need, and wealth of the locality and the social and economic value of the works to the area.

This involves a rather similar kind of need to get central sanction for the local works as pertains in the British system. There is insufficient interdepartmental coordination of the work.

Equalization Fund

Finally, since 1948 there has been an Equalization Fund, obtained from the proceeds of the local tax on business transactions. The total obtained is redistributed to the communes and *départements*. The money goes back according to a formula fixed by law, and partly in the discretion of a committee of nineteen, representing mainly the local authorities, and four officials of the ministries of Finance and the Interior. The formula of the law gives back a certain percentage according to the size of the local authority. Some get additions for having lost grants since 1948. All authorities are guaranteed a small average grant per capita of population, against which the communes richer than the national average must pay their excess to the Fund.

What still remains in the Fund is divided up by the committee of nineteen. This is accomplished by a formula: one fifth for the *départements* and four fifths to the communes. Each *département* gets its share according to area, population, value of the additional centime, length of roads. The four fifths is divided by the *départements* among the communes again on a reckoning of the comparative population, need, financial strength, length of roads, reconstruction needs, density, and a sum for comparative administrative costs. Something would still be left over—5 percent—to be divided as the *conseil général* thought fit.

VI. CENTRAL–LOCAL RELATIONS

The Administrative Courts at the Local Level

It is not intended at this point to cover this subject elaborately. Something more is said (pp. 521–524) in the section on the *Conseil d'État,* which is the supreme and the appellate court in administrative cases, including disputes between local authorities and the tutelary organization. But the *conseils de préfécture* are the courts of first instance in these matters: elections, actions for damages, litigation between local authorities and their officials, contracts, public works. Cases involving the powers of local authorities and the legality of their action are usually dealt with at once by the *Conseil d'État.*

The *conseil de préfécture* (until 1926 there was one in each *département;* since then there are grouping of some *départements*) is composed of four *conseillers* and a President. The latter has graduated from the *École Nationale d'Administration;* some are appointed by transfer from various central government services. These *conseils* act as advisers to the prefect on a few mixed administrative-legal matters he *must* put to them. But they are chiefly the first instance in the cases mentioned above: the *Conseil d'État* stands above it for appeals by the party dissatisfied with the judgment rendered by the local *conseil.*

Police in France

The police forces are under the joint administration of the central government and the local authorities. Covering the whole of France are two forces which are direct central officers: the *Sûreté Nationale* and the *gendarmerie.* The former is a special division of the Ministry of the Interior the latter, a military-type force of several score thousands under the Ministry of War. Under the *Sûreté Nationale* (the Scotland Yard of France) a few thousand plain-clothed inspectors and commissioners act for the security of Paris and the nation. Their police mobiles move wherever they are needed throughout the country, at the discretion of the central government, though it may be on call by prefects and mayors both to detect and help to quell crime and disturbance.

The *gendarmerie,* infantry, cavalry, and armored truck units are located in barracks in the various *départements.* They are at the call of the local authorities; they have authority to act for the nation at their own discretion; they also patrol the national highways outside the municipalities.

In Paris itself, and for the region of Greater Paris, there is a special police force directly under the jurisdiction of the Ministry of the Interior. (Similarly with Marseilles, Lyons, Strasbourg, Mulhouse, Metz, and Toulon, all either strategic points on the German-French frontier or naval bases.) The Paris *Préfécture de Police* is the managing agency under the Ministry; it includes a large corps of all kinds of police officers, amounting to about 16,000 persons, and its bureau of identification serves the whole country in the discovery and arrest of wanted criminals. The budget of the *Préfécture* is voted by the *Département* of the Seine's elected council (see below), but it is prepared by the prefect and cannot be reduced. One half the funds are contributed by the Ministry.

There is strong and sometimes unsavory rivalry between the *Sûreté* forces and the *Préfécture's* forces. Britain has avoided this kind of professional rivalry by having only one force for Greater London—the Metropolitan Police Force—which is under Scotland Yard, both being under the Home Office in a single, not a divided, hierarchy.

For special emergencies the central government disposes also of the *Garde Républicaine:* a Parisian *gendarmerie* of 20,000 or thereabouts.

The central framework of policing, then, is very substantial. In fact, the numbers already accounted for, amounting to almost 60,000 apart from the *Garde Républicaine,* is already more than the whole of the police forces in England and Wales—coping with a larger population. *But* the French need to cover an area over three times as great, and a people more divided and more passionate than the more stolid and docile British. Moreover, the Communist Party has twice since 1945 tried to foment immediate revolution or sabotage of plant, mines, and railroads.

In the municipalities, the mayors are assisted by one or several police *commissioners*—appointed by the prefect and paid by the municipality. They are the servants of the mayor, who is vested with the police authority. They assist the national prosecuting officials in combating crime. The larger towns employ local police officials under the commissioners and the mayors to carry out all the various branches of modern policing in urban conditions: *agents de police.* In the largest towns their institution is obligatory. The officers are under the authority of the mayor, but they need the approval of the prefect on appointment.

All the forces comprised in the preceding paragraph are employed on the basis of decrees of the central government setting out terms of salary and the organization of the force and the police department.

In the lesser rural places, there may be village police, at the discretion of the council. Such *gardes champêtres* (rural guards or police) are appointed by the mayor, subject to the approval of the prefect.

Police Organization for Emergencies. During the Vichy period and at the Liberation, the departmental framework had superimposed above it a regional organization of economic and police (or militant-military) authorities: at the Liberation called *Commissaires de la République.* (The maker of the new Civil Service recruitment method and the head of the *École National d'Administration* held such positions.) After the war the system was dismantled. But the Communist-fomented strikes of November 1947 caused people to realize that their nation was still in danger. For the separate departmental police structures could not be well or soon enough invigorated and coordinated to deal with violent subversive attempts.

The Minister of the Interior, Jules Moch, having put down the insurrectionary attempt, persuaded the Assembly to set up a new organization for emergency situations. Eight regions were established, each with an *Inspecteur Général de l'Administration en Mission Extraordinaire*—Inspector General of Administration on Extraordinary Mission—alphabetized as IGAME. They

assume total control of all military and civil security forces in emergencies, all the authorities being
obliged to put themselves completely at the service
of the IGAME. Each IGAME has a Letter of
Service for use when needed, in which the central
ministries concerned have devolved their powers
to him. The prefects of Toulouse, Lyons, Rennes,
Metz, Marseilles, Bordeaux, Lille, and Dijon are
the IGAME of the region around them, and
evidently crucial appointments. They have been
given special powers of reorganization of the
forces; the secretary general is in charge, under
them, of the arrangements. The system operated
successfully during the miners' strike of November
1948, once again converted by the Communists
into an effort at political destruction. The IGAME
are particularly important advisers of the Government on political and economic movements in
their wide areas.

Education

Education is almost entirely centralized. It stems
from the Napoleonic conception that all education,
at all levels, should be embraced by the university
—one and indivisible, as France must be one and
indivisible—for the whole people. We have seen
(p. 464) that the faculties, high and low, are
regarded as civil servants. This university (from
the original *universitas*) is organized in seventeen
regional *académies,* all under the authority of the
Minister of Education, assisted by the advisory
councils we have described (see p. 467). Each
académie is based on the regional university. The
head of the university is the *recteur,* appointed by
the central government. His qualifications are
academic. He is assisted by a *conseil d'académie,*
and with it, he has authority over the administration of all higher education within his region.

Within the regions, the *départements,* an *inspecteur d'académie* has devolved to him the
authority of the *recteur* for discipline and curriculum in secondary schools and for recommending teachers for appointment in primary schools.
He also organizes primary education, in a council
consisting of himself, the prefect, and the departmental Council of Primary Education, made up
of two inspectors of schools appointed by the
Minister of Education, four members of the *con-*
seil général elected by it, and two men and two
women schoolteachers elected by their colleagues.
The councils of primary education determines the
provision of schools, their curricula, and the
discipline and appointment of teachers. It must be
remembered that these powers are under tutelage.

This is vastly different from the British system,
in which the local authorities appoint the teachers,
even if the basic qualifications are laid down by
the Ministry of Education, and the latter's inspectors watch over the local authorities' maintenance
of standards of quality, numbers, and attendance,
subject to the loss of their grant.

The municipalities pay for buildings and maintenance (a large grant helps them); the *département* finds the money for the administrative expenses of education, excepting for the *lycées,* which
are a direct State expense (aided by funds paid
by the municipalities served by them). Municipalities may establish a college of their own, matching
the level of education of the *lycées.* Then the municipality administers its college; but it is subject to
inspection by the State.

There are, then, three outstanding features of
the French school system, administratively considered: (1) the teachers are State servants, not
local ones, paid and disciplined by the State; (2)
the local authorities have but an advisory share
in the administration, which is subject to the
regional *recteur;* and (3) all examinations that
count are State examinations.

The schoolteachers, especially in the smaller
communes and particularly the elementary schoolteachers, the *instituteurs,* are of fundamental importance in the development of the *laic* (non-
church and antichurch) and republican political
formation of the young minds.

Thus in the instrument that fashions the social
mind—education—and in the agency that sup-
presses crime and exacts nonviolence in the settlement of political, social, and economic conflict, the
central government of France has equipped itself
with a decisive domination over local separatism
and disturbers of the peace. A combination of
revolutionary history, a belief in the sovereign
power of logical systems, and the larger size of
the territory to be governed leads to greater centralization than in Britain.

Decentralization and Regionalism

For three quarters of a century and more, the mind of France has swayed between two conceptions of internal government: decentralization of more power to local authorities, a stream of tendency from Proudhonien thought that favored federalism, and, on the other hand, the fear of intermediate bodies that might arise between the individual and the State, to mar the former's loyalty and service to the national community, a Rousseauite tendency. (Though Rousseau also argued that only quite small states in federal union could give a democratic general will.) The decentralist sentiment has taken the combined form of decentralization and of regionalism. The latter is decentralization to areas larger than the present *départements,* with overtones of a return to the "natural" areas of the ancient provinces. It is argued that the communes are "natural" growths of communities; that the *arrondissements* represent the *ancien régimes'* natural *pays*—that is, countrysides around a chief town—but that the *départements* are arbitrary creations of the central authority.

Regionalism would allow of the release of authority to the local government of these; would evoke civic response and devotion; would allow of better technical provision of services that need large-scale organization for efficiency. Geographic features might form the basis of the regions: rivers, mountains, conurbations, and so forth. Thus, Frenchmen would cease to be merely *administrés.*

It is observed, jealously, that for education and police, for the Army and other local services, the central government ministries have given themselves a regional, not a departmental, territorial structure. No less than twenty-five legislative projects for regional decentralization were initiated in the Third Republic, though unavailingly, to produce more democratic consistency in what Paul Deschanel called "a republic at the summit and the empire at the base."

This cannot be, and will not be, because there would be greater accretions of regional political power to challenge the center. The disrupted history of France is not something that people would like to project into their future. *Local* participation in local government is continuous and strong. Within the *département* the problem of area is solved, or can be solved, by the formation of joint boards, *syndicats intercommunaux,* for special purposes. The regional dream of the geographers and the regional romanticism of literateurs must fail before the political realism of knowing that France needs social consensus.

Paris and the Département of the Seine

Paris rules France—in revolution or in its peaceful forfending. It, therefore, must be ruled. It has a special regime. It is governed as a *département-cum*-municipality in one, and by two prefects, the Prefect of the Seine and the Prefect of Police, both appointees of the Ministry of the Interior and continuously responsible to the Minister. The Prefect of the Seine is head of the *département;* he is "mayor" of Paris and he is the officer of the national government. He supervises all the services of the city and the *département* as does a mayor in other cities—but not over police. That police system we have already sketched (p. 504). The fire-fighting service is controlled by the Minister of War but paid for by the municipality and currently managed by the Prefect of Police.

Within the city are twenty *arrondissements.* Each has its "town hall" and its mayor. The mayors are appointed by the Ministry of the Interior and are subordinate to the Prefect of the Seine. The *mairie* is vested with powers over vital-statistics registrations, civil marriages, the census, registration of voters, schoolchildren and conscripts, the administration of the social services and employment offices.

The City of Paris has a municipal council composed of ninety members, elected in the *arrondissements.* But since 1945 the *arrondissements* have been grouped into six constituencies, each with from fourteen to seventeen councilors. The disciplinary powers of the Prefect and Minister (suspensions, replacement, dissolution) are more severe than in the other municipalities of France. They have not been used since the advent of the Third Republic, partly because the powers are in existence. Though it has a wide power of deliberation and decision—rather limited specifically in the decree laws of the middle of 1939 to the budget, the imposition of local taxes, loans, grants it wishes to make, new communal services, markets, highways, concessions of monopolies by the city, use of the city's property—even here the tutelage power is stronger than elsewhere in France. Before 1939 the city had the same wide power of discussion and decision as the other communes.

As for the *Département* of the Seine, it is governed with the assistance of a *conseil général*. This is composed of the ninety Parisian municipal councilors, as of right, plus another sixty councilors elected by proportional representation by five large electoral areas, each containing a number of suburban communes. These are elected for a straight six-year term at the same time as the municipal councilors are elected.

Since the *Département* of the Seine serves Paris as well as the suburbs, a most considerable urban complex of great population and wealth, the *conseil général* wielded enormous decision-making power, always subject, however, to the tutelary and executive authority of the Prefect and the Minister. Its powers were also limited, by specific inclusions in a list, in 1939. These include the budget.

The political importance of the capital to the nation and the fact that the parties take an interest of marked intensity in the government of its services mean that the prefects and the ministries of tutelage are responsive to the councilors' wishes, more than the strict letter of the law would seem to allow.

The public-assistance services of Paris are specially regulated by specific statutes, and they come under a director general (appointed by the President of the Republic) and its secretary general (appointed by the Minister of Public Health as advised by the Prefect of the Seine). The Transport Authority of Paris was created in March 1948 to take the various means of transport out of the influence of the elected assemblies, which were always conducting a political war over fares and service. It is controlled by the Ministry of Public Works, as a holding company, on the board of which some representatives of the municipal council and the *conseil général* sit. The chief officials of

the Transport Authority are personnel of the Ministry of Public Works.

Thus Paris is much more closely in swaddling clothes than the London County Council; for though the latter no longer owns and manages its own transport (trams, etc.) or its police, it is in charge of its education and its public assistance as well as having a list of permissions to act vaster than that allowed the *Département* of the Seine and the City Council of Paris. Also London is not subject to prefects and mayors responsible for execution of its decisions; these it executes through its own officers and committees.

Politics

The importance of the social and other services in the hands of the *départements* and the significance of the towns with them—together with the fact that the *département* is the basis of political party membership and organization for the national elections—and, further, that proportional representation reinforces the departmental area as the electoral basis of the party lists of candidates connect the local government of France closely with national politics. The result has been twofold: first, to give the important civic localities a power to influence the *tutelle* of prefect and ministers, and second, to encourage political parties to win and hold political power in areas long enough for these to be called their "fiefs." They correspond with the regional distribution of the strength of political parties as already indicated (p. 343ff.). The local distribution of party strength does not entirely follow that of the central parties, for local issues and locally conspicuous personalities break into their blanketed domination. In spite of national parties (which are loose, localized federations except for the Communists, the Socialists, M.R.P., and, to a lesser extent, the R.P.F.) and because a local mayor can be so popular and able, French local authorities are more vigorous and self-governing than the apparatus of *tutelle* would incline one to think. Yet the system is centralized, and it possibly must continue to be, because otherwise the "fiefs," especially of such extreme parties as the Communist and the R.P.F., might become recalcitrant or rebellious units.

Civil Rights and the Judiciary, Ordinary and Administrative

> The general will is always in the right, but the judgment which guides it is not always enlightened. It must be got to see objects as they are, and sometimes as they ought to appear to it; it must be shown the good road it is in search of, secured from the seductive influences of individual wills, taught to see times and spaces as a series, and made to weigh the attractions of present and sensible advantages against the danger of distant and hidden evils. The individuals see the good they reject; the public wills the good it does not see. All stand equally in need of guidance.
>
> —Jean Jacques Rousseau

Nature of Civil Rights

The generous array of civil rights enjoyed by the French match the American and British in scope. They spring from a written constitution, like the American. Their content may be studied in the documents provided in the *Appendix*, the Declaration of Rights of 1789 and that which now is the Preamble to the Constitution. The legislator in France has the authority to add or take away from these, for a revolutionary legislature promulgated them. In Britain rights originated before Parliament (p. 260). The respect of people for rights in Britain is primordial. Differing here very much from the United States, civil rights in France are not guaranteed by the Constitution (p. 330). In France as in Britain, the Parliaments, the Governments, and the judiciary have gradually molded the broadly and concisely stated rights by specific decisions on the balance of liberty, welfare, and order. There is a further conditioning, the *état de siège,* or state of siege, the power of the government to act in emergencies so as to overcome the

forces of internal subversion of external attack—the prerogative power (p. 40).

The judiciary is the continuous bulwark of these many liberties, and the security of the citizen who goes to them for a remedy is founded on their independence.

Each successive regime, in the thirteen since the Revolution, wiped out and relegislated civil rights and added *obligations*. It has been a sadly checkered history, and among its troubles has been an unwillingness to maintain an independent judiciary.

I. THE MAIN CHARACTERISTICS OF THE JUDICIARY

We list the main characteristics of the French judicial system.

1. No Elected Judges

French judges are never popularly elected. In certain special courts of the first instance—the commercial, social, agricultural—there may be a representative of the appropriate group, for technical knowledge or for humane approach, but the judges of the courts, the *magistrature,* as they are called, never emanate from popular election as in so many courts in the United States. Nor are they the appointees of political assemblies.

French practice today, then, is the result of French political experience of historical and unhappy nature. The judges of the *ancien régime* held their posts by purchase and inheritance. They could be independent of the monarch and the court, and we have shown how far they were (p. 281). But this did not insure justice for litigants; it was too class-biased and interested and not open to talent. The Revolution introduced the popular election of judges, subordinated the highest court —the Court of Cassation (concerned only with points of law)—to the legislature, and suppressed the judicial hierarchy. Napoleon replaced this debauched and horribly bloodthirsty arrangement with appointed judges (with slight exceptions).

Since his time, the election of judges has no place in French justice. This is in marked contrast with American practice. It differs from English practice not merely in excluding election, which the English system does, but in excluding appointment by the political authority—that is, the Government of the day—for this is English practice, though with many safeguards. In Russia all judges are elected by the Soviets: this means the Communist Party hierarchy.

2. Dual Hierarchy

The French courts fall into a dual hierarchy: the ordinary courts, dealing with common law, and the administrative courts, from the *conseil de préfecture* up to the *Conseil d'État.* The former are concerned with litigation among citizens and the application of the law to citizens. The latter are concerned with the acts of the administrative authorities in conflict among themselves, local or central, and the grievances that citizens may have against these authorities.

Separation of Powers. The reason for this distinction of the two hierarchies is the determination of the Revolutionary leaders not to have the judiciary interfering in the due march of administration,

not to suffer from the interferences which the *Parlements* (judicial bodies) visited on the monarchical administration. In their law reforms of August 16–24, 1790, they declared:

> Judicial functions are distinct and shall always remain separated from administrative functions.

As time passed, however, it was seen that the so-called "active" administration itself could abuse its powers and needed a corrective. Yet the corrective was not to be administered by the ordinary courts. Hence in the Year VIII—that is, in 1799— a new Constitution established administrative law courts—the most lasting institution in France.

Thus the judges of the ordinary courts cannot, as in Britain, quash the orders of the Administration. Nor can they, as in Britain, by their writs command actions or cessation of action, its correction, or the payment of damages. Recourse in such cases must be had to the administrative law courts. More will be said on this presently (pp. 519–524).

3. The Tribunal des Conflits

Since there are two hierarchies of courts, the border line between their spheres may sometimes become debatable. Hence there was created a Tribunal of Conflicts, original in France and special to her, to decide the respective competence. It is composed of men high in the hierarchy of the judiciary, having equal representation of judges from the Court of Cassation and the *Conseil d'État,* under the presidency of the Minister of Justice.

4. No Distinction between Civil and Criminal Courts

This is not to say that the courts do not bear different names, or that all law is confounded. The mere names of the criminal and the civil codes deny the latter point. But the same judges sit in both; or rather, in the civil courts, from which they are drawn for the trial, when necessary, of criminal cases. Similarly with the French public prosecutors, known as the *parquet* (see below, p. 512); they are occupied with civil as well as criminal cases, though attached to the civil courts.

5. The Magistracy Is One Corps

The judges, all of them except the *juges de paix,* constitute one profession. There is a single hierarchy—*la magistrature*—from the entrant at the lowest rank to the deans at the highest. The higher ranks are recruited by promotion from the lower; the lower ranks enter by the possession of required diplomas and the passing of examinations for the profession of judge. They are not elected by the people. They are not appointed by the government at its discretion. They are not given appointments, as in Britain, after years of distinguished service (more or less) from the ranks of barristers who have practiced before the law courts.

Recruitment of Judiciary. The recruitment method is as follows, as settled chiefly by the law of 1908: Admission to the judiciary is by competitive examination for the number of vacancies stated by the Ministry of Justice. Applicants must be at least twenty-three years of age; they must have taken their *licences en droit*—that is, the first law degree; in addition, they must have practiced in court in an apprentice stage for at least two years as advocate or *attaché* of the *parquet.* According to their order of merit in the examination, they are assigned to courts of first instance. The examination consists of solid tests in the laws, written and oral, set by high judicial officers. It is possible for certain other trained and qualified people to enter the judicial ranks: *Conseillers d'État,* professors of law, barristers who are admitted to plead before the Court of Cassation and the *Conseil d'État,* solicitors, and notaries with ten years of professional experience. Their appointment is, however, rare: it numbers today about one fourth of the total. The successful at the examination furnish the law officers for the magistracy—but this consists not merely of the judges on the bench.

This process supplies (1) the judges on the bench—the "sitting" judges; (2) the *parquet,* a kind of public prosecutor's office attached to each court—the "standing" magistracy, because they plead in court standing up; (3) the staff of the Ministry of Justice at the "civil administrators" level. All these offices are set out in a hierarchy of ranks, with the equivalencing of the ranks in (1), (2), and (3). A promotion schedule, formerly of twelve, now of ten levels is supplied by the Ministry. It starts at the *juge suppleant*—that is, the first rank supernumerary—who may be summoned to do odd judicial jobs or to fill vacancies on the bench or *parquet* for a time, and the *attaché titulaire*—that is, the first rank of the administrative hierarchy of the Ministry. The highest grade is the president of a chamber of the Court of Appeal in Paris. Beyond all classes are such positions as the President and Procurator of the Tribunal of the Seine, equally exalted officers of the Courts of Appeal, and the members of the Court of Cassation—some 120 posts.

This hierarchy of judicial officers is *separate from the recruitment of the Conseil d'État,* which has its own examinations and hierarchy.

Thus the French courts and *parquets* are manned by technically trained, rigorously chosen persons with a knowledge of the law. The law schools are proud of their products and jealous of their quality. All care has been taken to give them some knowledge of economics, political theory, and social science. The competition is very severe. In 1952 only 43 were admitted out of 331 candidates at the examination. The training includes an induction into the frame of mind a judge should have: the traditions of impartiality, thoroughness, desire for justice, the validity of evidence, jurisprudence.[1] The English barrister may have these qualities or not; it is hoped that he will have by the contentious practice of his profession and his knowledge of clients, judicial struggles, and the nature of judges in action before whom he has fought his cases. Sometimes they are and sometimes they are not such good judges. It is a moot point, which is the better method of appointment. Appraisal of the nature of the recruitment depends on the conception of judge and on the process of judgment in court that prevails differently in the two countries. On this something is said presently.

But one thing seems certain: the method of election of judges, as in the United States of America, has nothing to commend it. Its rare successes are entirely accidental, while its normal results are

[1] See A. Crémieux, *L'Avocat,* Paris, 1939, for a discussion of judicial qualities; also Pierre Bouchardon, *Le Magistrat,* Paris, 1922.

painful. The judicial function is *not* in the same category as the making of the laws, from the standpoint of popular ability to make a democratic —that is, an electoral—choice. It is argued by reformers, as in Germany, that the social sciences are insufficiently taught and required. Others, of course, urge education in psychology.

The men who are to be barristers—*avocats*— may have a law education in common with their university friends who are going on to be judges. But after the one has been recruited into the magistracy and the other into the *avocats,* their careers diverge. In England, often in America, some barristers (attorneys) rise to judgeships by appointment or election.

6. The Parquet

This institution, otherwise known as the *ministère public,* or men who act for the public weal, is a famous feature of the French courts. To each court there is a *parquet* headed by a *procureur,* or state attorney, and composed of a number of assistants to him. In the courts of first instance they are called *substituts;* in the courts of appeal they are called *avocats-généraux* or *substituts-généraux.* It will be remembered that they were recruited in the same way as the judges on the bench. The *procureur* is paid the same as the head of the court to which his *parquet* is attached. In almost all the courts up to the very highest it is a much-envied post because it offers remarkable opportunities for personal distinction.

The *parquet* represents the State in court, just as do the district attorney and the Department of Justice attorneys in the United States, and as the public prosecutor and his officers—men who are employed by the government, trial by trial—do in Britain. It alone conducts prosecutions. For this purpose it is loaned the services of the detective forces of the *Sûreté* and its officers decentralized throughout France. It embodies the dual interest of securing a conviction, yet also ensuring justice or fair play for the prisoner. Yet, again, the judge in France is not a man who leans back aloof, and neither to one side nor the other between litigants; he is one who conducts the trial, seeking justice, by means of unrelenting cross-examination.

The members of the *parquet* are irremovable and move upward in their own hierarchy. They are instructed by the Ministry of Justice, within which office they come under the supreme authority of the *Garde des Sceaux,* a political Minister who is Minister of Justice. Yet, in action, they may demur to the law embodied in the written instruction about action in the case and find themselves censured or suspended by their political chief (usually the hierarchy of the ministry) for their attitude. They have the customary right to seek rehabilitation by changing the mind of their superiors by means of reports asking for reconsideration. Their main business is in criminal prosecutions, to secure the repression of crimes. But they act also in civil cases which are of interest to the State, by submitting the point of view of the State on the law, and of the public authorities and of people incapable of presenting their own case. They see that the judgments and petty decrees are executed.

7. Abundance of Judges and Easy Access

The line of courts has the virtue of logical simplicity, of local accessibility. Combined with the fact that French courts never act with only one judge (frequent in Britain) but on the principle of collegiality—that is, with at least three judges on the bench—this must mean that there are many judges. We will see.

There are Justices of the Peace, *juges de paix,* in the petty courts of the cantons, or several cantons put together. (A Rousseauite vision of justice under the village oak: a great hope defeated!) They number some 3000. They have no likeness to the Justices of the Peace in Britain (p. 265). They receive a small salary. Appointments are made by the President of the Republic, on the proposal of the Minister of Justice. Names are usually put forward by the local parliamentary Deputy or other personage. They must have a certificate of some knowledge of the law. They have a limited and summary jurisdiction over minor offenses and civil disputes, the amount of the sum in issue limited to the equivalent of about $100. Since 1951 they are mainly conciliators—and very successfully so. If conciliation fails, the judge may try the case, the procedure of which is simple and without the *parquet.* In the rural areas, this is most important. Above the limit of the sum for which he may try a case, there is an appeal. His judgment includes small terms of imprisonment. Appeals are in the neighborhood of 1 percent.

We now turn to the true hierarchy of courts from the first instance—the true "correctional" courts, as they are called. These are the courts for which the judges are recruited by examination as stated above.

Courts of First Instance. Civil tribunals of first instance are found in almost every *arrondissement* in France—that is, there are about four in each *département*. They have a jurisdiction over all civil cases except those listed in the laws as belonging to other courts. They are appeal courts from the Justices of the Peace and the industrial courts [2] for arbitration in labor disputes (representatives of employers and workers man these). These courts also have jurisdiction in criminal matters— they include theft and embezzlement, but not serious crimes such as homicide. *There is no jury in these courts.*

Appeal Courts. From these courts there is one appeal—and only one appeal—to one or other of the twenty-seven regional Courts of Appeal. Appeals lie in civil matters where the amount involved exceeds $200 (roughly) and in the criminal cases. Twenty-four of the Courts of Appeal are in the provincial large towns and others are located in Paris, two in Algeria, and another in Corsica. These courts operate in two or more sections; each has at least five judges in its civil, criminal, and indictment division. Civil cases stop here, except for appeals on questions only of law to the Court of Cassation, which does not retry the case but settles the point of law and sends back the trial to the Court of Appeal, if the parties want it.

The graver criminal cases are tried by special Courts of Assize, on appeal or in first instance. These sit quarterly in each *département.* The presiding judge is brought in from the Court of Appeal affiliated with that *département;* his two associates come from the *arrondissement* court. It

is here, and only here, that the French courts admit a jury. The jury renders its verdict by majority vote if it wishes; it is not bound to unanimity. But in cases of a 6-6 or 7-5 vote, a unanimous agreement of the three judges may order an acquittal. The jury may submit extenuating circumstances, in which case, if first-degree murder, the judges may not go beyond lifelong hard labor or a twenty-year term and cannot give capital punishment.

It is clear from the geographical distribution of the courts that it is not possible to go beyond them to Paris; and it is not necessary, because there is no further appeal on the facts. In Britain many cases require hearing in London on first instance; and on appeal, there are four steps right up to the House of Lords. This is a great *temptation* to lawyers to urge clients to litigate.

The Court of Cassation. This leaves only the Court of Cassation as a final appeal court; but this does not retry the case, with all its paraphernalia of witnesses and pleading. Its own *parquet,* if not one of the parties, will ask its judgment on dubious points of the law. It is called *cassation* because it may "break" the law of the lower court, not the judgment. It is France's most distinguished court. It has three chambers: preliminary, civil, and criminal. It is composed of a President General, three presidents of section, and forty-five other judges.

In all, the number of judges in France (taking no notice of the *juges de paix*) is about 3600.

8. Collegiality and No Jury

The number of judges in England (omitting the Justices of the Peace) comparable to those mentioned above hovers about 150. This is an enormous contrast. It makes a substantial difference to the national budget, even though the French judges are paid (on an average) only about one third as much as English judges. The greater number is a result of the larger number of courts, and of the fact that no French court is allowed to give judgment, as in England, with only one judge making the court. The French insist on the principle of collegiality—that is, a multiple court—as a condition of justice. It is their way to rule out prejudice. Hence the first instances

[2] Called *conseil de prud'hommes.* They have expertise, naturally. There are also commercial tribunals of unpaid judges to deal with business disputes; the judges are elected by the businessmen.

have three, the higher instances have five, and some more with always an odd number; and the majority decides the case. The belief in the jury was lost with belief in the election of judges, and the tendency of present-day juries to be swayed by passionate pleading does not commend their spread beyond the courts in which they are now employed. Since the jury is not ubiquitous, it is just as well that the courts are manned by a collegial arrangement.

9. Independence and Irremovability

The most difficult feat in this world for those who anticipate or have received an adverse judgment is to believe that the judge is impartial. The next most difficult feat is to reconcile oneself to the independence of the judges, implemented by their permanence of tenure, their irremovability, in one's own case. Hence the propensity to election of judges, to their abuse and removal; all the more necessary is the resolution to assure their independence of mind.

These contradictions of spirit has caused great anguish and violent change of behavior in France ever since 1789. From the purchase of office, the Revolution moved to election, to break the *esprit de corps* of the judges. The Napoleonic Empire declared the principle of irremovability, but, in fact, the judges were dependent on the Emperor. Under the Charter, justice was said to emanate from the King, and the Judiciary was denied the dignity of being a separate "power" alongside the other two, the Legislature and the Executive. Even the former was depressed, and the Legislature is usually a more reliable guarantor of the independence of the Judiciary than an autocratic Executive is. The Republic of 1848 intended to put the judges rather in their present status. Napoleon III copied his ancestor, appointing dependent judges. The Third Republic's constitutional laws did not mention the Judiciary; the intention was to leave it as a public service, like the highways or education, but not to have it invested with the status and dignity of a "power."

The Fourth Republic seems to have abandoned this crass attitude. Yet the courts have not the "separated" status assigned to them by the history

of Britain and of the United States, in the first by unwritten conventions, in the latter as embodied in the written Constitutions of the Republic and the various states.

At each turn of change in the nineteenth century indicated above, the judges of the previous regime were expelled *en masse*. The Constitution of 1848 even declared irremovability incompatible with the responsibility of officials inherent in the republican system of government! The Third Republic, by a law of 1883, expelled the judges of the Napoleonic system and those, also, who had assisted the President MacMahon in the attempt to dominate the Chamber of Deputies by dissolution—in all 1000 judges. The Vichy Government proceeded similarly. At the Liberation in 1945, the Vichy judges were expelled and an ordinance of May 15, 1945, decreed irremovability. It applies to the "sitting" judges, not to the Justices of the Peace *or to the parquet* or to colonial judges.

The Third Republic was not, especially in its early days, altogether loyal to the independence of judges. In the constitutional assembly of 1946 the Communist Party proposed, as in their spiritual mother country the U.S.S.R., the *election* of judges —to insure impartiality! But other traditions— even though formerly honored rather in the breach —prevailed, and measures were taken to secure that the tradition should be observed. This was done by the establishment of the Superior Council of the Judiciary, the *Conseil Superieur de la Magistrature.*

The Superior Council. This *Conseil Superieur de la Magistrature* was organized in Articles 83, 84, and 35 of the Constitution. It was a reaction from the control of the judges by the Ministry of Justice, a position subject to political pressure, itself a sensitive political office. Judges could be ousted for physical and mental incompetence, *mala fide,* crass negligence. The passage of a law by a partisan Chamber secured this.

In the Constituent Assembly the conservatives and Radicals wished to vest the appointment and discipline of the judges in a body chosen by and from the judges themselves. The Communists inveighed against the danger of allowing the judiciary to become a caste alienated from the people.

They proposed that the disciplinary agency be elected by the Assembly, even from among its Deputies. They followed the line that may be read in Vyshinsky's *Law of the Soviet Union* (see pp. 807–08). The M.R.P. and the Socialists were for independence and nonremoval from popular control. All agreed, however, that sole control by the Ministry of Justice could not be tolerated, that supervision of the judges must be vested in an agency independent of the Executive.

The constitutional provisions are as follows (see text in *Appendix*): The Superior Council of the Judiciary is composed of fourteen members. The President of the Republic and the Minister of Justice are chairman and vice chairman, *ex officio*. The other twelve sit for six years. They stem from two sources: six are chosen by the judicial profession, and six are chosen by the National Assembly from outside its own membership by a two-thirds majority; there is no limit to the number of terms to which they may be elected. The six representing the profession consists of one member from the *juges de paix,* the courts of first instance, the courts of appeal, the Court of Cassation respectively, elected by their own body; the other two are appointed by the President of the Republic from the rest of the judicial professions. The six who are not National Assembly-elected are not reeligible.

The six-year term has a significance. It overlaps the term of a National Assembly, for the desire of the Constituent Assembly was to break into the circle where professional jealousies might spoil the course of competent justice rather than to put political pressure on the judiciary.

The parties have chosen, not politicians, but jurists, as its composition shows. One incident of the President's power is of great interest. In 1950, a Communist member broke with his party and offered to resign. The President of the Republic would not accept the resignation. Later this same member was expelled from the Council on the suspicion that he had passed to the party a confidential document of the Council, published by the Communist Party in 1948. In the filling of the vacancy, which requires a two-thirds vote, the Assembly's Commission of Justice never reached a decision; thirteen ballots, taken in a period of twelve months, produced no two-thirds majority.

The Council meets weekly at the palace of the President of the Republic. We pass over its important power to advise the President on his power of pardon and concentrate on its disciplinary power over the judges.

In this it takes the place of the Court of Cassation. But it also decides on promotions, taking over this power from the Ministry of Justice.

10. Promotion in the Judiciary

The arrangement made for discipline that could result in dismissal, mentioned above, is substantially satisfactory. A word must now be said on promotion. An English judge expects no promotion. The opportunity is rare indeed. He stays in the position to which he is appointed after his career as barrister is ended. He is therefore under no temptation to give judgments which may bring him promotion.

When, until 1945, promotion was fully in the hands of the Minister of Justice, a politician, the independence of justice was jeopardized, not only by the possibility (rarely used) of expulsion but substantially by the exercise of political influence in promotions. This came about, in part, because a substantial number of advocates before the law courts were members of the Chamber of Deputies and the Senate. They were powerful orators and powerful members in their political parties. They were alleged to be able to secure convictions or acquittals not available to less politicized advocates. Their political power with the Minister of Justice made a difference to promotions. As French judges are poorly paid, promotion is their very anxious concern. In other words, the independence of justice is to be obtained by irremovability *and* decent pay, in order to remove the judges from material temptation. It is not necessary, as all French professional salaries show, to make a man a millionaire in order to insure his integrity in his vocation, but salaries can be so small as to make higher ones a matter of temptation. It ought not to be so low, or the regulation of promotion process so open to influence, as to make any judge servile. But in the Third Republic some judges were afraid to reject the arguments of *avocats* who might well become the friend of a Minister of Justice or even become the Minister himself.

Therefore the Superior Council is endowed (Art. 84) with these powers:

> The President of the Republic shall appoint the judges whose names are submitted to him by the Superior Council of the Judiciary [with the exception of the *parquet*].

> The Superior Council of the Judiciary, according to the law, shall ensure the discipline of these judges, their independence and the administration of the courts.

> The presiding judges shall not be removable.

It is concerned with as many as 1000 posts a year. Its procedure is guided by a law of March 11, 1947.

Yet the Ministry of Justice is unreconciled to the powers of the Superior Council. It has succeeded in getting the right of countersignature of the President to warrants of appointment and promotion—though the power has not yet been used to upset the Council's decisions. The Government in 1948 attempted to reduce the powers of the Superior Council, but the project was not reported out of the Commission of Justice. The Council, on the other hand, has wished to extend its powers to the *parquet* and the *juges d'instruction* (see later, p. 517), and this project also was lost in the Commission. It is a parlous situation when the Ministry of Justice still prepares the dossiers on the judges for the use of the Superior Council because the latter body has an insufficient staff— yet the last word is with the Superior Council. The personal influence of the first President of the Republic, Vincent Auriol, for example, in exercising sober clemency in the pardoning of Frenchmen to be purged for wartime collaboration, etc., has been a creative influence, making for political moderation in matters judicial.

11. Procedure Is Judge-animated

In the law courts in the United States and Britain criminal cases are initiated by an attorney who prosecutes on behalf of the public. It is his business to make a case. The prisoner is defended by an attorney paid by himself or provided, if he is too poor, by the public funds. It is his business to prove that the prosecution has no case. Both sides rely on witnesses and other evidence to impress the judge and (if there is one) the jury. The judge acts as an impartial arbiter between the two rival presentations of the case. He may ask questions of counsel and witnesses and the prisoner in open court. But he is not an interrogator. Nor is there any previous inquisition, except in cases whereas a grand jury is required for an indictment.

The position is different in the French criminal courts. Before the case comes before the judge in court, there are preliminary investigations to prepare its presentation to the judges. This is in charge of the *juge d'instruction*. He has the power to order arrests of suspects and hold them until his investigation has indicated whether he should release them or not; he seizes documents and other objects of evidence; he interrogates suspects. This power goes back to earlier ages, being a process of questioning of an inquisitional nature designed to obtain confession. Though violence or constraint in any form is forbidden, the interrogation is powerful. Attached only to courts of first instance, the *juges d'instruction* do not form part of the most elevated ranks of the judiciary. They are under the supervision of the *parquet*. Such a man's ambitions are extremely pointed toward promotion. It is a sensitive point in the course of justice, especially since it is connected with the problem of arrest and detention.

The judge is, more than the English judge, a kind of party to the issue: he seeks the facts, whether there is a jury or not. It does not, however, follow that he will exercise a zeal for conviction any more than for acquittal or hand down a fair judgment. The French judge is skilled in the law; this means that he has mastered the codes in which French law and procedure have been embodied. Cases are cited, but they have nothing like the preponderance of value as in Britain and America, which are lands without codes and commentaries and where, therefore, the lawyers must argue from a multiplicity of cases. The French judge certainly is confronted by the *parquet* and the barrister for the other side, but he thrusts himself into the issue and, in the absence of a jury (for all civil cases), he is a judge of facts as well as law.

12. Absence of Habeas Corpus

Nothing resembling *habeas corpus* exists in France. It indicates the supremacy of the notion of the rights of the community over the rights of the individual. In the abortive constitution of 1946, Article 9 had attempted to remedy this lack. For it stipulated that

> No one may be detained unless within forty-eight hours he has appeared before a judge called to rule upon the legality of his arrest and unless this judge confirms the detention each month by motivated decision.

This was swept away from the new Constitution on the claim that the Declaration of Rights of 1789 satisfied the situation.

But the position is not pleasant. Warrants of arrest are issued by the *juges d'instruction:* the warrants have not always been precise. The *parquet,* the prosecuting office, may order the *juge* to effect an arrest, and the prosecutor is under the orders of the Ministry of Justice. Arbitrary action is possible. The notion of flagrant crime—caught in the act—has been given wide interpretation by the judges and the police, even allowing the charges made by a few people to be justification for such an arrest. The *juge* can hold the arrested person in preventive detention until he has finished his interrogation and collected the evidence he thinks will establish the guilt or the innocence of the accused. For how long? The criminal code (*instruction*), Article 113, is today still the form of 1865: the *juge d'instruction may* (*not* must) order provisional liberty if the accused asks it. There is no term set to the duration of preventive detention except that, when the penalty is less than two years' imprisonment and the accused has never before been convicted, he must be freed five days after the first interrogation—but this may last some time. Often it has lasted very long indeed, especially in political crimes, the very ones requiring freedom. There is no way to get the prisoner out of the hands of the *juge* automatically. The release, if given, is on bail. An appeal to a higher court takes much time. Meanwhile, the person is in jail with same conditions as a convicted man. Some cases during the last two or three years have aroused an outcry in the legal profession, the press, and the Parliament against seriously excessive detention, incompetent interrogation, and withholding of legal assistance to the accused in such wise, indeed, as to make innocent people suffer for years the possibility of a verdict against them.

Many officials, including the police, mayors, and prefects, have authority to make arrests. They must send the material to the *parquet* within twenty-four hours. This merely gets it transmitted to the *juge d'instruction*. It is his responsibility to let the prisoner free (on bail) if continued imprisonment is not indispensable. This leaves the matter to his judgment.

13. Political "Justice"

The constitutions of the nineteenth century provided for *impeachment*—that is, accusation and judgment in crimes of a political nature beyond the ordinary; accusation by the lower chamber, judgment by the upper. This was also the situation in the Third Republic. The Fourth Republic provides for this under Article 57, and in the following articles sets up a High Court of Justice. This deviates from the Third Republic, because there the Senate was a strong political body while now the Council of the Republic is both legally and practically subordinate. Hence, today the presentation of impeachment is made by the Assembly, by absolute majority, in secret session. Those who participate in the judgment are excluded from voting at this stage.

Judgment was lodged in a High Court of Justice, the law organizing which was passed in October 1946, simultaneously with the voting of the Constitution. It is composed of a president, two vice presidents, and thirty judges, all of whom are elected by the Assembly. Twenty are chosen from among the Deputies, by proportional representation of the political parties. Ten others are elected by a two-thirds majority in secret ballot—these must not be members of the Assembly, but may be (and some are) former Deputies. The presidents and vice presidents are Deputies—they are chosen by the latter method. Thirty alternates are elected similarly; so, also, three prosecutors (may be present Deputies) and six out of nine of a *commission d'instruction,* who prepare the case. These must be present Deputies. The other three are named by the Superior Council of the Judiciary; they include the chairman of the High Court.

The offenses are treason by the President of the Republic, and offenses in office by Ministers. Decisions are taken in secret; they require an absolute majority.

In March 1950 the Communist Party moved that three Socialist Party leaders be impeached for their connection with wrongdoing in wine imports in 1946. The Assembly rejected the motion. In November 1950, always the purest of the pure, the Communist Party moved the impeachment of Jules Moch (he had been one of their earlier three targets) for wrongful actions in the affair of the generals (see p. 437). They hated him because his security organization when he was Minister of the Interior had broken Communist violence during the strikes. The Deputies—in secret session—approved the motion by 235 to 203. The Cabinet took this to be merely a maneuver of Deputies who disliked Moch and the Government. It demanded a vote of confidence in public session, and obtained it. The secret motion was ignored.

This Court had been preceded after the Liberation by a special political court to judge the Vichy Government Ministers and officials. It had the same title as this permanent court. Its procedure may be learned from the trial of Pierre Laval, in *Le Procés Laval,* by A. Michael, Paris, 1946.

14. Cheapness of Justice

The courts are geographically close to the people; there is only one appeal on facts and law, and only one more on law. Moreover, French lawyers argue from the great Codes, not by the adducing of hundreds of cases from which the law today *may* or *may not* be gleaned. Hence the process as a whole is much cheaper than the seeking of justice in Britain or the United States. Furthermore, there is a rigid, official scale of charges for the services of the attorney and the notary.

It will not be forgotten that the French educational system, because it is not free and subsidized up to the university level, must make the judiciary far more accessible to the upper-middle and wealthier levels of society than to the poorer. Justice might be less cluttered with time-consuming red tape than it is and be removed from suspicion of conservative bias, if a more representative sample of the class and group levels and experience entered the judiciary.

II. THE CONSEIL d'ÉTAT AND THE ADMINISTRATIVE COURTS

Administrative Jurisdiction

We have observed that the French interpretation of the separation of powers requires that the Administration *per se* (not as officials committing *personal* faults while in office) be exempted from submission to the ordinary courts, but also that it ought not to be its own judge where citizens challenge its legality of action. They distinguish between the *administration active* and the *administration contentieuse.* The former is the everyday activity of the administration officials; the latter is administration in matters contentious, where a challenge has been lodged against the former. The latter is the sphere of the administrative courts, with the *Conseil d'État* at their summit.

The State Put on Its Defense. The implication is that, differently from Britain and the United States until very recent years (see p. 215), the French State has admitted and admits that the State as such can be sued for a fault of its officials acting in their official capacity, and that it will punish the offender and indemnify from its own funds the person injured. It supplies courts in which the cases may be brought; it makes them geographically accessible; and it makes the procedure very inexpensive, based on a scale of low charges set down by the *Conseil d'État.*

No Monopoly of Administrative Jurisdiction. Before we proceed to discuss the nature of this administrative jurisdiction, the student must clearly understand that the *Conseil d'État* does not concentrate in itself *all* lawsuits concerning the public administrative authorities. Many administrative activities have been established by the State in a private contract-*cum*-private-enterprise form: such as corporations for economic production and commercial operations, where the civil contract is used to rule the relationship between producer-administrators and their clients and customers. These are fought before the ordinary penal and civil courts, as already described. This sphere tends to grow with the growth in State activity, since by new administrative devices it is attempted to secure the flexibility and inventiveness of private business in such enterprises as the nationalized services (pp. 462–464). These and similar semi-inclusions of business sectors in the operations of the State have resulted in the building of an administrative edifice operating in the public interest and on public statutory standards that is exempt from the *Conseil's* jurisdiction and subject to the ordinary courts. Between the two sectors the line of demarcation is statutory rather than substantial, and it raises problems of definition, logic, and expediency in the process of practical solution, and this again raises questions of which judicial hierarchy ought properly to be vested with the jurisdiction in dubious cases. It is important to realize, then, that not all acts of administration which might be defined as "public" are channeled into the portals of the *Conseil d'État.* Yet it still has a tremendous jurisdiction, for there is, as we have seen, an exceptionally wide field of direct State activity in France.

Reminder of the Conseil's "Legislative" Functions. On other pages (384, 466) we have indicated the statutory powers of the *Conseil d'État* regarding the drafting of laws, of decree laws, and of rules of public administration. These interests keep the "judge-councilors" in touch with the living realities of law and administration, the execution of which they may later judge during litigation.

The Sphere of the Conseil d'État. We state this in two quotations, one from the decisive judgment by M. Romieu in February 1903, and the other from a comment made by the vice president of the *Conseil d'État.* René Cassin, professor in the Faculty of Law in Paris.

The judgment says:

All actions between public authorities and third parties or between these public authorities themselves and based on the execution, the nonexecution and the bad execution of public services are within administrative competence and belong, in the absence of a specific text, to the *Conseil d'État,* judge in common law of cases involving the general or local public administration.

Professor Cassin's statement is: [3]

It is, in truth, indispensable that the judge charged with judging cases against the State shall know how to avoid shackling the actions that are necessary in the public interest, by his anxiety to safeguard individual interests, even if they are legitimate. But it is also necessary that the judge should know how to secure the protection of those individual interests, injured by acts against which one can formulate no legal criticism whatever, by allocating considerable compensation for damages and interests, destined to assure protection to individuals who have seen their property or their person suffer as a consequence of the necessities of the general interest.

It is most important to bear in mind that the principles of its jurisdiction—that is, its view of its range of power in judging the Administration —are not stated in a statute but are self-made, developed by the *Conseillers* through a long history, even as the judgment given by M. Romieu and stated above was never stated in any enactment made by the parliamentary bodies. Its principles, some of which, will be discussed presently, are judge-made; the *Conseillers* have been and are creative judges in the establishment of a remarkable edifice of legal norms applicable to the acts of public officials.

Immensity of Difference from Britain. The traditional glory of the British system of justice is that all men and women, officials or not, come under the jurisdiction of one set of courts—the ordinary courts—and the same judges and under one system of law, basically the common law. This is the essence of the classic doctrine of the Rule of Law as enunciated by Dicey (see p. 4). The British believe that this keeps the officials from becoming a caste and assures that the officials will not be judged more tenderly by special courts that might be established to judge them. It can be seen that the riddle is to be solved by the composition, the independence, and the mentality of the courts:

---

[3] *L'Organisation Gouvernementale . . . de la France, Documentation Française,* Paris, 1952, p. 65.

these are the decisive things. Can *special* administrative courts be so devised as to be independent in their judgment of the individual against the public authorities? The French have thought so. Hence these courts. We have shown where the British tradition has its weaknesses and also the weaknesses of its criticism of the French system (p. 213ff.).

Growth of Administrative Jurisdiction. In 1791 the ordinary courts in France were forbidden to handle administrative functions and cases. In the Year VIII prefectoral councils (courts) and the *Conseil d'État* above them were created to judge administrative actions when challenged. At that time the *Conseil* was primarily a legislative and rule-drafting body—but its powers included administrative contentions. In time the *comité du contentieux* of the *Conseil,* under the Chief Justice, took over the increasing business of administrative cases, increasing because the procedure was cheap and prompt. So far, it only gave advice; the Minister did or did not carry it out. In 1848 it obtained the right to pronounce judgments. Liberals, such as de Tocqueville, were rather afraid of this new jurisdiction; they would have preferred to have the rule of the law as stated in the statutes and not subject to discretion before the ordinary courts, allowing the *Conseil* only cases founded on prerogative (see p. 40) and discretion.

Up to 1872 the *Conseil's* jurisdiction was limited to specifically stated classes of action. In 1872 it was given general and sovereign authority in administrative actions:

> The *Conseil d'État* has sovereign decision in actions of administrative contentions, and on demands for the annulment for exceeded power brought against the acts of the various administrative authorities.

Organization and Composition of the Conseil

In the same year (law of May 24, 1872) the *Conseil d'État* was also given its modern basic organization and composition, which, with some occasional amendments of the law of 1871, is now as follows.

There is a vice president (who is the effective president, since only when it meets on special occasions does the Minister of Justice of the President of the Republic preside over the *Conseil d'État*). Then come five presidents of sections. Below them are 54 councilors, then 45 *maîtres des requetes,* and beneath them, 44 *auditeurs* of the first and second class. In all, 149 members.

Two thirds of the ordinary *conseillers d'état* are recruited by promotion from the *maître des requetes,* the rest (and the 12 extraordinary *conseillers* out of the total of 54) are chosen from among the high levels of the Ministries, from the prefects. These extraordinary *conseillers* are nominated for periods of one year at a time, renewable. The *maîtres des requetes* rise from the class of *auditeurs,* but some come by transfer from various Ministries and some are legal specialists. The recruitment of the *auditeurs* we have already explained; they come from the students at the top of the examination lists of the *École Nationale d'Administration* (see p. 479). The members come from and go to the life of active administration; as administrative judges, they are not without a sense of pressing realities in the governmental process.

The great corps is recognized as the very élite of the nation's administrative personnel. It is truly distinguished and deserves its noble prestige.

The *Conseil* falls into five *sections.* Four are concerned with the administration and legislation covering various departments—Interior, Finance, Public Works, Social Affairs—because they are involved in the conduct of tutelage, advice, and the drafting of legislation and administrative decrees, etc. (see p. 384 and p. 466).

When matters before the *Conseil* affect two or more ministries, the appropriate *sections* meet together. The officials of the various government departments and the Ministers themselves may appear before the sections to put the departmental point of view. The *Conseil* may call in experts from the outside for specialist opinion on matters before it administratively. In the section that deals with the Interior the affairs of all the local authorities come; and education and justice. It is clear that sections must join when a local authority requests, for example, a loan for public works; this would need the opinion of the section that deals with Public Works.

The fifth section is the *Section du Contentieux.* This is the descendant of the *comité du contentieux,* the body that acts as a court of administrative justice. It consists of a president, 18 *conseillers* with the addition of a few from the administrative sections, some 30 *maîtres,* and 28 *auditeurs.* There is then a division into eight subsections, each with three *conseillers.* These *sous-sections* have assigned to them the various classifications of subject matter of government open to challenge, and they prepare a decision after hearing pleas and being offered evidence.

Jurisdiction

The State officials and the municipalities as corporate bodies are responsible for their actions; they can be sued in the administrative courts (we have already mentioned the first-instance courts, p. 504) and may be compelled to pay damages for any prejudice to life and property caused by "defective" action. *Defective* means lack of legal competence, violation of the prescribed forms, violation of a law, misuse of power—"the negligences, the omissions, the errors among the habits of administration when those habits are bad," in the words of a great master of administrative jurisprudence, Maurice Hauriou. The fault will entail condemnation and damages when the administrative fault is *lourde*—that is, weighty—meaning when it is beyond the *average* incompetence to be expected from the mass of men and officials. Here is an important discretion on the part of the *Conseil.* But it is tender toward the citizen, as we shall appreciate.

We have said that the State is suable and will pay. The limit is where the official was not truly acting in good faith for the public. For a *faute personnelle,* something done in office but not truly in pursuance of its purpose, the official himself is responsible, not the State. He will have to be sued personally before the ordinary courts for damages. Who decides what is, in a subtle case, *faute personnelle* or *faute de service* or *faute de fonction?* It is the *Tribunal des Conflits* (see p. 510). For

example, a teacher teaches his pupils to read (legal duty, but perhaps badly performed—an administrative case may arise), but meanwhile makes revolting remarks about God (a personal fault). Or an official posts an electoral list (legal duty, but may make some error in this, leading to an administrative case), but makes public the view that one of the electors has been excluded because of bankruptcy (this is a personal fault, suable by the bankrupt for damages). The decision in many cases is highly subtle, and there is a continuous concentration of legal minds on the dividing line.

Once the personal-fault issue has been settled and an administrative case is justified, the way is clear for a request for justice. There are various kinds of action. The case may be founded on *excès de pouvoir,* where the official has gone outside the bounds of his legal authority, based on the statutes and the regulations.

One kind of suit is *de pleine juridiction,* full jurisdiction over the annulment of the action of the official or the local authority when it occurs to prevent continuance, and if possible before injury occurs; also to give damages. If the act has caused injury, the action is for indemnification. The latter suit is a suit (*recours*) against *excès de pouvoir;* the former need not be *contentieux,* but the latter is, for the parties fight against each other's case. The suit may be merely for "annulation" (annulment) or amendment of an act (an *arrêté,* a decree, an order); or it may be for damages.

Excès de pouvoir may be plain violation of the law; or it may be subtle use of an official's or local authority's legal powers with the purpose of securing an end not permitted by the law: this is called *détournement de pouvoir* (embezzlement of power).

Annulment may come about on the grounds of no legal competence; wrongful form of action; or, as said above, cunning use of the law for a nonlawful purpose.

The public authority has in the jurisprudence of the *Conseil* been made responsible for "lack of foresight" or even for sheer unavoidable accidents, as in an explosion on a naval vessel, because in the present state of science it has been conceded that the fault of the service may not be assigned to specific cause. This theme has thus been expressed *à propos* of a leading case:

> When this vast machine, called the State, a hundred times more powerful and a hundred times more dangerous than the machinery of industry, has injured someone, those in whose interest it functioned when the injury was caused must make restitution; the principles of solidarity and mutuality upon which our constitutions are based, require it.

Though there are limits to the "self-interest" that the *Conseil* allows to qualify for the right to bring suit, the range of "interested" persons allowed is extremely wide. It includes electors, taxpayers, heads of families, inhabitants of municipalities, businessmen, landowners, civil servants, and members of corporations. Nor, except for what is said later on "acts of government," is there a limit to the official acts and the officials within the scope of entertainable suits.

Its General Principles. They are always in a process of development within the framework of the statutes made by the Parliament. Like the judges in the British courts, they cannot make themselves superior to the expressed will of the National Assembly, but their creative activity lies within the letter of the law; the vagueness of the laws is the horizon of freedom for the *Conseil*. Its general principles are those of the Declaration of Rights. Developed from these and alongside them is the principle of equality of all persons before the services performed by the public authorities, such as taxation and in respect of race, religion, sex. The impartiality of the services is required: the "indifference" or the objectivity and impartiality of the officials between businessmen asking the same privileges or charges when in cognate activities, also of all persons subject to financial and other duties they have to render to the State, by command of the law and the executive decrees. The *Conseil* is Draconic is its annulment of retroactive official actions, and takes this attitude toward the interpretation of statutes unless the one in question is explicitly creating retroactivity. And, of course, it maintains the principle of its open welcome to proceedings from any person with a "self-interest" against any administrative act, as a public right,

regardless of whether or not a statute directly establishes it.

A Case in Point: Five Candidates for the École Nationale d'Administration. Earlier (p. 441) we referred to the exclusion of five candidates from the list of would-be entrants to the Higher Civil Service. They brought a case before the *Conseil d'État* for annulment, and on May 28, 1954, this was pronounced on the grounds of legal errors and *excès de pouvoir*. The decision to strike the candidates off the list had been made by the Secretary of State, who, with the Prime Minister, is in charge of conditions of entry into the Service and establishment of the list of candidates for examinations of entry to the *École*. The form of the decision was an *arrêté,* a decree (see p. 466). The *Conseil* conceded that so long as the Secretary of State had this obligation, then (following the words of its own judgment, the *Arrêt Sieurs Barrel et autres*), he had the right to

> . . . appraise, in the interests of the Service, whether the candidates presented the guarantees required for the exercise of the functions to which the studies pursued at the *École Nationale d'Administration* gave access, and he could, in this respect, take account of facts and manifestations contrary to the reserve which candidates should observe. . . .

The *Conseil* set up against the need of such guarantees, the principle of the equal access of all Frenchmen to public office, as stated and reaffirmed in various Declarations of Rights. It found that the Secretary of State (1) had refused to communicate to it the dossier of two of the candidates at all, thus making it impossible for the Secretary to prove *his* contention that political opinions had nothing to do with his decision(!); (2) in the other cases had submitted a collection of personal data that had no bearing on the issue of striking off the list for political opinions; and (3) had left the clear impression through statements made in the press by officials connected with him and the director of the *École* that the motive was political. Hence, the withholding of the dossiers or the faulty maintenance of them (and the Civil Service statute requires that for a candidate already in the Service proper files must be kept *and* communicated) was a disobedience of the statutes, while the exclusion from office or candidature was an excess of power because it conflicted with the principle of equal access to office. The commissioner who reported the full argument before the *Conseil* had asked:

Is the measure by which a candidate is excluded from the operations of a competitive examination by reason of his political opinions or his membership of a political party founded on a correct juridical principle?

He answered:

For a Frenchman, to pose the question is to solve it. The principle of the equality of citizens in access to public office forms a part of the general principles which constitute the basis of our public law, because they are organically connected with the democratic regime, which is ours, with the body of concepts of equality and liberty which this regime supposes politically, socially, economically and which are intimately anchored in our minds and hearts since 1789.

He conceded that the State had its rights also: the necessities of the public office to be discharged, and the compatibility between the fitness of the candidate and these charges. But this must be shown not by what a candidate might think or his membership of a party, but by "a public act." Even the appreciation of this "public act" was in the jurisdiction of the *Conseil*. But no such acts had been adduced; the dossiers had been refused or were incomplete.

His statement of the position of the *Conseil* was this:

The power of making a decision conferred upon Ministers, whether on general principles of the law of public office or in virtue of specific texts (yet not limitative), is not subordinated by the law in any manner. It follows . . . that your control over the acts in question in the exercise of this power is the minimum control to which the administrative judge can allow himself; that is, that it is reduced to three points: the verification whether the act was taken in the public interest, that it was founded on a juridically correct principle, that it was founded on a materially exact basis.

The Secretary had failed in all three.

We might add that a corollary is that if the Government wanted the right to exclude for political opinions, it must secure legislation by Parliament clearly to this effect.

What the Conseil Cannot Judge. The *Conseil d'État* does not receive suits against foreigners or international authorities; against persons not exercising public authority (private persons); against the actions of the parliamentary assemblies, whether legislative or procedural; or against judicial acts of other law courts (that is, it does not discipline the administrators of justice). It is, of course, an appellate court over the restricted administrative jurisdiction of the lower administrative courts, and a suit may be entertained against the administrative (not the jurisdictional) behavior of these. It will not accept suits on the substance of public contracts, but it will accept them when against wrongful use of the rules relating thereto.

"Acts of Government." In addition to these limits, which are easily understandable, there are others classed in the general term: *actes de gouvernment,* governmental acts. What are they? They are not suable before *any* courts at all. What act is *not* an act of government, we might ask? It has been elaborated by an induction from the cases considered by the *Tribunal des Conflits, the Conseil d'État,* and the *Cour de Cassation.* They include acts of interior politics: the behavior of the Government in relationship with the Parliament; the legislative process; the discipline of the Armed Forces; even the state of siege (military emergency due to public disorders). Then there are diplomatic actions: annexations and their consequences; acts protecting French persons abroad (for example, refusal to intervene diplomatically to get damages for a Frenchman molested by a foreigner in a foreign country); instructions given to diplomatic agents; the validity of treaties and their official interpretation—the *Quai d'Orsay's* word is final. There are actions taken or occurring in time of war: murders, pillage, explosions, seizure of cargoes—unless covered by special legislation.

There are some French scholars and lawyers who argue that this list might well be cut down, even as in recent years measures expelling foreigners and acts modifying the legal situation of a colony have been acceptable as suits by the *Conseil.*

The general nature of the act of government is discernible: it is in the realm of prerogative, where the government is compelled to act in dire necessity by temporal or local circumstances, or facts of geography, or matters needing high degrees of discretion and confidence.

Decentralization of Administrative Jurisdiction. Until 1954 the concentration of administrative cases in the *Conseil d'État* was so great that it had a heavily swollen docket. The prefectoral councils (p. 504) in the localities were too few and too little vested with power in the first instance to relieve the *Conseil,* and so it took an average of from three to five years to obtain decrees of annulment from it. This meant not only that wrongs were not righted, but that since they were not, officials might in the interval before retribution be encouraged to illegal actions. By August 1, 1953, there were no less than 24,510 dossiers in arrears. This number was a vast increase over the arrears of earlier years, in part because the public becomes more conscious of its rights as the years go by, the activities of the State expand (especially had they done so during the war and just after), and the *Conseil's* own reach of authority encourages claims. But justice delayed is justice denied. Hence, a law of January 1, 1954, enacted a decentralization and some changes in the procedure at the center. The twenty-three prefectoral councils have become full-fledged courts of first instance in administrative cases. They take cases on two bases: (1) the residence of the act contested, modified (2) by the location of the official or act of materiel (e.g., goods) involved in the suit. The *Conseil* takes first-instance cases only from overseas territories, or put to it because the cases are presumed to be of transcendent importance or because they involve several administrative agencies—for example, where they concern the rights of civil servants or the validity of a governmental decree. Otherwise, it is a court of appeal from the lower administrative courts. In addition, it is still a body that sends out inspectors to make regular inspections of all administrative jurisdictions in France and the overseas possessions.

Execution of Judgments

Supposing the official or local authority, a policeman or a mayor, will not do as the judgment says?

Then his acts may be declared illegal. Supposing he still resists or slows down compliance? He may be made guilty of a personal fault, and damages may be exacted from him in the ordinary courts. But most judgments are at once given compliance.

Guarantees of Independence

The *conseillers* are nominated by decree in the Cabinet. They can be removed. The subordinate members, *maîtres* and *auditeurs,* cannot be removed except after consultation with the vice president deliberating with the sectional presidents; but they can be removed. Yet hitherto they have been practically irrevocable.

Thus the French have developed a method of making the State responsible for the unlawful trouble it may cause its inhabitants. It began earlier than the recent conversion of Britain in 1947 and the United States to State responsibility of this kind.

To temper the view that people may hold regarding "administrative justice," and to reinforce the point that justice depends on the mode of organization, the composition, and mentality of the courts, we may cite the opinion of Professor Henri Berthélemey:

> Let one be guarded against considering administrative justice as "exceptional" justice. . . . Administrative justice is not a dismemberment of the justice of the law courts. It is the judicial organ by which the executive power imposes on the active administration the respect for law. The administrative courts have not taken their role from the judicial authority; they are one of the forms by which the administrative authority is exercised. To put the matter even more precisely, it may be said that the administrative tribunals are, towards the acts and decisions of the administration, what the courts of appeal are to decisions of inferior courts.

Personal acquaintance with a number of *conseillers,* younger and older, and an insight into the preparation at the *École Nationale d'Administration,* warrants the judgment that they have a superb grasp of the law, the doctrine, the nature of the society served by their administration, and an assurance of their probity. They are not bureaucratic tyrants, but men of just and comprehending mind.

The Government of

Germany

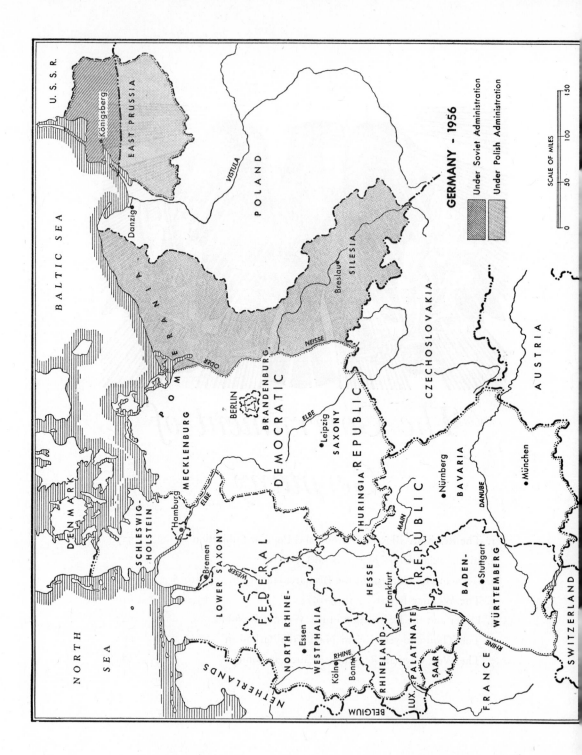

GERMANY - 1956

▨ Under Soviet Administration
▧ Under Polish Administration

SCALE OF MILES
0   50   100   150

The Reich of "Blood and Iron" and Popular Subjection

These doctrines [of Kant and Fichte] gave birth to revolutionary forces which only wait for the day to erupt and fill the world with terror and amazement. Then there will appear Kantians who even in a visible world will know nothing of reverence and who will mercilessly plough up the soil of European life with sword and axe and extirpate the last roots of the past. Armed Fichteans will enter the battle who in their fanaticism of the Will are not restrained by fear or self-interest, for they live solely in the Spirit and defy Matter, like the early Christians who could not be swayed by physical tortures or physical delights. . . . But even more terrifying than all of these will be the philosophers of nature once they actively enter upon a German revolution and identify themselves with its destructive work. . . . they will be able to invoke the demonic energies of old German pantheism, because that ancient love of war we find among the old Germans will once more awake in them and will fight not to destroy or conquer but merely for the sake of fighting.

—*Heine*

There are two possible ways of displaying the nature of German government. One is to take the present Bonn Constitution, only five years old, and *à propos* of each of its components, reach back to the German past. This produces too many complications of retrospection, while the present is transitional. The other way is the plain method of exhibiting the successive regimes Germany has had to the present. It is simpler. The student may, with this method, if he wishes, begin with the last chapter of this section and himself go back. But, as the making of government goes forward, casually, from a point in the past, a thousand years of national character is more important than five.

Violent and Disrupted Growth

After World War II no single unified German state existed. Defeat had split "Germany" into its Western regions with 50,000,000 people, and the Eastern, with 17,000,000, besides parts of its former territory annexed by Poland and the U.S. S.R. Three centuries of megalomaniac, militarist ambitions for empire reached their maximum success in 1942, when Hitler's Third Reich—designed to last a thousand years—stretched out to Stalingrad, Spitsbergen, and Greece, only to end with defeat and partition.

The new governments in Bonn and the Russian-dominated east are skin-deep. The governments of each avow eventual unification, and promise then to set up a new constitution. Germany's largest area and most creative state, Prussia, was formally dissolved in 1947. The political-party situation is utterly temporary in this predicament, yet it is fundamental to democratic government. Why, then, pretend that current institutions are definitive?

It is not enough to know what Germany momentarily is, but to guess what she may become, and for this it is essential to know what Germany so long was. It is essential to uncover layer after layer in the violent leaps of growth this body politic has made. In 1789 Germany was some 320 separate states; in 1815, 39; in 1871, 39; in 1918 it was 18 and later 17; from 1933 to 1945 it was practically one totalitarian state; in 1945 it reverted to 16 states, divided into two containers, the German Federal Republic centered at Bonn, with 11 states, and the German Democratic Government in the East, with 5 states, while Berlin, the former capital of Prussia and the Reich, was a separate governmental unit divided into a western and eastern sector hostile to each other. This is but a graphic preliminary index to the effect that German government, even in its basic element, territory, is less *being* than *becoming*.

Violent Change of Regime. A very able observer of contemporary Germany reports[1] this of German students:

"You English," one student told me, "are very lucky. You have solid traditions behind you. What have we got? The Kaiserreich or Bismarck? You would say they stood for materialism and power. Then the 1848 revolutionaries? They were, maybe, impractical romantics. Hardly the Weimar Republic, which failed, or the Nazis, who were criminals." Lack of tradition may contribute to that curious evasiveness of many Germans who maintain that they need not have an opinion of their own because "it has nothing to do with us."

German government is a succession of emergent stages, since 1815, each immature in existence and premature in decease. Even France has had only three regimes since 1871 (even counting Vichy, a wartime interlude!), but Germany today counts her fourth, of which one, the Bismarckian Reich, lasted 1871–1918 and did not achieve the consolidation of a tradition of nation, people, and State.

[1] Terence Prittie, B.B.C. correspondent, in the *Listener,* London, April 28, 1955.

The French, at least, founded a new State in 1789 and a unified fundamental current runs from that time to this. Germany revolted and reacted from regime to regime, like the Nazi and democracy and Bismarckian monarcho-oligarchy, with violence and the most extreme opposites.

Becoming, not being, is the characteristic of German government. We are forced to excavate. Out of this some persistent uniformities emerge. Each of the following chapters is a stratum excavated; but all are linked together to give the complete picture.

The strata are treated in historical order. Hence, reversely, this means:

The Bonn Basic Law set up in 1949 and its eastern rival

The Nazi regime, or Third Reich, from 1933 to 1945

The Weimar Republic, from 1919 to 1933

The Second, or Bismarckian, or Kaiser Reich, 1871 to 1918

The German Confederation from 1815 to 1867

Before this, almost lost in early medieval history, the hundreds of Germanic states in the Holy Roman Empire.

Characteristics. The characteristics of this Germanic area of Europe, between the French and Slavs and the North Sea, as a political society are:

I. No commitment to the democratic process; no popular revolution.

II. Recent unity of the area, produced by strokes of violence.

III. Evolution of Prussian predominance, military and political; its connection with difficult geographic-political features.

IV. Economic, social, and religious forces in Germanic society inimical to special unity and political democracy and favorable to an authoritarian State and popular subjection.

V. Its political outlook, a combination of metaphysics, romanticism, and a-moral realism.

I. NO DEMOCRACY; NO POPULAR REVOLUTION

Until 1919—that is, only until yesterday by the standard of the time needed for the development of social-habit morality—none of the Germanic states had democratic constitutions. In 1919, as a result of the German defeat in World War I late in 1918, the various states established democratic constitutions, and in 1919 such a constitution was established for the whole Reich—that is, these states associated in a federation.

This thoroughgoing modern democracy lasted until the assumption of the chancellorship (the prime ministership) of the Reich by Adolf Hitler in 1933, when it was viciously swept away. Even in the years 1919 to 1933, only fourteen years, democracy had been hamstrung by the *Reichswehr*, Germany's historic curse of the corps of career military officers, and by the counterrevolutionary movements of the nationalist parties, the Nazis (the National Socialist Democratic Workers' Party) and the Communist Party.

Before the rise of Weimar democracy, the *Reichstag*, the lower house in the bicameral federal government of 1871, was, indeed, elected by universal suffrage. But the Chancellor of the Reich under the Emperor (Kaiser), who was hereditary, was not responsible to the *Reichstag* by law or in practice (pp. 582–585). He governed by manipulating the political parties against each other and repressing the Socialists and underrepresenting them, and the implied threat of abolishing the *Reichstag* altogether, as Bismarck had emasculated the Prussian legislature in 1862 (p. 571).

By World War I and its aftermath the German people had had no experience of the opportunities, habits and difficulties of self-government. They were ruled from above, and protected from their own free political selves.

No revolution had, before 1871, enforced a sovereign parliamentary system. Parliamentary bodies had been established in the states, called Diets, but the hereditary rulers were sovereign, not the people; these were treated as subjects of the *Obrigkeitstaat*, the German technical name for the authoritarian State. Representation in the Diets was not by universal suffrage, but by Estates.

Similarly for the long period before 1815, or 1789; dynastic or ecclesiastical princes ruled by divine right, except in the Free Cities of the north, west, and south, where the upper bourgeoisie of trade and finance and big estates ruled.

The constitution which is safe for the people is that which the people have seized. Thus had the French, the English, and American people acted; the Germans, docile, waited for outside liberators, such as Napoleon or Woodrow Wilson in 1918. Why did the German people never revolt passionately enough to create a democracy? The answer is complicated and ambiguous.

The Throes of Antifeudalism

Until the middle of the nineteenth century, broadly speaking, the Germanic states were societies of serf-peasantry. Their lords, laymen, or bishops varied in culture and sense of duty. Towns were few, and their small middle class did not possess the firm self-confidence nurtured in the trading and domestic-manufacturing centers of England and strengthened by commerce and seafaring adventurousness—at least in the sixteenth century.

The serfs were subject to long military service; the landlords paid no taxes; the peasantry paid as much as one third to one half their income in taxation. Their servitude was as hard as in Russia (p. 735).

Lutheran Subjection by Massacre. The Lutheran doctrines of the individual conscience against the corrupted Church stirred the serfs more than Protestantism and misery had done in earlier revolts. In 1524–25 they rose with mass ferocity for the right to choose their own pastors (these were appointed by the landlords), the abolition of tithes, their servile bonds, and the right to hunt, fish, gather wood from the forests, and so on. The demands were properly supported by Scriptural quotations. Their device was a peasant's shoe—the *sabot* of the French peasant (whence *saboteur*). Fanatics, like Thomas Munzer, led the peasants and traveled from place to place igniting revolt.

Martin Luther did not support the peasants in

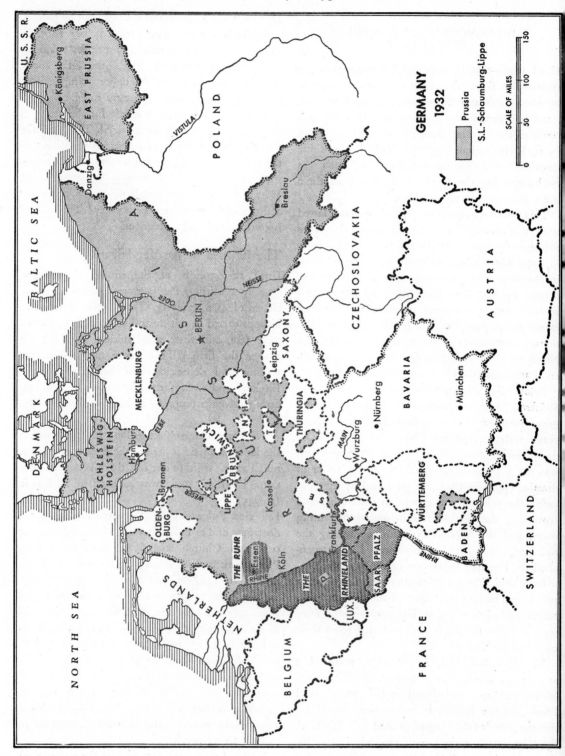

the revolt for which his doctrines and passion were partly responsible; challenged, he took the side of princely authority. He himself records that 47,000 peasants were slain by the princes' soldiers; later historians put it at 100,000 savagely slaughtered. These massacres were encouraged by Luther's exhortations to the princes to crush the revolt. As the peasant leaders had shrewdly seen, in Luther's Protestant *extremism* a new kind of autocratic authority was being nurtured against the individual.

Luther hated Western culture. He repudiated its tolerant values which he had seen in its Renaissance art forms in Rome. He returned to a hysterical non-Western German emotionalism, hostile to raising money for the building of St. Peter's. He gave to Germans a doctrine of utter subservience to civil authority. The small but powerful middle class shared his zeal for the individual conscience against Rome's authoritarianism, but for their own social stability they looked to the power of their individual local princes.

Luther's own words speak the doom of democracy in north Germany and the reinforcement of *particularism* (local sovereignty against the Empire or other union) in extreme terms.

> The princes of this world are gods, the common people are Satan, to whom God sometimes does what at other times he does directly through Satan, that is, makes rebellion as a punishment for the people's sins.
>
> I would rather suffer a prince doing wrong than a people doing right.

And again:

> It is in no wise proper for anyone who would be a Christian to set himself up against this government, whether it act justly or unjustly.
>
> There are no better works than to obey and serve all those who are set over us as superiors. For this reason also disobedience is a greater sin than murder, unchastity, theft, and dishonesty, and all that these may include.

His doctrine of obedience was crawlingly *abject*. He made himself the supreme and incontrovertible judge—the New Pope—of what was and was not Christian. But when the peasants submitted their twelve demands—all decent and fair,

especially in respect to the problem of their economic servitudes and rights to fish, hunt, etc.—he abandoned the poor and humble and suffering.

I choose only one representative passage from the three infamous pamphlets he wrote encouraging the princes, whereas to understand this frenzied blood-lust and hysterical emotionalism—in vulgar and obscene language, foul temper, and venomous ferocity almost identical with Adolf Hitler's—all should be quoted:

> Any man against whom it can be proved that he is a maker of sedition is outside the law of God and Empire, so that the first who can slay him is doing right and well. . . . For rebellion is not simple murder, but is like a great fire, which attacks and lays waste a whole land. . . . Therefore, let everyone who can smite, slay, and stab, secretly and openly, remembering that nothing can be more poisonous, hurtful, or devilish than a rebel. It is just as when one must kill a mad dog; if you do not strike him, he will strike you, and a whole land with you.

Luther was afraid for Germany. He had ready all the quotations from Scripture demanding obsequiousness as in Czarish Russia and its Orthodoxy. "Render unto Caesar . . ."; "Let every man be subject to the power"; "Be subject to every ordinance of man." He preached the view of punishment that was exalted by Nietzsche in the nineteenth century into a great political doctrine in the interest of the Superman. "It is to their [the princes'] advantage that the peasants have had a bad conscience and an unjust cause and that any peasant who is killed is lost in body and soul and eternally the devil's."

Faced with a similar situation in England a century later, John Locke declared *the very opposite:*

> If any men find themselves aggrieved, and thinks the prince acts contrary to or beyond that trust, who so proper to judge as the body of the people? But if the prince or whoever they be in the administration decline that way of determination, the appeal then lies nowhere but to heaven; force between either persons who have no known superior on earth, or which permits no appeal to a judge on earth, being properly a state of war. . . .

Unforgettable Cruelty Established Subjection. One hundred thousand slaughtered people was a very large proportion of the whole population.

But Luther told the peasants, "Christ says we are not to resist evil or wrong; but always yield, suffer it, and let things be taken from us." He told them that their Third Article, "There shall be no serfs, for Christ has made all men free," is dead against the Gospel, as St. Paul had commanded obedience; nor can a worldly kingdom stand *unless on inequality!* Hence, my lords, "Stab, smite, slay, whoever can."

Nietzsche, one of Germany's most "characteristic" political thinkers of the nineteenth century, recommends cruel punishment by authority, so that the horrible memory may forever prevent disobedience. "Something is burnt in so as to remain in his memory; only that which never stops *hurting* remains in his memory. . . ." He retails German tortures and concludes, "It was by help of such images and precedents that man eventually kept in his memory five or six 'I will nots'. . . ."

Furthermore, Martin Luther's teaching of obedience and oppression as the command of God led to a State-controlled religion. It did not, as in Britain, have moderation or allow for *political* dissent. The "religious" people, social groups, and classes became the allies of the Lutheran pastors, all in their abject servility to the princes. Martin Luther was the translator of the Bible into German; the act gave a universal language, German, to the "geographical expression," the hundreds of states. But it added to his servility-making influence. Luther was also Germany's first distinguished anti-Semite. To avoid debates about the Articles of Faith, he urged that Jews should be driven forcibly from Germany, their property confiscated, and their houses destroyed and synagogues set afire!

The Thirty Years' War: 1618–1648. When the growth of economic wealth between 1550 and 1600—mainly agricultural, but also in European commerce and urban arts—might have encouraged a new and successful assertion against the princes, Germany was afflicted by the Thirty Years' War, the war of religious factions, Protestant and Catholic. The Germanic states were of differing religious faiths: the west and southwest Catholic, the north and east, Protestant. Luther had divided them by his bloody ferocity. Moreover, the neighboring Danes and Swedes were Protestant and had an interest in fastening Protestant rule on the Germanic states, against the threat of the Catholic states of the southwest.

The war was dreadful in its barbarity, its hatreds, its destruction of homes in the towns and rural areas, in wholesale sacking and murder, in the rape of women, in bestial killings. It promoted ferocity and distrust as social habits; it set back the economy of the country; it subjected the masses again to the power of their rulers. Cannibalism was officially sanctioned, for food; polygamy, for population! Gustavus Adolphus of Sweden, who led the leagued armies of the Protestants, was aided by Cardinal Richelieu, the chief minister of Catholic France, by subsidies and by armies, since Richelieu's pro-French policy was *to prevent the unification of the Germanic states.* The barbarity (partly because the armies were mercenaries and often ruffians without faith or of diverse faith, whatever the faith of the prince or general they served) was so terrible as to stimulate Hugo Grotius to write his *Of War and Peace.* He said in the preface:

> For I saw prevailing throughout the Christian world a license in the making of war of which even barbarous nations would have been ashamed . . . and when arms were once taken up, all reverence for divine and human law was lost. Just as if man were henceforth authorized to commit all crimes without restraint.

It is estimated that in the terrible thirty years, the population decreased from 30,000,000 to 20,000,000. The greatest losses occurred in the villages. Many were totally deserted. Houses had been burned down; stock was destroyed. The remaining peasantry came more under the domination of the landlords than ever, for they needed to be rehabilitated. Their services and dues were increased. The loss of wealth to all classes was catastrophic. The landlords became even more dependent on the State, and they infiltrated the rulership. *What a tradition!*

While the Western countries, France and England, were increasing their wealth rapidly in the seventeenth and eighteenth centuries—by agriculture, commerce, and manufactures in an age of discovery, treasure accumulation, and colonial enterprise—the Germanic states were hard put to recover a more primitive level of prosperity. The rural and mercantile middle class that made the Revolution in Britain in the seventeenth century and produced the French bourgeois revolution of 1789 had no counterpart in Germany.

It is often said that the bloodletting of the Thirty Years' War so sapped the vitality of the German people that, once again, any proclivity to mass revolution was dissipated. It could be put down to the social consequences of the destruction of wealth (which was low compared with modern standards to begin with). It retarded the growth of a self-confident middle class. It caused dependence on the power of the State that was helpful in economic remedies. Nietzsche speculates, like so many Germans, on the sapping of German spiritual political resolution, by the War.

[In] certain places in the world there was almost bound to prevail from time to time among large masses of the population a sense of *physiological depression*. . . . Such a feeling of depression can have the most diverse origins . . . it may be blood-deterioration, malaria, syphilis, and the like (German depression after the Thirty Years' War, which infected half Germany with evil diseases thereby paved the way for German servility, for German pusillanimity).

The Lost Revolution

When the French Revolution broke out in 1789, the various Germanic states, above all Prussia, now second only in size and military power to her rival Austria, were ruled by firmly established autocracies. Here Church and State were in alliance to deny political liberties; legislative bodies had no more than advisory power. A stiff political censorship over books and newspapers was a marked symbol of narrow-minded authoritarianism. This despotism (even if anywhere it had benevolent popular intentions, under the influence of the French and English Enlightenment) was buttressed by the two great pillars of the State: a highly disciplined and routinized bureaucracy and a standing army, immense in relation to the population (p. 541) and officered by the Junker landed aristocracy.

After a momentary gasp of welcome for the Revolution because it offered the opportunity of weakening France internationally, the German princes, especially the Prussian, put into operation all the forces of suppression that reaction knows.

It must be remembered, also, that for centuries, "Germany" had been merely a geographical, not a social, idea. The fragmentation into small states inhibited the formation of widespread movements of people, organizations of thought and will. Territorial fragmentation shredded the urban middle class. That class was not, in any case, dynamic-minded or spirited for progress. Germans are given credit for remarkable imitative and developmental faculties but are denied originality. Education was not bursting with ideas as in England and France. In the seventeenth century the German universities had no such animation and ferment as Oxford, Cambridge, and Paris.

The one great hope of a revolution in two hundred years (1550 to 1789) had been lost. Why was revolution important to democracy in Britain and France? Precisely because it is, first of all, the obverse of Nietzsche's idea that an act of force by authority teaches subjects to be enduringly obedient; in a revolution the people teach the rulers that the people are masters. A revolution moves on a widely shared general faith. It signifies a people's self-confidence to rule themselves through their freely chosen leaders. It is a symbol of belief and will, to the point of self-sacrifice for its objects. Not enough Germans possessed these after the seventeenth century.

No centers of intellectual ferment existed, like London and Paris, of mighty magnitude compared to the total population, nor any such focus and incubators of political opinion, ideas, and will. Only the Free Cities of Western Germany were literate and liberal, but their populations were very small and their leaders were civil servants or academic men dreaming of a Germany, but not workers for it. No Hobbes, no Locke, no Dryden, no Pope, no Milton, no Fox, no Burke, no Bentham, no Montesquieu, no Voltaire (the King of Prussia tried to use him as a pleasant titivating lapdog at his court), no Rousseau, no *Encyclo-pédie* writers. All that Germany had was a late crop of metaphysicians: Kant, Fichte, Schelling, and Hegel, men who, instead of leading in the affirmation of right and wrong in the political arena of today and tomorrow, concerned themselves with "What is knowledge?," "What is the Universe?," "What is Duty?," "What is God?." Even the revolutionary poets or dramatists, such as Schiller, kept their doctrines for the stage. They enthused about the French Revolution but saw in it no incentive to do likewise in their own petty states. They turned conservative, romantic, medievally mystic. Only Kant, who had been ordered not to lecture on religion as the orthodox did not like his skepticism, maintained his admiration for the Revolution and Rousseau. As for Olympean Goethe, he steadily condemned the Revolution from the beginning. For he himself was a civil administrator, with princely benediction, in Weimar. He never believed in the ability of people to govern themselves, but always in benevolent and enlightened despotism and princely obligation. He took refuge in the doctrine that government could not cure the world's evils, but man must make himself noble, humble, and modest and stick to his own *métier*.

The peasantry were too wretched and crushed to respond to the Revolution's challenge. It takes wealthier burghers to lead a revolution, for they (as in France) resented noble and aristocratic privileges and exclusion from political authority. Armies were sadistic almost everywhere in Europe and in England at that time; but the German severities matched the Czarist ones (p. 736). The landed aristocracy that flogged the peasant on the estates did so also as officers in the Army.

The German people were for a time excited, not revolutionized from the outside, by the French Revolutionary armies and the Napoleonic invasion. Once Napoleon fell, they soon settled down again under the pressure of their rulers.

Liberalism was French, therefore patriotic Germans were antiliberal; liberalism was un-German.

The Failure of 1848

In the spring of 1848 revolution spread from Vienna to Berlin, Cologne, Frankfurt, Dresden, and other cities in Germany. This was part of the chain of European revolutions of that year. Middle class and working class were shoulder to shoulder in Germany also. The German rulers (including the most reactionary and feudal, the King of Prussia) were compelled to promise democrat reforms, already repeatedly promised and forgotten by the latter several times since 1815. But the fervent will was aborted. In the first parliament ever elected for all Germany, which met in Frankfurt-on-Main, the 800 members were the intelligentsia, officials, small professional and the business classes, not the solid middle class or peasants and workers. They were terrified of a popular armed guard or of the workers. While they debated brilliantly, the military and official class and Junkers, especially the Prussian, regained their ascendency and chased them away. They donated constitutions, tainted with Prussianism, which infected first Prussia and then the whole Reich of 1871–1918, since Prussia became master. **The Liberals Flee Germany.** Finally, in the years closely following the abortive revolution of 1848, and later when Bismarck persecuted the Catholics and the Socialists (1878–1890), too large a number of the more liberty-loving people emigrated instead of fighting the feudal regime in their own country. Between 1848 and 1854 alone 770,000 Germans in a population of about 34,000,000 left Germany, most for America where their civic virtues could flourish (represented by such names as Carl Schurz, John Peter Altgeld, and Wendell Willkie).

Such men were not available to lead a democratic revolution in 1918 when a lost world war, provoked by the German Reich, offered the opportunity. Is German force only available for collective, tribal obedience, to destroy the liberty of others?

II. HOW THE TERRITORY WAS HAMMERED TOGETHER

Two impressions have already been given, (1) that what came to be known as the German State or the German Reich in the nineteenth century was pieced together from many formerly existing sovereign territories, and (2) that the process was both violent and extremely recent. Let us look at this exercise in "blood and iron."

Germany—A Country without Natural Frontiers

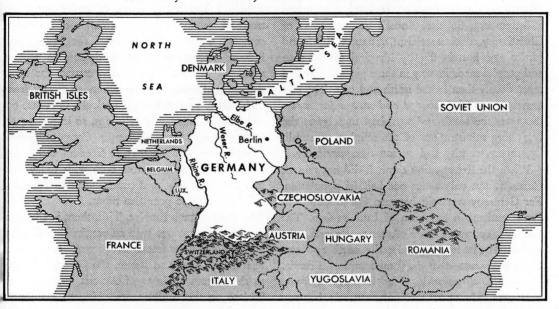

Piecing Together a German State

No "Natural" Frontiers. First, the area of Germany, except for the north, is geographically indeterminate: in the west the Rhine might or might not be a "natural" frontier, but Germany slopped over to its left bank into France. In the east, the Central European plain stretches all the way into the lands of the Slavs, Poland, the Baltic countries; and the east is the area in which, for plunder of the Slavs and then for mortal and permanent fear of them, Prussia and its cruel authoritarianism was born and nurtured.

In the west again the land merges into the Lowlands and the north of France. The southeast opens through Bohemia (Czechoslovakia) via Vienna into the Balkans. The north, at Denmark, leaves the way open to and from Scandinavia. There are temptations everywhere, especially as the North German Plain is not fertile, and there were dangers from without everywhere. No clear-cut geographical feature—not the sea, not the mountains, not the rivers—make something called "Germany" a neat, self-contained national community.

The northern plain, the central uplands, and the Alps in the south run into other areas that continue into other national communities: they dif-

ferentiate Germany internally without shaping her as one. That plain is divided by four rivers—the Rhine, the Elbe, Oder, and Vistula—and while these disintegrated the German people, yet they were not decisive enough to hold in populations until they congealed into separate national communities. Her rivers and mountains break up the land that might otherwise have been the basis for one community, with a great social capital, into several communities, differentiated by their economy, religion, terrain, and climate, connection with neighboring "foreigners" (the Rhineland with France, Austria with Italy, Bavaria with Austria, Prussia with Poland and Russia), and consequently by historic change and chance.

Disintegrated Areas. Roughly speaking, the areas out of which modern Germany made a State were these (taking the developing nations in the fifteenth century), broadly speaking: Austria, Bavaria, Saxony, Bohemia, Silesia, the various Free City States along the Rhine, the City States of the northern seacoast, Brandenburg, Prussia, and parts of Poland and Lithuania.

Roman law and cultural influence had overcome the barbarian Huns' attempts to destroy Rome. But Rome penetrated only into the south and west of these territories, as far only as the *limes Germanicus* Caesar's boundaries of Germany, from near Bonn on the Rhine to Regensberg (Ratisbon) on the Danube, covering Baden and Württemberg. So also, Rome's warmer view of Christianity, of sober stoicism, of natural rights and justice and human dignity identical for all men and peoples made its way in these parts earlier and more deeply than in the north and east. The east remained *un-Christianized and savage for centuries* after the south and west had undergone the beginning ministrations of the religion of humility, mercy, charity and *personal responsibility*.

When the Reformation came, it did not win all Germany but only about one half its population. For Germany was split between Catholicism and Protestantism, in the form of Lutheranism. The Catholic countries were Austria, Bavaria, the Rhineland (Baden, divided); the north and east were Protestant—that is, Brandenburg, Prussia, Pomerania, Brunswick, Mecklenburg, Saxony, Schleswig, Hanover, Hamburg—merely by way of illustration. Political authority *within* these areas was split into many "particularistic" principalities and dukedoms. Luther had led a mass German unifying religious movement. It ended by being deeply divisive and reactionary.

No Community Core. Out of these highly disparate areas a single State was finally forged. Every state and nation needs some creative and community-building center: the London area in Britain, the Île-de-France (Paris) Basin in France, Moscow in Russia. Pleasant attraction, and some compulsory allegiance, assimilates the rest of the country in time. Germany had too many capitals and no definite contours: the capitals of the "geographic expression" called Germany ranged between Vienna, Prague, Frankfort, Aix-la-Chapelle, and Berlin. For the "geographical expression" was not truly even such but rather an ideological or political expression—the Holy Roman Empire. Whereas other nations started with a nucleus of central territory and developed it, Germany was a congeries of regions, with no settled and final nucleus in one place. The gravity of political force rested now in one region, now in another, until after centuries it came to rest in the nineteenth with the harshest taskmaster of all, Prussia.

Visionary Frontiers. Until that time Germany reached out for a vast geographical area, itself varying at different times in its scope, the Holy Roman Empire. The vision of this Empire distracted Germans from the formation of their own compact social consensus from the inside, and induced impossible romantic dreams to replace political possibilities. Its scope caused the most damaging divisions among regions so distant from each other, so different in outlook, interests, occupations, climate, and religions, so impeding an early development of consensus. Communications could hardly hold together, in freedom and happy acceptance, so vast an area even with today's remarkable transport and communication facilities, let alone in those primitive times.

The Holy Roman Empire. This, then, is what occurred. Charlemange won an empire that covered all that we now know as France, Asturias in Spain, Italy down to Rome, the Germanic states to the eastern confines of Austria and south to Spalato on the Adriatic, stretching to Hamburg, Magdeburg, and the Bavarian mountains. This is the region of Roman and Catholic civilization and culture. The Germanic tribes had in A.D. 9 thrown back the Roman power; they had helped to sack Rome; they had been overcome by Roman spiritual superiority. But not, as will be noticed from the map, anything beyond the eastern line, say, the Elbe.

Charlemagne the Frank did what the Roman power had been unable to do, bring the various German tribes (*stämme*) into one dominion. The "Holy Roman Empire of the German Nation," as its title went, inaugurated in 800 with the crowning of Charlemagne in Rome, was split after his death, and the "German" part, including parts of the western Rhineland and Lorraine, had as its symbol the elective German crown. A German King would be crowned by the Pope, and this German King was at once King of Italy (its northern part) and the successor of the Caesars in the scope of his dominions.

As with Charlemagne, so with his successors, though in different ways; the dukes of the various German tribes (*Stämmesherzöge*) were the Emperor's feudal vassals. But these local rulers, in fact, repudiated any real subjection to the Emperor by the middle of the thirteenth century. The Emperors had all their work cut out to hold the

Italian domains to avoid subjection to commands from the Pope.

The Empire lasted from the year 800 to 1806, when Napoleon made away with it. In Voltaire's oft-quoted cynicism, it was neither holy nor Roman nor an empire, and, according to the jurist of international relations Pufendorf, it was "a monster of irregular body." Under Charlemagne it had combined the conception of a unified secular government, sanctified by a universal Church. It claimed all houses of government everywhere. But it could act only through local deputies of the Emperor, counts, holding authority from him. He was undermined by disruption into feudalism.

Up to 1356 the emperorship (*Kaisertum*) was in the hereditary succession in Charles the Great's family; then it became elective. The Electors were certain of the rulers of Germanic territories, of which there were seven. The election took place in Frankfurt-on-Main and the coronation at Aix-la-Chapelle (as German King), in Pavia or Milan (as King of Italy), and in Rome (as Roman Emperor). The Habsburgs, masters of Austria, managed to keep the imperial crown from 1438 to 1740, and then, after a short interval, to 1806. The Electors were established by an imperial law of 1356. They consisted of seven more powerful dynasties among all the scores of German principalities: four temporal Electors, Bavaria, Saxony, Bohemia, and Brandenburg or Prussia, and three ecclesiastical ones, the archbishops of Mainz, Trier, and Cologne. Two more were added in the seventeenth century.

Austrian Rulership over German Feebleness. The imperial power was, in form, immense: legislation in all matters, execution, foreign affairs. But it was no empire of "direct" rule over the peoples; at its best it could claim no more than to rule the princes. In fact, the empire was made powerless by the obstructive gadgets and various local "liberties." Its collateral institutions were the Electors and the *Reichstag*. The latter was (from roughly 1500 onward) composed of three "estates": Electors, princes, and cities. It legislated by treatylike agreements among the "colleges" or "estates" and the Kaiser. The College or Council of Princes (the many lesser princes) fell into the two divisions of spiritual and temporal lords. The Council

or College of Cities was at first cleft into Rhenish and Swabian divisions, and in the sixteenth century criss-crossed by another division, into the Catholic and Evangelical bodies. The *Reichstag* decisions were taken by majority vote in each of the three Colleges separately, all three then had internally to agree for a decision. With the criss-crossings, no decision was possible. Even if a decision were ever reached, the imperial heads—the Kaiser and his Imperial Chancellor—had no power of direct executive action: the princes had this and so could negate what had been decided.

The Empire had a supreme law court, the *Reichskammergericht*. Its practical power was limited because the princes enjoyed so many exemptions from jurisdiction. But, even so, it did transmit the Roman law to the Germanic states.

The succession to the emperorship (the Electors also had a right of removing an Emperor) offered an arena for intrigue and the foulest diplomacy and power pressures to the Electors.

The Empire, as such, had no army. The revenues necessary for the sessions of the government and the upkeep of the imperial offices and common action for defense or aggression were leviable on the princes and the cities. In war, the states supplied contingents for the Army. The levies were irregular, the payments were irregular and in arrears. This was no government—it was an illusion-making sham.

The Thousand-year Reich. The thousand-year-long experience gave the German political evolution various taints. One was a lasting obsession with the word *Reich*—that is, *Empire*, or far-*reaching* grasp. The term *Deutsches Reich* followed the Holy Roman Empire, not Deutsch*land*: not the equivalent of *England*, rather than *British Empire;* or *France*, rather than *French Empire*, at any rate, to begin within. It saddled the German people with a *Grossenwahn*—that is, political megalomania, chewing more than they could bite off. Hitler always talked of his Reich as "a thousand-year Reich"; the people yammered about the return of Frederick of Barbarossa—that is, the Holy Roman Emperor, a crusader with the red beard, who sought to establish peace and unity among the German princes and peoples, and they believed in the legend that he would arise from the

Kyffhaüser hills to be Germany's uniter against her enemies even as he had tried to be in the early twelfth century. The legend revolved around Charlemagne also.

At the same time it diverted their attention and will from the political necessities and possibilities that lay at their very feet: the making of sound political consensus. It allowed the continued existence of hundreds of local states, petty in the extreme, without any real political obligation outside themselves. Someone in the German states was always ready to ape Caesar after whom Charlemagne had fashioned his ambitions. Yet there were always local pretenders to hold onto their domains; and their votes as secular or ecclesiastical or Free Cities' electors of the Holy Roman Empire were designed to keep it weak or to support the dissensional strength of some new House—the Habsburgs, for example, who held or aspired to the emperorship. The claim was artificial; and it was the only bond of the "Germans" for a thousand years.

Coterminous Territorial and Religious Disruption

The religious settlement elsewhere left Catholic France and Protestant England with minorities of the other religion that could be assimilated or tolerated. In Germany it took on a territorial disruption: the princes and cities of the northeast and North Sea and Baltic, economically ruined, were Lutheran; the southwest and the middle and south cities of the Rhine were Roman Catholic, wealthier, in a more benign climate; the former anti-German (since to be German meant being, perhaps, Catholicized) the latter attached to the Empire, the land of Mozart, Haydn, Beethoven, and the Baroque. Charles V attempted to unify Germany by the sword and failed, for he was occupied with the Turks and the French also. Hence, in 1555 the Treaty of Augsburg divided Germany permanently on the principle that the religion of the prince was the religion of his country—*cujus regio ejus religio*—while all the princes were to be absolute and sovereign.

"Particularism" and "Separatism." With this curious ramshackle pretense the special characteristic of German statehood developed: *particularism* and *separatism*. What the Emperors had not been able to do, overcome the particularism of these feudatories (accomplished in England by the eleventh century, and in France by the seventeenth century) had later to be done by a harsher force in the late eighteenth and middle nineteenth centuries—Prussia.

Treaty of Westphalia. The German people did not wage the Thirty Years' War, but the German princes. The Catholic and the Protestant princes fought to prevent the empire becoming a reality, which would crush at least one of these religious persuasions. It was ended by the Treaty of Westphalia in 1648. This was enforced on the Germanic states by foreign powers: France and Sweden. Its territorial result was twofold: (1) the new areas of government were different from those decades before, hence the princely authority was without deep roots. (2) After Sweden and France had taken some of the total territory for themselves, the rest was fitted into *over 300 sovereign states:* say 200 temporal princes or counts, 63 archbishoprics, etc., and 51 free imperial cities; and between 1475 and 1800 tiny knighthoods. With a total population of around 20,000,-000, it may be estimated what was the average size of the 360 states, let alone the tinier governments.

There were other consequences. Each prince had his religious affiliation, Protestant or Catholic. The treaty enunciated the principle that whatever his religion was that of his people—that is, toleration for the dissenters was excluded. This was precisely the time when the people of Britain were successfully asserting the rights of dissent and when these were limiting the powers of the State. These new princes, so bolstered, entered into the heritage of Martin Luther's idolatory of Authority, *die Obrigkeit,* just when, a few months later, in 1649, the English cut off the head of Charles I in order to cut off the head of Authority. The peasants became ever more enslaved and subject to the cruelest exploitation. The system lasted throughout the eighteenth century—feudal territorial particularism. The burghers of Frankfort and Hamburg, without princely rule, could feel "German" as the other little governments could not, but their feeling of being German was connected with the nonexistence of absolute authority, a desirable condition, to be continued by particularism—that is, the denial of German unity.

Which Force? How could a way be found out of this territorial fragmentation and political absolutism? The foreign powers did not permit any of the larger rulers to grow at the expense of the rest. France was certainly not interested in German aggrandizement.

Prussian political and administrative ability and unscrupulousness finally won. For the rest of Germany was torn by different legal codes, customs barriers, currencies, stuffiness, and a sharing in the Enlightenment, the *Aufklärung*—that is, a cosmopolitanism envisaging humanitarian and liberal ideas of law, justice, and opportunity and toleration. This eighteenth-century cosmopolitanism, born and nurtured first in France, inspired Goethe, Lessing, the age of Bach, Handel, Gluck, Mozart, and Haydn, Herder, and Schiller. But in the last two, one already notices the onset of a violent and mystical romanticism, to counteract the tendency of cosmopolitan civilization.

Meanwhile there was weakness in the stagnation of crafts and domestic manufactures, in the decay of the universities, and a decelerated population growth. (1600 to 1800: France from 12,000,000 to 27,000,000; England, from 3,500,000 to 10,000,000; *but Germany,* only 20,000,000 to 22,000,000!)

III. THE PRUSSIAN STAIN

Before turning to the rise of Prussia, her capture of Germany, and her ruthless spirit, this warning is necessary. Within modern Prussia herself, there is a split personality: (1) East Prussia, a complex of ruthless militarism allied with authoritarianism and Lutheranism, and yet with mixed and rival interests, some "liberal," and (2) various territories given to or taken by Prussia which were of different character originally and remained so down to the present, the Rhineland and Hanover, for example. These were latter Catholic and/or liberal. These again were differentiated from the land of feudalism, militarism, and the Junker landlords, either by the features mentioned or (a late-nineteenth-century development) the dual pressure of big industry and the industrialists (who might be called modern "honorary" Junkers) and the working class in their factories and mines, who became socialist and democratic and were at fierce odds with the aboriginal Prussia.

One other matter is important. If it is impossible to talk of Prussianism as being the undifferentiated product of Prussia, we must also remember that the other Germanic lands were not altogether free in themselves of "Prussianism." But, and the proviso is very important, they were *largely free* of it. Indeed, their tone was to a considerable extent set by nearby Austria, which had been culturized by Italian influences: easy, musical, artistic, kindly, incompetent.

Its Pagan Origin

In the tenth century, in a land far to the east of Brandenberg, lived a tribe of pagans. It occupied the plain ending with the Baltic Sea to the north and the Silesian Mountains to the south. It covered both sides of the Vistula, east and west, from the Oder to the Memel. The name *Prussia* derives from *Before-Russia, Vor-* or *Bor-Russia,* thence, *B'Russia,* and finally, *Prussia.* This mixture of heathens, Wends, Letts, Swedish Goths, formed the root of Prussian state and the root of a whole world's troubles.

They pushed into the lands of Poland in the thirteenth century, for Poland had failed to Christianize them and had itself become internally enfeebled as a State. The Order of Teutonic Knights of Marienberg was invited to curb their murder and incendiarism. This Order had been founded in the late twelfth century, a consequence of the Crusades, which had mobilized the intention to eradicate heathenism in non-Christianized Europe as well as to win back the Holy Places. It was religious and military, a kind of military club or chartered company and political movement—in some respects not unlike the modern Communist Party of the Soviet Union.

The Prussians were cowed by the Order, but the Order did not then recede for other tasks; it reinforced its pressure to the east—the classic *drang nach Osten* of the Germans. It stayed on the subdued territory, both Germanizing it and Christianizing its people by force to the utmost. Germanization and cruel subjugation became syn-

The Growth of Prussia, 1300–1867

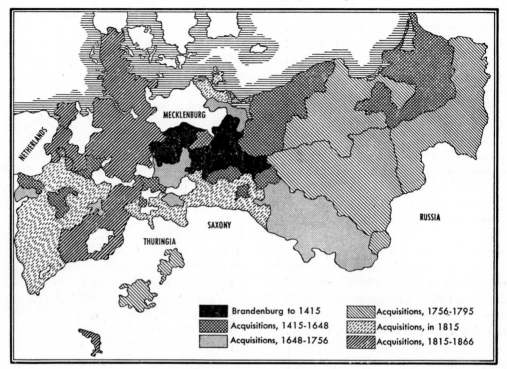

■ Brandenburg to 1415	Acquisitions, 1756-1795
Acquisitions, 1415-1648	Acquisitions, in 1815
Acquisitions, 1648-1756	Acquisitions, 1815-1866

onyms. The war was waged by the Order against the Baltic peoples, against the Slavs. It exterminated the Slavs and brought in Germans to till the land and to fight for it. The enmity has lasted 700 years, and fear of the Slavs could always be used by German statesmen to counter liberal votes.

The territory that was fully settled by Germans was what is known as East Germany. Elsewhere the Order and its followers exploited the populations through their clergy and merchants otherwise than by direct rule. The Slavs became serfs, bestially treated.

The Order ruled and annexed wider lands, in the teeth of resistance and frequent rebellion. In 1410, at Tannenberg, the mistreated Poles, Lithuanians, Russians, and Tatars defeated its armies. This failure was not accepted as the proper consequence of the resentment of other peoples against aggression and a lesson in self-control, but as being somehow due to "treason from within," the now familiar *"dolchstosz,"* or stab in the back.

Only the eastern part of the Order's domains were left to it, East Prussia; the west went to Poland. This left Prussia cut off by Polish land from the rest of Germany. Early in the sixteenth century, the Grand Master of the Order was converted to Protestantism. He married into the Danish royal family and was made Duke of East Prussia by the King of Poland. The line died out in 1618 and East Prussia was inherited by a relative, a Hohenzollern, the ruler of nearby Brandenberg, which lies between the Oder and the Elbe. This land, too, had been a border or *"märche"* against the Slavs; hence the rulers were entitled Markgraves, or margraves, of Brandenburg. Their pitiful, wretched capital was Berlin, little more than a military camp, hardly a big one until the eighteenth century.

Militarism and Bureaucracy

Brandenberg was peopled for the most part by converted Slavs. Even the names of its nobles show a Slav origin. The Hohenzollerns were merely unscrupulous military adventurers. The ruler in 1415 was made one of the Imperial Electors, so attaining German imperial importance. By the accession to them of East Prussia in 1618 they acquired considerable political importance.

The Treaty of Westphalia added eastern Pomerania to their domains. The territorial gulf between the frontier and East Prussia was narrowed. In 1655, Frederick William, Elector of Brandenburg (1640–1688), the then King William of Hohenzollern, known as the "Great Elector," invaded Poland and, capturing Warsaw (Poland was engaged in war with Sweden at the time, a neat opportunity for the Margraves of Brandenburg), forced out Poland as overlord of East Prussia. He picked up some small territories in the Ruhr. Thus the Hohenzollerns spread (with clefts between their dominions) east, center, and west. The Emperor of the Holy Roman Empire, Leopold, made Frederick William's son [2] a *King,* for services in the War of Spanish Succession (1701–1714): "King in Prussia," that land on the east side of Poland; hence his two titles, including the Electorship of Brandenburg. Prussia's royal insignia was the Hohenzollern's—Kings of Prussia through the rest of history. Long before this, the Grand Master of the Order, a Hohenzollern, had secularized and annexed the Order and its land of East Prussia: colonized land, as we have seen, of brutal exploitation of the Polish peasantry and unqualified absolutism.

By 1720 western Pomerania had been acquired and the possessions settled. The administrative genius of the King, Frederick William I, and his military abilities had further developed the competent if harsh managerial structure, training, morale, and subservience of the government.

The Bureaucracy Supreme and Militarized. In the development of a bureaucracy—a civil service—Prussia made brilliant progress in the seventeenth century, in part because it was ruled by three Kings with administrative talent of the highest order. From 1640 to the end of the reign of Frederick William, counted 100 years; of these the Great Elector and Frederick William ruled for seventy-five years. The intervening King was less able. Then followed Frederick II, the Great, for forty-six years. This sequence and longevity was a tremendous gift for administrative construction and strength, and a tradition lasting until today. The first part of it followed on the damages of

2 Frederick William I, 1688–1740, King of Prussia, 1713–1740.

the Thirty Years' War when the Junkers, the estate owners, were impoverished and needed State help.

By 1657 the Privy Council and departmental organization were rationally structured; the former, under the drive of the Great Elector, was an executive as well as deliberative and advisory organ. Provincial regents, *not* natives, were used to govern the localities for the King. They were later replaced by centrally appointed commissioners. These were in the early seventeenth century overtopped by War Commissioners to feed, equip, and restrain the mercenary armies. Then the armies were "nationalized," and so the War Commissioners became a regular part of the peacetime administration, raising money, recruits, and actively interested in a flourishing economy. Hence the local areas—towns, villages, and so on—were regulated by the State, through the War Commissioners, who utterly subordinated the city government councils and guilds. They needed money, and therefore they became the promoters of industry and prosperity—economic planners.

Centralization

Prussia, as a great German historian has said, "was then not a land with an army, but an army with a land." What the country gentry, as Justices of the Peace, did in England the military officers did in Prussia: these acted as inspectorial officers of all local governments, *provinz, kreis* (circle), and village or city (see pp. 595–596) and other civil officials for the central government, under the central aegis of the General War Commissariat that worked side by side with the Privy Council and a General Financial Directorate.

A very heavy centralization of administration occurred. The "county" (or "Circle") organization (*kreis*) was taken out of the hands of the original owners, the voluntary services offered by the local estate owners, and transferred to the appointees of the central government, the *Landrat,* its political agent. They came from the selfsame class. Some competence was now prescribed, but all pretensions of local self-government were abolished: tax commissioners dominated the guilds that ran town administration; with heavy taxes and deep and multifarious State control and promotion of crafts and occupations, they held the life of the towns in iron grasp.

A Civil Service arose: posts, taxes, customs, forests, salt promotion, mines, schools, Church.

By the year 1700, written and oral examinations were prescribed for the appointment of some officials, presupposing a university education. By 1723 a university training was specifically stipulated and instituted at the University of Halle. There was established, to develop the science and teaching of administration along with the legal education that was its basis, a Professorship of Cameralism at Halle and at Frankfort, "to teach the principles of agriculture and police,[3] also the institution of surveys of offices and estates, and also the efficient administration and government of towns."

Spartan Rigor. More important even than these foundations of administrative efficiency was the spirit in which the Service under the King was expected and regimented to work. Carlyle says of the regime that the King (Frederick William) as "the great manager," the "landlord," using the German word *Wirth,* and that "his reign was one of Economics!" It required punctilious obedience, earnestness, public honor, and integrity. The departments worked with a most intense spirit of administering other people, not of winning them into cooperation. Punishment for derelictions was severe; a rigorous system of inspectors kept all officials anxious. A spy system was ⟨o⟩perated, at the order of the King, by the heads of departments. Records and dossiers and files were kept; accounts had to be rendered to the last jot and tittle; the rules punishing bribe- and fee-taking was condign; personnel records were piled up against the day of punishment or promotion. A new Sparta was in the making.

Prussia created its arbitrary executive first, built and imposed its efficiency in the bureaucracy from above, with examinations and the rest, almost at the date of the Bill of Rights in England, and thenceforward never arrived at democratic institutions at all until the lost war of 1914–1918. In England first liberty and popular sovereignty,

then executive efficiency; in Prussia, first—and also last—executive efficiency and despotism. This Prussian evolution let loose upon Germany and the world a wolf nation.

Crushing of the Estates: No Parliament

As in France, England, and Spain, the several duchies and other divisions that composed the territories of Prussia had in medieval times developed their representative estates with Diets. They consisted of nobles, clergy and townsmen. At the Reformation the clergy were excluded; and also the same event increased the domains of the Crown, giving him additional power against the Estates, even though he had some interests in common with the nobles as a great landed aristocrat. The Estates still were tricameral: upper nobility, lower, and townsmen.

Between the nobles and burghers there was a perennial cleavage of interest and status. The grant of taxes, the amount, the period of the grant, the mode of collection, and the sharing of the burden between towns and countryside split this opposition to the royal authority. The towns were for short grants, small amounts, and self-administration. They wished the larger share to be borne by the peasantry. They desired taxes (excises) to stop the nobility from engaging in trade, brewing, and rural manufactures in competition with them. The nobility agreed, generally, in all except the repartition of the total needed between town and country, and any rule that would reduce their personal privilege of paying practically no taxes. They were concerned for two fundamental rights: to hold their serfs in subjection, and to deny any other social group access to public office, civil or military, high and intermediate.

It is not possible to retail the conflict between the Estates and the Great Elector to end this period of "dualism" of authority. He subdued them, for they preferred their own local and peaceful agricultural and mercantile interests to his, which was a great and growing independent kingdom, defense, and the obligation to go to war at the instance of the Holy Roman Emperor, for example, against the France of Louis XIV, against the Turks on the Austro-Hungarian frontier, against

---

[3] Meaning "policy," or government of the economy, morals, order and health, as is American "police power."

Tatars who broke in from Russia. The royal obligations and tastes meant a standing army and heavy taxation. The Estates in Prussia had even used Polish suzerainty to subvert their own royal chief!

The Great Elector handled this masterfully. One by one the Diets were reduced to nothing. The war of 1655 to 1660 between Poland and Sweden caused terrible devastation of Prussia: about one tenth of the population was lost by death, enslavement, and plague. The King billeted his soldiers on private homes. The protests against this and taxes was universal. The chief city of Königsberg,[4] very wealthy, organized resistance. In October 1662 the leader of resistance was arrested and flung into prison for life, rather a deterrent.
A Standing Army in Time of Peace: 1663. Then, in the Diet of 1661–1663, the Elector was *granted a small standing army!* This was the beginning of the end of the power of the nobles, because, through it, they lost their power of resistance that depended on alliance with the rich towns (even if these were temporarily impoverished). The Elector suppressed the townsmen by occupying Königsberg with his army in 1674. The day of bourgeois independence was finished. The Estates lost their virility: the countryside, as well as the towns, was sapped of self-government. The nobles were content with their high social position; their comparative freedom from taxes; their immunity from military billeting; their hold over their peasants; and their near-monopoly of governmental offices, in the Army, in the top civil administration, in local government and justice (as appointees).

Frederick William I (1688–1740), who came to the throne in 1713, further developed the splendid internal administration and the Army, the colonization of East Prussia, taxed the countryside with a general land tax, purified the fiscal administration further, alleviated the noble pressure on the peasants (*Bauernlegen,* peasant-smashing by dispossession of small proprietors). The Army was more than doubled, to reach 83,000. Its Potsdam Guard was composed of giants, imported if not native. It adopted the bayonet, the iron ramrod, and the parade-ground drill that awed Europe and

---

[4] Since 1945 *annexed* by Soviet Russia!

cowed the Germans. From 1717 elementary schooling became compulsory. Of this regime, in whose land he was born, Winckelmann, the classic historian, fleeing to Dresden said:

> I shudder at the thought of this country. It is oppressed by the greatest despotism that has ever been conceived. It is better to be a circumcized Turk than a Prussian. In a land like Sparta the arts cannot flourish and must degenerate.

The inborn cruelty of the King was translated and magnified into the character of a State. In his own words, "I establish my sovereignty like a *rocher de bronze* and leave the stink of the Diet to my gentlemen Junkers."
Raison d'État. The vulpine ferocity was contributed by Frederick II (1712–1786, King of Prussia, 1740–1786), known as Frederick the *Great.* (The Germans could not get Charlemagne, Charles the Great, out of their minds.) He inherited from his father an Army of 90,000, in an age when the English had rejected a standing army as hostile to political liberty. It had cost over 70 percent of the national budget and, compared in size with Russia's 130,000, France's 160,000, and Austria's 100,000, it was out of all comparative proportion to the population, for even in 1800, Prussia's population was only some 8,000,000 to Austria's 22,000,000, Russia's 38,000,000, and France's 28,000,000, while in 1754 it was about 5,000,000.

Like his father, who treated him worse than a dog, Frederick the Great must be given credit for sincerity when he said: "I am the first servant of the state!" The only question was what he thought the State to be, for whose benefit it existed, his ideas of virtue and happiness, and how far he was ready to consult representative institutions. He was the perfect administrator, a fine general, a brutal military adventurer, and became a Prussian and then an all-German hero, a model for Bismarck and Hitler and thousands in their generations.

"I am led by two things," he said. "Honor, and the interest of the state which has been given over to my conduct by Heaven." The trouble was twofold. He was something of a philosopher who had discarded his Calvinistic religion; this had left him with a freedom from scruple, due to nurture in his predestination, and a belief in other people's unfreedom. He lacked the dynastic feeling that might have made him keep faith with other princes.

He had no use for any but subordinates:

> Sovereigns of the first kind (who themselves rule) are like the soul of the state; the weight of government rests on themselves, like the world on Atlas' shoulders. . . . They have, like God (who makes use of knowledge superior to that of man to execute his will) penetrating and industrious minds to execute their plans and carry out in detail what they have proposed in the large.

Frederick employed this army and his Civil Service to seize other people's lands. The motive was none other than aggrandizement by naked and brazen aggression, without any ethics adduced but only *raison d'état*—that is, "the state needs it."

If the Revolutionary Catechism of the nineteenth-century Russian Nechaev (p. 752) is consulted, then the neatest summary of Frederician ethical nihilism is there available. He was merely a revolutionist like Lenin, but from above. In 1740 he broke the pledge of his father (collectively made with the other rulers of Europe) to uphold the rights of Maria Theresa to the imperial status and domains of the Habsburgs. He did this in company with France, which was anxious to abort the claims of the house of Bavaria to the imperial title and so suppress any rising power in Germany.

Frederick's prey was Silesia. He did not care for moral arguments—indeed, he had none. He proceeded on his own maxim: "First I grab, then I find a jurist who will provide the justification." When this was done, he applauded the conniver with the praise: "Bravo, the work is the work of an able charlatan." His invasion had started even before his ultimatum reached Vienna; and the blandishments included a promise that if he obtained Silesia he would thereafter protect the Empress's other domains. He greeted the shock to Europe's moral sensibilities (then not too noble!) with the cynical adventurer's observation: "I have infected Europe with the war disease as a harlot presents her lovers with certain painful souvenirs.

I myself am cured, fortunately, and watch the others to see how they will emerge from this cure." But he had not been cured, and his loathsome disease in time infected all Germany and contaminated all Europe.

Some other of his sayings (as alleged by his nephew who became Frederick William II): "By the word politics I mean that one must always try to dupe other people," and "Above all follow this maxim zealously, that to despoil your neighbors is to deprive them of the means of injuring you." If his *Political Testaments* and his *Anti-Machievel* (written in French, not German!) are consulted, they are the models of administrative propriety, self-immolation in work for the State, the provision of economic welfare, the embodiment of justice to his subjects, "the lawyer of the poor," as illustrated by the story of the bold miller who was ready to appeal for his windmill to the Imperial Court of Justice even against the King.

Yet all this is fully consistent with despotism and the treatment of his subjects as subjects, not as independent citizens, in the spirit and with the methods of an imperial ruler governing inferior colonial natives, much as the Kremlin treats its people today (p. 821), and with the wickedest perfidy in foreign relations.

What a strange turn for the State to have taken that emerged from the Christianizing efforts of the Order of Teutonic Knights, pledged to poverty, chastity, and obedience! Here was a return to the barbarous savagery of the guardians of the east *märche* against the Slavs. Under his path of conquest, the Prussia of the future was made by deliberate and artificial methods, made as a State —that is, as an area of single domination—but did not *grow* as a national community from the intermixture of its people and from the inward character they themselves possessed in their peaceful daily life. War had been and was further developed as the supreme national occupation: and with it went daily obedience, subservience, regimentation, severity, unscrupulousness, and the worship of the other pillar of the State, along with the high bureaucracy, the officer corps, and the glorification of all these ingredients of successful conquest.

In 1740 Frederick seized Silesia—now in the

teeth of all Europe's fear of this adventurer who broke all the rules of the international game. There were times in the Seven Years' War (1756–1763) when Frederick, the ally of Britain, fought by the coalition of Russia, France, and Austria, almost succumbed and faced the extinction of Prussia, but the divisions of his enemies left him the accumulation of his gains.

Perfidy, broken pledges, secret preparation to destroy other States that were blinded by lying blandishments, subornation of the officials of other countries by bribes, consistent spying were not only his practical methods, but were recommended by him to his successor, some in his *Political Testaments Written in 1752 and 1768.*

By these means, and the piece-by-piece demoralization of his victims ("eaten like an artichoke, leaf by leaf"), he had acquired Silesia, Saxony (1756), and then in 1772, by deliberate conspiracy with Catherine the Great of Russia (Prussian by birth and nurture), he divided up Poland, obtaining for Prussia the area of West Prussia, so uniting her western possessions directly with East Prussia. Later, in 1793 and 1795, Frederick's nephew, his successor, shared the remnants of Poland with Russia and Austria—the latter now intimidated by the marauding union of Russia with Prussia.

IV. MILITARIZATION OF LEADERSHIP

Immoral Consequences

Frederick the Great died amid universal detestation. He had enlarged the dominions, but diminished the people. The censorship was absolute and punishment severe; even in neighboring countries, wherever his arm could stretch, his gangsters beat up critics. He had prevented the rise of an intermediate powerful body of citizens between himself and his Junker-officered armies and army staff and the general body of the enslaved people: in the towns held down by taxation and military regimentation, on the land, purely serfs. The *Obrigekeitsstaat* was in full being. Religion did not oppose it: the Lutheran Church was dominated by the Kings of Prussia; the Civil Service was careful to exclude persons of other confessions.

Frederick the Great himself was a pagan, using both religion and toleration for their political use-fulness to his State. Literature was not nurtured in the Frederickian State, for the King personally detested its poor products and preferred French literature and language. His father and grandfather had no interest in the arts; his father thought that art and science were among the seven deadly sins. There were great German writers in Frederick the Great's time, some who fled from Prussia and dwelt in other Germanic states; Goethe, Lessing, Winckelmann, Klopstock, Herder, Kant; and such great musicians as Mozart, Haydn, and Gluck; but Frederick could not understand them. His French literary connections, especially with Voltaire, were an iron curtain between him and the artistic barrenness that his own dynasty had helped to create. Some of these writers hated Prussian despotism, even as Prussia hated *Kultur.*

The cult of *raison d'état,* as manifested in the evil trickery and force of Frederick the Great, came to be venerated by more than the Prussians, by the Germans.[5] Its practice brought in to Prussia in 1815 Lower Pomerania and part of Saxony, Westphalia, and the Rhineland; in 1866 Hanover, Hesse Cassel, and Schleswig-Holstein. By 1871 Prussia comprised two thirds of Germany's area and population. Who could withstand her?

The Prussian General Staff and the Officer Caste

In Britain, France, and the United States the civil statesmen dominated the Army. In Prussia the Army dominated the civil Ministers; they were members of an agricultural aristocratic class whose supreme landlord and warlord was the King of Prussia.

The Prussian General Staff Service was born somewhere in 1640, as suggested in the sketch of the origins of the Civil Service. It was the General War Commissariat, in partial operation in peace-

[5] Heinz Linge, Adolf Hitler's valet, says that when the *Führer* ordered him to burn his body after his suicide all his possessions were to be included—*except* the picture of Frederick the Great. "But do not—I repeat, do not—burn the picture of Frederick the Great which hangs over my desk." The valet continues: "That picture was Hitler's favorite possession. Through many a long night of work and in days of victory and defeat, the eyes of the great German emperor [*sic*—he was not an emperor! *Author*] looked down on him at his desk."

time, assembled when war was imminent, gathering together all the services needed for war. At the head was a Commissary General. The King was the generalissimo and Chief of Staff. The Civil Service, as we have seen, was militarized in outlook and discipline, and indeed, top officials were titled *Kriegsrat* or War Councilor. It sounds like a Viking and Berserk piratical gang of the Dark Ages, organized for prey and booty. It was pervaded by what was proudly called "Prussian" obedience. This was the machine that headed Frederick the Great's wars of conquest; "The nobles are good and valiant; they only need a national *ésprit de corps.*" It was, owing to the short range of firearms and bad transport, addicted to parade-ground evolutions in war and narrow-horizon battles. The ranks could mass and wheel their fire, but they were held firm by brutal discipline of the peasant infantry. The officers were mainly Junkers, and if not Junkers born, then they were given their *"von"* title for service and helped to acquire a Prussian landed estate. Not all the Junkers were rich; some were miserably poor, for Prussian land is sandy and unfertile and war's destruction and financing sucked away wealth. But they possessed the pride of status, owned serfs, controlled the Church and the administration of justice. Their chief occupation, other than the daily routine of their humdrum lives, was the Army, the Civil Service, and war. War was a brilliant attraction for them.

The Junkers as Rulers and Officers. They had been forced to do service for the King, unlike their counterparts in Czarish Russia who had escaped obligations (see p. 745). They lacked the grace and culture of the French nobles. They were foreign to those notions of political activity of the English gentlemen in county service, in the making and operation of Parliament, in overseas and colonial ventures. The Junkers found nothing in their existence to make them politically, economically, or socially liberal. On the contrary, the Slavs they used on their estates, which they themselves worked, were merely landless laborers, driven as masters drive conquered people in colonies. Somebody has called them "agrarian capitalists." There was more liberalism in East Prussia, however, among the Junkers than in Branden-

berg, Silesia, and Pomerania, because in East Prussia the original inhabitants had been wiped out and their land was given to German colonists, who were freemen and continued to be free farmers. In the other Prussian lands the inhabitants were not wiped out, but became serfs. The East Prussian farmers joined their compatriots in conservatism and militarism in the late nineteenth century for agricultural protection; until then they were comparatively liberal.

The Kings turned to these Junkers for political, administrative, and military support because they were industrious and efficient. He could not, as noted, look to the more considerable mercantile class such as practically advanced the cause of liberty and efficiency in England. The monopoly of government, civil and military, went to the Junkers. Here was a managerial class, nurtured in harsh landed conditions, requiring efficiency to survive, addicted to and willing to cultivate efficiency, but uncivilized. With Slav neighbors whom they hated and feared as well, they put away leisure and pleasantness and cast out their cultured deviants, to maintain their monopoly and to reach corporate hysterical self-control, called *stramm,* rigor. They despised the other Germanic nobility, for these, especially the Austrians, were charming and easygoing aristocrats, not an efficient managerial class.

These held the commanding positions in the Army. Their oath of obedience was never to a people or a nation or a constitution: it was always to the King personally. Close to the King were the dozen best pupils of the year graduating from the *Académie des Nobles* (observe the French name) under Frederick the Great. Next to the King was his Military Cabinet, of military officers and civil officials he especially trusted. At his right and left hands were the departments of recruitment, supply, ordnance, transport, and the commanding generals and military thinkers. This was the central core of the State down to 1919.

Though some liberal Junkerish reformers, after the defeat of Prussia by the French Revolutionary armies and by Napoleon, had some slight success with liberal social reforms, partly for general humane reasons, but *chiefly in order to build a more efficient Army,* they never did accede to, or desire, anything approaching political democracy. Indeed, they were the bitter enemies of this, even anxious to shoot down popular insurrections.

Scharnhorst's Army and Social Reforms. Reforms —the freeing of the serfs—were sought by Scharnhorst, a professional soldier, the son of a tenant farmer in Hanover, who took service with Prussia to become director of the Prussian Military Academy and chief adviser on the reorganization of the Army. Around him in the Quartermaster General's Staff (the general staff) were twenty officers, all from titled families. He secured changes in organization and tactics and the education of the officers. He stimulated a kind of party development: one, prolanded reform, and the other, anti-; not, let it be noticed, the growth of civilian parties that would direct the use of the Army but the growth of military parties that would direct the social changes for military purposes, and no further. This Christian, who believed that war was an evil, to be used reluctantly, tried also to get the nobility's privileges abolished and to send the cadets to the ordinary, not the military, schools, and also to discard the cruel punishments of the rank and file. He desired that the Army serve the nation, not solely the King. The Junkers opposed this loss of status and salaried service, for they had many sons and poor estates. They opposed universal military service because it armed the people: this was vilified as the act of Jacobins. They won the King's mind.

Stein. Another reformer was Freiherr vom Stein: again, no Prussian, and for a time planted on the Prussian King by Napoleon, yet, for Prussia's sake, a double-crosser of Napoleon. Stein was born in Nassau and studied law in four German universities including Vienna. He became a high civil administrator of war and the royal domains, and then commerce and mines, in the Prussian service.

Stein secured these reforms: the Edict of Emancipation in October 1807, abolishing the institution of serfdom throughout Prussia from 1810; free trade in land, the various categories of which (noble, peasant, etc.) were annulled; abolition of all hereditary distinctions and class qualifications for the pursuit of various occupations; local self-government in the towns (see p. 634); and a liberalization of entry into the Civil Service

(see pp. 592–593). But more general representative government was violently rejected by the King and Junkers, and the latter retained their judicial powers and their local police. The peasants were freed of feudal ties, but the Junkers compelled them to surrender their land by sale or enclosure, thus making them more helpless than ever.

General Militarization. The corps of officers was opened to commoners. But, alas!, this did not wipe out the caste. In a sense, the caste was strengthened. For the middle classes, now growing in commerce and soon to develop into powerful industrialists and financiers, came to regard a military commission as the highest social distinction, so dazzling was the military glamor now disseminated through the population. They preferred this to eminence in political life. The prestige they sought depended on their assimilation of themselves to look like the Junker aristocracy, the real thing.

Scharnhorst had the Ministry of War instituted. Thenceforward, there were three military centers of leadership, united (formally) by the King, the Supreme War Lord. These were the King's Military Cabinet; the Ministry of War; the General Staff of commanding officers and the many staff aides. One of the tragedies of German political evolution was that the Ministry of War was never, except for two intervals between 1918 and 1933, held by a civilian. He was always a military career man—that is, a military specialist, with the technical narrowness, the cultural one-sidedness, and the a-popular character of a man nurtured to preparation for war, a man whose only trade was war. Part of this tragedy was the institution of the special military schools which, designed by Scharnhorst and other liberals for improved education of men who were to be officers, came under the control of Junker martinets and so were converted into schools of military governors for Junker sons. Its top class "the Selecta" was given the title of General Staff, though the War Department was in charge of general staff matters.

Field Marshal August Wilhelm Anton Gneisenau, a Saxon, first in Austrian service, then an officer of the English army in the American War of Independence, joined the Prussian Army in

1786, further developed the general staff to handle flexibly mass armies—the *Landwehr,* made of universal service recruits. He, too, was a liberal humanist in politics, favoring constitutional monarchy and unification. But the King was in the grip of those among the Junkers who preferred not only to keep their privileges, but to make those who possessed them into a real caste by the expulsion of the physically unfit and those interested in science or culture.

There were in 1815 three elements in the war organization: the Ministry for War, which included the General Staff; the Adjutant General's department, which was a liaison office between King and the generals and also a military planning body; and the Military Cabinet of the King. They were ill related, and the Military Cabinet, ill defined.

The Best Brains, Military

From this time followed a succession of great military advisers, teachers, and organizers—Clausewitz, Moltke, Roon, and so on—who come down through the Revolution of 1848 into the Bismarckian era. Whereas in Britain and France the best brains went into civil statesmanship, in Prussia the best brains went into literature, the professorial life, the Civil Service, and the officers' corps. There was no Parliament to occupy them; and they did not make one. But the essential truth was that this was the Army of a special class, and the various elements of the central Army direction were always trying to become free of direction by the King's general civil advisers and Ministers.

The officers were always hostile to democratic reforms. Even a *Landwehr* had been enacted against the King's and their wishes. In 1800 the titled officers composed 60 percent of all, as the untitled had increased in number. In 1860 it was still as high a proportion. Even in 1936 noble families supplied 80 percent of the colonel generals in the *German* army, 33 percent of the generals, 30 percent of the lieutenant generals, and 22 percent of the colonels! The titled ones became all the more a closed corporation, especially as they had their education at cadet schools, while the others were heterogeneous in education and experience of the world. When reformers sought to broaden cadet education, they found themselves denounced as enemies of Prussia.

The system was admired by Czarist Russia, but was without any roots in the Prussian people. The liberal elements in the officers' corps were expelled: after 1848 they migrated to America. No one rose to rank, still less to high rank, in the regiments, without virtual selection by the regiment itself, though formally the King made the appointment. The Junkers were a proportionately declining class as German trade and industry began to soar after the Napoleonic Wars, for their estates were poor. They contributed to the State obedience and self-denial devotion, but they were not devoted to the nation as the people.

By 1833 the war organization had attained its form as maintained up to the war and downfall of 1914–1918: in other words, it ran the War of 1866, the War of 1871, and World War I. It consisted of the Military Cabinet and the King, the War Ministry, and the General Staff. The Military Cabinet and the General Staff, possessed of the most precious ingredient of influence, special knowledge, in a field that concerned the nation's existence, depressed the role of the Ministry of War.

All their brains were spent on four matters: (1) planning wars of defense and annexationist policy against imaginary enemies, and conducting war games, *Kriegspiel;* (2) considering the foreign policy that ought to follow from *their* plans and mastery of war technology; (3) undergoing technical training in the various special branches of the staff work—cartography, transport, gunnery, development and administration, communications, and so on, to the neglect of humane education; (4) the design of the smartest uniforms in the world. The newly growing railroad system was planned for *Blitzkrieg* by swift movement between the eastern and western borders: Slavs and the French.

Clausewitz. Karl von Clausewitz (1780–1831) was born and nurtured in an age when war had developed into the conflict of peoples, with ideology as their driving force. Thus in the French Revolutionary armies, thus also in the reciprocal enmities of the French, the Prussians, the Austrians, the Russians, and the Poles. War was no longer a game of chess with limited objects as conducted by the princes and aristocracies of the eighteenth century. Clausewitz taught the infernal doctrine that "War is a continuation of policy by other means." He was a Christian, but his profession was that of a soldier. He was devoted to the preservation of the State, less than the people. When war broke out the enemy must be smashed, *any means* of terror being proper to break the other State. Yet Clausewitz himself did not say that policy should be that of *seeking* war.

However, the severity of his doctrine that war is a continuation of policy by other means dehumanizes policy for the average soldier, and certainly for the Prussian statesmen with their rapacious heroes of the past, and for officers with a career to make. After Justice had been attained in the world, taught Clausewitz, Europe might have a common political order; until that time war was the *ultima ratio regnum*. He acclaimed not the State, as people, over the Army; but the Army as the guardian and leader of the State; again, not as people, other people, but only as the purposes and conscience of the little band of men at the top. In Clausewitz's own lifetime Alfred Krupp founded his gun factories at Essen; in 1846 he developed the first rifled guns that allowed a range enormously longer than smooth-bored guns; in the 1860's he supplied the breech-loaders; by 1870, 10,000 men were working in his factory.

In 1844 the Army shot down the weavers of Silesia who had risen in insurrection against their employers; in March 1848 they shot down the insurrection in Berlin, but retreating at royal orders, never forgot the humiliation at the hands of the ordinary burghers. The *Landwehr* showed some sympathy with the people, but neither this (which became ineffective) nor the regular soldiers went over to the people. In 1849 the Prussian army put down the pitiful embers of revolt in Saxony and South Germany. The solidarity of King, officers, and the Protestant Church was remarkable: the workingmen, even the middle classes, saw in them the incarnation of all that was reactionary.

A Class Army in Class War. By now the reaction of the Army was not merely the general reaction against democracy; it was class warfare against the middle class and the rising working class in industry. The Army also hated so-called "quill-drivers"—that is, writers, lawyers, literary men. Young philosophers, such as Karl Marx, left Prussia for foreign lands, he in 1843. The era of economic expansion that was now upon Germany ultimately produced a movement of the upper middle classes away from liberalism. For though they demanded political and social equality with the upper class, they were nationalists, and the combination of economic acquisitiveness with nationalism produced militarism. They, too, were not friends of the literary critics of absolutism, the people called in later times and other places "egg-heads." Chiefs of the General Staff, like the gifted Hellmut von Moltke (again a non-Prussian, born in Mecklenburg), were ardent friends of all-German unification but regarded democracy as "moral cholera," as Prussia's "worst enemy." They argued that German unification, necessary for the self-preservation of a land without natural frontiers and in an era when wars had become so terrible and exterminating, would have to come by the sword. Whoever favored nationalism and German unity began to be persuaded that the sword—that is, the Army—was its necessary instrument. Whatever their intentions, the reformers had not liberalized the State but militarized the people.

Bismarck, Greatest Junker. The final ascendency of the General Staff was attained in the years around 1862. For Otto von Bismarck became the King's chief minister and killed German parliamentarism by raising taxes by fraud and force against the will of the Prussian Diet. This is dealt with properly later (pp. 571–572). But the doctrine that best sums up his idea of politics for Prussia and Germany is perfectly expressed in his speech of 1862, the burial speech over the idea of a free parliamentary system:

It is true that we can hardly escape complications in Germany, though we do not seek them. Germany does not look to Prussia's liberalism, *but to her power* [italics supplied]. The South German States would like to indulge in liberalism, and therefore no one will assign Prussia's role to them! Prussia must collect her forces and hold them in reserve for a favorable moment, which has already come and gone several times. Since the treaties of Vienna, our frontiers have been ill designed for a healthy body politic. The great questions of the time will be decided, not by speeches and resolutions or majorities (that was the mistake of 1848 and 1849), *but by blood and iron* [italics supplied].

V. ROMANTIC NATIONALISM

Nationalism means the independent sovereign government of a group in its own frontiers, its independence being justified by a consciousness of long cultural belonging-together: it is a feeling of group self-hood. The same land, language, literature, much the same original physical characteristics and geographical concentration, and common historical experience help to create this feeling of likeness and mutual obligation.

The British had achieved this consciousness of kind, and a State to match it, by the fifteenth century. France arrived at its national consciousness partly through the views of Rousseau that the State had its justification in the general will of the people and partly in the dynamic embodiment of this view, when the Revolution engendered a passionate, creative consciousness in the masses of the democratic *patrie*. This had, in fact, given victory to the French soldiers over the old Prussian Army. It was the democratic element that infused French national self-feeling; it was a stout moderation in self-government and liberty that suffused the British.

But, with the Germans, it was the feeling of the rights of their nation *against* others and of nationalism as a mission of spiritual and physical expansion.

A famous German dictum runs: "When two revolutions encounter each other, the stronger devours the weaker." The two revolutions that encountered each other in Germany from 1789 onward were the democratic revolution and the revolution of the German states system (all 1800 of them) for national unity, or nationalism. Nationalism ate up democracy because, at least for one reason, the static forces of royal and class absolutism were too strong for the liberty, whereas absolutism could and did become the instrument of national unity.

The passion of nationalism in Germany had these characteristics.

(1) It was inspired by the humiliation of defeat by the French revolutionary invaders and by Napoleon's victories over them.

(2) It came late compared with other nations, in a time when it was taken over by mystic philosophers who endowed it with exaggerated meaning to Germans, flouting the demands of humanity and justice and charity, those values that emanated from or created Natural Law or Natural Rights embodied in Roman Christian civilization that had not sunk into east German character.

(3) Next, it was highly conscious of itself, because it arrived late; it was something about which to become hysterical or romantic.

(4) Further, it had been stimulated by economic considerations, since the multi-state system meant barriers to commerce in order to maintain the economic autonomy of the states. This did not inspire a slow and magnanimous growth of unity. It was too late for growth. The enforced attainment of unity through the planned power of absolute governments was the order of the day.

The Humiliation of Foreign Occupation

Prussia joined Austria to rescue the French monarchy from the Revolution. These allies were beaten at Valmy in 1792. Thenceforward, until 1815 Prussia was either at war or perfidiously evading her obligations to Austria by staying out in order to safeguard her Slav frontier. She took part with the Russian and Austrian jackals in the sharing out of Poland among them. The French held the west of Germany and the left bank of the Rhine for twenty years, from 1795 to 1815. Their feudal governments were overthrown and French revolutionary laws introduced—a permanent influence on this area. In 1806 Napoleon, having smashed Austria, founded the Confederation of the Rhine, by reorganizing the hundreds of Germanic princedoms and sharing them out among the bigger states, almost the boundaries of the twentieth century. He abolished the Holy Roman Empire in 1806, of which he had assumed the crown; now the sovereignty of the newly defined states was untrammeled.

Napoleon provoked the sulking Prussians into war and smashed them abjectly at Jena and Auerstadt in two weeks in October 1806. By the Peace of Tilsit (July 1807), merciful through Russia's friendly intervention, a small remnant of Prussia was saved from total disruption and complete dis-grace. The Polish thefts had to be disgorged; the army was reduced to 40,000; lands west of the Elbe were constructed into an independent West-phalia; a big indemnity was exacted. The remnant was allowed to remain a kingdom.

Nationalism Is Hatred, or Xenophobia. A terrible hatred arose for the French occupation authorities throughout the Germanic states, wildest in North Germany where they were most oppressive, and most bitter and nostalgic among the educated Ger-mans, the literary men, and the university stu-dents. The resultant passion will be conveyed in later pages. The Prussian King, after the burn-ing of Moscow and Napoleon's retreat, was finally forced into fighting by the Czar's pressure. A rising of some fanatical volunteers followed in the War of Liberation; it was not internal liberation, but nationalism. Many vicissitudes ended in the so-called Battle of the Nations—the very term is significant—in October 1813, in which Napoleon was defeated near Leipzig by the coalition of Aus-tria, Russia, and Prussia. Pursued, he reentered France; and the allies (with England paying and fighting in Spain) occupied Paris. The Prussian armies were in Paris for the first time in March 1814; for the second time after Waterloo, in 1815. It made for Prussian pride and for contempt of France and fear of her revengefulness; it began the French nineteenth-century account of wrongs against Prussia and then Germany. The Prussian army under Blücher had made an important con-tribution to victory at Waterloo; they came even to claim that the battle was *not* Wellington's.

The Political Reconstruction of Germany. The Congress of Vienna reconstructed Germany. The extension of the possessions of Prussia has already been retailed. She yielded Anspach and Bayreuth (in south Germany) to Bavaria, which was ex-panded further by the gift of Würzburg and the Palatinate.

Germany was now formed into only thirty-nine states, ten times fewer than the principal states alone of before 1806. Four of these were the Free Cities of Hamburg, Bremen, Lubeck, and Frank-furt. The rest were monarchies. The proposal to restore the Holy Roman Empire was rejected. In the Federal Act of June 1815 the thirty-nine states were organized into a confederation, with a Diet under the presidency of Austria located in Frank-furt. Excluded from this confederation were the Prussian lands of Prussia and Posen (not regarded as Germany!) and Austria's non-German areas. The significance of this peculiar union is dealt with presently (p. 567ff.). After Waterloo, Prussia obtained Saarbrücken and Saarlouis; she was de-nied Alsace for which her poets and romantic na-tionalistic philosophers yammered. In this con-federation the predominant states by far were Aus-tria and Prussia. Which would lead Germany?

Internal Religious Fission. The reorganization added another division to those already keeping Germany disunited. The ecclesiastical states had been ruled by Catholic prince-bishops. As govern-mental authorities they had been disliked. Now they and their people were in areas with Prot-estant princes. The bishops recovered their reli-gious prestige and became the leaders of Roman Catholic groups ready to make political group-ings and later nationwide political parties on a Roman Catholic basis. As we shall see, this had a profound effect in the Bismarckian *Kaiserreich* (p. 603) and gave birth to the Center Party of that era and subsequently of the Christian Democratic Party of the post-World-War-II period (see Chap-ter 7).

German Nationalism Came Late

German nationalism was romantic, total, and bru-tal, prepared to do things acceptable in the morals of the year A.D. 1000 but not A.D. 1900. This is a fact of world importance. The eighteenth century was, throughout Europe, the Age of Enlighten-ment. It showed a growing reliance on the dis-covery of Nature's laws and the extension of cos-mopolitanism, the idea of a world citizenship (as the Germans called it, *Weltbürgertum*). This was implied in natural law, and this, again, stemmed from the Roman thinkers and law and had be-come further humanized with time. The Ger-man populace entertained no *national* hatreds. In-spired by Greece and Rome, the German intelli-gentsia sought to revive classical humanism. But the Prussian Fredericks allowed toleration, not out of conviction but because they exacted obedi-ence first and last and could do so effectively with the aid of a standing army.

The partitions of Poland aroused the earliest

fury about the rights of nations. The humiliation of the French victories and then the jubilation at military triumph spurred on to unlimited exaggerations German romantic espousal of the nation as the superior of all forms of human life, whether the individual, *per se,* in relationship to the community or science, art, the economy, literature, the works of the mind.

This is of such controlling importance in the evolution and practice of German government, that some further analysis is essential.

The Volk

These men became inebriated with the idea of the lawless, law-imposing supremacy of the collectivity called the German *Volk:* Johann Gottfried Herder (scholar and court preacher), Karl Wilhelm Friedrich von Schlegel (poet and scholar), Johann Gottlieb von Fichte (professor), Ludwig Achim von Arnim (Prussian poet), Friedrich Wilhelm Joseph Schelling (professor of philosophy), Adam Heinrich Muller, and Georg Wilhelm Friedrich Hegel (professor of philosophy)—their lives spanning roughly the crucial period of the 1780's to the generation after the Napoleonic Wars. We can refer only to a few among these.

Herder (1744–1803). An East Prussian of poor parentage, Herder talked of "a nationality as a plant of nature," a "national animal," and the soul of the *Volk*—the folk. The word *Volk*, as in *Deutsches Volk*—that is, German nation or German people—has tones, however struck by these men, that are *deeper,* more tortuous and darkly indefinable, than the more conventional terms. *Tribal community,* in a sense of collective consanguinity, means almost the congealment of the individual in the passionate inward fervor of the blood-connected tribe. And this rooted historicity is of its essence. As a student of medicine turned to philosophy and anthropology, Herder became finally interested in the *nature-determined* evolution of ideas, poetry, civilizations. Herder declared:

> Do not nationalities differ in everything, in poetry, in appearance, in tastes, in usages, customs and language? Must not religion which partakes of these also differ among nationalities?

But what did this, if true, mean practically? That the German national spirit must find its territorial unity. It must no longer be contemptuous, with the *Aufklärung,* of "everything that concerns the fatherland." Let it be naïve, spontaneous, native. He even, in this intoxication with the *Volk,* claimed that the English are Germans and that in all the greatest things the Germans had even recently led the English. Here is megalomania. It is even more dangerous, for Herder, like German philosophers before and after him, argued that the primitive, subjective feelings, the subjective intuitions, were valid truth to be reasoned into validity and *let go.* He had learned this from the Königsberger Hamann, an antinationalist thinker, a believer in *belief* and tradition as valid shapers of truth. The way was being opened for the assault of the Will on men, regardless of Truth in that Will.

To secure this he proposes a completely totalitarian State: governmental command over one's occupation, ordering of trade and industry, farming and commerce by quotas. All foreign trade is a State monopoly but reduced to a minimum in the interests of self-sufficiency and strength in war. "Substitutes" are home-produced; luxuries are excluded. A great administrative and inspectoral system is in charge of this. "A firm plan" regulates all, even journeys abroad. The idea is to force other nations to yield to German demands for extended frontiers by intimidation without actual war: ". . . without bloodshed and without a stroke of the sword, and its operations would be more of a march of occupation than a war."

Anti-Laissez Faire. His *Geschlossene Handelsstaat,* the *Closed Commercial State,* published in 1800, utterly subjected the individual and his spontaneous groupings to the State or *Volk.* This work is the moral antipodes to Adam Smith's *Wealth of Nations.* The German philosophers (especially Adam Müller, p. 591) were the first haters of *laissez faire,* of individually directed enterprise, of the notion that the national wealth is the sum of the wealth of individuals created by them in the work and capital investment freely determined by them, and the human moderation of the English economist.

Fichte. Fichte answers the fundamental question of all governmental systems: What is life lived for? What ought people to want? His answer is "a higher level of national honor and a distinctly more decided national character," "the love with attachment of everything pertaining to the fatherland." What for?

The Addresses to the German Nation that Fichte gave in Berlin in 1807 were designed to stir the Germans to rise out of the defeat of Tilsit. They carried the gospel of expansionism and totalitarianism to a patriotic frenzy. The Latin languages were dead, while the German language alone (of all the Teutonic ones) was living and virile. It was time to discard all cosmopolitanism. For the Germans were the primitive *Volk,* the true *Volk;* its branches had no right to call themselves folk at all: *deutsch* actually means *original.*

> Only the German really has a *Volk* and is entitled to count on one, and he alone is capable of real and rational love for his nation. . . . The spirit which is to be produced by (education) includes the higher love of fatherland, the conception of its earthly life as eternal end and of the fatherland as the support of eternity. . . . Folk and fatherland in this sense, as a support and guarantee of eternity here on earth and as that which can be eternal here below, far transcend the state in the ordinary sense of the word, that is, the social order as comprehended by mere intellectual conception.

This is the ultimate in state-madness, surely? Other religions and States endeavor to understand and limit the State by "intellectual conception"; others allow for the individual's salvation in eternity and for this purpose leave him as great a degree of freedom as is possible with risks to the nation's self-preservation and collective welfare. Not this *German* State:

> What spirit has an undisputed right to summon and to order everyone concerned, whether he is personally willing or not, and to compel all who resist, to risk everything including his life? Not the spirit of the peaceful citizen's love for the constitution and the laws, but the devouring flame of higher patriotism, which embraces the nation as the mantle of eternity, for which the nobleminded man joyfully sacrifices himself.

Thus was the individual will, so weak, taught to find peace and satisfaction by drowning itself in the group, the German group!

"Kept" Professors. Fichte was appointed rector of the University of Berlin in 1810, the year of its foundation. This is the beginning of a long line of "kept" professors, appointed to preach philosophy or history justifying Prussianism. A liberal, applauded later by John Stuart Mill (p. 36), Wilhelm von Humboldt, had helped to found the university, the apex of the system of Prussian education that was to become famous for its intellectual severity and industriousness all over the world. But it was dedicated to the unliberalized support of Prussian authoritarianism, militarism, international ruffianism. Liberals were never appointed, or if this happened by accident, were chased away. Within three years Fichte was exhorting the King of Prussia to become the "Taskmaster for the Production of Germanity."

Schelling (1775-1854). Schelling born in Württemberg, leads on to Hegel. The State is not made by individuals; the intellectual substance of nature creates State and individual simultaneously, making individuals but "imaginary phantoms." (Hardly the point of view of John Locke or David Hume or George Washington!) The State embraces everything: science, religion, art. It does not exist "to ensure mutual assurance of rights." The German "displays the highest and the richest unity of which human nature is capable." He combines science (legislation), religion (public morality), and national heroism and art (the living rhythmic movement of public life), while other peoples keep them separate. Hence, foreign borrowings should be eradicated from the German spirit.

Patriotic poets, such as Hölderlin, von Arnim, and Arndt, set these *Volk* sentiments to verse and music, and the blood-lust into popular songs.

Deep Thinkers. This madness of *totality and depth* is seen in a more moderate form in Kant's metaphysics. It is the mark of the German thinker to be deep; he cannot stop on the surface of life or just beneath. He is the very opposite of the *flat* way of political thinking which is Anglo-Saxon. But where is depth to stop? It is a form of never resting, of always subverting, of insecurity except in extremes; of infinitism. Kant retained his fervor for the French Revolution and for a republic and for eternal peace among the peoples as these others did not, seeing in their peaceful development and their occasional friction a mutual stimulation conducive to moralizing them all. But, after all, his vast system started and ended in the apotheosis of DUTIES, not rights. It was the categorical imperative to duties that he conveyed to all peoples. The philosophers who followed, men like Nietzsche (p. 608) and Treitschke (p. 607) simply could not find it in themselves to argue and worship the liberal State or the equality, if not the inferiority, of the German nation among all other nations, to admit the value of other nations, or to counsel against war as the proper instrument of policy. Other views were not allowed expression in public in the nineteenth century. By denying that man could comprehend the world of reality outside his own mind, and asserting that Ethics were the product of his inner life not deducible from facts at all, Kant spurred on the view that one's own inspirations had the validity of truth, and others followed, inferring that inspiration was Will, sufficient to itself as the Good, embodied in group and leader.

Hegel. Of all German philosophers, Hegel has had the most influence on the greatest number of minds in Germany for his to become the prevailing political influence. He made more systematic the thoughts we have already presented. It is a Total doctrine. He does not build up from everyday men to a vision of the Whole, but begins with *his* Idea of the Whole universe and then places men and States within his fiction.

(a) *The Idea.* "All that is rational is real (or actual) and all that is real is rational." Then it might be right to be quiescent under authority, for the State is *real* as law, policemen, taxes, military service. But *is* the actual State before us *rational?* He skips the problem; he says he is only interested in the *essence* of the State, not its faulty forms, but its meaning in the universe. (Who, even of Germans, could grasp this?)

Somewhere in the sky there is an Idea or eternal and essential rationality or God. We should try to grasp this Whole, to become conscious of it and regard ourselves as mere nothings unless we sub-

ordinate our purposes, as we (capriciously) feel them, to it. Our purposes are mere caprices unless they are tamed to serve the *Idea,* to let it have its own way with us. If we grasp what the Idea is trying to do on earth at each stage of history—that is, everyday—and subject ourselves thereto, then we are free, and only such conscious subordination is freedom.

> The state is mind on earth, consciously realizing itself on earth. . . . In considering freedom, the starting point must not be individuality, the individual self-consciousness, but only the essence of self-consciousness.

But how can a citizen know the difference between his individual desires, thoughts, reasoning, and imagination and this *essence?* What is this essence? Who is to say authoritatively what it is?

> For whether man knows it or not, this essence is externally realized as a self-subsistent power in which single individuals are only moments.

The view of the individual, in this peculiar Hegelian religion or metaphysics, is in sharpest, abject contrast to the Western doctrine of the primacy and dignity of the individual.

> The state is the march of God in the world. The basis of the state is the power of reason making itself actual as will.

What a monstrous leap away from what is actual, that which we can appreciate with our five senses and understanding, to something that no one person really knows—the nature of God, and especially a God that one man, Hegel, has in mind!

> In considering the Idea of the State, we must not have our eyes on particular states or on particular institutions. Instead, we must consider the Idea, this actual God, by itself. . . . Man must therefore *venerate the state as a secular deity* and observe that if it is difficult to comprehend nature, it is infinitely harder to understand the state.

(b) *Duty Is Freedom!* Thus, excluded from regarding his own particular ends and ideas as sovereign and the State as an association arrived at by practical transactions to secure protection from violence in order that he may work out his freedom for himself, men are constrained by the Idea, by Reason, by God, to obey the secular representation of these, in the State. They are constrained to unconditional DUTY.

> The state is the actuality of the ethical Idea. . . . The mind of a nation [note the transition from *state* to *nation*—author] is the divine, knowing and willing itself. . . . This substantial unity [the state] is an absolute unmoved end in itself, in which freedom attains its supreme height. On the other hand, this final end has supreme right against the individual, whose supreme duty it is to be a member of the state. . . . Since the state is mind objectified, it is only as one of its members that the individual himself has objectivity, genuine individuality, and an ethical life.

This line of reasoning certainly allows the common man to work and speak, but such actions are only "personal," and must give way to the State's decrees.

> Since the laws and institutions of the ethical order make up the concept of freedom, they are the substance or universal essence of individuals, who are thus related to them as accidents only. Whether the individual exists or not is all one to the objective ethical order. It alone is permanent and is the power regulating the life of individuals.
>
> Thus duty is not a restriction of freedom, but only on freedom in the abstract, that is, on unfreedom. Duty is the attainment of our essence, the winning of positive freedom.

The upshot of the doctrine is plain: it puts the individual and all his groups at the mercy of the State.

Three other things are needed to appreciate Hegel's influence: the part assigned to leaders or heroes, the outlook on the separation of powers, and the value of popular representation.

(c) *The Hero Is Not Responsible.* Hegel taught that great men, Heroes, were those men Reason or the Idea had chosen, by its inscrutable processes, to take people the next necessary step ahead in the unfolding of the Idea's intentions. These men were not chosen by representative institutions; they just happened by birth. They, like no one else, could step forward, according to the quality of their Passion, and act. They were not responsible by prior election by the mass of mankind. They were not responsible for the pain they caused or the policies they pursued. Their justification was not in an elected trusteeship for others; it was in virtue of the Idea.

The view is developed in the *Introduction to the Philosophy of History.*

> Historical men—World-Historical individuals—are those in whose aims such a general principle lies (the development of the *creating* Idea, of Truth striving and urging towards consciousness of itself).

Like Caesar, Alexander, Napoleon, their

> own particular aims involve those large issues which are the will of the World-Spirit.

(When at Jena, he saw Napoleon riding by, he said, "There goes the World Spirit!") Does not this World Spirit sound like a romantic fairy story?

> They may be called Heroes, inasmuch as they have derived their purposes and their vocation, not from the calm, regular course of things, sanctioned by the existing order; but from a concealed fount—one which has not attained to phenomenal, present existence, from that inner Spirit, still hidden beneath the surface, which, impinging on the outer world as on a shell, bursts it in pieces, because it is a different kernel from the one which belonged to the shell in question. They are men, therefore, who appear to draw the impulse of their life from themselves. . . .
>
> Such individuals had no consciousness of the general Idea they were unfolding, while prosecuting those aims of theirs; on the contrary, they were practical, political men. But at the same time they were thinking men, who had an insight into the requirements of the time—*what was ripe for development.* This was the very Truth for their age, for their world; the species next in order, so to speak, and which was already formed in the womb of time. . . . World-historical men—the Heroes of an epoch—must therefore be recognized as its clear-sighted ones; *their* deeds, *their* words are the best of that time. ("Whatever is actual is *national!*")

But how can we know whether they are char-latans? or madmen? or for whose good they work? This is what Western institutions have sought—as we observed with David Hume (p. 32), to avert the operations of knaves. Hegel's only guide is no help at all: he leaves it to the *cunning or reason:* "it sets the passions to work for itself." Does it cause pain? Yes. Caesar, Alex-ander, and Napoleon had no happy personal fates. To others? Yes: "So mighty a form must trample down many an innocent flower—crush to pieces many an object in its path." Will Religion, Moral-ity, Ethics suffer in the process? Yes: but we should not fall into the "Litany of Lamentations, that the good and pious often—or for the most part—fare ill in the world, while the evil-disposed and wicked prosper."

Thus, all is out of human control; yet all is well! But there is imprinted on the consciousness of *all* men some apprehension of the Idea. Hence, surely, they ought to have an opportunity of stat-ing it? This would lead to equal and free votes to create the national will. Hegel does not accept this conclusion. Common men must not have the sov-ereign power to shape the will of the State; they may talk, but they cannot make the law. The law is to be made by that which is settled as the *de facto* stronger power—the monarchy. Even the representation may not be universal and individ-ual suffrage, but must be corporate, through estates or guilds, for this enables the containment of the individual wills in a higher *form,* otherwise the State would be pulverized into atoms, in ac-cordance with Rousseau's theory.

(d) *Separation of Powers.* His observations on the separation of powers will suffice to consum-mate the Hegelian outlook.

The powers of the state, then, must certainly be distinguished (to get rationality), but each of them must build itself inwardly into a whole and contain itself in the other moments. When we speak of the distinct activities of these powers, we must not slip into the monstrous error of so interpreting their distinction as to suppose that each power should subsist inde-pendently in abstraction from the others. The truth is that the powers are to be distinguished only as moments of the concept. If instead they

subsist independently in abstraction from one another, then it is as clear as day that no inde-pendent units can constitute a unity but must of course give rise to strife, whereby either the whole is destroyed or else unity is restored by force. . . . The vital point, then, is that since the fixed characters of the powers are implicitly the whole, as also all the powers as existents constitute the concept as a whole.

He was terrified by the destruction of the State implicit in the separation of powers, and by the example of the clash of powers in the French revolutionary government. The student is referred to the pages on the Russian Communist view of the separation of powers (p. 772): it is highly Hegelian!

(e) *Germanity and International Relations.* The history of civilization showed four successive periods: the Oriental, the Greek, the Roman, and the German. This last was the culmination. Hegel could think of nothing more original to come. It put Germany on top, and Prussia on Ger-many.

The Germanic spirit is the spirit of the new world, whose object is the realization of absolute truth as endless self-determination, of freedom which has its absolute form for content. The vocation of the Germanic peoples is to furnish the bearers of the Christian principle.

He was thus able to commend the idolatry of Frederick the Great. This deliberate and a-moral murderer, according to Hegel,

. . . comprehended the protestant principle from the temporal side and, while discounte-nancing religious controversies . . . he pos-sessed the consciousness of universality, which constitutes the uttermost depth of the spirit and the self-conscious power of thought . . . he can be called the ruler with whom there enters into reality the new epoch in which true state-interest receives its universality and highest right. Special appreciation must be de-voted to Frederick II in that he has intellec-tually comprehended the general purpose of the state, and that he was first among rulers who adhered to the general in the state, and did not allow the particular further validity if it was op-posed to the purpose of the state.

In other words, Hegel, the professor of philosophy at the University of Berlin after the death of Fichte, and thus holder of virtually a civil servant's position, approved whatever was in the Prussian State as it was. There are German scholars who charge Hegel with actual venality in this application of his general philosophy.

His own proposition that history moved in the stages of Thesis, Antithesis, and Synthesis, which then became the next Thesis, had no validity for him. For Hegel, history had culminated in Berlin with the imposed authoritarian Constitution of 1819. That is why Karl Marx had to stand Hegelianism on its head in order to help the cunning of reason one further step on. But this dialectical method is of little interest to us except for two reasons: its utter vagueness, an assertion to which individual men were enslaved, and, second, its incapacity to enable Hegel to predict the next stage and so enable men to control its process.

Hence war is not an absolute evil, for the transient (the State) is finite en route to the service of the Idea or the Essence.

War has the higher significance that by its agency, as I have remarked elsewhere, the ethical health of peoples is preserved in their indifference to the stabilization of finite institutions; just as the blowing of the winds preserves the sea from the foulness which would be the result of a prolonged calm, so also corruption in nations would be the product of prolonged, let alone "perpetual," peace. . . .

But the state is an individual and individuality essentially implies negation. Hence even if a number of states make themselves into a family, this group as an individual must engender an opposite and create an enemy.

States are not private persons but completely autonomous totalities in themselves, and so the relation between them differs from a moral relation and a relation involving private rights. . . . Now since there is no power in existence which decides in face of the states what is right in principle and actualizes this decision, it follows that so far as international relations are concerned we can never get beyond an "ought."

The nation-state is mind in its substantive rationality and immediate actuality and is therefore the absolute power on earth. It follows that every state is sovereign and autonomous against its neighbours. . . . If states disagree and their particular wills cannot be harmonized the matter can only be settled by war.

When politics is alleged to clash with morals and so to be always wrong, the doctrine propounded rests on superficial ideas about morality, the nature of the state, and the state's relation to the moral point of view.

Karl Marx. This same furor to grasp the Whole, to make a Total system, to subject all life and every individual in the meshes of one total net of history and existence inspired the economic-social-political philosophy of Karl Marx. As he said he stood Hegel upside down: Hegel said the Consciousness determines everything, including the economic, while Marx was convinced that the economic determined the Consciousness.

Building and Transmission of Political Values

A nation is a mass of average people, not a few talented men, geniuses, or eccentrics. But many among the masses admire their "betters" who are original; they get ideas and "inspiration" from them, excitement of taking sides. If the few acquire some force, the many are intimidated by them. Many more appreciate the common needs discerned and preached by the more creative minds. How do such developing doctrines of Right and Wrong spread? Through the schools, the Army, the press, and that mightiest and cheapest of all mass media, persons talking to persons, the most widespread pleasure human beings possess. In Germany the schools (p. 599) were deliberately parts of an authoritarian State. Politically, they taught not "character" as in the English schools of "gentlemen," but competence and obedience, even servility. Military conscription had started early, so that generation after generation the young men, universally, were regimented by Prussian sergeant-majors and schooled to obsequious sacrifice for the glory of the State, Prussia-style.

VI. THE GERMAN POLITICAL MIND

State Worship

Thus we have demonstrated the rise of Prussia and modern Germany from the original tribes and their resistance of Christianity and Roman culture so far as the east and north of Germany is concerned. We have traced the rise of the military expansionist a-moral State of Prussia and suggested the transmission of its influence through its force, success, and prestige. We have, in particular noticed the romantic, mystical, *unlimited* worship of the State by the philosophers, suggested their influence on the ruling groups in Germany, and observed the power of the latter over the nameless enserfed peasantry, and the physical crushing of the more enlightened middle class, alas, too small to prevail.

Incidentally, we have revealed the character of German political thought. It is (1) either narrowly, if efficiently, military and administrative; or (2) it is Total and Metaphysical, calling in some original *Volk* or some Idea as the authority and sponsor of governmental power unlimited by rational measure and moderation. It is arrogant, self-confident, sure of exclusive salvation. This polity, first founded on the extermination and enslavement of the Slavs or Catholic authoritarianism, converted its history into the plan of its future. No other country has this particular succession of nineteenth-century philosophers, so revolutionary in international affairs, so obsequious and mystically obedient to the Leader in domestic government, so ecstatic to lick the foot that kicks it.

Appraisal of German Characteristics in Government

(1.) Romantic Nationalism. All nations contain a mystique of collective life, of romantic nationalism. It is the desire for unity and self-preservation, a con-sentiment thereto. But is the unity absolute, like a mass of honey embalming the bees in every respect, over all movement of the spirit and behavior? Or is it to be the minimum integument, as voluntary as possible? Is it to be consent, retractable, of a social-contract nature rather than like an organic human body and mind? The German conception errs to an extreme view of the latter, to be a primitive horde rather than a collection of thinking individuals. It is, as Ferdinand Tönnies has suggested, a *Gemeinschaft,* a community, rather than a *Gesellschaft,* a society; and,

being German, he thought the former had a higher moral value than the latter.

(2.) Dionysian Spirit. Nietzsche has suggested that the German spirit is Dionysian, since it rather resembles the god Dionysus, the god of emotion, intuition, feeling, passion, insensate and intoxicated in its search for the ultimate mysteries of the Absolute. In ancient Greece, mad, drunken orgies, whipped up by music, sent its votaries into extremes of group self-forgetfulness. It could be suicidal, as were Bismarck, Hitler, Goering, and others. It reeks of the Nazi appeal to "blood and soil"; of "thinking with the blood," the "burning of the books," the threat by Goering to shoot with his revolver at the word *culture*. It is the flight from Reason.

Apollo represents clarity, precision, objectivity, not going beyond one's depth. It is rather a French and Anglo-Saxon trait; Apollonian.

The Dionysian appears in Luther's frenzied prophecies; in the Romantics; in Nietzsche, in Richard Wagner (p. 609), and Hitler, and is heavily present in Bismarck, as we shall see (p. 570ff.).

(3) Virtue Is Prior to Happiness. The German political thinkers are not Utilitarians (p. 34). Their calculus is not that of Pleasure and Pain, but Virtue and Vice; and Duty is the purpose of life, not Happiness. Of course, as between countries the distinction in this as other respects is one of degree. In Germany, the pursuit of Duty has made for a rigorous, strict ordering of life, subjection to authority, tremendous pressure on dissenters, a kind of subhysteria. A German father tends to treat his family as Frederick the Great did the State: "I am the first servant of the state!", and he wants something in return for his self-sacrifice.

(4) Family and State. All observers agree that the German family has been deeply nucleated, even neurotically so. The father has a status of authority, oppressive and coercive, almost of a drill sergeant's rigorousness. To him is owed *Ehrfurcht,* awe-laden submission, obedience without contradiction, and the largely passive acceptance of guidance and commands. He is the *Herr im Haus,* Master, to whom the mother defers just as much in opinion, judgment, and decisions for all in the house. This holds good for something like 70 percent of the German people, rather less so in the south and west. Passages of affection and easy and individualized brotherhood between father and children, even teen-agers, are frowned upon; equal comradeship and the liberty to say that father is in error, are rare. Even the mother is not allowed to go too far in sentimentally standing between the children and the father's acute authority and frequent physical beatings. Nothing like this severity of domestic despotism exists in Austria, in France (p. 296), in England (p. 27), or the United States—a fortiori.

To what is it due? This habit may have come first from the imposition of despotism by foreign rule or native feudal lords; the pressure from above has necessitated the same, for closer management of the family goods and its protection from oppression. Such severity may be the father's compensation for what he must endure at the hands of *his* lords. A harsh peasant life under grinding princes, themselves crushed between the French and the Slavs, may have enhanced the father's status. The more penurious the agricultural economy, as on the unfertile East German lands, the sterner the need for top decisions in the homes. Such families made such a State; such a State made such families, and the severities of military service added to the regimentation of the home.

Some psychologists suggest that to escape the rigor of the home the teen-agers enter the romantic *Jugendbewegung,* and then rush back again to the Leader as Big Father, to which all habituation has tended. How, then, can the German State be changed, unless the family is transfigured? How can this be done until the mother in the house achieves a higher status? Is the lack of self-leadership in youth to endure?

(5) Organizable. The practical upshot is that the Germans in politics and government and administration are amazingly organizable. Their leaders have been remarkable organizers, their Kings talented and devoted administrators. So have their trade unions or any social grouping, industrial or philanthropic, to which they have set their hands. They are inventive. They are researchers. They are dutiful, and place the greatest value on *tüchtigkeit,* meticulous competence. They are all keyed-up

to these qualities to a most intense degree. They have great vigor and endurance; and indeed, *ausdauern,* to last it out, is a quality of high social prestige. They bow to authority, to *Obrigkeit.* Perhaps they have all these qualities in too high a degree: it is dangerous domestically and internationally, to be so heedful of the excessively displayed sign: *Verboten—forbidden.* The English view has been that "Bad rebels make good laws." *The Germans and Charismatic Authority and Leadership.* In view of what has been demonstrated about the centuries of German subordination to royal and clerical and *father* authority, it is not to be wondered that a German sociologist, Max Weber, should have made charismatic leadership so momentous a feature of his doctrine, following the work of Rudolf Sohm on the authority of the early Christian Church. What is "charisma"? It is the gift possessed by rulers—a charm, a magic of personality, so impressive to men about him that they become his followers, and not for their personal utility's sake, not by a process of election for a limited term of office whence he is dismissible. Max Weber says:

> This [charisma] means that the "natural" leaders—in times of psychic, physical, economic, ethical, religious, political distress—have been neither officeholders nor incumbents of an "occupation" in the present sense of the word, that is, men who have acquired expert knowledge and who serve for remuneration. The natural leaders in time of distress have been holders of specific gifts of the body and spirits, and these gifts have been believed to be supernatural, not accessible to everybody.

His examples are men inclined to "seizures"—frenzied behavior, Achilles, Berserkers, Shamans who go into ecstasies. Such leaders give the impression to their followers of having a divine mission.

The connection of this charismatic leadership, which only works if it is directly accepted because it is recognized, with Hegel's Heroes of the Cunning of Divine Reason in the world, is obvious and most striking (p. 555). Indeed, the terms in which Max Weber argues his thesis are an immediate and valid introduction to the rule of Adolf Hitler, not only over the mass of German political illiterates but over the educated upper classes of professional skill. He talks of the "blond beasts" (!) kept in Byzantium, kept in order to impress by their seizures or manic fits; of Shamanist ecstasies and epilepsy. The parallels with Hitler are too penetrating to be ignored (p. 652 and 653). But the English with their cool blood and utilitarian sense (p. 37) are but moderate in their following of charisma. For they have for centuries been nurtured away from acceptance of the "inscrutable" mission: they finished with that with Charles I, and thinned out their monarchy (p. 39) as their churches, suspicious, as the Germans are not, of any *Mysterium Tremendum.* The Germans are medievally prone to charismatic leaders. Hitler adored Mussolini, his charismatic precursor in 1922.

Here is another aspect of that worship of the Will—acknowledgment of the overriding rights of the artist-statesman—and the Germans have come to believe that they are a nation of *Künstler,* artists, a *schöpferisch* nation, a creative people, in which the artist can defy all ordinary ethics for art's sake.

(6) A Mixture of Extremes. The English, the French, the Americans have two superb qualities for government: common sense and a kind of golden mean. The Germans are a people of extremes: sentimental and yet ruthless; musical and yet administrative; people of small states and yet of unscrupulous brutality for empire; pious and yet bestial; worshiping God and yet trampling religion under a filth of paganism. There is an element not explained by historic happenings. Moreover, "Germany" comprises a vast range of different communities, north and south, east and west: their differences add up to something like social heterogeneity inside a single State imposed by force, not made by up-growing, contributive consensus. This cuts into the party life, and since this had been incoherent in the past, it has laid open the people to the authorities' command of "Divide and rule!" The only answer to this, if democracy is wanted, is "Combine and assert yourself!" This has been difficult through the mixture we have suggested.

Let this section be concluded with Nietzsche's classic description of this abnormal political psychology of tortuous and rather chaotic mixture.

The German soul is above all manifold, varied in its source, aggregated and superimposed, rather than actually built: this is owing to its origin. . . . As a people made up of the most extraordinary mixing and mingling of races, perhaps even with a preponderance of the pre-Aryan element as the "people of the center" in every sense of the term, the Germans are more intangible, more ample, more contradictory, more unknown, more incalculable, more surprising, and even more terrifying than other peoples are to themselves:—they escape *definition,* and are thereby the despair of the French. It is characteristic of the Germans that the question: "What is German?" never dies out among them. . . . It is characteristic of the Germans that one is seldom wrong entirely about them. The German soul has passages and galleries in it, there are caves, hiding-places, and dungeons therein; its disorder has much of the charm of the mysterious; the German is well-acquainted with the by-paths to chaos. And as everything loves its symbol, so the German loves the clouds and all that is obscure, evolving, crepuscular, damp, and shrouded: it seems to him that everything uncertain, undeveloped, self-displacing, and growing is "deep." The German himself does not *exist;* he is *becoming,* he is "developing himself." "Development is therefore the essentially German discovery and hid in the great domain of philosophical formulas—a ruling idea, which, together with German beer and German music, is laboring to Germanize all Europe.

That un-Christianized, un-Romanized tribal underman is still the temptation to defeat the light.

Bismarckian Unity over Liberal Germans

Out of these three reverences [for Heaven, for Wisdom, for Mercy] spring the highest reverence—reverence for one's self, and those again evolve from this: that man attains the highest elevation of which he is capable, that of being justified in reckoning himself the best that God and nature have produced— nay, of being able to continue on this lofty height, without being once more, through self-conceit and presumption, drawn from it down to the vulgar level.
—*Goethe,* Wilhelm Meister's Travels

The Reich of 1871 was made by Bismarck's "blood and iron," the trampling down of liberalism and humanity, the surrender of the liberal *élite* of Germany to Bismarck's success. That new State was preceded, then, by a ramshackle one: the Confederation of the Rhine.

I. THE CONFEDERATION OF THE RHINE, 1815-1866

The Confederation of the Rhine was imposed by the foreign powers in the Acts of Vienna, 1815— it was not home-made. Its form is what Germans call a *Staatenbund,* a states' alliance, not a *Bundesstaat,* a federal union like the American. Its members were the thirty-six princes and the Free Cities of Hamburg, Lübeck, Bremen, and Frankfurt. It was "governed" by a federal assembly or Diet, *Bundesversammlung* or *Bundestag,* established in Frankfurt. Its members were ambassadors from the various member states, which were unequally represented, Austria, Prussia, Hanover, Bavaria, Saxony, and Württemberg having 4 votes each, and the rest, 3, 2, or 1. The smaller states together could veto the will of the *Bundestag.*

Its powers concerned war and peace for all the states; the protection of states' rights; aid to any state attacked with danger to Germany; the reduction of customs barriers between the states; promotion of the development of constitutional government in the states; the guarantee of equal civil and political rights to all Christians and some slight improvement in the status of Jews.

This was the alternative to (1) restoring the Holy Roman Empire, with Austrian supremacy; (2) the division of Germany into southern and northern confederations under Austria and Prussia, respectively; and (3) a *trias,* Austria, Prussia, and the rest making the third state. Russia and Austria were afraid of each other; the other states were afraid of both.

The *Bund* (the federal authority) was without legislative, executive, or judicial powers over the citizens in the states; its decisions became effective when the state governments accepted them. It became the device to *prevent* German unification by its counterbalancing of votes and no *popularly* elected assembly. Its main service was to apply the Austrian Foreign Minister Metternich's policy of repressing liberal, especially students' movements throughout the states, in accordance with the conservative policy of the Holy Alliance.

The States and Their Governments

Happily protected from Big Brother Austria and Big Brother Prussia, the princes promoted *Klein-staaterei,* "small statery," or "particularism," or separatism. They were enthusiastic supporters of the Holy Alliance and Hegelian authoritarianism, now expressed in the political science of conservatism by the *Restauration* school of Haller and Stahl. The basic idea was that history and tradition make the law, not one's brains applied to contemporary problems. The ruling classes and their hired professors made bad use of the works of Edmund Burke (p. 35).

They had constitutions, but imposed ones, *ok-troyiert,* a translation of the French *octroyée,* "imposed." They were monarchies by divine right; the Crown by his grace allowing designated classes to advise in government, in the bicameral estates, with their highly limited franchises. Ministers were appointed by and responsible only to the Kings and sat in and dominated the legislatures, which were kept to brief sessions. Civil servants were given leave to be members of these bodies, some even leading the "opposition." The whole of these smug and stuffy polities were run by officials, petty professional men, and professors, dependent on the Court for jobs and prestige. They were not challenged by middle-class capitalists or managerial employees or industrial masses —not yet existent. In Nassau, qualifications for membership of the chamber were so intricate that of 100,000 population only 73 candidates were qualified, and these supplied the pool to fill 30 seats. The government overruled the chamber when it did not vote by absolute majority.

The Rechtsstaat. Instead of responsible ministries, the surest guarantee of the Rule of Law (p. 4), the German states developed the still-abiding (p. 597) idea of the Legal State, or *Rechtsstaat,* the judiciary having much to do with this. It is to be traced in Kant's *Principles of Politics* and Wilhelm von Humboldt's *Nature and Purpose of the State* and even in Hegel. It meant equality before the law, judicial impartiality, judicial control of administration. The middle classes could not win

more than this before 1848 without violent insurrection against the princely governments; and their social and economic interests were satisfied with the *Rechtsstaat.* But the judges, being civil servants (p. 597), were rather more zealous for the State's authority than for the individual.

"Autolimitation." The German doctrine of "autolimitation," the self-control of the sovereign, supplemented the *Rechtsstaat.* But this is not enforced responsibility; it is only "moral" or *ex gratia,* hardly a guarantee.

Liberal Ferment

It would be unfair to give the impression that no liberal or reformative forces fermented in these states, including Prussia and Austria. The French Revolution of July 1830 gave the German states a shock. Some of the more despotic princes were actually forced to flee. In some the constitutions were liberalized or newly granted. In Baden freedom of the press, everywhere else subject to censorship, was allowed, against the will of the Confederal Diet. Turbulent meetings occurred in all parts. The ferment died and rose again and again to the climax of 1848, to be discussed presently. But no victorious revolution occurred to press decisively the establishment of responsible government.

II. PRUSSIAN DEVELOPMENT

Prussia was governed by a king and the Ministers chosen at his discretion, and was without any central legislature at all. The Crown had promised such a combined Diet in 1810, 1811, 1814, 1815, and 1820. Frederick William III evaded these promises, regarding all who looked to constitutional liberty as Jacobins, one of the most frequent and undeserved epithets in use in Germany since the French Revolution. The only "representative" bodies were the various provincial Diets of the lands united to make Prussia, and these were permitted only a voice in local affairs. The time-honored yoke on monarchs, fully exploited by the English liberals—the control of the purse—did not apply to the Prussian King, because the taxes and excise already enacted by seventeenth-century Diets, and the efficient administration of the domains and monopolies, as well as care to avoid international conflict, allowed him a sufficient budget. The very competent civil service (see p. 592) conduced to royal freedom and popular subjection.

East Prussian liberals—that is, peasant proprietors and big estate owners and the Catholic Rhinelanders—continually pleaded for an all-Prussian Diet. They were regarded as traitors. The various Diets themselves used to send delegates to a central committee in Berlin; it was tolerated but not consulted, and its discussions were *not public,* even as were those of the provincial Diets. For centuries the proceedings of the British House of Commons had been an open secret and, more recently, officially open to the public; since 1789 the French assemblies had deliberated in public. But the German people were told nothing.

Character of the Kings. In a monarchy of this nature, political evolution much depends on the character of the King. In 1840 Frederick William IV ascended the throne. This man was eccentric to the point of madness; in the end he became altogether a lunatic. Above all, he was madly romantic, especially about the creation of Germany as a single State. He detested liberalism but thought kindly of the medieval type of Estates. But this he could not achieve. For the Junkers on whom he relied would not countenance the representation of the Third Estate, which would have brought together liberal lawyers, professors, and civil servants, particularly those who had been given a strong liberal-constitutional bias in their habits of mind in their native neighborhoods *west of the Elbe,* influenced by the French Revolution and Napoleon's incursion. It would also have introduced into the legitimate counsels of the state, the Roman Catholics of the western regions.

Indeed, in 1830 an open conflict had broken out between the Prussian government and the Roman Catholics of Posen (the Polish state stolen from Poland) and the Rhineland, numbering some 6,000,000. The Roman Catholic bishops prohibited mixed marriages. The state, as intolerant as the Church, refused to allow its secular authority to be limited. This was the conflagration point of conflict inherent in the position since the addition

of these dominions to Prussia. The Archbishop of Cologne was imprisoned in 1840, the Bishop of Trèves banned from his see, the Archbishop of Posen forced to resign by the Pope because he had preferred not to fight. The Roman Catholics were regarded as "un-German"; and the fact that some of them were Poles added to the malice, because Poland was a national enemy of Prussia.

On coming to the throne Frederick William called off this fight; and so enabled Prussia to gain the undeserved reputation of being a tolerant host to both Protestants and Catholics, a very important factor in swaying many people toward the possibility of Prussia's leadership in a Reich in which the people were so divided between the two faiths.

Junker Assistance of Unity

The Junkers now assisted the cause of unification, even if unconsciously. They were monopolists of administration and the Army; their efficiency was progressive both on their land and in the state. Two movements, one before the reign of Frederick William IV and the second during his time, marked their governmental competence and then their yielding to as much liberalism as the King himself was prepared to concede.

Zollverein. The first was the establishment by Prussia's initiative and example of the *Zollverein* or customs union. Its value for Germany as a whole (though this first advance was much more limited) was best described by the political economist Friedrich List in a report to the *Bundestag* of the Confederation on behalf of the German Commerce and Trade Association in 1819. List was one of the philosophers of German nationalism, inclined to an enclosed national economy supported by external tariffs, rather like the model of Herder (p. 552). He said:

Thirty-eight customs and toll boundaries in Germany paralyze internal communication and produce approximately the same effect as if every limb of the human body was tied up so as to prevent the flow of blood from one to the other. In order to transact business between Hamburg and Austria or between Berlin and Switzerland, one must cross ten states, master ten systems of customs and tolls and pay transit duties ten times. Whoever is unfortunate enough, however, as to live where three or four states join, must spend his whole life among foreign customs officials and be a man without a fatherland. This situation is most lamentable for those who wish to carry on enterprise and business. They look across the Rhine with envious glances and see one great nation stretching from the Channel to the Mediterranean, from the Rhine to the Pyrenees, from the frontiers of Holland to Italy, carrying on trade along free rivers and open roads without once encountering a customs official. The powers of the Germans, who at the time of the Hansabund, carried on world trade under the protection of German men of war, are being destroyed by 38 systems of customs and tolls.

The Confederation did nothing.

In May 1818 Prussia, however, had decreed free trade within its own borders among all the various provinces. The principle of free trade was declared, to be promoted by arrangements appropriate to the policies of other countries. Prussia then proceeded to negotiate such treaties with her neighbors; a limited customs union came into existence by December 1828, including the middle German states. By January 1834 the Prussian *Zollverein* was in existence. It included eighteen German states with over 23,000,000 population. For some time there were excluded the three Hanse towns, the two duchies, and three other states in the north, and in the south, Nassau, Baden, Frankfurt, and Austria. Austria remained excluded; the others were negotiated, wheedled, or intimidated in the late 1840's.

The developing commerce and then industry of the later 1830's and 1840's powerfully stimulated the commercial classes and the "liberals" of all kinds to join this lesser unity if the greater one were not yet obtainable. It was Prussian tactics to keep Austria out, for she already dominated the Confederal Diet and was a rival for the union of Germany. Prussia had won her way because she had something to offer the commercial classes who were liberal. The princely governments yielded to the demands of their commercial classes, because they preferred to give them this satisfaction rather than take the risk that these turn "Jacobin." Moreover, they believed the economic union to be a lesser evil and an impediment to a full political union. Even the Prussian machinators of this beneficial system regarded it as a way of putting off, not of bringing on, the union of Germany, certainly the *Grossdeutsch* union, the Great German Union, which would include Austria. They favored what had come to be called the *Kleindeutsch* solution—that is, German union, led by Prussia and excluding Austria.

The Austrian government could not even remove its own internal customs until the Revolution of 1848. Prussian civil servants thus opened a way across Germany to the North Sea ports. They saved money on customs administration. They helped to engender further nationalist feelings by the example of union; by its origin and decade-long management, it led to Prussian primacy.

The Railroads. The second Junker action concerned the Eastern Railway. In the 1830's the railroads brought the straddling lands of Prussia into a more coherent system. The Junkers were won over to a degree of constitutionalism by their need for the Eastern Railway, the *Ostbahn,* running from Berlin to East and West Prussia. If this railroad were not built, then Berlin might be politically pulled *westward*. The state had to undertake its building, because private enterprise found it not worth the capital. Eagerness for the line made the Junkers greater State-enterprisers than ever (even "socialistic"), more "nationalistic," pretending that they were the champions of Germanhood in the Polish east and of Prussian integration on an east-west axis. It also made them the promoters of a constitution for Prussia. This was accidental. The former King had promised not to raise the needed loan for building the *Ostbahn* without the consent of a representative legislature. The Junkers therefore pressed the King to establish a united Diet (or *Landtag*). It was against his will, for it would not be the medieval arrangement of his psychopathic maunderings. But all the provincial Diets were assembled together in April 1847.

The resultant *Landtag* consisted of two assemblies: one of nobles, with 72 of high rank; and the other of the Three Estates, 231 nobles, 182 town representatives, and 120 peasant representatives, respectively. This was *merely a consultative body*. It could exercise only powers over new taxes or increase of old ones. Its power to approve loans concerned only those made during peacetime. Its sessions were to be secret, although verbatim reports were made for subsequent publication. It had no power over the Executive. The King told the *Landtag* that it was not convened to express opinions but to represent the rights of the Estates and the throne. As for constitutions, he said:

> No written piece of paper will ever come between me and the Lord God in Heaven to govern the country, a second providence, as it were . . . to make away with the old fealty.

The "mongrel creation" could not even ask for the redress of grievances unless the petition were carried by a two-thirds majority of the curia of the nobles, separately, and of the other three curiae in joint session. The franchise was, of course, extremely restricted.

The *Landtag,* just the same, was headstrong. It formed into parties. It demanded regular sessions, and that no taxes be leviable without its consent. Its demands were refused. It was here that Otto von Bismarck, Germany's dreadful Fate, came forward as an extreme and unscrupulous supporter of the monarchy. He had advocated welching on the royal promise to avoid the calling of a *Landtag.*

The Rhinelanders were the most obstinate opponents of the *Ostbahn;* they were supported by the Third Estate of both the rural and urban areas in East Prussia. The former had commercial and religious interests different from the Protestants, the Polish Catholic persecutors; the latter were not ready to pay taxes for the further advantage of the Junkers. The loan was refused: the most remarkable manifestation of civic courage in Prussian post-French Revolutionary history and not to be successfully repeated till the late 1880's. The *Landtag* was dissolved. Later in 1847 the King was meditating concessions to its demands. The Junkers were prepared to follow. On this, supervened the German Revolution of 1848.

III. THE MARCH OF IDEAS AND REVOLUTION

The proletariat of Germany was not yet in existence in 1848; the peasantry were still servile, if no longer serfs; the middle class had no experience or mass support; Prussia had its Junkers and these had the Army. The Revolution failed. Why it failed must be unraveled, because it is the decisive reason for the Bismarckian Constitution of a united Germany with the continued domination of Prussia and the continued domination of Prussia by the Junkers and the rise of Hitler down to 1945.

Little Industrialization. Germany was mainly rural. Prussia's population was still, in 1846, 72 percent rural, its towns very small. The population of all Germany had risen steadily since 1815: it was then 24,500,000, and in 1846, 34,000,000: if the Austrian areas in the Confederation are also counted, the figures would be 33,000,000 and 45,000,000, respectively. There had been but a slight, yet a perceptible, development of urban workers (in domestic manufactures) and journeymen workers (organized in guilds). The areas most industrialized were Westphalia, the Rhineland, Silesia, and Bohemia and Saxony, engaged in mining, metallurgy, spinning, milling, and cutlery. Apart from state-founded iron works in Berlin, calico printing started by the state of Baden, sugar refineries, and shipyards, large-scale workshops did not exist. The main industry, conducted in the homes, was textiles. The weavers faced serious competition—even ruinous—from English mills. In the 1840's the Ruhr mines developed and the coalfields in Silesia; the famous firm of Krupps began at Essen; clocks and toys were made in Thuringia as by-industries.

But enough economic advance had been made to produce a desire for radical change.

Social Protest

Aping the Young Italy movement, a Young Germany movement arose in the 1830's, to overthrow the native *Obrigkeitsstaat,* the Hegelian constitutions. The Confederal Diet counterattacked them; their press was quashed. They demanded popularly based responsible government and unification. At once the anti-Semitic theme was invoked, for some minds like Heine and Börne among the leaders and Rüge and many others were Jews, but a tiny minority: they were vilified as Young Palestine. All were hounded by spies and forced to leave the country, only, through their sojourn in Paris to send the waves of socialistic thought back, especially to western Germany. Another current joined (and ultimately diverted) this stream of humane rationalism: the Marxist ideas. These Young Hegelians took the second horn of the Hegelian dilemma: all that is rational *should be* real; the dialectic of history must not stop with Frederick William III's constitution. Feuerbach's attack on pietistic religion, the prevalent Prussian state of mind, brought in the materialistic view of historic causation. Instead of Hegel's "The State is the march of god in the world," he circulated the idea that "Man is what he eats."

Karl Marx acknowledges his debt to Feuerbach, like Engels, thankful for the sense of liberation from Hegel's spiritual chloroform. Arnold Rüge brought together such thinkers in his magazine, in a later form known as the *Deutsche-Französische Jahrbücher.* Karl Marx was later a copublisher of it in Paris. It urged Germans to give their energies to public affairs, not to be swamped in private matters and Prussian pietism; for the French had won self-government by political *courage.* It should not continue to be believed that because liberty was French and English, it was therefore unpatriotic for a German to seek it.

Karl Marx and the German Class Government. *The Communist Manifesto,* published in 1848, was produced by the pre-1848 circumstances already sketched. Its first paragraph is most apposite:

A spectre is haunting Europe—the spectre of Communism. All the powers of old Europe have entered into a holy alliance to exorcise this spectre: Pope and Czar, Metternich and Guizot, French Radicals and German police spies.

Marx was a Jew, but not a professing one; he had departed from the faith of his father, a lawyer, and his mother, the descendant of rabbis. He married a gentile, Jenny von Westphalen, the daughter of a Prussian government official, a neighbor and friend of the Marx'. This Ludwig von Westphalen was a cultivated man of the humane, eighteenth-century Enlightenment. On Marx, he exercised a beneficent influence toward humanity and the development of one's character. Marx's birthplace (1818) was Trier, in the Rhineland. This region had been strongly pervaded by French revolutionary influences: "Liberty, Equality, Fra-

ternity." Marx's father, whose original name was Levi, was a rationalist and had been encouraged in his French Enlightenment views by Napoleon's introduction of social and economic equality of opportunity in the Rhineland. This, as well as inward conviction, had promoted in him the impulse to loosen his religious associations. When Napoleon was defeated, the Prussian restrictions on the Jews were re-established: no Jew could practice law. Levi was forced to change his name to Marx and to be received into the Lutheran church.

Karl Marx was the child of the French Revolution; Lenin its grandchild, through Marx. A student of law and philosophy first at the University of Baden (hearing Schlegel's [p. 552] lectures on Homer) and then at Berlin, he became the fierce opponent of the Hegelianism that hung like a luminescent yet impenetrable cloud over German learning. He joined the loose grouping of Young Germans and Young Hegelianer, and threw himself into practical politics. In 1842 he joined the *Rheinische Zeitung,* a democratic journal published in Cologne in the Rhineland; in 1843, the Prussian government suppressed the paper. Marx migrated to Paris, the center of European radicalism, his connections including Proudhon, a socialist of the type of Fourier (p. 291), Bakunin (p. 752), and Friedrich Engels. Engels was also a Rhinelander, who dwelt normally in Manchester, England, as the representative of his father's German textile business; he became the collaborator and the financial benefactor of the scholar-politician Marx.

The German Class Structure and Marxism. It is of the utmost importance to know, for the evolution of Germany, the special contribution of Marxism to it. First, such countries as England had nothing like the rigor of the class structure as it existed in Germany, and especially Prussia. Marx was confronted by (1) a rigid economic class structure—we have noted that the bureaucracy, for example, was not open to any but the Junker type and higher bourgeoisie, and that certain occupations until recent date were legally closed to certain groups. This is even to omit the general social and educational effects of inequality of wealth. This was a strong *hereditary* class fabric, forbidding social mobility, unconnected with native, individual ability or social service-ability. (2) There were religious obstructions: Marx experienced the exclusion of Jews from certain occupations. (3) As we shall see, there was established soon a franchise for the Prussian *Landtag* of 1849 onward, on a crude class differ-entiation: the three-class system, by which the representatives were equally divided between the grossly unequal three categories of taxpayers: top, middle and lowest. This supervened on the divi-sion of the Diets into two Chambers and four Estates.

This structure was without flexibility: its rigor goes far to explain the Marxian revolutionary antagonism to the status quo and his turning of Hegel upside down in order to show that all his-tory, all political struggles, the State itself, was the *emanation of class distinctions,* and only class dis-tinctions.

Second, Marx was so obsessed with the need of seizing power to overthrow such a system that any instrument of power was acceptable. He inevitably agitated the cult of violence, so that his working-class followers placed themselves on the same basis as the Prussian militarists, especially their greatest modern exponent, Bismarck.

Third, another instrument was the State. The only issue was: Who was to control it, not, as with some of the French socialists, to dissolve it. Hence, Marx was Bismarckian and more: to produce the greatest area of unification in Germany, with Prussia as the instrument, since it was efficient. He romantically believed that *after* unification the workers would take over the accomplished fact. So he was anti-Austrian; anti-Polish. This gave supporters to Bismarck.

The later development of Marxism and German Social Democracy is treated presently (p. 603).

There were other streams of socialism; for ex-ample, that of von Baader, a Catholic social phi-losopher of Munich, or Lorenz von Stein's *Social-ism and Communism in Modern France* (1842), or Wilhelm Weitling's Christian communist doc-trines—he was a German tailor apprentice who had lived in Paris. These taught a Christian approach; but Marx differed for he had been Prussianized by admiration of Prussian efficiency and militancy, and he reacted obsessively against

Hegel, the antithetically obsessed apologist of Prus-sian authority.

1848: The Problem of Unification

A widespread sentiment of unification, of nation-ality, pervaded Germany. Political leaders blended it with a longing for liberal government. The two leading Germanic states were fundamentally hos-tile to each other: Prussia, largely Protestant, rising and efficient, with the dutiful Junkers at the core; Austria largely Catholic, with an easy, happy-go-lucky aristocracy, in Prussian terms, sloppy, *Schlamperei.* The Diet had a mechanical equilib-rium of votes, but the states' system was instable in men's minds. Prussia had enemies in the Poles and guarded the Rhine against France, a heavy burden. Austria needed more power to help hold her Slavs and Magyar and Italian lands. The *Zerrissenheit,* of "fragmentation" of "Germany" provoked great mental anxiety.

The Revolution of 1848 started in Paris and ran on to Vienna and Berlin. The west German people forced liberal ministers on their terrified rulers. But no liberal leaders were available to produce really free states. Vienna forced Metternich to flee, but the German liberals who hoped for unifi-cation now felt that Vienna had gone too far.

The Prussian Revolution

Workmen, moved by distress, and by liberal and socialist ideas, rose in insurrection in Berlin. Mod-erate demands were made by the Berlin Municipal Council: a people's militia, withdrawal of the Army, a constitution. The King, who detested Hohenzollern militarism, ordered the Army to withdraw. The palace courtyard was invaded. In the fierce fighting, 225 were killed or died of wounds. The King was forced to take part in the parade of burial of the martyrs and to don the black-red-gold colors (to be the flag of Weimar in 1919 to 1933). The King proclaimed:

To my people and the German nation. . . . Salvation from internal and external danger can come only from the union of the German peo-ple and the sovereign princes under one polity. . . . I take over today the leadership for the days of danger. . . . I have embraced the old German colors this day and placed myself under the honorable flag of the German Reich. *Prussia will merge itself immediately in Germany!*

The demands for a Constitution were declared accepted, and a Rhineland liberal was made Prime Minister.

What were the demands of the heterogeneous "liberals"? The most radical were the arming of the people; a German parliament based on popular franchise; universal suffrage; freedom of religion, of teaching, and of the press; trial by jury; a unified German citizenship; taxation according to ability to pay; general education; the right to work and the protection of labor; fair relations between employers and employed; responsible and unauthoritarian Ministers and administrative officials; the abolition of social and economic privileges. In South Germany the leaders followed the Jacobin pattern of building a network of political clubs. In the west the "Federation of the Just," Karl Marx's creation, later called the Communist Party, was in operation.

The Frankfurt Parliament. In March 1848 fifty-one self-appointed leaders met at Heidelberg to plan and organize the calling of a national—that is, a German—assembly. Later that month 500 delegates met at Frankfurt for the same purpose. They were *not* elected or delegated by "the people." This was known as the *Vorparlament* or "pre-Parliament." Three hundred and fifty were monarchists, 150 republicans. The south Germans, with the program mentioned above, took the lead. These were not social revolutionaries but moderate constitutionalists.

The *Vorparlament* arranged for the election of a German National Assembly, not on the basis of universal suffrage but according to the very limited franchises that prevailed in the states. In May 1848, amid rapturous hopes at the courage and promise of the deed, the Assembly met at Frankfurt. Its composition doomed it as a German savior; it had no single resolution.

Its composition was this: 46 merchants, bankers, manufacturers; 60 landowners; 49 university professors and 57 teachers; 157 judges and civil servants; 66 lawyers; 20 mayors; 118 higher officials; some diplomats, librarians, doctors, ministers, many writers—this academic segment numbered some 570. The total body numbered 831. Four

were master workers, 11 were post office officials, etc. All the great historians and political theorists were there; the great jurists, with the Ministers.

They fell into Right, Center, and Left groupings. The Extreme Right was led by Austrian officials; the Right by Prussian officials, making one seventh of the entire Assembly; the Center was occupied by the historians and political scientists, mainly from North Germany. The Left Center, itself split, came from South Germany: it numbered about one seventh. The Left mustered 56 deputies; they had been the leaders of the local revolutions. There were 47 in a grouping of the Extreme Left, including Arnold Rüge (p. 566).

A Failure. The Frankfurt Parliament failed to create a united and popularly governed Germany for several reasons. The princes had the force, not they; and the former could not be *persuaded* to relinquish their particularistic sovereignty. Indeed, backed by the Prussian Army, they soon killed off the revolutionists. The liberals were afraid of a parliamentary Prussia as dominator of Germany, thinking Prussia had gone too far Left! They were hostile to the masses and preferred Austrian liberalism. Prussian militarism in the suppression of the insurrections frightened them. They preferred Austrian easiness to Junker efficiency. Their mixed motives, including a sentimentality for the Holy Roman Empire, paralyzed their will to liberty. Then their nationalistic outlook betrayed their liberalism, for the Assembly warmly supported the Austrian Army's suppression of the Czechs of Bohemia, and later Prussia's suppression of the revolt of the Poles of Posen—for a unified Germany ought to be a big Germany. Its vote of 342 to 31 in commendation of the latter demonstrated that these men did not understand that the liberty of Germany would be lost if they condoned their governments' suppression of liberty elsewhere. Furthermore, the Assembly commended one more German nationalistic venture: the revolt of Schleswig-Holstein against their suzerain, Denmark.

Germany was in a nationalist uproar and another wave of insurrections occurred—this in September 1848. The Assembly had to ask the Prussian King to send his Army to restore order.

A frenzy of pan-Germanism had seized the Assembly. There were, however, strong counter-currents that sought the larger brotherhood of free peoples.

A Proposed Constitution

The Assembly carried on its debates toward the making of a federal constitution. It was to be so shaped: (1) a German Reich, at the head of which would be "the Emperor of the Germans" (not an Emperor of *Germany*), hereditary sovereign; (2) a countersigning responsible ministry; (3) a bicameral parliament, one house representing the people, the other the states (modeled on the U.S. Senate), the former not subject to dissolution; (4) federal revenues were to come from tariffs and indirect taxes, with state contributions, if these still left a deficit; (5) a supreme Reich court, reminiscent of the U.S. Supreme Court, was to interpret the constitution as to controversies among the states and between government and parliament.

Austrian Failure. In Vienna, the Austrian counter-revolution triumphed. Two members of the Frankfurt Parliament were arrested, and one of them, Blum, was executed, a famous advanced democratic member of the Assembly. Austria's imperial German star had already begun to fade, because the Assembly had already legislated the exclusion of any union of a part of the Reich with a non-German area—that is, Austria's Magyar and Slav dominions. The *Grossdeutsch* solution was further shelved when the Austrian Constitution of March 1849 was promulgated, because it united the Magyar dominions, and the others, in one empire. The *Kleindeutsch* (Prussian) advocates were winning by Austria's own default.

Rejection by All. The Frankfurt constitution was acceptable to twenty-eight states—*if* it were amended to give the Emperor a right of absolute veto; to make elections open instead of secret; to give more powers to the upper chamber. The Assembly could not find a majority for these. Austria, Bavaria, and Hanover rejected the constitution.

By 290 votes to 248 abstentions, the Assembly offered the crown to the King of Prussia. The delegation was greeted with contempt by the Ministers, the flunkeys, and the Junker officials and abused by their organ, the *Kreuzzeitung*. The King rejected the offer: "a crown of filth and mud" offered by the representatives of the people. He would accept the crown only from the princes and lawful sovereign authorities. He later summoned such to a conference, but none appeared. The Assembly was a hollow shell. Risings occurred in various parts of Germany: local or Prussian troops crushed them. The governments—Prussia, Austria, Saxony—recalled the deputies from Frankfurt, though they had not sent them. The deputies obeyed. A rump of 65 moved to Stuttgart; they were driven from inn to inn and finally scattered by bayonets.

The people did not rise to support the National Assembly. They slunk off with their tails between their legs. Their motives had been too confused: work, wages, land; Prussian leadership; Austrian; unifiers; romantic radicals; social revolutionists; moderate "official" liberals; general zeal for change.

The Prussian *Landtag* of March 1848 concerned itself with the framing of a constitution, and its Left wing with constant harassment of the royal power and the liberal Ministry. It attempted to annul "By the grace of God . . ." from the royal title, and abolish all titles of nobility and distinctions of rank. The Army, full of prestige from its Polish and Schleswig ventures, surrounded the *Landtag*. The excuse of popular tumults was used to dissolve it; the soldiers lifted the Speaker into the street as he sat in his chair; the *Landtag* dispersed. The King imposed a Constitution, the conspicuous features of which were its bicameralism—the upper chamber (*Herrenhaus*), a house of lords; the lower elected by the three-class system—and a nonresponsible Ministry.

By this year the British had a well-rooted sovereign Parliament based on a fairly wide franchise and a responsible Cabinet system; the French, their Second Republic. But the Russians were ruled by a despotic Czar and a kow-towing Church.

IV. BISMARCK

The liberals had failed. Their ideals defeated, only force and expansionism remained to solve the problem of German unity. It was for Otto von

Bismarck to erect a German Reich by such means in place of the Confederal Diet which, under the reactionary Prince Schwartzenberg of Austria, had resumed its status.

On all of Germany Bismarck stamped Prussian absolutism, efficiency, and the a-moral military ruthlessness of Frederick the Great. His motto was: "Our solution is not Union at any price, but rather the prerogative of the Prussian crown by every means." He did it for Prussia's glory and to preserve the social and religious views of the Junkers: the King, the Junkers, the Army and the Civil Service for the younger sons, landed estates and feudal authority for the eldest; the Lutheran's kind of Christianity, neither meek nor charitable; the submissiveness of tenants and laborers; no self-government for the workers in town or country-side; the snobbery of class and title; contempt for tradesmen, manufacturers, Jews, Catholics, and all the nations around, except Czarist Russia; no concessions to democratic socialism. The grim corollary was the suppression of Liberty, Equality, and Fraternity with saber and gun and without scruple. These Junkers intermarried or rose into the higher nobility; some into bourgeois families, like Bismarck's father—the deviants, like artists or liberals, were cast out.

Bismarck was born on the family estate in Brandenburg on April 1, 1815, three years before Karl Marx, of a family established for 400 years. He was a Prussian brute of strong girth and sensitive nerves, ruddy of face and hair, with light gray eyes; a fabulous drinker of beer and love-maker in his youth, rough, coarse in speech as the case required or sharp with quips and aphorisms. He very closely resembled Nietzsche's "blond beast" (p. 608). He had a powerful personality; the quickest wits; great self-restraint to hit his target, no more and no less, as the occasion required; subtle diplomatic calculation—and no morals. He was the perfect *Realpolitiker,* measuring out the necessities, not tempted by glamor. But, above all, he sought Power, durable power. Since he was able to overawe or overargue the King, he was virtually absolute king of Prussia and then Germany until 1890.

He resigned from the Prussian judicial service early, detesting subordinacy. He restored the parental estates to prosperity. He read and traveled widely. He assimilated and purged himself of Hegel, David Strauss, and Feuerbach and rose above philosophy and its scruples. In doubt, some statesmen have chosen charity; but Bismarck chose Frederick the Great. He found no firm morality, either, when he espoused the Pietistic Christianity of his neighboring Junkers, when, seemingly devout, he was thereby allowed to marry Johanna von Puttkamer, the daughter of the most pious among the group that met for domestic services. It seems to have left his conscience free for *raison d'état* alone, though (like Charles I of England) he was a most devoted husband and father.

The Ultramonarchist

In the *Landtag* of 1847, he was so ultramonarchical, insisting on the divine right of monarchy and the Christian nature of the State (!) that he attracted the attention of Frederick William IV. During the days when the King bowed to the will of the Berlin insurrectionists, Bismarck's name was proposed for office. The King knew his extremist temper well enough already to write: "Only to be employed when the bayonet governs unrestricted." He applauded the King's refusal of the Imperial Crown offered by the Frankfurt Parliament. He counseled the wildest repression of the revolution. He was not thought of as a deputy to the *Landtag* (he represented only as an alternate) or the Frankfurt Parliament: he was too extreme. But he became one of the first and most energetic supporters of the newly founded Conservative Party and newspaper, the *Kreuzzeitung,* the very name of which (*The Cross*), is reminiscent of the Order of Teutonic Knights out to Christianize pagans and Slavs—that is, the rest of the German population. He was then the advocate of the Christian State, meaning hierarchical authority and duties of social welfare rendered *ex gratia* by the nobility; the corporate organization of economic occupations (as in the Catholic doctrine as suggested of French Catholic parties on p. 355); and the continuance of the powers of government, jurisdiction, and control of their peasants by the nobles. He returned to the *Landtag* in his own right in 1850, assisted by the new three-class franchise.

Prussian Envoy at the Confederal Diet. Bismarck was appointed to Prussia's envoy to the Confederal Diet in 1851. This was the consequence of his ultraconservative speeches against liberalism and Prussian independence in the *Landtag*. By these he won the King. But even more so by his majestic dignity in the Olmütz clash between Austria and Prussia. The episode is significant in the evolution of German unity.

Austria was violently opposed to a meeting of the smaller states of Germany at Erfurt in March 1850, called by the Prussian chief Minister, Josef von Radowitz (of Hungarian descent, and a career officer in the Hanoverian and Prussian armies), to plan a united Germany with Prussia at its head. The Austrian Prince Schwartzenberg, Metternich's disciple and Prime Minister, at this time compelled the Prussian government, most humiliatingly, to desist from sending troops to help the Elector of Hesse in a fight with his liberals for a constitution. Here Prussia was forced to promise not to discuss German unity except when *all* German states were present. Bismarck, surprisingly, sided with retreat, in a speech that brought him to office.

Great States, he said, acted only "for State egoism, not romanticism," and ought not to fight for "things that do not belong to their own interests." Prussian honor consisted not in risking a war with Austria and Russia, the mediator in the conflict, or French invasion of the Rhineland, but in severing herself "from all humiliating associations with democracy," which might be strengthened in the course of a lost war! These democrats only wanted a "war of principle," a "war of propaganda," to help parliamentarism in Hesse, Württemberg, and Saxony—the Poles, Frenchmen, Italians, all of whom would be killing their brother Austrians! The Army had already surrendered to the "proletarians," in March 1848. The best war was not that against Austria, "the representative and heir of an ancient German power, which often and gloriously had wielded the German sword," but against the *Landtag*—by dissolution!

Bismarck became Prussian envoy to the Diet at Frankfurt, where by 1856 he well learned that German unity required Austria's ousting by war. The *Camarilla* (the legitimist conservatives who

had proposed his appointment) and the King did not like revolutions, even by the Prussian King against the Austrian. Bismarck, therefore, proposed relaxing the censorship to gather the *Landtag's* sympathy for Prussian liberalism and German leadership. He was "put on ice" (his phrase) as envoy to St. Petersburg to disembarrass the government of his ugly extremism. His new assignment taught him high and sinister foreign policy. Unwilling to risk a French invasion by Napoleon III (p. 306), ally of Italian freedom, he advised the King to abandon Austria in her losing fight against the Italian forces, though other advisers urged Prussian intervention.

The "Great Divide" of 1858–1862

States are made by the wills that dominate, and Bismarck's will, astuteness, and physical vigor dominated the King and his successor. In the Prussian elections of 1858, in spite of the three-class system of voting, the moderate liberals won 210 seats against 59 for the Conservatives. William I, then Regent, was persuaded of the need for an increase in the size of the Army, consistent with the growth in population. The *Landtag* was not averse to this. But it required that the cost be reduced by the reduction of service from three to two years, and that the *Landwehr* (home service reserves) should be kept separate, under its own officers, in order to have a popular counterweight to the army of Junkerdom. The King rejected this demand as a violation of the royal prerogative. The *Landtag* made temporary concessions, demanding that the final form of its appropriation be with its provisos.

High tension between Crown and *Landtag* developed. On his coronation in 1861, the new King, William I, a career Army officer, repeated his insistence on "divine right." The elections saw the return to the *Landtag* of a party more to the Left than the moderate liberals, *the newly organized Progressive Party* (p. 602). It insisted on the provisos to the Army appropriations. Von Roon, Minister of War, felt inclined to yield, but the King would not.

A situation had arisen like that between Charles I and Parliament (p. 39) and the parallel was frequently quoted. The King, an extreme conservative, torn between conflicting sentiment—he did not wish to rule unconstitutionally—meditated abdication. The Army chiefs organized the forcible destruction of the *Landtag*. In this dilemma, von Roon recommended the appointment of Bismarck, "the mad Junker," as Prime Minister. William I admired Bismarck's diplomatic astuteness. Bismarck promised to carry through the struggle with the *Landtag*—in opposition to the majority in it. The King tore up his letter of abdication, thus virtually giving up his sovereignty with his conscience to Bismarck. Bismarck's interests lay in both gains: a large and efficient Army, for his policy, now absolutely clear and even expressed to the King, was to overcome Austria and also to defeat liberalism. When the King, still advised by some to go over Bismarck's head and make peace with the *Landtag,* said to Bismarck, "They will cut off your head and mine," the latter answered, "And after, sire?" "We shall be dead." "Can we die more honorably—I, like Lord Strafford, Your Majesty not like Louis XVI but like Charles I?"

Bismarck gloried in the fight. He accepted no compromise on the Army's demands, even over Manteuffel, head of the Military Cabinet, who was ready to make some concessions. He would have the whole cake, or resign—and the King was afraid to let him resign. This was a decisive moment. The King was won over by the argument that *surrender on the smallest issue meant the subversion of the monarchy!* Bismarck went out of his way to provoke the liberal opposition—he wanted and needed an open fight. The censorship was sharpened; provocative articles were inspired; the Civil Service was purged of liberal sympathizers; government officials were ordered to press the voters; votes of confidence were engineered and hostile ones muzzled from various municipal councils; even reactionary remarks were attributed to the King, for public consumption. Bismarck meant to tame the "House of Phrases." **"The Gap in the Constitution."** Bismarck produced the theory of "the gap, or lacuna, in the constitution," a German cliché. Hence he could not be removed. Second, all laws, according to the Constitution of 1850, required the agreement of the Crown, the *Herrenhaus* (the upper chamber), and the *Landtag,* the lower chamber. What was to happen when the three could not agree? The Constitution did not say. "There is no provision of the Constitution which tells us which of the three must yield when the three fail to agree." No appeal to theory was useful. "For me the necessity is sufficient that the State exists. . . . Necessity alone is the decisive factor." The taxes must be collected! The *Landtag,* western Prussian industrialists, Rudolf von Gneist, the great jurist, famous historians and political scientists appealed to Bismarck to respect the political-moral order, the *Rechtsstaat.* The Progressive leader in the *Landtag* characterized the behavior of Bismarck as "government without a budget, the rule of the saber at home and abroad. I consider him to be the minister most dangerous for the liberty and happiness of Prussia."

Bismarck dissolved the *Landtag* once more. The opposition was returned, even stronger. He continued to collect the taxes. Only one democratic member of the *Landtag* proposed a public strike against their payment. Ferdinand Lassalle, the democratic socialist leader, contrasted the situation in England in such a pass with that in Prussia. In England the tax collector would have been resisted. His officers might have killed the citizens who would not pay. But he would have been brought before a court and there condemned for murder. His defense that he had been merely executing orders would fall, since they were illegal. Citizens killing the tax collectors would be acquitted because they had merely offered resistance to illegal force. The knowledge that they would be thus protected would cause them to resist. But in Prussia, the resisting citizens would be jailed by the courts for resistance to lawful authority, and any murderous soldiery would be protected by their orders from above. *For the courts were not independent,* as the English had been at least since 1689, and had fought to be, long before that. In Prussia, the courts belonged to the State, not as in England to the nation. He emphasized his bitterly reactionary policy with the speech on solutions by "Blood and Iron" already quoted (p. 550).

Liberalism was overthrown, because the liberals did not resist the tax collector and fight to sustain the *Landtag*.

"The Men of Light and Leading" Lost to German Politics. The economic development of Prussia, with a surge of industrialism and commerce, gave the Prussian state, with its traditional "planned-economy" outlook and administration, power to supply services to businessmen, as we shall see. This dissuaded the liberal forces among the industrialists and merchants and financiers and the entrepreneurs of transport, utilities, and shipbuilding from struggling for a parliamentary government truly responsible. Furthermore—of cardinal significance—businessmen and capitalists worship success. They pay homage to the social framework of prestige. Military success, dictatorship by a powerful and cynically winning rogue, a glamorous Crown, was now their model. Elsewhere the already-well-established liberality of the constitution could contain the new economic entrepreneur —so in England, so in the United States, partly so in France. But not in Prussia and then Germany. In other countries the liberal constitution was a condition to be observed; in Prussia, Bismarckianism was a loophole for the leader. Moreover, henceforth there was small attraction for men of ideals, ambitions, and brains to enter the service of political life, into statesmanship. German politics was run by such people as Bismarck, or weaker successors, and by the Army and the civil servants. Germany's brains and character went into wealth-producing, hence the almost miraculous economic progress, and into professorships, still tamed to the oligarchy's service, and, subordinately, into local administration.

Three Wars Deliberately Made for Unity

The taxes were collected; the Army was provided for; von Roon, Bismarck's military chief made the Army ready for the three wars Bismarck progressively foresaw he must deliberately make to mobilize German nationalistic sentiment for unity and to abase the liberalism of parliament.

Bismarck used all the power of his personality over the King to dissuade him from participating in any of Austria's proposals for reorganizing the *Bundestag*, even though the assembled princes had sent an envoy to beg him to follow his legitimist loyalty to Austrian leadership. Bismarck cunningly counterproposed a federation, led by Prussia, with a parliament *elected by universal suffrage*.

Schleswig-Holstein. He determined to seize the duchies of Schleswig and Holstein (p. 568). They had a large German population and occupied a most strategic situation, linking the North Sea (and the world) to the Baltic and Russian waters. The duchies were under Danish suzerainty, that situation having been endorsed by the great European powers—including Britain, Russia, France— in 1852. The people of the duchies sought to preserve their limited autonomy against a new Danish constitution. Then two dynasties became rivals for the suzerainty, on the death of the King of Denmark. Holstein was a member of the German Bund, and Austria took the side of one candidate, Bismarck of the other. The Great Powers opposed Bismarck's evident ambitions. The King and the court were zealous for the claims of autonomy by the duchies; the small states and the liberals were also. Bismarck inveigled Austria into joint war on Denmark; a victory was won; an uneasy treaty of joint administration (Gastein, 1865) prevented war between the two allies; Schleswig was entrusted to Prussia, and Holstein to Austria.

Austria. The next step was to fight and defeat Austria and pick up all the stakes. This was done in July 1866. The King was nerve-wrackingly argued into connivance; his Prussian conservative friends deserted him; Napoleon III was tricked into remaining neutral by some kind of promise that he would receive some Rhineland territories; an alliance was made with Italy which would hold down Austrian forces. Bismarck picked a quarrel with Austria over the interpretation of the Gastein Treaty on Schleswig-Holstein, sent Prussian troops to maintain order in Holstein, and annulled the treaty. Austria asked for "federal sanctions" of the Bund, against Prussia. Bismarck declared that a Bund vote favoring Austria would be a declaration of war against Prussia. When Austria was upheld by a small majority, Bismarck denounced the Prussian pledge to the Bund, declared it dissolved, and demanded that the other states join *his* Confederation—without Austria. His temptation to the liberals, a *Reichstag* with universal franchise, was dangled.

War followed. The South German states and Hanover, Hesse, and Nassau fought on Austria's side. Within three weeks they were defeated at Sadowa (or Königgratz). These states, defeated along with Austria, owed an indemnity to Prussia in money and territory. Bismarck conceded these in return for a mutual defense alliance with them, against any attacker, and the placing of their troops under Prussian command in time of war.
Despotic Consequences of War Gambles. The gambler had won the crucial tricks. Prussian hegemony was assured, a victory of the spirit. It drew with it the moral acceptance of German "liberal" leaders and the people to a very large degree. Bismarck (through the King) asked the *Landtag* for an act indemnifying himself for the collection of taxes without due process of law. The *Landtag*, now conservative through elections won in time of war, voted the indemnity by a substantial majority, with congratulations, although the King refused to give guarantees asked that the behavior would not be repeated. The Bitch Goddess Success had won: for the victories of unity the Deputies had reversed their demand for parliamentary government. The opposition, the Progressive Party, split into two: the rump remained true to liberalism and declined in strength, and the National Liberal Party waxed in numbers and declined in political morality.

The North German Confederation was founded. The *Reichstag,* elected by universal franchise, met in February 1867. It adopted a Constitution, with minor changes in the draft formulated by Bismarck, by a majority of 230 votes to 52. Alongside the *Reichstag* was the *Bundesrat,* with 43 votes, the representation of the princes. Its main features became those of the German Reich of 1871, and therefore its terms need not be analyzed here.

The *Zollverein,* shattered during the war, was now reconstructed, but with interesting changes. *All* the German states (excluding Austria, of course) were invited to make treaties to enter it. It would include the southern states. All were now to be included in a *Customs Parliament,* composed of the Deputies of the North German *Reichstag plus* deputies from the southern kingdoms. These latter were forced to accept, or lose the economic advantages. The Customs Parliament met in 1868, and North Germany and South began to cooperate in economic government, which is so large a portion of all government.

Austria was allowed easy terms. She seceded from the Confederation. The south German states were allowed to remain outside the newly established Confederation, in sovereign independence. Prussia annexed Schleswig-Holstein and the north German states—Hanover (see p. 601 and p. 602), Hesse, Nassau, and Frankfort—thus giving Prussia a clear territorial link from the Rhine to Poland. This annexation was achieved at the cost of Bismarck's wheedling and browbeating his King, who was not anxious to have his dominions extended by the inclusion of hostile states. He had, on the other hand, strongly vindictive and annexationist intentions toward the southern kingdoms, but was fought off by his Prime Minister. He did not want a hostile South German group who might some day find their way back to the Austrian camp; he respected the legitimacy principle in the particularist kings (p. 576); he could not risk Napoleon III's intervention even then.

The southern states were won over after the war by Bismarck's revelations to them of Napoleon III's demands, which Bismarck pretended to entertain but left dangling in inconclusive negotiation: for the Bavarian Palatinate, for Rhenish Hesse, and for Mainz, the southern fortress.

Bismarck now had economic and military unity for all the states; and political unity for the north. Thus, German military and economic needs preceded German polity. Parties came to be "interest groups."
The Franco-German War, 1870–1871. By 1870 Bismarck had taken advantage of the provocative behavior of Napoleon III of France, who nagged for territorial gains (for example, Luxembourg). Then he used a quarrel over which of two rival candidates for the Spanish throne should be supported. Bismarck supported (against his King) the candidate of Hohenzollerns (a Catholic and a Swabian), perhaps a future ally on the southern

borders of France. Napoleon threatened war if the candidate were not withdrawn. Again Bismarck browbeat his King, into a withdrawal of a promise to this effect, and published an abridged account of the whole matter in a telegram from Ems. The French Court stumbled into a declaration of war, July 15, 1870.

The German armies of the south joined with the north, as arranged under the recent treaty. The speed of mobilization was so great, and the railroads so efficient, that they were at the French frontier before the French generals were awake to their danger. The German soldiers were never so good a *nation* as when warring on other people. They were courageous, enduring, obedient, and they were led by von Moltke and the general staff with good guns and keen strategy. By September 1870 Napoleon III was taken prisoner; all German victories culminated in Sedan; and Paris, besieged, surrendered in January 1871.

The Bismarckian Kaiserreich

The Bavarian government initiated the movement of the South German states to enter, each by treaty, into the North German Confederation, and so make it into a Reich, and the Bavarian King proposed the assumption of the imperial title by the King of Prussia, to which all other states agreed.

With the exception of Bavaria, the legislatures of the southern kingdoms accepted the Constitution with small opposition. In Bavaria the Catholic Ultramontane opposition was strong; 46 voted against, and 102 for, some Ultramontanes absenting themselves. The Reich was accepted in fear, not love.

On ratification of the peace treaty between France and Prussia in 1871, the ceremonial of acceptance was enacted in Versailles, in its Hall of Mirrors—that is, in the very arcanum of French glory under Louis XIV. William I (surrounded by his cheering retainers with drawn swords, and

Bismarck, first of all of them) was pronounced *German Emperor*—not Emperor of Germany. The symbolization was of remarkable interest. There was no *Germany* as a community out of which an emperorship had emerged, but "blood and iron" had triumphed where national good will had failed or *had not been allowed enough time.*

Alsace, taken by France from the old German Empire in 1648, and Lorraine, reunited to France in 1766 after 800 years of quasi-independence under the Holy Roman Empire, were annexed. They were very useful to Germany's defense. They were not to be partitioned among the adjoining German states but kept as a *Reichsland,* an imperial province, governed under a special regime by a kind of viceroy (*Reichstatthalter*). The booty was a common possession cementing German unity. It became the center of French designs for revenge on Germany—and this again stimulated German unity.

What Was This New Reich Built For? It was not built to further Liberty; Bismarck hated Equality; and the conception of Fraternity was for Germany chiefly military tribalism. It was not a rising standard of living that inspired the movement for unity, except in the search for wealth by the upper commercial and the new industrial classes, and now, perhaps, wealth as a means, in Bismarck's policy, of greater international strength. It could only be for mere national self-preservation against Prussia's neighbors, the kind of oligarchic and feudal society of the Junkers in Pomerania, and Bismarck's own pride and lust for office. It had still to be filled with worthier human principles. Meanwhile, Bismarck was created a Count for the Austrian victory, and Prince, for the unification of Germany at the victory over France. The "little men," accustomed to feeling comfortable under rulers whose authority was independent of the choices made by men of free conscience, hailed the "Iron Chancellor" and enjoyed the moral protection of this grim metal.

German Government in the Bismarckian Reich, 1871-1918

I want to make music the way I like it or else nothing at all.
—*Bismarck*

I. A MONARCHICAL CONFEDERATION

The Reich was, formally, "an eternal alliance" of the King of Prussia, in the name of the North German Confederation, with the Kings of the southern states for the protection of the territory, the laws, and the promotion of the German *Volk*. Its designation was "the German Empire," that traditional title going back to Charlemagne's edifice.

It was not a federation of peoples; nor the emanation of one matured nation. It was founded on the sovereignty of the princes and Kings. This was Bismarck's clear intention. To be otherwise would have meant the introduction of the "Jacobin" principle of destroying legitimacy, which Francis I had rejected in . . . and Frederick William IV had rejected in 1848. It would have admitted that Prussian legitimacy could also go the way of the rest. Bismarck detested "particularism" but admitted it as the existing force which must be given rein.

Whatever may be the origin of this factitious union of Particularist elements, its result is that the individual German readily obeys the command of the dynasty to harry with fire and sword and with his own hands to slaughter his German neighbors and kinsfolk as a result of quarrels unintelligible to himself. To examine whether this characteristic be capable of rational justification is not the problem of a German statesman, so long as it is strongly enough pronounced for him to reckon upon it. . . . The dynasties formed everywhere the points about which the German impulse toward segregation set its crystals in closer array.

This explanation appears in his *Reflections and Reminiscences,* a candid and modernized version of the kind of political testaments the Hohenzollerns had left for the guidance of their heirs. He carries the point further, thus:

In order that German patriotism should be active and effective, it needs as a rule to hang on the peg of a dynasty. Independent of dynasty, it rarely comes to a rising point, though, in theory, it does so daily in parliament, in the press, in public meetings. In practice the German needs either attachment to a dynasty or the goad of anger to hurry him into action: the latter phenomenon, however, is by its own nature not permanent. It is as a Prussian, a Hanoverian, a Württemberger, a Bavarian, or a Hessian rather than as a German that he is disposed to give unequivocal proof of patriotism. It is not difference of stock, but dynastic relations upon which in their origin the separatist elements repose. . . . The preponderance of dynastic attachment, and the use of a dynasty as the indispensable cement to hold together a definite portion of the nation calling itself by the name of the dynasty, is a specific peculiarity of the German Empire.

The Reich, therefore, would at the beginning merely make a State strong enough only for foreign defense and the abolition of various economic and judicial absurdities. "One must keep more to the Confederal system in form, but in practice give it the nature of a Federation with elastic, innocent, but far-reaching phrases." It took Bismarck long, angry, and anxious negotiations to win over Bavaria, Württemberg, and Baden.

Four conspicuous features characterized the nature of the Federation, which is regarded as of a *confederal* nature: (1) the states were treated unequally so far as the powers they relinquished to the federal authority were concerned; (2) the Reich was much dependent for its revenue on the states' good will; (3) the states managed the administration of federal legislation through their own civil servants, necessitating a kind of Reich diplomatic handling of law fulfillment and sanctions, called *Reichsaufsicht*, or "Federal supervision"; and (4) the states were represented unequally in the Federal Diet or *Bundesrat*, the upper chamber of the new Reich (as of the 1867 *Bund*).

"Reserved Powers"

The variation of the powers of the states may be thus summed up. Bavaria was conceded the complete independence of her railway system, her posts and telegraphs, the taxation of beer and brandy, legislation regarding settlement and citizenship, the regulation of trade, her civil and criminal code (except instruments of credit and commerce), and her consulates. Her army was to be separate (a claim renewed in 1919 [p. 649]), though to be reorganized uniformly with that of the other states. In time of war the army was to be subordinate to the Reich commander in chief. She need not make any contribution to the German Navy, as that was regarded as important only to the north of Germany. But she had to submit to an oath of loyalty to the Federal Army, to inspection of her army by the federal commander,

and the determination of the total Reich military expenditure on arms by the federal authority, or be excluded from the economic advantages of union, which meant railroad connections with the north and tariff unity. Württemberg was permitted authority over her posts and telegraphs and her armed forces, and the latter concession applied to Saxony.

Finances of the Reich

A German political scientist (A. Hensel) said: "The State is only the sum of its financial capacities, and financial authority constitutes the faithful reflection of political sovereignty." The American federal system was so constructed as to give the federal authority adequate revenues of its own; and the amendment permitting an income tax (Amendment XVI of 1913) was passed in pursuance of the general opinion that its growing functions required great financial freedom, allowing it to be independent of the states for its funds. That federal strength and independence, from a monetary point of view, is fundamental in the character of American federalism. The states are equally free. As Hamilton said (*The Federalist*, XXX), "Money is, with propriety, considered as the vital principle of the body politic; as that which sustains its life and motion, and enables it to perform its most essential functions."

The finances of the Bismarckian Reich differed immensely from the American arrangement. The Reich was given four fields of finance: (1) tariff duties, (2) taxes on consumption, (3) postal and telegraph services, and (4) "in so far as they cannot be supplied by those revenues, they [the common expenses] are, until Imperial taxes are introduced, to be met by contributions from the single states of the Confederation in proportion to their population." Notice, no direct taxes were included! Yet the phrase "Imperial taxes" might have been held to include these.

The *Reichstag* intervened to cramp this liberal grant. Actually, the *Reichstag* maneuvered to make the contributions from the states the center of financial gravity. These were known as *Matrikularbeiträge*. In 1879 Bismarck bartered his need for tariffs against State financial support, by the so-called "Franckenstein Clause" that declared

Bismarck's Constitution and the Weimar Constitution

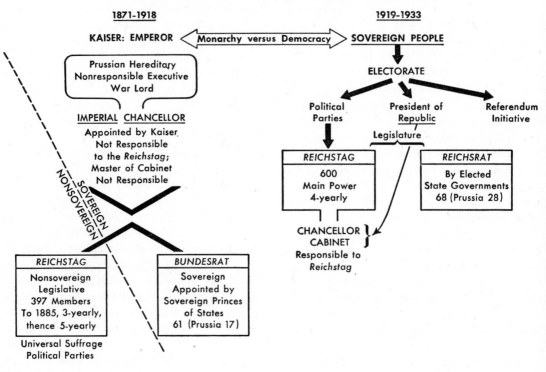

1871-1918

1919-1933

KAISER: EMPEROR ⟨ Monarchy versus Democracy ⟩ SOVEREIGN PEOPLE

Prussian Hereditary
Nonresponsible Executive
War Lord

ELECTORATE

Political
Parties

President of
Republic

Referendum
Initiative

IMPERIAL CHANCELLOR
Appointed by Kaiser,
Not Responsible
to the *Reichstag*;
Master of Cabinet
Not Responsible

Legislature

SOVEREIGN
NONSOVEREIGN

REICHSTAG
600
Main Power
4-yearly

REICHSRAT
By Elected
State Governments
68 (Prussia 28)

REICHSTAG
Nonsovereign
Legislative
397 Members
To 1885, 3-yearly,
thence 5-yearly

BUNDESRAT
Sovereign
Appointed by
Sovereign Princes
of States
61 (Prussia 17)

CHANCELLOR
CABINET
Responsible to
Reichstag

Universal Suffrage
Political Parties

that anything over a certain sum raised by tariffs and a tax on tobacco would be *given* to the states in proportion to their population. Thus the *Reichstag* had established a certain power for itself by limiting the revenues to the sum stated, thus limiting the power of the Government, and simultaneously had obstructed a growing revenue with growing trade. It was in the main a concession to the Center Party (p. 602). The *Reichstag* obtained the power of *annually* fixing the sum. Therefore, even with revenue from tariffs, the Reich might still be in deficit on the expenditures it wanted to make—and so it would have to come to the various states for proportionate contributions! It could at one and the same time be paying something (the excess over the amount allowed by the *Reichstag*) to the states, and getting deficiency contributions from them.

The Reich became, in fact, more and more tied up with the deficiency-contribution system of financing itself. The aim of the states was to get as much as they could draw from the Reich in return for the smallest sum that they could be

squeezed to pay to it. From 1883 to 1898 the states were happy, because the surpluses they received were greater than the deficiency payments they had to make. But by 1894 they began to be burdened. They then attempted to get their levels of payment "bound" or limited to a fixed proportion. But the Reich's expenses were increasing; the states were asked for more; the Reich refused to fix the sums once and for all, or for several years.

Hence the Constitution had to be amended in 1904 and 1906. The Reich obtained (virtually) the power to raise *any* taxes—that is, direct ones also—in addition to the rest. And the deficiency contributions from the states were more explicitly fixed in the Reich financial powers than before. It was a hampering system, produced by Particularism and by the spite of impotent political parties against the monarchical system.

The Budget of the Reich. The main point to be noticed is that annually a power was available to the *Reichstag* to cause the Chancellors anxious moments. But, above all, the military aspects of the budget were so important to the monarchy that

Bismarck got them exempted from this *rule of annuality*. The *Reichstag* allowed him army appropriations for seven-year terms. He had wanted permanent grants; the seven-year arrangement was *to him* a concession to parliamentarism! It was an abdication of the *Reichstag* parties, except for the Progressives and Social Democrats, who always voted against the budgets. Later, naval appropriations were also provided by Septennates. It might be remembered that the dependence of the Reich on tariffs, which were not fixed annually, also deprived the *Reichstag* of its power over the Government. The most it had ever asked was a three-year review of the military budget; Caprivi, in 1892, reduced the Septennate to five years.

Substantial Federal Powers

The total powers assigned to the Reich were substantial: citizenship and nobility; tariffs and commerce; weights and measures; coinage and paper currency and banking; patents and copyright; foreign commerce; railways, roads, and canals; navigation on rivers common to several states; posts and telegraphs; mutual execution in civil law matters and contracts, crime, commerce and bills of exchange, and legal procedure (a big drawing power for the middle classes); military and naval affairs; power over the press and the right of association (added in 1871); diplomatic representation and the power of declaring war and peace. But it had no *general-welfare* clause.

It was a Reich of *enumerated* powers, as in the United States, with the residual authority lying in the states. There was no limitation on the power of government in favor of the people, as in the U.S. Constitution. The Reich and the states shared all the sovereignty. The powers untouched by the Reich Constitution and left to the states were, it can be deduced, considerable: for example, church, education, industrial law, the mines, agriculture, health administration. The Reich and the states had concurrent jurisdiction regarding association and health administration.

The numbers in the Armed Services were settled by the legislature of the Reich: the states contributed the states' contingents; their commanders in chief were sworn by the Emperor, the Kaiser.

From this time forward until 1918 the reserved powers of the southern states were eroded, and a powerful body of legislation increased the authority of the Reich as a whole compared with the states. Special concordats were made to contribute to uniformity in such matters as education, public health and plague control, railroad fares, roads and motor transport, legal procedure and phrasing, etc. Great codes of law were made uniform for the Reich: criminal, commercial contracts, bills of exchange (a great instrument of credit and commerce), civil law.

The war of 1914–1918 speeded up this centralizing trend, especially the close cooperation of the Civil Services of the various states and the Reich and state government departments. Still, those who desired true unity were irked by the tedious administrative negotiations and legislative struggles to make progress.

Administrative Power and Federal Execution. In the United States the federal government is endowed with the power to execute the law by its own officers throughout the states. The Supreme Court has prohibited any state action directly or indirectly obstructing direct federal action on persons. In the German Empire, administrative action was positively left to the states' civil services. But as this would have subjected the Reich to heterogeneity and potential incompetence, the Reich was granted a power of "superintendence" over all the enumerated powers. This was divisible into two types of activity: (1) one was the provision of such detail in the laws as to make uniformity almost a necessary consequence. The *Bundesrat* took powers (since it was the ambassadorial representative of the princes) to provide rules made under the laws for specific application.

Still, it was necessary also to vest in the Emperor (2) "the care of the execution of Imperial laws," and this was exercisable through the office of Imperial Chancellor, the Prime Minister under the Emperor. We shall presently see what this meant in practice. If disputes arose over the interpretation of a law or order of the *Bundesrat,* this body—not (as in the U.S.A.) a supreme court manned by judges—was the final arbiter between Reich and states. If a judgment of the *Bundesrat* was not followed—then the ultimate resort was given in Article 19, allowing federal execution (or *Bundesexecution*) against the refractory authority.

Is it not extraordinary to reflect that in the German Reich even the collection of the tariff duties and other indirect taxes were left to the officials of the states, excepting that imperial officials were put in supervisory positions in the states' revenue services? The Reich's own Civil Service was confined to such supervisors and foreign affairs, postal and telegraphs, consular service, and naval and military affairs (with the reservations already noted).

Superintendence meant that in some matters the Reich made contact with the branches of administration it wished to control more meticulously. We have mentioned the method in the customs; similarly in railroads and military matters. Commissioners, controllers, inspectors observed the practices. They were allowed to propose improvements; but had to avoid rebukes, commands, and prohibitions. Reform had to proceed by way of a report to the Reich, which then sent a proposal to the state in question. All the instances in a state had to be exhausted first, including the judiciary, then the *Bundesrat* would be asked to be the intermediary. It took a long time in the period 1871–1918 to make progress, though some was made, in the enforcement of the laws. Even when the will to cooperation developed, ignorance and incompetence frustrated good, uniform management.

Where certain branches of administration required instantaneous action—for example, diseases of men and animals—the *Bundesrat* allowed direct rights to the departments in the states to give orders. In other cases—for example, tax administration, emigration, insurance—the federal departments employed supervisors in the states, and the Reich administrative courts developed uniform interpretation of the rules.

Difficult Reich Regulation. The *Bundesrat* was not the kind of body to regulate administration simply for the technical best. It was a court of peers, not a common superior. Large states were not subjected to a majority vote of the rest. Small states were made to toe the line, but not necessarily for the best technical result. If no compromise could be found, the willful state was free to do as it pleased. The Imperial departmental officials lost

their confidence, as they were unsure of the *Bundesrat's* support.

This is a most instructive light on the confederal nature of the Reich.

Prussia, above all, could not be subjected to Imperial regulation. For, in the end, she could not be coerced by the federal troops: she herself was in command of them! She also controlled the *Bundesrat's* vote (p. 581). But, being the maker of the Reich, her own officials were extremely sensitive to the ideal of doing their best, and they consulted the Imperial departments before taking action. Yet, what a complicated system! The Imperial Chancellor was at the same time the Prussian Prime Minister—that is how the Emperor, the highest Executive authority, fixed it. And the Imperial Secretaries of State were made members of the Prussian Cabinet and representatives of Prussia in the *Bundesrat*. What became of "superintendence" and "supervision" in such circumstances? This immunity by hegemony encouraged the other states to be disobedient, and the complaint of partiality was often made.

Article 19 of the Constitution said:

> If members of the Reich do not fulfill their federal obligations they may be compelled to do so by execution. Execution is to be resolved upon by the *Bundesrat* and carried out by the Kaiser.

But Prussia could not be coerced. The southern kingdoms could hardly be coerced, for they had together enough votes to prevent this. The smaller states could be pressed to improve their administration a little without "execution."

In the United States federal coercion of the states was unnecessary because the Constitution arranged for the easier method of orders sanctionable directly on disobedient persons by its own law-enforcement officers. In a later time, in the U.S.S.R., federal coercion of the Republics was unnecessary as everybody was a slave.

State Representation in the Bundesrat

"We, the people" of the United States enacted the Great Compromise to the effect that the nation as a unity was to be represented by numbers in the House of Representatives, while the states, as enduring entities were to be represented, regardless of the size of their population, by equal numbers: two Senators each.

The disparity of magnitude of the states in Germany had since 1815 stamped unequal representation on them in the federal council, the *Bundesrat*. It could be made viable, because in 1867 and 1871, the smaller states had at least the immunity from federal power that they ran their own administrations. They also contributed so little compared to Prussia and the three bigger southern kingdoms. The problem of representation of the states had been an obstructor of federal unity until Bismarck solved it. If Prussia had demanded a representation in proportion to her population, she should have had about 48 votes out of 58, because her population was over 80 percent of Germany's. But even 30 votes would have put her in a permanent majority. She was safeguarded by the provision that no constitutional amendment—in the power of the *Bundesrat,* not the *Reichstag*—was valid if 14 votes were *cast against it.* This also safeguarded Bavaria, Württemberg, and Saxony, who had 14 votes between them. By amendments in 1879 and 1911 the final distribution was: Prussia, 17; Bavaria, 6; Saxony and Württemberg, 4 each; Baden and Hesse, 3 each; Mecklenberg and Brunswick, 2 each; the other seventeen states, 1 each; Alsace-Lorraine, 3—making 61 in all.

The *Bundesrat* was a congress of princes, who appeared through their delegates. Votes that were not instructed were not counted. States with more than one vote were obliged to cast them uniformly. The latter provision, arising out of the power position of the princes, maintained the superior power of Prussia. It had already given rise to the demand by western Prussians and other liberals that the Prussian vote should be split up, so that Prussia should be merged in Germany, but the time had not yet come for the reform (p. 618).

On the matters on which some of the states had "reserved powers," they were not allowed a vote in the *Bundesrat.*

The Superior Place of the Bundesrat in the Government. This body was the center of the Constitution, fixed there as much to safeguard Prussian sovereignty as to found itself on that of other princes. Legislative power was exercisable by the *Reichstag* and the *Bundesrat* acting in agreement. Both had the legislative initiative.

The presiding officer of the *Bundesrat* was bound to put bills on the agenda when any member of the Reich exercised the right given to all by the Constitution to propose them. The Emperor did not, *per se,* possess this right of proposal, but bills could be introduced as *präsidial* (presidential) but to be treated as Prussian measures. Once the *Bundesrat* had passed a bill, then the Imperial Chancellor, now acting as the agent of the Emperor, could introduce bills into the *Reichstag.* Such bills were then expounded by members of the *Bundesrat* or its special commissioners in the *Reichstag.*

Constitutional lawyers of the Reich agreed that *the sanctioning power of the law lay in the Bundesrat.* The final action on all bills, even when they had originated in the *Bundesrat* itself, was taken in that body, even if they had returned from the *Reichstag* without any amendments.

Moreover, the *Bundesrat* was endowed with the power to supply the detailed regulatory provisions in any statute whose outlines were too general, if no named agency was vested with the power, or wherever defects in the laws had been disclosed in practice.

The balance of power in the *Bundesrat* was determined by Prussia's position; by that of the Emperor and Imperial Chancellor; the technical conditions of policy-making; the desire to maintain friendliness among these newcomers to the Reich; the power of the *Reichstag.*

Prussian Hegemony. With 17 votes out of 58, Prussia had a primacy over all other states, so long as she could manipulate a few states. The small states were very dependent on her because her railway system and military predominance at once attracted them and intimidated them. The shutting down of a railroad station in their territory was a sanction. Yet the southern states (mustering 16 votes) and some others could overcome Prussia. Therefore, the latter always worked for preliminary agreements outside the *Bundesrat.* It became almost a convention that that body should not be the scene of contested votes. The southern states usually went along with Prussia, because her power was greater than her votes; and their own political status, their reserved rights, and monarchical regime were, in fact, supported by that power. The larger states were willing to side with

Prussia to reduce the small states to negligible quantities. The Imperial Chancellor, they could see, at every session, was President of the *Bundesrat,* and he was chosen not by them but by the Emperor.

II. THE CHANCELLORSHIP

Decisive Power in Emperor and Imperial Chancellor. The Kaiser or Emperor was President of the Federation. He was, hereditarily, the King of Prussia. All the authority attaching to the emperorship, then, was added to that of the Prussian Crown. The kaiserdom was an all-German institution with a Prussian soul. And the Prussian *Landtag,* which made law and controlled the administration of Prussia (to some extent), was itself warped conservatively and Junkerdomly by the three-class system of voting and the failure to redistribute the seats conformably with the growth of population in the western and democratic and socialist parts of Prussia (p. 589).

A "Chancellor-System"

The Imperial Chancellor was, usually, simultaneously the sole responsible Minister in the Reich and Prime Minister of Prussia. He did not have to be these officials combined. But that is the way Bismarck wanted it, and some of his successors joined the offices because their Kaiser and King so desired it. It put central power in the hands of Prussia. As Imperial Chancellor, he was head of the Imperial departments, besides being president of the *Bundesrat.* Hence, the Prussian Prime Minister (as Imperial Chancellor) could use the Imperial departments to draft legislation which he could introduce as Prussian bills. The departments could hardly avoid Prussianizing their proposals. The other states received the bills rather late for change or discussion. *All the Imperial Chancellors, excepting Hohenlohe, a Bavarian friend of Prussia, were Prussians, and all from the ruling social caste.*

When the evolution of business made it essential to appoint Imperial Secretaries of State (see p. 584), Prussia appointed them as her own representatives in the *Bundesrat.* In 1907, for example, 9 of the 17 Prussian representatives were Imperial Secretaries of State; and among the other 8, several were Prussian officials. Thus the constitutional initiative of the *Bundesrat* was usurped by Prussia. The committees of the *Bundesrat* became practically Imperial departments, guided by Prussian officials in Imperial mantles, to develop the ordinances and rules executing the statutes.

The self-same Chancellor and Secretaries of State also led the *Reichstag.* Hence the *Bundesrat* was pressed to yield to these Ministers in order to avoid discomfiting them before the popular body the *Reichstag.* This gave the *Reichstag* more power than had been bargained for—if only the *Reichstag* had been less pliable in the hands of a nonresponsible Chancellor.

By 1880 a convention had grown up that the Emperor might veto a bill; this also restrained the *Bundesrat;* for princes did not want to humiliate a greater prince before an elected assembly.

Particularism remained strong, largely through Prussia's own needs of a policy (as we shall see) antagonistic to large sections of the population especially her Roman Catholics and industrial proletariat, and her Junker agriculturists (p. 589ff.). But a strong feeling of tension for greater unity developed.

The Nonresponsible Imperial Chancellorship

Authority emanated from the Crown, the Prussian Crown, then the Imperial Crown: this was the fruit of liberal submission to Bismarck's kind of Reich.

Nothing in the Constitution required that the Chancellor be responsible to the *Reichstag.* He, the Constitution, said, "shall be appointed by the Kaiser"; and the officers of the Empire were dismissible by the Emperor. Prussian and state practice and doctrine were hostile to parliamentary responsibility. It had been rejected again and again by the Kings and princes and their Ministers when the legislatures had demanded it, the most signal example being that of Bismarck himself in 1862. It will also be remembered that the highest authority was located in the *Bundesrat.* Even the National Liberals, cowed and tamed and tempted still pleaded for ministerial responsibility. But their demand only eventuated in Article 17 of the Constitution, which said that the laws would be pro mulgated by the Emperor but required the signature of the Chancellor. In other countries, democratic practice had produced parliamentary subjection of Ministers through such a clause, because the parliamentary leaders had forcibly seized authority over the Crown and Ministers. In Germany, in Prussia, the parliamentary leaders had failed: we already know the reasons.

The Bismarckian chancellorship was what may be described as a "Genius system": its conduct depended on the talents of a man like Bismarck. This was his greatest disservice to Germany. It is the acutest expression of his own deficiency, pride. For personal pride cannot be erected into a permanent system of government, seeing that men are mortal.

The chancellorship was vested in a single person; it was said to be "responsible"; it was a servant of the Kaiser. It was, therefore, a prescription like certain public contracts, which are so specified as to fit only one firm, although the law calls for open competition of bids by rival contractors.

The Tactics of Irresponsible Government. "Responsibility" meant that whatever the Kaiser did or said, he was not to be officially and publicly praised or blamed. Praise and blame were to be concentrated on his Chancellor. Yet the Chancellor could not entirely avoid the development of answerability to the *Reichstag* and the *Bundesrat*. Was he always to act like Bismarck in 1862? This would have been impossible for the peaceful and stable and serene march of government. It would not even have satisfied the sole consideration of Prussia's internal and foreign strength. The Constitution required that elections take place no later than sixty days after dissolution. There were leaders in the country (see p. 601ff.) who might have caused a liberal furore, if not uprising. Therefore, the Chancellor (be he Bismarck, and still more any of his line of weaker successors) could not govern without a majority for laws and taxation.

As early as February 9, 1872, Bismarck said (even if guilefully): "Every minister is obliged to keep his policy in harmony with the majority of the people which finds its expression in the representative assembly." The trick, then, was to find a majority amenable to the Chancellor. How this was done will appear later (p. 605). It may be said in anticipation that in 1888 the various expedients had been so exhausted that Bismarck contemplated a *coup d'état* to overthrow the Constitution, and in 1890 Kaiser Wilhelm II "dropped the Pilot."

The Chancellor had to use the most adroit methods to buy himself a majority through party blocs, which were paid some concession of economic advantage—tariffs, subsidies, markets abroad through foreign policy, the building of a Navy, the acquisition of colonies, the lowering of tariffs, a beating down of the Catholics, an assault on the Social Democrats, etc.—for votes at the expense of the momentary minority. It was accomplished by the-nation-is-in-danger appeal—against France, against Russia, against Britain. A time came when these were exhausted, and World War I was thrust on the German people, who were very romantically ready to undertake it.

Bismarck explained, ingenuously, why the Kaiser and he were needed:

> But a Parliament which consists of an appreciable number of groups, 8 or 10, which has no consistent majority or recognized leadership, ought to be pleased if there exists the ballast of a royal government, a royal will in the vessel of State. If this did not exist, all would fall into ruin, and chaos would reign.

A Nerve-wracking "Genius System." The chancellorship was a nerve-wracking post. The management of the legislature and the elections (which would return to Berlin weal or worry for the Chancellor, and over which he had considerable control through the management of local government officials and over the press and the educational system) was already a tough job. But the Chancellor had also to manage the King and the courtiers—the King-Kaiser had a will of his own, and by Prussian tradition was ruler, truly the personal ruler, taught to answer to "God," however this term was interpreted. The interests of all Germany and those of Prussia had to be adjusted to the advantage of the latter. The King had to be dominated, and yet not thought to be weak.

The Chancellor, Bismarck admits, found it desirable to have public criticism of the King, in order that his vanity, and above all the influence of his courtiers, the *Camarilla,* his flatterers and the women at Court, should be challenged. "In proportion as I became better acquainted with Court circles, [I] had to defend the interest of the State from their influences and also from opposition from departmental patriotism."

Yet he was determined that "a real responsibility in high politics can only be undertaken by one single, directing Minister, never by a numerous board with majority decisions," on the ground that the slightest departure from the one line became magnified by the number of people it went through. The assumption was that the right line could be found by one person alone, and only one person. The British Cabinet system gives the lie to this assumption, for it invented party oneness to answer the problem posed (p. 147ff.). Bismarck was always governing not *with* but *against* parties.

The system proved to be fatal to Bismarck, for it lasted for him only until a willful new King had ascended the throne, too young to be seduced by the memory (as King William I always was) that Bismarck had rescued him from either abdication or dethronement in 1848 and beyond. The Chancellor had no longer a psychological leverage over the sovereign, and was not prepared to lead a civil war against his King with the aid of the parties who might have joined him had they forgotten the injuries he had done them (the Social Democrats and, perhaps, the Progressives).

Here is his own analysis of the psychological and spiritual burden of responsibility where parties still exist and where Christian values retain a value (not so in the USSR):

> My health at that time had long been impaired, not by the work I had to perform, but by the continuous sense of responsibility for the great events which placed the future of my country at stake.

This came from the inability to foresee *with certainty* whether the road was right.

> The question whether his own estimate, his political instinct is leading him rightly, is difficult

enough for a Minister whose doubts are set at rest as soon as he feels himself sheltered under the royal signature or a parliamentary majority: a Minister, one might say, of Catholic politics, who has got absolution and is not troubled by the more Protestant question, whether he has got absolution from himself.

He complains of the harassing effect of uncertainty; of the agitating effect on the conscientious and honorable man; of the doubts and anxieties; of the feeling of honor and responsibility; of being left alone, boycotted by former friends, with his anxieties of office.

In the end Bismarck said, and he may have meant it, "Were it all to come over again I would be republican and democrat." It may have been merely resentment at his dismissal. But it may have been the deeper conviction, that a role between democracy on the one hand, with collective responsibility, and naked despotism at the point of the sword was the hardest form of government even for a man of his genius.

The Chancellor's Secretaries. In 1879 the Substitutes Law enabled the Chancellor to appoint associates to share his work without sharing his responsibility. A large part of the daily routine had been performed since 1867 by the Prussian Ministers, and this was coordinated by the Chancellor's Department then created under Rudolf von Delbrück. The amount of Reich business grew prodigiously. Separate departments had to be established: Foreign Office, Admiralty, the Treasury, Posts and Telegraphs, Justice, the Railway Department, and others. The Substitutes Law enabled his departmental deputies to countersign documented decisions on their own responsibility. An ulterior motive was the linking of the Prussian departments with the Imperial ones.

No Cabinet was formed thereby. The Chancellor was not the Prime Minister, he was the sole Minister. The Chancellor was given authority to *ask* for appointment of a substitute: substitutes could not be appointed except on the Chancellor's request. He could take over their tasks and authority delegated to them at his own discretion. The substitutes certainly grew in their departmental discretion. But the main power especially of supreme policy was the Chancellor's.

An Imposing Tradition: Leadership and Stability.
This quite-long tradition of (1) leadership by the Chancellor and (2) stability of the Executive must be borne strongly in mind. It is more significant in its effects on the shaping of the Executive (Chancellor and Cabinet) in the democratic period of the Weimar Republic (1919 to 1933), and the terrible anxieties under which the German people labored when for the first time in their history they were then asked to govern with an instable parliamentary executive dependent on free political parties in the *Reichstag*. They wilted under the removal of what Bismarck had called "the royal ballast"!

The Chancellors after Bismarck

These were Caprivi (1890–1894); Hohenlohe (1894–1900); Von Bülow (1900–1909); Bethmann-Hollweg (1909–1917), and Hertling (for eleven months in 1918). We omit Prince Max von Baden who served one month in 1918 to tide over the transition to democracy.

Caprivi. Count Caprivi who followed Bismarck, was the son of an old Prussian family, whose career was the Army, in which he served with high distinction in the wars of 1866 and 1870. He was Secretary of the Admiralty from 1883–1885. He became Chancellor at the age of fifty-nine, a man without parliamentary experience and without a party and unknown to the public. He could not manage the *Reichstag* and resigned in 1894. Within the lines of policy drawn by the Kaiser, he was a dutiful but undistinguished Minister.

Hohenlohe. Prince Hohenlohe was a Bavarian pro-Prussian of mixed Catholic and Protestant descent. He had served for a short time in the Prussian Civil Service; was a member of the Bavarian *Reichsrat;* a free-lance politician because he believed in a union of Germany and liberalism; Prime Minister of Bavaria in 1866; a supporter of the Federation and negotiator with Bismarck and the southern states; an anti-papalist; a member of the *Reichstag* since 1871; a supporter of Bismarck's anti-Ultramontane policies; German Ambassador to Paris; a Secretary of State for Foreign Affairs under Bismarck (during his illness), and a popular governor of Alsace-Lorraine.

Bülow. Prince von Bülow was born in 1849 (died 1929) in Prussia of a Holstein family who had served in the Federal Diet at Frankfurt so well as to impress Bismarck. The latter induced Bülow's father to enter the German ministry as Secretary for Foreign Affairs in 1873. Prince Bülow fought in the war of 1870; entered the Prussian Civil Service after studying law (the usual way in the Prussian and German Civil Service [p. 592]), and entered the diplomatic service. He received promotions for excellent work, reaching Rome by 1894. (He had married an Italian princess.) In 1897 he was appointed Secretary for Foreign Affairs by Hohenlohe. In 1900 he became Imperial Chancellor.

In political outlook as far as foreign policy went, he was fully a disciple of Bismarck's *raison d'état*. The chief factor in his appointment was the belief of the political figures in the entourage of Kaiser Wilhelm II that someone was needed who could guide this hysterical megalomaniac German who had dropped Bismarck. He was a charming broker and diplomat, but uncreative in the sense that Bismarck was. He was an able parliamentary speaker, but not a man of creative policy. He incurred the passionate enmity of the Kaiser in 1908 in an incident inherent in the Kaiser-Chancellor relationship. The Kaiser gave an interview to an English newspaper, virtually suggesting that Britain had won the Boer War by following the Kaiser's strategy. The Kaiser had been, like most Germans, highly hostile to the British during that war. Bülow declared he had not seen the interview, sent to him by the Kaiser, thus throwing back the "responsibility" on the Kaiser for a most unfortunate international incident, because it had aroused the passionate wrath of Britain at a time when there was already serious trouble between the nations because Germany was building a menacing navy. Bülow fell, to the pleasure of the Kaiser, less than a year later, when the conservatives in the *Reichstag* rejected a tax on inheritances, and the liberals rejected a number of indirect taxes.

Bethmann-Hollweg. He came of a Prussian banking family. He rose in the regular Prussian Civil Service, became Minister of the Interior in 1905, at the age of forty-nine, Secretary for the Reich Home Office in 1907, and vice president of the Prussian Cabinet. He succeeded Bülow in the chancellorship. He was a humdrum Minister, in difficulties with the Conservative-Liberal bloc who had caused Bülow's fall. He received strength in the elections of 1912, because the Social Democrats and National Liberals so increased their representation that the Right came to his support. He conciliated the Catholics (p. 603), established a new and more representative constitution for troublesome Alsace-Lorraine; tried but failed to liberalize the three-class system of representation in Prussia (destroyed by the biased *Landtag*); and carried Germany into World War I with the atrocious classic that the German guarantee of Belgian independence was only "a scrap of paper"—pure Frederick the Great, Hegel, Treitschke and Bismarck, taken up for the first time by the challenge of a foreign Great Power instead of the German people themselves. He muddled through the war until, in July 1917, Hindenburg and Ludendorff interfered with his conduct of policy to such an extent that the Kaiser, now terrified of losing his military leaders, let him resign. He was a wooden administrator in an age that demanded a supple man of political talent with the ability to lead political parties.

Hertling. Count von Hertling was the last card played by the crumbling Reich in the effort to avoid *political* destruction by military defeat in 1917–1918. He was a Bavarian, a Catholic, a professor of philosophy, a member of the Center Party (for some time the leader of this predominantly Catholic interest party) and Bavarian Prime Minister, 1912–1917. A *Reichstag* Deputy for over thirty years, he was appointed Chancellor in November 1917 and wished to negotiate as best a peace as possible with the Allies to end World War I. The Generals stopped him. He could not resolve to introduce responsible parliamentary government, which might have helped his main cause. He resigned in September 1918.

Government by Officials, not Statesmen. The general picture is clear: these men were officials, had risen by official lines of promotion; they were not statesmen of wide outlook; they were not responsible leaders of great and free political parties, ascending by ability in the political arena to sovereign power by winning a majority. For parties were not allowed to arrive at sovereign power,

since the system excluded ministerial responsibility.

It has been established [1] that the prior positions held by 76 incumbents of Reich ministries (what passed for a "Cabinet") fell into the following categories (1890 to 1918):

	Percent
Members of *Bundesrat*	65.8
Reich Civil Service up to Minister	48.7
Local officials	63.2
Judiciary	14.5
Colonial officials	6.6
Quasi-colonial officials	5.3
Others	25.0

One hundred and seventy-seven appointive positions had been held. The appointments to the *Bundesrat* have been indirectly explained in the discussion of this body. Many had held several of these positions; naturally, because judicial and local officials were starting positions for many in the Civil Service, who then were promoted for efficiency or family relationship (Junkers) or economic and social status. Colonial officials are few, because Germany had no colonies until the 1880's, small even then and afterward.

As regards elective positions held members of the *Kaiserreich* Cabinets, the position was this:

	Percent
Reichstag Deputies	30.3
Mayors, etc., in local government	11.8
Party officials	4.0
Trade-union officials	1.3

Another index is the officeholders in relationship to the election results, where party affiliation was known:

	Cabinet Members	Voters
Left	1.3	28.5
Center	10.5	30.9
Right	26.3	28.9
No party	61.8	—

The "no-party" group were not without political views: the appointments to the Civil Service and local government service and the judiciary were carefully organized to keep out Jews, Social

[1] See Max Knight, *The German Executive, 1871–1933,* Hoover Institute Studies, Stanford, 1952.

Democrats, lower-middle-class elements and working-class candidates (even if they could afford the preliminary legal training) and those who in any way betrayed anything other than a *Reichstreu* (that is, a "Prussia-loyal") state of mind. If they were not Junkers, they were Junkerish, as we show (see p. 592ff.).

Bavaria was grossly underrepresented; Prussia provided some 60 percent of the Ministers; about 65 percent were of the hereditary or created nobility or aristocracy without a working-class representative, the rest being middle class largely assimilated to the aristocracy; a very large percentage had served as regular officers in the Army; the predominant careers were Civil Service, then law (which as it included judges who were of a Civil Service status, must be added to the class of civil servants); some had come direct from military careers.

This is a numerical index of the ability of the Junker-Prussian outlook to capture the government of Germany. This Prussian domination will now be seen as it operated in the *Reichstag* and in the Prussian *Landtag*.

III. THE REICHSTAG

The vote was accorded to German male citizens at the age of twenty-five. This age was the qualification for eligibility as a Deputy to the *Reichstag*. It was direct, secret; without proportional representation. The second-ballot system was established, in which an absolute majority was ensured in each district by a run-off election contest between the two leading candidates at the first ballot, if no candidate had then obtained an absolute number of the votes cast. The Right and Center parties usually combined to beat the Left-wing candidates at the second ballot. The term was three years to 1888, then five years.

The results of the elections were very nonproportional, not merely owing to the facts implied in the observations already made but because attempts to adjust the seats allotted to the various parts of the nation were deliberately obstructed in order to overrepresent the "parties of order" and authority—that is, the Conservatives. The number of Deputies was fixed at 397 in 1869; so it stayed until the Revolution of 1918! This was what may be called "passive Gerrymandering": the population moved away from the rural areas and naturally increased in the urban, industrialized areas, but no redistribution occurred. The parliamentary consequences may be thus represented, below, for the election of 1912.

The underrepresentation of the Social Democrats is very marked; they should have had about 132 seats instead of only 110; so is that of the Progressives. The extreme Right was favored, so was the Center, which could, for religious reasons, keep its votes together in the southern states, in

Composition of the Reichstag in 1912

Electorate 14,400,000
Votes cast: 12,200,000

Parties	Thousands of Votes	Seats	Percent of Votes (circa)	Percent of Seats (circa)
Conservatives	1,126	43	10.0	11.0
Reichspartei	367	14	2.8	3.7
National Liberal	1,663	45	14.0	11.25
Progressives	1,497	42	12.8	11.0
Center	1,997	91	15.5	23.0
Poles	442	18	3.75	4.0
Social Democrats	4,250	110	33.0	28.0
Guelphs	85	5		
Danes	17	1		
Alsace-Lorraine	162	9	1.2	2.2
Anti-Semites	105	3		
Others	497	16		
		397		

Bavaria especially, and these were also heavily agricultural areas.

The full significance of the parliamentary system is, however, to be appreciated only after some account is given of the economic development and problems of Germany, and the reciprocal action of parties and Chancellor, and the parties among themselves. This will be undertaken as soon as the main features of the government of Prussia have been appreciated.

The Government of Prussia

The Constitution of January 31, 1850, was an imposed constitution. Its central institutions were the Crown, the House of Lords or *Herrenhaus,* and the House of Representatives or *Abgeordnetenhaus.* The two houses constituted the *Landtag* or Diet.

The hereditary King did not yield his sovereignty, as we appreciated in the discussion of the Bismarck episode in 1862; and the grant of a Constitution by one who proclaims he rules by divine right is not the same thing as the establishment by revolution of the people's right to sovereign power.

The Constitution only admitted the responsibility of the Ministers to the King, not to the *Landtag.* The King appointed them and dismissed and disciplined them. His, combined with theirs, was the initiative in the legislative and executive leadership. Statutes required the consent of both Houses and the *King's consent,* the veto being preserved in full strength, not forced to wither as in the British system. His Civil List was his in perpetuity, not granted merely for the reign. This also took care of the Emperor of the Reich (the same person, of course). The titles he could grant could be made available for Imperial services, since as Emperor he had no such power of granting titles. All the Imperial Court were the personages and officials of the Prussian Court.

Ministers had the right to appear in either assembly and speak at their discretion, with a right to the floor when they demanded it. They were in the assemblies about as often as British Ministers in the House of Commons, since they had to manage the *Landtag's* votes, though they need not and did not resign if outvoted.

The *Minister President*—that is, the Prime Minister—was recognized as the leading figure in the

making and direction of policy. His Ministry was an aggregate of the Ministers but possessed nothing of the nature of collective and popular responsibility of the British Cabinet. It was almost entirely a Ministry of departmental experts, the men normally having risen through the ranks of the Civil Service. They tended to go their several ways, while the Minister President made general policy in consultation with the King and powerful members of the Court, the so-called *Camarilla,* to which further reference is made shortly.

Aiding the Ministries was a highly educated and trained career Civil Service, the developed successor of that the origins of which in the seventeenth century we have traced (p. 541). Its top posts were largely in the hands of the Junkers (see p. 595). It was immune from parliamentary pressure, as Ministers were not responsible to the *Landtag.*

The *Landtag* was required by the Constitution to be convened at least once a year. The House of Representatives could be dissolved at any time, and new elections were then required to be held within sixty days, with a recalling of the *Landtag* within three months. On several occasions, the House was dissolved even before it met because the Ministers and King were not pleased with the election results.

The *Landtag's* consent was required for laws, taxes, loans, and the annual budget. But the taming action of Bismarck in 1862 was not forgotten, and the Government knew how to manage the elections. The professors of constitutional law had obediently excogitated the view that, as the House had not the *sole* right to repeal a law, it could not have the right to refuse money for administration, because this would be tantamount to emasculating a law that required finance for its execution!

The *Landtag* could initiate legislation; but the Government took charge of this right, not lamentable if it had emanated from election and been responsible. But the *Landtag* could amend, and this was the point of tension between it and the Government.

The *Herrenhaus* or the House of Peers was composed at the will of the monarch, for its composition was not settled in the Constitution but vested in the King. It was composed (1854) of the princes of the blood; hereditary nobles whose ancestors had been princes of the Holy Roman Empire; hereditary members created at the Crown's discretion; some life members, some being high State and Court officials, and the others appointed by the King at his pleasure on nomination by the large landowners, the universities, the church, and some cities—hardly a Jacobin body. It numbered a little over 300; predominantly an assembly of large landowners. It was a support of the Crown *versus* the people; but it was often a brake, sometimes an enemy of, the Crown when it pursued a liberal policy. It could be brought to heel by the creation of the necessary number of life members —so in 1872, when Bismarck's bill for local self-government was carried against its opposition by this device.

The House of Representatives had the budget and money bills presented to it first, to be accepted or rejected as a whole by the House of Peers (as the convention went in Britain); otherwise the two Houses had equal powers. The upper House exerted an immense power on financial legislation. **The Three-class Election System.** The House of Representatives was composed of 433 members, elected for five years. The suffrage was most cunningly devised to impede democracy and liberalism. Election was *indirect*. The first stage was election of "electors" in original electoral districts (*Urwahlbezirke*), where one elector was chosen for each 250 people. Such elections were carried out by voters classed into three categories according to the amount of taxes they paid. The largest

there was no reference back to the original electors. **Biased Results.** Here are some of the results. The Class I taxpaying group consisted of but a few men, in some places only of one; Class II was often twenty times the number, and Class III a hundred (sometimes hundreds and even thousands) as numerous. In the election of 1900 the Social Democratic Party gained a majority of the votes, but of some 400 seats obtained only 7. In 1908 there were 293,000 voters in Class I, 1,065,240 in Class II, and 6,234,079 in Class III, or, respectively, representing 4 percent, 14 percent, and 82 percent of the population. In Cologne, the Class I of 370 men chose the same number of Deputies as 22,324 working men. In Saarbrücken and in one Berlin precinct, a single person was Class I.

This monstrous system, described by Bismarck even, as "the worst electoral system ever created," was further marred by the lack of any major redistribution of seats since the year 1858. Thus, the 3,000,000 population of four large Prussian constituencies still could be represented by only 9 Deputies, whereas another 3,000,000 spread over 40 constituencies, sent back 66. In the election of 1903 the Conservatives, with 143 representatives, had obtained only 324,157 votes, but the Social Democrats who polled 314,149 votes obtained 0 representatives.

Junker Overrepresentation. Let us bring together the figures relating the Conservative Party and the Junker representation, for it is essential to observe the marked influence of the quintessential Junker core on Prussia and the whole Reich.

	No. of Deputies	Junkers	Conservatives		Free Conservatives		National Lib.
1903	433 of which	65 of which	61	and	3	and	1
1908	433 of which	65 of which	60	and	4	and	1
1913	433 of which	59 of which	54	and	4	and	1

payers who altogether paid one third of the taxes made Class I; the next largest taxpayers contributing another third made Class II; the rest composed Class III. Each class elected by separate vote a third of the electors to which the constituency was entitled. Then all the electors so chosen met together and elected the representative by absolute majority vote, with run-offs where necessary. By-elections took the form of the electors coming together to pick another man to fill any vacancy:

The Junkers, then, made up over one seventh of the entire Assembly, though stemming from but a few hundred families. Almost all were Conservatives. After the elections listed above, the Conservative Party held 143 seats, 152, and 148 making just over one third of the total of the House. The Junkers thus constituted about 40 percent of all the Conservatives. Over 84 percent of Conservative strength in seats came from the 7 eastern provinces of Prussia, and the Junkers there constituted half of the Conservative representation. Moreover, the Conservative group in the *Reichstag* of 1908 was composed of 29 large landowners, 19 bourgeois landowners and peasants, 2 big industrialists, 9 officials and professional men, and 3 men of the middle class; while the party committee of the Conservatives contained 6 Junkers out of its 11 members—this was the steering committee.

One other feature of the system is worth note: elections to the *Reichstag* were by secret ballot; for the Prussian House, voting was oral and open. In the latter situation, with small electorates on the Right, government pressure was powerfully exertable, and exerted. The *Herrenhaus,* overwhelmingly Conservative, contained Junkers to the extent of 30 percent; plus noble landowners.

Consequences: Political Reactionary Conservatism. Prussia was almost brutally Conservative, indeed, reactionary; and her *Bundesrat* members represented the tone of the eastern portion of Prussia. Her government was practically, we have shown, the government of Germany as a whole, through the predominance of the Chancellor and the King, the group of Ministers and courtiers. Her industrial population did not get its opportunity to exert even its potential class-affected liberalism and sense of social justice, because the Constitution repudiated the principal of parliamentary responsibility, and public representation of the voters' sentiments was warped by the electoral laws.

However, if the principle of shooting down opposition is not openly put into practice as the major and reputable way of dealing with parliamentary opponents, what is a Government, supported by a core of reactionaries, to do when faced with millions of popularly given votes? It is public hypocrisy and international shame for a nation that claims it is cultured (and *Kultur* was the fetish of the Germans) to ignore and flout them. At least some tactics must be developed and concessions made in the face of mounting public pressure from the strong and vociferous political parties that had begun to grow in the middle of the century under the twin incitement of unity and liberalism.

Hence, it is of moment to consider how this system of belated and qualified absolutism—or call it, constitutional monarchy—behaved in action.

We may consider this problem by paying attention to the main features of economic development; the main chief characteristics of civil and judicial administration; the evolution of political parties and the respective tactics of the monarchy, its advisers, and the parties, leading to the military and social breakdown after the defeat of 1914–1918.

IV. ECONOMIC DEVELOPMENT AND GOVERNMENT

Toward the outbreak of the War of 1914–1918, Germany had a population of 67,790,000. This was a remarkable increase over the 42,500,000 of 1871 and was largely due to economic progress, the main features of which were very rapid industrialization and scientific improvements in agriculture. Both were spurred on by amazing applications of chemistry, natural technology, and research to machinery, processes, and fertilizers. The increasing population,[2] in its turn, stimulated economic enterprise. The schools continued to mold a highly docile, obedient, even *untertänig* (that is, servile), and highly competent working class. In 1871, 63.9 percent of the population was rural; in 1910, only 40 percent; urban population rose from 36.1 to 60 percent.

Capitalism

The capitalists, who from about 1850, ventured in industrial development became National Liberals or Conservatives; and they allied themselves with the Prussian monarchy because it had proved itself successful by war and the repudiation of the liberals in the achievement of unity. In the Prussian *Landtag* the liberals had surrendered for a mess of unifying potage, industrial opportunities, and nationalism. Political parties degenerated into mere critics and negativists in the legislatures, and therefore no longer attracted the finest brains and characters. Brains went into industry. The parties became doctrinaire, and found that they could

[2] Emigration was much reduced: from the annual average of about 135,000 between 1881 to 1890, to 53,000 between 1890 and 1900, and only 22,000 a year between 1901 and 1910.

do best for themselves by offering the voters not policy for the State but concessions to interests. They became "interest groups" covered with a thin and extreme halo of ideology.

Government and Tariffs

German industry was stimulated by the French indemnity of 1871, by unity, and by organized talent. Germany was made into one business area by the Reich statutes unifying business law, legal procedure, and credit operations creating a common coinage, joint-stock companies, free mobility. But when overspeculation in 1873 led to a crisis, the industrialists appealed to Bismarck for protective tariffs. Bismarck preferred the society and agriculture of East Prussia, but considerations of national power caused him to give the industrial magnates tariffs. The motive of war-making capacity was so conspicuous as to arrest the European free-trade movement that had developed since 1846. Bismarck needed heavy industry under tariffs rather than the international economic division of labor. Tariffs were repeatedly raised. This help of the State was in the full tradition of German evolution—for, as we have pointed out (p. 542), there was no break between Prussian State-activity policy as embodied in Cameralism of the seventeenth and eighteenth centuries and the State-economy theories of the nineteenth century, such as had occurred in Britain and France and the United States.

"State Socialism"

Adam Müller had taken this attitude toward what the Germans called *Smithianismus.* (The quotation is from his *Elemente der Staatskunst,* or *Elements of Statecraft,* first published in 1812):

The State is not merely a factory, farm, insurance company, or mercantilistic society; it is an inward combination of the total physical and spiritual needs of the whole internal and external life of a nation to a great energetic perpetually-moving whole. . . . Order, freedom, security, law, the happiness of all, are sublime ideas for those who conceive them idea-wise; the State, however great and sublime, however comprehensive, however much it rests in and upon itself, does not disclaim to be considered, among

other things, as though it existed only for one of those purposes; it is, however, too big, too full of life, to devote itself to one of these purposes exclusively and solely to please the theorists; it serves everything they want, it serves every conceivable purpose, because it serves itself.

Friedrich List's chief work, *Das Nationale System der Politischen Ökonomie,* published in 1841, derived from both Adam Müller and from Alexander Hamilton's "American System." He reached high influence some thirty years after his book was given to the world, just when German industrialists, agrarians, and a power-lustful government were ripe for a justifying doctrine. He was an extreme opponent of international trade and national economies harmonizing with maximized world trade through the division of labor and the subsequent exchange of goods produced in their best-endowed localities. Equally bitter was his hostility to free trade, as this quotation illustrates.

Which country would destroy its fleet, disband its armies, demolish its fortresses in the hope of perpetual peace? None!

. . . at a time when technical and mechanical science exercises such immense influence on the methods of warfare, where all warlike operations depend so much on the conditions of national revenue, where successful defense greatly depends on whether the mass of the nation is rich or poor, intelligent or stupid, energetic or lethargic, etc., etc.—at such a time, more than ever before, must the value of manufactures be estimated from a political point of view.

Quite a Leninist-Stalinist idea (p. 778)! List claimed Holland, Switzerland, Belgium, and Denmark as German lands, by reason of origin and international position. (This is a softener of German consciences bent on invasion in the twentieth century.) He proposed emigration to all the Americas (less to U.S.A.) to be made into "supplementary regions" for German manufactures. Here is the Kaiser's "place in the sun"; Hitler's *Lebensraum,* and the Pan-German League (p. 606). He denounced Adam Smith's *cosmopolitan* economy; its pursuit of wealth, its *materialism,* instead of the nation's strength; its *individualism,* instead of nationalism.

Industrialization

Occupations developed thus (in percentages of the occupied):

	1882	1907
Agriculture and forestry	42.3	34.0
Industry and crafts	35.5	39.7
Commerce and communications	8.4	13.7
Public and private service	5.8	6.8
Domestic service	8.0	5.8

German per-capita income increased 450 to 645 marks between 1896 and 1913, for a greatly expanded population.

Government and Industry. The remarkable feature of German industry was the extent to which the State contributed to its growth. Industry began with large-scale corporations—iron and coal, chemicals and dyes, electrical and glass, textiles, armaments, motor cars and engineering, transoceanic shipping, railroads—all bound up with banking and commerce and aggressive financing. The educational system produced the technical experts and white-collar employees it needed. The able and daring entrepreneurs—whose brains were denied to liberal politics—built the nexus of cartels, combines, and trusts of a monopolistic character. The government did not regulate or break them, as in the United States, for the masses of consumers had no political power. Indeed, the government connived with business to bolster it against the proletariat; both industrialists and Junker agrarians were given tariffs, first in 1879. The cartels produced the armaments and war supplies. German investments and manufactures were directed to Russia, so that the German government might influence that nation's policies, rather than let Britain and France in. The German government was terrified of the Slavs.

The *Direktors* and *Generaldirektors* of industry and finance were inextricably linked with German militarism. They were not *laissez fairists* but, if the government were monarchical, they gave it nationalistic obedience, while they themselves were despotic monarchs in their own firms, *Herr im Hause.* The professors of economics did not challenge them. The idea was disseminated that *Macht* was Right; that economic cartelism was like German unification. The government, to save waste, even compelled the formation of trusts, as in potash, coal, and iron.

State Welfare for the Workers. A mass of industrial workers grew fast. They raised the twin problems of factory conditions and social welfare, and the problem of the price of food, and thereby that of the protection of agriculturists. This will be discussed *a propos* German political parties (pp. 600ff.).

But we must remember that, to the German captain of industry, the government was a servant of industry rather than the political servant of a whole nation.

V. THE ADMINISTRATIVE MACHINE

The British specialized in Parliament; the Prussians and then the Germans in Bureaucracy. The former gave liberty, the latter governmental efficiency with imposed values. It is not desirable to speak of bureaucracy if we mean only the existence and operation of public officials, for where these are openly appointed and always subject to the commands and discipline of a free parliament, *bureaucracy* is but a term of vilification by those who happen to dislike the administrative activities founded on the law made by free legislatures. But the word *bureaucracy* is a proper designation of the Prussian and German Civil Service and local government officials, because they were recruited from a deliberately restricted social group and used to enforce policies that were not created and authorized by free representatives of a free people.

Here we insist only on the main features of the bureaucracy. It was a characteristic counterpart of Big Industry, Junker Agriculture, the *Offizierkorps,* a nonresponsible Chancellor heading a corps of promoted officials and not of leaders of free political parties, and a protesting, but obsequious, people, accepting welfare provisions but not sovereign master of their enactment.

The Civil Service

The Prussian Civil Service, to which our remarks are mainly addressed, was the model for the Service of the Reich and some of the other states, as well as itself serving the State that was some two thirds of the population of the whole Reich, containing the main manufacturing centers.

In 1881, to take a date a decade after the Reich was in working order, the Prussian Civil Service numbered 152,000 in a population of 27,500,000; and the Reich Service numbered 452,000 with a population of 45,400,000. The latter figure included the Reich, all the states, all the local authorities of the states; thus, the Prussian figures are included in the Reich's as are the other states'. The figure then represented some 1 in 44 of the occupied population. By 1911 there were 1,159,000 officials in a total labor force of some 32,000,000, or about 1 in 30.

The Frederickian Civil Service (p. 547) crumbled under defeat by Napoleon as had the old-fashioned parade-ground-drilled Army. Freiherr vom Stein proposed considerable decentralization to relieve the central departments of excessive work and responsibilities and to get the ventilation of popular consultation. He proposed to get rid of multiple-executives (commissions or colleges) at the head of the departments and replace them by single Ministers, for responsibility and despatch.

For Prussian administration, which was highly book-learned and subject to the strictest rule of accountability and discipline upward, had suffered an inner withering, precisely because discipline was too strict, and because in the course of time the considerable practical apprenticeship required by regulations had become perfunctory. Officials lived in "the printed, not the real world"; they had become a "clerical caste."

The tasks and monarchical spirit of the Prussian State required high discipline and obedience of the Civil Service. There was no parliament or elections to invigorate it by open criticism or a change of Ministers produced by popular replacement. Officials did not look outward to the public, their consumers, but to the Ministers and King, upward, their masters and employers. The political theorists actually assigned to them an *irresponsive* and aloof status. Hegel had declared (*Philosophy of Law*): "Here [in the officialdom] is found the conjunction of universal and particular interests, a union which constitutes the conception and the internal stability of the State." And Adam Müller

added: "The politicians and the Civil Service produce the State."

Critics accused the Civil Service of the following bureaucratic qualities. It lived and acted by self-worship. It moved on the principle of the infallibility of its superior officials, with the corollary of uncritical execution of orders. It was intimidated by fear of what was contained in the secret conduct reports that decided rewards and punishments, salaries and titles. "Subordination," says a critic, "is the Holy Ghost which speaks with fiery tongue and permeates and illuminates everyone."

The Judiciary (pp. 597-599) was recruited by the same legal education at the universities as the higher civil servants; after three or four years of service in the law courts, the common entrants separated in their careers. They were like-minded.

This machine was, of course, involved in the defeat of the liberals; it was opposed to the people, the *canaille*. Furthermore, the civil servants and the military officers intermingled; the former were often recruited from those who had served in the *Offizierkorps*. The secret reports we have referred to remained in being until 1919; not till then could an official inspect his report and challenge it in a proper disciplinary court.

The public officials' technical efficiency, in the narrow sense of the word, was far superior to that of France, England, and the United States through to the latter part of the century. But it lost to them in responsiveness and inventiveness to the welfare of the consumer.

No Open Competition. A university education and years of apprenticeship to the age of twenty-seven or twenty-eight implied the restriction of the Service to the wealthy. But the practical rules of admission made certain of more than this: a potent class bias. The candidate had to be "friendly to the State"—that is, a conservative—a person of family standing, a member of a students' *corps* and/or a reserve officer, and a member of the State church.

The Civil Service moved away from the practical studies of Cameralism (p. 542), for the *Rechtsstaat* (p. 562) was in the ascendant. Therefore, the law studies were given priority, only to nourish punctilious and legalizing administrative martinets. They earned Bismarck's contempt, if Hegel's admiration, who said, "The sense of State and the most conspicuous education are found in the middle class, to which the State officials belong."

Decade by decade the legal element in studies and preparatory practice in the law courts was given priority in the rigorous examinations, though heavily criticized by public fretting under the Service. This happened precisely in the era when the State assumed new economic and social duties and initiative, and when parliamentary parties could sting Ministers if not eject them from office. By 1879 the Prussian *Landtag,* after a long inquiry, tried to introduce political science and economics into the first law examination; the government permitted it only *after* the preparatory service with the judiciary. But all were dissatisfied with the law studies. The rules lasted to 1918, while the debate between social science *versus* legalistic preparation lasted even beyond. For German law studies had become sterile mastery of the Prussian and other codes, without the "case" method or sociological seminars to stimulate discussions of law in the making and application. The students were detached from their Olympian caste of professors and lost time in taverns, dueling and loafing. For the social sciences they went to "crammers." In 1906, the preparatory service was increased from three to four years. The system operated until 1920. Its main lines were these. The student took law *and political science* for three years at a university. It ended by his first law examination. It was but a short time, but the government was anxious to have men enter the Service when they are still young. If the examination was passed, the recruit entered preparatory service for four years. For these administrative officials, there was one year in the law courts, and it could even be reduced to only nine months. The recruit must then get acceptance by a *Regierungspräsident,* the chief official of each of the fifteen great areas of local administration. Without this, no career was possible. The central ministries were not too anxious to be made the first selectors of their younger men; some people were afraid that if the central departments were responsible, then political influences would be brought to bear. The

latter fear, except from an opposition standpoint, was ludicrous, since the choice by the local authorities was heavily political, in favor not only of conservatism but even of reaction, though less so in the western part of Prussia than the east. We return to this point presently.

There was, then, no open competition for entry.

The recruit—the designation was *Referendar*— entered three or three and a quarter years of practical apprenticeship, under the severe eye and sanction of the *Regierungspräsident.* The time was divided among the *Kreis,* local government areas, with the *Landrat* at its head—twelve months; a small popularly elected municipal authority, three months; and fifteen months in the *Regierungsbezirk,* in the executive and the committee branches. Within this local experience the *Referendar* varied his service in urban and local areas, as deputy to a *Bürgermeister* of a city, in various branches (such as education or the finance divisions), by indoor work and missions requiring travel. Almost continuously an older official was in charge, advising, teaching, supervising, and reporting on moral and political conduct. It was only when the *Regierungspräsident* was satisfied by all the assembled reports that the final examination was taken whereby the *Referendar* could enter the Service. An extensive practical study was required of the *Referendar* as proof of his maturity.

This examination was written and oral, and comprised Prussian private and public law, constitutional and administrative law, economics, and political science. A dissertation on undisclosed topics was required on each of two days—reference books were allowed. The third day was devoted to a verbal report. An oral examination followed. One failure only was permitted; a second failure entailed exclusion from the Civil Service.

Thus, the examination was practical and technical. It was assumed that the student had acquired a philosophy and capacity for humane reasoning at high school and during his university and practical experience. But certainly since high school he had been immersed in administration and law, not in general studies. The German judgment and strength of speculation and analysis; the former was more formalistic and technical; the latter more functional and critical; the former pedantic, the latter, urbane and inventive; the former starting work at between the ages of twenty-one and twenty-four, the latter at nearly thirty. As Professor Schumacher of Berlin said: "I suffered very much under the oppressive feeling that I was entirely chained up just in the years when I most strongly felt the impulse to act . . . the thwarted desire for activity produced as a substitute that pretentious bearing toward others that has so often given offence." Most of those who had left the Service agreed with him. The civil servants came to independent responsibility for decisions and action very late.

Junker Strength in the Civil Service. The strength of the Junkers and other nobles in Prussian administration was truly extraordinary. It is to be estimated by available statistics.

In the period 1888 to 1914, of the twelve *Oberpräsidents* of the provinces, never more than three were commoners, usually only one; the rest were Junkers or other nobles. In the first part of the period from 50 to 40 percent were Junkers; later there were fewer of them compared with other nobles; they retained a greater predominance in the eastern than in the western provinces. Of those serving as officials to these highest officers, namely, *Oberpräsidialräte* (assistants and deputies), some 25 percent were Junkers, and they were usually assigned to serve men who were not themselves Junkers. Other assistants to the *Oberpräsidents* were the *Regierungsräte* and *Regierungsassessoren;* they fell in percentage of the total of such officers from almost 56 in 1888 to nearly 15 in 1914. In the office of *Regierungspräsident,* of which there were variously thirty-four or thirty-five, the Junkers occupied about 40 percent of the positions, and other nobles about the same percentage, leaving by 1914 between 16 to 50 percent of places for commoners. Associated with these were advisers and deputies, *Oberregierungsräte:* the total number of officers was from 113 in 1888 to 176 in 1914; in 1895 Junkers held their maximum percentage, namely, 18, while in 1914, it had sunk to nearly 10 percent.

Governmental Significance. The importance of these figures lies in two factors: first, the percentage of Junkers and the percentage of other nobles

was out of all proportion to their percentage of the population; and, second, these controlled access to the practical term of service of the Civil Service recruit and, thus, to the final examination. Moreover, the commoners who were let in had to be "satisfactory"—that is, politically acceptable.

The next in the local hierarchy of local government-central government officials were the *Landräte,* their number being about 490. The Junkers held nearly 30 percent of these places; and other nobles about the same and a slightly growing number; while only some 40 percent went to commoners. Some Junkers who were *Landräte* were also members of the Prussian House of Representatives; as much as 30 percent of them in 1888. There was a wholesale dismissal of these in 1894 by the Government, because so many of them had voted against the Government's bill for the construction of a canal from West to East Germany as injurious to East German agrarian interests, which meant their own. The Junkers in the House ran to about 70 out of a total of 400.

It must be remembered that the *Landrat* was an official of dual power: a representative of the central government and the executive officer of the local circle (*Kreis*) government area, which had its elected council and executive committee (see p. 632). He had very many opportunities for political influence, seeing that votes could be swayed by the kindness of the central government toward the local government functions and services of the area, and because the central government officials were election officials and, for the government, election manipulators. The *Landrat* position was a steppingstone to that of *Oberpräsident,* and this to high office in the central ministries. The *Landrat* position was sometimes a place for those who had worked in the ministries but had not been able enough for top promotions. Some were men who could have gone higher in Berlin, but preferred to hold office where the estates belonging to them or their families were situated. The Junkers occupied no less than 50 percent of these offices in eastern Prussia. In the later period of the Reich, some 12 percent of those who served in East Prussia were nobles from the western areas.

While a large number of officials in these levels

were commoners, they were men who tended to
be assimilated in outlook to the traditional holding
group. Their appointment could not be avoided,
except on a serious risk of administrative (and
therefore the general political) incompetence of
the State. For there were insufficient Junkers; not
all wanted to serve; and many of those who did
serve the State went into the Armed Services. The
temptation to enter the Army as a career rather
than the Civil Service came from the fact that the
prestige was even higher, and the educational expense was very much less, since it took place at
military cadet schools and began and ended at
earlier ages. The government charged smaller fees
in the cadet schools than those demanded by the
universities.

The Grip of the Antiliberals. The government
relied on its officials for quasi-political services as
well as technical administrative ones. For the
prestige of the monarchy needed to keep the
competence high. The introduction of commoners,
even of high economic and social class, and the
service of some of the Junkers inevitably outside
the area of their own estates and the aboriginal
home of the Junkers, tended to introduce something of a liberal (but *not* democratic or proletarian) tinge into the administrative outlook. Snobbery and official advancement, fear of the Social
Democrats, enabled the Junkerdom officials to
"feudalize" large numbers of the bourgeoisie, not
least the new financial, manufacturing, and commercial magnates. For example, the number of
commoners belonging to the Conservative Party
in the Prussian House of Representatives was
about equal to that of the Junkers in it, and some
had become Prussian propertyowners.

The Junkers and their congeners did not enter
the departments that were of the new technical and
social-welfare kind. They tried to dominate the
more "political" ministries: War, Interior, Finance,
Foreign Affairs, Church, Agriculture. In the Ministry of Foreign Affairs, employing 120 higher
civil servants by 1914, the number of nobles (including Junkers) in the Reich period made up
about 80 percent of the total employed; while the
Junkers, plain and simple, occupied a sixth of all
the posts, because, it is said, they were too coarse,
too little diplomatic to be entrusted with foreign

representation. The Ministry of the Interior was
held by Junker chiefs steadily, and molded to a
highly conservative form. The number of Junker
assistants was some 16 percent of the total. In the
War Office, the Junkers held 10 percent of the
offices, and the highest.

In the Royal Household, Junkers held some 50
percent (and sometimes 55 percent) of the high
posts, in closest proximity to the King—and the
Imperial Chancellor. The percentage was about
the same in the Military Retinue.

Under William I—and Bismarck—this system
of administration marched fairly smoothly under
their direction; they were very much, though not
altogether, part of them. Wilhelm II was more
German and spread-eagle, and often found himself
at odds with his Chancellors, Prime Ministers, and
official Cabinet. Tensions resulted, as we shall see,
between these agencies and the higher civil servants.

Brilliant Local Government. It will be gathered
later (pp. 631–639) that in this period the administration of the urban and rural areas, especially of
the cities, exhibited much progress, as might be
expected where the art of technical administration
had so long been cultivated, and where a love of
one's own city had for so long meant much more
to a Germany than love of Germany. It was, above
all, in city administration where traditions sometimes went far back into the Middle Ages, that
civic dedication and services exhibited their greatest efflorescence. This was another branch of
large-scale business; and here, also, something of
self-government through elected councils in cooperation with appointed or centrally ratified
burgomasters, called on the pride of the citizens
and diverted them from the governing class's
monopoly of high domestic and foreign policy.

"Acquired Rights." The public services thus described, with a social élite at the top, and with
dutiful commoners in the middle ranks and
former soldiers in the lower ranks, had a well-
marked series of so-called "acquired rights"—
economic, rank, title, uniform, disciplinary penalties, jurisdiction, and guarantees—that marked it
off from the rest of the population. These details,
of great importance in securing disciplined devotion to the masters at the top and some disdain for

the popular representative bodies and the political parties composed of the mass of Germans, appear later (p. 628). The civil servants were the faithful and punctilious servitors of the monarchy and the Chancellor and Ministers—and these were *not* the choice of the public. They were a buttress of the *Obrigkeitstaat,* demonstrating by their political aloofness and competence that there existed something different from popular voting, which could be called "a sense of state," and that technical competence could not be expected from the untrained and "irresponsible" people and political leaders.

The Camarilla

Around the person of the King and Emperor, and sometimes intruding between him on the one side and, on the other, the Imperial Chancellor and Prussian Prime Minister and the publicly known Cabinet, was the *Camarilla,* composed (or on the way in, or recently out) of the two *secret* Cabinets, the one Civil and the other Military. These were the King's most trusted secretaries, three in the former and eight in the latter, appointed personally by him. Under Wilhelm II, the Chancellors became sick at heart at the incense-burning to the Emperor; the flattery and obsequiousness that had its influence in increasing the megalomania of the man; the rejection of candor; the encouragement of the royal vanity, the exploitation of the royal weaknesses summed up in the term *Byzantinism.* It was fatefully fraught with the impulses toward World War I, and this toward World War II.

The Judiciary

No revolution settled, as in England or the United States, that the courts should be separate from the Executive. This was done by the Prussian Kings' own fiat. In 1752 Frederick the Great had said in his *Political Testament,*

> I have resolved never to interfere with the course of trials; in the courts of justice the laws must speak and the sovereign be silent.

He did, however, interfere from time to time, especially in the case of the miller Arnold (1779–1780), where he dismissed six judges for a decision that was according to law, but, according to

right reason, oppressive to the miller against his landowners. The King soon regretted his reversal of the court, for everyone began to appeal to him directly. He then had the laws codified, at any rate, to guide the judges and to unify the several courts that had sprung from feudal and provincial evolution. The judges themselves and the royal Ministers of Justice in the various states developed a sense of judicial duty, involving impartiality, independence, and incorruptibility. They were, of course, in descent from the tradition of Roman Law that had been "received" by the Germanic states about four centuries before, and so were appointed as servants of the State by the Crown. The schools of law of the developing universities furnished the candidates for royal appointment, though the Crown was not strictly bound to such sources.

The judicial career in Germany was and is of the nature of the Civil Service, indeed, with the same basic preparation (p. 594). The principle of the separation of powers was not established, as elsewhere, by revolution. It did, however, develop by tradition among the Kings; and throughout the nineteenth century the judicial officials themselves developed the concept of the *Rechtsstaat* (p. 562), to do right to all parties and to keep officials within the bounds of the law. The Prussian Constitution of 1850 said (Articles 86ff.): "The judicial power shall be exercised in the name of the King by independent tribunals subject to no other authority than that of law." Other articles guaranteed equality before the law; that no one should be deprived of his lawful judge; that exceptional courts should not be permitted. Judges were appointed for life and were removable only by judicial sentence; their appointment was limited to those alone who had the statutory qualifications. The Weimar Constitution carried on the institution of independence, for in Article 102 it stipulated that the "judges are independent and are subject only to the law"; similarly in the various *Länder* constitutions.

The experience of the rendering of judgment during the Weimar regime, particularly in matters concerning public order and constitutional-democratic behavior, was, however, scandalous (p. 650, p. 656, and p. 659), and critics pointed to two faults. The first was the exaggeration of the virtue of impartiality, consisting in interpreting the law in a formal way and without the judge's sense of justice and statesmanship, letting the destroyers of the Weimar democracy flourish. The second was a direct charge of "class justice"—that is, of judicial decisions deliberately, or through unconscious class bias, in favor of nationalist and militarist subverters of a social democratic tendency in the Constitution. There was ample ground for both complaints. The first one was often buttressed by the charge (to a considerable extent true, though unequally among the various judges) that law training in Germany left the judges formalists and without the common sense of practical life.

The Bonn Constitution, drafted by a large body of men themselves practicing or teaching law, has taken much of the discretion to be undemocratic or antidemocratic out of the hands of the judges, unless they deliberately betray their sworn trust. This will be seen by its text in Articles 92ff, and particularly in Articles 97 and 98. Judges are independent and owe a duty to the law alone. They can be removed only by decision of their fellow-judges, based on statutes regulating such procedure. They can be removed from office or transferred if, in or out of office, they violate the principles of the Basic Law or the constitutional order of a *Land*. The status of judges in the *Länder* is regulated by their own laws, but the Bund can enact general rules for these.

Organization. The administration of justice until the federal arrangement of 1871 was the affair of the states; after it, that situation still pertained. But soon the hierarchy of courts then came, in some matters, to be subordinate to the *Reichsgericht* at Leipzig, especially in the interpretation of laws unifying the judicial profession, procedure in the courts, and the interpretation of the great Reichwide codes (p. 579).

The profession of *Justizbeamte* (magistracy), or *Richter* (judge) is distinct from that of attorney, much as it was in the Reich and the Weimar Republic. The entrant now (as then) comes in from his law course, takes an entrance examination, has three years as *Referendar*, or apprentice in the courts, takes a final State examination. He is appointed as *Gerichtsassessor,* or court assessor— that is, as an apprentice still with minor duties, and with an allowance but not a salary. Though the level of pay is not high, the profession has great public prestige and the arrangements for pension and security are sound. There is, as in France, a regular system of public attorneyship, called the *Staatsanwaltschaft,* like the procuratorship in the U.S.S.R., although in Germany it has not the dictatorial, punitive functions of the latter: it is like the French *parquet* (p. 512), to maintain justice and integrity in the judiciary's attitude and work. Some of the latter become judges. Attorneys, in contrast to the judges, are dismissible.

In the highest criminal courts alone do juries participate. All the judges serve for both civil and criminal jurisdiction. The *Staatsanwaltschaft* prepares cases for the court in a similar way to the *Juge d'instruction* in France (p. 517).

Generally speaking, the courts rise in a hierarchy thus: the Office Court or *Amtsgericht;* the *Landesgericht,* regional; the *Oberlandesgericht,* supreme regional Court; and the *Reichsgericht.* In all these courts, except the *Amtsgericht,* several judges sit together; in the former, a single judge. All these are fully trained judges of career. There are no elective judges and never have been in the German system, though there have been in France during the Revolution of 1789, and there are still such in the United States, and none but such in the Soviet Union (p. 845) though "elective" there has a peculiar meaning. The Office Judge sits alone for minor and intermediate matters; for more serious affairs he has two lay judges with him, called *Schöffen.* These are chosen by the judge and a judicial-administrative committee annually from a list submitted by the municipalities, and acceptance is an obligatory civic function. This latter provides an element of human understanding beyond that of the expert judge's outlook.

Appeals from the Office Judge go to the *Landesgericht* and in serious criminal matters to the *Oberlandesgericht.* The *Reichsgericht* to 1918 was composed of judges nominated on a ratio basis by the various states. The number of judges is large: in 1883, 7006; in 1915, 10,600; in 1927, 9361; in 1941, 14,031. The public prosecutors' offices employed in the neighborhood of 2000 attorneys. Altogether in 1927, Prussia alone had nearly 46,000 persons (judges, attorneys, officials, etc.) concerned with the administration of the law —and under authority of the Ministry of Justice.

Germany is noted for its "specialized" courts, in addition to its administrative courts, of which the Weimar *Oberverwaltungsgericht* was the apex and exemplar. There were and are such courts as the Commercial, the Labor, Tax, and Social Security Courts, manned by a professional judge flanked by two laymen with a knowledge of the branch of affairs in the court's cognizance. The laymen are chosen by the clienteles—for example, labor unions or businessmen's associations or chambers of commerce. There is a line of appeal from them to the ordinary courts.

The administrative courts (*Verwaltungsgerichte*) go upward from mixed bodies of officials and people nominated by the local or provincial elected assemblies, to the highest court (see above). Neither under the Empire nor Weimar was there a *Reich* supreme administrative court, only those of the *Länder*.

Education

German education in her schools and universities was most industrious, highly intellectual, technically competent, patriotic in the monarcho-Volk sense (p. 551ff.), and of a decided class-discriminatory character. It was rooted in the Lutheran

cultivated, and all teachers were carefully selected for their conformity to and zeal for the Fatherland. The anti-Socialist themes were strongly stressed by force of decree. Teachers were always reported on by the *Landrat* and his school inspectors, often clergymen, for they were considered to be State officials. They were penalized if they showed their support of any but conservative politics. Civics was taught in the upper classes of the secondary schools, but this was not a free exercise in the discussion of alternatives to the Prussian State and the other Germanic monarchies. Teachers had a remarkably authoritarian status over the pupils and their families.

All universities were, and they still remain, institutions of the government. (There were a very few "High Schools" for economics and political science, and so forth; but they did not count, when it came to professional careers.) All professors were and are State appointees. The upper- and middle-class students who could afford attendance at universities joined the *Studentenkorps,* whose patriotism, prestige, and snobbery were necessary to professional or public positions often attested by a *mensur,* a duel scar on the face.

Attendance at the universities was impossible unless one had graduated from a high school. The class inequality, and with it the political outlooks, may be gathered from the figures of attendance at the various levels.

1912: Attendance in Schools and Universities

Elementary (*Volksschulen*)	10,300,000	and 26,000 private
Middle schools	274,000	and 80,660 private
Gymnasium; *Realgymnasium; Realschulen,* boys and girls	420,000	
Universities	70,000	
Technical high schools and professional schools	26,000	

severity of public instruction of all for religious and secular good order. It was studded with some of the most brilliant names in pedagogy; and what is characteristic, the German educators and the students were pedantic, all pedagogues, "enlightened despots." By 1794, though the beginning goes back to 1763, the Prussian government, had enacted and organized a compulsory system of universal elementary education or a State-accepted equivalent. From the post-Tilsit era (p. 54), the patriotic element in the schools was sedulously

All were compelled to go to school from the ages of six to fourteen. The middle schools were like the elementary schools, but included French and English languages. The *Gymnasium* was the secondary school for classical studies; the *Realgymnasium* taught mathematics, natural sciences, modern languages, and some classics. The *Oberrealschulen* taught mathematics, natural sciences, and so on, but no classics at all. There were many private and preparatory schools leading to the *Gymnasia,* another class-selective sieve.

Thus only 1 in 25 of the elementary school population went on to secondary schools; less than 1 percent went to the universities.

The Press

Frederick the Great even wrote newspaper articles or paid or forced others to do so to support his policies. Like his predecessors (Frederick William I, "the populace should not reason") he used the censorship. After the main Metternichian repression had relaxed (p. 561), the rising bourgeoisie and nascent political parties set going hundreds of newspapers. By 1885 there was one newspaper per 14,731 population, by 1914 one per 15,381; the average circulation had risen from 3069 to 4221 in these years. One half the newspapers, roughly, through the monarchical Reich and the Weimar Republic, were party newspapers. If we take the year 1913, the Conservative papers were 22.6 percent of the total; Liberals, 14.4; Catholic, 11.6; Socialist 2.2 or 87 in number, but of enormous circulation of the chief ones, like *Vorwärts.* The rest, nonparty, amounted to 49.2 percent. They were run as business propositions. They were hostile to the Social Democrats and unfriendly toward the Progressives. The Socialist papers were often persecuted by legal actions by the government for *lèse-majesté*—that is, insults to the Kaiser and Government (less than sedition and not known in Britain or the United States)—or for violating the sphere of interest the law regarded as proper to editors.

Men, like Bismarck, planted articles with their friends on the *Kreuzzeitung* and other papers. Some newspapers were almost official, so close was the relationship between them and the various "political" ministries, such as the Chancellery, Foreign Affairs, or the Ministry of the Interior; their intelligence divisions were in close contact with and gave out special "scoops" to them. Journalists were subsidized from secret funds. The news-gathering bureau, Wolff's Telegraphic Agency, was a private firm, but it had communications privileges from the government, and in exchange it disseminated news planted with it by the government.

After the special regime of the press in wartime (1914–1918)—strict control—the press went back to its freedom and party alignments. The democratic press, like the *Frankfurter Seitung,* the *Berliner Tageblatt,* the *Vossische Zeitung,* received a great accession of political strength. The Communists now came into the field with their press, their evening Berlin paper having the largest circulation of any there. The great Rightist papers, excepting the Nazi *Völkischer Beobachter* and its Berlin affiliate, came into a great chain forged by the reactionary nationalist, Hugenberg.

VI. THE DEVELOPMENT OF POLITICAL PARTIES

General Characteristics

The German political party system that developed after 1848 acquired certain general characteristics that may be mentioned at once.

(1) Not Sovereign. Parties were cut off from the direct exercise of power and sovereignty. Therefore, the general German tendency to find refuge in elaborate and distant philosophy was especially pronounced in them, in their need for subtle justification. They became at once *Weltanschauungsparteien* and *Program-parteien,* the former term meant that they developed complete and even metaphysical systems, to back their claims. They did not descend from the level of philosophy to that of the expedient policy. The latter meant that they had to formulate programs that had not the ring of reality about them; they took grandiose looks toward the horizon, very distant—once again as justification and allurement to the electorate. It was in the light of their programs that they criticized the monarchical policies and other parties.

(2) A Catholic Party. One of these parties, the Center Party, or *Zentrum,* very large as will be seen from the figures of elections we give, was ostensibly based on a religious creed, the Roman Catholic, aiming to hold together *all* economic and social classes, rich or poor, noble or commoner, agricultural or proletariat, and all regions, in one common bond. Its fate and works we shall see—but it was certainly very *separatist.*

(3) "Interest Parties." These parties were more sharply interest parties or pressure groups for economic segments or classes than anywhere else in the world. They had come into existence in a time of heightened class-consciousness, and vigorous if incipient organization in terms of the Industrial and Commercial Revolutions and the universal sectarian, separatist, divisive influence of Karl Marx and all the diverse anti-Marxians. Even the Catholic Center Party was a special-interest group.

(4) National Minority Parties. In addition, there were several "national" groups, small enough to be called "splinter parties." Their names appear in the election statistics (p. 587). They were in almost permanent opposition.

Political Consequences

The result was to nurture the German masses in grandiose sentiments. They lost time better spent in the practice of everyday compromise of extreme claims, harmonizing cooperation, and reciprocity of concession and good will, which are essential to the democratic process of self-government. The parties, under conditions they could hardly help, put off the day of the democratic second-best by sticking to their ideologies fully, except for special forays for class booty.

The table on p. 587 shows the political parties and their votes; the *Konservativen* at the far Right, the *Sozialdemokraten,* at the far Left. They must be described.

The Parties of the Right issue from the feudal and Romantic philosophy we have already described (p. 552ff.). They were feudal and agrarian to begin with; then the industrial, commercial, and financial *nouveaux riches* bought their way into this aristocratic, agrarian class.

"The Cross." In 1848 the Junker civil servants, their politicians like Bismarck, and the high officials of the Prussian Evangelical Church started the *Kreuzzeitung,* the *Newspaper of the Cross,* to be a meeting ground for high conservative opinion, agitation, and group effort. Groupings of "Fatherland Societies," "Unions of Prussians," and "Societies for King and Fatherland" became nuclei of organized agitation. They aborted the democratic Constitution. Many were hostile to unification, and of the "Iron" Bismarck. They were friends of autocratic Austria and Russia.

In 1861 they founded the Prussian National Union to combat Bennigsen's National Liberal Party, founded in 1859. The reactionary eastern agrarians split off and even refused to indemnify Bismarck in 1862 (p. 571). They became the Conservative Party. The pro-Bismarckians organized as the Free Conservatives. Both wings together never surpassed about two ninths of the *Reichstag* or Prussian *Landtag.*

When Bismarck dispensed with the support of the National Liberals both Conservative groups went to his aid. They voted for tariffs, for persecution of the Socialists. They coalesced with the Center rather than the National Liberals, for the former were more authoritarian and agricultural than the latter. With them they helped establish the Accident Insurance Law. Bismarck bought them with his increasingly high tariffs on agricultural goods, when American grain was so low in price as to make them otherwise insolvent. Thus the German masses ate dear food for the Junkers' sake and to be self-sufficient in war. The Conservatives reciprocated by accepting the Septennates (p. 577). In 1891 they conceded an income and industrial tax in Prussia; it was painful, but it relieved Prussia of too strong a grip by the Reich. They defeated more liberal education for Prussia. They were anti-Semitic; they were anti-Polish, supporting the cruel measures of the government to settle Germans on Polish lands. They were hostile to local self-government reforms (p. 632); and, paradoxically, they opposed the *Kulturkampf* (p. 602), because they feared that suppression of the Catholic Church might lead to suppression of theirs, of which they were the leaders. **A Farm Bloc.** *The Bund der Landwirte,* joined them in 1893, for tariffs, chambers of agriculture, control of stock-exchange operations. They opposed an east-west canal, fearing the loss of labor to the industrial west.

The party had disproportionate influence at Court and with the Chancellors, for these, also, were anti-Left and anti-Center. The Central Association of German Industrials and the Navy League, established in 1898, gave it financial support.

Alliances of Conservatives and Center—that is, Protestants and Catholics, both Christians—encouraged colonial expansion; and Bismarck conceded this, which he thought nonsense and a dangerous provocation to England and France, as a bait to the chauvinistic masses, the high-born imperialists, and the manufacturers. They supported the building of a fleet that threatened Britain's very life; and, rejecting Britain's pleading diplomacy from 1897 to 1905, would not desist. Thereby, they brought the Triple Entente of France, Britain, and Russia finally about their ears. They defeated the reform of the three-class distortion of the Prussian franchise and the just redistribution of seats. They had the major responsibility for leading and encouraging Kaiser Wilhelm II and his later Chancellors in international adventures and megalomaniac schemes of militaristic expansion in Africa, the Balkans, and Asia Minor, leading directly to World War I.

They were supported by Court Preacher Stocker's Christian Social Party, founded in 1878, a Tory Democratic group, later only vitriolically anti-Semitic. This brought in the lower and middle-middle class of Jew-baiters and seekers after a social-welfare State.

The National Liberals. Rudolf von Bennigsen, a Hanoverian liberal, founded the National Liberal Party. He was able to balance the liberal and the unification *motifs*. The party split in 1861 (p. 571) into nationalists and Progressives; the Bennigsen group condoned Bismarckianism. Even after 1881, it had 14 percent of the voters. It did obtain small concessions in *Reichstag* administrative and financial control; in local government; in free trade (till 1878); liberalized administrative law. Its mercantile clientele and industrial magnates found these pleasant. But the party became increasingly nationalist and imperialist: conceded a navy; strict press sedition laws; bigger army appropriations in the Septennate; persecution of the Catholics; persecution of the Socialists. A group of southern protectionists left it; in 1880 another group hostile to the Septennate left it. The main body joined in electoral coalitions with Conservatives and Center, against the liberals and the Left. Being big industrialists, its members acceded to Bismarck's social-welfare policy for the workers as a seduction from socialism. Their later leader was Gustav Stresemann (p. 641), who made them the most intensely annexationist group in World War I.

The Center Party. In the fullness of time the Center Party opened the way for Hitler's Third Reich of abominations (p. 664). It was established in 1852 to defend Catholics against attack by the Conservative Prussian government (p. 563). The Rhinelanders, about 70 percent Catholic, returned Catholics to the Prussian *Landtag* who cooperated with Prussian Liberals. 1866 tore away their Catholic friends of Austria. They were "great Germans." Bavaria was their last great bulwark. It was a special-interest group: against the democracy of the working classes; against Prussian Protestantism. It claimed what Catholics in the minority everywhere claim: social and educational independence, local self-government, and a social policy like that of the M.R.P. in France (p. 355). It was always a very strong party: to 1907, it held 20 percent of the votes; even in 1912, it had 12.3. Many of its followers moved Left, to the Social Democrats.

The Kulturkampf, 1870–1887. Bismarck detested the Social Democrats (as much as Hitler's Nazis did later). Catholics comprised one third of the total population in great blocs. In 1870 Bismarck started their suppression on the ground that the German states must not dismiss those Catholic teachers and priests who refused to accept the dogma of infallibility of the Pope recently promulgated. He happened to need National Liberal support, and was being opposed by Windthorst, the leader of the Center, who was also leader of the Hanoverian party that resisted Prussia's annexation in 1866 (p. 574). Bismarck refused to dismiss the teachers; and, on the ground that the Church was interfering in State matters, he counterattacked by stripping the Church of all sorts of privileges (such as religious marriage; registration of births, deaths, and marriages; exclusive right to appoint to priesthoods) and by interference with education for benefices, expulsion of the Jesuits, and a power of removal by the State of priests who had broken tricky rules he had created. The clerical authorities resisted in every way. The Archbishops of Posen and Cologne and the Bishop of Trier were arrested; the first was deposed by the judiciary and the State.

The Center Party, the Polish party, the Right-wing Conservatives, and the Catholic people sustained the opposition. Bismarck turned the screw tighter, by State appointments of unfilled offices and the withholding of funds to contumacious parishes and revocation of the constitutional autonomy of the Church in Prussia.

A Catholic tried to assassinate Bismarck in July 1874;[3] the Pope summoned all Catholics to resistance and denounced Prussia's laws.

Where was the dissension to end? Imitating Henry IV in 1076, the King of the Germans, a fierce and barbaric fighter for his royal power and excommunicated, who was forced into submission by Pope Gregory VII (Hildebrand) at Canossa in Italy, Bismarck shouted, "I will not go to Canossa!" But he needed money—that is, Center Party votes for more customs duties for the Reich. The National Liberals were asking for office for Bennigsen and two others, too high a price for protection. He believed that the Center, not the National Liberals, would support his meditated social-security schemes. He dissolved the *Reichstag* in 1887 after there had been two attempts on the life of William I, blaming the Social Democrats for the second that had seriously injured the King. The National Liberals lost votes heavily. Bismarck made a financial bargain with Windthorst, getting his customs duties, with the excess above a certain line going to the states (p. 578). The "May Laws" were repealed and the fight dropped. The two archbishops were obliged to resign, abandoned by the Pope.

Conservatization of the Center. Many workers and lower-middle class seceded to the Social Democrats: the former fell from 22.1 percent in 1887 to 18.6 in 1890; the latter rose from 7.1 to 19.7 percent respectively. The Social Democrats would be persecuted; the Center would still be Bismarck's friends.

The party became supporters of tariffs, Navy, Army, colonies, and social security. But it included too many interests to be without internal tensions. The Left wing demanded reduction of brutality in the colonies. The Right wing was militarist; the Left, under Matthias Erzberger (p. 611, p. 644) less so. It was anti-Semitic and imperialist. It joined Conservatives to outvote death duties for the Reich in 1909. Its workers' and peasants' representatives supported the social-security policy; the Catholic

industrialists of the Rhineland preferred the Prussian aristocracy and the Conservative policies. The party sponsored Catholic trade unions to detach workers from the predominant free-trade unions that followed the Social Democrats.

The Social Democratic Party. The *Sozialdemokratische Partei Deutschlands* was first organized in 1869, merging two movements, one built by Ferdinand Lassalle, the other by August Bebel. The movement in time became deeply Karl Marxian, dropping its Marxian slogans only after World War II.

Lassalle was a Jew, an upper middle-class, educated lawyer and a liberal politician. Various workers' groups, fostered by liberals, appealed to him because the liberal parties would not join in their demand for universal suffrage. In March 1863 he proposed they found a workers' political party, and two months later the *Allgemeine Deutsche Arbeiterverein* was established, one of the ancestors of the Social Democrats.

Lassalle suffered deeply under the disabilities and German public hatred of the Jews. He was a radical, though inherently an aristocrat. For his radical pamphlets, he was jailed in 1849. He taught the poor not to suffer from "damned wantlessness," but to rely on their associated efforts to get from the upper classes that charity which those classes would never give them. Their first target must be universal suffrage, for 90 percent of the votes could not be ignored for long. Thus his way was *not* revolutionary but parliamentary. His brilliance awakened the German working class. But his political outlook was Prussian—that is, for a strong State and against the do-nothing one of the liberals, what he called their "nightwatchman State." Hence he was an associate of Bismarck's! He was monarchical; he supported Bismarck against the *Landtag*. Marx and Engels hated him, though they also supported active and strong State power, for his was to be by democratic votes.

The Marxian ancestry derived from August Bebel and Wilhelm Liebknecht, the former a woodturner (and as a genuine workman, the darling of Nikolai Lenin, p. 754), the latter a middle-class intellectual, exiled by the Prussian police after the 1848 revolution. They seceded from Lassalle's organization, and in 1869 founded

---

[3] Compare the Catholic theories of regicide in France in the sixteenth century, p. 287.

the Social Democratic Party at Eisenach. In May 1875 the two organizations joined at Gotha, where a program closely following the *Communist Manifesto* was accepted. It must be remembered that the *Manifesto's* last pages contain a parliamentary program of immediate reforms.

The Social Democratic Party had a strong international flavor and was charged by other parties with "fatherland-hatred." It joined the First International (p. 307) and was inspired in 1871 by the Paris Commune.

Diverse German Socialisms. Germany is not traditionally the land of free enterprise, but of State action; the "socialist" mentality was very widespread.

A Christian Socialist Party existed, under the wing of the Conservatives (p. 601). Its liberals left it in 1896, and organized the National Socialist Union, under Pastor Friedrich Naumann; it rejected the *laissez faire* of the Progressive Party and looked to social welfare and justice promoted by the State, by democratic methods.

There were Socialists-of-the-Chair, the *Katheder-Sozialisten*—that is, professors opposed to the social consequences of *laissez faire,* with an outlook like that of the English Christian Socialists and Tory Democrats. In 1873 the leading economists (mainly *historical* economists, and political, not merely analytical) and 160 lesser ones founded the *Verein fur Sozialpolitik* for research, discussion, and publication of social-security and social-welfare measures by State action. They were derided by the Socialists for their political timidity, and by Treitschke (p. 607) for trying to do away with the masses of laborers who were necessary to serve the more cultured and socially higher placed.

The Trade Unions. By 1869 labor unions had the right to organize. They developed in three movements: Socialist, Catholic, and liberal-fostered. After 1890 their growth was rapid, thus:

	Free *(Socialist)*	*Progressive* *(Hirsch-Duncker)*	*Christian*
1891	278,000	66,000	0
1905	1,345,000	117,000	188,000
1913	2,574,000	107,000	343,000

They exhibited the same astounding technical talent for organization as did the directors and employees of the cartels and trusts, very interested in the provision of social, educational, recreational, and employment services. These managerial-type union leaders were a strong conservative brake on socialist political will power.

The Employers. The heavy industrialists, such as Krupp, von Stumm of Saarland industries, or the Rhineland coal and steel masters, were bitter haters of the unions. They gathered their forces in 1876 in the *Zentral Verband deutscher Industrieller* to resist the workers, to fight for tariffs, and to limit if not defeat social-welfare laws then being sponsored by Bismarck with his "Prussian socialism." The professors denounced them, and called for labor arbitration and joint management of industries.

Repression of the Socialists. Bismarck had hated the self-help of the workers since the March uprisings in 1848. The Paris Commune gave him a terrible shock (p. 308). He detested their internationalism. By 1877 he noted that the Social Democratic Party had 9 percent of the votes and 12 seats in the *Reichstag* (40,000 votes in 1867). One hand bore a sword, the other bribes, to destroy the Socialists.

Authoritarian Welfare State. Against the resistance of the liberals, he established compulsory insurance for industrial injury, for sick funds, for old age and disability. This occurred between 1884 and 1887. His own plan was even more comprehensive and would have been entirely State-administered. But the funds were given over to the administration of employers and workers. The Center Party assisted this development. The will of the workers to democratic government was partly suborned.

Simultaneously, in October 1878, with the support of National Liberals, Conservatives, and the *reichspartei* against the Progressives, Center and Social Democrats—221 to 149 votes—the antisocialist laws were passed, the expression of Bismarck's political atavism. The government was given, and forcefully used, the power to suppress independent labor organizations, Socialist activities, Socialist meetings, and the Socialist press, and could use extraordinary legal measures to arrest, try, and condemn Socialists. The law was renewed every two years up to 1890, the dismissal of Bismarck. For more than twelve years, a modern, civilized State persecuted its workers. More than

1500 persons were arrested; the press was suppressed; industrial victimization was brutal. But an underground was organized, and by 1890 Social Democratic votes were quadrupled. In 1891, now free again, it produced a highly Marxian program at Erfurt. By 1914 its newspapers sold 1,500,000 daily; it polled 4,500,000 votes, one third of the total; its periodicals on practical and theoretical problems were world renowned. It was Lenin's idol (p. 602)!

Revisionism. But the Social Democratic Party was now in trouble with itself, for Marxian predictions of social revolution had not come true yet. Hence, was it to follow the kind of ideas now being pronounced by Lenin, a conspiratorial and revolutionary movement, or was it to become like the British Labour Party (about to be founded) or Fabian, as proposed by one of its leaders, Eduard Berstein who had been to London?

The party was a negativing party: it always voted against the budget; refused the presidency of the *Reichstag;* would not attend Court; cooperated only with the Progressives in the Assembly. Hence it became more of a *Weltanschauung* party than any other. It was forced into estrangement from the rest of Prussia and Germany, to make a socialist *society* of its own: agnostic, sectarian in economics, with its own cultural, educational, and youth leagues. But it was weakened by the rising standard of living and the nationalism and militarism around them.

An extreme group formed on the left: Rosa Luxemburg (from Poland), Karl Liebknecht, son of the pioneer; Clara Zetkin. In 1919 these would found the Communist Party.

VII. GENERAL OBSERVATIONS ON GOVERNMENT TACTICS AND POLICY, 1871-1918

This Reich collapsed in World War I, leaving the German people the task of finding a constitution for themselves, the task they botched in 1848. They again failed, struck down by Hitler. Then in 1949 a new beginning was needed.

Government by Transient Coalitions

Since Bismarck had conceded universal suffrage to win friends for unification, he was forced to play the parliamentary game. This was done by playing off party against party and managing the elections by cries of "Socialism!" or "Clericalism!" or (very frequent) "The nation is in danger!" The nation's enemies were the French, especially in Alsace, or the Poles, for, indeed, his policy of underbuying Polish landowners in Posen to settle Germans, the imposition of German schools, and his denial of local self-government had inflamed the Poles. It was in the elections before each Septennate that maneuvering was most intense.

The Presumption of Force. The method of trading with the various parties and then jilting them, as inferrable from our previous description of the political parties, introduced a general cynicism and intensified the dislike of the parties for each other. It engendered contempt for the political process, and intensified German fear and contempt of foreign enemies. The Germans were taught that international problems could only be solved by *their force.* Finally, Bismarck ran out of a program; one man's inventiveness is much less fertile than that of spontaneous parties grouping free people. And his scope was limited because he was a Junker. Then, in 1888, he is reported reliably to have contemplated a *coup d'état* to abolish the *Reichstag* and universal suffrage!

Dependence on the Character of Chancellor and Kaiser

Wilhelm II (1859-1941) came to the throne in 1888 at the age of twenty-nine. He was educated in England and in the Prussian *Offizierkorps.* This was an incoherent nurture fitted on top of a most hysterical and incoherent character. He meant to be an absolute ruler. He was seeker of popularity; a glamorous Supreme War Lord, always being photographed in resplendent uniform on horseback at parades and maneuvers. He was a frenzied orator in private and public; exuberant and all-interfering. His withered left arm seemed to compel him to a lifelong search for compensation, for the injury to his high-strung and volatile personality drove him to exhibitionism. His Calvinistic tutor had imbued him with the idea that God had chosen him to lead Germany to further greatness. He wore a thick, fierce, upturned moustache, with two spikes like bayonets, to match the spike on the Uhlan helmet he liked to wear. Attila and the Huns, the shining sword, the Death's Head Hussars in fur shakos—these were his oratorical and martial accompaniments constantly. "There is only one master in the Reich and that is I, and I shall tolerate no other," he declared shortly after his accession. He believed in more social welfare for the people—this he learned from Stocker's national socialist group. He believed that MY PEOPLE deserved the dropping of the antisocialist laws.

The personalities of Kaiser and Bismarck clashed; the latter was dismissed in 1890.

Frenzied Imperialism

By the middle of the 1890's, the German Navy was seventh largest in the world; by 1914, it was second only to the British. Admiral Tirpitz, close personal friend of Kaiser Wilhelm, had gathered 1,000,000 members into his Navy League. The capitalists were reminded of the past glories of the Hansa League. The masses thrilled that German ships could protect German colonies. A tribal frenzy was whipped up. Only the Progressives, the Socialists, the Poles, and the Guelphs opposed the Navy appropriations.

By 1882 great organizations, the *Kolonialverein* and the *Gesellschaft für Deutsche Kolonisation,* had been promoted by zealots seeking expansion in East and West Africa. They cried out for emigration opportunities for "our young men." Bismarck was swept along, but Wilhelm helped propel the current: to the Far East, the Pacific, the Near and Middle East, and then North Africa, through annexations by the State—not Bismarck's policy of colonial commercial corporations. Chancellor Bülow expressed envy of Britain's world prestige and claimed "A place in the sun"; for colonies were to be a vehicle for "the German soul." This was hardly more than disturbing bravado, for, though by 1914 the colonies included about 12,000,000 natives, only less than 25,000 white settlers lived there; and it is estimated that German taxpayers' subsidies for them were more than six times the amount of profits German merchants and investors made. Germans who left Germany preferred the United States and South America.

The world was terrified by the boasts by the Kaiser and his friends about Germany's mighty Army, his "shining armor," his "mailed fist," and his interference in Morocco and the Balkans; his plans for the hegemony of *Mitteleuropa* (worked out to a blueprint!) and the Deutsche Bank's financing of the Berlin-Bagdad railroad; the contempt for the British in the Boer War; and the scorn of the peace conferences at The Hague, designed to foster international arbitration.

Mass Imperialist Propaganda. Mass organizations exalted the "little German" into a "big shot." A fanaticism was heated up about *world* policy and *world* Reich: *Weltpolitik* and *Weltreich.* These phrases were German inventions, as was *Realpolitik,* realistic politics—that is, unethical tactics and aims. It was not the Junkers and the officers alone who succumbed, but the German middle classes and the workers also. The delusions of grandeur thus nurtured by the *Reichstag* leaders, the Civil Service, the Army, the Navy, the industrialists, the shipowners, the Foreign Office, the League of Agrarians, the most important newspapers of the Center and the Right, the Pan-German League (started 1891) and its associates, the leagues for the Navy, the Army, the colonies, Young Germany, the Union of Industrialists, and the rest produced an arrogance and sense of superiority that led directly to war, and when it was lost to inconsolability that then destroyed the Weimar Republic. The Pan-German League aimed to include Holland, Belgium, Luxemburg, Hungary, Poland, Romania, Serbia, Austria, and parts of Switzerland in a Central Europe belonging to Germany!

A Faulty Foreign Policy. Bismarck's foreign policy was tricky and duplicity itself, but its lines were simple and its scope measured and limited. He needed a long breathing space for this Reich, internally weak as it was from its infancy. He made an alliance with Austria and Italy, the former to offset Russia, the latter to offset France, whose *revanche* he feared. Then he reinsured himself by the Reinsurance Treaty with Russia—a secret treaty—whereby Russia would remain neutral if France attacked Germany, while Germany backed Russia's Bulgarian interests and even a descent on Constantinople, should it come; the status quo in the Balkans could be changed by Russia only by arrangement previously with Germany.

Austria and Russia could not be friends, because their competition for the Slavs of the Balkans embittered them daily. In 1881 and 1884 it had been possible for Bismarck to bind the three emperors together in the Three Emperors' Alliance. In 1887 this alliance could no longer be renewed. Bismarck's great worry was Austrian expansionism in Central Europe. He feared that this would finally set Italy and Russia against Germany if Germany should give rein to Austrian pretensions, and he was profoundly uninterested in Austria's non-German (Hungarians, Czechs, Slavs, etc.) peoples—they were "not worth the bones of a single Pomeranian grenadier." He coupled the Reinsurance Treaty with his Austro-German Treaty, guaranteeing Austria's present frontier only. The purpose was to keep the status quo, and if any movement occurred, to put Germany in the position of being necessarily consulted and of being mediator. Germany needed peace among these contestants for the Balkans, for Bulgaria, Serbia, Turkey, Bosnia Herzegovina, Albania.

He was not interested in colonies *per se;* he did not seek a "world policy." He sought the peace of digestion for Germany within its existent frontiers.

Secret Diplomacy. But under the Kaiser, foreign policy was guided by him, his favorite, Count von Eulenberg, Friedrich von Holstein, a civil servant, and the General Staff. There was no way of smoking out devious and irresponsible tactics, as is possible in democratic governments. Holstein, in the Foreign Office, even secreted crucial documents from his master, the Kaiser and the Chancellor! He pursued by his private correspondence a policy of zigzagging between Britain, Austria, and Russia, adding to the fears of all and the friendship of none. He conceived a hatred for Britain, yet did not renew the treaty with Russia! All German diplomats were brutal like Bismarck and imputed to all other nations the Machiavellian hypocrisy and aims by which they themselves were animated. Their spirit is summed up in Chancellor Bethmann-Hollweg's notorious admission in 1914 that the treaty (signed by Germany) of Belgian independence was but "a scrap of paper," and that the admitted breach of international law was subordinate to the principle "necessity knows no law." With weak governments in Russia and irresponsible ones in Austria, both internally unstable, and a race rivalry between these over the Balkans, each was ready to fight the other out of sheer fear. It was the responsibility of the Kaiser to reassure Russia and restrain Austria. Once the Reinsurance Treaty was not renewed in 1890, the scourge of war was bound to fall on mankind sooner or later.

The additional social services and social-security measures provided by the Kaiser was hardly a compensation for 1914. Edward VII of Great Britain, who had tried long and patiently to come to an understanding with Germany, knew his nephew Kaiser Wilhelm II very well:

> But since his cowardice is even greater than his vanity he will tremble before these flatterers, when, under pressure of the General Staff, they will call upon him to draw the dagger. He will not have courage to bring them to reason and will pitifully submit to them. He will release the forces of war not as a result of his own initiative, not in warlike *élan* but—out of weakness.

By 1914 the Kaiser was trapped in his own delusions as he signed the mobilization order. With his generals closely pressing in on him, he said, "Gentlemen, you will live to rue the day when you made me do this!" This was *Der Tag!*

Treitschke and Nietzsche

The professors and philosophers had inflated the Germans' ego. One was Heinrich von Treitschke. Born in 1834 in Dresden of a Saxon army family, he soon turned from youthful liberalism to ultra-Prussianism. He became the Hegel of his time, but more crude, more directly brutal. He was the idolator of Prussia. In Machiavelli, he discovered, "the physician of an iron age," even as Marx had discovered that "Force is the midwife of every old society pregnant with a new." The main theme of his history lectures at the University of Berlin was, "The State is Power." If the nation is right, as German historical economists taught him, if every nation is right to its own peculiar form of economy, then it should also have its own kind of State. Treitschke was elected to the *Reichstag* in 1871; all society crowded to his lectures. He told them that John Stuart Mill's liberalism was feeble and erroneous; that Herder (p. 552) and Hegel (pp. 554–557) who discarded "natural rights" had a better understanding of human destiny. For the individual's life was a trifle compared with that of the State; and the State was the highest human law; religion was its slave, and the Army its quintessence. "War was an institution ordained of God," and even a trivial insult should be answered by war.

He vaunted the Aryans; he hated the British who were so religious and peace-loving! The best thing in *their* history had been their blowing Indians to bits during the Mutiny, by shooting them off the mouths of cannon! He praised Germans who knocked Croats on the head; he advocated German expansion because Prussian culture was the best in the world. The moral sublimity of war lay in the individual's renunciation of his ego for a patriotic idea.

Friedrich Wilhelm Nietzsche (1844–1900) was a nobler, more poetic spirit, but still a hater of Christian values, of democracy, of utilitarianism, and a fomenter of megalomania for all in spurring men on to become Supermen.

In his *Anti-Christ* he said:

Christianity is the revolt of all things that crawl on their bellies against everything that is lofty: the gospel of the lower orders.

This had produced a miserable, wretched weakness of will in Europe. For people were not killing each other; there was no fear of creative willing men. People forgave. Instead of a Master Morality, Europe was smitten with Slave Morality; the disease was Christianity.

The people invented democracy, a device of the weak to curb the strong of Will and Power. A new morality was being prevented: its creators would be natural aristocrats. Men must become Hard! Then they could resist majorities. "Dionysius *versus* Christ; here is the contrast" is the antithesis in which he sums up his doctrine, and by Dionysius he means "sensuality and cruelty." With what purpose? To transvalue all present values and produce the Superman. For this world "is a world will to power—and nothing else!"

Society has no right to exist for itself, but only as a scaffolding and base by means of which to select a higher race of beings, elevating themselves to higher duties and higher existence. "Let the blond beast that lies at the core of all aristocratic races appear," and devour the dwarfed, stunted, envenomed Christians and utilitarians.

He sneered at Bentham and his disciples (pp. 34–35), for these wanted no new thought, but only English morality—that is, "the greatest happiness of the greatest number," comfort and fashion, and a seat in Parliament; for them "this is the true path of virtue."

Instead he wanted an egoism that would deny one morality for all and impose a distinction of rank. Nor would any cruelty be forbidden; nor need the aspirant aristocrat acknowledge responsibility to those around him.

What kind of existence, in the end, did he and Treitschke want? What specific character of man? To what ultimate end? They did not say. This was as far as they traveled. They fled from Reason, unsettling men's minds. They disseminated military, regimented madness. So did Hitler's high-school teacher, then at the beginning of his teaching career. Yet Nietzsche suffered from that duality of the German mind, at once saying that the future of German culture rests with the sons of Prussian officers and again despising them for inability to act except as a member of a Race.

I feel inclined, I even feel it my duty, to tell the Germans for once in a way all that they have on their conscience. Every great crime against culture for the last four centuries lies on their conscience. . . . And always for the same reason, always owing to their bottomless cowardice in the face of reality, which is also cowardice in the face of truth; always owing to the love of falsehood which had become almost instinctive in them—in short, "idealism."

Racial Cruelty. If they could not say what kind of man this lunacy was to produce and fit their State to, they could vent their hatred on what they were taught to despise. Count Gobineau, a Frenchman had set off the neo-German anti-Semitism and pure racialism in his *Essay on the Inequality of the Human Races,* published in 1854. Gobineau was an enemy of the French Revolution and sought the theoretical basis for reversing its libertarian and egalitarian ideas and reestablishing an aristocracy and absolute monarchy. His work was picked up by Richard Wagner, the musical genius, who was a strong anti-Semite. It was elaborated in an anti-Semitic direction by the man who became his son-in-law, Houston Stewart Chamberlain, in his farrago of nonsense, entitled the *Foundations of the Nineteenth Century,* first published in 1890-91. Pure races, he taught, would produce the Superman; and the purest is the Teutonic—the exclusive makers of today's civilization and culture. Thus innocent people could be hunted down with arms, a keenly delightful blood sport.

The German nation, and all its parties, even the Social Democrats (though in least measure) became trigger-happy, and went off to war in 1914 —a war for which they were chiefly responsible because they did not change their own form of government—and disgracing defeat.

Bismarck's Heritage

Besides the beginning of German unity (a great gift), the Bismarck Constitution had reinforced two elements in German governmental habits. (1) The people were accustomed to a *stable* Executive —that is, pretty stable government—certainly in comparison with France. They continued to expect it and were later appalled when democracy made it difficult to obtain. (2) As Georg von Bunsen said: "Bismarck made Germany great and Germans small." The people and their political parties were denied experience in government—

that is, choice between alternative interests and the sacrifices they entail, and self-control and the art of compromise with good grace. They never made a *decision* in the Bismarck system. They were sheltered from final choices and exercise of controlled will. When their authority-given social, economic, and political status was taken from them and replaced by popular sovereignty, neither they nor their political parties were educated and enured to bear the strain. It is not surprising that Erich Fromm, a German of the post-Bismarckian Germany, should write the book *Escape from Freedom.* They had not the civic courage to rise above the defeat of 1918; they fell below it, back to militaristic megalomania.

More self-consciously than elsewhere, the German people treated themselves as "little men," yet with race-inflated egos straining to assault other nations with the claim to be supermen. The pressure of the world on their individual consciences— the Slavs, the French, the tedium of life, the changing economy, and the curse of labor—they evaded, repudiating personal responsibility for the answers given by their government in their behalf. Government, for them, was the incarnation of the tribe, on which they loaded the obligation of their conscience to say whether men's actions are moral or not. The order, diligence, response to command, dutifulness that had over the centuries been trodden into teachers, church, fathers, and the "little men" caused them to accept the orders of their government as the unquestionable orders of God and to be ready to drench other peoples in blood as a glorious and orgiastic moral holiday.

The Weimar Republic: 1919-1933

Let Man be noble, helpful and good,
For that alone distinguishes man
From all other beings known to man.
                                        —*Goethe*

I. DEFEAT AND NO REVOLUTION

The Course of Collapse

Only the Social Democrats had reservations about zeal for the war: they calmed their consciences by the thought that it was defensive against Czarist Russia. But the whole group voted Aye for war credits, to Lenin's horror, for it was supposed to be Marxianly pacifist. Its extreme Left (14 out of 92 members) were dissatisfied and later dissented.

The German people were told little by their leaders about the course of the war, least of all when the *Blitzkrieg* tactics failed at the Battle of the Marne. Hence, the passage of time with no decisive victory frayed their nerves. For though the *Reichstag* occasionally met, no such candid debates occurred as in Britain and France.

Military Dictatorship and Planning. The conduct of the war brought about two most significant consequences. (1) The generals, under Paul von Hindenberg, a Prussian who had fought in Bismarck's war of 1870 and was no Chief of Staff, and General Erich Ludendorff, commander in the field, got the Emperor and Germany under their thumbs. They became the arbiters of the whole civil life of the community, since total mobilization of all persons and resources became necessary once a six-week war had failed. It was not to their interest to tell him or the people when they were being defeated.

(2) With their managerial ability, superhuman

dutifulness, and obedience, a most remarkable feat of civil and military organization was accomplished. The British Navy had blockaded Germany effectively enough to provoke floods of self-pitying tears among the Germans, who simultaneously and literally almost starved England to death by submarines. For Germany's agricultural lands, even though treated by the wonders of her chemical industry, and the discovery during the war by her scientists how to make nitrogen from the air, far from sufficed to feed the population. Oils, fats, fibers, metals were lacking in her own economy. Substitutes—*Ersatz*—had to be found and, for a long time, were. Rationing was introduced. Above all, for the planning of supplies in relation to strategic needs, Walther Rathenau—a Jew!—member of the General Electric firm of Germany, set up an organization to produce synthetic and substitute materials and measure out supplies to wants. Man-power planning was involved in its entirety.

This *Kriegswirtschaft* developed into *Planwirtschaft* and *Planwirtschaft* into *Gemeinwirtschaft,* through various stages of experience and thought: from war economy to planned economy, from this to "common economy" or "socialization from above." The term *planning* soon entered into the literature and had a profound influence on post-war Germany when it blended with Socialist socialization and with the stream of Plans from Sovietized Russia.

The German people, the parties, the Army officers, and the Governments had no mercy for the lands they defeated. Excepting for the Socialists, who rejected annexations and indemnities, they were megalomaniac and brutal expansionists by conquest. The Treaty of Brest Litovsk with defeated Russia, made in 1918, is a sign of what victorious Germans would have done to the rest of the world within their power.

Collapse; No Revolution. By the fall of Russian Czarism in February 1917 the Left-wing Socialists (now calling themselves the U.S.P.D. or Independent Socialists) were joined by the Majority Socialists, for Russian defeat canceled their argument about a "defensive" war. A Left-wing leader of the Center Party, the party of Catholic Christians, Matthias Erzberger, horrified by the defeats he had learned about on a tour outside Germany, led some of his party to join them and the Progressives in a resolution favoring a reasonable peace. The Supreme Command blessed it. But simultaneously they sponsored *Vaterlandspartei,* a mass organization to fight it in public; it was led by Tirpitz and Wolfgang Kapp, a forerunner of Adolf Hitler and leader of the military *coup* against the newly founded Weimar Republic in 1920 (p. 643).

The lie of German invincibility came home to the people, especially to the hard-driven workers and the hungry, poor families and to the men in the Navy (cooped up in harbor) late in 1917 and ever more so in the following months. Strikes broke out. The cleavage between classes became too evident in the bread lines.

Some liberal professors and leaders proposed constitutional reforms; even universal and equal suffrage for Prussia (p. 589). Even the more liberal National Liberals saw the point. Too late! "Quickly!" barked the Supreme Command, "get a liberal-looking government and make the essential reforms, for then we will get easier terms from that democratic madman President Woodrow Wilson and the English and French hypocrites! Quick! Before a *real* revolution breaks out and the armies just walk away homeward; before the State breaks down!" They meant *their* State— that is, the authoritarian monarchy.

This, then, was a collapse, *not* a revolution. The military caste and the ruling classes could later represent this defeat as *"a stab in the back,"* not a defeat; for the Germans in the Army had performed prodigies of valor, but the Social Democrats and the Center Party had led the people to treason. These were later vilified as "November Criminals" (the month of surrender in 1918), the perfect setting for Nazism. This stab-in-the-back legend was a lie as enormous as it was deliberate, unless it was a militarist's natural delusion.

Prince Max of Baden, a liberal South German and Catholic nobleman, was made Chancellor September 28, 1918. He made a cabinet of Socialists, Progressives, and Center—the opposition. Ludendorff was dismissed; a Bavarian general, Groner, replaced him; Hindenberg, the "wooden Titan" was spared, for a rainy day. The Constitution was amended to make the Chancellor responsible to the *Reichstag,* and the laws were signed by the Emperor. The Kaiser was forced to abdicate; for all parties detested Wilhelm II personally, though only the Socialists were antimonarchist. Hindenberg, Groner, and Max of Baden, and the Kaiser himself, objected to abdication; but fear of an army and popular revolt forced him into exile. The armistice was signed November 11, 1918.

The Majority Socialist, Fritz Ebert, once a saddle maker, now leader of the party, became Chancellor; another Socialist Minister, Philip Scheidemann, proclaimed the Republic from the royal palace, to the deep chagrin of Ebert.

There was no mass rising to expropriate the Junkers, the officers, the big industrialists, to disperse the General Staff and the *Offizierkorps* and chase away the monarchical civil servants and judiciary, as had happened in Russia in February and November 1917. Government had been transferred peacefully to the Majority Socialists. The U.S.P.D. and the newly sprung-up Communists fomented Workers and Soldiers Councils (like the Soviets) all over Germany in the states whose dynasties and Ministers had fled. But the Majority Socialists had an enormous majority in them. Germany was still too well organized and cultured to permit of the victory of a German Lenin and Trotsky.

Ebert declared "I hate Revolution like sin,"

emergent as he was from a movement deeply and devotedly democratic and constitutional. He and his party moved toward a constituent assembly and a duly acceptable majority constitution. The party and the trade unions were not "blond beasts" or appliers of "blood and iron," that they had fought for years, but democratic humanists: "little men." **The Freikorps, Seeds of Nazism.** The U.S.P.D. and the *Spartacusbund* (Communists), encouraged by Russian agitators and subsidies, pushed the Majority Socialists further to constitutionalism. From October 1917 to March 1918 they fomented mutinies and insurrections throughout the nation, to force the Soldiers and Workers Councils on the body of the nation.

The government was forced—now knowing what a horrible dictatorship of a minority had been at work in Russia, not *many* miles away from Berlin—to suppress the revolts. They bargained with General Gröner to *maintain the Army intact,* if it would defend the government—that is, the tiger would defend the lamb! Thus the *Offizierkorps* was preserved to be a "State within a State." It retained its glamor, returning with laurels in parade: with the glamor of victory! The Free Corps—that is, officers and men volunteering for suppressing the revolts—under Socialist Minister of the Interior Gustav Noske, numbered 4000 in December 1918 and 400,000 in May 1919, for into it poured the unemployed, the *déclassés,* the soured veterans, the young men who had not had their fill of the brutality and comradeship of the "front-line" trenches. They committed many atrocities with their "lynch justice"; the officers' tribunals were even trusted to judge the lynchers of Communists and Left-wing Socialists. Karl Liebknecht and Rosa Luxemberg were killed in brutal ways. A bestial cruelty spread over Germany, like that of the Peasant War (p. 530) and the Thirty Years' War (p. 532). Those who lost the war against armed opponents were now winning against unarmed fellow Germans: it was a sheer delight. For these atrocities the Majority Socialists were not responsible. They fed the people, restored production, got the wages paid, and steered Germany to the Constituent Assembly at Weimar, toward the first democracy Germany had ever known.

The Democratic National Assembly, 1919

The National Assembly elections took place on January 19, 1919. Universal suffrage, including women, was established; voting age, twenty; for 423 Deputies, with proportional representation. (The Assembly chose twelve Deputies to represent Alsace-Lorraine.)

"National" Return of the Political Parties. The political parties reformed themselves. The adjective *national* made a conspicuous and specious appearance in their designations. The Conservatives became the *Deutschnationale Volkspartei* (the German National People's Party); the National Liberals became simply, *Deutsche Volkspartei* (or German People's Party); the *Zentrum,* for a short period, became the *Christlich Demokratische Volkspartei* (the Christian Democratic People's Party) and then reverted to the Center. It may be remembered that *Volk* (p. 552) has a national-tribal significance to Germans, not by any means in the sense of a democratically self-governing aggregate.

Of great constitutional-strategic importance, if only for a few years, was a new party, the *Democratic Party,* formed from the old Progressive Party and the Left wing of the National Liberals, as well as many liberal intellectuals and academically distinguished people. These were the closest to the outlook of the Liberal Party in Britain: democracy, fairness, a moderate dose of social welfare, controls over the excesses of industrialism, but no class-representation or class-warfare narrowness. It was republican and nationalist, the latter rather by contrast with Marxian internationalism than in an intense militarist-chauvinist sense.

The *German National People's Party,* which had been mainly responsible for the war, now had the gall, in the election campaign, to reject responsibility for the past and to hope that some day the monarchy would return, while promising to co-operate in Governments that would assure stability, law, and order. It roundly condemned the revolution as the gravest crime, and advocated the defense of private property, German equality in international relations, Christian orthodoxy (it had just been the chief maker of a war), and German racial loyalty—that is, *Volkstum.* It "surrendered" world politics; it was prepared to accept socialization of basic industries, provided that did not reduce their productivity.

Nor did the German National People's Party accept the republic, though it did not deny the new suffrage. It combined nationalism with *laissez faire.* It regarded the revolution as "useless"—all that was worth while could be accomplished without it!

The *Center* made an onslaught on the Social Democrats—who were the Government—as being a class party and, of course, as being an atheistic foe of the Catholic masses' independent educational institutions and social-welfare policies. After all, millions of Catholic workers voted Social Democrat. To them the revolution had been "regrettable," because it was not a necessary consequence of German needs nor could it help improve German political conditions. A republic was not necessary. Indeed, the Constitution as amended before the Social Democrats took over would suffice. But they accepted, they *said,* the facts of the day.

The *Socialists* developed their democratic and socialist line; the Communists and U.S.P.D., who had violently opposed an early calling of the Assembly while they "educated" the electorate, boycotted the campaign and propagated Marxism respectively.

There were 36,000,000 on the electoral registers; 30,000,000 voted. The results were:

Parties	Votes	Seats
German Nationalists	3,121,500	44
German People's	1,345,600	19
Center (with Bavaria)	5,980,200	91
Majority Socialists	11,509,100	165
U.S.P.D.	2,317,300	22
German Democratic	5,641,800	75
Various	484,800	7

The "various" parties included an Economic Party, the German Hanoverian Party, and some other "splinters." To the Center Party has been ascribed the votes of what later became the Bavarian People's Party (21 seats in election of June 1920).

Unstable Coalition Cabinets. Some general characteristics of the new system of government must be emphasized. The closest to a majority of the votes cast was the almost 38 percent of the Majority Socialists. Even with the addition of the 7.6 percent of the U.S.P.D.—had it been reliable—there was no solid majority. The elections ushered in an era of coalition cabinets, by their very nature unstable. This instability (see table, p. 641) was a sorely trying phenomenon to a people hitherto habituated to a stable Executive, if a nonpopular one, and in years that were so peculiarly fraught with mobile, changeable, and difficult social and economic and foreign policy problems that would try nations with long experience of free parliamentary government, as for example, France and even Britain. Just over the border was always the example of a government that made short shrift of opposition—Soviet dictatorship with power to make long-term plans, and morbidly frightening to *all* Germans. The succession of Cabinet crises was terrifying to the German electorate; for freedom works best where there is considerable social consensus and where individuals are themselves independently stable enough to withstand the anxieties it must produce in thinking or sensitive people. The Germans were not individually stable; they were not habituated to take the anxieties of freedom in their stride; and, as the splitting into six major parties shows (even omitting the "splinters" and the Communists), the age-old division of the public mind was as deep as ever.

The First Government. Ebert was elected President of the Republic by the Assembly by 379 to 277, the Conservatives voting against. The office of Chancellor being vacated, a new Cabinet was needed. The Majority Socialists had first claim. They asked the U.S.P.D. to join with them, on condition they accepted the parliamentary system and abandoned a policy of a *coup d'état,* which came to be known in Germany as a *Putsch.* They refused. The Majority Socialists were thereupon obliged to make a coalition with the Center and the Democrats, the Chancellor being Philip Scheidemann. The posts were shared, one half to the Socialists and the rest between the two other governmental parties.

The Assembly, which met at peaceful Weimar, away from Prussianism, was guarded by the forces of a regular general, Maercker, from insurrectionists.

The Assembly took until July 31, 1919, to draft and discuss freely the new Constitution. It passed by a vote of 262 to 75 abstainers. The parties took the following attitude in their voting: *For:* Social Democrats, almost unanimous; Democrats, almost unanimous; Center, some abstentions. The abstentions made up the 75 abstainers. *Against:* German Nationalist, People's Party, U.S.P.D., and Bavarian Peasants: in all over 90.

While the Assembly deliberated, a civil war was being fought, though on a declining scale of intensity.

Woe at the Peace Terms! Considering German behavior in making and conducting the war—with its inhumanity of *"spurlos versenkt,"* sunk without a trace, as its symbol of U-boat warfare, which had finally brought the United States into the war as her enemy, the terms of peace, made at the Paris Conference while the Weimar Assembly was debating the new Constitution, were mild, indeed. There were heavy reparations; the return of Alsace-Lorraine to France; a corridor for the Poles to the sea in East Prussia; an army limit of 100,000 men; no possession or manufacture of certain heavy weapons; submission to Allied inspection and control; delivery of certain leaders as war criminals; Allied occupation of the Rhineland for ten years; the demilitarization of the Rhineland. But, if Germans were the Master Race and invincible and superior to all other peoples, how was this tolerable, or even just?

The responsibility was unloaded on the Socialist and Center parties, who were accused of treason to the Fatherland. The Cabinet was opposed to the treaty by 8 to 6, Chancellor Scheidemann being the most vehemently opposed of any. But General Gröner, now Defense Minister, a strong nationalist, *demanded* acceptance, observing that a resumption of the struggle was impossible. The Cabinet, under a new Chancellor, also a socialist, signed. The Assembly accepted it by 237 votes against 138, 5 abstaining; the other 50 stayed away from the Assembly, a cowardly act. It was finally ratified by 209 to 116; for others ratted, on July 9, three weeks prior to the voting of the new Constitution. The synchronization of Weimar and the so-called *Diktat* of Versailles was a bar sinister on the new Republic.

Bavarian Secessionism and Militarism

Bavaria, the birthplace of Nazism, was the scene of sinister events. *Landtag* elections in January 1919 put Kurt Eisner and the U.S.P.D. in a minority of 3 in 180 seats, the Bavarian *Volkspartei* having 66 and the Majority Socialists 61. Before Eisner resigned, a reactionary student, son of the nobility, murdered him, and the life of the Majority Socialist leader was attempted. A sharp civil war ensued. Led by Ernst Toller, noble idealist and playwright, the tiny body of the U.S.P.D. proclaimed the "Soviet Republic of Bavaria," defying the Socialist Government of Berlin and acknowledging loyalty to Soviet Russia. The Communist Party of Bavaria then set up *its* government also. The Majority Socialist Government called in the Free Corps and federal troops to chase away the rivals. The savagery on both sides was horrible. In one week—April 30 to May 8—557 people were killed. Hostages were murdered, men and women shot without form of trial, civilians were beaten and killed. The rebel leaders were beaten to death or executed or, like Toller, given long prison terms. The youth of Bavaria went berserk-nationalist, maddened with anti-Semitism, since the Communist leaders included Jews. The fact that Bavaria was a land of Catholic (80 percent) peasantry and small middle class must be taken into account. Bavarian "particularism" (p. 576 and p. 577) now as always cried *"Los von* Berlin," to be free of Socialist and democratic Berlin, which stood for a united Germany. Bavaria became the sanctuary for the militaristic, nationalistic, and anti-Semitic underworld, the incubator of men like Hitler.

II. THE INSTITUTIONS OF WEIMAR

A Most Democratic Constitution. The man chiefly responsible for drafting the Weimar Constitution was Hugo Preuss, constitutional lawyer and professor, Minister of the Interior, representing the Democratic Party in the Cabinet. He was a distinguished student of Prussian constitutional history and of modern comparative government. He drafted and redrafted, and the Assembly debated, amended, and accepted, the most democratic constitution in the world in 1919. It contained an institutional answer to every democratic problem and difficulty raised in the practice of the last one hundred years and thoughtful inventions designed to cope with a long future. The members of the Assembly were of well-mixed occupations and politically experienced.

The main features of the Constitution were (1) transfer of popular sovereignty to the people; (2) the establishment of a Republic; (3) the development of more unity in the federal structure and processes; (4) the formulation of a modern bill of rights, including economic and social rights; (5) the institution of proportional representation as the basis of an almost sovereign *Reichstag;* (6) the introduction of a cabinet system, responsible to the *Reichstag;* (7) the severance of the Cabinet from the presidency of the Reich, and the dire basing of the latter on direct, popular election; (8) a Reich Economic Council, as an advisory body, alongside the Government and *Reichstag;* (9) use of the referendum and initiative; (10) constitutional amendment by special procedure and referendum; and (11) judicial review of constitutionality by a special court. It thus established the "Open Society"—that is, a democratic means of progress with popular policy and as democratic a way of changing course on the perception of error.

We dwell on some of these arrangements.

(1) and (2) The Republic

There were parties on the Right and some in the Center who fiercely hated popular sovereignty and the Republic. They were supported by the *Offizierkorps* and the General Staff. In the end, these joined Hitler for this reason, among others. The Communist Party was hostile to the regime, because it did not admit the "dictatorship of the proletariat." As the election tables show (p. 642), both the extremes grew in the late 1920's to be formidable enemies of the Republic and popular sovereignty; in the 1930's, their opposed endeavors overthrew these bases. The several states were committed to a republican (*freistaatlich*) constitution also, following the model of the U.S. Constitution in this stipulation, for the constitution of the parts is an organic contribution to the constitution of the whole body politic. It is not unimportant to appreciate that the substitution of the black-red-gold flag for the Imperial black-white-red was generally disliked, even among the antimonarchists; it produced no symbolic resplendence in place of past glory but, as it fluttered, reminded of defeat, which Germans were not spiritually courageous enough to take in their stride.

(3) The Länder in the Reich

Article 61 of the Constitution, ardently espoused by Bavaria, allowed Austria into the Reich after her "affiliation" or *Anschluss.* This became inoperative (though not annulled) under pressure from the Allied governments—a historic error on their part. When Dr. Heinrich Brüning, Chancellor and leader of the Center Party, attempted in 1931 to evade the ban by making a customs union (the historical model is evident, p. 563), the Allies again banned it and were supported by the International Court of Justice. Hitler secured *Anschluss* by open and contemptuous force in 1938, a long step toward World War II (p. 671).

The Bismarckian Reich had consisted of thirty-nine states. The states in the new Constitution were restyled *Land* and *Länder*—lands. They numbered eighteen; by the end of Weimar they numbered seventeen; and their areas had been tidied up by the inclusion of some small principalities into the larger adjacent *Länder.* Thus, early, the Thuringias entered into one Thuringia; Coburg melded with Bavaria; Pyrmont and Waldeck in 1928 were embodied in Prussia. The *Länder* were still of remarkable diversity in population and resources.

Now the pressures for unity of the *Länder* were much greater and far more successful than in 1871. For, first, the Constitution had been made by a sovereign assembly, not by sovereign and particularistic princes. Second, this body was elected by the people *en masse,* and the Constitution made by the single one-chambered Assembly. Third, the separatist movements, chiefly Bavarian, could be contained and, furthermore, were undermined by the unity of the political parties in the separatist areas with the nationwide party organization outside of which they were parts. A momentary "Free from Berlin" cry gave way before these factors, and the centrifugal forces were further damped down by an almost universal appreciation of the needs for continuing the centralized economic system of wartime, especially as the ideas of planning and socialism were in the ascendant. Preuss was no particularist: he was by origin (Jewish) no Junker, and, for a larger justice, was ready to make Prussia, even carved up, merge in Germany. Social policy and democracy and economic progress were in the foreground of objectives: centralization was the means. It prevailed over the tentative separatism of the Rhineland and Westphalia, whose bourgeoisie, industrialists, and Catholics saw an advantage in getting away from a possibly socializing Prussia!

The separatism of the states, including Prussia, caused the establishment of a second chamber, the *Reichsrat*: Bavaria, Württemberg, Baden, and Hesse insisted on this against Preuss. Yet greater unity by far than in the Bismarckian Reich was achieved.

The *hereditary* predominance of Prussia as Reich executive was abolished, for the presidency was made elective by the whole population.

Centralizing the Federation. The reserved rights of the South German states were abolished. The legislative competence of the Republic was immensely expanded; it virtually was given all the powers of government. An extensive list of fundamental rights endowed it with power. Then came a list of exclusive powers. Third, concurrent powers were enumerated, to be exercised by the Reich as it decided, overriding state laws as soon as it made any enactment conflicting with them. These concurrent powers were given in "free" form, and in "conditional"—that is, where "there is need to promote social welfare or maintain public order and safety," or where it needs to lay down "general principles" to which the states must conform.

No other federation in the world exhibited so wide and deep a vesting of powers in the central government. Furthermore, exercise of the *Reichs-* *tag*'s discretion under the "conditional" grant of power was not reviewable by any court of law. Both Prussia and Bavaria protested against the power of "conditional" or "normative" laws to be binding directly on citizens, but in vain. The hand of the Reich was everywhere. Indeed, it almost looked as though the Reich were a unitary State with decentralization to regions. For the powers were massively used, especially as the period 1919–1933 was one of almost continuous and severe economic crisis (see p. 639).

In the Second Reich, disputes over a conflict of federal-state jurisdiction were decided in the *Bundesrat*. Now they came before the Supreme Court of State (p. 617).

Reich Administrative Competence. Still the Reich was not endowed with its own direct power to administer its laws directly on persons. The power of execution was definitely vested in the states; but the power of the Reich to *superintend* was spelled out. Thus (Article 15), which is of great interest for federal theory:

In so far as the Federal Laws are exercisable by the state authorities, the Reich can issue general instructions. The Reich is empowered to send commissioners to the state central departments and with their agreement to the subordinate authorities. The state governments are obliged, at the request of the Reich government, to amend any deficiencies which have become apparent in the execution of the Reich laws. In the case of differences of opinion the Reich government as well as the state government can call for the decision of the Supreme Court of State, unless some other court has been provided for by Reich law.

The resultant practice took four forms. (1) One was to include in the Reich laws great detail on administrative methods, and to add the agencies through which difficulties were to be settled, or to associate certain Reich departments with the administering authorities, or to require regular information from the states on administrative progress. (2) Another, which was quite rare, was the appointment of Reich inspectors of state administration. (3) A third was direct superintendence of such matters as the running of electri-

power systems, railroads, canals, etc. (4) In some cases—for example, unemployment insurance, factory inspection, the employment services—the Reich assumed direct management.

The *Reichstag* (not as before the *Bundesrat*) was given the power of making administrative rules. Where such rules affected the execution of Reich laws by the states, the assent of the *Reichsrat,* the federal chamber, was required. The rule-making power was used to create or extend the power of a large number of Reich administrative departments—for example, social welfare, coal commission, labor exchanges, juvenile welfare, emigration, etc.

The power of the Reich was assisted by the chronic financial distress and therefore the willingness of the states to save money by centralization. And, of course, the Reich had direct administration in foreign affairs, military affairs, railways, posts, telegraphs and radio, and customs.

Justice. The old duality of judicial administration was continued, which meant a heavy decentralization of jurisdiction to the states, with a supreme court for the Reich. But two innovations were made. First, the Constitution established administrative courts, whereas, earlier, these had been a matter of judicial custom, and it was stipulated in the Constitution that they were intended to be for the protection of the citizen against the administrative authorities.

A Court of State was established—the *Staatsgerichthof*—later organized by a Reich statute as Article 108 required. It was charged with impeachment of the *Reichpresident,* the Chancellor, and the Ministers for criminal violation of the Constitution or laws of the Reich (on arraignment by the *Reichstag* with at least 100 members in favor); with controversies about maladministration of Reich statutes by the states; with constitutional conflicts within a state not having a court of its own for this purpose, and between states, and states and Reich; and with several other matters to do with the expropriation and transfer of the railroads and with communication systems between states and Reich.

For impeachments the court was part of the ordinary supreme court; for other matters, it followed the same practice until a Reich Administrative Court was established. The court was composed of career judges, a barrister, chosen by the German Bar, five members chosen by the *Reichstag* and five by the *Reichsrat*—for impeachments. For the other cases, there was a mixture of judges of the administrative courts, of the supreme court, and some members chosen by *Reichstag* and *Reichsrat.*

The court was established at the more special insistence of Prussia which, as we shall show, had lost its power in the old *Bundestag* and needed protection of its authority by such a court removed from separatist politics.

Representation of the States. Preuss had wanted to have a Chamber of States chosen by the state legislatures (which would have been divisive of representation), sent without state instructions. The new body, of course, was bereft of the sovereign-ambassadorial character of the departed *Bundestag,* for sovereign power was vested in the people, acting through the *Reichstag.*

The *Reichsrat* was composed of representatives of the states. Each state was given at least one vote. Then (by amendment, March 1921) the larger states were allowed one vote for each million inhabitants, while any surplus each had which equaled at least the population of the smallest state counted as another million. The original figure was 700,000. The amendment was made in order to increase Prussia's votes, so that, for purposes to be explained presently (p. 618), her number of votes could be divided exactly by two.

Preuss wanted to give the smallest states only a combined representation. The states resisted, and something of the old inequality, but still with separate representation, was established. Progress was marked by making it depend on the population census. The eighteen states (after 1928, only seventeen) varied in the middle 1920's from Prussia with 38,000,000 population to Schaumburg-Lippe with 48,044. Prussia had 27 votes at first, later 28—in a total of 68. Bavaria with 7,400,000, had 11 votes; Saxony with nearly 5,000,000 people, 7; and the rest followed with 3, some 2's, and ten 1's.

The governments of the states designated their representatives—as many of these as they had votes, at their discretion. The difference from the Second Reich was that the state governments were now responsible to the state legislatures and electorates. Most states were represented by high officials, though they could choose to send ministers. A flavor of ambassadorship for their states still prevailed. Even the title was used, or "plenipotentiary."

Were they to be bound by instructions or could they vote at free will? Preuss tried to stipulate the latter. The stipulation was dropped. The states gave instructions. When a Social Democratic plenipotentiary of Württemberg voted at his party's command contrary to instructions, he was officially reprimanded by his state president. How different, then, is this from the status of an American Senator!

Prussia's Plenipotentiaries. The Constitution was silent on whether state representatives must vote uniformly. They did. But Prussia was subjected by the Constitution to special rules on this subject. The constitution-makers wished to disrupt the power of Prussia, in the interests of a truer federation, and to subordinate Prussian illiberalism (hitherto!) to German policy. The ambition to make Prussia "merge in Germany" was alive. Hence (Art. 63), "One half of the Prussian votes are accorded to the Prussian provincial administrations according to Prussian statute." The latter was enacted in 1921. Thus, fourteen representatives were severally elected by the Provincial *Ausschuss* (the executive committee of the largest local government area). The law also rewove what had been sundered. In the *Reichsrat* committees, Prussia's vote was to be cast by a representative appointed *by the Government*—and much work was done in committee by that body! Furthermore, the law required the discussion of topics before the *Reichsrat* "in common" between elected and appointed members, "for the purpose of securing a uniform vote."

In several cases Prussia's vote was divided. Hence, her influence was canceled, or sometimes her interests as a whole were damaged by interprovincial differences. Political party ties minimized these fissiparous tendencies; so also did

informal consultations outside the *Reichsrat* and direct Prussian pressure on the Reich Government, for Prussia was still two thirds of the whole Reich.

Prussia no longer presided as of right (through the Chancellor) as before 1918. The Government of the day presided, and the committees were presided over by a Minister.

The Powers of the Reichsrat. This was much weaker than the *Bundesrat* had been; and far weaker than the U.S. Senate. Its smallest power was its right to be kept informed of Reich affairs by the Reich departments, and to be heard by the latter on important matters. Its next higher power was the requirement of its consent to administrative rules for the enforcement of the Reich laws by the states. Its most important power was its right to initiate legislation, to challenge bills passed by the *Reichstag,* and to be consulted by the Government before it introduced bills in the *Reichstag.*

These were all-important powers, especially the last. But the Constitution gave the power of passing statutes *to the Reichstag alone.* As a rule the Government and the *Reichstag* had their own way against objections by the *Reichsrat* in those cases for which its previous assent was needed. Most of the differences arose regarding the Reich-and-state division of powers. Yet the *Reichsrat* also won victories. The power we speak of included financial legislation. As for the *Reichsrat's* right of initiative, this did not include finance bills. This was no power when it encountered the Government's disagreement; then the Government merely had to put the bill and the *Reichsrat's* arguments for it before the *Reichstag.*

If a statute was declared urgent by both Houses, the Reich president had the right to override the demand of one third of the *Reichstag* for suspension prior to a referendum. Both Houses agreed in 1925 that a Devaluation of the Currency Act, arousing bitter internecine feelings, was urgent, so avoiding a referendum.

If the *Reichsrat* challenged a *Reichstag* bill, the law had to be reconsidered by the latter and revoted. If, still, agreement proved impossible, then within three months the President could invoke a referendum on the points of disagreement. If the President refrained, the law fell. If a two-thirds majority of the *Reichstag* defied the *Reichsrat*'s challenge, then the bill, as passed by the *Reichstag* had to be presented to a referendum.

This challenging power gave the *Reichsrat* great influence. It was hard for the lower House to get a two-thirds majority or even a mere 51–49 majority in the presence of many small parties.

The power of the *Reichsrat* on the budget was the same as on ordinary bills; even greater, for the *Reichstag* was not allowed to increase or create new expenditures without the assent of the *Reichsrat*. Yet this power it did not use on important chapters of the budget.

The power of the *Reichsrat* was exerted through these items, but also because it was composed of distinguished officials.

Unitary Finance. The old deficiency-contribution system (p. 577) was jettisoned. The Reich obtained full power to raise taxation and other revenues for its uses, with some care for the damaging effects on the states if their historic revenues were trespassed on. Nor was this all: the Reich was allowed the right to establish norms to regulate the state's raising of revenue to (1) prevent loss of income to the Reich or damage to its commercial relations, (2) to prevent double taxation, (3) excessive or obstructive charges on public communications and institutions, (4) tax discrimination between imports *versus* home products and commerce between the states, (5) export bounties, and (6) to protect important social interests.

The result was a series of laws in which the Reich had *first call* on all revenues, with permission to the states and municipalities to tax according to a most carefully regulated Finance Settlement Law. A Reich Financial Court decided controversies about the consonance of state taxes with the substance of Reich statutes. The *Reichsrat* decided whether a state or local tax was, in fact, good or damaging to the Reich revenues or incompatible with the national interests. Thousands of federal tax and customs officers worked in the Reich offices within the states to secure the effectiveness of the Reich's domination.

The State Constitutions. The Constitution, pursuant to Preuss' theory that the Reich must be built up as a popular state *from below upward,* prescribed that states must have a free-state constitu-

tion—the representatives to be elected by free, universal, equal, direct, and secret suffrage, with proportional representation, a parliamentary-responsible government. This permitted a bicameral system. Bavaria was a permanent and bitter objector to this article.

Territorial Reorganization. Perception of the administrative loss involved in eighteen separate state organizations had long suggested territorial reorganization, especially during the war when regional military and supply arrangements had to be superimposed. A struggle between unitarists and separatists resulted in the former's desire to have no state smaller than 2,000,000 in population being shelved for a mild compromise in Article 18. Briefly, it permitted the amendment clause of the Constitution to be used to alter the territory and contour of the states to "serve the maximum economic and cultural utility of the nation." If one state involved in such a rearrangement itself desired it as demonstrated by a local referendum, and as "required by paramount Reich interests," an ordinary statute could effect the change. One third of the voters in such an area could ask the Reich to institute the appropriate referendum. The article enabled the unions already mentioned (p. 615). Some other attempts failed: to make a separate state of Upper Silesia, when a 10-to-1 vote of the people favored staying in Prussia; to separate Hanover (p. 574) from Prussia, when the one-third initiating vote could not be obtained.

The article is an interesting idea in a federal system, unparalleled elsewhere. By the time Hitler arrived in 1933, long conferences had been proceeding between the states for a thorough-going reorganization of areas but had not reached fruition. Hitler abolished the *Länder* (p. 671).

Reichs-exekution. Article 48, a fateful one in the final downfall of the Reich (pp. 657–659), included the ancient practice of Reich power of sanctions to compel a state to carry out its constitutional obligations. It was a power vested in the President, to be implemented by armed force if necessary. Of course, the responsible Ministers were needed to countersign. The power had been vested in the *Bundesrat* in 1871–1918. The President's decision was challengeable under Weimar by appeal to the Court of State or other courts.

Unitarism versus Separatism. The centripetal forces were strong. Above all, it was considered especially anomalous that two great state organizations—Prussia in Berlin and the Reich in Berlin—coexist. The great urban complexes that crossed state lines provided awkward problems. Unitarizing policies (especially Reich direct administrative responsibility) were strongly advocated by the Social Democrats and Communists and the Democrats and Center. The two Left-wing parties subordinated structure to the social policies in their program; the Democrats wanted universal civil rights equally effective; the Center (excepting its Bavarian wing) needed to gather Catholic votes everywhere. The *Reichstag* Deputies were a unitarizing force, being the bearers of the tradition of unity. The Reich Civil Service ached for an administrative efficiency that is technically the same everywhere to be instituted everywhere; and unitary government saved all sorts of nerve-wracking and delaying negotiations.

Yet the anti-unitarist sentiment was lodged mainly and most obstinately in Bavaria. It claimed that the high unitarism of the Republic had been snatched at an exceptional revolutionary time, and that the *uniqueness* of the state traditions and of self-government demanded independent statehood, and therefore far-reaching changes in the Constitution. It even demanded the right to have separate diplomatic representatives abroad; to deal with a state of emergency in its area before the Reich was called in; to cut down the "conditional" lawmaking powers of the Reich; to reduce the Reich power in administration. The whole unitary financial system was challenged. The *Reichsrat* should be like the old *Bundesrat*—and so on. Back to 1871!

The German Hanoverian Party assisted the movement. The German Nationalists were anxious for the 1871 constitution, also.

Bavaria was very restive and insurrectionary throughout the Weimar Republic, resenting "socialist" Berlin. The government of Bavaria was, from Kurt Eisner's assassination, in the hands of the Bavarian Catholic clergy. In 1923 the Bavarian government even nurtured plans for civil war with the Reich (p. 649), and Hitler tried it.

It will be appreciated that the simultaneous existence of high unitarism in a federal system with state governments run by political parties in systems that did not have the comparative stability of the separation of powers (fixed Executive) as in the American system, made the running of the Reich and states a clashing and bewildering affair for all in official positions and for the Republican mass electorate, called to sovereign responsibility and authority for the first time.

The Nazis were incubated in Bavaria; they took legal power in Thuringia, Oldenberg, and Mecklenberg in 1931. The Weimar assumption was of cooperation between Reich and *Länder;* but the social dissensus betrayed it, until Hitler imposed his own sweet brand of consensus, for his fanatical will demanded total centralization.

Prussia also keenly resented Reich power, for the party composition of her own government of 38,000,000 people out of a Reich total of 62,000,000 was not the same as that of the Reich. In fact, Prussia became *very liberal!* This we discuss presently (p. 658). Various solutions of the Prussian difficulty were in the air in the 1920's. (1) a completely unitary state; (2) reestablishment of Prussian hegemony; (3) Prussia to be governed by the Reich—to be a *Reichsland;* (4) the division of Prussia into several states.

The Reichstag. Generally, this was a parliament like the British or French, following Western democratic customs. It worked through parliamentary committees, as in France, rather than Britain. It was master of its own procedure. Its rules gave hostages, of course, to the minority; and this made its sessions untenable as soon as the Communists and the Nazis (the latter, especially) became strong enough to obstruct business. As Goebbels, Hitler's psychotic propaganda chief, said (April 30, 1928):

We enter Parliament in order to supply ourselves, in the arsenal of democracy, with its own weapons. We become members of the *Reichstag* in order to paralyze the Weimar sentiment with its own assistance. If democracy is so stupid as to give us free tickets and salaries for this bears' work, that is its affair. . . . We do not come as friends or even as neutrals. We come as enemies. As the wolf bursts into the flock, so we come.

Investigating committees were an innovation over the previous regime, and were furiously resented by the Governments, unaccustomed to such challenges so usual in the United States, Britain, and France. The method of interpellation was developed. The extreme parties were, as in France since 1945, strengthened in the extremeness of their public demagoguery and incitement by the immunity of parliamentary Deputies from arrest for actions connected with their position as Deputy (Articles 36 to 38). As in the Bismarckian *Reichstag,* but with more vim, it supervised the Government by question and, even more so, by interpellations (p. 439).

Its authority was tremendous. It was master of financing; of the making of war and peace, of treaties and alliances; of impeachment of President and Ministers; and of the Government itself since the latter required the confidence of the *Reichstag;* the continuous control of administration through debate, questions, committee deliberations.

Until 1930 it was a relatively calm chamber; businesslike; free of tumults, such as are not infrequent in the French Chamber; and provided more of a sense of stability than the much older French parliamentary system. From 1930 the onset of the Great Economic Depression could not be handled by the German political parties, and government by emergency decree (see p. 625 and p. 657) was massively used by Chancellor. Dr. Heinrich Brüning, of the Center Party. Then this period slipped into the madness of pre-Hitlerism with an utterly schizophrenic *Reichstag.* The spectacle of an impossible *Reichstag,* and the prospects of one dissolution after another—a diet of dissolutions—in the attempt to get the public to make up its mind on a viable majority, became psychologically insufferable to millions of Germans, and the Nazi movement, as well as the Communists, made the most of it.

The members of the Reichstag of 1928, the last in "normal" times, fell into the following occupational groupings, by percentage of the total. The analysis, following the figures of a gifted German scholar (Otto Kircheimer), demonstrates the "double" representation (but the phrase is tricky!) of the German people, through officials of "pressure groups" as well as party leaders.

	Percent
Politically appointed officials and Ministers	16.3
Permanent civil servants	3.6
Party officials	20.0
Journalists, writers, publishers	12.9
Proprietors and managers in industry and finance, and officers of business associations	8.3
Agricultural proprietors and officers of agricultural associations	13.7
Retail business, artisans, officers of such associations	6.5
Trade union, cooperative, social insurance unions and agencies	10.6
Workers and white-collar employees	0.2
Free professions and housewives	7.9
	100.0

(4) The Fundamental Rights and Duties

The rights, including economic and social rights, of citizens were set out in great scope and some detail in Articles 109 to 165 and classified into four great sections on: (1) the Individual and Social Life (including articles on marriage, motherhood, education, youth, meetings, association, local government, the rights of civil servants, actions against the public authorities for illegal behavior, the obligation of military service); (2) Religion and Religious Associations (prohibiting a State church, allowing complete liberty of worship, disjoining the exercise of a religion from the rights to office, etc.; (3) Education and Schools; (4) Economic Life, organizing economic liberty within the principle of justice (meaning obstruction of exploitation and the establishment of social welfare and security). The latter permitted socialization with compensation, and the cooperation of the workers in the administration of business enterprises (p. 706). The right of economic combinations was established for workers and employers alike. There was then no charter of rights wider in scope or more modern in the design.

(5) Proportional Representation

The pre-Weimar electoral system had been so unjust that the Weimar Republic established the most just imaginable. Its principal innovation was

Proportional Representation, or P.R. We must not make the mistake of believing that this system was the chief cause of the multiparty system in Germany. The causes of this, we have had ample reason to appreciate, were historical and social. But it is still true that the "splinter parties" were encouraged to remain firmly organized, and to be intransigent, since the system gave them their almost meticulous mathematical share of the seats by a sweeping together of all their voting adherents all over the Reich. It also strengthened party leadership *too much* for the blending that is essential in a democracy. No quantitative index of centralization and decentralization in a party system can be stated; the general opinion of enlightened observers is that the German parties were *overcentralized,* and that P.R. strongly assisted this.

If P.R. is desired, constituencies must be multimembered. Proportionately the size of the area would be increased thereby, to avoid an unwieldy legislature. This has a potent effect on the organization that selects the candidates. It desires to poll its maximum strength throughout the district, and, therefore, it is careful to pick the strongest, not the weak, candidates who come to its notice. The "machine," the "bosses," become more powerful, and the party more rigorous instead of flexible; it is less individualized. Second, in the list of each party's candidates, it will matter very much to each individual candidate whether he is put at the top or at the bottom of the list. The voters tend to go for the man at the top. Again, the party selectors are given added power.

The Lists. The whole population of 65,000,000 was divided into thirty-five districts. The average size of a German electoral district (*Wahlbezirk*) was about 1,700,000 inhabitants, or 1,150,000 voters. (The British constituency is much smaller— one twentieth the size.) The largest was the whole of Württemberg, 2,500,000 inhabitants; the smallest was East Hamburg, 1,000,000. These districts were then grouped into sixteen conjoint districts (*Wahlverbände*); in some cases, only the original one, in others, a combination of two or three. The average number of seats per electoral district was 11.

Parties competed at the election by rival lists.

The name of the party had to be designated on the list, because after a few years it was found that the voters could not otherwise distinguish the mere names when there were so many. The lists each received a number, 1, 2, 3, etc., according to the strength of the party in the existing *Reichstag.* The party was not required to name on its list more than the first four names; after that it could be blank. This meant that if the party got more votes than would fill four seats, *it* could name the additional Deputies at its discretion up to the votes cast for its list.

Lists could combine within a conjoint district, so giving the parties the benefit of any remainders over the quota per Deputy throughout the country. It was an intended and real benefit to small parties.

Finally, each party set up a list of candidates for the whole of Germany—its *Reichslist.*

Electors had one vote each. They could vote for a list and nothing but the list. They did this by marking a cross at the top of a list on the ballot paper. Their votes went to that list, not the candidate. For each 60,000 votes a party was entitled to one Deputy. Thus, if it got 260,000 votes, it had four seats, and 20,000 surplus votes. The wastage of the 20,000 was avoided by the combination of surpluses in each conjoint constituency. Surpluses left over from these, again, were swept together over the whole Reich, and for each 60,000 leftover votes, each party *Reichslist* had seats distributed to it, any fraction of 30,000 and over giving them an additional seat. What precious justice!

A concession was made to the argument that P.R. would encourage small parties: no party could obtain more members from its *Reichslist* than it obtained in the constituencies.

On the "snapshot" theory of representation, the system was well-nigh perfect. It made no provision for by-elections; the lists provided "substitutes" in case of future vacancies.

Effects on Parties. The system militated against the development of parties with an electoral majority. The Social Democrats, together with the U.S.P.D. would, it is thought by many close students, have obtained a majority, with the former German system of run-off elections, which differed from the French second ballot in that *only the two leading parties* could contend in the second vote. The lagging parties were then compelled either to abstain or to choose between the two top contenders. Since they would have needed some non-Socialist votes, the resultant policy, given the basic democratic nature of the Majority Socialists, would have been a moderate development of the welfare State on free, democratic lines. This might have made the splintered opponents unite also.

The system nourished the rise and resistance of parties, some of which remained small, others becoming tremendous. The Communists were encouraged to challenge the Social Democrats *all over the country,* using their usual foul tactics to pick up votes everywhere. The Nazis, first running with General Ludendorff's German Racialists as the New Freedom Party in 1924, were able to cull 32 seats in the *Reichstag,* for 6.5 percent of the votes—yet they did this mainly by gathering their surpluses all over the Reich, not by possession of substantial strength in a few nucleated places. Left to a second-ballot system, they might have failed to get a single seat. The electoral system enabled the Nazis to dispense with an illegal *coup,* when, under such men as Brüning, the Reich would have crushed them, knowing well their later intentions. The Nazis could always argue that a vote cast for them anywhere, seemingly in sterile ground, would be accounted to them. The Nazis obtained the publicity that was their very life by being in the electoral running; and their Deputies brought in a salary income and were provided with free travel throughout the Reich, *en route* to destroying the regime that paid them.

Other splinter groups were encouraged which otherwise would have been snuffed out. They were the Economic Party of the German Middle Classes, and two or three (it varied) Farmers' Parties (see table, p. 642). The other parties, then, to meet the interests and experts on the splinter group lists, had to offer similar candidates, though they (a public official or a farmer, a trade-union officer, an artisan, and so on) were not necessarily of statesmanlike quality.

Large or small, the parties became "bureaucratized" in this sense: they fixed policy and candidacies at the center. They did not renominate men of independent mind; they were not at the mercy of men of this type. These inside leaders came to be known as *Partei-bonzen,* party bonzes, after the Buddhist priests of Japan and China. The presumed transactions inside the temples disgusted the younger voters with the process of democracy, especially the trading of priorities on the party lists for potential blocs of votes from specific interests, *Kuhhandel,* "cattle trading."

The large constituency, and the predominance of the party, with "star" candidates at the top of the list, did tend to make of the election campaign an affair of broad slogans and parades, rather than small face-to-face meetings of candidates working for their own constituencies as in Britain or in France under the single-member constituency system.

Now, we must not slip into the error that modern States can be run without party coherence, and we have noticed that even in Britain, which maintains the single-member constituency system, party headquarters and the leaders have dominant power in elections; but on sufferance of a contingent revolt by the local caucuses. Nothing got in the way of a kind of party juggernaut in Germany. Even down to September 1930 the majority system with second ballot would have given *the democratic parties a definite majority in the Reichstag.* The justice of P.R. kept Nazis and Communists alive ready to murder each other and together to murder the Reich.

(6) and (7) The Executive: The President and Cabinet

The multiplicity of parties, to some extent encouraged and perpetuated by P.R., spelled the failure of stable Executive government and gave Hitler and his Nazis extraordinarily inflammatory propaganda material. But it is necessary also to look into the laborious and sincere attempts to organize a sound Executive system.

The Presidency. The National Assembly rejected the Swiss method of composing the Executive— that is, to choose Cabinet and President at one and the same time from the legislature and by the legislature. It was considered that Germany was too big, too complex a culture and varied an economy, to expect quiet harmony in the electing body. The Conservatives added that such a method would savor of anarchy and might facilitate the rise of a dictator. The U.S.P.D., following Russian models, stood by the Swiss idea—a new form of Soviet! Preuss objected to the American system of complete vesting of the Executive power in one man, virtually directly elected by the people, because he objected to the separation of powers: it severed the Executive from the Legislature, and meant that the former would be spiritually sterile and the latter would lack executive stimulus and knowledge.

What then? Germany's magnitude and her international status and the diversity of domestic interests, required a *personal incarnation*. Hence, the feeble French method of choosing the titular Executive was to be avoided. Yet there must be an Executive responsible to the legislature. And somehow, some of the glamor of the British monarchy must be provided. Again, the Executive must be a counterpoise to the Legislature—with a strength the French Executive did not possess. Hence, the Constituent Assembly created a presidency directly elected by the people. This idea was supported by the donation to that President of the authority to appoint the Ministers (who would be responsible to the assembly, of course). The argument (Preuss') ran:

> A leader who issued from popular election, therefore, is most probably a man experienced in political tactics and can, when in doubt, more accurately weigh up the relevant political and technical circumstances, and make a decision, than where there is parliamentary selection.

Never was a prophecy more tragically belied by events! For it did not follow that the *German* use of popular election would produce the kind of man promised.

He was to be elected by the German people, eligible at the age of thirty-five. He must be a citizen. The term of office was seven years with indefinite reelection. When Hitler stood against Hindenberg in 1932, he not being a German but an Austrian citizen, his friends in the government of Brunswick gave him that status. A law in 1920 spelled out the details of the electoral method. It included the second-ballot method, in case at the first election no candidate polled more than half the votes cast. A simple majority was sufficient for election at the second ballot, where, however, the number of candidates was not limited and new candidates could also come forward.

There is no point in listing the functions ascribed to the President, for each required ministerial countersignature (by the Reich Chancellor or a Reich Minister—Article 50), to be valid, thereby throwing the responsibility on the Cabinet and thereby requiring the Cabinet to shape policy leading to decisions.

Powers of the President. The President was elected by the people, to give him strength. He could stand up against his Ministers, therefore, with the explicit or implied argument that his authority was as good as theirs. The National Assembly had produced a split Executive, each part drawing its authority from the people, when it came to tests of will between them, the Cabinet itself having its power intermediately through the *Reichstag*. It can be seen how much the operation of a constitution, then, would depend on a respect for its general spirit. Was it to be the will of the *Reichstag*, or of a single man and his advisers who might not be members of Parliament at all— the "kitchen cabinet," in short? This became a fatal question for Germany, as we shall see, when a militarist-monarchist Junker, Hindenberg, of Bismarck's generation and caste, became President.

Some of the powers of the President were, using Mussolini's adverb, "exquisitely" political. They need attention: foreign representation; commander in chief of the Armed Forces under ministerial responsibility; dissolution of the *Reichstag*; appointment and dismissal of the Reich Chancellor; emergency powers.

Dissolution. We shall see later how some of these functions were handled by the second President of the Republic, Hindenberg, in such wise as to bring about its downfall. Attention may be called to the dissolution power and the emergency power. Article 25 gave the President the power to dissolve the *Reichstag,* but only once for the same cause. New elections were to take place at the latest on the sixtieth day after dissolution. It was an echo of the British monarch's power to dissolve at the request of the Prime Minister (p. 154) in order to clarify the relations between Cabinet and House of Commons by appeal to the electorate. It was designed to strengthen the Executive by use of an instrument at the *Government's* disposal and avoid the feebleness into which the French Executive had fallen by the desuetude of its power of dissolution (p. 418). Unfortunately, the power came to be misused. The Reich President (Hindenberg) accepted the advice of his confidential friends, such as von Pape and General von Schleicher, and of his own son and *his* friends, to oust a Reich Chancellor whom he disliked (Dr. Brüning), though the Chancellor still had a parliamentary coalition with a majority, and then appoint a new Chancellor and give *him* the advantage of dissolution in the hope of winning a parliamentary majority for *him*. It happened twice in 1932, for the two men mentioned above. As these men were enemies of the Republic and not adamant enough against or as wily as Hitler, the majorities let Hitler in in January 1933. The instances throw a harrowing light on another of Dr. Preuss' vain prophecies about the presidency:

He who has issued from the people's will, may be expected to be able to judge more clearly and more accurately circumstances and persons, than a monarch who is separated from the people by birth and breeding, and can only see with the eyes of the narrow social circle surrounding him, and hear with their ears.

A representative of a caste, in his dotage, did precisely what Kaiser Wilhelm II had done.
Emergency Government. Article 48, on the state of emergency, dealt with two situations: (1) *Reichs-exekution* against states not fulfilling their obligations; and, then (2) came the situation of such fateful moment:

The President, if public security and order in the German nation should be considerably disturbed or endangered, may take all necessary measures to reestablish such public security and order, and, if necessary, intervene with the aid of armed force. To this end he may provisionally abrogate, in whole or in part, the fundamental laws established in Articles 114, 115, 117, 118, 123, 124, and 153.

These articles contained the guarantees of civil liberties. There were certain *Reichstag* checks on the use of this power when of any duration—but it was open to the President (with countersignature) to take action at once where he judged delay to be dangerous.

Such a power appeared in the Bismarckian Constitution. It is an echo of the prerogative (p. 40) power remaining in a monarchy to act in case of public danger. It was certainly a part of Prussian monarchical authority and had been plentifully applied in the recent past.
Its Danger. The trouble was that the words *public security and order* came to be interpreted *broadly,* not as immediate and present danger of physical violence but as political situations which might eventually lead to such—that is, exercises in probability, based on subjective party fears. For example, distressful economic conditions in general opened the way to abrogation of civil rights, and the use of decrees for the making of legislation for which parliamentary majorities could not be obtained owing to the disintegration of the party membership of the *Reichstag*. Once again, as with the constitution of Prussia in 1862, there was a "lacuna in the constitution," namely, the right interpretation of the article. Gaps in a constitution can only be remedied wholesomely where experience and social consensus provide wholesome conventions. The conditions were adverse in Germany to a democratic convention to plug up the gap. There must always be gaps in constitutions and laws—the imagination cannot include all future situations. Good will is needed in the interstices of laws. Germany did not have it as we shall see presently.

The President took an oath of office which read:

I swear to consecrate all my energy to the welfare of the German people, to increase its welfare, to avert injury to it, to preserve the constitution and the laws of the Reich, to fulfill my duties conscientiously and to deal justly with all.

The Constitution further subjected the President to the recall. Before the expiration of his full term, the *Reichstag* could move for the removal of the President from office, which would then be decided by a referendum. The *Reichstag* resolution required a two-thirds vote of those voting. He would be at once suspended from office, and could submit himself for reelection within a short period. If reelected, a new term of seven years started for him—and the *Reichstag* would be automatically dissolved. The power was never used.

The first President was Ebert, who died in February 1925; the second Hindenberg, elected in April 1925 and reelected in April 1932.

The Cabinet or Government. Just as Germany's monarchical past caused the presidency to be given a status not compatible with responsible ministries, so her experience of chancelloric leadership helped to shape her cabinet system (though her party disintegration destroyed it).

Articles 52 to 59 created the Reich governmental system. We present only the main features. The government of the Reich consisted of the Reich Chancellor and the Reich Ministers. The Chancellor was to be appointed and dismissed by the Reich President; on the Chancellor's proposals, the Ministers were to be appointed and dismissed by the Reich President. They required the confidence of the *Reichstag* for the conduct of their office; and any of them had to resign when by explicit resolution the *Reichstag* withdrew its confidence. The Chancellor was endowed with the chairmanship of the Reich Government, with the duty of conducting its affairs according to an order of business established by the Government and approved by the President.

The Chancellor's Leadership. It was for the Reich Chancellor to determine the policy and assume responsibility for it to the *Reichstag*. *Within* this line, the individual Ministers were to conduct their departments and assume responsibility for these before the *Reichstag*. Thus, the leading position of the Chancellor was made clear. The Ministers were obliged to lay before the Government for discussion and decision all drafts of law and differences of opinion on functions concerning several departments. The Government was to reach decisions by majority vote (rather stultifying the leadership of the Chancellor!). The Chancellor had a casting vote.

There was much muddle in the thinking of the National Assembly on the system it set up. For example, one view was that the Ministers were not dependent associates of the Chancellor but had an independent responsibility to the *Reichstag* for departmental administration. What did this do to collective responsibility and coordination? It was desired, apparently, to allow the Chancellor and *Reichstag* to get rid of individual Ministers without overthrowing the general policy of the Chancellor. But, if collective responsibility is thus disintegrated, then each man ceases to take an interest in collective policy! Preuss also thought that Ministers need not be chosen from Parliament, but from anywhere! This was a mistake in theory; it became a tragic mistake in practice—Ministers of Defense could be (some were!) generals, professionals, not civilians who were Deputies. Mad! The rabid dog killed the Republic.

A most interesting set of rules were developed for the conduct of cabinet business.[1]

The system functioned with German meticulous administrative smoothness inside the general lines of policy, when it was possible to make these in firm outlines. But it was at the mercy soon of economic crisis, military sabotage by the *Offizierkorps*, who found their way in at the back door through the nonparliamentary Ministers of Defense—Generals von Seeckt and von Schleicher (p. 644 and p. 657). It was buffeted by the multiplicity of intransigent parties.

(8) The Reichswirtschaftsrat

Partly spurred on by the rise of Soldiers' and Workers' Councils, but also by the democratic experience of "pressure groups" and Germany's own tradition of Economic Parliaments (of the *Zollverein*, p. 563) and a later-day proposal by Bismarck to establish an Economic Parliament, the Constitution set up by Article 165, a body representative of occupational groups. There is not space enough here to explain the composition of the Economic Council or its scope of functions in any detail. It must suffice to say that it came to be composed of representatives of the occupational organizations, with a few representatives of "consumers" and the "public interest." Its function was to give its advisory opinion on drafts of social and economic legislation introduced by the Govern-

[1] See H. Finer, *Theory and Practice of Modern Government,* first edition, New York, 1932, Vol. II, pp. 1092ff.

ment. It could draft such laws, which had to be presented to the *Reichstag* by the Government even if it disagreed with the Economic Council, giving an exposition of its own point of view. Originally, this body was to have been the apex of a great understructure of advisory workers' councils. This understructure was never fully built; but works councils were established in factories with twenty and more employees. The Reich Economic Council did some useful work in the analysis of social and economic conditions; but the hopes placed in its usefulness as a nonpolitical and technical forum in which the economic groups would help reason to be heard were vain. The *Reichstag* generally cold-shouldered it. Popular representatives believe they know more than anyone else where the facts of life are concerned, and believe that they ought to deal with suppliant "lobbies" where the will to policy is involved.

(9) The Referendum and the Initiative

The referendum was made available as an arbiter between *Reichstag, Reichsrat*, and the Reich President. Constitutional laws might require a referendum if the President backed the *Reichsrat's* right of objection to the *Reichstag's* project. For ordinary legislation, the popular initiative was available at the instance of one tenth of the voters. The proportion of voters was within reach of the substantial parties, but too big for spoilers among the splinter parties to get what they wanted by referendum when they could not get it by electoral votes ordinarily, and was also beyond reach of crank movements. For the success of the initiative, a majority was necessary, not only of the voters who had participated, but of the registered electorate. If the bill so referred was an amendment to the Constitution, then not only did this condition obtain but also a majority of the registered voters had to be in favor. These provisos made it possible for one or two big parties to defeat an initiative by getting their followers to abstain from voting.

In the period 1919–1933, either initiatives were attempted. Three alone got the necessary 10 percent of requestors (and some were disqualified because only the *Reichstag* could initiate *financial* referendums); two went to referendum; none was

legislated. As predicted by some scholars, the instrument was used for insincere agitation by extremists, unhappy with the existence of the Republican regime itself. One, in 1926, was designed to expropriate the former ruling houses in the states. It provided an opportunity for nationalistic propaganda revolving around the benefits of monarchy and the sanctity of private property and the Fifth Commandment. It failed. In 1928 the Communists started a campaign against the building of a "pocket" battleship, designed to evade the terms of the Treaty of Versailles, and to help the Soviet Union's international position. It could not get out sufficient petitioners. In 1929 the Nazis initiated a protest against the final American reparation plan; they agitated enough for sufficient petitioners, but suffered a resounding defeat at the referendum.

All these attempts at referendum did was to subject the land to more agitation than the regular *Reichstag* elections and party meetings, etc., and to attempt to tear out from the general policy of the parties and the legislature some page for separate adoption. Both were politically bad. The founders of the Constitution had not really come up to date with democratic experience: the more coherent, organized and responsible-minded the parties—and this was the case in Germany—the less is *direct* legislation needed.

(10) Constitutional Amendments

The Constitution was made a rigid one: amendments required a two-thirds majority of the legal membership of either House for their initiation. It was possible to amend the Constitution by referendum. This could be instituted if one tenth of the qualified voters petitioned to this effect. To be accepted, a majority of the *electorate* must vote for the project. If the *Reichstag* decided to amend the Constitution against the protest by the *Reichsrat*, the Reich President could hold back the amending law if the *Reichsrat* demanded a referendum within two weeks.

This arrangement was not liked by the states, as far as the referendal aspect was concerned, because it admitted the whole united populace to a power over the states' autonomy. They would have wished full equality of the *Reichsrat* with the

Reichstag. But the *Reichsrat* obtained only the power of initiation or objection in the form given above.

(11) Constitutional Review and the Courts

The Constitution had no words literally establishing judicial review of constitutionality. But the courts, supported by the Right, Center, and the Socialists, assumed that the *Rechtsstaat* required it, in the absence of any prohibition. The jurists supported it by the constitutional article saying that judges were independent and subject only to the law. In 1921 and again on a Revaluation (currency) Law in 1925, the power began to be used, but not massively.

The Civil Service under Weimar

The Constitution itself introduced vital changes in the recruitment and status of the Civil Service and the various Civil Service laws of Prussia (a pioneer), with the other states following suit. It does not require reiteration that the Service at all levels remained highly competent and devoted; on the whole, it became more efficient than ever, because it benefited from the accumulation of thought about public administration, to which the Germans were extremely important contributors, and because the civil servants, now released from the climate of regimentation of the monarchy and Bismarckism, themselves took a hand in the cultivation of the civil servant's mind and morale through the Civil Service Associations and the courses they arranged with the universities and local colleges for after-work continued study.

We concentrate attention on the Higher Civil Service policy of the Weimar Republic. Its Magna Carta was written into the Constitution's bill of rights (Arts. 128–131). It opened public office to "all citizens without distinction, in accordance with the laws and according to their ability and attainments." This was a striking contrast, not to the principles laid down in the Constitution donated in 1850 (p. 588) but to its practice, which restricted the Civil Service, more especially the higher ranks, to a single, small, social class.

Diversification. The practice of the Republic under this caused the entry of a much more diversified sample of the population, Catholics, Jews, atheists, as well as liberals and socialists, now getting their opportunity. The existing monarchical appointees were retained; they had their rights; they were not purged. A purge had been proposed at the time of the Kapp *putsch,* but only a few isolated punishments followed. In fact, the Civil Service had then served the republican government, true to its character of obedience to the legal authorities. Many were ensconced in the Service biding their time. But the fact was that the Reich Governments were composed of coalitions of several parties, the Center and Right parties soon predominating. Hence a consistent and continuous policy of purgation of antirepublican elements, who might give away governmental secrets to the parties of the Extreme Right, and later the Nazis, could not be carried out. At any rate, substantial numbers of persons who were genuinely sympathetic to the Weimar Republic duly received appointments on their merits.

How were these merits now appraised? The system of recruitment to the Higher Service was fundamentally that established by the early years of the twentieth century (p. 593). A Prussian Act of July 8, 1920, introduced some changes designed to energize and widen the outlook of the recruits, who came, as before from law education. The preparatory service was reduced from four years to three. It now began with judicial practice of only six months. In the written examination at the end of the course a quarter of the time was assigned to *public* law—that is, constitutional and administrative law; and in the two days' oral, one day was given to economics and political science. Thus, the time of education on social rather than positivistic legal studies and the time now devoted to nonjudicial practice of a preparatory nature were increased. The *referendars* were now especially coached while in the preparatory service by officials appointed to be their mentors, for the arrangements of this kind, begun in 1906, were extended. Furthermore, the recruits were given special leave for the purpose of attending lectures at the Institute for Further Education in Political Science, and here they met to discuss current problems.

In 1930 an agreement was made between the

Reich Government and the states to improve legal training. For it will be remembered that this latter was the crux of dissatisfaction by both practical officials and statesmen, as well as teachers, with the German method of preparation for the public service. The spirit of the agreement strongly emphasized the historical, economic, and business management outlook, especially the relation between economic phenomena and the legal order.

As previously, the Higher Service was a superior category of its own, entered by its own educational access, and still almost entirely closed to entrants by promotion from the grades below. It still, therefore, was the preserve of the community's wealthier persons. Besides the Higher Service, there were the great and numerous classes of the middle and lower Civil Service, access to which was fully open to secondary school graduates and elementary school graduates respectively, by examination, with some privileges for ex-army and ex-police career men in some positions.

The basic thoroughness and excellence of the German schools provided a great supply of well-instructed, conscientious, honest, dutiful officials, not too accustomed to think for themselves. The origin of most civil servants made them responsive to the *middle-class* outlook in German politics, the respectable, nonproletarian, and fixed-income group mentality and interests (pp. 593–595).

Service Status. The Constitution required that civil servants be "servants of the whole people, not of a party." The Reich Civil Service Act of 1873 required that "Every civil servant is obliged to fulfill conscientiously, according to the Constitution and the laws, the duties of the office conferred on him and to prove himself in his behavior inside and outside the office worthy of the esteem which the profession requires." Thus was it sought to keep the officials at the service of something called "the nation"—not subject to the pressure of parties and other interests; to put him in a position of impartial yet positive service to the whole people, in the midst of the political conflict as to what the people ought to be and become. The Prussian Supreme Administrative Court had for decades been developing from one disciplinary case to the other the detailed rules to make this workable, and continued this work.

Civil servants were *constitutionally* guaranteed their "duly acquired rights," in order to protect them against *legislative* and party assault, and compensate them for their obedience. The rights included rank, title, salary, pension, leave, and economic security if invalided by accidents at work. It was the province of the Reich Supreme Court to decide how this independence could be maintained in individual cases of inability to perform the job, economic stringency for the national economy, etc., in relation to the guarantee of life tenure to retirement age.

The Constitution and the Reich Civil Service Act further developed the code of Civil Service ethics that had been put together gradually and organically since the middle of the seventeenth century. This included obedience, loyalty, subordination; impartiality of service for the common good; eschewal of selfish and personal interests; candor; proper manner and conduct toward the public.

Discipline was maintained on the basis of the Constitution, the Reich law, and the intelligent selection of traditional practices. There was a well-organized disciplinary procedure, in various steps of seriousness, with the departments and then the administrative courts (highest instance, the *Reich Disziplinarhof*) as the instances where meticulous care was taken to secure individual justice and dutiful public service. In the departments, the procedure was quasi-judicial, not arbitrary. In this procedure the civil servant obtained a right, denied him since the rise of the Prussian State, to have discovery of the reports made on him by his superiors. Violations of the rights of the public in the course of official duties were challengeable in the administrative courts; the liability was assumed by the government; it then dealt appropriately with the official for his fault.

Political Rights. The Weimar Republic was an exercise in freedom. The Constitution gave to all civil servants the guarantee of "freedom of political opinion and of association." This had come about *de facto* in the fall of the monarchy and the advent of democracy. But the principle had to be limited by the obligations of the Service, matched by the economic rights provided for officials. The right to strike was denied. The official was obliged to be discreet in his political activities. It was even laid down in cases that it was a disciplinary offense to cooperate in any way with "a revolutionary creed or movement." It was difficult to make this latter principle effective, so long as such movements were not banned from legal contest at elections. The Prussian Cabinet in June 1930 prohibited civil servants from belonging or supporting the Nazis or the Communist Party. It was rather late.

It was also an error of misplaced liberalism for the Constitution to permit all civil servants and the military to stand and serve as Deputies in the *Reichstag* and State legislatures, with facilities for leave during the campaign for election. The British government has firmly stood out against such liberty, realizing its deleterious consequences (p. 211); the French government has fallen victim to them (p. 474), as did the German government. For the taint of politics, and inevitably "revolutionary" or "reactionary" politics, must spread when election prospects are open to civil servants.

In fact, a certain back-tracking became necessary soon after the Constitution went into effect, owing to the Kapp *putsch,* the disorders in Bavaria. In July 1922, by constitutional amendment, the Act on the Duties of Officials to Protect the Republic required civil servants to "support the constitutional republican form of government in their official duties"; and to abstain from all activities which could not be reconciled with being a servant of the public. The act classified a substantial number of Higher Civil Service posts as "political offices," delegating to the states the power to do similarly. Such officials could be retired for a time in the interest of consolidating the republican form of government. This enabled the Republic to deliver itself of some Right-wing officials who had entered the Service under the Kaiser and to replace them by more liberal elements.

Educational Reforms

The Weimar supporting parties were themselves divided in aim regarding educational reform. The Catholic Center certainly differed severely from the Socialists, even on the place of private schools alone. But the preparatory schools and private schools for the *Gymnasia* were abolished. *Every-one,* of any class, must attend the first four years of elementary school, from age six to ten; the schools were renamed *Grundschulen,* or foundation schools. This was a response to the idea of the *Einheitsschule* (like the French *école unique*), where all classes should meet in one kind of school, and all have an equal chance of entering high school at ten. But many religious private schools were allowed to remain open. The fees for secondary education were reduced, and more scholarships made available for gifted students. Yet the cost of maintenance was still a tremendous obstacle to education being open to the talents. Some further professional opportunities were opened by the institution by some cities of evening secondary schools, and by the *Aufbauschulen,* which took students from elementary schools for intensive courses at the age of twelve and gave them a secondary education acceptable by the universities. After *Grundschule,* the students were compelled to attend continuation or trade school for some hours a week to the age of eighteen in working hours.

1931–32: Attendance at Schools and Universities

Elementary	7,600,000 and 50,000 private
Continuation and trade	1,500,000
Secondary all kinds, including *Aufbauschule*	790,000
Universities	68,000

Thus, the inequality was modified, but far from radically over the Bismarckian period.

Though the Constitution (Article 148) required that the pupils should receive a copy of the Constitution, the civic sentiment that was to be developed as stipulated in the same article was not treated with really potent republicanism either in textbooks or oral teaching. Teachers were still very authoritarian, though not political, alas!

III. THE LOCAL GOVERNMENT SYSTEM

It is awkward to describe the changes in local government in Germany in the successive stages of 1871 to 1918, 1918 to 1933, and since the rise of the West German Republic. Therefore, I have decided to insert here a description of the operation of the system about 1930, before the changes introduced by Hitler, which are noted on pages 674-675. To lead up to an appreciation of the system in its evolution, a very short historical sketch is now given. The general structure and spirit prevalent in the period 1919-1933 were extant in 1885-1918, except that in the later period universal franchise replaced the old limitations on voting, party government played a more vigorous and (with Communists and Nazis) sometimes destructive part, and the needs of central financial stringency forced a shrinking of local financial autonomy, with all its meaning in the loss of full self-government. Though the system, 1871-1919, was highly authoritarian, it still allowed of great *local* initiative, so that its achievements were solidly honest and brilliant, at a time when the government of American cities was so sunk in corruption that such men as Lincoln Steffens were forced to write *The Shame of the Cities* and other muck-raking books, which, however lurid, were still moderate compared with the actual filth.

The Development of Local Government

Prussia is described here, because it was so large a part of Germany; the other states had similar systems, but the differentiae cannot be adequately noticed here.

By 1806 the system of Prussian administration (p. 541) had disemboweled the local areas, provinces, counties, and cities of self-government. In rural areas local administration—roads, poor relief, police, cleanliness—was in the hands of the nobility and large landowners. In the cities, a small group of people, nominated by the various guilds, governed the affairs of the area, but the real power was exercised by royal officials. The *Landrat* in the *Kreis* (the Circle) was the real force in that area: the owners of the manors made up the Circle Assembly and elected that official, but he was appointed by the Crown and owed his primary duty to it. This overcentralized State broke down under the impact of Napoleon's assault (p. 550). Baron vom Stein and Hardenberg sought a way out, and, believing that lack of local popular cooperation had petrified the administration, proposed local

self-government. They could not achieve a universal form of the local units, but the Municipal Edict (*Städteordnung*) of 1808 at least reformed the government of the towns. This established a government by burgomaster, *Magistrat* (an executive commission), and a town council, all variously elective, with a wider franchise. The administration of justice was taken over by royal officials. The towns obtained wide powers and financial independence. Supervision by the central authority was retained, but moderated. In 1831 this too-great liberty was modified: the franchise was widened, but the qualification of councilors was raised and central control, especially over local taxation, was intensified.

Similar reforms were applied to the communes in the rural areas and the circles, the districts, and the provinces. For instance the *Landrat* became a representative of the *Kreis* as well as remaining a royal official; and the large and small landowners and *Gemeinden* received rights of representative election to the assembly, and wide financial powers. *Regierungs-Bezirke* were established and their central official governing bodies modernized. Similarly with the provinces from 1815 onward; provincial assemblies of nobles, citizens, and peasants were revived, and a Chief President, *Oberpräsident,* was to exercise the royal power of surveillance and welfare administration.

"Self-government." Reaction set in from the 1820's and continued until after the liberal elements had been destroyed by Bismarck's monarchical absolutism and wars of German unification. In the 1870's it became clear that the possession of German local government by the upper class alone was not merely unjust (if the broader circles of the population were to be drawn to a loyalty to the Imperial system and a continuance of the monarchical principle) but incompetent. It was important also to busy the population with lesser things than Imperial high policy. Professor Rudolf von Gneist suggested, for reasons of the *Rechtsstaat* (p. 562) and governmental competence, the establishment of local *self*-government, in the English *elective* sense, though he wanted more central control than then existed in England. But this was to be achieved by the mixture of officials with elective laymen in the local government councils. It was still a principle of "deconcentration," *not* "decentralization." One of the incentives to reform by men like Gneist was to have councils in which the political capacities of the people could be developed. (For England, *post hoc ergo propter hoc!*) By a series of statutes, for the circles in 1872, the provinces in 1875, and applicable at different times to the various parts of Prussia (ancient, newly acquired, etc.), reforms were instituted. In 1891 a Rural Commune Order was passed, rounding out the system.

These reforms were not the result of a strong *popular* movement; hence the system was not truly decentralized. The initiative in local affairs was left to the officials, as the position of the burgomaster or the *Magistrat* shows (p. 632). Furthermore, in the cities, the three-class system of representation prevailed (p. 589).

In this system, the burgomaster was appointed for periods of twelve years by the local councils, giving him a dominance over the councils whose period of office was so much shorter. Also, in this main level of local government, he was *never appointed unless* persona grata *to the central government.*

The Chief President of a province had the right to suspend resolutions of the provincial assembly, which was a body representative of the circles—chiefly officials and the wealthy—if the resolutions were *ultra vires*. Also, loans and taxes above a certain amount required the approval of the central authority. This, and the group of centrally appointed officials who conducted the day-by-day administration (except in the towns), secured strong central control.

Below this unit was the government district (*Bezirke*), to administer certain central services and to exercise a general supervision over the subordinate local government officials who had central government duties to perform.

The Circle (*Kreis*) had a *bona fide* local self-government role, though its three electoral colleges were designed to cushion government against the impact of the people as a unified popular mass. Its executive chief, the *Landrat,* was a professional official and exercised central control of its resolutions and financial activities. He and a committee of officials were *supervisors of the rural and urban municipalities,* the rural ones being subject to extremely close control of all their transactions. The establishment of functions by these and the cities required the approval of the Circle or district committee, an officially appointed body.

Thus (1) central supervision prevailed over the scope of duties of local authorities, services (such as elementary education) for which financial provision was "obligatory," and most aspects of the raising of taxes, loans, dealings in property. (2) The foremost part played by appointed officials—for example, the burgomaster, etc., and the *Magistrat,* in the elected bodies introduced a spirit of authoritarian legality and technical managership to guide and control the popular representatives. (3) The officials of the higher local-central government areas were central appointees, exercising a *tutelle* over the lower levels.

Areas. Between the level of the national government and that of the city or county, the various states displayed varied patterns of territorial subdivisions. Prussia was divided into (*Provinz*) provinces responsible for maintenance of provincial roads, agricultural education and improvement, institutions of poor relief, and institutions for the handicapped. The Prussian provinces (largest, Rhineland, 6,000,000; smallest, Schleswig-Holstein, 1,400,000 in 1900) were divided into districts (*Bezirke*), simply an administrative subdivision. The districts, in turn, are divided into circles or counties (*Kreise*). Other states, being smaller than Prussia, were divided into provinces and thence into counties; some only into counties.

Officials of Lower Levels of Jurisdiction. At the city or county level a single individual was charged with the dual role of chief administrative officer for the province within that local unit as well as executive chief of the local self-governing unit.

The administrative chief of the province was the *Oberpräsident,* or Chief President, appointed by the Crown or central government, as the agent of the central authority over against the provincial assembly, invigilator of the *Bezirke,* presiding officer over the provincial boards for education, church affairs, public health, recruitment of army, etc. But for its self-government the province had a

German Local Government Units

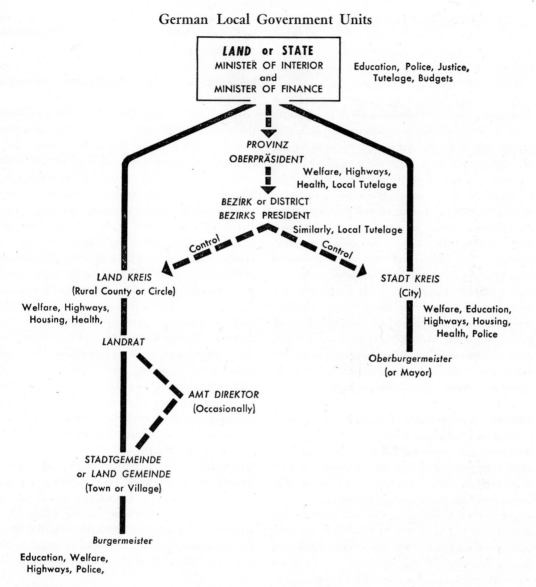

locally elected representative assembly, the (1) *Provinziallandtag*. Chosen by this assembly, and acting both in the capacity of a "cabinet" and that of a legislative house somewhat coordinate with the assembly, was the (2) executive committee, or *Provinzialausschuss*. Also chosen by the assembly, but subject to the confirmation of the central ministry, was the provincial director who, acting as the chief executive officer and presiding officer of the committee, held either the title (3) *Landesdirektor* or *Landeshauptmann*. These three (1, 2,

and 3) elements were provincial officials concerned with the affairs of the province. Distinct from them were the *Oberpräsident* and the *Provinzialrat*, the chief president and his provincial council, wholly state officials concerned with state business arising within the confines of the province.

The basic (omitting manorial estates) unit of German local self-government was the *Gemeinde* —that is, the commune or municipality, every foot of German soil.

A union of *Gemeinden* constitutes a *Kreis*, or

county. The *Landkreis* is the rural county—that is, it is a county made up of essentially rural *Gemeinden*. The *Stadtkreis,* or city county, is really a city separated from *Landkreis* supervision, and given *Kreis* status.

Being vested with both county matters and delegated provincial administration, the government of the *Kreis* consisted of a *Landrat,* or county prefect appointed by the central Ministry of the Interior from a list of nominees supplied by the *Kreistag,* the representative assembly. In addition to this task of nominating the chief executive officer, the *Kreistag* also appointed the members of the *Kreisausschuss,* or executive committee—a kind of cabinet for the chief executive. The *Kreistag,* of course, concerned itself with legislative matters of local interest and competence, but the state-appointed *Landrat* and his committee, the *Kreisausschuss* chosen by the *Kreistag,* managed the task, mentioned above, of executing and administering local *Kreis* matters on the one hand, and, on the other, administering a portion (a rather large portion in the Weimar Republic) of the affairs of the larger jurisdictions of which the *Kreis* was a part.

Divided Responsibilities. The "police" aspects of public-health administration were state affairs in the hands of the state officials of the larger areas of local government; the close environmental services and hospitals were a function of the towns. The more important roads were in the authority of the larger territorial authorities: province, circle, and district; the streets in that of the cities; the rural communes had authority over petty roads and streets. Education, at the secondary level, was the affair of the State, administered by the provincial

chief president, in all its branches; while elementary education was in charge of the district officials. The cities had devolved powers over secondary and elementary education, as permitted by these higher authorities, and, furthermore, the municipal councils deputed members to join with officials and co-opted persons to be committees for the supervision of the schools. Local authorities joined in unions for the provision of poor relief—in the provinces and lesser areas—but its actual administration was vested in the municipalities. The towns were allowed much latitude on the provision they wished to make for the various classes of the destitute. Police organization was devolved by the state to the district president and his committee. Under his authority, the *Landrat* was the responsible police official for the circle. In the rural communes, the local police came under the orders of the local mayor or several burgomasters or a joint commission for a number of them. The burgomaster was head of the police in the smaller towns; the towns providing the money and general conditions, the former exerting state executive authority over the force. In large towns the police were state-appointed, including the chief of police. The local authorities paid from a half to a third of the cost, according to the measure of decentralization they enjoyed.

The Cities. If one bears in mind the distinction, already noted, between the *Stadtkreis,* or city charged with *Kreis* functions and jurisdictionally separated from the *Kreis* of which it would otherwise be a part, and the other counties, the *Landkreise,* it is necessary once more to revert to the basic unit, the *Gemeinde,* in order to discuss the cities.

Numbers of Gemeinden of Various Population Categories in Prussia *

Gemeinden	Population	1925	1934	1937
Rural *Gemeinden*	Under 2,000	48,272	47,116	46,573
Rural cities (*Landstädte*)	2,000– 4,999	2,247	2,289	2,321
Small cities (*Kleinstädte*)	5,000–19,999	920	966	996
Medium cities (*Mittelstädte*)	20,000–99,999	216	211	220
Large cities (*Grossstädte*)	100,000 or more	45	52	53
Total		51,700	50,634	50,163

* Excluded from these figures for purposes of keeping the data comparable are the communes of the Saar, and the manorial precincts of which there were 11,856 in 1925. After the 1929 acts dissolved most of them, there were still 247 manors in the late 1930's. These are excluded also. The decrease in the total number and in the number included in the lowest population category, as well as the increase in numbers in the other, more populous categories, is a reflection of consolidation and rationalization in the Third Reich.

The existence of cities depends on the grant of the states, made by both general enabling statutes and special enactments. Prior to Hitler, nine of the German states had a single act (*Gemeindeordnung*) regarding municipal government, but in the other states there were separate acts (*Städteordnungen* and *Landgemeindeordnungen*).

City Associations. Freedom and power being of prime concern to the municipalities, the cities banded together after the turn of the century the better to pursue their interests in the German Union of Cities (*Deutscher Städtetag*), founded in 1905, for the larger, and the National League of Cities (*Reichsstädtebund*), founded in 1910, for the smaller cities. Within these were state and provincial associations.

The German national leagues conducted many research and advisory functions of the state leagues in the United States. The American Municipal Association had, in 1954, a secretariat of less than ten persons, but the *Deutscher Städtetag* had in 1931, in their extensive Berlin offices, a secretariat of over 60. Before the National Socialist regime, the German municipal leagues were powerful and aggressive lobbies. In the crucial days of 1931 and 1932 they were pressing for one national municipal government ordinance, a *Reichsstädteordnung*.

Governmental Bodies

The Weimar Constitution required that all governmental bodies have universal, equal, and direct suffrage, and endowed the local government authorities with "the right of self-government." The provisions formally opened local government to popular initiative, and democratic forces took command with considerable vigor.

In 1932, all local self-governments in Germany had legislative assemblies elected by a broadly based franchise and serving without pay. (The exception of the three-class system until 1919 will be remembered [p. 589].) The councils of the large towns met regularly from once a week to once a month, more often in the larger than the smaller. The local authorities of the larger *areas,* the assembly, did not meet so often; the average among Prussian circle authorities being about three times a year. Council meetings were open to

the public. The seats in the council were hotly contested along party political lines. Turnout at the polls varied between 60 to 80 percent from town to town and in time. Seats in the councils were allotted according to the principle of proportional representation, which would not harm a city council as it did the *Reichstag*.

Under the Reich and Weimar Constitution, civil servants could sit on the council. Civil servants even predominated in the upper house, where cities had a bicameral legislature. They were disqualified from proceedings that affected their self-interest.

Bicameral City Government. Whereas the other states (nearer to France) developed municipal government with stronger councils, the Prussians tempered their local self-government with professional excellence. Several Prussian cities still had bicameral governments in 1932. The three largest —Breslau, Frankfort-au-Main, and Hanover—had *Stadtverordnetenversammlungen* (the popularly elected lower house) of 88, 85, and 74 *Stadtverordneten* (councilmen) respectively.

The *Magistratsverfassung* was a bicameral system (akin to that of New York City), in which the legislative power was divided among two chambers: (1) a directly elected city council presided over by a chairman chosen by the council, and (2) a *Magistrat* or administrative board composed of lay and professional members elected by the council and presided over by the burgomaster who was selected by the city council. Local ordinances needed to be enacted by both chambers. Collegial *Magistrat* was the chief executive organ of the city as well as a legislature. The burgomaster presided over the *Magistrat*. In legal theory he was only *"Primus inter pares";* in practice his personality and ability decided the administrative center of gravity.

Councils had at least eleven members and no more than 100, according to the population of the town. Election to the council was open to qualified voters over twenty-five years old. In most cities, members were elected from the city at large and sat for a term of four years. Prior to 1919 half the council seats had to be filled by resident homeowners, but this provision was abolished along with the ban on council seats for bureaucrats. It was, of course, also at this time that the franchise was broadened to "universal, equal, direct and secret suffrage."

Observers in the 1890's did not expect democratization but planned for the stability of the city councils and the enduring predominance of the permanent career civil service. The Weimar system brought in wider social groups.[2]

The nearly automatic reelection gave way to sharply contested elections, a fairly high turnover in the council membership, and, consequently, councils much less skilled at their business. But the Prussian officials were not violently assailed, although by 1932 patronage had begun to show around the edges. During the 1920's, the rowdyism of the Left and Right extremes damaged local administrators.

The council divided itself into standing committees along substantive and functional lines, such as finance, welfare, and so forth, and into *ad hoc* committees as transient needs arose. Proportional representation was carried to committee assignments, which were made in accordance with party strength.

Its membership selected by the council, the *Magistrat* consisted of paid professional civil servants as well as unpaid, honorary members. The

[2] *Aix-la-Chapelle, 1912*

Manufacturers and directors of works	13
Businessmen	8
Government officials	4
Architects	3
Rentiers	3
Physicians	2
Lawyers	2
Agriculturists	2
Engineers	1
Druggist	1
	39

Magdeburg, 1924

Merchants, shopkeepers, business managers	16
Skilled craftsmen (e.g. carpenters, etc.)	9
Labor-union officials or employees	8
Schoolteachers and administrators	6
Wives and other women not employed outside the home	7
Clerks, bookkeepers, secretaries	5
Postal and railway officials and employees	3
Editors and reporters	3
Lawyers	3
Unskilled laborers	2
Engineers	2
Rentiers	1
Physicians	1
Miscellaneous	2
	68

latter group, like the unpaid members of which the council was constituted, served for four years. The number of such was set by the particular municipal code governing the city. The career bureaucrats who joined them in the *Magistrat* were appointed for twelve-year terms. Appointment was subject to confirmation on authority above the city level. The number of these paid *Stadträte* in any municipality was determined by local ordinance.

This group, chaired by the *Bürgermeister*, was a collegiate executive and at the same time the upper chamber of the legislature.[3]

Its paid officials were the chief administrative officers of the city; the *Kammerer*, a chief finance officer, the *Stadtsyndikus*, the charge of legal and general administrative matters, the *Stadtbaurat*, of chief technical officials, and so on. The powers of the *Magistrat* vis-à-vis the council were but slightly reduced by the revolution of 1918.

In its coordinate legislative capacity it was the prime force, with the power of setting the agenda and preparing bills. It was exceptionally competent in preparing the budget, for its individual members were chief officers in the departments, and, collectively, formed the executive committee with the initial control over the total budget, and had finally a virtual veto over the lower chamber.

It was a very powerful group indeed by its control of finance, including revenue and expenditure, auditing and accounting; control of personnel administration and of administrative management; custody of the city's documents and records; control over all municipal property (which is extensive in the case of German municipalities); the official representation of the city in concluding contracts with private companies as well as in dealings with other governmental units; and, entirely independently of the council in this regard, the enforcement and administration of state and national laws and regulations.

[3]	Size of the Magistrat			
	1925	Paid	Unpaid	
City	Population	Members	Members	Total
Altona	227,419	7	5	12
Breslau	554,801	17	15	32
Dortmund	320,256	12	17	29
Hanover	422,435	15	13	28
Potsdam	64,093	8	11	19
Wiesbaden	102,557	10	12	22

The *Bürgermeister* was chairman of the *Magistrat*, but was also *individually* empowered as chief executive to exercise a partial veto over that body. Like the *Magistrat*, he too was an agent of the state as well as of the city. He was required to

who shared the executive power with the mayor within that collegiate body were merely administrative subordinates (*Beigordnete*) of the mayor under the *Bürgermeisterverfassung*. Pictorially, the power structure is thus:

Distribution of Power in German City Governments

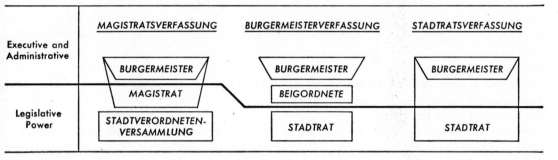

render assistance to the state's attorney, to serve, if necessary as a magistrate of the district court, and, in fact, to handle "all functions relating to county, district, provincial, or state administration" not elsewhere assigned.

Unicameral City Government. In some of the provinces of Prussia, notably Westphalia and the Rhine Province and in the states of Hesse and Saxony, the prevailing type of city government was the *Bürgermeisterverfassung*. Rural communes in general followed this system. In Bavaria and Württemburg could be found the *Stadtratsverfassung*, a rather recent (1919) development. In both these systems the legislative functions were restricted to a single chamber, the *Stadtrat* or *Gemeinderat*. In the *Stadtratsverfassung*, the burgomaster was seated within the city council itself as its presiding officer and was subjected to a constant responsibility thereto. The council consisted not merely of elected members, but also of the principal administrative officers of the city. Since the council itself was the chief organ of administration, the executive power of the *Bürgermeister* was somewhat lessened as compared to the *Bürgermeisterverfassung* wherein the *Bürgermeister*, separate from the council, and the unitary chief executive, had power comparable to those of the *Bürgermeister* and the *Magistrat* combined in the *Magistratsverfassung*. The chief administrative officers who were members of the *Magistrat* in the bicameral system and

In all systems of local government in Germany, the executive power stood at some advantage to the legislative during the period of the Weimar Republic. Even in the *Stadtratsverfassung*, in spite of the fact that the office of *Bürgermeister* was encased within the council itself, the office was a powerful one, as it certainly was in the other two systems.

The advantages and disadvantages of these three types of city government are those of bicameralism and unicameralism.

Much preparatory work was assigned to administrative committees. Private citizens with economic or other interests affected by the regulation and rules involved were sometimes co-opted to these administrative committees. In the *Magistratsverfassung* joint committees, consisting of members of the council, members of the *Magistrat*, other paid officials, and private citizens might be charged with the administration of matters delegated to it by the two chambers. Such a committee is known as a "deputation." Except in the case of school deputations, which were under the supervision of higher authorities in the school system, administrative committees were responsible to the *Magistrat*.

The *officials* of the municipalities—that is, the local officials truly defined—saw to it that by the 1930's the associations of cities organized statewide systems of recruitment procedures, examinations, scales of pay, professional rights, and opportunities of transfer by way of promotion from smaller to larger authorities. The procedures and the officials were highly competent.

Municipal Powers

Local authorities are, of course, strictly without inherent sovereignty of their own, creatures of the State, rather deconcentrated than decentralized entities (p. 241). But the General Local Government Laws gave the *Gemeinden* the right to make laws within the scope of "the welfare" of the commune—that is, a general enabling power.

Autonomous Powers. The Supreme Administrative Court of Prussia pronounced in 1885 that the "commune can accordingly embrace within the sphere of its operations everything which furthers the welfare of all, on the material interests and the intellectual development of the individual . . . limited only by state supervision."

Anything, then, which the commune wanted to do—as long as it was based on sound finance and did not run counter to some specific or general end of the state—fell under what in Germany were called "autonomous powers." Except in periods of economic stress the right "even to do occasionally something foolish" obtained as long as the financial instability was not the result of administrative dishonesty, an element singularly rare in Germany.

Delegated Powers. In line with what was said earlier about the "dual" functions of local executives and administrators, the city also exercised "delegated powers." These included school administration, collection of state taxes, conduct of elections, and the police.

The distinction between the two classes of power might be made by deciding whether a particular activity is taken up by a municipality on its own initiative or, on the other hand a municipality "is in general obligated to carry out orders in a given branch of administration . . ." Those matters which produced a high degree of interference from above merely for administrative improvement are delegated powers, but those matters which seldom receive the attention of the State, and then only for cause, are autonomous powers. However, a state might interfere freely with activities undertaken by virtue of autonomous powers

if the city demonstrated an inability or lack of interest such as to botch its administration. State interference might range all the way from the rendering of advice to the dissolution of the city government. In the middle 1930's all "autonomous powers" became "delegated powers" with a mere twist of the National Socialist fist.

During the period of the Weimar Constitution, an increasing degree of state interference in local matters occurred, especially in the field of taxation (p. 619).

Nevertheless, for range, originality of services, and brilliance of administration, German local government was the best in the whole world.

Some notion of the extensive activities of German municipalities can be had by realizing that a sample of 204 German cities indicated in 1930 that on the average, 23.7 percent of the land within the corporate limits (exclusive of streets) belonged to the city, much of it given to farming, to buildings for rent, and public parks.

Social-service institutions maintained in goodly number by German cities included: consultation offices for marital problems; infants' and mothers' homes; nursery schools; kindergartens; children's training homes; recreation centers; youth hostels; social-guidance clinics; asylums; camps for the a-social; transients' homes; workshops for the physically disabled and for psychopaths; treatment centers for venereal diseases, tuberculosis, alcoholism, and cancer; convalescent homes; placement agencies for institution-eligible mental patients; hospitals; and old-age homes.

Municipal Enterprise

Enterprises for the service of the community include: street construction, lighting, and cleaning; sewerage systems; supplying of light, water, and even milk; street railways and bus lines; administration of municipally owned real estate; promotion of housing, erection of dwellings; opening up of new subdivisions, leasing of vacant city lands in very small tracts to citizens for little gardens (*Kleingarten*); poor relief and care for the young; establishment and administration of cemeteries, crematoria, parks, playgrounds, athletic fields, bath houses, restaurants, docks, breweries, factories, slaughterhouses, market halls, savings banks, and pawn shops; and theaters, concert halls, museums, and other agencies for the encouragement of art and learning.

Normally the state and the Reich did not interfere in the internal fiscal matters of the city, but evidence of unsound finance brought intervention. Especially, in the great economic depression that started in 1929 Reich decrees compelled the cities to introduce drastic economies in the compensation of their officials, in educational administration, welfare and relief activities, housing undertakings, practically depriving the municipalities of financial autonomy.

As early as 1920 the financial problems of the Reich forced it to pre-empt several fields of taxation that had formerly been more widely tapped. The state and local governments relied primarily on two taxes: the real property tax and the business tax raised from the profits of commercial or industrial enterprise. It was allotted, also, a proportion of national revenues.

The finance of local government is most briefly representable in the following table, for 1924, of revenues in large towns in Prussia and in Bavaria. In the latter, the sums are from additions to the state taxes on land houses and businesses.

Source of Revenue	Prussia, Percent	Bavaria, Percent
Profits on municipal undertakings	11.0	21.0
Income and corporation tax	24.2	15.3
Exchange tax	6.7	5.1
Land and buildings tax	17.1	10.5
House rent tax	8.9	—
Business tax	20.1	17.0
Other taxes *	12.0	12.6
Earnings of communal property		11.0
Surplus from last year		7.0
	100.0	99.5

* Increment value, entertainments, dogs, visitors, sale of liquor, and many others.

IV. THE WEIMAR CONSTITUTION IN OPERATION

The tragic and simple truth is that the people and parties of Germany, operating through the *Reichstag* and the Cabinet, were too weak to withstand the convulsions that afflicted the world in the period 1919 to 1933 and the special forms these took in Germany. Even far-longer rooted democracies staggered under the pressures. Germany's plight may be considered under three heads: economic, international, and constitutional.

The Economic Difficulties

There is a considerable correlation between the ups and down of the economy and the viability of the Weimar Republic.

The economy went back to private industry, because the Socialists were not electorally strong enough to carry their program of nationalization of the basic industries. The maximum they enacted was a Works Councils Law in 1920 to give the elected delegates of the workers in plants with over 20 employees the right of cooperation with management in plant safety and welfare, the right to organize, the enforcement of collective agreements, and the right to have members on the board of directors to receive information about labor matters, wage records, future employment, and the balance sheet. This boiled down to not very much, especially as economic conditions became hard and the German employers, now installed in their mighty enterprises again, dealt harshly with their workers when it came to choosing who should be made unemployed first.

There was nothing in the path of arrogant, despotic big business and finance except the Republic and the trade unions, thus tamed; and the trade unions were ponderous organizations, replete with property and funds.[4] Their *élan* was gone. It is a material point.

Inflation. In the period 1918–1923 catastrophic inflation occurred. The German mark, exchanging at 4.2 to the American dollar in 1914, was at 8.9 in 1919. It was reduced to 4200 *billion* marks to the dollar by November 1923, having reached this by unpredictable spurts of hundreds, thousands and millions, or 2.3 trillion paper marks for one gold mark![5]

[4] Membership of all German trade unions for 1921 and 1931 was:

Year	Free	Christian	Hirsch-Duncker	Total
1921	7,568,000	986,000	225,000	8,779,000
1931	4,418,000	578,000	181,000	5,177,000

[5] Spring 1922, 290 marks per dollar; November 1922, 9150; October 1923, 12 billion; November 1923, 120 billion.

Germany almost forthwith after the defeat intensified the wartime inflation, for markets had been lost, production was disorganized, and money was required to cope with the adverse balance of international payments and reparations and then to finance resistance against the separatist movement that had been started in the Ruhr in 1922–1923. Ten cabinets between February 1919 and November 1923, coalitions of Socialists, Left and Center, and People's Party, preferred inflation to taxation to meet the difficulties. The industrialists and financiers abetted the policy, for they made fortunes out of smart buying operations as the mark zigzagged in its fantastic fall.

The internal debt was almost wiped out. It meant that the middle class lost its property, the value of its pensions, its savings, its interest receipts. This class hated the system of government in which it happened, and especially it hated the workers, to whose lot they were afraid they might fall from their own traditional status. The workers suffered because wages did not catch up with rising prices. All who had come out of the war needing employment—young people, uprooted soldiers—were riven with insecurity. The conditions drove the middle class into the arms of the Nazis and anti-Semites.

From 1923 to 1929, through the genius of Hjalmar Schacht (a financial genius and a political poltroon, p. 655), the recovery of world markets, the immense forgiving of reparations by the Allies, and the German government's fulfillment of the Treaty, economic good times were achieved. The Socialists, during these years, were outside the coalitions, which were composed of Democratic Party, Center, People's Party and Nationalists—upper-middle class and big business, headed by Chancellor Marx (a Catholic) or Hans Luther (a nonpartisan Chancellor). Swift and remarkable recovery was made in industry with modern technology. By 1928 real income per capita had again reached prewar level. America supplied the capital. The trusts blossomed with most ingenious organization ("Rationalization"), financing, and management. It was the emergence of technocracy, with a new managerial class (aided by white-collar assistants lifted out of the working class), in steel, cement, electricity, and I. G. Farben in chemicals and dyes as especially brilliant examples.

The labor unions also built gigantically and meticulously; they amalgamated in the *Allgemeinev Deutscher Gewerkschaftsbund* with 6,000,000 members. They had nothing in common with the Communists and were rather fearful of too heavy cooperation with the Social Democrats. They represented integrity and orderliness, not the *élan* of democratic defense against the Right.

Thus, Germany positively festered with her grievances, her megalomania, and her problems of the feared and hated Russians and Poles and the despised French. Russian tactics and the Comintern's machinations gave grist to the Right wing and to Hitler's sadistic mass agitation. It must always be remembered that the Russian border was only 750 miles from Berlin, and that by land.

Political and Constitutional Dynamics

German *Zerrissenheit,* earlier geographic and religious, was now a shreddedness on the party level. A multiplicity of parties mattered more when sovereign power was in their hands than when it was in Bismarck's.

Fragile Cabinets. As the table on page 641 shows, Cabinets were short-lived. They were now like the French, almost, with an average of eight months, or twenty-one Cabinets from February 1919 to January 28, 1933. The most durable was the Socialist Heinrich Müller's of twenty months ending March 29, 1930. If this were subtracted, then the eight-month average must be reduced.

The Nazis mirrored the effect of stability on the German mind, so used to a stable, aloof Executive. This is from a Nazi pamphlet on its program of 1930:

Chaos and bewilderment! . . . Government against people, parties against parties, concluding the most curious and impossible arrangements, parliaments against governments, workers against employers, consumers against producers, merchants against producers and consumers, house-proprietors against tenants, workers against peasants, officials against the public, working class against the "bourgeoisie," Church against State, all fighting the temporary opponent with blind rage, and all with only one thing in view—their own personal interest, their power, their *own* good, the interest of the purse.
. . . In vain do they attempt to produce order,

The Twenty-one Cabinets of the Weimar Republic

Chancellor	Duration	Participating Parties
1. Scheidemann (S.P.D.)	Feb. 13, 1919–June 19, 1919	7 S.P.D., 3 Dem., 3 Cent. 1 nonpartisan
2. Bauer (S.P.D.)	June 19, 1919–Oct. 3, 1919	7 S.P.D., 4 Cent.
3. "	Oct. 3, 1919–Mar. 26, 1920	6 S.P.D., 4 Cent. 3 Dem.
4. Müller (S.P.D.)	Mar. 27, 1920–June 8, 1920	5 S.P.D., 3 Dem., 4 Cent.
5. Fehrenbach (Cent.)	June 20, 1920–May 4, 1921	2 Dem., 5 Cent., 3 People's, 2 nonpartisan
6. Wirth (Cent.)	May 9, 1921–Oct. 22, 1921	3 S.P.D., 3 Dem., 2 Cent., 2 nonpartisan
7. "	Oct. 26, 1921–Nov. 14, 1922	4 S.P.D., 2 Dem., 4 Cent., 1 nonpartisan
8. Cuno (nonpartisan)	Nov. 22, 1922–Aug. 12, 1923	2 Dem., 2 Cent., 2 People's, 1 Nationalist, 4 nonpartisan
9. Stresemann (People's)	Aug. 13, 1923–Oct. 3, 1923	4 S.P.D., 2 Dem., 3 Cent., 2 People's, 1 nonpartisan
10. "	Oct. 6, 1923–Nov. 23, 1923	3 S.P.D., 2 Dem., 3 Cent., 2 People's, 1 nonpartisan
11. Marx (Cent.)	Nov. 30, 1923–May 26, 1924	3 Dem., 3 Cent., 2 People's, 1 Bav. People's, 2 nonpartisan
12. "	June 3, 1924–Dec. 15, 1924	3 Dem., 2 Cent., 2 People's, 2 nonpartisan, 1 Bav. People
13. Luther (nonpartisan)	Jan. 16, 1925–Oct. 29, 1925	2 Cent., 2 People's, 5 Nationalists, 1 Bav. People's, 2 nonpartisan
14. "	Jan. 20, 1926–May 18, 1926	3 Dem., 3 Cent., 3 People's, 1 Bav. People's
15. Marx (Cent.)	May 18, 1926–Feb. 1, 1927	3 Dem., 4 Cent., 3 People's, 1 Bav. People's
16. "	Feb. 1, 1927–June 28, 1928	3 Cent., 1 Bav. People's, 2 People's, 4 Nationalist, 1 nonpartisan
17. Müller (S.P.D.)	June 28, 1928–Mar. 29, 1930	4 S.P.D., 2 Dem., 1 Cent., 1 Bav. People's, 2 People's, 1 nonpartisan
18. Brüning (Cent.)	Mar. 29, 1930–Oct. 7, 1931	4 Cent., 1 Bav. People's, 2 People's, 1 Dem., 1 Nationalist, 1 Wirtschaft, 1 nonpartisan
19. "	Oct. 9, 1931–May 30, 1932	2 Cent., 1 Bav. People's, 1 Staatspartei, 5 nonpartisan
20. Von Papen (nonpartisan)	May 31, 1932–Nov. 17, 1932	No party—"Barons"
21. Von Schleicher (nonpartisan)	Dec. 2, 1932–Jan. 28, 1933	No party—"Barons" and "experts"

for nothing is incorporated organically in society, in the higher wholeness of the nation. . . .

The Political Parties. *The German National Party* fought the Republic inside and outside the *Reichstag* to *kill*. Its clientele was the upper and middle bourgeoisie, the Junkers in the Army, administration, business, and agriculture, especially East Prussian. It was finally captured by the cruelest antisocialist, antidemocrat Dr. Hugenberg, a tycoon of many industries (including press and films), and he and his voters by the Nazis. Its top strength was in December 1924, with 20.5 percent of the voters when the nationalistic and militaristic currents were again flowing openly and potently and before Hitler captured its electorate. It was at the back of every violence and illegal attempt to get back to Bismarck.

The German People's Party contained the conservative, nationalistic remnants of the National Liberal Party (p. 602). Its clientele consisted of middle-class persons in business, commerce, manufacture, officials, and salaried technicians, and managers of the great industries, big industry, commerce and finance, and many Protestant clergy. It took part in every Cabinet coalition, the Grand Coalitions, to Brüning's in March 1930, led by Gustav Stresemann (p. 656). He fought it hard to carry his followers along the path of Treaty-fulfillment. It was nationalist only next to the German Nationalists. Its maximum strength was shown in June 1920, just under 14 percent of the votes. By 1924 and 1928 it was down to 8 percent, and declined. Its leaders were very influential among the generals, Ministries, and Cabinets.

The Center Party was largely its old self (p. 602), its basis being Catholic Christianity, with a heavy stronghold in Bavaria. It was democratic,

German Reichstag Elections: 1919, 1928, 1932, 1933

	January 1919	May 1928	November 1932	March 1933
Total number entitled to vote	36,767,000	41,225,000	44,374,000	44,686,000
Total number of valid votes cast	30,400,000	30,753,000	35,472,000	39,343,000
Percent of valid votes cast	82.7	74.6	79.9	88.0
Nationalistic parties:				
Nazis	—	810,000	11,737,000	17,277,000
Nationalists	3,121,000	4,381,000	2,959,000	3,137,000
People's Party	1,346,000	2,680,000	662,000	432,000
Several small parties combined	—	1,371,000	105,000	—
Total votes for nationalistic parties:	4,467,000	9,242,000	15,463,000	20,849,000
Percent of total number of valid votes cast	14.7	30.0	43.6	53.0
Percent of total number entitled to vote	12.1	22.4	34.9	46.6
Nonsocialist republican parties:				
Democrats	5,642,000	1,506,000	336,000	334,000
Center	5,980,000	3,712,000	4,231,000	4,425,000
Bavarian People's Party	—	946,000	1,095,000	1,074,000
Several small parties combined	275,000	2,472,000	259,000	498,000
Total votes for nonsocialist republican parties:	11,897,000	8,636,000	5,921,000	6,331,000
Percent of total number of valid votes cast	39.1	28.1	16.7	16.1
Percent of total number entitled to vote	32.4	21.0	13.3	14.2
Labor parties:				
Social Democrats	11,509,000	9,153,000	7,248,000	7,182,000
Independent Socialists	2,317,000	3,265,000	5,980,000	4,848,000
Communists	—	—	—	—
Total votes for labor parties:	13,826,000	12,418,000	13,228,000	12,030,000
Percent of total number of valid votes cast	45.5	40.4	37.3	30.6
Percent of total number entitled to vote	37.6	30.1	29.8	26.9
All other parties—10 to 20 parties, each receiving less than 100,000 votes:				
Total votes for all other parties:	210,000	457,000	860,000	136,000
Percent of total number of valid votes cast	0.7	1.5	2.4	0.3
Percent of total number entitled to vote	0.6	1.1	1.9	0.3

but only among most of its members, in spite of itself. It was strongly nationalist and militarist. Its policies otherwise were as before—that is, social-welfare measure but not socialism. Its clientele was extremely diverse: farmers in the Catholic regions of Germany, Catholic bourgeoisie, big businessmen among Catholics. It never approached a majority, and therefore its Christianity was never really tested. It participated in every coalition from 1918 to 1932, supplying four outstanding Prime Ministers. Its top strength, including the Bavarian Party, was in the Weimar Assembly, 18 percent; then it fell to a steady 15 percent. It best resisted erosion by the Nazis who hated it, referring to the clergy with loathing, as "black moles." It was a stabilizing influence. The party later voted in favor of Hitler's Enabling Act, which put the Weimar Constitution out of existence. Its Bavarian subsection was reactionary and separatist (p. 649).

The German Democratic Party was the offspring of the Progressives, a party of economic and philosophical liberalism and parliamentary democracy, a sincere parent of the Constitution. It was followed by business people, banking leaders, men of commerce, many Jews, officials, teachers, professional people, intermediate and small farmers, journalists, company executives. It faded away, leaving its followers among the more passionately positive parties, though it gathered no less than 18.6 percent of the voters in the elections for the Weimar Assembly.

The Social Democrats' Marxist spirit was diluted after the shedding of U.S.P.D. and the rise of the Communist Party; it was stoutly democratic socialist. It had sufficient strength to help produce the Constitution, to prevent the extremer cruelties of economic exploitation, and to maintain and even expand social security, social services, and educational opportunity, but *not* to transform a capitalist and class-privileged society. Its voting strength was 38 percent in 1919; through 1924 it sagged to 20 percent; it rose to nearly 30 percent in 1928, and even in 1930 it was 24.5 percent. The party was followed by a solid mass of skilled and semiskilled workers and employees, some democratic middle-class elements, even seceders from the Communist Party. It was soundly liberal, honest, and humane, a lover of international peace, though intent on the righting of the real wrongs done to Germany. It could not stop the building of the first "pocket battleship," which was begun as it took office again in 1928, since it seemed this would take work away from people already hurt by unemployment. The Right wing regarded the Social Democrats as the traitors of Versailles, the Communists, as the "lackeys of the Bourgeoisie" and "social Fascists" to be destroyed. The party was least to blame for lack of governmental resistance to the Nazis, because it held office only until 1919, and again in 1928-1930. It held office in Prussia almost continuously from 1919 to 1933. It also had a kind of militia, the *Reichsbanner,* but this was not brutal as the Nazi S.A. (p. 648) and Communist toughs were.

The Communist Party, the *Kommunistische Partei Deutschlands,* was founded in December 1918. It was moved by the Marxist principle of class war and Leninistic tactics of destruction of the democratic and capitalist bourgeois State by force. All its tactics were tactics of negation and division. It entered the *Reichstag* as a weapon of class war, exploiting every kind of grievance from the standpoint that the cause is capitalism, class exploitation, or imperialism—except in any action taken by the Soviet government. It constantly badgered the Socialists to form a united front with it.

Of course it refused to cooperate with any Government. Its strength was in the areas of heavy industrialization and mining. Starting with 2 percent of the voters in 1920, it steadily rose to 17 percent in 1932 (November) and still had 12.3 percent in 1933. It took away voters from the Social Democrats, and seduced young men and women from both the Social Democrats and potentially from the Nazis (!) as these developed. It continually fomented strikes; kept up its armed bands from 1918; was nourished and directed by Soviet Russia.

Chronic Civil War. The Right-wing groups meant to kill the Republic. One *coup* or murder after another was carried out.

(1) Dr. Wolfgang Kapp. In the spring of 1920, 60,000 men were ordered retired from the Army in accordance with the Versailles Treaty. Rancorous officers, of high rank, plotted with Kapp, a leading figure of the notoriously reactionary chauvinist Fatherland Party (p. 611) and General Ludendorff and the commander of the Berlin region's troops to overthrow the Government. The Nationalist and People's parties fomented the *coup.* The rebel General von Lüttwitz demanded of the Government complete subjection to his will! The Government sought the arrest of the conspirators, but they escaped and set in motion the plot. The Government left Berlin, called out all workers on strike. The police supported the insurrection; the government buildings were seized; Kapp declared himself Chancellor, Lüttwitz, Minister of War; a perfect Junker, von Jagow, the Berlin police chief, Minister of the Interior. General Von Seeckt, head of the *Truppen Amt* which was the General Staff under a pseudonym, and other high officers would not take office in the Government; but they had not fought the insurrection, von Seeckt preaching the doctrine of Army neutrality (to preserve the Army's ultimate leading position in the nation).

Kapp let loose all the Army forces in the Reich against the liberals. But the workers' stranglehold on economic life, the loyalty of most high civil servants, the refusal of the *Reichsbank* to deliver funds to him, and his incompetence brought about the abject defeat of the *Putsch* (German for *coup d'état*). The Communists did *not* oppose Kapp; they even opposed the Socialist Government, for

Moscow's subversive sake, until the Government was winning. The Army was split—the eastern commands for Kapp, the south and west for the Government, where the *Länder* were also for the Government. The fomenters of the *coup,* including the Right political parties, told Kapp and Luttwitz that it was all over. (Stresemann was ambiguously involved!). In four days all was over. Kapp died in prison, awaiting trial; Lüttwitz was retired; Ehrhardt, leader of the murder-syndicate troops lived on to become a notorious political murderer in Bavaria. Von Seeckt became chief of the Army command, the secret and sinister builder of the *Reichswehr.*

(2) *Communist Insurrection.* The Kapp *putsch* led to an abortive Communist *coup.* Carl Legien, the gifted leader of the trade unions, sought a union of Socialists, unions, U.S.P.D., and Communists to curb the officer class and Junkers once and for all by socialization, break-up of the Junker estates, liberalization of the Civil Service, and full democratization of the Army command and rank and file. The Extreme Left stood out on Marxist-Leninist grounds. The last great opportunity was missed. In March 1921 the Communists, encouraged by Russia, encouraged some unemployed workers to fight with weapons left over from the Kapp *putsch.* They failed. In 1923 Radek of the Comintern encouraged the Communists to take common action with the Nationalists against Socialists. The rising Nazis and the *Reichswehr* stopped this. But the agitation (intended to improve Russo-German understanding!) did cause great strikes (against the pleading of the trade unions), climaxed in August 1923 with a rising inspired by Moscow. In Hamburg the workers, honest men but Communist dupes, rose and were cut down, for no arms were available for them nor mass support and the Communist leadership knew it beforehand! What did they care for workers' lives?

(3) *Erzberger.* Matthias Erzberger (p. 603 and p. 611) was involved in a libel suit when he was Minister of Finance by Karl Helferrich, one of the economic gods of the conservatives. The judiciary, pre-Weimar vintage, judged that there was libel, but that some of the charges were true. He resigned. In August 1921 one of the officer murder-syndicates murdered him. One of his murderers, Ernst von Salomon, lived on, to bespatter the Western Powers, after World War II!, with sneers in his *Fragebogen* (New York, 1955).

(4) *Walter Rathenau.* In June 1922 Rathenau was murdered after violent nationalist incitements had inflamed the population, "Shoot down the Jewish Rathenau, the God-accursed Jewish sow." He had collaborated with the Center Chancellor in proposing that Germans would honor their Treaty obligations in paying reparations.

(5) *General Staff and* Reichswehr. The Army emerged from the defeat determined to seize an equal place at least with the constitutional Government. It began this by preserving the Officers' Corps as the Government's big brother against revolution from the Left (p. 612). By a series of political intrigues and a web of chicanery disloyal to the Republic, they cooperated with Hindenberg, the President, to let in the Right—but all they obtained was Hitler. This is analyzed later (p. 656ff.). But by the late 1920's many of the younger officers had been seduced by Nazi propaganda; for greatness offered them war and a career.

Hitler and the Destruction of the Weimar Republic

At long intervals of human history, it may occasionally happen that the practical politician and the political philosopher are one. The more intimate the union, the greater are his political difficulties for such a man does not labor to satisfy demands that are obvious to every philistine; he reaches forward toward ends that are comprehensible only to the few. Therefore his life is torn between hatred and love. The protest of the present generation, which does not understand him, wrestles with the recognition of posterity, for which he also works.

—*Hitler,* Mein Kampf

I. THE MAKING OF A MADMAN

Adolf Hitler

Hitler was born in April 1889, in Braunau-am-Inn, on the border of Upper Austria. His father was Alois Schickelgruber, the bastard of a peasant woman, the father taking the name Hitler late in life when the putative grandfather admitted paternity. Young Hitler had contempt for his father's lowly occupation as a minor customs official, because it was quiet and respectable, even as young Bismarck had despised a Prussian judgeship (p. 570)—it was all too tame! He excelled in history and geography, otherwise being an indolent student. This elementary history that Hitler learned consisted of the world and Germany as seen by a teacher who worshiped Bismarck, Treitschke, and Teutonic achievement. It compounded together all the farrago produced by Herder, Hegel, Fichte, Treitschke, and the Pan-German mass societies, and in this Hitler came to believe with lunatic fervor.

No Doubts on Values. Having in infancy imbibed the gospel of Germanism, Hitler soon ceased to think, doubt, and examine, if his own account is to be believed. He chose to read only those works that satisfied the values so sucked up. He says:

> When studying a book, a magazine, a pamphlet, those who master this art of reading will immediately pick out that which in their opinion is suitable for them—because it serves their purposes or is generally worth knowing—and therefore to be remembered forever. . . . When life suddenly presents some question to be examined or answered, then this manner of reading will immediately take the already existing picture as a standard. . . .

He goes on (in *Mein Kampf*) to explain that the mind must be formed in this way, or else a person engaged in public controversy will get confused. He was not concerned with *true* arguments but with avoiding being confounded. It was not a matter of one's private reputation but of a political leader's effectiveness. "From my youth I took pains to read in the right manner, and in this I was happily assisted by my memory and intellect."

Here Hitler is in the most characteristic current of the German mind in government, for it elevates the subjective over the objective element, personal waywardness over dispassionate reflection on competing facts. He averred his belief that "all creative ideas appear in youth, provided they are present at all."

> . . . the genius of youth whose inexhaustible fertility pours forth thoughts and ideas without being able to digest them because of their abundance (is in contrast to the greater thoroughness of old age's wisdom). Youth furnished the building material and the plans for the future; maturity takes and cuts the stones and constructs the building provided the so-called wisdom of old age has not suffocated the genius of youth.

Long before the age of twenty-four Hitler had formed "an image of the world," requiring little addition or change. It was "the granite foundation for my actions."

This is like the attitude of Georges Sorel and other insurgents of the nineteenth century against Western civilization; it is like Lenin's way (p. 756); it is the way of Marx, who conceived the *Communist Manifesto* long before it was published when he was thirty. "Philosophers may seek to understand the world, but we seek to change it!" They did not want knowledge and reflection to get in the path of their insurrectionary *élan,* even if knowledge was truth.

Megalomania and Hatred. Hitler picked up his intellectual equipment, as the servant of his will, in the Pan-German school of history, a home on the Bavarian-Austrian border that reminded him of the strength of Prussia and the need to bring back Austria into Germanity, and in Vienna, where he lived in a poor man's hostel, picking up a few cents here and there as a vendor of his own picture postcards and odd jobs. In Vienna he allowed full vent to anti-Semitism, because the Jews there were well off, because he read of Karl Marx, the Rhineland Jew, because the Jews of Poland and Galicia came into the city from their village and city ghettos of Russia and Poland, the Jews of the beards and vastly different features and habits from his blond friends while he was a flophouse crank.

In Vienna also was focused the bitter racial and national animosity of the conglomerate Empire:

Germans, Magyars, Czechs, Slavs. He was eaten up with rancor. He had fought his father to the death not to become a civil servant. He had artistic pretensions, but at the age of eighteen failed the entrance examination to the Vienna Academy of Fine Arts. He went home to his mother. She died when he was nearly twenty. He returned to Vienna and spent his embittered years, as we have noted. He worked as a casual laborer, idled in the cafés, reading all the newspapers, full of the controversies of the time and the journalistic presentation of his pet ideas—*idées fixes.* He blamed the rest of the world for his fecklessness and failure, especially the socialists and trade unionists; and he fused socialism with the Jews who were in its vanguard. He devoured the writings of the racialists, such as Gobineau and Houston Chamberlain, for they proved to him that he was infinitely superior, innately so, to the Jews and the socialists who were international conspirators to subvert the world. He was a degraded being, without status, class, or profession. He went to Munich—and even there he was feckless and further nourished his paranoia.

War, His Salvation. World War I was for Hitler, as for millions of Germans, a joyous opportunity to get rid of a neurosis, that of tedious existence.

> To me those hours came like a redemption from the mortifying experiences of my youth. Even to this day I am not ashamed to say that, in a transport of enthusiasm, I went down on my knees and thanked heaven from an overflowing heart. . . .

It was more than a confession; it was a program.

He gave up his Austrian nationality by joining the German army. He was in the trenches four years. He won an Iron Cross. He was not promoted to officer's rank, because his captain reported him as "hysterical." He became a corporal.

Like so many scores of thousands of other men in Germany (and in all countries), he could not go back to civilian existence: he had never had one. As Clausewitz (p. 548) had said: War is a continuance of politics by other means. Hitler decided to make politics his substitute for the war that was finished—and, in the end, to fight that war over again and win it. But he was inwardly resolved to do more. He transferred his artistic longings into a craving to remodel the world. In fact the medium in which he could work in Germany was less severe and exacting than canvas, paint, paper, and pencil.

He was chock-full of all the alibis for the defeat: Jews, socialists, a weak populace, the "stab-in-the-back," the "November criminals," traitors. He was swept up by the reaction in Bavaria, as he was stationed in Munich. He yelled with joy when Eisner was put down (p. 614) and the *Reichswehr* and Free Corps murdered the Communists, Socialists, and idealists. General Ludendorff, fresh from his failure in the war and his success in pinning the responsibility for its liquidation on the Social Democrats, was near by. *Reichswehr* intrigues mounted against Weimar. Whereas the Abbé Siéyès needed a sword and produced Napoleon (p. 301), the *Reichswehr* needed a spokesman, a fanatical tongue. They found Hitler and used him as "education" officer. All his rancor mounted into his screaming Pan-German voice. A large proportion of any audience responds to conversion to a higher life: it responds to the noble in it. When this is in the form of insistence on justice for one's own nation, which has just been defeated and subjected to harsh (even if just, and even generous) terms compared with the crime, then self-pity is added. Hitler had a compelling voice.

He joined a group of people, called the German Workers' Party, as a spy. It was headed by a locksmith named Anton Drexler, who mixed frenzied nationalism and militarism with ideas of socialist extremism—something like the anti-Semitic Stöcker's group in the 1890's (p. 603). Hitler came to spy and stayed to pray. For the group of forty had been part of the Pan-German Society (p. 606) and of the Fatherland Party. He joined the party as Member No. 7 of its inner "cell" in July 1919, a link with the *Reichswehr,* an enemy of the Republic. The socialistic element came to be represented by a group under Gregor Strasser.

The Nazi Party

Nazi is the abbreviation of the title of Hitler's party, whose formation we shall now follow. Its German name was *Nazional Sozialistische Deutsche Arbeiter Partei.*

Hitler despised Drexler's petty ideas and used the party organization for incendiary propaganda on a wide scale. He ascribed the victory of the Allies largely to their aptness at propaganda, a false conclusion. A program was elaborated with the help of Gottfried Feder, a civil engineer; the notorious forgery of slanders on the Jews called the *Protocols of the Elders of Zion* (also used by the Czarist police to stir up discontent-diverting pogroms, p. 761); the romanticism of a monarchist and Nordic-loving minor poet named Dietrich Eckart. They produced a twenty-five-point program; and Eckart, the Nazi slogan *Deutschland, Erwache!*—Germany, Awake!

Its chief points were: the union of all Germans in a Greater Germany (self-determination justified it!); equality of rights for Germany; annulment of the Treaty; return of Germany's colonies; for Jews and others not of German blood, loss of citizenship and participation in political life and the press; contempt for the parliamentary system, based on party considerations and not "moral character and abilities"; State duty to provide jobs; equal rights for all; the common welfare above individual; a ban on income not derived from labor, thus leading to abolition of "interest-slavery"; the confiscation of war profits and the nationalization of the trusts; a share in the profits of industry for the workers; the creation and preservation of a healthy middle class; the socialization of the department stores and their transfer on easy terms to small businessmen; State benevolence toward small business; State benevolence toward the peasantry, by expropriation without compensation of land, the abolition of mortgages, and of speculation in real estate; assistance to education, public health, and physical training; a national Army in place of the professional one. The party was "Christian" but not tied to any particular sect. A unitary regime must be established for Germany.

The N.S.D.A.P. In April 1920 the party's name was changed to the National Socialist German Worker's Party, or N.S.D.A.P. It had picked up the Swastika as an emblem—a Hindu fertility symbol—from a reactionary secret military society, the Thule Society, which published a vilifying newspaper, the *Münchener Beobachter,* later run by the obscene murderer, Julius Streicher, one of the high-level friends of Hitler.

The Embryo Führer.[1] Hitler soon sold the points about nationalizing the trusts and land reform for the funds necessary to capture Germany, when he could do as he liked. He had his insignificant, flat, and asymmetrical nose fixed into a firmness of profile. He and his friends, but he above all, went into the attack on the Republic and the Jews with an obscenity, an irresponsibility, a brutality that fascinated and captured vast audiences of Germans. He gave them what they had an appetite for.

He was helped by the Bavarian police; he rose to be master of the party; he cast out the original members who tried to hinder him; he built the Storm Troops, with their uniform of brown shirts. The S.A. started in November 21 by men of the Free Corps, put down opposition at meetings, broke up the meetings of other parties, intimidated decent citizens, fought the Communists, and gave the middle class the impression that the restoration of Germany by military means was in the making.

Hitler's Associates.[2] Among Hitler's associates was a Bavarian tough, Captain Ernst Roehm, the head of a group of Bavarian terrorist officers. Roehm built up stores of arms and brought in Free Corps men and kept contact with the *Reichswehr*. Another recruit at the top was Captain Hermann Wilhelm Goering, a career officer in the Prussian Army, a wartime aviator of distinction. He transferred his nerve-shot desire for thrills to politics. He was gross, obscene, cruel, a drug addict, a madman for uniforms. He could not tolerate postwar Germany, with its triumph of the workers, and went to Sweden as an exile. Picking up a fortune there by stealing someone else's wife, he returned to Germany and found Hitler greatly to his taste. He became organizer of the S.A., second to Hitler alone in the movement. From the Thule Society, via a business career and a lieutenancy gained during the war, came Rudolph Hess, to be Hitler's private secretary. A theorist was supplied in Alfred Rosenberg, born a German of middle-class merchants in Estonia. He was educated in Czarist Russia. He fled at the Bolshevik Revolution—to Munich, a ferocious hater of Jews and Bolsheviks. Rosenberg captured Hitler's imagination completely—on the theme of his work that appeared in 1930, *The Mythos of the Twentieth Century*. Hitler did *not* read the book, but he

[1] The title *Führer*, or leader, was that of the head of the new party, Hitler; he aspired to be and became *Führer* of the German nation, as Mussolini in Italy was then plotting to become *Duce*, or leader of Italy.

[2] Among those in the immediate entourage of Hitler who were outstanding rather as barbarians who descended on a pastoral people (like Vikings and outlaws on ancient and innocent settled peoples in the distant past) may be mentioned Goebbels, Goering, Bormann, Himmler, Ribbentrop, Hess.

Joseph Goebbels was born in 1897 in the Rhineland. He was the prize pupil in a Jesuit seminary; he received his Ph.D. from Heidelberg. He aspired to journalism. In 1922 he joined the Nazi Party as leader of its student movement. In 1926 he was made by Hitler party organizer of the Berlin sector. He started a newspaper, the *Angriff* (Assault), became head of the party propaganda machine. In 1933 he was made Minister of Enlightenment and Propaganda. He was a brilliant and corrupt genius in the art of propaganda; a wizened cripple. In April 1945 he and his wife committed suicide in Hitler's bunker, while their young children and dogs were put to death beforehand.

Hermann Goering, born 1893, in Rosenheim, Bavaria. Entered the regular Army; in World War I he was a renowned air ace. A profligate, a voluptuary, and dope addict, he left Germany after the war, hating the Republic. While in exile in Sweden, he stole his host's wife. He joined the Nazis and took part in the Munich Putsch, and then fled to Italy. On his return, he became the leading Nazi member of the *Reichstag*, second in influence only to Hitler. He acquired many offices, where brutality and administrative drive were needed, head of the *Luftwaffe*, of the Four Year Plan, a desperado of the ugliest character. He took honorific titles like "Master of the Hunt." He was in the close line of succession after Hitler; but as World War II went against Germany, especially when the *Luftwaffe* failed to destroy Britain, he lost favor, and in the last days of Hitler the latter ejected him from office and from the party and threatened to have him tried for treason to Hitler. He committed suicide in Nürnberg while awaiting execution by the Allies.

Joachim von Ribbentrop was born in 1893 in Wesel, Rhineland, of an Army officer's family. He had a very cosmopolitan education and many travels, serving as businessman, journalist, etc. He was in the Army in World War I, but not in the fighting line; he served in spying and diplomatic missions under men like von Papen. After 1919 he made money by financial speculation and corruption of customs officials to secure the import of French champagnes. He became a champagne salesman and married the daughter of the chief German firm in this line. He was a supporter of Stresemann and acted the English gentleman. He was a member of the *Herrenklub*. In 1928 he went over to the Nazis; in 1929 he met Hitler; in 1933 he brought about the meeting between Hitler and the *Herrenklub* at which the bankers relieved the Nazi's financial distress. Hitler made him his Foreign Minister, after a period as Ambassador to Britain. He exercised the most baleful influence

gathered that racial blood was the supreme good; that the Teutons were first as bearers of culture through their blood; that a pagan-Nordic religion ought to supersede Christian humility; that heroic deeds should be done to expel the Jews from the earth and raise Germany to the pinnacle of world empire by violence. Rosenberg was given a weekly newspaper to edit, the failing *Volkischer Beobachter*—a "guardian for the *Volk*" (p. 552).

The Abortive Coup of 1923. In 1923 three groups in Munich thought the time was ripe for seizing the government of Bavaria and by force severing it from the Reich. They were the Prime Minister's (Gustav von Kahr), Ludendorff's, and Hitler's. The first had forcibly taken over the government

supported by the archreactionaries, the Bavarian People's Party (p. 642), from the Social Democrats. The second had been brewing the overthrow of the Republic with Army officers out of work and some in active service. Hitler's movement had made formidable gains. Kahr and Hitler became enemies, because the former wanted his revolution, not the upstart Hitler's, but to placate Hitler he ordered the military formations of the Social Democratic Party suppressed and too anti-Semitic measures ended. Berlin sensed revolution. In October 1923 various *Reichswehr* units outside Bavaria had rebelled. The Reich Government took action under Article 48, on a state of emergency, giving the local *Reichswehr* general in Munich

over Hitler, having immediate access to his presence at any time. He was executed at Nürnberg.

Hans Frank, in World War II the bloody Governor of Poland, was born in 1900 in the Palatinate. He came of an impoverished lawyer's family, his father being disbarred for swindling. He knew poverty. He took an easy wartime high-school diploma, and was drafted as he did not volunteer. In April 1919 he joined the *Freikorps* and made friends with *Reichswehr* officers, meanwhile studying law and economics in Munich. He joined the earliest Nazi cell, the Thule Society; became acquainted with Hitler; was made a Storm Troop leader. After the Munich *coup* failure, he fled for some time; then returned to take his law degree and enter the Civil Service. In 1927 he became *Reichsleader* of the Legal Department of the Nazi Party.

Wilhelm Frick was born in 1877, his father a teacher, his forebears, farmers. He studied at nearby Kaiserslautern and then at Munich, to be a lawyer. He took his doctorate at Heidelberg in 1901. He rose in the ranks of police administration in Munich. Here he connived with the Nazis and arranged that force should not be used against them by the police. He was sentenced for treason, but released on parole. In May 1924 he became a member of the *Reichstag,* after which he devoted himself entirely to Nazi activities. He was the party's tough lawyer. In 1930 he became Minister of the Interior in the Thuringian government, and here in 1932 he enabled Hitler to become a naturalized German, through some legal trickery, Hitler having been refused this status elsewhere. In 1934 he was made Reich Minister of the Interior. Executed at Nürnberg.

Heinrich Himmler was born in Munich in 1900, his father being a school supervisor. He received a classical education in high school, not being very bright. He did a desk job during War World I. At loose ends at its close, he joined the Nazi Party while he was a factory worker, intent on learning scientific agriculture. His farming ventures were failures. In 1925 he became business manager of the Bavarian section of the party, and general administrative factotum. In 1929 he became leader of the S.S.; in 1934 he fought Roehm's S.A.; by 1933 he had 100,000 armed men (S.S.) at Hitler's disposal; thence he graduated to be head of the *Gestapo* and Security Police and a complete spy organization. He committed suicide as he was about to be arrested by Allied officers at Germany's collapse.

Martin Bormann was born 1900, at Halberstadt. His father was a postal official, formerly an army trumpet sergeant-major. Bormann joined the *Freikorps* in 1919. He was imprisoned in 1923 for his share in the *coup* of that year. Released in 1925, he became chief of staff to Rudolph Hess, the Deputy *Führer,* and a member of the *Reichstag.* After Hess's flight to Scotland in 1941, a gap occurred in his chief's position; and in October 1942 Bormann was made Deputy *Führer,* and had great influence with Hitler, especially in the conduct of the anti-Semitic measures. He died, it is thought, during the final onslaught on Berlin. Hitler had made him his executor; he was a jealous rival of both Goering and Himmler, and ordered the execution of Goering. He was known in comradely circles as "Hitler's Mephistopheles"; in command of the party machine, he never left the *Führer's* side lest others capture his ear. He wanted to escape Hitler's bunker, and govern after the latter's downfall.

Rudolf Hess was born in Egypt, 1896, of a German business family resident there. His mother came from Bavaria. There was a history of mental disturbance in his ancestors. At twelve he went to Germany for his secondary education. He left school for another in Switzerland to learn commerce; then joined a business house in Hamburg. In World War I he was a front-line fighter, twice wounded. Later he joined the air force. In 1918 he joined in the anti-Semitic, reactionary groups in Munich, taking part in street fights against Left-wing politicians. Then, he enrolled in Munich University, taking history and social sciences, and was overwhelmed with Haushofer's geopolitics. He joined the Nazis; sustained a head injury in street fighting; led a student Nazi battalion; served for months in prison as punishment for his part in the Munich *coup,* and there acted as Hitler's secretary to whom the *Führer* dictated *Mein Kampf.* He became personal adjutant and secretary to Hitler, remaining as such until 1933. He rose to be Deputy *Führer,* with a hand in every important decision in the party; he joined the Hitler Cabinet soon after the Roehm massacre. In May 1941 he stole a plane and flew to Scotland alone, convinced that he could get a peace concluded with Britain. His plane crashed; and he was kept a prisoner during the war, and later brought to trial at Nürnberg, where he continued to behave as a person of unsound mind. He was given life imprisonment.

appropriate powers. Kahr was defiant of the decrees. The *Reichswehr* general would not suppress
the Nazi newspaper when ordered to, even as
Kahr had refused. He was dismissed. Kahr appointed him to the Bavarian army! Free Corps
toughs were now assembled to liberate Germany
"from international Jewry and Bolshevism" and
to march with Kahr on Berlin—as Mussolini, just
a year before, had marched on Rome.

The Beer-hall Putsch. Meanwhile, the Communist
rising had been suppressed (p. 644), and "Bolshevik" excuses for Bavarian secession had been met.
There had even been negotiations between the
Chancellor, Stresemann, and Kahr, to restore the
Bismarckian status of Bavaria (p. 577). They
backtracked. Hitler became panicky that the bargain was at the expense of his movement. He
determined to force their hands. So he and his
Storm Troopers invaded a beer-cellar meeting at
which Kahr, the rebel general, and other notables
were speaking. He announced that the national
revolution had begun. Kahr and the others were
captured and threatened with murder by Hitler,
who threatened suicide unless they began a march
on Berlin. They refused. They were released after
Ludendorff had been brought in and they had
given a promise of cooperation. Immediately they
took action against Hitler, cooperating with General von Seeckt, in charge for the government in
Berlin, which declared the movement treason.
Von Seeckt meant business, for he needed the
reputation for defending public order as the basis
for his restoration of the strength and political
status of the Army.

On November 9, Hitler set out on his march
with Ludendorff, Goering, various adventurers
and assorted Nazis, and other elements. He was
true to his usually successful policy of going the
limit of his bluffs to cow his opponents. The
Reichswehr barred the way, for which Hitler never
forgave it, in the end getting his revenge by
humiliating and besmirching it (p. 680). In the
ensuing scuffle, sixteen Nazis were killed; Ludendorff marched on, narrowly escaping death. But
Hitler, a coward, ran away. He was arrested two
days later and brought to trial with Ludendorff,
the rebellious general.

Before the court Hitler did not plead innocent

but boasted of his guilt. The judges, members of
bourgeois officialdom and also Nationalists, let
him use the courtroom as a political platform for
the Nazi cause. He turned on the rebellious general who now repented his rebellion, seeing what
a megalomaniac Hitler was. Hitler declared: "I
aimed from the first at something a thousand
times higher than a Minister. I wanted to become
the destroyer of Marxism!"

> The man who is born to be a dictator is not
> compelled; he wills it. He is not driven forward,
> but drives himself. . . . The man who feels
> called upon to govern a people has no right to
> say: If you want me or summon me, I will co-
> operate. No, it is his duty to step forward.

His peroration concluded with the appeal to the
"divine judgment" from the judgment of the
court.

> *That* court will judge us, the Quartermaster of
> the old Army [Ludendorff] his officers and sol-
> diers, who, as Germans, wanted and desired
> only the good of their people and Fatherland;
> who wanted to fight and die. You pronounce us
> guilty a thousand times over; the goddess of the
> eternal court of history will smile and tear to
> tatters the brief of the state's attorney and the
> sentence of the court; for she acquits us.

He had always hated the bourgeois world and,
like Lenin (p. 754), wanted to tear it down,
regardless of what to put up in its place. But a
part of it, the *Reichswehr*, he would use as allies,
for *his* purposes, not theirs.

The court found Ludendorff not guilty. Hitler
was found guilty of high treason and was given
the minimum sentence of five years in prison. He
should have been deported, according to the law.
He spent only eight months and two weeks in
prison. This leniency may be compared with the
terrible sentences and punishment given the so-
called "Reds" in 1919. He was released so early
because the Bavarian Minister of Justice paroled
him—in spite of police reports that tumults would
begin again if he were released and not deported.
In prison Hitler and several other Nazis had the
time of their lives. They were well fed, were allowed great liberty, wore their own clothes, received visitors, and were deluged with gifts. Here

in the prison at Landsberg, Hitler had the leisure to dictate to Rudolph Hess and another intimate his book of policy and megalomanic self-praise: *Mein Kampf*.

While he was in prison, the Nazi movement languished and a part of it got into affiliation with a *Völkisch* movement in North Germany led by Count von Reventlow, a veteran Junker Conservative of the most reactionary type. They later severed connection. Hitler let the Nazi movement languish and tolerated the dissensions that arose between his several followers: for by dividing, he could rule, and why should they rise to success, when he was not present to make his personal fortune by it?

"Legality." He now learned, and avowed, that, given the present situation of the government and the loyalty of the *Reichswehr,* he must give up the *putsch*. He could allow the S.A.—the Brown shirts—to be built up, but he must pursue the path of legality. As he confessed in 1933, on the tenth anniversary of the beer-hall *putsch:*

> This evening and this day made it possible for us afterward to fight a battle for ten years by legal means; for, make no mistake, if we had acted then I should never have been able to found a revolutionary movement, and yet all the time maintain legality. One could have said to me with justice: You talk like all the others and you will act just as little as all the others.

He meant that *after* the *putsch* he could argue down his opponents in the party to the effect that to win power was impossible merely by a *coup;* and that to master a whole State, as he also said in 1936, "the new State must be built up and be practically ready to one's hand . . . the conditions must be created which would exclude the possibility of a second failure." When he tried again in 1933, "all that there remained to do was to destroy the last remnants of the old State—and that took but a few hours."

This "legality" was itself a cunning deception. It did not mean exercising decency and fairness in democratic political behavior. He used lies, duplicity, threats, blackmail, extortion, and fighting in the streets intended to kill or intimidate. Democratic legality assumes government not by violence but by persuasion; and even more, there

is a point where some kinds of "persuasion" are so brutal psychologically as to become inadmissible. The Nazis, with ill-concealed glee, overlept the point.

Ten Years of Building. For ten years the party built itself into a great nationwide movement. The *putsch* had given Hitler the status and glamor of Hero and Martyr. The Nationalists and People's parties were won over. The Army was courted at the big rallies and the younger officers suborned in private. For the time being the two incompatible tendencies in the party—Hitler's dictatorial German militaristic delusions of grandeur, and the antibourgeois socialistic-nationalist movements of the brothers Otto and Georg Strasser and the homosexualist Captain Roehm—did not break out into open fighting. Later (July 1934) Hitler had the leaders of the latter murdered.

A Lunatic

What kind of government did Hitler want? Once again, the fundamental problem of government arises: for what purpose? For what kind of human existence, mundane and beyond death?

Hitler was a lunatic, and he succeeded in winning over three quarters of the German people *in all strata of society,* but least so among the industrial workers. What is meant by a lunatic? There are many people in insane asylums sincerely convinced that they are Napoleon or Julius Caesar or others of those great men, those Heroes, as eulogized by Hegel (p. 555). They fanatically believe that they are born to reconstruct the world, that they know how to do it and why, that Providence or God sent them on this mission and will enable them to accomplish it, and that they alone have the genius to do it. They are ready to stop at nothing in ethics or brutality—Force—to achieve success.

This was precisely the state of mind of Hitler; all his speeches attested it; all his table conversation demonstrated it; all his acts of policy manifested it. He fell into the psychopathic class of schizophrenics known as extreme Narcissists—that is, self-worshipers, entertaining illusions of omnipotence. Every challenge to their passion of omnipotence is compensated for by hatred and an increase in the feeling. Some think wonderfully in symbols and do not regard this as distortion. Some believe that an outside force—God—is putting the ideas into their minds. They believe in the power of their spoken word. The world is full of grand meanings; those who entertain them speak in the language of prophecy—that is, certainty and a sense of ruin if, as we see in Jeremiah and Isaiah, the people do not obey the Prophet.

National Connivance. This is Hitler's case. But why did he succeed in putting the world into a madhouse instead of letting the world put *him* in one? Because his delusions were plausible and pleasing to some millions of people in Germany. Nazism responded to the profoundest wishes of the Germans. It touched the Junkers in their estates. It ensured the Army officers of their position. The industrialists sensed the economic monopoly of Europe. The middle class could be assured of its status as an educated *élite,* defense against Bolshevism, the slings and arrows of outrageous capitalism, the preservation of its culture. As we shall see (p. 654), middle-class "intellectuals" now had no roots anywhere else. The "little men" got jobs, houses, and fun.

Hitler had the infernal genius of taking advantage of other people's weaknesses—as he admitted, deliberately—and with scorn for Christian ethical scruples. He regarded lies, fraud, guile, torture, betrayal (not of himself by others!), blood lust, as proper means to his end and, instinctively, it may have been, his final ends. He believed in the power of his own will to outlast and overcome any other. He was willing (like Lenin, p. 757) to go his own path alone, to fulfill his intuitions without dilution. "Providence leads me with the sureness of a sleepwalker."

Hitler Understood the German People. Hitler's armory of gifts for dominating the German people included among its foremost, an uncanny understanding of their national psychology. Somehow, by native intuition, improved by close observation or by direct fellow feeling, he knew that they were, as Wheeler Bennett says, "the most inhibited people in Europe." The phrase chimes in with what we have said of the influence of the German Father—doing his duty of providing a livelihood for his family, protecting it, but also exacting complete, uncritical obedience, which was duly rendered. And it chimes in with what we have to say about the "social bracing" that tended to keep the internals of a German immature (p. 682). This new Father realized he could develop this arrogance of the Germans, which was their compensation for everlastingly paraded inferiority complex and a patching-over of their want of self-assurance and responsibility to themselves personally. They could be led along the path of iniquity by two main tactics. The first was to help them indulge in Pan-Germanic daydreams of world glory and conquest, for an undisclosed end; the second was to arouse vitriolic hate in all classes, hate against capitalism, against big estates, against life in the cities, against the Jews, against Versailles, against the Poles, the Slavs, the Russians, the Communists, bourgeois respectability, democracy, equality, the French, the Americans, international financiers, the whole world! The public, he discerned, was too ignorant and self-confident, to see the inconsistencies of the competing hatreds.

Ideological Delusions. What, then, was his delusion? That he had been sent into the world to save Western civilization from destruction by contemporary forces, being Bolshevism, the Jews, and cowardly Christianity. We have already traced the German origin of these notions (pp. 552–557, 607–608). Two other writers confirmed and fanaticized these maunderings: Schopenhauer and Spengler.

Schopenhauer (1788–1860) was a well-educated son of a wealthy Hamburg merchant. He suffered mental derangement as a youth, attempting suicide. He became, after studying philosophy in Fichet's time (p. 553), a morbid student of morbid cases in Berlin's hospitals. He was in pathological animosity against his mother, his own temper being insensate. It took until the age of fifty-six before his *World as Will and Idea* (written at thirty) was fully recognized. His notes on sex are regarded as unprintable. Hitler made great acknowledgments of his influence. His main gift to Hitler was the primacy of the Will in human behavior, not the Intellect or the Conscience, and it is Will at the level of animality. Man cannot rise outside his physical primitiveness, to virtue, truth, and compassion. The ego will not let him. Progress to nobility and magnanimity was, then, a delusion. The doctrine raised the question whether politics could be otherwise than "Nature red in tooth and claw." This was a nasty type of "realism." (Schopenhauer's way out was, for the individual, through art or ascetic renunciation). Schopenhauer charged Hegel with being a charlatan, since Hegel was so Idealist. But mix Hegel's Heroes of History (p. 555) with Schopenhauer's disgust with men, and Hitler's murderousness is visible.

Oswald Spengler (1880–1936) was a German high-school teacher of history, a deep thinker who believed it possible to evolve a complete and absolute theory of the human race's cycle of civilizations. His *Decline of the West* was published in 1914. Hermann Rauschning in his *Voice of Destruction* reports Hitler as actually quoting Spengler verbatim on his flight from Reason and Rationalism into subjective, creative cruelty. Spengler says:

> Man is a *beast of prey* . . . and the paragons of virtue and thinkers of social ethics who wish to be or rise above that are merely beasts of prey with their teeth drawn.

Hitler repeats:

> In my *Ordensburgen* a youth will grow up before which the world will shrink back. A violently active, dominating, intrepid, brutal youth —that is what I am after. Youth must be all these things. It must be indifferent to pain. There must be no weakness or tenderness in it. I want to see once more in its eyes the gleam of pride and independence of the beast as eradicated in thousands of years of domestication.

Spengler saw no Reason, no equity, *no final goal.* But Germany alone was able to lead Western Europe in its Faustian culture that had superseded that of Greece, Rome, and the Arabian. For Britain was decadent, while the Germans were young and Prussian—that is, were "socialistic," that is, anti-individualist—and had impetus. Prussia represented the principle of "all for all," with every individual being the servant of the whole, the State, the *Volk,* regardless of social position. This was challenged by Marxism, which was a reaction from the industrial slavery of Britain's industrial system. Prussia was built on command and obedience; Britain merely on rich and poor.

Geopolitik and the Destruction of Russia. As destiny had placed Germany on the borders of Asia—that is, Russia, a culture violently opposed to the West—Germany must master Russia, not for happiness' sake but for *"greatness."* Why would the Germans do this? Because Germans possessed the

> . . . unbounded necessity to serve, to follow, to venerate no matter who or what, faithful as a dog, blind in [their] belief despite all objections. . . . In no other country is a cause, a leader, a caricature of one even, so sure of unconditional following [as in Germany]. . . .

So "the eternal cosmic pulse" was bringing back Caesarism to remake civilization. It would use demagogy, not diplomacy, "an orchestra of brass instruments instead of the old chamber music," for the former was needed for the masses with their outbreaks of will. Praise be to the Lie as a tool, praise to the manipulation of mass "religiosity." Here, then, were Nietzsche's "blond beasts" (p. 608). A party was necessary, and with it a single person could nurture "this cosmic something." "The real international is imperialism," one race over all others by way of war.

The subject was carried further by Professor Karl Haushofer, head of the Geopolitical Institute at Munich, whence his ideas were carried to Hitler by one of his pupils, Rudolf Hess, his close companion and later Deputy Leader of the Nazi Party. The great civilization-redeeming empire would be a land empire, based on the Heartland, the Citadel of World Empire, of Central Europe and Asia. Hitherto empires had been sea empires, for the sea allowed of easy transport. Now, however, modern transport gave the primacy to the land empires, no longer challengeable from the sea. This meant that the Heartland would be held by Russia or Germany. Considering Russia's fertility of population it would be Russia.

Hitler decided it would be Germany—provided Christianity, the religion of cowards (p. 608), were wiped out. He would do what Genghis Khan had done, for all the Germans needed was a leader like himself, not a mealy-mouthed type like Kaiser Wilhelm II who consorted with Jews like Ballin, head of the Hamburg-Amerika Line. A complete revolution in German government would provide the dynamic power for German's *Lebensraum,* and Thousand-year Reich, like Charlemagne's.

The Russians would be pushed back beyond the Urals, the Ukraine colonized, and the Russians enslaved, especially if all Germans in Europe were gathered together into the Reich. Will could do anything; destroy all opposition; reach any goal. Will enabled minorities to rule majorities. The Russian people were low animals; the Russian government was Marxist. They must be annihilated. But Hitler admired the Communist Party, being monolithic; it was a wonderful model. He admired Stalin, "the crafty Caucasian," who was "a beast but a beast on a grand scale."

Since we, who read this book, are not insane, *we* do not surrender to the temptations of our daydreams, when we find the world very complicated with ideas and persons who oppose us we do not seek to end our "insecurity" by the annihilation of all opposition. Hitler did; he forsook the Golden Mean, and hence was insane.

II. THE CRISIS OF THE WEIMAR REGIME

Hitler could overthrow the Weimar Constitution, if he could find enough people to vote for him for *some* among the many reasons men vote; if he were not met with total opposition. If they were confused, weak willed, politically ignorant, overcome by economic cares, threatened in social status (like the middle class), he might pick up some associates, some for personal profit or ideology or grudges against persons and classes. Their vaguer ends might be like his: *Volk,* authority, military grandeur. Then he could win more. Others could be frightened by his uproar and his armed troopers. Then a fairly large mass of following would convince the millions of doubters. This is what happened.

The Classes Who Followed Hitler

Hitler now converted his theory of one-sided reading to one-sided pleading to the distracted, divided, confused people. As he explained to a French journalist in 1936:

> I will tell you what has carried me to the position I have reached. Our political problems appeared complicated. The German people could make nothing of them . . . they preferred to leave it to the professional politicians to get them out of this confused mess. I, on the contrary, simplified the problems and reduced them to the simplest terms. The masses realized this and followed me.

In other words, he did *not* tell them the truth, but preached an evangel. Who followed him to make up his great vote of 1932?

The Middle Class. This formed the backbone of Hitler's following. Specifically who were they? Small industrialists, retail and wholesale merchants, lower civil servants, white-collar employees; *less so* the teachers, clergy, higher civil servants, professional persons, the bigger men of industry and business.

Their Élite. Among these, some special groups became the *élite* of the Nazi movement. Some special groups of the middle classes became the leaders of the Nazi movement, its *élite*. The administrative group among this *élite* came to the extent of some 53 percent from the Civil Service, from the professions, and from business. *None came from among the workers.* Only 7 percent came from among farmers, which can include the Junkerish type. No less than 14 percent came from military careers. As for the Nazi propagandists, they came to the extent of 51 percent from those with the profession of "communications"; 16 percent were Nazi officials by career (administrators were in this group to the extent of almost the same percentage); and the next three categories were civil servants and the professions, each with 9 percent, and business with 8 percent. Again, no workers, and but 1 percent, farmers. Another class in the Nazi *élite* consisted of "coercers"—that is, "soldiers" and "police" in high positions. Here we have the data for the father's occupation. The Nazi *élite's* "soldier" components were from fathers who had as occupation: military, nearly 41 percent; landowners, nearly 7 percent; the professions, 25 percent; the civil service, 13.2 percent; business, 13.2 percent; and peasantry, 1.3 percent. The police had respectively: military, 19 percent; *no* landowners (the police were urban products, the soldiers considerably rural products); professions, nearly 24 percent; the civil service, over 33 percent; business, 19 percent; peasants, nearly 5 percent.

Their age (of these selected *élites*) in 1934 was 61 percent under forty for the propagandists; and nearly 48 percent under forty for the administrators; and the mean age of the military men was fifty-two and of the police forty-seven.

What, generally speaking, did this mean? It meant that the middle-income skill groups of modern Germany—the engineers, lawyers, managers, technicians, foremen, salaried employees, who regarded themselves as a social *élite* and were the kind of people to entertain German national arrogance and were also badly liable to unemployment or impoverishment in Germany's economic crises—could detach themselves from other parties and find a use for their services in a revolutionary movement of the authoritarian Nazi kind. It meant also that another group, sometimes called "alienated intellectuals"—teachers, journalists, artists—could find peculiar spiritual satisfaction, and certainly rewards in wealth and power, by attaching themselves to a movement, destined to revolution and the authoritarian rule, when the existing society failed to satisfy them. And German society did fail to satisfy these young men of this kind of career, because thousands upon thousands found no work or hope of it in the way they might have liked, in the conditions of unemployment and social disruption and uncertainty that prevailed in Germany in the 1920's, when so many of them had returned from the war to chaos and hopelessness. They chose the easy way. The chaos was partly made and sustained by the Nazi movement.

Big Business. Big Business joined toward the 1930's, when another Socialist-led Cabinet had just left office. It did not need Hitler in the middle 1920's, for it was making money fast and enjoying power. The businessmen did not like the movement's diatribes against hereditary class rule and social snobbery or prolabor demagoguery. But, the Hugenberg group and steel and coal barons joined him in the Young Plan referendum (p. 656), out of extreme nationalism. In October 1930 Hitler, these industrialists, and the Nationalists made an alliance called the Harzburg Front, openly to destroy the Republic. One of its members was Dr. Hjalmar Schacht, the banker (p. 640), who had been a founder of the Democratic Party. In the presidential election of 1932 some of the businessmen helped Hitler's candidature. Most, with Hugenberg, went with Hindenberg. In January 1932 Hitler had made an understanding with the *Industrie Klub* of the big businessmen, in which he sloughed off his radical associates, like Gregor Strasser (p. 647), and promised to leave business alone if he became Chancellor.

The businessmen threw in their lot with Hitler with reluctance; they thought they could use him to subvert the Republic and then get rid of him. It did not work.

The Peasants. Landowning peasants and middle-sized farmers were flattered by the "blood-and-soil" creed of the Nazi Party. The Socialist Party, being urban, did not help them in the depression of 1929. Free Corps leaders helped them resist the tax and loan collectors. The Nazis promised higher tariffs and so higher prices; reduced taxes; preservation of small farms against "speculators" in land. The Nazis infiltrated the *Reichslandbund*, the farmers' pressure group. The Bavarian peasant was pro-Nazi blindly. Most landless farm laborers followed Hitler; as well as the small and middle-sized farmers of East Germany. Less so the larger farmers.

The Workers. Would members of the working class follow the movement? There certainly was a tug in its nationalism and militarism. The workers were part of the German recipients of the *Völkish* and "socialist" doctrine in the nationalist lore, and they were obedient people. We have shown how their trade-union membership and zeal for the Republic dwindled with bad times. Fear of Russia and its type of Communism was used. Some Communists joined the Nazi Party, moved by nationalism and their own failure against the Republic. Some workers believed in the socialistic side of the Nazi twenty-five-point program, following Gregor Strasser. Skilled and semiskilled workers were afraid of the technological devices introduced by the trusts and cartels. Large bodies of the unemployed workers joined in the period 1929 onward. "Little man, what now?" they asked in the words of the then-famous novel. They voted for Hitler from despair and then gratitude. It has been estimated that about 15 percent of socialist voters joined Hitler.

Youth. It is a fact of vital importance that between 1924 and 1930 no less than 7,000,000 voters came on the electoral register for the first time on reaching voting age. Several millions more, between twenty-five and thirty, were immature, also, in the past politics of Germany. They knew only what the extremes screamed at them. Many wallowed in Nietzsche and Schopenhauer and such pessimistic-dissolvent poets as Stefan Geörg. They rejected bourgeois existence, morals, and religion. They wanted a leader to some romantic goal, especially the reassertion of Germany's greatness in face of the disgrace of military defeat. Some lapsed into Nihilism, the disgust with the nonexistence of perfect justice in the world. Their inclination to vague philosophizing and the sentimentalities of the youth romantic movements like the *Wandervogel* led them toward a miasma of ruin rather than rational leadership.

The Big Lie. Hitler's great stand-by with all groups, carried out at the monster rallies and in the Nazi press was *propaganda,* the avowed, longed-for key to political success, on which Hitler had long reflected. It is summed up in his doctrine of The Big Lie as it appears in *Mein Kampf:*

> The size of the lie is a definite factor in causing it to be believed, for the vast masses of a nation are in the depths of their hearts more easily deceived than they are consciously or intentionally bad. The primitive simplicity of their minds renders them an easier prey to a big lie than a small one, for they themselves often tell little ones but would be ashamed to tell big ones. Such a form of lies would never enter their head. They would never believe of others so important a possibility as the complete reversal of facts. Even explanations would for a long time leave them in doubt and hesitation, and any trifling reason would dispose them to accept a thing as true. Therefore something of the most impudent lies always remains and sticks, a fact which all bodies and individuals occupied with the art of lying in this world know only too well, and hence they stop at nothing to achieve this end.

This was a deliberate outrage on the "little man," who is respectable. It could flourish to the degree it did only in an immature political society.

The Brew from 1929 to March 1933

The country now teemed with quasi-military formations, crammed with violent young men: Communist Red-front Fighters; Socialist and Democratic *Reichsbanner* (Black-Red-Gold); Nationalist *Stahlhelm,* Hugenberg's veterans; the Nazi Storm Troopers (S.A.) and its Élite Guard, the S.S. or *Schutz-Staffel.*

From 1918 to 1922 political groups of the Right *killed* 354 opponents; the Left, 22. Murders occurred every year. In 1930, the murders rose to 20. These were only the acknowledged figures. Hundreds of woundings were inflicted. The pre-Weimar judges consistently favored the Right-wing toughs.

In the elections of May 1928 the Right suffered losses, whether Nationalists or Nazis. For the economy was good and international status was improving. A Cabinet of Socialists, Democrats, Center, Bavarian People's Party and one nonparty Minister took office, under Herman Müller, a Socialist. Even as it issued the slogan, "The foundations of the Republic stand firm and unshakable," it was in mortal danger. For Hugenberg's *Stahlhelm* issued a declaration of open war on Weimar. It, with Hitler, the Pan-German League, and Hugenberg Nationalists, joined in the referendum appeal against the Young reparations plan. It included a clause declaring the government would be punished for treason if they accepted the plan! Stresemann, of the People's Party, who had formulated the payments plan (immensely scaling down German obligations), defeated the referendum. The Rhineland had been evacuated as part of the reparations bargain. The Hitler-Hugenberg agitation obtained only less than 6,000,000 instead of the 21,000,000 votes needed. The more decent Nationalists, genuine conservatives, abandoned Hugenberg's party. Stresemann died in October 1929.

Then occurred the Great Economic Catastrophe (p. 659). The coalition split on the issue of reducing unemployment payments, all parties except the Socialists being in favor.

Brüning's Emergency Regime. Brüning, leader of the Center, began to govern by decrees under Article 48 (p. 621). He had graduated from Catholic trade-union administration and entered the *Reichstag* in 1924. He was an opponent of the murdered Erzberger (p. 644). He was no lover of the Republic; had, indeed, been a member of a promonarchist subversive group. Gravity and God were written all over his emaciated features and blue-white skin. He was Schleicher's nominee. Schleicher's general political views were Nationalist but anti-Hugenberg, Junkerish-Conservative— that is, rather Bismarckian. He wished to oust Socialists (remember Bismarck's antisocialist laws, p. 604) and the Republic. Hindenberg was very content with the nomination.

"Presidial Cabinets." Hindenberg, now senile, was persuaded to accept the theory of "presidial" cabinets, meaning cabinets having the confidence of the President but not necessarily of a positive vote of the *Reichstag*. Brüning's, Center and Right, had much fewer than one half the *Reichstag's* votes. He conceded to the Nationalists (for their entrance into it) financial subsidies to East Prussian landowners, called *Osthilfe*, actually asked for by Hindenberg and his son and adjutant, Oskar, since both had estates.

Brüning issued decrees for coping with the economic depression and unemployment: administrative economies, higher taxes, agricultural tariffs. The Socialists charged that the government and the Hindenberg-Schleicher *camarilla* were violating the Constitution with their nonresponsible cabinet and Article 48. But the answer was that a "threat to public order and security" under Article 48 meant political and economic conditions that might *eventually* produce such a threat. The vast majority of the *Reichstag* voted no confidence in the government.

The Nazi Wave. Though a middle-party majority was dominant in the *Reichstag*, Brüning dissolved it. In the new elections of September 1930 the Nazis reaped the harvest of all the troubles and cross-current of forces already narrated. It rose from 12 to 107 Deputies. The Center rose slightly. The Communists rose from 54 to 77. The Nationalists declined. The Socialists declined. The Nazi ranks included criminals, common lawbreakers, gangsters, and murderers. Henceforward the sessions of the *Reichstag* were little but continuous subriots. From January to the end of September

1931 political street fighting in Prussia alone cost 45 lives.

For the Socialists the alternative to Article 48 was Hitler. They even had to tolerate his decrees cutting the social services and official salaries, increasing taxation and tariffs on foodstuffs. He built armaments; he tried a customs union, and *Anschluss* with Austria, which was vetoed by the Allies and The Hague Court.

Hindenberg's Second Term. The economic decline could not be sufficiently palliated. But the Republic as formal basis still existed. In March 1932 Hindenberg's first term ended. Elections were due. His massive figure and square face, with jowls and hair *enbrosse,* had represented the dignity and monarchical Bismarckian tradition, indeed, the German Father (p. 559). He was the War Hero, even if he was no great military talent. In the election of 1925 the first ballot gave him 10,500,000 votes; a Socialist, 8,000,000; a Center candidate, 4,000,000; a Communist, 3,000,000, and General Ludendorff, 300,000. At the second ballot the Weimar groups combined on Wilhelm Marx, the Center candidate; the antirepublican parties on Hindenberg. All depended on the Communist votes. They deliberately threw their votes to their own candidate, thus putting Hindenberg in: the Communist got 1,900,000 votes; Hindenberg, 14,-660,000, Marx, 13,750,000. Stalin dug the grave of millions of Germans and many millions of his own people. He helped elect a destroyer of the Republic, who, even if unwittingly let in the invader of the Soviet Union, Hitler.

In March 1932 Brüning tried to continue Hindenberg's presidency by a vote of the *Reichstag* with the numbers required for a constitutional amendment. All refused. Foiled in the attempt to ward off Hitler's planned campaign, the election took place. The Weimar parties took shelter under Hindenberg's wing. The votes, in millions, were:

	First Ballot	Final Ballot
Hindenberg	18.7	19.36
Hitler	11.34	13.42
Thalmann	4.98	3.70
Nationalists	2.56	

Clearly, *some Communist votes had been split between Hindenberg and Hitler;* and the nationalists had gone over to Hindenberg. The campaign for Hindenberg was conducted with the utmost zeal and success by Brüning.

Exit Brüning. Within six weeks, Schleicher and the *Reichswehr* induced the doddering Hindenberg to dismiss Brüning by the slander that Brüning intended to decrease the subsidies to East Prussia. Their strategy was to come to terms with the Nazis, now the biggest nationalist and anti-Weimar force in Germany. They persuaded Hindenberg to call Brüning a Bolshevik for wishing to slightly increase wages; and to divide certain insolvent East Prussian estates to relieve unemployment.

The Cabinet of Barons. Schleicher and *Reichswehr* and *camarilla* now put forward Franz von Papen as Chancellor. He was a charming aristocrat, a rich Westphalian Catholic, a colonel in the Army, a man who had been expelled from the United States for plotting sabotage during World War I of American armaments. He belonged to the extreme Right wing of the Center Party (p. 613), a ferocious anti-Weimarist, a Prussian Diet Deputy from 1921 to April 1932, and a leading member of the *Herrenklub,* the Berlin club of the nobles and high officers.

The strategy was to hold off Hitler by a Junker Cabinet. All the top nationalist forces found him very acceptable; but he was not commended to the *Reichstag.* Hitler stayed out, pursuing hysterical denunciation of everything and everyone but promising toleration in exchange for *no ban* on his Storm Troopers and a promise of new elections soon. Schleicher hoped to tame or smash the Nazis.

The Cabinet of Barons included all the utterly reactionary *Herrenklub* notables; the militarists; men of Krupps and the dyes trust; Junkers. Schleicher was Minister of War, his first public political office.

Back to 1871. The Cabinet was disavowed by every force in the nation, except the minorities who composed it. Here were the Junker Hindenberg and von Papen trying to perpetuate the social domination that had led to 1871 and World War I.

An election was called for July 31, 1932, the *Reichstag* being dissolved with the Bismarckian excuse that it no longer reflected the national will.

Von Papen restated all the anti-Versailles and anti-republic animosities; detestation of "the charity State"; "cultural Bolshevism." He removed the ban from the Nazi Storm Troopers—were they not "sound" Germans? The Nazis cried out against cuts in unemployment pay and new taxes. In two weeks 100 were killed and 1200 injured in street political fights.

Rape of Prussia. At this same time von Papen overwhelmed Prussia. This state had become more liberal than the rest of Germany since 1919. Its two thirds of Germany's population had had socialist and liberal coalitions for more than thirteen almost-uninterrupted years, with Otto Braun as Prime Minister, moderate democratic socialist. The Minister of the Interior, Severing, was socialist, and head of the Prussian police, the largest force in Germany.

This was a prize for von Papen and his baronial strategists. He demanded, under the constitutional power to get Reich laws enforced everywhere (p. 619), that the Prussian *Landtag* elect a new minister-president to save the state from economic collapse. For the Otto Braun government was now a kind of caretaker, awaiting a new coalition, after the recent Prussian elections. This was hard to secure, for the *Landtag* had resolved that a minister-president needed an absolute majority of the *Landtag* for office, and with the multiplicity of parties this left too little time to negotiate. (The resolution was passed to prevent a Rightist *coup.*) Prussia and the other *Länder* protested against von Papen's interference and his threats to send in a Reich commissioner and cut off financial aid.

Von Papen then induced an "emergency" under Article 48. He let loose the Nazi and other squads by removing the ban on them. Then, signed by Hindenberg, the fundamental civil rights were suspended. A Reich commissioner was appointed by another decree. The grounds were that the government of Prussia could not dominate the Nazis! Otto Braun and Carl Severing were dismissed, the rest of the Cabinet suspended; Severing was physically ousted from his office; General von Runstedt appointed commissioner; the civil service was purged of "republican" officials; the judiciary was purged and intimidated.

The Center and Social Democrats appealed to

the Constitutional Court. This, full of conservative judges, refused to declare that von Papen's emergency decree was "lacking in urgency," though he refused the court precise charges against Prussia on the ground that state secrets would be divulged! An injunction was refused; final judgment was delayed until October 1932, by which time von Papen had full grip on the State, though the Reich had not a legal toe to stand on. But the Reich courts had always sustained any use of Article 48; this built up the authority of Hindenberg, its chief user; they held that the Executive must be allowed its way because Germany's experience of democratic government was so short.

The Left Fails. This was the final moment for the defensive revolution of the Left. It did not come from the Socialists. They were older and slower than the Nazis, and "legal." The *Reichstag* leaders were between fifty and seventy years of age; most of the Nazi *élite* were under forty. The trade unions did not repeat the general strike against Kapp (p. 643) of a decade earlier: Schleicher dissuaded them by blandishments. The Communists were interested in destroying the Republic; let the Nazis win; and then, *sancta simplicitas!,* smash the Nazis. Nor could the rest of the Left trust the Communists, who had so often deceived them.

Hitler's Victory

The Allies had almost wiped out reparations, conceding to von Papen what they had denied to Socialists and even Brüning. The Nazis still denounced them. The barons and officers promised egalitarian and welfare economics and the banning of the Nazi troopers, curbs on business property, and a radical revision of the Constitution. Hitler's propaganda machine held parades and monster meetings everywhere, promising the movement's Left-wing socialistic program. Widespread nationalization and inflation would come to the help of the poor, the middle class, and the 6,000,000 unemployed—mankind would not be crucified on a Cross of Gold!

Hitler won.[3] The Nazis held 230 seats out of 608; the Communists, 89. The Right-wing parties lost heavily, those which had thought to trap Hitler. But the Nazi vote was no greater than at the presidential election—was their vote saturated? The Socialists lost; the Center gained.

Hitler was invited into the Cabinet, for, as the barons had calculated, he had not nearly a majority. Von Papen stayed in office, though he had but a handful of supporters. Some of Hitler's followers urged acceptance, fearing a *coup* against them, and coveting the flesh pots after so many years of hard work and small reward. He refused anything but the chancellorship. Hindenberg sent him away from his interview, despising the nobody of a corporal. The *camarilla* offered him the vice chancellorship. He refused. They let him in again to convince the President. The old Junker resented being told that Hitler's position was like that of Mussolini after the March on Rome (October 1922);[4] he refused to allow into office a party so biased in its national policy; charged him with breaking his pre-election promises to support a Hindenberg-chosen Cabinet; told him (Hitler!) to behave like a gentleman. Von Papen published the interview, humiliating Hitler.

The government then proclaimed summary judgment of terrorists. Nazi bullies murdered a Communist worker, bestially. Hitler publicly

---

[3] Until he was made Chancellor of Germany in 1933, Hitler never held public office. He did not stand for election as a member of the *Reichstag,* though the Nazi Party and he made every election in which they participated an inflammatory national plebiscite for the *Führer.* This was all the more feasible as the Nazi Party appeared as one of the electoral lists required in P.R., and because all the candidates for it were chosen carefully by the party election organizers under Hitler and all were sworn to unconditional obedience to him. Indeed, until 1928, he was legally forbidden to speak in several of the German states, including Prussia. The first office he sought was the presidency, in the election of 1932, when he was beaten by Hindenberg.

Clearly, there is much wisdom in the British practice of single-member constituencies, where each aspirant to parliamentary life must fight his own individual battle before the public, even though he is a faithful member of the party; and wisdom also in the constitutional convention that a member of the Government (and Cabinet) must be a member of Parliament. This is the way to focus responsibility and force a man to reveal his character in a smallish forum in critical competition with several hundred able and popularly elected members of other and rival parties. The German system encouraged irresponsible ranting all over the nation. It is not irrelevant to remark that until February 22, 1932, Hitler was not a German citizen; then a conniving Nazi government in Thuringia gave him citizenship, and this qualified him as a candidate for the presidential election, p. 649, *fn.*

[4] For this, see H. Finer, *Mussolini's Italy,* New York, 1935.

aligned himself with the murderers and promised that those sentenced to death would not be executed. They gloated that Hindenberg was old enough to die soon. Some Left-wing Nazis joined the Communists; the Strasser wing (Rosenberg, Frick, and Feder) urged entry into the Cabinet. Goering and Goebbels supported Hitler in the policy of all—or all, one way or the other (*Entweder . . . oder . . .*) Von Papen determined again to dissolve the *Reichstag*. Goering, President of the *Reichstag,* tried to allow the tabling of a no-confidence motion, but von Papen tabled the decree of dissolution first. The no-confidence motion was passed 512 to 42 against von Papen.

Von Papen, owner of great mines in the Saar, persuaded his industrialist friends to stop paying money to Hitler. The Nazis were stricken by this tactic, for they could not otherwise support their thousands of full-time functionaries, especially in election after election, von Papen's strategy. Now Hitler claimed in the campaign that he was fighting reactionaries; that the plutocrats (who had been paying him) were vultures. As in the former campaign he spoke everywhere, moving to as many as three meetings a day by plane. Violence again broke out. The judges freed the Nazis and jailed the Communists. The middle class was outraged by the Nazi ultra-Bolshevism.

Nazi Recession and Triumph. The Nazis lost 2,000,000 voters; their percentage fell from 37.4 to 33.1. The Communists rose by 11 seats to 100; its votes to nearly 17 percent. The Nationalists improved. Was this a Nazi recession? They had risen so fast that its members thought it could fall just as swiftly. There was no money in the cash box. An insurrection was demanded. Luck came to their help. Schleicher grew jealous of von Papen. He was in touch with the Nazis and wanted a government including them. He maneuvered von Papen into a meeting of all parties to find who would support the latter. Only the Right would, and it was less than one sixth of the *Reichstag*. Von Papen resigned, feeling that he would certainly be recalled when the President had seen the other parties and failed. The fool even advised Hindenberg to see Hitler again; the latter would not give Hitler emergency powers, mis-

trusting him. Schleicher edged von Papen further out on the argument that his return would put them back again to more dissolutions. Hindenberg thrust the chancellorship on Schleicher. The latter could not get the support of the Center and the Socialists though he dropped the more unpopular of the barons. The Nazis were split on Schleicher's offer of some ministries, Schleicher playing for the Left-wing Nazis. The leader of the Left wing thereupon quarreled with Hitler and left the party. It seemed as though the party were about to split; also, it had lost some strength in *Länder* elections. However, on Hitler's threat to commit suicide, the party regained cohesion. This took the wind out of Schleicher's sails. But his Cabinet made some progress on the economic front.

All forces concentrated on Schleicher's downfall; the revengeful von Papen and the barons; the industrialists who returned to Hitler, wishing to secure the downfall of the welfare State which Schleicher still supported; the movement of Nazis into the Communist Party, ordered by Hitler if he were denied the chancellorship; the Junkers and the Agrarian League against the government's low tariff and food import policy. The lamentations of the latter were carried by Oskar Hindenberg to his father, the President.

Starved of funds, the Nazis were almost in dissolution. But von Papen induced Thyssen, the banker Schroeder, and others to save them by paying off the Nazis' debt of 12,000,000 marks. Hitler promised to enter the Cabinet without the chancellorship. The Nazis succeeded in improving their vote in the *Land* elections in Lippe. Schleicher tried to get a dissolution and new elections, as he declared, to get a more pliable *Reichstag* which would avoid the disclosure of certain East Prussian land-subsidy scandals in which Oskar Hindenberg was involved. Von Papen forestalled Schleicher, and the President called von Papen back after Schleicher had been refused his request. He resigned January 28, 1933.

Schleicher had recommended Hitler as his successor, not von Papen. The Center was ready to tolerate Hitler, if he behaved himself! Von Papen agreed to be Vice Chancellor. The conditions were that (1) the *Führer* (p. 664) (of the Nazis) must leave the presidential power inviolable; (2) Hitler was not to confer with the President without von Papen's presence; (3) the Nazis would take only three ministries. The Ministry of Economics went to Hugenberg, the bitter enemy of labor. The Ministry of War, at Hitler's insistence, went to General von Blomberg, a Nazi enthusiast. The leader of the *Stahlhelm* was made Minister of Labor. The *Führer* was appointed Chancellor on January 30, 1933; he took the oath to preserve the Constitution and to govern by legal means. That same night Hitler and Hindenberg took the salute together at the Chancellery in Berlin. A torchlight procession illuminated the scene. For everyone else, darkness fell, pitch-black: for Hitler was a genius of treachery. He had plausibly promised the obsequious millions jobs, houses, health, vacations, more children, hope, and victory over the former victors. He gave them all these—but not victory, or liberty, the former failure aroused their one regret, the latter they did not understand.

6

The Thousand-year Reich: Nazi Totalitarianism

If I had the Ural mountains with their incalculable store of treasures in raw materials, Siberia with its vast forests, and the Ukraine with its tremendous wheat-fields, Germany under National Socialist leadership would swim in plenty.

—*Hitler,* Nürnberg Rally, September 1936

If I were to come to the *Führer* and say "My *Führer,* I have to report that I have annihilated another 15,000 Poles," he would reply, "Magnificent, if it was necessary."

—*Hans Frank,* Hitler's Governor of Poland, *Diary*

I. SUBVERSION OF THE CONSTITUTION

Whose Guilt? It is always difficult even for a people who have won liberty by revolution to be quite confident that their democratic government will see them safely through war and economic distress. But the Germans had never won liberties for themselves. Against their concrete economic needs or class status or nationalist pride, weighing most heavily, what significance could self-government, a mere phantom, a puny infant, have?

Still, even in the elections of March 1933, over 45 percent of the voters (an 88-percent poll) voted for the Weimar parties. The trouble was that the democratic citizens were divided in policy, so confusing the electors; that the voters were never given the clear choice between Nazis and Weimar, but bewildered by the conservative parties and the Communists. The question that could not be easily answered was: Is this the moment to take a stand, even by force, against the Nazis? In 1939 Heinrich Himmler, chief of Hitler's police forces, history's most callous mass murderer, asserted that

the first country that had to be conquered if war came was Germany itself. Mass morality was subverted in small doses until it was too late to resist.

The Germans nourished a sense of international and domestic injustice, class against class. But no man, to rectify injustice, ought to choose a vicious leader. This, for a democracy, is as crucial a principle as the dictum that no man ought to be a judge in his own cause. The German people cannot be excused the iniquity of Hitler, even if they did not imagine to what lengths he was about to go as soon as he had dictatorial power. Yet they had heard murder being advocated and they saw it in the streets for years, perpetrated by Nazi toughs.

The persistence of will of the minority of Junkers and the economic magnates allied with that class linked the ages of Frederick the Great and Bismarck with the present to deliver over the German people and its own begotten *Offizierkorps* to Hitler. The persistence of the will of that original ruling group is amazing. It cropped out again in Hindenberg's mistrust of Hitler and again in

662

the attempt in July 1944 to assassinate Hitler. In all of them it took the short-run view of comfort and convenience, and ignored the cruelty in Hitler's nature that might be exercised *against* someone else! It offers a profound lesson in responsibility for government. There is remarkable political validity in the well-known question: "Am I my brother's keeper?" Yes, on pain of one's own death, moral and physical, if not at once, then ultimately.

Those who felt the need to assail Hitler had to face two problems. The first was what Ribbentrop, Hitler's foreign-affairs expert, called the "Führer's *ad infinitum*" decisions. He meant Hitler's determination to go to any extreme necessary to accomplish his purposes, always cold-bloodedly one step further than his opponent. This raised the second problem, the *ultima ratio regnum,* the final thing that rules, the shedding of blood. Hitler had no reverence for life; he had a clearly demonstrated blood-lust. A correspondent of Wheeler-Bennett put the point decisively in saying:

> The S.S. are armed; we aren't. No one is going to give us weapons either; and if anyone did, we wouldn't know how to use them. We aren't just killers. *We revere life.* That is our strength —and our weakness.

Hence, *ad infinitum* decisions always favored Hitler. Anything others would do, he could always do, more crushingly. The answer is Cromwell's; Robespierre's; George Washington's.

The Dictatorship Is Built

Whatever the Nazi program might have been in the past, dictatorship was inherent in it. Hitler's instincts now came out, and the dictatorship was built: the totalitarian police state, meaning the assumption by one man—the *Führer,* or Leader— of State authority over every aspect of human life, implemented by the ready use of force limited by no rule other than the will and purposes of the Leader, with the total annihilation of dissent or disobedience.

The March 1933 Election. First, the nation was forced into another election, the conditions of which were organized to give the Nazis the majority they needed to subvert the Weimar Con-

stitution formally. Propaganda chief Goebbels, educated as a Jesuit, a brilliant intellect, and an utterly unscrupulous personal adventurer, chief of all "alienated intellectuals," organized a plot to set the *Reichstag* on fire. This was accomplished on February 27, 1933, by S.A. men who entered through the *Reichstag* Speaker's (Goering) entrance. The fire, as arranged, was framed on the Communists. It served two purposes: to allow fear and hate propaganda for elections that Hitler wanted in March, and, second, to give a basis for the suspension of the constitutional guarantees. The success was enormous; a large part of the public were convinced that the fire was the signal for a Communist revolution.

The Decree for the Protection of People and State was issued under Article 48 the next day. Hindenberg was a party to it. It cut the heart out of opposition to the Nazis, for it suspended personal freedom, free expression of opinion, freedom of the press, association and meetings, secrecy of the mails, posts, telephone and telegraph, judicial control of search warrants and protection of property. This was the decisive act of dictatorship. The police and the S.A. were let loose on the opposition.

The election gave 17,280,000 votes to the Nazis, a rise of over 50 percent on their showing in 1932! It was almost 44 percent of the voters. They were flanked by their allies, the Nationalists, with 8 percent of the votes. Between them they had a majority of the *Reichstag:* 288 plus 52 in a house of 647. The Socialists polled 7,200,000; the Center 4,420,000; the Communists 4,850,000. Nearly 40,-000,000 people had voted—that is, over 88 percent of the electorate.

The Constitution Destroyed. Hitler proceeded swiftly. On March 24, 1933, the *Reichstag* met. It was asked to pass the Enabling Act for the Relief of the Distress of the Nation and the Reich. Let the propaganda note be observed! It involved the amendment of the Constitution:

> Reich laws can be enacted by the Reich Cabinet as well as according to the procedure in the Constitution. [This was made applicable also to financial legislation and the raising of loans.]
>
> The Reich laws enacted by the Reich Cabinet may deviate from the Constitution in so far as

they do not affect the position of the *Reichstag* and the *Reichsrat*. The powers of the President remain untouched.

Provision was made for immediate promulgation of these Cabinet laws; and the power of the *Reichstag* over treaties was annulled. Hitler's speech threatened the opposition with their lives.

A two-thirds majority was needed. It was as simple as ABC. The Communists with 81 seats and 26 of the Socialists were kept out of the *Reichstag* altogether—by exile, imprisonment, or certain threat of murder. The 94 Socialists present bravely voted against the bill. All depended on the Center —the party of Catholic Christians. *They voted to a man for the bill.* Their leader, Brüning, pretends that another leader, Monsignor Kaas, had been given a promise of a letter by Hitler to withdraw the suspension of the constitutional guarantees, if the party voted for the present act. Hindenberg pressed them to vote. The letter, continually promised, never came. The Center voted for Hitler, knowing well enough what kind of a scoundrel he was; none even abstained. He, and his cabinet, were masters of the Constitution; for they could ignore the legislative assemblies. The act was twice extended (January 1937 and 1939), and prolonged by decrees in 1943. The *Reichstag* was kept as a propaganda façade. The *Reichsrat* was later swept away (p. 671).

The rest was very simple. For Goering was now Commissioner for Prussia, in charge of the Prussian police, and Goebbels was in charge of propaganda, with the new medium of the radio at his complete command. Hitler could do anything he liked by *Regierungsgesetz,* by decrees.

Total Executive: Der Führer

The *Reichsrat* was abolished by decree in February 1934—that is, the palladium of the German historic states' particularism, so intent always on their sovereignty, was simply wiped out. No *Länderkonferenz* (p. 619) this time; no charity toward Bavaria, the incubator of Nazis and nurturer of Hitler himself.

Hindenburg died on August 1, 1934. Hitler had no use for a split Executive. By a decree the next day, he merged the chancellorship and the presidency, to become *Führer* and *Reichkanzler*—thus absorbing all the presidential powers. Hitler on this occasion used a plebiscite to ratify the change. Not that he needed it; but he wished the *Volk* to give its decision. Only 16 percent of the people voted NO or spoiled their ballot papers. In July 1935 the title was changed simply to *Der Führer,* on the ground that Chancellor sounded like a civil servant, whereas *Führer* indicated the "beloved" leader of his *Volk*.

Banning of Political Parties. On July 14, 1933, the *Law Prohibiting the Formation of New Political Parties* made the Nazi Party the only political party in Germany and enacted it a criminal offense to maintain or form any other party. On December 1, 1933, Party and State were legally united by the *Law to Safeguard the Unity of State and Party*. It was made a corporation in public law, with its constitution determined by the *Führer*. His party representative was to be a member of the Reich Cabinet. The party members and the S.A. and affiliated organizations were recognized as the "leading and moving power of the Nazi State" with special obligations to the leader, the people, and the State. The public authorities were commanded to assist the party members who had power to render justice and legal redress—for Hitler was now afraid of the lawlessness of his own toughs and their continual depredations on the public. The law was later amended to list the many units of the Party: S.A., S.S.; the Hitler Youth; the trade, teachers, lawyers, doctors, veterans, civil servants, and technicians unions—all were absorbed by force and hopelessness. The law of December 1934, gave penal protection against attacks on the State and Party—that is, criticism. Thus, the Executive swallowed up the Legislature, and the civil rights were swept away. All was at the mercy of Hitler.

Gleichschaltung, or Forceful Infiltration. The changeover from the Weimar institutions and economy to the Nazi was very swift. It was accomplished by what the Nazis called *Gleichschaltung,* or coordination. It meant that Nazis, loyal party members, were immediately included in the directing institutions of the government and the economy and cultural institutions. They displaced members of the civil service and judiciary; they pushed out the democratic governments of the states and the local authorities, who had been duly elected; they put their own commissars or watchers in the chambers of commerce and agriculture and on the factory councils and boards of directors of enterprises. Sooner or later, the laws were decreed to give formal validity and enhanced control.

The Purge of June 1934

The campaign for the *Reichstag* election of 1933 was undertaken by Hitler without any program: "The human purpose is decisive," he shouted, denouncing the last fourteen years of other governments and asking for four for himself. Hindenberg had acted on the belief that Hitler would be able to acquire a majority at the election. In this, Hitler failed. He was still not dictator; still on sufferance, even though Goering had command of any number of thugs (auxiliary police) in Prussia and was fast purging the Civil Service. The governments of the states had within a few months been overcome by *putsches* carried out by Nazis under central direction (the laws would come later). The trade-union offices had been smashed open by the S.A. and looted; the officials were beaten and put into concentration camps; their property sequestrated. The same thing happened to the Social Democratic Party's buildings, presses, newspapers, and property. The other parties (Nationalists also!) had been forced to dissolve. Hitler treated von Papen contemptuously, breaking his promise not to talk with Hindenberg except in von Papen's presence. Hugerberg, the Nationalist sponsor of Hitler, was ejected from the Cabinet. A former Chancellor (Hans Luther) was made to resign from the *Reichsbank*. These men had been caught by the animal they had sought to catch—"the beast of prey with the ferocious gleam in his eye."

Yet the dictatorship was not settled. The nation teemed with violence. The Secret State Police (the *Gestapo*, under Goering then) and Nazi toughs held up, beat up, and murdered in all directions, for personal as well as political reasons. The concentration camps of Oranienburg and Dachau were full and groaning. A dangerous ferment was at work inside the Nazi Party for more and better paying jobs, and new recruits to

it—careerists—made this the more vehement. Jobs was the ferocious quest.

Hitler Goes Rightward. Hitler was in difficulties. He needed a revolution under his *own* guidance, not a permanent insurrection. Like Lenin in 1920 (p. 774) he needed settled discipline in his State. Many of his Nazis took the anticapitalist antifinancier policy of 1925 seriously. They continued to attack the big men in the German economy, since they had to keep their middle-class following and (1) to secure a reduction in the unemployed and (2) to start armament production for their policy of *Weltmacht oder Untergang*.

Apart from his war plans, Hitler had not the slightest interest in the conduct of the economy; he was no genuine socialist; and he did not give a damn about administration. He was dictator to supply the will power, the cunning, and the high policy. But he intervened from the middle of 1933 to stem the attacks on the big men of the economy. He appointed one after another of them to the highest economic departments. He dissolved the middle-class economic pressure organizations. He damped down all talk of economic and political revolution. At the demand of Hindenberg, he even restrained the Nazi "German Christians" who were disrupting the Protestant Churches.

There was as yet no improvement in the economy; 6,000,000 were still unemployed; even at starvation wages no more employment had been organized.

Death of the Left Nazis. Two men were the foci of the continuing revolution that Hitler needed to congeal. One was Captain Ernest Roehm, chief of staff of the Storm Troopers, who had blazed the way of violence for Hitler, intimidating the timid and neutrals to vote Nazi lest they should suffer once Hitler was in power. The other was the sincere believer in the socialist as well as the national revolution promised by Hitler, Gregor Strasser (p. 647). Both denied the revolution was accomplished. To them, Hitler was just another associate on equal terms, and not the god he claimed to be. They continued, even more stridently, to attack the *Reaktion*—that is, the capitalists, the Junkers, the generals, the Conservatives, the high civil servants, the dignified and substantial bourgeoisie—everything that had class, for they were *declassés.* Goebbels, in the Ministry of Enlightenment (!) and Gauliter of Berlin was with them in this. Their followers wanted the fleshpots; jobs, official cars, expense accounts, women.

The issue was settled, as before, by a quarrel involving the *Reichswehr,* and this time the *Reichswehr* put the noose around its own neck and in Hitler's hands to pull. Roehm answered No! His Storm Troopers numbered 2,500,000 hungry men, now being heavily armed. He wanted his men in the uniforms and role of the *Reichswehr* including officers' commissions. The *Reichswehr* numbered only 200,000; its high officers contemptuously spurned being Nazified by gangsters. Hitler tried blandishments on Roehm, and brought him and Rudolf Hess into the Cabinet under the Law to Unify State and Party, as Chief and Deputy Chief of the S.A., *ex officio.* He was at his wit's end to get rid of the S.A.

The approaching death of Hindenberg brought matters to a head. The dotard wanted to restore the monarchy—a wish long shared by many of the top groups. Hitler naturally wanted himself to be President and Chancellor simultaneously, and no monarchy, for then the Army's oath of allegiance would be transferred personally to him. And *the personal oath was a factor of immense importance* to Germans, especially civil servants and even more so to the officers whose career was supposed to be built on honor. Therefore, in April 1934, Hitler made a bargain with the generals and the admirals. Roehm would be disposed of; the Army would be intact; Hitler would be *Führer.* Any army officer could at that time have strangled Hitler singlehandedly; but he served the generals' interests.

Goering, Roehm's friend, had been made a general and was now an enemy of Roehm. Himmler, chief of the S.S. was made head of the Gestapo as well. Hitler, making a profession of peacefulness, offered the Allies a reduction of the S.A.—perfect duplicity. A horrible docket of vice regarding Roehm and his associates was drawn up: financial trickery, homosexuality, embezzlement, moral corruption. In June, Hitler ordered the S.A. to take leave till August. Roehm was given sick leave. Hitler vacillated: Roehm was the only man with whom he was ever friendly enough to use *du.*

Von Papen forced the situation, supported by Catholic dignitaries. He denounced this Nazi Marxist Revolution; Nazi incitement of youth; Nazi personal careerism instead of traditional Prussian public service. A great scandal resulted. Hindenberg and General von Blomberg personally confronted Hitler with the choice: appeasement or a state of emergency decreed by the President with power transferred to the Army! Blomberg had Roehm expelled from the league of officers, and declared the Army's attachment to National Socialism, the President, and Hitler.

Murder as an Act of Government. Goering, Himmler, and Hitler now took the necessary evasive movement of efficient murders. Goebbels, till then, on Roehm's side, now ratted also. With Hitler in personal and hysterical command, Roehm and others were cut down, as they still were in bed. Everywhere—in Munich, Berlin— shootings and bludgeonings went on for over two days. Over 400 people were thus butchered, including many non-Nazis who needed to be put out of the way: General Schleicher and his wife; Gregor Strasser; Catholic leaders (Brüning had already fled); von Kahr of Munich (p. 649); von Papen just escaped, but not so his secretary. Innocent people were murdered through mistake, as the victims were checked off from greasy lists. The S.S. firing squads were chosen deliberately from among those of good family in order to besmirch the landed gentry and nobility in iniquity and future connivance.

Hitler explained to the *Reichstag* that he had not been able to allow the Army to be molested; that he had so promised the President; that there could be only one bearer of arms, the Army— "and there is only one bearer of the political will, and that is the National Socialist Party."

Germany was now doomed. Hitler's quintessential barbarism was evident and fortified. His scorn of judicial trial for the slaughtered was in ominous terms:

> In this hour I was responsible for the fate of the German people, and thereby I became the supreme lord of justice of the German people. . . . And everyone must know for all future time that if he raises his hand to strike the State, then certain death is his lot.

Hitler *was* the State. For the tamed S.A. was his; the Army became his as soon as Hindenberg died (p. 664), for General von Blomberg smoothly countersigned the accession to the Führership, along with Schacht, von Papen (!), the career diplomat von Neurath, and Schwerin von Krosigk, a financial expert among the Junkers. Himmler was rewarded with the monopoly of the S.S. and in 1936 made chief of all police forces, repressive and detective and security, and thereby acquired power to cow the generals also.

> I swear by God [they swore] this holy oath: I will render unconditional obedience to the *Führer* of the German Reich and People, Adolf Hitler, the Supreme Commander of the Armed Forces, and will be ready, as a brave soldier, to stake my life at any time for this oath.

For nationalism, for class privileges, for social standing, they sold themselves to a vicious dictator.

As Stalin, in 1931, said, when he had finished with the Old Bolsheviks by murder, "Life is better, life is happier," implying the nation was (p. 781). Three months after, at the annual mammoth party rally at Nürnberg (intending to rejoice the German heart and intimidate all others), Hitler said,

> Revolutions in Germany have always been rare. The Age of Nerves of the nineteenth century has found its close with us. In the next thousand years there will be no other revolution in Germany.

II. TALENTS OF THE DICTATOR

Hitler's attitude to mankind was roughly as follows.

(1) Hatred of Man

He despised the Germans. They did not deserve his genius; but, if it should happen that they could, then it would be because they obeyed him energetically and unconditionally. This alone would be their redemption. If they failed him in his adventures, then they deserved to be wiped out. He believed in social Darwinism, the survival of the human fittest, the Nietzschean coming of the Superman: Model? Himself. Thus, it was not democratically philanthropic, but misanthropic.

The common man, with his easy good nature, small lies, unheroic muddling, feeble Christianity, he hated. Once he was like them—in Nazi language, *Dreck*—when he was on Skid Row in Vienna, and they were *Dreck;* but now he was Chancellor while they remained *Dreck.* The Superman not only regards himself as a superman, but to him other men are not men but submen.

> The majority of people are simple and gullible. In every nation there is only one statesman once in a blue moon, not a hundred or more at any one time, and secondly the masses have an instinctive prejudice against every outstanding genius.

This man-hating nihilism was summed up in the Nazi slogans of hatred: Root out! Attack! Awake! Power! as incitements to assault; and Faith, Labor, Sacrifice, Fight as commands to German *subjects.* They aroused the hysteria of malice; and the frenzy of the supremacy of the Aryan "race" in all science, art, culture, inventions.

(2) Nonresponsible Government

We have already suggested the bestiality to which this must lead. It, of course, implies a system of government strictly nonresponsible and pervasive of every aspect of human thought and activity, the *Volk,* the tribe over the individual, "thinking with the blood" not the brain, a "flight from Reason," a hatred of culture.

> The State in its organization, beginning with the smallest cell of the community up to the highest leadership of the entire Reich, must be built on the principle of personality. . . . There must be no decisions by majority, but only by responsible persons . . . at every man's side there stand counselors, of course, but *one man decides . . . authority of every Leader towards those above.*

At the summit, then, the responsibility is to the leader's own conscience, to the man he sees in the mirror.

(3) Charisma

His own qualities as a leader are deducible from his writings, his speeches, and above all his actions. And his speeches were part of the latter.

He had the power of fascinating audiences by the force of his oratory and the conscious desire to do it, not for reasoning, but for conviction. He was prepared to reduce nations to serfdom to build something called a "New Order." He did not quail at wholesale extermination of peoples— no matter how extreme and obscene were the brutalities necessary thereto, particularly, the Jews, the Poles, and the Russians, regarded by him, openly, as subhuman.

This essential contempt for the human mind was accompanied by homicidal lusts. In his orders to the generals on the march into Poland in September 1939 Hitler said:

> Our strength is in our quickness and brutality. Ghengiz Khan had millions of women and children killed by his own will and with a gay heart. History sees only in him a great state builder. What weak western European civilization thinks about me does not matter. . . . I have sent to the east only my "Death's Head Units," with the order to kill without mercy all men, women and children of Polish race or language. Only in such a way will we win the living-space that we need. Who still talks nowadays of the extermination of the Armenians?

Propaganda Techniques. He could dramatize himself, suiting the approach he needed to the persons to be cuckolded, whether wheedling charm, ingenious lying, bursts of tears, or throwing fits of exhibitionist rage. He was helped by the piercing, riveting eyes.

He was a splendid tactician, especially in timing, except that the play of luck must be taken into account. Among the instruments were, as already suggested, elaborate care for impressiveness by propaganda, to provide a sense of the inevitability of his coming victory. So in the parades; so in the monster rallies with their marching, shouting, martial and sentimental music, torches, searchlights; so also in the exhibition of films to the statesmen of other nations in order that they should see what Nazi radical and surgical force had already done to those countries that had withstood the *Führer's* will. The noise of his propaganda diverted the people's attention from the atrocities of policy.

Hitler kept himself to himself and kept his own counsel, with the most astute measurement of his words. He stood over his associates, partly not to be involved in discussion and reasoning, and therefore the dilution of his will, but partly also to be able to undermine anyone, or use anyone of them singly, for his purposes, without their being able to form a cabal against him. He was the only one in his regime who knew the complete pattern of policy and its operational stages: all the rest were kept in the dark except for their special fragments. He liked to play his associates off against each other. He could *force* through situations that his despised experts hesitated over—up to a point in World War II, when his generals and his economic experts went finally unheard and the facts fell in on the superhuman *Führer*.

(4) Lust for Power and Praise

His lust for power was equaled only by Lenin's and Stalin's. Yet it did not subordinate itself to the interests of Germany, as theirs did to even a semblance of Marxian philosophy. It was allied with and partly a product of his personal hatred against the German world itself: the middle-class world, with its respectability and inclination to comfort. We are reminded of Nietzsche's contempt for the English Utilitarians (p. 35). Its other facet was a passion to be flattered. He acquired his associates to tell him constantly that he was a Hero in Hegelian poetry (p. 555); and his arrogance was so overweening that his advisers dared not bring him bad news. In the end, this was his downfall.

He speaks like Hegel and Nietzsche: conscience is, for him, "a Jewish invention, a blemish like circumcision" (p. 608).

(5) No Administrator

Hitler was neither an administrator nor an expert, and he despised both. His habits, arising out of his biological nature, which had caused him to hate his father's respectable humdrum service as a customs official or had developed in his years of loafing about trying to be an architect, were far from regular, businesslike, and punctual. This was his *Künstlernatur*—his artist's personality. He could not sleep—not because his conscience disturbed him. He kept very late hours. He drank no liquor, not even tea. He was a vegetarian. He suffered from dyspepsia, or stomach-ache. He was liable to colds and such sicknesses, and was mortally afraid of them. He was a health crank, and he feared death for all his brave talk. He patronized quacks who kept him going on injections of vitamins and so forth, unless they were merely injections of plain water. He preferred, by far, his few associates of the first fighting days of the movement (those who had not been killed off by him), like Goering and Goebbels, Bormann, Hess, Ley, his photographer, his publisher, his chauffeur, to the elegant diplomats and bankers who were needed to run the Nazi economy and foreign office.

He liked women but kept to two: a young niece who committed suicide (it is alleged) in 1931, and then Eva Braun, who was his mistress to the day of her death in the Berlin bunker; he married her before they committed suicide.

The most remarkable fact about Hitler is that his advisers, however well established socially or financially or professionally, were *afraid* of him.

III. THE NAZI SYSTEM OF GOVERNMENT

The Weimar Constitution was not formally overturned. The doctrine, put to the courts by Nazi attorneys, was that its articles stood, except where canceled by incompatible Nazi legislation and decrees. If action were undertaken by the government, as for example, in expropriating the Jehovah's Witnesses and depriving them of civil service jobs because they would not give the salute *Heil, Hitler!,* then the speeches of the *Führer* were invoked to show that the new spirit of Nazism overrode the Weimar articles.

The Führer's Authority

Hence, there was no constitution except the physical and psychological one of the *Führer,* summed up in the term *Führergewalt,* the authority of the *Führer* from whom all government stemmed. Of course, this meant that there were no popular controls, no separation of powers, no independent law courts. Hitler blended the three forces of *Volk:* (1) the people tribally considered, (2) the *Beweg-*

ung, the Nazi movement party, and (3) the State. He correspondingly operated through three chancelleries: that of the Reich, of the President, and of the NSDAP.

The Cabinet was called, typically, the *Reichsleitung,* the Reich-leadership. There was not a single limit to the powers of the State now vested in Hitler.

The *Führer* himself arranged for his succession; the people or *Reichstag* had nothing to do with changing what God had ordained, his accession. The Succession Act of August 1934 provided that he appoint a deputy leader. He did so when he started World War II. Hess and Goering were named; then in 1944 Goering, being out of favor with his master, was replaced by Martin Bormann, the deputy leader of the party. Admiral Doenitz took the place of both in Hitler's will before the *Führer* killed himself.

"The Cabinet." The members of the *Reichsleitung* recognized that they were Hitler's mere executive officers; and they, of course, emphasized this especially when, at the Nürnberg trials, they argued that they had no responsibility for preparing World War II or any of its horrors, such as the extermination of Polish men, women, and children. They denied that their duty to cosign Hitler's decrees implied their agreement with or cooperation in making the policy they embodied. The inability of Hitler to get a good grip on the administrative departments and his so-called "subleaders" resulted in a serious disintegration of policy fulfillment and much organized and destructive departmental jealousies. Soon there were no cabinet meetings, and coordination was left to Heinrich Lammers, the secretary of the Reich Chancellery, and the grouping of ministries through higher interdepartmental levels, such, for example, as under Goering for the Four Year Plan.

Some department or departments drafted the decrees, and, with the signature of the *Führer,* they acquired the force of law. This lawmaking power, first granted in the Enabling Act, was made unlimited by the *Reichstag* elected in November 1933. Then, the Nazi Party had been the only one permitted to take part in the election. It had resulted in 43,000,000 of 95.2 percent of the

Dictatorial Authority in the Third Reich: Hitler Downward

FÜHRER, STATE, AND NAZI PARTY

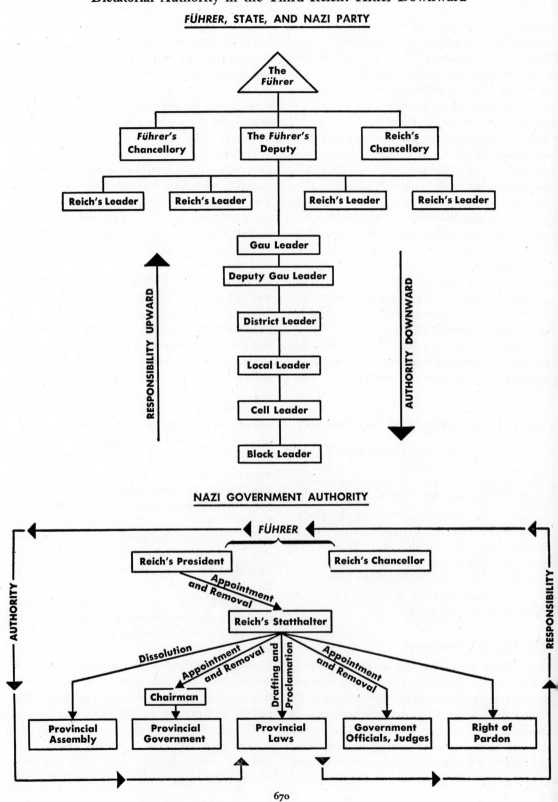

NAZI GOVERNMENT AUTHORITY

whole electorate voting Nazi, with 3,400,000 people still having the pluck to make their votes invalid.

The Reichstag. The philosophers of the Nazi State still had the gall or self-deception to call their dictatorship-by-blood-and-torture, a "democracy-led-by-the-*Volk*." There prevailed in Nazi Germany what had prevailed in Mussolini's Italy and existed in Stalin's Russia: a pathetic illusion among the leaders that if the people were forced to vote for them, then, somehow, this expressed popular approval. Also, of course, elections were used to whip up party energy and morale. Jews were excluded from the franchise, not being of pure German blood. There were *Reichstag* elections in 1933, 1934, 1936—and finally in April 1938. As the number of Deputies depended on the number of voters, and as these grew in number under Nazi pressure, the final *Reichstag* was composed of 813 Deputies. This was a valuable thing for the Deputies, for they received salaries. They were nothing more, of course, than a body for cheering the *Führer*. The candidates were chosen by the Nazi Party director of elections. The list was headed by Adolf Hitler. All the elector did was to mark it *Ja*, with the intimidating eyes of the S.A. on him.

Plebiscites. The Nazi Reich used plebiscites also—technically known as *Volksbefragung,* or appeals to the people—pretended to represent the "purity" of Nazi democracy. The device was authorized by a law of July 14, 1933. However, the device was characteristically perverted into a popular appeal only *after* the *Führer* had taken the measures he wanted: withdrawal from the League of Nations, the *Führer* Succession Act, and (April 1938) annexation of Austria.

There is no point in naming the sixteen Reich ministries which had been established to accomplish the fell purposes. Most were filled by Nazi bigwigs. In addition, there were Ministers without Portfolio, such as Rudolf Hess (p. 649), Frank, reformer of the courts and later brutal governor of Poland, Lammers, already mentioned, Meissner, the latter's counterpart in the Reich President's chancellery, Schacht, the wily banker, whose financial know-how was needed, and another oppressor, Seyss-Inquart, governor of the Netherlands. Most of these twenty-two men had no qualifications for government except party status.

Trevor-Roper,[1] using the Nürnberg documents, has shown that the *Reichsleitung* was not a cabinet, but a court of adulators of Hitler. They did not dare talk back to him. The system reposed on the dutiful, competent, steady activity of the thousands of Reich, state, and local civil servants, even though they were hurt by the expulsion of many able but non-Nazi members (p. 672). Goering was very capable, and even more ruthless; Speer, in charge of armaments production; and Frick, as Minister of the Interior, Schwerin-Krosigk (pure Junker, of generations of state service) as Minister of Finance, and Lammers were very able.

Extravagant Inefficiency

The administrative extravagance, the backstairs conflicts, the chaos in some branches, were supportable, so long as the budget and taxation were not submitted to a true representative assembly for criticism and authorization, and so long as the true standard of living of the people could be forced down by State-regimented labor at wages settled by the State's force. Moreover, such a system was sufferable for a short time, while national glory and then early successes in the conquest of Europe sounded sweet in the ears of the multitude.

Federalism Abolished. By successive acts, this was accomplished. The *Länder* were given a government like the Reich and the former Ministers were swept away by Nazis. Elections were abolished. In April 1933 a law set up State Governors (*Reichsstaathalter*) to be appointed by the *Führer;* they were his regents in the government of the *Länder*. In order to wipe out any vestiges of the age-old particularism, an act of January 30, 1934, transferred the powers of the states to the Reich. Henceforward, the *Länder* governments were nothing but deconcentrated agencies of the Reich, and the Reich a unitary State. The Reich Minister of the Interior governed the *Länder* governors. The *Länder* officials were officials of the Reich. The *Reichsrat,* last remnant of state separatism and their political substantiality, was abolished in Feb-

[1] H. Trevor-Roper, *The Last Days of Hitler*, London, 1949.

ruary 1934. In an act of January 1935 the annihilation of the states was carried to its conclusion: the governors were made the executants of the orders of the various Reich departments, reduced to intermediate administrative officers between the latter and the local government authorities. The *Länder* were territorially remodeled to allow of eleven regents. Later the *Führer* graced Austria with seven, and the Sudetenland with one. The jobs were paying and glamorous and went to deserving party veterans. As we shall see (p. 675) the regents often held the position of chief local party officer, called *Gauleiter,* and so combined a high decree of political power.

The *Länder* Diets disappeared; the laws of the Reich were applied everywhere; the old, indirect form of federal administration was replaced by that of officials who were Reich civil servants. The *Reichsleitung* could have abolished the regencies altogether, leaving nothing but the Reich Government in direct contact with the government of the rural units and the cities. It left the wasteful intermediary level in order not to provoke a resentful recrudescence of particularism.

Prussia was a *Land* like the rest; but of this state the *Führer* himself took the regency. He exercised it through Goering, as Minister-President. The Prussian departments were merged with those of the Reich. At last, Prussian identity had been subordinated to the Reich's; and this was further accomplished by a subdivision of the provinces and their criss-crossing by the Nazi Party's own territorial districting, the *Gaue.* As will be seen (p. 685), the results of World War II were to grind down Prussian statehood still further.

The Civil Service

The Nazis had two interests in the State and Reich Civil Services: they wanted jobs, and they were determined to have civil servants on whose loyalty they could completely rely. They were not lackadaisical, as the Weimar Republic was, about either; for their party creed overtopped all ethics.

As a matter of fact, the German Civil Service, especially the Prussian, lent itself more than any other Civil Service elsewhere in the world might have, to the faithful subservience to Hitler. From the time of the Great Elector (p. 541), competence

and total and intimidated obedience had been the two outstanding qualities cultivated in it. It hardly cared what master it served—it served.

Nazi Purges. When the Nazis entered power, only 4 percent of all civil servants were members of the party. The party leadership was split between those who wanted a complete purge with the jobs available in thousands for the *Altkämpfer,* the old fighters, and those, like Wilhelm Frick, Minister of the Interior, himself a career civil servant, who scorned this solution in the interests of "a State and administrative apparatus of a population of 68 million people organized down to the smallest detail with its unendingly numerous and multifarious tasks of government and economy."

The Civil Service Act of 1937 set up a new order for the Civil Service; before and after it, there were purges. Social Democratic officials were ejected if radical; placed under observation if moderate; the heads of the Prussian provinces and the higher officials were discharged, with pensions. Some were among those murdered in 1934.

In the higher—and that is, the decisive—levels of the Prussian service 28 percent (of 1663) were dismissed as "unreliable," Jewish, or the like (12.5 percent), or demoted to lower positions for "administrative reasons" (15.5 percent). In the middle levels, only 3.46 percent altogether were affected. All officials having to deal with "political action" or personnel, the presidents of the *Regierungen* and *Kreise* (see pp. 630–634), the police chiefs, and their aides were affected. The "well-acquired" rights of the civil servants were abolished by the law or in practice, and heads of departments were ordered to dismiss all civil servants they considered politically unreliable, so that, within four years of taking power some 80 percent of the highest administrative positions had been taken over by the Nazis.

A more drastic changeover was undertaken in the police forces, admitting to that service Nazis of vicious character.

Unconditional Obedience. The Civil Service Act produced changes in the status of officials, designed to make the Service abjectly pliant to the *Führer's* will. While enacting many conditions of service hitherto established only by the Administrative Courts, the Nazis repudiated the principle of official neutrality (p. 172). The civil servant was enjoined

> . . . to intercede unreservedly at all times for the National Socialist State, and to be guided in his whole conduct by the fact that the National Socialist Party in indissoluble union with the *Volk* is the bearer of the German idea of the State.

The official was commanded to be an active participator in the Nazi movement, an example of loyal fulfillment of duty. Work in the party was facilitated. Ministers exhorted officials to send their children into the Hitler Youth. The courts backed up this political participation by condemning civil servants in trouble because they had avoided political activities. They were pursued for critical remarks about the regime.

The civil servant's duties now required that he report any criticism of the regime. The category of "political" officials was, in theory and in practice, much extended. Their oath was not merely to a constitution and the laws but *to the man:* Hitler:

> I swear I will be true and obedient to the *Führer* of the German Reich and Volk, Adolf Hitler, respect the laws and fulfil my official duties conscientiously, so help me God.

Then the statute and those who implemented it tried the usual gambit of a totalitarian State: they wanted the officials to be unconditionally obedient, yet to be leaders, "to form human destiny"! This, when all their rights were subject to political punishment—to lose their security of tenure, titles, pension rights, protection against disadvantageous transfer, vacations.

The right of a civil servant to examine his official record was abolished. The Administrative Court explained that it violated the Nazi conception of civil servant and stated: "The leadership principle does not admit the questioning and criticism of the rulings of his superiors by the civil servant." This court, like the inferior instances, no longer served justice to officials with Weimar's independence.

Why the Civil Service Obeyed. It would have been possible for the Civil Service to cripple the Nazi State by resignation *en masse*. But this entailed, under German law, the loss of pension rights.

Furthermore, some higher officials who remained in the Service, did so, *they said,* because the younger people begged them to, in order to protect them from harsh treatment or to mitigate the full horrors of Nazi viciousness by intervention and counsel. The pension system under the Nazis was equally a material factor in inducing the continued service of those whose conscience was revolted. Of course, masses of the Service did not worry for whom they worked. There was also, always, the risk of death for open resignation; for spies were everywhere in office.

All officials were compelled to belong to the Nazi Party German Officials' Association. They were spied on outside the office; and *inside* the departments and local government system, the spy system was beautifully organized by the Secret Police and unofficial informers. Even the Ministers put their spies to track down each other. Moreover, official categories and the legal and regulatory allocation of authority and duties were grossly overridden by the party chiefs when the exigencies of production needed it.

The Nazi ideal view of a civil servant was expressed in April 1942 in an article in the law journal, *Akademie für deutsches Recht,* by the Ministry of the Interior's secretary of state:

> The German civil servant must furthermore be a National Socialist to the marrow of his bones and must be a member of the party or of one of its formations. The State will primarily see to it that the Young Guard of the movement is directed toward a civil service career and also that the civil servant takes an active part in the party so that the political idea and service of the State become closely welded.

In spite of all the pressure of the party on the administration and the judges, official and judicial inertia became very grave once the success of World War II had passed its crest.

The Judiciary

Something may be said here of the judges, since they were officials (p. 597). There was little reason to make serious changes in the judiciary, for it was composed of the most conservative and nationalist of public servants (p. 598). Yet the Nazi problem here was that the men had been trained to stick to the law! It was solved in part by the appointment of very many new subservient judges.

The subordinate, subservient role of the judge, so diametrically in contrast to that played by the courts in independent or quasi-independent control of the potentially arbitrary Executive and officials in free countries comes out clearly in some of the pronouncements of the Nazi leaders. The dominating conception is that set out by Nazi attorneys in the Jehovah's Witnesses Cases referred to already.

> National life needs a container in order to be able to use the forces active within it. . . . This foundation of national being is the constitution . . . the fundamental order in which a people forms itself in the State. . . . A constitution is not a number (or assemblage) of individual constitutional laws but an enclosed whole made up of all the principles of the Movement we possess a catechism of political world outlook which provides a criterion and principle in the decision of questions of constitutional law.

Judges were therefore expected to interpret the laws according to the "unambiguously expressed will of the *Führer.*" They were *ordered* by the Reich Minister of Justice, Thiereck, and the Party's Law Leader, Hans Frank, to give judgments on the basis that "law is that which serves the German nation." Their ground of judgment *must* be "How would the Leader decide in my place . . . is this decision compatible with the National Socialist conscience of the German *Volk?*"

In consequence, the judges were fully assimilated to civil servants as regards obedience to orders from above. They were dischargeable for political unreliability. They were despoiled of their traditional freedom to make their own rules of procedure and rotate the membership as they felt right for the conduct of cases. All lawyers had to belong to the Nazi association of lawyers, with its political tests, as a condition of being allowed to practice. No judge or state attorney could be appointed except with Nazi Party consent. They were continually bullied and bombarded with circulars from the Minister of Justice—"thereby to give the judge the inner security and freedom to come to the right decision." The effrontery of the phrase takes away one's breath: a Hitler tactic!

Obliteration of Local Self-government

The Nazi regime overlaid the traditional system of local government by the Municipal Code of 1935. It intertwined the high technical competence of the municipal officials with the "leadership" principle of Nazism. The preamble said the Code was

> . . . intended to call forth the highest possible service of the communes in close cooperation with the party and the government, enabling them in the true spirit of the creator of municipal self-administration, Baron vom Stein, to contribute to the fulfillment of the national ideal: to have a united people permeated with a national spirit, where common interests are put above private interests, and to create a real people's community guided by the best men of the people, giving even the lowliest fellow-citizen interested a feeling of solidarity.

This code subjected all municipalities to supervision by the *Reich* Ministry of the Interior. Their budgets required advance approval by the Ministry of Finance. The Ministry of the Interior appointed the mayors and councilors of cities with a population over 100,000, while in smaller cities appointments were made by the Reich *Land*-governors or other Reich officials. The burgermaster was chosen by the Ministry of the Interior from among three candidates proposed by the local Nazi Party delegate. Thus appointed, the burgermaster was given exclusive and full responsibility to govern the municipality. The councilors became merely advisers chosen by the Nazi Party delegate, himself appointed by the *Führer's* deputy, the local Nazi leader. "Political reliability," capability, and character were the criteria of selection—on paper. The burgermaster was to consult the council but could act as he wished. Why, then, the councilors? To obtain from the population "a sympathetic understanding for the measures taken by the mayor." Indeed, the code *required* the councilors to express disagreeable criticism (an example of so-called "self-criticism" raised to a system in most dictatorial regimes that frightens people to death, p. 887). It was observed by German experts that the councilors failed the system; they had no will or stomach for it.

Of the 51,000 German *Gemeinden,* the burgermasters or other chief executives were replaced by 50,000 Nazi Party members soon after the party's rape of authority. Of course, many of the 50,000 were officials who had now joined the party for the sake of continuing their jobs.

The Nazi Party

The Nazi Party was made the "bearer of the State concept." It consisted of member groups and affiliated associations. The former embraced the Storm Troopers, the S.S. or Élite Guards, the Hitler Youth, and the organizations of students, women, motor and flying corps. The latter included the unions of officials, lawyers, technicians, teachers, professors, physicians, and the German Labor Front, the Nazi simulacrum of trade unions.

At the height of its success, the party had managed to muster no less than 9,000,000 dues-paying members. Like the Communist Party of the Soviet Union, on which it was to a great extent consciously and admiringly modeled, its top management provided for a party parallel to the organs of Reich government. Hitler was at the top of both, but the deputy leader was the *Führer's* top counterpart in the party. The party had a cabinet and meticulously organized departments paralleling the various activities of the State, to make sure that the policy of the party became the commands of the State. These proliferated with paid officials.

The party's territorial organization overlaid the administrative units of the government for more effective control of *Länder,* cities, and villages. Below the top clique of party officials were the leaders of the districts—*Gauleiter. Gau* was an ancient German word for tribal area, especially military. Goebbels was *Gauleiter* of Berlin, a choice appointment. Below these were other subareas, *Kreise,* "places," *Ortsgruppe,* and in the cities, the capillary organization, what the Communists call the "primary cell," the Blocks, with their wardens (*Blockwarden*), the spies, blackmailers, and informers that kept Germans trembling and servile.

Like the Communist parties, the Nazi Party claimed to be the vanguard of the nation, its teacher of national consciousness and duty. It gave a *Volkisch* outlook and orientation on world affairs, really on the meaning of existence. This

was a most important part of its work, done through innumerable publications, through the party's Chamber of Culture and the Reich Propaganda Ministry. For the masses, ill educated and confused, the party demonstrated how each little thing that happened to man's person or mind was related to and significant only by the outlook of the party. It was producing a new religion. The party selected cadres, leaders. It infiltrated all offices, and the appropriate level party functionary endorsed appointees to governmental office to make sure of party loyalty.

Education for Leadership. Germany had been one of the earliest countries to organize youth into political groups affiliated with the political parties, long before the Nazis were born. The Nazi movement had its Hitler Youth. In 1936 this was given status as one of the member-groups. It mobilized children from the age of six to the age of eighteen: *Jungvolk, Jungmadchen, Hitlerjugend,* and *Deutsche Mädchen.* All children were obliged to join and be indoctrinated in the deification of Hitler, to take part in the camping and marching and drilling, and to be saturated with the poison of the racial and nationalistic doctrines of the Nazi philosophers.

Hitler had established a number of Adolf Hitler Schools, National Political Institutes of Education and *Ordensbergen,* Order Castles, to train young people for political leadership. The lower levels of the schools were opened to boys of age twelve for a six-year course, the recruits being chosen by the party from the Hitler Youth. The schools admitted some 300 youngsters a year. Their teachers were top Nazis; their studies: race biology, history, and current affairs. The political institutes were substitutes for the Prussian cadet schools, and were used to train Storm Troopers, the Élite Guard, and leaders of the compulsory labor service. The Order Castles go back to the Order of Teutonic Knights (p. 539), then the subjugators of the Slavs, now the subjugators of Germans who did not believe as Hitler and Himmler believed! One out of four of the graduates of the political institutes were received by them. Here they were even more physically tuned up than at the younger levels; athletics, parachute jumping, arms, political education, racial biology, international politics (of

Eastern Europe, especially) were to be drummed in in a six-year course. How ridiculous, even on Hitler's own presupposition, that *leaders* could be thus developed! It is obvious that only murderous executants could be produced by this method and in this regime. It is in a free democracy that leaders are produced, even as Hitler himself was allowed his ascent in a democracy.

Criminal Courts and Concentration Camps. The special criminal courts must be put in the setting of the party. The *Volksgerichtshof* or People's Court was given permanent status in 1936, after already functioning since 1934. It was charged with "counterrevolutionary activities," the definition of which was exceedingly elastic (see Communist practice, p. 842). Of its five judges, only two were trained in the law; the other three were S.S. personnel. The usual guarantees of procedure, counsel, etc. were not available. The proceedings were secret, the punishments cruel. The Nazis, to exhibit their will power, reintroduced executions by the axe. Concentration camps housed numerous victims, with brutal treatment. Arrests occurred on the slightest pretexts and in circumstances of utmost cruelty. "Preventive custody" was legalized —that is, commitments to concentration camps— on a hundred different excuses, summed up in the phrase "healthy sentiment of the *Volk.*" The "little men" shut their eyes to wickedness.

Gestapo, etc. The police was organized as the strong pillar of the Nazi State. Head and center of the repressive forces was the *Gestapo* (*Geheime Staatspolizei*) or Secret State (or political) Police. This was established in April 1933 as a Prussian government force by and under Goering. Then a year later all the Reich police forces were amalgamated under Heinrich Himmler. In February 1936 the Gestapo was put under Himmler, with his title of *Reichsleiter*, Reich Director. It was now vested with authority to order all other State agencies to obey its commands and to extract information from them and was made immune from any sort of administrative or judicial control.

Alongside the Gestapo were the S.D. or Security Service, another police service, counteroperating opposition and crime. With the Gestapo, the Reich was provided with a highly skilled body of police administrators, most of them young people of

great talent, now given a remarkable employment opportunity for their detective and repressive abilities. They were highly trained. The "little men" had *always* been registered by the police.

The law of February 1936 vested vast powers in the Gestapo. It was to "uncover and fight all tendencies and occurrences dangerous to the State, and for this purpose to undertake all measures considered necessary and expedient." In pursuit of this assignment, a network of agencies and men was developed, finally pervading every element of the Nazi State: the party organization, the common people in their families and at work, the Government, the Army. It had a stranglehold on the party, and thereby on the whole nation. In the last two years of World War II Himmler, its chief, a rival and then the superseder of the Reich's wartime spy service, grew to such power that his associates were persuading him (and he was almost ready) to challenge Hitler himself for the vicious Fuhrership of the failing Reich.

The S.S. Alongside, but not organically a part of, the Gestapo was the S.S. or Nazi Élite Guard, the black-uniformed and armed, Storm Troopers, of the highest rank and most careful selection by physical and Nazi "moral" standards. All the top officers of the Gestapo were *ex officio* officers of the S.S. This, however, was the militia of the Nazi movement. *It was Hitler's counterforce to the Reichswehr.* The S.S. were instructed to regard themselves as the quintessential embodiment of Nazism, the superman of Hitler's lunatic imagination. They were to be the breeders of the *élite* of the Thousand-year Reich. Their own press carried the doctrines of the "blond beast" and Alfred Rosenberg (p. 648) to fantastic extremes. Meanwhile, to give them experience, they surrounded the *Führer,* as his final bodyguard and honor guard and guard to the high party leaders at their ceremonials. The S.S. were used by the Gestapo to be their bloody hands in the work of repression.

Modern Terror. Between the Gestapo and the S.S. and their associated connivers, the application of terror was conducted with all the ingenuity which hitherto had been given by Germans to scientific and cartelized industry, to techniques of public administration. Their purpose was the destruction of the human spirit, accomplished through torture. They had machines, drugs, and always utter callous, bestial, and even inquisitionist cruelty at their disposal. Their professional pride lay in the extraction of confessions; their monument was erected in their concentration camps. At first the concentration camps housed Germans—Jews, Social Democrats, trade unionists, Communists, non-party critics, Catholics whose principles made them anathema to Hitler. Then the "submen," the *Untermenschen,* were herded in as the Reich went to war and disarmed its opponents. The concentration camps became human stockyards for Russians, Poles, Baltic peoples, and again Jews.

We can still see the piles of emaciated bodies, worn down by work, until they fell, beaten and flogged, the once-men, the once-women, the once-children, heaped up like mere firewood or offal. The judges of the Hitler regime at Nürnberg calculated that from 1933 to 1945 close to 8,000,000 had entered the fifty concentration camps, and of these less than 600,000 lived to tell the tale.

Of this most vile crime, two things must be known by the student of government. First, it was the consequence of the insane philosophy of the Superman and his terrestrial trustee and representative, the Nordic and Teutonic people, indeed, of the German *Volk.* This *hubris,* this arrogance, this vulgar narcissism, inspired adult men, strong, chosen for their physique, to walk over to children three years of age and men and women in their declining years and beat or shoot them to death. Second, until 1939 in Western Europe, and in December 1941, in the United States, all dedicated to Christianity and Humanity, no finger was lifted to remove this curse, though its foulness was well known. The principle was "Hear no evil, see no evil, speak no evil" until Hitler made war on these nations. The millions of German people, citizens, who survived the regime and the war, still pretend they knew nothing about the subhuman wickedness that was perpetrated, but it has been fully proven that they knew or guessed. The other nations forgot that morality and immorality do not stop at frontiers; the German people were willfully thick-skinned. But . . . was it not genius that the gas chambers were administered without any *written* orders?

The Ingenious Government of the Jews

The Jews offered the Nazis the pleasure of lingering torment-infliction and a kind of sexual lust. The Germans had always been anti-Semitic (p. 532 and p. 603). In the Weimar system the Jews had been allowed political and economic equality. Though the objects of prejudice, they were, in peace and in war, good citizens, amply nationalistic.

The Nazi movement propagandized Hitler's antipathy to the Jews into a mass blood-sport. On his advent to office, the cunning pretence of serving racial purity attained its full opportunity against a people without arms to retaliate or law courts to give protection.

By ingenious steps "Non-Aryans" were expelled from public office, from all professions, from the public schools. The true Aryan students tormented their schoolmates among the Jews while the schools were still open to them. Jews were excluded from the officially organized guilds that regulated all forms of cultural activity and therefore from their practice. To remain in the press, it was required that Aryan parentage be proven all the way back to the year 1800. Jewish employees were dismissed at the instance of the *Gauleiters.*

The "Nürnberg Laws" of September 1935 "for the protection of German blood and honor" took away all political rights and citizenship from the Jews, and made sexual intercourse between Jews and Aryans "a racial scandal," a crime. What, then, was a Jew? Anybody with four or three Jewish grandparents. Mixed marriages were illegal. The concentration camp was punishment for violation of the law.

The property of the Jews was by various legal chicanery seized. In November 1938, after a Polish Jewish youth had had the courage to kill a member of the German Legation in Paris, the party organizations let loose "a spontaneous eruption of the people's wrath": every single store throughout Germany and Austria and the 529 synagogues were sacked and pillaged. All homes of Jews were vandalously looted. Seventy thousand Jews of all ages were put into concentration camps, with indescribable brutality and many deaths. The Jews had to pay for all the damage; a collective fine was levied on the community; their property had to be sold at confiscatory rates. They were then given monthly pittances from the sequestrated funds. By July 1939 Jews were, by various decrees, eliminated from economic life; and the Jewish community had to provide all schooling and poor relief. The schools might only train for emigration.

During World War II the German armies, police, and administrators smothered, beat, shot, worked, starved, and gassed to death 6,000,000 Jewish people, more than one half of whom were infants and teen-agers. Government as human stockyards! The "little men," become party members, obeyed orders to accomplish this.

IV. NAZI POLICY

The instruments indicated above were fashioned to serve a policy. First, the nation was organized to become an economic *Autarky*—that is, to provide for itself the maximum possible products necessary for sustaining a war. It was almost like a transcription of the maunderings of Herder and Fichte (p. 553) and Friedrich List (p. 563). A Four Year Plan was started in 1936 for this purpose, and the purpose became the dominant policy for all departments and levels of government. Goering was in charge of it, later followed by a genius accidentally discovered by Hitler, a building constructor at work in the Reich Chancellery—Alfred Speer. The consequence was the absorption of the unemployed, of which there were 6,000,000 in 1933. It is easy to absorb unemployed if (1) the standard of living makes no difference to the organization of the economy and the people, and (2) if liberties are ignored. The standard of living in Germany went down as a result of putting a whole nation to fashion arms, productive capacity, and to growing foodstuffs, fibers, etc. But private property remained; the employers' authority was enhanced, since the employers were regarded as "subleaders" in the Nazi plan; their rate of profits rose; the family budgets, on the average, were impoverished. But more people had jobs, and more people had better incomes than their unemployment doles of 1928–1933.

Enserfing of Industry and Labor

All were subjected to the power of the State. The "Estate" of Trade and Industry grouped the various branches of manufacture, commerce, and crafts, and these again were even more meticulously organized in subbranches than ever before in a land long adept at organization. The leaders were appointed by the State, which set production quotas, fixed prices, wages, marketing, qualities and quantities. The size of businesses was government-determined, and the smaller businesses, which had been propagandized into expecting defense by the Nazis, were ground out for larger firms. Price-fixing and the rationing of materials and credit were firm controls in the hands of the government. Even the businessman lost his freedom; but he was paid for it. Yet Weimar had given him more of both, to his late regrets.

Labor had become enserfed. It was soon put under conscription; made to go where the Reich directed it; forced to work the hours demanded; forced to stay on the jobs the Plan needed. It was given a semblance of representation in the so-called "Labor Front," under an infamous Nazi, Dr. Ley, a Nazi zealot put at its head by Hitler. Membership was compulsory and came to include all the workers. Strikes were now impossible and forbidden. The worker was to exemplify the Nazi creed of the Dignity of Labor—but under orders from above and as a *Gefolgschaft* or "following" of the employer, who was "the leader of the shop community." The workers were at first allowed to choose their representatives (for minor works' management affairs), but as soon as the workers showed independence in such elections—that is, did not elect Nazis—elections were stopped. They had the compensation of a twelve-hour day, and *Kraft durch Freude,* or Strength-through-Joy. This latter was a vast organization of leisure-time activities of every kind: cultural, recreational, vacational, tourist, hobbies, lectures, etc. It was paid for by *compulsory* dues from workers and employers and was another instrument in the Nazi seduction of liberty.

"Blood and Soil"

In agriculture, the Nazis carried out their principles of *Blut und Boden,* the fundamentality of work on the soil for the wealth and health of the *Volk* and the purity of the blood of the *Volk* by rural occupations and fresh air away from the sinful cities. The farmer's estates were not to be freely sold but to pass down to his son or nearest male heir. The owner was given a kind of title of nobility—Hereditary Farmer. Soon the war plans made these "nobility" into executors of State orders as to production, prices, and the rest. They were compensated by being provided with plenty of slave labor brought in from conquered Poland and Russia and France.

Religion

There was complete regimentation in the interests of the conquests needed to produce Hitler's Great Reich. The schools and universities were made instruments of Nazi doctrine—and many professors, whose earlier works had entitled the West to think they were men of character, assisted the Nazis. In the main, the Protestant Church was seduced, and such resisters as Pastor Niemöller, almost a Nazi in political terms of nationalism and militarism and Germanism as any, were imprisoned. Finally, the Gestapo cleared up the remnants, while the mass of the clergy satisfied Hitler with good behavior, for they were Germans before they were Christians, and they remembered Martin Luther (p. 531). As for the Roman Catholic Church, whose only begotten political party, the Center, had let in Hitler through von Papen, and through Monsignor Kaas, leader of the party group in the *Reichstag* of March 1933, Hitler had an admiration for its principles of papal infallibility, its hierarchic organization, and its strong discipline. He ardently wished such qualities on himself. He was rather scared of its international strength. The Church (through von Papen's negotiation) made a concordat with Hitler, in which it was allowed freedom of worship, religious education in all schools and opening of confessional Catholic schools whenever parents demanded this, and Catholic social and cultural organizations. In return, the Church forbad political activity by its priests and orders. The Nazis soon violated their side of the pact, especially after Cardinal Faulhaber of Munich preached sermons against racial dogmas and German chauvinism and exclusive Teutonic salvationism. Steadily, grindingly, the Nazis persecuted the clergy. One clever method was to accuse a priest of immorality or violations of the laws regulating the economy, especially regarding the currency. This gave the regime the advantage of judicial trials that were transformed into propaganda demonstrations. Thousands of the clergy and faithful laymen were consigned to the concentration camps.

Paganism Preached. In place of existing religions, the Nazis, especially people like Rosenberg, tried to establish a Nordic and Aryan pagan creed, freed at last, as Nietzsche would have had it, from the sniveling Judaic-Christian, the Asian servility to the doctrine of charity and peace of the Sermon. The S.S. Élite Guards became bearers of the cult of Thor and the Vikings, the Teuton festivals and sun rites. (General Ludendorff and his wife were pioneers in this also.) As World War II began, German youth was beginning to be affected by this rubbish, perfect pabulum for *Wandervögel*, playing mandolins on the mutilated bodies of unarmed children.

The Nazi heroes were: Arminius, who turned back the Roman Legions; Widukind, leader of a tribe of Saxon pagans who *resisted* Charlemagne's attempts to Christianize them; and that list of German men of force and blood and iron and the *Volk* thinkers, and the Superman and "Western decline" thinkers we have so often named. Their devils were their socialist and Catholic opponents, Sigmund Freud, Germany's liberal newspapers, especially the *Frankfurter Zeitung*.

V. WORLD WAR II, THE GENERALS, AND UNCONDITIONAL SURRENDER

As German strength promised to grow and grew, Hitler carried out his lunatic plan to make Germany the World Reich. The sequence is well known. In May 1936 came his rearming of the Rhineland, the Treaty of Versailles. This was accomplished against the advice of the General Staff, who feared action by Britain and France. Hitler's intuition told him rightly that the West would not intervene. He himself was in a fright-hysteria in the first forty-eight hours after his *coup*. Austria was undermined, and he seized it in March 1938. Next he smashed Czechoslovakia (1938) on the plea that the Sudetenland and

Germans were being maltreated, breaking all his obligations to the Prime Ministers of Britain and Czechoslovakia. Again, the generals had been timid and Hitler successful. All this was accomplished after the most unthinkable luring-on of the heads of these states and their browbeating and contemptuous vilification by Hitler himself, most so for the representatives of Austria and Czechoslovakia who were so maltreated as to need medical assistance. Then Hitler resolved to recover Danzig and make away with the Polish Corridor. By this time, the Berserk nature of the brute brought in British guarantees to Poland. Hitler safeguarded himself by a pact with Stalin—rule of the land he intended to dismember and colonize with German overlords to whip Slav subhumans into slave labor.

The generals begged him to wait. He went ahead (1939), and overthrew Poland in a few weeks. The generals were appalled by the deliberate wanton cruelty inflicted by Hitler's direct orders to exterminate all, for they had been educated in military ethics regarding the treatment of prisoners of war and of civilians. But they did not carry their protests to resistance. They were frightened of the West's intervention, and Hitler did not expect it. Yet it came—his first great mistake. The generals quieted their consciences; for rewards were handed out to them; and Hitler's intuition on Poland had been right.

Hitler wanted an offensive against the West in November 1939, the period of the "phoney" war; it was mounted and ordered. The generals protested. Their representative, the Chief of Staff, General von Brauchitsch, was sent to confer with the *Führer* on this.

Hitler's Hold on the German People: Why?

The incident is fundamental to an understanding of the hold of Hitler on the government of Germany—that is, on 70,000,000 people. When the General had made his report, this, in Wheeler-Bennett's knowledgeable words [2] is what occurred:

Every insult, every accusation, every manifestation of hatred and contempt which Hitler cherished for the *Generalität*, he now spewed forth

[2] John Wheeler-Bennett, *The Nemesis of Power*, London, 1952, p. 472.

upon von Brauchitsch, who quailed before the torrent. When, at the end of what Halder, with consummate restraint, describes as "a most ugly and disagreeable scene," the *Führer* abruptly terminated his own tirade by leaving the room, the Commander in Chief tottered back to his car and fled back the eighteen miles to Zossen [headquarters], where he arrived in such poor shape that, at first, he could only give a somewhat incoherent account of the proceedings.

. . . All desire to oppose, let alone resist, the *Führer* had been knocked out of him in this fateful encounter.

We return to the significance of this incident later.

Most of the generals detested Hitler. They were of a superior social class; they had expertise; they loved their Germany sufficiently not to take technically unjustified risks; and they had been nurtured at home and schooled, certainly in social and religious conservatism but still with a sense of social propriety, justice, and decency. Hitler believed in his intuition; knew he was hated; knew he was disbelieved and opposed; yet had the generals kowtowing to him, because they had no political strength. They detested the S.A. and the S.S. They were the only remaining force strong enough to overthrow him. His Gestapo knew this.

The Generals hoped the West would make a negotiated peace; they did not want their Reich in ruins. They wanted a repetition of 1918, to be intact (p. 611). They made contact with numerous civilians, above all Goerdeler, mayor of Leipzig, Center Party, socialist, trade-union, and even Communist leaders, to take Germany over, if once Hitler could be killed. They instituted contacts with the West, designed to secure first some gains over the Weimar situation; later, to keep areas gained by victory; and later still, not to be *crushed* for the sins of the German Armies and people. They hoped that Hitler's Western offensive would fail. It succeeded dazzlingly, Norway and the Low Countries being taken by perfidy and brutality and military brilliance, and France by martial tactics with tanks and the *Luftwaffe* of surpassing genius, after six years of hollowing out Nazi agents and her own easy virtue. The generals fawned; and all the bells of Germany rang out for three days!

The Russian Debacle

Then, against the advice of the generals, Hitler made war on Russia—perfidy immeasurable. The generals were mainly inclined to the Bismarck policy of friendship with Russia (p. 606). Hitler meant to take away the Ukraine and exterminate all the Communists. Army orders made by him were to kill all "political commissars" taken! All went swimmingly until the reverse before Moscow in 1941 and 1942. The lands taken in Poland and Russia were despoiled, the people made subhuman slaves. The commanders were forced by Hitler to persist in drives and last stands against their own better knowledge of terrain, climate, and opposition. He drove them forward.

The tide turned after Hitler's intuition failed at Stalingrad in February 1943. Yet his will pressed the nation to continue its efforts, though the generals and responsible-minded conservatives saw that Germany, now that the United States was in the war, must be ultimately crushed—for the bombers were making havoc of the cities. Goering who had boasted, as head of the *Luftwaffe,* "If a single bomber gets through you can call me *Meier* [a derogatory Jewish name]," was now being called *Meier.* Yet none of the generals or officer corps had the courage singlehanded to kill Hitler. They, like all Germans, accepted existent authority, if it was nonpopular.

The Russian Error and Crime. Germany may well have lost the war that might have been won when Hitler lost the opportunity to win to his side the millions of Russians, soldiers and civilians, who surrendered to the advancing German armies in 1941 and 1942 (p. 785). These vaguely believed that the Germans were liberators from the dread oppression of Stalin. But especially and *personally* incited by Hitler, on ideological grounds and for reasons of land-grabbing (which amounted to the same thing in the end), the fleeing Russians were treated as *Untermenschen,* to such indignities and cruelties, that they were glad enough to return to their own native brutes of masters. Under the influence of Hitler's anti-Russian lunacy, even General Vaslov, a Russian renegade with a powerful Russian army that was anti-Stalin, was treated with exemplary Nazi perfidy and betrayed, never used. The outraging of the Russians may have cost

Hitler his war, his Reich, and his life. It was as direct a consequence of his character as was the whole Nazi structure.

The Army was dispersed; the chiefs arrested by the Allies; the heads of the Nazi organizations picked up. They were tried and condemned at Nürnberg. They had left chaos.

The Generals, Junkers, and Others

Several plots were made; Hitler foiled them. The conspiracy that gradually took shape of the elements mentioned above was caught in two sticky webs: (1) disagreement on the shape of Germany after the war and what would be an acceptable peace from the Allies, for the Army at any rate wished to preserve its being and authority intact (as in 1918); and (2) the reluctance of some of the generals to break their oath sworn to Hitler personally, and fear that some pro-Nazi generals, like Keitel (known as *La-Keitel* or *lackey*) or von Kluge (known as *der kluge Hans, clever Hans*) would not help or would betray. Also, the position of the generals was materialist. Wheeler-Bennett sums it up well: [3]

> Technically able and physically courageous, they yet lacked the moral courage and, in the main, were wholly wanting in spiritual resistance and intellectual independence. The majority were out to make their professional and social careers in the most material sense. Marshal's batons and Knight's crosses, gifts, estates, and building permits, silenced such pangs of conscience as may, from time to time, have assailed.

The blows rained on Hitler from all sides. By July 20, 1944, the opposition conspiracy managed to smuggle a bomb into one of Hitler's conferences. Officers had been alerted everywhere to take action in a well-designed plan to take over power *the moment Hitler was dead.* There could be no assured action till then, so strong was his personality and the force of the personal oath to the live Hitler! The bomb was placed by a cool, brave officer, Klaus von Stauffenberg, a Bavarian aristocratic career soldier inspired by Christian motives. (He had been seriously wounded and mutilated in the African campaign.)

The explosion occurred; but owing to sheer

[3] *Ibid.,* p. 536.

accidental circumstances, it only wounded Hitler (even blowing his pants off him and setting his hair alight), though it killed several others who stood or sat around him. A shocking purge occurred the next day. Some accounts estimate that nearly 5000 were slaughtered, among them 2000 officers. Perhaps the total was something like 2000 or 3000. Wheeler-Bennett actually names about 200, and his list includes the pride of German military, political, and aristocratic society, distinguished administrators, and Catholic, Prussian, and labor leaders. "It is my wish that they be hanged like cattle!" screamed Hitler, full of his normal blood-lust. They were; so were their families, down to young children. The films of the executions were shown to others, to intimidate. Generals, like Beck, died—by slow strangulation, suspended from meat hooks. Not even respectful criticism was made against the *Führer's* determination to have Germany, all Germany, go down in ruin, because he was now to suffer the punishment of defeat, with no alibi about a "stab in the back" (p. 611). The officer who had acted in Berlin to smash the plot, Otto Remer, became a neo-Nazi leader in 1947 (p. 709).

This time—differently from 1918—the Army surrendered unconditionally as soon as Hitler was dead in his Berlin bunker.[4] Before this happened, Hitler's court had dispersed. They all had been fighting for their own heads—Goering, Himmler, Bormann, Speer—in the months since Stalingrad. Nobody had been permitted to mention the word *defeat;* no preparation had been made for transition to peace after defeat. Goebbels, sustained, as the *Führer* was, by horoscopes drawn by astrologers and echoing his master's voice that "Germany did not deserve the *Führer,*" he was so great, died with him, also by suicide.

The Hero and His Following

All this phase of German government, the undermining of Weimar and the ascendency of a bestial tyranny, had been made possible by the demonic force of one man. But, how can one man seize 70,000,000 people? As we have seen, when forces

[4] Cf. H. Trevor-Roper, *Last Days of Hitler,* New York, 1950.

are divided against themselves, a strong, affirmative, and uncompromising one gets its chance. It can take advantage of people's distress, if they are, like the Germans, without civil courage to last out an economic depression. But a *Führer* must convince a few people who can then pass on the authority he obtains, and the arms he is ready to use, to subleaders, who will then dominate ever-growing members beneath them, especially as so large a proportion of modern electorates are utterly ignorant of the nature of government. How, then, did Hitler get hold of a few? Partly by material prospects.

The Id versus the Superego. But how could he dominate the generals, men like von Brauchitsch, well brought up, ethically structured, sustained by social friends, family, connections with a holy church, professionally schooled? The answer lies in the very conditions, those just mentioned.

Hitler stripped them of their socially built ethical and professional structure, the ego and superego that had raised them above the instincts of their Id. His own dragging up had given to his Id no ethical structuring, no moderation. The original force of his Id, the primitive, chaotic instinct, without class, with culturation, without taming, remained in him with a hysterical force. When in a rage, with the froth of fury on his lips and blazing eyes, he denied the values of those who confronted him—and in addition undermined their belief in their own structure by showing that his own military intuition, for example, got results while their professionalism *failed*—he shattered them by his primitivism, by knocking away their social iron braces. They went back to their Ids, like babies lost faith in their egos and superegos, and were bereft of their socially constructed strength. This is why a von Brauchitsch could be incoherent. They were fascinated by the sadism he had revealed to them in themselves; and so they were disarmed.

And most of the Germans were in the same case. They all liked someone else to do the dirty work for them, to satisfy their primitive rage for sensations, the work their Ids coveted: smashing down other people, breaking windows in other people's houses, insulting and maltreating the strong and the weak, twisting the arms of passers-by, buffeting old gentlemen, stealing some nice pieces of property, shouting out how grand and glorious, how brave they themselves were, strutting and boasting, wearing gaudy uniforms, raping and ravishing whenever they got the chance, fighting and beating a common enemy, finding a common enemy on whom to fix their blood-lusts, commanding them to *Ehrfurcht* like their lost fathers. For underneath what they had been taught at home, and resented, and at Church and rebelled against, and at school and were impatient with, was the elemental aggressiveness of the German human animal. It was a relief to have a statesman take over these fell burdens of intellect and conscience. For this they gave him their votes. But with Hitler, a vote was a portion of sovereign power, which when in his possession he kept permanently, treating the donors as he had said he would treat, not *them,* they thought, but *other people* as the victims of his blood-urges. They were mistaken and their Germany was ruined. Can they be built into political adults, to have self-assurance and a sense of responsibility toward themselves?

Can they be taught that Decency and Truth ought to dominate their will, for they had been nurtured by their philosophers in the exactly opposite creed since the end of the eighteenth century?

The German Kaiser-State and society of 1871–1918 may be represented as a steel network, leading up to and dependent on the Kaiser's authority. It was a firm, taut, wired structure. In it were held the upper leading and directing groups of society as in a brace. All individuals were braced in their positions, principles, and duties. They owed obedience, but they were protected against assault from without and responsibility to make decisions within. They were not free personally to fight their personal, rabid, primitive passions that still raged underneath the social heritage, the "cake of custom," everywhere. Let a

destroyer, a *nihilist,* cast off the brace he hated because he never enjoyed it though he envied it, and there was moral chaos, and for many of the people all the time, and some of the people some of the time, ferocious enjoyment in atavistic abjectness of shouting and brutal great-man-ism, in masochism and sadism.

Can they be taught to care that the moral decisions made by a government in their name is their personal responsibility? Will they learn no longer to regard themselves as "little men" and cease to be smugly happy under the authority of a nonresponsible rulership? Can it be brought home to them that it is not right to accept jobs, homes, vacations, and power, unless the atrocious cost to those who are made to pay their lives for it is counted? Is there a man or men who will teach them that evil must be resisted at its first, trivial appearance, lest the conscience be seduced step by step to total unholiness; that the potential end must be projected, and if it be immoral, must be contested in its first beginnings? For the implied sins of the governed in these questions were the sins of the German people. Tautly structured to work and obey, over the centuries by the immense pressure of other peoples on their easily overrun frontiers, they transferred and vented their tenseness and insistence on others in their own nation and on other nations. The cure of the world lies in the cure of these weaknesses in the Germans.

After the suicide of Hitler, Goebbels arranged the announcement of his master's death over the radio: with music from Wagner's *Twilight of the Gods,* the slow movement of Bruckner's *Seventh Symphony* (composed for the death of Wagner). But the announcement, made by Admiral Doenitz, did not mention suicide; the lie was broadcast that the *"Führer* had fallen, fighting at the head of his troops." It was pretended that he died fighting Bolshevism. The regime began in a lie and ended with a lie.

7

The West German Republic: Rebirth at Bonn

Nothing is so good, absolutely, as a good character.

. . .

The highest maxim of morality and freedom is: Act so that you employ the humanity in your own person as well as in the person of every other individual always as an end and never as a means.

—Immanuel Kant

The reconstruction of German government was the product of German will and the predominant resolution of the nation that Hitler had allied against his aggressions. The former was, at any rate for the time being, in a democratic frame of mind, and the latter were determined to have a Germany whose self-rule would purge it of militarism and keep it stable and decent.

The stages by which Germany came to be torn into two, West and East, by which the East itself became diminished by Soviet and Polish annexation, and by which two separate constitutions— one for the West German Republic and the other for the German Democratic Republic—came into existence can only be briefly noticed.

I. FROM DEFEAT TO THE CONSTRUCTION OF THE WEST GERMAN REPUBLIC, OR THE BONN CONSTITUTION

True to his sadism and hatred, Hitler left Germany in chaos. His cohorts had made no provision for the transfer of government to other parties or to the Allies. They raced off as fast as they could from their offices and went into hiding. Nor did

the German people make even a gesture of revolution to provide a new set of authorities. Some of those who had emerged from the concentration camps and others (as in Hamburg), who had, outside them, maintained anti-Nazi associations gradually emerged to offer their services to the democratic Allies. They were in too many cases rebuffed, especially by American military officers, as much from political prejudice and crass ignorance as on principle. Once again Germany was freed by outside arms. The people had, on the whole, connived with Hitler. No alternative governing class was extant. The cities were reduced to rubble; the Russians had added the rape of Berlin; transport and communications, the banks, the utilities were shattered; government was dissolved. There milled around in German territories 66,000,000 Germans, 8,000,000 foreigners who had been seized by the armies and put in labor and concentration camps, 8,000,000 soldiers of the Allied Armies, scores of thousands of refugees from Poland, the Baltic, and Russia, glad to flee from Communist rule, and 10,000,000 Germans who had fled or been ejected from their Central European settlements, such as Hungary, Yugoslavia, Romania, Czechoslovakia, East Germany, Silesia, etc.

It took the Allied Powers, assisted by an ever-swelling number of German leaders and officials, until 1947 to sort out this cataract of peoples.

Allied Principles of German Government

At the Yalta Conference (February 1944) and then more circumstantially at the Potsdam Conference (August 2, 1945), the Allied Powers had laid down certain principles of German government. The former resolved to extirpate Nazism and militarism but not to destroy the German people, and yet, in the phrase which had been earlier expressed, to demand "unconditional surrender." The latter arranged for (1) a joint government under continued occupation of Germany by the four Commanders in Chief (U.S.A., U.S.-S.R., Great Britain, and France) for matters concerning Germany as a whole, in order to (2) fulfill policies that have come to be sloganized as the Four D's. These were Demilitarization, De-Nazification, Democratization, and Decentralization. Nazi officials, leaders, institutions would be swept away, the war criminals punished. Decentralization was designed as a way of taking back government to the people and so nurturing them in self-government, and as also a means of weakening the strength of the German State. As for the economy, the main principle in the American mind, at least, was the dissolution of the great economic units—cartels, trusts, combines—while the British were interested in dismantling the war factories (and perhaps competitive manufactures) and socialization. The Russians had grimly different plans in mind.

There were wilder, more radical policies, such as the Morgenthau Plan, to reduce Germany to nothing more than an agricultural economy. They were impossible, unless a century-long occupation of a cruel sort was contemplated and feasible. Nor is it a valid criticism of the principles above noted that their inherent belief that reform of the principles and machinery of government and re-education in the schools would democratize the Germans was vain. If this was vain, all alternatives were vain.

Trial and Collapse of the Control Council

The map (p. 526) reveals the change in the *Länder* territory. Germany was divided into four zones. The American included the *Länder* of Bavaria, Württemberg-Baden, Hesse, and Bremen. The British comprised Hamburg, Lower Saxony, North Rhine-Westphalia, and Schleswig-Holstein. Again, these *Länder* were not coterminus with those existing hitherto in Germany. The French zone embraced the Rhineland-Palatinate, Baden, and Württemberg-Hohenzollern. Into this, as into the British zone, parts of Prussia had been merged. The Soviet was accorded Mecklenberg, Brandenberg, Saxony, Saxony-Anhalt, and Thuringia. This swallowed and disintegrated most of Prussia. The *Länder* were demarcated shortly after the capitulation of Germany on May 5, 1945. The division left nearly 18,000,000 in the American zone; 24,000,-000 in the British; 5,600,000 in the French; and 2,000,000 in the western sector of Berlin. Berlin itself was governed jointly by the four Allies. In the western area lived altogether, then, nearly 50,000,000 Germans. The Russian zone contained 17,300,000 and nearly 1,200,000 in East Berlin; or about 18,500,000 altogether.

In each zone the commanders operated the government and the economy with their own military and administrative national experts, and in association with political and bureaucrat leaders they could individually trust. For example, in the American zone, municipal and state councils and officials were utilized as *agents* of the military command. These "agent-governments" got enforcing power for their ordinances from the military command. By the end of 1945 the "Ministers-President" of the included *Länder* joined in a Council of *Länder,* the *Länderrat,* for the whole zone, and these secured parallel action in the zones in many matters. The decisions required unanimity and approval by the American deputy military governor. In September 1946 the American and British zones were linked in a bizonal administration, the Americans and the British being the only two politically elevated enough to accomplish such a sensible democratic arrangement. The French and Russians stood out.

The Russians, in their zone, proceeded by relentless force to socialize the economy, to divide up the large estates, and to crush all forces that were not Communist (see pp. 713–715).

The American, British, and French zones developed their sincere answer to the Potsdam principle of restoring self-government to the Germans, commencing with the local authorities. By August 1945 political parties were permitted to organize and function at the *Kreis* level; by the spring of 1946, for the whole zone; a little later in the French and British zones. Political life picked up: in the American zones there were communal elections in May 1946, municipal elections in May, *Land* constituent assembly elections in June, followed in each by *Landtag* elections in November. The other western zones followed shortly. From that time forth, German unfettered electoral opinion and will were restored and nurtured; it was German and it was free, working through German instrumentalities. Their actions, of course, remained liable to Military Government's veto. The *Länder* now had their own constitutions, freely made, and top political leaders, one of whom, Konrad Adenauer (p. 690), ultimately became Prime Minister of the Bonn government.

Partition of Government. Meanwhile, the Control Council fell victim to the "cold war" between Russia and the West. It managed to secure uniform laws on finance, taxation, labor relations, agriculture, military dismantlement—and, above all, the formal abolition of the state of Prussia in February 1947. But the future of Germany as a whole, and the role of Germany as an ally or as a neutral, tranfixed the Council. By the beginning of 1947 the three Western powers had agreed to unify the economy of their zones. A last attempt was made to establish a united Germany in the Moscow Conference of March-April 1947. It broke down because the West wanted a loose federal system and the Russians wanted centralization; through different interpretations of the word *democracy*—that is, through different intentions; and, connected with the federalism issue, the desire of the West not to have a central "police" force. Those who follow the Russian way with their zone (p. 713ff.) will appreciate that an agreement on these subjects could not possibly be reached, given the different way of life of Soviet commissars and Western statesmen. Nor did the U.S.S.R. ever intend to loosen her grip on East Germany. At this conference the American representatives spelled out what they meant by *democracy* as applicable to Germany. It is a statement of enduring significance, because (1) it was acted on; (2) it represents a most acute summary of the lessons that American political scientists (they developed the principles) had learned from watching the deficiencies of the Fascists, Nazis, and Communists, and their attempts to arrive at bedrock of techniques for democracy omitting the inessential differentiae. They must be reproduced.

Democracy. All levels of German government in the U.S. zone must be democratic to the extent that:

1. All political power is recognized as originating with the people and subject to their control;

2. Those who exercise political power are obliged to regularly renew their mandates by frequent references of their programs and leadership to popular elections;

3. Popular elections are conducted under competitive conditions in which no less than two effectively competing political parties must submit their programs and candidates to public review;

4. Political parties must be democratic in character and must be recognized as voluntary associations of citizens clearly distinguished from, rather than identified with, the instrumentalities of government;

5. The basic rights of the individual, including free speech, freedom of religious preference, the rights of assembly, freedom of political association, and the other equally basic rights of free men are recognized and guaranteed;

6. Control over the instrumentalities of public opinion, such as radio and the press, must be diffused and kept free from governmental domination;

7. The rule of law is recognized as the individual's greatest single protection against a capricious and willful expression of governmental power.

In addition, German governmental systems were required to provide for an independent judiciary, one not subject to the Legislative and Executive arms in general and the police activity in particular. Though authoritarian government was banned, it was permissive to organize government on the cabinet system—that is, the linking of the Legislature and Executive—and not essential to establish the American separation-of-powers system.

Then the requirements set out the elements of the federal system—the intention being expressed thus: "The functions of government shall be decentralized within that structure to the maximum degree consistent with the modern economic life." Even the designation of the federal units was given attention: they were to be *not Länder* but *Staaten,* a rather futile attempt to reinvigorate the political psychology of German "particularism" (p. 576). The basic centrifugal feature was that the states should have the primary powers, reserving power not so delegated to wither federal or state authorities to the people.

It was a valiant attempt artificially to inseminate democracy in a hitherto nondemocratic people. It was right to make the attempt even if either (1) it should not succeed, or (2) there emerged from the German mentality and circumstances themselves a democratic and enduringly viable regime.

From the collapse of the Moscow Conference, the Control Council was doomed. When the economic merger of the western zones was consummated, the Russian representative in Berlin asked and was denied an explanation of what he called a "unilaterally established unified western economic state." He walked out; and on April 1, 1948, General Lucius Clay, then chairman, refused to convene any more meetings of the Council.

The Political Mentality of the West German People

The Americans more than any other Occupation authorities sought to de-Nazify and re-educate to democracy the German people. What has been the fate of such efforts? What has happened to the German political mind? Some general notions may be mentioned at once.

Broadly speaking, the German people were sorry rather than penitent and converted: sorry that they had lost the war, disturbed that they had lost their leader, sorry for themselves that they had been visited with destruction. As many as possible pretended that they had known nothing of the cruelties of the Nazi regime; claimed that they had followed it out of ignorance or out of fear of violence to them. They could not take upon themselves the remorse of guilt against the many millions who had been Nazi victims—it was not *their* guilt. They started the aftermath of the war with stupor and hunger and abject obsequiousness. They could not, as after World War I, pretend or be truly persuaded that the war was lost by a "stab in the back." They could not put the erection of a new system of government to the discredit, as they then did, of those who built a democratic system of government. This, at least and probably, was saved for the future good of their nation. There was widespread German recrimination and accusations to Military Government regarding connivance in Nazi brutality—leaving a legacy of hatred.

Mistrust of Politics: Ascendancy of Officials. Above all, there arose three firm psychological traits. (1) Youth, finding no extant leadership, and past leaders having been deceivers, tended to withdraw from politics. Since one generation had been made away with in the concentration camps or war, the middle ranks of the population were lacking as political guides. Hence, leadership fell back to those who had led in the Weimar Republic, largely—that is, older and sober men. (2) The Nazis and Nationalists, *for the time being,* went under cover of other names and other parties. (3) A so-called "skepticism" or sobriety (*Nüchternheit*) attitude was cultivated: of "I won't be caught by propaganda!" as put out by *anybody.* As far as foreign policy was concerned the *"ohne Mich,"* "without me," attitude was developed. A great deal of petty self-seeking and trivial, bourgeois security and prosperity became uppermost in political and social behavior. So intricate were the problems of the transition and the reconstruction, as well as the making of claims of restitution of losses inflicted by the Nazis or losses by the civilians through the war damage, and losses inflicted on former Nazis, that the State had to rely, even more than traditionally, on the bureaucracy and to favor a strong, if democratic, Executive. The military class was for the moment shattered by Hitler's executions in 1944, death in battle, execution and imprisonment on sentence by the Nürnberg tribunal, and the German process of de-Nazification and dissolution of the Army. The Junker basis was destroyed by the break-up of the estates in the eastern zone under the Russians.

De-Nazification

At Nürnberg (November 20, 1945 to August 31, 1946) the Allied tribunal, and in the respective zones, special tribunals, the main strokes of justice against the Nazi criminals were delivered. The chief Nazi leaders were hanged; two committed suicide. Others were given life imprisonment; others from ten to twenty years. Unfortunately Schacht, von Papen, and Fritsche were acquitted altogether. Some Nazi organizations were convicted: the S.S., the Leadership Corps, the *Sicherheïtsdienst,* the Gestapo. The General Staff, the Reich Cabinet, the S.A. were acquitted. Nevertheless, the broad purpose, to fasten legal liability on political leaders for making war and practising inhumanity in the name of the authority of the State was achieved: it is a lesson that may have weight in the councils of nations. It had one possible disadvantage: the common German man and woman, regarded this as sufficient expiation for crimes in which they themselves had connived, in three senses as defined by the philosopher, Karl Jaspers, namely (1) political, that they had allowed Hitler to act in their name, in cruelties and in the making of war; (2) moral, because they had not had strength and nobility of conscience; and (3) metaphysical, because they had not remembered their duty to be responsible that justice should be done to all mankind. These tended to be forgotten in the punishments meted out for the other kind of guilt, the criminal guilt.

In the American zone 1539 persons were convicted and 444 given death sentences, but only 250 executed. The British sentenced 665 people and executed 250. As time went on, and memories grew milder while Russian aggression grew more menacing, many sentences were commuted, and some of the convicted were released. The head of Krupp's armament works was granted release! The rising tide of German nationalism contributed to this tremendous leniency of the Western powers; but the leniency was never enough to satisfy the Germans.

They themselves were given the task of further de-Nazification. They were spared the direct attack on the Nazi Party and its affiliated organizations. This and the permanent prohibition of the party were accomplished by the Control Council. For the rest of the task the Control Council laid down the criteria that Nazis and persons hostile to Allied purposes and war criminals (Nazis and militarists) were to be removed from office and positions of responsibility. A most highly complicated series of categories were elaborated. This was at once met by the almost complete solidarity of the German people to defeat the fulfillment of the program. It was pretended that practically every Nazi had to the last man been terrorized into being a Nazi; that there was no element of voluntarism about it. As Allied policy changed from "no fraternization" to friendship, it was the denouncers of the Nazis, the Nazi victims, who suffered by ostracism!

The damning figures are these. Thirteen million names were registered. Of these only 3,450,000 were chargeable according to the criteria set out by the Allies; 2,488,000 were amnestied without trial. Only 945,000 were actually tried; of these one third were amnestied or the proceedings stopped. This left about 600,000 out of 13,000,000 convicted. Of the 600,000, only 1600 were major offenders! The maximum penalties were the labor camp; only 9600 of all the 13,000,000 got this. The rest were let off far more easily. Not a single death sentence was imposed.

Soon the bureaucracy and the judiciary helped their friends who had been ejected from office to get back, once they had been cleared by the de-Nazification boards, while acting officials were dismissed. In the 402 members of the *Bundestag* of 1949, 13 percent were former Nazis. In the *Landtagen,* the situation is worse.

It was, in fact, even impossible for the Russians, who are without humane ethics, to abstain from using the services of thousands upon thousands of administrative, judicial, educational, and economic experts, without which the State cannot function. The Civil Services were not de-Nazified substantially before the Bonn regime started. The Allies needed anti-Communist friends and assistants and some of these were former Nazis. Some Allied officials and officers were very unsure of their own political beliefs, regarding the Nazis as just another political party like those they thought they understood at home! The Germans were fairly solid, having either "pressed" their dreadful past or having never been able to realize that it was dreadful—most having the idea that history began, or ought to begin, only with 1945.

The Bonn Constitution: Creation and Features

Until the end of 1949 the upsurging political parties needed previous licensing by the military authorities of the zones. When de-Nazification petered out and the first elections of the Bonn *Bundestag* were to be held, the system of licensing was abandoned. Henceforth the only limit on parties became that of the German law courts, where Nazi characteristics are proscribed (p. 701). Hence, in the nascent period of the Bonn Constitution most political parties already known in Germany, excluding the two extremes, were in operation, though the Social Democrats were not in good standing with American military and administrative personnel who were steeped in ignorance about "socialism," when the Social Democratic Party is the soundest devotee of democracy among the German people. New parties, such as those representing the refugees and those expelled from non-German states, were permitted also.

An accord among the Allied powers of the west in June 1948 led to the unification of the German zones in the west, though obstructed by the French until then, and even afterward by various practical obstacles. For the accord provided for the steps to be taken to allow the Germans to erect a free and democratic form of government and to re-establish their unity (the Russians had cut off their zone and gone their own way, p. 717). Someone has called the making of the Constitution a Caesarian operation on the German people. He meant that those called on to make the Constitution were reluctant to do so, since they might thereafter be stigmatized by German nationalists as new "November criminals" (see p.

611), especially as many politicians were terrified by this act of cutting off West Germany from East Germany, and thus being the condoners of German partition.

The Allied Powers did not choose elections for a constituent assembly, but called for one to be composed of delegates chosen by the *Landtage* of the *Länder*. The German leaders preferred to call it the Parliamentary Council. This would be convened by the joint call of the eleven Ministers-President (each heading a *Land*). The constitution to be produced by the Parliamentary Council would need to be ratified by the voters. But the German leaders discarded popular ratification, to avoid popular recriminations. The main preliminary guide to the Council provided by the Allies was that the system to be established should be "federal"—that is, a loose federation. The Ministers-President were given formulas on the constitution, on territorial reorganization, and on the reservations of sovereignty to the Occupying Powers according to the Occupation Statute.

The Ministers-President elaborated a comprehensive and subtle draft. It was to be called a Basic Law or *Grundgesetz*, not a *Verfassung* or constitution, although the former term had the same meaning as the latter in German constitutional tradition, to avoid some unexplained moral inhibition. The constitution was regarded as one *for all of Germany*, not merely the West, in order to avert the accusation of partition. They stipulated ratification by the *Landtage,* not the people.

The Parliamentary Council met in Bonn, September 1, 1948. Its 65 members were chosen by the *Landtage,* being about one delegate per 750,000 inhabitants of the western area, while each *Land* had that proportion of the 65 which its population bore to the population of West Germany. Thus Baden, 2; Bavaria, 13; Bremen, 1; Hamburg, 2; Hesse, 6; Lower Saxony, 9; North Rhine-Westphalia, 17; Rhineland-Palatinate, 4; Schleswig-Holstein, 4; Württemberg, 2; Württemberg-Baden, 5. The composition by political parties was: Social Democrats, 27; Christian Democrats and Christian Socialists, 27; Free German Party, 5; Center Party, 2; German Party, 2; Communists, 2. Some parties that had entered the scene since 1946–47 (the electoral basis for the *Land-*

tage's selections) were not represented; some, like the C.D.U. was over strength. Five observers from West Berlin were present. Of the 65 delegates, all were members of the *Landtage;* and of them, no less than 51 were also civil servants; most of the remainder were professors. There was no lack of meticulous gadgetry in discussion and drafting. The then *Oberbürgermeister* of Cologne, Dr. Konrad Adenauer,[1] Catholic political leader in the Weimar Republic and now leader of the Christian Democrats, was unanimously elected President of the Council. Other internationally known figures included Carlo Schmid, professor of international law, and Professor Ernst Reuter, the courageous and ingenious mayor of Berlin. Debates were unbound by instructions; the party affiliations, not the association with the respective *Lander,* determined attitudes. The acutest conflict revolved around centralization; the Social Democrats favoring it, the Christian Democrats being hostile. Inspiration came from many sources, including the Occupation authorities and German constitutional experts.

Main Conflicts. We have already mentioned the C.D.U.-S.D.P. split on federalism. In the centralist position the latter was joined by the Free Democratic Party. The opposers of the C.D.U. secured that, broadly speaking, the second chamber should not be of the dominant state-powerful type over the lower chamber. The American authorities were strongly on the side of the C.D.U., convinced of the desirability of a *weak* federal authority. They were persuaded by the kind of arguments for federalism and the separation of powers needed in the nascent U.S.A. in 1788, namely, to keep government weak for the sake of a *durable* and *democratic* (that is, atomized) system. This caused the S.D.P. to go into opposition. It refused to follow the American ideas, believing that they

[1] He was born of a middle-class family in Cologne in 1876. After study of law and economics he was a public prosecutor and then entered the civil service of Cologne. He progressed to the position of *Oberbürgermeister* in 1917. In 1918 he was appointed a member of the Prussian upper house; under Weimar, president of the Prussian upper house. He was forced to leave politics in 1933, since he was a member of the Center Party, anathema to the Nazis. During Hitler's rule he was arrested twice by the *Gestapo.* U.S. Military Government restored him to Cologne and politics in 1945, though the British interfered for some time.

would result in too weak a government. The Allied Powers were sensible enough to recede on this issue, especially touching the respective financial powers of *Länder* and Bonn. The Basic Law was voted by 53–12; all were in favor—that is, all excepting 6 Christian Social Union delegates, angry that the federalism was not much looser; 2 of the Deutches Party; 2 Center; and *all* the Communists—that is, 2.

The Allied Powers had tried to get the Civil Service banned from the legislature; the Germans maintained successfully their traditional permission to enter it. The Allies wished for a substantial reorganization on a more rational basis of the boundaries of the *Länder;* the Germans would not recede from what now still remained of the historic areas. The Allies wished the inclusion of West Berlin fully in the Basic Law government; this would have given the S.D.P. a majority of votes in coming elections. The Germans excluded this, wishing no provocation to the Russians, while the C.D.U. maneuvered for a majority in the coming *Bundestag.*

Ratification took place in May 1949. The approval of two thirds the *Länder* was required for this. This was obtained, for all approved, excepting only Bavaria. This *Land,* surely as much a problem in German federalism as Prussia had hitherto been (pp. 616–617), rejected it by 101–63 (members of the *Landtage*), most of the C.D.U. being opposed because the unitarizing features were too strong. Another vote took place later, to accept the law because it was binding by the ratifications of the other states. This time it passed by a majority of 97–6, the *former* friends, the S.D.P. and the F.D.P., now becoming neutrals, as it were, by abstaining!

There are people in Germany, such as the extremist nationalist Pastor Niemöller, who argue that the Basic Law was forced on the German people. This is nonsense. What exactly would have been the Constitution if it had been drafted in the complete absence of the Occupying Powers and by a popularly elected constituent assembly we can never meticulously tell: but it most likely, since the C.D.U. and the S.D.P. would have had the overwhelming majority of votes (far more so than the Weimar making parties did), that we

Organization of the Federal Republic of Germany

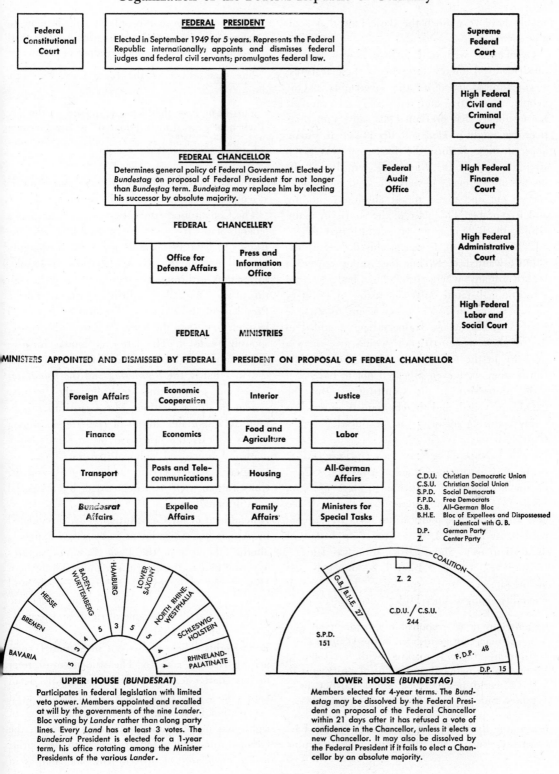

Federal Constitutional Court

FEDERAL PRESIDENT

Elected in September 1949 for 5 years. Represents the Federal Republic internationally; appoints and dismisses federal judges and federal civil servants; promulgates federal law.

Supreme Federal Court

High Federal Civil and Criminal Court

FEDERAL CHANCELLOR

Determines general policy of Federal Government. Elected by *Bundestag* on proposal of Federal President for not longer than *Bundestag* term. *Bundestag* may replace him by electing his successor by absolute majority.

Federal Audit Office

High Federal Finance Court

FEDERAL CHANCELLERY

Office for Defense Affairs

Press and Information Office

High Federal Administrative Court

High Federal Labor and Social Court

FEDERAL MINISTRIES

MINISTERS APPOINTED AND DISMISSED BY FEDERAL PRESIDENT ON PROPOSAL OF FEDERAL CHANCELLOR

Foreign Affairs	Economic Cooperation	Interior	Justice
Finance	Economics	Food and Agriculture	Labor
Transport	Posts and Tele-communications	Housing	All-German Affairs
Bundesrat Affairs	Expellee Affairs	Family Affairs	Ministers for Special Tasks

C.D.U.: Christian Democratic Union
C.S.U.: Christian Social Union
S.P.D.: Social Democrats
F.P.D.: Free Democrats
G.B.: All-German Bloc
B.H.E.: Bloc of Expellees and Dispossessed identical with G. B.
D.P.: German Party
Z.: Center Party

UPPER HOUSE *(BUNDESRAT)*

Participates in federal legislation with limited veto power. Members appointed and recalled at will by the governments of the nine *Lander*. Bloc voting by *Lander* rather than along party lines. Every *Land* has at least 3 votes. The *Bundesrat* President is elected for a 1-year term, his office rotating among the Minister Presidents of the various *Lander*.

LOWER HOUSE *(BUNDESTAG)*

Members elected for 4-year terms. The *Bundestag* may be dissolved by the Federal President on proposal of the Federal Chancellor within 21 days after it has refused a vote of confidence in the Chancellor, unless it elects a new Chancellor. It may also be dissolved by the Federal President if it fails to elect a Chancellor by an absolute majority.

should have very much the Basic Law that actually emerged.

Germans as well as the Allied Powers had almost identical interest in securing these features:
a government based on the sovereignty of the
people; an effective and responsible government;
arrangements that prevented the lapse into practices that might produce another Hitler. In pursuance of these factors, the Executive was given
strength *vis-à-vis* the *Bundestag* but denied the
lax use of emergency powers; the civil rights were
spelled out and made almost absolutely binding
and irrevocable. The place of the courts in maintaining the Rule of Law was strengthened. Above
all, a constitution had been produced, because the
C.D.U. wanted it, having the voting power in
West Germany; whereas the S.D.U. had preferred
a transitional statute only, amendable by ordinary
voting power, in order not to seem to exclude
East Germany, whose voting strength, added to
that of their western friends, would give them a
majority in the nation as a whole. To save the
future, they were even prepared not to have civil
rights imbedded in the Constitution. But the
C.D.U. prevailed, and thereby gained almost certainly enduring majority for the duration of the
Basic Law in the West.

Notable Features. The Basic Law (pp. *xxvii–xliii*)
or Bonn Constitution is an ingeniously worded
document, with 146 Articles in place of Weimar's 183. Its Preamble recognizes that it is "to
give a new order to political life for a *transitional*
period." It has acted, it declares, "on behalf of
those Germans to whom participation was denied."
Its spirit ought to be exhibited, because it is part
of the answer to the question: "Has German
mentality changed since Hitler's demoralization?"

> Conscious of its responsibility before God and
> before man [not mentioned in the Weimar Con-
> stitution—*Author*], inspired with a resolve to
> preserve its national and political unity and to
> serve world peace as an equal partner in a
> united Europe. . . .

begins the Preamble. Then, with an eye on East
Germany, Russia, and the future, the Preamble
ends:

> The entire German people is called upon to
> achieve, by *free self-determination* [notice this!
> —*Author*], the unity and freedom of Germany.

The final article of the Basic Law, No. 146,
states:

> This Basic Law shall become invalid on the day
> when a Constitution adopted by the German
> people by means of a free decision becomes
> effective.

Were they saying that, the Occupying Powers
absent, the Basic Law would be different?

The Constitution establishes not a unitary but a
federal State. Its units are the *Länder* and the
Bund. It is a democratic republic, sovereignty
emanating from the people. The flow of popular
sovereignty is through the legislature, and through
this to the Chancellor, as Prime Minister, and the
President of the Republic. The former is elected
by the *Bundestag,* the lower House, and owes responsibility to it. The latter is chosen for five
yearly terms by the two Houses of this bicameral
system—that is, the *Bundestag* and the *Bundesrat*
—in joint session, thus discarding the Weimar
system of direct election. The Constitution contains an important tableau of civil rights, among
which appears the safeguard of free and democratically organized political parties. These are
safeguarded by appeals to the law courts; and the
Constitution itself is safeguarded by a special
constitutional court.

Amendment of the Constitution. This is regulated
by Article 79. Amendment is by a law expressly
altering the text of the Basic Law; it requires
approval by two thirds of the membership of both
Houses. To maintain the federal structure and
Articles 1 to 20 of the Constitution intact—no
amendment at all is possible of rights and prohibitions therein established.

Basic Rights. These are set out in Section I, comprising Articles 1 to 19. The student must refer
to this charter textually for the interesting detail
(pp. *xxvii–xxix*). Some main characteristics need
explanation here. The first is that the charter of
rights has now assumed such importance in the
German mind that it appears *first* in the law, prior
to the machinery of government, not later as in

Weimar. Symbols are important to express an attained conviction and to help build the habits of the following generations.

Though the rights contain as much concern for the nationalization of enterprises as did the Weimar Constitution, and concern for economic and social welfare, there is now a highly emphasized attention to man as an individual. Thus Article 1 actually begins with

> (1) The dignity of man is inviolable. To respect and protect it is the duty of all state authority.
> (2) The German people therefore acknowledge inviolable and inalienable human rights as the basis of every human community, of peace and justice in the world.

Here is evident, as were the discussions on their form and wording, the effect of Hitler's brutalities on the German people and other people, and the discussion of human rights by the United Nations' Commission on Human Rights. The flavor of relative rights has been thinned out to give more emphasis on rights as absolute—*against* the State. Moreover, there are no Fundamental Duties, as in the Weimar Constitution. Both the Christian Democrats (former Center Party) and the Social Democrats learned that democracy is prior to welfare and is the condition of any social justice and church rights.

Nor is this all. Article 1 goes on to say:

> (3) The following basic rights are binding on the legislature, on the executive and on the judiciary as directly valid law.

Weimar did not do this, taking the alternative course of declaring that subsequent legislation would spell out the detail of the rights. But here, the rights are substantive law. Naturally, they are liable to suffer in interpretation; but they are enacted. To safeguard the injured individual, the Basic Law in Article 19 enacts some safeguards. If any person's rights are infringed by public authority, he may appeal to the courts; the ordinary courts, unless some other authority is competent. This gives the judiciary and the person a standing not possessed under Weimar: it took bitter experience to show what guarantees were

necessary. Furthermore, laws that restrict basic rights (by formulation of them as stipulated in several of the articles) may not do so for individuals but must apply generally; and the law must name the article affected. Its basic content may not be injured. This is *the best* a constitution can do. The rest is up to the judiciary and the other authorities. Only a constitutional amendment could pervert or convert these.

An attempt is made (Art. 18) to thwart the attempt of future usurpers like the last one, Hitler, to undermine the rights essential to the democratic process itself.

> Whoever abuses freedom of expression of opinion, in particular freedom of the press . . . freedom of teaching . . . freedom of assembly . . . freedom of association . . . the secrecy of the mail, of the postal services and of telecommunications . . . property . . . or the right of asylum . . . in order to attack the libertarian democratic basic order, forfeits these basic rights. The forefeiture and its extent shall be pronounced by the Federal Constitutional Court.

The purpose is to obstruct the abuse of democratic freedom by those, like the Nazis, who employed them to destroy those rights for others (see p. 663ff.). It is an answer to the problem posed earlier, whether there is not a point of mutilation in tactics and demagoguery as serious as the use of physical violence in the democratic process which must be stopped (p. 651).

There are several *unconditional* rights. They are absolute, touchable only by constitutional amendment, and not assailable by Emergency Laws and Decrees. This averts the disastrous actions of Hindenberg and Hitler (p. 663) of suspending such rights. They are: no legislative discrimination on account of descent, race, language, homeland, origin, faith, religious or political opinions; no forced labor except by judicial sentence; no retroactivity of criminal legislation; no death penalty or physical or mental ill treatment of detained persons; no detention or its continuation without authority of a judge, nor keeping under arrest for longer than the end of the day after arrest, unless by judicial warrant; a relative or confidential friend of the arrested must be notified *forthwith* of the judicial warrant of detention; freedom of religion and conscience; parental right to decide on religious education for children; fair compensation for expropriation or socialization; right of petition; supremacy of international to domestic law, the rules being *operative as immediate rights and duties for individuals* (remember the trials for "crimes against humanity," etc.); the unconstitutionality of actions designed to disturb the peace or prepare for aggressive war.

Attention, then, must be drawn again to Article 1, on the inviolability and inalienability of certain rights: for this is designed to *bind all governmental* authorities, even though the Constitution amended the various rights we have cited and others. It is the equivalent of "due process." These rights are *put above the Constitution.* This is the essential progress over Weimar: there are some things the State is *not allowed to do at all,* as in American but not in British government. It is noteworthy, also, that the Basic Law makes these rights enumerated parts of the Constitution, whereas the Preamble of Rights in the Fourth Republic (p. *xvii*) is but a Preamble. There is, then, a sphere of *unamendability* in the Basic Law. The courts are the protectors of rights even if affected by an amendment. Still, it will be noted that, first, there is no *habeas corpus* writ—that is, compulsory release from detention if a judge says the law warrants detention. Second, the Constitutional Court is composed of appointees of the two Chambers, chosen by them by simple majorities— it *could be* packed. Nor can there be a formal safeguard against a party that packs the Chambers with two thirds of a membership which then connives to revise the Constitution, as Hitler did. For protection one must rather look to the courts, to the federal structure, to the *Bund* machinery of government, and to the several political parties.

Omission of Two Institutions. From the Basic Law two institutions on which the Weimar democrats placed great emphasis have been omitted: the *Reichswirtschaftsrat* and the plebiscites. The former had not proved so valuable as was expected (p. 627), for interest groups had preferred direct negotiation with the parties and the *Reichstag,* and so had the latter.

The experience of the referendum and the initiative (p. 627) had proved to be in no wise constructive, but only demagogic and subversive of good sense.

Addition of the Constitutional Court. Judicial review of the laws and executive orders for their constitutionality had been operative in the Weimar system, but (p. 629) rather by implication than direct grant of power to the courts in the Constitution. The influence of American Occupation Authority, as also American influence gleaned by German scholars, the bitter experience of lost liberties, and now, the firmer establishment of basic rights and the federal arrangements, conduced to the creation of a court to guarantee the Constitution—as in France (p. 333).

With the Supreme Bund Court, its inferior instances, and the law courts of the *Lander,* there is also provided the Federal Constitutional Court. It is composed of federal judges and other members. These are elected one half by the *Bundestag* and one half by the *Bundesrat* from persons not being members of either of these bodies or of the government of the *Bund* or *Länder*—thus ensuring some independence of mind. The statute regulating the Constitutional Court was passed in March 1951. It sets up the court in two senates, dividing out the work among them by topics found in the Constitution. These have twelve judges each. Judges must be at least forty years old, and be qualified for judicial office or have passed the examinations for the Higher Civil Service and be distinguished in the knowledge of the public law and have practical experience. Once chosen they may not practice any other occupation, with the exception of teaching law in a university. Four of the judges for each senate are chosen from the higher federal law courts for the term of their office, which is a life career. The other eight are chosen for eight-year terms, with re-eligibility. One half of the numbers are chosen by *Bundestag* and *Bundesrat,* respectively. Those elected by the *Bundesrat* need a two-thirds majority of its total membership. The Chambers take turns in picking the President of the court. The quorum in each senate is nine judges. If either senate wishes to depart from the ruling of the other, the matter is settled by a joint meeting of the senates.

The Legislature. "This democratic and social federal state" (Art. 20) has the sovereignty of the people exercisable through elections, plebiscites,[2] and legislative, executive, and judicial organs. The political will is formed by the participation of political parties—the most explicit statement of the role of parties in any existing constitution (not matched in the Weimar system) with the exception of Soviet Russia, which, however, is intent on the role of the *only* party, the Communist (p. 854). We touch on this again in the section on current political parties.

The legislature is bicameral, with the *Bundestag* as the lower and popular chamber and the *Bundesrat* as the "federal" chamber; the former is popularly elected; the latter is composed of delegates

It operates by the method of parliamentary commissions such as we have seen in operation in France. These work more smoothly and less embarrassingly to the Government and the orderly march of governmental business, partly because one party, the C.D.U., has had command of a majority of the *Bundestag* since 1949 (see electoral statistics, p. 703). There is now a regular daily period for questions, ten Deputies being needed to support one. For interpellations, an endorsement of thirty members is required, in order to abate agitation by smaller bodies.

We present now an occupation analysis of the 1953 *Bundestag* conveniently distributed by political parties. It appears in the *Handbuch des Deutschen Bundestages,* 1954.[3]

Occupation	C.D.U.	S.P.D.	F.D.P.	G.B./ B.H.E.	D.P.	No Party	Total
Government officials and employees	51	28	7	7	2	—	95
Teachers	14	11	3	2	1	1	32
Employees:							
Free enterprise	12	14	7	3	4	—	40
Political parties	2	15	—	—	—	1	18
Trade unions	17	17	—	—	—	—	34
Other organizations	15	5	4	2	—	—	26
Manufacturers and businessmen	32	11	11	1	2	—	57
Artisans and craftsmen	15	19	—	—	1	—	35
Farmers	38	3	7	2	3	1	54
Physicians	2	2	1	1	—	—	6
Lawyers	20	7	8	6	—	—	41
Clergymen and church officials	7	2	—	—	—	—	9
Journalists and publishers	7	17	1	1	—	—	26
Miscellaneous free professions	7	5	2	1	1	—	16
Regular Army	2	—	—	—	—	—	2
Housewives	9	6	2	1	—	—	18
Totals	250	162	53	27	14	3	509

C.D.U., Christian Democratic Union; S.P.D., Social Democratic Party; F.D.P., Free Democratic Party; G.B./B.H.E., All-German Bloc; D.P., German Party.

named by the *Länder* legislatures. The *Bundestag* is the superior legislative power; the latter has lesser powers, to be noticed almost directly.

The Bundestag. It has a four-year term, though it may be dissolved earlier (p. 699). It enjoys the full range of parliamentary privileges and immunities; the right to set its own procedure, to decide the commencement and termination of its sessions; to establish investigation committees; and so on. It has authority over disputed elections, though there is a final appeal to the Constitutional Court.

Over one half of all the members are between thirty and fifty years old. The proportion of officials and employees is very high—the "managerial"-employed type who administer associations and corporate representative bodies. The members who are party functionaries amount to 20 percent, 70 percent, 30 percent, 75 percent, and 30 percent of the total group in the *Bundestag* of the parties listed above, respectively. It is a very highly educated parliamentary body.

Another grouping of a sociological nature is

[2] But provisions for these are scarce in the Constitution.

[3] Cotta, Stuttgart, 1954, p. 167.

made by v. d. Heydte-Sacherl, *Soziologie der Deutsche Parteien,* p. 297. Its results are:

Courts. As for the ordinary courts, most of the jurisdiction is at first instance, in federal matters,

Grouping	Percent of Party Membership				Percent of Population So Occupied
	C.D.U.	S.P.D.	F.D.P.	B.H.E.	
Agricultural	15.6	2.0	12.5	3.7	23
Industrial and artisans	7.4	10.6	2.1	—	38
Technical	2.5	4.0	2.1	—	3
Business and commerce	21.3	25.2	27.1	22.2	16
Household, health, and social	0.8	2.7	2.1	7.4	6
Administrative and law	31.5	29.1	35.4	44.5	7
Intellectual and artistic	9.0	19.2	6.2	18.5	2
Not defined	0.8	0.6	2.1	3.7	5
Independent, but no occupation	11.1	6.6	10.4	—	—
	100.0	100.0	100.0	100.0	100

In its first two years following the election of 1953, 347 bills were submitted to the *Bundestag:* 174 by the Government, 166 by the political parties (or groups), and 7 by the *Bundesrat.* Of these, 145 were passed and promulgated, and 57 were awaiting promulgation. These included some very important measures, such as basic fiscal reforms; family allowances; a rent law; assistance to agriculture; pension increases; and social-security measures—and the law to establish an Army on a voluntary basis to meet Germany's obligations under the Paris Treaties signed in February 1955.

In the two-year period 47 weighty interpellations were debated on high policy, and 144 of lesser importance put by groups or individual members. There were in all 13 hours of questions during which 395 questions were asked and answered. No less than 15,500 petitions were processed by the *Bundestag.* It is a very serious, hard-working assembly, tending to draw to itself thereby the loyalty of the population.

The Bundesrat. This body, representing the *Länder,* is, as traditional in German practice, composed of *unequal* representations of the *Länder.* Each has at least 3 votes; but those with over 2,000,000 inhabitants get 4; with over 6,000,000, 5. We have given their distribution earlier. They must be members of the governments of the *Länder,* which appoint and dismiss them. They must vote as their governments instruct. Hence, the elections in the *Land* governments must be watched, because they determine the complexion of their governments and so the political party strength in the *Bundesrat.*

conducted by the *Land* judicial authorities. Appeals lie to the federal courts. A Supreme Federal Court makes decisions where the uniformity of justice in the higher federal courts is involved: the judges to this are appointed by the Bund Minister of Justice and a committee of *Land* ministers of justice and an equal number of members of the *Bundestag.*

The older practice of having special courts for special purposes is retained. There are the administrative courts—and, also, courts for finance, labor, and social affairs.

In constitutional matters, a *Land* may assign its internal constitutional disputes to the Federal Constitutional Court. Any court must suspend proceedings on any issue before it where the interpretation of constitutional rights is involved, and apply to the *Land* court on the constitutionality under *Land* constitutions or the Federal Court where the Basic Law is involved, and this applies where a *Land* law is in conflict with the Basic Law or a federal law. A *Land* court may not deviate from a decision of the Federal Court or any other *Land* Constitutional Court, without previously obtaining a decision of such courts.

Extraordinary courts (like the Nazi People's Courts, etc., p. 676) are outlawed; nor may anyone be prevented from appearance before his lawful judge.

No Separation of Powers. Some American advisers to Military Government pressed strongly for the institution of the separation of powers as in the United States, in order to ward off the excessive power of the Executive. German tradition won.

The Constitution, like that of Weimar, preserves parliamentary responsibility and the blending of Executive and Legislature. The exceptions are (1) that civil servants have been excluded from the *Bundestag* and (2) the courts are guardians of the constitutional order against the trespassing of either Legislature or Executive.

Budget of the West German Government, 1955-1956

	Millions of Marks	Percent
Expenditures		
Ordinary		
Defense and Occupation	9,186	33.0
Social services, allowances	9,327	33.6
Aid to Berlin	800	2.9
Food subsidies	273	1.0
Debt service	913	3.3
Reparations and indemnities	680	2.4
Investments	528	1.9
Administrative services	2,468	8.9
Contingencies	2,020	7.3
Extraordinary		
World Bank Subscription	20	0.1
Investments	1,569	5.6
Total	27,784	100.0
Revenues		
Ordinary		
Customs and excise	18,454	66.4
Income tax	4,280	16.4
Special income tax	161	0.6
Coal tax	100	0.4
Postal receipts	230	0.8
Landbank	40	0.2
Mintage	4	
Bills of exchange	906	3.3
Loans to meet social charges	2,020	7.3
Extraordinary		
European Recovery	20	—
Loans	1,568	5.6
Miscellaneous	1	—
Total	27,784	ca. 100.0

II. FEATURES OF THE BONN CONSTITUTION

The Territorial Foundation

The sovereignty of the area is shared between the *Bund* and the *Länder*. The former may be trans- lated as *federation* (see p. 561 and p. 577ff. for the- oretical discussion). The eleven *Länder* we have already named. All of them are "artificial" in the sense that they are not what history had produced as separate states then joined in the Weimar Con- stitution. The reorganization of the areas was made by the Occupying Powers and was very substantial. The marked inequalities of population were so greatly reduced that, given the extinction of Prussia as a single state, the special protections and "reserve" powers of some of the states were no longer necessary. Like the Weimar Constitu- tion, an article of the Basic Law (Article 29) still provides for eventual reorganization "with due regard to regional ties, historical and cultural con- nections, economic expediency and social struc- ture." If this is ever undertaken it must be so within three years (already passed) by federal statute initiated by popular request and referen- dum.

The Federal Balance of Power. The powers of the *Bund* are enumerated; the rest of the powers lie with the *Länder*. But the manner of distribution is that of the Weimar Constitution (see p. 616), exclusive to the *Bund*, concurrent for *Länder* and *Bund*, and general standards set for the *Länder* by the *Bund*. The exclusive powers (Article 73 and Article 105) are spare (foreign affairs, citizen- ship, weights and measures, coinage and commu- nications, customs and fiscal monopolies). But the concurrent powers exercisable by the *Bund* if (Art. 72) "a matter cannot be effectively regulated by . . . the individual *Länder* . . . [if] a *Land* law might prejudice the interests of other *Länder* or [all of them] . . . [if] the preservation of legal or economic unity demands it." This lets in the *Bund*, as the text shows (p. *xxxiv*), to almost everything. As such it was strongly opposed by the Occupying Powers—but in vain, for the Germans were as interested in centralization as the whole corpus of the American Constitution as interpreted by the Supreme Court on the basis of congressional legis- lation has become.

The traditional stipulation that federal law overrides *Land* law appears. The *Kompetenz- Kompetenz* power (p. 581) to increase its powers by constitutional amendment is available to the *Bund*.

The Administration of Bund Statutes. The Basic Law signalizes a recession from the Weimar arrangement of much direct administration by Reich officials of Reich law (p. 617). The *Bund* is now restricted to its own civil service administration in foreign affairs, federal fiscal system, the railroads, posts, telegraph and telephone. *Outside this,* by Articles 83ff, the *Länder* administer, by their own officials, all *Bund* legislation. Even more: only in the case of certain enumerated taxes may the *Bund* assess and collect; otherwise this is a *Land* function. The right of supervision is assigned to the *Bund* in Article 84: the methods are those of the Weimar Constitution (p. 617): administrative regulations, *Bund* commissioners to the *Land* departments at top and lower levels. Failing successful cooperation this way, the *Bundesrat* (the "federal" Chamber) decides if there has been default. Against this an appeal may be made to the Federal Constitutional Court. There are further devices to secure uniformity of *Land* action on federal legislation too involved to reproduce here.

The power of *Federal execution* (p. 619), the right of the *Bund* to send forces into the *Länder* to secure compliance with the Constitution, is attenuated to this: Article 37 allows the *Bund* "necessary measures" to enforce compliance with *Bund* instructions, but, instead of leaving it merely to the President of the *Bund* (as in Weimar the Reich President) alone to take action, now the approval to the *Bundesrat* is required.

Imminent danger to the free democratic basic order of a *Land* (as of the *Bund*) may be met, where the *Land* will not or cannot combat the danger, by *Bund* commands to the police of the *Land* and other *Länder*.

The Financial Power. The evolution of Weimar toward a coordinated budgetary and taxation system for *Bund* and *Länder* together sets the pattern for Bonn. This, which came to be called the *Finanzausgleich* (more a "single design" than merely equalization of burdens to help the financially weaker states), gives the preponderance of fiscal authority to the *Bund*. This was commended not only by the conception of the unified economy but because on the *Bund* certain special afterwar burdens were placed, such as Occupation expenses, refugee and expellee subsidies, war-damage

compensation, support of those made destitute by the war.

The Basic Law assigns revenues to the *Bund* and the *Länder* respectively (see p. *xxxix*), to the former chiefly customs and government enterprises, like liquor, matches. It allows the *Bund,* as necessity requires, to take taxes on income, inheritance, and property. And the *Bund* may also raise excise taxes that are primarily assigned to the *Länder,* such as tobacco, beer, coffee, sugar, and business transactions. The tethering of the *Bund* to the *Länder* as in the Bismarckian Constitution (p. 581ff.) is outworn.

Stability of the "Federal" Structure. Pursuant to the desire to keep Germany without excessive unitary strength, Article 79, on the mode of amending the Constitution does *not permit any amendment at all* of the existence of the *Länder,* their basic cooperation in legislation, or any of the basic bill of rights and the foundations of democratic government that they enjoy and must observe. The *Bund* may keep them republican, democratic, and social. They are entitled to an equitable employment in the top federal service of *their* officials. The *Bundesrat* must be given all bills initiated by the Government before their submission to the *Bundestag*. It may initiate laws. As for the authority of the House in legislation, a distinction is made between *Foederativegesetze* and general legislation. The former, stressing the federal element, are laws that especially concern matters in which the *Länder* have a direct interest; the latter are those which concern the *Bund* as a whole. For the former, the *Bundesrat's* consent is essential for enactment. To secure solution of deadlocks between the Houses, a joint arbitration committee of both proposes a text. The Houses decide. This, then, is a defense of the *Länder* rights. Such "federalistic" matters are among others on territorial changes; constitutional amendments; *Bund* demands for a share of income and corporation taxes; the creation of new federal agencies.

In "general" legislation the *Bundesrat* has only a suspensive power. Within a week of receipt from the *Bundestag,* it may reject a bill. If this is by an ordinary majority, then the *Bundestag* may rebutt the veto by an ordinary majority; if by a two-thirds majority, then it must all have a similar majority to triumph. Then the *Bundestag's* will prevails. In these matters, the *Bundesrat* is much weaker than the Council of the Republic in France (p. 445ff.).

The *Bundesrat*, rather like the United States Senate, has some Executive functions also. It participates in the impeachment process concerning the *Bund* President; its consent is needed to the *Bund's* use of the emergency laws; it appoints a half of the members of the Constitutional Court.

It is but a shadow of the *Bundesrat* of 1871. But it still represents those obstinate entities, the *Länder*. And being composed of high officials, it has great weight of authority. Naturally, the political parties seek to dominate it as they do the *Bundestag*. A party that captured both with a considerable majority could, if it wished, subvert either pole of the federal system, the center or the *Länder* strength.

The Executive

This consists of the President, the titular executive, and the Chancellor and Ministers, the parliamentarily responsible authority.

The President of the Bund. The Bonn draftsmen were fully cured of what may be called "Preuss' Folly" (see p. 624)—that is, a President elected by the people at large and endowed with substantial powers. They were cured by the use made of elective authority and his powers by Hindenberg (p. 657ff.).

The President has a term of five years instead of seven and is re-eligible but once. He is elected by a special body called the Bund Convention, or *Bundesversammlung,* a tribute to the ingeniosity of professors of constitutional law. It is composed of the members of the *Bundestag,* plus an equal number of persons elected by the parliaments of the *Länder* by P.R. The latter arrangement is bound almost to duplicate the party composition of the *Bundestag*. The new procedure would have resulted in Hindenberg's defeat for the presidency.

All the acts of the President, allowed to him as the personal embodiment of the *Bund,* need the countersignature of the Chancellor or a Minister with jurisdiction over the particular matter.

It will be seen, when the status of the Chancellor is discussed, that the President has been shorn

of four powers that he had under the Weimar system, with destructive effect to it. (1) He no longer has the power to appoint a Chancellor endowed with all the powers of government until overthrown by a parliamentary vote of censure. (2) He can no longer dismiss a Chancellor, whereas he was able to *formerly* even though the latter had not been parliamentarily overthrown. (3) He can no longer dissolve the Parliament with the countersignature of a Chancellor who had not yet obtained a vote of confidence (the von Papen and Hitler cases, p. 660; p. 663). (4) He no longer has the power to institute at his discretion, and with countersignature, a state of emergency (p. 625). His arbitral power in the choice of a Chancellor (such as the President of France has, almost *in excelsis*) no longer exists, for the Chancellor is he who gets an absolute majority in the *Bundestag*. But if, after the third ballot, the nominee for Chancellor has only a relative majority, the President may, on his own discretion, decree a dissolution, when he may secure influence over the Chancellor. However, he does propose the nominee for the chancellorship to the *Bundestag:* and here he does not require countersignature either. Hence he has *some* discretion, which might be used in collusion with a favorite party leader. Adenauer of the C.D.U. and Kurt Schumacher leader of the S.P.D. until 1952, when he died, were not averse to such collusion, as each are men of firm, centralizing resolve.

The Chancellor and the Government. It has always been a characteristic of the Germans to have and wish a strong and stable Executive. Weimar foundered partly owing to its absence. Hence, the reintroduction of *the primacy* of the Chancellor in the Council of Ministers. The Chancellor "determines the policy lines and assumes responsibility for them." Furthermore, he has authority to propose who his Ministers shall be, the President then appointing them; equally, he can get them dismissed individually or otherwise. There is no such constitutional stipulation requiring "collective" responsibility as appears in the French Constitution (p. 423) or as a convention in British government. The Bismarckian constellation, carried through Weimar, dominates—of course, subject to the tremendous anti-authoritarian influence of parliamentary responsibility and the pressure of free members in free parties. Each Minister is responsible for his bailiwick within the general policy of the Chancellor, with power of the ministry as a whole to settle differences among them. But the constitutional arrangements for a vote of no confidence in the Government concern the Chancellor and not the Cabinet as a whole or the individual Ministers, although the former would have general consequences, of course.

The *Bund* Chancellor is elected by the *Bundestag* (without debate) when the President of the *Bund* has proposed a nominee. If he gets a majority of the whole membership, he is elected, and the President appoints him. If he does not, then within fourteen days after this vote, the *Bundestag* may elect anyone at its choice by an absolute majority. Failing such an election, there can be a third ballot, and in this the plurality decides. If the elected person receives an absolute majority within seven days thereafter, the Federal President must appoint him; if not an absolute majority, the President may appoint him *or* dissolve the *Bundestag*.

What is the political meaning of this? It takes power from the President and lodges it in the *Bundestag;* and it thereby presses on the responsibility of the members of the *Bundestag* to make a positive choice. In case of difficulty, it calls in the electorate to decide. It offers guarantees to the people and the nation that they have the responsibility and authority to decide, not the President.

Such a government and such a Chancellor proceeds with its work until the *Bundestag* votes a want of confidence in it. This process is now known as the "constructive vote of no-confidence" in contrast to votes of no confidence in other constitutions and in the Weimar system, where the legislature could vote out a Government without any responsibility for offering an alternative. When the *Bundestag* wants to get rid of a Chancellor (and his Government), it must do so by electing his immediate successor with a majority of its members, then requesting the President of the Bund to dismiss the cashiered one; whereupon the President also must appoint the person newly elected.

Dissolution. There is an alternative. If the Chancellor, himself asking a vote of confidence, does not get it by a majority of the membership of the *Bundestag,* he may ask the President for a dissolution, who must obey within fourteen days. But if the *Bundestag* does elect another Chancellor in this time by a majority of its membership, then the right of dissolution lapses.

This is an ingenious device to bring the *Bundestag* to a sense of its responsibility for any instability of Governments it might cause: the destroyers of a Chancellor might not come back, while reconsideration by the parties may find a second or third choice to carry on the Government. The French suffer because they would not discipline themselves in this way (see especially p. 418).

The "constructive vote of no confidence" is rather reminiscent of a famous turning point in the British convention of cabinet responsibility. In 1873 the Liberal Government under Gladstone was defeated in the House. Disraeli, the Conservative leader, refused to take office, having only a minority to rely on. Gladstone insisted that the conventions, hitherto obeyed, "required that an opposition which has in this manner and degree contributed to bring about what we term a crisis, is bound to use and show that it has used its utmost efforts of counsel and enquiry to exhaust all practicable means of bringing its resources to the aid of the country in its exigency"—in other words to take office. For politics is not just a game as too many French Deputies have seemingly come to believe.

The new German device certainly endows the Chancellor with peculiar strength and transgresses by excessive weight on the side of the Executive. It is braced by the denial of right to the *Bundestag* to raise expenditures or taxes over the Government's veto, a transcription of British convention (p. 128).

Emergency Situations. In spite of the difficulty of getting rid of a Chancellor, or with a second or third choice who is disliked, the state of parties could prevent the laws, including the budget, from being passed. Hence "a state of legislative emergency" is necessary and provided for. But it is vastly different from the notorious Article 48. (1) It is not a *general* emergency, but only "for a bill"

—the one in question. On this bill and this alone, the *Government* (not merely the Chancellor) may ask, and the *Bund* President *may* (if the Government's request has been approved by the *Bundesrat*) declare a state of emergency, if the *Bundestag* has rejected the bill, though the Government has declared it *urgent*. The state of legislative emergency holds good similarly if the Chancellor combines the bill with his motion to receive a vote of confidence, as previously described (p. 700).

If, then, when the state of legislative emergency has been declared, the *Bundestag* again rejects the bill or passes it in a version unacceptable to the Government, the bill is deemed enacted so far as the *Bundesrat* approves; also enacted with similar *Bundesrat* approval if the bill is not passed by the *Bundestag* within four weeks after its resubmission, by dilatory tactics, etc. During the term of office of a Chancellor any other bill rejected by the *Bundestag* within six months after initial declaration of a state of emergency as set up according to the previously described procedure may be passed in that time. After expiration of this time, no further declaration of emergency is open to that same Chancellor in his continuing term of office. Moreover, the Constitution itself cannot be amended or wholly or partly repealed or suspended by a law enacted under the foregoing provisions.

There has thus been abolished the crude opportunity of subverting the constitution that was so amply taken to end the Weimar Republic or the means of raping the free government of one of the constituent *Länder* as von Papen did to Prussia in 1932 (see p. 658).

Political Parties and Elections: Formal

The makers of this Constitution knew only too well that the conduct of democratic and responsible government requires the services of political parties. Their suppression by the Nazis and the ugly spectacle of the monopolistic Communist Party a few miles away over the eastern border of Germany rammed home the lesson. Hence the constitutional prescriptions on the nature of parties in Article 21. This insures their multiplicity; their freedom; the democratic principles of their in-

ternal organization; public accounting for their sources of funds. Thus equipped, however, the parties cannot act licentiously:

> (2) Parties which, according to their aims and the conduct of their members, seek to impair or abolish the libertarian democratic basic order or to jeopardize the existence of the Federal Republic of Germany, are unconstitutional. The Federal Constitutional Court decides on the question of unconstitutionality.

Details of the organization of the parties and the immediately foregoing paragraph are yet to be regulated by *Bund* laws.

This is, indeed, a very far-reaching attempt to preserve democratic government against the brutes who take advantage of "legality" to pin a dictatorship of Right or Left on the subjugated body of democracy.

But the constitution-makers thought that even more was required than this. In Article 9, which falls within the Basic Rights, the right of free association is guaranteed, but there is a limitation:

> (2) Associations, the objects or activities of which conflict with the criminal laws or which are *directed against the constitutional order or the concept of international understanding* [italics added] are prohibited.

This is a direct outlawry: they are *ipso facto* illegal.

The statute on political parties has not yet been enacted, but is under formulation. The "corsets" (German journalistic phrase) to hold parties firmly to democracy contain the following "stays": that the starting of new parties is free; they must register officially with their program and rules; to be qualified as members of a party, persons must be qualified to sit in the *Bundestag* or *Landtage;* youth organizations, are, however, permitted; parties must have a voluntary, federal structure, building from below; leaders of superlocal party organizations may be elected only for two-year terms, though they are re-eligible; important decisions of parties must be taken in full party conference of members or their duly elected delegates, and this includes the setting up of party election slates; members must not refuse to take a seat or give it up, at their own discretion or at the request of others; they are not bound by the will of other people or organizations, even, inferentially, their own group; accounts of receipts and disbursements are to be made public in detail; parties that are hostile to the Constitution are to be dissolved.

On October 23, 1952, the Federal Constitutional Court decided that the *Sozialistische Reichspartei,* a Nazi-type party, was unconstitutional according to Article 21 of the Constitution. The grounds of its judgment were the program, the attitudes in propaganda, and the internal constitution of the party.

> If the internal constitution of a political party does not correspond with democratic fundamental principles, then, in general, the conclusion follows that the party will carry out in the State the structural principles which it has established for itself, and will discard the essential components of a free democratic constitution, that is the creation of the will of the State as a result of the free play of political forces, in favor of an authoritarian system.

The court added that when the degree of repudiation of the democratic structure reached the point where enmity to democracy was clearly manifest, the party must fall under the ban of Article 21. The court argued also that the unconstitutionality of a party swept away the right to sit in the parliaments of its elected members.

Elections. The German *Länder* went directly back to Proportional Representation as soon as elections were permitted and parties licensed by Military Government. This was the most tempting device to all parties: in postwar uncertainty and reconnoitering to make sure of all the seats due them by the gathering together of minority votes. It was an error of Military Government not to insist on the single-member system, seeing that P.R. had helped the "splinter parties" to survive and make a destructive nuisance of themselves in 1919–1933. It was too late to break the habit by 1949.

The Basic Law merely prescribes (Art. 38) universal, free, equal, direct, and secret elections for the *Bundestag* but does not prescribe P.R. (as in Weimar) or any other system of election, which is therefore left to be determined by a *Bund* law. (But some of the *Länder* constitutions prescribe P.R. for *their Landtage*).

However, the encounter of the incentive to security of *Bundestag* strength and of the wisdom of keeping out "splinters," especially of the extreme Right and Left, resulted in the curious compromise in the Electoral Law of June 1949, perpetuated with small changes in that of June 1953, in which the simple-majority system in single-member constituencies is mixed with P.R. This is the system put very simply. The total number of Deputies to the *Bundestag,* 400, is divided among the various *Länder* according to their population. The voters of each *Land,* then, return their proportionate number of Deputies. (This happens anywhere, whatever the division of the whole nation into districts.) Then (1949) 60 percent of the Deputies from each *Land's* share were elected in single-member constituencies, and the other 40 percent by P.R. for the competing party lists on a statewide basis. For example, North Rhine-Westphalia had 109 members in the *Bundestag;* of which 65 were to come from single-member constituencies and 44 from the statewide lists. The latter were divisible among the competing parties in proportion to the number of seats their lists received.

In 1949 the voter was faced with a single ballot paper, that for the single-member seat. After those who had won their seats in the single-member elections had been elected, thus personally, all the votes for the various parties were counted up, thus enabling the total number of seats to which the party was proportionately entitled to be found. From this number per party was deducted what the party had already won in direct personal successes, and the rest were divided among the men on the respective lists. Parties getting more seats in the personal districts could keep them even if they exceeded the number of seats justified by P.R. Hence, instead of 400 members, as fixed, 402 were returned.

Any party polling less than 5 percent of the total vote per *Land* could have a share in the P.R. pool *only* if it had won at least one personal district.

The voters voted for party lists, not for local personalities as had been hoped.

For the elections of 1953 the law was amended, passing by 202 to 175. The C.D.U. wanted a complete system of single-member districts only, with

German General Election Results, 1953 and 1949

	1953	1949
Eligible voters	32,101,602	31,179,422
Voters participating	28,479,654	24,495,613
Valid votes	27,551,376	23,732,398
Percent of total	86	78.5
Bundestag seats	487	402

Party *	Votes	Approx. Percent	B'tag Seats	P.R. List	Votes	Approx. Percent	B'tag Seats	P.R. List
C.D.U./C.S.U	12,444,055	45.2	243	71	7,359,084	31.0	139	24
S.P.D.	7,944,953	28.8	151	106	6,934,975	29.2	131	35
F.D.P.	2,629,169	9.5	48	34	2,829,920	11.9	52	40
D.P.	896,230	3.3	15	5	939,934	4.0	17	12
K.P.D.	607,761	2.2	—	—	1,361,708	5.7	15	15
B.P.	465,641	1.7	—	—	986,478	4.2	17	6
Z.P.	217,078	0.8	3	3	727,505	3.1	10	10
D.R.P.	295,746	1.1	—	—	429,031	1.8	5	5
G.B./B.H.E.	1,616,956	5.9	27	27	—	—	—	—
G.V.P.	318,476	1.1	—	—	—	—	—	—
D.N.S.	70,726	0.3	—	—	—	—	—	—
W.A.V.	—	—	—	—	681,888	2.9	12	12
S.S.W.	44,585	0.1	—	—	75,386	0.3	1	1
Independents	—	—	—	—	1,406,489	5.9	3	—

* Key to the name of each party:

1. C.D.U./C.S.U.: Christian Democratic Union (and Christian Social Union, Bavaria)
2. S.P.D.: Social Democratic Party of Germany
3. F.D.P.: Free Democratic Party (Democratic People's Party, Baden-Württemberg)
4. D.P.: German Party
5. K.P.D.: Communist Party of Germany
6. B.P.: Bavarian Party
7. Z.P.: Center Party
8. D.R.P.: German Rightist Party—or Party of *Law* (*Recht*: a tricky German pun)
9. G.B./B.H.E.: All-German Bloc
10. G.V.P.: All-German People's Party
11. D.N.S.: German National Concentration, or National Union
12. W.A.V.: Economic Reconstruction Party
13. S.S.W.: South Schleswig Voters Association

run-off elections. The S.P.D. were generally retentive of the 1949 arrangements, being as the minority (see above for figures) strong for P.R. Few changes were made. Instead of the 60–40 relationship of personal seats to P.R. seats, a 50–50 ratio was established, not on principle but for convenience. The size of the *Bundestag* was raised from 402 to 484 seats. The *Länder* were divided into 242 constituencies: these provided so many personal seats, and P.R. lists per *Land* the rest.

Now the voters were confronted by two ballot papers and two votes, one for the personal candidate in the single-member district and the other for the party lists. In other words, he could vote for the former because he liked him; and vote for a rival party list. In fact, few, almost to negligibility, made the distinction: they went for party lists.

Parties getting no personal seats get no share in P.R. Parties getting less than 5 percent of second votes on the lists get no share in P.R. Party nominations (according to the Constitutional Court's decision) must be by a secret ballot of a party convention or committee elected by it. With the nomination, the parties must offer documentary evidence that they have a democratically elected executive, a written constitution and a program—unless they already have at least five Deputies in the *Bundestag* or *Länder* parliaments. If not they require between 500 to 2500 endorsing signatures for party lists. This represents a drive against petty parties. The Constitutional Court would not allow the imposition of the 500-endorsement for *individual* candidatures.

The names and electoral strength of the political parties may be gleaned from the following table of elections for 1949 and 1953, as well as electoral participation, which, in 1953 was a bigger percentage than at any time in German history, including Weimar, but excluding the intimidated voting under Hitler.

The seats won by the personal and the P.R. or "reserve" lists may be gleaned by subtracting the figure of the latter from the total given in the table on page 703.

The C.D.U. has again unsuccessfully attempted to enact the single-district system.

The Parties in Movement: General

The present parties resemble, as they descend from, those of Weimar and the Reich of 1871 (see pp. 612–613 and 641–643, and pp. 601–605).

As, since 1871, each party forms itself into a *fraction* (p. 343) or group in the *Bundestag* for purposes of parliamentary procedure (representation, etc.); the minimum number is 15, for recognition. As before, also, "pressure groups" operate (discreetly) although the parties are highly interest groups. They are still in 1955 not their firm selves, as some are inflated beyond their "normal" strength (the C.D.U.) being the refuge of conservatives still afraid to unmask themselves, while others, like the neo-Nazi, S.R.P., have been dissolved (or are infiltrees) by anticipation of legal action against them. The one new party, destined to eventual redistribution is that of the refugees and expellees, the All-German Bloc, founded in 1950. As will be later appreciated, actual membership in parties is rather weak, excepting for the S.P.D., since people are afraid to invite the penalties of taking sides (p. 721). The ideological character of the parties (see p. 600) is still strongly marked. Only a small breach has been made in the strength of the central party machine that had been so dominant in the P.R. electoral system in Weimar (see p. 621); but it is nevertheless a healthy breach. Nazi-type Right and Communist Left are reduced to mere fragments; the middle prevails overwhelmingly. Party discipline in *Bundestag action is firm*.

The Parties: Severally

The Christian Democratic Union. The C.D.U. is the heir of the Catholic Center (p. 602 and p. 613). But it drew in many Protestants in the first years of Bonn, a "believers" movement against Nazi paganism. The latter, like the Right wing of the Catholic Party, were middle class in status and outlook and soon found that they could achieve the maintenance of the bourgeois society, freedom, and private enterprise in parties of their own, when they need not submit to the influence of the Catholic clergy. For a time the C.D.U., then, had strength not only in its regional strongholds of the Rhineland and South Germany but also in the Protestant northwest—that is, lower Saxony and Schleswig-Holstein, as well as Württemberg. By 1951 a large number had peeled off in response to the Evangelical Church's antirearmament policy of Pastor Niemöller and his friends. Some joined the S.P.D. The Protestant Christians did not like the C.D.U.'s Catholic dominance and its potential dissuasion of its leadership to bring back the East German area to Germany; they would gain a majority over the Catholics thereby, while Konrad Adenauer would lose his. The Protestants went over to the Free Democrats and the D.P. Also, refugees (most are Protestant from the East) left the C.D.U. to make their own party.

It may be gathered that, involved in this clarification of the C.D.U. clientele, the Protestants looked to see that the unity of Germany, which was first on their list, should not become second to Adenauer's unity of Europe, which was first on his. The Protestants remembered that in united Germany there is a Protestant majority; in the West the two religions are about equally balanced, while the Catholics there are better church members and so electorally superior and have mass organizations of welfare, youth, etc., etc. Yet Adenauer's policies of European unity and his lieutenant's (Ludwig Erhard) policies of free enterprise, a rising standard of living, and currency reform (anti-inflation), and the strength of his Minister of Finance, Fritz Schaeffer have rallied Protestants to the party.

The party lacks inner solidarity, because it is not, especially in North Germany, a party of mass membership. This makes its finances weak; and makes the character of the leader or leaders the prime factor of cohesion. Hence, the significance of the talents and character of Konrad Adenauer; hence also, since he is eighty years of age, the pessimistic outlook for its continuing unity, seeing

Members of the C.D.U. and F.D.P.

	Percent C.D.U. *	Percent F.D.P. †	German Adults Percentage
Workers	21.2	16.2	31.3
Employees and officials	21.9	32.0	12.3
Businessmen, artisans, free professions	23.5	36.6	5.6
Farmers, independent	12.4	—	3.5
Pensioners and rentiers	8.7	8.3	16.0
Students	0.8	4.3	0.3
Housewives	11.5	5.6	22.1
Domestics	—	—	8.9
	100.0	100.0 ‡	100.0

* For Rhineland † For Wiesbaden
‡ Figures are approximately accurate.

that those who are close to him do not tower as he does. Hence, the C.D.U. is prey to the inner tensions that afflicted the Center: its Christian scope includes out-and-out capitalistic persons and welfare-State men and women on the Left (Karl Arnold and Jacob Kaiser), as does the French M.R.P. (p. 357). The latter are supported by the Christian trade unions.

The party is followed by the Catholic middle classes, especially the peasantry of the rural areas. Its Right wing contains the wealthy and big industrialists and merchants. It allies for election purposes with the D.P. and F.D.P. It attracts a much higher percentage of the women's vote than men's, especially in the upper age group and the young. In Bavaria as many as 60 percent of those who voted C.S.U. were women; and nearly 53 percent of *all* women voters in Bavaria supported the C.S.U. Over two fifths of its voters are above the age of sixty. Eighteen of the 40 women Deputies are C.D.U. and 18 S.D.P. It is strongest in Rhineland, Baden, Westphalia, Schleswig-Holstein, and Bavaria; weakest in Hamburg, Lower Saxony, Bremen, and Hesse. Two thirds of its Deputies are natives of the *Land* they represent. Its Deputies' occupation may be gleaned from the table (p. 695); men follow it less than women; middle aged men much more than those under thirty.

The occupational distribution of *members* of some of the parties is as the following tables portray. An occupational distribution of the German adult population is added for comparison.

The C.S.U. is the Christian Social Union, the Catholic Party of Bavaria, working in alliance with the C.D.U. It is the offspring of the former Bavarian People's Party (p. 642; p. 649). It is a centrifugal, particularistic party of backward Bavarian peasants and ignorant Bavarian petty bourgeois, the minds that nurtured and preserved Hitler's movement in its early years. It is still the temporary home of nationalists and Rightists. It has lost strength seriously since 1946: then it had 104 of 180 seats in the *Landtag;* in 1950 it fell to 64 in 204.

The Center Party. The Center Party (Z.P.) is a separate and Leftish social-welfare Catholic Party, also a descendant of the Center Party. In economic matters it sides roughly with the socialists; in education, culture, and church politics with the C.D.U.; its clientele is the lower middle and working class of the North Rhine-Westphalia area. It spurns adhesion to the C.D.U.'s wealthy wing.

The Social Democratic Party. S.P.D. inherited the mass support of the democratic working class from 1932; its bureaucracy soon reconstituted itself; its membership is big, and pays regular dues. The trade unions [4] maintain their declaration of no affiliation to a party, but, in fact, the good trade unionist votes Social Democratic unless he is a

[4] The reconstituted trade unions are greatly helpful to the Social Democrats. There are no longer three types of unions (p. 604), but only a single German Federation of Trade Unions (the A.D.G.). In 1955 its membership was about 6,000,000, equal to about 30 percent of all eligible workers. The total is composed of about 93 percent workers, 11 percent employees, and over 6 percent public servants. It is very powerful economically and politically; though it is politically independent (not like the British unions), it confesses it is not politically neutral.

strong Catholic. It has rightly benefited from its democratic good will of the Weimar period; it never connived, as the Center did, with a vote for Hitler's Enabling Act.

It has discarded the Marxian phraseology of the class war, following the Reformists (p. 605) of the early nineteenth century into the way of the British Labour Party and so, with a Fabian, parliamentary, and democratic social-welfare and nationalization policy, has attracted middle-class and intelligentsia voters. For, partly, the exhibition of "Marxism" in Russia and Eastern Germany was sickening. It would follow the policy of quasi-public operative corporations for the basic industries as in England. It has strongly supported the "codetermination" policies (*Mitbestimmungs-recht*). The Works Council Law of 1952 gave the workers a one-third share in the supervisory boards of management, throughout industry. The law of 1951 on codetermination allowed the unions and workers to appoint five out of eleven members on each such board, the eleventh being a neutral. One of the three executive directors of the firms is appointed by the unions to be charged with labor's welfare.

Its first postwar leader was Kurt Schumacher, crippled in the concentration camps of Hitler, an almost Robespierrean character, enforcing the purity of the party and its internal discipline. S.P.D. is the second largest party in the State. Were Germany united, it would approach a majority. It has pursued a ferocious policy of unification; of anti-Americanism; of ambiguous *rapprochement* with Russia; against German rearmament; adverse to the Paris Pacts; sharpened beyond conscience, perhaps, by the memory of Hitlerism and the resoluteness not to be reputed as anti-nationalist. Schumacher's fierce energy was directed toward making the party something different from its stodgy Weimar self, but the party officials are men with decades of attachment to the old ways. He is followed by Erich Ollenhauer, a life-long party leader. S.P.D. remains a democratic party of urban workers and their wives, social-security recipients, intellectuals, and some civil servants, the intellectuals very few and mainly occupied in political leadership.

The party is suspicious of the Catholicizing of politics, though it is not the sectarian atheist of the past. It has had affiliations with Protestant party groupings. Yet it must avoid loss of Catholic voters.

This means that its present 28.8 percent of the total vote is practically its saturation point, and therefore, that it cannot expect to get office. For this, it would need to coalesce with the C.D.U., and lose its identity of policy, though it might do this always to avert a Rightist return, in defense of the democratic system. Its nature as a *Weltan-schauung* might let it coalesce with the Refugee, etc. Party, which would be no help to office (see figures, p. 695); nor, even could it conscientiously form a coalition with the F.D.P., etc., could it reach with them above about 40 percent of the seats. This confinement of opposition makes it an exaggeratedly sharp critic with an inclination to negativism.

Its greatest strength lies in Hamburg and Bremen (over 39 percent of the total vote), Hessen, North Rhine-Westphalia and Rhineland-Palatinate; its lowest (about 24 percent) in Bavaria and Baden-Württemberg. One half the Deputies are natives of their *Land*. A much larger percentage of men than women vote S.P.D., and it attracts the younger and middle-aged voters more than the older population; and the men and women among the young are equally represented in its clientele. More middle-aged men than women vote S.P.D.

Occupations	Percentage Membership S.P.D., All-Bund
Workers	45
Employees and officials	22
Artisans, professions, students, teachers	12
Peasants	2
Housewives	7
Pensioners and rentiers	12
Domestics	—
	100

The Communist Party. K.P.D. was one of the parties earliest licensed—a tribute to Western democratic sincerity. It was compelled to sever connection with the S.E.D. of Eastern Germany (see p. 714) by the pressure of the Military Government that increased with the growing malignity of the U.S.S.R., especially after the Berlin Blockade of 1948. It has not been banned, though the Constitution would justify this, and has taken part in all elections. Its policy is that of Moscow, as in the French Communist Party. Its strength lies in the Ruhr, Mannheim, and Hamburg proletarian districts. It suffers from Russian and Communist German brutality in the Russian zone, from the plain stories brought in by the refugees and expellees, by increasing knowledge of the benightedness of the U.S.S.R., whose professions are more easily gauged from only a few miles away. In local elections, 1946–47, it won about 10 percent of votes; by 1949, its votes had sunk to 5.7 of the total cast for the *Bundestag*—that is, less than 1,400,000, with 15 seats; by 1953 it obtained only 2.2 percent of the total votes and won no seats at all, in fair and open fight. It reached 3.9 percent of the vote only in Hamburg and Bremen (its best showing), and 2.8 percent in North Rhine-Westphalia. It attracts the youngest voters and the oldest less than the middle age groups, and women only very feebly. It has four Deputies in the *Landtag* of Bremen only.

The Free Democratic Party. F.D.P. is most reminiscent of the Weimar German Democratic Party (p. 642), the party of commerce and strictly free enterprise. It has been favored by the anti-authoritarian postwar trend; by coalition with the governing party of the C.D.U. against the Social Democrats; and by connection with the miraculous economic revival assisted by American gifts and benign encouragement. In it there is a blend of the Weimar Party mentioned and the more liberal section of the National Liberal Party of Bismarck's time and the German People's Party of Weimar (p. 641). It is a party of the Right; it is perhaps attached to democratic government; it is certainly anticlerical and attracts those Protestant Right-wingers who might otherwise be in the C.D.U. It has a very inferior record for de-Nazification. In the *Bundestag* of 1949 its Deputies contained most of the 50 former Nazis in the house. Its clientele is Protestant upper-middle class, professional workers, many white-collar workers, substantial farmers; but is more urban than rural; it is rural in North Wesse, Oldenberg, and Württemberg. It is the most considerable of the parties of the Right,

the other parties that preceded it being as yet too nationalistic to survive, but it is the most nationalistic of the three biggest parties. It laps beyond the Right and the Left borders of the C.D.U. In Hamburg and Bremen and Baden-Württemberg its Weimar democratic (Stresemann, p. 641) tone is heard; in most of North Germany and Hesse it approaches the extreme Right, the Hugenberg (p. 655) type. It has given the Bonn Republic its first President, Theodore Heuss, who is a disciple of the Christian, Protestant, nationalist, welfare, responsible-government outlook of Friedrich Naumann (p. 604). Should the party move to its Right-wing bias, it would lose its South German voters, who are robustly democratic. It therefore has to allow much independence to the various contingents from the different *Länder*. It appears to be moving Rightward, and many former Nazis have infiltrated it. Its percentage of votes for the *Bund* elections in 1953 was nearly 10 percent; its best showing was in Hessen, 23.7 percent; Hamburg, 17.8 percent; Baden-Württemberg (where it is known as the German People's Party), almost 14 percent, and it is nearly as strong in the Rhineland-Palatinate. It is mainly supported by middle-aged voters; least by the young. It has benefited by economic prosperity and the growing antiforeign, nationalistic sentiment; jumping in voting strength by 80 percent from 1946–47 to 1949, and falling, with Adenauer's successes, in 1953. Its 48 seats have given it a strong place in the Adenauer coalition Cabinet, where it is extremely restive, especially anxious to secure German reunification fast, even by deals with Moscow that would harm NATO.

Others. The W.A.P., or Economic Reconstruction Party, was entirely Bavarian and of a Hitler-demagogic type. It ceased to exist as a separate entity in 1951, losing to the Refugee Party. The Bavarian Party was a particularistic organization, seeking some sort of near-independence for Bavaria and monarchy for that state. It had 4.2 percent of the votes in 1949, not enough to appear at the *Bundestag* elections of 1953. The D.P., or German Party, has affinities to the Free German Party in its character. It is the posterity of the Hanoverian or Guelph "state" party (p. 613). The *Land* of Lower Saxony corresponds to its dreams of a return to Hanoverian particularism, for it has been detached from Prussia which annexed it in 1867. It is Protestant and democratically conservative, rather Torylike, not separatist, and has a strong rural clientele of tough peasant conservatism. It has broadened out from its original postwar appearance as the Lower Saxony *Land*-party: its strength is in Lower Saxony and northwest Germany. It was "colonized" by former Nazis, and so became nationalistic. Yet it joined in coalition with Adenauer, in spite of his fulfillment and European policy, as someone has said, given a "European lacquer," and the paintbrush was its antisocialism, to bar the S.P.D. from power. They sucked in the W.A.V. and exceedingly Rightist elements. This, also, is one of the sponges that is sucking up the Nazi surge, and in disguised form. Hesse and North Rhine-Westphalia are the totalitarian areas for this and the F.D.P. parties.

The Refugee Party, or the All-German Bloc (G.B. and B.H.E.). Something like 8,000,000 refugees and expellees flooded into Germany of the West, largely in Schleswig-Holstein, but more and more spread over the whole *Bund*. They might have become a politically organized force even before 1949, but they were refused licenses, and then later, standing only as personal candidates, they had not the preconditions of getting their own party lists. But in 1950, the B.H.E. came along very strongly. In 1953 it got nearly 6 percent of the votes. But to be refugees is to have a political need in common only in a few matters. It is not of the Right or the Left, distinctly; in Schleswig-Holstein, where it polls about 11 percent of the vote, it works with the middle-class parties; in Lower Saxony with the S.P.D. government, and elsewhere at various times with the S.P.D. and the F.D.P. and C.D.U. They are unified when it comes to prompting and voting for assistance in money and housing and jobs, etc., to make their lot more near that of their German hosts, some of whom would have expelled them (as air-raid evacuees in Britain were sometimes spurned by the places of refuge, a phenomenon witnessed during World War II in every country), and others who would have given them the scantiest help consistent with Christianity as professed, and patriotism as preached.

Industrial workers found work; so did the officials, professional workers, and businessmen. There are, however, many peasants and middle-class and elderly refugees, uprooted because they have lost their possessions. These are the basic clientele of the B.H.E. But they have no Left interests; and have no commonalty with the propertied people of the Right. They might be a mass that would follow a neo-Nazi movement; and, indeed, many of the banned S.R.P., a Nazi movement, voted for the B.H.E. candidates. About 50 percent of the refugee mass have found places in the normal parties. The leader of the party, Waldemar Kraft, formerly an S.S. officer of rank!, has become a Minister in Adenauer's Cabinet, and preaches loyalty to Bonn and against radicalism. It is in the *Landtage* very much a direct interest group, and mixes with any parties, on behalf of its clients, without ideology or ideals. This party is likely to dwindle in proportion as its program of refugee welfare and social integration is successful. To meet this, the party's name has been changed to "all-German" bloc (*gesamtdeutscher Block,* but the appropriate "all-German" program to match this has not yet appeared.

Neo-Nazis? Right-wing parties, of extreme nationalism and anti-Allied resentment soon sprang in Hesse and Lower Saxony in the years 1946 to 1948, getting about 3.25 percent of the local votes. From 1949 these parties acquired strength and confidence, for economic conditions became better, releasing people's attention for politics, and the licensing of political parties was assigned to German officials. The *Deutsches Rechtspartei* won 5 seats in the *Bundestag,* all from Lower Saxony, and was joined by 3 other Deputies, its group in the *Bundestag* calling itself the National Right. It spoke with the tongue of the extremist German National Party of Weimar days (p. 641). Its leader claimed the return of Eastern Germany, denounced those who had punished the Nazis, charged the Allies with crimes against humanity for bombing German cities, demanded German equality with other European countries, preached "Germany first," with a gibberish of profit-sharing. The leader was found to be a Nazi *Gauleiter,* who had faked his own death and taken a new name.

In June 1949 another such party, the Socialist Reich Party (*Sozialistische Reichspartei*) was established, in the city on the Rhine where Neville Chamberlain had flown to Hitler in 1938. It sought together former Nazis and officers, eastern expellees, and prisoners of war. It had Hitler's audacity and all his methods. It was led by the Nazi Party lecturer, Fritz Dorls, another Goebbels; Hitler's favorite, General Otto Ernst Remer, who had moved the bomb-laden briefcase far enough away from Hitler to save his life (see p. 681); Count von Westarp, a member of the S.S. Élite Guard, and others also of high Nazi Party rank. They intended to give Germany "the good side" of Nazism: *Volks-sozialismus,* beginning with an immediate withdrawal of the Occupation troops and restoration of German sovereignty. America was the enslaver; Russia, a friendly power; Germany was to be neutral in a war between these two. It is said that the Communist Party helped on the S.R.P. with finance and by not heckling its meetings. Its greatest success was 11 percent of the vote in May 1951 in the *Landtag* elections of Lower Saxony, which had great unemployment and a very heavy concentration of refugees—but its strength was in formerly Nazi areas. It did well in other elections —Bremen, 7.7 percent of the vote; by-elections in Hesse, Schleswig-Holstein, and Bremen, with from 9.5 to 11.9 percent of the vote—all straws in the German wind. Then in May 1951 Adenauer's Government seized the Federal Constitutional Court with its unconstitutionality, as a successor of the Nazis and an intended destroyer of the liberal democratic Constitution. It took the court a period of eighteen months to reach the decision that the S.R.P. was unconstitutional. By then the party had dissolved itself. Its group in the *Bundestag* was expelled. Remer was sentenced for criminal libel and fled; so did Dorls. The remaining elements sprang up in municipal elections in Lower Saxony in other guises: getting 20 percent of the votes.

A *Reichspartei* was set up; joined by members of the D.R.P. It was rather like the S.R.P. in outlook and membership. It also was charged before the Federal Constitutional Court so far without a ruling. It could not muster enough votes to get on to the *Bundestag* lists. But an affiliation of itself and other such groups put up 138 candidates, 39 being former Nazis, above all, the chief assistant to Goebbels. They got no higher than about 1 percent of the votes; they won not a single seat.

The real trouble with neo-Nazism does not consist in parties openly appearing as Nazis, with or without the exact appellation; it consists of Nazis who infiltrate in to other parties, like the F.D.P. and the D.P., to warp their policies and bide their time until they can come out again into the open.

We estimate the future, after a consideration of the fate of the east of Germany under the rule of its Russian Communist and German Communist masters.

The Civil Service and Local Government

The Civil Service. The Law that now regulates the Civil Service of the *Bund* (and almost identically is matched by *Land* legislation, much of it of pre-Nazi vintage, of course) is the statute of September 1953. It will be remembered that most of the administration of Germany is in the hands of the *Länder* officials, both for their own *Land* legislation and for a very substantial part of the *Bund's* legislation. It is a return, with small exceptions, to the Civil Service as regulated under Weimar, with the disgusting Nazi additions (p. 672) extracted, particularly the *personal* oath to the *Führer,* the right of political activity, and the Nazi denial of (1) the right to see one's personnel file in case of adverse findings and (2) the subordination of professional "acquired" rights to Nazi political maneuvering of functions and jobs. The political neutrality and the sense of colleagueship of civil servants have, since 1945, resulted in the reinstatement of substantial numbers of former Nazi officials in office; but it must be considered that these, under other political and administrative leadership, are largely deprived, for the time being, of power of political and personal harm. Offenders and major offenders are excluded for always. On the whole, if one does not take an absolute view of Nazism as being membership of the party, the main danger is more from "bureaucracy," in the sense of rather authoritarian attitudes to the public and the legislatures, etc., than Nazi convictions. Most are sincerely loyal to the *Rechts-staat,* the rule of law, and the basic rights. The number of officials of which one now takes account is in the neighborhood of 400,000 established civil servants and 365,000 employees and workers in the *Bund* service (including railroads, posts, and customs) as compared with the Reich's 1,517,000 and 1,461,000 respectively in 1942. (The *Bund's* population is about 70 percent of the Reich's.) [5]

The Constitution itself requires the preservation of the "traditional principles" of the Service. The Allied Powers were anxious to end the monopoly of legal education as access to the Higher Civil Service: the statute allows economics, financial science, and social sciences but *excludes political science,* which Military Government asked for. The suspicion is, for the time being, justified; once the Constitution gets set, the curriculum might be reconsidered.

The Allied Powers fought a hard and persistent battle to remove officials from the electoral battles and from sitting in the legislatures (one may recall the Place Bills in England, p. 70, and Article I, 4 (2) of the U.S. Constitution). In the British zone, British practice was introduced: civil servants were not permitted political activity. The American and other Military Government authorities compelled the inclusion in the Election Law of 1949 of the provision that *federal* officials must give up office if elected, but they were still allowed to campaign for election. This law was generalized in one made by the Allies to all levels, federal, state, and local. But still nearly 15 percent of the *Bundestag* of 1949 were or had been officials.

The statute deals with the subject for the *Bund* officials. Its terms are interesting (Article 52, 53):

> The official serves all the people, not a party only. He must fulfill his duties impartially and fairly and care for the welfare of the whole of society in the course of his official activities.

[5] The total of officials of all kinds (including teachers, judges, railroads, ports, and customs) for Federal government, *Länder,* and local authorities is, *circa,* in Higher Civil Service, 251,000; Upper Middle, 708,000; Simple and Middle, 1,267,300. The total amounts to about 4.5 percent of the employed population.

> The official must by all his behavior acknowledge the free democratic foundations of the State in the sense of the Basic Law and to take sides in maintaining it.

These are direct official duties, enforceable by way of discipline in the administrative office and in the administrative law courts; they are enforceable also in the courts that guard the Constitution.

> In the course of political activity, the official must preserve that moderation and reserve which issues from his status as servant of the State as a whole and concern for the duties of his office.

This does not, as some proposed, take away his political rights; it extracts partisanship. But Article 57 has made a change in German tradition:

> The official must resign his position, if he accepts election as member of the *Bundestag.*

This applies to officials, employees, and judges, not to workers. The persons concerned are not cut off from the Service, but are "suspended" without loss of seniority and other rights. The acceptance of Civil Service office by a Deputy causes the loss of his membership of the *Bundestag.* But membership of a *Land* parliament is compatible with office in the *Bund.*

The Allied pressure to open the higher jobs to outsiders and promotion from below rather than keep the traditional exclusive regular entrance at specified educational levels, was resisted by German tradition, for after 1945 the civil servants were themselves in high authority during the remaking of the German State, and they still are. Entrance is at four levels: the Higher Service (see pp. 628–629); the Elevated Service, of a responsible executive character; the Middle Service; and the Simple Service (custodians, postmen, messengers, etc.). The first requires the university studies already referred to and three years of preparatory service, with final examination; the second, secondary school or equivalent schooling and three years preparatory service, with special examination; the third, successful graduation in primary and early secondary school, plus one year's apprenticeship; the fourth, elementary schooling and some apprenticeship.

The *Bund* civil servants' oath of office may be noted:

I swear to preserve the Basic Law of the German Federal Republic and all the laws in force in the *Bund* and conscientiously to fulfill the duties of my office . . . [with or without] so help me God.

Local Government. The Constitution, in Article 28, lays down certain principles of a republican, democratic, and social *Rechtsstaat;* and among these are the rules that at *all* levels of local government universal and equal election shall prevail, and that these bodies be guaranteed, even provided with, "their own responsibility" to govern all the affairs of the local community. The *Bund* is guardian of these rules. But this still leaves the *Länder* with the initiative. The Occupation Authorities each tried to remold the traditional systems of their zones, in the image of their own institutions, mainly to break down overcentralization. They were strongly resisted and had little effect. But, as compared with 1871–1933, the elected councils have been strengthened over against the burgomaster and *Magistrat;* and the officials of central government tutelage have suffered some reduction of their power. It is not possible to enter into details.[6]

Judiciary

Under Bonn, the system sketched still pertains, except for the changes made in the Federal Constitutional Court (p. 695), with which the similar structure of the Weimar system may be compared (p. 617; p. 628). Under Weimar a Supreme Federal Court, the *Reichgericht,* had been established and operative; the present Constitution in Article 95 sets up an analogue. It is concerned with getting uniformity of principle in the higher federal courts, to which appeal is possible on federal matters from the *Länder.* Its judges are appointed by the *Bund* Minister of Justice jointly with a committee of *Land* Ministers of Justice and an equal number of *Bundestag* Deputies.

German legal thinkers and members of the profession are still exercised by the problem of keeping the judges apart from the active administrators. Hence in the statute of 1953 on civil servants, judges are *not* included, and the commentaries point out that the judges are not officials but "public law holders of office." This is to emphasize the *idea* of the separation of powers. A special law on the status of judges is therefore to be made. In the preparatory memoranda on this subject, it is observed that the Constitution excludes judges from the status of officials. This is extremely important for the citizen and democracy, for it has a bearing on the state of mind of the judge— whether he inclines to being the protector of civil rights or leans toward the authority of the State, in his judgments, and German judges have, in the past, been overly State-minded. Partly, the constitutions of the *Bund* and the *Länder* meet this necessity by putting the appointment of the judges in the hands, not of the Ministers of Justice alone, but associating with them nominating committees elected by the legislatures. It is proposed to meet the partisan effects of this arrangement by having representatives of the judges and the State and free attorneys as members of the selection committees. It is also proposed to make judicial and legislative office incompatible. The term *conscience* has been dropped from the present Constitution as that to which the judge is subordinate: he is under the subordinacy of the *laws,* and nothing else; *conscience* offered him too much scope. The authority of the Minister of Justice in matters of discipline and *promotion* is continued, and such is also recommended by the professions. It has its dangers of political interference, but with judicial and Civil Service exclusion from the legislature, it has not all the blemishes this had in France; and, furthermore, the deconcentrated departmental and field organizations of the judiciary assist the Minister's personnel department in making its decisions.

Berlin

The former stronghold of Prussia and capital of the Reich is split into two sectors, the eastern, Russian-dominated, and the western, freely affiliated with Bonn. In the former live a little over

[6] For a good account, see E. H. Litchfield (ed.), *Governing Postwar Germany,* pp. 64–82, by Roger H. Wells, Cornell, 1952.

1,000,000 people; in the latter, a city of refuge from the East (Russia itself, also!), live about 2,250,000. In December 1948, while Four Power occupation still persisted even if but a shadow, elections gave the S.P.D. 64.5 percent of the vote, the highest vote by far of any party in all German political history under free and honest conditions. The Soviet declared the elections invalid! and in November 1948 set up their own city government for the eastern sector. By May 1949 the Western Allies released Berlin from controls. The government of the western sector took a constitution based on that of Bonn. The city council became a *Landtag* (though Berlin could not become the twelfth *Land* of Bonn) and its *Magistrat* became a Senate; the area has the rank of a *Land*. The legislative body allows for 200 members; only 133 attend, for the eastern sector, under the S.E.D. (p. 714), Soviet dominated, does not participate. The Senate is the executive body, consisting of a Chief Mayor (brought to fame by Ernst Reuter, died 1954), a burgomaster, and thirteen Senators. The *Bund's* laws become valid in Berlin when accepted by its own government. The *Bund* takes responsibility for the financing of all *Bund* laws operative in Berlin—in other words it must heavily subsidize this area, which is economically dependent on the larger body politic. The S.P.D., though it has lost its earlier strength, is still by far the largest party and has the lead in the government. The latest elections, held in December 1954, gave these results: S.P.D., 44 percent and 64 seats; the C.D.U., 30 percent and 44 seats; the F.D.P., 12.7 percent and 19 seats; in all 127 seats. The D.P. scored 4.8 percent, but obtained no seats; the K.P.D., 2.7 percent; the B.H.E., 2.5 percent. A coalition of S.P.D., C.D.U., and F.D.P. governs.

As will be seen subsequently, the Soviet Government, in March 1955, declared the German Democratic Government over East Germany a sovereign state, calculating that this would force the Western Powers and West Germany, and, indeed, any sovereign State, to recognize the independent power of this authority. Later, on September 20, 1955, the Soviet made a treaty with East Germany giving it freedom in its domestic and foreign policy. But the Soviet, of course, had inserted in this treaty, that her troops would remain "temporarily" in East Germany but "will not interfere with the interior affairs of the German Democratic Republic and with the social-political life of the country." Then, this treaty gave the East German Government control over its borders around and in Berlin. This, for the first time, gave this Government power within the city itself. Pursuing their brazen insolence even further, the Soviet authorities, in December 1955, allowed the East German Government to begin to regulate the intercourse between the West (and West Berlin) and East Berlin, thus making it possible for the East German Government to claim that Berlin was the capital of the German Democratic Republic and to cause such annoyance to personal and commercial traffic with East Berlin as to force the Western Powers to negotiate with the German Democratic Republic as an independent State. The other three Powers immediately and energetically rejected the newly created status, holding the Soviet Government responsible for all occurrences in Berlin, on the basis of the original Four Power agreement. This is an excellent example of the Soviet's readiness to do mischief with any force at its disposal, in order to bring other people under its domination, an example in foreign policy of cold, deliberate Leninist and Stalinist tactics of "power-politics."

The Bonn Government in Action

The *Bund* President, Professor Theodor Heuss, is a member of the F.D.P. He is a political scientist and follower of former Friedrich Naumann (p. 604), and earlier was professor at the Berlin High School of Politics—a liberal, belonging to the Democratic Party during Weimar (p. 642). He was expelled from office by the Nazis. The government has been under Konrad Adenauer (p. 690) and has been a coalition of the C.D.U., the F.D.P., and the D.P., resulting from the elections of September 1949. After the elections of September 1953, the B.H.E. was also included. On this second occasion, Adenauer obtained a vote of the *Bundestag* of 304 against 148 opposed, with 14 abstentions and 21 absentees. Under these auspices, and giving big industry and free enterprise rein, production has risen 138 percent over that of 1936, a year given to intense economic effort under

Hitler and sovereignty and democratic institutions have been achieved. A mighty housing and rebuilding plan has been fulfilled. Exports are booming. The Chancellor has not been aloof from immixture in the politics of the *Länder,* for they appoint the *Bundesrat.* Hence, interventions for the purpose of securing that coalition, led by the C.D.U., which would give him the kind of delegates that suited his policy.

In spite of almighty difficulties, the educational system has been rehabilitated. Its general lineaments are those of the Weimar system (p. 630). The class inequalities begin to operate at the high-school level, owing to the fees to be paid and the cost of maintenance. The university student body has *doubled* in size, and therefore is more than three times proportionately to the population compared with 1932.

The press has recovered, though none of the newspapers has yet achieved an international reputation. The general character is much as in the Weimar time (p. 600). The radio and television systems are owned and managed by the *Länder.*

Bonn was chosen as the federal capital, for this was Adenauer's native city. It is situated in North Rhine-Westphalia, the most considerable of the *Länder,* where also is situated Cologne, of which Adenauer was so long the distinguished burgomaster, itself the site of the great Cathedral of his faith, and among the great iron foundries and coal mines of the Ruhr. Despite anxious demands, Frankfurt, so long a part of German liberal history was rejected by 200 to 176 votes.

The *Länder* are governed by coalitions according to the constellation of parties in their own elections.[7]

III. THE GERMAN DEMOCRATIC REPUBLIC

The Russian hold on East Germany at the onset of the victorious invasion began with terror, rape,

looting, and murders by the Russian soldiers. Its next phase was official and brutal seizure of every kind of industrial, transport, and communications equipment, public utilities plant, and stocks of all kinds, without previous benefit of the arrangements later proposed in the Potsdam Agreement. Far-reaching arrests of Nazis, anti-Communists, scientists, and useful intelligentsia were undertaken. The administrative machine was more thoroughly destroyed than in the western zones, because the way of Stalin was well known, and democrats and socialists fled along with Nazis. These were replaced by German Communists under orders of the Russian military and security authorities—with appalling inefficiency, cruelty, and corruption at the beginning.

The Soviet Military Administration was established in June 1949, then under Marshal Zhukov. A departmental organization was elaborated, and under it, military governments were set up in each of the five *Länder,* modeled on the central one, and headed by a colonel-general. Moscow not infrequently circumvented the central government by direct connection with the *Länder* ones—a favorite device to keep the center in order and anxiety—and stocked all the levels of administration with Moscow-chosen teams of secret police, trade missions, etc. Later on, it established joint stock corporations of German and Soviet firms.

Between the spring of 1945 and the fall, the Soviet authorities created a German parallel organization to their own: the German Central Administration. The central authority and the *Länder* were staffed with German civil servants and technicians, of course, by the Soviet central administration, and from among Communists in controlling positions and others whose political character was acceptable. The German Central Administration was advisory only until the end of 1946, when it was allowed to take immediate and commanding authority over the *Länder.* In February 1947 its power was increased, by an official agreement between itself and the *Länder,* whereby it obtained the right to integrate all economic functions of the latter. Between June 1947 and September 1948 a segment of the German Central Administration was given (by the Russians) all economic authority over the whole area. This

---

[7] Thus, taking the latest election figures available: Bavaria, S.P.D., B.P., B.H.E., F.D.P.: with the first-named leading; Rhineland-Palatinate, C.D.U. and F.D.P.; Lower Saxony, C.D.U., D.P., B.H.E., and F.D.P.; Bremen, S.P.D., C.D.U., and F.D.P.; Baden-Württemberg, S.P.D., F.D.P., B.H.E.; Hamburg, C.D.U., F.D.P., D.P., B.H.E.: North Rhineland-Westphalia, C.D.U.; Hesse, S.P.D., B.H.E.; Schleswig-Holstein, C.D.U., B.H.E.

exercised the fundamental functions of government; was staffed with the most trustworthy and servile German Communists, as the chosen instrument of Russian domination, dedicated fully to the Russian type of planned economy and the strictest centralization. This was in glaring contrast to the governmental principles of the western *Länder,* where decentralization was a basic principle and the robust practice, enjoyed by the *Länder* and the Occupation Authorities.

The German Communists and Party Government

Simultaneously with the erection of the machinery, Moscow planned and built the political motivating force of the so-called "Socialist Unity Party" (*Sozialistische Einheitspartei Deutschlands*), the German Communist Party engorged by its swallowing of the Social Democratic elements that had sought their own separate party.

The German Communist Party in the eastern area was composed of German Communists who had escaped to Russia during the Nazi regime and Communists who had survived inside and outside the concentration camps, and converts these made among the general population, prisoners of war taken by the Russians, and refugees. The leaders had been well known for many years in German politics: Wilhelm Pieck, Walter Ulbricht, at their head. The Russians had the advantage of being without scruples as to the self-government of the 17,000,000 Germans outside Berlin who had fallen under their domination: they were to be Russianized—that is, molded utterly to fit the purposes of the Communist Party of the Soviet Union. Therefore, almost at once after the overrunning of the area in 1945, political parties were permitted (exactly the opposite occurred in the western part of Germany, p. 686), though the only two allowed to show their heads were the Communists and the Social Democrats. Naturally, the Social Democrats became the vastly stronger party, for to it flowed those who wanted no part of the Communists or rejected two other parties soon allowed by the Soviets, the Christian Democratic Party and the Liberal Democratic Party, as they were too conservative or tainted with Nazism.

The way was, however, clear for the domination of the Communist Party, for it was given every facility by the Russian administration, and it labeled itself as the "liquidator of Nazism," intimidating its opponents of any hue by vilification implied in its alleged mission, and forming anti-Fascist (*Antifa*) all-party groups which it then devoured in the name of a zealous policy of socialization, of the break-up of the large estates, and de-Nazification. This kind of progress was too slow for Moscow, and in 1946 brusque and brutal pressure was exerted to produce the fusion of the two parties, Communists and Social Democrats, for the success of the latter and its disdain for the former was intolerable to totalitarian dictatorship. By April 1946 the fusion had been consummated in the Socialist Unity Party, and the former two separate parties dissolved. The joint heads of the new party were the Communist Wilhelm Pieck and the Socialist Otto Grotewohl. A very large proportion of the members of the Social Democratic Party resigned or were ejected from the party, while most of them in Berlin stuck to their own separate party, in association with the Social Democratic Party of the western area. The too-well-known process of Moscow then proceeded to oust Social Democrats from official positions in the new party, to grind away or seduce their characters, to stigmatize the firm with Stalin's brand of "deviationist." The organizations of the population, like those the Nazis set up (p. 675) and like those set up by the French Communists (p. 350), were developed in order the better to deliver the people into the party's hands: trade unions, youth, farmers, women, cultural societies, Nazi victims, German-Soviet friends, etc.

By October 1946 the party itself was estimated to have nearly 1,300,000 members. But, in the elections of that month, with all the familiar pressure and propaganda and intimidation (see the chapters on the Soviet Union), the party obtained only a mere absolute majority with the votes counted in of the farmers' association, while in Berlin (for the all-Berlin city council) the Social Democratic Party polled nearly two and a half times the number of votes, and all non-Communist votes together (for the other parties also) amounted to 80.2 percent of the total cast!

	Elections to the Parliaments of the Five *Länder*			Elections to the Berlin City Assembly		
	Votes	Percent	Seats	Votes	Percent	Seats
Socialist Unity Party (S.E.D.)	4,625,925	47.4	249	405,992	19.8	26
Social Democratic Party (S.P.D.)	—	—	—	999,170	48.7	63
Christian Democratic Union (C.D.U.)	2,398,035	24.6	131	454,202	22.2	29
Liberal Democratic Party (L.D.P.)	2,410,146	24.8	113	192,527	9.3	12
Farmers' Mutual Aid Association (Vdg.B.)	282,940	3.2	10	—	—	—
Total	9,717,046 *	100.0	503	2,051,891	100.0	130

* Or 85.8 percent of all entitled to vote.

Henceforth, *free* elections, even to this extent, were taboo.

The Imposed Länder Constitutions

The *Länder,* far from being given any autonomy, as in West Germany, were more firmly devised as merely local agents of the center, in accordance with the project of the Socialist Unity Party for the future German constitution. This was made public in November 1946: the various parliamentary bodies of the *Länder* followed this almost word for word and invariantly.

The project provided and the *Länder* adopted these bases of a constitutional order. (1) The legislature was unicameral and sovereign. (2) The Prime Minister was to be elected by that body. (3) The legislature appointed and dismissed the judiciary. (4) The legislature maintained a control over the Government—that is, the Prime Minister and the Ministers he selected. (5) The legislature was elected by universal suffrage and P.R. (6) No President was established for each *Land.* (7) No constitutional court or judicial review was created. The similarity to the Soviet Constitution is obvious; as also to the French Communist Party's proposal for the constitution of the Fourth Republic (p. 324ff.). As in Russia, the party and the Russian military and police system excised from behind the democratic façade all semblance of democracy.

The "Monopolistic Party"

The growth in the membership of the Socialist Unity Party was accelerated by bribes and penalties: the bribes in the form of jobs, dwellings, food (in permanent scarcity), vacations, reduced railroad fares, bonuses, and so on; paper for printing presses, automobiles, other transport to meetings. The "bourgeois parties" were subjected to the smear of being pro-Nazi. The C.D.U. and the L.P.D. were prohibited from publicly assailing the Government. Their most outspoken and gifted leaders, men like Jacob Kaiser, were ostracized from their party by Soviet orders. They were bullied to drop their own independent policy and forced to separate entirely from their western party connections. So far did totalitarian cunning go, that, in order to bamboozle the ordinary elector into the belief that he was living in a democracy, they were forbidden to dissolve themselves, the better to maintain the semblance of a "free" multiparty system!

This nefarious cunning was nothing compared with another trick, intended to confuse the voters who might have stuck together as an anti-Soviet bloc. The S.E.D. actually spawned two new parties: the Peasants and the National Democratic Party, designed to draw away voters from the clientele of the C.D.U. and the L.D.P., namely the middle class and the peasants. It was possible also to draw some former Nazis into these also. They succeeded to some extent; though German suspicions limited the effect intended. Meanwhile, the Russian and Russian-directed Communists pushed the various non-Communist parties into one bloc; while they themselves absorbed the various mass organizations already mentioned, to create the National Front of Democratic Germany. The incentive of anti-Nazism now (1948) gave way to that of Germany's unification—and poisonous enmity of the western parties and the policies of America and the NATO powers, and, of course, the rise of the West German Republic.

A set-back to this policy had occurred at the first open Soviet launching of it. In June 1947 a Soviet-sponsored meeting of the Ministers-President of *all* the German *Länder* at Munich, to discuss unification, ricocheted on the sponsors, for the Ministers-President of the West refused to discuss that very problem. Those from the Russian area went home almost immediately. The Soviet-supported German governments then tried other devices, like a congress of *all* German political parties. But it was boycotted by the West, except for its Communist Party, and by the chiefs of the C.D.U. in its own territory. This congress, held in December 1947, was followed by another (both in Berlin) in March 1948, the hundredth anniversary of the 1848 Revolution (p. 567). Its party composition was as one-sided as the earlier meeting: its venom was spent on the Western Powers and their political party associates in West Germany, and its zeal on the policy of German unification. It established a permanent (Communist-directed) council to secure a popular initiative and referendum for unity for all Germany and a German constitution for West as well as East. The West forbad any canvassing in its zones, but in the East 8,500,000 names were obtained for the referendum. The sponsors produced a constitutional project that was adopted in March 1949 by the council of the congress just named, which, then had the effrontery to announce that it was "the only legitimate representative of the German people."

The next trick was to call elections to a third congress, People's Congress, using the time-matured German conception of *Volk* (p. 552), called a *Volkskongress*. The electoral appeal was even more of a snare. So many seats were officially allocated to the S.E.D.; so many to the "bloc parties"; so many to the "mass" organizations. All appeared on one ticket. The voters were allowed only acceptance of the whole list, or rejection. The voter was then mentally coerced by the referendal declaration at the head of the list, introducing the candidates: "I favor German unity and a just treaty of peace; I therefore vote for the following. . . ." To offset the potential spoiling of the ballot papers—one way of exhibiting opposition—the East German Government decreed that spoiled and unmarked ballots were to count *pro!*

Even all this rigging in favor of the Russian hand in the German Communist glove did not help much. For the Government list obtained only 61 percent of the votes, while almost 34 percent was opposed. In East Berlin, the figures were, respectively, only 58.1 to 41.9.

The resultant congress met and drafted the "Constitution of the German Democratic Republic" (pp. *xliii–lv*). It was to be put into effect if the German Federal Republic in the West could not be prevented from coming into existence. This occurred in September 1949; hence the Soviet Military Governor called a meeting in October 1949 of the permitted East German party leaders, to erect the constitutional machinery—"to be responsible to the German people and not to any High Commissioners." Two days later, on October 7, the committee of 330 of the *Volkskongress* became the People's Chamber of the German Democratic Republic, opened in a tantrum of venomous denunciation of the Western Powers and their republic in the West. The S.E.D. was allotted 90 seats; the mass organizations of stooge parties, 150; the C.D.U. and the L.D.P., 90 divided equally. Notice the exquisite tact of allotting only 90 seats to the modest S.E.D.!

The principle of unicameralism was now abandoned. By the side of the People's Chamber, the Democratic Republic aped the "federalism" of the Western Republic (that was more than sincere, even centrifugal) and the "federalism" of Big Brother Stalin (p. 817), with a *Länderkammer,* a Chamber of Provinces, elected by the members of the five parliamentary bodies of the *Länder* (October 7, 1949). Of its 34 members, 18 were from the S.E.D. and the trade-union federation.

These two Chambers, in joint session, elected Wilhelm Pieck to be President of the German Democratic Republic. The election was Soviet-unanimous. Otto Grotewohl was chosen Prime Minister. His party controlled all East Germany by holding the Ministries of the Interior, Justice, Planning, Industry, and Education, and the first of these was master of the police and of all administrative levels downward. Behind Grotewohl stood Walter Ulbricht, the Deputy Prime Minister and general secretary of the German Communist Party and the S.E.D. C.D.U. and L.D.P. were fobbed off with trifling ministries.

The Soviet Military Administration was "transformed" into a Control Commission, and some of the former's functions were devolved to the German government, including *foreign affairs,* a trump-joker card superior to the powers allowed the West German Government.

This truculent fakery was denounced by all the powers, German and Occupationary, of the West, except, of course, the German Communist Party. Above all, the crude cheating by the establishment of a government not voted for by free parties was patent and roundly condemned.

Leading Features of the Constitution

The Constitution of the German Democratic Republic is not only as "democratic" as the Weimar Constitution, but far more so! Its detailed expression of this must be read in its own terms (pp. *xliii–lv*). The only thing it lacks to be the perfect democracy is the free right of the people to free elections to choose and cashier and discipline the legislators and Executive by unhindered, unintimidated, and unhampered freedom of opinion and the right of association—that is all, for all the freedoms implied in the preceding phrase are denied by the party system we have just described. Even its elaborate bill of rights prohibits "Incitement to boycott of democratic institutions or organizations . . . [etc.] and any other discriminatory acts [that are directed against equality] are felonious crimes." The "elected" judiciary makes sure of the totalitarian interpretation of such clauses. As in Russia, only "democratic" organizations may nominate candidates for elections; and only political parties and mass organizations "which . . . aim to bring about the democratic organization of public and social life in the entire Republic [which includes the West as well as the East!] . . . "may nominate to elective office. Religious action and education must not be misused for anticonstitutional or political purposes. The method of election follows that already portrayed (p. 714)—that is, it is controlled by the S.E.D. for the S.E.D. The strongest political party in the Chamber of the People, *not a majority* of this body, designates the Prime Minister, who then appoints his Council of Ministers. Each party, having at least 40 members of the 400, must be represented in the Cabinet, in proportion to its

numbers, unless it should choose to remain outside. All non-Communist Ministers are "assisted" by S.E.D. Deputy Ministers. The Government may be overthrown by the device of the "constructive vote of no-confidence" as in the Bonn Constitution—but this could not happen without the S.E.D. and its tools being overwhelmed.

As in the Soviet Union's Constitution, the elements that construct and sustain "federalism" are missing, and for these one should see pages 817ff. Above all there is no limitation to the legislative powers of the central government; no residual powers remain with the *Länder.* The old German phrase *"Reichsrecht bricht Landsrecht"* (p. 579) is given a new meaning, to crush the independent life to the last breath out of the *Länder.*

The "federal" chamber, elected by the various *Landtage* according to the seats that have fallen to the various parties, has no power but to suspend for a short period what the *Volkskammer* wants to do, even then overrideable by a simple majority.

The judicial system almost identically follows the Soviet system, including the special tribunals (p. 843), and the intervening Public Procurator (p. 843). There is *no* theory or practice of judicial independence or control over the Legislature or Executive. As in the Soviet Union, the *Volkskammer* is a dimly decorative appendage to the Executive and the dominating party: it meets for about ten days once each year.

In 1952 the *Länder* were abolished (like Hitler's action in 1935, p. 671); and the *Länderkammer* was thus left floating on air—Communist Party air.

In October 1950 elections were held for the *Volkskammer.* They followed the system already described, and the well-known practices of the Soviet Union. Threats were uttered against the person of abstainers, to be checked off on the registers. The issues were falsely represented as peace, unity, and demilitarization of the German people. One "Unity List" fixed by the Communists was presented. The guarantee of the secret ballot was abrogated by a "spontaneous" (dear to the Nazi and Fascist regimes who were past masters in the official arrangement of "spontaneity") movement of factories, offices, apartment and workers' housing estates, for "open" voting. Those who insisted on their guarantee were in danger. No elections were held in East Berlin that had so rebuffed the Soviet masters before; no foreign correspondents were permitted to watch. A total of 12,331,905 people voted, or 98.4 percent of the electorate. Of these a result nearly comparable to that of Soviet Union elections was obtained: 99.5 percent voted for the "National Front" set up by the S.E.D. and, within it, the core of Communists.

The ensuing government was composed of 15 seats for the S.E.D. and its friends, and 6 trivial places for all the other "tolerated" parties, some even being filched by a tricky statute from the C.D.U. and the L.D.P.

The *Länder* governments, like the central executive, became the master of the legislatures. The central budget (as in the Soviet Union) absorbed all the budgets of *Länder* and local government units. In July 1952 the five *Länder* were abolished and local government was devolved instead to 14 *Bezirke* (districts) and each of these was divided into around 15 *Kreise* (Circles), the former with elected assemblies, the latter with elected councils.

Behind all this, the S.E.D., represented by its small nucleus of members on the Politbureau, personally prevades the top level of the state offices and controls the Party and all antiopposition and police activities, following identically the model of the Communist Party of the Soviet Union. The general secretary of the Communist Party is in the Politbureau and is Deputy Prime Minister. The local assemblies are elected on "unity lists" even as the central government is. The only mitigation of Soviet-style party unity is the tensions produced by the attempt to combine Moscow-trainees with German Communists, and the proximity of the Western Powers and Western republic and the open sore of Berlin. The S.E.D. has now some 66 percent Communists to the 33 percent of Social Democrats in its membership of about 1,250,000. It is, of course, a Marxist party in the image of Moscow. As such the people are terrorized by the German police army of 120,000 officers and men, with another 40,000 special police for air, sea, border, and transport and numerous Russian spies, M.V.D. agents (p. 885), informers and the rest, and a half dozen concentration camps, of which four bear infamous names of Hitler's human stockyards. Some 185,-000 had inhabited these camps up to 1950 when they were dissolved, of which nearly 100,000 had died, 37,000 deported to the U.S.S.R., about 37,000 set free, and 14,500 sent to German prisons.

In the administration of this system, the Soviet rulers were not ashamed to make use of efficient Nazis by the hundreds. They are peculiarly able to manipulate the Communist definitions of "social-political danger" for the working classes and the laws regarding "the endangering of society," these rules closely following the Soviet criminal code on "counterrevolutionary" crimes (p. 842).

Included in the German Democratic Republic's armory are all the processes for the capture and demoralizing and mutilation of German minds, including the onslaught on the Churches that have not been banned outright.

Two things the Russians have forced the German tools to do are of ultimate value to a united and democratic Germany. One is the break-up and redistribution of the great estates, including the seedbed of the Junkers. The other is to demonstrate to the Germans everywhere the hell it is to live in a Communist State. The first succeeded in creating 200,000 newly formed small farms. But these farmers as well as the rest are subject to agonizing pressure for production at State-determined rates through the kind of instruments at work in Russia. Tax rates are especially hard on the large and middle farmers.[8] A communizing of industries has proceeded in the enterprises not seized by the Russians—that is, about 40 percent to German government and 20 percent to Russian firms. The rest are steadily coming into German government hands.

How much the East Germans like "their People's Democracy" is indicated by two well-known phenomena. By the end of 1953 nearly 2,500,000 had fled to the West, a steady informed referendum in which not votes but bodies are tallied. On June 17, 1953, the workers of East Berlin rose against their oppressors, the ostensible and first cause being a 10-percent rise in work quotas. Widespread riots occurred in the rest of East Germany, against Ulbricht, Pieck, and Grotewohl—

8 Small farms are below 10 hectares; large, over 20 hectares.

"Beard, Belly, and Eyeglasses are not the will of the German masses!" they shouted. Russian tanks put them down but showed who was really master and government. On March 26, 1955, this state was declared by the Soviet Union to be a "sovereign Republic," but that Soviet troops would remain to safeguard "security" and the Potsdam Agreement, in other words the S.E.D. State. The Soviet intention, carried forward at the Four Power meetings in Geneva in July and November 1955, was to thwart the Western Powers' policy of German reunification, for if East Germany were "sovereign" the U.S.S.R. could represent that reunion was possible only by direct negotiations between West and East Germany, the latter counting not as 17,000,000 people against 50,000,000 but 1 to 1, while the Soviet would no longer have any responsibility.

IV. BEYOND THE RESTORATION OF DEMOCRACY

On May 5, 1955, the Occupation regime begun ten years before, ended; the German Federal Republic became a sovereign state. Chancellor Adenauer said:

> The German people have paid harshly for the horrors which were committed in their name by blind and evil leadership. These sufferings have transformed and purified the German nation. Today, everywhere in Germany peace and freedom are felt to be the greatest treasures, as was the case in the best periods of her history.
>
> I see, in the accession of the Federal Republic to the North Atlantic Treaty Organization and in the implementation of the treaties which the German Federal Republic has entered into with the nations of the free world, the expression of the need to overcome the narrow-minded nationalism which, in the past decades, was the root of our disaster. . . .
>
> Within the community of free nations Germany will be an able and reliable partner and in this community we wish to employ our efforts for the safeguarding of freedom and human dignity. These noble aims will guide Germany now that she is called upon, together with the other member nations, to take her share of responsibility for the preservation of peace in the world.

What is the augury for the ability and willingness of Germans to *remain* free men?

The situation is still obscure, complicated, and anxious. A German historian said after the collapse, "Germans stood perplexed and distracted at the grave of their past." The period of physical destitution is but recently over. The boat is not yet on an even keel; a keel has only recently been provided, and hitherto that boat was steered in a lake made by the victors of World War II. Now the boat is on the open seas; the crew democratic, and better fed.

The Junkers and their link with the Army, Prussian politics, and the military tradition are broken and scattered, their estates given away. Who can, or will ever want to, give them back? The horrifying war damage has, for the first time, brought home to Germans the ravages of modern war and seems to have inspired some doubts whether nationalistic aggrandizement really pays. Frederick the Great and Bismarck are being scrutinized with critical moral judgment, not blindly worshiped. Yet an Army is to be built, and, to secure its subservience to democratic principles and civilian statesmen, the *Bundestag* has enacted that one of its own committees will supervise the selection of officers of the rank of Lieutenant-Colonel upward; the S.S. of this rank are excluded; the conduct of all recruits is to suffer severe investigation. In East Germany the Soviet Union, with shocking blindness, has consciously built a German army, called the People's Police, 100,000 strong, a fifth of whom are officers and N.C.O.'s, a cadre army, ready to expand, like von Seeckt's (p. 644). It has been deliberately reimbued with the spirit of Prussian glory and all its symbols and standards and victorious memories! Conscription is announced. On January 19, 1956, it was officially converted into an army. Two thirds of German youth in the Russian area are members of Communist Youth: outside this there is no economic opportunity or educational advancement open to them.

An impetus to racialism still prevails; but so far, wanting a charismatic leader and his attendant murderers, it is held within bounds. Perhaps there is even shame for it, especially as Adenauer and President Heuss made monetary recompense to

Israel and individual Jews to acknowledge the assumption of collective guilt and remorse. Yet one of the Ministers (Seebohm) is an active anti-Semite, and the *Länder* have *not* met their financial obligations to Nazi persecutees but have reinstated Nazis.

A democratic government is in operation, its guarantee of basic civil rights being formally stronger than almost anywhere else in the world. Founded on free political parties (public opinion polls showed 22 percent interviewed in 1951 preferred a *single* party; in 1955, only 14 percent), a stable and strong government has, for six years, functioned beneficially with Adenauer at its head. Who will replace the octogenarian, his skill, his resolution, and appeal to the people? No man of his stature appears on the horizon; the C.D.U. might waver and split into its various tendencies when Time takes him.[9] The political chiefs are supported by a bureaucracy which maintains the old service-value system of Weimar and pre-Weimar: the supraparty service of the State, with detachment from partisan politics, and a noticeable disdain for "demagogues," meaning political parties and the parliamentary "talking-shop." Its skill is masterly, as shown in dealing with the millions of claims and cross-claims in war damage and loss, rehabilitation of citizens injured by Nazis, or because Nazis, etc. With the population it shares the general "philosophy of exculpation" of guilt for the war and Nazi excesses. It is democratic, with a preference for the C.D.U., less so for the S.D.P. What it would do on the return of a strong party of the Right is still a problem. It is professionally hostile to the officers of the Army and to rearmament.

The public asks normality, security, and private enjoyment; and boasts "sobriety," a cautiousness

against being incited by Left or Right extremists who took advantage of its previous gullibility. This is especially noticeable among the younger people. It is demonstrated in what is called "privatizing," aloofness from politics. Unwillingness to assume leadership and make commitment by youth is hardly healthy; but it is far more wholesome than the frenzy that overcame youth, the ex-soldiers, and ex-officers in 1919 (p. 613). This time the Allied Powers left them without strength, and suppressed potential revengists. Yet insistent upsurges of nationalism, malicious defiance of charges of war guilt, growing praise of Prussian glamor and glory keep breaking out with worrying strength and insistence. And the fever of nationalism is rising again. It was very strongly manifested in the campaign against the internationalization of the Saar, which was rejected by a vote of 67.7 percent of that *Land*'s voters against 32.3 percent, in October 1955. This passion was reaffirmed in the elections for its *Landtag* on December 18, 1955. Then the voters supported the parties seeking political reintegration with Germany: the Christian Democratic Union, with 25.4 percent of the votes; the Right-wing Democratic Party (led by a former Nazi), with 24.2; the pro-German Social Democratic Party, with 14.3. There were 36 percent of the votes cast against reintegration, thus divided: Christian People's Party, 21.8 percent; the Saar Social Democrats, 5.8; the Communist Party, 6.6. (In all about 576,000 voters. The pro-Germans failed in the effort to get 75 percent of the 50 seats needed to revise the Constitution.) The *one* tradition the Germans have is Nationalism and the Authoritarian State as representing the tribal *Volk*. Self-pity is much deeper and more widespread than acknowledgment of guilt.

It is, nevertheless, highly probable that the German people will endure as a free democracy, even if a rather authoritative and bureaucratic one. In the East-West international struggle this is rather a merit; Germany can do its duty to NATO more reliably than can France. But the German people are still torn whether to create an Army, which means an *Offizierkorps* and a General Staff. This is the cross the Germans must especially bear. Chancellor Adenauer has personally taken over the task of building an Army to comport with Ger-

---

[9] It would seem that Adenauer would like the mantle to fall on his Foreign Minister, Heinrich von Brentano. He was born in 1904 of a family well known in Germany's intellectual and literary history, resident in Offenbach-am-Main. He graduated in classics and law and took over the family's law practice. His brother had to flee from the Nazis—he remained quietly in his profession. In 1945 he rose to leadership of the C.D.U. in Hesse, was elected to the *Bundestag*, became chairman of the C.D.U. group. He participated in the Committee that wrote the Constitution. He is an active leader in the European Movement and a member of the Coal and Steel Community. In June 1955 Adenauer gave him the position of Foreign Minister.

many's international obligations, frequently acknowledged in the Basic Law, one that is loyal to the Constitution yet shorn of the old Prussian sergeant-major rigor and brutality and infused with democratic civility. Germany is not permitted by treaty to manufacture certain arms: missiles, warships, atomic and bacterial weapons, warplanes, etc. She has no need for colonies in an age —except for Soviet empire-building—of imperial dismantlement. She has learned how bloodily she can be mauled by aggressions on the Slavs. She has been given truly noble treatment by the democracies. Perhaps her *Volkish* paganism may be appeased by reasonable consideration for individual rights. Perhaps, in sips, Germans may take the heady wine of freedom, for once, like gentlemen.

Two dangers lie ahead. The big industrialists escaped decartelization and socialism, for American international policy and industrial culture frustrated both. The Thyssens, Stinnes, Hugenbergs, Krupps (not with these names, except Krupps) have risen again, as haughty in their firms and politics as in Weimar's fall. Their enduring and sincere loyalty to democracy is doubtful; they prefer an uncontrolled technocracy to the restraints of democracy in the economy and nation.

The second is the deep, intense, and almost universal feeling for German nationalist unity. The struggle for reunification of East and West may throw men into the waiting arms of Russia (as in the past, p. 606 and p. 644); and/or might even overthrow democracy for a leader who will take back the lost provinces, Germany's birthplace and glory. The German friends of the West may be the friends of the West's power and not of its democratic culture, of its material and military gifts and not of its moral virtues.

The gravest question is whether the German people and leaders can lift themselves out of a tragic error of belief, that the Will is to be followed, whatever its good or evil. This addiction to intemperate and ethically reckless behavior was in part nourished by the Romantic philosophers of the *Volk* (p. 552). It had its root in the view that artistic creativeness must be free of any trammels of Reasoning or concern for anything but the artistic impulse, Art for Art's sake alone. About taste, there is no debating or reasoning. But Germans applied this to men and women in politics, worshiping the creative, the *schöpferisch,* the genius-beings, the Heroes. They imputed the privilege of the unfettered, unethical Will, free of attempts at Truth and Goodness, to their government, the *Obrigkeit,* or to whoever, such as Bismarck or the Kaiser or Hitler, happened to seize it and them. They have to learn that the True and the Decent must stand above the Will, and that their shape and compulsion are discoverable by reasoning, this side of their total schemes of metaphysics, on the theme of "Live and let live." If they do not, they will again destroy their liberties and ravage the peace of other peoples.

The Government of the
U.S.S.R.

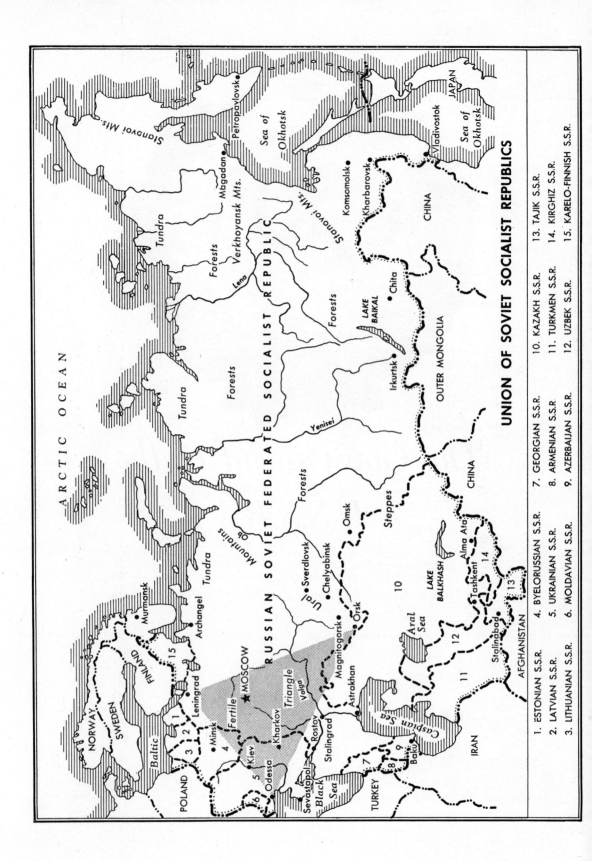

UNION OF SOVIET SOCIALIST REPUBLICS

1. ESTONIAN S.S.R.	4. BYELORUSSIAN S.S.R.	7. GEORGIAN S.S.R.	10. KAZAKH S.S.R.	13. TAJIK S.S.R.
2. LATVIAN S.S.R.	5. UKRAINIAN S.S.R.	8. ARMENIAN S.S.R	11. TURKMEN S.S.R.	14. KIRGHIZ S.S.R.
3. LITHUANIAN S.S.R.	6. MOLDAVIAN S.S.R.	9. AZERBAIJAN S.S.R.	12. UZBEK S.S.R.	15. KARELO-FINNISH S.S.R.

"Orthodoxy, Autocracy, Nationalism": Russia

We felt, then, that the true moral core of the people of Russia was a *broken-heartedness* to which nothing can be compared. . . . Russia, tensed to the breaking point, is savagely, cruelly, organized for sorrow. . . . What is atrocious is this, that the only thing which means anything to him, the Russian, the one and only idea he has in his head, the sole love he has in his heart—all seems combined to break it at any moment. . . . The inferno of the Russian soul is the breaking up of his family. The landlord can do this with one word. That is why the poor man abases his soul before him. He is owned *down to his very entrails.* If his wife or daughter are taken from him, he has nothing to say; if his little child is seized, he must pretend that all is well.

Finally he himself is seized; one day, seized, shorn, and put in chains, he will be made to march to the mines, the factories, the army, and he can say nothing. His bereaved wife is forced to enter the bed of another man. She, too, is a property, and that property must not be unemployed; it is necessary, that like the soil, she produces year by year, that she yields new serfs and conceives in despair.

> —*Michelet*, Les Martyrs de la Russia
> (early nineteenth century)

Despotism tempered by assassination: that is our Magna Carta.
> —*A Russian Noble* to a Hanoverian Ambassador,
> 1801, on Czar Paul I's assassination

The phrase used as the title of this chapter was coined by a despotic Minister of Education to the despotic Czar Nicolas I in 1832, to depict the government of Russia under its "truly Russian conservative principles"—Czardom. Since 1917, the Bolshevik *coup,* the only differences are that instead of a Czar, (1) a dictatorial clique is autocrat, (2) orthodoxy is not that of the Russian Church but the Marxist-Leninist Communist Party, (3) its nationalism is far more brutal and ambitiously imperialist than the Holy Russia of the hereditary Czars, and (4) the Western World has taught the Russian rulers the objectives, the scientific, technological, and managerial means of a raised material standard of living for the Russian people.

I. A TRAGIC WORLD PROBLEM

The Union of Soviet Socialist Republics, the U.S.S.R., is a dictatorship that relies for popular obedience—incalculably more than any other government on earth—on naked and brutal force, accompanied by thinly veiled threats and the

absolute monopoly of the propaganda of its justifying doctrines. It is very callously government
of the people; it is not government *by* the people;
and it is psychologically doubtful whether it is
government for the people. On principle, the
dictators repudiate what they call "bourgeois"
democracy, which is the system by which men rule
themselves in the countries this book has already
described.

The government of the U.S.S.R. holds in its
rough fists the power of some 210,000,000 prolific
people, in an area of some 8,000,000 square miles
comprising one sixth of the land surface of the
whole globe itself. It is an area of tremendous
mineral and agricultural resources. By the end of
1961 (at three Five Year Plans' distance from
1946) the Soviet Union will approach the United
States in the products of heavy industry, for its
government has come into the possession of the
inventions and technology first created and developed by the Western world, the lands of democracy. So mighty a force controlled by a small body
of men, uncontrolled by their own masses and
inflamed by a self-righteous will to govern, of
fanatical intensity, in the name of doctrines that
reject the principles of the democratic way of life
of these other peoples with murderous hatred,
constitutes a mortal problem for other nations and
an inhuman tragedy for the Russian people. For
those rulers have no care for the individual soul
here and now but for the retention of their own
power in the name of something to be attained in
a distant future which they preach is Communism.

"People's Democracy"

The Soviet leaders—and therefore all the little
leaders and the spokesmen and every organ of the
press—claim they are a "people's democracy."
What do they mean? (1) They have instituted
elections on the basis of universal suffrage; and
they claim they are genuinely seeking to draw in
the masses to the participation in government.
They show that not even when the local *Zemtsvos*
(p. 747) were at work since the 1870's or in the
period of the *Duma* (p. 762) was there such a
popular basis as now in all the Soviets (committees
or councils) of government. (2) They claim that,

as they have abolished private property almost
entirely (p. 889), there is not in Russia, as in other
lands, that obstacle to the exercise of political
rights and the enjoyment of civil and social rights,
which economic inequality produces in spite of
constitutional declarations of equality. They claim
they have the purest democracy—the means of
communication and campaign funds are not in the
hands of the propertied. (Whose then? it may be
asked. For some alternatives are worse than
others.) (3) They observe that their constitution
allows of the "recall" of Deputies to the legislative
and executive offices by the electorate. (4) They
point to the attitude of the Communist Party, as
"the vanguard of the proletariat," conscientiously
devoted not only to the good of the people but to
teaching the people what is for their good. They
could use the phrase supplied by Sidney and
Beatrice Webb in that most peculiar work of old
age, *Soviet Communism: a New Civilization?* and
call the party, "a vocation of leadership." They
have completely convinced the Russian people that
the government in the United States or any other
democratic country is *not representative of its
people,* but Wall Street-dictated!

Sodom's Apple: The Dictatorship. It is a beautiful,
polished apple, but inside that red skin are acrid
ashes. For the Government has despotically discarded the spirit and institutions of democracy.
There is only one political party: it has the monopoly of elections in every particular from the choice
of candidates to the provision of funds, meeting
places, propaganda. No other party is permitted
in law or fact to exist to offer rival ideas of existence or policies of daily expediency. The prohibition is contained in the Constitution, in other
laws, and in the stipulations of the Criminal Code
of associations, on "counterrevolution" and "sabotage." Free association and free speech are thus
outlawed; but these are not "political," they are
primordial. If they are "granted," as in Russia,
they are broken reeds; they must be seized by the
people to be reliable rights. The Russian people
were not allowed by the Bolshevik leaders to seize
possession of their own rights (including that of
setting up and cashiering their governors), but
those leaders used the people to wrest the authority

from the Czar and usurped it, to offer only crumbs, backed up by revolvers and machine guns, to the people.

Responsibility in Government

The Bolshevik leaders, headed by Nikolai Lenin (otherwise Vladimir Ilyitch Ulyanov, 1870–1924), permitted "representative" government but not "responsible" government. As the experience of Bismarckian Germany (pp. 582–609) demonstrated, it is possible to have universal suffrage, yet to deny the Legislature the sovereign power to designate, discipline, and eject the Executive, on terms of responsibility for policy itself. A democracy requires a responsibility *downward* from the top levels of government to the people. It is a responsibility that is *external* to the Executive itself. The Soviet leaders may say they are responsible, they might even feel so; but they have certainly erected a system that does not *constrain* them to responsibility. Their system in this respect is that of Adolf Hitler (p. 662ff.), and he partly modeled himself on Stalin's Party, the "crafty Caucasian." The Soviet leaders' idea of responsibility in government is that of the masses and the subordinate leaders *upward* to them.

"Burocratism, Not Democratism." Lenin, who made the party and the succeeding regime after the *coup* of 1917, rejected "responsibility" in these terms in *One Step Forward, Two Steps Backward* (1905):

Burocratism *versus* democratism, that is, precisely centralism *versus* autonomy, such is the organization principle of revolutionary social democracy against that of the opportunists. The latter principle strives to go from below upward, and therefore defends as far as possible and wherever possible autonomy and democracy. . . . But the organization principle of revolutionary social democracy strives to go from the top downward, and defends the enlargement of the rights and plenary powers of the central body against the parts.

He added: "The spontaneous struggle of the proletariat will not become a genuine class struggle until it is led by a strong organization of revolutionaries."

In other words a principle of *nonresponsibility* was deliberately adopted, so that the Bolshevik pure in heart and clear in mind and responsible-in-conscience should rule others for the good the *leaders* thought they ought to be subjected to, not a good self-chosen by the masses. For the revolutionaries against the iniquity which was Czardom distrusted the peasants and the workers, and Lenin was one of the former. As Tkachev, one of Lenin's mentors, declared:

Neither in the present nor the future can the people, left to their own resources, bring into existence the social revolution. Only we revolutionists can accomplish this. Social ideals are alien to the people; they belong to the social philosophy of the revolutionary minority.

Lenin and Stalin and their associates held this creed, and carried it through to the task of government *after* the political revolution.

Thus, Karl Marx's "dictatorship of the proletariat" was transformed into the "dictatorship of the Communist Party" and, by Lenin and Stalin, into the "dictatorship of the top man in the party" for the time being: *de facto* not *de jure.* Lenin referred to himself as *starik,* the Russian for *old man,* a typical ingratiation of a crypto-dictator; and Stalin was called *khozain, the Boss.*

Thus, Soviet "responsibility," even if admitted, is of the species known as "moral," not externally-enforced; it lies in the conscience only of the ruler. Its best justification, in principle, is that the ruler has been born and nurtured in humanity; it might prevent corruption. Or some terrible social catastrophe might for the time of the catastrophe justify its operation. Or the principle might call for the ruler's subordination to an ethic: the Marxian one, for example. But is it not obvious that corruption and caprice and personal power-lust is only too easily substitutable for humanity or beneficence in emergency, the pretended ethic? It happened that the Russian environment was one of corruption, brutality, chicanery, terror, murder, and mute, suffering, illiterate *mouzhiks,* and revolutionaries always on the run before the police and police spies. This led to the abandonment of principles of humanity; it produced undeviating acceptance of that re-entry to barbarism, "the end justifies the means."

The Western democratic system does not believe in the perfect conscience of rulers, even elected ones. As David Hume declared: in government we must build as though all men are knaves (p. 33)—that is the probability, *in the long run,* even though our governors may be righteous, hard working and self-sacrificing now. Though one must rely much on the moral standards of those who govern (whether rulers or electors), since too many checks and balances would stop government altogether, democracy requires potential punishment by loss of career, frequent elections, and so on, to keep governors from being stale, irresponsive, and despotic.

The fundamental difference between governments depends on the answer practically available to these questions. Can the will of the government be changed by the available disciplinary power of the electorate? Can the electorate, against the will of the government of the day, force the latter's powers away? Can they make the government change tack to please the consumers rather than the governors' own consciences? That is the point. The Soviet system says "Decidedly and on principle: NO!" The democracies practice externally enforced responsibility.

This does not exclude the fact that there may be some responsiveness, if not responsibility, in the Soviet system. For can a mass of 210,000,000 people always and in everything be coerced? Even their prejudices and inertia must in some degree be respected, or they will not produce (as in the Russian farms!). There may be an opposition of sullenness and sulkiness and "go-slow," even if there is no opposition party in the field at elections. Hence, *the* party has to make some concessions, rather than bear the burden of pure coercion, even to wholesale carnage.

The Conditions of Democracy

We have seen what the conditions of democracy are in respect to the establishment of it in Germany after World War II (see, *now,* p. 686). One of these, not mentioned there but taken for granted, is private property. The community, properly, has some rights to modify it, by due process of democratic law. But the Soviet extreme where all the means of production, exchange, and communication are governmentally possessed, cripples all other liberties; for it cuts down the material basis of an organized opposition.

The Soviet system has no popularly made and ratified constitution. It has no rival parties. It denies the principle that decisions are made by a freely associated majority. Its civil liberties are granted, not popularly seized. It rejects the separation of powers. It allows no time for legislative deliberation. Its elections are "fixed." Local government is coordinated by Moscow and the party. It denies that political good is to be discovered by the free evolution of individuals; but asserts a "closed society" with commandments regarded as eternally settled by a self-appointed minority using force at its own discretion. It is not reluctant to use force, as in a democracy, as a final, reluctant factor; but is ready with force without reasoning and patience. It does not say, Is force right?, but, Is force expedient?

The government of the U.S.S.R. is the product of the Revolution of November 1917. It will be necessary to trace the course and nature of the Revolution; the course of events in World War I and the fate of Russia in that war, and the resumption of a revolution that broke out but was aborted in 1905. In 1917, in fact, two revolutions occurred. One was a "liberal" and democratic revolution in March 1917 soon led by Alexander Kerensky, which confirmed the overthrow of the Czar. The second was the Bolshevik Revolution of November 1917 (in the Russian calendar, October). Then occurred the so-called "Ten Days That Shook the World." The Bolsheviks, under Lenin, Trotsky, and Stalin, overthrew the nascent provisional liberal government by another revolution, the kind that by dictatorship and police methods could not be reversed.

A system of government was imposed, taking its character from the revolution's character. The character of the revolution was created by Russia's history as a human society and the personality and mind of the revolutionary leaders. They jointly fastened on the country a tyranny that seems to be proof against any kind of opposition that can be mustered inside it.

The Written Constitution of 1936—Imposed! The revolution produced a single one-party monopolistic State, and autocracy. The parliamentary institutions are only a façade. The true constitution of the Soviet Union is the constitution of the Russian Communist Party. This imposed one constitution after another, the latest being the written Constitution of 1936 (see p. 789ff.).

The decisive seizure of power was made by self-chosen men. Only later were Soviets popularly elected. Even when they were, no opportunity was allowed by the self-imposed of a free and open election among competing parties to create the constitution-making body. A dictatorship of a few people fastened its constitution upon the country. Whereas, in democratic countries, a constitution is a promise of the people to itself, a pattern of applied scruples which limits the authorities, in the Soviet Union the Constitution is an instrument of power of the ruling and self-chosen clique. The Constitution does not limit them, unless one is deceived by its formal language. And we know that behind it is the one monopolistic party, upon which the dictatorship clique is founded and which alone is in the position to head or amend the Constitution it imposed.

II. WHY THE REVOLUTIONARY USURPATION WAS POSSIBLE

How was it possible for a few score men, animated by Lenin in theory and planning and Trotsky in practical strategy—that is, only two men—to win supreme authority, with all the appurtenances of power, armies, officials, government-buildings apparatus, funds, and the rest, over 200,000,000 people? It depends on the men and on the character of the people. It is to this that we must now address ourselves, an inquiry into the nature of Czarist Russian society, as fundamental to Soviet government as to the *coup* that enabled it to seize the reins.

Although the analysis may not identically follow the themes, these may at once be itemized. (1) Russia's great size always militated against *popular* revolution and assisted autocracy. (2) Its size and climate did not conduce to the growth of a close-knit, spontaneous community of Russia. (3)

Its neighboring peoples were of such different ethnic character, religion, and interests that autocracy and cruelty over masses of peasants was fostered by "foreign danger." (4) The expansion from the original "Russian" centers between the Neva's mouth and Kiev and Moscow was at the expense of "foreign" peoples—Russia was composed of extremely heterogeneous "national" strains. (5) The economic development of resources in so vast an area of opportunity required State help, hence furthered autocracy. (6) Owing to the autocracy's needs, no intermediate bodies of citizens came as a connecting link between the millions of peasant serfs and the Czars, except the landlords, who were subordinated by the Czars for venal reasons and used as police over the serfs. (7) The area was severed from the influences of Western civilization by geography and climate and for over two hundred creative years—1250 to 1450—by Tatar invaders (p. 733), lying athwart the western lines in potential cultural infiltration. (8) Russian Christianity was servile and became a conscious tool of the Czar, the "Little Father." (9) There was no training of wide circles of the population in elementary self-government and self-confidence. (10) Facing millions of *mouzhiks,* peasants, abject in inertia with few alert urban proletarians, and assisted by the habits and institutions of absolutism, a few, conscious, willful, resolute men seized the latter with opposition when it broke down before World War I's trials, total war, then unprecedented. (11) To the peasants, bestially poor, *land* was freedom, and the revolutionists promised it to them, only to take it back when they had power. (12) Above all, pervading everything, was the great sodden mass of peasant-serfs, ignorant and brutalized beyond the most benighted hill-billy, beyond Western conception!

Illiteracy

Since illiteracy may get lost in the analysis that follows, let it at once be noted that the Russian people of 1917—over 80 percent peasants and only less than 20 percent city dwellers and urban industrial workers—were abysmally illiterate. The basic meaning is the inability to read and write. What is the chance of self-government in a community of any size without this, at the very minimum? But they were unschooled in the most elementary sense. The figures reveal this. In 1897 the census showed 79 percent of the people unable to read and write: 29 percent of the men were literate and 13 percent of the women; 45 percent in the towns and *only 17 percent in the rural areas.* It is reliably reported that this figure declined little by 1917. Among Army recruits in 1913, the illiteracy was 32 percent—this among the younger men of the population, whereas it had been nearly twice as bad twenty years earlier. But with them, as with the rest of the population, the so-called "literate" took no notice of their low standard or the fact that since schooldays they had never read or written anything and could hardly even write their names. In 1911 whatever the provisions of the law or of accommodation, 49 percent of the children between eight and eleven *did not attend school;* for those below this age the attendance was even worse. Only 1 out of 4 children between seven to fourteen attended school in the rural areas. The *Zemstvos* (provincial and city councils) and the Church provided schools; and there were schools maintained by private societies. But compulsory education (and with it the funds to furnish it) in elementary schools was not enacted until 1908—only for children from eight to eleven, and even then not to be executed fully until 1922! In 1911 it was attempted to expand this, but the Czar's Cabinet rejected the *Duma's* bid. By 1915 there were some 364,000 students in secondary schools; the ratio of secondary students to population in the middle 1890's was 1 in 564.

There were virtually no universities until the beginning of the nineteenth century, whereas enlightenment and political doctrine and animation had flowed from these in England, France, and Germany for five hundred years before that. It is true that the University of Moscow was founded in 1755—but for decades it lacked teachers and students! When the universities did begin to assume strength in the later nineteenth century, the student body was still an extremely small fraction of the persons of university age: no more than 36,000 at all the universities together, mainly in technical faculties. There were some 50,000 others at various higher schools and institutes. The main

features were the brilliance of some teachers; the overwhelming number of poor students, those who came from middle and lower social groups, and eked out an existence while studying; their very widespread assumption of a liberal, a radical, and often a revolutionary attitude toward their terroristic and obscurantist government; the governmental intervention in university administration, the appointment and dismissal of teachers for political reasons, the persecution by the police of liberal students, drafting them into the Army or denying them the right to study (which meant the denial of the right to enter a profession), and student mass insubordination and strikes.

How can illiterate masses be anything but misled if they have not the most elementary tools for finding the facts that would enable them to resist deception and submission. The primary schools were choked with the Church's orthodox attitudes; and the Czarist Ministers of Education had contrived or been forced throughout the nineteenth century to deny educational facilities, to indoctrinate them, to keep the minds enslaved.

A Vulnerable Food Supply

Russia is a colossus in size, but fairly puny in agricultural strength. Most of Russia lies far to the north of the U.S. northern frontier, the 49th parallel. Nearly two thirds of the Soviet Union lies (like Canada) in Arctic tundra or stunted forest. Altogether, three fourths of the Soviet Union is too cold or too dry for the production of food. Its eastern portion, Siberia, etc., has the most continental climate in the world. Even on the northern edge of the present productive area, artificial drying of crops is necessary. Hence, only the "Fertile Triangle," between Leningrad, Odessa, and Orsk in the Urals, is the "breadbasket" of Russia—that is, about 10 percent of all the Soviet Union alone is arable. The United States enjoys 25 percent of its area in arable condition. This is a controlling "political" fact. For Russia has always suffered a terrible struggle between food supply, fertility of population, and the military and policy demands of its government. Coercion alone (p. 916ff.) will not make wheat and corn and cattle grow and thrive.

The Growth of European Russia, 1000–1945

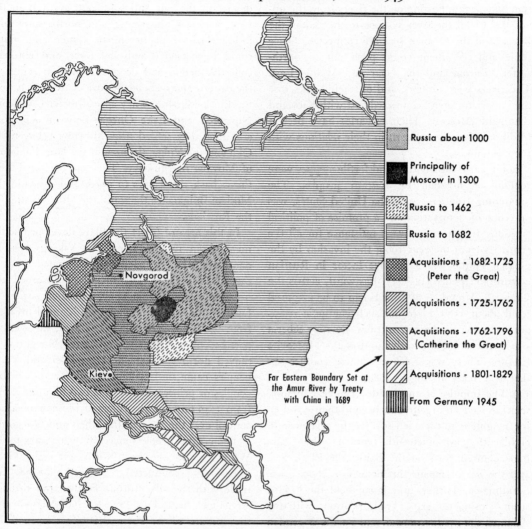

Russia about 1000

Principality of Moscow in 1300

Russia to 1462

Russia to 1682

Acquisitions - 1682-1725 (Peter the Great)

Acquisitions - 1725-1762

Acquisitions - 1762-1796 (Catherine the Great)

Acquisitions - 1801-1829

From Germany 1945

Novgorod

Kiev

Far Eastern Boundary Set at the Amur River by Treaty with China in 1689

The Geography of a State

(1) **The Beginnings of a State.** Russia is three times the size of the United States, itself difficult to govern well because of its size. Russia's geographical unity is based on four horizontal natural zones extending from the Pacific and the Mongolian Deserts to the European frontiers between the Barents Sea and the Black Sea. The northernmost is the barren and frozen Tundra at the Arctic; next is the forest; next, the steppes and the fertile plains of black earth and chestnut soil; finally, comes the desert region of the south. This linkage east-and-west has given rise to political and geographical speculations that Russia is a single unit —Eurasia. The Kiev state, the first Russian state, was formed along the Dnieper River; for the rivers enabled the ebb and flow of Russian culture. It led to Byzantium (Constantinople), to the Black Sea. From the glamorous Greco-Roman Eastern Empire, Kiev and Russia learned her absolutist political tradition and received the Greek Orthodox (not the Roman) religion.

The Volga facilitated trade to the Caspian and to Persian and Arab culture; and to the center of the land and to the Volga from the North came the Varangian Norsemen, who founded the Russian State, again floating on the rivers from the upper Baltic. All the river systems to the Baltic, the Black, and the Caspian seas are connected, hence trade and settlement could push out to northeastern Europe and the Near and Middle East. The rivers were unifiers, and on their banks rose the important towns, connected first with Kiev and then with Moscow. Their estuaries have been a traditional Russian concern in their relations with their neighbors.

Southward, the inviting and fertile steppes were regions of invasion by Eastern peoples. The "marching frontier," as in the United States, was an economic temptation and a promise of political freedom. It met with savage resistance for all the centuries from the year 1000; the invasion by the Golden Horde was a decisive factor in Russian culture and polity (p. 733). Eastward, across the Urals, the Kingdom of Sibir began to be acquired from about 1580. Here not such energetic resistance was met by the native tribes. By 1637 Siberia was a special administrative unit of the Muscovite Empire. There was a Russo-Chinese conflict settled by a treaty in August 1689.

(2) **The Impulse of an "Inside" People.** "Inland" societies have an urge to pass beyond their enveloping neighbors to the open sea. By the seventeenth, eighteenth, and nineteenth centuries, the Czars had acquired ports on the Baltic, the Black Sea, and the Sea of Japan. But none was "open" sea. Scandinavia, Turkey, and Japan held the key or straits closing the exits. Trade relations with the Atlantic, the Mediterranean, and Pacific depended too much for Russian pride and fear on the good will of these countries. They could be used for invasions of Russia herself. Hence, the ambition since Catherine II (1729–1796) to acquire the Dardanelles, and several wars to achieve this; so also wars with Sweden, in the Crimea; and western intervention in the civil war of 1918–1922.

(3) **Force to the Utmost.** Assuming that a people wants a land, and assuming that certain rulers want it for riches and government, the larger it is, the greater the hardship in its conquest, for human power in early times is of human muscle and stamina. Hence, terrible drives by the Grand Dukes and Grand Princes to conquer this ever-

receding frontier. Cold in the north and east, deserts in the east and southeast, swamps in the west, forest in the center and north, snow-and-mud-blockaded plains in the center and south could be mastered only by force and enforced collective action and defense. The first center of the eastern *Slavs,* about the fifth century, was near the Pinsk Marshes. They spread to Kiev-Moscow Novgorod and Lake Onega. Between A.D. 1000 and 1200 they settled near Moscow, between the Oka and the Volga, the area of the later Kingdom of Moscow or Muscovy. They ejected the Finns threw back the Tatars to north and east and the Moslem Bulgars. In the south the Mongols stopped the Russians.

In this area of forest the Slavs developed settlements from 1240 to 1440. The Vikings (led by one Rurik) had invaded and dominated them in the ninth century, but they had absorbed the invaders.[1] Kiev Russia arose, a well-off society of farmers and traders. About 1240 Mongol invaders from the south split this state's area, the western part becoming Lithuania, while the Novgorodite moved north and east, and the Oka and Volga peoples came under the Mongol Khan, whether peoples or princes. In the next two hundred years from 1240 onward, the rulers of Moscow obtained control over the areas of the Khan and Novgorod.

The central people moved by waterways to the White Sea in the Far North. Ivan the Great (1440–1505) conquered Novgorod in 1478. The trade with the adventurous English ran through Archangel, because the Swedes and Poles covered the middle route. Peter the Great opened his "window on the west," St. Petersburg on the Baltic, to replace Archangel; in this, also, Riga helped. While the Western powers sailed round the world in the sixteenth century, the Russians were straining across the wastes to the Pacific. The strain was directed and exploited by the Czars. They took tribute from the tribes; levied taxes on the fur dealers; developed exploration. Wax, honey, pelts, hides, timber, works of craft, tea were won and imported. Later the government turned to mining. In the nineteenth century the Russians were at San Francisco and recoiled from

[1] *Rus* is alleged to derive from *rothes*men, meaning, *oarsmen.*

Alaska only in 1867. The process required intelligence, governmental drive, protection, obedience, and physical stamina.

(4) The Golden Horde: Asiatic Despotism. The Mongols conquered Kiev Russia in 1227. They left a lasting mark on its rule in their two hundred years of domination. The conquerors were known as the Golden Horde—the "golden family" of Genghis Khan being their ancestors. A fact of towering importance resulted: Russia was cut off from the West to stew in her own primitive cultural juice. For two hundred years, until well beyond the middle of the fifteenth century, she was isolated from her previous civilizing connections with Byzantium and Bulgaria, and this in the very period when the Renaissance and the Reformation were in the making, wherein the rulers in the West played so potent a part. If a ruler, one man, were converted, society was on the way to conversion.

Second, the Golden Horde were skilled takers of tribute. Provided the princes of Moscow paid, the Mongols supported their power. The clergy supported both for their own dominance. Moscow was forced to set up censuses, tax gatherers, and techniques of coercion to raise the tribute. Its absolutism and brutality were nourished; the grimness and humiliation of Tatar brutality produced its reaction, its imitation, and its habits of transmission. The Khans of the Horde and the lesser Moscow princes played politics against the Grand Prince, and this again exerted a callous pressure on him which he visited on others. The princes and grand dukes of the various Russian rulerships acquired title to rule by appeal to the Khan, who sanctioned the favorite with a *yarlyk*—that is, authority. As the Russian rule of succession left the right to govern open to family dispute, whoever paid the Khan more was likely to get the *yarlyk* and Tatar Armies to support it. Ten times between 1259 and 1408 the Mongols raided deep into Muscovy and took terrible vengeance on tribute defaulters. The Orthodox clergy, conniving for their own power, and themselves the owners of great estates requiring princely protection, taught the people that God had sent the Mongols as a trial to wicked mankind. This teaching had political importance of decisive effect also.

In 1480 Ivan the Great was able to overthrow the rule of the already-crumbling Horde, after horrible clashes between the Tatar soldiery and Russian soldiers and peasantry that supervened on Tatar internal quarrels. He seized the dependence and tribute for so long conceded to them. Thenceforward, Muscovy progressed south to Kazan, taking over one hundred years, and thence to Astrakhan by 1556. Turks and Crimean Tatars barred the way to the Crimea—even raiding and burning Moscow in 1571; even as far north as Kharkov in 1710 and 1718. From their center the Czars could not police such a distant frontier as the Volga and the Crimea, for the steppes offered little water or food, while the Crimean Tatars could play off Russians, Poles, and Cossacks against each other.

Ivan the Terrible (1530–1584) preferred to use his forces against the Poles and the Baltics. It took from 1687 to 1783 to master the Crimea, by several wars. But for two hundred years settlers had seeped down to use its good earth, defended by government garrisons and military colonists, elaborately organized since 1650.

(5) Colonization and "Men of Service." The princes, from 1500 onward, pursued a strong and steady policy of colonization. Land was given to important men, and with it serfs and rights to manufacture and mine. Military colonists—that is, conscripts—worked the land, etc., becoming later "state peasants"; others were bonded peasants or serfs. Other areas were peopled in part by fugitives from government lands or from their owners; some left out of adventure, others for religious reasons. *The climate did not allow them to go very far;* if caught, they were enserfed. Such colonists were the creators of the Cossack "host"— *Kazak* is the Tatar term for light horseman. They were steppe frontiersmen, used by the State to fight the nomads of the south and east and middle Urals, with quasi-independent self-government. Peter the Great brought the Cossacks under the direct sway of St. Petersburg—a cavalry militia under the War Ministry with an annual grant from Moscow. They became the Czars' brutal oppressors of liberal movements. In 1905 they sang: "We don't need a constitution; we don't want a republic; we won't betray Russia; we'll defend the

Czar's throne." The Bolsheviks after 1917 turned their knouts upon the Cossacks.

The colonization by the State pushed out to Siberia in much this way; by serfs to Siberian mines; by mass political deportations; by forced colonization. In the 1880's disastrous famines caused great migrations. The Czars renewed the systematic colonization. The Bolsheviks offered youth the equivalent of "Go west, young man!", in Siberian mining and manufactures, a tremendous magnification.

(6) Size and Climate. The seizure of an area, its settlement and assimilation, its exploitation, its policing—all involve intense efforts of will and anxiety by a few men at the top. The process was hardest and harshest in Russia, far above the sovereignty-making travail of the nations of the West. It accounts for the tyranny, nationalism, and religious orthodoxy of a thousand years. It proceeds before our very eyes in the body- and mind-breaking dictatorship of the centralized U.S.S.R.

Even Russia west of the Urals alone is an unwieldy area. Its size and climate have had three consequences on Russian political culture. (1) The Russian people expended their strength in making a State over so vast an area, leaving little for a refined culture. Russian life was and is brutal in the extreme; physically brutal, where beatings and floggings are everyday occurrences; where men and women curse bestially; where to be a gentleman is an accident. Obscenities and physical uncleanliness and filthy drunkenness are part of the Russian heritage. Morbidity, inertia, and political indifference go with it.

(2) A quality of immoderation is alleged to be the result of the immense expanses on the human spirit. On this Nicolas Berdyaev says: [2]

There is that in the Russian soul which corresponds to the immensity, the vagueness, the infinitude of the Russian land, spiritual geography corresponds with physical. In the Russian soul there is a sort of immensity, a vagueness, a predilection for the infinite, such is suggested by the great plain of Russia. For this reason the Russian people have found difficulty in achieving mastery over these vast expanses and in reducing them to orderly shape. There has been a vast elemental strength in the Russian people combined with a comparatively weak sense of form.

(3) The climate is one of extremes: cold indescribable; heat; mud. Two consequences follow. First, the weak have died. The Russians are a physically very powerful people, and, spiritually, they have created a habit of suffering the powers that be. They survive by submitting to the laws of their climate and surmounting the hunger of the centuries. Second, the climate closes in each household and each village from the rest for long periods. This has produced a numb kind of patience; endless Dostoevskian self-examination that usually produces a feeling of guilt; and an "It doesn't matter," a *nichevo*, response to external misfortune, since one is in the hands of uncaring Nature. This isolation has meant the frustration of a *larger consensus!* Without continuous communication of ideas, common feelings, collective values, the community cannot be built from below but is the more easily imposed from above. The mutual trust and distrust of men requires that the senses of men come into direct contact. This was for long impossible in an area of Russia's size and climatic disruption of communication. Even today the railway and road system of the U.S.S.R. favors the government's machine gunners against the atomized farm dwellers and city groups who cannot associate their efforts. In the 1850's the Russian railroad system compared thus to the British; the former had 660 miles, the latter, 6635; by 1891 Russia had 22,000 miles, Britain about the same—but the areas were as 1 is to 40 west of the Urals alone! By 1890, the United States had built 160,000 miles; but then she was peopled by free men who had arrived with education, culture, and free institutions.

(7) Imperialism and Ethnic Diversity. "Russia" came, by force as well as by peaceful settlement, to include 169 ethnic groups, one quarter of whom have the yellow tinge of Asia. In ten major divi-

[2] *The Russian Idea*, New York, 1948, p. 2. In Edward Crankshaw's, *Russia and the Russians*, New York, 1947, the reader will find a most significant, long, and circumstantial verification of Berdyaev's thesis, written with an artist's talent and the knowledge of a direct observer.

"A comparatively weak sense of form"! We shall have much to say on this later—for it is in forms that liberty is secreted and guaranteed.

sions the ethnic groupings are Indo-European, 36; Caucasians, 40; Semites, 6; Finns, 16; Samoyedes, 1; Turks, 48; Mongols, 3; Tungus-Manchurian, 6; Palaeo-Asiatics, 9; Far Eastern, 4. Russians, White Russians, and Ukrainians make up some 75 percent of the total population.[3] These constitute the eastern Slavs, as against the western Slavs, who are the Czechs, the Slovaks, the Poles, and the southern ones: Bulgarians, Serbs, Croats, and Slovenes.

The Ukrainians have a distinct language and culture and strongly consider themselves the heirs of the Kievan Russia—that is, the first pre-Muscovite Russia. They originated as western Slavs, were at one time part of Lithuanian dominions during the Golden Horde (p. 733), and then had Western Catholic religion. As settlers and Cossacks (p. 733), they seeped into the area of the Black Earth. They had before and for long since been molded by the West, by German law and Western chivalry, city life, Latin Renaissance, trade. Their first university originated in 1625! Their universities of Lemberg and Kiev were centers of culture superior to that of Moscow, and they nourished a Ukrainian Party bent on secession. In World War I and World War II they showed little allegiance to Russia that had oppressed them by a fierce policy of assimilation; indeed they set up exile resistance groups (p. 785). The Baltic states, infiltrated since Peter the Great's attempt to secure a "window on the west," are not Slavs (Latvia, Estonia, Lithuania) but of a kind of Finnish ethnic origin. Latvia and Estonia are 80 percent Protestant, the rest Orthodox; Lithuania is 85 percent Roman Catholic; and in the early centuries they acquired a far higher level of culture than Moscow through the influence of Catholic Poland and Protestant Sweden. From the reign of Catherine the Great, who invented the term *Russification,* Russian pressure on these and other peoples became more consistent and steadily brutal. Since the Russian Orthodox Church became highly nationalistic and blended with the despotism of the Grand Princes of Moscow, the western Slavs, the Baltic, and Moslems and pagans were involved in territorial as well as religious wars of the cruelest nature. The Thirty Years' War (p. 532) bore down from Sweden on the Baltic to Poltava in the Ukraine as late as 1709. Russian soldiers were taught to regard themselves as God's chosen, crusading for his own land "Holy Russia." The Czars fought and tortured to conquer and assimilate the surrounding peoples.

III. CLASSES IN RUSSIAN SOCIETY AND GOVERNMENT

Until 1917, and even today almost, Russia was a land of "peasants," and this in the pejorative sense of illiterate, uneducated, stupid, earth-bound, of lowest productivity, deepest superstition, and most brutalized. In 1900 four fifths of the people lived on farms in very small villages. Moscow and St. Petersburg had the largest urban societies, although there were a few other towns of over 100,000.

There is a constant use of the word *culture* in past and modern Russia; it is an admonition to acquire what was and is lacking. It was not existent generally even fifty years; it is rare today; and a hundred years ago it touched only a small upper fraction of the population. It is not the inborn nature of the peasant that was and is to blame for this primitiveness but the rule by government and landlords. This produced a stark, deep abyss between a few hundred thousand at the top and a hundred millions at the bottom of the pit.

The classes were nobles, landowners, and serfs and then, from after 1870, a relatively very small but growing class of industrial and commercial entrepreneurs and proletarian workers. The latter

[3] In 1945 the political division of the U.S.S.R., which gives only a wholesale idea of the ethnic variety, was as follows:

Union Republic	Population in Millions
R.S.F.R. (Great Russians)	109.0
Ukraine	40.6
White Russia	9.4
Azerbaidzhan	3.2
Georgia	3.6
Armenia	1.3
Turkmen	1.3
Uzbek	6.3
Tadzhik	1.5
Kazakh	6.1
Kirgiz	1.5
Karelo Finnish	0.5
Moldavia	2.4
Lithuania	3.0
Latvia	1.8
Estonia	1.0

may, for the moment be ignored, in any thought of Russia's fundamental governmental evolution, though in the lands of the West, this bourgeoisie of the cities was the most powerful influence for culture and political liberty.

(1) The Landlords

These numbered some 260,000 families. One half of these owned four fifths of all the serfs in Russia, for the *peasantry were serfs* down to 1865 (and even beyond)—real serfs, without figurative language. Landlords held from scores to thousands of serfs. The 260,000 families compares with about 100,000,000 people about 1900.

At the apex of society were a few princes connected with the Romanoff family that held the throne, and about two hundred families of old aristocracy by blood, lineage, and service. Then came families ennobled for public service, on attaining a certain rank. The first two groups composed the nobles, known as the *boyars*.

The nobles and landowners were the pillars of the Czarist autocracy, deliberately so established. The Czars found they could intrust order, justice, police, local government to about a quarter of a million men, with safety and convenience to the central government. It was wicked, brutal, and incompetent and so was liable to morose passive resistance, to stagnation, and occasional wild outbursts of murder and arson by the peasants and resentments building up to future revolution. A Czar once said: "The nobles are the gratuitous police chiefs for the central government."

The Serfs

Serfs fell roughly into two basic classes. A little more than 50 percent were landlord serfs, bondsmen, and about 45 percent (in the seventeenth century) were State peasants. Outside these were miscellaneous groupings of servants to landowners with more or less of servile status. The bondsmen were liable to the full burden of serfdom. The State serfs were people who had been taken by the government and set to work on government lands, mines, forests, and so forth. From early times, let us say, from 1500 onward, much of the colonization of Russia, the extension of the frontiers, was largely accomplished by the Prince or the Czar (later the Emperor), undertaken as a direct State enterprise. People were ordered into the Army, but they were also ordered into forced labor.

The Nature of Serfdom. State serfdom meant that the government ascribed you permanently, or for lesser periods, to government service as a courier, a musketeer, a frontiersman, to serve in the regular Army, to construct public works for the government, to work in its mines, its workshops, and its lands and forests. The condition of State serfs was rather better than that of the landlord serfs.

Stalin's father was a serf! The serf's burdens are factors in the Bolshevik Revolution and the subsequent nature of its rule.

The landlord had immensely stern rights over his serfs. He could punish them for any infraction of duty, except by capital punishment. Yet he could and did flog them with knout or *nagaika* (rawhide, wired or held with metal rings) until they died. He had the right of settling disputes among the serfs, though criminal cases went to the law courts. In the case of "audacious behavior" on their part, he could commit them to hard labor in Siberia. He had the right to choose from among the serfs those who were to be recruits for the Army. (Until the end of the nineteenth century it meant a twenty-five-year obligation.) He could sell them as recruits to the Army or to other people who did not want to send their own serfs.

Marriages needed the permission of the landlord, and payments had to be made to him in respect of the permission. (The landlords abused the peasant women.) Serfs could be sent anywhere in the service of their lord. They could be made to do any kind of work. (Much early Russian craftsmanship and early industry, especially in textiles, mines, forests, woodwork, and so forth, began with the serfs of an owner being turned away from their ordinary agricultural work into their owners' industrial occupations.) They were compelled to do at least three days' work a week on the lord's land. Plenty of them were made to do four or five; some were made to do even six, although that was an exception. The rest of the time was their own.

Thus, the owner had tremendous control over the lives of their persons. He could sell the whole family to anybody anywhere or break it up, with or without land. Gogol's *Dead Souls* describes the landowners gambling with each other with the souls of the serfs, as stakes. The system was callous and brutalizing.

Yet with all the amount of labor, the serfs were not good economic producers. The land was not theirs. They resented the injustice: their point of view was that the land belonged to those who worked it.

Unfree till 1861. The serfs passed on a proverb: "My body belongs to the Czar, my soul belongs to the Church, and my back to the local squire." Until 1861 (only yesterday in the evolution of government) the serfs were more enslaved and victimized than in France even before 1789 (p. 282). In England, feudalism and serfdom had begun to decline after 1350; in France, in 1789; in Germany and Austria, after 1815. But, with slight local exceptions, the Russian white slaves of white landlords were not emancipated until 1861 —and even then on terms which kept them servile almost to 1917. A century, and even more, makes a decisive difference in the character of modern governments, on comparison, for governments are made of their constituent people. Not even by 1917 had there developed in Russia a class of sturdy, robust, freedom-loving yeomen like John Hampden in Britain. When this appeared possible, by 1917, in the form of *kulaks,* Lenin and Stalin killed them to preserve their autocracy (p. 780).

Serfdom was developed between 1500 and 1700; whereas elsewhere in Europe this had occurred between 1100 and 1300. For the Kings of Muscovy needed the strength of the magnates to resist the Mongols from the south; they needed to overcome rival princelings; they needed "men of service" to fight the Ukrainian and Polish Slavs and their Roman Catholicism (more hated by the Orthodox than other religions, except the Jews, even today). For even in 1609 the Poles captured Moscow and ruled it till 1613. There were many such "times of troubles" before this, from outside and from internal insurrection.

From about 1450 to 1650 people who may have been free or were servants by contract were converted into serfs by the denial of their "right of departure." They were virtually "ascribed." The big "men of service" to the Czars were given land,

the small ones were ascribed to these masters. The magnates owed services, military and governmental, to the Czars for the gift. Runaway serfs could be recaptured; this process became a great affair of the State. The land of steppe, forest, and immeasurable cold made escape almost impossible. Those who succeeded in getting to the Crimea or the north and Siberia attained a much freer status; here there was less serfdom, being more distant from the center of government and police.

Peasant Frenzy. From time to time in the seventeenth century, especially in the lands from the Volga over to Moscow, there were ferocious peasant uprisings led by very forceful leaders (Stenka Razin, 1670–1671; Bulavin, 1707–1708; and Pugachev, 1773–1778), resulting in the murder of landowners and gentry, in arson and pillage. Pugachev, in Catherine's time, was rampant for six years before he was subdued. The risings included non-Russians—that is, anti-Russians. Marching on Moscow (as pretender that he was the true Czar, the supposedly murdered husband of Catherine the Great) Pugachev proclaimed: [4]

We grant to all hitherto in serfdom and subjection to the landowners the old cross and prayers, heads and beards, liberty and freedom always, to be converted against recruiting levies, poll taxes or other money taxes, with possession of the land, the woods, the hay meadows, the fishing grounds, the salt lakes, without payment and without rent. And we free all those hitherto oppressed by the very fact of landowners and the bribe-taking officials and judges, those who were hitherto gentry on their lands and estates, these opponents of our rule and perturbators of the Empire and ruiners of the peasants. Seize them, punish them, hang them! Treat them in the same way as they, having no Christian feeling in them, treated you, the peasants. With the extermination of these and the malefactor gentry, everyone will begin to enjoy a quiet and peaceful life which will continue forevermore.

Such risings never, apparently even at the greatest, numbered more than about 200,000. Men could never link up until the Bolsheviks linked them, with modern communications, in 1917. Re-

[4] Quoted from B. H. Sumner, *A Short History of Russia,* New York, 1943, p. 157.

peatedly between the years of the great insurrections, there were many murders of landlords, their bailiffs, and there were executions of peasants for murder if flogging with the knout failed to kill.

The peasants were especially incensed when, in 1750, Catherine the Great was foiled by a palace revolution of nobles in her attempt to exact services from the landlords for the lands the State had given them. "They are not commanded to do any service; why should we do any service to them?" The liberal doctrines of the West that touched Catherine were trapped in Russia, becoming fetid.

A thousand serfs provided a landlord with a very comfortable living, although their methods were Biblically primitive. The lords could be absentee or enter the military or administrative services. They had little incentive to emulate the agricultural innovations of the English and French gentry of the eighteenth century. Nicholas I (1825–1855) commented, in the era of proposed reform just after the impact of the French Revolution: "Serfdom is the indubitable evil of Russian life, but I think it is still more dangerous to interfere with it." His Chief of Police added:

> The landowner is the most reliable bulwark of the sovereign. No army can replace the vigilance and the influence which the landowner continuously exercises in his estates. If his power is destroyed, the people will became a flood endangering in time even the Czar himself. . . . The landowner is the most faithful, the unsleeping watchdog guarding the State; he is the natural police magistrate.

Lenin once said: "If 125,000 landowners can govern Russia, why cannot a couple of hundred thousand Bolsheviks do it?" Whoever could release (or promise to) the land-passion of the peasants could bolster his way to supreme power; whoever could then dispossess them of it, could rule, as the landlords and Czar had done. Lenin did this in November 1917.

The Mir: the Village Commune. The peasants, as serfs to 1861, and thenceforward whoever was free lived in a *collective village* agricultural economy, called the mir. This had originated in the fifteenth century. (The Bolsheviks resuscitated it under Stalin in 1926, p. 907.) In the village, on an estate,

each family had its garden plot, cottage, and stock. Beyond were meadows, forest, and common lands that belonged to the State or were claimed by the landowner but used by the villagers. These common lands were managed by a council of village elders. The mir was the customary association of householders. The household, with its very closely nucleated family, played a decisive part in the life and fate of all individuals in the village. The elders decided what was to be sown, the distribution of strips by location (which might be miles away), the use of common stock, distribution of the harvest, the building of common works, such as roads and bridges, minor policing and keeping the peace, and the periodical redistribution of the land according to the changing size of families. The elders also picked the recruits for the Army and passed on the names to the landowner. In the village economy, the landowner played some part, but most decisions and enforcement fell to the villagers themselves.

The mir was the village tax collector, beginning in the sixteenth century. The landlords were responsible for collection from the village as a whole, passing on the receipts to the governmental collectors. This poll tax, of so much per head, was levied as a total on the village. (It was not paid by landlords or clergy.) For its administration, a classification of State peasants, townsmen, and landlord serfs was drawn up. Once on the register in this way, freedom of status and place were hard to achieve. Gift or manumission by the lord could emancipate; or freedom might be achieved by purchase. Those who left the village (one could try to run away) left a bigger tax burden for the rest. Hence internal passports were introduced— identity books showing place or origin—to be given by the village elders. This immobilized people in the mir, reinforcing the agricultural stagnation.

Reform, 1861. The humane influences of the West, the nascent development of industry (textiles in Moscow and St. Petersburg and iron mines in the Urals and around Kharkhov), affected the bureaucracy and some landowners. The new industrialists argued that serfdom was so unproductive because no more productive uses for labor had been introduced; they offered the better opportunities. Also, the Crimean War (1854–1856) had demonstrated how disgracefully inefficient were the peasants in the Czar's uniform; it was thought that peasant inertia might be overcome by freedom. The French Revolutionary impulse to emancipation had been swamped in the reaction against the rising of the Czar's liberal officers of the guard in the Decembrist Revolt (December 1825, p. 749). Now new impulses, material and ideological, triumphed.

According to the edict of emancipation, serfdom ceased; the landlord lost the right to serf labor and duties. He himself retained the land around his mansion. The cottage and the garden plot remained the individual family's. But *the mir was continued*. The common lands now belonged either to the lord or to this peasant commune. The peasant was free of the lord but not of the commune. The mir's share in the common land was obtained by paying the lord or State for it, by payments arranged over a period of forty-nine years through a government peasants' land bank. True, peasant freedom would not have arrived until the annuities were paid off, practically speaking. This need to pay the annuity and low productivity per acre with a most prolific population kept the peasant in an abject debtor status. In many places the government's—that is, the landlord class's—assessment of the value of the land was extortionately above market value; and the government gave excessive portions of the pasture, meadow, and woods to the landlords.

This freedom was a remarkable reform and was, in fact, the seed of the revolutions of 1905 and 1917. But the impression must be retained that *social* serfdom still persisted; the peasants were still called "bare backs." By 1900, the reform was beginning to take deep hold; but this, again as an influence on government, is but yesterday. The peasants were intensely dissatisfied. Most of the land was still in the hands of a few people. Just before 1917 about 1,000,000 gentry and nobility (including families) owned 100,000,000 acres, while a 100,000,000 peasants owned only 400,000,-000 acres—a person-to-person ratio of 25 acres to 1. They suffered intense land hunger. The internal economy of the village was disturbed. As time went on a (roughly) threefold grouping de-

veloped: *kulaks* ("fists"), who were well off and sometimes employed others; a "poor peasant" class with pitifully small holdings and almost no implements or stock; and a middle peasantry. In 1907 the reactionary Prime Minister Stolypin instituted greater freedom of individual purchase, in order deliberately to foster social differentiation and secure the loyalty of the *kulaks* to the autocracy. By 1916, when some two thirds of the cultivatable land was held by the peasants, the *kulaks* (a very vague term), comprising about one tenth of all peasant households, owned a third of peasant-owned land, in holdings of 50 acres or more. The land had been sold by the nobles through a state bank system. By that time, also, one out of every two peasant households had acquired its own land. Half the peasant population was, then, still in the mir system altogether. The poll tax had been abolished in 1886; annuities were annulled in 1905.

Still the conditions of the peasantry were serf-like: poor, illiterate, medievally superstitious, ignorant infamously and pathetically. About the date of the Revolution of 1905 the total income per farm was valued at $100 to $250; nearly 70 percent of it was needed for food, of a crude kind at that; the rest went for clothing, lodging, kerosene and candles for lighting, nails, etc.

Vodka. By 1914 four fifths of the national revenue came from indirect sources, a notoriously regressive way of raising government funds. Of the total revenue, nearly 30 percent was raised by the State's monopoly of vodka. This extremely potent liquor was particularly bad for the health and morals of a peasant population that had a life of despair and was inclined to wild drinking bouts and subsequent brutalities.

The Upper Class

From the first assumption of authority over their serfs, the upper class had become a people of almost another world—in speech, education (though very unequal), interests, ambitions, dress, manners, character. They controlled or served the government, local and central; were hand in glove with the police; most remained on their estates. Some of them developed critical minds suspicious (sometimes revolutionarily so) of Czarism and its bureaucracy. They gave birth to the "conscience-stricken" gentry and some who wished in the nineteenth century not to remain "superfluous men." From these stemmed liberals and revolutionaries, such people as Pushkin, Turgenev, Tolstoy, Bakunin, Herzen, Kropotkin, and many who entered the student terrorist groups, in spite of Karl Marx's nonsense about the class determination of a sense of justice. Yet most had no conscience; and of those who did, most were passive.

They occupied high office in Moscow and St. Petersburg; they were provincial governors and the local representatives of the central ministries; they provided delegates for the provincial governors' consultative councils and the lesser governmental authorities in the narrower districts. After 1865 they took an important share in the elected *Zemstvos* and their executive boards, being given on these a far larger representation than peasants and townsmen. Some of them became liberal and moderate leaders in the Octobrist and Constitutional Democratic parties (p. 763) connected with the *Dumas* of 1906 onward. Some formed the Union of the Russian People and their terror squads, the Black Hundreds.

No link existed between them and the peasantry, except that of authority, exploitation, and murderous hatred—and except for occasional eccentrics, such as Count Tolstoy. They spent their receipts from the land sold to the peasants on luxury and gambling. Their capital did not go into the land. By 1904 a third of the land that they still owned was in pawn to the state-run Notables Land Bank. They were, all in all, wastrels, even if they were charming and graceful. They did not possess themselves of the State and govern it as a liberal aristocracy as the English lords did. This we now see.

IV. THE AUTOCRACY AND ITS CHURCH

From, say, 1450 to 1917 Russia was the world's outstanding example of an unlimited autocracy. Its character was Asiatic rather than European in its despotic, villainous nature. It has even been labeled a theocracy—that is, rulership in temporal affairs in the name of a spiritual doctrine by divine right.

Orthodoxy, autocracy, and nationalism—these three strands blended into a more solid absolutism than in any other community of the modern world. The Asiatic influence entered through the Mongolian incursion; through Byzantium, which was not only Christianity's Eastern capital but the center of an Oriental rulership that does not admit of representative institutions or the sharing of power between rivals.

Stalin was fully Asian; Lenin, from Kazan, with Mongol features, was a baleful mixture of East and West; Trotsky, the Jew from Odessa, was Western. Stalin, of the East, had Trotsky exiled and murdered.

The early popular assemblies and assemblies of nobles and high landed gentry (the *boyars*) had lost political significance because (1) serfdom developed, and (2) the gentry connived with the princes to get protection from other princes and the Mongol and earlier invaders. For life was dangerous—from 1228 to 1462. Northern Russia was invaded 133 times by foreign powers, including 48 times by Tatars, and there were also 90 feuds among princes.

An attempt was made by the nobility about 1550 to establish a *Duma* (parliament) in which their representatives would be able to limit the Czar or Emperor, who had become semisacrosanct and absolute. It was played out by 1640, the very year in which the English started a civil war to suppress the powers of their King. From that time until 1906 no central, elected, representative check on the Czar's authority was ever in being.

Ivan the Terrible first took the title Czar in 1547. This king had pursued for a decade a deliberate policy of murdering all neighboring nobles of importance, together with mass deportations, to make it known that he was master and to disperse potential opposition from the capital. For this, the poor praised and obeyed him. He began the policy of "selection" or forced service for the government, general conscription for the State's purposes. He was popular also because he conquered Kazan and reached the mouth of the Volga, so obstructing future Mongol incursions. The subjection of an autocrat, as English history shows clearly, requires the union of classes against him. But in Muscovy, *boyars* (nobles and magistrates) and *mouzhiks* (peasants) were at history's critical moments mutually hostile: each sought the authority of the Czar against the other.

The title *Czar*—that is, *Caesar*—was taken from both the leader of the Mongol Horde and from the Byzantine Emperors; with it went the blood-sucking Mongol tribute-government and the Byzantine autocracy, guile, and bestial cruelty. Peter the Great replaced *Czar* by the western *Emperor*. *Czar* returned. The symbol was the Byzantine two-headed eagle; the crown jewels were alleged to be its jewels. After the fall of Constantinople to the Turks in 1454, Ivan the Terrible's predecessor married the last descendant of the Byzantine Emperor. This was a dazzling ancestral connection to multitudes of *mouzhiks*. Furthermore, on the overthrow of Constantinople, the Russian autocrat assumed the headship of the Byzantine Church, which was taken under the wing of the Russian Orthodox Church. A decisive event had occurred: the monistic interweaving of the secular and spiritual authority of momentous cultural consequences.

The Czar's style was "Czar Autocrat, chosen by God." Hence the link with Julius Caesar. *Autocrat* is the Greek word for *Imperator,* and this meant in Rome not only supreme ruler but also commander of the Army. Rome had personified the Divine in Augustus—all to impress the subject peoples with their Caesar as a deity. This, transferred to the Russian Czars, was *charisma* (p. 559), indeed!

We have already suggested that all men were under obligation of State service. The French *corvée* of so many days' work a year on the roads or transporting military supplies were a triviality compared with Czar-decreed "service" in anything the government ordained, the Army, public works, mines, on the land, roads, exploration, frontier duty. All land was owned by the Czar; you lived at his good will. The State became omnicompetent: we have seen that the climate and colonization and defense against neighbors brought this about—Sweden, Finland, Poland, the Ukraine, the Baltic states. Military policy became the directing, paramount rule of State activity and methods.

There was no question of *laissez faire;* the State protected Russian products by tariffs; mining and manufactures were undertaken by the State, and later the State pressed forward the revolution in industries and railroads. In the seventeenth century the State fostered economic productivity by giving serfs to the landlords who used them in factories, some very large, even before the introduction of mechanical power.

The Church and the Faith

Thus, omnicompetent and omnipotent, the Czar, was supported by the Church.[5] Something must be said on this now, with a reversion to the Czar's institutions later. The Western Church was far from admitting anything like the absolute power of the national kings of Europe; least of all the Roman Catholic Church, whatever its actual connivance. The Western Church advanced the doctrine of the "keys of the kingdom" of St. Peter and the "sword" as two separate powers, the former belonging to the Church, the latter to the Crown. The Church even claimed to moderate temporal rule by its ethic, else it could not rule over people spiritually. Tremendous conflicts agitated Europe from 1100 to 1900 over the distribution of power; and whether the victory went to the Catholics or the Protestants, to the Church or the State, both suffered a limitation of its claims to authority over men. Nothing like the Reformation occurred in Russia. Nor was there the Renaissance that raised the spirit of the individual against authority in the light of the moving classic appeal. The western and northwestern peoples had stubborn, individual consciences and self-confidence, not the Russians.

The Russian Church taught the Christian doctrine of obedience, also used by the West, but unlimitedly and crudely, to secure submissiveness. This took strong hold on a land-bound serf society, without education and without the inspiration of universities and city men of business, crafts, and commerce. Alternative doctrines could not enter from the West, for the Mongols had set

[5] Christianity, in the form of Greek Orthodoxy, was embraced by Vladimir I of Kiev in 988. It was forcibly imposed on the pagan people by royal armed officers; but the people either kept their primitive superstitions in harness with their "Christianity" or deeply infused the latter with their belief in magic.

up their golden curtain. This superstitious influence lasted for centuries, without any rival system
of religion or philosophy. It taught orthodoxy and
unification of political power because it sought
these in Church matters.

Emphatically, the prevailing religion is a potent
ingredient of a society's government because it
teaches obedience and the value of the individual
soul. The Russian Church taught abject, obsequious, subservient obedience, without revolt.

Chapter 13 of the Epistle to the Romans and
the first Epistle of Peter were the fundamental
doctrines of the relationship between the spiritual
and the temporal power. It is hard to speak of
these *separately,* because the Church yielded both
sides of power to the Czar.

> Let every soul be subject unto the higher
> powers. For there is no power but of God: the
> powers that be are ordained of God.
> Whosoever therefore resisteth the power, re-
> sisteth the ordination of God: and they that re-
> sist shall receive to themselves damnation.

Damnation? Those who know anything of the
history of the relationship of the Catholic Church
and the souls of people in the early centuries know
that the Church separated the body and the soul
and, for the sake of the soul, were prepared to
kill, torture, and burn the body, and to deprive
those who sought assurance of salvation of this
unearned for comfort.

> For rulers are not a terror to good works, but
> to the evil. Wilt thou then not be afraid of the
> power? do that which is good, and thou shalt
> have praise of the same:
> For he is the minister of God to thee for good.
> But if thou do that which is evil, be afraid; for
> he beareth not the sword in vain: for he is the
> minister of God, a revenger to execute wrath
> upon him that doeth evil.
> Wherefore ye must needs be subject, not only
> for wrath, but also for conscience sake.
> For for this cause pay ye tribute also: for they
> are God's ministers, attending continually upon
> this very thing.
> Render therefore to all their dues: tribute to
> whom tribute is due; custom to whom custom;
> fear to whom fear; honor to whom honor.[6]

[6] Romans, 13:1–7.

Let us look at the next passage:

> And who is he that will harm you, if ye be
> followers of that which is good?
> But and if ye suffer for righteousness' sake,
> happy are ye: and be not afraid of their terror,
> neither be troubled;
> But sanctify the Lord God in your hearts: and
> be ready always to give an answer to every man
> that asketh you a reason of the hope that is in
> you with meekness and fear:
> Having a good conscience; that, whereas they
> speak evil of you, as of evildoers, they may be
> ashamed that falsely accuse your good conversa-
> tion in Christ.
> For it is better, if the will of God be so, that
> ye suffer for welldoing, than for evildoing.
> For Christ also hath once suffered for sins, the
> just for the unjust, that he might bring us to
> God, being put to death in the flesh, but quick-
> ened by the Spirit:[7]

What would a robust American on the frontier
have answered to *"Ye shall stand all these things"*?
What did the English Puritans say and do?

The power of religion is greater than that of the
hydrogen bomb in politics. For it indicates the
ends that man ought to pursue (including his
economic interests) and the means thereto that
are justifiable in the national community. The
Russians were taught spiritual servility and morbid
low-spiritedness.

The clergy was (1) monastic, or black, and (2)
local, called the "white" clergy who lived with the
peasants and who could marry—illiterate and
superstitious. The former had been colonizers,
teachers of the arts and handicrafts. They produced no theologians, but many saints. Their
orders degenerated.

The essence of this Orthodoxy was *sobornost,*
the notion of the congregation as a primal, collective body, not as individuals. Pentecost, when the
spirit of Christ descends to the whole community
as one, is its symbol. It is contrasted with the
Western Church symbol of the Last Supper, when
Christ sat with the individual Disciples on equal
terms. Its other aspect is known as *kenoticism,*
the suffering of humiliation, the patient persistence
under the burden of the Cross, the bearing of

[7] I Peter, 3:13–18.

burdens, the self-ascription of sin, meekness and asceticism, in the example of Christ. The humiliated Christ was identified with the Czar, *Papashy,* the Little Father of Holy Russia, the "child who must die for his people." Russian religious art bears this out. The Orthodox believer is the Messiah of all peoples, the whole world with Russia, Holy Russia, as its savior. The preoccupation of the giant writers of the Russian nineteenth century with the social and moral responsibilities of Christians is prodigious; the works of Tolstoy and Dostoevski are Christian apologias. They have *no limits* as the West has and had; most of all the Protestant sects. It is a warm mysticism; but a dark one. The peasants mingled it with devils, demons, evil powers, superstitious charms, and deep cursing. It craved the whole. As Berdayev said:

> In the West is conciseness; everything is bounded, formulated, arranged by categories, everything (both the structure of the land and the structure of the spirit) is favorable to the organization and development of civilization. . . . In virtue of their religious-dogmatic quality of spirit, Russians—whether orthodox, heretics or schismatics—are always apocalyptic or nihilist.

It is All or Nothing in politics. It produced obedience. It made anti-Semitism easy to agitate as a diversion from the mismanagement of the Czar and the exploitation of the landowners. Russian peasants could be made to believe that Jewish people need the blood of Christian children for the celebration of the Passover!

The only great perturbation in the Russian Church—called the Roskol—occurred in the seventeenth century. "Old believers" stuck to the old and perverted texts; the others, supported by the State and supporting it, purified the Church's practices and texts, but the central doctrine remained intact. However, many sects developed with their own kind of Orthodoxy, and the State put them under severe disabilities. None formed a church which could undertake free and tolerated rivalry with *the* Church. Peter the Great, in 1700, transformed the historic Church-State relationship. For centuries the Russian Metropolitan had been chosen by the Patriarch of Constantinople, many being Greeks. In 1440 the Russian and the Greek churches were severed. The bishops were appointed by the Czars and their council elected and consecrated the Metropolitan. The Church had lands and serfs. Peter abolished the Patriarchate (formerly the Metropolitan) and set up a Holy Synod to rule the Church. This was the bishops plus officials appointed by the Czar and headed by an official called the Procurator-General. The Church was under a despotic secular master, fully subordinated to the needs of the State. The clergy served in governmental positions; were called into imperial councils; worked hand in glove with the police; administered estates; dominated the censorship of publications; and for far into the nineteenth century ran the public schools. They inspired people and government with Messianism. When Byzantium, the Second Rome, fell in 1453, the Russian monk Timofei wrote to Ivan III, Czar of the Muscovite State, saying:

> Of the third new Rome . . . Of all kingdoms in the world, it is in thy Royal domain that the holy Apostolic Church shines more brightly than the sun. And let thy Majesty take note, O religious and gracious Czar, that all kingdoms of the Orthodox Christian Faith are merged into thy kingdom. Thou alone, in all that is under heaven, art a Christian Czar. And take note, O religious and gracious Czar, that all Christian kingdoms are merged into thine alone, that two Romes have fallen, but the third stands, and there will be no fourth. Thy Christian kingdom shall not fall to the lot of another.

The Moscow Orthodox kingdom was totalitarian: all in the State, all for the State, nothing outside the State. Its powers were not limited; its powers were not separated; it had no social-contract basis. It was a Caesaro-papacy.

V. THE CZAR'S INSTITUTIONS

In the middle of the sixteenth century, the Czar ruled with the help of a kind of Privy Council, a *Duma,* of *boyars* (p. 736). The Czar was too strong to permit the development of independence in the latter, to lead to a parliament. The *boyars* would not rely on the populace to obtain such power. There were no burghers adequate to the liberation that they had produced in the West. The *boyars* needed royal power and arms to hold their own lands far away from Moscow. They connived, and the Czars ruled by *ukaz* or *nakaz,* decrees, initiated by his officials or suggestions from the *boyars,* but always under his own undivided authority.

Several councils of magnates, clergy, and lesser landowners were called in the sixteenth century to relieve the Czar of excessive administrative strain, and from 1550 to 1614 these councils played some part in policy-making. Then the "time of troubles" broke on Moscow; the Poles occupied the city and set up a Polish Czar. When he was overcome, the *boyars* judged that, to avoid personal rule that had brought on this disaster, a central representative institution ought to be created. Between 1612 and 1622 an assembly of the land, the *Zemsky Sobor,* was summoned annually. It consisted of the magnates, upper clergy, selected members of the Army, the bureaucracy, and the middle landowners, rather like the French Estates General of 1614. It petered out by 1653. Some *boyars* and "service" nobility, preferred an autocrat who would sustain their serf privileges to a Diet that might lead to anarchy, as in Poland, owing to the exercise of a veto power by the old nobility.

The ending of the "time of troubles" had been rounded off by the choice in 1598 by the landowners and middle nobles of Boris Godunof, the first of the Romanov dynasty, to be Czar. This dynasty lasted until the murder of Czar Nicholas II in 1917.

The succession was a mixture of acknowledged primogeniture and horrible murders, in which the high nobility serving in the Czar's Guards played executioner, and in which husbands, wives, and sons were murdered by the ruler to affect the succession. From the time of Catherine the Great (a German petty princess), the Czars were descendants of German families. They called in German experts; and so intensified the nationalism of the Russian people who detested the "Germans" and "Westerners"—who brought culture and science.

Peter the Great

Peter the Great "Westernized" the Czardom, up to a point. The birth date of Peter the Great is 1672; he began to reign in 1682, and reached his majority in 1694, to die in 1725. Of those years, 1695 to the end of his life, he was at war for twenty-eight years. Peter's war necessities provided the fulcrum that enabled him to reform his Army, his bureaucracy, to subordinate his Church, and to introduce Western science and manufactures.[8] In 1697 Peter toured Europe. He worked in the Amsterdam yards as a shipwright. He took with him young people to become saturated with Western ideas. He detested the Russian idea, insofar as it was one of low productivity, incompetence, superstition. When he said, "I have not spared my life for my fatherland and people," he was saying what Frederick the Great was going to say a few years afterward: "I am the first servant of my people." His was a firm attempt at a benevolent and competent autocracy. About the same time Louis XIV declared, "I am the State." But it was also about the same time that William III of Orange swore submission to the Bill of Rights. These comparisons are of some interest.

Peter the Great wished to turn the "Russian beast into a human being," to turn him from "childhood to adulthood." He reformed the status of the nobility and the bureaucracy. Officialdom was especially numerous, as local assemblies did not exist, and Russia was a big country. The sparser the population, the bigger the proportion of bureaucrats. You can rule ten people almost as easily as two if they are close to you. In the absence of local elected assemblies, more officials and police were necessary. The hierarchy was the nation: the province, with provincial governor; beneath it, the districts, called *uisyed;* and below them the cantons, called *volost;* and then the communes. In the towns—there were not many—there was a town organization. The military and the tax-gatherers assisted the hierarchy.

Abortive Education and Civil Service. Peter the Great reinvigorated the idea of service by the landowners with remarkable austerity, even planning and decreeing the establishment of a school for them in economics and civics (in other words, the Cameralism of Prussia (p. 542) or the Colbertism (p. 283) of France or the Mercantilism of England (p. 12, p. 284) of that epoch—roughly speaking).

[8] Cf. Robert Bain, *Pupils of Peter the Great,* London, 1897.

The school never started: the nobility's children were not interested in learning. This, it must be remembered, was more than two hundred years after the foundation of the schools for the gentry and the middle class in England that, among other things, prepared their scholars for service in the interests of the Commonwealth, and engendered that spirit which took the Puritans to New England.

Moreover, Peter the Great had registers made of the children of the landowners, and appointed officials to call up the various young men to their duties, such and such a proportion for the Civil Service and such a proportion for the Army and the newly established and much hated (by the nobility) Navy.

The service of the State was formalized in a Table of Ranks (1721), which, in the separate categories of Army and Navy and Civil Service, ranged the services into fourteen ranks or classes, leading to the highest positions in the service. All, whatever their social status, were compelled to prove their ability and to learn their job by starting at the bottom. Noble rank could be attained, if not possessed at the beginning, and it could be improved if already possessed, by service and on the attainment of a certain point in the fourteen-level hierarchy.

Lenin's father rose to nobility as inspector of schools some one hundred and fifty years after the inception of this system.

Apart from some private schools (and there were as yet no universities) or those maintained by the clergy, the landowners obtained their education in their apprenticeship to the military or Civil Service and in the Cadet School in Moscow.

This system of ranks lasted until 1917—of course, service carried a salary with it. It looked as though it opened the career to the talents. But, the wealthy entered the service high up and then were more speedily promoted; and social boycotting of newcomers helped to preserve the status of the landowners. Yet, there was seepage in of men who had become able outside the ranks of the hereditary officials; and they, owing their position to the State's favor, were particularly subservient to the autocracy.

Departments. For the central government eight departments, in the form of collegiate bodies, were established. This was the Prussian model. With three or five at the head of a department instead of one, Peter could be sure that secrets would not be kept from him.

Senate. A Senate was established. It was a "kind" of Cabinet, of nine members, a superior executive body under the Czar's immediate authority, appointed by him. It controlled and directed all administrative activities of the government; supervised the eight departments; established the budget; acted as supreme judiciary—exhibiting the nonexistence of the separation of powers. It directed the provincial governors, and through them the landowners and the city governments. A large secretariat assisted it.

A Strong Apparatus. Peter the Great created the following things extending the strength of the State: a fleet, a standing Army, the tables of ranks, the collegiate departments and the Senate, an Academy of Science, the system of internal passports, and the poll tax. He developed shipbuilding, state factories to make military supplies and revenue-producing commodities, mining for iron. He built St. Petersburg and made it the capital. The poll tax had to be paid under the authority of the householders in the village communes; this tended to stabilize and solidarize the communes, both as an economic unit and as an administrative unit useful to the central government.

Most of this was borrowed from Sweden and Prussia, carried by German advisers. But there was no Protestant influence and the "Rule of Law" to modify the crushing despotism. The Russian beast was not turned into a human being; he did not follow Peter the Great and shave off his heavy beard.

To the Year 1917

Only slight institutional changes were made down to 1917 in this system: collegiate boards became ministries; and the Ministers remained the sole appointees of the Czar, his servants, without collective responsibility in their councils. The departments were uncoordinated through incompetence, and by designed "divide-and-rule" policy, and through the prevalence of spies who reported to the Czar and their ministerial masters against other Ministers. No parliament existed to invigorate the officials, and the Czars were inept. There was a war of all against all in the departments. They were sterile and rotten.

A Council of State, set up in 1810 (after the Napoleonic model in France) was a body of advisers to the Czar: it developed and prepared decrees and worked with the departments. These directly administered the highly centralized life of the provinces. They developed ideas, passed them on to the Council, which then worked them up and also guided the high level policy of the nation. The 35 to 60 members of the Council were appointed from the high nobility, the clergy, and the high "service" bourgeoisie. In 1905 this Council was converted into the second chamber of the newly established *Duma*. There was never a responsible ministry.

No Independent Judges. Until 1864 independent courts did not exist, on principle. There was no facing of accusers or jury trial or open day in court, with rules of evidence. Hence, there was hardly a legal profession as in the West, which became the bulwark of popular liberty and enemy of autocracy, such as Sir Edward Coke in England (p. 39). In 1864 the Czar instituted a combination of French and English courts. But the government constantly interfered in cases; it put whole regions under a "state of siege" with military tribunals whenever it feared disobedience and agitation. Then the police handled the cases deemed "political"—that is, opposition to the Czarist system, and the cases were dealt with administratively. Cases likely to excite public opinion of any kind were handled in *camera*.

The Police: the Okrana. The police were always powerful, for, as it has been observed, this was a regime of autocracy, tempered by assassination but also by corruption. After the Decembrist uprising in 1825, the secret police organization was reorganized and extended. The *Okrana* was the third section of the Czar's Chancellery. Nicholas I, its creator, circulated the deception that he needed such police in order that the people might get around official obstacles to communicate their thoughts to him, "the Little Father." The police would bring their messages. The *Okrana* employed spies and *agents provocateurs:* they worked with informers—janitors, workmen, clergy, schoolteachers; they had a branch that tracked down Russian political dissenters abroad, Geneva, London, Brussels, Zurich, etc. Teachers reported on their students, as, for example, on young Lenin, when he wanted to enter the University of Kazan. The skilled provoking agents were planted in political groups and, later, in trade unions, to incite people beyond the very narrow limits of legality and so openly to commit themselves. A hostility developed between the police and other departments, as the former spied everywhere and produced that anxiety which reduces men to submission to a Czar. Informers and denunciations became universal.

While, in England our admiration for skill would be fastened on Sir Robert Peel, on Gladstone, on John Quincy Adams and Lincoln in America and Thiers in France, our interest would, in Czarist Russia, be focused on Azeff the doublecrosser of revolutionaries and police, and a spy who duped Lenin and was even a member of the *Duma* in order the better to hide his tricks in the open. Tentacles everywhere?

The Censorship. Printing filtered in via Poland to Moscow by the middle of the sixteenth century. Until Peter the Great only the Church printed books; between 1700 and 1750 only eighteen works a year were published; and between 1750 to 1800, about 160 books a year, including imports. Some had been prohibited and some confiscated on complaint of clergy, noble, or official. Yet, already in 1550, Western Europe was showered with books and pamphlets. In 1650, before Russia began to print, Milton's plea for press freedom in *Areopagitica,* inspired the road to freedom. But in 1804 State and Church in Russia established a preventive censorship. All material, printed at home or imported, was required to go to the censors before being put on sale. Particularly during the revolutionary times of 1815, of 1830, of 1848 in Europe, especially in Poland and the Baltic, was the gag thrust firmly in the mouths of those who turned to the masses with appeals against the Czarist cruelty, corruption, autocracy, suppression of other nationalities, the misery of serfdom. But from time to time, liberal-minded bureaucrats let radical doctrines pass—some were of the "conscience-stricken gentry" (p. 740); they had friends like Pushkin or Kropotkin. From 1856, the era of liberal reforms, the censorship was changed to being punitive: publication needed no previous permission, but fines, prison, or suspension and seizure would follow on offenses. This system included the daily press; imports, however, required a license. Karl Marx was allowed; Spinoza and Hobbes were excluded!

Local Government Reforms. In 1864 elected *Zemstvos* were established in the provinces (*Gubernie*), districts within them (*Uezed*), and the municipalities.

Up to this time all forty-one provinces had been governed from St. Petersburg by governors appointed by the Czar. He was assisted by a bureaucracy and a local council appointed from among the nobility and landowners. In the capital city of each province, the regional officers of the central ministries—Education, Interior, etc.—also operated. The provincial committees, appointed from the nobility and the big towns, helped plan the budgets, raise taxes, organize peasant forced labor for government works. There was no local autonomy. In the villages the mir elders managed affairs and picked an executive board. Social conditions in health, welfare, roads, poor relief were shocking, and education almost nonexistent (p. 729). In the cities, government was conducted by corporate bodies headed by a city officer appointed by St. Petersburg, and manned by appointees from the wealthier bourgeoisie and gentry. A strict tutelage was exercised over them by the provincial governor and inspectors.

In 1864 the thirty-four fully Russian provinces were given the right to administer certain functions through elected *Zemstvos*: health, education, welfare, agricultural development, trade, industry, roads, bridges, harbors, fire-fighting and insurance, local police, stock-breeding—as far as a limited tax base would allow. The provincial authorities planned and guided and ran the institutions; the smaller areas did the direct administration.

The district assemblies were directly elected; then these chose delegates to the provincial assemblies. In district or province, the chairman was the marshal of the local nobility elected by the *curia* of the nobility. The elected assemblies chose executive boards. They and their chairmen *required central approval*.

The electorate (already indirect for the provinces) was not equal and universal. It was divided into *curia*. The owners of real estate outside the cities were assigned their number of representatives; *in* the cities, theirs; then came the peasant communes. Regardless of the number of voters in these groups, the law fixed their representation: the nobility and the larger landowners dominated.

Yet they did remarkable work, for no other institution in Russia had attracted such large numbers of unselfish workers: they tapped the sentiment of guilt among educated and progressive men and women. For example, in 1895, after thirty years of operation in *Zemstvo* provinces there was a hospital bed for every 6500 people; in non-*Zemstvo* provinces, only one for 41,000 people. Education showed similar progress. They spent their revenues in order of importance on education, health, welfare, agriculture, veterinary service, roads.

By the 1880's they were feeling their confidence, power, and pleasure in liberty to create. The liberal members joined nationwide unions and conferences. So did the technical officials, the teachers, the physicians, the lawyers, the accountants, the engineers, etc., and were known as "the third element"! The All-Russian Union of *Zemstvos* advocated constitutional monarchy (in the large, as they now knew it in the small!); after 1900 they affiliated with fourteen unions of technicians in the Union of Unions, to educate and confer on liberal reform.

The Czarist government was early resolved to emasculate this liberal growth, and the *Zemstvos* had their own local difficulties also. The *mouzhiks* were hostile to health and education; they were hostile to a tax in place of forced public labor; they did not like land experts. Some landlords were saboteurs of education and culture (concerts, lectures, the theater) for *mouzhiks* and workers. Hence, some *Zemstvos* were very backward.

The central government gave the governors power to reverse *Zemstvos* decisions; required central government approval for appointment of the technical officials (supplied by the growing universities, and men of liberal social and political views of the *Narodnik* outlook, p. 751), and allowed their rejection on grounds of political "undesirability." (Lenin's father, an inspector of schools, was one of these, subject to central approval!) Teacher-training colleges, libraries, lectures, were strangled by the central departments. The governors were given power to exclude elected people from office and substitute others. The upper limit of taxation was put at 3 percent of the value of the real estate being taxed. The autocracy meant to stifle this new life.

These bodies, left alone (better still, encouraged), might, with the growing railroad communication, the universities, and the press, have produced intermediate bodies of men of good will and liberalism, to link Czardom with people, to temper the former and nurture the latter in self-government. But Nicholas II blocked the *Zemstvos* "senseless dreams" of representative government. Later the Union of Unions joined the moderate political parties that brought about and acted in the *Duma* of 1906.

The city *Zemstvos* followed much the same course as the provincial ones and were hampered in the same way. The bourgeoisie ran a remarkable range of public utilities in the towns. They did not want revolution, nor did they find the Czarist autocracy or the serfdom pleasing. They hastened the fall of the Czardom by their educational ventures; but joined not Lenin's Bolsheviks, but the Octobrists (p. 763) or the K.D.'s (p. 763), the constitutionalists.

In the land, in 1889, *Zemski Natchalniks,* land captains, were established by Czarist decree. They displaced the local justices of the peace, who were elected by the mir, to take first-instance notice of minor civil and criminal cases. They were made supervisors and correctors of every phase of peasant existence, with a power to sentence village elders and judges, without trial or appeal, to prison or fine. They were appointed by the provincial governor from lists supplied by the local gentry, with a right to appoint others if they thought fit. The peasants, once again thrown back into abysmal servitude, hated the land captains, some of whom, later, joined Czarist reactionary parties to wreak horrible cruelties on the peasantry.

To Lenin's Successful Revolution
of November 1917

To whom will the people appeal one day against the silence of the great? What explosion of vengeance is being prepared against the autocracy by the abdication of such a cowardly aristocracy? What is the Russian nobility doing? It adores the Czar and makes itself an accomplice in all the abuses of the sovereign power in order to continue, itself, to oppress the people, whom it will flog as long as the god it serves leaves the whip in its hand (note that it is the nobility that created this god). . . . An oppressed people has always merited its suffering; tyranny is the work of peoples. Either the civilized world will, before fifty years have passed, fall again under the yoke of the barbarians, or Russia will undergo a Revolution more terrible than the revolution whose effects are still felt in Western Europe.

—Marquis de Custine, Journey for Our
Time, pp. 93-94. July 1839

I. THE INVITATION TO TERROR

Illiteracy; bestiality of human relations; rural dispersion and dense collective pressure; superstition and suffocating religion; poverty and coarseness; no free government; the abasement of serf by lord and police, and the degeneration of the gentry; no intermediate bodies of civic leaders between the scattered millions and the few thousand at the Czarist apex—to men and women of conscience, these were an incitement to terror and revolution, the more so because the masses were afflicted with a hardly assailable and movable INERTIA produced by the factors mentioned above.

Why did the autocracy concede any reform at all in the 1860's? It could not altogether resist certain forces. The upper class was divided in conscience; made so by the news of the cultured world outside Russia (and some studied abroad) or by the litera-

ture that the Russian geniuses of the nineteenth century were writing (pp. 750–753).

On December 14, 1825, officers of the Guards attempted to seize the Czar. Their purpose was to set up a government on the Napoleonic or the American model. Loosely organized in secret societies like the other young men of idealist Europe, they had acquired their ideas while on foreign service against Napoleon. They were mercilessly executed or sent to Siberia with such brutality as to quash revolutionary attempts or even thoughts for a long time. The very liberal idealism of the thousands who followed them was their undoing. But the intolerable evils of Russia— prompting such works as *Who Can Be Happy and Free in Russia?*—shocked the sons and daughters of the upper class still. The Czarist response was to exile them as soon as they exhibited the slightest publicity of their views. No mention of the evils of serfdom, "Baptized property" in Herzen's phrase, was permitted. Almost every writer to be referred to in the next few pages was persecuted or exiled.

Nevertheless, some concessions had to be made. Within the bureacracy itself officials could not look on the mass servitudes without relenting. The universities could not be altogether suppressed. The country was too big to be ruled by perfect terror. Industrial and commercial people, the technicians, the students pressed, with their new-found knowledge and experience of fairly free human relationships, for change. Some concessions were therefore made; and some, as we have seen, were limited after they had allowed the *Zemstvos,* and so on, to taste blood.

The government met terror with terror; and its terror and frustration engendered terrorists. From the 1880's assassinations were undertaken by revolutionary groups; the government reacted with its "state of emergency." This process, leading to the revolution of 1905, and then to the two revolutions of 1917, one in February and the Bolshevik *coup* in November, will be described after a glance at the strange nature of Russian political thought.

Representative Russian Political Thought

There is no native Russian Marx of the magnitude of Karl Marx; indeed, there is no great Russian philosopher at all of the class of those we have named as representative of Britain, France, and Germany. The nineteenth century produced some splendid pamphleteers, and the rest, Pushkin, Leontieff, Gogol, Dostoevski, Tolstoy, Turgenev, Goncharov, and Chekhov, expressed themselves through fiction, like Wells, Shaw, and T. S. Eliot. All were tormented by their native society.

Strange words, indeed strange to Western ears since the Middle Ages, are needed to characterize Russian political ways of thinking. They are: *Apocalyptic; Eschatological; Maximalist* and *Totalitarian; Messianic;* and *Nihilistic.*

Apocalyptic means the revelation of the final future, an idea of the last judgment, a celestial judgment on the activities of men, their righteousness, and their evil.

Eschatological (from the Greek *eskos*) means *last things,* fundamental, the opposite of that shallow or "flat" attitude of English thought: it means

the four last things—death, judgment, heaven, and hell, theologically speaking—which, as we have seen, involve it in political thinking.

Messianic concerns the savior and liberator who will come, the Messiah, the first of that kind recognized in Western civilization being Christ.

Maximalist means both *including everything* in a philosophy, so that it does not deal just with the "political" aspect but is inclusive of *everything* in human behavior and life. For the Russians a political ideal will embody art, culture, religion, science. The political will orders life in all respects. *Maximalism* also means going to extremes in the logic of any principle. We have seen that this is a tendency, visible in Saint-Simon, Fourier, Proudhon, and Comte, and a German tendency in Hegel —and these made a very substantial impact on Russian political philosophy in the first three quarters of the nineteenth century. Involved was an absolute metaphysical scheme, rather than the piecemeal, unphilosophical, utilitarian way of the Americans and the English.

Totalitarianism, another characteristic of Russian thinking, can be roughly equated with its *maximalism.* Political activity and political change require that everything conceivable in society be fitted into the sphere and obligation of the State. This thinking was protest, rather than construction. It became deep, dreamy, unoperational, without quantitative utilitarian limits (p. 34), because it was developed by men not immersed in the practice of government but idle on estates or imprisoned in Siberia or in exile—such were Alexander Herzen, Mikhail Bakunin, Kropotkin, Plekhanov, Lenin, Trotsky. They became sectarian, bitter, and destructive or utopian.

The French Revolution's "Liberty, Equality, and Fraternity" and belief in the human nobility first stirred the intelligentsia, to be overshadowed by the Decembrist slaughter. In the succeeding decades Hegel was the philosophic hero, and Russia would have been better off for his prescriptions than with what she had in Czarism; the "conscience-stricken gentry" took the *passive* element in Hegel: all that is actual is rational. Why change? In the 1860's the *active* element of Hegel caused ferment: "Since I am rational, *I* will be the hero to make the rational effective on earth!": it was the current that in the 1880's (even earlier) joined with Marxism—the Hegelianism turned on its head (p. 557).

In the 1860's the populist socialists arose; the *Narodniks*—for the "peasantry" or "people," the "toilers"—to become revolutionary in the 1880's, concerned rather with social, agricultural revolution than political, but driven to terror, since constitutional change in Europe seemed to produce so little so slowly.

The Nihilistic Strain. This was almost co-eval with the *Narodnik* movement. It does not mean bomb-throwing; and the word came into the West from Russia. Its impulse was a cosmic sense of injustice, best represented in the novels of Dostoevski. "What, in this world," he asks, "can justify the tears of a child, an innocent child?" He thinks that nothing can, except a convulsion not only of society and government but of all human nature. Hence, the world, of government also, should be fled till all men are Christians of either *his* personal kind or Tolstoy's (who freed his serfs, from a sense of guilt). This, then, is rejection or nihilism; it is total, because it requires *everything* to be included in the political; and it is profoundly pessimistic, another characteristic of Russian thinkers, including, curiously enough, Lenin and his friends.

An aspect of this was Prince Kropotkin's "philosophical anarchism" (*not* bomb-throwing). In his *Mutual Aid,* he transferred the results of his philosophizing about Nature—insects, animals, growing trees, etc.—to human society: Nature developed by the uncoerced, helpful relationships among its beings. Therefore why not, as in the mir, dispense with government and coercion and achieve a socialism based on uncoerced, unlegislated mutual help—no police, no bureaucracy, no armies but only fraternal men and science? The reader is in a position to answer this undue revulsion from government.

In 1879, when Lenin was nine years old and in the year in which Trotsky and Stalin were born, a total gospel, of Messianic character, had arrived in Russia in the form of George Plekhanov's *Contribution to the Development of the Monistic Theory of the State or of Materialism,* or, in plainer words, Karl Marx for Russians. Its author had been founder of a group called "The Liberation of Labor." It gave Russian radicals what they had been conditioned by government and previous thought to need: a complete, a revolutional, a *willful* doctrine. Above all, it was "scientific." Natural science had entered Russia late, from the middle of the nineteenth century only, if we omit the efforts of Peter the Great and his St. Petersburg Academy of Science. We know that in the West natural science, philosophically regarded, helped to disintegrate the divine right of kings and produce the "social-contract" theory of authority; it also quantified political ideas. In Russia the mass impact of its highly developed results produced credulity and dogmatism. Marx was total and materialist-scientific. This maximalism was swallowed whole and fanatically. The governmental conclusions were Draconic.

The Narodniks and Beyond. The names associated with this movement are Alexander Herzen; the historian Chaadaev; the philosopher Michaelovsky; Mikhail Bakunin, international stormy petrel; Tkachev and Nechaev, career revolutionaries. Herzen (1812–1871) swore as a boy of thirteen to achieve what the Decembrists had failed to do. He served in the bureaucracy; he was soon exiled. He was a "Westerner," looking to the liberalism of the West to save Russia's soul. France and England disillusioned him; he became a Slavophil—that is, he looked to Russia's own indigenous mir culture, purged of governmental distortion, to save Russia and the world. Others joined him in 1862 to form an organization that later obtained the name of the Society for Land and Freedom; it, again, was an offspring of a movement called "To the People," the *Narodniks,* the intelligentsia, especially the students who moved among the peasantry with tidings of a new world, politically, economically, socially. The peasants denounced them to the waiting police. (See the description in Turgenev's *Virgin Soil* and, for the coining of the term *nihilism,* see his *Fathers and Sons.*) Herzen grieved over the brutalization of the peasant. His journal, *The Bell,* was smuggled into Russia. It said:

When you see him [the *mouzhik*] appear in the law courts, all you can see on his face is incomprehension—he cannot even understand the words they use—fear; and when he goes away acquitted he cannot even feel happy in the existence of justice because he does not even know what it is.

There were many nuances in the doctrines of these movements. But, generally, they held that the existing order must be overthrown, some said by social revolution, others, by political revolution. Russia could get to socialism without passing through capitalism. They expected little from "capitalism," for they saw in the West a petty and comfort-loving bourgeoisie, and this was not good enough for *them;* they needed something nobler. In the course of time the peasant would work wonders in the mir, and the *artel,* the collective-contract group that made nails, shoes, clothing, domestic utensils, and furniture with great aesthetic quality. Here would flourish democratic communism led by the village elders. The *Narodniks* believed that the peasants were communists and pacifists by instinct. Anti-*Narodniks*—Westerners—scorned these beliefs; they thought the peasants were ignorant, stupified with religion and drink; they pointed to the emergence of *kulaks.* Some *Narodniks* relied on heroic leaders, such as Bakunin. Others hoped for peasant evolution, somehow. Some looked to peaceful redistribution of the land, called the "Black Redistribution"; others saw that an uprising would be needed. Bakuninites had a revolutionary will; were even antigovernmental anarchists (hence hated by Karl Marx who expelled Bakunin from the Internationale in 1874); men like Herzen had no revolutionary will.

Nechaev: The Revolutionists' Catechism. Police persecution led to terrorism. Nechaev (1874–1883), was a young friend of Bakunin's, a lowly born schoolteacher, imprisoned for the last ten years of his brief life. At the age of twenty-two he murdered a fellow student of the University of St. Petersburg who had betrayed his ideas. (See Dostoevski's *The Possessed.*) His doctrine is a fundamental step in the overthrow of Czarism and the Leninist-Stalinist-Politbureau's dictatorship. It is so identical with Lenin's doctrines that it must be regarded as creative. It is the coldest-blooded revolutionary creed conceivable. Some direct paragraphs are material.[1]

1. "The revolutionist is a doomed man. He has no personal interests, no affairs, sentiments,

[1] See complete translation in Max Nomad, *Apostles of Revolution,* Boston, 1939.

attachments, property, not even a name of his own. Everything in him is absorbed by one exclusive interest, one thought, one passion—the revolution."

2. "Should he continue to live in [the world], it will be solely for the purpose of destroying it the more surely." Hence a break with all the laws and moralities of that world, which he considers his ruthless foe.

3. "He knows only one science, the science of destruction. . . . The object is but one—the quickest possible destruction of that ignoble system."

4. "Whatever aids the triumph of the revolution is ethical; all that which hinders it is unethical and criminal." Hence a hatred of present-day morals.

5. He is merciless to the State and the privileged educated classes. The war between him and them is merciless. He must be ready to die and to stand torture.

6. There is no love, friendship or honor—they are subdued by "the one cold passion of the revolutionary cause": inexorable destruction.

7. Cold calculation overcomes even personal hatred and revenge, as it does sentimentality, friendship and such passions.

8. The only permissible friendship or enmity is measured by loyalty to the measures required by revolutionary success—the all-destructive revolution.

9. Revolutionists act together, or take separate responsibility, as acts of destruction require.

10. The revolutionist and his associates must regard themselves and each other as expendable: some will not be initiated, they are to be used; some will be initiated, they are to be asked their assent to their expendability.

11. Rescue of an unsuccessful revolutionist must depend on his usefulness, not on friendship.

12. "Everybody and everything must be equally hateful to him"—he is in society only to destroy it. He penetrates everywhere, "into the Third Department and even into the Czar's Winter Palace," an impostor, to destroy.

13. Society is listed in categories of those who are to be destroyed, according as their death will be useful to the revolutionary cause, and to this only. The first category contains those who are dangerous to the revolutionary organization itself; the second, men who can be spared awhile

so that they may provoke the people to revolt; the third, rich and well-connected people, to be used and exploited; the fourth, "ambitious officeholders and liberals of various shades"— they are to be used, mulcted of secrets, compromised. A fifth category are "doctrinaires" in the revolutionary camp, who must be forced into extreme statements, to destroy the majority and make the rest into real revolutionaries. The sixth includes women, to be made use of and worked up into abandoned revolutionary feeling, and used—"fully initiated and having completely accepted our program."

14. The revolutionists have "no aim other than the complete liberation and happiness of the masses, that is, of the people who live by manual labor. The only road to this is an all-destroying popular revolution." Therefore, they will further the evils and calamities of society to provoke the people thereto.

15. No western revolution is intended, for such bows to property rights and so-called civilization and morality, and has replaced one political form by another. "Only that revolution will be beneficial to the people which will destroy at the very root every vestige of statehood and will annihilate all of Russia's state traditions, institutions and classes."

16. "Our business is destruction, terrible, complete, universal, and merciless." The movement of the people will then itself in future generations produce a future organization—we will not foist one on the people from above. (Here Lenin and Stalin parted company sharply from Nechaev and his associates.)

17. Therefore "let us join hands with the bold world of bandits—the only genuine revolutionists in Russia," against the nobility, the bureaucracy, the clergy, the merchants and capitalists ("guilds" or "curia") and against the parasitic kulaks.

18. "To consolidate this world into one invincible, all-destroying force is the sole object of our organization; this is our conspiracy, our task."

Nechaev helped to organize the assassination of Alexander II. He had preferred to stay in prison rather than accept the offer of rescue by a friend, wishing that friend to concentrate rather on the murder of Alexander II. Ten years after the murder of Alexander II, Lenin's brother was executed for following in Nechaev's footsteps in a plot to kill Alexander III. The cultural connection with Lenin is significant.

Some anarchists were terrorists; some were patient evolutionists. Some radicals were Westernizers; others, Slavophils. The former obtained their impetus from Peter the Great, the French Revolution and French culture; the Decembrists were Westernizers. They scouted the mystic belief in Russian indigenous culture; they thought it stank. Plekhanov became one of these. The Slavophil doctrine was the spontaneous and holy regeneration to spring spontaneously from the peasant commune and Russian Christianity, once Czarism was purged. They hated the Petrine reforms, the Germans, the Protestants, the Prussian state. Tolstoy and Dostoevski ("the Russians are God-bearers") were of this kind, despising the hard, efficient bourgeois of the West. From the *mouzhik* would issue godly light, holiness; the dirtier now, the better some day. Lenin was first a Slavophil, then a Westerner with Marx, and then a mixture of Marx and the peasant-Slavophil. Trotsky was a Westerner. Stalin was an Oriental Slavophil.

There is terrible foreboding, in the poets and novelists of the second half of the nineteenth century. The pessimism foresenses an apocalypse, some rightful, ruinous, cleansing cataclysm in Russia, a judgment on the historically accumulated sins against God's law in Christ. It seemed to them the *only* way to a better Russia.

There had never been an age of chivalry in Russia, love with valor, courage, truth, and charity—that is, humanity. Russians had been taught submission to the will of God through the Czar. They had no Renaissance after the fall of Constantinople, such as inspired the great feats of art and letters in the West, but subjugation by the Czar and Church; no Renaissance had taught them the virtue of disobedience. They hardly knew compassion, let alone humanity. If so much inhumanity prevailed, it prompted equal inhumanity to purge it. Let this be compared with Western Puritanism: "Life is real; Life is earnest . . . Act, act in the living present!" Russian society never reached anywhere near the standard of Western bourgeois civilization before Marx taught its leading radicals to detest it for something utopian. Granted its faults of economy and culture, western achievements, justice, freedom, personal dignity and freedom from fear, moderation, legal and social guarantees or personal rights, the right to participate in the formation of the nation's law of right and wrong, were and are tremendous. It was a tragedy for the Russian people that they did not enter this heritage before they were seized by Lenin and Stalin.

Vladimir Ilyitch Ulyanov: Otherwise Nikolai Lenin

Character, Ideas, and Revolution. One of the *Narodniks,* and then a convert to Marxism, was Lenin. His character and doctrines can be merged with the events of 1890's and the revolutions of 1905 and 1917.

He was born into a typically Czarist and Orthodox family in Simbirsk on the Volga in 1870. His family, with two brothers and two sisters, was happy and mild. His mother was of German descent and read aloud to the family those classics of which we have taken note: their social criticism was an open secret. Lenin's father seems to have had Mongolian blood in him. (At the end of the seventeenth century, 17 percent of the upper classes of Moscow were of Mongolian descent.) He was a teacher; was promoted; returned to Simbirsk as inspector of schools, one of the "third element" already mentioned (p. 747); and was made a noble for public service. He specialized in mathematics and meteorology. Physically, Lenin resembled his father. Lenin's elder brother, Alexander, and he were the most brilliant and assiduous boys at school. The family were "liberals"; nothing revolutionary marred their progress until Lenin's sixteenth year.

Alexander inclined to mathematics and science, Lenin to the humanities. In the 1880's the terrorist organization, *The People's Will* (*Narodnaya Volya*), with the slogan, "One Alexander after another," had killed Alexander II. In 1883 Lenin's brother entered St. Petersburg University. In 1887 Lenin's father died, making Alexander the head of the family, which, we know, was highly nucleated (p. 738) in Russia. Deeply affected already by his father's death, he joined with other students in a plot to kill Alexander III, not realizing that

The People's Will was now dormant. He, a student of natural science, made the amateur bomb. The students were seized; Alexander, unnecessarily self-incriminating, was executed with some others.

Within one year, young Lenin, at sixteen, suffered this double trauma; and he deeply loved his brother. The liberal neighbors practically outlawed the family. Lenin later judged the bourgeoisie as "unreliable and treacherous." Top of his high school class, he went to the University of Kazan in June 1887, under police vigilance, since the police were aware of his brother's guilt ("attainder of blood" in the sixteenth and seventeenth centuries: "guilt by association" in the American 1950's). He studied law and political economy. He was sober, aloof, and nobody called him "buddy." He was expelled very shortly for presence at a students' protest meeting, "for deceit, dereliction, and even discourtesy." He lived on his mother's estate, getting first-hand experience of peasant and serf labor. He later returned to Kazan to read in the library. After much intercession with the educational friends of his father, his mother got Lenin permission to study at the University of St. Petersburg. Here, in one year only, he not only mastered the four-year course in law but finished up first of the whole class. At twenty-two he was ready for the practice of law, having received the official certificate of loyalty and character.

Lenin's character is the soul of the Russian revolution and then of Soviet government. He practiced law briefly, not with special note, in the office of a bourgeois lawyer, and on amicable terms. In 1891 he became politically-minded as a result of events during a terrible famine, one of Russia's periodic curses. He became a *Narodnik* (p. 751). He accepted terror on principle ("a form of military operation which may be usefully applied or may even be essential in certain moments of battle"); the only problem was its expediency.

Lenin's interests however were captured by the movements of socialism in the West, especially in Germany where Bismarck was trying to destroy the Social Democrats (pp. 604–605). August Bebel, the workingman leader, was Lenin's ideal. Lenin's mind was a slave to Plekhanov's works:

they had abandoned the peasants and preached Marxian theory, the arrival of capitalism, next its overthrow, and then Communism. For Plekhanov, the Westerner, Lenin had "respect, reverence, infatuation." He now turned from the *Narodniks* to the industrial proletariat and wrote pamphlets on this theme.

He lived an austere and dedicated life of socialist teacher in St. Petersburg, marrying Nadya Krupskaya, daughter of a noble of provincial Civil Service origin, expelled from the service for liberalism. Krupskaya also taught. Both entered the Marxist groups about the factories; the workingmen's libraries set up by the *Narodniks,* and workingmen's classes. They had to work underground; the Marxists and Social Revolutionaries (p. 763) moved through the "liberal" and "sympathizers" groups. Here Lenin's first contribution to the revolution and the U.S.S.R. became apparent: unremitting, back-breaking industry in handwriting his pamphlets, in teaching, in study, in mastery of the facts. *Then,* he declared "The role of the intelligentsia is to make leaders from the intelligentsia unnecessary." Two other elements developed. He conceived a stone-cold antipathy to the petty bourgeoisie; this included the peasantry, for they were interested in private property, while he was interested in socialism. Again, he developed clear-cut, uncompromising, Nechaev-style separateness of his own revolutionary organization: the working class must organize a socialist labor party of its own. Marx and Engels did not like this turning away from the peasantry in Russia. Lenin was rejecting universal brotherhood. In the course of time, Lenin reversed himself on the value of the peasantry in revolution, but not on the separateness of the proletarian spearhead.

He looked with distaste on the latest police maneuver: permission to publish Marx and articles on Marxism, about 1894. The police sought to embroil the revolutionaries in study and polemics, and so to keep them from terrorism, especially as Marx-Plekhanov taught that socialism could come only after capitalism had fully developed. It had hardly begun in Russia! (p. 760). He continued with his hectograph pamphlets, warning that the revolution must not be retarded.

Rise of the Bolshevik Party. In 1895 he was allowed, after pneumonia, to travel abroad. He visited socialists in Switzerland and Kautsky in Germany. He returned to Russia, made contacts for the Union of the Emancipation of Labor (established by Plekhanov); he set up the St. Petersburg League of the same name among the tobacco, textile, and metal workers, till then *Narodniks.* Julius Martov, a Jewish socialist, then worked with him; but later Martov was hostile, being a *liberal,* not a dictator.

Henceforward, Lenin became a master and teacher of all the tricks of conspiratorial outwitting of authority and political rivals. He became a master of secret codes (in invisible ink); of smuggling of forbidden literature; physical evasion of police; tricks of writing and print to pass on messages. These details are weightier than Russia's constitutional clauses! For they demonstrated an unbreakable, ruthless will, backed up by superior ability and absolute self-sacrifice. From 1894 to 1895 Lenin was in Siberia, sentenced when the police caught him printing a paper called *The Workers' Cause.* Whether in the St. Petersburg prison awaiting sentence or in Siberia, he managed to keep in touch with the outside world, to learn and to direct. In Siberia he wrote, *The Development of Capitalism [in Russia].* For it, he read 299 works in Russian, 38 studies in German, French, and English and in Russian translations for facts, statistics, and theory. He translated the Webbs *History of Trade Unions;* he wrote articles and reviews. He stayed away from other exiles, unwilling to share their personal and ingrown quarrels. This period of "withdrawal," as Arnold Toynbee has demonstrated, gives a leader a definition of personality, a firmness of conviction, and an objectivity (and perhaps ruthlessness) of character essential to an "event-making" individual leader.

In 1899 all socialist groups everywhere were split by the advent of the "Fabian" ideas or "revisionism" or, as Lenin called it, "economism"— that is, the appeal of gradualist political and economic gains (see p. 605). "Economism" was hated by Lenin. Out of Siberia, he went to Plekhanov in Geneva and then to London, resolved to crush "economism" for the sake of the Marxian revolution in Russia. The two quarreled over the leadership of a newspaper they were to start: Lenin at once conceived the most bitter hatred for Plekhanov, because the latter had contrived to get two votes on the board of three. "Young comrades court an old comrade out of the love they bear for him, and suddenly is injected into this love the atmosphere of intrigue. The enamoured receives from the object of his love a bitter lesson, to regard all persons without sentiment, to keep a stone in one's sling." Lenin was now thirty.

Iskra (*The Spark*) "which would light the conflagration" was published. Lenin printed it in Germany, making it inaccessible to Plekhanov's votes in Geneva. He meant to make the newspaper into *his* party. It appeared once a month or so; 2000 copies were circulated; two thirds were confiscated at the Russian borders. Some got through. In the early issues Lenin taught the absolute need for a *vanguard* to make a revolution; Peter Tkachev's (friend of Nechaev) doctrine that the proletariat could not spontaneously make a revolution. Tkachev was influenced by the French revolutionary socialist Auguste Blanqui (p. 308), by a Jacobin theory of leadership. "Social ideals are alien to the people. They belong to the social feelings of the revolutionary minority." It was to leadership like Nechaev's (p. 752) that Lenin tended. He demands clear-cut theory—no disputable fuzziness; revolutionary activity by a dedicated group; no freedom of discussion. Principle was essential: "the role of vanguard can be fulfilled only by a party that is guided by an advanced theory."

In 1903 the various Marxian groupings, of which there were many with many scattered members, were transformed in a meeting in London into the Russian Social Democratic Labor Party. Lenin prepared for this meeting with the assiduity and skill of a consummate political boss, to pack it with his kind. He gathered 33 delegates out of 51 in his favor, the *Iskra* doctrine. A battle occurred over Article 1. Lenin's draft was that a member is

> one who recognizes the party's program and supports it by material means and *by personal participation* in one of the party organizations.

Julius Martov proposed a milder form: "by regular personal assistance under the direction of one of the party organizations." The revolutionaries saw the difference. Lenin meant to oust the "opportunist" intellectuals, who would debate but not take active part in inciting the workers. He wanted a party of professional revolutionaries only. Martov *and the majority* challenged Lenin's virtual demand "that they abdicate their right to think"; Trotsky supported them. Martov won 28 votes; Lenin 22. Lenin, however, won control of *Iskra* and made this into a factional paper, his faction. He called himself and his friends the *Bolshevik* Party—that is, the "greater" or "majority" party, because Martov and the Jewish Socialist Bund group had walked out from the voting as Lenin had opposed their voting as a bloc, since he hated tight groups within an organization he meant to dominate. He saddled the majority of the opposition to him with the label *Menshevik*, "smaller" or "minority"!

Lenin always hastened to split his party and go his own way, in a persistent minority of one if necessary, to impose his revolutionary will. He never hesitated to undermine a decision taken by the party. At one time he supported the central caucus against the local groups; when the former went against him, he revived the appeal to the latter. Everything went according to the fanatical intent of the tactics of conspiracy and revolution.

He had formulated the fatal principle of a centralized party hierarchy.

> I assert: (1) that no movement can be durable without a stable organization of leaders to maintain continuity; (2) that the more widely the masses are drawn into the struggle and form the basis of the movement, the more is it necessary to have such an organization and the more stable must it be; (3) that the organization must consist chiefly of persons engaged in revolution as a profession; (4) that in a country with a despotic government, the more we restrict the membership of this organization to those who are engaged in revolution as a profession, the more difficult it will be to catch the organization; (5) the wider will be the circle of men and women of the working class or other classes of society able to join the movement and perform active work in it.

Trotsky and the Polish-German Left-winger, Rosa Luxemburg, saw where this was tending. Trotsky predicted:

The organization of the party takes the place of the party itself; the central committee takes the place of the organization; and finally the dictator takes the place of the central committee.

Rosa Luxemberg warned against Lenin's fallacious transfer of the discipline of the barracks and of the factory to the political action of the working class: she hoped rather for the "voluntary discipline of social democracy," not the "corpselike obedience of a dominated class." But Lenin, Nechaev-style, said: "Give us an organization of revolutionaries and we will turn Russia upside down!" He meant to have "burocratism"—that is, organization from the top downward—not "democratism"—that is, autonomy of "opportunists." Lenin stuck to these principles through hope and despair. He thereby abandoned the fundamental spiritual drive of Marx and Engels: "the freedom of each produces the freedom of all," democracy as expressed in the *Communist Manifesto*.

Lenin abandoned democracy; *before* it, he wanted revolution, and this needed dictatorship in the party; *after* it, he wanted communism, and this meant dictatorship. Whatever he may have suggested from time to time, he abandoned democracy in the name of a state of society in the future which he did not define or place within limits of time. The following passage is most significant (from *The State and Revolution*, 1917):

> Democracy is by no means a limit one may not overstep; it is only one of the stages in the course of development from feudalism to capitalism, and from Capitalism to Communism. Democracy means equality. The great significance of the struggle of the proletariat for equality, and the significance of equality as a slogan, are apparent, if we correctly interpret it as meaning the abolition of *classes*. But democracy means only *formal* equality. Immediately after the attainment of equality for all members of society *in respect* of the ownership of the means of production, that is, of equality of labor and equality of wages, there will inevitably arise before humanity the question of going further from formal equality to real equality, that is, to applying the rule, "From each according to his ability; to each according to his needs." BY WHAT STAGES? BY MEANS OF WHAT PRACTICAL MEASURES HUMANITY WILL PROCEED TO THIS HIGHER AIM —THIS WE DO NOT AND CANNOT KNOW.

This allows only for equality, not liberty; it is narrowed down to economic equality only; it is committed only to the abolition of classes; it asks no referendum for its own principle of righteousness (Lenin's): "From each according to his ability, to each according to his needs"; it proposes to fasten this ascetic ideal on a people by revolution; he is unsure whether the ideal can be attained!

Lenin was surprised by the *spontaneous* outbreak in Russia in 1905 (led by Trotsky!) and the emergence of the Soviets then. But he thereupon devoted himself to the study of war, revolution, street fighting, the Paris Commune (p. 308). Outvoted on *Iskra,* he started a paper to fight it, *Vperod* (Forward), later renamed *Proletari,* by which he led and controlled his own Bolshevik faction. To run this and other party ventures he accepted money obtained by "bandits," who raided banks and arms depots and stole or forged banknotes. This was, as quoted from Marx, "looting the looters." One of his great suppliers was Stalin, organizer of raids in Tiflis and Baku. The party congress of 1906, with a majority of Mensheviks and some Bolsheviks, prohibited these raids, as doing moral harm to the party. Lenin continued his course. At later congresses Stalin was expelled for his raids; the party almost unanimously condemned Lenin's behavior; forced him to hand over the "dirty money." In 1912 Lenin contrived to get the Mensheviks expelled for "plotting to liquidate the party," by such bans on stolen moneys.

We must appreciate the immense contribution one person can make if he is that kind of person— thoughtful, forceful, trained, ascetic, determined, unslackening, fanatical, merciless, and capable, because of these qualities, of fascinating blind followers without scruple. The Mensheviks he called "softs"; some succumbed to the "hards"; and the "hards" idolized the "hardest." The "hardest" despise the "hards," the "hards" despise the "softs" to the point of demanding abject obedience on pain of liquidation. They hold that violence is good if successful.

We may conclude this analysis of the statesmanship character of Lenin in the various terms used about him by that acute Russian observer Berdyaev, as it appears in the latter's *Origin of Russian Communism*. He observes that Lenin possessed the qualities of the Russian people, not the intelligentsia, for he showed "simplicity, wholeness, boorishness, dislike of rhetoric," and he was practical and suffused with the nihilism of morality. To the qualities of Nechaev, the conspirator, he added those of the Grand Princess of Moscow, ideas that were inflexible alongside a daily opportunism and astuteness. He had learned to labor, to exert discipline over himself, to learn all that he must as his objective exacted, to concentrate on the constructiveness required in each situation in which he found himself. He was a despotic imperialist in pursuit of a maximalist revolutionary aim, whole and unqualified.

Berdyaev sums up:

> Instead of the Third Rome in Russia, the Third Internationale was achieved, and many of the features of the Third Rome passed over to the Third Internationale. The Third Internationale is also a consecrated Rome, and it is also founded on an orthodox faith. The transformation of Russian Messianism comes about by the identification of the Messianism of the Russian people with the Messianism of the proletariat and the proletariat everywhere.

Marxism-Leninism-Stalinism

What was in Lenin's mind about the nature of the State, of government, and of man? He absorbed Marxism and in some respects deformed it. We state his attitude in tersest propositions with comment in parentheses:

1. The State is *nothing but* the organization employed by the bourgeoisie to exploit the proletariat. For the former are the owners of the means of production and the latter are compelled to work for the former at the former's term for a bare living. The history of man has been the history of class war. Abolish class and you abolish the State, and with it coercion.

(But the State, or Government, would still be needed to settle differences between the members of a single class?)

2. The relationship of men in production—that is, their economic fortunes and demands—

is the decisive element in the formation of their consciousness, that is, their idea of legality, jurisprudence, morality, religion, and "all the rest of ideology." The economic relations are independent of men's wills as they enter the world.

(But, at the least, inborn character *as a whole*, and not merely the economic elements in it, determine "consciousness." This is individually contributed as well as socially molded; creative, as well as the creature of the existent economy. It will always surge out again, with each new person born into the world.)

3. There is a dialectic of happenings in the government of man: his governmental forms change with the change in economic production; the slave State, the feudal State are each the spawn of their own preceding economy. Industrial capitalism must inevitably give way to another form, communism, and this will produce *no* State.

(Is it inevitable that it will go your predicted way in every country? How do you know in so sanguine a conviction? Is your alleged "science" of sociology so well founded?)

4. In capitalism, the rich must get richer; the poor, poorer; the rich fewer, the poor more numerous. Their hostile consciousness of class reaches a point where the latter squeeze out the former and then go on, through a temporary dictatorship, to communism. Then men will act on the principle, uncoerced, of "From each according to his ability, to each according to his needs."

(But this was and is untrue to Western history. The least criticism of the propositions is that a very large and well-off middle class comes into existence; that wealth gets more diffused; that free trade unions control the rich as much as *they* are controlled. The free vote in responsible governments produces change without revolution.)

5. God is but a figment of the imagination produced by a picturesque representation of the economy; it is an opiate for the working class. There is no immortality.

6. Capitalists live on what they rake off as "surplus value" over and above what they allow the workers to have, whereas the worker is entitled to *all* the produce of labor.

7. Freedom is the most desirable condition of

man; he will get there by overthrowing capitalism, which distorts his nature and its nobility, and communism will assure this freedom to man.

8. Their gospel, pleasurably quoted by Lenin in *State and Revolution* from Engels' *Anti-Duhring,* was this. The first act in which the State really comes forward as the representative of society as a whole—the taking possession of the means of production in the name of society—is at the same time its last independent act as a State. The interference of the State power in social relations becomes superfluous in one sphere after another, and then ceases of itself. The government of persons is replaced by the administration of things and the direction of the process of production. The State is not abolished, *"it withers away."* For the "special repressive force" is no longer needed, when the workers are not held in subjection. (*When* they are not. But Lenin's claws seized them!)

(But this assumed that nobody will have a lust for power, a desire to pass on advantages to his family, other ideals of what to do in the economy that may be unorthodox, that men are equal, and even identical in their life aims. If they do differ, then an arbiter and coercion would prove still necessary.)

Lenin added certain emphases:

9. The revolution is not to be waited for as the inevitable accompaniment of the advent of capitalism, but depends on the revolutionary will. "The dialectic must be helped!": thus Stalin also.

(This produced Lenin's theory of the dictatorial and conspiratorial and terroristic party [p. 756]. It surely meant that government would not be abolished, but made all-pervading and brutally coercive. Malenkov even declared after the death of Stalin that the proposition that the "State would wither away" was *"a rotten theory"* [*Central Committee Report,* 1952 Party Congress].)

10. All philosophers, for example, like Mach, that have a spiritual element in their teaching are not merely men with a difference, but men with a "guilty conscience," that are sinful. The one philosophy is that which denies the operation of the "spirit" as a guide or dominator of living matter.

11. Wars emanate solely from the imperialism that capitalist-dominated States must inevitably pursue in order to get better markets and investment opportunities in colonies than the maturity and competition in the homeland afford. There are no other causes of war—for example, "armed opinions."

(But it might be argued that the modern international economy is precisely the one to bring nations together, if the economic aspect is the only one that operates. Even Marx observed that nineteenth-century capitalism tended to break down the separateness of nations. See Herman Finer, *America's Destiny,* Chapter 2.)

12. There must be inevitable wars between States that convert to communism and capitalist States; they cannot live side by side in peace; the capitalists would encircle and seek to destroy this threat to their polity, for they would be afraid that their own workers would rise and make the Marxian revolution.

13. Finally, what would follow the wresting of power from the bourgeoisie? Here Lenin let himself imagine that all the economic institutions would come under the supervision and management of the workers themselves. His romanticism about the workers' ability must be given in full; from *State and Revolution* written in 1917:

We want the socialist revolution with human nature as it is now. Human nature itself cannot do without subordination, without control, without managers and clerks, but there must be submission to the armed vanguard of all the laboring and exploited classes, the proletariat. The specific bossing methods of the State officials can and must begin to be replaced immediately, within twenty-four hours, by the simple functions of managers and clerks, functions which are now already quite within the capacity of the average townsman and can therefore be performed for a workingman's wage. . . . We must reduce the role of the State officials to that of simply carrying out our instructions. They must be responsible, reputable, moderately-paid "managers and clerks" (of course with technical knowledge of all sorts, types and degrees). . . . We have but to crush with the iron hand of the armed workers the resistance of those exploiters, to break the bureaucratic machine of the modern State. And we have before us a highly technically fashioned machine freed of its parasites. . . .

The accounting and control necessary for this have been *simplified* [Lenin's italics] by capitalism to the utmost, till they have become the extraordinarily simple operations of watching, recording and issuing receipts, within the reach of anybody who can read and write and knows the first four rules of arithmetic.

So, says Lenin, when this job is properly learned, the State will wither away. Within twenty-four hours of making the Revolution, he began, and Stalin and successors continued, loud lamentations that the workers needed long training and coercion before they could be made over into capable officials and managers and the dictator is needed to give the training and apply the force.

II. TOWARD THE REVOLUTIONS OF 1905 AND 1917

Who Was Trotsky?

His born name was Lev Davidovich Bronstein, of a well-off Jewish farming family in the Ukraine near Odessa. His revolutionary feeling was first aroused by the oppressive and servile relations between his father's bailiffs and the local peasants, farmers, and servants. He was a vivid person, of warm-hearted and humane instincts, acute intellect; he was a brilliant student and a remarkable literary artist. He read the classics of the West, including John Stuart Mill, Mignet's *French Revolution,* and Bentham (p. 34), which he called "a philosophy of social cook-book recipes." He was an enthusiast and impulsive: Lenin a callous chess-player and "hard." At seventeen Trotsky entered revolutionary activity; in November 1899 (after over two years in prison without a sentence) he was sentenced to four years in Eastern Siberia, not in open trial. There he studied Lenin, nine years older, with tremendous admiration. Trotsky, like Lenin, earned his living in Siberia by writing—but literary essays rather than Marxist economics. Escaping from Siberia, he took the name of Trotsky, traveled to Vienna and London, where he met Lenin, who employed him on *Iskra* and missions. But they disagreed strongly, for Trotsky did not accept Marxism as Messianically

and fanatically; and he was a brilliant writer, an artist, and so detested Lenin's hammer-blow, browbeating style. "The style is the man." He was the tribune of the people; a remarkable orator in the classic French Revolutionary tradition, a resourceful drafter of resolutions and proclamations. In 1905 Trotsky was the leader of the insurgent Soviets. But he rejected Lenin's callous centralism and bitter conspiratorial dictatorship—though quite as ardent for the socialist society. His mind, however, was not transfixed by Revolution Number 1, to overthrow Czarism, but dwelt, as Lenin's did not, on the shape of government thereafter, Revolution Number 2; the second was to modulate the nature of the first, and it was to be democracy. His alliance with Lenin in May 1917 assured Lenin's triumph, but the subjection of the Russian people. Insofar as any one of the triad was responsible for the conduct and success of the November Revolution 1917, it was Trotsky, and not Lenin, and still less the lurking Stalin.

The Proletariat

Russian industry took on fairly swift growth from the 1860's. In 1860 mining and manufacturing accounted for some 800,000 workers; in 1913, over 3,000,000. In the critical years 1905 to 1914 about 4,500,000 workers were employed in all industries and transport. The swiftness of growth from those who flowed into the towns from the recently liberated serfs was disturbing and full of anxieties for workers and employers. Moreover the units were large-scale ones, since the employers and the Russian State had learned lessons from Germany and Britain. By 1914 manufacturing enterprises with 500 workers each comprised 56 percent of all workers; those with 1000 and more employed 40 percent of all industrial workers. In textiles and metals, especially, did large units prevail, and these became politically radical. In 1900 only 14 percent of the German workers were in firms of over 500 workers; only 8 percent in those over 1000.

The workers were recruited from the freed serfs. The capital came from the landowners' redemption funds. The bureaucracy desired strength and revenue for the State: it supported loans from France and Britain and Germany, whose biggest firms sent in plant and technicians.

They were actuated by profits and the desire of their rival governments to have Russia as a foreign ally. Between 1890 and 1899 industrial production of the most diverse kind increased at the rate of 8 percent per year!

Housing was overcrowded and shocking; wages were low; hours were limitless until 1897, when the law limited day work to 11½ hours, and night work to 10; but factory inspection was hardly enforced. Women and children were exploited. Strikes were prohibited, but began to occur on a large scale after 1900.

Political parties now arose (see p. 763), more organized than the movements like the *Narodniks*. Marxism found a fertile ground in the factories and mines, developing and exacerbating all discontents.

The autocracy would not yield one iota. Nicholas II told the *Zemstvos* delegates in January 1895: "Let everyone know that . . . I shall safeguard the principles of autocracy as firmly and unwaveringly as did . . . my father." The censorship was intensified; students went on mass strikes (between 1899 and 1904, some 10,000 students were arrested, expelled, or banished of a total student body in those years of some 100,000!). The Lenin-Plekhanov-Martov organization (p. 755) in St. Petersburg and then Moscow aggravated the dissensions. On this, later, followed the Russian Social Democratic Labor Party, Lenin's party, with its nucleus of Bolsheviks.

Assassinations

From 1900 the terrorists had begun new attacks. In 1901 there was an attempt to kill the Procurator of the Holy Synod, which failed. In 1902 a student killed the Minister of the Interior. In April 1902 another unsuccessful attempt was made on the Procurator of the Holy Synod and the military governor of St. Petersburg. In July 1902 a worker tried to kill the governor of Kharkhov and missed him. On May 5, 1903, a railway worker killed the Governor of Ufa, one of the provincial territories. By 1904 bombs came into use. In July 1904 the Minister of the Interior, Plehve, was killed by an expelled student. In June 1904 the Governor-General of Finland was killed by the son of a financial officer helped by the spy Orloff. There

were many other attempts. (Six or seven attempts had been made on Alexander III.) A crescendo of reciprocating violence, terror, and assassination rent the nation.

In January 1904 the Japanese War began. Some allege that the Czarist government began it deliberately to divert revolutionary agitation. In September 1904 all radical and revolutionary groups, with the exception of the Social Democrats, met in conference in Paris. (For *Social Democrats* one must read *Revolutionary Communists*.) Programs were developed by the conference for a constituent assembly, for radical land reform, for a modification of the autocracy. This, of course, brought government retaliation on the Union of Unions.

The police met terror by counterterror; by proclamations of a "state of siege." They diverted peasant wrath, which in the year 1902 had plundered 90 manor houses, and mass strike impulses by organizing pogroms, horrible in bloody and drunken bestiality, against the Jewish quarters of such places as Kishinev.

The police had tried to abort the trade-union movement by establishing police-led unions. They succeeded only in teaching the workers the value of organized effort against employers and government, and provided masses of followers for the Social Revolutionary and Social Democrat leaders. They inspired further underground activity.

The Revolution of 1905

In January 1905, when the nation was still seething with the news of the surrender of Port Arthur to the Japanese, a strike occurred in some printing works in St. Petersburg. It spread fast. Father Gapon, a "white" clergyman, directed the movement. On Sunday, January 9, 1905, since called Bloody Sunday, he led a peaceful procession of workers to the royal palace, hoping to get some benefits for the workers (and asking for an elected constituent assembly) and to demonstrate that the Little Father was their friend. They carried icons, pictures of the Czar, and chanted hymns. Soldiers stopped them and shot them down indiscriminately. Socialists estimate that 500 were killed and 3000 wounded; the police say only 150 and 200. Gapon fled, but disseminated a message to the Czar, running in part:

The innocent blood of workers, their wives and children, lies forever between thee, oh soul destroyer! and the Russian people.

The wicked, callous crime took many of the Russian people from the Middle Ages of divine right to the twentieth century, even the twenty-first. The magic of monarchy was gone. Liberal Ministers resigned; police were dismissed. The Grand Duke (uncle and brother-in-law of the Czar) was killed by a Social Revolutionary's bomb. **Toward the Duma.** On urgent advice, the Czar promised, in February 1905, an elected assembly to assist in law making. The Union of Unions and other liberal organizations counterdemanded a *constituent* assembly. A Peasant's Union was organized in July. The nation seethed with reform meetings. All liberal groups in Russia and outside were jubilant at Russia's acknowledgment of defeat at the hands of Japan. Strikes raged; troops in the East went on strike and formed their own committees of action. Violent uprisings occurred in the rural areas. In June occurred the classic mutiny on the *Potemkin* of the Black Sea fleet. Henceforward the disloyalty of the Armed Forces must be reckoned with.

Brutal reaction set in: the nobility, the lower middle class, small tradesmen, clergy always, minor governing officials, even formed a party called the Union of the Russian People, which was governmentally patronized. They were nationalist reactionaries, stung by the Japanese defeat; haters of the Finns and Baltic peoples and the Jews. They organized the brutality of the *lumpenproletariat,* the lower classes who have no ideological purpose.

The revolutionary parties struck back. Strikes developed into general strikes, with political purposes. In the face of decrees of a "state of emergency," the workers in October stopped all work over the entire country. They demanded a democratic republic, a political amnesty, the disarming of troops and police. Their demands were endorsed by the technicians unions and the professions. The first Soviet arose in St. Petersburg, a congress of Workers' Deputies, October 13, 1905. It was a kind of insurgent parliamentary body, with one delegate for each 500 workers, the elections being fixed by the *Narodniks,* Social Revolutionaries, Social Democrats (Mensheviks and Bolsheviks). The spearhead were the Mensheviks; the leader was Leon Trotsky, the hero of the St. Petersburg Soviet. Under his inspiration and tactics, the Soviet behaved as an independent authority *vis-à-vis* the Czar's. It founded a newspaper— *Izvestia (The News).*

Thus, the Soviets were spontaneously emergent councils of workers and peasants, inspired by their own leaders and by professional politicians of a mixed Left wing. The name is now full of *mystique,* or charisma. Trotsky afterward declared them the Great Rehearsal for 1917. They learned something about organization.

When the workers, for bread, had to return to work, the Army and police began punitive expeditions. Trotsky was given the very unusual opportunity of an open trial. For nearly three months of proceedings, he inflamed public opinion by his remarkable defiance of rhetoric. He and fourteen others were condemned to Siberia for life; others got shorter sentences. (In March 1907 he was back, having escaped.) In 1905, 2000 manor houses had been burned by peasants, the owners murdered or chased away.

Lenin was disappointed: the workers had revolted and found a form of organization without him! He had not reached St. Petersburg from Geneva in time. The Social Revolutionaries had not expected such leaderless ability of the workers. The sacro-sanctity of the Czarist system had received an incurable wound. Trotsky summed up the gains by the dictum, "La Revolution est morte; vive la Revolution!" It was confirmed that a disastrous war is the opportunity of revolutionists.

The Duma and Its Parties

A parliamentary body was announced; the first since almost 300 years before. It was a shackled mongrel, with little power.

In April 1906 the Fundamental Laws set up a *Duma* of two chambers. One was a State Council (a Senate), an appointive body, one half of officials appointed by the Crown and the rest elected by the clergy (6), the *Zemstvos* (56), the nobility (18), the universities (6), commerce and industry (12), and the Finnish parliament (2); and the second was the lower parliamentary House, the State *Duma.* It could make legislation, but only on the

Czar's initiative. The two Houses must agree before a law was valid; and the Czar could veto the legislation. If the *Duma* did not pass the budget, the last budget prevailed; thus the *Duma* could not force the government by the power of the purse. This Czarist evasion had been learned from Bismarck's struggle with the Prussian Parliament in 1862. The *Duma* could not make laws regarding loans: an enormous foreign loan was immediately floated, so that the Czar had the money he needed free of *Duma* control. Ministers were not responsible to the *Duma,* but only to the Czar. The Czar could dissolve the *Duma* at his wish.

The franchise was indirect, based on *curia* or colleges of voters: large landowners; lesser landowners and clergy; city voters; peasantry; 26 large cities; industrial workers; lower-middle-class intellectuals in cities; the smallest landowners. The large landowners voted directly for provincial assemblies of electors, who then chose *Duma* members. The lesser landowners and clergy elected first to *volost* (district) assemblies, who then elected to the provincial electors, who then elected to the *Duma.* The city voters (bourgeoisie and substantial taxpayers) elected to the city assembly which then elected to the *Duma.* The peasants had one representative for each ten householders to a local assembly; two of these there elected went up to the *volost;* this again selected electors to the provincial assemblies, who then chose the peasant representatives to the *Duma.* The industrial workers elected to the city assemblies, etc., first through the factories, where plants of at least 50 workers were election units; but the bigger factories were given less representation than the smaller, being more radical. The numbers of the *Duma* and the proportion allowed the various groups were changed from *Duma* to *Duma,* in order to overrepresent the clergy and the Right-wing parties, quite callously and openly.

Political parties had developed and were now given firmer organization for electoral purposes and *Duma* tactics. They may be briefly mentioned.

The Union of Russian Peoples. This was proautocracy; Great Russian chauvinist; anti-Semitic. Its terror organizations were known as the Black Hundreds. Its terrorization, raping, pillaging, and beatings-up were assisted by the police and the clergy, vodka, and the government. It kept the *Duma* in an uproar.

The Octobrists intended to work with and develop the constitutional possibilities of the Czar's manifesto of October. They were conservative landowners, but ready for civil liberties and representative government under the monarchy; more land for the peasants, peasant credits; labor welfare and the right to organize and strike; increases in educational facilities; independent justice; more equitable taxation; and the rule of law for officials. They were strongly antirevolutionary and anti-Marxist.

The Konstitutional Democrats were led by the liberal history professor Paul Miliukov, who had been exiled. He organized the Union of Unions (p. 747). These K.D.'s or Kadets looked for a limited monarchy and a responsible Ministry; universal and equal franchise; civil liberties; extensive land reforms. They hoped by a "correct siege" of the Czar to compel reforms, given time. Their following consisted of liberal landowners, industrialists, and the professional classes.

The Narodniks were the most moderate of the Left-wing parties (p. 751). They demanded the division of all the land among the peasants. They advocated autonomy for Russia's minority nationalities in a "federal" arrangement. They included commerce and industry in their nationalization plans. Of course, they expected all political liberties on an equal basis, with a unicameral system.

The Trudoviks were chiefly peasant rank and file, led by intellectuals. The urban workers were at this time in the Social Revolutionary and Social Democratic parties. They sided with the K.D. political program, but looked to the development of socialism. Among their leaders was Alexander Kerensky, a liberal Leftist lawyer, born in the same town as Lenin. He resembled the English Fabian socialists. Lenin and his associates hated him; and in 1917 chased him out of the prime ministership he had acquired in the first, the liberal revolution, of February 1917.

The Social Revolutionaries were founded in 1878, descendants of the *People's Will* movement. They were extreme socialists, touched by Marxism; extremely agitational; had terror as an avowed paragraph in their published program and had used it. They were anti-autocracy, anti-industrialist, propeasantry, and proletarian. The *Narodniks* were willing to cooperate in a monarchy; these sought a republic. Officially, they boycotted the first *Duma,* convinced it would be a fake.

The Russian Social Democratic Workers' Party was the Communist Party.

There were also several "nationalities" parties, such as Poles, Finns, etc.

The Fate of the Duma. The first *Duma* lasted from April to July 1906; the second *Duma* from February to June 1907; the third from November 1907 to June 1912 (a full term); the fourth (and last) from November 1912 to February 1917, its power having virtually departed from it with the advent of World War I.

By the third *Duma,* the franchise had been twisted by the government, and its electoral interventions directed so as to raise the Rightist clergy from 6 to 45. Every campaign was a reign of terror with suppression of the opposition press. During the election of the second *Duma,* with government connivance with the Black Hundreds, 16,922 people were killed, of which 7331 were murdered. Government officials of all ranks numbering 3611 had been killed; and 13,381 citizens had been executed or killed by courts martial, troops, brigands, and the Union of Russian People.

Membership of the Duma and the government's success at manipulation may be seen in the following table, which also indicates the distribution of political strength.

Duma, as others suggested, as a forum of insurrection and disturbance; exactly like Goebbels and Hitler in Germany in the 1920's (p. 620).

The government's Ministers, chief among whom was the notorious Stolypin, toyed with the *Duma;* dissolved it; laughed at it. The *Duma* took itself seriously, and rattled the government with its interpellations and parliamentary investigations of the police, governmental terror, and emergency decrees, the Army, land reform, the judiciary, the budget. More and more its disgust with the Czarist bureaucracy was intensified, frustrated as it was by the absence of a responsible Ministry. It was increasingly impotent, except to rail, and increasingly alienated. Yet it lived for too short a term to educate the masses to a new kind of authority, at once liberal, self-governing, and socially reformative. Too late!

The masses of peasants *were utterly inert*—excepting for their hunger for land. The proletariat was heavily involved in trade unions or near-Marxist policies.

III. WORLD WAR I AND THE FEBRUARY AND NOVEMBER REVOLUTIONS

The incompetent and chauvinistic Russian diplomats blundered into a war with Germany and Austria over the Slavs in the Balkans. The nation was hotly romantic for the war. The *Duma* Bolshevik Deputies were transported to Siberia, without popular protest. Lenin urged *complete de-*

	First Duma	Second Duma	Third Duma	Fourth Duma
Popular Socialists and Trudovniks	85	120	14	10
Social Revolutionaries	2	37	0 *	0 *
Social Democrats	17	65	14	14
Other Socialists	7	—	—	—
K.D.'s	184	99	53	58
Progressists	—	—	28	47
Poles and Other National Groups	32	93	?	—
Octobrists	38	54	150	97
Nonparty	112	50		
Moderate Right			150	185
Right and Monarchists	7	10		

* Boycotted the *Duma* elections.

Lenin, from afar, was at first fanatically opposed to participation in the "bourgeois" assembly. Then he became as fanatically favorable, to use the

featism—and in all countries—for to him and his associates, the war was an imperialist war, engendered by the economic needs of the "ruling circles." He was devastated when the German Social Democrats voted for war credits (p. 610). The Mensheviks condoned cooperation in the war, maintaining that at some point of time a moment would come when civil war would break out of itself out of the workers' own consciousness. They cooperated with the Kerensky group in a "defensive war" against German and Austrian nationalists and capitalists. Lenin regarded the war, in Marx's prediction, as the lubricant on the wheels of revolution. The Mensheviks supported the newly arisen workers' factory committees for improved production, a new access to leadership, and fomenting revolutionary consciousness of the workers. The Bolsheviks preferred the party's conspiratorial groups to the committees.

The Russians were badly organized, badly equipped, illiterate, at war. The "peasants in uniform" had not the slightest idea of the State for which they were fighting; the cause was not theirs. There was gross incompetence in the administrative direction and military supply. Most recruits got real rifles only from the hands of their dead comrades. People and *Duma* (kept out of affairs) questioned whether the terrible carnages of Russian soldiers were not due to treason by the Court, for the Czarina was a German princess, and a principal Minister, Sturmer, was of German descent. The casualties mounted: 7,000,000 were suffered (counted): 750,000 dead; 2,500,000 wounded; 3,500,000 prisoners and missing. There was wholesale disorganization of transport and food supplies, and nursing the wounded was almost unknown. In 1916 surrenders *en masse* began. By October 1916, the Army was demoralized; officers were afraid of being killed by their own men (they were landowners, and Ivan was a serf!). New classes refused to obey the draft. A campaign against war and for liberty was even developed by the upper and middle classes. The Left-wing parties, with the Bolsheviks, had vastly increased activity in St. Petersburg in December 1915. But Lenin was in Geneva, Stalin in Siberia, and Trotsky in the Bronx, New York.

February 1917

In this state of disintegration of morale and organization, food riots began on February 23, 1917, a week after the *Duma* had opened. They began peacefully but took on momentum as the workers joined in against the terrible privations and the sufferings of their families by the war. The police fought them; they fought back. On February 27 the troops went over to the insurrectionists. The rising was then put down. A crisis was on hand: the *Duma* organized a governing committee from its Left parties; in its walls the Petrograd Soviet of Workers' Deputies suddenly arose—anyone who happened to regard himself as a Social Democrat or Social Revolutionist or Plekhanovist. This Soviet now became the focal point of the final, the November, Revolution. Ministers and officials were arrested. *The Czar was forced to abdicate* at the *Duma's* demand and fled with his family (later slaughtered by Bolsheviks).

This was Russia's real revolution, for the authority of a thousand years was gone. It was not Lenin's revolution; it was not the communist revolution; it was not the revolution of the Bolsheviks or even the Mensheviks. It was a Left-wing bloc, loose but ardent, that sent Czarism to perdition. The peasants began to seize the land, *their form of freedom.*

The mighty focus of authority was gone; the *Duma* was too young to have won over the impulses of order and obedience and confidence. Now, with only 1500 casualties, the Petrograd Soviet stood as the claimant of authority against the Provisional Government—that is, Ministers chosen from among the Center and Left-wing of the remnants of the *Duma,* led by Kerensky and including Social Revolutionaries. The Soviet included *all Left parties:* but most active were the Social Revolutionaries, the Mensheviks, and the Bolsheviks. In a period of what Trotsky has called "dual powerlessness," caricaturing the official designation of "dual power," the Soviet challenged, bullied, and directed the Kerensky Government from its inception (its first leader was Prince Lvov, a liberal noble of *Zemstvo* fame) to the *coup* of November 7. Kerensky was a member of the executive committee of fourteen of the Soviet.

The Petrograd Soviet organized soviets throughout the nation and brought nationwide conferences of delegates of workers and peasants and soldiers to the capital. These were "elected" by local soviets, of which by August there were 600, with sup-posedly 23,000,000 members.

Lenin arrived at the Finland Station in April, having been supplied by the German General Staff (anxious to disintegrate the Russian enemy) with a sealed train through Germany, Sweden, and Finland. Swiss socialists had negotiated this transport of what someone has called the *bacillus asiaticus*. Trotsky arrived in May from the Bronx *via* Halifax, Canada, on a British ship, after being released from internment at the instance of the Russian government! Now entered the sharpest revolutionary and most fanatical wills of all to agitate and seize the minds of the population.

Sailors at Kronstadt coined the winning slogan, "All power to the Soviets!". Lenin wavered on this, as the Soviets were of mixed political com-position. He first preferred the workers commit-tees, as more likely to be incited as vehicles of revolution. Later, he changed about.

Lenin's fanatical character and single-track mind won power for the Bolsheviks. He never ceased the propaganda of ending the war at once, without indemnities or annexations, without any condi-tions, even, and the land to the peasants! *Izvestia* subverted Army discipline by publishing first the Kerensky's Government decree that soldiers in the field were entitled to full civil rights compatible with discipline and implying the right to form committees, to choose their officers, and to decide whether commands to fight were "defensive" or "offensive" operations. Nor were Army units favorable to the February Revolution to be sent away from the capital or to be disarmed.

The Germans kept up their pressure at the front. *Pravda* (*Truth*), edited by Stalin and Molo-tov, harried by Lenin, persisted with the Marxist-Leninist thesis of war being caused only by bour-geois greed. The Kerensky Government and the Social Revolutionaries were denounced as un-trustworthy bourgeois because they would not make immediate peace. In his April Theses (*Pravda*, April 7, 1917), Lenin's speech to the Bolshevik delegates to the All-Russian Conference of Soviets was reported. He claimed that the first stage of the communist revolution was accom-plished, having given power to the bourgeoisie; now the second stage was at hand, "which must

place power in the hands of the proletariat and the poorest strata of the peasantry." He harangued frenziedly for incitement to revolution and the seizure of power. When he was called "a lunatic" by a delegate, he declared his preference to be in a minority of one rather than have faith in the Government. He declared the need of immediate nationalization and socialization of all means of production, including the land, which would be managed by local Soviets of peasants and farm laborers, the poorest peasants having their own Soviets (always class against class and subclass against subclass!). A mir system would apply everywhere. The title of the party must be dropped; it was now like "soiled linen"; the Com-munist Party would express its character best.

While the others promised land to the peasants by legal procedures, especially after the election of a Constituent Assembly in November, which all parties agreed to, including the Soviets, Lenin abetted the immediate seizure of the land by the peasants. As Trotsky said: "The peasants did not read Lenin; Lenin clearly read the thoughts of the peasants." He merely said, "Let the land be seized with the maximum orderliness." He needed the peasant masses to support the small urban prole-tariat as the lever by which he could heave him-self into power. By April 29 his gimlet mind and will, incessantly drilling, had got the All-Russian Conference of Bolsheviks to accept his *Theses*.

Meanwhile, the Russian Army had suffered a complete debacle, by July 8. This was shortly after an abortive four-day attempt at revolution in Petro-grad, a bloody attempt by revolutionary soldiers and populace clamoring for food. The Bolsheviks did not instigate it, Lenin thinking the time was not yet ripe. But they were drawn into it. Trotsky and others were arrested or fled. Lenin fled to Finland, a few miles away. Thence, he sent in-structions to the Bolshevik and Soviet committees steadily, incessantly, insistently.

The last throw of Kerensky and Russian liberty occurred in September. He tried to bring an army under General Kornilov to Petrograd against the revolutionaries, against whom there was a reaction after the June *coup*. This army would save Petro-grad from an imminent German advance; and crush the Bolsheviks, whose prestige and incitement were now winning mass adherence. But the soldiers would not form rank; and the railroad workers would not move the trains. An intense reaction in favor of the Bolshevik developed, for fear lest the Czarist system should return in the wake of the generals.

The peasants took over the land; the soldiers made for home to get their share. Conferences of Peasants' Deputies met in Moscow. The Social Revolutionaries were dominant in these. Kerensky in May obtained an 800 vote against Lenin's 20, when they elected an executive committee. But the Social Revolutionaries' hold on the peasantry was failing, because they preached *legality* and led the better-off rather than the far-more-numerous poor peasants to whom Lenin appealed. These now conducted a horrible pillage and carnage against the landowners and against the peasant *kulaks*. Troops sent in by Kerensky to suppress the slaughter, arson, and destruction joined the peasants not in uniform. These were Lenin's pawns—*Bauern* as the Germans call them—peasants, in the chess game of revolution.

The trade unions of the proletariat and the Bolsheviks were not on good terms. They were what Lenin vilified as "economists"—that is, for democratic and gradual economic reforms, for better working conditions. He wanted a communist revolution; and always scorned the Samuel Gompers, the Arthur Hendersons, the Ramsay Macdonalds, who had no "revolutionary consciousness" but were content with less hours and more pay. The workers' committees also interfered with management—often now, foolishly—for supplies were unavailable and there were no markets for their products. They seized hold of the management. Lenin himself wanted to dominate industry, directly. (It took Lenin and Stalin many years to get back to "one-man management.") As soon as he obtained power, he had a short way with the trade unions.

The Bolsheviks were small in number until May and June. In municipal elections few Social Democrats were elected compared with the Social Revolutionaries. At the June meeting of the All-Russian Congress of Soviets, only 100 Bolsheviks were among the 800 to 900 delegates. But Lenin's sedulous propaganda and his clear-cut slogans of Peace and Land and All Power to the Soviets won over more and more followers.

The *Duma* was formally dissolved in September. The Government's authority was now no better than the Soviet's. Popular elections were set for September 1917 for a Constituent Assembly. The Soviet and the Bolsheviks agreed. The latter boycotted, as tactics, a kind of delegate "preparliament" of *Zemstvos, Duma* members, etc., called by Kerensky. In September, Kerensky went further to try to bolster "liberal" authority. A wide liberal-socialist Coalition Government was formed. The Republic was proclaimed. The Right-wing organizations, military and political, were disbanded. Top officers were purged. On September 4, he freed Trotsky and others from prison. He appealed for Bolshevik help—for the war continued. Meanwhile, Bolshevik membership had tremendously increased: from January 1917, when it had 24,000 members, it increased to 200,000 in August—mainly in the cities. The Soviets were armed; the Red Guard was being created. Lenin trained his vehement enmity on the Mensheviks, Social Revolutionaries, and other "liberals" and "opportunists" in the Soviets.

Kerensky left the use of force against the fomenters of force too late. He did not understand their unscrupulous fanaticism.

By the end of September Lenin judged that the time for a successful Bolshevik *coup* had come. Hitherto he had cried, "Wait!" but now insistently, "Be ready to attack!" By October 17 (Russian style) his messages pointed to all the signs of disintegration; the failure of Kornilov, a mutiny in the German Navy.

> This shows that the world workers' revolution has begun. Doubts are impossible. We stand on the threshold of the world proletarian revolution; therefore, let us go. If we do it now and take power now, and we have the revolution elsewhere, they will stand on our side and prevent us from being overcome as we might be by the bourgeois governments that surround us.

He was frenziedly resisting the members in his own party who suggested that the decision be postponed until the second All-Russian Congress of Soviets to meet later in the year, October 25.

Lenin was able, on October 10, in the Central

Committee of the Bolshevik Party, to get approval of the rising by a 10 to 2 vote (Zinoviev and Kamenev, old comrades in exile of Lenin's, were against him; later on they were murdered by Stalin).

Seven members were chosen from among the Bolshevik Party to form a Politburo for the revolution: Lenin, Trotsky, Zinoviev, Kamenev, Stalin, Sokolnikvo, and Bubnov. It must not be forgotten that several Bolsheviks were publicly and vociferously opposed to the rising. There was not at this time, nor until 1920, a shutting down of opposition by expulsions, purges, or executions. They could still vote for Lenin or against him. There was still formal equality of membership; and two opposed the revolution.

As a matter of fact, party discipline was rather loose *among the top leaders*. Throughout the development of this party since 1903, whether in the Menshevik or Bolshevik faction, the practice of Continental politicians to reserve "my special opinion" ("dissent") had prevailed among the restive, highly self-conscious revolutionaries and sectarians. Lenin himself had always insisted that *he* could reserve his special opinion even to secession. Others did likewise. As a matter of fact, Lenin and Kamenev had resigned from the party on October 10, Lenin probably to enforce action, Kamenev because he did not want the revolution to take place. No action was taken on the resignations. Trotsky, in a speech on October 16, denied that a rising was planned. Lenin was even afraid he was being double-crossed by Trotsky; but Trotsky's action was merely a protective smokescreen over an open secret. The whole organization revolved around Trotsky. On October 16 the Central Committee of the party appointed five members, including Stalin, to join the revolutionary committee. It never functioned.

How much Lenin's personality meant is shown by the fact that on October 16 and 24 he appeared in person at the committee in order to browbeat it into taking the resolution to act. Trotsky's book, *Lenin,* says;

> The chief debates at the sessions of the central committee were naturally devoted to the struggle with that section of the membership who were totally opposed to the uprising. I re-

frain from mentioning here the four speeches Lenin made on the theme, "Is it time to seize the power? Shall we keep the power if we seize it?" Lenin wrote them down, and later wrote some pamphlets about this. It is utterly impossible to picture the united spirit of these intense and impassioned improvizations to the hesitating and the doubting, the course of his thought, his will, his conviction and his courage. Here the fate of the revolution was decided. The session broke up late at night. All felt somewhat as though they had gone through a surgical operation.

The Military Revolutionary Committee. To prepare the overthrow, a Military Revolutionary Committee of the Petrograd Soviet was elected. Trotsky was leader of the committee. Neither Lenin nor Stalin played any practical part in the rising. The subleaders were chosen; the positions reconnoitered; Red Guards were organized; arms distributed; the Petrograd troops won over; the Petrograd commander of the garrison was controlled by "commissars," by Soviet military committee representatives.

The "October" Revolution: October 25, or November 7 (New Style)

Lenin appeared at the center of the Petrograd Soviet and the Bolshevik Party, from his hiding place, on the evening of October 24, and Trotsky opened up their offensive that night. All positions were soon occupied, with little fighting. Kerensky had not become really alarmed until October 23, but legal measures against the leaders of the threatened rising, the Bolshevik chiefs and their press, were all too late. He had practically no forces to resist a *coup.* He left the Winter Palace at 10 A.M. on October 25 to get military help; he never obtained it; he never returned.

At 10 o'clock, the same time on October 25, the Revolutionary Committee announced the deposition of the Provisional Government. It took all day on the 25th to round up the Ministers and various officials and occupy the government offices. There was almost no bloodshed. By 2 A.M. on October 26 all the personnel adverse to the revolution in the Provisional Government were arrested and in prison. The Bolsheviks were in command of Petrograd. Later they secured Moscow; but it took them until the following April (1918) to make sure of other cities in the central areas of Russia. As for the Ukraine, Georgia, and other various regions, a civil war, lasting until the middle of 1920, was needed for their subjugation.

A "Walk-over." The second All-Russian Congress of Soviets had met. Of its 650 Deputies, elected by most equivocal methods, there were 390 Bolsheviks, 80 Mensheviks, and 150 Social Revolutionaries. Practically no opposition to Lenin's *coup* had come from the bourgeoisie and their parties. The Army command was at the front, facing the Germans; they did not advance on Petrograd. The garrison of soldiers and sailors there supported the Bolsheviks; only a woman's battalion and some cadets fought them in the Winter Palace until overcome. Anti-Bolshevik troops had no transport.

The chief opposition to the *coup* was from the Mensheviks, and some Bolsheviks, and the Right-wing Social Revolutionaries, who withdrew from the Congress of Soviets, leaving the Bolsheviks in command. They regarded it as "a crime against the revolution" to seize power by violence without waiting for the Constituent Assembly.

The Bolsheviks then passed resolutions declaring peace; abolishing private ownership of land; establishing a government called, not "ministers," but the Council of People's Commissars because this sounded more revolutionary—*Sovnarkom* for short. The final settlement of the land problem was to be undertaken by the forthcoming Constituent Assembly (!), until which time the mir system holding all the land, which was nationalized, would function. The Bolshevik-dominated Congress was a kind of legislative authority; 101 members were elected by it, as a general executive; and 15 men, with Lenin as chairman and Trotsky as Commissar for Foreign Affairs and Stalin as Commissar for Nationalities, made up the *Sovnarkom*.

The Right-wing Social Revolutionaries and Mensheviks formed Committees of Salvation to fight against the Bolsheviks. The trade unions were split among Bolsheviks and their opponents. Soon Lenin merged his Central Committee of 101 with Peasants' Deputies. Trotsky declared that now the Bolsheviks had the enunciation of a party program in the language of power—but hardly yet a State.

Crushing the Constituent Assembly. In mid-November (over many days) the Constituent Assembly was elected by P.R. and lists of candidates, with universal suffrage. Such had never happened before in Russian history. The parties were many and not well known. Radkey [2] shows that there were supposed to be 808 Deputies and some 42,000,000 votes. Only 703 Deputies assembled. Of these, *168 only were Bolsheviks;* 39 were Left-wing Revolutionaries; *380 Right-wing Social Revolutionaries;* 18 Mensheviks; 17 K.D.'s and "bourgeoisie"; 81 "national groups," almost entirely anti-Bolshevik.

The Bolsheviks had steadily supported the election and authority of a Constituent Assembly. Now Lenin elatedly and arrogantly laughed it out of court. He wrote that "a republic of Soviets is a higher form of government than democracy." (Theses on the Constituent Assembly, *Pravda,* December 16, 1917.) For this was the *only* form of assuring the least painful transition to socialism! Any attempt to regard the Assembly from the "formal juristic standpoint" would be *treason* to the proletariat. It had better accept the Soviet Revolution unconditionally!

The Assembly met January 16, 1918. In preparation for it the *Sovnarkom* drew up a Declaration of the Rights of the Toiling and Exploited Peoples. To it were added some resolutions requiring the dispersion of the Assembly of itself. The Assembly, heavily threatened, some Social Revolutionary leaders arrested, and the K.D.'s outlawed, their press quashed, nevertheless met. It *rejected* the *Sovnarkom* resolution after debate by 237 to 138 votes. The Bolsheviks withdrew—Lenin's tactics of all or nothing. The Left-wing Social Revolutionaries withdrew. The Central Committee of the Bolshevik Party, in session elsewhere, ordered a sailor to tell the Assembly to close the meeting because the guard was tired! It adjourned for twelve hours. It never met again, because Soviet guards were posted outside. Not enough people were on hand to fight its battle, indeed, their own battle for freedom and social justice.

[2] See D. H. Radkey, *The Elections to the Russian Constituent Assembly of 1917,* Cambridge, Mass., 1917.

Why a Successful Revolution?

Why was the Bolshevik Revolution feasible in Russia and not in the Western countries, when Russia did not fulfill the Marxian prediction that it could only be the outcome of class war founded on the clash of the propertied class with the industrial proletariat? Where the Marxian analysis applied in economic class terms, the Revolution did not come; where capitalism was only nascent —in Russia—it *did* come.

The explanation is simple. The stark polarity of two classes appeared in Russia and not elsewhere. But it was not the duality of the industrial workers and the capitalist owners of industry—it was a duality of the Czarist government versus the workers plus some of the peasants. Between the top layer of government and the few million workers there were no living bridges, no intermediate and tying-in social and economic bodies. Here were two "classes"; and the first had lost moral authority and political strength by reason of justifiable social criticism and defeats in war. Here there were two "classes": a few governmental administrators, and many workers plus peasants in uniform. The latter class was ignorant of politics, administration, and society—and therefore could be propagandized without the capacity to be critically resistant to promises, because it had no experience in the personal sacrifices necessary to make them come true. It was not told how much personally it would have to pay for the brave new world promised it in terms of advantage to it. It did not yet have the self-confidence of the Western proletariat.

In the West the formation of two hostile classes in Marxian terms was never consummated. For there was a middle class: and in each class there were both economic groupings that broke the coherency of the class and suggested alliances with groups in other classes. There were also spiritual values that brought about cross-class loyalties and intraclass disloyalties. Furthermore, the bitterness of class hatred that Marx postulated was modified —indeed, made to look silly and malignant—by the cooperation of classes in political parties and parliaments and local councils in social and economic reforms and political liberties commonly developed. Industrialization brought wealth and education—and this counteracted the Marxian prediction that the rich would get richer and richer and fewer and fewer while the poor would get poorer and poorer and more and more numerous until the latter "bumped off" the few rich.

Willingness to Murder. Even so, the Bolsheviks could not make their revolution stick without a continuing and brutal terror—*against* the class supposed to be the revolutionary one. Indeed—so ignorant, so benighted, so inexperienced, so without political consciousness—could it be called a "class"? They suppressed the *free* consciousness of the Russian workers as expressed in their trade unions.

The West had transferred power from the holders of wealth to the holders of votes, rich or poor. The political value of the free and equal vote depended on the faith that its authority would be respected as the instrument of deliberate and considered social transformation, as much as men could freely tolerate. History shows it was justified, and that Karl Marx was horribly in error about both human nature in general and the relationship between economics and the human spirit in particular.

Now there was a new "Orthodoxy, Autocracy, and Nationalism" installed. Lenin was deified by millions of Russians because his claims made by monopolistic communications could not be contradicted by rivals, and he gave the impression of caring for the workers' interests. He was Caesar-Pope in one. His embalmed body—he was wounded by a Social Revolutionary in August 1918 and died of cerebral hemorrhage by natural causes on January 21, 1924—was laid in the mausoleum in Moscow's center. Some so worshiped his will and hammering arguments that they copied his handwriting. He was followed by Stalin, referred to by Lenin as "an impure brute." Lenin had left terror as a legacy; it now came to be established as the totalitarian sledgehammer of a future sketched by Lenin himself in the hands of no thinker, no man of sensitive humanity, but an Ivan the Terrible, a genius at administration, and no boggler at murder. The masses were still suffering from *crass inertia,* ignorant of the universe and their own small world.

Revolutionary Development of the Dictatorship, 1917-1955

To slacken the tempo would mean falling behind. And those who fall behind get beaten. But we do not want to be beaten. No, we refuse to be beaten! One feature of the history of old Russia was the continual beatings she suffered from falling behind, for her backwardness. She was beaten by the Mongol Khans. She was beaten by the Turkish beys. She was beaten by the Polish and Lithuanian gentry. She was beaten by the British and French capitalists. She was beaten by the Japanese barons. All beat her—for her backwardness: for military backwardness, for cultural backwardness, for political backwardness, for industrial backwardness, for agricultural backwardness. . . . This is why we must no longer lag behind. . . . We are fifty or a hundred years behind the advanced countries. We must make good this distance *in ten years*. Either we do it, or they crush us.

> —Stalin, *to the First All-Union Congress of Managers of Socialists Industry, Feb. 4, 1931*

Problems

Lenin and his colleagues had the Russian Empire, with nearly 150,000,000 people, at their feet and on their shoulders. The problems they had to solve were these:

1. How was the economy to be organized and motivated? The eventual answer was socialization; collectivization of the farms; heavy industrialization as the goal; inequality of reward, according to quantity and quality of labor.

2. Was the State to be strong or weak? A guild system at its representative base, and with open elections, was urged by the Left Social Revolutionaries. This was a kind of syndicalism. As this was like anarchism, and the economy required concentration of authority, it was forcefully rejected and the strong, mass State was established.

3. Could true local self-government be permitted, an extension of the *Zemstvo* experience, in the name of liberty? No! Because socialist production and "equality" came first. Hence, the local soviets, so proud in the first rapture of the revolution, were subordinated to Moscow (p. 828).

4. Similarly with federalism. Communists had long been promised federalism as a solution to accommodate the Russian minority nationalities, suppressed by Czarism over the centuries. But for Bolsheviks, it was too reminiscent of the Swiss democratic government's weaknesses and many knew Swiss government at first hand. Federalism and local government were, they thought, merely devices by which the classes in bourgeois countries checked and balanced each other on the long way to the socialist revolution. But here, now, in Russia, the workers' State had been established. What need was there for a territorial division of powers? The greater the centralization of power, the

greater the "liberty" of the workers. A unitary State under the mask of a federal State was created (p. 817).

5. Nor need there be a separation of powers in the classic sense—for, again, this was a device needed only in lands that had competing classes, limitations developed by them to obtain rights or immunities from the power of government (p. 807). Lenin said his problem was "one of power." For him, now, the problem of law was the act of "class" will, a special kind of cudgel, nothing else; absolute, undivided, and unlimited. The people were now to govern themselves—they needed no safeguards of civil rights and no localism to safeguard their rights. Nothing then *against* the State! For the revolutionary creed assumed that *all* men in the same class had *identical interests,* that dissenters were senseless or saboteurs; "individual idiosyncrasies" were laughed off or killed off. Even the *vote* was no *right,* as in the West; it was a "social function." For against whom should a *right* be employed in the process of building communism?

6. For the workers the party was the representative of this State, the "caretaker," the "vanguard." It itself needed inner centralization, on Lenin's principles of "democratic centralism" (p. 868), already built up in the course of arriving at power. It "substituted," in Trotsky's aggrieved complaint, the party for the people, and the top clique for the party. It put dictatorially developed communism above liberty, equality, and even fraternity, a vague and undated overriding ideal.

These problems were not met all in convenient order but criss-crossed in the midst of social, economic, and foreign dissensions and struggle. They were solved always with the conscious and predestined application of massive terror. The process of governmental evolution took the course narrated in the ensuing pages.

These answers to the main problems of statecraft confronting the Bolshevik leaders were embodied in the various constitutional documents, as acts of dictatorial authority, never by free vote of the people. It could be properly said that the answers were prejudged, since Lenin was undisputed leader. At any rate in "constitutional" form, they were successively embodied in these evolving

documents: the Declaration of the Peoples of Russia, November 2, 1917; the Declaration of the Rights of the Toiling and Exploited People, January 1918; the Constitution of the Russian Socialist Federated Soviet Republic, July 1918; the Constitution of the Russian Socialist Federated Soviet Republic, May 1925; the Constitution of the Union of Soviet Socialist Republics, put into force, July 1923, by the Central Executive Committee of the Congress of Soviets, when the warring national minorities had been vanquished by external and internal Bolshevik forces, ratified by a Congress of Soviets in January 1924; and, finally, the Constitution of the Union of Socialist Soviet Republics, adopted by the All-Union Congress of Soviets, December 1936. The last named is reproduced with its subsequent amendments in pages *lvi–lxv,* the full-fledged verbal answer to the problems of constitutional structure and process raised by the Bolsheviks usurpation of power and their own ideology.

Six Stages of Soviet Government

The dictatorship has assumed shape and methods through six stages:

> I. War Communism—from the Revolution to the end of 1921;
> II. New Economic Policy, or N.E.P., thence to 1927;
> III. Five Year Plans: 1927 to World War II;
> IV. World War II: 1939 to 1946;
> V. Postwar reconstruction to Stalin's Death: 1946 to 1953;
> VI. The Alleged Thaw of Collective Leadership: Malenkov-Khrushchev.

The Communist Party of the Soviet Union assumed its tasks and character to meet and make the different situations implied. The capital was moved from St. Petersburg (Leningrad) to Moscow; from Peter the Great's "window on the West," from Western culture back to the savage heart of barbarous Muscovy.

I. WAR COMMUNISM TO 1921

The Soviet Commissars issued declarations of rights of the people and the nationalities; the Constitution of 1918 was promulgated from above, with high centralization. Soon Lenin revolted against this earlier romanticism of workers' ability to manage factories and called for "self-discipline." Property was nationalized, labor militarized, but the actual grip on the economy was feeble and incompetent.

Lenin enforced the acceptance of the Brest-Litovsk Treaty, imposed by the German armies, against Trotsky's "no peace, no war" policy and against Bukharin and the "Left" Bolsheviks, who wanted a "revolutionary war," and against the Social Revolutionaries. Russia was thereby deprived of about one third of her territory, resources, and industry. Lenin preferred this to probable loss of power. But the "bourgeois" victory of the Allies over Germany in November 1918 gave Lenin back Russia's losses and settled him in authority.

Soon Czarist generals and Russian troops, sometimes aided by French, British, and Czech soldiers and sailors, by Poles and Germans, from Siberia, Archangel, the Caucasus, the Don, began a war on Moscow; this was intermixed with a war of Russian non-Czarist opposition to the Communists, and the revolts of Ukrainians, Finns, the Baltic peoples, and the Caucasus against the new dictators. The rural areas rebelled against the forced exactions of produce, to which the Bolshevik Party zealots responded by urging the committees of "poor peasants" to denounce the *kulaks*. Agricultural production was only one half even the miserable level of 1913; industrial output was only one fifth.

The Commissars were at their wits' end for survival; they instituted two main measures, for even the Red Army was composed of heterogeneous elements, zealots, careerists, and Czarist officers. The *Cheka* (Extraordinary Commission for the Overcoming of Counterrevolutionary Activity) was set in operation, Lenin's counterpart, but more ruthless of the *Okrana* (p. 747). Stark terror was the mark of this stage. The Civil War was not its cause; Trotsky had put the normal Bolshevik doctrine in a nutshell: "We shall not enter the kingdom of socialism in white gloves on a polished floor." By November 1920 the White troops had been completely defeated.

The opposition was dealt with by a series of decrees beginning in June 1918. The Mensheviks and Right-wing Social Revolutionaries were excluded from the party and all Soviets, as "notorious counterrevolutionaries." The Left-wing Social Revolutionaries left the government and the Congress of Soviets, dissatisfied with the peace treaty and objecting to *judicially* imposed death penalties. They had also assassinated the German Ambassador to force a continuation of the war, and fomented insurrections. Their leaders were arrested; thirteen former members of the *Cheka* were shot. The *Kadets* had been outlawed. With growing Bolshevik successes in the Civil War in 1920, the *Cheka* persecuted any opposition even more ferociously. After December 1920 Mensheviks and Social Revolutionaries were excluded from the Congresses of Soviets: in 1922 their leaders were subjected to mass trial for conspiracy —eleven were sentenced to death, others imprisoned. The external opposition was crushed. The secret police and terror were further developed; the Red Army (Trotsky's brilliant creation) was pervaded with political "Commissars," for the Lenin Government did not intend to suffer military disintegration as the Czarist Army had under Lenin's tactics. The trade unions were subjugated.

The governmental slogans called for a new communist world, for defense of the fatherland, "the citadel of the world revolution." They engendered a period of intense revolutionary inspiration, especially among the urban proletariat and soldiers. The fanatical promise of "pie in the sky" tomorrow morning evoked tremendous zeal and enabled the dictatorship to win sway over the country, and within it to center power in a few.

By 1920 the word *plan* had come into use; it was the Leninist alternative to capitalism; private property turned on its head, as it were, with the already-existent large-scale enterprises of the capitalist world as ready models. Plans were produced for the factories and mines, and this led to the Commissars' insistence that the technicians, whether Czarist or not, be not interfered with by the Works Committees. The workers still believed that they were in a free land. Hence, a Workers' Opposition arose. It was counterattacked. By the spring of 1921 massive discontent against the Bolshevik objectives and policies came to a head among the workers, the peasants (afraid that the government would take back their land), and the Navy. In March a mutiny at Kronstadt occurred. It was crushed with a ferocity the Czars had not surpassed, especially as the sailors demanded liberation from the Commissars and clamored for *real* Soviet rule!

The party was purged of the dissolute, the dishonest, the criminal elements, the self-seekers. This problem was henceforth recurrent.

From July 1921 through 1922 American Relief Administration, under Herbert Hoover, led various charitable organizations in feeding about one twelfth of the Russian population which was stricken with famine.

II. N.E.P., MARCH 1921-1927

Lenin ordered a retreat against colleagues unwilling to concede. The N.E.P. set a fixed tax on peasant produce, the surplus remaining with the peasants. Consumer goods were increased, as the factories were released from war production with the winning of the war. Though all industrial plants were under government regulation, freedom of business was permitted, to replace the "black market" and "bag men." Party organizers were admonished that ringleaders of revolution were now less important than organizers of order and managers of the economy; this they must learn and teach their followers.

The total mastery by the party of all institutions of authority now developed. Lenin died (January 1924) and Joseph Vissarionovich Djugashvili (alias Stalin) took over the reins. Before he died Lenin had bequeathed to the party and to Stalin the dictatorship of fire and steel (Stalin).

At the Eleventh Congress of the party (March 1922) Lenin and his close associates were under open attack by a group leading a miscellaneous and strong opposition, the "Committee of Twenty-two." They fought back (some expulsions occurred), and Lenin laid down a rule of discipline supported by murder:

Then discipline must be more conscious and is a hundred times more necessary, because, when a whole army retreats [meaning N.E.P.—*Author*], it is not clear to it, it does not see,

where it will stop, it sees only retreat; then sometimes a few panic voices are enough to start everyone running. Then the danger is immense. When such a retreat is being carried out with a real army, machine guns are brought out and, when the orderly retreat becomes disorderly, the command is given: "Fire!" And quite right. . . . At such a moment it is indispensable to punish strictly, severely, unsparingly the slightest breach of discipline.

He advocated machine guns against Mensheviks and Social Revolutionaries—and expulsions from the party. Stalin among others supported Lenin's severity. Had there at that time been *free* elections in Russia, the Bolsheviks would have been cast into the wilderness.

III. STALIN AND THE FIVE YEAR PLANS, 1927-1946

By the time Lenin died, Stalin had moved into positions of party and governmental authority that soon put all Russia at the mercy of his ugly character and his administrative genius. His career and significance are now material, for in a dictatorship the State's constitution is the physical and spiritual constitution of the dictator.

The Rise of Stalin

He was born on December 21, 1879 at Gori, near Tiflis, in Georgia, the Caucasus, of Georgian parentage. His father was born a chattel slave to a landlord; freed, he became a failure at independent cobbling. His mother was the daughter of a serf, married at fifteen. Stalin's father was a typical peasant brute, who gave his son cruel beatings. When he died—Stalin was only eleven—the mother worked as a washerwoman. Her son was the only one left of four; the others had died soon after birth. She sent her son to an ecclesiastical school, ambitious for his success. He was most proficient. Riots against their Russian teachers and officials were endemic in the highly nationalistic Georgia against enforced Russianization. Stalin—pet name, Soso—participated. This was a land of Oriental pessimism about human life, of lingering serfdom, of primitive superstitions, of brigands and blood feuds, of bestial cruelty, of revenge. In

1894 Stalin graduated to the Tiflis Theological Seminary where, between the ages of fifteen and twenty, he rebelled against the discipline and creed of the Greek Orthodox Church (p. 740) and assimilated at close quarters its incense-covered knavery. The pupils did not mind religious dictatorship so much as its application *to them.* They sought out the emancipating works of their generation in free libraries: Darwin, Buckle, Mill, Renan, Hugo, and the Russian Nicolas Chernyshevsky who blended Feuerbach's materialism (p. 566) and Fourier's socialism (p. 291); his novel *What to Do?* was the socialistic classic. The students became atheists; went on strike against the Russian authorities (the former principal had been assassinated); sought out revolutionary groups. Stalin was an ungenerous, jealous debater; astute; stubborn; grudging; revengeful; and bore slanderous tales.

He joined a moderate social democratic group in Tiflis and acquired the rudiments of Marxism, for reasons of social status, and "the harsh intolerance and Jesuitical discipline that cursed me mercilessly at the seminary." He mingled with the workers of the industrial revolution in the railway workshops and oil plants of Tiflis.

He was expelled in May 1899 for nonattendance at examinations, after cell-confinement for reading forbidden books. Thenceforward, without academic qualifications, he became a professional revolutionist, a member of the radical intelligentsia rooted in a backward, sly, lazy, and inert, class-ridden people. Lenin and Trotsky came of social groups that retained some Western fastidiousness and humanity; Stalin rose among brutes. His light came from the pages of Lenin's *Iskra.* He was Lenin's adorer, an enemy of Mensheviks, who were the large majority in Georgian revolutionary leadership—until Stalin had them purged as part of his Russification policy in 1921.

It is as easy to grasp and manipulate the primitive theses of Karl Marx as it is to apply Freudian psychoanalysis to other people. Such primitive notions Stalin gleaned from the deadly closed mind of Lenin. *He was nothing of an original thinker himself:* his articles are copies of Lenin's; beyond the revolution, he was sterile.

He became a member of the radical under-ground, with all the tricks of escaping arrest, using false names, organizing strikes, always on the run, and he became a master of *committee work.* Taking the pseudonym of Koba (The Indomitable) from a famous Caucasian brigand, he developed and deployed his talents for cajoling, balancing, undermining, overpowering, betraying, to keep on top. He was one of the *praktiki*—not an ideologue. This he showed as a member of the Social Democratic Committee of Tiflis, to which he was elected in November 1902. The police finally caught him in April 1902, a propagandist among the Batum factory workers. He "sat" in local prisons or Siberia until February 1904, having escaped two years before his time. He had been elected a member of the All-Caucasian Federation of Social Democrats; and now he became a loyal member of Lenin's Bolshevik faction, recently founded (p. 756). He was especially insistent on Lenin's dictatorial party doctrine.

> Is it not understood that he who works in one of the party's organizations, he who fights together with the party and submits to its organization, cannot follow any tactics or principles of organization other than those held by the party?

He was even "harder" than Lenin; and the master's praise of committee men was honey to Stalin.

Lenin caught sight of Stalin in the year of Soviets, 1905, in an ultra-Bolshevik pamphlet, a year when Stalin played no unusual revolutionary activity. Then Stalin took a position rather like Kerensky's *Trudovniks* (p. 763). But he was blood-lusting, whereas the Mensheviks were not.

> Only on the bones of the oppressors can the people's freedom be founded—only the blood of the oppressors can fertilize the soil of the people's self-government.

Stalin made his first journey outside Russia in 1905, to Finland, to the party congress in Tammerfors. Here he met Lenin, was disappointed by Lenin's personal modesty but entranced by the force of his intellect. He was on the opposite side from Lenin in siding with those who favored boycotting the *Duma* (p. 764). In April 1906 he made his second trip outside Russia, as Caucasian party delegate to the Stockholm Congress. The other ten Caucasians were Mensheviks. He evoked Lenin's scorn as a narrow-minded "practical party-worker," because he advocated outright gift of the land to the peasants, whereas Lenin, seeing much further, demanded nationalization. (The Mensheviks proposed municipalization.)

Stalin's prominence now came from his organization of the party raids on arsenals and banks (p. 757). He was the liaison-man between the Caucasian Bolshevik Executive and the raiding squads, commandant, organizer, and staff consultant. In May 1907 he made his third short trip outside Russia to London, as a party delegate. These three visits, of course, were spent indoors. This was his first encounter with Trotsky, who was sharply hostile to armed raids and therefore to Stalin's fame and conceit. Stalin reported to his local party that Trotsky had exhibited "beautiful uselessness."

Stalin was rooted in Russia, and one of its most backward parts of a religion-steeped serf-ridden society. He visited Cracow and Vienna by the time of the Revolution; but, again, inside meeting halls. He knew the Caucasus; he knew Russia less well; the European, English, and American peoples he knew not at all, nor could he be influenced by their conscience and spirit. He was deeply engaged in the deadly strife between a local peasantry and their proletarian offspring and the parvenu industrialists and oilmen of Baku. In those years Lenin and Trotsky were immensely fertile; but Stalin had not as his hero and guide any picture of Man in Communism.

He exhorted the *Duma* Bolsheviks to obey committee instructions, not to become legislators; he developed trade unions and a general conference of these among oil and other workers, and incited to strikes. It was a life of terror, police spies, betrayals; he saw imprisonments and executions with *sang-froid:* the war of all against all, Hobbes' war! The police got him in November 1908; he escaped from Siberia by February 1909. He was made Caucasian correspondent of the party periodicals published abroad. He inveighed against the exiles' ignorance of the Russian "reality"; he double-crossed the Georgian Mensheviks. He opposed the suggestion that underground work

should be "liquidated" since the *Duma* allowed open political parties; he denounced leadership from abroad. He urged nationwide integration of party work. He was again arrested in March 1910. He left Siberia in June 1911 but did not return to the Caucasus, because banned by the police.

In January 1912 Lenin broke with the Mensheviks at a meeting in Prague, and secured the *co-option* of Stalin who had *not* been *elected,* since he was unknown. The Central Committee established a Russian Bureau, with Stalin and three others. Lenin did this trick because he had himself deliberately discarded his own associates, for fanatical purposes, and because he wanted *komitetchiks* to take advantage of a felt surge of revolution in Russia.

Stalin was meanwhile rearrested for being in St. Petersburg, a city forbidden to him by the police. He escaped in the spring of 1912. Co-option to the Central Committee had given him a *fateful seniority,* for in 1917, while Lenin was still absent in Geneva, Stalin laid claim to leadership of the party! This act shows, indeed, how insignificant was the Party at that time—a loose group of discontented nobodies.

He was a party nonentity. Before leaving for Siberia, he edited the first number of *Pravda,* a newspaper started by Trotsky in Vienna, but its title and good will shamelessly stolen by Lenin. Lenin managed to pry Stalin out of the editorship and put it into the hands of a younger and more "sensible" man, Molotov. For Stalin had opposed Lenin's policy of a strict gulf between Bolsheviks and Mensheviks in the *Duma.* In Cracow and Vienna, for some six weeks, Stalin was met by Lenin, who coached him in a nationalities policy (p. 818). There was also a short meeting in Vienna with Trotsky. Trotsky was at that moment a fierce critic of Lenin, and Stalin sided with Lenin: for Trotsky was trying, as he had for many years, to bring together Mensheviks and Bolsheviks. Stalin said of Trotsky: "He has proved himself to be a noisy champion with faked muscles," for he had failed in his endeavors. Trotsky remembered Stalin's "yellow eyes" and their "glint of animosity."

In February 1913 Stalin was banished to Siberia and kept there until 1917. Lenin's attempt to rescue him had misfired, because the member of the Central Committee he trusted to do the job happened to be an agent of the secret police who had completely duped Lenin! In Exile, Stalin did not, like Lenin and Trotsky write, mainly because he did not *think*: his was a mind of domination that needed people and practical situations for its practice.

Stalin and the Revolution. Stalin returned to St. Petersburg in March 1917—a month *after* the liberal revolution had occurred. He resumed his seniority in the party, deposed the trio that edited *Pravda,* and carefully circulated in the no-man's land between Right and Left Bolsheviks. Only the Georgians knew him, and they were always Mensheviks. He was advocate of a bourgeois democratic government; against immediate cessation of the war; evaded the overthrow of the Kerensky Government; sided with reconciliation between Mensheviks and Bolsheviks; swayed from side to side. Lenin returned, berated *Pravda* with fiery contempt for being vacillating; Stalin obediently contradicted himself.

In April 1917 Stalin was for the first time *elected* a member of the Central Committee of nine. His job was liaison with the Soviets, councils, trade unions. He developed his nationalities doctrines. When Lenin went into hiding, Stalin used *Pravda* to avoid provoking the counterrevolutionary forces. In the critical October days, Trotsky took the decisive leadership; Stalin was not evident. Indeed, he had opposed Lenin's demand for an immediate insurrection, was reprimanded by Lenin, and tendered his resignation. On its refusal, he immediately became the ardent supporter of Lenin and Trotsky. He followed the minds that had ideas, the hands that could chastise him. Hedging? He was of but small effect in the Civil War, putting obstacles in the way of the great Commissar for War and maker of the Red Army, Trotsky. He was a joyous applier of Red Terror and a penetrating inspector of armies and transport.

Now, he arrived at positions that gave his peculiar conspiratorial and punitive talents ideal scope. As Commissar of Nationalities he was given power to make peace with Finland and maneuver the national minorities into submission. He re-lieved Lenin of routine party chores. As a result of his inspectorial reports and trouble-shooting in transport, he was appointed to the commissariat of the Workers' and Peasants' Inspectorate, whence he could move at will into any foul administrative situation. He was a member of the five-man Politburo. In April 1922 he was also appointed General Secretary of the Central Committee of the Communist Party (Bolsheviks). It was an appointment fateful for the great globe itself.

For Trotsky and the policy-makers did not pay sedulous attention to meetings and organization. Stalin was a boss; they were not. He was in charge of the Politburo's agenda, records, dossiers, documentation, the calling of witnesses it needed, the fulfillment of its decisions throughout the hierarchy now growing all over the Soviet domains. As Sir Henry Taylor said (*The Statesman,* London, 1832):

> Wise men have always perceived that the execution of political measures is in reality the essence of them.

Stalin had the support of the party's fundamental principles of centralism and bureaucratism; the conduct of the purges; appointments and promotions in his sole hands. It is difficult to undo such work. This was the basis of his ascendency. Lenin alone could rein him in. Lenin died just before he decided to get rid of Stalin, painfully disturbed by his brutishness—and his intrigues even against Lenin!

In his testament Lenin said:

> Comrade Stalin, having become General Secretary, has concentrated enormous power in his hands; and I am not sure that he always knows how to use that power with sufficient caution.

In a postscript of January 4, 1923, written after Stalin had shown bestial cruelty and Great-Russian chauvinism in dealing with his own home state of Georgia, Lenin added:

> Stalin is too rude, and this fault . . . becomes unbearable in the office of General Secretary. Therefore, I propose to the comrades to find a way to remove Stalin from that position and appoint to it another man . . . more patient, more loyal, more polite and more attentive to comrades, less capricious, etc. This circumstance

may seem an insignificant trifle, but I think that from the point of view of preventing a split and from the point of view of the relations between Stalin and Trotsky which I discussed above, it is not a trifle, or it is such a trifle as may acquire a decisive significance.

Lenin's widow and those colleagues who knew about the will were too merciful, too humane, to use it to displace Stalin. Their mercy eventually condemned them all to death and many millions more.

But Stalin was *not* suicidal. Actually, on March 5, 1923, Lenin wrote to Stalin, to break off all relations with him.

Thus the man of brutality, coarseness, and violence, perhaps sadistic with hatred against his cultured (upper-class) colleagues, consumed with ambition, was in a position to kill them off, as he did. His jealousy of Trotsky was insane, founded on Trotsky's revolutionary ability. Returning from the party Congress of May 1907, Stalin's report to his Baku Communist newspaper said:

Somebody among the Bolsheviks remarked jestingly that since the Mensheviks were the faction of the Jews, and the Bolsheviks that of the native Russians, it would become us to make a pogrom in the party.

For the Jews were the moderates. A strange jest, for a Socialist!

Stalin embraced "Great Russianism," as had the Slavophils (p. 751); he liked the barbarity in its home-made variety. Since he stuck at no murder, however great the scale, while his associates had still some compunction and believed in debate and collective decisions and a certain tolerance, he triumphed, while they died.

In November 1922 the party began to face the fundamental problems of what form their ambitions should take on the way to communism. They thereby prepared ideas for Stalin. They were, first among all things, afraid of overthrow from the "capitalistic" world, especially since Lenin's and Trotsky's expectations that the workers in other countries would come to their aid by revolution (but not Stalin's) had failed. Lenin laid down the policy of planning for heavy industry as first priority.

Unless we save heavy industry, unless we restore it, we shall not be able to build up any industry; and without heavy industry we shall be doomed as an independent country. . . .

Heavy industry needs State subsidies. If we cannot provide them, then we are doomed as a civilized State—let alone as a socialist one.

The alternative of private enterprise, and private property, with State control was discarded. Bread to the cities and land to the peasants had been contradictory in timing, been promised to the industrial workers and the peasants respectively.
Right and Left Oppositions. Bukharin and friends composed a "Right" opposition, arguing that the peasantry should not be harshly treated, and that industrial progress should be accordingly gradual. The *kulaks* might prosper, but be taxed, whence the investment for industry would be gathered. Industry must provide the incentive of consumer goods for the peasants. The urban proletariat must also bear part of the burden of abstinence and hard work for heavy industrialization. They noted that already the peasants would not send food to the cities, as the "scissors" of supply and demand caused high prices for the cities and serious industrial unrest.

The Left-wing opposition (Zinoviev and Kamenev) urged expropriation of the *kulaks'* surpluses, State and collective farms, mechanization, swift industrialization.
Fast Means Force. But Russian agriculture was too primitive to produce enough to supply investment-surpluses, what has now come to be called "Operation Bootstrap," in backward economies. TIME is the critical factor in "primitive accumulation" of investment capital. Foreign investors would not lend money; all the Czarist foreign debts had been repudiated. Russian industry was young—it could not supply all the savings required. The per-capita production in 1927 was but one tenth of that of the United States. It hurts more to give up 1 unit of income out of 100 than out of 1000, and far more than in the proportion of 100 : 1000.

The Commissars and Stalin (who wavered while the various oppositions were incriminating themselves by frankness) finally decided on speed and therefore on force, fraud, and hunger: a large proportion of 2,000,000 *kulaks* (including families) lost their lives, in bestial cruelty to young and old. For as Stalin declared to the business directors in February 1931:

> We are fifty or a hundred years behind the advanced countries. We must make good the lag in ten years. Either we do it or they crush us.

"Socialism in One Country"

Trotsky had preached the "permanent revolution" —that is, that for Russia's sake she would have to foment revolution continually in other countries, in order that the workers there might come to the aid of Russia's primitive economy, otherwise Russia would be encircled and the Bolsheviks destroyed by capitalists. It went along with the traditional economic and political internationalism of Marx and the Bolsheviks (how sincerely is another question, once Moscow's own interests were satisfied). This policy has never really been abandoned. But now Stalin came forward after 1924, not only with command over the party *apparat* filled with his *apparatchiks*—his men in the machine—but an idea contradicting the "permanent revolution." He hated the West and the old Bolshevik's brains and urbanity. He was so ignorant a Slavophil that he was original about "socialism in one country"! With this idea, he fought Trotsky's hold on the imagination of the party, their most beloved. He scouted the slander that the peasants would resist collectivism; ignored the warnings of class hostility that would come out of too hasty socialization. He ignored the warnings about the losses that must be suffered from high speed in a primitive administrative and industrial machinery, or that economic inequalities would result to affront Karl Marx and the ethos of the Bolshevik Revolution. He picked Trotsky's brains on sketches of economic planning learned by Trotsky in his command of the Red Army. He gathered supporters from about the nation, and planted them where they were helpful.

By 1926 he proclaimed that the Russian revolution was self-sufficient. The slogan "socialism in one country" was the very wine of existence for the party rank and file. It gave them a sense of Messianic purpose; satisfied their Russianism; relieved their waiting upon other countries; and a reason for the exertion of power *over* others. Here was a pro-Muzhik and pro-Russian *mystique*. It brought Stalin immense support against Trotsky, whom he called "adventurer," and gave him a reputable justification for terror to destroy all opposition. The vicious circle was forged: heavy industry is needed for a good society, and this requires national self-preservation; this demands a dictatorship; but once the new industry is achieved, a dictatorship is essential to preserve it.

Five Year Plans: Piatiletka

A succession of Five-Year constructive plans were now developed to meet all the needs of production and consumption in all fields of economic endeavor. It required a civil war from above on the peasantry, and quick industrialization. The process is sometimes called the Stalin Revolution.

The peasants' farms were collectivized forcibly, though the party pretended they had persuaded them. It was pretended that only *kulaks* had a capitalistic mentality, or "petty bourgeois" as the phrase went. Such mentalities would be *politically* hostile to socialism and favor private property and political liberty. But the party found that most peasants, even the poorest, had these ambitions. Hence, it was fiercely resisted. The government and party did not care for intelligent or willing peasants: it would supply the brains and energy through experts and the operators of motor tractors, etc. What should be grown and cultivated would be decided by the central planning brains. If individual property in the land persisted, then the Soviet government would be obliged to try to handle 25,000,000 separate households, stubborn units. It was much more convenient to have only 240,000 collective farms. (After World War II reduced to about 94,000, p. 915.) To achieve this, Stalin became a new Ivan the Terrible (p. 733).

The policy was involved in the personalities of the old Bolshevik leaders and Stalin's domination of the party. By 1923 Trotsky had already cause to complain that the secretarial hierarchy had supplanted the whole party! Stalin had infiltrated his party secretaries down to the county inspectorial levels. He packed the Central Control Commission of the party (p. 876). At the end of 1925 his faithful crony, perhaps more cruel than Stalin,

Molotov, was made a full member of the Polit-buro. By 1926 the Politburo was entirely Stalin's! Trotsky was no longer Commissar for War; Tomsky had been ejected from the headship of the All-Union Trade Union Council; Bukharin had been expelled from his leadership of the Comintern. In October 1926 Trotsky was maneuvered out of the Politburo by Stalin. In 1927 eighty-three leaders of the opposition to Stalin publicly complained about his failures in China and Britain, in the slowness of industrial progress, in various peasant concessions. Trotsky and Zinoviev were expelled now from the party itself! In December 1927 the Congress of Soviets, now dominated by Stalin, expelled seventy-five members of the chief opposition; others had been locally expelled or imprisoned. Trotsky was deported to Alma Alta beyond the Urals. Others, like Zinoviev and Kamenev, recanted. All these were "softs"; Stalin and his new friends were "hards." "*He* will strangle us," Bukharin is reported to have whispered to Kamenev. The "softs" had themselves to blame. Thus, when in the Congress of May 1924, Trotsky was forced into his defense by charges that he was leading all the Left opposition to Stalin and Stalin's stooges in the Politburo, Trotsky conceded:

> The party is in the last analysis always right, because the party is the single historic instrument given to the proletariat for the solution of its fundamental problems. I have already said that in front of one's own party nothing could be easier than to acknowledge a mistake, than to say: all my criticisms, my statements, my warnings, my protests—the whole thing was a mere mistake. I, however, comrades, cannot say that because I do not think it. I know that one must not be right *against* the party. One can be right only with the party, and through the party, for history has created no other road for the realization of what is right. The English have a saying: "Right or wrong—my country." With far greater historic justification we may say: right or wrong, on separate political issues, it is my party.

But Lenin and he and Stalin had made the road, not history. Yet he was ready to tread it, and be trodden down for it. The individual ought never to place himself or herself *outside* history—the self should remain in it, molding it by conscience, mind and will.

What did the peasants want? Fewer taxes; freedom to hire laborers; long-term leases (as the sale of land had been prohibited); freedom of investment in the land. In 1924 they had even risen in Georgia, Stalin's home base, against oppression. By 1927 Stalin struck the peasants with all his organized power, blaming famine or *kulak* "disruption." The party was cruelly purged in 1928, to increase the fanatical impetus at his command.

> We must smash the *kulaks*, eliminate them as a class. . . . We must strike at the *kulaks* so hard as to prevent them from rising to their feet again. . . . Do not lament the loss of the hair of one who has been beheaded. . . . We must break down the resistance of that class in open battle.

The peasants, not merely the *kulaks*, slaughtered more than half of Russia's horses, nearly one half of large cattle, two thirds of all the sheep and goats. Dreadful famines afflicted the Ukraine "breadbasket" of Russia, while the industrial workers were fed. Even Stalin finally was forced to order his forces to slacken; in a speech entitled "Dizzy with success!", he used the dictator's traditional trick of putting the blame of the local executants. Now, he pretended to be the *muzhik's* protector! Every device of propaganda and animation was used. The present generation was "the manure of the future." Pie was visible in the sky—tomorrow! The *Komsomols* (p. 874) were flung into the countryside, like the *Narodniks* of the 1870's (p. 751), to preach, not revolution and the seizure of the land, but obedience to the government for benefits to come in the Land of Socialism. The vastness of the Plan was contrasted with the decadence of the West, especially when 1929 brought depression there (p. 639, for Germany, for example). No begging of a dime for a cup of coffee in the U.S.S.R.!

Socialist Construction. The younger generation was given a militant feeling of constructive crusadership. Idealism was engendered and exploited. Jobs and careers, educational opportunities, must come with the process of modernizing and expanding industry. The arts were harnessed to this "positive" adventure.

Stalin's persecutions gave zest to the single-minded plans. On Stalin's demand, the Politburo, with only Bukharin dissenting, had Trotsky exiled in January 1929. Spectacular and menacing trials were staged in the early 1930's of alleged saboteurs and "wreckers." Among those arraigned and convicted were members of the Industrial Party, a group of the intelligentsia and workers who advocated that the trade unions should be free and powerful; technicians connected with coal production in the Donets Basin; fourteen Menshevik professors and officials, including Professor Groman of the *Gosplan* (p. 893); the English Metro-Vickers Company engineers and technicians. A leader of the Industrial Party was Professor Ramzin, physicist, of the Moscow Institute of Thermodynamics, charged with working for the French General Staff! All these were variously accused of sabotage, of conspiring with foreign powers and Mensheviks abroad to overthrow the Soviet regime, when the wrecking may just as well have been the inability to reach the production levels set out by impossibly ruthless and optimistic planners. Some were later reinstated, as their expertness was indispensable; some were shot; some were in prison for many years. The intelligentsia was cowed.

It must be borne in mind that, until the purges of 1935 and beyond, various Old Bolsheviks fairly openly contended with Stalin's clique and ideas. Yet a steady succession of lesser purges went on.

The Russian revolutionists of the nineteenth century had developed the idea of the "propaganda of the deed"—that is, that their views should be spread by dramatic acts, such as assassination or sabotage. Now, arrived in dictatorial office, they reversed the situation, teaching their illiterate public to be loyal to their purposes by a new "propaganda of the deed," spectacular and sensational trials, more false than just. Thus they stimulated defensive and authority-identifying passions among the millions of mystified serfs and workmen.

Rise of the Soviet Intelligentsia. At the advent of the Soviet regime, the Czarist experts and managers had been chased away. Lenin soon brought them back, cured of his own romantic idea (*State and Revolution*) that the workers could easily learn how to manage industry, the banks, etc. He even spurned the Bolshevik want of "culture." Still it was the ideological tactics of the party to exalt the plain worker and to pour contempt on the intelligentsia. To be skilled they had to be schooled. To be schooled they had to be recruited and rewarded. The United States and Britain had to be emulated in making the peasant into a person of work discipline: precision, tempo, habit, routine. A managerial hierarchy needed to be selected and trained. Absenteeism and unpunctuality had to be cured. After the terrorization of the engineers and experts in 1930 and 1931 by Stalin, a worship of the intelligentsia was produced by his abrupt about-face, since industry sagged under the terror. Medals replaced mud-slinging. Men and firms were spurred on to compete, by "socialist competition" to overfulfill their Plans and quotas. Stakhanov (p. 903), the coal miner who exceeded all norms, was transformed into a national hero, and his productivity into a movement. Careers were created for the ambitious, hope for the peasant and the lower working class who wanted to make something of their lives. The prospect of raising the standard of living and of the "career open to the talents" by the use of industrial science and technology were powerful emancipating motivations: Stalin could not achieve his Plans or enforce his dictatorship by coercion alone. In the West, it is regarded as a most praiseworthy ideal to raise the standard of living; and the Russian people were peculiarly benighted beasts of burden, laboring deep under the curse of Adam. Two million party members could not then succeed against 180,000,000 people by force alone.

This was the era when Georgi Malenkov was sent to the Moscow Engineering School and when Nikita Khrushchev graduated from the Industrial Academy, a school of business administration. A mass movement of education was under way. The new generation became stocked with Soviet-educated engineers, managers, accountants, statisticians, economists, technical specialists, administrators of all levels; medical men, social workers, tractor drivers, and so on. Soon also the same was true of the composition of the Commissars and the

Politburo (since 1953 the party Presidium). The class structure of the party now changed (the rules were amended to assist this) from workers and peasants to the new intelligentsia (p. 863). Differential pay rates were set up, to stimulate incentive. An unequal society was seen to have its economic-production advantages. The *motif* of an inevitably hostile capitalist world was used to keep the workers sweating and to offset the Leninist promise that "the State will wither away." The party, the military organizations, and the secret police permeated all industry and social organizations to secure "fulfillment" and avert sabotage; the trade unions were subjected to being their instrument. Workers, managers, party members, the children in the family, were taught to denounce each other, and they obeyed, anxious lest they themselves might be punished—which happened often.

Suddenly, with the advent of Hitler in Germany (p. 661), the Soviet that had fomented trouble wherever it possibly could, became the friend of peace, of "collective security," of the doctrine that "peace is indivisible." In 1935 it joined the League of Nations, dubbed by Lenin earlier as the "plague of nations." The foreign Communist parties, long united in the Moscow-dominated Comintern, were now instructed to be peaceful and democratic and to join so-called "popular fronts" with the liberals against the reactionaries, the anti-Soviet parties.

The Great Purge, 1935–1938. Many younger Russian Communists detested Stalin, and not because they were interested in Trotsky. They read the sacred texts of Marx, Engels, Lenin, and the nineteenth-century revolutionists. They, as individual minds, disagreed with Stalin's dictatorship, brutality, and the hypocrisy of the party careerists, their inhumanity. In the Politburo some members pressed for some liberalization, return to open debate. But on December 1, 1934, Kirov, a member of the Politburo, a young favorite of Stalin's and head of the Leningrad Party, was killed in his offices by a Young Communist, merely one of thousands who violently resented what Stalin had made of the revolution. Stalin was in a frenzy of alarm and personally interrogated the culprit. Then a storm of investigation, purges, shootings, and imprisonments began, with transportation to

Siberia—in the tens of thousands. In June Stalin had decreed collective responsibility of all families for treason by any member. Terror spread everywhere; denunciations occurred by day and night. Trials of the Old Bolsheviks took place. Sixteen Old Bolsheviks were tried; then seventeen others; then Marshal Tukhachevsky and six of the top generals of the Red Army; and finally, in March 1938, twenty-one more of the famous Old Bolsheviks. These included all the members of Lenin's politburo excepting Stalin himself and Yagoda. The latter was the chief of police who had procured the evidence in the trial of Zinoviev and Kamenev and of Yezhov. The latter had been chief of police who had replaced Zinoviev, who was charged with falsifying evidence—the same happened soon to Yezhov.

Actually some millions of persons were arrested and imprisoned during this dreadful time into 1939, because in June 1934 Stalin had decreed collective responsibility of families for treason committed by any of their members. It reached a point where it is alleged that a member of every family in Russia was in jail at some time. The malpractices of informers, party men, police, and so on were so widespread that these themselves followed their victims into jail, sometimes even meeting them there. For, in the end, the situation was so tragic and ridiculous that Stalin's minions had to throw the blame for crimes and misdemeanors on alleged infiltrators into the party! Torture was, of course, used whenever it was thought worth while. "We were obliged to handle some of our comrades roughly," explained Stalin to a later Congress. "I must confess that I, too, had a hand in this."

The phase may be concluded by a short statement from the *Official Short History of the Communist Party* (p. 347):

> The trials showed that these dregs of humanity, in conjunction with the enemies of the people, Trotsky, Zinoviev and Kamenev, had been in a conspiracy against Lenin, the Party and the Soviet State ever since the early days of the October Revolution. . . . The trials brought to light the fact that the Trotsky-Bukharin fiends, in obedience to the wishes of their masters—the espionage services of foreign States—had set out

to destroy the Party and the Soviet State, to undermine the defensive power of the country, to assist foreign military intervention, to prepare the way for the defeat of the Red Army, to bring about dismemberment of the U.S.S.R. . . .

These Whiteguard pigmies . . . These Whiteguard insects . . . These contemptible lackeys of the fascists forget that the Soviet people had only to move a finger, and not a trace of them would be left. The Soviet court sentenced the Bukharin-Trotsky fiends to be shot. The People's Commissariat of Internal Affairs carried out the sentence. The Soviet people approved the annihilation of the Bukharin-Trotsky gang and passed on to next business.

The totalitarian State of Stalin reached its highest point: now there was no opposition at all. (Even Trotsky, in exile in Mexico, was murdered in 1940 by a stranger, his head smashed in with an axe. His children by two wives were killed.)

The 1936 Constitution

The party had learned the value of putting the medicine in jam. Hence, in February 1935 (see pp. 791–792) the Seventh Congress of the party moved the election of a constitutional drafting committee to amend the existing Constitution. The purpose was a show of democracy, both for home consumption and for exhibition to the gullible of other lands. For the League of Nations' debate on whether the Soviet government could be regarded as a "self-governing" State had shown considerable doubt about this. Some nations had voted against the Soviet's admission, which was desperately wanted as a defense against Hitler and Mussolini and Japan.

Time and Human Teachability. We have said that Stalin was a pessimist about human society. He was predisposed by nature and his childhood and subsequent revolutionary career to the use of murderous violence as an instrument of "progress." Lenin had had some romantic, optimistic notions, as shown by his belief in the proximate advent of the communist society. The issue was one of TIME—TIME and the Teachability of men. Stalin took the view that in the time which he had at his disposal men were not teachable. If the objective were to be reached, those who could not be taught must be coerced and humbugged.

He acted like a wrathful God—remote, always praised, and mercilessly avenging.

Free Men Enserfed. The standard of living that had been slowly rising in the middle 1930's was reduced in the Plans. The workers were tied down to their work, as the serfs had been tied to the land in the sixteenth century and onward. In October 1930 deserters and absentees from their jobs had been subjected to punishment by the loss of a job for six months. In 1932 the regime of internal passports had been reinstituted: the Czarist arrangement was restored; and those who flitted from one job to another, because they preferred one rather than another, were subjected to deprivation of their ration cards and lodgings. Yes, goods were rationed! It was part of a planned economy in an era of scarce goods. The various firms constrained to fulfill their plans undermined the labor regulations by illicit inducements and by not reporting absenteeism, etc.

In December 1938 every worker was assigned a "labor book"—the record of his employment. He could not be given employment without it, and the book had to be deposited with the enterprise. Violations of labor discipline, stated by the bosses and managers, involved loss of living quarters (when housing was scarce and squalid) and the reduction of social insurance benefits. Managers were subject to penalties for conniving at violations of discipline. (The party cells in the firm watched, caught, and informed on them.) In 1940, severe punishments were enacted for unpunctuality, for larceny, for hooliganism—the definitions were elastic. In June 1940 no change of employment was allowed (compare the ancient abolition of "the right of departure" to the serfs) except by express permission of management—the penalty was imprisonment. Offenses in defense industries carried long years of forced labor after trial by court martial. Finally, in October 1940, the system of State Labor Reserves was established: each year the government drafted 1,000,000 boys to be technically trained in the shops, factories, and railroad schools for from six months to two years, after which they were forced to work at any government-directed works for four years. This has not been dismantled to date, or any of the other rules just mentioned.

At the same time, something in the neighborhood of 8,000,000 to 10,000,000 prisoners of every kind were confined in "forced labor" camps under the direction of the Security Police, who became the nation's biggest single industrial, mining, lumbering, and public-works entrepreneurs, with this same labor.

Imposed Inequality. The intelligentsia of industry were further extolled and privileged. The gap between the wages of the unskilled and the skilled widened apace, until it was far greater than in the Western industrial economies. Differentials, piece rates, bonuses were used to encourage brains and muscles. The norms for piece work were pushed upward. "Shock workers" were given medals and special pay and preferences of commodities and services. The promise of the widest and freest opportunities for education was violated by the charging of fees at the high school and university levels, thus giving the advantage to the better off workers, the aristocracy of the factories, the party, and the military forces.

Total Absolutism. The nation was saturated with floods of State-monopolized propaganda; news came through State sources and these only. The educational system was attuned to prepare capable technicians and obedient and, if possible, credulous not necessarily convinced, Communists or Stalinists. Party, police, the Army, and the administrators of the State were organized by the highest levels of the party to check and balance and spy and report and betray each other. A dynamic system of anxiety for one's self and family and insecurity in one's job, whatever it was, was established. This anxiety was made operative by the imposition of impossible tasks on subordinates; but as the tasks could only be performed (to avoid accusation of sabotage) by some rational but illegal or irregular connivance (for example, obtaining raw material for the plant outside the prescribed channels and forms), the unfortunate violator was laid open to criminal charges, and certainly to betrayal by observers.

New Economic Theories. The teaching of economics was subjected to careful review, to contradict Karl Marx, now inconvenient. Teachers were warned to inform their students that certain theories were dogma. (1) There must be surplus value in the socialist State, because the worker must expect to pay taxes out of his produce for defense and for general administration of the nation. (2) Communism has not yet come and would take a long time. Meanwhile, distribution could not be based on the principle of equality, but according to the diverse productive efforts of men at work. Inequality must prevail until communism came, and it would be a communism of abundance. (3) The State could not yet wither away as Engels and Lenin had promised, because the Soviet Union was surrounded by Fascists, Nazis, capitalists, imperialists, prepared to destroy the Soviet Union at the least sign of weakness.

A return to many conventional ideas and practices in society and government, which had earlier been made the excuse for revolution and terror, now became fashionable and praiseworthy.

The early impulses of the People's Commissars had been destructive of the conventional family. Ideas of free love had mingled with objections to the strictness of the marriage ties in unsuitable marriages. The position of women had earlier been almost equated with that of serfdom, and an impediment to the revolutionary *élan* of the younger generation. The Soviet government lauded youth, and berated the nations which deferred the right to vote until twenty-one. The codes of 1918, 1921, and 1926 made divorce extremely simple, and marriage also.

But laws passed in 1936 and 1944 abolished *de facto* marriage; made divorce more difficult; abortion, which had been romantically legalized, was subjected to restrictions; the legitimate union is favored over the nonregistered. Large families are given endowments. The conventional bourgeois family had returned; Stalin, once a theological student, was aware of its usefulness as a subordinable economic and political unit, wherein the discipline and habits of obedience and acceptance of authority can be efficiently nurtured. Children who were encouraged to seek freedom from their families were, in the middle 1930's, suddenly subordinated to the family again. Now, the criminal codes under Stalin underwent tremendous change: *individuals could be guilty,* and it was their personal fault, not society's. How otherwise could authority be maintained in a "revolution from above"? The few occasional "individual excesses" in a socialistic society, predicted by Marx, had nothing in common with the incessant millions of individual excesses in Stalin's state. The *environment* was not to blame; men were bad!

IV. WORLD WAR II, 1939–1946

Part of the Bolshevik revolutionary creed was the outdating of the national State, of patriotism ("the worker has no fatherland" affirmed the *Communist Manifesto*), and the declaration of the nobility and imminence of an international socialist order. Soviet historians rewrote Russia's history from a Marxian point of view. The Czarist regime was denounced for its black attempts to subject the national minorities on the borders—"for Great-Russian chauvinism." But on the advent of Hitler, the Fatherland was proclaimed as Russia's supreme glory. The Armed Services were flattered, even while they were being spied on by the Security Police and the party commissars. The Czars were now extolled for bringing civilization to such lands as the Ukraine, Finland, Poland, the Baltic states, Georgia, and the lands beyond the Urals; they had not been conquered, but *liberated!* The foreigner was projected, in the Chinese phrase, as "a foreign devil." The superior culture of Sovietism—first in honor, in socialism, in the overthrow of class distinctions, in the freest constitution in the world, in love of peace, art, science, medicine, invention—was universally and efficiently inculcated and a hatred of encircling foreigners, bent on destroying it, was imbued in a people constantly alarmed by rumors of spies. The country was pulled together by the State Defense Council, headed and inspired by Stalin.

V. POSTWAR RECONSTRUCTION, 1946–1953

The Soviets survived World War II by a remarkable effort of arms, supply, morale and strategy, and endurance. Once again, as in November 1918, the regime was saved by Western "bourgeois" Allied help, for it could not have survived a straight fight with Nazi Germany. One of the most remarkable phenomena (not adequately noticed by any other writers) of postwar Russia was the sigh of relief evident in the speeches of the leaders, Stalin included, that *the people of Russia had stood by the regime during the war!* Evidently they had expected that once again, as in 1917 and Czardom, war might lead to revolution in Russia. Actually, tens of millions of Soviet citizens did surrender to the German armies, willingly, as armies of liberation—but the Nazis enslaved them, and most fled back to their fate, preferring a Russian to an alien treatment as subhumans. With colossal cruelty, the government resuppressed the returned and returning Russians. In this daily and nightly brutality, Khrushchev (p. 882) played a foremost and bloody part in the rebellious Ukraine. A powerful industrial and agricultural plan was undertaken, for the destructiveness of the Nazis had been incredible in scope and minuteness.

At once the regime swung into severing the Russians from the rest of the world by a foreign policy of alienation and heavy Marxian orthodoxy. The "cold war" pursued in East Germany, which remained occupied (p. 713), and the Baltic and the "satellites" Rumania, Bulgaria, Czechoslovakia and Albania, and (though opposed) in Yugoslavia, through the Cominform which had replaced the Comintern (suspended during the war), in China especially, was made to rage. It remains a paradox to maintain Russian historic nationalism, even Czarist imperialism, with the worldwide propaganda of Marxian class war against "imperialists," but the memories of the "Great Patriotic War" are constantly exploited. Russia is the foremost force in the world that is hostile to Existentialism and the friend of domestic and foreign activism. Stalin reassumed civil dominance.

VI. POST-STALIN

Stalin's swan-song was sung at the party Congress of 1952 (p. 879). He produced there a portentous set of theses for the future. The doctrine of inevitable wars between Communist Russia and capitalist encirclers was there; insistence on heavy industry. But above all, there was dissatisfaction with the produce of the collective farms. In this respect he made some curious answers to theoretical criticisms that had been raised by some temerarious spirits. For he admitted that the farmers were something of an alienated class, and he suggested that the *artel* form of property and production ought eventually to be made over into the image of the State production through the factories, in State farming (p. 915). The two principal speakers with Stalin were men who had intimately worked with him during the past fifteen years: Malenkov and Khrushchev. Malenkov took over the leadership at Stalin's death (pp. 881–882). He seemed to be the bearer of new tidings: amnesty for political prisoners, "peaceful coexistence" with the outside world, more consumer goods, some liberalization of the repression of thought and expression. He fell to Khrushchev's strokes in February 1955 (p. 882). He returned to strict Leninism, obliterating Stalin as much as possible. For he was *one of the new intelligentsia* produced by Russia's educational development already referred to, and hardly a sincere admirer of Stalin's personality and methods. He returned to the policy of heavy industry; sought now to solve the desperate plight of agricultural production, arising out of a fast-increasing population and crude methods of cultivation and poor incentives to produce (p. 918). This feeling of economic weakness, aggravated by the constant drain of equipment for the "cold war" seems to have encouraged one of Lenin's classic "zig-zags" in foreign policy, once again a "thaw," once again an appeal for "peaceful coexistence"—for the moment a breathing space for further but steadier development of heavy industry and the making of mischief among the new nationalisms of the Middle and Far East against the world's democracies.

How, in fact, is the regime sustained? The chapters that follow explain this. Here, however, we may emphasize the use of one of the most famous theses of Marx and Trotsky and Lenin and Stalin, on the use of war by bourgeois governments to divert the attention of people from their misery at home. The best quotation, thoroughly representative, is from Zhdanov's speech of September 1947, inaugurating the Cominform. (He is believed to have been *murdered,* in August 1948, to prevent him succeeding Stalin).

The capitalist world has also undergone a substantial change [as a result of World War II]. Of the six so-called great Imperialist powers [Germany, Japan, Great Britain, the United States, France, and Italy], three have been eliminated by military defeat. . . . France has also been weakened. . . . As a result, only two great imperialist world powers remain—the United States and Britain. But . . . after the war, Britain became increasingly dependent, financially and economically, on the United States. . . .

[There follows a caricature of the British economy.]

Whereas before World War II the more influential reactionary circles of American imperialism had adhered to an isolationist policy and had refrained from active interference in the affairs of Europe and Asia, in the new, postwar conditions the Wall Street bosses adopted a new policy. They advanced a program of utilizing positions won abroad during the war, but to expand them to the maximum and to replace Germany, Japan, and Italy in the world market. . . . The purpose of this new, frankly expansionist course is to establish the world supremacy of American imperialism. With a view to consolidating America's monopoly position . . . the new course of U.S. policy envisages a broad program of military, economic and political measures designed to establish United States' domination in all countries marked out for American expansion, to reduce these countries to the status of satellites . . . and to set up regimes within them which would eliminate all obstacles on the part of the labor and democratic movement to the exploitation of these countries by American capital. ["Labor" and "democratic" means in Communist semantics, pro-Soviet Union—*Author.*]

But America's aspirations to world supremacy encounter an obstacle in the U.S.S.R. . . . in the new democracies [meaning the Soviet-dominated States of Europe—*Author*] and in the workers of all countries, including America itself, who do not want a new war for the supremacy of their oppressors. Accordingly the new expansionist and reactionary policy of the United States envisages a struggle against the U.S.S.R., against the labor movement in all countries, including the U.S.A., and the emancipationist, anti-imperialist forces in all countries. . . .

At the same time, the U.S.S.R. had been pursuing only the path of peace and reconstruction.

This attitude toward the United States is only a variation of the regular and fanatically held thesis of Lenin and Stalin and the Communist Party from the days of Marx and of Lenin's theory of imperialist war (p. 759). It is always directed against the strongest resister of the traditional form of Russian imperialism with Communist expansionism to urge it toward the maximum goals of the globe itself, far, indeed, from the muddleheadedness of the Czars. Lenin, Stalin, the Communist International preached and really meant that wars between Communist States and "capitalist" States are inevitable; for the former would not look with indifference on the triumph and example of communism, while for the Communist International (Moscow-dominated; *Theses,* 1928 Congress), "Revolutionary war of the proletarian dictatorship is but a continuation of revolutionary peace policy 'by other means'." The only thing to watch in this necessary and inevitable revolutionary world war is the correct tactics suited to the time. Stalin said, following Lenin (Fourteenth Congress of the party, 1925):

> Revolution does not usually develop in a straight ascending line, as a continuous rise, but in zigzags, in advance and retreats, in an ebb and flow, hardening the forces of revolution in the course of development, and preparing the way for its final victory.

Hence, the Soviet rulers have never ceased to horrify the Russian people by alarms of imminent onslaught on them, while protesting their own lily-white innocence.

On a people who, like all others love peace and their motherland, the propaganda is most influential; all the more so, on a people, like the Russian, who have but recently emerged from primitive peasant subjection only to be cunningly prevented from learning the truth about other nations by the deliberate interest-begotten prejudice of their dictatorial rulers. They needed fifty years of beneficent liberalism and the most candid education; they had thrust on them a dictatorship that put out the people's eyes. Such a "closed society"—closed to free thought, to newly elected governors, to the spontaneous values that develop in creative individuals, closed to internal debate and the contention of wills—is bound by such tactics to force "open societies" (admitting new ideas, new values, confessing that truth is not yet totally known) to arm to defend themselves. This again is evidence of their "aggressive" intentions. For the Soviet peoples can know the rest of the world only through the press and radio in sole possession of the Communist Party and its other self—the Government.

Main Lines of Foreign Policy

The foreign policy of the Soviet Union is simple. It blends Czarism, Slavophilism, and Communist fanatical Messianism. Czarist ambitions over the centuries were for warm-water ports and the maximum feasible subjection of neighboring peoples (p. 732). The Slavophils (p. 751) had unbridled passion in the mission of Holy Russia to take over all Europe for Russian Orthodoxy and Order against the ideas of the French Revolution. Russia was the horrible specter of Europe during the whole of the nineteenth century, because her vast population and barbarism terrified. She was feared and reviled as "the policeman of Europe." Her part in the Holy Alliance and the periodic murder of the Polish people is well known. She even reached out to India. She frightened the young United States to formulate the Monroe Doctrine. She claimed the amalgamation of all the Slavs of the Balkans down to the Mediterranean and the Adriatic, world without end.

To this arrogant Messianism, the Communists added their passion, persistence, determination and total unscrupulousness generating a Soviet imperialism *far beyond the dreams of the most frenzied Slavophil or Czarist megalomaniac.* Its momenta are (1) a belief in "inevitable" war between communism and "bourgeois" governments, and (2) the need to revolutionize other lands, partly in genuine conviction of social justice, partly for self-defense through "permanent revolution" (p. 779). It is dangerous to think this is *"only"* Czarist imperialism!

Its means, which are used in combination or

with varying alternative strength, and with tactical (and conscienceless) aggressiveness or relaxation, are: (1) direct force (Korea, the Baltic, Finland, the Balkans, etc.); (2) the seizure of satellites (Czechoslovakia, etc.) through internal subversion and force; (3) subversion of those it regards as foes, through infiltration of political parties and trade unions and by espionage, etc.; (4) incessant incitement against "colonialism"—since Lenin taught that the colonial peoples were the Communists' most powerful leverage in population and resources against the bourgeois nations, especially in the Middle and Far East (China and India); (5) insistence on "national sovereignty" for all nations in order to induce resistance against alliances with the United States, in NATO, or other defensive arrangements against Soviet infiltration —but always allowing a "workers' government" to undermine "national sovereignty"; (6) denunciation of world government as a bourgeois trick to undermine national independence; (7) reluctant entrance to the UN and massive use of the veto, claiming that the U.S.S.R.'s ideas of social justice would otherwise be swamped by those of other nations; (8) *no inspection* of atomic weapons by an international body unless under conditions that preserve the veto in case of resolutions to punish violators; (9) disarmament, but in terms giving Russian standing armies a decided advantage; (10) an Iron Curtain around Russia and her satellites; (11) bitter indoctrination of her own people with belief that there is "capitalist encirclement" and only Russia wants peace; (12) deployment of "peaceful coexistence" of all political systems, when it suits the moment; and, more recently, (13) economic aid to underdeveloped nations to win them away from reliance on and gratitude to the Western democracies, though that aid is wrung from the toil of Russian workers.

All the time there is the ferocious intention of the Communist Party to survive and expand, to set up buffers and defenses around itself, to embroil other countries in exhausting wars, and, if possible, to destroy, subvert, and dominate wherever the cost is well within its resources. The

dreadful power of the hydrogen bomb gave momentary, intimidated relaxation of the "cold war," but as soon as it was found (Geneva, July 1955) that the Western Powers might never use nuclear weapons, for conscience's sake, the "cold war" was resumed with tremendous vigor by Khrushchev, Bulganin, and Molotov.

This embittered foreign policy is the external facet of the Soviet Communists' resolution, whatever the obstacles and however long it takes, and whatever it costs in blood and corruption, to remake the world's population in the image of Lenin. Another curious expression of it is seen in the obstinate and ignorant support of the biological theories of T. D. Lysenko, Russian expert in seeds. He was canonized by Stalin and Malenkov and Party and State for the doctrine (which is proven scientific heresy) that acquired characteristics can be inherited, and his science critics were officially banned and punished. The reasons for the coronation of this utter nonsense were (1) the Soviet boast that Soviet science led the world, and (2) the ruthless desire to bolster the Communist Party's belief that if the Party used enough force and propaganda long enough, even to wholesale extinction of the kinds of people they did not like, it could change the inner nature of the Russian people to fit the pattern. Lysenko has been proved to be a fake, in spite of some adventitious successes in improving some seeds. The creed that government is able, and therefore right, to eradicate fresh, oncoming, individual lives that do not conform to the Communist pattern has been proved erroneous in thousands of past generations under many other "monistic" and cruel governments (Hitler's ideal was the same)—and elsewhere, in opposition, it led to the rise of democracy that lets the mold of government be plastically responsive to the inborn nature of diverse individuals as they enter society in their new generations of every day in a "pluralistic society." The Communist way is merciless to the individual; the democratic way is founded on mercy and care for individual dignity. The works of political Lysenkoism will now be seen.

The Constitution of the U.S.S.R.:
Forms and Operation

We have no right to expect of the classical Marxist writers, separated as they were from our day by a period of 45 or 55 years, that they should have foreseen each and every zigzag of history in the distant future in every separate country. It would be ridiculous to expect that the classical Marxist writers should have elaborated for our benefit ready-made solutions for each and every theoretical problem that might arise in any particular country 50 or 100 years afterwards, so that we, the descendants of the classical Marxist writers, might calmly doze at the fireside and munch ready-made solutions. But we can and should expect of the Marxist-Leninists of our day that they do not confine themselves to learning by rote a few general tenets of Marxism; that they delve deeply into the essence of Marxism; that they learn to take account of the experience gained in the 20 years of existence of the socialist state in our country; that, lastly, they learn, with the use of this experience and with knowledge of the essence of Marxism, to apply the general theses of Marxism correctly, to lend them greater precision and *improve them.*
—Stalin, *Report to Eighteenth Party Congress, 1939*

The true constitution of the Soviet Union is the constitution of the Communist Party. Yet the professed forms must also be appraised, sickened though the heart may be that the pea is now under this thimble, now under that.

I. ITS GENERAL CHARACTER

The prevailing Constitution is that of 1936. It is *imposed* or *donated* like that of Prussia in 1850 or that of the Czar in 1905; it is not a pattern of rights won by the people for themselves. It is not anything like society's creation of a political consensus, but the exertion of will over society by a small minority.

Why should a dictatorial party even bother to enact a constitution? The vaster the society, the greater its scope of functions, the more necessary is a formal distribution of rights and duties; to get a grip on responsibilities and functions, men must know who is vested with each one specifically. The Constitution removes such matters from the realm of the arbitrary; the Communist Party provides the mobile mixer.

The makers of the Soviet Constitution know full well the prestige value, the influence, of the word over the minds of men; for they know the part the fight for constitutions in Europe and America and in Russia (1905 to 1917 and its Constituent Assembly) played in the development of liberty. They load their international critics with the onus of proving that their Constitution is not designed for liberty.

The Economy and the Judiciary

Two other institutions besides the constitutional distribution of functions affect the lives of Soviet people: (1) Private property in the means of production and distribution is abolished; (2) the judicial system is not "independent."

(1) Articles 4 to 7 repeat, with some variation, the Declaration of the Rights of the Toiling and Exploited People (notice the propaganda-filled terms!) of January 1918 and the succeeding Constitutions.

> The economic foundation of the U.S.S.R. is the socialist system of economy and the social ownership of the instruments and means of production, firmly established as a result of the liquidation of the capitalist system of economy, the abolition of private ownership of the instruments and means of production, and the elimination of the exploitation of man by man.

> The land and its resources, factories, mines, housing, etc., all belong to the State, with the exception of income from work and savings, the objects of domestic and household economy, personal use, and comfort.

Hence, Soviet people have not the material means of creating mass-units of workers, firms, and enterprises that might resist the will of the government.[1] They cannot freely own and use the press and the radio or have factories for the manufacture of arms or put to shame the products of the State's planned economy. The substantial degree of private property essential to bring about association and so political liberty is forbidden. Nor may private persons employ others, though the cunning term *exploit* is used. Hence resistant groups having group interests and self-confidence cannot develop. The consequences for the conduct of election campaigns is obvious (p. 810).

(2) The judiciary is "elected," the lower courts by the people, the higher ones by the various Soviets of the ascending territorial levels (Chapter IX of the Constitution, p. *lxiii*). Article 127 gives this assurance: "No person may be placed under arrest except by decision of a court or with the

[1] The right to private property in personal things and income must be remembered, lest it be thought that *everything* is socialized (p. 832).

sanction of the procurator." But all this apparent guarantee of independence and legality is aborted by the definitions of "counterrevolutionary crimes" in the Criminal Code, and crimes against State property, plant (p. 842). The phrasing leaves open to the arbitrary will of the government precisely that which in the Western experience of democracy has been most carefully excluded from the Executive's prerogative, "political" opposition. Elsewhere the security for free minds are given by (1) precise definitions of treason, sedition, etc., (2) independent judges; (3) *habeas corpus* (p. 4). The Soviet Union lacks all these three requisites of freedom. But it adds "cruel and unusual punishments" by way of interrogation of accused under torture; and the establishment of "special" tribunals for "political" crime.

The Monopolistic Party

The Constitution of 1936 openly admits the exclusive domination of the Communist Party, a slight change from the *de facto* rulership after 1917. Stalin even vaunted this in his speech to the Congress of Soviets. It is a classic passage.

> I must admit that the draft of the new constitution does preserve the regime of the dictatorship of the working class, just as it also preserves unchanged the present leading position of the Communist Party of the U.S.S.R. [*Loud applause.*] If the esteemed critics regard this as a flaw in the Draft Constitution, that is only to be regretted. We Bolsheviks regard it as a merit of the Draft Constitution. [*Loud applause.*]

> As to freedom for various political parties, we adhere to somewhat different views. A party is a part of a class, its most advanced part. Several parties, and, consequently, freedom for parties, can exist only in a society in which there are antagonistic classes whose interests are mutually hostile and irreconcilable—in which there are, say, capitalists and workers, landlords and peasants, *kulaks* and poor peasants, etc. But in the U.S.S.R. there are no longer such classes as the capitalists, the landlords, the *kulaks*, etc. In the U.S.S.R. there are only two classes, workers and peasants, whose interests, far from being mutually hostile, are, on the contrary, friendly. Hence, there is no ground in the U.S.S.R. for the existence of several parties, and consequently for

freedom for these parties. In the U.S.S.R. there is ground for only one party, the Communist Party. In the U.S.S.R. only one party can exist, the Communist Party, which courageously defends the interests of the workers and peasants to the very end. . . .

They talk of democracy. But what is democracy? Democracy in capitalist countries, where there are antagonistic classes, is, in the last analysis, democracy for the strong, democracy for the propertied minority. In the U.S.S.R., on the contrary democracy is democracy for the working people, *i.e.,* democracy for all. But from this it follows that the principles of democratism are violated, not by the draft of the new constitution of the U.S.S.R., but by the bourgeois constitutions. That is why I think that the constitution of the U.S.S.R. is the only thoroughly democratic constitution in the world.

The speciousness of the argument is worth notice. Was Stalin ignorant of Western realities? Was he enjoying a joke at the expense of the Russian people? Was he knowledgeable and simply lustful of power? The tone is relentless.

The Form of the Constitution

The State the Constitution serves is the Union of Soviet Socialist Republics. The Constitution falls into thirteen chapters, the titles of which may be seen in pages *lvi–lxv.* They fall into three broad classes of affairs: the authority of the State; the Russian State as a federation or union; the basic rights and obligations.

Its Making. It was cogitated to "pass out some honey cakes" during the Great Purge by Stalin (p. 782) and to impress democratic governments at a time when the Soviet enemies, Hitler and Mussolini, were in high fettle and when (later) a horrible civil war had burst out in Spain, under onslaught by Franco's Fascists. Stalin's commendatory speech said:

The international significance of the new Constitution of the U.S.S.R. can hardly be exaggerated.

Today, when the turbid wave of fascism is bespattering the socialist movement of the working class and besmirching the democratic strivings of the best people in the civilized world, the new Constitution of the U.S.S.R. will be an indictment against fascism, declaring that socialism and democracy are invincible. The new Constitution . . . will give moral assistance and real support to all those who are today fighting against fascist barbarism.

The Communist Party, not any free political grouping outside it, had decided in February 1935 to initiate constitutional change. Stalin, of course, was the pioneer. The Congress of Soviets obligingly elected a constitutional commission of thirty-one, under Stalin's presidency. Subcommittees drafted the minutiae; on May 15, 1935, the draft was approved by the main commission.

It would be missing the nature of Soviet government to omit Vyshinsky's tribute to Stalin on this proceeding: [2]

As President of the Constitutional Commission, Stalin also presided in the subcommittees on the general questions of constitutional and editorial matters. Thus Stalin carried on the general guidance of the work of creating the draft of the new Constitution of the U.S.S.R.—as well as the immediate work on editing the final text thereof. He is the creator of the new Constitution of the U.S.S.R.—the Constitution of victorious socialism, justly called the Stalin Constitution by the Soviet people.

He reported it to the plenum of the party: it was approved unanimously. A Congress of Soviets was convened to "consider and confirm it." (No alternative seems to have occurred to Vyshinsky as being conceivable.) The Presidium of the Central Executive Committee of the U.S.S.R. (the collective presidency of the nation, emanating from the Supreme Soviet) approved it.

In June 1936 it was published, as a draft, and, according to Vyshinsky, "in this discussion millions of people took part"; it was "read with delight"; and hundreds of thousands of written comments came in to the various government offices and newspapers. No record is offered us whether any of the delighted millions rejected the draft or the process of its formulation. The former Chief Public Procurator, whose work we have been quoting, cannot conceive this possibility either. He glows with retrospective and salaried zeal.

[2] Vyshinsky, *The Law of the Soviet State,* 1948, p. 121.

In the discussion by all the people of the draft of the fundamental law of our state—the Stalin Constitution—Soviet democracy found its most brilliant expression. Only in conditions of a socialist state of workers and peasants is it possible to draw many millions of the masses of toilers into the task of working out a constitution.

We know that to draw millions into the discussion requires freedom of choice. In the Fourth Republic, the French people could even reject their draft constitution; not so the Russian people!

The Congress of Soviets considered the draft in twelve meetings and on December 5, 1936, *unanimously* approved it. Of course, in the prevailing rein of terror, no delegates hostile to Stalin could represent opposition groups. The people played no part, except, it is alleged, to send to the party various suggestions. But these may well have been invented by the party.

Stalin's Commendatory Arguments. Stalin argued that Soviet progress over 1917 had resulted in the complete victory of the socialist system in all spheres of the national economy. Capitalism had been banished; the exploitation of man by man ended. There were no crises, no unemployment, but every opportunity to lead a prosperous and cultured life.

The class structure had been transformed. The capitalists, *kulaks,* and merchants had given way to workers, peasants, and intelligentsia, none any longer exploited by private entrepreneurs, all working with equipment "possessed jointly with the whole people." But Stalin did not answer the fundamental question: for *whom* and for *what* did they work? His assumption was that the working class cannot exploit itself; true, perhaps, if the working class is, in fact, free to decide what it shall produce, how to produce, and how to divide the product. So, also, with the peasants. But the Communist Party, he had said, was on top.

The intelligentsia, he calls a "stratum," not a "class," because it serves the people, and its origin is 80 to 90 percent in the workers and peasantry. He was bolstering his fallacy that there was no longer a division of interests in Russia, therefore no need for free political parties. He even slipped into the phrase that the "guidance of society by the State is in the hands of the working class the most advanced class in society"—that is, *one* class, not the peasants.

Socialism, Not Communism

The Constitution was not utopian but represented that which was already achieved; not communism, but socialism: "From each according to his abilities, to each *according to his work";* and *not yet,* "From each according to his abilities, to each *according to his needs."*

He poured scorn on "bourgeois" constitutions on the ground that they tacitly proceed from the premise that society consists of antagonistic classes. This is untrue to history and contemporary facts. Democratic constitutions did not start from any such premise but from strongly held diversities of value and interests, not those of class but of individuals and their free groupings. But Stalin could not admit that *individuals* existed, for Lenin's *State and Revolution* declares:

> We are not utopians, and we do not in the least deny the possibility and inevitability of excesses by *individual persons,* and equally the need to suppress such excesses.

Citizens must not dare to be their individual selves; all men are identical; this is the inarticulate major premise for Soviet Communism. There is something pathological or criminal about individuality.

Internationalism. Stalin once boasted that, "profoundly," the Constitution proceeds from

> the proposition that all nations and races, irrespective of their past and present, irrespective of their strength or weakness, should enjoy equal rights in all spheres of the economic, social, political and cultural life of society.

He erroneously alleges that bourgeois constitutions distinguish between nations and races. He vaunts the "multinational" State of Russia, "single, federated." The national culture of the peoples of the U.S.S.R. was "national in form and socialist in content." We shall see (pp. 817–825) that this is mockery, for the world outside and for Russia. There was no equal and voluntary affiliation between Great Russians and the lesser nationalities; the planned economy and the monopolistic party, in principle and practice, emasculate national diversities, called "bourgeois nationalism."

"Consistent and Thoroughgoing Democratism." Stalin claimed the Constitution is the most democratic on earth because:

> It is not property status, not national origin, not sex, nor office, but personal ability and personal labor, that determines the position of every citizen in society.

He has forgotten his own repeated assertions (p. 854) of the domination of the one party and its determination of standards of right and wrong, reward and punishment. Democracies may have their shortcomings about merit and reward, but at least their correction is not cut off in a single-party strait-jacket.

Similarly, with the curious praise of civil liberties and rights in Stalin's Constitution. Stalin scorns the civil liberties of the democracies because they are, in practice, spoiled by the inequality of property rights. But the free combination of *small* amounts of property and the free votes of the labor force enables men to develop their freedom and welfare *in their own way*. Where there is no private property at all, the rights of men are altogether in the hands of those who, in practice, decide what shall be done with that property: in the Soviet Union, a small clique. Stalin argued that Soviet rights were real because they were not merely declared but were enacted in statutes—for example, the right to work is ensured by the planned economy. But all such rights are *donated* at the will of the party, at the moment engaged in the most murderous purge in history to keep people from defining rights other than as Stalin decided.

Stalin, later in his speech, complained that foreign critics had characterized the new constitution as a "Potemkin village." [3] His answer really confirmed the criticism that it was this and also a "scrap of paper." For all he could offer was the assertion that the Soviet government had overthrown the capitalist regime and increased production, especially industrial, and improved the people's standard of living.

Thus, Stalin's speech is an excellent appraisal of the political state of mind of himself and his associates at the head of the party. It is revealing, when subjected to historical and philosophical thought, of thick-skinned deception. How self-deceiving Stalin could be is visible from his contradiction of his own assurance that class differences no longer existed in Russia, expressed at the Party Congress of 1952:

> Naturally the workers and the collective farm peasantry still represent two classes differing from one another. But the difference does not in the slightest weaken their friendship. On the contrary their interests lie along the same line, the line of consolidation of the socialist system and the triumph of communism. It is therefore not surprising that no trace has been left of the previous distrust, much less of the countryside's hatred for the city.

Yet—it is the city which would be made to flourish by the government and the party. And, he continued, now that capitalism has gone, there are and can be no antitheses between the mental and manual workers—ignoring the data of his own factories.

Having said these things, he then admits the problem of eliminating the various distinctions "is an extremely serious problem for us." If one entirely socialized the activities and property of the village, then prices and sales between city and country and sales by the farmers of their own produce would disappear, and there would be more harmony. So also if the "majority of the workers" raised their cultural and technical standards to the level of the technical and engineering personnel—up would go production to heights unattainable by other countries. But this still does not deal with the tensions of class differences brought about by Soviet economic policy itself.

II. ORGANIZATION AND DISTRIBUTION OF AUTHORITY

Sovereignty

"All power in the U.S.S.R. belongs to the working people of town and country as represented by the

---

[3] Villages faked by Potemkin in 1787 to deceive Empress Catherine the Great, when she inspected his colonizing works in the Crimea. Potemkin was a Field Marshal and Catherine's Minister and lover. Yet his colonizing was still remarkable for all the deceptions.

Soviets of Working People's Deputies" (Article 3). Thus, all others than "workers" could be excluded, however society began to evolve. Exercise is through Soviets. Also Article 1 stipulates a *socialist* State. But this is a truly elastic term, tactically employable against any movement in or outside the party; for words produce habits and bear the force of the legitimate to obedient-inclined people.

The justification of this location of authority is taught in all the schools, to those also who are going to be lawyers and judges. It is Vyshinsky's (pp. 161–164):

> The Soviet State is a state democratic after a new fashion—a democracy of a higher type. . . . In our country that authority is actually in the hands of the toilers—they in reality govern the State and all the affairs of the State.

He offers a kind of justification of this because voters in Western nations depute active government to the Executive and Judiciary; an untruth of fact, a fallacy compared with real conditions in Soviet Russia, where the party usurps *all* decision. He omits the legislatures and the relationship of party control of them in Europe, England, and the United States. He sneers at local self-government in the Western nations, alleging that it is "completely subordinated to administrative organs of State authority," but that Russia's local Soviets— "the mighty foundation of all the Soviet State organization"—are free links in an unbroken chain to the top. Evidently he would not or could not tell the story of local government as in the present work. The Soviets in Russia are completely subordinate in principle to the higher levels of government (pp. 825ff.) and, in practice, to the maximum possible.

He and Stalin are evidently repeating the slogan "all power to the Soviets" which was one of the winning forces in 1917; but he knows that they are almost at once degenerated into vehicles of Communist Party "cells" or "primary *aktivs*" (p. 867ff.).

The Various Levels of Soviets and Their Authority

The Soviets govern the various levels of Soviet state life as follows:

(1) The supreme organ of state power of the whole U.S.S.R. is the Supreme Soviet (or Council) of the U.S.S.R. It is bicameral, in order that the "nationalities" may be represented, as such, and consists of the Soviet of the Union and the Soviet of Nationalities. According to the Constitution, it is elected every four years in *toto*.

(2) Within the Union there are sixteen *Union Republics* (pp. lvi–lvii). Each has a single-chamber Soviet—the Supreme Soviet of the Union Republic, elected for four years.

(3) Within Great Russia—that is, the Russian Soviet Federative Socialist Republic—there are twelve *Autonomous Republics;* two in Georgia; and one each in the Azerbaijan and Uzbek union republics. Each of these has a Supreme Soviet, which is the supreme legislative organ of the area.

(4) There are nine *Autonomous Regions,* of which six fall in the area of the R.S.F.S. Republic, and one each in Georgia, Azerbaijan, and Tajik. These have Supreme Soviets also, established generally by the Union Constitution but given status in detail in the Constitution of the Republics with devolved authority.

(5) There are ten *National Areas,* of lesser authority and scope than the autonomous regions— they all fall within the R.S.F.S. Republic. They have devolved and superintended authority.

(6) There are, then, *Territories; Regions; Districts, Cities,* and *Villages*—variously shaped in the Republics, in various numbers and varying in authority.

All of these bodies have elected authorities. Emanating from them, *by election by them,* are executive councils, called Presidium and also Councils of Ministers; or there are less exalted names as the magnitude of the governmental unit decreases in importance.

It is to be noted that the Soviets at all levels do not conduct the direct administration as one might suppose from Lenin, Stalin, and Vyshinsky. They choose (and are supposed to) control the executives they elect, including the administrative staffs who are career experts working under the direction of these executives. The legislative and executive powers are not separated by separate election of the Soviet and the executive, as is the case in the American system with Congress and

The Structure of the Soviet Union Government

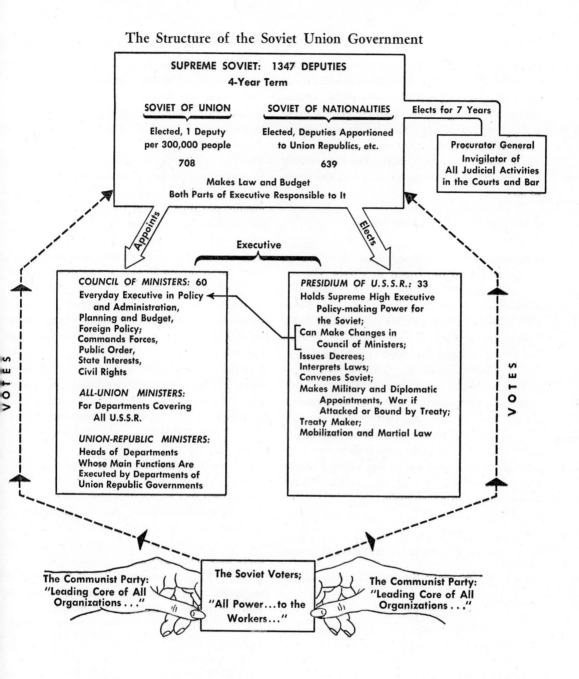

SUPREME SOVIET: 1347 DEPUTIES
4-Year Term

SOVIET OF UNION   **SOVIET OF NATIONALITIES**   Elects for 7 Years

Elected, 1 Deputy per 300,000 people   Elected, Deputies Apportioned to Union Republics, etc.

708   639

Procurator General
Invigilator of
All Judicial Activities
in the Courts and Bar

Makes Law and Budget
Both Parts of Executive Responsible to It

Appoints   **Executive**   Elects

COUNCIL OF MINISTERS: 60
Everyday Executive in Policy
   and Administration,
Planning and Budget,
Foreign Policy;
Commands Forces,
Public Order,
State Interests,
Civil Rights

ALL-UNION MINISTERS:
For Departments Covering
   All U.S.S.R.

UNION-REPUBLIC MINISTERS:
Heads of Departments
Whose Main Functions Are
Executed by Departments of
Union Republic Governments

PRESIDIUM OF U.S.S.R.: 33
Holds Supreme High Executive
   Policy-making Power for
   the Soviet;
Can Make Changes in
   Council of Ministers;
Issues Decrees;
Interprets Laws;
Convenes Soviet;
Makes Military and Diplomatic
   Appointments, War if
   Attacked or Bound by Treaty;
Treaty Maker;
Mobilization and Martial Law

VOTES   **VOTES**

The Communist Party:
"Leading Core of All
Organizations . . ."

The Soviet Voters;

"All Power . . . to the
Workers . . ."

The Communist Party:
"Leading Core of All
Organizations . . ."

the presidency, or state legislatures and governors. There is not even the separation operative in the British system, where leaders of the various parties are distinguishable from the general membership of Parliament even during elections as being almost certainly marked out to become the Executive—that is, the Cabinet. Furthermore, the Soviets elect and remove the judges in the courts of law.

The Agencies of Authority in the Union

The major areas of sovereign authority are the Union itself and the Union Republics. The rest are well integrated into the economic, social, constitutional and foreign policy of these, and even the Union Republics are fully subordinated to the Union, except Great Russia which, in practice, rules the others and the Union (pp. 822–825).

If the authority of the U.S.S.R. itself is appraised, we shall have established the major truths about the government of the Soviet Union as regards its lesser units of government. Some attention is later paid to the latter, even though our main concern is to make clear not so much the concrete scope of powers as the essential nature of authority. We therefore turn to the U.S.S.R. and its organs of government.

III. INSTITUTIONS OF THE UNION OF SOVIET SOCIALIST REPUBLICS

The Union of Soviet Socialist Republics is governed by

1. The Supreme Soviet;
2. The Presidium of this Soviet elected by it, whose chairman is the President of the Soviet Union;
3. The Council of Ministers (until March 1946 called the Council of People's Commissars), chosen by joint session of both chambers forming the Supreme Soviet.

1. The Supreme Soviet

The Supreme Soviet is the exclusive exerciser of the legislative power of the Union. The Presidium is not characterized by any such brief definition of duty, but it is accorded fourteen powers that jointly make it the Chief Executive or give it something like the status of the British Cabinet. The Council of Ministers is "the supreme executive and administrative organ of state power of the U.S.S.R." It is something less than a cabinet in the British sense, more of a joint coordinating and planning administrative body over the separate Ministries. It is of lesser politico-executive authority than the Presidium, which, in a sense, is its mentor and director and controller on behalf of the Supreme Soviet.

It will be seen that the number of ministerial departments in the Soviet Government is far larger than that in Britain, France, and Germany, and of the chief departments in the federal government of the United States. This would be extremely unwieldy if it were not for the guidance of the smaller, better knit, Presidium. If the latter did not exist, it would be administratively inefficient to divide the operations of government among so many Ministers, even with a council and a chairman and several vice chairmen, to attempt coordination. It still is, in practice, incoherent administratively; the State is responsible for too much.

It is essential now to give the detailed distribution of functions, and characterize the kind of government that results therefrom.

Distribution of Authority. The two Chambers of the Supreme Soviet—the Soviet of the Union and the Soviet of Nationalities—proceed from election, every four years. The nature of the election process is crucial to an understanding of the nature of the authority of the government and of the masses. But that phase of the subject is postponed until page 808ff. The present number of Soviet Deputies is 708 in the Soviet of the Union and 639 in the Soviet of Nationalities.

Legislative Power. The Supreme Soviet exercises legislative power over all the subjects allotted to it in Article 14 of the Constitution which see. We may say with little error that the Supreme Soviet is *unlimited* in political powers. Since these include all social and economic affairs and every kind of right and obligation known to man, its power is unlimited in scope. It surpasses Blackstone's account of the absoluteness of the British Parliament (p. 98).

Typical Organization of U.S.S.R. Territorial Administration

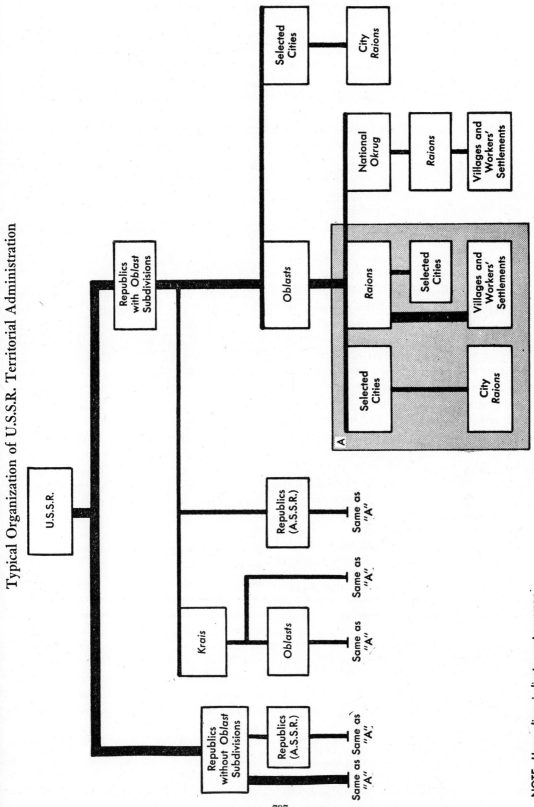

NOTE: *Heavy lines indicate most common administrative relationships*

797

However, the term *legislative power* gives cause for thought. The Soviet rulers and constitutional lawyers boast that they have no such thing as the separation of powers. Why, then, single out the *legislative* power? There would be no point discussing this question were it not for the persistent attempt by Soviet apologists to argue that they have got something essentially different in organization from other States, especially the democratic ones, in *form*. It all turns out to be only that "the sovereign will" of the people is meant, in general, and that "no other organs of authority have the right to issue acts having legislative force." (Vishinsky, p. 311.) This *is* a separation of powers. Yet the authority of the Supreme Soviet is confused, because, (1) it has more than the power merely to make laws; and (2) other organs are given the power by the Constitution to make "instructions" (Presidium), and "decisions and orders on the basis of and in fulfillment of laws of force" (Council of Ministers). These have, in fact, been of greatest "lawmaking" scope throughout the history of the regime. Indeed, it is only by the pretension that these other organs have no lawmaking power "independent" of the Soviet, and that the Soviet has the right to call Ministers and Presidium to account, that a Vyshinsky can maintain his position.

Other Powers. Let us now set out *the powers of the Supreme Soviet* and then of the other organs.

The Supreme Soviet has the legislative power. (They may have meant "the power of a legislature" in bourgeois States, without knowing just how to say it.)

It elects in joint session the Presidium, composed of thirty-six members, and this body is "accountable to the Supreme Soviet in all its activities."

It appoints, when it deems necessary, investigating and auditing commissions on any question.

It forms the government of the U.S.S.R. at a joint session—the Council of Ministers. The Government and individual Ministers are obliged to answer orally or in writing any questions asked by Soviet Deputies.

It elects the Supreme Court and the special courts of the U.S.S.R. for a period of five years.

It appoints the Prosecutor of the U.S.S.R.

(equals, roughly, the Attorney General) for a period of seven years.

Thus the Russian Supreme Soviet has a wider scope of authority and a deeper and more ramifying power than any legislative body on earth. It is vaunted as such by Soviet statesmen. What is the reality? Its role must be further examined, in order to answer this question.

Elections. Elections are to occur every four years, it is stipulated. Somewhere the Soviet spokesmen have sneered at Western parliaments, paraphrasing Rousseau's classic error about British Parliament in the eighteenth century—that the electorate exercised its sovereignty, and exhausted it, once in seven years. (The Commons was then septennial.)

This is the history of the Russian Soviet. There was no All-Union *direct* election until the first one held under the 1936 Constitution in 1937. World War II prevented the holding of an election in 1941; it was held in February 1946. Further elections took place in 1950 and again in 1954.

Before the Stalin Constitution, from 1918 on, elections were *indirect*. The electors in the cities and the villages chose their Soviets. Then the full assemblies of these chose delegates to a district congress. This, again, sent delegates to territorial or regional congresses. Finally, these congresses elected delegates to the Republic Soviet and the Union Soviet. They did so on the basis of 1 Deputy for each 25,000 city electors, and from the provincial Soviets the peasantry sent 1 Deputy per 125,000 inhabitants. This meant that the city electors had the advantage over the rural voters by about 2 to 1 (allowing half of 125,000 as *voters*)— if that mattered with the party in control.

Thus, there were no All-Union election campaigns, but only local campaigns for the local Soviets. Now and again, the Central Committee of the existing Congress of Soviets (first established November 7, 1917, and called a "Congress" because delegates of the *local* Soviets congressed to it) called a meeting of a new Congress. In roughly the first twelve months of Soviet rule four Congresses were called; from July 1918 to December 1922, another five; thence until December 1936, another eight. To 1921 Congress was (by the then Constitution) convenable every three months; later every six; from 1921 to 1927 (by a change in the law) it was convenable only once in two years. The apparent uselessness of Congresses was explained by the one that introduced the two-year rule thus, "What is needed is profound work of construction, which requires a concentration of attention." The local Soviets need not be disturbed by elections to Congress; if people stayed at home they would become more experienced in government. The last Congress before the 1936 Constitution was called almost four years after that of 1931. Between 1917 and 1936—that is, in twenty years—the total time for which all Congresses were in session was only *104 days* altogether. In "bourgeois" democracies, legislatures sit for *150 days each year,* or 3000 days compared with the Russian 104. Since 1937 the intervals between Soviets have been four years, excepting for the understandable hiatus of World War II. Yet in the democracies the Parliaments functioned steadily through the war.

Powerless versus the Executive. A basic safeguard of the people has been the winning of an independent power of the legislature to convoke itself by a proportion of its own membership (France, p. 379; Germany, Art. 39 (3), p. *xxx*). The U.S. Congress has an automatic right of session guaranteed in the Constitution. The British check is financial (p. 48).

What Standing Has the Soviet? The present Constitution treats of the convocation of the Supreme Soviet in Article 46. It requires that sessions of the Soviet be convened twice a year—by the Presidium. In addition, extraordinary sessions may be convened by the Presidium at its discretion or on the demand of one of the Union Republics.

Now the only *independent* power to get the Soviet called, apparently, independent of the will of the Presidium, is that of any one Union Republic. But the Republics are dominated by the authority of the leaders of the Communist Party in Moscow, who are chiefly Great Russians. Hence, in fact, the only power able to stand out against the Presidium would be those who hold command of Great Russia. No combination of other Republics could aspire to thwart the will of the Presidium, and so make the Soviet independent in the use of its legislative authority, against the

strength of Great Russia in population and power, or its command of the Communist Party. This applies to both Houses, because the Constitution stipulates that they must meet simultaneously.

In the Soviet Union, the financial check does not exist, because the Plans transcend each year, and much of the revenue of government flows in as a part of the contribution from each firm and sector of the economy.

Scanty Sessions. Unless the Presidium wishes to call a session nothing can force it to. From 1938 through 1954, the record is this: there were three sessions in 1939; in six of the years there were two sessions; in nine of the years, there was only one session. The longest-lasting session was twelve days, the shortest three, while the average is about five days.

How much time does it take the Supreme Soviet to be a "democracy of a higher type," according to Vishinsky's fulsome phrase? The British Parliament, the U.S. Congress, and the French and German assemblies (and most other truly democratic parliaments), sit for about 200 days per year. Their genius is not less than that of Soviet Deputies in the proportion of 200 is to 5! The plain truth is that the Soviet has no function beyond the *unanimous* acceptance of the work of the Presidium and the Council of Ministers, to listen to their spokesmen, to proffer some perfunctory remarks about the laws submitted, and to burst into rounds of ringing applause. What more can be expected of their industry in five days?

During 1955 the Communist leaders evidently decided to persuade the world that the Supreme Soviet was truly significant. Special sessions were called on August 4 (2 days) to hear Bulganin on the Geneva Conference and on December 26 (4 days) to hear reports on the November Geneva Conference and the dictators' tour of the Far East. The Warsaw Treaty and the U.S.S.R.–West German Agreement were made subject to parliamentary ratification. The Supreme Soviet has made contact with the worldwide Inter-Parliamentary Union.

The Supreme Soviet of the U.S.S.R. has been dumped into the position the Kings of England designed for Parliament before Charles I had his head taken off by the resisting Parliaments; that the *États Généraux* were consigned to by the Kings of France while they even existed to 1614; and the Czar put the Russian *Duma* in 1906! Strange commentary on "popular sovereignty"!

The Soviet's Proceedings. The Various Ministers report on their work and propose bills. There are three commissions: Legislative, Budgetary, and Foreign Affairs, elected in each house to consider bills submitted by Ministers. The brevity of the sessions makes initiation of laws by the Commissions an impossibility—had they the temerity. Each group of fifty Deputies has the right to pick a reporter to participate in discussions or debates. (Even to use such terms makes the present writer feel a dupe!) These reporters are accorded an hour's first speech and then thirty minutes for a summation after debate; their coreporter, a lesser time. A Council of Elders (senior members), following European parliamentary practice and especially representing the various Republics and Regions, is ostensibly in charge of the agenda and proposals for the choice of the Presidium and officials.

Occasionally, the Commissions do suggest amendments to bills and to the budget. They are extremely trivial; nothing like the amendments proposed and often carried by the Opposition in democratic legislatures. In Russia, they are probably planted by the party leaders. In 1955 the Budgetary Commission was given the data a little earlier—but the score or 20 of speakers behaved just as before, they caviled trivially, boasted and applauded, and the military budget was not even disclosed.

The objects of discussion and legislation vary a little from session to session. However, the collection of decisions and ordinances made by the Council of Ministers and the Presidium far outnumbers the laws (a dozen or so per session) made by the Soviet. Whether the former are "laws" or not is entirely academic. They have the force of law, and without waiting for the Soviet's confirmation. Their substance would not in other lands be regarded as merely Executive Orders or "statutory instruments," but fully statutes.

The two Chambers meet separately for the first meeting of the session, to be addressed by one of their seniors, to select a chairman, to adopt the agenda and time table, and select the Commissions. At the next meeting the Chambers meet jointly to hear the budget report. Here the *Party* Presidium attends, as well as the Soviet Presidium, the Ministers, and chiefs of the party, mostly conspicuously draped about. It is a gala occasion, and there is much cheering and laughter. Then the Houses meet separately to discuss the budget. Following the party rules regarding "criticism and self-criticism," which are pseudo-compulsory, some members offer critical remarks and remedial suggestions, evoking promises from the Ministers of improvement in the future. The Minister of Finance concludes this phase of the session by a final report to each House on the budget, taking notice of the foregoing discussions, whereupon each House *unanimously* approves the budget.

The decrees made by the Presidium, that often contain dismissals and appointments of important personnel in the ministries up to the Ministers themselves, are presented by the Presidium to each House and are adopted *unanimously* without debate. Laws presented are accepted without substantial discussion.

The concluding meeting of the session is again a joint meeting. This elects the Presidium, on the slate presented unchallenged by the Council of Elders, and it does so unanimously. So also does it ratify the Council of Ministers, several of whom have most probably been appointed by the Presidium in the interim between sessions of the Soviet. Finally, demonstrative resolutions—concerning the Plans of World Peace—are pronounced for public and foreign consumption.

There is never any tension of a Ministry in trouble with an Opposition or its own followers in revolt. There is never an imminent sense that as the result of a debate, the Ministers may be ejected. Fear, in Russia, afflicts the Soviet Deputies, not the Ministers, except among themselves.

A few formal characteristics of the Supreme Soviet must still be added, to avoid a charge of incompleteness.

The Deputies of the Soviet. Despite the impotence of the Supreme Soviet, the Soviet spokesmen persist in a romantic theory of the Soviet Deputy. This is what Vyshinsky says he is (p. 353):

A deputy of the Supreme Soviet is no professional politician or "legislator." He is a person connected with socialist production, science, and so forth. He is an agent of the bloc of communists and non-party members, a man of lively experience and work, a champion of socialism. He does not "fence" with glittering speeches but strives as a deputy to put all his constructive experience into the creation of laws bound to assure socialism's further strengthening and development.

And he recites all the "rights" a Deputy has—to prepare laws, to ask questions, and so on.

Of course, the Deputy is supplied with all the panoply of privileges enjoyed by members of true parliaments in other nations. It is hard to answer why he should have these. He has inviolability of person. He gets 1000 rubles a month and 150 a day during sessions of the Soviet, and free travel at any time. During the sessions he is afforded the best hotel accommodation and the best seats at the theaters and opera.

Vyshinsky charges "bourgeois" Deputies with an "absence of principle." They, he avers, frequently go over from one party to another during their elected term. This we know to be untrue. What *is* true is that they are not sworn to stay by the policies of a few leaders, nor are they under material or terroristic compulsion to do so.

The two Chambers have equal powers. If they are in deadlock, it is broken by their dissolution by the Presidium and new elections. But the party makes them like-minded through the process of election and choice of the candidate and any subsequent talking-to that might be desirable. They convene and adjourn simultaneously. A simple majority vote in each is required for the passage of legislation.

Social Composition. It is highly important at this point to take notice that the percentage of party members and candidates has increased. In both Houses together from 76.1 percent in 1937 to 81.0 percent in 1946, to 83.4 percent in 1950, and 78.0 percent in 1954.

In these circumstances, having regard to the actual practice of "democratic centralism" in the party, the total body of the Soviet especially when acting in public, and in view of the rules forbidding the formation of "factions" or "fractions" by the party rules, makes the Soviet a rubber stamp. Furthermore, to take one statistical illustration: in the Soviet of the Union of 1950, over 72 percent of the "workers'" Deputies were paid officials in the party, administration, the Armed Forces, etc. They could hardly be "independent." Over 40 percent of the "peasant" Deputies were similarly employed, and over 50 percent in addition were chairmen of collective farms—and these are not chosen freely of wishes.

In the Soviet of 1954 there were party and government employees to the proportion of nearly 42 percent of the total membership and business executives making nearly 35 percent: in all, 77 percent themselves governmental executives with an interest in *not* criticizing and controlling the Presidium and the Ministers.

The figures of the social composition of the party given later (p. 866), show how the Soviet intelligentsia has supplanted the "worker" and the peasant.

2. The Presidium

We state the powers and status of the Presidium, as the Constitution does.

First, its general character: it is a collective or collegial presidency, as though the Founding Fathers of the U.S. Constitution had, indeed, accepted some of the proposals to have three of five or seven members to compose the chief Executive, instead of the single one actually adopted. It is the lesser self of the Soviet in numbers and its greater self in actual power, and practically this in the authority delegated to it. Its chairman is often referred to as the President of the U.S.S.R., especially in international affairs and in Soviet State ceremonials and celebrations. But he has been nothing but a kindly nonentity, decorative, and useful to the party leaders to blandish some large body of the Russian people or to propitiate a section of the ruling groups. Thus, the post has been held by Kalinin, an Old Bolshevik Party man, a peasant, who served from 1919 to retirement in 1946; from 1946 to 1953 by Shvernik, who had been chairman of the All-Union Central

Council of Trade Unions since 1930—that is, for over fifteen years. Most recently it was conferred on Marshal Voroshilov, one of the Soviet old guard, a Stalin protégé and comrade-in-arms since the Civil War. Shvernik gave way to Voroshilov after the death of Stalin to return to his post at the head of the Sovietized trade unions.

The Interpersonal Web of Party and State. At this point it is essential to indicate the personal interconnections between party and State, shown acutely in the Presidium and the Council of Ministers. The Presidium is elected by the Supreme Soviet, and, considering that the latter is the official master of the former, the party sees to it that the Presidium consists of none but party members (whereas the Soviet has, as we have noted roughly 16 percent of nonparty Deputies). Then there is an interlacing between the top directorate of the party—that is, its Party Presidium (formerly the Politbureau)—and the Soviet Presidium and the Council of Ministers. This we display for the most recent situation in the illustration on the opposite page, essential to the appreciation of the Presidium from anything but a merely formal point of view.

Status and Powers. The Presidium is elected in a joint sitting of the Soviet of the Union and the Council of Nationalities every four years. The Constitution made the membership thirty-seven; but in an amendment of March 1946 the number was reduced to thirty-three, so distributed: a chairman, sixteen vice chairmen, fifteen members, and a secretary.

The practice of the system has been to elect to the sixteen vice chairmanships the chairmen of the Presidiums of the sixteen Union Republics. It is at once an obeisance to the idea of federal union of nationalities and also an earnest of Union integration. As already foreshadowed by the observations of interpersonal party membership of governmental and party bodies, some members of the Soviet Presidium are members of the Party Presidium, in 1950, six; and in April 1954, four. Members of the Council of Ministers are not elected to the Presidium, since it is realized that they have what should be independent functions.

With peculiar constitutional preciosity, the chairmen of the Soviet Chambers are not elected as the Presidium, since they are supposed to be the watchdogs over the latter.

Its powers are far-reaching. It:

convenes sessions of the Supreme Soviet;

interprets the laws in force and issues instructions on their administration;

dissolves the Soviet in conditions of bicameral deadlock and fixes new elections;

may conduct referenda at its initiative or at the demand of one of the Union Republics;

may rescind decisions and orders of the Council of Ministers of the Union, and of the Union Republics if they are not in accordance with the law, and this includes the law of the Constitution;

between sessions of the Supreme Soviet, relieves and appoints Ministers at the instance of Chairman of the Council of Ministers—later confirmable by the Supreme Soviet;

awards decorations and assigns titles of honor of the U.S.S.R.;

exercises the right of pardon;

appoints and replaces the Supreme Command of the Armed Forces of the U.S.S.R.;

between sessions of the Supreme Soviet, declares a state of war in the event of an armed attack on the U.S.S.R., or if it is necessary to fulfill international treaty obligations of mutual defense against aggression;

declares partial or general mobilization;

ratifies international treaties;

appoints and recalls plenipotentiary representatives of the U.S.S.R. to foreign states;

accepts the documents of appointment and recall of diplomatic representatives of foreign States accredited to it.

Between the expiry or the dissolution of the Soviet until a newly elected Supreme Soviet is formed, the Presidium preserves its authority. The new elections are arranged by the Presidium within a period of not more than two months from the cessation of the Soviet. The newly elected Soviet is convened by the Presidium not later than a month after the elections.

We emphasize, among all these powers, the interpretation of the laws and the Constitution; the rescinding of ministerial and Republic decisions; the appointing and dismissal power; command of

Integration of the Communist Party (C.P.S.U.) and Soviet Government, December 1955

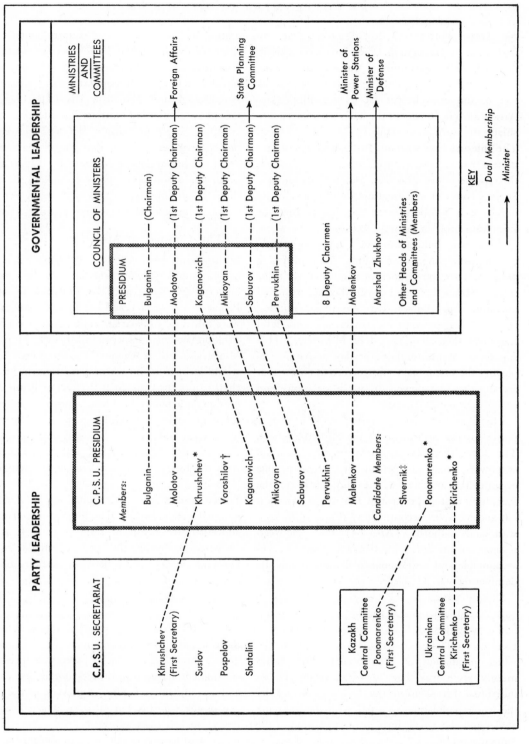

the Armed Forces; the declaration of war and diplomatic representation. They have been mightily used. "The Presidium of the Supreme Soviet of the U.S.S.R. is accountable to the Supreme Soviet of the U.S.S.R. for all its activities," says Article 48. The brevity of the latter's sessions emasculates the word *accountable*.

The Internal Iron Curtain. In the absence of free parties that take turns in office and shed light on their predecessors' practices, and as the Supreme Soviet's power of investigating the Ministers is not usable, it is not possible to appraise further the Presidium's role in making decisions.

It seems to hold a kind of Cabinet or policy-making, directing, coordinating, and initiating position above the Council of Ministers, yet to be removed from the actual day-by-day departmental executive responsibilities. It is at once a continuing substitute for the Supreme Soviet, a higher level Executive than the Council of Ministers, and a supervisor of ministerial everyday activities employing the disciplinary and corrective power that accompanies the power to quash decisions and orders and to oust Ministers.

The Presidium is not vested with a formal power to veto laws made by the Supreme Soviet. The Soviet theorists' antipathy to the separation of powers would not permit them to allow one organ to veto another. All they did was to put the Presidium on top, practically. For to the powers it has and its Soviet accountability is added the constitutional authority (Art. 65) that "between sessions" of the Soviet the Council of Ministers is accountable and responsible to the Presidium. Its dominating status is clear.

Stalin reported to the Congress of Soviets in 1936 that an amendment regarding the Presidium had been suggested. It was that the President of it (we have called it chairman) be elected by the whole population of the country. His rather muddy prose was that "there must not be an individual President in the U.S.S.R. elected by the whole population on a par with the Supreme Soviet and able to put himself in opposition to the Supreme Soviet."

He referred to historical experience to support the view that a "collegium" is "the most demo-cratic." It "safeguards the country against undesirable contingencies." It is true that where the Executive or cabinet, especially if it be one man, has the backing of the popular vote (for example, Napoleon I and Napoleon III, Hindenberg in Germany, Hitler in various presidential votes, etc.), a dangerous tension develops between a power-lusty person, conscious of his mass votes, and the other organs of government. It is so much easier for a monopoly party to govern if it reduces the number of organs of State power possessing independent and direct popular strength.

3. The Council of Ministers

It has already been indicated that from November 8, 1917, until March 1946, the Ministers in the Soviet system were called, by Trotsky's invention, People's Commissars, and the departments earlier were called Commissariats. The day-to-day administration became respectabilized into Ministers, Ministries, and a Council of Ministers. There would seem to be no warrant for referring to the chairman of the Council as Premier or Prime Minister as some books do. There is no such precedent for it in Soviet history. To go back to the times of the Czar and even the *Duma* is fatuous—at any rate, the title is not official, and hardly accords with the rough ethos of Soviet governmental behavior.

Powers and Status. The Constitution (Art. 64) designates the Council, "The highest executive and administrative organ of state power." It is declared to be "responsible and accountable to the Supreme Soviet"—and between sessions of the Soviet, accountable "to the Presidium." This strengthens the official supremacy of the Presidium.

Until the Constitution of 1936 was established, the Council (under a different name) had undergone a fluid variation of its powers comprising a shifting emphasis on its decree-making, legislative, and administrative medley of powers. In the practice of the Constitution of 1924, it acted legislatively, no less than administratively. Since 1936, referred to as an "organ of state administration" and with the insistence of Stalin that legislation be restricted to one body, the Soviet (though it is not), the Council is more limited in authority—to execution of the laws already made and giving the various Ministries powers and the Council as a whole certain authority.

We reserve a general evaluation of role until after the presentation of the constitutional powers of the Council have been enumerated. These are:

ART. 66. The Council of Ministers of the U.S.S.R. issues decisions and orders on the basis of and in pursuance of the laws in operation, and verifies their execution.

ART. 67. Decisions and orders of the Council of Ministers of the U.S.S.R. are binding throughout the territory of the U.S.S.R.

ART. 68. The Council of Ministers of the U.S.S.R.:

(a) Coordinates and directs the work of All-Union and Union-Republican Ministries of the U.S.S.R. and of other institutions under its jurisdiction;

(b) Adopts measures to carry out the national economic plan and the state budget and to strengthen the credit and monetary system;

(c) Adopts measures for the maintenance of public order, for the protection of the interests of the state and for the safeguarding of the rights of citizens;

(d) Exercises general direction in the sphere of relations with foreign states;

(e) Fixes the annual contingent of citizens to be called up for military service and directs the general organization of the Armed Forces of the country;

(f) Sets up, whenever necessary, special Committees and Central Administrations under the Council of Ministers of the U.S.S.R. for economic and cultural affairs and defense.

ART. 69. The Council of Ministers of the U.S.S.R. has the right, in respect to those branches of administration and economy which come within the jurisdiction of the U.S.S.R., to suspend decisions and orders of the Councils of Ministers of the Union Republics and to annul orders and instructions of the Ministers of the U.S.S.R.

It would be otiose in this text to sketch the departmental reorganizations from 1917 to 1954 suffered by the Ministries and the Council. They have been many, responsive to the rise and fall of State functions undertaken for the occasion, the development of socialist planning, and so on. They have been responsive also to the lessons of experience regarding the comparative merits of large or small departments, clientele departments, holding-company type departments, and so forth. It must suffice to say the Council has almost always been far larger than its closest counterpart in other countries. Thus, distinguishing the Ministries that have jurisdiction throughout the Union as All-Union Ministries, and those which operate through the appropriate ministries of the Union Republics as Union-Republic Ministries, one finds the numbers have evolved as follows:

Ministries

	1924	1936	1947	1949
All-Union	5	8	36	28
Union-Republic	5	10	23	20
Total	10	18	59	48

	1952	1953	1954 (as 1952)
All-Union	30	12	30
Union-Republic	21	13	21
Total	51	25	51

There is no point in burdening the text with the list of Ministries, but the footnote [4] lists them

[4] 1952: (Constitution of 1936, as amended): *All-Union Ministries:* Aircraft Industry; Automobile and Tractor Industry; Foreign Trade; Navy; Munitions; Geological Survey; Procurements; Machine and Instrument Construction Industry; Ferrous Metallurgy; Nonferrous Metallurgy; Merchant Marine; Oil Industry; Communication Equipment Industry; Railroads; River Fleet; Communications; Agricultural Machinery Building; Machine Tool Industry; Construction and Road Building; Machinery Industry; Machine Building Enterprise Construction; Heavy Industry Enterprise Construction; Shipbuilding Industry; Transport Machinery Industry; Labor Reserves; Heavy Machine Building Industry; Coal Mining Industry; Chemical Industry; Electric Equipment Industry; Power Plants; Paper and Wood Processing Industry. *Union Republic Ministries:* Internal Affairs; Armed Forces; Higher Education; State Control; State Security; Public Health; Foreign Affairs; Cinematography; Light Industry; Forestry; Lumber Industry; Meat and Dairy Industry; Food Industry; Building Materials Industry; Fishing Industry; Agriculture; State Farms; Trade; Finance; Cotton Growing; Justice.

1935 (for a few months); *All-Union Ministries:* Coal Industry; Oil Industry; Metallurgical Industry; Chemical Industry; Machine Building; Transport Machinery and Heavy Machine Building; Power Plants and Electrical In-as in (1) 1952, and then in (2) 1953, after Malenkov had succeeded Stalin as Chairman of the Council of Ministers (after which they reverted to much like 1952!) and had halved the size of the Council for increased efficiency. The list is interesting as illustrative of the scope of Soviet governmental activities, for most of the Ministries are nothing but the organizations of nationwide industrial and economic enterprises.

In addition, there are some administrative committees, such as the State Planning Committee, headed by a chairman, and the State Committee for Construction—and there were others of such devices at various times—and also interdepartmental *ad hoc* committee arrangements that are given some mention where they have special significance later—for example, the State Planning Committee (*Gosplan*).

The departments of the Ministers are responsible for controls and enterprise too complicated and detailed to allow of their amalgamation in two or more departments. For it would be difficult to find a man who could be responsible for the breadth as well as depth of the Soviet planned controls and management.

The various Ministers come and go; little is known about any but the top men, such as the Chairman and Deputy Chairmen of the Council.

The Chairman is important; he may be the first man in the Soviet and Communist Party hierarchy. The holders of this exalted position have been Lenin, Rykov, Molotov, and Stalin, in direct succession until Stalin's death in March 1953. Then Georgii Malenkov left the position of First Secretary of the party to become Chairman of the Council. He did not last long, for on February 8, 1955, he was ousted as the result of a shift in the policy and personality balance within the Communist Party leadership. He was demoted to being Minister of Electric Power Stations, and

the chairmanship was taken over by Nikolai Bulganin, until then Minister of Defense. The main speaker to the Supreme Soviet, then in session and utterly taken unawares by this and other changes, was Nikita Khrushchev, First Secretary of the party. The circumstances and significance of the change politically are dealt with *à propos* the leadership of the party (pp. 881–883).

The Deputy Chairmen are high-ranking personalities of the party, most of them members of the Party Presidium, formerly known as the Politburo.

Between the death of Stalin and as a consequence of personal changes made on and after February 8 through March 1955, the organization of the top of the Council of Ministers appears thus. There is (1) the Chairman. Then (2) there are five First Deputy Chairmen. Then comes level (3) consisting of eight Deputy Chairmen. This makes a body of fourteen in all. The Chairman and the five First Deputies are all members of the Party Presidium; so also is Malenkov still a member of the Presidium, though he was no longer anything but one of the eight Deputy Chairmen. (But in December 1955 he was promoted to be a First Deputy.) The Chairman and the five First Deputies form a special little nucleus, called the Presidium of the Council of Ministers. It developed out of an earlier informal "presidium" or "bureau," something like an "inner cabinet" in Western democracy.

This is evidently the dynamic, propelling, supervisory thought and coordinating organ among the still-large number of Ministries. They are interlaced personally with the Party Presidium, the Soviet's Presidium, and the Supreme Soviet itself, thus injecting a stream of tendency in them.

The main interest is the curious subordination to and division of functions between the Soviet Presidium and the Council of Ministers. The men at the head of the many Ministries are not "amateurs" in the sense that Ministers in the parliamentary governments are. They are professional and career experts, who have been trained for the specialized responsibilities of the specific departments and have risen by promotion in them. They have not been recruited from those who have worked in the "political" field, though some may, by character and aptitude, acquire a mastery of

dustry; Defense Industry; Construction; Transportation; Communications; Merchant Marine and Inland Shipping. *Union Republic Ministries:* Internal Affairs; Foreign Affairs; Defense; Domestic and Foreign Trade; Agriculture and Procurements; Culture; Light and Food Industry; Building Materials Industry; Lumber and Paper Industry; Finance; Public Health; Justice; State Control.

The nomenclature slightly differs from that of the U.S.S.R. Constitution in the *Appendix* because it has been compiled from other sources.

politics and tactics. Hence, the special significance of the Council of Ministers and of the Supreme Soviet to give general orientation and impulse of policy to the fifty or more segments into which the total scope of the Soviet government is divided. Moreover, the First Deputy Chairmen usually have *no departmental responsibilities,* though sometimes they may have coordinating or supervisory duties over several departments constituting a big segment of Soviet economy. They are left free to think and orient the expert heads of departments, and to make linkage with the Presidium and Party Presidium. They and the rest of the Council reach high place not through the Soviet but through the party hierarchy.

Darkness. The motivations and tactics of the men in the Presidium and the Council of Ministers is shrouded in mystery, for no rival parties demand and get answers from each other, for electoral appraisal, even on financial appropriations. The process of antiseptic and educative publicity is excluded. Nor can so-called "criticism and self-criticism" supply the deficiency (p. 887). When Malenkov was made to resign as Chairman of the Council, he made a statement telling of his deficiencies in government and policy (p. 883), but we do not know what he thought of those who forced this course on him. Candor in the Soviet Union is *ex gratia,* and for the government's benefit; in the democracies, candor is enforced, *ex principe* and for the people's benefit.

The Separation of Powers?

Soviet apologists seem under emotional compulsion to explain their behavior in terms of abnormal nobility, pouring contempt on Western democratic institutions. It is possible that Presidium and Ministers experience conscientious responsiveness to the Russian people. But we have seen enough to appreciate that the ever-operative power of discipline over them stemming from the people is lacking, obstructed by the leadership principle and party.

Vyshinsky's *Law of the Soviet Union,* the gospel for Soviet lawyers, has the gall to claim (because Ministers are required by the Constitution to answer questions within three days of their being put by Soviet Deputies):

The place of the Council of People's Commissars [Ministers] in the system of higher State organs, and the method of its formation, differ radically and in principle from the role of a cabinet of ministers and a council of ministers in bourgeois countries. The most recent development of the bourgeois state shows how the significance of legislative organs—of parliament and of legislation itself—is declining and the authority is ever more and more concentrated, being in the hands of the government with its vast bureaucratic machinery and ever-increasing responsibility.

He then supports this judgment by the well-known works of Ramsay Muir, Lord Hewart, Bryce, etc.

This is worse than caricature. Most criticisms of French and American government are usually to the effect that the legislatures are *too strong* as compared with the Executive. Vishinsky pretends that the legislatures have no power in the establishment of the Cabinets. He ignores the power of party. He sneers at "collective responsibility," saying the Cabinets and Prime Ministers have been made by capitalists.

This is the basest misinformation of the Russian people, not only about other countries but about their own government. Is such prejudice and closed mentality, like Lenin's, forever excluded from understanding?

Montesquieu and John Locke advanced the theory of the separation of powers (p. 289 and p. 32) to divide power among semi-autonomous agencies in order to preserve the liberty of persons and groups against the solid might of government. The Bolshevik official theory retorts that this was only a limitation of power by economic classes for the advantage of those economic classes. Locke and Montesquieu are not guilty of this charge. It is still true that the institution of checks and balances benefits all individuals no matter what class they belong to; for example, where the law courts order a man's release from detention by the Executive. Within classes men and women have lawsuits with each other; groups contend about policy and laws.

Vyshinsky asserts (p. 314):

Delimitation of functions, given out as separation of powers, is nothing more than the hegemony of the executive power over the legislative, a limitation of the rights of parliaments.

The description of any one day in the relationship of Executive and parliaments shows that this is nonsense. It is used to support the Soviet apologists' justification of all power to the Soviets *via* the one party. It is false to the Russian people to pretend that the President of the United States can appoint enough additional judges when the Supreme Court is hostile to his policy; that Parliaments are merely "chattering"; it is truer to say the Executive's teeth are chattering.

It will be noticed that those who have no doubts about human destiny and values, who believe they have all the truth about man once and for all time, abjure the separation of powers. Those who, like the makers of the American Constitution, and the lands that either gave birth to that policy or have learned from it, understand man's fallibility, especially in positions of power, have sought the separation, in order to force men to think well before they can take authoritative action, and until then keep it weak.

The reason is simple. The Bolsheviks wanted undivided power to destroy Czarism; and then "monolithic" (p. 856) power to dictate their form of socialism.

Paragraph 5 of the Party Program says:

The Soviet Government, guaranteeing to the working masses incomparably more opportunities to vote and recall their delegates in the most easy and accessible manner, than they possessed under bourgeois democracy and parliamentarianism, at the same time abolishes all the negative features of parliamentarianism, *especially the separation of legislative and executive powers* [*italics added*], the isolation of the representative institutions from the masses, etc.

What, then, does the Communist Party and its constituent assemblies put in place of the separation of powers? This, says Vyshinsky (p. 318):

From top to bottom the Soviet social order is penetrated by the single general spirit of the oneness of the authority of the toilers. . . . The unity of the authority of the toilers, embodied in the highest organs of that authority, expresses the democratic nature and the sovereignty of the Soviet people. . . .

In the U.S.S.R., authority has its beginning in the genuine popular sovereignty personified by the Supreme Soviet of the U.S.S.R. This is not incompatible with limiting the jurisdiction of authority as between organs. [NOTE! *Author*] Such limitation flows out of the extraordinarily complex functions of the Soviet state machinery governing both people and economy.

He regards the overthrow of the separation of powers by the bourgeoisie (which he alleges occurs, but against the evidence) as leading to "fascism." But the Soviet regime overthrows the separation on *principle*. Is it then fascist? He would say, "No! because" we "use our power for the benefit of the workers!" If the answer to this were, "How do you know it is for the benefit of the workers, since you never allow them the free opportunity to say Yes or No?", his answer could only be that the party knows what is best for the "workers and peasants and intelligentsia."

This is the vicious dictatorial circle again in evidence.

It would, then, seem idle for Vyshinsky to spend pages on trying to define the difference between "statute," "decree," and "statutory interpretation" —the terms we have met in the allocation of powers to the Soviet, the Presidium, and the Council of Ministers. Yet he does so. But we have seen that in actual fact, the Soviet has no power to will statutes; it is dominated by the Presidium, and behind it, the One Party.

There is no separation of powers, then, in the Soviet Union. For (1) the legislature is impotent; (2) the judiciary is under the control of the Presidium and the Ministry of the Interior and Procurator (elected by the Soviet, under controls); and (3) the "interpretation" of the laws and decrees, etc., which in other countries is vested in the judiciary, is, as we have seen, vested in the Presidium in the U.S.S.R.

IV. ELECTIONS AND THE RECALL

Is it the proletariat, including the peasantry, that dictates policy through elections, as the Constitution requires, or is it the party that dictates in the sheep's clothing of "democratic" elections?

Elections to the Supreme Soviet are regulated by

Chapter XI of the Constitution of 1936, and the Election Law of January 9, 1950 replacing that of October 11, 1945 (replacing the law of July 9, 1937, itself replacing earlier rules, to which some reference will be made later). These laws were passed by the Supreme Soviet with practically no discussion whatsoever!

Basically, the principles of election are these: universal; equal; direct; and secret ballot; at age eighteen for either sex as electors, at age twenty-three for candidates; regardless of race, nationality, sex, religion, educational qualifications, residence, social origins, property qualifications, or past activity. Excepted are insane persons and persons sentenced by a court of law to be deprived of electoral rights.

Some Preliminary Observations

Soviet theorists never fail to boast that their institutions are nobler and more progressively innovating than those of Western democracies. As to the electoral system they have made virtues of the following matters.

(1) **Age Eighteen.** It used to be vaunted that the age of eighteen was chosen because men and women are at work at that age, and that if Soviet workers could be trusted with factory and farm responsibilities then they could be trusted to participate in the government of their nation. Vyshinsky and others have charged the Western democracies with keeping up the age of voters, beginning at over eighteen, often at twenty-one, some countries at some times even going as high as twenty-five. The purpose is to cheat *Youth* of the vote, when youth has the passion and convictions for change.

(2) **Workers as Citizens.** The emphasis was put on the fact that voters were *workers* rather than merely citizens, for in democracies the voters could include rentiers, idlers, and exploiters of the labor of other people.

Up to 1936, indeed, certain categories of Soviet people were excluded from voting. They were persons employing hired labor for the purpose of deriving a profit therefrom; persons living on unearned income; private traders and middlemen in trade or commerce; ministers of religion by profession, and monks; employees of the Czarist

police, gendarmes, secret service, and members of the dynasty, etc. It was estimated that these exclusions disfranchised about 5 percent of the electorate. They were the logical result of the revolutionary convictions of the party, the impulse toward a class-free society plus rancor.

The obverse of this was the declaration in the Constitution of 1924: "All persons who earn their livelihood by engaging in productive, socially useful labor, and all persons who are engaged in household work . . ." are entitled to vote.

Stalin pointed out in his speech on the draft constitution, in answer to alleged critics who wanted the exclusions maintained, that the exploiting classes had been abolished. "If our propaganda work is conducted in a Bolshevik way, the people will not let hostile persons slip into . . ." them.

(3) **Active and Passive Franchise.** Up to 1945, the law allowed voting at eighteen and also candidature. Vyshinsky's boast (p. 616) of this fact follows a long hostile review of age qualifications in the democracies and fascist countries, to show that the age of eligibility is higher, in order to avoid "the most impulsive part of the population and the most dangerous to the bourgeoisie in terms of revolutionary moods." Alas for Vyshinsky's philosophy that at this age [18] he has by general admission already attained complete intellectual and political maturity"! For in the U.S.S.R. law of 1945 the age for candidates was raised to twenty-three. There is little wrong with this act. What is dubious is the defense of whatever the government decides to do, making tactics a matter of boasts of noble principle.

(4) **Nationality.** Another boast has suffered eclipse. The Constitution of 1924 contained a special note: "Persons who have not become citizens of the R.S.F.S. Republic shall enjoy the right to vote and be elected." This gave rise to paeans of wonder that the Soviet fatherland allowed the proletariat to vote, whatever their nationality! But Stalin's Constitution requires that the right to vote and be elected is restricted to "all citizens of the U.S.S.R."

(5) **No Disqualifications.** Vyshinsky rightly observes that the democracies have some restrictions on the right to vote. Here and there property qualifications, race qualifications, if not in law then in practice, educational qualifications, do to

some extent reduce the number of people who may vote. These limitations have practically disappeared. Even by 1914 they were not inconsiderable. Perhaps the chief present restriction is the actual disfranchisements of Negroes in the southern states of the U.S.A. By the time the Soviet revolution had occurred, sex disqualifications had been abolished in several countries, or have gone since that time.

The Conduct of Soviet Elections

The Voters' Lists. These are compiled by the executive committees of the various city, city ward, and rural Soviets for the general population, and by the military commanders in military units in active service. A month before elections, the lists are posted at the Soviet offices for public inspection, to permit challenge for errors, and the local officials are constrained to rectify errors promptly. Appeals by aggrieved persons are possible to the local courts.

Electoral Districts. The Supreme Soviet is a bicameral body. In the Soviet of the Union, the constituencies are delimited to allow of some 300,000 inhabitants in each. In the election of 1954, this produced 708 districts, and as many Deputies.

In the Soviet of Nationalities the constituencies are thus arranged: 25 in each Union Republic; 11 in each autonomous Republic; 5 in each autonomous province; and one in each national district. Each of these constituencies elects one Deputy. The number of constituencies and of Deputies is 639.

These electoral areas are large, as large as a Congressional district in the United States, and four or five times as large, counting population, and usually very much larger territorially, than British constituencies. Because the electorate numbers about 121,000,000 people and that vast areas are but sparsely populated, the mere work of driving the voters to the polling booths is fearful, let alone explaining intellectually why they should vote. It clearly necessitates a powerful and large propaganda organization. This is the Communist Party and the regime's State-owned and State-manipulated mass media of communication.

To assist electoral organization, precincts are formed of 1500 to 3000 inhabitants where the city or village unit has more than 2000 population. Smaller settlements than this are separate precincts up to a population of 2000, with some exceptions where the settlements are smaller or nomadic. Vessels at sea, military units, hospitals, and so forth are constituted electoral precincts. No voter is neglected, even passengers in long-distance trains on election day.

The Nomination of Candidates is carefully regulated in the election law. Who has the right to nominate? Not eight voters as in the British system; or simply the candidate as in the French.

> The right to nominate candidates is secured to public organizations and societies of the working people: Communist Party organizations, trade unions, cooperatives, youth organizations, and cultural societies—(Art. 141)

and (the Election Law adds):

> the right to nominate . . . is exercised by the central bodies . . . and their republic and local organizations and by general meetings of workers and employees at enterprises and institutions, in military units, peasants on collective farms, and state farm workers and employees at their places of work.

When these, one or two or more of them, in large or small conference, have somehow assembled in these large districts and chosen a candidate, they submit the nomination to the electoral commission already described. It must be accompanied by the minutes of the nominating meeting and signed by the members of its executive or presiding group, called, in the law, the presidium. Thus, there could be several nominations reaching the election commission, if there were no concerted action among the groupings mentioned in the law. The minutes of the organization must show the name, the time, the attendance at the meeting, and the personal description, name, age, etc. of the candidate.

In addition, the candidate must announce his agreement to run under the aegis of the organization. The registration of candidacies must be fulfilled not later than thirty days before the elections.

The electoral commissions must register these candidacies and publish them within twenty-five days of the election. All the so-registered candidates must be included on the ballot. Default by an electoral commission is appellable to the central electoral commission.

The electoral commissions print the ballots and send them out to the precincts not later than fifteen days before the elections. These are in the language of the population of the various districts. **The "Freedom" of Candidature of the Soviet Union.** How liberal the Soviet election law looks! No deposit of £150 must be laid down as in Britain; no 20,000 francs as in France. No primary laws have to be complied with as in the U.S.A. As this is a simple single-member-constituency system, there are no awkward and confusing lists, as in France, or worry about the justice of P.R. Nothing seems to stop a new party or organization from making a nomination by petition (not necessary under this system) supported by a substantial proportion of the votes cast at the last elections in the district. As Vyshinsky says (p. 695): "The Soviet voting system assures that every citizen possessing the right to vote may participate completely in elections." A mere change of domicile about the time of the election will not cause a loss of rights to vote, because a certificate from his local commission will secure the person of the right at the destination.

Vyshinsky looks upon the nominating method in the U.S.S.R. and glows with satisfaction over its noble rectitude:

The Stalin Constitution directs basic attention to the factual assurance of rights and not to their formal proclamation. The right to nominate candidates in the U.S.S.R. is a truly democratic right, guaranteeing in fact the attraction of the entire population of the country into this responsible political work. (p. 710)

Attraction! Let us see. For at the Geneva Conference of November 1955 M. Molotov recommended it for all Germany!

How an Election Is Managed. There is only one political party, the Communist Party. Within every economic, social, and cultural organization this party has its nucleus of party workers and officials, and at the directing head (for example, in the factories, the mines, the cooperatives, and

so on) party workers, "tried and tested" as Stalin was fond of saying, have been planted or have arrived by promotion, sometimes for technical efficiency and sometimes by intimidation.

The leading role in the nomination of candidates is played by the party, both openly as a unit and hardly less so in the management of the other organizations.

What is its attitude toward the choice of candidates? If we may judge from results, as well as from occasional observations made during election periods and the dicta of the party Congresses, it acts thus.

1. It makes quite sure about the overwhelming predominance of Communist Party members in the Soviet.

2. It attracts nonparty, but not antiregime, persons. For this it forms a so-called "bloc of Communists and non-Party people," the latter following the cause, however, of Lenin and Stalin, with no doubt about it.

3. It picks out those people who have done some spectacular action in the spirit of the Soviet regime. Thus, prize-winning teachers or a research worker or inventor or a brilliant example of the new technical intelligentsia or a physician or cultural leader, especially in the more backward areas. Of course, the well-known local and national leaders and military-political figures.

4. The candidates are chosen, as may be appreciated from the foregoing paragraph, to awaken the interest and the gratitude of the masses, in this, the first generation of elections, in the glorious achievements of the regime. Few devices for propagandizing and exciting the often apathetic masses anywhere are so dramatic and moving as the live person of a candidate. Whatever the merit of the dictators' desire to bring out 100 percent of the electorate, the desire is there, and the variety of candidates is adapted thereto.

Vyshinsky says:

The Soviet election system is a mighty instrument for further educating and organizing the masses politically, for further strengthening the bond between the state mechanism and the masses, and for improving the state mechanism and grubbing out the remnants of bureaucraticism.

He characterizes the results of the election of 1937 as demonstrating that "the entire population of the land of the Soviets are completely united in spirit."

In fact, the major pronouncements of the party, including its own description of itself in Statute 1 of the Statutes of the Communist Party (p. *lxvi*), so far as persuasion of the masses and a kind of dragooning into new paths desired by the regime, is given its intensest and most noisily dramatic theatricality at the elections.

BUT—THERE IS NEVER MORE THAN ONE NOMINEE ON THE BALLOT FOR EACH ELECTORAL DISTRICT. THERE ARE NO RIVAL CANDIDATES. The party has managed to pick the man or woman it wanted, if two or more candidates have been favored by different opinions in the party, sometimes about which among party rivals themselves would like to be a Deputy, the conflict is ironed out within the privacy of the local executive of the Communist Party, and especially among the full-time and paid party workers. As we have already seen, the role of the Deputy in the Supreme Soviet is in startling contrast to that of a member of a democratic representative assembly, for in the latter, the Deputy is a free wielder of a portion of the nation's sovereign power, and his own career depends on his use of his power in originality and force of character and independence, even if this operates only as a tension between him and his party caucus. A democratic member of a popular legislature is despised, sometimes openly, always secretly, if he is a Yes-man, or a toady. But the Soviet Deputy is in principle, and dares not otherwise be in practice, a Yes-man. The democratic representative is elected by his constituents, against real, bitter rivals, to be a creative member of the lawmaking body and a critic of the administration.

Stalin let the cat out of the bag in an interview given to Roy Howard of the Scripps-Howard newspapers before the elections of 1937. He said:

You think there will be no election contests. But there will be, and I foresee very lively election campaigns. There are not a few institutions in our country which work badly. Cases occur when this or that local government body fails to satisfy certain of the multifarious and growing requirements of the toilers of town and country. Have you built a good school or not? Have you improved housing conditions? Are you a bureaucrat? Have you helped to make our labor more effective and our lives more cultured?

He pretended to expect competition among party and nonparty organizations. But it has not materialized. The party bureaucracy has seen to that. Stalin's district always voted 100 percent of the register and 100 percent. Yes.

The Campaign and Voting. In spite of the nonexistence of rivals to their slate, the Communist Party and the various auxiliary organizations of the party, like the Young Communists, the *Komsomols* (perhaps because they are fighting against the requirements of their own standards) put in an immense effort to bring out the voters and to seem to offer them a reason why.

The day of the election, a Sunday, is known two months ahead. An immense agitation is set afoot and made to sweep the land. The leaders of the party and the Council of Ministers make speeches at selected chief cities and issue a manifesto. The press and the radio incessantly excite the population. Leaflets and posters are circulated in tens of millions of copies. Decorations and signs go up in all the streets and meeting places. The party organizes "agitators," at the ratio of 1 to every 20 or 30 voters in the cities and to every 10 or 12 households in the villages. Agitation points are opened in the wards. These *agitpunkts* (note the German term) are located in the nicest buildings—houses of culture, clubs, schools, and so on. They are obtained to further the cause. The expense of these seems to be on the party, though the State, through the election commission, furnishes a contribution. It is contrived to drive the workers in factory and farm—as a sideline—to greater than normal production at this time, as a kind of electoral donation to the nation. The trade unions, the cooperatives, the schoolteachers, all with a voice and standing, macrophone the message of the gods in Moscow. In 1954 there was quite a significant collective letter signed by Politbureau, Ministers, and outside party personages, renouncing *multiple* nominations, which their worshipers had made, though the law does not permit them.

The polls are open at 6 A.M. and close at midnight. The electorate votes for both of the Chambers of the Soviet at the same time. The ballot is secret. Before 1936 it was open—and deliberately so, to unmask "class enemies." The voter at the polling premises receives from the officer of the election commission a ballot, after his credentials have been checked. The paper contains the names of the candidates—no! in Russia, *the* candidate. The law requires the voter to cross out the names of those candidates he does *not* want to elect, leaving the one he wants untouched. This is an easy process in Soviet Russia; for as there is *only one name* he does not have to do anything with the ballot except to drop it into the box in full view of everybody. He can go into a private partition and use a pencil—the only place where a pencil is to be found. But if he does so, it means that he may cross out the name of the one candidate. If he does go into the partitioned-off place and come out with the ballot folded: he is under suspicion! The voter can spoil the ballot; or he can invalidate it by writing in Stalin or Malenkov or some other favorite, and some do, whether by design or ignorance.

The total effect of the two months of propaganda, and the knowledge of what happens to voters who go wrong, and the conditions in the polling booth (it must be remembered that the election commissions are dominated by the Communist Party), and the marching of whole staffs of factories and offices and schools carrying banners to the polling—is to produce a nearly 100-percent participation, and nearly a 100-percent vote favorable to the candidates of the party. Thus: Elections to Supreme Soviet, March 18, 1954:

Total electorate: 120,750,816. *Total voting:* 120,727,826, or 99.98 percent of the electorate.

For the Soviet of the Union: 99.79 percent of voters cast votes *for* the official candidates. A total of *247,897 votes were cast against* the "people's block of Communists and nonparty persons." Only 680 votes were declared invalid.

For the Soviet of Nationalities: 99.84 percent of voters cast ballots *for* the official candidates;

187,457 votes were cast against; 609 ballots were invalid.

This is, indeed, an awe-inspiring triumph!

In view of the foregoing true account of Soviet elections, it is of interest to note what Vyshinsky says about campaign expenses. He denigrates the raising of funds in democratic countries as undignified and as a deprival of the rights of the workers, who are too poor to pay for the concrete means of fighting a campaign. "In capitalist countries an election campaign takes on the character of a commercial enterprise" (p. 712). The richer win, he says. What does the Soviet Union do?

Every organization which has nominated a candidate registered with the district electoral commission, as well as every other citizen of the U.S.S.R., is guaranteed the right to campaign for that candidate without hindrance, at meetings, in the press and by other means in accordance with Article 125 of the Constitution.

Article 125 says that

civil rights are ensured by placing at the disposal of the working people and their organizations printing presses, stocks of paper, public buildings, the streets, communications facilities, and other material requisites for the exercise of these rights.

In other words, the State, through the local electoral commissions, pays the expenses. BUT NOT, BE IT NOTED, FOR RIVAL CANDIDATES TO THOSE HANDPICKED BY THE COMMUNIST PARTY WHICH HAS A CONSTITUTIONAL STATUS. THIS IS, INDEED, THE NEMESIS OF THE ABOLITION OF PRIVATE PROPERTY AND FREE MULTIPLE PARTIES.

The Recall

The Communist Party partly salves its conscience for the discarding of the separation of powers ("a negative limitation") by "freedom" of election. To this it adds the recall. Let us state the latter in the formal constitutional terms (Art. 142):

It is the duty of every deputy to report to his electors on his work and on the work of his Soviet of Working People's Deputies, and he may be recalled at any time upon the decision of a majority of the electors in the manner established by law.

This stipulation is applicable all the way down to the lowest level of Soviets.

It is the Communist Party's answer to what Lenin always inveighed against: "burocratism." He meant the assumption of authority and action by officials and the loss of power and activity by the masses (p. 826). It will not be forgotten that the recall is largely an American state government invention.

Yet the Soviet practice of recall again belies its magnificent profession. It was used in a special party drive after the elections of 1930–31, in the village and city soviets of Great Russia. It is estimated that in the years 1931–1934 about 37 percent and nearly 18 percent in the village and city Soviets, respectively, were recalled, for inactivity or inefficiency or abuse of power or deviation from the class line. Thereafter, the number recalled declined almost to negligibility, whether because Russia then entered into a period of stress and purge, so that the party was told to hold fast to the *status quo,* or because it was considered good to keep people in their elective office long enough for them to learn the job. Perhaps the better answer, corroborated by some who have fled Russia, is that as the party is in control of the nomination of candidates, a recall would be an admission that it could be in error! In the early days of the regime, the recall was used to eliminate Mensheviks and Social Revolutionaries, who, in Vishinsky's elegant terminology "had sneaked into the Soviets," and then, in the years specifically referred to, the party was effectuating Stalin's revolution from above in industrialization and collectivizing the farms, so the recall was used as a means of changing the Deputies and local officials for this heavy fighting purpose. Then, in Stalin's words (December 5, 1937), the electors did "throw to the dogs the Deputy who has turned aside from the path." *The* path, it will be remarked.

All the Other Soviets

Something like the electoral process we have described proceeds in the Union Republic Soviets and the Soviets of the lower tiers of government, and in off years. The Soviets have as their off-

spring—midwifed by the Communist Party, with many changelings—the various executive bodies—that is, the councils of ministers, and the city and village and regions, etc., executives, each with great bodies of career officials under them. Inside the areas of the Union Republics, autonomous republics, and so forth, set out in the Constitution are some 4400 district Soviets; 1440 city Soviets and 459 "borough" Soviets within some of the latter; 2300 settlement Soviets and nearly 75,000 village Soviets. The total number of Soviets in the entire nation is more than 83,200, and the number of Deputies is nearly 1,500,000.

These thousands of Soviets serve, of course, in the first instance, as the administrators of local public affairs in their neighborhoods: in education, health, agriculture, local industries, social insurance, public works, utilities, cultural activities and amenities, and the consequential budgetary provision. But, in the present point in the development of the polity, they are the vehicles of activating an interest and developing experience in government in a population which until 1918 hardly possessed these at all. The elected Deputies associate other citizens by co-option onto executive or advisory committees, and this increases the circle of active citizens. The proportion of the *nonparty* Deputies increases in the Soviets of lower rank [5]— necessarily, as the party could not possibly alone supply all the offices in government and industry, etc., with the numbers it now contains. Also, the party leadership does not increase the nonparty membership to a point where its Communist and separatist mentality would be diluted. In 1937 the two Chambers together had 23 percent nonparty members; in 1946, 19 percent; in 1954, 22 percent.

Furthermore, since the party has no open rivals in the elections, and its machinery of government is the vastest in the world today, or ever known to history of the world, it is essential to have a mobile, dynamic critical element in continuous operation. The local Soviets and the elections for them offer the opportunity of conducting and inducing criticism of officials, not at a high level of

[5]	*Soviet of Union*	*Soviet of Nationalities*
1937	19.0	28.27
1946	15.5	22.50
1954	20.0	24.00

policy but at points where the local Russians or other nationalities have experienced pain and inconvenience. This process is useful to the upper levels of the Communist Party hierarchy, since it can use the criticisms elicited to inspire *a sense of insecurity and anxiety* in party officials at the lower ranks and administrators in the Soviets, and so hold them to obsequiousness: a regular device of the Soviet regime. It makes them shake in their shoes.

Conclusions

The party perverts the electoral system for the Soviets into a mere public demonstration. The Presidium and the Council of Ministers exercise authority, downward. The election of and the meeting of the Soviets is nothing but an inciter of the population. In the long run, such agitation may produce a body of people who, educated as the professional and technical intelligentsia, may worry the men at the top by taking the elections seriously. The candidates themselves are already increasingly from this intelligentsia. Will they always remain stool pigeons? Meanwhile, the party, but 3 percent of the population, is in sole command. Insofar as the central and local Soviets enjoy any liberty, it is not that given in principle, but the accidental latitude of the practical administrative inability of the party to dominate totally.

What Does the Regime Get Out of the Electoral System? It gives the people the illusion that they are free. It makes them conscious of the oneness of the nation, driving toward consensus. It makes an extraordinary occasion for bringing home the purposes of the regime to millions who are still abysmally ignorant. It forces the actual abstainer, or potential dissenter, to ask himself, "Can I be right against 99.99999 percent of all the people?"

It is impossible to govern so large a land through career officials alone. Some collaboration must be secured from the clients of government. The point is most obvious in education, public health and everyday work. The strain of not having electoral collaboration is greater than the strain of manufacturing it.

More fundamentally, every man in government seeks a justification for his activity in life. Lenin sought his justification in countless books and speeches. Men in government want others to accept their actions as right. They cannot tolerate in their consciences or pride the application of naked and unjustified force. They feel the irrepressible desire to obtain either approval in the behavior of those they command or open approval. The dictators of the U.S.S.R. seek their justification in Marxism, even when they dilute and contaminate it. But this requires "democracy," and the "dictatorship of the proletariat" to develop the political consciousness of the masses. Even foreign nations who are condemned as "capitalist" form part of the public opinion within which the dictator prefers praise to condemnation—even if his own people were never reached by such disapproval from abroad.

The logical conclusion of the inner need for self-justification is elections. Yet that justification, having relieved its conscience so far, then takes a further step—the men at the top of the party know best what is right and wrong for "society." If they personified "society" as the living masses actually before them, their action might be different. But it is a future "society" that lures them on. Hence, the self-righteous manipulation of the elections.

The Opposition of Apathy and Inertia. The Communist Party, in line with this, must agitate by itself, whereas democratic countries *several* parties perform the work of awakening. It fights against no other party, but it fights against mass apathy and latent opposition. *Every single person is another potentially hostile person.* We have already spoken of the frightful popular *inertia* that is a legacy of 1000 years of absolute Czardom. The rulers fight the harder to be convincing, though they superficially ask first for obedience. If, then, elections are to be held at all, it needs a 100-percent participation and a 100-percent approval. One absentee, one rebuff, in a hundred million, is a reproach. It produces shame and questioning at home and disgrace abroad. Lenin did not believe in neutrals: "Those not *for* me are *against* me!" But this is far from making a democratic and responsible government out of those who have reached the highest levels of party—which means government—by fraud, guile, and murderous force or through pleasing those who did.

The rulers may soothe their consciences by the

illusion that though they have managed the elections, nevertheless no force in the world could make 100,000,000 go to the polls unless they really believed in the rulers.

"In my opinion," declared Stalin to Roy Howard, "our new Soviet Constitution will be the most democratic Constitution in the world." Clearly, it is not so yet. Hence, it is curious that apologists still embroider Stalin's declaration in December 1937: "Our universal elections will be carried out as the freest elections and the most democratic of any country in the world."

Federalism and Public Administration

The imperialists always looked at the East as the basis of their prosperity. Did the innumerable natural riches of the countries of the East . . . not serve as an "apple of discord" for the imperialists of all countries? This explains why the imperialists, warring in Europe and *talking* about the West, never ceased to think about China, India, Persia, Egypt, Morocco, as the real issue all the time concerned the East.

It is the task of Communism . . . to deprive world imperialism of its most "reliable" rear, of its "inexhaustible reserve."

—Stalin, November 1918

I. SOVIET FEDERALISM

The Union of Soviet Socialist Republics pretends to be a "multinational" State or federal union. In reality, it is a highly unitary State, tending strongly to obliterate the national features of its national minorities after having liquidated their independent government and economy. A truly "federal" union, or "multinational" State, as Stalin called it in 1936 (p. 792), perhaps as a semantic evasion, must exhibit at least two features. They are: (1) an admission in principle that the "national" units possessed sovereignty—that is, political independence of will—before associating and *still possess some afterward;* and (2) institutions imbedded in the Constitution to make the retained sovereignty a concrete reality. Neither of these conditions exists in the Soviet Union.

Federalism in the U.S.S.R. in Principle

When Lenin and then Stalin created a dictatorship of the proletariat, with an unpredictable tenure, they thereby subordinated federalism. They either misunderstood federalism or deceitfully abused it (p. 771). The rest followed in expedient subjection of the minorities.

Lenin's ideas of federalism went back to Switzerland where he and so many other Russian exiles lived (there he was much worried about the growing baldness of his red head), and to some remarks by Marx. Bolsheviks needed a *strong* dictatorship; hence Swiss federalism was an object of condescending contempt. As for Marx, he had reacted violently against the ideas of Fourier (p. 291) and against Proudhon's *Féderalisme Économique* which expressed a persistent trend in French socialist thought that favored the break-up of the Great State and of free association between small economic units. But, then, Marx was as violently attracted by the spontaneous rise of the Paris Commune in 1871. Could this spontaneity of many such communes, then federated, be the shape of the coming dictatorship of the proletariat? Lenin was finally (*State and Revolution,* 1917) violently opposed to the "federalists"; he rallied Communists with the invective that Proudhon and the Commune were "anarchist"—always the other extreme! Lenin had already (1903) rejected the representation in the party of a *Bund,* the all-Russian Jewish politico-trade union organization as a self-contained but freely associated unit.

Yet the popular word *federalism* was bandied

about by Communists, partly with romantic ideas, partly as political cunning. When the issue had to be settled in the Bolshevik State, it was settled as the issue of the separation of powers was: by the preference of centralized power over all local and rival bodies.

The often-referred to (and overpraised) small tract by Stalin on *Marxism and the National and Colonial Question,* inspired by Lenin, makes many gestures of acceptance to the elements of nationality—language, folkways, costume, and the rest. But it is adamant, even if tactfully so, that socialism overrides nationality. This implies that the institutions of socialism—or, for that matter, any other strict system of government flowing from an intolerant major premise of policy—modify or entirely annul the individuality of the states within the workers' federation.

The first impulse of the October Revolution was expressed in the declaration of Rights of the Peoples of Russia (November 2, 1917). It declared an end to the incitement of the peoples of Russia against each other that had been systematically practiced by the Czarist regime. This must be "replaced by one of voluntary and honest union of the peoples of Russia." It based itself on the right of the peoples of Russia to "free self-determination" —an inalienable right. It then set down the following principles: the equality and sovereignty of the peoples of Russia; the right of the people of Russia to free self-determination, to the point of separation and the formation of an independent state; the abolition of all forms of national and national-religious privilege and disability; the free development of the national minorities and ethnic groups inhabiting the territories of Russia.

No State had ever been so liberationist with its formerly held territories. Nor was the Soviet Union, thenceforward.

The Constitution of 1925 was called the "federated soviet republic," a State "based on a federation of the national Soviet Republics." It even permitted "secession."

By bitter war and guile and purges, the Soviet dictators, working through the Red Army and the Communist Party, subjugated the insurrectionary provinces and states by 1922, compelling them into the Union on the basis of treaties that left them no

sovereignty in fact. The Constitutions of 1924 and 1925 proclaimed a voluntary union, but destroyed the concrete guarantees of the minority nationalities' independence. The two vaunting quotations must be given, in order that they may be contrasted with the institutional reality.

The Constitution of 1925 says:

The will of the peoples constituting the Soviet republics which recently assembled in the Congresses of their respective Soviets and there unanimously decided to form the "union of Soviet Socialist Republics," is a reliable guarantee that this Union is a *voluntary association* [italics added] of peoples enjoying equal rights, that the right of each republic to secede from the Union is inviolate, that admission to the Union is open to all socialist Soviet republics whether now existing or hereafter to come into being, that the new federal state will prove itself a worthy pinnacle . . . to permit nations to dwell peacefully side by side in fraternal collaboration, that it will serve as a reliable bulwark against world capitalism and will make a new decisive step toward uniting the workers of the world into a World Socialist Soviet Republic.

This declaration was not entirely unsophisticated from an international point of view. The powers assigned to the government in Moscow were deadly from the point of view of the independence of the nationalities. For they covered almost everything, but above all they covered the whole of *economic and social existence.* According to Marx, however, these very "production relations" of the economy determine everything else, the law, the social mores, even the religion, hence, certainly federal freedom!

From 1925 to 1936 Moscow, always the home of Great-Russian chauvinism against the Russian minorities, ground down the nationalities and occasional revolts and resentments on their part, under the collectivization (even Eskimos were subjected to this!) and the uniform regimentation of the industrialization plans and the educational uniformities they demanded.

In 1936, speaking in praise of the new Constitution, Stalin said:

That [1924] was the period when relations between the peoples had not yet been properly adjusted, when survivals of distrust towards the Great Russians had not yet disappeared, and when centrifugal forces still continued to operate. Under those conditions it was necessary to establish fraternal cooperation among the peoples on the basis of economic, political, and military mutual aid by them in a single, federated, multinational state. The Soviet government could not but see the difficulties of this task. [Difficult only if one's will were set on rigid economic unity established in a short span of time, instead of by general persuasion over a long span of time—*Author's comment.*] It had before it the unsuccessful experiments of multinational states in bourgeois countries. It had before it the experiment of old Austria-Hungary, which ended in failure. Nevertheless, it resolved to make the experiment of creating a multinational state, for it knew that a multinational state which has arisen on the basis of socialism is bound to stand every and any test. [Notice this admission!—and faith—*Author's comment.*]

Since then fourteen years have elapsed. . . . This period has shown beyond a doubt that the experiment of forming a multinational state based on socialism has been completely successful.

The Communist Stereotype. Stalin then explained the success. There were no exploiting classes. These were the chief organizers of strife between nations. His regime had got rid of classes and therefore of exploitation which cultivated distrust and nationalist passions in other countries. Power in the hands of the working class is the foe of all enslavement and the vehicle of internationalism. (But we know that the workers did not have power in Russia, that this was concentrated in the hands of a dictatorship by the leadership of a party founded on tyranny and terror.) There had been mutual aid, economic and otherwise, between the nationalities for fourteen years. There was, "finally, the flourishing national culture of the peoples of the U.S.S.R., culture which is *national in form and socialist in content.*" Hence, all these factors had caused mutual distrust to disappear, friendship to develop, and thus "real fraternal cooperation among the peoples has been established within the system of a single federated state!"

The guile of this explanation is obvious: it is still compatible with the disemboweling of the political independence of the nationalities. Only minor picturesqueness was, in fact, left to the minorities. Their independent being was destroyed by the party's onslaught on religion, on the national diversity of the economy, on political opposition anywhere, its insistence on Russian historical teaching that elevated the culture of Great Russia, the nonexistence of national armies and independent diplomatic status and representation, a single currency and banking system, and one Red Army subject to the political indoctrination that we have already noticed.

The Fake of "Secession." One other pretension must be unmasked, in order that ignoring it may not leave the student open to the accusation of gullibility. Always since 1917 the declarations and constitutions have proclaimed the right of the nationalities to secede. But they have never been allowed even to murmur, much less secede. Actually in his speech on the draft constitution, Stalin pokes fun at the right of the smaller units to secede—"they would fall prey to the imperialist powers." *A fortiori* with the bigger national groupings. It will be recalled that the Criminal Code makes it treason to advocate the dismemberment of the Soviet Union! The matter is summed up by Stalin himself, vaunted "liberator" of nationalities:

We are *for* the separation of India, Arabia, Egypt, Morocco and other colonies from the Entente, for the separation in this case means the freeing of these suppressed countries from imperialism, the weakening of imperialist positions, the strengthening of revolutionary positions. We are *against* the separation of the border territories from Russia, because separation means in this case imperialist slavery for the border territory, the weakening of the revolutionary capabilities of Russia, the strengthening of imperialist positions. . . . The question of separation is to be decided according to concrete international conditions, dependent on the interests of the revolution.

Revolution means the domestic and international needs of the Communist Party of the Soviet Union.

It is admitted, of course, that the national minorities were not, when the Soviet took over, "sovereign." They had been subjected, crushed, assimilated partly, Russified, by generations of brutal Czarist rule. But the Soviet was vaunting that its policy would be more magnanimous and liberating than the Czar's.

The Institutions of Soviet Federalism

The guarantees of continued independence, up to a point, in a federal association for the previous sovereign units should lie in the following institutions:

(1) Control over the amendment of the Constitution, called in the literature of federalism the *"kompetenz-kompetenz,"* namely, the competence to vary the competence of the central government and the units;

(2) The assignment of powers to the center as compared with the residue left to the Republics, etc.;

(3) The special representation of the Republics, etc., in a legislative assembly chamber of their own, with veto and deadlock powers over the chamber representing the nation as a unity;

(4) The existence of a court that stands above the Union and the Republics to decide disputes between them regarding their respective rights;

(5) The existence of two independent sets of law courts, one for the Union, the other for the Republics;

(6) Independent financial resources;

(7) Exclusive control of foreign relations by the Union;

(8) Independent political party organization in the several republics.

The Situation of These Guarantees in the Soviet Union

(1) **Constitutional Amendment.** This is vested in the Supreme Soviet, which, by a two-thirds majority in each of its chambers, may adopt an amendment.

If the Soviet of the Nationalities were truly founded in free political organizations of the states—and if, as in the United States, the republics were guaranteed an *equality of representation* unchangeable except with their individual consent—then there still might be some warrant of

independence in the republics. We know that this does not exist.

What is of more importance in the constitutional guarantee over the amending power to safeguard minority independence is that the revisions by the Soviet be ratified by the people. In the United States, in Australia, in Switzerland, amendments must not only be ratified by popular referendum (the Soviet government and the Communist Party could easily supply this) but *a majority of the states* is required to ratify, in addition to a mass majority. In the United States, three quarters of the state legislatures or special conventions must ratify. It is a difficult process. The smallest state in the Union may obstruct a change in the U.S. federal powers, against the will of the whole nation, by standing in with any twelve other states out of the forty-eight who object. Not so in the U.S.S.R.

(2) **Assignment of Powers to the Center.** In the U.S.S.R. the Constitution leaves the republics and autonomous regions, etc., virtually no independent sphere of authority at all. The powers assigned to the Union are enumerated in Article 14 (p. *lxvi*). Everything that makes for the power of a State over the life of a community is included.

We make merely a few observations on this assignment of powers.

The national economic plan is paramount over the economy of every area. It is impossible for the areas to develop a spontaneously desired economy, even if they had such a wish. Classes (j) to (q) of the powers permit the fixing of an intensively uniform economic system of production, distribution, commerce, and finance on every acre of all the nationalities, down to the last camel in Kazakhstan and the last gallon of petrol in Baku.

The U.S. Supreme Court has said, in a case involving economic power over the several states, "a power over a man's income is a power over a man's will." In the U.S.S.R. the distribution of powers is so absolutely to the advantage of the center, and the socialistic economy is so rigid, that a forcible control is exercised by economic decisions over all other aspects of the area's life. It carries with it, for example, trade-union freedom, social-insurance benefits, leisure time.

Now, it is true that in all other federal systems in the world, the trend in the past fifty years has been toward economic centralization. This is chiefly due to the advantages of a nationwide division of labor, which then requires a nationwide coordination of the economic activities so divided. Examples are, the regulation of one labor market over the entire economy, and therewith a uniform law on social insurance, unemployment assistance, unemployment placement services, and so on; and the need to unify all communications.

Yet, this integration has proceeded by gradual persuasion, and there is still, *by resolute principle,* substantial autonomy of policy, law, and administration remaining with the states. They have through the federal institutions and their own state political party strengths, helped to decide how much power they shall concede for what reasons, and on what principles of advantage and disadvantage. Authority has proceeded upward, not despotically downward. The final consequence has been to keep the national legislature and administration sensitively responsive to the "grass roots" in industry, commerce, and agriculture.

The Soviet rulers have deserted their own principle of federalism, if they ever genuinely meant it, for that of unitarism. Soviet federalism remains only the federalism of accident—that is, whatever independence of the economic operations and life of the localities exists is not because Moscow wants and recognizes that it ought to be, but because Moscow's administrative incompetence and the human failures of the Communist Party officials and membership (as we have seen) result in unwanted loopholes in centralization. What is irksome is the guilefully noble profession of freedom contrasted with the gruesome facts of centralized despotism.

It will be noticed that even where the Union is not assigned actual powers of lawmaking—as in (q) to (t) it is master of the "principles" of land tenure, etc., of education and public health, of labor legislation, and in (w) concerning marriage and the family.

The student is advised to sum up in his own mind which of the powers in the list assigned to the Union in Russia still remain in America with the several states. It is not difficult, and it is revealing.

Foreign Relations. In the Constitution of 1936, as originally drawn, Article 14, clause (a) ran, simply:

> Representation of the U.S.S.R. in international relations, conclusion, ratification, and denunciation of treaties . . . with other states.

An amendment in February 1944 added the words—"establishment of general procedure governing the relations of Union Republics with foreign states." This passage was included to preserve the authority of the Union because some *apparent* concessions had been made to the Union Republics that looked like autonomy in foreign affairs and maintenance of their own armies.

Two new articles had been added to the Constitution in February 1944 that seemed of startling moment to foreign observers. They are Articles 18a and 18b, respectively. They read:

> Each Union Republic has the right to enter into direct relations with foreign states and to conclude agreements and exchange representatives with them.

> Each Union Republic has its own Republican military formations. [And Article 60(f) gave the Union Republic Soviet the power of determining the organization of these formations.]

The whole world was set agog by these "gifts" of independence. Some learned observers speculated that Moscow wished to recover the shaken allegiance of such areas as the Ukraine and White Russia, as World War II approached its end. Others thought it a bait for potential satellites among states on Russia's border. Moscow certainly used the gambit at the Yalta Conference to claim representation of sixteen sovereign States on UN! She actually obtained one each, seat and vote, for the two areas mentioned! Otherwise absolute authority over foreign policy and military forces remained with Moscow. When the British Government (probably in merry mood) proposed diplomatic relations with the Ukraine in 1947, the rejection was icy.

In this respect one other fact is important. In Article 22 of the Constitution appear the listing of the "autonomous republics that lie within the Union Republic of the Russian S.F.S." Originally it included some that during World War II cooperated with the German armies which invaded that territory. As soon as it was physically able, the government of the Soviet Union demonstrated its rigorous fists. The Volga-German, the Kalmyk, the Checheno-Ingush, and the Crimean Autonomous Republics were dismantled as autonomous areas (decrees of 1941 to 1945). The first-named were of German descent: *en masse* they were transported beyond the Urals before they might cause trouble behind the Russian lines. The other two minorities were cruelly hauled away to Siberia.[1]

(3) Special Representation in the Soviet of Nationalities. Such a representation and the equal (and sometimes, as in the United States) superior power of the "federal" chamber over the numerically representative one constitutes the guarantee that the states as states will not be swamped by majorities. In the United States the status of the Senate constituted the "great compromise" making union possible.

We have already seen that the Supreme Soviet is bicameral. The representation of the territorial units has already been stated. It provides a different representation for the Republics, regions, areas, etc., than does the numerical representation of 1 Deputy per 300,000 inhabitants. Merely to observe that each Union Republic regardless of population has 25 Deputies reveals the respect paid to each such Republic, for their population is extraordinarily diverse. The figures when consulted reveal this startlingly, running down from Great Russia with over 110,000,000 people, to the smallest, Karelo-Finland, with about 500,000 people; while in between range the Ukraine with some 42,000,000, White Russia with something over 10,000,000, and several with 6,000,000, some between 3,000,000 and 4,000,000, others under 2,000,000. There is no point in pursuing the designed special representation down through the other lesser areas within the Republics. They merely reinforce the principle.

Stalin, in his speech on the Constitution of 1936, explained the need for the bicameral arrangement,

especially as some critics had (allegedly, for one never knows whether such statements are merely fake or genuine) suggested *a unicameral system, as in all the other Soviets* from each Union Republic downward. He said:

> In addition to their *general* interests, the Nationalities of the U.S.S.R. have *also their own particular, specific* [italics added] interests connected with their national characteristics. Is it possible to disregard these specific interests? No, it is not possible. Is there necessity for a special supreme organ which would reflect precisely these specific interests? Yes, absolutely. There can be no doubt that it would be impossible without such an organ to administer such a multinational state as the U.S.S.R. Such an organ is the Second Chamber—the Soviet of Nationalities of the U.S.S.R.

All "National" Parties Crushed. This is a sound declaration. But what has been the practice? There are *no* free political parties in the Republics or autonomous and national regions. They have all been crushed. Hence it is impossible for the "nationality" of the areas to break through the Iron Blanket of the Communist Party with all the instruments of terror at its disposal. Again and again, the Ukraine, Georgia, and Kazakhstan—mere examples—have been subject to the bitterest wholesale purges and "brain washings."

In the United States and other federations the political parties in the various states build up from the grass roots—counties, provinces, etc., cantons—federally, by voluntary association. Such locally rooted parties determine Washington's policy for the Union, create the platform and find the candidates by free debate, contention, and pressure and counterpressure using their free power. The national parties, Republican and Democratic, are actually disintegrated internally by regional differences of ideas, culture, economic interest, and moral values.

In Russia, instructively, the elections for both Houses occur on the same day. The nominating process is identical. The two Chambers have the same length of office—four years. There is no process of partial reelection as in the U.S. Senate.

Nor is that all. We have seen that the Soviet Presidium is in authority while the Supreme Soviet is *not* in session, for about 360 days out of

---

[1] We now have an account of this brutality given by former Lt. Col. G. S. Burlitski of the M.V.D., who escaped from Russia, though he held such high and privileged office. He testified before the U.S. Congressional Committee on Communist Aggression. See *The New York Times*, June 29, 1954.

365 per year. The Presidium is made up of the Union Republic Leaders: but these are the high officials of the Communist Party in each of their areas.

Furthermore (though this is practically academic), the Presidium has the power to dissolve both Chambers and call for new elections if the two Chambers get into a legislative deadlock.

In the United States free parties in the states enhance the constitutional guarantees of the "indestructibility" of the states. The states even enact the laws of election for Congress as *they* like. In the U.S.S.R. the single party renders such constitutional guarantees nugatory. Of course, it is not denied that since the territory of the U.S.S.R. is far flung (much further flung than the U.S.A.), regional diversities must be taken notice of. It is no use that the Plan requires the culture of roses be undertaken in Irkutsk. But this is a different consideration from the safeguard of rights of nationality and region-hood by political institutions.

(4) Determination of the Distribution of Powers in Case of Dispute. In all federations, a judicial body or a quasi-judicial body settles any dispute between Union and states or provinces or cantons. The purpose is to safeguard the weaker of the two disputants, and to do this by removing the jurisdiction from a political elective body that has a prejudiced interest in the judgment. The most notable instance of this is the Supreme Court of the United States; it has presided over the most momentous of such controversies. We have seen similar powers exercised in Germany by the Constitutional Court (p. 694).

The U.S.S.R. Constitution leaves nothing to chance. Let us consider the assemblage of articles that bear on this point: Article 14 gives the U.S.S.R. jurisdiction thus:

(d) Control over the observance of the Constitution of the U.S.S.R. and ensuring conformity of the Constitutions of the Union Republics with the Constitution of the U.S.S.R.

Then Article 20 says:

In the event of divergence between a law of a Union Republic and a law of the Union, the Union law prevails.

No law court is vested with judicial review of the Constitution. Instead, the Supreme Soviet Presidium is assigned the power [Art. 49(c)]— gives "interpretations of the laws of the U.S.S.R. in operation." And in section (f) "Amends decisions and orders of . . . the Council of Ministers of the Union Republics if they do not conform to law."

This is decisive. But two other articles are relevant.

Article 15:

The sovereignty of the Union Republics is limited only in the spheres defined in Article 14 of the Constitution of the U.S.S.R. Outside of these spheres, each Union Republic exercises state authority independently. The U.S.S.R. protects the sovereign rights of the Union Republics.

But the "protection" is through the Presidium, not through a court with "independent" justices.

Article 16:

Each Union Republic has its own Constitution, which takes account of the specific features of the Republic and is drawn up *in full conformity with the Constitution of the U.S.S.R.* [Italics added].

The last phrase includes the "leading role of the Communist Party."

(5) One System of Law Courts, Not Two. In the several states of the U.S.A., two sets of law courts and of judges operate. The codes of laws differ substantially from state to state, in accordance with state legislation and customary or common law. The courts in their procedure are molded locally, with certain basic exceptions regulated by the Bill of Rights in the federal Constitution. The judges are appointed by the state governor and legislatures. All this *without interference by the Union.* On the other hand, the Union has its law courts and judges, its district courts and appeal courts, and the Supreme Court, with their own procedure, administering federal law and the Constitution. Appeals from state courts go to the federal courts where a federal constitutional right or obligation has arisen—on appeal. Similarly, in German federalism (p. 698).

In the U.S.S.R. the law courts are more closely integrated. The Procurator of the U.S.S.R. appointed by the Supreme Soviet appoints the pro-curators of the Republics, territories and provinces, and confirms those of the cities and rural areas. All these bear responsibility to him for their activity, and none to the local organs. One party "elects" all the levels of judges to apply one body of laws (p. 843ff.).

(6) Financial Resources. The surest guarantee of day-by-day federal diversity is the possession of independent power to raise taxation with tax sources either unlimited or trivially limited only, and the power of formulating expenditures without external restriction. This freedom obtains in the United States absolutely, except that U.S. Government instrumentalities may not be taxed, lest they thereby cause a reduction of the power granted to the U.S. Government by the Constitution.

But in the U.S.S.R. the one economic plan dominates all the economies. Article 14 (k) leaves no doubt about taxes and revenues—these are entirely under the jurisdiction of the U.S.S.R., for itself, for the Union Republics, and for all the lesser territorial units of government. There is only one consolidated budget. We have also seen that there is no actual power in the Soviet of Nationalities (like that of the U.S. Senate) to differ from the Soviet of the Union about the budget, on behalf of the national areas as such.

(7) Administrative Power. Administrative power throughout the Union and indirect power through the Union Republics for some functions and others respectively is enacted by the Constitution and the laws.

The All-Union Ministries direct the branch of governmental administration entrusted to them throughout all the territory of the U.S.S.R. directly or through their deconcentrated regional offices and officials. The Union-Republic Ministries—which are Ministries of the Soviet Union government—operate by devolving authority and functions in their own discretion to the corresponding Ministries of the Union Republic governments. They are bound to the scope of action, the number of activities, and so on, as set down by the Presidium of the Supreme Soviet.

These Ministries do *not* reveal that the heavy force of administrative centralization is in the hands of the Council of Ministers in Moscow, because they seem to decentralize. But the devolution of immediate administration to the Union Republic Ministries is not a gift of freedom: it is but a convenience of administrative deconcentration for Moscow. The Council of Ministers there has its hands on all the strings, including the continual changing of the scope of local activity and its methods. The authority is Moscow's. Responsibility does not stop with the Union Republic, but its Council of Ministers owes responsibility to Moscow. One ludicrous result of this pseudo-decentralization is to locate the Ministry of Foreign Affairs in the list of Union-Republic Ministries, to support the specious granting of freedom of diplomatic action to the Republics in February 1944. This was a pure fiction.

(8) Exit "Nationalism." There are, of course, no independent political parties in the various Unions Republic, etc. The secretaries (the full-time officials) are everywhere planted by the Central Committee of the party, sometimes from conniving nationals, sometimes from among the Great Russians. "Bourgeois-national" ideas, literature, party composition, historical teaching, and so on are stigmatized by the local party. This has been very evident in the Ukraine, Georgia, Kazakhstan, and other areas (as may be appreciated savorously from their reports produced for the Nineteenth Party Congress in October 1952).[2]

It is *Marx "uber alles"*: the "socialist" policies of Moscow over everything. Great Russian membership of the party and representation at congresses and in the Central Committee are more than in proportion to the preponderance of population of the area in the Union, which is great enough already. The purges contributed deliberately to the eradication of the "national"-minded in the areas mentioned, and further in White Russia, and Armenia, and Turkestan and so on. U.S. Supreme Court Justice W. O. Douglas declares (December 1955), from first-hand observation that in Central Asia, with 16,000,000 Turkmen, there is segregation in the schools, special courts for Russians, economic and cultural discrimination, ruthless suppression of all nationalism and liberty. In

---

[2] See *Current Soviet Policies,* translating these (Praeger, New York, 1953).

the Russian-built arsenals there, the Russians get 30 percent more salary than the Asians for the same jobs.

The observation of Zinoviev, made in September 1920, to the Leningrad Soviet is achieved: "We take these products [petroleum and cotton from Azerbaijan and Turkestan, respectively] which are necessary for us, not as the former exploiters, but as older brothers bearing the torch of civilization." The policy announced in the 1920's known as *korenizatsia,* from *koren,* a root (in other words, "grass-rootsism"), has been overcome by the party's needs and policy. By the time the smaller nationalities are able to produce their own party leaders, the educational system and the economic system and All-Union oppression will have produced party members who stand outside the grass roots.

Crushing, incessant intervention by the Soviet Government in the development of science, in the conformity to its policy in music, literature, painting, and its heresy-hunting in these fields and historical writing, leaves nothing to the minorities but their different language, and even that is being undermined. About the last vestige of cultural difference, apart from the weather and local products to eat and wear, is language. Stalin, the former Commissar of Nationalities, leaped to the defense of this and in two essays on *Linguistics* (actually proving nothing) asserted that language was not one of those aspects of culture that was determined by the economic processes of production, but was a common factor among classes. It is not un-Marxian for a Georgian to order shishkebab in Georgian or a Kalmyk, to continue to make love in Kalmyk. A joke is current in Russia that Great Russia has left the nationalities their language, but abolished their nationality. The schools everywhere are forced to teach the predominance of Great Russian culture.[3]

Thus, the totalitarian economy; the uniformity of political and administrative institutions; the monopoly of the Communist Party and the over-representation of its Great-Russian membership; the *under*representation of the higher educational schools in the lands of the minorities; Moscow's domination of culture, art, press, and radio; the centralization of the police and the armed troops; the suppression of freedom of worship—these make the policy of Russification wider, deeper, more ferocious, and more efficient than under the Czars.

II. PUBLIC ADMINISTRATION

It is not possible to discover how many officials serve the central and local departments, as the census of 1939 (the last) does not discriminate, and the officials are inextricably blinded with the managers and directors of what, in other lands, would be business firms.[4]

Until 1934 the departments were run by boards and not single Ministers. It made responsibility inprecise, but was used because Communist officials individually lacked experience and to keep a check on Czarist residues. Stalin, following Lenin's counsel (December 1918), set up a single Minister as head of a department, but put advisory councils of 40 to 70 officials in operation with him. Then in 1926 the former boards were reintroduced, leaving a hierarchy of Minister, administrative board, and advisory board. The administrative board consists of from four to seven Deputy Ministers and operates in all matters of policy, fulfillment, personnel, inspection of local offices, development of administrative procedure. If the Minister disagrees with the board, he may act alone. In any case, he takes responsibility. Either may appeal to the Council of Ministers and (!) the Central Committee of the party. The board does foster thought and interdivisionalism, and it integrates the vast num-

[3] Cf. G. S. Counts and N. P. Lodge, *"I Want to Be Like Stalin,"* New York, 1947, p. 58ff. This is from the approved textbook in teacher training of the Soviet Union, Chapter four, "Our Beloved Motherland."

[4] Britain has some 500,000 nonindustrial civil servants, less also, postal carriers. The U.S.S.R. has four times the population. Her equivalent officials would then be about 2,000,000. *But* the U.S.S.R. also multiplies its direct State administration of the national activities by some five times more than Britain. This would give a body of officials at the top of about 10,000,000. It could be a third of this with good overhead planning; it is probably more, since the administration is raw and crude.

Even the figures in N. De Witt's, *Soviet Professional Manpower* (Washington, 1955) do not help us, owing to the muddle and gaps in Soviet official statistics. There the *total of all* professional and semi-professional manpower for 1954 is given (p. 347) as about 6,350,000.

ber of sections in these headships of great nation-wide monopolies; it is a school of administration in a very, very primitive nation, administratively speaking. Lenin inveighed against the incompetence and the lack of culture (equals elementary education and business habits) in his very last article, called "Better Fewer, but Better." Stalin was distracted by the problem of enforcement and fulfillment (p. 887). His Commissariat of Inspection had proved inadequate. In May 1934 he again bitterly declared, "we used to say, 'technique decides everything,' but now it must be replaced by a new slogan, 'cadres decide everything' . . . if we do not have cadres we shall be lame on both legs."

Civil Service

Recruitment of Officials. Each department supplies itself with Civil Service recruits. No central organ, such as Civil Service Commissions, selects and appoints. The head of the department normally decrees each appointment. This fosters departmentalism and permits a lowering of the standards set up by the Soviet government for applicants as departmental need and caprice decides.

The technical nature of the jobs determines the education required for appointment. The "administrative" appointments are filled by those with university training in law or "engineering" and business administration. The other positions are filled from the universities and institutes and high schools that give specialized training. There are no competitive examinations but only a qualifying test, if that, and reliance on the grades and reports of the candidate's teachers. Students who desire to enter branches of the service of their choice ask for admission into the appropriate schools. When this is given and a job arises at the end of the course, the student must take it and stay for at least three years, subject to criminal prosecution, unless he is excused.

The State Commission on Civil Service. This body formulates organizational structure and procedure for the departments of all kinds; establishes job classifications and specifications for all officials; and controls, in detail, the fulfillment of its regulations. For no agency can effect any change in its own structure without the Commission's approval. It fixes staff ceilings and has powers to streamline numbers. But it has no power over appointments.

Training. The departments, All-Union and Union-Republic, have units entrusted with orienting officials in their public responsibilities; they are supposed to inspect their work and see that they get proper instruction at the lower levels of the hierarchy. This has been declared to be a better procedure than dismissal forthwith for inefficiency. Instructors are appointed to these units. The departments and local Soviets sponsor, subsidize, and conduct after-recruitment seminars, lectures, courses, and so on at the nearby schools of different levels, at correspondence schools, and within the various agencies themselves. This activity seems to be very zealous and is perhaps really serious, though there are complaints of superficiality.

Incentives and Controls. It goes without saying that the ideological element in the education and continued cultivation of Soviet officials is heavily and constantly stressed. The party sees to this. Salaries are in the top three categories with banking and construction, on the whole higher than the comparable jobs outside, and within the Service are differentiated by premiums and bonuses as well as salary differentiation. The whole Service has, rather like the traditional Prussian Service and the Czarist, insignia, ranks, titles, and *uniforms*—a most remarkable spectacle all over Russia. These distinguish officials of the State from other workers and promote the cult of and obedience to the "intelligentsia" and "experts." There are also many Service awards, such as Hero of the U.S.S.R., the Order of Lenin, the Order of the Red Banner, and lesser medals. These entitle to privileges in housing, free transport, vacations, theaters, goods in short supply.

Ministry of Finance and Ministry of State Control

The Ministry of Finance controls public administration by "control through the ruble"—in other words, branches of the Ministry invigilate the departments (like the U.S. Bureau of the Budget or the Treasury in Britain) to lower costs on *matériel* and immoderate expenditure on salaries. For this purpose all organs of Soviet administration must register their staff lists with the Ministry; these have been authorized by the Council of Ministers and the Ministry of State Control. A similar procedure applies to the Republics, territories, etc., and their staffs and Ministries of Finance or equivalents, all the way down to the cities' organs. The Ministry checks the authorized establishment and budget against the facts, and for this it has special inspectors in all finance departments to the level of the *raions*.

There is a branch of the Ministry of State Control in each of the Union Republics—rather like a resurrection of the Commissariat of Inspection and the party's Control Commission (p. 876) that together sought since the early 1920's to secure fulfillment and good practices in administration. It was set up in 1940. It has three functions:

(1) To exercise control over the production, economic and financial activities of the state, cooperative and communal organizations, enterprises and institutions and to exercise strictest check on the records and handling and expenditure of funds and supplies in their possession.

(2) To check the fulfillment of decrees and orders of the U.S.S.R. government.

(3) To submit to the U.S.S.R. government reports on fulfillment of the state budget.

Although the protection of Soviet property and the control of production appear to be the major tasks of the Ministry of State Control, an important aspect of its work—and more pertinent to administration in the traditional sense of the term—is *practically and effectively to supervise the performance of all functions of the state.*

To perform its role, it has been granted broad rights, in particular the right to carry out audits and checks in the Ministries and departments, Soviet, cooperative, and public organizations. The inspectors of the Ministry of State Control are authorized to demand and obtain the necessary documents, data of official records, and other material showing the operations of the controlled agency or institution. They also may issue to officials of the Ministries, departments, enterprises, organizations, and institutions orders that they

submit explanations and information on questions relating to the check-ups and audits. In turn, the inspectors are bound to study those documents "in accord with the plans for audits and checks" and to report on their findings to the organ by which they had been authorized.

Whenever specific violations and failure to carry out decrees and orders of the government are discovered, the Ministry of State Control is entitled to issue commands to the respective enterprises and institutions, by way of the reports sent to the Ministers and directors of central institutions, orders from the Ministry of State Control, and in special letters.

It may take disciplinary action against officials for negligence, carelessness, wastefulness, lying to State Control agencies, leading to fines, reprimands, demotions by the Deputy Minister, or dismissal with permission of the Council of Ministers. It has devised its own internal divisional organization to match the departments, each with a Controller General, and each of these has controllers inside all important enterprises of all kinds.

The M.V.D.

The M.V.D. (p. 885), distinct from these controls, has its own agents in every department and office. There is a special section in each department staffed by the M.V.D., keeping careful watch on all officials. It is assisted by the *seksots* (p. 886), private informers. They may make arrests and the M.V.D.'s special boards will hear and sentence. This can hardly inspire inventive enterprise, though it may have a short-run bludgeoning effect on obedience and limitation of sabotage.

The party (p. 867) mans the top offices, and through its various groups of members keep a control over all that goes on. Required by Party Statutes (p. *lxxii*) to do this, top party leaders also keep up a constant outcry against the undue interference by party members in the conduct of administration. The dilemma is obvious: the party ascribes responsibility and then complains about the use of authority. In the local Soviet executive departments party watchfulness takes the form of visits by the Soviet Deputies; regional executive committees may form "revision brigades" for periodical inspection of the work and "fulfillment" of the bodies at the lower area levels, and they are experts themselves or go accompanied by them.

Local Administration

The executive committees (and their departments) of the Soviets of Working People's Deputies are the organs of state administration in the territories (*krai*), regions (*oblast'*), autonomous regions, national and administrative areas (*okrug*), districts (*raion*), city districts, district Soviets within large cities, and villages. These committees are chosen by the respective Soviets and are accountable directly both to the Soviet which elected them and to the executive organ of the immediately superior Soviet of Deputies.

The departments of the executive committees are in charge of "direction of the cultural-political and economic construction" on the territory of the given unit. The constitutions of the Union and Autonomous Republics provide for the organization of the departments in the executive committees of the Soviets of the Deputies, with the exception of the village soviets where the executive and administrative organ consists of the chairman, vice chairman, and secretary elected by them. These departments are of two kinds: obligatory and facultative, according to the particular conditions of a given territorial unit.

The following are the obligatory departments of the executive committees of the territorial and regional soviets: (1) department of land, (2) finances, (3) trade, (4) health, (5) popular education, (6) local industry, (7) communal economy, (8) social security, (9) roads, (10) general, (11) arts, (12) administration of the Ministry of Justice of the Union Republic, (13) administration of the industry of construction materials, (14) administration of the local power industry, (15) administration of automobile transport, (16) a planning commission, and (17) the sector of cadres at the office of the chairman of the executive committee. With the approval of the Union-Republican Ministries, other departments may be formed on the territorial and regional level if they are necessitated by the particular conditions of the territory and region (for example, departments of light industry, textile industry, fisheries, etc.). The Ministry of Interior has its territorial or regional administration attached to the respective executive committee.

The district executive committees consist obligatorily of the following departments: (1) land, (2) finances, (3) trade, (4) health, (5) popular education, (6) social security, (7) roads, (8) general, (9) a planning commission, (10) the sector of cadres at the chairman's office. The establishment of the departments of local industry, communal economy, is facultative and may be effected in accordance with the requirements of the district economy and on the approval of the immediately superior organs. As in the case of the territorial and regional executive committees, the Ministry of Interior has its district administration attached to the district executive committee.

The city executive committees have no departments of arts and roads, and the departments of land and local industry are facultative. To the district Soviets within large cities apply the same provisions as to the city Soviets and their executive committees.[5]

Appraisal

The impression conveyed by the literature in Russian is this: (1) The internal organization as well as the general departmentalization is seriously inefficient, and staff and line rules are violated. (2) Directorates are grossly out of proportion to staffs. (3) Offices and actual staffs are wildly redundant; it has been reported that between 1952 and 1954, no less than 1 in 5 of all officials were dismissed for redundancy! In 1955, official newscasts claimed a further reduction of 0.9 percent from the total administrative expenses of 3.1 percent of the Union budget alone! (4) The office staffs are gravely out of proportion to the productive personnel—when they have been dismissed by one department they "wander" to another. But the evil is basic: it takes a century to convert a peasant people into one that has the precision, knowledge, experience, and sense of trusteeship that make a

[5] E. E. Evtikhiev and V. A. Vlasov, *Administrativnoe pravo* [*Administrative Law*], Moskva: Iuridicheskoe izdatel'stvo ministerstva iustitsii SSSR, 1946, pp. 30–31.

Typical Oblast Soviet of Workers' Deputies

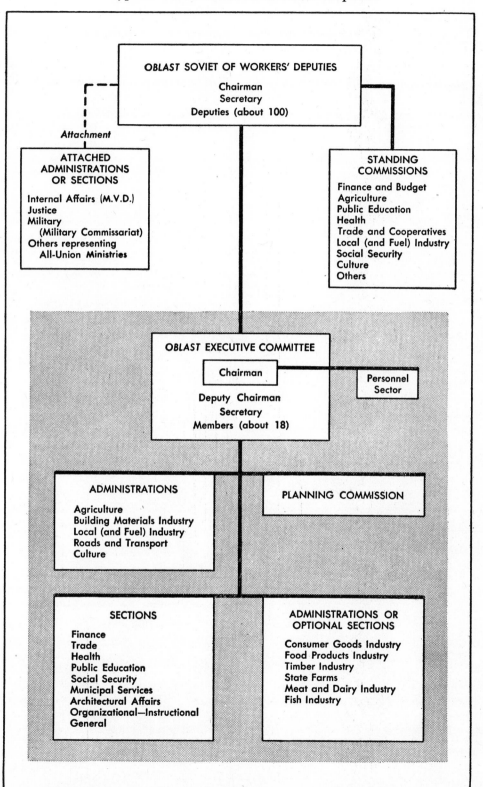

OBLAST SOVIET OF WORKERS' DEPUTIES

Chairman
Secretary
Deputies (about 100)

Attachment

ATTACHED ADMINISTRATIONS OR SECTIONS

Internal Affairs (M.V.D.)
Justice
Military
(Military Commissariat)
Others representing
All-Union Ministries

STANDING COMMISSIONS

Finance and Budget
Agriculture
Public Education
Health
Trade and Cooperatives
Local (and Fuel) Industry
Social Security
Culture
Others

OBLAST EXECUTIVE COMMITTEE

Chairman

Personnel Sector

Deputy Chairman
Secretary
Members (about 18)

ADMINISTRATIONS

Agriculture
Building Materials Industry
Local (and Fuel) Industry
Roads and Transport
Culture

PLANNING COMMISSION

SECTIONS

Finance
Trade
Health
Public Education
Social Security
Municipal Services
Architectural Affairs
Organizational—Instructional
General

ADMINISTRATIONS OR OPTIONAL SECTIONS

Consumer Goods Industry
Food Products Industry
Timber Industry
State Farms
Meat and Dairy Industry
Fish Industry

capable and stream-lined Civil Service. The atmosphere of coercion and party orthodoxy is not likely to breed sensitive, resilient, frank, and inventive officials; just the contrary. If the party and the Ministers want to control all life in detail and absolutely, then swollen staffs at the top—controllees over controllers—must result. It certainly paralyzes enterprise; and it must be the most wasteful administration outside the Far East and some Latin American countries.

It is extremely worthy of note that in June 1955 First Secretary Khrushchev was seriously demanding early and significant *decentralization* of public and business administration.

Civil Rights and Duties and
the Judiciary

To carry on a war for the overthrow of the international bourgeoisie, a war
which is a hundred times more difficult, prolonged and complicated than the
most stubborn of ordinary wars between states, and to refuse beforehand to
manoeuvre, to utilize the conflict of interests (even though temporary) among
one's enemies, to refuse to temporize and compromise with possible (even
though transient, unstable, vacillating and conditional) allies—is this not ridiculous in the extreme? Is it not as though, in the difficult ascent of an unex-
plored and heretofore inaccessible mountain, we were to renounce beforehand
the idea that *at times we might have to go in zigzags,* sometimes retracing
our steps, sometimes abandoning the course once selected, and trying various
others?

—Lenin, *Left-wing Communism*

Few nations have, since the French Revolution of
1789, made so much ado about the civil rights
embodied in the constitution as the Bolshevik
Party since its advent to power and its first Declaration of Rights of January 1918 (p. 769). We
concern ourselves with the Basic Rights and Obligations in Chapter X of the Constitution of 1936
(see pp. *lxiii–lxv*). We need only recall Stalin's
sneer at all other nations' rights as ineffective because of inequalities of property and income. The
Soviet rulers claim that they provide "effective"
rights.

I. THE RIGHTS AND DUTIES OF
THE CITIZEN

1. Work, a Right and a Compulsion

Article 118 guarantees work with payment according to its quantity and quality. It is supported by
the socialist economy, which is able to avoid crises

and unemployment. Social insurance covers sickness and temporary loss of work.

Yet a planned system does not avoid collapses in
production plans or transitions from one phase of
production to another. Instead of crises there is nonfulfillment of plans in quantity and quality. This
occurs often and seriously in the U.S.S.R. (pp. 896–
897; p. 903). For the central planners cannot plan
exactly how to keep all employed, without breaks,
at the maximum of their productivity. The economy produces less than it might; Soviet per-capita
income is very small (p. 901). But the significant
feature of an economy is *not* that people are employed but *the magnitude of the rewards they
obtain for their work.* It is possible to be *enslaved*
to work and still be on a low level of subsistence.
This is the actual situation of all but the aristocracy
of Soviet workers (pp. 901–903), to a considerable
extent through the managerial faults and plans of
the Communist Party rulers and their administra-

tive officials. We have seen already that Russians are forced to work at the products, the norms of quantity and pay by punitive measures, decreed by the government.

2. The Right to Rest and Leisure

The right to rest and leisure is enacted (Art. 119). A seven-hour day is promised—it has hardly ever existed. Annual vacations with pay are promised. But they are withdrawn unless the workers obey the factory production-expediter unconditionally. The sanatoria and the rest homes, etc., go to the intelligentsia and "heroes of Soviet labor." It is precisely the workers in the lower ranks who need the right, but they are precisely those in the Soviet Union who do *not* get priority of treatment.

The democratic countries, where free enterprise and free trade unions function, all the benefits referred to in the Soviet Constitution are acquired by the workers by their own strength, savings, cooperative societies, mutual-benefit arrangements with vacation camps, travel corporations, and so on. They are not the compensation for coerced labor as in Russia.

As to crises and depressions, the democracies since World War II (and some before) have full-employment policies and the institutions to prevent them or palliate their consequences.

Soviet workers have social insurance; so have workers in democracies; but in the former the funds and terms of benefit are not decided, as in the latter, largely by the freely applicable pressure of the workers' unions through free political parties that determine the enactments of the legislatures and control the administration. Hence, the promise in Article 120, the right to maintenance in old age, sickness, and disability, is nothing new and suffers the serious blemish that it is donated and administered by taskmasters for work that is *unchosen* compared with democratic conditions.

It is not intended to denigrate any effort at making the life of the worker happier, but not to be deceived by unfulfilled professions.

3. Private Property

Article 10 of the Constitution legally protects the right of personal property in income (*from toil*), savings, in the person's dwelling house and auxil-iary domestic economy, in the articles of the latter and personal use and comfort. It protects the right of inheritance of these. This latter point was in debate when the Constitution of 1936 was being drafted; Stalin averred the government had decided to concede this. Hence there is much inequality in the living standards of Soviet citizens and their children. There are people who own cars, diamonds, precious jewels, furs, homes, better clothing—very unequally. But property as the means of production is State owned.

4. The Right to Education

The right to education, most beneficent of all, is guaranteed by Article 121. It offers universality, compulsion, and *free* education to the seventh grade (from age 5), scholarships, etc. It is most laudable, in principle. Severe practical limitations on its fulfillment have always prevailed since 1917 and prevail now. As late as 1930 Stalin told the Congress of the party:

> The main thing now is to introduce compulsory elementary education. Up to the present we have been forced "to economize in everything, even in the schools," in order "to save and restore heavy industry" [Lenin].

It is possible to calculate from Soviet announcements that only 1 child in every 4 actually gets beyond the fourth grade and perhaps only 1 in 100 actually completes a full secondary course. Why is this? It is not due to especially severe standards for promotion, compared with Britain, France, or Germany or even the United States. Rather, schools and teachers [1] are not provided; industrial production is preferred. In the rural areas parents keep their children from school, and the inspectors do not enforce attendance efficiently. Children are not legally permitted to enter industry under fourteen (!), but plant managers, anxious to fulfill their imposed quotas, employ many. The State Labor Reserves system (p. 783) is hardly an example of the "right to education." In "higher" education (mingling secondary, university, and technical),

---

[1] In 1930 the primary and secondary students per teacher were 36; in 1950, 23. Teachers work from 30 to 22 hours a week, the former in the elementary, the latter in the upper grades. Other activities bring up the total to 40 hours.

Soviet schools have less than one third the numbers in American schools of equal rank, despite Russia's far larger population. It is still immensely better than Czarist education provision (p. 730), but the constitutional guarantee has been amended by the preference for industrialization.

Yet education constitutes a major achievement of the Soviet dictatorship, in spite of its many imperfections of quality and coverage, class inequalities, and total social regimentation.

Inequalities. As the higher schools have limited facilities, preference is given to the children of the leaders of the party, the military, the families of the press and literature, the technical intelligentsia of industry, commerce, and public administration. In Moscow the children of the security police, the M.V.D., have exclusive model schools.

Rural children are supposed to attend school from age seven to eleven; city children from seven to fourteen. The rural areas especially have been neglected, with some sound attempt at remedy only since 1943.

Secondary education must be paid for, except for occasional scholarships for youngsters bright enough to be usable by the State, though this itself may be a benefit to the individual. In October 1940 fees were introduced; though not very high, they are deterrents to social mobility. For the last three years of secondary school, the fees amount to about 6 percent of the wages of an unskilled worker; 3 percent of the wages of a more skilled worker; about 2 percent for white-collar worker. It takes no account of the child's cost of living.

To enter "higher education," a secondary-school degree is necessary. At the university level, the fees amount to double the proportions of income already mentioned above: 12 percent; 6 percent; 3 percent respectively. For the richer Soviet people, such fees may be negligible; not so for the poorer, especially if the university is distant from home. A university degree requires roughly five years of study.

Exempt from fees are: orphans, totally incapacitated persons or their children, war orphans, regular Army soldiers up to the rank of captain, the children of "distinguished" people and retired officers of the Armed Forces.

Children on collective farms are obliged to begin farm work at the age of twelve. Unless one has been through elementary school, it is almost impossible to get into secondary school. It seems that only 15 percent of places in the graduating class in secondary schools are reserved for children who first come into these schools at the age of fourteen. It is believed that a social selection occurs at the secondary-school stage, allowing only the smaller percentage into secondary schools and sending the rest to the elementary-*cum*-junior-high.

There is a grave lack of space, of good textbooks, of qualified teachers, of apparatus. The latest Five Year Plans *promise* education raised to seventeen years in the big cities, and later such education universally. Yet, in 1955, the party and government took much pains to make propaganda to the effect that young people should not insist on higher secondary and university education, but should prefer to go early into productive work.

The curriculum of the schools is rather like that of the Western world, but with a far heavier emphasis on the natural sciences.[2] At the university level, technical specialization is rigid and intense. But the whole system is acridly suffused with the political teaching of Marx, Lenin, Stalin, and party doctrine, from the earliest moments of learning consciousness. All teachers are under party invigilation and must take a conspicuous lead in personal demonstration of their "fulfillment" of the party's programs. Meetings of indoctrination and conferences, often run by the Agitation-Propaganda section of the *Komsomol* students, must be attended lest suspicion of disloyalty should be alleged. "Objectivity" is derided and punished. Teachers and finest students must remain "divided men"—that is, carry in one mind the data of science and the revelation of the party. The teachers are under continual anxiety of party punishment, with loss of job or demotion. They sometimes give students marks under political pressure.

[2] The superb study of Soviet education in Nicholas De Witt, *Soviet Professional Manpower* (National Science Foundation, Washington, 1955), shows that the Soviet Union had almost drawn even with the United States in producing a total of 500,000 professional trained engineers, and the Atomic Energy Commission warned in November 1955 that the Soviet Union would outstrip the U.S.A. in this respect by producing 1,200,000 trained engineers and scientists in 1950–1960 to 900,000 in the latter.

Some good students are ruined by the political judgment of their superiors. A liberal education, designed to encourage the strength of individual values and the intellect, is heresy.

Yet it would be wrong to depreciate the educational advances made in the U.S.S.R.—that is, the magnitude and quality of the schools. The teachers and pupils work very hard and achieve a sound grasp of their subjects. They have no time for idleness or exhibitionism and "soft" subjects.

5. The Rights of Women

In every respect the rights of women are accorded in Article 122. Women, nevertheless, are few in the higher ranks of the party or in the management of trade unions. They appear in the Soviets, but these have little power. They constitute about 50 percent of all the professions in the U.S.S.R. Most are in teaching, in the social and health services, perhaps rather more so than in the democracies—think of Britain, America, Scandinavia, Germany![3] They play a far larger part in heavy and "sweated" labor on farm and in factory and mines than in the lands of the West. Women in Russia have been traditionally beasts of burden, except among the old nobility and bourgeoisie. The Communist declaration of the opportunities of women was the promise of a remedy. The party has condemned women to their old status of labor, with the exceptions noted.

6. Equality of Person

"Equality of rights of citizens . . . is an *indefeasible* law" in all fields of economic, government, cultural, political, and other public activity, irrespective of nationality or race (Art. 123). This bans distinctions between *individuals* apparently, for we have seen that national minorities are leveled under the Iron Blanket (p. 819ff.). However, there is no legal or economic prejudice in terms of color or ethnic origin. This is a contrast with some nations. Otherwise all Soviet people are unfree and unequal equally, except Communist zealots.

[3] But the total Soviet professional women number about 830,000 while in the U.S.A. there are over 2,250,000 in a roughly similar classification.

What of anti-Semitism? In the late 1930's Jews were 4.34 percent of the membership of the party, as compared with their population percentage of only about 1.8. It was a reaction from Czarist oppression. A decline then set in, especially severe during the purges. In 1930 Jews constituted 10 percent of the delegates to the party Congress; in 1938 their percentage at Republic Congresses had fallen to 2.5. The decline has probably gone much further.

The Central Committee contains 1 Jew; the Party Presidium, 1; the Council of Ministers perhaps 2 or 3 out of about 60.

During 1947 the party whipped up a campaign against "rootless cosmopolitans," meaning Jews and Zionists. During the Russian invasion of the Baltic lands and Poland in 1939–1941, the M.V.D. had treated the Jews perhaps even worse than Hitler did. For Stalin's men hated the merchants and, above all, the democratic labor leaders—the same kind of men as Trotsky, Martov, and the Mensheviks had been, liberal and humanitarian. In January 1953 some doctors were charged with having caused the death of Scherbakov and Zhdanov, while serving the Kremlin. These doctors were Jews. It was alleged that they had sought to ruin the health of certain top defense officers to weaken the nation's defense. They were linked with the Jewish Joint Relief Agency; agents of the U.S.A. and British Intelligence! The Procurator General disseminated material for a campaign of "political vigilance" against "antinationalism."

Suddenly, April 4, the government declared that the whole story had been concocted in the Ministry of State Security. Honest and respected figures had been vilified "as a provocation." The regime nobly discoursed on the virtues of legality. A Deputy Minister and a former Minister were disciplined by ousting from his job and the Central Committee, respectively. Somehow the matter was tied up with Lavrenti Beria, head of the security services, and the rivalries around Malenkov. The anti-Semitic element was extremely conspicuous and was fomented in Czechoslovakia simultaneously.

Generally, there is utterly arbitrary discrimination in all the fields mentioned between citizens, but not from race and nationality in themselves, altogether at the caprice of the various levels and individual officials of the Communist Party.

7. Religious Freedom

Article 124 proclaims freedom of conscience; separates Church from State and school; gives equal rights of religious celebration; and *freedom of antireligious propaganda* to all. This article, and its predecessors in earlier constitutions, have been accompanied by forcible expression of freedom of worship, and since 1940 a concordat of obsequious subjection of the Orthodox Church to the State.

Marx coined the Soviet's axiom: "Religion is the opiate of the people." The Communist leaders carried out its inferences with exceptional brutality to overcome the pronounced superstition and politicization of the Czarist Church (p. 741). Lenin gave the Soviet regime its guiding lines:

> All contemporary religions and churches, all and every kind of religious organization, Marxism has always viewed as instruments of bourgeois reaction, serving as a defense of exploitation and the doping of the working class. . . . The struggle against religion cannot be limited to abstract ideological preachments . . . this struggle should be brought into connection with the concrete practice of the class movement directed toward the elimination of the social roots of religion. . . . The party of the proletariat must be the spiritual leader in the struggle against all kinds of medievalism, including the official religion.

The only problem was how to cope with so sensitive a factor in Russian mentality.

From November 1917 to February 1922 a formal and an unofficial onslaught was made on the Church. By law, its property was confiscated; the priests were deprived of various civil rights, as "nonworkers," including the franchise. Religious instruction in any school was prohibited, as also in any organized group of those under eighteen. In the future, church marriages and divorces were not legal. The believers to whom the Soviets could lease the churches were given administrative persecution. Priests were executed, exiled, imprisoned; churches desecrated; valuable sacred articles were confiscated—to help famine-stricken areas—by bloodshed when the Patriarch Tikhon refused to

give them. A schism was fostered inside the Church; the anti-Tikhonites were recognized, but on breaking into factions they were dropped.

More cunning methods were tried from February 1925, when the Militant Atheists' League was founded; the tactics of scurrilous blasphemy and rationalist contempt, backed with charges of political disloyalty. Taxes were clapped on new churches; sermons were censored; religious teaching in church was prohibited. In 1928 the sale of Easter food and Christmas trees and ornaments was forbidden. On resistance, the churches were closed and demolished *en masse* or converted into silos, schools, and movies—that is, the bases of a socialist society! A decree of 1929 banned social activities in the churches; the monopoly of these was for the party. An amendment to the 1929 Constitution replaced "freedom of religious worship and antireligious propaganda" with "freedom of religious and antireligious propaganda." The Atheists' League permeated the trade unions and spurned the members who held onto religion. Schools were commanded to be actively antireligious. By 1932 the Atheists had 5,500,000 members and plans for 15,000,000 and the extinction of religion by 1937.

It became expedient to change tack in this obstinate fight. For Stalin needed admission into the "collective security" of the powers against Nazis, Fascists, and Japan. Then, to avoid religious influence in the first elections after the 1936 Constitution, a new wave of religious and atheistic persecution was ferociously launched, with arrests, charges of espionage and sabotage for foreign lands (Fascists not democracies, at the moment); then followed the Purge (p. 782).

As World War II was seen to be nearing, it became expedient for Stalin's clique to pretend to be more humane than Hitler. Hence the Atheists were now vilified and disbanded. Antireligious propaganda and persecutions were relaxed. It was found expedient also to disseminate the ideas that religious practice might support morality against drunkenness, brutality, crimes of the Ten Commandments' kind, family solidarity, and dutifulness. And Soviet society is at all levels horribly brutal and drunken. It was suggested that a "national" Church was preferable to "international" Catholicism; and easier to control if it were centralized, with the hierarchy back.

In World War II, on Hitler's invasion, the periodicals of the Atheists were suspended. The Acting Patriarch called on all to fight to save Holy Russia. The Bishops of Leningrad and Kiev were received by Stalin. The Council of Bishops and the election of Sergius, as the new Patriarch (banned since the death of Tikhon in 1925) were permitted.

The government in 1944 set up its own councils to conduct relations with this Church and others. The theological seminaries were opened for the training of priests and the publication of religious works was resumed.

Decrees in August 1945 and August 1946 canceled most of the earlier persecutory decrees. The parishes were again allowed to acquire buildings and objects of worship, with almost a right of corporate organization. The local soviets were ordered to assist (no longer ban!) the parishes in their building efforts. The tolling of church bells, forbidden since the early 1920's, was permitted. Taxes on monasteries' land and buildings were lifted. An international convention of the Orthodox Church was assisted to meet in Moscow in July 1948.

The Armenian Church and the Baptists have similar charters to the Russian Church. Lower in the hierarchy of permitted religions are the various Protestant sects, then the Moslems and the Jews. Those churches most helpful domestically and internationally to the government have the priority of standing and latitude.

Of course, no members of the party or a *Komsomol* may be other than a professed atheist. There is also the greatest care that all leading civil and military official positions, even in schools, shall not be occupied by believers.

Today there are some 80 bishops, 26,000 open churches, 3500 chapels, 33,000 priests, and 90 monasteries. In 1953 there were 325,856 churches in the U.S.A. In Moscow, with between 5,000,000 to 7,000,000 (no census since 1939!), there are 55 churches, whereas in New York City there are over 2600. Moscow has only one synagogue.

Religious instruction in school or church is prohibited. Religious literature is scanty. The opposition to religion, especially among the *Komsomols,* is obstinate and contemptuous. Army men and families hardly dare attend worship. Women vastly outnumber the men as church-goers, and the elderly women at that. The priests, it is reported, are unctuous.

What Is Religious Freedom? The Russian Church is fully subordinate to the dictatorship—even more than it was to the Czars. It is not allowed to exercise full freedom of worship, even now. For the latter, in the West, means full rights to public expression as regards governmental affairs, justice, social evils, above all, the political faults of governmental leaders. Rites and hymns are not all of religious freedom; this requires the preaching of social behavior as it embodies the spirit and ethic of the Faith. *This is decidedly not permitted in Russia.*

The Church does not answer by counterattack, as it does elsewhere. It serves the ends of the regime by taking the party's message to places in the world where it might otherwise be suspected. The Patriarch has been sent on missions to the satellite countries. He received Pastor Niemöller of Germany; in December 1954 he made an appeal to France against German rearmament. He may persuade people by the mere status of the Church that the Soviet government is entitled to be appraised as humane.

8. Freedom of Speech, of Press, Etc.

Freedom of speech, of assembly, meetings, street processions and demonstrations is guaranteed: *but* (Art. 125) "the socialist system" limits these rights. This bevy of rights requires commentary.

All meetings need the license of the Soviet executive committee (equals "Ministry") of the governmental level appropriate to the area from which the persons to attend are drawn.

All associations are legal only when they have obtained from the government a charter. They may be dissolved by the government. In neither case must the government justify its action before a law court: the Ministries concerned are sovereign.

Inviolability of the home and correspondence,

and the security of the person, are altogether subject to the police and judicial system (pp. 843–851).

We pay special attention to freedom of opinion. **The Monopoly of Communications.** The heart of the right to free expression lies in the actual control of mass communications. In democracies, we have seen that the press is in the hands of private owners, with a minimum State control over what and how they present news and views. This has its faults; but these are immeasurably outweighed by the social advantages, from the standpoint of freedom of opinion and the advancement of truth by the open competition of values.

In the Soviet Union every vehicle of opinion is owned by the government or the Communist Party. No independent, nonofficial person can obtain the following requisites for freedom of expression: (1) newsprint, for it is owned and dispensed according to Plan, by the government; (2) printing machines, subject to the same conditions; (3) room in which to conduct writing, copying, and printing operations; (4) transport facilities for dissemination and sale; (5) no one may employ the labor of others, except the government; hence, any operation requiring more than one person or a single family (say, because this would keep the clandestine operations safe from discovery) are impossible. Any operation which entails a noise that may be overheard is in peril, because of the presence of official and unofficial informers.

The "Private" Author. The private author is free to write what he likes, providing it is never discovered by design or accident to contain material distasteful to the Party Presidium, which, let it be remembered, has its inspectors and control officers everywhere vigilant. If the author wishes freedom of expression, he must get a publisher. But the State runs the publishing houses. The author, therefore, is subject to the control, politically, of a publishing board, which is carefully planted by the party. Assuming that he then gets published, he may come in for very large rewards (p. 902).

But he is also subject to the criticism, not only of the public, which may or may not buy his works at its own discretion, but of the various party organs. For example, the various party organizations will write reviews in the press; and this function may be undertaken by the lowest and the highest organ. The Communist-planted professional associations, such as the All-Union Congress of Soviet Writers and the Union of Writers, are the instruments of the party views on how much freedom is permitted in any branch of art or the intellect, music, painting, the novel, poetry, sculpture, architecture, the drama (especially), the natural sciences, philosophy.

The Iron Blanket on Thought and Feeling. It is not possible, within the present scope, to trace the interesting history of this Iron Blanket thought control and emotion control. It responded to the ugliness and repressiveness of Lenin's and Stalin's nature. Briefly, indeed, we will say, that the hero, of whatever branch of art and the creative mind, has been forcibly dictated to be "positive"—that is, must extol Communist virtues. He must not be "negative"—that is, must not show qualities to be admired that are contradictory to the view of man as held by Karl Marx, as materialized and brutalized by the needs of collective farms, sweated industry, and adulation of the party leaders. He must not be "formal"—that is, he must not treat of social relations or the characters of men and women without connection with politics. He must fight "alien ideologies," such as "bourgeois nationalism, formalism, naturalism, and cosmopolitanism." In other words, he must write so as to flatter the nationalism of Great Russia and put down Ukrainian patriotism, etc. He must take sides—that is to say, one side, the Communist side. He must not let his characters be their own individual selves, with their internal conflicts of character and outlook, for example, showing that a Communist Party man and hero may be a wicked husband, a rapist, a thief, or coward in personal relations. He must not be "cosmopolitan"—that is, see the point of view of Western democracy. Beware of criticism, also, of "the dark sides of Soviet life"!

The attitude of the party leaders toward freedom of opinion and expression may be appreciated from one famous episode in which the constant efforts of the party to control creative literature culminated in a decree abolishing certain journals in Leningrad that had transgressed, in August 1946. Explaining the Draconic decrees, Zhdanov, then spokesman of the party and looked to as the successor of Stalin, admonished the First All-Union Congress of Soviet Writers in a 10,000 word Communist diatribe. Extracts will suffice to give the determined essence of the party's policy.

Lenin had said (1905):

> Literature must become Party . . . the socialist proletariat must promote and develop the principle of *Party literature* and bring this principle to life in the most complete and integral form possible. . . . Down with non-Party writers! Down with supermen writers! The literary cause must become part of the general proletarian cause. . . .

This, Zhdanov dutifully quoted, heartily approving its theme that "our literature cannot be politically indifferent, cannot be 'art for art's sake.'" His own addition was this:

> . . . creative genius belongs to the distant past. It is alien to the realities of contemporary life and cannot be tolerated in the pages of our journals. Our literature is not a private undertaking designed to please the diverse tastes of a literary market. We are under no obligation to provide space in our literature for tastes and tempers which have nothing in common with the morals and qualities of the Soviet people. What of instruction can Akhantova's works give to our youth? Nothing but harm. These works can only sow despondency, depression, pessimism, and an inclination to run away from the urgent problems of society, to leave the broad highway of social life and action for the narrow little world of personal experiences.
>
> Comrade Stalin called our writers engineers of human souls. This definition has profound meaning. It speaks of the enormous responsibilities of Soviet writers for the education of the people and for the education of Soviet youth. It says that wastage in literary work is intolerable. . . . the Central Committee hopes that the Leningrad writers will find in themselves the strength to block all attempts to divert the literary detachment of Leningrad and its journals into the channel of ideological indifference, lack of principle, and political neutrality. You stand on the advanced line of the ideological front and you have enormous tasks of international significance. This should heighten the sense of responsibility of every genuine Soviet writer toward his people, his state, and his Party, and the consciousness of the importance of doing his duty.

Zhdanov observed how brilliant had been the works of prosocialist writers in Czarist times. For example, Chernyshevsky and others who practiced "militant art." But the foolish Zhdanov seemed not to understand, or to believe his audience of writers understood, that such men had been free and were writing *against injustice.* Nor did he realize that those who had been reprimanded had attempted to do just that, but that Soviet Communism was a machine determined to crush freedom and therefore extinguish life.

There can be no wonder that the party press has simultaneously with its denunciations of its Soviet writers for the inferable backslidings—very dangerous even to the lives of the writers—to rebuke the writers for their lack of creativeness, the boredom with which they infect their readers and audiences, and the "unreality" of their characters. It complains also of the lack of good authors. The party blows hot and cold on the "criticism" vented through the vehicle of the works of art; and that vented by the professional and party critics. Periods of shocking strictness are followed by a sharp turning against the critics so far cozened and rewarded, and then a similar vindictiveness against their victims.

Malenkov, at the Nineteenth Congress of the party, expressed disgust with Soviet art and literature.

> The ideological level is not sufficiently high. . . . [There are] many mediocre and drab products and sometimes simply hackwork which distorts Soviet reality. . . . It would be wrong to think that our Soviet reality does not provide material for satire.

He complained of "falseness and rot." Is this a keynote speech? Does it portend even a little more freedom in literary and artistic creativeness? The intelligentsia that has developed in the Soviet schools and universities is more and more dissatisfied with Soviet literary products. Apparently, Malenkov was voicing the intelligentsia's disgust, he himself being one of the intelligentsia, unlike Stalin.

Can the dictatorially planned and managed lives of 210,000,000 people be so conducted without uniformity of spirit? If there is a let-up in the latter, would not the dictatorship be headed for disintegration? Will the new cry for something "bold and creative," for something "lyrical," for "real difficulties, misfortunes, joys and sorrows of living Soviet people," the "stream of life," the "clash of forces" triumph over "the dull, superficial, colorless, schematic portrayals of conflict," as *Pravda* called (Khatchaturian's phrase) "the institutional guardianship over composers"? Or will, in Shostakovich's words, "the Union of Soviet Composers' 'guard' over composers prevent them from searching for the new, from following independent, untrod paths of art"?

It would seem that the latter is to win. For when, in 1954, Vera Panova wrote a novel called *Seasons of the Year, Pravda* complained that the Five Year Plans, the collectivization of agriculture, socialist competition, and the Great Patriotic War had been omitted.

Then beware the movement of the free, original, discerning soul of Proust, Joyce, of Virginia Wolf, of Hemingway! At the end of 1954 Marguerite Higgins reported from Russia the story of the American Marine Guard at the Embassy in Moscow who got tired of Russian plays and movies. "I soon gave it up," he sighed. "A fellow can take just so much of this business of boy meets tractor and girl meets quota."

The Censorship. All printed material is censored by *Glavlit,* the Chief Office for Literature and Publications. This was established in June 1931 as a division of the Ministry of Education. Its purpose, runs the relevant decree, is

to ensure political-ideological, military, and economic control in every aspect over articles, manuscripts, photographs, illustrations, etc., which are intended for publication or circulation and by radio broadcasts, lectures and exhibitions.

The Office has the authority to prohibit the publication or dissemination of such things if they are inconsistent with the interests of the government. It has authority to exercise (1) preliminary

and consecutive censorship, (2) to confiscate material that should not be circulated; (3) to grant licenses allowing the establishment of publishing firms, to close them down, to allow publication of newspapers or periodicals, to allow or forbid importations or exportations of literary material; and (4) establish *an index of works which may not be published or circulated at all*—once again, the dread *index expurgatorious.*

The Office may try again, after publication, if something has slipped past its vigilance, or the party has in the meanwhile changed its line.

The Office has its officials located in all the publishers' offices, the editors' sanctums of periodicals, in typographic plants, in the telegraphic agencies, the customs and postal offices, etc. Its stamp is required on every publication, its consent to every lecture and every broadcast. The Criminal Code backs up the censorship office by a fine and correctional labor up to three months—if "innocent" of counterrevolutionary slant. We later define this elastically incriminating term (p. 842).

Furthermore, the programs of theaters and concerts need approval by the All-Union Committee of Arts of the Council of Ministers.

Exempt from the censorship are the publications of the Government Printing Office and of the Central Committee and Presidium of the Party, and the local publications of the party's committees down to the district level.

The Press. The Soviet press, being entirely in the hands of the Communist Party and the Soviet Government, is consciously used as the instrument for the organization, education, and communist upbringing of the masses. The basic slogan provided by Lenin and always quoted in all Soviet discussions of the press states: "A newspaper is not only a collective propagandist and collective agitator; it is also a collective organizer."

The Soviet press is not a business venture. It is not an instrument to express the opinions of individual publishers or to reflect or mirror public opinion. It is the major social force to be harnessed to facilitate the attainment of the society's defined goals.

The basic features of the Communist attitude toward the press are: (1) The Soviet press must be free of capitalists, careerists, and "bourgeois anarchistic individualism." (2) The Soviet press should be *not* "objective or negative." Its approach to any set of facts must include the element of *parteinost'* (partisanship). It must evaluate them from the point of view of the revolutionary proletariat. (3) Social processes, not personal events, are news.

The Soviet press is developed according to a definite plan. The first Five Year Plan, launched in 1928, included a precise program for the growth of the press during the following five years, and each of the subsequent Plans has included a similar program. This planning has enabled the government to effect the closest integration of the ends the party pursues in mobilizing public opinion and the means it has at its command to achieve those ends.[4]

The component parts very closely follow the territorial-administrative structure of the Soviet State and the Communist Party. At each level of the territorial administrative hierarchy there is an appropriate press apparatus to serve the government, party, and public organizations. At the apex of the Soviet press pyramid stands the "Central" (All-Union) press, consisting of twenty-five newspapers with 7,500,000 circulation (1949). In the middle are 462 Republic, territorial, and regional papers of the "provincial" press, with over 10,000,-000 copies at a single printing. At the base of the pyramid are the district, city, factory, and farm papers of the local press sector, with a combined circulation of over 13,000,000 copies. Below this, as a kind of foundation for the entire structure, come several hundred thousand wall newspapers found in every shop, office, and farm.

Of equal importance with the horizontal division of the Soviet press, however, is its vertical structure. The horizontal levels of the press hierarchy are carefully subdivided along functional lines into separate groups of newspapers, such as those of the party, governmental, trade-union, agricultural, and industrial press. Some of these are general newspapers—*Pravda* (the party paper) and *Izvestia* (the government's paper)—directed to all citizens throughout the U.S.S.R.

Some are directed to citizens of their respective Republics. Others are directed to special audiences.

The total number and circulation of Soviet newspapers is not large in relation to the size of the population.[5] This is largely compensated for, however, by careful planning of the distribution of available resources and by utilization of wall newspapers. The party has precisely designed each newspaper to serve a given area, to reach a specific segment of the population, and to fulfill concretely defined functions. It is this organization of the press that makes a reality of Stalin's slogan that the press must be a "transmission belt between the Party and the masses."

The Soviet newspaper is a device through which the party and government transmit decrees and decisions in which they present, explain, and justify their policies. Throughout all the material, domestic and foreign, there runs a constant, single, simple theme: the righteousness of the Communist Party and its allies, the error and wickedness of all nations and men who are not its abject friends. Through the press, instructions are issued to local organizations. Their work is subjected to criticism. The press is a kind of house organ of the party and government units at all levels. It is a clearing house for the exchange of advice and information and no problem relating to the improvement of production is too small to deserve a column of discussion.

The newspaper editor must be the representative of the party, and he is consequently appointed by it. The party rules provide that the editors of the party press organs at each level of the territorial hierarchy shall be appointed by the corresponding party committee. The editor of any Soviet newspaper, by virtue of his position as editor, is at the same time a responsible official of the organization

---

[4] One unplanned use of the press is the widespread use of the paper to make cigarettes, the filling being very inferior "tobacco," known as *"makhorka."*

[5] The Soviet newspapers, 1913–1955 expanded thus:

	1913	1928	1939	1949	1955
Number of newspapers	859	1,197	8,769	7,200	7,100
Millions of circulation at single printing	2.7	9.4	38.0	31.0	47.0

From Alex Inkeles, *Public Opinion in Soviet Russia,* Cambridge, Mass., 1950, p. 144, except for 1955, which embodies data released by the U.S.S.R. on May 5, 1955, the latest figure gives one newspaper per 4.5 persons as compared with U.S.A. with 785 English-language dailies with average circulation of 54.6 million.

that publishes the paper. Although a certain degree of technical competence is absolutely indispensable for a newspaper editor, the predominance of political considerations in the training and retraining of editors persists. The top editors receive their training in the editorial department of the Institute of Literature and Languages of the Central Communist Academy; the less important ones are trained by the branches of the Communist Institute of Journalists.

Great emphasis is placed upon the participation of nonprofessional journalists writing for the newspaper at irregular intervals in those areas in which they have special competence.

The basic problem that editors of Soviet newspapers face is that of correctly interpreting the instructions which come to them from above. Another problem is that of striking a correct balance between material originating in and written about the area served by their paper and material reprinted from the central press and *Tass* wire service.

Direct censorship is less important here than party influence through: (1) the selection and training of editorial personnel; (2) the issuance of broad directives governing the content and operations of all newspapers or particular groups of papers; and (3) the utilization of formal supervisory machinery.

In addition to being the collective propagandist, etc., the Soviet press serves also as an instrument of mass or public control, as a medium for official and popular criticism of the government and party. "Criticism and self-criticism" (p. 887) are the foremost responsibility to the press. A large portion of its total space goes to printing critical appraisals issued by the party and the government. Moreover, the press must secure close ties with the masses, and the worker and peasant "correspondents" are the eyes and the ears and the mouths of "proletarian public opinion," as well as its commanders. The communications which the editors receive from their net of nonprofessional correspondents are supplemented by "letters from the average Soviet citizen" who wishes to register a complaint, express a grievance or opinion, make a suggestion, or ask a question. These letters are largely "fixed" and are paid for.

Radio is, of course, entirely in government possession and operation, and there are only 1 in 4 individual radio sets to "wired speakers," or 4,000,000 to 16,000,000. The latter are loudspeakers in homes, schools, farms, factories, streets, and here the radio studio chooses the program. There are rather less than 500,000 TV sets in comparison with 32,000,000 in the U.S.A.

In view of the faithful and factually based account of the Soviet press given here, the reader may well ponder the answer given in an interview with the board of editors of *U.S. News and World Report* (Nov. 11, 1955) by the leader of a Soviet press group visiting the United States. The first question was, "Is there freedom of the press in the Soviet Union?" Boris Kampov-Polevoy (Secretary, Union of Soviet Writers, member of Supreme Soviet, Stalin Prizewinner) answered:

> Unquestionably. The tone of the question indicates that you doubt this. I must tell you that I, who have worked in our press for twenty-five years, do not know of any limitation on the freedom of our press. The only thing which we are not allowed to write is war propaganda in any form.

This is a direct untruth, and the subsequent answers were partial or complete supporting untruths or evasions. What can be the explanation, taking the most charitable view of this brash and false assertion? Only this, that those who have been elevated to journalistic jobs by the party, especially the higher ranks, are so in harmony with the Communist doctrines of the Politbureau that they regard themselves as free—they have no need to dissent.

It is a world tragedy that the Soviet government can thus shut off the truth about other nations from the Soviet people's mind.

What Rights?

One thing may be added about rights. There is *no right of freedom of movement* about Russia. All people over the age of sixteen must have internal passports. This is regulated in detail by a regulation of 1940. Those aged fifty-five and over get indefinite period passports (irony!). Between sixteen and fifty-five, passports are for five-year periods. It is practically impossible to change addresses without a passport, for any change of residence requires presentation of the passport with the militia on arrival, if the change is for more than twenty-four hours, and deregistration on removal!

The net effect of these rights is the offer of a deception. They are in the gift of an authoritarian and brutal government that regards its ends as justifying any means, and these "rights" are used as means. They are not rights in the sense of something seized by the people for themselves and administered by themselves and enforced on the government that is the servant of the people. Rights donated by a despotic master are not rights, but crumbs from the dictator's table.

The Obligations of the Citizen

These are grimly real. They are the obligations to:

abide by the Constitution . . . , to observe the laws, to maintain labor discipline, honestly to perform public duties, and to respect the rules of socialist intercourse (Art. 130).

safeguard and fortify public, socialist property . . . and persons committing offences against [it] are enemies of the people (Art. 131).

[serve in the military forces, under a law of universal service] (Art. 132).

defend the country—[not commit treason, etc.] (Art. 133).

II. LAW COURTS AND JUDICIARY

We have noticed the constituents of justice as administered by the judiciary of a State in Britain, France and Germany: they amount to independence of all other authorities and impartiality between the parties before the court. The Soviet Union provides badly for these factors, most of all in "political" crimes, those where independence is of utmost importance, being fundamental to the rest of the State's functions.

Counterrevolutionary Crimes

Hence it is important to take note of the width, vagueness or elasticity of the "crimes" concerning

the political process itself. This is dealt with in various articles of the Criminal Code, first promulgated in 1924 and later amended. The fundamental definition is in Article 58–1. It runs:

Any act is considered counterrevolutionary, if it aims at the overthrow, subversion, or weakening of the power of the workers' and peasants' soviets, and workers' and peasants' governments of the U.S.S.R., Union Republics, and autonomous republics, which have been elected by the soviets by virtue of the Constitution of the U.S.S.R. or the Constitutions of the Union Republics, or if it aims at the subversion or weakening of the external security of the U.S.S.R. or of the fundamental economic, political, and national conquests realized by the Proletarian Revolution. . . .

The key words in this paragraph cover even the slightest criticism of any act of the government and party, so open are they to interpretation by the judges. It would not even be necessary to act; omission from action—for example, failure to achieve one's quota under the Plans—could be interpreted as sabotage, not honest bad judgment. "Intent" is in the mind of the person; the Communist Party does not stop at the act, or it does, at its discretion.

The Code contains specific counterrevolutionary crimes. One is *treason*. This includes escape or flight abroad, as well as acts prejudicial to military power, the independence of the State, the territory of the U.S.S.R. betrayal of secrets, passage to the enemy. There is armed action against the government. There is *contact with foreigners* with "counterrevolutionary" intent. There is espionage, which includes "economic information" which is not a State secret but whose disclosure is forbidden by law or the orders of the heads of offices, institutions or enterprises. There are *acts of terror,* against the government or the organizations of the workers and peasants, not necessarily for political purposes. Ironic that the dictatorship that emanated from the avowedly terroristic parties of the 1870's (p. 751) should be so punitive? The scope of the attacks has been widened to include those who write letters to the press (p. 841) for the benefit of the regime, and *Stakhanovites* (p. 903). There is *destruction of public property*—with "counterrevolutionary" intent. But almost all property is public, and the intent includes interference with the "normal activities" of all forms of the State economy, which is almost every incident in Russian daily life. There is, of course, *sabotage:* this even includes "incorrect planning," "unjustified" delays in building plant, "irrational" use of railroad cars ". . . the default or deliberately negligent execution . . . of his definite obligations."

The punishments are extremely severe, some carrying the death penalty.

The Soviet Judiciary

This is instituted in Chapter IX of the Constitution, Articles 102–117.

There is provided a system of courts, in a hierarchy, running down from the Supreme Court of the U.S.S.R. to the Supreme Courts of the Union Republics, the Territorial and Regional Courts, the Autonomous Republics and Autonomous Regions, Area Courts, and the People's Courts—*and the special courts.*

The Supreme Court is the highest judicial organ; it is charged with supervising the judicial activities of all the judicial organs.

In all the courts, cases are normally tried with the participation of "people's assessors." But there are frequent exceptions enacted by law. The people's assessors are the closest approach to the participation of a jury, but are still far from this basic Anglo-Saxon practice.

All the courts, including the special courts, are supposed by the Constitution, to be "elected." This is the term used in the Constitution. It has, however, been used in the usual sense of the term— that is, popular election—only thrice, in 1948, 1951, and again in December 1954, to elect the judges of the People's Courts, by a process presently described. All the other courts have been "elected" only in the sense that the judges have been named to their posts by the soviet assemblies at the various levels. We have already analyzed the abject subservience of the Supreme Soviet in all matters. At all levels, the Presidium and the Council of Ministers or local executive, present the judges wished-for (decided on) and the Soviet accepts them with praise and applause. Hence in all cases except that of the People's Judges, the

judges in the Soviet Union are appointed by the Executive, in a system where the legislature is totally a dressed window.

The Soviet propagandists who use the word *elected* mislead themselves, and the rest of the world, if they profess that there is popular control of the judges through election. We do not argue that there ought to be. Better ways of assuring justice than popular election of judges are varieties of Executive appointment. But it is necessary to be clear on what Soviet practice really is. For in 1948 the Soviet Minister of Justice described the very few judges who are elected by state legislatures in the U.S.A. as "appointive"!

The Constitution stipulates that the Supreme Courts of the Union and the various Republics and Territories and Areas, as above mentioned, are "elected" by the respective Soviets for *a term of five years.* But the People's Courts "are elected by the citizens of the district on the basis of universal, direct and equal suffrage by secret ballot for *a term of three years*"—just like the Supreme Soviet, in fact, except as to length of term.

Cases are heard in public universally—unless otherwise provided for by law. But the exceptions are numerous and notorious, as we shall see; the constitutional stipulation *sounds* nice. The accused is guaranteed the right to be defended by counsel—but the counsel is in the hands of the State and the party, as we shall see. The "Judges are independent and subject only to the law." But, as we have seen, there is no separation of powers in principle and none in practice. The judges have no independent defense of their independence of mind, even if they wanted the latter and craved and needed the former. They are the creatures in principle and practice of the Soviet Executive.

As there is no separation of powers, and the judges are in principle and practice a branch of the State's administration, a system of administrative supervision is imposed upon them. This is vested in the Procurator General of the U.S.S.R.— the apex of a corps of Procurators for all the levels of the judiciary. The highest levels down to the Autonomous Regions are appointed directly by the Procurator General of the U.S.S.R. for terms of five years. The area, district, and city procurators are appointed by the Union Republic Pro-

Soviet Judicial System

SUPREME SOVIET OF U.S.S.R.

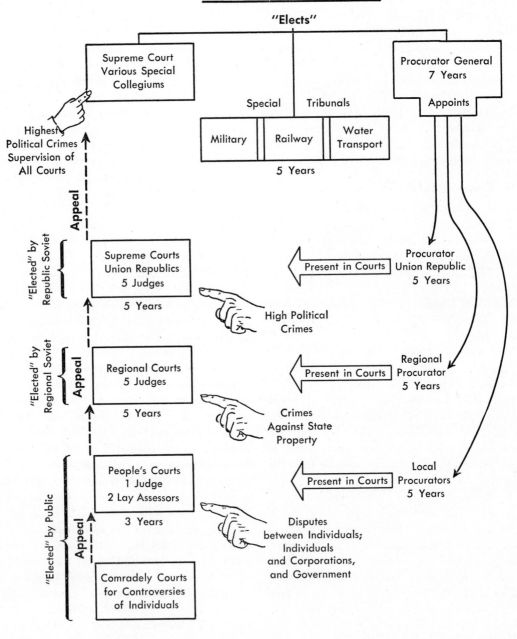

"Elects"

Supreme Court
Various Special
Collegiums

Procurator General
7 Years

Appoints

Special | Tribunals

Military | Railway | Water Transport

5 Years

Highest
Political Crimes
Supervision of
All Courts

Appeal

"Elected" by Republic Soviet

Supreme Courts
Union Republics
5 Judges
5 Years

Present in Courts

Procurator
Union Republic
5 Years

High Political
Crimes

"Elected" by Regional Soviet

Appeal

Regional Courts
5 Judges
5 Years

Present in Courts

Regional
Procurator
5 Years

Crimes
Against State
Property

"Elected" by Public

Appeal

People's Courts
1 Judge
2 Lay Assessors
3 Years

Present in Courts

Local
Procurators
5 Years

Disputes
between Individuals;
Individuals
and Corporations,
and Government

Comradely Courts
for Controversies
of Individuals

Bar and Bench Disciplined by
Ministry of Justice of U.S.S.R.

curators for five years, subject to the approval of the Procurator General of the U.S.S.R. He himself is "elected" by the Supreme Soviet for *seven* years.

These Procurators are under the authority only of the Moscow office; they function independently of any local organs; in other words they are tied direct to the Politbureau!

The office of Procurator is somewhat similar to that of United States Attorney or State Attorney in the U.S.A. or the Public Prosecutor in the British system or the Procurator and *Parquet* (pp. 511–512) in the French system. It undertakes the bringing of people to justice before the judiciary. But it also has the supreme power of supervision over the execution of the laws by all Ministries and their subordinate institutions, and by public officials and all the citizens of the U.S.S.R.

The Imperialist Character of the Judiciary. Some generalizations must first be made, to understand the functioning of the U.S.S.R. judiciary.

First, Lenin, under the stress of experience, found it obligatory to retreat from the romanticism he and his Communist associates had indulged in (when they were cogitating revolt!), that anybody could be, that everybody ought to be, a judge. "We must," he had said, "ourselves act as judges. The citizens must take turns participating in the courts and in the administration of the country." This notion came down from naïve Rousseauite ideas that all men were noble, if only the effete, conventional institutions around them were abolished; and that every man had solid, good sense in judging a case if the evidence were put before him. Law and justice are rather more complicated than this. We shall see that the People's Judges and assessors are left very small discretion, and that appeals are numerous from them.

Second, and far more important, is the Soviet conception of law and the judges. This is the definition given in the textbook prepared by the Institute of Law of the Academy of Sciences of the U.S.S.R. (p. 12, following the definition made by the Scientific Worker-Jurists in 1938):

Law is the composite of norms [rules of conduct] strengthening the rule of a class and the order which is advantageous and pleasing to it,

which norms are published and sanctioned by the State and made operative by the compulsion of the State.

These are the marching orders of the judges and the assessors. How simple this makes the task of the Russian judiciary compared with the lights by which the judges in democracies are guided! For instance:

. . . the common law consists of a few broad and comprehensive principles, founded on reason, natural justice, and enlightened public policy, modified and adapted to the circumstances of all particular cases which fall within it. [Chief Justice Shaw, in a Massachusetts case in 1854.]

Third, following from this, and of supreme significance, is the true role of the Soviet judicial system. It is *not* regarded as an independent power *vis-à-vis* the Executive, the Legislature, and still less of the Communist Party leadership.

It can best be envisaged as the performance of the judicial function in a colonial territory by an absolutely dominant old-fashioned, imperial master. The system of law is imposed, according to the policy of the imperial ruler, without consultation with the native population. Then, in judging cases *between individuals* (contract, torts), the judge may be perfectly upright, perfectly independent, perfectly uncorrupt. He may mete out even-handed justice between the litigants, on the basis of the law prevalent. This law, as regards such interpersonal matters of theft from each other or assault or rape or fraud or breach of contract or obscenity or trespass or even family relations (for example, a parent's right to thrash an errant youngster) may be sensible, humane, not retributive, but corrective, rehabilitating, and educative. This is generally true of the Soviet system and is a considerable advance on the Czarist judiciary and its code of laws. The Soviet propagandists have made a tremendous fuss about this at various times, anxious for their good repute in the world.

The moment, however, the march of the economy and the domination of the dictatorial system of "socialism" is touched by any case, the colonial nature of justice grimly emerges: the defendant is not on a par with the colonial power.

No Habeas Corpus is a direct product of the system of party and Executive dominance.

The Judges

In the People's Courts, cases are heard and decided by one judge and two assessors. The judges are popularly elected and may be re-elected; candidates must be over twenty-three. This position is then a full-time job. A judge needs no formal training, but there are courses of lectures provided by the various Ministries of Justice, and he learns some more on the bench. Furthermore, there are easy-to-read textbooks. He is assisted by two assessors. These also are elected at the same time as the judges. Some 50 to 75 assessors are elected per judge; and the assessors are laymen and laywomen, acting in rotation part-time, each serving ten days a year. The assessors have identical powers of judgment with the judge. Decisions are made by a majority of the three on both facts and law.

Elections were held in 1948, 1951, and December 1954. The candidates are submitted by much the same groups, dominated by the Communist Party, as in Soviet elections.

It is sought to get the comparatively better educated people, the intelligentsia. In 1948 nearly 70 percent of the assessors held Soviet decorations. In 1954, 99.92 percent of the eligible voters took part in the elections; of these 99.54 cast their votes for the Communist bloc of party and nonparty candidates of judges, and 99.98 percent for the assessors. There was but one candidate for each place. (In Moscow alone 185 judges and 15,000 assessors were elected.) The candidates in 1948 included no less than 53 percent who were not members of the Communist Party. It corresponds to the need, given the small proportionate size of the party and the tremendous demands on its energies, to bring in other people to the service of the State, and also, to the "parental" theories of Soviet criminologists and penologists of tutoring the people in the meaning of justice. The popular campaign, with its boasts and promises and accounts rendered of justice done, conduces to this latter end. As the red placards, red flags mark the polling places and the music blares forth, it enables the regime to announce on the loud speakers:

"The Soviet Court—the Most Democratic Court in the World," that the "bourgeois court is the court of the rich," a "tool of suppression" and a "tool for exploitation of the working people."

Law Training

The universities have their law faculties. But the courts are not filled by those who have graduated in them. As far as we are able to discover few, indeed, of the Supreme Court and Republic Union Courts judges have had legal education. Some 70 percent of the provincial court judges have had little training. Only about 40 percent of the judges of the lowest courts have had some training, usually by correspondence, although some have attended the two-year schools. From about 1930 many students have attended the regular four-year university courses even more the two-year and correspondence courses.

Those who wish to graduate in law at the universities have a curriculum of four or five years with an average instruction of 1000 hours per year. This is distributed thus: 12 percent on Marxism-Leninism and political economy; 15 percent on Latin, history, logic, foreign language, etc.; 63 percent on twenty-three law courses. The political subjects occupy twice the time they do for science students.

This kind of training does not make for "independence" of justice. It is totally pervaded with the Communist theory of the State and of law—that is, the objectives of the State—as much as any zealot of the party leadership. To make the dependence more certain, the "elections" are for periods—that is, the electing body has a clear right to throw a judge out in five or three years. Moreover, the recall (p. 813) is stipulated and practiced. How convenient for the Executive to have at its disposal a legal and theoretically justifiable instrument of removing incompetent judges. We have seen that the judges in Britain are appointed from the Bar; this supplies the Bench with independent-minded militants for legality. The judges are irremovable. In France the judges are appointed by the Executive, but are irremovable. In both countries, however, there is something in addition to this: the law schools are free schools, and there are several of them, and they teach and thrive in an environment of freedom of discussion and teaching, the renewed research of truth, and the admission of free and active dissent to any kind of doctrine that might like to call itself "official" or "reason of State" (pp. 39–40). In the Soviet Union the law schools are strait-jacketed like any other school, like any individual, by the principles of the regime. The law students learn more of the dictatorial necessities than we have even attempted to demonstrate in this work; and it is their supreme law.

In these law schools, this is the official interpretation of "judges are independent":

> The independence of the judges referred to in Article 112 of the Stalin Constitution does not and cannot signify their independence of politics. The judges are subject only to the law— this provision expresses the subordination of the judges to the policy of the Soviet regime, which finds its expression in the law. . . .
>
> The demand that the judges be guided by the policy of the Communist Party is considerably wider than the demand for strict observance of the principles of legality, because the law itself gives grounds and leaves latitude for the application of political criteria. . . . (From the Moscow *University Herald*, November, 1950.)

But we know that *politics* in Russia embraces every aspect of man, now and future. And authoritative commentaries add:

> The action of the courts must be coordinated with that of the whole Soviet and Party apparatus.

The practical effect of such injunctions is that in the tension between individual and State, the State is preferred; that cases are given priority on the docket according to propaganda needs; that facts emerging in judicial proceedings of interest to party and State (the M.V.D., for instance) are passed on to them; that the locus of a trial is changed to suit propaganda purposes or make sure of conviction.

It will be appreciated, also, that the independence of the judges is undermined by the presence everywhere of informers and party spies. It is further subverted by the ambition for promotion and the requirement that the aspirant satisfy his Soviet masters.

Counsel

The great safeguard of persons charged with crime or civil wrong is independent counsel of their own choice. Such counsel ought to be a profession independent in training, recruitment, payment, professional mores, of the State. This exists in the Western democracies as we have shown. Such a body of counsel does not exist in the Soviet Union.

Counsel cannot be employed in the preliminary investigations, before the case comes before the court, though this process may be decisive. The attorneys enter the profession on graduation from a Higher School of Law, or they may come only from secondary schools of law provided they have had a year's experience as judge, as procurator, as investigator, or legal adviser of a public institution. People without formal training at all who have had the mentioned experience for at least three years are also admissible.

They are organized in law offices in the main district cities. Their president is appointed by the regional bar association, called the College of Advocates. These associations are run by executive committees which are elected by the members, with the party taking control of the election. These bar associations are the disciplinary bodies, and the admission-to-the-bar authorities. The Ministry of Justice requires that these associations are satisfied of the applicants' "political" as well as professional qualifications.

Attorneys may be expelled by their association for conviction of crime, unprofessional behavior, and breaking the association's rules. Appeal against this is up to the Ministry of Justice, a powerful political grip over the attorney, as he cannot appeal to the courts. (What good would it do, if he could?) The Ministry of Justice itself may cancel an admission made by a bar association on its own initiative. The bar associations have heavy disciplinary powers up to expulsion. This firmly subjects the profession to the dictators.

The fees are set by the Ministry of Justice. They are paid to the College of Advocates. Then the colleges (regional) pay a salary to the attorneys from the funds. The colleges, through their local offices, assign the attorneys to clients. The Ministry of Justice maintains close daily supervision of this process.

The colleges' internal rules require that a lawyer be under obligation *first to the State*. He must even help the prosecutor! The moment the case has a "reason of State" aspect (the very ones that require the maximum independence and militancy on behalf of the client), the Soviet defense counsel becomes little more than an echo of the prosecutor. The most he can do is to try to get the sentence moderated. In the words of the Deputy Minister of Justice in June 1951 (*Literary Gazette*, June 8):

> Bravely and consistently defending the accused, the lawyer must be guided by the principles of Socialist justice. He must present his arguments for the defense without departing from the standpoint of a Soviet defense attorney. . . . A Soviet lawyer cannot confine his task merely to the interests of the client, but must always think in the first instance of the interests of the people, the interests of the State.

Who could possibly feel safe and secure with such a defender? Nobody is.

Appeals and Jurisdiction

The People's Courts have wide jurisdiction, covering all civil cases in which individuals sue each other, minor suits in which the State and para-State institutions are parties, and criminal cases *except* where State interests are involved. As State interests soon become involved, the exception takes to other "nonpopular" courts those where it is desirable that the strength of the State should be especially limited. Its power of punishment goes all the way, but not to the death penalty; cases involving the latter go to higher courts.

The regional court or territorial court, the judges, flanked by assessors, are appeal courts from the People's Courts and courts of first instance for the graver cases. The latter include the beginnings of crimes against the State: counterrevolution in its various forms; theft of property from the State; law-breaking by officials; the more important cases in divorce, rape; civil cases implicating State and para-State agencies.

Appeals lie from these to the Autonomous Republics and Union Republic's Supreme Courts. In the Union Republic's Supreme Courts, there is a first instance jurisdiction in important criminal cases. In these cases, the Procurator has intervened to remove the case from the lower courts. Their jurisdiction includes, especially, offenses committed by administrative and judicial officials at the higher levels of the government. They act also in civil cases, where a Ministry or other central agency or a Soviet executive committee at the higher level in the Republic is involved, and where the court takes cognizance of cases withdrawn from the lower courts for their legal complexity or their political and public importance.

The Supreme Court of the U.S.S.R. consists of 78 judges and 35 people's assessors. Its chief function is to take appeals from the lower courts and to give final interpretation of the laws compelling the lower courts to follow suit. As a court of first instance, it functions rarely and only for the trial of the highest officials charged with State, military, economic, or service crimes, or cases which have been sent before it by the Presidium of the Soviet of the U.S.S.R. for their legal complexity or political importance.

Removal of Venue. The main interest in the distribution of functions lies in the fact that the Procurator or the Ministry of Justice can easily get trials removed to the court where it may make the most public impact. It is doubtful whether this means the loss of such a guarantee of justice as is provided for in the U.S. Constitution (Amendment 6) ". . . by an impartial jury of the State and district wherein the crime shall have been committed," for there are so many other cards already stacked against the accused.

Perhaps truly local courts might be more just to one of the subject nationalities of the "multinational" State in the Ukraine or Kazakhstan, or Byelo-Russia, than a trial in Great Russia. Mere expediency settled by the high administrative powers can settle where and by which court the trial shall be conducted. It is hardly a question of the unhindered operation of a local jury—there is none. But it is possible to get more pliable judges; and to avoid inflaming local populations who may know the accused. It may be done in the interests of competence, but hardly in the interests of magnanimity.

In appeal cases, the higher courts have three judges, without assessors. Why are the assessors left out? Because, the authorities say, appeals require serious legal qualification and experience. Why this does not rule out assessors in the People's Courts it is hard to see.

Non Bis in Idem: No Double Jeopardy? Western democracies embody in their justice the principle that when a final verdict has been reached, the acquitted person will not be tried a second time for the same offense; the convict will not have his punishment increased. Furthermore, there are statutes of limitation. In the Soviet system, any judgment may be reversed at any time; any crime may be ferreted into at any time, at the instance of the Procurators at the higher levels and the presidents of the Supreme Courts of the Union Republics or the U.S.S.R.

The Soviet State does not admit that the "interests of the State or of the workers" shall be injured by a judgment, or allow one which violates the law, in spite of the work of the original and appeal courts. This, by the way, gives the Procurator General of the U.S.S.R. a power of invigilation and correction going all over the U.S.S.R. and deep down into the smallest cranny of the judicial system. The highest courts of the republics and the Union take cognizance of these cases. *The parties are not admitted to these hearings!* Nor can they be represented by counsel. It might give an advantage to them. The courts so seized may do whatever they like with the judgment. The Procurators at the relevant levels *may* attend the hearings.

This is "double jeopardy," indeed; but not for the Soviet State, for it does not intend to be half-safe.

Many Special Jurisdictions. The Rule of Law, in its purest form, embodies the principle that all cases involving any private individual, any official of State and local authorities, alike, shall be judged by the same courts, the same law, with the same procedure. The closest to its practice is in Britain. Close to this comes such countries as France, where a differentiation is made only into common courts and administrative courts.

In the Soviet Union, the law is segregated into the ordinary courts we have touched on and—as the constitution puts it—the special courts. They are all All-Union courts. There are military courts for *all* crimes by the Armed Forces (this is reminiscent of the "benefit of clergy" in medieval times), or for espionage, treason, "diversionary acts," and terroristic acts, purchase, storage, or sale of firearms, divulgation or loss of State secrets and documents, arms and ammunition, etc., theft of firearms, regardless of whether a person is in the Army or not. Thus, at once, the tranquillity of the citizen's mind is violated by this subjection to a military court. The judges and assessors are elected by the Soviets in the usual way. As soon as any of the above-mentioned crimes are involved, the culprit is withdrawn from the ordinary courts.

The correctional labor courts are courts set up since December 1944 to try prisoners in the camps and the officials of these camps, the former for crimes therein committed, the latter for any offenses not touching their service obligations. The military personnel here, for *any* crime, and the civilian officials for service crimes, are tried in the courts of the Ministry of the Interior's own Armed Forces. These latter courts try all offenses of these Armed Forces, service offenses of the State Security agencies, of the militia, the civilian officials of the camps and prisons, and civilians who have committed any in the usual gamut of anti-State crimes.

The military courts are headed by the military section of the U.S.S.R. Supreme Court. This has primary jurisdiction over offenses committed by all the top officials, service, administrative and judicial, connected with the Armed Forces. It takes cases sent to it by the Presidium—they are the most important political anti-State cases. It does not need to use its assessors; it may act with only three judges. The Procurator may protest its judgment; there is no appeal from it. It takes appeals from the lower military courts. It supervises the application of the law by the lower military courts.

There are railroad courts and water transport courts. This arrangement is evidence of the sensitiveness of the Soviet regime to its transport network: it remembers the damage done by the Old Bolsheviks to the Czarist regime by subversion of the railroad workers: they stopped Kornilov's march on Leningrad! Furthermore, the tautly planned economy depends on the far-flung network of lines and boats. The courts embrace cases of labor discipline, damage or destruction of *matériel* by violation of nonobservance of the traffic rules, human accidents from the same cause, of endangering traffic safety or regularity by such cause, delaying turn-about of vehicles, and so on. The penalties are most severe. They do not depend on malicious intention or criminal intent. The severity is partly owing to impatience with the peasants and near-peasants who have been drafted into work of this kind, and the readiness of the government to break men and women in the interests of the fulfillment of their Plans.

These courts have jurisdiction over ordinary persons for crimes of a counterrevolutionary nature and property damage and theft, etc., against the State connected with transport. The Supreme Court has special divisions over the local water and transport courts.

Discipline of the Judges

Though the party has been careful to choose the judges according to their political zeal and reliability, it is still possible that, in action, they may be stirred to an undesirable deviation, or may be incompetent from any point of view. A judge *may even be too zealous,* and stir up party and civilian hornets' nests.

Besides the invigilation of the Procurators and the rules sent down by the Supreme Courts, the judges are subject to the Ministry of Justice at the All-Union and the Union-Republic levels. Their local and central officials revise all cases. They cannot possibly do this for all cases; but they make periodical samplings. They visit the courts, point out defects, submit rules for improvement, examine the pretrial investigatory process. The Soviet newspapers are full of demands for legality, and fulminations against judges and procurators who are dilatory or break confidence or use improper methods of investigation. This is especially so, since the discovery that the nine doctors of the Kremlin had had confessions forced out of them —it being politically expedient in the fight with Beria, to make all this public. One shudders at the number of grotesque miscarriages of justice, even admitted by the Soviet authorities themselves.

By a Decree of the Presidium in July 1948, the responsibility of judges was stipulated in clear terms: "violation of labor discipline [*You've got to work!* Italics supplied], a defect in judicial practice caused by negligence or deficient discipline of the judge, or commission of acts that cannot be reconciled with the dignity of a Soviet judge." The higher courts judge the fault, tier above tier, to the disciplinary division of the U.S.S.R. Supreme Court. This is done at the instance of the Ministries of Justice or the presidents of the various courts. As a result the Minister may ask for a recall of the judge; and he will get it.

If judicial crime is involved, the Procurator sets the law in motion.

Innocent unless Proven Guilty? It may be that in ordinary cases the rule that a man is innocent until the prosecution proves his guilt to an impartial judge operates in the Soviet courts. But it is disputed that it ought to be, by some Soviet jurists as a principle, and it is clear that the accused are given treatment by the investigator as though they were guilty. In political cases, the presumption is heavily against the accused, and he is very lucky to get off. The whole procedure of arrest, the spying, the informer system, the promotional pressure for securing convictions, and the quick public jubilation by the party and State press that class and national enemies have been found, all militate against the presumption of innocence.

Arrest and Investigation

The code of criminal procedure prohibits arrest and detention except under the law and by legal procedure. The Procurator or judge discovering such detention must immediately free the person held illegally. Detention is permitted for suspicion of committing a crime, subject to preliminary investigation, in order to prevent evasion of the suspect. It can only be used if the suspect is caught directly preparing or committing, or just after, the crime; when the injured or witnesses point out the culprit; when clues are found on him or in his home; when he has attempted flight or during it; when he has no permanent residence or occupation; when his identity is not established.

The prosecutor's office conducts preliminary investigations. There is no limit to the time this may take. Meanwhile there is detention, without privilege of legal help.

There is no way whereby any civilian friend of the suspect can get him before a court for impartial treatment, *for there is no habeas corpus writ* procedure. In cases that suit the State and the party—if they get to hear of them—there may be disciplinary intervention against a dilatory or negligent investigator. There is no external check on the methods of investigation. People have been in jail for months, even years, as a result.

This has special dangers for those arrested on suspicion of counterrevolutionary crimes, etc., for which "preventive" arrests is permitted. In minor cases bail may be acceptable. But more important ones, especially those touching the safety of the State, State property, and so on, bail is not available. The various decrees do set down maximum terms for various detentions: but once the "enemy of the State" theme is involved, the culprit is in the toils, notwithstanding the severe penalties on the judicial authorities for delays.

The M.V.D. In the cases previously referred to, the defendant appears in court, and he and his counsel may argue. There is another court where there is *no appearance of defendant:* the Special Conference of the M.V.D. (see p. 885). This acts as a kind of administrative court (like the Senate of the Czars used to for Trotsky, Lenin, Stalin, and such prisoners) for "socially dangerous" culprits, with power to banish, exile, or imprison for up to five years. They get into the forced labor camps. The courts supply them with work; so do the police.

Finally, each Soviet at the *raion* level has a special committee that may levy fines and consign to limited periods of forced labor for various misdemeanors.

The Inviolability of Homes and Correspondence. Closely connected with the judicial process are these immunities, guaranteed by the Constitution. But the militia has the right to enter private dwellings in pursuit of suspects or escapees, *without judicial warrant.* The investigators may at their own discretion enter homes and make searches at their complete discretion and without warrant. They will be held responsible by the Ministry of Justice for abuse of power. This, itself, is a stimulus to invent or plant objects to cover derelictions of duty. The seizure of any required documents, including letters, is included. If the investigator wishes to get hold of postal or telegraphic correspondence, he asks the permission of the Procurator's Office; this received, the post office delivers to him what he asks for. This, notice, is not an independent judge's warrant; it is a prosecuting official's approval.

Summary

The law of crimes against the State is the broadest and vaguest in the world. The judges are not independent. The Procurator's Office manages the courts. The Ministry of Justice manages the judges. The arrested person is at the mercy of the investigator and the ministerial hierarchy. The special courts are jurisdictions of particular severity. The M.V.D. is subject to no rule of law at all. The accused has no independent attorney at any time. The judges are trained in a system of law that makes them the creatures of the Executive.

No Soviet person can have tranquil and serene faith in justice where the interests of the party and the State are touched.

Yet the government has the nerve to say (*Pravda,* April 6, 1953), after the false witness in the doctors' case had been announced:

No one will be allowed to violate Soviet legality. Each worker, each collective farmer and each member of the Soviet intelligentsia can work in confidence and tranquillity, knowing that his civil rights are under the trusty protection of Soviet socialist legality. The citizen of the great Soviet state can be sure that his rights guaranteed by the Constitution of the U.S.S.R. will be held sacred and protected by the Soviet Government.

Every day the press violently denounces incompetence and corruption. Beria was made away with by a tribunal composed of a military marshal, the chairman of the Central Council of Trade Unions, the First Deputy President of the U.S.S.R. Supreme Court, a general, a member of the party's Central Committee and First Secretary of the Moscow Party, the chairman of the Council of Trade Unions of Georgia, the President of the Moscow city court, the First Deputy Minister of the Interior of the U.S.S.R. Only two of these were judges. The trial took place under the law of December 1934, which does not call for a special tribunal of this kind but merely requires in cases of treason and terroristic crime, prompt trial without appeal or pardon, and with immediate capital punishment in the event of conviction. The Procurator's Office instituted the proceedings.

Since Stalin's death, Soviet air has rung with promises by the Party and the Government to improve judicial safeguards for the citizen and to make milder the criminal law; indeed, much was said on this score before the death of Stalin, also. The latest of such promises and professions have been gathered by Professor Harold Berman of the Harvard Law School from interviews conducted in Russia recently and reported in *The New York Times*, December 16, 1955. All that Russian people and foreign observers can comment on these is that when they really take effect they will be welcome, but so far they are but vague promises. We learn that the M.V.D. troops have been transferred to the control of the Soviet Army (1953), and that the three-man courts of the M.V.D. have been abolished. The Army has replaced the M.V.D. as directors of some labor camps, and there has been, it is alleged, some improvement in their administration. Military tribunals are revising those sentences made by the M.V.D. courts.

A new criminal code and procedure is in the making, to be released imminently. It does not change the grim nature of Soviet police State. The law of "counterrevolutionary" crimes remains intact. Arbitrary arrest and forced labor will still exist. But peasants will not be criminally liable for nonfulfillment of work days; managers may sell surplus equipment, and will not be punished for minor negligence. The doctrine of "analogy"—that is, conviction for a crime because it is analogous, though not identical, with the one prescribed in the law—will be set aside. Severity of punishment for some counterrevolutionary acts will be reduced —from ten to five years' maximum. People accused of crimes will have counsel as soon as indicted by the prosecutor. The period within which the prosecutor can re-call a case for rejudgment will be cut from five to two years.

It might be remembered that the Army can be just as severe in its judgments and no less arbitrary than the M.V.D.

There is no guarantee of justice for the individual without a free parliament based on free elections conducted by freely organizable political parties. All the rest is a delivery into the hands of the dictatorial leaders.

The long lectures delivered on ethics, morality, and the beneficence of Soviet justice by the judges in court may educate the public, but it would be better if they purified the system.

The Communist Party of the Soviet Union

Are the decisions of the leading bodies carried out or are they pigeon-holed by bureaucrats and chair-warmers? Are they carried out properly, or are they distorted? Is the apparatus working conscientiously and in a Bolshevik manner, or running with the motor idling? . . .

A proper check on the fulfillment of decisions is a searchlight which helps to reveal how the apparatus is functioning at any moment, exposing bureaucrats and chair-warmers to full view. We can say with certainty that nine tenths of our defects and failures are due to the lack of a properly organized system of check-up on the fulfillment of decisions.

—Stalin. *Report to Seventeenth Congress, 1934*

I. THE SOVEREIGN RULER

The sovereign ruler of the Soviet Union is the Communist Party. Its power has no limits in principle but only in human inability to achieve all it wants by coercion and persuasion.

The party's principal characteristics receiving analysis here, though not necessarily in the order set down, are:

1. It is monopolistic; there are no other parties.

2. It is self-righteous, exclusively and fanatically so.

3. Its vocation of leadership is united with the militia of terror.

4. It is deliberately small in size—an *élite*.

5. It engenders obedience and represses opposition.

6. Its social composition has been varied with the leaders' purposes.

7. It has a planned apparatus (*apparat*) covering the entire empire.

8. It operates on the principle of "democratic centralism."

9. The motivations of its membership are mixed.

10. The Party Presidium—until 1952 called the Politbureau—is the apex of the dictatorship.

11. It exploits auxiliary organizations to effect its mission: Security Police, *Komsomols,* the schools, trade unions, etc., etc.

Size and Structure

In 1952, at the Nineteenth Congress of the party, membership was 6,882,145. This amounts to about 3 percent of the population. We shall use the round number 7,000,000, though Khrushchev announced in December 1955 it had risen to 8,000,000.

When the membership was about 2,000,000 in 1937, Stalin declared that the leading forces of the party were thus disposed:

In our party, if we have in mind its leading strata, there are about 3000 to 4000 first-rank leaders whom I would call the Party's corps of generals.

Then there are about 30,000 to 40,000 middle-rank leaders who are our Party corps of officers.

Then there are about 100,000 to 150,000 of the lower-rank Party command staff who are, so to speak, our Party's non-commissioned officers.

The higher of these alternatives add up to nearly 200,000 party officials, or 1 per 35 members of the party. These are full-time, or nearly so. They are paid, in part, from party funds, and, in part, by the jobs they hold in some branch of the government, industry, farming, or other officially organized branches of Soviet life. They may be paid from State funds for what are practically sinecures on the State payroll. The public is not told.

Information from former party officials who have fled from the Soviet Union gives the impression that there may be as many as 600,000 party officials, or about 1 in 10 of the total membership.

The party has "substituted" itself for the Russian people in the conduct of all phases of its life. The word *substitutism* was first used by Trotsky as a reproach to Lenin for assuming dictatorship of the party (p. 772). This had been the bane of Russian political development: "an orthodox theocracy" in place of the people themselves.

The Monopolistic Party

Stalin's boast in his speech on the Constitution (p. 790) was only another of many. Another statement, of 1926, oft-repeated is:

The highest expression of the leading role of the Party here in the Soviet Union, in the land of the dictatorship of the proletariat, for example, is the fact that not a single important political or organizational question is decided by any soviet or other mass organization without guiding directions from the Party. *In this sense* it could be said that the dictatorship of the proletariat is *in essence* the "dictatorship" of its vanguard, the dictatorship of its Party, as the main guiding force of the proletariat.

The growth of parties *outside* this one is made impossible by the Criminal Code's dispositions on "Counterrevolutionary" crimes, etc. (p. 842) and the force in the hands of the party. Furthermore, the constitutional obligations of the citizen (p. 842) give the courts and the prosecutors ample ground for extinguishing nascent opposition. The right of association (Article 126 of the Constitu-

tion) is exercisable only in "conformity with the interests of the working people"; and is subject to the Communist Party, which in that article is ascribed the right to be the "leading core of all organizations."

No parties may be formed *inside* the one party. Lenin's fury at the Kronstadt mutiny in March 1921 was vented in a decisive resolution of the party, at its Tenth Congress:

All class-conscious workers must clearly realize the perniciousness and impermissibility of fractionalism of any kind, for no matter how the representatives of individual groups may desire to safeguard Party unity, in practice fractionalism inevitably leads to the weakening of team work and to intensified and repeated attempts by the enemies of the Party who have fastened themselves upon it because it is the governing Party, to widen the cleavage and use it for counterrevolutionary purposes.

In the practical struggle against fractionalism, every organization of the Party must take strict measures to prevent any fractional actions whatsoever.

Examination of Party decisions and policy and errors must in no circumstances be submitted for preliminary discussion to groups formed on the basis of any sort of program, etc., but must be submitted exclusively for discussion directly to all members of the Party. . . .

The Congress therefore now declares dissolved, and orders the immediate dissolution, of all groups without exception that have been formed on the basis of one program or another [such as the Workers' Opposition, the Democratic Centralism group, and so on]. Non-observance of this decision of the Congress entails absolute and immediate expulsion from the Party.

In extreme cases the party's Central Committee could expel culprits from the party; and with a two-thirds resolution of the Central Committee from the Committee and Control Commission itself. The victims spoke of the party's "mailed fist," as first Lenin, and then Stalin from 1924 used the rule to gain ascendency. Stalin acted with complete "legality" in the use of these rules, but it was of the order of "legality" used by Hitler in

Party Echelons and Levels of Soviet Government, 1954

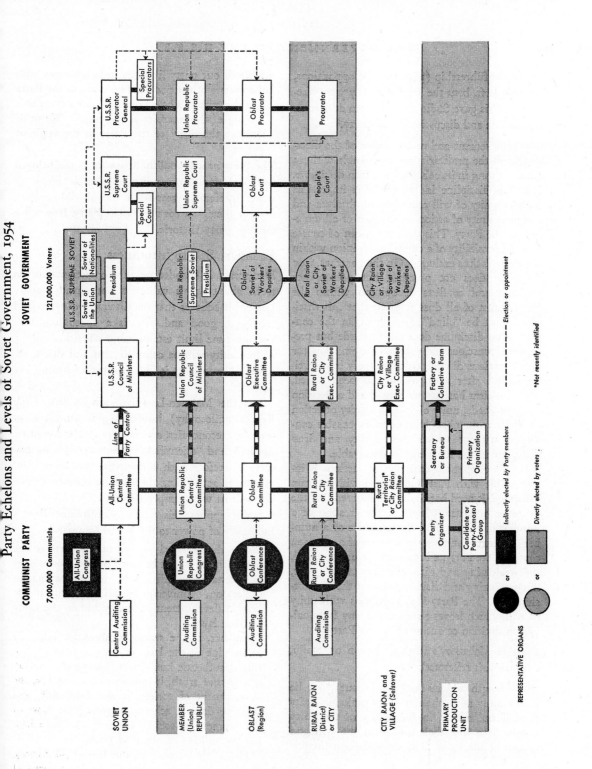

rising to the führership (p. 651). The oppositions, Right and Left, bent the knee, for they were like-minded.[1] This gave Stalin the power to declare an end to debate and discussion in the party.[2]

> The achievement and maintenance of the dicta-torship of the proletariat are impossible without a party strong in its cohesion and iron discipline. But iron discipline in the Party is impossible without unity of will and without absolute and complete unity of action on the part of all mem-bers of the Party. This does not mean of course that the possibility of a conflict of opinion within the Party is thus excluded. On the contrary, iron discipline does not preclude but presupposes criticism and conflicts of opinion within the Party. Least of all does it mean that this disci-pline must be "blind" discipline. On the con-trary, iron discipline does not preclude but pre-supposes conscious and voluntary submission, for only conscious discipline can be truly iron disci-pline. But after a discussion has been closed, after criticism has run its course and a decision has been made, unity of will and unity of action of all Party members become indispensable con-ditions without which Party unity and iron discipline in the Party are inconceivable.

> It follows that the existence of factions is in-compatible with Party unity and with its iron discipline. It need hardly be emphasized that the existence of factions leads to the creation of a number of centres, and the existence of a num-ber of centres connotes the absence of a common centre in the Party, a breach in the unity of will, the weakening and disintegration of discipline, the weakening and disintegration of the dictator-ship. . . . The Party is synonymous with unity of will, which leaves no room for any factional-ism or division of authority in the Party.

Even in Malenkov's funeral oration on Stalin, the principle is reiterated:

> The strength and invincibility of our Party lie in the unity and cohesion of its ranks, in unity of will and action, in the ability of the Party members to fuse their will with the will and desires of the Party. The strength and invinci-

bility of our party lie in its indivisible ties with the masses of the people. The unity of the Party and the people is based on the Party's invariable serving of the interests of the people. We must treasure the unity of the Party as the apple of our eye.

The Party as a Monolith. *Monolith* is the beloved metaphor for party unity. "A single block of stone," preferably granite; it was also Mussolini's favorite metaphor for the Fascist Party. It is still a force in party rhetoric.

Fanatical Self-righteousness

Democracy is founded on the conviction that the truth about man's values is not already totally known. It believes that the discovery of truth and falsehood, good and evil, is a continuing task without time limit establishable when knowledge of humanity will be complete, cut and dried, ab-solute. Democracy is the institutionalization of doubt.

But the Marxian-Leninist view is that (like Regel's philosophy) historical generalizations in sociology, economics, and politics can be complete, finished, and "scientifically" demonstrable by his-tory. Therefore such knowledge should be con-vincing to action, and therefore to obedience. The disobedient were simply perverse.

Stalin applies this to the Communist Party's monopoly of power to think and command.

> Hence the practical activity of the party of the proletariat must not be based on the good wishes of "outstanding individuals," not on the dictates of "reason," "universal morals," etc., but on the laws of development of society and on the study of these laws.

> Further, if the world is knowable and our knowledge of the laws of development of Na-ture is authentic knowledge, having the validity of *objective* truth, it follows that social life, the development of society, is also knowable, and that the data of science regarding the laws of development of society are authentic data hav-ing the validity of objective truths.

> Hence the science of the history of society, despite all the complexity of the phenomena of social life, *can become as precise a science as, let us say, biology,* and capable of making use of the laws of development of society *for practical purposes* [Italics added].

---

[1] Their state of mind is accurately portrayed in two works of "fiction": Arthur Koestler, *Darkness at Noon,* New York, 1941, and Victor Serge, *The Case of Comrade Tukaev,* New York, 1951.

[2] Joseph Stalin (J. Fineberg, editor), *Leninism, Selected Writings,* New York, 1942, pp. 96–97.

So, therefore

> Hence the party of the proletariat should not guide itself in its practical activity by casual motives, but by the laws of development of society, and by practical deductions from these laws.

The passage is quoted from an article purported to have been written by Stalin in September 1938 for the *History of the Communist Party of the Soviet Union* and appears in *Leninism* under the title of "Dialectical and Historical Materialism." It is a crude summary of Marxist and Leninist theory and exhibits not the slightest philosophical talent. (No sooner was Stalin dead, than his successors denied his authorship of the *Short History!*) **Stalin Is Truth, or Whoever Is de Facto on Top.** Yet, elsewhere, Stalin points out that Marx lived fifty years before the Russian Revolution. He could not, therefore, be expected to foresee all the complexities of practical everyday problems arising in the Soviet Union. *Therefore, Marxism must be interpreted* to fit the problems actually to be solved, and he recommends his followers to do so. In doing this, then, an arbitrary element enters into the interpretation of Marxism and any other "ism," for example, Leninism, by the one man who may be at the top of the party. That Stalin regarded himself and, personalities apart, any successful successor of his as entitled to say what the laws of historical sociology *precisely* said for *practical* purposes at any juncture is deducible from (1) the passages on the organization of the party and the singleness of its will, (2) his purges of opponents, (c) the practice of "centralism" in the party instead of its qualifying term *democratic* to which we devote attention later (p. 868). Stalin put the matter nicely, if gruesomely, when he twitted his defeated opponents thus at the Seventeenth Party Congress:

> Here, too, [in general policy] as in other spheres, there is no little confusion in the views of certain members of our party. Sometimes, while fighting against the Right deviation, they turn away from the "Left" deviation and relax the fight against it on the assumption that it is not dangerous, or hardly dangerous. This is a grave and dangerous error. This is a concession to the "Left" deviation which is impermissible for a member of the party. It is all the more impermissible for the reason that of late the "Lefts" have completely slid over to the position of the Rights, so that there is no longer any essential difference between them.
>
> We have always said that the "Lefts" are also Rights, only they mask their Right-ness behind Left phrases. . . .

Life must be pretty hard in a land that allows only such a narrow, straight, sharp line between Left and Right—definable by one man. That same man had scoffed only a few moments before: "At this Congress . . . there is nothing more to prove and, it seems, no one to fight. Everyone now sees that the line of the party has triumphed." Everyone, that is to say, not yet "liquidated" or dead.

Thus, the party, then, assumed what has come to be called the "closed society"[3]—that is, the existence of the shape of the good society, now known once and for all, regardless of the variations in human personality and of values noticeable by other philosophers in mankind's past, and regardless of the new variations and creativeness in the perception of truth and beauty and goodness in the succeeding people newly born day by day. This is the opposite of the "open society," roughly equatable with the democratic way of life, that is interested in accommodating social institutions and set forms to the free evolution of new individual characters as they enter this life and develop their potentialities. The Communist way is the way of a common stereotype impressed on subjects by authority, a ready-made character.

It follows from Leninism and Stalinism that the record of the past must be forced to conform with the propaganda needed today. Hence, the Soviet practice of expunging from known history the men and events they do not like their people to know. Trotsky, his ideas, personality, and services to the Bolshevik have been converted into the picture of a national and party traitor. Beria, with four pages of praise in the *Soviet Encyclopedia,* is recommended for excision by sharp scissors or a razor blade and an article on the Bering Sea provided to replace him! Yet, even such tricks can hardly deceive all the people all the time; for some

---

[3] See Karl Popper, *The Open Society and Its Enemies,* New York, 1951.

memories are transmissible. But this is what the dictator tries.

The Vocation of Leadership— and Terror

Some of the early Czar-fighting Bolsheviks were undoubtedly involved completely and conscientiously, in genuine dedication, to the Communist ideal. Such men as the *Komsomol* who murdered Stalin's friend Kirov (p. 782) felt such a true and total call as well. It is difficult, indeed, to argue solely that some or all of these were merely lustful for power, regardless of the aim of a better society. It is daring to make such an assertion of Stalin even, shocking as his methods were. But we do know enough about some of them and the many members of the party (so does the party!) in whom motives are very mixed: They want power, prestige, delight in business, recognition as one of the Soviet *élite* and "socialites." Some merely like the leaders, or some among them. "Careerism" is one of the most frequent charges within the party, not always sincere, either.

But the party's doctrine, solemnly and repeatedly pronounced is that one enters the party in order to lead—whom? The masses. We draw attention to Stalin's speech on "iron discipline," which was a paraphrase of the Party Rules of 1934. In the redraft of the statutes of 1952, the doctrine of leadership runs:

> The Communist Party of the Soviet Union is a voluntary, militant union of Communists holding the same views, formed of the people of the working class, the working peasantry and the working intelligentsia.
>
> Having organized the alliance of the working class and the working peasantry, the Communist Party accomplished, through the *great* October *socialist* [4] revolution of 1917, the overthrow of the capitalists and landowners, the organization of the dictatorship of the proletariat, the liquidation of capitalism and abolition of the exploitation of man by man, and ensured the construction of a socialist society.
>
> The chief tasks of the Communist Party of

the Soviet Union now are to build a communist society by gradual transition from socialism to communism, to bring about a constant rise in the living standards and cultural level of society, to educate the members of society in internationalism and establishment of fraternal bonds with the working people of all countries, and to strengthen in every respect the active defense of the Soviet country against aggressive actions of its enemies.

The passage excludes what was evident before the words *domination, vanguardship,* but retains that of *militancy.*

Coercion versus Welfare. The problem is to shepherd some 210,000,000 men, women, and children of the most diverse nationalities, cultures, language, economic occupation, and level of civilization into a highly artificial economy and culture, omitting for the moment any belief in the shape of Communism-to-Come. We take only the more immediate target; its attainment is a Titanic one. Seven million members could not altogether *enforce* obedience over one sixth of the earth's land area. Weapons would lose servants; threats would diminish long-run incentive.

A large part of the population finds its welfare in the economic and cultural advance and the new opportunities for talent and skill. It has broken reliance for these on private property and enterprise by force to the utmost. It has to persuade or force the insurgent freedom of the human spirit looking for such welfare through unfree channels, and also to cope with deep inertia, ignorance, and sloth. The vocation of the party, then, is to curb, guide and eradicate if necessary, any deviations from the path the party has decided for the nation. The task is more than persuasion, it is conviction without reservations. It would like everybody without exception to believe as it believes—perhaps more than this!—and accordingly identify their whole individuality with the purpose. If this is unattainable, it must have obedience, if not applause, then complaisance. For this the party starts with an enormous advantage and one tremendous disadvantage. They arise out of the same phenomenon: the economic, cultural, and literary backwardness of the mass of the people. The triumph of 1917 demonstrated that (pp. 765–768). It has

---

[4] The two words italicized constitute the full extent of amendments proposed by the Party Congress to the draft of the statutes prepared by the Central Committee of the party! Such spontaneous unity is little short of miraculous telepathy.

been easy to win prestige by raising the level from its shocking depths. But the obverse is a people whose superstition, ignorance, crass managerial incompetence, primitive habits, and suspicions deter intelligent collaboration. Hence, the *militancy*. It has to fight backwardness, and for a most extraordinary forwardness, of a degree that puts an intolerable strain on the human nature of even its best.

Moreover, since men may form a kind of opposition party merely by closing their minds to persuasion and command, it has to ferret out, expose, and eradicate, latent opposition and apathy. Apathy is Russia's great opposition party to the Communist Party, passive resistance, nonviolent noncooperation. Its own standards have to be lowered from the utopian to the possible level.

Education of the Masses. The leaders have never ceased to require of the party a going-out to the people, to work for them, to serve them; it is incessantly drummed in. Of course, what is meant by *service*, its sincerity, in the absence of free and open choice of leaders and policy by elections, is a question. But the doctrine is reaffirmed almost fearfully. Stalin put this into the peroration of the *Short Course of the Communist Party*, the breviary of the zealots. He smoothed its path by recounting the myth of Antaeus, some of Poseidon and Gaea, goddess of the Earth. Until Hercules lifted him from the earth, he was invincible. So must the party be invulnerable by contact with the people.

We may take it as a rule [says Stalin] that as long as the Bolsheviks maintain connection with the broad masses of the people they will be invincible. And, on the contrary, as soon as the Bolsheviks sever themselves from the masses and lose their connection with them, they become covered with bureaucratic rust, they will lose all their strength and become a mere cipher.

Lastly, the history of the Party teaches us that unless it has wide connections with the masses, unless it constantly strengthens these connections, unless it knows how to hearken to the voice of the masses and understand their urgent needs, unless it is prepared not only to teach the masses, but to learn from the masses, a party of the working class cannot be a real mass party capable of leading the working class millions and all the laboring people.

A party is invincible if it is able, as Lenin says, "to link itself with, to keep in close touch with, and to a certain extent if you like, to merge with the broadest masses of the toilers—primarily with the proletariat, but also with the non-proletarian toiling masses."

But, as already noted, do the leaders go out with *their* ideal in mind; with what the people *want* or what they *ought* to want; is it an ideal over and above the leaders? Is it a base lust for domination rather than service of a Utopia?

The "Transmission-belt" Principle. The impulse to connection with the masses is sometimes put in the mechanical metaphor of the party as transmission belt between leaders and people. If it is not permitted on principle that the people be let freely to answer the question of genuineness and competence, at least this principle may offer some check on the capriciousness of the "vanguard" of the proletariat. The upper echelons of the party can always use the criterion as a principle of criticism and reward and punishment of the lower levels. Some sense of responsibility is introduced by it. Yet it does not, of course, prevent the chastisement of the people by the party for their own good.

The Party as Élite

Only 3 out of every 100 of the Russian people are members of the Communist Party. This is a great distinction. Yet we cannot be sure that many more would like to be members, for the party has at all times militantly fomented the desire to join its ranks.

Its attitude is dual. (1) A mass demand for entry would be flattering and enhance its power to manage the State. Yet (2) it believes that the undue increase of numbers would bring in too many who were not pure of heart or single-minded or militant. To be an *élite* is to have character without dilution. There are few people of this kind in any vocation. Furthermore, members of the party have onerous duties (p. *lxvi*). Lenin preferred even a party of only *one*, so long as it was self-sacrificial in its conviction and will power.

Democracies Are Less Particular. Democratic governments worry, but much less than the Communist Party, over the qualities of conviction of their members. For the possibility of losing elections and the existence of robust rivals in threatening competition keeps up the level of competence and wholesomeness. Their politics are less dogmatic about mankind's history and future; they are not so severe about the worthy and unworthy; their catechism is less absolute and sanguine.

The Communist Party is otherwise; it has to do from within what party rivalry does to democratic parties. It has to use purges, and exercise careful control of entry (pp. 861–866). For it needs fanatics only, of the Nechaev Revolutionists' Catechism variety (pp. 752–753). It has to winnow these out of the candidates who seek entry because it is the only access to high political activity, to administrative office, to the high positions in the socialized economy, to being Deputy in the Soviets, leader of clubs and groups in cultural activity, the Armed Forces, the diplomatic service, a Soviet Union "somebody."

The smaller the proportion of the people allowed to enter, the higher the value of a scarce commodity. As we have said, there is not a large proportion of people anywhere of such intense conviction, fanatical loyalty, uncritical obedience to "the Party line," mad perversion of logic and neglect of facts to preserve faith, uncompromising lines of action, brutal enmity toward opponents, self-sacrificial work under shame and punishment, subordination of all ethics to the aim.

Yet a minimum number is still required, though they possess these qualities in small degree, since the tasks are multifarious; this compromises the purity of Bolshevik "virtue."

Engendering Obedience and Repressing Opposition

This is the work of persuasion and rewards and inquisition, detection, and terror.

First, let us notice that the nearly 7,000,000 members and candidates of the party are made up of about 350,000 primary party units or "cells"—that is, an average of 20 members per cell. Such a unit is established, according to the Party Rules, by members in any institution or enterprise with not less than three members of the party. These are, as it were, the capillaries of the body politic

of the party. Now above these are the territorial organizations, which, coming downward on the primary units, numbered in October 1952: the All-Union Party Congress and Executive, 15 Union Republic *apparats*, 8 *krai*, 167 *oblasts*, 36 *okrugs*, 544 cities, 4886 *raions*. Then spread out the primary organizations. More will be said on this network later (p. 867ff.).

Functions of the Apparat. The functions may be classified thus:

1. To spread the essential doctrine of Marx-Leninism, the basic philosophy as a kind of religious sociology, by means of classes, lectures, speeches, articles, and behavior.

2. To spread the policy of the government, explaining the harmony with the essential Marxian doctrines and the current facts of international and national existence, yet making identity with Marx impossible and inadvisable, thus extolling the genius of the leader—Stalin, Malenkov, or any expedient duo or trio of them.

3. To recruit members and watch the quality of the party.

4. To invigilate all economic enterprises of any kind, and see that the management not only does not sabotage but that it fulfills its assigned Plans and output, both in quantity and quality and without violation of the rules which have been established by the Plans and laws.

5. To dominate all elections to all the Soviets, to secure leading positions on them; to select which of the nonparty people should be elected thereto; to dominate the executive bodies of the Soviets at all levels.

6. To dominate and manage all the institutions of the State as to policy pursued.

7. To invigilate all governmental administrative departments and secure the complete fulfillment of the tasks assigned to them with efficiency.

The tasks of the primary units should be studied in Statute 57 (p. *lxxii*) of the Statutes of 1952.

The *agitational work* is conducted through party schools, party newspapers, public lectures and conferences, wall newspapers, the radio, speeches, pamphlets. Nonattendance at meetings, not only for party members but for any person who is dependent on the State for something—for example, a scholarship or promotion to a higher job—is most dangerous. At some moments it might even be construed as "counterrevolutionary." The *Agitprop aktivs* organize the parades on the Soviet anniversaries: the Revolution; Lenin's birthday; May Day; Stalin's birthday, and so forth. The work is much more intense than the propaganda of democratic political parties, penetrating every block of apartments, without respite. And every happening in the world and the streets is related to the party's hopes and philosophy, incessantly, all tending one exclusive way, like the religion of Europe before Gallileo and the Reformation.

Recruitment of Members. No one knew better than Lenin did, that in the party, as in the administration of any human purpose, the vital element is personnel. Its basic concern is always to transmit, and preserve from long-run corruption, the fanaticism that was originally revealed to the founder, by means that cannot quite equal his in originality and purity. As Stalin was in command from 1924 to 1952, he was the genius of administration of the conspiratorial and totalitarian party of Leninist spirit and purpose. It does not mean that he was a good man. Others, with his wicked purposes, have been fools. His pre-Revolutionary career taught him the need of *komitetchiks* to make the Revolution and of *apparatchicks* to keep it productive in the radical reconstruction of society.

His doctrine on the importance of cadres enunciated several years before, appears in its fullness in his Report (as Secretary) to the Eighteenth Party Congress in 1939.[5] He said (in part):

The party cadres constitute the commanding staff of the party; and since our party is in power they also constitute the commanding staff of the leading organs of State. After a correct political line has been worked out and tested in practice, the party cadres become the decisive force in the work of guiding the party and the State. A correct political line is, of course, the primary and most important thing. But that in itself is not enough. A correct political line is not needed as a declaration, but as something to be carried into effect. But in order to carry a correct political line into effect, we must have cadres, people who understand the political line

of the party, and who accept it as their own line, who are prepared to carry it into effect, who are able to put it into practice and are capable of answering for it, defending it and fighting for it. Failing this, a correct political line runs the risk of being purely nominal.

And here arises the question of the correct selection of cadres, the training of cadres, the promotion of new people, the correct allocation of cadres, and the testing of cadres by work accomplished. . . .

The proper selection of cadres means:

First, valuing cadres as the gold reserve of the party and the state, treasuring them, respecting them.

Secondly, knowing cadres, carefully studying their individual merits and shortcomings, knowing in what post the capacities of a given worker are most likely to develop.

Thirdly, carefully fostering cadres, helping every promising worker to advance, not grudging time on patiently "bothering" with such workers and accelerating their development.

Fourthly, boldly promoting new and young cadres in time, so as not to allow them to stagnate in their old posts and grow stale.

Fifthly, allocating workers to posts in such a way that each feels he is in the right place, that each may contribute to our common cause the maximum his personal capacities enable him to contribute, and that the general trend of the work of allocating cadres may fully answer to the demands of the political line for the carrying out of which this allocation of cadres is designed.

He then went more deeply into the problem of overcoming inertia in the appointment of young people. For the "old cadres" were few, valuable as they were with their tremendous experience in leadership, their grasp of Marxist-Leninism, their knowledge of affairs, their capacity for orientation. "But they were already partly going out of commission owing to the operation of the laws of nature." (He must have laughed inwardly at this, considering how many he had assisted to go out of commission!) The young men had a sense of the new.

The tasks he outlined were consigned to the Cadres Administration of the party's Central Committee and its field offices throughout the country.

[5] Reprinted in *Leninism, Selected Writings*, New York, 1942, pp. 463–465.

Admissions. The presently applicable rules, which were adopted October 1952, run as follows:

> Persons to be admitted to the Party must be sponsored by three members of the Party of at least *three* years' standing who have been acquainted with the candidate in their joint work for a period of not less than one year.

> For those coming into the Party from the *Komsomols,* the recommendation of the latter's district committee counts as equal to the recommendation of one Party member.

> Members and candidates for the Central Committee of the Party may not make recommendations [Query: To maintain the independence of the local units *vis-à-vis* the center? Most probably; also to prevent the central members from competing with each other for a local clientele.]

> Admission is discussed and decided by a general meeting of the primary organization; the decision has force only when ratified by the "district" Party committee or the city committee where there is no such district subdivision. The recommenders need not be present during these discussions.

> The candidates for admission must have attained the age of 18. If the candidates are under 20, candidates may join only via the *Komsomols.*

How does one become a candidate? Admission to this stage is by the same rules as apply to final membership; if successful, the status of candidate lasts normally *one year.*

The stage of candidature is essential "in order that the candidate may acquaint himself with the Program, Statutes, and tactics of the Party," and so that the Party may verify his personal qualifications.

The Rules open the Party to successful candidates, and qualify admission with the phrase "workers, peasants, and intelligentsia who are politically aware, active and devoted to the Communist cause."

Some other rules are important. The first is that "admission is granted exclusively on an *individual* basis." This rule was imposed because local units showed a tendency to be lax in the admission of groups at one time, without exact scrutiny.

No distinction between classes is any longer made. The stages of previous differentiation are most instructive. From 1917 to 1921 no distinctions were made between workers and peasants, with two party recommendations and approval of the local meeting. The party was chiefly of urban workers. In December 1919 a two-month candidacy was set up for workers and peasants; for others, six months. In 1921 a great purge was necessary, of "rascals, bureaucrats, dishonest or wavering Communists, and of Mensheviks who have repainted their façade but who have remained Mensheviks at heart" (Lenin).

To obstruct antiproletarians, in August 1922 the rules placed candidates in varying categories; workers and Red Army; peasants and artisans not exploiting the labor of others; others, like office employees, etc. The number of references and their own length of membership were easier for the former than the latter, and candidature for the first category was shorter than for the others.

In December 1925 preference was given to workers at the bench as compared with others. Their sponsors were fewer and of shorter standing. Thus, a predominantly large urban following flocked in, reducing the proportion of peasants. Soon, it was seen that there were not enough educated people for the control of industry and public administration or able to assimilate the ideology. After the purges of 1932, new rules were drafted in 1934. Thus:

1. Industrial workers of not less than five years' production record;
2. Industrial workers with less than five years' record; Red Army men from workers or collective farmers, and *engineers and technicians* working in the shops or higher organizations of industry;
3. Collective farmers, members of crafts or artisan artels, and elementary school teachers;
4. Other employees.

Group 1 needed three recommendations of members of five-year standing and a candidacy of one year. All other groups had a two-year candidacy. Group 2 needed five recommendations from members with five-year standing; Group 3 the same, *plus* a recommendation from the tractor-station political representative or the district party committee. Group 4 needed five recommendations from members of ten-year standing! Thus, the intelligentsia of industry were advantaged, as the

Soviet handling of industrialization of the nation required, but the rules were too thorny for ready admissions.

The purges of 1934–1938 swept out "class enemies," "careerists," incompetents, ignorant and unmalleable collective farmers, and workers newly arrived in factories.

In 1939 the Eighteenth Congress of the party thoughtfully reconsidered its rules of admission. For the years of purge had revealed wholesale maladministration. Persons had been admitted without personal interview; records were faulty or nonexistent; the rules had been ignored, for various motives. Now the issue was how to gauge Communist loyalty. Zhdanov treated this question. He reported that two years earlier Stalin had said that "If we continue further along this path [that 'tried and theoretically-trained Marxists' should compose the party] we should have to leave only intellectuals and learned people generally in our Party." Who wanted such a party? asked Zhdanov and Stalin. Neither of them! The formula must be Lenin's: "A member of the Party is one who *accepts* the program of the Party, pays dues, and works in one of its organizations. Lenin's formula did *not* say *mastering* the program, but only *accepting* it."

Zhdanov continued:

Mastery of the program implies the ability to explain its underlying principles. *Accepting* the program means subscribing to its principles, agreeing with it and being ready to defend it. It is clear that by demanding that candidates for membership should *master* the program, that is, should be able to *explain its underlying principles,* we frighten people away from the Party. There is no theoretical justification for such a demand. . . . Many candidates have hesitated to apply for full membership of the Party for fear of being subjected to a political examination and, what is more, often by ignorant people. . . .

Hence the abolition of the Rule that new members must have mastered the program as well as accepted it.

There is more in the abolition than Zhdanov disclosed. If members do not show an aptitude for the ideology, what will sustain the regime in the long run? If they do, bright young men, like the *Komsomol* who killed Kirov, will read the philosophy, as thousands throughout Russia then did, as *their* mind and conscience spontaneously demand, and then sentence the party dictators for being disloyal to the ideology. They may be more communist than the Communists. The party was always plagued by this possibility, and Stalin had to write tracts to answer these critics who regarded *him* as the deviationist! Ultraroyalists have been more royalist than reigning kings, to regicide! (p. 287). A sharp light is thrown on this by observers in the Soviet prisons during the Great Purge. Soviet youth had to read the radical classics of the nineteenth century in order to *master* the ideology. Some began to ask, Where was humanity? Would Herzen have thought this right—would he have condoned the murder of the *kulaks?* Some informers alleged that those who were "disloyal" out of political conviction were more to be distrusted than "careerists"! "He thinks too much; such men are dangerous!" To the leaders, faith, loyalty, fear, personal comfort are more reliable than intellectual conviction. The thoughtful may desert; the uncritical may be fools.

Hence, (1) an opening of the way to the new technical and professional and academic intelligentsia developed in Stalin's regime, and (2) reference to those "who are politically aware, active and devoted to the Communist cause."

As the table on page 866 shows, the intelligentsia is now the largest sector of the party; the workers second; the peasants, a bad third.

In the Party Congress of 1952, Malenkov spoke strongly for restricting admissions to the party, preferring quality to numbers. When Khrushchev became First Secretary of the Party he chose a policy of substantial increases, particularly in the rural areas. His personal interest in recruiting new members favorable to his own regime is obvious, especially in view of his need to win authority in and for the party. Hence, a rise of some 300,000 members per year from 1953 to 1956.

Expulsions. Expulsion from the party is political outlawry; it will most probably bring economic degradation, civic persecution, and family disgrace.

Expulsion of an ordinary member is decided (Rules, October 1952) by the general meeting of the primary party organization he belongs to. The resolution needs confirmation by the district or city committee of the party. This again needs confirmation by the province or territory party committee or by the Central Committee of a Union Republic. Until the latter confirmation has been expressed, the member retains his card with all rights.

The primary party organization cannot resolve to exclude from membership (or reduce to candidate status) any member of the Central Committee of the Party of the Union, of a Union Republic or a territory, province, region, city, or district. No—of course not! It might permit of the organization of opposition and a revolt of the lower tiers of the party against the intermediate and upper and even the highest tiers, to great Stalin or Malenkov or Khrushchev himself! This would be party democracy, indeed.

Expulsions at these higher tiers take place by a two-thirds vote of a plenary session of their own central committee.

The leaders of the party suffer anxiety about expulsions because there must be "cleansings," *chistka;* and expulsions could be used, have been exploited, to coerce members for personal reasons, as blackmail, often to prevent criticism of themselves at congresses, meetings, and in the press. It is essential to protect members from malice, excessive zeal, corruption.

The Rules of October 1952 say:

When deciding the question of expulsion . . . the maximum care and comradely concern must be exercised, and a very careful examination must be made whether the accusation leveled against the Party member may be justified.

Minor misdeeds should be punished by Party educational measures and other means of influencing the individual [warning, reprimand, etc.] and not by expulsion. . . .

One such lesser punishment is reduction to candidate status for up to one year.

The aggrieved may appeal against expulsion, etc., to the same bodies as judged him.

Purges. The problem of expulsion raises the question of a massive change in the party composition and mentality, as contrasted with the normal continuous business of purifying the party in detail on its routine basis. The purge is an instrument, parallel with the policy of admission, of answering grave new social, economic, and political questions that plague the party leadership. Which elements in the population are more likely to be loyal members of the party, adept at community indoctrination? Who will be able to keep a disciplinary eye on the Armed Forces? Who can be trusted to carry out the managerial and secretarial duties of the party? What kind and variety of mass following, what representative character, must the party achieve? How, through specification of membership, can a control be obtained over the multifarious economic operations in town and country? What proportion of membership is needed to maintain the balance of Great Russia and the national minorities in Russia's peculiar federal arrangement?

The table [6] showing the rise and fall of party membership indicates the severity of the chief purges. In the five years, 1933–1938, the party was

[6] *The Growth in Numbers of the Party and the Purge Effects.* There are various versions of the statistics of growth of the party: in the *Short History*, which is official, but also in the reports of the Congresses that are also official. They do not quite square with each other. Yet the main facts are clear. In the following table, the candidate members are severed from the members, so that the full effect of the purge and special calls for the enlistment of new members, may be more forcefully manifest. An asterisk * is placed at the figures where the purges occur, and an E, where special enlistments begin. Round numbers are given at January 1, except where noted.

Year	Members	Candidates	Total
1905	8,500		8,500
1917	23,600		23,600
1918	115,000		115,000
1919	251,000		251,000
1920	431,400		431,400
1921	576,000		576,000
*1922	410,430	117,924	528,354
*1924	350,000	122,000	472,000
E1925	440,365	361,439	801,804
1926	639,652	440,162	1,079,814
1927	786,288	426,217	1,212,505
1933	2,203,951	1,351,387	3,555,338
*1934	1,826,756	874,252	2,701,008
1938	1,405,879	514,123	1,920,002
1939	1,514,181	792,792	2,306,973
E1940	1,982,743	1,417,232	3,399,975
1941 (Feb.)	2,515,481	1,361,404	3,876,885
1945	3,965,530	1,794,839	5,760,369
1947 (Sept.)	—	—	6,300,000
1952 (Oct. 1)	6,013,259	868,886	6,882,145
1956	—	—	8,000,000

purged of over 25 percent of its members! The purge of candidates comprised 55 percent! The party then renewed itself; for by January 1939 candidates and members totaled 2,306,973 again; and within a year, rose to 3,399,975. Of the latter figure, 40 percent were new entrants in 1938–1940, the beneficiaries of the more open access (p. 862). The intelligentsia was let in, perhaps changing the nature of the regime (p. 863).

In 1939 Zhdanov excoriated the mass purges; the party had been strengthened by them (he *had* to say) but faults had been committed. Everyone was measured by one criterion, without consideration of individual qualities. Lenin's principle of the individual approach to people had been violated. (The principle deserves notice!) Noisy people, flattering and pompous, remained in the party, and even threw others out; while quiet and passive but loyal men and women were expelled. But there were often good reasons why the "passive" elements were passive; they had other duties, quite laudable. Or some people could not answer brainracking questions of political theory. Careerists had made progress by expelling people. Vigilance had been turned into slander. Some believed that, since the party had 2,000,000 members, it could well afford to throw out some thousands. Zhdanov argued that antiregime people had thrown out members in order to increase bitterness in and against it. (But this makes it a difficult problem to know how such people were ever admitted in the first place.) Personal enemies were expelled, though they were good Bolsheviks, even better than those who did the expelling. Also, the general formula of "class enemies" or people having connection with such or the "grandmother principle" of expelling people because of their ancestors had been applied, without discrimination—the "biological approach."

Hence the need for the greatest individual care in expulsion.

During the surge of opposition from various quarters in the early 1930's the party had for the first time specified openly the reasons for expulsion. What were they? These: class-alien and hostile elements; double-dealers who conceal their real view and disrupt the policy of the party; overt and covert violators of the iron discipline of the party and of the State; degenerates who have coalesced with bourgeois elements; careerists, self-seekers, and bureaucratized elements; morally degraded persons whose improper conduct degrades the dignity and besmirches the banner of the party; passive elements who are undutiful and have not mastered the program, rules, and the most important decisions of the party.

These categories have been relied on wholesale by the local purgers.

There need be no doubt of the party leaders' sincere concern for *individual* consideration of expulsion. The party must have members; it must have loyalty; it cannot have disgruntled people circulating in the community; it must give the appearance of honor and dignity and justice in its own ranks. The party itself, especially the leaders, have the serious problem of making an instrument that will be active and undertake great self-sacrifices to be a militant leadership, and it must be sure of these against the malicious elements in the party. The greater the top leaders' solicitude for the individual, the more the individual will be beholden to them, and the more likely will he be to exercise the criticism and the self-criticism which is a party duty, and upon which the possibility of maintaining honesty, competence, and wholesomeness in the party depends.

Hence, there was developed quite a party doctrine of the treatment of *the individual member in the party.*

Stalin, the genius of Bolshevik Party *apparat* administration, had said at the Central Committee that some of the party leaders suffered from a lack of concern "for people, or members of the Party, for workers." They did not "study" the members. They had no "individual approach" in appraising members. "Whether he remains in the Party or is expelled from the Party is a matter of life and death to the ordinary Party member."

Zhdanov insisted that the merits as well as the demerits of a man's character must be appraised. In rejecting the "biological" approach to expulsions, he made the important point that

our whole work of building socialism, our whole educational work is designed to remold the minds of men. . . . This way of judging people abstractly, in accordance with a ready-made standard, instead of studying them in all their connections and manifestations, condemns one to passivity, to a pessimistic view of people —profoundly hostile to Bolshevism.

Hence the party dropped the "categories"; insisted on lesser penalties and the possibility of rehabilitation; laid down the rule of individual care; and even of humanity.

Social Composition of the Party

The gist of the situation is as follows, in approximate figures:

"Class"	To 1929	1932	1940–45	After 1946
Workers	61.4	43.5	32.0	20.0
Peasants	21.7	18.3	18.0	25.0
Nonmanual	16.9	38.2	50.0	55.0

The peasants include those at work in the M.T.S. (p. 913) and other noncollective farmers' groups. The nonmanual are the "intelligentsia." The difference between pre-1929 and the war and postwar years is most significant.

Age. The members of the party have become older. In 1927 almost all were under fifty; in 1952 no less than 15.3 percent of the Congress delegates were over fifty. In 1927 about 54 percent were under thirty, in 1946 only 18.3 percent were under thirty-five. The proportion of higher age in 1952 is above the last figure.

Education. The progress of education of the party delegates to the Congresses is indicative of the general progress in the party. In 1939, 26.5 percent had higher education; in 1952, 58 percent. This last percentage was equal to 709 delegates and of these, 282 were engineers, 98 teachers, 18 economists, 11 physicians, 7 lawyers, 68 agronomists. As regards the whole party, these figures are significant: by 1947, with its vastly increased absolute numbers, nearly 7 out of 100 members had higher education and almost 21 in 100 had finished secondary school, whereas in 1939 the figure for middle or secondary school was 14 percent, and in 1928 only 8 percent. Before that date only about 1 in 200 had higher education, and only a little more than 6 in 100 had "middle" education, while nearly 5 in 100 were illiterate. Once again, let us emphasize the rise of this new

Soviet-produced intelligentsia. It was welcomed by Stalin at the Eighteenth Party Congress (1939) thus:

> This theory [disdainful and contemptuous attitude to the Soviet intelligentsia, regarded as an alien force] is now out of date and does not fit our new, Soviet intelligentsia. Our new intelligentsia demands a new theory, a theory teaching the necessity of a cordial attitude towards it, solicitude and respect for it, and cooperation with it in the interests of the working class and peasantry.

The Credentials Committee of the Congress of 1952 added to the welcome:

> The presence among the Congress delegates of such a large number of specialists in various branches of economy and culture shows once more that in our country educated people who know their work well and are capable of advancing it are highly valued and boldly promoted.

Women. Women have increased their membership in the party steadily, from 8.2 percent in 1924 to about 21 percent in 1950 and beyond. They come much more from the cities than the rural areas. Women serve as party secretaries (meaning "executive") in 1 out of every 7 primary party units; they hold 1400 such positions in the higher echelons up to Union Republic. Only two are found among the 125 members of the Central Committee and four are alternates; none serves on the Presidium. Women comprised 12.3 percent of the delegates to the Congress of 1952 and 9.1 percent in that of 1939. (Much less than their proportion of total membership.) Most, of course, come from Great Russia, as the Asian and Caucasian do not allow their women political activity and the Baltic States spare them it.

Nationality. Great-Russian membership is dominant, being between 50 and 60 percent of the total. It is not out of line with the proportionate population of this area. This is a deliberate policy of the party, for it needs personnel to send to the Asiatic fringes and troubled areas, such as the Ukraine; it needs to plant Great Russians there, to offset their "bourgeois nationalism." In Asia, backward, native personnel hardly exists. Stalin's Georgia has required many brutal purges. In the Ukraine the party membership in the cities in 30 per 1000 population; the national average is 30; the *Moscow average is 68;* the Ukraine average, including the rural areas, is less than 19. In the Congresses the Great-Russian delegates have more than their population-ratio superiority. More members and greater acceptance by them of the party in the fringe areas would be better for the fulfillment of Soviet plans of all kinds.

City and Country. Obviously, the party is largely urban. Workers and intelligentsia together amount to some 75 percent of the total. But 66 percent of the people live on farms. The collective farmer and his wife are still ignorant and stubborn about their way of life and their view of justice to the agricultural toiler: they think they are getting a bad deal—and they are (p. 906). One of the reasons for the policy of much larger collectives (p. 914) is to bring them more within the scope of the relatively small party membership in rural areas.

Summary of Party Composition. It is today predominantly a party of the Soviet technical, managerial, foreman, State officials and party directors, professional intelligentsia. It has moved away from its original worker strata. This is the rising element in the Soviet Union. It is heavily urban and weakly rural. It is a man's world. Great Russia dominates it.

The party is now composed *not* of the masses, to whom it is commanded by the statutes and Congress injunctions to go out and to develop their socialistic and communistic consciousness to the end that each may receive according to his need. This suits the leadership's purposes of rapid industrial advance, substantial equipment of the nation with productive capacity, and the maintenance of armed force sufficient to ward off destruction and even to expand territory and influence to distant lands which will be its allies in diplomacy and, if necessary, supply manpower and strategic footholds and raw materials in case of war. The screw will be tightened for foreign economic aid.

If about 5,000,000 party members are urban, then they are in relation to about 40,000,000 non-

agricultural workers, or as 1 is to 8: it is a controlling proportion.

II. THE IRON GRIP

The Nationwide Apparat

We concern ourselves only with the central and top organization that operates downward through to the 350,000 primary units and the lesser congresses and executives, and the force of central domination or "democratic centralism."

The Central Committee. This is the highest body of executive and legislative force in the party; it replaces the "democratic" legislature of the party, the Congress, in between the latter's sessions; in reality it dominates the latter, and is, in reality dominated by its inner clique, called the Party Presidium, formerly Politburo. Its departmental organization is treated with that of the Party Presidium. It numbers 125 members and 110 alternates. In 1930 this body employed 767 full-time workers. Purely guessing, it employs today about 2000. (I multiply by 3, as the membership increased roughly three times.) Perhaps Stalin's figure of 3000 to 4000 front-rank leaders (p. 853) includes this guess of 2000. That quotation indicates also the full-time officials who spread throughout the Soviet Union.

Of the primary party organizations, up, in districts and cities, about 180,000 need paid directors. The larger organizations need extra paid workers with the *Komsomols,* general propaganda, party schools, press liaison, and direct press publication. The total would begin to reach the 600,000 mentioned by knowledgeable refugees.

The functions of the Central Committee are thus set out in the Rules:

36. In the intervals between Congresses the Central Committee of the Communist Party of the Soviet Union directs the whole work of the Party; represents the Party in its relations with other parties, organizations, and institutions; organizes various Party institutions and directs their activity; appoints editorial boards of central organs of the press, which function under its control and confirms the editorial boards of Party publications of large local organizations;

organizes and directs undertakings of social significance; distributed the manpower and resources of the Party, and administers the central fund.

The Central Committee guides the work of the central Soviet and public organizations through the Party groups within them.

The Republic, territorial, regional, area, city, and district levels have direct party-to-public functions and are supervisors over the next lower tier. We offer only one example, that of the regions, of which there are 167, standing intermediate between 544 cities and 4886 district organizations below them, and 36 area organizations above. Rule 48 says:

> The regional committee organizes various offices of the Party within the region and directs their activities; sees to undeviating fulfillment of Party directives, the development of criticism and self-criticism and the training of Communists in an uncompromising attitude toward shortcomings; directs the study of Marxism-Leninism by Party members and candidates; organizes the Communist training of the working people; appoints the editorial boards of the regional Party press organ, which functions under its direction and control; directs the activity of regional Soviet and public organizations through the Party groups in them; organizes undertakings of regional importance; distributes within the region the manpower and resources of the Party, and administers the regional Party funds.

Inner Party Organs. The "parliamentary" body of the regional organization of the party is the "conference." This is made up of delegates elected by the city and district organizations. The conference elects the regional committee; the regional committee elects a bureau of up to nine persons, including three secretaries of the regional committee. These secretaries are confirmed by the province committee, the territory committee, or the Central Committee of the Union Republic. The conference also elects the Inspection Commission, a unit to be found in all levels down from the All-Union Party, to check the actual fulfillment of party resolutions and tasks. This is one of the most frequently repeated injunctions at Party Congresses, indicating that the Russian people have still

not learned completely the need to carry out their resolutions adopted by their votes when in an enthusiastic mood.

The coherence and hierarchical nature of the party may be inferred from the foregoing. More will be gleaned from the succeeding sections of the discussion. It may merely be added that the primary party organizations are "chartered" by the district or city committees.

The Territorial Secretariats. The secretaries of the various party bodies at the different levels require a minimum number of years' standing in party membership as a compulsory qualification. For Union Republic, province or territory, it is five years; for the regions, three years; for the cities and districts, three years; in the primary organizations, it is one year.

Democratic Centralism

The Communist Party is not an organization with democracy at work within its own operation. It is a dictatorship within itself, its intention and nature masked with the specious slogan "democratic centralism." We have seen how this principle developed through Lenin's building of it and Stalin's usurpation (pp. 756–757).

The Statutes of 1952 (pp. *lxvi–lxxiii*) preserve in identical terms those of 1939 and 1934 on "democratic centralism," thus:

> 21. The guiding principle of the organizational structure of the Party is democratic centralism, meaning:
> (a) Election of all Party governing bodies from bottom to top.
> (b) Periodic accountability of Party bodies to their Party organizations.
> (c) Strict Party discipline and subordination of the minority to the majority.
> (d) The decisions of higher bodies are unconditionally binding upon lower ones.
> 22. The Party structure rests on a territorial-production basis: *the Party organization serving any given area is regarded as superior to all Party organizations serving parts of this area* [italics added], and a Party organization serving an entire branch of production is regarded as superior to all Party organizations serving sections of this branch of production.
> 23. All Party organizations are autonomous

in deciding local questions, *provided that the decisions are not contrary to the Party's decisions* [italics added].

Where is the democracy? If (a) and (b) principles were fully, genuinely, and continuously obeyed in the spirit and the letter, the party would be a democratic organization, as parties are in the Western democracies. Insofar as they are not, the party is dictatorial. It will be shown that *they are not honored, but deliberately perverted.* If this is the case, then the principles (c) and (d), binding the lower organs, *produce a despotism.* In practice, as we shall show, *they do.*

Who are the real rulers? The Congresses and conferences of party delegates are supposed to be the sovereign bodies. But between the Congress of 1952 and 1939 a gap of thirteen years yawned; before that, five, to 1934; before that four to 1930. Between 1917 and 1927 the Congress met almost annually. To 1952, the Rules called for triennial meetings. In the intervals, the Central Committee acts in sovereignty. The lower tier conferences used to be convenable annually; since 1952, each eighteen months. The *apparatchiks* still complain they have too much everyday work to attend more often.

Congress and conference admissions prove that the decisions are made by the executive committees of these bodies, and even more so, by the "bureau" of a few members including the party functionaries. The members of the various *aktivs* even are far too burdened to take the initiative in developing policy for the meetings and higher legislative bodies. About 1 in 10 of the *aktivs,* some say only 1 in 35 of the membership participate in policy discussions.

Even so, the Secretariat of the Communist Party in Moscow guides and coerces all these lower levels, especially as they are zealots and all the more amenable to "influence." There is a special organ of the Central Committee for this purpose (perverted to it), the Party Control Committee, with the following powers (Statute 35):

(a) Verifies the observance of Party discipline by Party members and candidates; calls to account Communists guilty of violating the Party Program and Statutes or of breaches of Party and State discipline, as well as violators of Party ethics (those guilty of deception of the Party, dishonesty and insincerity in relation to the Party, slander, bureaucracy, moral turpitude, etc.).

(b) Examines appeals against decisions of the Central Committees of the Communist Parties of the Union Republics and of territory and province Party committees concerning expulsions from the Party and Party disciplinary measures.

(c) Has its representatives, *independent of local Party bodies* [italics added], in the Republics, territories, and provinces.

Congresses and conferences and meetings have thus been perverted into *claques.* For the "planted" secretaries at the lower tiers are closely involved with Ministers in Moscow and other capitals, and the local Soviets and supervise job-giving in all important positions throughout the economy and in all party ancillary agencies. The "first" secretary at the territorial level is planted by Moscow's "recommendations" on the party members there; he, in turn, is needed to "confirm" all secretaries in echelons below. The first secretary of the Union Republics must be approved by the All-Union Central Committee. The secretaries everywhere maneuver the meetings and their various elections, among them, the committees in charge of admissions and expulsions.

We cannot give statistical proportions to these and the ensuing observations. Even the party headquarters perhaps has not a precise picture. But highest levels and all levels complain about these derelictions, as they always have. Officials are admitted wholesale, rather than individually. Co-option replaces election. Attendance at meetings is slack. There is widespread fear to voice criticisms of bad practices. The ideological abilities of the membership is deteriorating. Committees and secretaries are alienated from the masses. Party rules are violated. Party officials conceal the truth, even conspire with others to hush up misdemeanors, crime, nepotism, patronage, bureaucratism, and appointments to jobs without even seeing the candidates. The *apparatchiks* go their own way.

The dilemma of a dictatorship is apparent in Malenkov's painful analysis at the 1952 Congress:

It is the duty of all executives, particularly Party officials, to create conditions in which all honest Soviet people may boldly and fearlessly criticize defects in the work of organizations and institutions. Meetings, gatherings of the *aktiv*, plenary sessions and conferences in all the organizations must really become broad forums for bold and trenchant criticism of defects.

What? When the word *honest* has to be slipped in? When penalties for "deviations" may be the forced-labor camp for life? When the officials, as anywhere in history or in the world today, will shun responsibility unless it is forced on them by an authority genuinely vested in the masses? When the officials are terrified by the punishment that may be meted out to them by their bureaucratic superiors for even an honest mistake?

The party rules for its members to criticize and self-criticize may be cited, with discussion left for later (pp. 887–888).

> Statute 3: . . .
> (g) To develop self-criticism and criticism from below, to expose and seek to eliminate shortcomings in work, and to fight against a show of well-being and against being carried away by success in work. Suppression of criticism is a great evil. He who silences criticism and substitutes ostentation and boastfulness in its place cannot remain in the ranks of the Party.
> (h) To report to leading Party bodies, right up to the Party Central Committee, shortcomings in work, irrespective of the persons involved. A Party member has no right to conceal an unsatisfactory state of affairs or ignore wrongdoings which damage the interests of the Party and State. He who hinders a Party member from carrying out this duty must be severely punished as violating the will of the Party.
> (i) To be truthful and honest before the Party and never permit concealment or distortion of truth. Untruthfulness of a Communist toward the Party and deception of the Party are grave misdeeds incompatible with Party membership.

The grapevine and the party press prove to the Russian public that the first secretaries of the city and district committees are the expendable scapegoats of the top leaders for public grievances, true or peevish. The scapegoats defend themselves by all sorts of chicanery and illicit rewards and punishments.

Thus, the minority is not subordinated to the party majority, but the very small minority at the summit subordinates the majority. This is centralism and not democracy. The Politbureau is irresponsible.

Inner Party Democracy. So anxious were the leaders about the loss of democratic vigor that at the Congress of 1939 the caption "inner party democracy" was put in place of "party discipline" to head the clauses on the latter subject. They had to reaffirm in the Rules the *constitutional rights* of party members. Thus:

> 4. The Party member has the right:
> (a) To take part in free and businesslike discussion, at Party meetings and in the Party press, of matters of Party policy.
> (b) To criticize any Party functionary at Party meetings.
> (c) To elect or be elected to Party bodies.
> (d) To insist on personal participation in all cases when decisions are adopted concerning his activities or behavior.
> (e) To address any questions or statements to any Party body, at any level, right up to the Central Committee of the Communist Party of the Soviet Union.

Nor was this all; these rights were *written into the party members' duties:* see this, *now, verbatim,* especially in the Party Statutes, Article 3 (p. *lxvi*)! Such duties must be fulfilled, subject to reprimand, demotion, or expulsion. They ask for honesty, unqualified devotion, appointments without favoritism, a single standard of law-abidingness in party and State and economy. They were devised to be the medicine of failing party morale. The reward is office and relative relief from terroristic outlawing.

The Dilemma of Dictatorship. The party faces a grave dilemma. For *élan* and energy in all the institutions of the State and the economy and education, the party needs militant conviction in its members. Militant conviction can never be other than the child of freedom of choice. But the party does not want this freedom—unless by Nature's dispensation such freedom should exhibit itself as free acceptance of the philosophy and policy of the party and its discipline. To secure freshness and energy it must seek freedom; yet it must curb freedom if the leaders are to remain on top. It attempts to secure continual militancy and upsurging interest and intellectual concern by setting down certain rights for members of the party. Then, because the exercise of these rights is so perilous (through the party's own dictatorial faults) it seeks to convert these rights into duties.

It would seem that Stalinism, spawned by Leninism, withered the morale of the party members as his deification and despotism flourished.

It is the "inalienable right of each Party members" to take part in "free and businesslike discussion of questions of Party policy, of local or All-Union scope." For party discipline must be "conscious, not mechanical. . . ." *But,* broad discussions must not be such as to lead to attempts by an "insignificant minority" to impose its will on the party majority! I suppose, also, that "businesslike" limits the use of oratorical effects? If at least several provincial or Republic echelons think it desirable, such broad discussion may take place. But that is exactly the broad, concerted assailment that the Moscow leaders would kill stone dead! Discussion is also allowed when there is no firm majority on major questions in the Central Committee—which, surely, must be never! Men usually need encouragement to be critical; top Soviet party leaders brandish grim deterrents.

The Party's Auxiliaries: Trade Unions, Red Army, Secret Police, Etc.

Wherever men's primary common interests may give them an independent mass interest and cohesion, the party's tentacles send out their penetrating and divisive grip.

The Trade Unions. The Bolsheviks, on attaining power, soon seized the trade unions and made them into the instrument for "strengthening the socialist state, the defense of the country, and the building of socialism." They were too young, inexperienced, and out-terrorized to resist. Their famous old leader, Tomsky, one of the Old Bol-

sheviks was ousted from office, subjected to a purge trial, ejected from the Politbureau, and committed suicide.

Some 90 percent of all the workers are members of unions. The unions are not fighting organizations for the economic and civic benefit of the worker. He must pay dues. Why does he join? For no free movement anywhere in the world has anywhere near this proportion of the workers. What is the magic? Trade-union members alone get certain benefits, as enacted by the State. They get twice the sick benefits of nonmembers; 50 percent more disability benefits; preference in jobs and promotions; housing (p. 921); libraries, clubs, playing fields, holiday resorts, run by the unions. These also dispense hospitalization, legal advice, and money loans and run nurseries and kindergartens (so many women are workers). This is connected with civil rights (p. 834).

The unions function under the principle of "democratic centralism." True elections have been met by annulment and punishment of the daring. Strikes are not outlawed—but they are clearly "sabotage" or "counterrevolutionary" (p. 842). There are no strikes. The Statutes of the U.S.S.R. Trade Unions list nine functions. The first is to secure fulfillment of the Plans, improve quality, and lower the cost of production. All men are paid according to their falling short of the standards set by "shock workers." The party members and *Komsomols* set the increasing pace and stigmatize the laggards; for this they are made Heroes of Soviet Labor and get privileges in theaters, vacations, housing, and bigger pay by far. They plan piece work and rates; help introduce improved techniques; sign "collective agreements" (fake!) with management and government officials to fulfill Plans. They administer the social-insurance system, assure safety, and help settle disputes.

The worker's fate is in their hands, fully. The trade unions are, by their Statute, subjected to the Communist Party's firm "leadership." The party's "cells," all the way up from the smallest plant, organize the domination of the unions. The workers are thus split between trade-union members and nonmembers; "heroes" and "disgraces"; the highly privileged and the sweated; party members and nonentities; and lack the political power that is inherent in the right to strike.

The Armed Forces. Never was the image of Napoleon Bonaparte absent from the mind and anxieties of Lenin, Trotsky, and Stalin; nor is it from the worries of the current leadership. They knew that revolutions can be usurped by military leaders, as Napoleon entered as "the sword" on the Eighteenth Brumaire (p. 301), to reap the benefit of the reaction of the people from the intolerable drives of revolutionary fanaticism. They *must* always be on top of the military, whom, however, they needed in great supply and morale, first to kill off their enemies at home and always to defend them against foreign assault. The dictators were always afraid of the discipline, hierarchy, command, pride, the dignity of professional ability, and the deadly weapons that constitute an army.

The party subverted the discipline of the Czarist Army (p. 766). Then, fighting for its own authority, it restored appointment in place of election of officers. It went on to appoint political commissars to supervise operations and instill Bolshevism into the soldiers and sailors. The idea to employ these was Trotsky's. It was genius, learned from the armies of the French Revolution. At times the operations of the Civil War needed the joint signatures of the commissars with those of the Army commanders, for many of the latter were Czarist, re-employed. Many of the commissars were the bravest of "shock troops."

Naturally, Lenin had to pretend that the Soviet government was the inventor of political morale building for an army. In March 1919 he told the Eighth Party Congress:

> If this war is waged with much greater energy and with exalted gallantry, it is only because for the first time in history an army has been created which knows what it is fighting for.

But Cromwell's Ironsides, the New Model Army, the Puritan Army, had 300 years before, fought, literally, with the Bible in one hand and gun in the other *against* a royal despotism, not to establish a dictatorship. So had the French armies at Valmy, etc. It was too inconvenient to recall. The

Army actually rose in 1921; other troops shot down the peasants. Others were bodily transferred into factories, mines, and transport.

Steadily a Regular Army was created, fed by conscription. Czarist officers gave way to those trained under the Soviet government. By 1934 nearly 70 percent of the officer corps was composed of members of the party and the *Komsomols*. Besides party activities, the Army was indoctrinated by special schooling for many hours per year in Communism. The Political Administration of the Army was given special attention by Stalin to root out Trotskyites and replace them by his stalwarts; Marshal Voroshilov, a dull buddy of Stalin's, became Commissar of War and another trustie was made head of the Administration. By the middle of the 1920's the Armed Forces were gripped by (1) political commissars who ran schools and watched the command; (2) party *aktivs* to indoctrinate and recruit members; (3) the Security Police (O.G.P.U., then N.K.V.D., then M.V.D.). Their lines of command were separate, and each spied on the others; the last-named were anonymous.

Soldiers and sailors of worker origin were filtered into the most crucial fighting units, such as the Air Force, Signal Corps, tanks, and transport. These could control the infantry, over 90 percent being peasants. In 1937 Marshal Tukashevsky and seven generals were executed in the Great Purge; the corps of officers was "cleansed" (p. 864). Some heads of the Army administration committed suicide. The young generation of Bolsheviks was massively promoted. Pay was greatly multiplied; titles were invented and distributed; handsome uniforms were designed. Discipline was made much more cruel. The political commissars came back, with joint holding of command with the officers. Then they were abolished, because they had hampered operations in the Finnish War of 1939. *Zampolits* replaced them, Assistant Commanders for Political Affairs—only to conduct propaganda and education. The party was torn between the need to tame the generals and yet have an enterprising Army to meet World War II. They feared the Nazi Army, the Nazi Party, the S.S. troops immensely—and rightly, for the Russian armies deserted *en masse;* whole ethnic regions welcomed the Germans; Communist Party men had often to press the Red soldiers into battle at the point of the tommy gun.

In July 1941 the political commissar system was reintroduced; as the situation improved, the single Army command returned, with the *zampolits* only. Tremendous efforts were made to recruit men into the party. It is estimated that in 1941 over one half of the Soviet Army were members of the party and *Komsomols* and even larger proportion than that among the officers. The political personnel of the Army in 1939 was five times the number it attained in the Civil War—34,000.

Stalin took over command of all Russia's forces when war broke out. His role was mere playing. It is undeniable that his steadiness, endurance, morale, and either ability or luck enabled Russia to hold out and finally conquer Germany. He sent the government to Kuibishev; but he stayed in the Kremlin, now as chairman of the Council of Ministers and head of the State Defense Committee, with Molotov, Voroshilov, Beria, and Malenkov as members. He ordered "scorched earth." He ruled on dismissals, and the promotion of Marshals Zhukov, Vasilevsky, Rokossovsky. Production was started beyond the Urals. Former heretics were released from prison and given commands or high places in industry. Patriotism came back; hierarchy, *élite* guards, exclusive officers' clubs, separation of junior and senior messes were established. In March 1943 Stalin took the title of Marshal, following the victory of Stalingrad; after victory, he was acclaimed Hero of the Soviet Union and Generalissimo; no uniform was more resplendent than his.

The war over, Zhukov was consigned to oblivion in the Ukraine and his name wiped out of the press, with the other military victors. There was to be no chance of a Decembrist rising (p. 749)! The party was discreetly purged of many soldier recruits. Marx came back over nationalism; historians who had been given prizes for the former were ejected.

The groping hand of the party went right into the entrails of the Armed Forces again. At the top is the Main Political Administration, being simultaneously part of the Defense Ministry and the Military Department of the Party's Central Committee. It has political teachers and inspectors throughout the Forces, to indoctrinate and report on morale; it runs schools for such teachers, etc. The heads of the various field units of these must have their appointments sanctioned by the party's top officials. Various grades of *zampolits* functions from divisional commands down to companies, using all the oral, writing, and visual techniques of influence. The M.V.D. investigates all recruits; recruits get intensive pre-Army talks. The company political officer, called *politruk*, sucks up to them and picks all their thoughts and sentiments. In the Army, two two-hour sessions per week on Soviet politics are conducted. The officers are also brought into school; their promotion depends on the reports made by the M.V.D., the party *aktiv*, the *zampolits*.

The M.P.A. does the work in the forces otherwise imposed on party members for all other phases of Soviet life in the neighborhood. The Central Committee of the party appoints the party secretaries in the military districts and Army groups. The M.P.A. appoints at the lower levels. More concerned with detection is the M.V.D. It works with informers. It examines ingoing and outgoing mail; keeps dossiers on all; makes interrogations. Its clearance is required for all promotions. A dreadful spirit of anxiety and suspicion is infused by the four separate agencies of the party: Party, *Komsomols*, *Zampolits*, and M.V.D. Four separate loyalties glare darkly at each other with insecurity: Army, M.P.A., M.V.D., and C.P. This is how the dictatorship rules.

The Officers and Generals. The Soviet officer is torn between his professionalism and discipline and the political attitude pressed on him at the pain of losing his promotion or even being broken by the M.V.D. en route to a forced-labor camp. The rank and file try to absent themselves from the indoctrination or by sleeping through lectures, etc. The result is hardly conviction. But Khrushchev and the rest would say, "It is better than nothing!" The officers have very high social privileges in education (p. 833), food, pay, housing. Will the resulting resentments among the rank and file produce disbelief in the "equality" legends of the party, and so in all other analogous matters?

At the Party Congress of 1952 it was announced that 86.4 percent of the officers in the Army were party or *Komsomol* members; the top command is completely party. The officer corps is the Soviet social *élite*.

Will the Army Swallow the Party? As soon as Stalin died, the Malenkov-Beria-Molotov *troika* (since then one of the horses has been shot dead, and another hamstrung!) brought the top commanders into the Government. Marshal Bulganin was made First Vice Chairman of the Council of Ministers and Defense Minister. Voroshilov was made president of the Soviet Presidium and a member of the Party Presidium. Marshals Zhukov and Budyenny were made alternate members of the Party's Central Committee and member of the Soviet Presidium and First Deputy Defense Minister, respectively, and Marshal Vasilevsky, First Deputy of the Defense Ministry also. On the ousting of Malenkov from the chairmanship of the Council of Ministers in February 1955, the Army was given greater apparent melding with the regime. Bulganin was promoted to be Chairman of the Council of Ministers—that is, prime minister in the State; Zhukov was made Defense Minister; and Marshal Konev was made First Deputy Defense Minister. What did this mean? Ignorant journalists in the United States suggested that the Soviet regime had been taken over by the Army; *if* so, it is an Army that has been Communized. But we merely state that the party has made sure that the Army is still its, by bringing the Marshals *away* from their troops to the Kremlin where they can be seen, face to face, and liquidated when necessary. Other comments appear later (p. 883). Since Stalin's death, the Army has come in to dominate the M.V.D.

Komsomols, or Young Communist League. The intention of the party, as of all *dogmatic* movements whether "reactionary" or "revolutionary," is to catch the minds of youth while they are in immature formation and fill them with an account of man's nature and history, ideals and purpose, so biased and penetrating that they will never be able to recover by their individual contemplation of realities. They know that the individual's five senses—the "gateways to the soul," as William Blake called them—will, as youth

grows, perchance escape. But they have nothing to lose but youth's brains for trying.

At the 1952 Party Congress the secretary of the *Komsomols* reported that the *Komsomol* membership was 16,000,000 as against 8,000,000 in 1939. Between 1939 and 1952, moreover, over 4,000,000 of the Y.C.L. had joined the party. The membership is open to those between fifteen and twenty-six. A younger grouping of Soviet youth is the *Young Pioneers,* aged nine to fifteen. They now number 19,000,000. Within the 16,000,000 there were comprised 75 percent of all the students at universities; 61 percent of those in industrial schools; 65 percent of elementary and secondary pupils. Thus 25 percent of university students do *not* belong; 39 percent industrial pupils; 35 percent of the rest. It is an impressive majority; and it is an impressive minority, considering the ancient apathy and the contemporary pressures respectively. The *Komsomol* Secretary (N. A. Mikhailov) declared in 1952:

> Soviet, Stalinist youth burns with a desire to devote all its strength, mind and will to the service of the homeland, the Communist Party, the cause of communism—the great cause of Lenin and Stalin. . . .

The deliberate kindling of this flame is instructive; it can never be left untended.

The Party Is on Top. The party does not allow the younger generation, as in democracies, to grow up freely, hoping that the next generation may be better than the present leaders. How could they? Hence the party statutes make the *Komsomol* Central Committee subordinate to the Party's Central Committee, and the local party organs take charge of the *Komsomols.*

What is the Young Communist League? The Statutes so describe it:

> 62. The Young Communist League is the active aide of the Party in all State and economic work. Young Communist League organizations must be channels for active application of Party directives in all fields of socialist construction, especially where there is no primary Party organization.

> 63. Young Communist League organizations have the right of broad initiative in discussing and submitting to the appropriate Party organi-

zations all problems in the work of industrial enterprises, collective farms, State farms, and offices connected with the aim of eliminating shortcomings in their operations and rendering them help needed to improve work, organize socialist competition, carry out mass campaigns, etc.

The organization developed by careful tending out of the "free" socialist youth organizations which began, bravely and romantically, to flourish at the onset of the Revolutions of February and November 1917. The Bolsheviks struck dismay into the heart of free and aspiring youth; many youngsters committed suicide in the N.E.P. period. The Bolsheviks knew how to exploit the idealism of adolescence. They used the urban youth to propagandize and foster industrialization and collective farms; to overcome illiteracy; to liquidate the *kulaks,* to help gather harvests in emergencies, to run the M.T.S. (p. 913), to be "shock brigadiers" in farm and factory, taking advantage of their desire to exhibit prowess. They went into the Militant Atheists' League to laugh or beat out religion. Those who could not sustain the brutality died or lost their minds. Others replaced them.

The party sought not everyone, or proportionate class composition, but the more politically *conscious* of the whole population. In 1936 Stalin declared that those were needed who would "master knowledge, to study, study in the most persistent way." The utmost pressures were and are applied at school, at work, with the inducements of uniforms, medals, command over other youngsters, group joy, family prestige, and even jobs, job preferences, hero worship, academic favoritism, visits to great cities, etc. to get members and keep them loyal and active. Stigmatization pursues the reluctant.

Since a *Komsomol* assassinated Kirov (p. 782), terrible chastizement visited the *Komsomols.* But others were put into its directing positions and were grateful for the jobs. Yet, during World War II, large-scale defections occurred to the Germans. The party persisted: if fees are charged for secondary and university education, the free place is an instrument for getting and disciplining members in enduring habits.

By October 1945 the membership had reached 15,000,000, through recruiting in the Armed Forces during the war. By April 1949 the number had fallen to 9,300,000 from expulsions for slackness, absenteeism, ideological neglect, nonpayment of dues. The "inner party democracy" rules were liberalized (p. 870); candidacy was abolished. The membership rose to 16,000,000. But almost every first secretary in the cities and towns are planted on the *Komsomols* by the party, though it has decreed that these be elected by the young people. Their duties follow those assigned to members of the party (p. 860). In addition:

to be honest, truthful, to restrain comrades from committing foolish acts, to respect the laws . . . to struggle with drunkenness, hooliganism, with the remnants of religious prejudices, with an unsympathetic attitude toward women.

About 1 in 4 are enrolled in the schools of Marxist philosophy.

The *Little Octobrists* organize children between five to eight; the Young Pioneers those between nine and fifteen. They develop the techniques needed to make them want to be like Stalin through brigades with elected leaders under the direction of *Komsomols.*

A *Komsomol* needs the brigade's recommendation for entrance to the party; and it is sought, for the chances of getting into the party are something like 16 is to 7,000,000. The record in the *Komsomols* is decisive for the young man or woman's whole future, in every public aspect of it, and little is left private in the Soviet Union. The social party pressure never ceases from the day of a child's birth; it is excruciating.

The *Komsomols* have their daily paper, the *Komsomolskaya Pravda,* the younger ones, the *Pioneer Gazette,* and many magazines, etc. They run libraries, clubs, theater and movie groups, workshops—and Soviet elections.

Yet the party leaders complain about their violation of labor discipline, religious "relapse," superficiality of Marxism, deceitfulness, lack of original literary work; card-playing; excessive drinking in *Koktail-Khalls,* jazz dancing and even zoot suits, and all the varieties of serious juvenile delinquency and crime.

The war refugees prove the general truth of the

complaints. It is the regime that has made it impossible for so many people to live other than as hypocrites. Observers suggest that perhaps from 10 to 20 percent of the 16,000,000 are honestly convinced of their cause. That is very substantial. About half the eligible by age are *not* members. They are mostly farming people; industrial workers who hate the humbug and inequalities of the regime; and alienated intellectuals (dangerous!). They learned too much about the world outside Russia during their war wanderings and from the Germans; they resist party propaganda. But it is impossible to quantify the preference for Western values that is known to exist.

III. TOP LEADERSHIP: THE DICTATORIAL CLIQUE

The continuing legislative-executive representative of the Party Congress is the Central Committee (p. 867). It is supposed to hold not less than one plenary meeting each six months. It is too large to take continuous action.

The Party Presidium

The Politburo, since 1952 the Party Presidium, replaces the Central Committee, for the Rules of the Party run:

> 34. The Central Committee of the Communist Party organizes a Presidium to direct the work of the Central Committee between plenary sessions and a Secretariat to direct current work, chiefly as concerns verification of the fulfilment of Party decisions and selection of cadres.

The Party Presidium is *the* arcanum of Soviet government, a supreme directing and aloof sovereign. It is the quintessentially political leadership in the core, and at the apex, of all activities and thoughts of Soviet and Communist statecraft, the bearer of the revolutionary power, totally, vested in the Congress and passed on through the Central Committee. Each Congress sets its size. When Stalin died, March 6, 1953, the Presidium "elected" by the Central Committee became ten members and four candidates, the latter with the right of presence but no vote. It is rather smaller than Cabinets in most democratic systems. We return to it presently (p. 878).

Organs of the Central Committee

(1) The *Central Committee* consists of 125 members and 110 candidates. It elects: (2) *The Presidium* with ten members and four candidates; (3) *a Secretariat* of five; (4) *the Party Control Committee.* In addition, the Congress itself elects (5) *the Central Inspection Commission.* This is the group of day-by-day apparatus that controls the whole land. Of these organs the Party Presidium is master, and its General or First Secretary, through personal membership on the Presidium, the Boss of Russian politics, once Stalin, then Malenkov, followed by Khrushchev. The system was not altogether invented by Stalin, but he was its chief architect and inspiration.

The relationship of the organs needs some notice. The *Central Committee* contains the *élite* of party officialdom: party secretaries of the central apparatus, the Union Republics and chief territories; the principal Ministers of the Union and the chairmen of the Councils of Ministers of the Union Republics; military commanders, high police, departmental officials especially the Foreign Office, the party's intellectuals and theorists. They are all otherwise busy men. Hence, apart from other causes, they cannot act as a functioning collective miniature of the Congress. Frequently, party and State ordinances and laws are signed and cosigned by the Central Committee, but the Committee is not, in fact, a decision-making body; its infrequency of meeting means abdication even in deliberation. Thus, it has declined since the 1920's, when it was mentioned in the great controversies over the substance of its functions, especially that in Article 31c, whereby "it determines the tactical line of the Party on fundamental questions of current policy." We have yet to see whether the post-Stalin insistence on "collective leadership" (pp. 884–888) restores it. Certainly during 1954 and 1955 its imprimatur appeared on several statements of policy, agricultural and political; but whether this was more formal than substantial, we do not know.

The Party Control Committee. The Party Control Committee's functions have been noted already (p. 869). It was established in 1920 in order to bring to bear the complaints of the public against party officials (then called the Control Commis-

Party Control and the Central Government, 1954

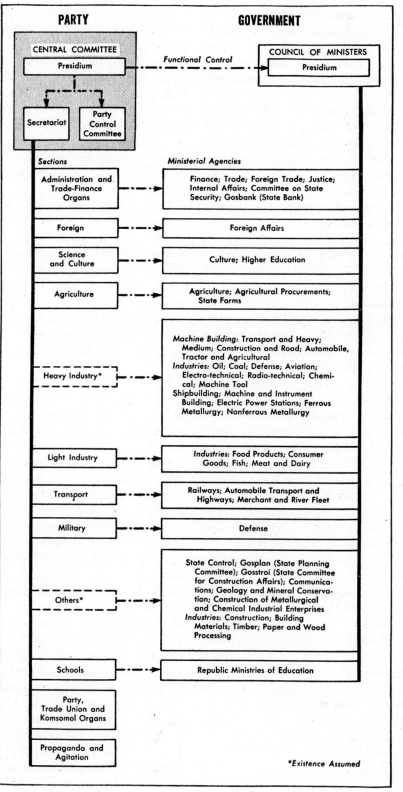

PARTY

GOVERNMENT

CENTRAL COMMITTEE
Presidium

Functional Control

COUNCIL OF MINISTERS
Presidium

Secretariat

Party
Control
Committee

Sections

Ministerial Agencies

Administration and
Trade-Finance
Organs

Finance; Trade; Foreign Trade; Justice;
Internal Affairs; Committee on State
Security; Gosbank (State Bank)

Foreign

Foreign Affairs

Science
and Culture

Culture; Higher Education

Agriculture

Agriculture; Agricultural Procurements;
State Farms

Heavy Industry*

Machine Building: Transport and Heavy;
Medium; Construction and Road; Automobile,
Tractor and Agricultural
Industries: Oil; Coal; Defense; Aviation;
Electro-technical; Radio-technical; Chemi-
cal; Machine Tool
Shipbuilding; Machine and Instrument
Building; Electric Power Stations; Ferrous
Metallurgy; Nonferrous Metallurgy

Light Industry

Industries: Food Products; Consumer
Goods; Fish; Meat and Dairy

Transport

Railways; Automobile Transport and
Highways; Merchant and River Fleet

Military

Defense

Others*

State Control; Gosplan (State Planning
Committee); Gosstroi (State Committee
for Construction Affairs); Communications; Geology and Mineral Conservation; Construction of Metallurgical
and Chemical Industrial Enterprises
Industries: Construction; Building
Materials; Timber; Paper and Wood
Processing

Schools

Republic Ministries of Education

Party,
Trade Union and
Komsomol Organs

Propaganda and
Agitation

*Existence Assumed

sion). But Stalin perverted into his tool for pressure on the *apparatchiks* throughout the nation. It obtained authority over the control commissions of the local party units. It was linked with the Secretariat's organs that controlled appointments at the lesser levels. It ceased to report back to an independent Central Committee, for Stalin had packed this with his friends. It is commander of the party collegium of each Union Republic party organization, and also has a supervising officer, appointed by the Central Committee, at Union Republic headquarters.

The Central Inspection Committee. This Committee invigilates for efficiency, economy, and accountancy the treasury affairs of the party, the collection and disbursement of dues, profits and loss of party publications, and expenditures. It regulates the size and operation of the lower level party inspectorial commissions and staffs—for they get salaries. It is the authority and guide on party record cards and files. The purges showed that the local organs were (and are) shockingly lazy, inefficient and even corrupt, in the matter of dossiers—even causing distress and death through their loss or neglect.

The Secretariat. The Secretariat is empowered "to direct current work, chiefly as concerns the verification of the fulfillment of party decisions and selection of cadres." How innocently laconic! It means the management and regulation of every phase of human existence in Russia. So far as is known, the Secretariat's organization of 1948 (it went through various organizational changes over the years) still obtains. It is headed by the Secretariat of five, with their staffs. Directly under it are eleven divisions:

1. Party, trade union, and *komsomols*
2. Propaganda and agitation
3. Special section
4. Main political administration of the Armed Forces
5. Heavy industry
6. Agriculture
7. Planning, finance, trade
8. Foreign
9. Light industry
10. Transport
11. Administration.

The Special Section is presumed to be concerned with the secret police. The Administration divisions acts on the placement of officials in the important State positions. No official of the higher service as we have treated of it concerning Britain, France, or Germany can in Russia be appointed except after verification of ideological credentials by this division. The Foreign division watches over the appointment of Foreign Service officials, the connections with foreign Communist parties and assembly of data on foreign policy for party decisions.

The various other divisions concerned with the economy keep a penetrating watch over fulfillment of Plans and the placing of the best technically and as party loyalists in strategic positions. The local parties assist this. This raises the question of "fulfillment" of decisions, on which Stalin was a great teacher and taskmaster of Russian traditional inertia. It is raised later (p. 887). It also involves the related *problem of self-criticism,* also treated later (pp. 887–888).

The Presidium

Little is known about its internal operations. It can be supposed that since the members are of different origin, experience, and technical expertness, there is some division of labor among them. We list the suddenly swollen Politburo before Stalin's death and then the members in its form shrunken to what it had been a little earlier, to show the variety in the membership.

There is wide geographic representation, especially the crucial Ukraine, the "soft under-belly" of the Soviet Union. The State and party interests are well blended.

Single or Collective Leadership. We are in no position to say whether one man, an inner clique, or all together take the initiative in deliberation and decision. Lenin did work by argument and collective decision—up to a point. Stalin's way with the opposition demonstrates that there was debate in the Politbureau, even violent, but that he liquidated the various oppositions. The men who are now at the top are all Stalin's men; they worked with him and were promoted by him. As soon as Stalin died, Malenkov, who was First Secretary and then Chairman of the Council of

Stalin's Presidium and Members' Interests		*Post-Stalin (April 1954; Changes in Order of Importance, February 1955)*		
1. Stalin	Party and universal	Khrushchev	22,	interests
2. Abdrianov	Party, Leningrad	Bulganin	5	do
3. Aristov	Central Committee	Kaganovich	8	do
4. Beria	Security, Party	Molotov	17	do
5. Bulganin	Military and Minister	Beria	4;	executed
6. Voroshilov	Military; Ukraine Party	Voroshilov	6	interests
7. Ignatyev	Security; Uzbek	Mikoyan	15	do
8. Kaganovich	Economic; ministerial	Saburov	20	do
9. Korotchenko	Ukraine Prime Minister	Pervukhin	18	do
10. Kusnetsov	Trade unions	Malenkov	12	do
11. Kuusinen	Karelo-Finn Soviet	Suslov	21	do
12. Malenkov	Party personnel; general			
13. Malyshev	Shipping; Minister			
14. Melnikov	Ukraine party secretary		*Candidates*	
15. Mikoyan	Trade; Minister	Kirichenko (First Secretary, Ukraine Central)		
16. Mikhailov	*Komsomols* chief			
17. Molotov	Foreign affairs; general	Shvernik	24	do
18. Pervukhin	U.S.S.R. Council of Ministers	Ponomarenko	19	do
19. Ponomarenko	Secretary, Central Committee, Minister of Supply, First Secretary, Kazakhstan			
20. Saburov	Gosplan; Minister			
21. Suslov	Secretary, Party Central Committee			
22. Khrushchev	Secretary, Central Committee; Agriculture			
23. Chesnokov	Intellectual Press			
24. Shvernik	Trade-union president			
25. Shkiryatov	Party Control Committee			

Ministers, emphasized to the confirming Supreme Soviet on March 16, 1953:

the strength of our leadership resides in its collective, cohesive and monolithic nature. We regard the strictest observance of this supreme principle as the guarantee of correct leadership of the country and a most important condition of our further successful progress along the path of building communism in our country.

But was this the Presidium's protest against Stalin's excessive, browbeating egocentricity? Or was it a cunning move of self-protection from another contender—such as the new First Secretary, Khrushchev? Or was it the strategic substitution of the party as a whole for the dead man, who had come to embody Soviet communism as the evoker of political and economic obedience, until the new leaders should be established in his stead? We take this question up again presently.

The First and Last Resort. It is surmised that the Presidium functions thus. (1) Initiative comes from within itself. It cogitates whether the good of the nation requires the amalgamation of collective farms into very large ones, whether to preach "peaceful coexistence," whether more articles of civilian consumption shall be produced rather than heavy industry and arms. (2) Yet much material for decision must come to it from the Council of Ministers at the All-Union level and the Union Republics. The whole party apparatus must spurt with problems and anxieties. The Presidium is the highest authority for deciding values and priorities. Someone must produce ideological directives like that of Stalin at the 1952 Party Congress on "Economic Problems of Socialism in the

The Rise and Fall of Soviet Leadership

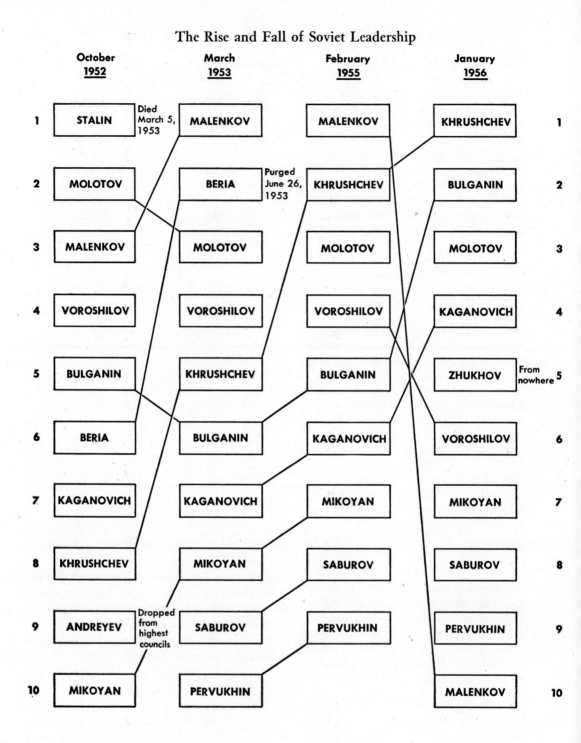

	October 1952	March 1953	February 1955	January 1956	
1	STALIN	MALENKOV (Died March 5, 1953)	MALENKOV	KHRUSHCHEV	1
2	MOLOTOV	BERIA (Purged June 26, 1953)	KHRUSHCHEV	BULGANIN	2
3	MALENKOV	MOLOTOV	MOLOTOV	MOLOTOV	3
4	VOROSHILOV	VOROSHILOV	VOROSHILOV	KAGANOVICH	4
5	BULGANIN	KHRUSHCHEV	BULGANIN	ZHUKHOV (From nowhere)	5
6	BERIA	BULGANIN	KAGANOVICH	VOROSHILOV	6
7	KAGANOVICH	KAGANOVICH	MIKOYAN	MIKOYAN	7
8	KHRUSHCHEV	MIKOYAN	SABUROV	SABUROV	8
9	ANDREYEV (Dropped from highest councils)	SABUROV	PERVUKHIN	PERVUKHIN	9
10	MIKOYAN	PERVUKHIN		MALENKOV	10

U.S.S.R." [7] When the facts of trial and error and popular reaction are presented, it must decide the issues by reference to its notion of destiny. Even survival may depend on a right answer to the question: What will the scarcity of consumer goods do to public morale; for it has been deemed right and necessary to decree that the daily motivations of 210,000,000 people shall be geared in detail to the economic initiative that comes from above, in Plans.

Its Secretariat staff in the several divisions give it information; so do the Ministries of State; and this is weighed by the ministerial experience of the Presidium's own members, for most have held some ministerial responsibility. In addition the party's many levels, its inspectorial and control bodies, pass on their findings.

Is this as manageable and sound as the impact of parliamentary assemblies and responsible Ministers in a flux of free parties operating day by day? It is less manageable, less sifted, less trustworthy. No independent-minded critics exist to offer a disinterested and fearless commentary. Stalin once claimed (at the 1930 Party Congress):

> Our Party does not by any means live and work in a vacuum. It lives and works in the very thick of life, subjected always to the influence of its environment. . . .

Inside the Kremlin? With so few of the members ever having been out of Russia at any time in their lives? Perhaps their only possibility of success so far, bought at the cost of so many lives, has been that they have been insulated from the rest of Russia and the world, and therefore never face the pain inflicted by their decisions, nor in actual fact, the incompetence of their millions of servants. Yet Malenkov and, even more so, Khrushchev have moved about in Russia; and in 1954 and 1955, the heavenly twins, Khrushchev and Bulganin, disported themselves in Jugoslavia, India, Burma, and Afghanistan.

Is Deliberation Possible? It is difficult to imagine the kind of debate that can go on in the Presidium, considering the fate of former members. Who dares to speak first, or then firmly criticize, when

an opinion may lead to disgrace and downfall, and even execution? Thus of twenty-seven members of the Politbureau who in all held office between 1917 and 1949, two were murdered (Trotsky and Kirov); five were executed (Bukharin, Kamenev, Krestinsky, Rykov, Zinoviev); one committed suicide (Tomsky, who might otherwise have been executed); three disappeared (Rudutzak, Kossior, and Chubar, the last two during the purges of 1938); and one, Voznesensky (who suddenly shot into the Politbureau from academic economies and headed the *Gosplan*), was dropped, where to, no one knows. This leaves Lenin with a natural death, though probably hastened by his being wounded by a bullet in 1921; and Stalin, Sverdlov, Kalinin, Kuibyshev, Ordjnikidze, and Zhdanov, about whose death in 1948 there is some mystery.

The rest live: Molotov, Voroshilov, Kaganovich, and Malenkov—but not Beria. And Malenkov was unceremoniously ousted from the chairmanship of the Council of Ministers (p. 883).

Beria. Beria's story is sad. He, Molotov, and Malenkov were the successor triumvirate to Stalin's throne; he for State Security, Molotov, the oldest Bolshevik alive, for foreign affairs, and Malenkov, heir to the leadership of the party. At the Supreme Soviet session just after the death of Stalin and the reorganization of the Government, Beria paid a warm tribute to Malenkov, saying,

> I think I express the Deputies' common opinion when I express firm confidence that the Soviet government headed by Comrade Malenkov will direct the entire work of building communism in our country as Lenin and Stalin taught; that it will serve the interests of our people with supreme fidelity.

He moved Malenkov's appointment to the chairmanship of the Council of Ministers. Then Malenkov replied with the observation that the government would be "collective," as already quoted.

Earlier at the funeral of Stalin, Malenkov had lauded the "unity, the monolithic nature and cohesion of the ranks of our party." Beria had lauded Malenkov and "the cohort of leaders tested in battle," trained and rallied around him by Stalin, the vivid expression of the complete unity

[7] See L. Gruliow, editor, *Current Soviet Policies*, New York, Praeger, 1953.

and singleness of leadership of the party and the State.

Within four months Beria was arrested (about June 26, 1953) and charged with plotting against the Bolsheviks in 1919 and 1920 in Baku and Georgia for the British Secret Service, having treasonable connections with other foreign powers; murdering various members of the party; sabotaging the party farm policy; fomenting discord among non-Russians and Great Russia; attempting to seize power in the U.S.S.R. In brief, "criminal anti-Party and anti-State activities."

Within six more months, in December 1954, without public trial, he was executed with six alleged accomplices.

In such circumstances it would seem that free and frank discussion and collective policy-making is at least difficult. Who will speak first? Who will speak frankly?

Malenkov–Khrushchev Case. This, even as the Beria case, demonstrates the importance of the Party Presidium and the fact that where there are two bodies with slightly different responsibilities, even though most of the men of each body are the same, a clash will surely arise between two hierarchies, for they see life through different problems and pressures.

Georgi Malenkov was born in 1902 in Orenberg, in Cossack land, of a Cossack subaltern's family. He joined the party in 1920 after some months as a political commissar with the Red cavalry. After the Civil War he attended the Moscow Higher Technical School, where he was party organizer of the student organization and studied engineering and management. In 1925 he became personal secretary to Stalin; in 1930, organizing secretary of the Moscow section of the party. Four years later he was appointed a member of the Organization Division of the Central Committee and head of the Personnel Department. In 1939 he became a member of the Central Committee of the party (elected by Congress) and was one of the five Secretaries. In 1941, still Stalin's man, he was made candidate member of the Politbureau and one of the members of the State Defense Council with Stalin (p. 785). For his expediting of aircraft production during the war he was awarded the Orders of Lenin and Hero of

Socialist Labor. In 1941, he inveighed against "bureaucracy"; industrialists were fired, including Molotov's wife, of the cosmetics trust. In March 1946 he became a full member of the Politbureau and one of the Deputy Chairmen of the Council of Ministers. Thus, he held three strategic positions: Politbureau, Minister, and Secretariat. On the death of Stalin, he was accepted as the first among the pretenders to highest authority: became First Secretary and then, on the proposal of Beria, Chairman of the Council of Ministers, whereupon, soon after, he relinquished his secretaryship of the party.

It is believed that Malenkov represents the newly thinking intelligentsia produced by the Soviet educational system, and that he was responsible for a certain "thaw" in Russian policy, a new life for all, being his slogan, amnesty for political prisoners, better housing, more consumer goods, a relaxation of international tensions.

Nikita Khrushchev was born in 1894 of a miner's family on the border of the Ukraine. (Malenkov perhaps came of a lower-middle-class family.) With little elementary education he became a pipefitter in the Donbass mines. He joined the party in 1918 and fought in the Civil War in the Ukraine, and then went back to the mines. The party schools gave him adult education. He was promoted to be party secretary of a *raion unit*. After four years of Ukraine Party work he was helped to enter the Industrial Academy of Heavy Industry. Here he dominated its party committee. Stalin let him into the high ranks of the Moscow Party organization, soon to be second only to Kaganovich therein, and in 1934, First Secretary with some other posts for the region around Moscow. These were key posts. In 1935 he was made a member of the legislative body of the Union. He assisted in the building of the famous Moscow subway. The Great Purge opened the way for him upward; he acquired the significant nickname of "the promoted one." In 1938 he became a candidate member of the Politbureau, three years *before* Malenkov; in 1939 became boss of the Ukraine Party; in 1940, full member of the Politbureau, six years before Malenkov. In World War II he did military-political and guerrilla duties at the front in various places in the resistance to the Nazis. In February 1944 he was actually chairman of the Ukraine government (40,000,000 people), and for three years, with very bloody hands, he restored the unruly land to party subjection and punished the "deserters." He returned to Moscow in December 1949 as First Secretary of Moscow Party *oblast,* and then became Third Secretary of the party (Malenkov then was *Second*) and became increasingly the party spokesman on agricultural affairs, especially effecting the amalgamation into the *agrogorods* (p. 914).

He must have looked askance at the younger man who had had a less tough life and certainly far less rough-and-tumble experience out in the field. His life was pitted against Malenkov's, certainly when he became the First Secretary of the party when Malenkov went to head the Government. Both (like their colleagues) in exceptional measure wallowed in the brutality of Stalin's Great Purge. Khrushchev led the cruel collectivist war in the Ukraine in 1929, and the *Yezhovschina* (p. 782), Yezhov's murders. Malenkov was in the very party focus, with Stalin and Vyshinsky, during the Yezhov purges. Khrushchev has since revealed himself as a guileful, fanatical, and braggart Stalinist, boorish, rough, vile of mouth, as well as ignorant of world history and conditions outside Russia.

The tangle of intrigue and murder concerning Beria's probable attempt to come out on top with his control of the Security Police, and the clash of personal ambition and fear and policy is too dark and twisted to be unraveled here or perhaps by anyone even in Moscow and Leningrad.[8] In December 1955 six more of Beria's former associates in Georgia were executed.

The Supreme Soviet met on February 7, 1955, in ordinary session. Suddenly when the meeting had been expecting a routine speech on foreign affairs by Malenkov, the Prime Minister, another member of the party, the Chairman of the Soviet, read a statement by Malenkov. It was his resignation. The reasons given were : (1) to strengthen ministerial leadership; (2) to have a chairman of the Council of Ministers more experienced in gov-

[8] See Harrison Salisbury, *American in Russia,* New York, 1955.

ernment; (3) his "lack of experience in *local* work (my italics; Khrushchev could claim this work in the field); (4) no experience in administering a branch of the national economy at the ministerial or directorate level; (5) guilt that *he* had for agricultural failures—though Khrushchev had really been in charge of this. But Malenkov was not purged—yet. He was demoted to being Minister of Electrical Power Stations, still remaining a member of the Presidium. The Supreme Soviet was utterly flabbergasted; but Deputies must have learned on which side their bread was now buttered, as they watched Khrushchev sitting and listening. At the later session the latter submitted the proposal to appoint Bulganin Prime Minister —in the name of the Central Committee of the party.

For many months before Khrushchev and various associates had criticized Malenkov in public, without needing to mention his name, for failures in the promised housing, for preferring consumer goods (not materialized) to heavy industry; for food shortages. Furthermore, in Malenkov's tenure, East Germany had risen, a strike had occurred in a prison camp, insufficient rattling of the Soviet sword and too much "peaceful coexistence" had been prevalent. The policy of Stalinist toughness with the world and of heavy industry must return.

The Presidium and the Military. The new Prime Minister, Marshal Bulganin, is *not* a military professional at all. Born a year later than Khrushchev, he is an early post-1910 Bolshevik; was a Chekist organizer and police official; graduated on the early Planning Council; got an engineering education; became Director of Electrical Industry and mayor of Moscow (at Moscow with Khrushchev and Kaganovich!); then had a military course; became Prime Minister of the Russian Republic in 1937; head of the State Bank in 1938; and Deputy Chairman of the U.S.S.R. Council of Ministers. He became the party representative in the Army and Minister of Defense in 1941. He is no professional soldier.

Has the Army swallowed the party? The answer so far is No. For the government of the Soviet Union requires an immense and comprehensive policy. Zhukov and his military associates seem not to have one that can rival and overturn that of the party. Zhukov cannot rule Russia by blowing his bugle from the walls of the Kremlin. Who would respond and for what policy? The only time a military man can govern a nation is when he has the mind of a *statesman,* like Napoleon I and Cromwell or George Washington. This does not obtain in the Soviet Union, except in the party leaders. Moreover, Konev and other Marshals are at serious professional and political odds with Zhukov. *"The"* Army is split.

From Vozhd to "Collective Leadership" to Vozhd. The maintenance of consent and social discipline, day after day, in regular work, exacting work, with all the burdens of life, of over 200,000,-000 people, certainly requires the dominance of genius—of all the individuals contributing, or of a few, or of one. The Soviet rules are possessed with a "revolution from above," regardless of the spontaneous way of life the masses might themselves choose. They are therefore committed to being genius enough to find a destination, to discovery of the Machiavellian tactics, the fear, the playing on noble impulses, and the exercise of unremitting force to the point of bestial abolition of all who stand in the way, even their immediate associates at the Presidium's council table. With the passing of Stalin, the age-long warning that it is well nigh impossible to fill the place of a dictator came true, especially the *peaceful* transfer of authority.

Stalin approximated this genius, though he had to leave many things undone for lack of brains and commensurate power. The post-Stalin rulers appealed against this "un-Marxist [even 'Fascist'] cult of the single leader." Stalin's personality and erstwhile extolled "genius" was washed away by a vigorous return to the greatness of Lenin. *Pravda* drove the lesson home fully on August 21, 1953:

Decisions taken by a single individual are always or almost always one-sided. The Party teaches that only the collective political experience and the collective wisdom of the Central Committee of the Communist Party, founded as this wisdom is upon the scientific basis of the Marxist-Leninist theory, assure the correct leadership of the Party and the country. . . . The collective nature of the leadership means that all basic decisions are taken after all the circumstances have been understood and all the aspects of a question have been discussed. The principle of collectivity is the greatest force in the Party leadership. As experienced as the individual leaders may be they cannot replace the experience and knowledge of a collective team. . . .

It was constantly hammered home by the regime's literary flunkeys and every means of communication. Perhaps there is still "collective leadership" by the Presidium and of the party and that of the Council of Ministers: personally identical, except for Khrushchev's First Secretaryship, which grows daily in public significance. If there is, no one really knows what the distribution of influences actually is. But, so tight is the desired social and economic discipline of the Soviet people that it calls for clear-cut leadership, a single line, without deviation; if leadership *is* collective the social body will lag, be bewildered, and lose efficiency, perhaps disintegrate.

Since June 1954 the Politbureau members are listed alphabetically—to save questioning. Otherwise the order of seating at functions tells the story of pre-eminence.

Who dares to speak first in council, when an error may mean political and physical death, as the Presidium meets? These men sleep with revolvers at hand. Can the weight borne by Stalin be carried by any one single person? It depends upon the person. No one knows the caliber of Bulganin or Khrushchev. Will the party, then, lose cohesion? Will it lose its grip on the numerous intelligentsia? Will criticism and self-criticism cease to flow, in the absence of a murderous tyrant? Or will it come in such spates as to cause the dissolution of the loyalties in the regime? Are there original policies, of the magnitude of heavy industrialization, collectivization of the farms, and war that will give such a fanatical spirit to the ideology that the dictatorship of the Presidium can be maintained? This seems doubtful. Have the top commanders bitten off more than they can chew?

The lost Malenkov sent up the despairing cry again in the election period, March 1954:

Cooperation in the work of Party organs is the only guarantee that decisions will be correct, the only means of insuring Party organizations against mistakes, distortions, and the arbitrary will of individuals.

In autumn of 1955, the Soviet periodical, *Soviet State and Law* declared that "collective leadership" means majority vote in a collective body.

Of the nine members left in the Politbureau, with the passage of Comrade Beria, this may be ventured. Voroshilov is senile. Ponamerenko operates in Kazakhstan, for Khrushchev's agricultural plans. Molotov concentrates on diplomacy. Malenkov and Mikoyan have been demoted and lost prestige. Peruvkhin and Saburov were friends of Malenkov's, but they are "engineers," not political leaders. Shvernik has been moved into and out of the trade-union leadership, as suited the party. Bulganin is probably too old to withstand the will of Khrushchev. This leaves only Khrushchev and Kaganovich in the forefront of leadership, and these have long cooperated. A curious collectivity it is, if it is collective leadership. Kaganovich is a Jew, and so cannot be first in leadership. Yet he was the principal person entrusted with authority during the foreign tours of Bulganin and Khrushchev.

Toward the Twentieth Party Congress

A Communist Party Congress was called for the middle of February 1956. It will be a vital one for Khrushchev and the U.S.S.R., for it is to be the first after the death of Stalin and after the demotion of Malenkov and the incursion of Khrushchev into the highest position in the party and thereby, the State. He has been making his preparations. He knows he must have a Congress that will elect a Central Committee that will select a Presidium with him at its head. For he cannot be absolutely certain that it will do this with full dedication to him. Hence, a number of evident maneuvers. "Collective leadership" and "inner party democracy" have been re-emphasized—the delegates must have the illusion of their free and solicited participation in decision-making. This has been stressed, also, in the apparent raising of the role of the Supreme Soviet in 1955, and the amelioration of the police regime by measures already noted. Furthermore, Khrushchev and Bulganin, the latter under the former's substantial wing, have traveled abroad; made a kind of peace with Marshal Tito; insulted

the Western Powers, especially America, Britain, and France in the Far East, fomenting hatred and violence, raking up old grievances (e.g. the Crimean War of 1856); been adamant on the continued disunion of Germany; rebuked Molotov for stating that socialism was not yet achieved in the U.S.S.R. They also recommended the "cold war" after a period of false smiles in July 1955. They can thus go to the Congress with an assertion of Soviet determination to win the world for Communism.

Energetic practical measures on a party level have also been taken. Numerous and widespread changes have been enforced in the party secretaryships at various levels and in different regions, and Khrushchev's nominees planted in the vacant places. He returned from his Far Eastern campaign of vilification of the West and Russia's leap into the Middle East with arms, with many Communist laurels.

IV. TERROR; FULFILLMENT; SELF-CRITICISM

The wider the scope, the deeper the levels of government control of an authoritarian nature, especially to integrate each moment the human cogs in the *exact* place and undeviating duties of the economy, the more extensive the area of terror.

The M.V.D. or Ministry of Internal Affairs

At its head is this Ministry, comprising four sections: (1) to deal with high party and governmental leaders; (2) to cope with "counterrevolutionary" activities in economic affairs and to gather information about foreign nations; (3) the Secret Political Administration to deal with opposition, deviation, the Church, the intelligentsia; (4) the Special Section for action inside the armed formations—with its own independent hierarchy directly under the Minister. Additional sections are concerned with counterintelligence, transport, foreign espionage. These divisions have their field organs through farms and precincts, apartment houses, factories, offices, regiments, and agencies abroad.

Its officers are the very *élite* of Soviet society. Recruitment is most exacting. The personnel directors try to recruit by "claiming" likely persons; those claimed are practically bound to accept the "honor." They are sent to special schools in politics and technology of criminology, spying, interrogation, torture, and confession-enforcement. The reign of pure technique is unhampered by humanity.

Seksots. The M.V.D. makes further use of informers, *seksots,* fanatical party and *Komsomol* members, or people who are subject to the M.V.D.'s hold. The informer's family is under threat, especially as the Criminal Code makes large use of the principle of family incrimination. They are forced into increasingly dirty methods, and when squeezed dry, often imprisoned. The life of the M.V.D. depends on its dragnet scope; this spreads terror and anxiety. Everyone's best friend, at work and at home, may be a betrayer, as one's own child may be. Hence, the greatest care by everyone about what they will say, for it is possible to turn the most innocent remark, a pleasant joke, even a silence into "counterrevolution." The party and government stir this up with announcements that foreign spies and saboteurs have been captured, tried, and executed, men who have infiltrated by land, sea, or parachute.

Methods. Dossiers are amassed. Some arrests are made for suspected crime; some to frighten the population. Some take place simply on "objective" symptoms—"Old Bolsheviks" or foreign-born, Ukraine writers, former prisoners of war (very suspect and harassed), even the M.V.D. itself! The M.V.D. arrests without any court warrant. Terror is added by arrests and searches at the dead of night. No legal process interferes with the interrogation in prison that can continue indefinitely. The prisoners may go to a general jail or be held in solitary confinement, whichever brings in the maximum information and confession. Some are tortured; some drugged; some starved; some not allowed sleep. The confessions are tricked out of the victim. If no guilt is present, then perhaps "objective" guilt—that is, effect without intention—may be charged. The professional pride of the M.V.D. demands a confession, or it may be fear that they themselves may be accused of sabotage. At the end of the Great Purge, thousands of the M.V.D. were themselves imprisoned for being "infiltrated class enemies." The trial is not in open court but by a police committee; the sentence may well be to a forced-labor camp so harsh as to make death preferable.

The M.V.D. was preceded by similar organizations: the N.K.V.D. that followed the O.G.P.U., that followed the *Cheka,* that followed on the Czarist *Okrana.* The first head of the O.G.P.U. was the sinister Djerjinsky. He was followed by Yagoda, himself condemned to death with the "Rightists" Bukharin, Rykov, etc., in March 1938. He was made to confess that he had murdered his immediate predecessor, Menshinsky, and had tried to murder his successor Yezhov, had assisted in Kirov's assassination, was responsible for the murder of Maxim Gorky and his son, and had planned a *coup,* with foreign spies, to assassinate Stalin and the Politbureau! Yezhov was appointed earlier, in 1936, to continue the purge, until he was ejected and his place taken by Lavrenti Beria. It is estimated that between 1934 and 1939 about 7,000,000 at least (some venture 14,000,000) had been imprisoned as purge victims. The Balkan and Baltic lands gave the N.K.V.D. more grist, so did the returning surge of civilians and soldiers who were moved by or deserted to the Nazis or returned from duty abroad.

Beria was the close friend of Stalin, a Georgian like him and head of the Georgian Communist Party till 1938. In World War II he administered the deportation of the minorities (p. 822). A member of Stalin's Politbureau, he became one of the first post-Stalin triumvirate, for he held in his hands, as Stalin's bequest, all the terror and police forces. These comprised the merger of the Ministry of the Interior with the home, frontier, and transport troops, the general militia, who are regular uniformed police, military fire brigades, and forced-labor camps, and the Ministry of State Security, with its secret police and investigators of political crime. It is alleged that Stalin had merged them at Beria's instance, himself having kept them apart as a check on each other for his own domination of both.

His colleagues ousted and executed Beria, before he did this to them. The terror is unabated. It now comes under the M.V.D. as before for routine police functions; while the K.G.B. or Committee for State Security took over the "security" functions in March 1954 by a decree of the Soviet Presidium. The Committee (of career police officials) is attached to the Council of Ministers; it *is* a committee, with a career police official, I. A. Serov as chairman. It is calculated that 1 in every 5 Soviet persons are in imminent danger of arrest some time in their lives. The sense of guilt is ubiquitous; for the law makes so many ordinary activities into crimes, even winks at them when they help to fulfill Plans, that a misdeed lurks in everyone's conscience; and each abrupt change of governors requires an adjustment of conscience.

Fulfillment

The Russian people were neither intelligently malleable by the Czarist regime nor experienced in modern social and economic affairs; they represented a rather inert or resistant mass to Lenin and Stalin. They were not habituated to fulfill their resolutions or the government's. *Oblomov,* the hero of Goncharov's novel, and the "superfluous men," talking and doing nothing, altogether lazy, were the symbols of apathy. It will take over half a century from now to make a real impression on this. Stalin set himself to pounding the table, dragooning, making tormented demands for "fulfillment," even lauding Americans for their capacity in this respect! The trouble is still widespread and deep seated. Malenkov declared (1952, Party Congress):

> One of the most widespread and deep-rooted defects in the practical work of the Soviets, economic and Party organizations is poor organization of the factual fulfillment of directives from the center and their own decisions, and absence of proper check on their execution. Our organizations and institutions issue far more decisions, directives and orders than required, but take little care to see whether or how they are being carried out. After all the essence of the job is to carry them out correctly and not bureaucratically. An unconscientious, irresponsible attitude toward carrying out directions from the executive bodies is a most dangerous and vicious manifestation of bureaucracy. Experience shows that even good officials begin to grow spoiled and bureacratic when left to themselves with no control or check on their activities.

> It is a most important task of the Party to take every measure to increase checking and following-up on decisions throughout the entire system of leadership, in the work of all organizations and institutions from top to bottom.

This damaging criticism is true, as all foreigners at work in Russia have verified.[9] Malenkov proposed the remedies, again, for the thousandth time: (1) increase the *personal* responsibility of all heads of organization for checking; (2) improve central and local inspection; (3) reinforce the personnel of inspection in authority, experience, and political alertness; (4) reinforce every kind of party intervention to verify fulfillment from above *and* below, in order to develop an atmosphere "in which decisions and directives will be carried out punctually and meticulously in Bolshevist style."

Self-criticism

In place of a free parliament and free, rival parties, as the grand inquest of the nation speaking openly at the minimum because they are soliciting power, the Communist Party, to secure fulfillment, has had to ask and then *command* its people to exercise *self-criticism,* or *samokritika.* It is the offshoot of their romantic obstinacy in ignoring the hard teachings of human nature. They have boasted of this great invention. But it is no more than a bad substitute for the open criticism of customers in a free economy or of the free and equal voters through sovereign and competing parties. In the Russian case, it is nothing but confessions obtained by wheedling or coercion. All experience shows that compulsory confession, even among servile men with a Russian inheritance of servile confession, is ineffective.

The party asks in its Rules that everybody become an informer and confessor. But the Soviet system is no market-and-price economy where a complaint is taken as an *impersonal,* technical matter only. It is no government in which, as in democracies, the *function* is criticized with personal malice reduced to a limited minimum coverage. There neither the customer nor the parliamentary or public critic nor the criticized official

[9] For example, Brigadier General Deane, *The Strange Alliance,* New York, testimony from the head of the Lend-Lease mission during World War II to Moscow.

need fear social boycott, political outlawry, penalties against his family, prison for alleged "sabotage."

Hence, self-criticism and criticism fail to do the job asked by the party; instead, the top men must complain of bureaucracy, degeneration, corruption here and there; arrogance, smugness, of *aktivs* perverted into "a show, a place for self-praise," a dulling of vigilance, negligence, forgetfulness of capitalist encirclement. Malenkov said, "It is a mistake to think that criticism from below can develop of itself, spontaneously!" But the top of the party itself is not under pressure from its followers of being fired. The best encouragement to those in the ranks to criticize is always to reward men for criticism not to purge them. But it is this latter that the top leaders mete out to real criticism.

Men need encouragement, not deterrents to do the nasty chore of criticism.

Conclusion

We observe that the rulers of Russia so far have been professional revolutionaries, some with technical knowledge of various departments of the society and the economy, some with special knowledge of foreign affairs. None has had a parliamentary life on a decent, tolerant basis; all have been involved in murder and the attainment of high place by threading their way up by brutality, with brutality, through brutality, and the mercilessness and faithlessness of "the end justifies the means." Of other lands, alas, they have no firsthand touch, for their information in and outward has always been distorted.

The Soviet Socialist Planned Economy

All economic enterprise in the Soviet Union is planned and directed from the top. The motive and initiating power in the production and distribution of goods and services is not the spontaneous and dynamic choice of workers and managers but pressure and command exerted downward upon them.

A century ago, when Marx's *Communist Manifesto* let loose a specter on the world, books on government would not have included the economic system. Today *society*—that is, all phases of human behavior—has become more intimately blended in "the State." Of this trend, the Soviet Union is the conscious, full-fledged example. The State has swallowed the economy whole.

The State it is that uses all the cruelty and wickedness following from the rejection of democratic principle; this is the *essential* sin against the Western light. The other aspect, the economy, is still very unpleasant, but less unpleasant than the former evil. Men and women are denied the right freely to determine the work they should undertake; how that work should be organized; what principles of reward should be used in the division of the product of industry. A free society could decide to do the same in the economy; but there would be a point where the limitation of private property, free enterprise, free contracts to employ other people, principles of distribution too divorced from the effort contributed, would diminish the *power* of individuals over the political will of the

State. This is the situation in Soviet Russia: the subjugation of the economy to the dictator's political values.

There is no private employment; no private enterprise; no private property—the tolerated exceptions are practically negligible. The State owns all the means of production and resources; it is the universal employer; the sole entrepreneur; the establisher of the goals of work and wealth. It guides, directs, drives, and disciplines an immense labor force and enacts the main stereotypes of what shall be consumed, worn, eaten, and how much shall be saved. But there is far more *practical* flexibility than the planners want—for so many people and so many products escape the inflicted stereotpe.

The Labor Force

In 1950, the Soviet labor force, over the age of twelve, was, say, 115,000,000; of this 63,000,000 were male and 53,000,000 female. The percentage of *non*agricultural workers is about 36 percent, or about 40,000,000. (The population in 1954 was about 210,000,000. In 1897 it was 125,000,000; in 1939, 170,500,000; in 1950 nearly 200,000,000.) These are the upper limits of estimate made by Western scholars, in the absence of up-to-date forthright figures produced by the Soviet government itself. It deliberately (by law) conceals its statistics, for defense and propaganda purposes.

Soviet *industrial* production is conducted by (1)

State factories, mines, etc., (2) industrial cooperatives, (3) individual artisans, working alone.
Agricultural production is conducted by (1) collective farms (or *artels* or Kholkhoz), (2) State
farms (or Sovkhoz), (3) communes, and (4)
joint cultivation associations.

The prevailing organization of production in the
industrial is in State factories, mines, etc. Industrial cooperatives play a role in certain consumption goods. But only about 2,000,000 out of about
40,000,000 in nonagricultural production work in
industrial cooperatives. Individual artisans are
very few. The industrial cooperatives produce furniture, boots and shoes, textiles, leather goods, toys,
and so on; run stores, restaurants, refreshment
stands, and so on. They come under the governmental Plans and the authority of the specialized
departments. They get supplies from the State
firms. Members buy a share; manage the business
cooperatively; get wages and a share of the surplus.

Not Communism

Socialism and communism may take any number
of forms, with the most diverse objectives: democratic, aristocratic, dictatorial, theocratic. Marx defined communism as the common holding of all
productive property; the determination of the objects of production by the whole community, without distinction of master and worker; distribution
according to the principle of "need," not according
to each worker's contribution. This was Lenin's
promise, to which the party committed itself. The
Soviet Union breaks this promise.

Productive property is, it is true, held by the
State. But is this the "community," if the State is
dictatorial and excludes the masses from the right
of freely voting on the process of production? The
dictatorial government decides what shall be produced. Master-worker status is abolished: this is
communistic; yet not the community but some dictators actually enserf the workers rather than employ them. And, as noticed (p. 793), the principle
of "to each according to his needs" has been postponed to the era of unlimited abundance! *Now* it is
"to each according to his work"—Taylorism in
excelsis, but without free trade unions! It is a punishable offense to teach in school or otherwise that

the day of communism is *now* and not in the
utopian future, unspecifiable.

Main Problems of Any Economy

What goods shall be produced and in what relative quantities? When shall the variable degree of
consumption be enjoyed, now, or shall commodities be conserved for future generations? How
shall goods be produced? Who decides? In what
kind of organization, with what technology: large
units, small units, mass production, with machinery—or otherwise? For whom are the goods and
services intended? To whom are they to be distributed for consumption?

Free enterprise answers these questions by leaving it to free decision among intending producers
and desiring consumers, the former keen on staying alive by producing better and cheaper than
rivals, the latter looking for the best use of every
one of their all-too-meager pile of cents. The price
in the market tells the producer what he can afford
to allocate for land, labor, capital, to make the
goods. Men without resources to allocate, owning
only their own muscle and skills, try to get the
maximum from the entrepreneur (and, thence, the
consumer) by their strength combined in labor
unions. The system has great strengths: the perpetual strain for invention, innovation, jobs to
satisfy the consumers; inefficiency limits its consequences to the falling out of the separate firms or
sectors showing incompetence. It also has demonstrated weaknesses: connivance against competition; fraudulent recommendation of goods to the
consumer; ignorance and lack of coordination that
cause investment and employment to fall off, causing distress and loss of productive capacity; social
insecurity (pp. 831–835). But it takes the chance
that it has its own medicine inside itself. Only
where the competitive medicine does not work,
the legislatures representing the millions of workers by hand and brain add, collectively, a dash (in
the twentieth century everywhere a considerable
dash) of regulation in the interests of social values,
longer views neglected by free enterprisers, stability and security, welfare of the weak and un-
lucky, and the common defense.

The Soviet State rejects this economic system

root and branch, on the main professed ground that it permits and encourages the exploitation of man by man—its errors lie in its false conception of *exploitation*. It rejects the idea that the wealth of the nation is the free result of an arithmetical sum of the goods of the individual workers and employers; to it the national wealth is a formula prepared by a self-appointed small group of directors over all.

I. SOVIET INDUSTRY

The Law of Planning

Since 1918 the various Constitutions and declarations have contained piecemeal clauses promising a "state national economic plan." The Constitution of 1936, Article 11, runs:

> The economic life of the U.S.S.R. is determined and directed by the state national economic plan, with the aim of increasing the public wealth, of steadily raising the material and cultural standards of the working people, of consolidating the independence of the U.S.S.R. and of strengthening its defensive capacity.

"Defense Is Prior to Opulence." It is as well to notice the *"defense" and "independence" aspect of planning*. For, if the nation is kept closed off from free information about the nature and way of life of other nations, it is not difficult for a dictatorial regime to disseminate a picture of them so aggressive against the U.S.S.R. that the industrial and economic objectives chosen by the leaders can be justified in their terms, and a military spirit of energy, subordination, and self-sacrifice demanded of the worker. This is what the Russian planners have consistently and urgently done since the beginning of the Plans, by development of national fears and phobias about "capitalist encirclement." Thence the other aims of the Plan become subordinate to industry for national preservation; and consumer goods need be produced in less quantities, and real wages can be low.

From December 27, 1927, at the Party Congress, began a massive and radical industrial revolution, the first Five Year Plan, in Russian, the *piatiletka*. Indeed, by December 1920 Lenin was fulminating

for "electrification," and in February 1921 a General State Planning Commission, *Gosplan,* had been established to elaborate it. By 1925 a network of planning officials was appointed across the country, and, under the aegis of *Gosplan* and the central ministries, studies and surveys were made of aims, resources, priorities, methods, public information, and the corresponding organization of labor. The first Five Year Plan was put into operation late in 1928, its targets raised to "optimal" heights in April 1929, to be fulfilled in four and a quarter years by the end of 1932. The next Plans were 1933–1937 and 1938–1943. But the latter was interrupted by World War II and replaced by war "planning."

In February 1946 Stalin set new goals:

> As regards long-term plans, our Party intends to organize another powerful upswing of our national economy that will enable us to raise our industry to a level, say, three times as high as that of prewar industry. We must see to it that our industry is able to produce annually up to 50 million tons of pig iron, up to 60 million tons of steel, up to 500 million tons of coal, and up to 60 million tons of oil. Only when we succeed in doing this can we be sure that our Motherland will be insured against all contingencies.

The Plan envisaged not merely a single five-year stage but three five-year Plans, giving larger and vaguer but still guessed-at results by 1961—supplies of all heavy kinds that would put the U.S.S.R. close to the United States in heavy industrial goods and rolling stock. That target is interesting; it indicates something of the process that goes on in the mind of the planners.

The fifth Five Year Plan was published and discussed (to a certain applausive extent) in October 1952 at the Nineteenth Party Congress.[1] It is intended to surpass the per-capita industrial output of the wicked capitalist economies. The Plan directives fall into four great sections: industry; agriculture; commodity turnover (commerce),

[1] The general directives and form of the Plan are printed in Leo Gruliow, editor, *Current Soviet Policies,* New York, Praeger, 1953, and a briefer account appears in J. H. Meisel and E. S. Kozera, *Materials for the Study of the Soviet System,* Ann Arbor, 1953.

The U.S.S.R. Budget for 1954 *

Expenditure		Billions of Rubles
I. The National Economy		216.4
of which:		
Heavy industry		
Light industry	79.7	
Internal trade		
Agriculture procurement	14.2	
Agriculture and forestry	62.5	
Transport and communications	21.5	
Local economy		
Other	38.5	
II. Social and Cultural Measures		141.4 †
of which:		
Education	67.2	
Health and physical culture	29.3	
Social security	24.7	
Social insurance		
Family allowances	17.8	
III. Defense		100.3
IV. Loan Service		10.5
V. Administration		
VI. Other		94.2
Total		562.8
of which: investment		121.1
surplus		9.7

Revenue	
Turnover tax	234.4
Deductions from profits	92.8
State loans	15.9
Increase in savings bank deposits	9.5
Agricultural tax	4.2
Other direct taxes	41.5
Social insurance premiums	24.7
Other revenue	149.5
Total	572.5

* Source: *Economic Survey of Europe in 1954,* United Nations, Geneva, 1955.
† The discrepancy in the addition of the items under II is in the source.

Defense figures must not be taken to be the equivalent of the budgeted amounts for the same rubric in democratic countries of free enterprise; for much defense installation and production in the U.S.S.R. is hidden in such items as Heavy Industry, Transportation, while the item indicated in "Other" includes the expenditures by the Ministries of the Interior and State Security—that is, the police, the militia, etc., directly auxiliary to the men in the Armed Forces.

transport, and communications; and further improvement of the material well-being, health, and cultural level of the people.

The Plan came before the Supreme Soviet for approval and was further presented in the form of implementary laws and budgets. But, as we have seen, this process is no legislative process: it is a mere exhibition in the few hours during which the delegates are met.

Enterprise from the Top. The Party Presidium makes the highest political decisions. The Council of Ministers (its top nucleus consists of five members of this same Presidium) feeds the Party Presidium with continuous data of success and failure in the on-going Plan with ideas for remedy and progress. The *Gosplan,* which is the technical-administrative brains, feeds the Ministers, the Council, and the Party Presidium. Hence the

Party Presidium's state of mind, its hopes and fears, its appraisal of allies and enemies and their intentions and striking power, are the first issue in planning; foreign "danger" and security, its first priority. Thence follow the allocation of all resources and the kind of skills and the amounts to be developed in the industrial and agricultural labor force, all the way down to morale-building, consumption, house room, health, etc.

The broad ideas of the Party Presidium are circulated well in advance of the next party Congress and Supreme Soviet's sessions. Hence, the local party organs may dilate on difficulties they will encounter if they try to carry out the projected directives. Some adjustment is therefore possible. But the main lines are accepted as command by the party officials and Congress and Soviet. Almost every Ministry (p. 805) is the head office of a gigantic and monopolistic branch of the colossal economy. We already know how the branches are coordinated by the Council of Ministers (p. 805ff.)

The Gosplan. The State Planning Commission became the State Planning Committee in January 1948. At that time a part of its function was separated from it, namely, the rational organization of the allocation and distribution of raw materials and machinery. This was put into the hands of the Committee for the Material-Technical Supply of the National Economy, *Gossnab*. Thus the *Gosplan* was left with the planning of production, the financial statement and arrangements following from this, and verification of fulfillment.

It is profitable to describe very briefly the *Gosplan*, on the basis of the statute for it issued in a decree of the Council of Ministers, February 1938, even though various of its details have changed.

It is composed of eleven members, individually approved by the Council of Ministers from "among the leading planning workers, the most prominent scientific workers and specialists." As a body it is under the Council of Ministers.

It works out, and submits for consideration to the Council of Ministers, the long-term, the yearly, and the quarterly plans; submits its findings to the Council on the plans of like nature submitted by the various Ministries and constituent Republics; verifies fulfillment; thinks out problems of the socialist economy on its own or at the request of the

Council of Ministers; appoints expert commissions on economic problems; elaborates the methodology of socialist plannings; supervises socialist accounting. Its principal function is to insure, in the Plan, correct relationships in the development of the various branches of the economy and measures for the avoidance of disproportion.

It is responsible for coordinating the work of the complementary branches: extractive and manufacturing; agriculture and industry; transport and the national economy; increase of production with increase of consumption; providing finance and materials for production; correct geographical distribution of enterprises in order to abolish unnecessary freight hauls in relation to raw material sources and markets.

It is the universal verifier of the work done by the executive enterprises; it puts up to the Council of Ministers problems and suggested solutions arising out of fulfillment functions.

As we have seen, for the above purposes, it has its central apparatus, sectors, and groups, and in the Republics and lower territorial levels its agents, who are direct subordinates of the *Gosplan*.

At the center the *Gosplan* has a department integration of the national economic plan; another for capital construction; a department of the budget and credit; a department for distribution of enterprises and regional planning.

It has today about forty sectors. As a sample, we mention only fuel; chemical industry; food industry; railway transport; foreign trade; culture and cadres (education, amusements, sport, and vocational training); local and cooperative industry. Each sector is responsible for all matters to do with the planning of its branch of the economy and verification, quantitative and qualitative, of fulfillment.

In addition there are sectors for training planners, registration of inventions, internal administration, publications—the journal *Planned Economy* is of especial importance.

Each sector has several branches of sections: they cannot all be enumerated. A typical one is the Sector of Chemicals: basic chemicals, organic chemicals, rubber and rubber articles, special chemistry. The more minute specialization of administrative organs in the sectors, and so on, must be sought elsewhere.[2] But, if there are some forty sectors and each has three sections, we have some 120 units of administration, planning, execution, and managerial verification.

Statistics. One thing needs to be added at this point: the central statistical arrangements. Without statistics, planning is impossible. Not until 1931 did the *Gosplan* have its own statistical office. Before that the various departments, the Republics, and the Council of Ministers as a whole had statistical agencies. In 1931 the U.S.S.R. Central Statistics Administration was reorganized into the Central Administration of Economic Accounting within the *Gosplan* to "work out and ratify the system of indices of accounting for the entire national economy in accordance with the requirements of economic planning." Since then the Central Statistical Administration has become a separate agency under the Council of Ministers. This is probably in order that its operations may be independent of the body that is responsible for *results* in planning and so under the temptation of making the figures and the indicia an accomplice of its potential incompetence and deceitfulness.

The Plans

The Plans then are made in Moscow for 210,-000,000 people. They are time plans: for five years. *But* within them lesser plans, for better prediction and control, are made: for a year, for a quarter-year. They are Soviet *law,* with penal sanctions. They are extremely detailed, running into thousands, indeed scores of thousands of units of planned figures. Yet there is a watchful flexibility. For two things at least cannot be settled to perfection: foreign troubles (say resistance against aggression in Korea, therefore the need to supply North Koreans and Chinese) and the weather and consequent harvests.

The consumers, the local firms that produce, have little influence on the Plan, so far as their values and *will* are concerned. They are bound to have some "objective" influence on the Plan, seeing

[2] Alexander Baykov, *The Development of the Soviet Economic System,* Cambridge, 1947, p. 448 and p. 466ff. The latter gives an almost terrifying picture of the detail to which organization must go in all-embracing and meticulous economic plan.

that human nature cannot be suppressed too much, that, for example, general food consumption could not be cut down for five years to a calorie consumption of 250 per day. Even when some firms, by luck or contrivance overfulfill their assignments, the planners are not always pleased. There is suspicion that the overfulfillments are publicized in order to put pressure on "socialist competition," to extract more out of the enterprises.

The closest controls are exerted in the blueprint of heavy industry and agriculture; much less over the production of consumer goods by the cooperatives.

State Banking

The center of credit financing is the *Gosbank,* the world's biggest single bank. Its president has Ministerial rank, reporting directly to the Council of Ministers. It handles all the short-term banking requirements in the U.S.S.R. and credits and loans up to one year. It draws its resources from the Government, which, in turn, draws them from taxes, the surplus of receipts from economic transactions over the cost, savings, and public loans that are practically compulsory, supported by unilateral propaganda and a tone of menace. As it lends at 1 or 2 percent domestically, it can afford to lend to foreign governments at low rates and still do well. There is no gold backing for the mass of paper money it administers.

Ministerial Quotas. Each Ministry is assigned its task in figures of production and the materials assigned to it, plus the labor and the regionalization of the operations. The production of each product is related in the time and program to other products of which it is either the raw material or a semifinished part. The timing of production must be fairly exact, as well as delivery at the factory or farm needing it—*otherwise there is unemployment* among the would-be recipients.

Each product is not a simple thing. There are many varieties of rubber, of coal, of steel. One kind will not satisfy the uses of any other kind. In each process, labor must be delivered in its special skills and experience. Hence, the whole educational system must be geared thereto, and it is. Every item in a projected product must be manufactured to time or the Plan is spoiled. If it is determined to make 5,000,000 motor car tires in the year, and the cotton or other fiber to be used is enough for only 2,000,000 tires, the repercussion on transport and agriculture (tractors) is obvious. Hence, the planners and the ministerial executants are on the rack of multiple variables, one maladjustment leading to many others. They are constantly on the alert, and the more severe about infractions.

"Balances." The massive control figures are known as "balances." A balance is for any desired commodity, say pig iron, the amounts now known to be in stores, the amount to be produced, imported, exported, consumed for any period of planning; and the commodity is linked with other commodities, according to the will of the planners. Thus, for 1 ton of pig iron, about 1.8 tons of iron ore and something in the neighborhood of 1 ton of coke will be necessary.

These balances enable the planners to settle what quantities of each commodity must be produced if other quantities they have determined to have are to be produced; and how much they demand depends on what their inventory of commodities in store, etc., shows them is necessary. These inventories are known as "natural" balances. Corresponding to them are "synthetic" balances—that is, the financial indicia of the "natural" balances, when prices have been attributed to the various commodities—and they can be expressed in a financial relationship to each other: for example, the price of pig iron, of a ton of iron ore, of a ton of coke.

The financial indicia are (by pricing that is largely *arbitrary* in the *Gosplan*) arbitrary to guide production and consumption the way the Presidium broadly wants it. They make some goods and services plentiful and others scarce, some forms of labor highly paid and others poorly compensated. The pricing is undertaken for two reasons: for simplicity of the exercise of controlling power by the government over the producers and consumers, because thereby it can penalize the use of some goods and relax on the use of others, bought out of the funds at the disposal of an enterprise or of a family. Furthermore, the pricing makes accounting precise and so does two things: (1) it indicates statistically to each enterprise how

well it is fulfilling its target, and (2) whether it is bringing down its cost of production to below a figure set for it by the government, a method of governmental discipline for improved productivity.

Labor "balances" link up with commodity and financial balances—what we have, what we need, the amounts and kinds of labor that go to each kind of commodity or service, the cost of it in rubles.

In 1950 "natural" balances for 1500 commodities were elaborated by the government. The supply inventory was offset by a utilization inventory for each commodity. Hence: production requirements; construction requirements; supplies used in the production of the commodity itself; retail supplies; exports; additions to State reserves; supplies left in the stores of distributors at the end of each period.

Thus the broad balance of the whole economy is drawn up: consumption over the next five years; production; what commodities in production and consumption; in what relative quantities; what is the rate of conservation to be included in the calculation, and what stocks or reserves; what tax to be exacted from the firms and individuals for general administration and defense of the nation —and so on.

Ministry Down to Firm

Each Ministry has its planning orders. Each Ministry is a big business organization, with many plants under it. To do its job properly, it has an internal organization, roughly, of technical, planning, finance, supply, sale, construction, manpower, and accounting sections. These are the staff aid to the Minister's job of getting the plants under his jurisdiction to fulfill his orders as planned.

Beneath the Ministry is a linkage of organs to the individual plant or mine or construction job. Simplified to the basic organization, there descends from the Ministry these levels. *First,* a *Glavk,* or chief administration, a delegacy of the Ministry, controlling the plants, etc., in a region producing certain types of products. *Second,* there follows a *trust* or *combine* or a group of plants associated in a single administrative combination. *Third* is the *enterprise,* and this, according to the nature of the product, might be merely an individual factory or it might be a trust or combine, in the latter case one level of the form would be omitted. Whether the two-tier or the three-tier organization is used depends on the commodity and its technical production characteristics. Schwartz[3] offers the example of the Magnitogorsk Combine. It manages iron mines, steel mines, coke chemical plants in and about the city of that name. Above it is the *Glavk* descending from the Metallurgical Ministry. There are many other *Glavks* and combines belonging to the Ministry. Below the Combine are its various enterprises. Sometimes the *Glavk* stage is skipped.

The Enterprise or Firm. This is managed by a director, who, responsive to his own assignment and the determination of the party and the government to maintain "one-man management" as a way of personalizing responsibility and heightening technical competence, is vested with complete power of management and control.

To make definite the responsibility of the enterprise, the law makes a legal entity able to sue and be sued in the courts, for the fulfillment of its obligations, to the government, to the banks, to the employees, to other enterprises with which it makes contracts of sale and purchase and deliveries. The functions and status of the enterprise are set down in a charter approvable by the relevant Minister or the whole Council of Ministers.

Each enterprise (I sometimes refer to it as "the firm") is endowed by the government with fixed capital, such as buildings, machinery, various equipment, working capital in raw materials and money in the bank, and an account in the State Bank, from which it can get credit. The U.S.S.R. government Ministry of Finances takes no liability for the firm's debts. The firm now has the wherewithal to manufacture, mine, or trade. It has its bank account. It must make up its own accounts, to show profit and loss and balance sheet. It has its production targets set for it by the Ministry. The director knows from whom he must buy and to whom he may sell and at what prices. Now—let him do business and produce!

[3] Harry Schwartz, *Russia's Soviet Economy*, New York, Edition 1954.

Before 1934 the director of a firm would get orders from several superior authorities, actually from the various Ministries and their subdivisions. Thus, "This is your plan," from the State Planning Commission. "This is where you sell and at these prices," from the Ministry of Internal Trade. "This is where you will buy!" from various raw-materials-producing Ministries. That was the so-called "functional" method of management. Clearly, it produced a multiplicity of orders, a confusion, and added to the difficulty of easily locating inefficiency. It gave rise to collegial management, several directors each responsible for some specific line of orders from above, and a kind of factory parliamentarism.

In 1934 Stalin declared that this could no longer be tolerated. The system was abolished and replaced by the so-called "production-territorial" system: the firm and the director take *all* directions from a *Glavk*. It is the *Glavk* that takes the various orders from the sectors of the Ministries and coordinates them and then issues decisions to the firm or through a *trust* to the firm.

The director is heavily dominated by the *Glavk* and the trust; the trust by the *Glavk*. The *Glavk* has engineer-expediters who supervise one or more firms—they spur forward fulfillment and supply technical assistance.

The Director. The director is appointed by the Ministry under whose jurisdiction his product falls. Below him are two kinds of aides: staff aides, engineers, planners, budgetary experts; these are advisory to the director, not joint managers as of old. Then there are the men in the line: shop chiefs. From them downward there are foremen. The shop chiefs manage all the activities within the shop, employ and dismiss workers; the foremen boss the workers and pass down the director's program in their orders.

The director of a Soviet enterprise may not sell his capital. But some do, illegally, and are severely punished. (In late 1955 the rule was slightly relaxed for surpluses, allowing a certain useful flexibility.) His payroll is fixed for him. Often he does not directly sell his goods to other producers or the public or buy his material where he might get it, for these functions are performed by a Ministry agent, or the *Glavki*. He has no flexibility, except within the factory; and how he achieves this will be apparent soon.

He is not only controlled by the agencies to which we have already referred, but when he needs short-term credit, and when he draws his pay-envelope money, he is audited for "fulfillment" by the State Bank. On these occasions, the Bank will see that he keeps his expenses within the work plan assigned to him, and that he has met his arrangements for meeting his obligations to other plants. Since only small cash payments go from one firm to another, and the rest are bookkeeping transactions through the Bank, the latter is a very potent controller of fulfillment.

Now, it can be inferred that the freedom of enterprise of the director is almost nil. In this he differs as the night from day in comparison with the managing director of a firm in a free-enterprise system. The latter must always seek customers; the former has his planned customers; the latter must seek credit, capital, raw material, plant, out of resources he must find or induce other people to find for him, and prove his worthiness to receive, by demonstrations of profit-making ability. The Soviet firm director has all these provided for him in conditions in which he can hardly make a mistake of production and sale and insolvency.

At the most, he has two possibilities of entrepreneurial mobility: (a) daily decisions on the small, unforeseeable problems arising within all his cut-and-dried ministerial donations and obligations, and (b) to cut down the cost of production by invention, innovation, and so make a profit— that is, the difference between what he gets for his produce at prices and quantities fixed by the government, and any beating down of the dictated cost of production.

The best study so far available on the directors of Soviet firms offers the following conclusions. In heavy industry, the directors are almost entirely members of the Communist Party, in spite of occasional efforts of the leaders of the party to get nonparty recruits. In the lower management, there is considerably less proportion of party members, as little as one third among the chief engineers or technical directors, foremen, and departmental superintendents. For these posts are either technical or of a subsidiary "political" nature. These figures relate to the 1930's. It is probable that the percentage of party membership is higher now, as the party has taken into its fold so many more of the intelligentsia.

This marches with the improvement of the education of the higher personnel of the firms. In 1934 directors have had more than primary education in only 50 percent of all cases; but by 1939 the proportion with higher education had risen to more than 80 percent. The heads of *Glavki* and engineers are between 80 to 90 percent men of higher education respectively—this includes, of course, their engineering training. In 1933 only 2 percent of the foremen, the lowest managerial level, had higher education, and only 7 percent technical secondary education. By 1940 the government was able to lay it down as a firm rule that only those with at least a secondary technical education might be appointed foremen in heavy industry, unless they took an examination set by a commission of the whole firm.

There is great brevity of tenure of managerial positions. The bulk of directors hold the same post for from one to five years. Nearly one third held the same job for less than a year. It would seem that the turnover is due to transfers rather than to promotions or demotions; due, again, to rapid development and change of the firms. But nervousness among the ministerial and industrial leaders, who have to manage the enterprises by pressure and guidance from the top, and jittery changes of job through discovery of incompetence, account also for this feverishness.

Dynamic Factors

How is the factory, etc., kept going and in line with the Plan? There is (1) governmental control from above by the officials of the various Ministries. This we have dealt with already. There are (2) certain technical controls—chiefly cost accounting and contractual relations among suppliers of various goods. There are (3) party controls.

A brief reference to (2) and (3) is necessary. (2) *Cost accounting* (*khozraschet* in Russian) is the minute analysis of cost of production. It now applies to each firm as a whole, which is a legal separate entity, and so produces detailed analytical budgets. There are also shop-accounting systems being set up, sofar as the separation is feasible.

This technique of financial analysis has been in operation, in highly ingenious forms, for over a century in the Western economies. But Russia is a most uncultured and in many respects a very illiterate land. It is producing the first full generation of substantial supplies of accountants and administrators. Hence, every now and again the land resounds with a new *mystique,* promising salvation to the economy's weak points, brought about by the absence of free consumers who could decide by their willingness to pay a price for goods, the solvency and efficiency of the firm.

Cost accounting is another way of locating responsibility for costs. By minute analysis, two things are accomplished: the costs may be imputed and seen, and therefore a train of remedial thought may be set off; and the mere attempt to establish costs rivets the mind of the director and others on the problem of reducing costs.

It seems rather ridiculous to do this, in view of the fact that the director is in a strait-jacket of fixed prices and quantities and orders from the *Glavk* about how to manage his business. It does, however, force the director to give attention to the problem of lowering costs. This is important for the whole national economy, which is a very immature, raw one, and is constantly being accused by the party leaders of wastefulness of all the components, including labor, of goods produced. It is also important to the director and the employees, because since 1936 a measure of profit sharing has been in operation as a flexible incentive for higher production. A word on this may be said at once.

The Director's Fund. In any year the profit product of a firm goes to the following destinations. About 60 percent of it went back to the government as part of its budget revenues. The rest of the profit was used to expand working capital and capital investment in the firms and Ministries that had realized the profit.

However, in 1936–1941, and then after World War II, from 1945, some of the total profits are allowed to be kept by the firms, in the Director's Funds, variously calculated for three different groups of industries. Let us take as an example the situation in 1950 in metallurgical production and other labor-intensive firms. The Director's Fund consists of 5 percent of the planned profit and 45 percent of unplanned profit. The amount obtained in this way is ordered to be spent thus: 50 percent for expanding production and for constructing and repairing housing for the workers in the plant in amounts above the planned capital investment. This is a satisfaction to the workers. The rest goes to improvement of workers' living conditions, bonuses to particularly efficient employees, tours and vacations, rest homes and sanatoria and emergency lump-sum grants for exemplary workers. The budgetary estimates for the use of the fund in this way needs the agreement of the labor union's factory committee.

Since the employees and workers stand to gain from profits, it is to their interest to press the director and the accountants to keep analyses of cost that may be the monitors of their attempted reduction.

Profit? This raises a curious question. How can there be profit, and, conversely, how can there be insolvency or bankruptcy in a Soviet firm? One would think that a *planned* economy of such meticulous calculation would match costs and revenues, and so all balance sheets would come out even. The profit we speak of is the calculated amount of surplus that the firm will have, as determined by the planners above it: it is the difference between the revenue for the *fulfilled* quantities and qualities sold and the costs of production. The difference could be lost by nonfulfillment; it can be increased by overfulfillment; it can be increased further by reduction of the costs of production.

How could the difference be lost? By bad management; by labor slacking; by spoiled goods that will not be accepted by the contractors (firms contract with each other, by law, in order that there may be one more force and pressure on the firms to fulfill); by bad morale and bad organization that causes a waste of working time; by unexpected changes in consumers' demand.

How can it be overfulfilled? By good organization; adept administrative team work; by clever advertising to get a bigger turnover; innovations of technique and labor-saving; Stakhanovism, and so on. So one firm can be bankrupt, and the director and his associates may be demoted. Or the director can be in line for promotion, for public honors, and for special premia that are paid to directors for fulfillment and overfulfillment, especially as to quality, that implies *careful* work.

To Animate Monopolies

In the Soviet Union all production is in the hands of great, nationwide, legally protected monopolies. The consumers must take what is offered them by authority of their leaders, or nothing, for no alternative form of production is permitted. Hence, the controls over production must be exercised by the party, as the "vanguard" and "militia" of the "masses"; and by enlisting the masses in this process. Soviet planning can err twice as a system of producing the national wealth: once because the decisions of the party leaders do not please the public (so that goods and services offered are not *welfare* in the consumers' opinion), and second, within the choices that the leaders have made and decreed inefficiencies of management may occur.

The party operates to see that, at least, the second fault does not materialize. At the Eighteenth Party Conference, 1941, Malenkov delineated no less than fourteen tasks for party organizations; they imply a collateral interest in and pressure for good management in every entrepreneurial direction.[4]

Whipping Up the Workers. This is implemented by the various levels of the party organization. They appoint an industrial secretary for each kind of industry in their area to organize party control and spur forward "socialist competition." The party unit in the factory participates substantially in selecting factory personnel and ousting lax workers. (The student may notice what a coercive power this gives the party over the population!) Small groups of party members at work in a plant are appointed as production and business *aktivs*. They are the "front-line" fighters (what in England might be called a "ginger group," to heat

[4] *Cf.* Alexander Vucinich, *Soviet Economic Institutions,* Stanford, 1952, p. 13.

people up), to lead party efforts of supervision and to permeate with their ideology. Also, the party unit sees to it that meetings of various organizations (trade unions, sports clubs) are not held during work hours.

This little phalanx of party unit workers, with chosen experts—"technical brigades of specialists" —from among them, sharply impinge on the one-man management. It is linked outside with the rest of the party and upward, whence it can get any skilled help that it lacks in the vicinity. It can force a change in decisions on processes of operation, redistribute manpower, throw over foreman and shop chiefs for others proposed by the party.

The party maintains a continual stir around the director's head. It will not let him ignore cost accounting, it besets the managerial staffs that delay in introducing government-recommended innovations. It makes suggestions that have an unpleasant weight. It points out the good and evil of factory occurrences in "wall newspapers" or works bulletins. It conducts committee or shop or *Komsomol* or trade-union meetings with harangues and debates. It mixes the various levels of workers and party men at conferences or sets up meetings of members of the technical or professional staffs.

While these activities are directed to getting the plan for which the director has managerial responsibility fulfilled by the workers, the party factory unit is helping the director, and it makes his task easier. Though the party unit is not permitted to "induce" the director to change his decisions, except where the law allows alternatives, some nevertheless interfere substantially, sometimes against the law. Sometimes they practically replace the manager.

Yet the responsibility of the party for achievement is different from the director's. His is continuous, and the law will rigorously enforce it. The party's responsibility is controllable by the party, and this is not so set and established and continuous a responsibility. It is in and out; sometimes very effective; but sometimes out when it should be in and in when it should be out.

A New Governing Class. As the technical and professional intelligentsia has developed under Soviet auspices and has entered the high ranks of the party itself, and as it has weighty representation in the factory, a locus of resistance to party control has developed. This significantly affects the problem of, For whom does the economy exist? If the intelligentsia is in command, and its salaries and premia are so much higher (p. 902) than those of the middle and lower workers, under what impulse is it *ever* going to concede these advantages for the sake of "communism"? It merely looks like a new governing class that tries to pass on its advantages to its own children.

The party also operates through its control of the trade unions which have duties of production fulfillment and improvement required by their charter. They work through "public inspectors" and "production conferences."

Consumer Reaction. The public is invited to send letters to the editors of various newspapers. This is another—and a weak—substitute for consumers' sovereignty. The "worker correspondent" and the "peasant correspondent" are public institutions. They are invited to "informative" conferences by the editors. Also for spontaneity! For the party has the responsibility of calling conferences of letter writers, and of planting party members among them locally, even cultivating them in seminars. Some editors pay fees for letters! The party claimed that in 1939 no less than 2,000,000 correspondents had written in in this *"mass* participation," with almost a hundred times greater population. The party is in the dilemma of wishing to give the impression of mass participation and mass acceptance of the regime, yet is impelled to organize the writers, to indoctrinate them, so that they may become the additional servants of Plan fulfillment.

Labor

Under the first Five Year Plan began the organized efforts of the government to increase the labor force. The collectivization of the farms made more peasant labor than ever redundant; the peasants drifted to the towns. *The abolition of unemployment pay* for anything save hospital-certified ill health helped bring the unemployed into work. The children and wives of workers were "directed" to employment by orders of the Ministry of Labor and Transport. Specially needed worker-technicians, and so on, became legally removable from their work to other jobs needed in the Plan.

An immense propaganda was let loose all over the country on the glory of the Plan, its meaning for the nation, the need for industrial workers, the opportunities available to them. The gatherers of labor for the factories and mines were given powers to make special contracts with the collectivized farms for groups of workers. The self-improvement opportunities and educational facilities were advertised and in fact instituted, in special schools and in training courses on the job and around the factory. Special rewards were introduced for skilled and exemplary workers.

The trade unions were now used as trainers, discipliners, cultivators of the workers. The *rationed foods* were more advantageously available for the industrial workers than on the farms; and ration categories were created according to production ratings of various towns and industries: the highest being for Moscow, Leningrad, Baku, the mines, metallurgical workers, engineerings, chemicals, and so on. The industrial plants had their own gardens and farms, another advantage in a time of terrible scarcity. The scarce consumption *enabled the government to save and invest in the capital* is needed out of Russia's own resources.

Russia had an enormous surplus of peasant labor—that is, many millions of peasants could be entirely removed from the land without any total reduction of product, since so many did nothing or very little, as the complementary tools, fertility, size of plots, and knowledge did not permit of a higher productivity. They had the normal range of ambitions for a better standard of living, advancement, improvement of their skills, opportunities of education, and the exercise of their abilities. The Soviet opportunities opened up by developing industry were very welcome to many, just as the opportunities of the New World had attracted scores of millions of Europeans, among them Russians, to migrate from their native land.

This normal attraction of a better standard of living is fundamentally the cause of the rising size of the industrial labor force in Russia. Coercion is a subordinate cause, and affects the tempo of increase rather than its basic surge, and also, the assignment to specific jobs against the will of the workers rather than the fact that they would like a job and an education.

The numbers so increased:

Year	Millions
1928	11.6
1929	12.2
1930	14.5
1931	19.4
1932	22.9
1933	22.3

The standard of living was very low compared with Western standards. Great lapses occurred from the legal five-day seven-hour week. The last ounce of energy was squeezed out of the workers. In 1933, when farm supplies increased, rationing was abolished, so that the differential wages could buy freely, and provided more incentives between skills and input of work. Then (p. 783) industrial conscription was developed, mainly indirect, partly direct.

Rates of pay in the various categories are fixed in the Plan. The different categories of skills are paid by different rates of basic pay for certain norms of production. There are premiums and bonuses for the exceeding of the norms as set down with the basic pay. A constant effort is made to raise the norms. In this the shock workers and *Stakhanovites* play a pioneering and high-pressuring effort.

Labor and the Intelligentsia in Soviet Industry: Work and Rewards

Three questions are of interest: (1) How did the Soviet government raise its total industrial work force from 3,000,000 to 40,000,000 in 1950? (2) How do they pay workers of various strata? and (3), What are the social relations of the various strata in the factory or mine, etc.?

Some Data on Wages, Salaries, Etc. In order to indicate the wide inequality of compensation for work, we offer the following figures. They are for the year 1950. In 1954 these figures would be raised by about 10 percent for current validity.

The average income *in towns* was 500 rubles per month, or 6000 rubles per year. This includes all kinds of workers, the intelligentsia, the skilled manual, the unskilled, etc. If the employees and skilled workers of exceptional earnings were excluded, the figure would be 450 and 5400 rubles respectively.

In the mechanical engineering shops, the highest category workers get a basic wage of just over 757 rubles per month. There are then seven other categories, in descending order: the fourth gets 425 rubles per month and the eighth, only 291. The span between workers in the first and eighth category *in wages* is approaching three times.

In this mechanical engineering plant, however, the eight categories of workers are managed by the intelligentsia. An ordinary engineer earns a basic rate of between 600 to 900 rubles per month, while the senior engineers get between 900 and 1100. The span between the senior engineers and the lowest grade of worker, then, is *at least four times. At least*—because the intelligentsia are eligible for bonuses confined to them.

In 1954 a competent carpenter in a small woodworking shop earned 600 rubles a month for a six-day and forty-eight-hour week. A medium-skilled translator and editorial worker for a publishing house in Moscow earns 1500 rubles per month and commission, making 3000 altogether. Thus he earns ten times (and more) the pay of the lowest category worker in the engineering shop. A trained female nurse earns 800 rubles a month, for two twenty-four-hour spells per week.

We turn to the salaried employees, again in 1950. A starting salary for a teacher at a rural elementary school is 325 rubles; his principal gets 450 rubles. A starting salary for a teacher in a city secondary school is 525 rubles; his principal gets between 650 to 1000 according to size of school. Kindergarten teachers get 225 in the country, 500 in town; the education and seniority make a difference. Professors at teachers' colleges earn 625 to 800 rubles per month, according to qualifications and experience; their directors are paid from 850 up to 1250.

A stenographer earns from 385 to 450 rubles per month, in a big office perhaps 10 percent more. Office cleaners get 260 to 285; furnace men, 310 to 335; janitors, 310 to 335.

Bonuses—Incentives to Production. We offer a mere indication of how the premium or bonus incentives are used for the directors and other intelligentsia of the various firms.

The multifarious directors, engineers, managers, technologists, accountants, production control, staff aides, shop chiefs, foremen, etc., and the principal assistants to these are classified into three categories. The first grouping gets as much as 22 percent maximum bonus on basic salary for fulfillment of plan; the second, 15 percent; the third, 15 percent. For surpassing fulfillment, 2 percent; 1.5 percent; 1.5 percent respectively, in addition, for each percent of overfulfillment. These rates vary between kinds of enterprise, some getting more because the government wants to encourage them more than it needs to do others. Within each category in each industry there is a further differentiation. The individual's rank in his individual job will get him more or less than others in the same kind of job: for example, bonuses of 37 percent, 30 percent, 22 percent, and 15 percent go to the highest officials, managers, and principal engineers in the mechanical engineering occupation. The top men get their bonuses direct from their organizing Ministry; the subordinate employees are paid them by the director of the firm.

A director could get a bonus by sharing the general director's fund, plus his percentage for fulfillment, plus a share for keeping down the use of fuel and power, plus overfulfillment bonus. But—no one may have more than a 150 percent bonus from all sources over the basic salary.

The first-class enterprises are allowed up to 37 percent bonus for fulfillment and an additional 4 percent for each percent of overfulfillment; the second-class, 30 percent and 3 percent, respectively; the third class up to 22 percent and 2 percent respectively.

A director of a class-one enterprise might have 2000 rubles per month basic salary *plus* 37 percent for overfulfilling and economizing *plus* 4 percent bonus for each percent overfulfillment. Say the latter is 35 percent overfulfillment. His pay goes up by 3540 rubles per month, but will be cut to 3000 because of the 150-percent limit.

These rates of pay contrast sharply with the "sweated labor" in his shop.

In the most valued trade schools a principal earns from 1200 to 1500 rubles monthly; his assistant principals who specialize in culture and educational matters and particularly party education earn 1100 to 1400; so do his senior foremen-instructors. His assistant principals who teach the professions earn 930 to 1050. These rates are paid in the first of three categories of industries; the

less important are paid less. The librarians in these schools earn from 425 to 600.

It is now simple for the student to see how far the salaries will go in buying the commodities set down in the earlier table. He can also make up a family budget and make comparisons with the living expenses of an American worker. A Zim automobile, rather inferior to an Oldsmobile or Pontiac, costs 24,000 rubles; a twelve-inch TV set, 1200 rubles.

Artists' and Writers' Earnings. These are set down by government decree. In 1944 they were as follows. In addition allow an additional 25 percent for the rise in pay rates since that low wartime figure.

For a short story, if 75,000 copies are published, from 1000 to 1500 rubles. For best sellers, with 75,000 copies at least, 2000 to 3000 rubles for every twenty pages. The sum of money is for each 75,000 published. A scientific article is paid 1500 to 3000 rubles for each 10,000 copies. A university textbook is paid for at 1500 to 2500 rubles per twenty pages and per 25,000 sold; an elementary school textbook, 1000 to 1500 rubles per twenty pages for each 400,000 sold. Once a book or article is accepted, the editions are immense.

Over and above normal royalty payments there are the annual prizes for each category of the arts: music, literature, drama, and the social and natural sciences. The prize money is: first, 100,000 rubles; second, 50,000; third, 25,000. There are many lesser prizes in these and other spheres.

Social Relations in the Factory. We have already remarked on the advancement to a position of relative wealth and social distinction of the intelligentsia—that is, the managerial, professional, and technical staffs. This is the product of the joint operation of the three forces since the advent of the Plans: worship of improved technique, worship of skilled cadres, the contempt for equalitarianism.

Since the first two demands imply a fairly lengthy and thorough education, it is all the more difficult for ordinary workers, and especially women who form a very large proportion of the unskilled labor, to break through to the top. A large proportion of the present generation of unskilled workers, or, let us say, nonintelligentsia workers, never had the opportunity to acquire the formal education and, therefore, are condemned to be the "exploited," as it were, during their lifetimes. The exceptions are distinguished *Stakhanovites,* who can get promotion. This managerial intelligentsia obtains very substantial premia for overfulfillment of their norms—as much as 25 percent above their basic pay. It is suspected of driving the workers to achieve this. It has housing, food and clothing, and amenity privileges and is better able to pay the higher education fees and give its children cumulative social advantages of employment value (p. 833).

The technicians set the norms of output, not the trade unions. These are raised by the criterion of the average output, not of *all* the workers but of the "advanced" ones, for the below-average producers far outnumber the advanced ones, and so the point of striving has been raised. The skilled workers get the higher rates and bonuses; the semiskilled and unskilled falling below the norms are relatively worse off. There seems to be a party intention to perpetuate and even aggravate this differentiation.

We have used the terms *Stakhanovite* and *shock troops.* What do they mean? On August 30, 1935, Stakhanov, a miner, hewed 102 tons of coal in his shift of six hours and thereby earned more than an average miner's one-month pay. It was not done by merely more intense hewing, but by an improved hammer, adaptation of cutting to the different coal seams, and a new division of labor among principal and accessory operations and skills. Russia has never since diminished the furore this example caused or to insist on the significance of such techniques of higher productivity or to reward by medals, prizes, higher pay rates and premiums, the workers of all kinds who emulate the original Stakhanov.

The "shock" workers or "shock" brigades are of a different nature. They get certain jobs done in a record time by team work and more intense effort, the methods and techniques remaining the same. For certain jobs they have value in the fulfillment of Plans; and they set an example to the worker of average pace.

Pressure. All this gives the impression of furious haste and pressure in the Soviet factories and workshops. The impression is correct as the Plan-fulfillment norms are set high, and the penalty for nonfulfillment is local and public disgrace and perhaps worse. The pressure is necessary also because this is the first full generation of industrial workers who have come from primitive farms. It takes some generations to create a state of mind that understands punctuality, regularity, a steady pace, and technical subordination to the needs of the purpose the factory fulfills.

Stakhanovism involves a technical ingredient in output, not merely stamina and experience. Hence the reorganization of work on its basis tends again to give the superior pay and position to the trained and educated workers. A more recent application of Stakhanovism is a readaptation of the older "brigade" system of work. The work of a whole shop or plant is reorganized with its internal division of labor and processes by the technicians and foremen, and then the group as a whole swear an oath to fulfill or overfulfill whatever their norm is. *The governing class is increasingly the engineers, technicians, and the bosses.*

We must remember that the State Labor Reserve system (p. 783) means that these young, forcibly levied and trained 1,000,000 youngsters a year cannot choose their work freely or the location of it. The labor-reserve authorities sign the contract with the employing plant, and the workers *must* stay where placed for four years.

The Pathology and "Eyewash" of the Soviet Factory, Mine, Etc.

The directors and workers resist being treated as totally Plan-subjected robots. Their chief evasions are as follows:

1. *Shturmovschina.* A common practice of Soviet workers is called *Shturmovschina.* It means taking it easy on the job the first ten days of the month, picking up effort the second ten days, and then going into a mad rush the last third of the month to fulfill the norms in view of the drastic penalties for failure. Clearly it involves a general connivance among all the strata of the firm or a powerlessness of the directors and foremen. The authorities are baffled by it. It requires only a little imagination to realize the inefficiencies involved in such practices.

2. *Thieving.* There is *very widespread theft* of

goods and tools from the plants. It requires connivance and careful planning, considering the number of party and legal-official supervisors. This is in spite of the constitutional injunction about the preservation of "socialist" property and the terrible severity of punishments laid down in the law. Watchmen are unfaithful; bookkeepers falsify stock accounts; officials are ready to take the rap in league with their thieves, but to profit while the stealing is good. Some use the materials and tools to make goods for the black market; others dispose of the goods.

3. *Anti-Stakhanovites.* Go slow; play dumb; keep to the rules so meticulously as to slow down production. These are practiced as spite action against the higher paid and bonus-receiving tiers of skilled workers and foremen.

4. *Blat*, pronounced *blaht*, means *pull, influence, beneficial conniving*. It is a widespread practice that gives some workers an advantage over others; it enables the director or the foremen or the plant as a whole to get hold of raw materials, tools, labor, when the law and official machinery have somehow made this impossible or difficult. It is sometimes done to enable mere fulfillment of the planned norms, sometimes to overfulfill and earn rewards for the person or the whole shop. It applies especially to the firm's industrial procurement difficulties. The Plan organization may be defective or the orders for delivery have not come through or the contractual quota deliveries have not materialized, and so on. Hence by *blat,* perhaps relatives or social friends or mutual connivers, the supplies are obtained.

5. *Strakhovka* is the "insurance" or "safety" factor; it is the figure added to demands of material or labor quotas for the fulfillment of a production task. It produces a greater ease of mind and organization in the desperate race to fulfill a task. It causes a building up of hoards of supplies from fear of lack of deliveries in time.

6. *Swindle* is indulged in to pretent to fulfillment of Plans, when such is not the case. The *total* of all the targets of production is fulfilled: but the wrong assortment of items is covered up. The value of goods is falsified in the accounts. Funds are misappropriated. For example, money is spent on wages which was planned for the plant to go to repairs, overhead costs, or was not planned but is alleged to have suddenly become necessary. Why the additional amount on wages? Because labor is otherwise difficult to entice into the plant, or because the workers in the plant are practicing a go-slow policy.

7. Finally, the *lowering of the quality* of goods is perhaps the most universal and continuous and vociferous complaint by high and low throughout all Russia. This is the difficult factor to trace back and reform: it stems from lack of incentive, want of skill, and inferior machinery.

A joking cartoon in *Krokodil* tells a truthful secret shared by all: "Let's report that we have fulfilled half of the Plan by 200 percent."

Premiums. Factory behavior, involving the use of *blat* and swindles and so forth are motivated by the desire to obtain premiums and public distinction. It is demoralized further by the fact that if a factory is 1 or 2 percent below the norm—that is, underfulfilled—it may lose 30 percent in directorial rewards and in the content of the Director's Fund. Further, among workers everywhere there is the desire to "featherbed" and "live a quiet life"—to take it easy. Hence the various devices are used by workers and foremen and directors to decelerate the drive and lower the heights of the central planners in Moscow and their party organization efforts.

Incentives in Production

Two factors powerfully assist Soviet production, despite hard conditions, badly ventilated, badly lighted, and very inefficiently equipped factories (though some factories, as in the metal industries —for example, ball bearings—are extremely up to date). The first is the opportunity Soviet industrial development has given to the formerly underprivileged classes to become professional workers. In 1929 Soviet professional personnel was by social origin thus: workers and descendants, 9.7 percent; peasants and descendants, 18.9 percent; artisans, intelligentsia, white-collar, proprietors and descendants, 71.4 percent. By 1940 the figures had sharply changed to: 30.1 percent; 19.5 percent; and 50.4 percent, respectively. The first two classes together, with far greater absolute numbers, had reached about 50 percent against some 28 percent.

This progress, and the hopes of more entertained with certainty, is a powerful spur to satisfaction with the regime, hard work, connivance in the Party directives, and contempt for the democratic countries. By now, the descendants of the Soviet Union's own created first generation of social promotees from the first two classes swell its numbers. The second factor is the rise in the percentage of professional personnel who are members of the Communist Party. In 1929 the percentage was only 7; in 1947 it had risen to about 33 percent—and in that year the percentage included 38 percent of all engineers, 19 percent of all doctors, some 19 percent of agricultural field professional workers, and 16 percent of professional workers in education.

Summary. Two things stand out in this account. First, the inequality of conditions of the various workers in pay and social status. *This* is the Socialist State, and such practices raise legitimate doubts about the true purposes of the party leaders. Second, the practice of widespread breach of "socialist" ethics by almost all strata in industry, and the actual violation of the law, where the law of the Plan is so stringent and detailed in its prescriptions. This makes almost everyone a lawbreaker, and thus anxious and insecure, liable to be informed on, and dreadfully punished, among other things, to forced labor, the convict branch of Soviet industry, on which something is said at the end of this chapter.

Procurator and M.V.D.

The Procurator's office is charged especially with the protection of socialist property, the maintenance of work discipline (which comes under certain obligatory services), and the safeguarding of labor. The agents conduct periodical inspections of the smaller establishments and, in the larger ones, keep officers on the premises or near by for continuous and close control. They are the recipients of information from various quarters and in their turn make known to the trade-union activists the various kinds of illegalities brought to light, so that, again, these may know what illegalities to look for and report.

The M.V.D. and their *seksots,* their surreptitious informers, spy on the workers.

Soviet Industrial Production

What success has the Soviet socialist-dictatorial pursuit of high industrial production had? The labor force in industry and its administration and distribution has risen from some 4,000,000 in 1917 to 40,000,000 in 1955. This is an excruciating revolution in the space of thirty years, if we omit the disruptive World War II years. It cannot but be inefficient, wasteful of resources and human beings.

Since the U.S.S.R. regards economic statistics as one of the weapons of war, foreign statisticians have had to do much guessing about the figures the Soviet government actually publishes. They are in dispute with that government and in dispute among themselves. But the order of magnitude is somewhat as follows. If 1927–28 is taken as a base of 100 for Soviet industrial output, then it was 172 in 1932; 430 in 1940; and 646 in 1950.[5] From 1940 to 1953 the rise in Soviet industrial output [6] (based on prices-base of 1926–27) was worth in 1940, 138.5 billion rubles; in 1950, 240 billion rubles; in 1953, 345.5 billion rubles. Of these latter figures, the percentage devoted to *consumer goods* was 38.8; 27.5; and 27.9 in the respective years. Crude steel manufactured shows this comparison:

Thousands of Metric Tons of Crude Steel

Year	U.S.S.R.	U.S.A
1929	5,003	57,336
1953	38,000	102,000
1960 (planned)	60,000	117,000

With European production, the NATO powers far exceed the U.S.S.R. But the U.S.S.R. plans more military use for its steel than do the democratic powers, concerned for their people's comfort. Hence, in all strategic materials the strength of the U.S.S.R. is far, far greater than the comparative general index of its production.

In general the productivity per hour of the Russian industrial workers is estimated at but 40 percent of that of an American. Some believe it is

[5] A. Bergson, editor, *Soviet Economic Growth,* New York, 1953, p. 232.

[6] *Trends in Economic Growth,* Joint Committee Print, 83d Congress, 2d Session, 1955, U.S. Government Printing Office, p. 257.

less. The tables of consumption and earnings (p. 918 and p. 919) confirm the estimates. In some industries Russian man-hour productivity is better than this. In oil production it is 63 percent; in iron, 55; in railroad equipment, 56; in tractors, 64; in agricultural machinery, 60; automobiles, 61; cotton spinning, 61. It is surprising to notice[7] that Russian workers work some 5 percent less time, perhaps much less than this, than those in the United States (except in coal mining). Here is Russian "unemployment": the firms cannot yet use the labor force more substantially because the Plans do not call for it, because the capacity and resources and organization are not yet capable enough.

It is a tremendous achievement. But the quality is very poor. "Operation bootstraps" over peasant workers at high speed is to blame for inefficiencies as much as "planning" and dictatorship. Yet so much progress is deemed to have been made that, in late 1955, the Khrushchev regime began an extremely ambitious policy of economic and technical assistance to the Middle and Far East, a blow in the war of "peaceful coexistence"! So, the Russian peasants and workers will eat and dress ever less well!

II. SOVIET AGRICULTURE: THE COLLECTIVE FARM OR KOLKHOZ

The Agricultural Process and Plan

The peasantry of Russia, numbering some 68,000,-000 to 75,000,000 in 1950 (according to different bases of calculation), numbered 60,000,000 in 1939 and 71,000,000 in 1926. The agricultural labor force was: in 1950 from 62.7 to 65 percent of the total; in 1939, 66.6 percent; and in 1926, 81.8 percent. Its proportion has therefore remarkably declined.

This labor force is organized in 97,000[8] "amalgamated collective farms" (October 1952, reported by Malenkov at the Party Congress) instead of 254,000 "small collective farms" which existed on January 1, 1950. This number, 254,000, was the net result of the campaign of collectivization that was undertaken in 1929, at which time the number of farms was in the neighborhood of 25,000,000 individual farms.

Not all of this labor force is in the collective farms. A small proportion are in the State farms—that is, the *Sovkhoz*—and a very few peasant farms still just exist.

We have already explained why and how the *kulaks* were crushed and dispersed in the years 1929–1931 and collectivization forced, with the help of the poorest peasants (p. 779ff.). The law forbad the renting of land and the hiring of labor by peasants. A sweetener for them was the inclusion of the *kulaks'* liquidated property in the collective. The government decreed that the basic form of collective farm was the *artel*—that is, common ownership with socialized stock, seed, machinery, etc., in the form of a contract between government and farms that it drew up for the *artel*.

Peasant Individualism. The peasants—all of them—manifested a powerful instinct for private ownership of the land, cattle, and so forth, like peasants all over the world. The instinct is as powerful today, if we may judge by (1) the government's inability to extract from the peasants the cooperation it has enforced with bitter coercion over twenty-five years, and (2) that at the slightest opportunity the peasants slice off the maximum private plots for their own family and lavish their care on these far more than in the common operations. The Soviet government has even been compelled to allow a considerable private property in the dwelling house, some stock, and a private plot to each peasant family and does not dare stake everything on the collective. The Soviet government ferociously forbids the stimulus of private property to production on the political ground that it would thereby have prepared a class of individualists who would demand political liberty to protect their economic liberty. They cannot allow so heinous a sin!

In the period of war on the peasantry for collectivization, the peasants slaughtered their cattle and horses, not yet made good after twenty-five years. In doing this they unwittingly put themselves at the mercy of the government for, having lost their draft animals, they all the more subjected themselves to the motor tractors, etc., mo-

---

[7] Bergson, *op. cit.*, p. 205.

[8] By the end of 1954 reduced further to 93,000.

nopolized by the government, in a ransom technique worse than that of any capitalist.

The Agricultural Plan is made with the estimates of the past in mind, and the planners' noses are always turned to the skies for signs of the weather. *Gosplan* and the various Ministries set crops and acreages, plan the irrigation works, and so on to be undertaken; set out the amount of farm equipment to be supplied; predict and order the growth of the herds; make plans for afforestation, antidrought measures, and so on. The plans are long-term and short-term. They are very special and important for certain crops—for example, cotton, oilseeds, and other industrially necessary plants. The Plan goes down through the Republics and the provincial and territorial tiers of Ministries and agencies and is applied to each farm. The Ministry of Agriculture heads an enormous organization of its agents throughout the Union. It maintains agronomical research in a thousand stations and has all the staff services of statisticians, entomologists, foresters, and the rest.

Collective Farm Constitution and Democracy. The collective farms are constituted on the basis of the Standard Articles of Association of the Agricultural Artel of February 17, 1935.[9] This was "approved" by the second congress of the *kolkhoz* shock workers and confirmed by the Council of Ministers and the Central Committee of the Party. (This is a law—yet it was not evolved in the Congress of Soviets!) Since that time there have been minor amendments and several admonitions against the violation of its articles by the peasants.

Each farm has a charter based on the above-mentioned articles. The land belongs to the State, but the collective is given permanent use of it. A government document confirms the right and assigns the boundaries of the farm. The land is inalienable: it cannot be bought; it cannot be leased.

The collective owns all the means of production except the large machines. These latter belong to the State and are operated by the Motor Tractor Stations—M.T.S. The means of production mentioned above includes all cattle, tools, farm buildings, flour mills and other simple processing equipment, and seed, fodder, and so forth.

[9] See Meisel and Kozera, *op. cit.,* pp. 217–219.

Private Property. Each collective farmer may own a dwelling house, garden tools, a garden plot, some livestock, and the buildings needed to shelter the latter. The government decrees the amount of livestock that can be held; it varies slightly from area to area. For example, in the areas that are chiefly engaged in raising crops, the limits are one cow, two calves, one or two sows and their offspring, up to ten sheep or goats, unlimited poultry and rabbits, and up to twenty beehives. Where alternatives are mentioned, the local farm administration has the discretion.

Farm "Democracy." The collective is constrained to work to the annual plan set down by the authorities above. This takes account of the shares of the produce that will remain with the farmers and the obligations of delivery and taxation they have toward the State. This division of the product will be discussed presently (p. 911). The collective is ordered to maximize production, minimize the cost, and conserve the farm's assets; improve the efficiency of the members; and establish and maintain certain civic services, such as newspapers, books, barber shops.

Always bearing in mind that the farm operates in a stiff legal framework and under the vigilance and harassment of agencies of fulfillment—the party and the government—to which attention will be given shortly, we know that the farm is vaunted to be an example of "Soviet democracy." For the charter lays it down that the authority over agricultural operations is a general meeting of the members. It elects officers, and members; dismisses and expels these; approves work plans, budgets, and the division of the product. The everyday management committee is elected by the general meeting; it exercises the collective's authority between the general meetings. It consists of from five to nine members, according to the size of the farm. Its chairman is elected by the meeting, and his is the highest individual executive authority. Because general meetings are infrequently called, the highest policy authority is exercised by the committee and the chairman, in practice, almost invariably the latter.

Almost the entire labor force on the farm consists of the *kolkhozniki* and their families, *plus* the mechanized units at the special times of the year when they are needed, *plus* hired specialists from time to time, and extra hands at critical seasons.

This is the general framework of the collective. We now turn to the actual working of the system. It inspires four questions: Who actually says what shall be produced? What is the result of collective farm democracy? What is the result in productivity? And if it is not acceptable to the Soviet rulers, what remedies do they purpose?

Who Actually Decides What the Farms Produce?

The government's agricultural authorities; the party units; and the Motor Transport Station personnel.

Although the *kolkhoz* is not subject to *direct* management by the government, as is typical of the factories, the so-called "guidance" by the government is extremely close and intensive. Though the charter of the collectives vests the right to establish the rules of procedure and working order in the general meeting—that is, the by-laws of the *kolkhoz* work and management and discipline— the various Republic governments have laid down model rules, setting minimum standards.

The farm must obey all the plans, directives, and crop rules established by the planning authorities in Moscow, then more specifically blueprinted for it by the Soviet authority in the district (*raion*). This is *law* imposed on the *kolkhoz,* though the charter says that the general meeting decides this. It cannot decide otherwise.

The principle of distribution of the produce of the farm among its members, and between the farm as a whole and the government, are not determinable by the collective, but is unilaterally *commanded* by the government.

A farmer cannot be expelled from the collective unless the order is approved by the *raion* Soviet department.

The Hand of Esau. The village soviet has the authority to take part in the guidance of the work of the collectives. These soviets, which are locally elected and therefore include some of the farmers (but dominated by the Communist Party in the decisive positions of power), read the collective's minutes and can request the annulment of de-

cisions that are illegal. What is "legal"? The Soviet chairman has a control over the production plan's fulfillment. He verifies the collective's adherence to the charter rules. The members of the village Soviet group themselves within the collective farms (there may be several village soviets within any one big collective) into activist nuclei to drive production and expose mistakes.

The *raion* soviet is even more important as a master of the collectives. Its executive committee approves the charter, can expel members, nominates the members who are to be elected by the *kolkhoz* to its audit commission (explained below). It analyzes the annual income and expense accounts of the *kolkhoz* with all its inferential opportunities of commanding influence. When the collective makes the contract for service with the M.T.S., the Soviet's approval is needed. It has complete power to cancel any decisions whatever of the collective general meeting and the collective's board of management if it considers them unlawful. It controls the board of management's obedience to the charter regulations.

Ministerial Commands. The Ministry of Agriculture in Moscow exerts its local power through the agricultural department of the district soviet. It:

decides on crop rotations;

draws up production and work arrangements;

"advises" on "socialist competition";

ordains the production quotas for corps and work rates;

classifies the collectives in nine categories as prescribed by Moscow on the basis of individual skill and the quantity and quality of the work assigned to each farm;

manages all electrical power and lighting;

is employer of the chief agronomist of the Soviet, who is an appointed official taking orders from Moscow sifted down through its territorial administrative tiers; he works through the M.T.S.; he controls sowing, according to Moscow's plans; enforces farm deliveries of decreed quantities of produce to the State; compels the collectives to make the contracted payments to the M.T.S.; continuously assists the collectives with the setting up and the solution of management and production affairs; through his personnel (like the U.S.

county agents) applies the principles of proper crop rotation, mechanization, scientific agriculture, and conducts various media of agricultural progressive "education."

M.T.S. The Machine Tractor Station, referred to as M.T.S., is the local unit that gives mechanical service to the collectives. Its characteristics will be described later (p. 913). But its functions are far wider than its mechanical activities in sowing and reaping. It helps the collectives and advises on organization and economic policies, helps them to formulate their production plans, and train skilled farmers. It overlaps several of the accounting and production planning function of the *raion*. It is said that this overlapping is deliberate, as is part of the Soviet leaders' design to have one institution and set of officials with slightly different interests to check and balance the other, and so divide and rule. But the official agricultural authoritative link between Moscow and the collective is the *raion* soviet: it is the link also between Moscow and the M.T.S.

As in the management of the factories, the Procurator's office at the district level invigilates the farms also.

The farmers are dependent on the government to include in the national production Plans, the mechanized equipment and tools, cement, wire, steel, etc. they will need.

In September 1946, always in a state of anxiety about its farmers, the U.S.S.R. Council of Ministers established a new organ at the center to accompany those already existing for the conduct of farm affairs—the Council of *Kolkhoz* Affairs. This was set up in a document called "against violations of the *kolkhoz* charter," the result of a nationwide set of reports on the fractious and wayward behavior of the peasantry. (These peasant shortcomings, from the standpoint of the Soviet rulers, are dealt with later.) [10] It coordinates the actions of the government to subordinate the collectives to its rules and production plans. It has inspectors attached to the Republic Soviets and local soviets who may arrange inspectorial periods over any culpable collective, call in all the various enforcement agencies to correct and punish violators of the laws and plans. The members of this Council are high members of the All-Union Central Committee of the party!

What Is the Result of Collective Farm Democracy?

What, then, is left of democracy in the collective farms? Almost nothing. Why does it exist, why was it so established? Why was there not planted directly in the farms a government director, as in the factories? Perhaps because at the stormy and murderous establishment of collective farms, it was not thought of, since the Soviet rulers were themselves infected with mir (see p. 751) romanticism or habit. Or perhaps, direct State management was too drastic a measure, threatening less cooperation from the peasants than the "democratic" system gives. Or maybe they could not find at once all the expert managers needed—they were already in difficulties for skilled men in industry. This is consistent with a recognition that the peasant had his "petty bourgeois" prejudice in favor of private property, and the collective looked a little more like that than a complete administration by officials appointed from the outside. In the meanwhile, it has been thought, the peasants' consciousness might be gradually transformed from capitalist to socialist ideals and values.

The "Democracy" of the Kolkhoz. According to the charter, the *kolkhoz* is governed thus. The supreme authority in the collective is the general meeting of all its working members over the age of sixteen. It elects its chairman, a managing board, an audit commission. It admits new members, expels those who have violated the rules; draws up annual estimates of income and expenditure; formulates the annual production plan, the financial plan, and the plan of capital construction. It makes annual contracts with the M.T.S. It sets down norms of output and the ratings of the various jobs on the farm. It draws up the rules of internal farm order. It makes agreements with outside organizations. For the employment of "hired labor" and for loans from the State or Agricultural Banks, its approval is necessary.

The meeting decides all these problems, the quorum being at least one half of the members.

---

[10] Reproduced in Meisel and Kozera, *Materials for the Study of the Soviet System,* Ann Arbor, 1953, p. 388.

The expulsion of a member requires a quorum of two thirds the membership.

The general meeting holds sessions twice a month. For the continuous conduct of business it elects an executive committee of between five and nine persons; it is the board of management of the farm, to effectuate the decisions of the meeting. It is a complicated business, and so the executive appoints managers, brigadiers for various sectors of the work, stewards of livestock farms, accountants, and so on. It composes the brigades and small inner-brigade groups (*zvenia*) who work together as teams on given jobs of sowing, reaping, tending, and so on. It prepares and submits to the meeting *the norms of output and piece-work rates* for the various kinds of work. It acts in a sense as manager in current operations, seeing that the brigades carry out their assignments, punishing the slackers, stimulating "socialist competition."

Its chairman is also chairman of the collective as a whole. He directs the work of the board, convenes the general meetings, selects the appointed officials, directs the financial affairs according to the charter and the meeting's decisions. He is also the collective's representative in its external transactions.

The audit commission audits the books of the collective and reports to the general meeting.

The general meeting can at any time remove the chairman by a vote, on the grounds that he is not carrying out the meeting's policies. Similarly with the board of management.

This looks like an ideal, small, democratic collective enterprise.

We have seen, however, that the various central and local governmental controls petrify and suppress and supplant the democratic elements of the collective by externally fixed decrees and administrative and police surveillance. The Soviet rulers take out the vitals of democracy which is nothing if it is not free decision. It accomplishes this also by setting the party members on the conduct of collective farming.

The Place of the Party on the Farm. The regional party committees have agricultural departments which are entrusted with the manipulation of the peasantry. The immediate work is done by the district party committee—the *raikom*. It is tre-

mendously powerful and penetrative. It controls all the organizations like the Soviets, the M.T.S., the farms, and so on. It indoctrinates party leaders, interprets the rulings of the higher level authorities, plans agitation, education, propaganda in the villages, maneuvers the selection of the key members of the *kolkhoz*. It guides the work of the primary party unit in the collective itself.

It is uphill work for the party; the peasants have taken to the membership of the party much less readily than urban workers. In 1939, after the most strenuous efforts, only 9 percent of the total membership of the party came from the collectives. During the World War II many young peasants in the Army were induced to join. In 1947 it was announced that rural Communists constituted about 27 percent of the party membership at that time. But this is far from saying how many farmers on the collectives are members. For a considerable proportion of these were administrative and technical personnel in the rural areas, and the paid officials of the farms, people on the State farms, and the M.T.S. workers. The party is highly discontented with the party membership by the collective farmers themselves. It indicates that they still have the "petty bourgeois" mentality. Khrushchev, in 1948, observed that in 28,207 collectives in the Ukraine (a most important agricultural region) only 11,895 had party organizations *at all*.

The *Komsomols* have entered in places where the party is nonexistent or weak.

What does the party do through a primary unit or a district unit so far as it can? It

(1) maneuvers the meetings to get its choice of persons elected—the right persons;

(2) organizes and manages the cultural work, lectures, discussions, propaganda, political education;

(3) manipulates socialist competition and urges on to higher productivity;

(4) disseminates the party doctrine and translates this into peasant terms;

(5) incessantly invigilates the collective, all its works and operations.

In order to accomplish these purposes, the party members buttonhole amenable peasants who, though not Communists, are not unsympathetic—

and so establishes an *aktiv*—the nucleus of activists, of zealots. "Sympathizers" and onlooking fellow travelers among the peasantry come within its orbit. These are satellite voters at the meetings. The *Komsomols* are let loose (as the refugee accounts amply portray) on the mobilization of cultural activities and socialist competition, exactly the activity for the younger generation aching to establish themselves as individuals different from their parents. They deploy their activities in private as a party unit (a huddle to determine the plays) and then call public meetings or rallies open to the whole collective.

Just as the party has its political commissars, its *zampolits,* in the Army battalions, and so on, so it has its equivalent in each collective: the secretary of the primary party unit appointed by the *raikom.* *He* is the real chairman of the collective, so far as the reality of decision making on any important issue is concerned. He can engineer the discharge of any chairman through farm party caucus. The chairman has no power of effective retaliation against him, unless he should have committed some violation of the law—which sometimes happens.

The collective is held in the grip of professional party organizers who come from district headquarters and the chief members of the collective's executive committee and the brigade leaders. The expert agriculturists (like the U.S. county agent in function from a technical farming standpoint) are more often than not the leading members of the party, and even secretary of the primary party unit.

We now know who says what shall be produced, and that the effect on farm democracy is to make it practically null and void.

What Is the Result in Productivity?

We turn now to the question, What is the effect on the productive process and productivity of the system? This involved an answer to certain other questions, such as the method of payment and the contentment of the peasantry with the collectivized form of production in general.

How Is the Peasant Paid for His Work? The produce of the farm is shared among the following entities. (1) The State takes *a tax in kind*—

that is, a delivery quota of a certain amount per acre of arable land or, for certain crops, absolute amounts, or livestock by fixed numbers per acre of all agricultural land. The government pays for these but at *a much lower price* than they would fetch on the open market. (This is equal to rent!) The burden is almost constant, whatever the harvest—in bad years the peasants suffer. This is the collective's first commandment: Pay this tax. It is varied to provide incentives to produce.

(2) The collective pays the M.T.S. for its services in kind—at a price determined by the government, not by free bargaining.

(3) The government gets repayments of seed loans and such like loans in kind.

(4) What now remains in the collective's produce is divided into two parts as decided by the general meeting (remembering the party caucus of activists). One part is sold to the government or to the cooperative organizations that sell to consumers or on the open market. *This is the source of the farm's money income.* The price of these sales are much higher than the price at which the government takes its kind. The free markets bring in the highest prices—producer to consumer. The other portion of the production remaining is divided among the members in kind. So is the money income, after the State's income tax and after the fire and other insurance are paid and a sum of 15 to 20 percent has been set aside for capital and repair purposes. What then remains of the produce in kind *plus* the net money fund is divided among the farmers.

"Work Days." The principal of division is the "work days" put in by the farms, days actually put in. Each person gets the total produce divided by the *total of farmers* $\times$ *the work days* $\times$ *the number he has worked.*

All work days are not equal. The work day is not merely chronological. In 1948 the government set down nine different work-day rates for the different jobs on the farm. The least-skilled work is rated as one half a work day; the most skilled and onerous jobs are rated at two and a half work days. Thus rewards are given to quality and quantity of work. Furthermore, in order to introduce what is evidently so sadly lacking all the way through the Soviet economy, "personal responsibility" and incentive to higher productivity, the government set up incentive pay, per brigade, and then per *zenia*—that is, the smaller group within the brigade, the "link." Each of these units is given a 1 percent addition to the work days for each percent of production exceeding *its* planned output. There is a penalty for default. Where the output falls below the assignment of the Plan, for each 1 percent there is a deduction of 1 percent up to a maximum penalty of 25 percent. Beyond that the peasant would be practically dead, and not capable of revival even by the party *aktiv*. This arrangement tends to keep the brigades cohesive and constant, making for better work rhythm and method.

The method of pay, then, is that of piece rates and is far from the promised egalitarianism of agrarian communism. This is a grim retreat by the party from its professed ideals before it took power. Even during the 1920's the division of the product was according to the number of working members of each family, the problems of internal discipline being settled by the farmers in the collective spirit of the old mir times. Even the model charter of 1930 did not stipulate anything other than generally forbidding the principle of the number-of-workers-per-family and requiring a consideration of the actual work days.

In February 1933 seven vertical categories of skill, amount, and intensity of labor were decreed. The top category could get four times the pay of the lowest one. Economic differentiation and an economic rank and title were thus fixed on the village people. The placing of the jobs in the categories was left to the collectives: *they* modified it, according to their neighborly and equalitarian spirit.

The Soviet leaders intervened because the collectives were charitably giving too large an income to peasants who may have worked more and longer, but who actually produced less than others. The government sought to remedy the system by ordaining bonuses to those who fulfilled or overfulfilled their quota. They thereby penalized the under-the-average producers, as the supplements were taken out of the joint "kitty."

Hence in 1948 the nine-category system and a government decree demoting some of the high category jobs. A skilled collective farmer in category nine obtains five times the income of a *mouzhik* in the lowest category. (Query: is he a *Soviet kulak?*)

A further attempt at differentiation has been undertaken in recent years. The government has set up smaller teams, the *zveno,* of seven to fourteen people (the brigade ranges from thirty-five to seventy-six, with regional variations), once again in order to identify skills, and even individual piece work. But farm work is more collective than factory production, less amenable to identification of responsibility for good or bad work, at any rate in detail. It would require too many audit officials, "production accountants," to be economical. It cannot be *so micrometric.*

Brigades are assigned each a special task. They compete for prowess. There are inter-*kolkhoz* socialist competitions.

"Individualistic Philosophy." If the land does not belong to the peasant and he cannot sell or consume the produce as he personally wishes and he must grow things as the government demands, why should he not be slack? There is, says the party leaders, a "survival of individualistic psychology," in spite of Little Father Stalin's divine attributes as pictured throughout the land and in the schools.

Two drastic measures have had to be undertaken by the government in recent years to make the farmer work on the collective: (1) to set minimum work days, and (2) to reduce the care and energy he spends on the private plot of ground.

Minimum Work Days. First, in May 1939 the government introduced a 100-work-day minimum for cotton growers, a 60-work-day minimum for grain growing in the central areas, and an 80-work-day minimum in all other areas. It recommended also that those who do not satisfy the minima should be *excluded* from the collective—a terribly drastic penalty. In 1942 the minima were raised: 150, 100, and 120 respectively. In addition, the nonfulfillers of the minima were subjected to very harsh specific penalties: sentence by a court to a maximum of six months' corrective labor on their collectives, while 25 percent of their work-day payment was kept by the collective. (This is *to be* made milder in 1956.)

The result of the setting of minima is that as the workdays are reckoned not chronologically alone, but are weighted according to the category, those in the high categories can the more easily fulfill their obligations.

Violations of the Government's Agricultural Order. Secondly, the peasants concentrate too much on their own private plots for the government's satisfaction. It was found in 1937 that about 13,000,000 physically able peasants worked less than fifty workdays for the collective—spending their time on their private plots, with all ingenuity raising its product. They encroached on the collective land and appropriated more for their plots. The exact amount is not exactly determinable, but it might be in the order of a half to three quarters of an acre per family. In many places—especially away from the nucleated villages—the tending of private land had become the primary, though not the exclusive, occupation of the farmers! With this went the appropriation of other items of *kolkhoz* property. Something like half the total of eggs, poultry, and milk are currently produced on the private plots.

The government made an onslaught on these practices, urging the local soviets and party units —(who, clearly, must have connived or been slack) to recover the property. It counterattacked also. The breeding of livestock was promoted on the collective, so that there was less reason for it to be conducted on the peasant's own plot: up to 1939 over half of all the stock was privately owned. Furthermore, the government ordered and *enforced* the cultivation on the private plot of so many fruit trees of various kinds. Also farm boys of twelve to sixteen were now compelled to join the collective labor force; before that they were the chief tenders of the cottage plots. Worst blow of all, the produce of the plots was now included to be delivered to the government up to a certain percentage, *at government-settled prices.* The peasant sees his income from private produce on the open market crassly diminished.

No government is so cunning and uncharitable as the Soviet government in finding means to force mankind into the line of action it ordains.

The Remedy for Unacceptable Production: Mechanization

Still productivity is most unsatisfactory (p. 917). In a variety of ways the government has sought to increase agricultural produce, especially in view of the larger population, and especially in order to be able to count on a surplus of manpower on the farms that it could use for agriculture. We have already observed that the State Labor Reserve system has been taking away something like 1,000,000 farm youngsters each year since 1940.

The M.T.S. were the one vital answer, so far as equipment was concerned. These stations were instituted in June 1929. On January 1, 1941, the Soviet government directed over 7000 Motor Tractor Stations, employing some 2,000,000 persons (hence the inflation of the number of rural population in the party membership). The Plan for 1952 onward is that by 1956 the number of tractors should be increased by 50 percent. They now do approximately 82 percent of the collectives' ploughing, 52 percent of the sowing, and 34 percent of the harvesting. An M.T.S. station serves several collectives, five or six each.

The M.T.S. service the collectives. They are managed by a director at the top, appointed directly by the Ministry of Agriculture, from those skilled in agriculture, mechanics, and financial planning. He has a staff of agronomists and engineer-mechanics, bookkeepers. There is alongside the director a deputy "for political work." They are party appointees, and their task is to keep the whole M.T.S. in political tone and to invigilate fulfillment by the M.T.S. as well as the collectives. They are assisted by the *Komsomols* in keeping the workers under surveillance and making suggestions for appointments, and helping to secure more training facilities.

The officials carry out the orders of Moscow, sent through the district soviets. The work plans of the M.T.S. need the approval of their agricultural experts.

These are the intelligentsia of the countryside, so far as the M.T.S. are concerned. It should be added that some of the agricultural experts of the M.T.S. are elected as collective farm chairmen.

The workers in the M.T.S. consist of the operators of the machines, the repair workers, truck drivers, electricians, communication workers, and so on—skilled men. They cooperate with the subordinate administrative and clerical staffs, among them "dispatchers" who control the tractor brigades whose field of action may be very distant from headquarters.

The peasantry man the tractor brigades. They are temporarily attached to the M.T.S. and are on leave for the purpose from their collective. While they are with the M.T.S., they are under its management alone. Some are tractor brigadiers, taking the tractors to the place of use, choosing their assistants, doing the job, and returning the machines. They are men of importance locally and have weight with the *kolkhoz*. They are the center of a work-net of farm brigades, and are of the social standing of the workers of the M.T.S. Under them are the senior and junior tractor operators, and various servicers—water, fuel, tool, and food bearers, and general handymen.

The M.T.S. is a most powerful influence in the life of the collective farms, a spearhead of modernity, mechanization, science, and planning determination among the rather primitive and still deeply superstitious rural millions.

Each year the collective contracts with the M.T.S. for its services, including the fee to be paid. The agreement is formulated by the government—its latest form is that of January 27, 1948. It specifies the plan laid down by the State; the types of work, the terms of fulfillment; the volume, quality and periods of work; the agrotechnical measures, accountancy, controls, finances, involved in the relationship of M.T.S. and *kolkhoz*. It is a legal contract.

The effect of the arrangement is to make the M.T.S. the planner and controller of the work of the *kolkhoz*. It is a kind of external collective directorate over all the work and plans and methods of the collective farms with which it does business, partly by the use of its own contractual authority and derivative influence therefrom, partly as an executant and colleague of the local agricultural sections of the soviets. The M.T.S. director's decision, and his agronomists' decision can be overridden by the soviets'.

The wage and salary payments in the M.T.S. hierarchy follow the piece-rate systems with their various categories prevailing in industry.

The M.T.S. are the nuclei of the party at a very high level of power and effectiveness in the rural areas. They contain party primary units and some of the best, most zealous minor party chiefs, headed by the M.T.S. Deputy director for political affairs. He and the party members have the same animating, activating, ideological functions as the party units in the factories.

Through the M.T.S., the party, the *Komsomol,* the party leadership, and the State officials try to put yeast into the heavy dough of the peasantry. The alternative is to make them soar on the air of freedom and private holdings. The government will not do the latter, even though it might immensely raise productivity.

It acts through constant agitation by the party and the local soviet technical and M.T.S. intelligentsia, through peasant clubs, speeches, lectures, wall newspapers, and so on, explaining the necessities, retailing the delights. Each officeholder or leader in a brigade, a *zveno,* the party, whatever it is, is supposed to stimulate the others who are associated in some other connected part of the work of the farmer and the needs of the State. The various agrarian strata, experts, and *kolkhozniki* join in conferences. Beyond this the government, as we have seen, puts its hands into the very entrails of farm management and backs this up with penal measures. The government has established local rural schools for the leading figures of the village: chairman of the farm, brigadiers and stewards of livestock farms, members of the executive committees, party and *Komsomol* members. Some 30 percent were not members of the party. These schools are to a large extent for peasantry with no formal schooling. The idea is to advance the older generation by schooling for two or three years from October to March of each year.

The Giant Farm as a Help? Since 1950—and causing tremendous perturbation in the highest levels of the party—the remedy for rural backwardness has been thought to be the increase in the size of farms. The ideas involved are these: [11] that a larger size would permit the application of the relatively scanty party forces to operate on so many more nonparty farmers. By creating a central dwelling center, agricultural cities, or *agrogoroda,* the peasantry would be shaken out of their rural darkness and inveterate habits, and become more progressive, city-wise. They would overcome the substantial distances between the hamlets and "inhabited places" produced over the centuries. New housing could be built, with better community and amenity arrangements. It was thought also that the M.T.S. equipment and personnel could be used more economically, with better crop rotation. In the same way, the administrative and accountancy officials could be reduced. A better specialization of important crops, such as fruit, industrial crops, horticulture, could be carried out.

By the middle of 1951 the number of collectives was down from 252,000 to 123,000, and by October 1952 to 96,000 (1955, 93,000)—that is, on the average the *kolkhozy* were increased in size threefold. Whereas a Moscow-region *kolkhoz* had consisted of about 42 households, the number rose to 152 households.

The scheme has run into serious difficulties. It was carried out, perhaps mainly originated, by Nikita Khrushchev (p. 882). He has had to retreat and zigzag twice since his reforms took concrete shape. The mistakes that ensued from the enlargement of the collectives have proved to be many. The farmers had to walk or be transported further to the fields than before, losing time and temper. The peasant private plots are said to have been diminished in size, and are a considerable distance from where the farmers dwell. They were tempted into by-occupations, such as making bricks for the farms, with resultant distraction of effort and costs high above the delivery price from the construction firms. The party found that peasant conservatism caused a fall of produce. Some main harvests fell; cattle were reduced; fodder supplies decreased with serious effects on the quality of cattle and milk supplies. An attempt has been made to remedy the situation by decreasing the agricultural requisitions from farms and garden plots; more tractors have been sent out; more propaganda has been put in.

The State Farms: Sovkhozy

They are State owned and operated by the officials and workers of the Ministry of State Farms. Those now remaining are the residue of the grandiose schemes that floated in Lenin's mind for a very much larger proportion of such agricultural management, especially for experimental and demonstration purposes. They cover about 10 percent of the sown area in the U.S.S.R. and are mainly devoted to the raising of special crops, grain, sugar beets, livestock, dairy products, cotton, though this last crop has come under a special Ministry of Cotton Growing.

There are some 4,000,000 State farms and they are large, many going beyond 5000 acres. They employ about 13,500,000 workers and employees. Just before World War II they produced nearly a third of all the milk received by the government from Soviet agriculture, and about a quarter of all the meat and wool. Besides this there are substantial percentages (though lesser) of sugar beets, cotton, and grain.

Here the government meets all the expenses and takes about three quarters of the produce. The machinery belongs to the farm.

In the difficult period of collectivization, State farming was considered a desirable alternative to peasant farming, and it was between 1928 and 1932 that the number and acreage increased tremendously. But it was found that State farms necessitated excessively high costs of production. For they were too large for efficient management. Their crops were insufficiently diversified to allow economical rotation and other common techniques. Labor was hard to get, as the farms had been started in areas of sparse population. They lost governmental popularity.

They seem to be still entangled in difficulties, despite the increase in their number through Russia's acquisition of the Baltic areas. They are still overspecialized; have high labor turnover; many were unprofitable. The provision of a garden plot for the workers, and of better housing, still left the farms shaky. The labor problem is difficult of solu-

---

[11] See *Pravda,* Feb. 19, 1950, "Against Distortions in Collective Farm Organizations." In Meisel and Kozera, *op. cit.,* p. 568.

tion, because work cannot be spread among the different peak periods of a *variety* of crops. Hence a rush for extra hands at some times, and a wasteful assembly of men in idleness during some parts of the year. An additional turn of the screw has been given by the M.T.S. and the police.

At the same time, the assembling of the dwellings from the villages to the *agrogorods* has been slowed down.

It must be remembered that even where the party is able to announce a total increase of production over the level reached before World War II, the rapid increase in the Soviet Union's population (estimated, say, at 3,000,000 net per year) means that since 1945 another 27,000,000 people need food. One new approach is a copying of Russia's traditional approach, *to expand the area cultivated now to the outer fringes* of the desert land on the Caspian, Siberian, and Turkestan desert land. This is to be brought under the motor plough by urban so-called "volunteers," by *Komsomols* in the thousands. In 1954 thousands undertook this miserable task, with poor results. Land is not enough to make a boy a successful farmer. In 1955, after another even more energetic campaign, an even greater failure occurred, owing to drought, as predicted by critics.

It ought to be added that the M.T.S. are by no means the brilliant and impeccable right arms of the collective farms. As we have seen, they are *the* power among the farmers: their refusal to act or spiteful action against the farmers would be ruinous to the harvesting and the sowing of the crops. They take from 10 to 20 percent of the produce—with variations dependent on the harvest. There are many breakdowns of the machines; bad repair work; machines improperly serviced; badly tended and operated, and left unsheltered in inclement weather. After all, many of the workers and technicians are recently off the farm or from the unskilled members of the urban workers and are not yet used to handling delicate machinery. The machines are often not in repair when they are needed in the spring or autumn. They are not so sturdy as American farm machinery.

The various criticisms were still being echoed at the Party Congress of October 1952: pilfering, coercion on the chairmen by party officials to get produce for themselves free or at low cost, enforced exchange of their own low-grade livestock for better animals. The organization of the brigades and *zvenos* (less favored of late) is on an impermanent basis too often, management is inefficient, the work-day method of distribution is insufficiently precise. The instructions for farming are not interpreted by the officials or the party according to local conditions and possibilities, but followed with a ruinous uniformity. And above all—though "antiscientific, reactionary ideas in agricultural science have been exposed and defeated," the party has not yet filled the minds of the farmers and even the officials with the new, scientific and successful principles. Even the agronomic experts have not yet the command of science they should have. The cultivation of the State farms is based on brigades, as in the collectives. Pay, however, is based on piece-work wages, at so much per hectare of work on the various crops.

The State farms are maintained, despite the difficulties, because prestige would be lost in their abandonment. It is asserted by some that as this is the model of Soviet ideals of farming—factories of the land—their continued maintenance and improvement is a necessary model which the *kolkhozy* may one day follow. The advent of the giant collectives may seem like a step to universal State farms, but hardly yet.

The Relative Poverty of the Various Collectives

There is a tremendous variation in the total income of collective farms, owing in the first place to the difference in the crops they raise, to the prices assessed by the government, and to the varying fertility of the farms in so far-flung an area as the Soviet Union. It is not possible here to disentangle these factors from the effect of the number of farmers on a collective, and this varies immensely, and the differences in the number of working days put in in different places. But we have figures relating to 1939 and 1940 of the income groups. Thus, income from all sources, kind, and money: [12]

---

[12] From a Soviet Source, reprinted in Harry Schwartz, *Russia's Soviet Economy*, New York, 1951, p. 277.

Income Group	1939 Percent	1940 Percent
Under 700 rubles	21.8	29.1
701–1000	19.8	23.0
1001–2000	51.2	44.7
2001–3000	6.3	2.8
3001–4000	0.7	0.3
4001 and over	0.2	0.1

The mass of the peasantry is very poor, as poor as the very lowest grade of factory worker. The difference between the two columns comes from the fact that it was in 1939 that the government took measures to discourage private farming. In 1939 the lowest 20 percent of the collective farmers averaged 488 rubles in a year, while the highest 0.2 percent averaged 4882 rubles—that is ten times as much. Not much egalitarianism there! [13]

III. THE RUSSIAN STANDARD OF LIVING

For a comparison of the standard of living of the U.S.S.R. and the United States we print (p. 918) a table showing the cost of commodities, based on the ruble-dollar rate as established March 1, 1950, and the working time cost needed to buy consumer goods.

Why So Low?

The contrast, so amazingly glaring, between the two economies (p. 24 also) is not due merely to the inefficiency of the great, overweighty, creaking machine of centralized planning and the ill success of the agricultural policy. *It is due also to the recency of Russia's emergence from a primitive rural economy,* and the included fact that it is only fourteen years ago that the Industrial Revolution was really inaugurated. Even then, a dreadfully destructive war, from June 1941 to June 1945, devastated the land, despoiled it, disorganized its labor force, and took the lives of at least 7,000,000 soldiers.

Both the urban and the rural workers are in a parlous condition, including the high intelligent-

[13] *Voprosy Ekonomiki,* Moscow, May 1955, declares that the total money income of farms was 49.6 billion rubles, 2.4 times what it was in 1940. This is equal to 528,000 rubles per collective farm. At 200 families per farm, this means about 3000 rubles per family per year. From this about a third must be deducted for taxes, insurance, and cost of production, leaving 2000.

sia. The city population may reach a tolerable standard of living in twenty years' time; the agricultural population will take much longer to make a decent living. Starchy foods, like wheat and potatoes, will still make up some 70 percent of Russian total calories as compared with 35 percent of diet in the United States. The party pressure will still be grinding on all; and the intelligentsia will be more firmly entrenched as the (perhaps) 10 percent of the population that gets by far the better deal out of the planned economy, while peasants and semiskilled and unskilled workers, with a large proportion of women among them, will do the sweated labor as on colonial plantations. There is hardly a white shirt to be seen in Russia—yet one can live in gray shirts.

It is not useful to try to count the social services provided by the government in mitigation of the poverty. The people pay for them in taxes and the quality is truly inferior.

Agricultural Crisis. The conduct of agriculture by the government, though indirectly, has subjected the Russian people to a serious crisis. The number of livestock fell thus:

Animal	1928	1953
Cattle	66,800,000	56,000,000
(Cows	33,200,000	24,300,000)
Sheep and goats	114,600,000	109,900,000
Horses	36,000,000	15,300,000
Hogs	27,700,000	28,500,000+

The population has increased by some 30 percent in the same time. Milk yields per cow have for years been only half the average in the United States; a Soviet acre gives 12 bushels of wheat and an American one, 17; corn, 17 against 40! The decline in milk and meat edibles from 1930 to 1955 has been in the order of 30 percent. Grain yields have been only equal to that of 1928 per capita. The postwar Stalin-Khrushchev onslaught on the peasants attempted to coerce them into giving better supplies of grain, milk, meat, and fruits and vegetables. For the policy of industrialization requires good diet for the workers, and the diet has been poor while education has raised expectations. The workers had hitherto been fed by tax-coerced deliveries from the farmers, some of whom were left on the margin of existence (compare the prices below with the average pay scales (p. 901). Khrushchev devalued currency and forced the farmers into selling more. He put heavier taxes on the produce of their private plots. His *agrogorod* reorganization caused a disorganization and diversion of labor and interests. He was criticized by other members of the party and by one Presidium member, but he persisted and failed (p. 915) but diverted the blame to Malenkov, head of the State (p. 883).

Between September 1953 and August 1954 Malenkov's short regime produced new policies, so

Prices or and Average Working Time Required to Purchase Selected Consumer Goods in the U.S.S.R. and the U.S.A., March 1951 *

Commodity	Unit	U.S.S.R Price in Rubles	Average Cost in Work † Hrs.	Min.	U.S.A. Price in Dollars	Average Cost in Work ‡ Hrs.	Min.
Rye bread, black	kg.	1.70		35	n.a.		
Wheat bread, white	kg.	4.80	1	38	0.35		14
Beef, chuck roast	kg.	17.45	5	56	1.61	1	3
Fish, fresh	kg.	21.05	7	96	0.90		36
Butter	kg.	35.35	12	1	1.81	1	12
Tea	100g.	12.95	4	24	n.a.		
Lard	kg.	28.00	9	31	0.48		19
Sugar, granulated	kg.	11.50	3	55	0.22		9
Potatoes	kg.	0.90		18	.10		4
Carrots	kg.	1.28		26	.14		6
Beer	½ litter	3.00	1	1	.16		6
Suit, men's wool	each	919.00	312	35	37.95	24	58
Dress, cotton	each	125.00	42	31	2.96	1	57
Shoes, men's leather work	pair	196.00	66	40	5.98	3	56
Stockings, women's rayon	pair	20.00	6	48	n.a.		
Stockings, women's nylon	pair	n.a.			1.29		51
Public transportation	one	.80		16	.12		5
Movie ticket	one	5.00	1	42	.90		36
Items Hard to Buy in U.S.S.R.							
Eggs	10	11.90	4	3	.52		21
Milk	liter	3.25	1	6	.20		8
Mutton	kg.	18.75	6	23	1.77	1	8
Coffee	kg.	70.20	23	53	1.84	1	13
Makharka (cheap tobacco)	50g.	.72		15	.09		4
Toilet soap	100g.	1.70		35	.07		3
Cigarettes	25	4.30	1	28	.23		9
Durable Goods							
Sewing machine	one	705.00	239	47	97.00	63	49
Tea set	one	105.00	35	43	6.95	4	34
Kergas stove	one	85.00	28	55	11.35	7	28
Radio, 6 tubes	one	810.00	275	33	28.00	18	25
Radio-phonograph	one	1,055.00	358	50	37.00	24	21
Pocket watch	one	280.00	95	14	2.50	1	39
Woman's wrist watch	one	395.00	134	21	17.00	11	11
Table clock	one	245.00	83	20	4.35	2	52
Man's bicycle	one	780.00	265	18	36.50	24	08

* *Source:* U.S. Department of State. Food prices based on data provided by the U.S. Bureau of Labor Statistics. Manufactured goods prices taken from Sears, Roebuck catalogue, Spring–Summer, 1951.

† Calculated on the basis of estimated average hourly earnings of 2.94 rubles for nonagricultural workers.

‡ Based on average hourly earning of $1.52 in manufacturing.

Cost of Feeding a Family of Four *

Item	Quantity	Sweden (Crowns)	W. Germany (Marks)	Italy (Lire)	U.S.S.R. (Rubles)
White Bread	2 kg.	2.00	1.60	280	6.40
Meat	500 gr.	3.00	2.00	450	7.50
Milk	1 liter	0.45	0.38	80	2.60
Butter	200 gr.	1.40	1.20	200	5.60
Potatoes	2 kg.	0.40	0.32	75	1.20
Vegetables	1 kg.	0.80	0.45	100	2.00
Sugar	200 gr.	0.30	0.28	52	2.00
Coffee, Tea	10 gr.	0.28	0.40	20	0.81
TOTAL		8.63	6.62	1257	27.51
Average Daily Wage		20.00	12.00	1600	26.00
Percent of Daily Wage Spent on Food		42.80	55.10	78.90	107.50 †

* Source: Bulletin of the Institute for Study of U.S.S.R., Munich, June 1954, p. 8. Soviet data based on the official exchange rate of the ruble is even more worthless. The dollar is now valued at 4 rubles in the U.S.S.R., the Deutsche Mark at 95 kopeks, and the Italian lira at 0.6 kopek. If we accept this rate, the 40,000 lire received by the average Italian worker per month would be equivalent to a mere 240 rubles. This is excellent propaganda, since the average Soviet worker receives 640 rubles monthly.

On the other hand, if we convert Italian prices into rubles according to the Soviet exchange rate, the effect is precisely the opposite. A liter of milk would cost 48 kopeks (80 × 0.6), whereas it costs 2 rubles 69 kopeks in the Soviet Union. Sugar would cost 1 ruble 56 kopeks (260 × 0.6), while its official price in the Soviet Union is 10 rubles. The results are similar whatever product we might take.

Therefore, the real value of the lira, dollar and Deutsche Mark is much superior to the official Soviet exchange rate. If we measure the kopek value of the lira by a comparison of the costs of the sixteen major consumption goods in both countries (bread, potatoes, butter, fats, vegetable oils, meat, herring, milk, sugar, eggs, cigarettes, cotton cloth, broadcloth, men's and women's shoes, men's suits and women's cotton dresses), the lira proves to be worth at least four kopeks. In April 1954 the Italian consulate in Moscow calculated, including rent, medical and other services, that the real value of the lira is not less than 3 kopeks.

The average Italian worker's monthly wage corresponds, then, to 1200 rubles—not 240. In other words, his real wage is almost twice that of his Soviet counterpart.

A comparison of purchasing power is also indicative. An average quality wool suit costs 1500 rubles in the U.S.S.R.; a much better suit costs 26,000 lire in Italy. The monthly wage of a Soviet worker is equal to half the cost of the suit; the Italian worker could buy 1½ for his monthly paycheck. A good pair of men's shoes sells for 250 rubles and 5000 lire. The average Soviet wage could purchase 2½ pairs per month; that of the Italian worker could purchase eight.

† Therefore the wife must work as well as the husband.

decreed. The price of government-enforced deliveries was raised *on the average* by 11 percent. The obligatory deliveries were decreased in amount, to give farmers the incentive of growing more for the free market. Deliveries from the private plots were decreased. Back taxes were canceled. Deliveries were reckoned per acre, not a rising percentage of produce, so that farmers would not feel that if they increased production, the increase would be taken from them. More access to pastures for "private" livestock was allowed. More building materials and fertilizers were planned and delivered. The size of the private plots was increased. More feed was provided; more machines. It was still insufficient. Warlike measures were introduced. By 1956 the government planned to expand the area of grain cultivation by 70,000,000

acres, an addition of 20 percent of the Soviet sown area, or the equal of America's total. Even double this was proposed later! The former figure would produce an additional 600,000,000 bushels; the total American is but 1,000,000,000. This was to be achieved by the traditional Russian method of "expansion," by ploughing up virgin land in Kazakhstan, western Siberia, the north Caucasus, the Volga, the Urals. For this venture the *Komsomols*, the office agronomists, the Motor Tractormen were mobilized as "volunteers." One hundred and fifty thousand skilled men and families were moved, to live in tents and prefabs; tractors and equipment were supplied, etc. Naturally, the environmental facilities were bungled. The "volunteers" were insufficient; many complained of the bitter hardships. It is estimated that to do the job

—if indeed soil and climate can be conquered at all—requires a movement of some 2,000,000 people. The new lands failed in 1955, and very badly. Only a good harvest in the Ukraine saved the situation to some extent. In January 1956 a retreat in policy was announced.

The situation is truly parlous. For the government has long run counter to the human incentives of the farmers, and it has brutally exploited them by the staggering difference between what it pays for the enforced deliveries and the price at which it markets them.

Yet Russia is basically a poor agricultural land. It is afflicted by cold, aridity, variability of climate, and the poor quality of the soil; its Fertile Triangle, covering the Ukraine is only 10 percent of its area, whereas the United States has 25 percent of its area arable.

Most of Russia lies north of 49°—that is, it is like the wastes of Canada. It is possible for a government to take the land and give coercive orders to the farmers, but does this make them into good, intensive farmers? A dictator's force cannot change geography. At least the campaign in what might prove a national catastrophe may keep the dictators peaceful for a few years. In June 1955 Khrushchev publicly declared the need for going back from the *agrogorod* policy to smaller farms was necessary because they were too big to manage and the land was too widely scattered. Removals of party and State officials for agricultural failure have been proceeding wholesale. *Pravda* scourges party leaders for "talking not leading" in the new program. A campaign is afoot to begin the growing of maize and combine hog raising with it; it flies in the face of Nature in the Russian soil and climate. The United States was charitable enough to let Soviet farm experts visit American farms and consider allowing the sale to U.S.S.R. of seed and machinery. **Distribution.** Soviet produce is distributed partly through (1) the peasants' open markets, from the residue of their harvests after their compulsory payments have been made to government and the M.T.S., (2) the State trading system, and (3) the cooperatives.

The State trading organization, under the Ministry of Trade of the various Union Republic Councils of Ministers, distributes the goods in the quantities that the U.S.S.R. government has determined shall be for consumption that year. The Ministry of Requisitions takes deliveries from the farms. The other Ministries that administer the various branches of production have administrative divisions of sales—for example, for sugar, tea, dairy products, liquor, tobacco, meat, light, etc. *Chain Stores.* Throughout the nation there are chains of stores run by the retail sales division of the Republic Ministry of Trade, mainly serving the urban centers. The administration of each product and store chain is in the hands of a unit called *Torg,* administered by officials appointed by the Ministry of Trade of the Union Republic where the stores are located. They get their goods delivered by the warehouses belonging to the various sales units of the Ministries that produce, as indicated above. Some stores, however, that sell special products—for example, drug stores—are owned and managed by the Ministry of Health. Some other Ministries have their own retail stores. *"Cooperatives."* Consumers "cooperatives" supply the rural areas. In 1948 there were some 28,000 cooperatives of this kind with 32,000,000 farmer members. These units are located in the villages; the members take shares in them. The cooperative thus formed runs the village shops, according to the wealth or poverty and tastes and size and diversity of the village. The cooperative shops buy supplies from the U.S.S.R. central organization of cooperatives called the *Tsentrosoyuz.* It is the summit of a system of elected delegates: from the village upward to a district cooperative union, to the regional cooperative, and so on upward.

Nothing, however, could be further removed from the free cooperative association or democratic self-government begun by the Rochdale pioneers of consumers cooperatives or the present practice in Britain, the home of the movement. For, as usual, the Soviet government and the Communist Party have expelled the democracy and instituted unbreakable bonds over the units, in ways with which we have already become familiar, in the factory and on the farm.

The cooperatives often act for the farms in selling their produce to State organizations and the State; it also buys goods from some industrial wholesale suppliers.

Some 2,500,000 persons are engaged in trade, compared with three times that number in the United States. There are many times fewer stores in Russia. The shops are incompetently managed; they are badly stocked with wrong assortments; they are often bereft of the merest necessities, let alone comforts known to the Western democratic customer. They are beset with waiting queues and annoying rules about priority of customer service. There are continuous and universal and bitter complaints about the lack of goods, their low quality, their lack of lasting power, and the crudeness of the sales people.

Housing. Housing is managed by the local Soviet administrations, who own and build and manage the houses; by the factories who provide housing for their workers (to be vacated when the worker leaves that particular job); and by some cooperatives, which own some private houses from bygone days. In August 1948 the Presidium of the U.S.S.R. Soviet decreed that any citizen might have the right to buy or build a house for himself, in personal ownership, in the city or outside, of one or two stories and with from one to five rooms. The lot for this purpose is assigned, on unlimited lease, by the local Soviet executive departments, according to the planning and rebuilding blueprints approved by the U.S.S.R. government.

Housing is a more-than-usually black spot in the Soviet economy, a byword for crowding, dowdiness, lack of toilet and washing conveniences, rickety steps, bad construction, unpainted, cracked plaster, leaking roofs. We quote the profile sketched by Harry Schwartz: [14]

> Privacy was and is a rare privilege for those living in Soviet cities and towns. . . . [The] typical housing available for a small or medium-sized family in a Soviet city was only one room, in an apartment containing three to six families, all sharing the kitchen and bathroom, if any.

An average family of four has less than 240 square feet of living space—that is, one room of 10 $\times$ 24 feet, or the equivalent in separate rooms. This helps to explain the stranglehold of the factory over the worker. It has his roof and bed. This explains also the privileged position of the intel-

[14] *Russia's Soviet Economy*, New York, 1951, p. 384.

ligentsia, the Red Army officers, the party officials, the M.V.D.

Soviet Transportation and Society

The Soviet government has made important additions to the railroad network in length of line and spread since it assumed the power formerly possessed by the Czarist system, which had made a State development project of railroad transportation (p. 734). Yet it is far flung, uneven, oriented to the industrial areas that are widely dispersed. This is properly so.

But the rail network is not made for passenger traffic, and hardly could be. The villages and hamlets are widely strung out, and the population is far too poor to take trips as part of the amenity of living. Most railroad passenger traffic consists of the movement of commuting workers to the industrial plants near by. Even motor-bus transport is extremely weak in comparison with the United States or Western Europe and Britain.

This is most important as a factor in the political strength of the government in relationship to the population. The Communist Party, with a hard core of about 7,000,000 of the population as members, can travel as it wants, with all priority. The railroads and other forms of transport are guarded and kept alive in work morale by the M.V.D. officials and militia. Their revolvers are much in evidence. These are the only forces in the country that articulate political feeling by personal contact. And the other media of communication, the radio principally and the press, are soundly in the hands of the party (p. 837). The organization of challenging mass opposition is impossible from inside Russia.

On the other hand, this is awkward politically for the party. It suffers from the inability to permeate the population as it would like to do. To control the mind it is necessary not only to be present by the side of the mind to be affected, but to stay there. The party cannot afford so much personnel in permanent residence. It has not the facilities of transport to service enough itinerants for long enough periods to keep its controlees loyal enough to accomplish works of party salvation. This, in part, accounts for the party's zeal in creating the *agrogorods* three times the size of the existing collective farms, to bring the dispersed population within hearing and influential distance of the party officials and their city culture.

A government's use of coercion is in proportion to the inability to prevail by persuasion. The effectiveness of persuasion is dependent on communication, of which personal transport and face-to-face confrontations are exceedingly important causative elements.

Hence, an extra dose of coercion and its ability to get conformity in face of a great inchoate mass of population that cannot meet to link up the forces of nonconformity and resistance.

Labor

The whole of the labor force in the Soviet Union is subject to Pharaoh's compulsion of work, in some form or another. It may be a forced levy from a rural area; assignment to jobs from the Labor Reserves and from the higher schools; compulsory change of job from one place to another. Much that would seem to be voluntary for the worker is in fact cruelly obligatory, because a refusal to undertake what he is bidden to do could be construed as sabotage or enmity to the regime, and he knows that brutal penalties would immediately be invoked.

Besides this, there is the system of convict or penal labor of massive proportions, and horrible work and living conditions, under the administration of the State Security Police, the M.V.D. Its spirit is one of most vindictive class war, "an unerring weapon against class enemies, pitilessly suppressing them and mercilessly dispensing justice," [15] in the words of André Vyshinsky, former Procurator of the U.S.S.R. and thereafter permanent representative of the U.S.S.R. to the United Nations.

People are accused of constituting a danger to society, through criminal connections or family

relations, for infractions of labor discipline which has a thousand cunning facets invoking police arrest. Furthermore, as we have seen, there is no open procedure or judicial courtroom practices, where the M.V.D. is concerned.

There is no absolutely accurate statistical summation of the amount of forced labor in this convict sense. Estimates range around the number of 8,000,000 plus or minus 10 percent: a very sizable labor force. Another measure of the importance of slave labor to the Soviet economy is that in the 1941 Plan the amounts for capital investment allotted to M.V.D. (then the N.K.V.D.) equaled *over 12 percent of the total of all projects in the U.S.S.R.*

These forced laborers are used in cutting timber; building roads and railroads; digging and constructing the great canals; mining coal, gold, chrome; manufacturing bricks; etc.—and this in the areas of most inclement climate. Many are hired out to other enterprises by their jailer-managers.

Atrocious Conditions. The conditions in the camps constitute the most abominable atrocities against human nature that human beings can devise. The rations amount to something like a pound of bread a day and a warm meal of cereal, with tiny scraps of dried fish or meat or bacon. Even to mention these quantities is to give too kindly a statement of the cruel conditions. The food depends on the achievement of arduous norms. The camps are beds of disease, dirt, vermin. Plain criminals lord it over the "economic" and "political" criminals. The medical services are monstrously incompetent and inadequate. The camps are living deaths. The forced workers produce more than they eat, and then they may expire. The possibility of release after the frequent three-year detention is quite haphazard: it is in the hands of the M.V.D. administration without appeal.

Though the original impetus to the forced labor camps was political rather than economic—that is, "to correct" the mind of class enemies—once they became labor units they entered into the Soviet's economic system. There are always disagreeable jobs in unpleasant regions to which labor will not

---

[15] *Cf. Report,* Ad Hoc Committee on Forced Labor, United Nations and the International Labor Office, Geneva, 1953, p. 84. See also for the various estimates, *Trends in Economic Growth,* Joint Committee on Economic Report, 83d Congress, 2d Session, 1955, Government Printing Office, p. 235ff.

freely go. The Soviet has a steady supply of these pitiful, powerless individuals who have infringed the meticulously drawn or the vague law, the interpretation of which depends on a system that knows no independent courts of justice.

Spetsi. Besides the labor-camp inmates, there are millions of other people whose labor is exploited under indirect coercion. These are known as *spetsi:* men and women banished to live in certain ordained places as a penalty for having come up against Soviet law. Because they cannot live and work where they like, but only in the harshest conditions of geography, climate, and type of work, they are cruelly exploited.

Contemporary Appraisal

All these physical and spiritual forces form a gigantic machine, constructed in a simple, purposeful way, directed by the hand of one single man, the Russian Czar, who with one motion can start it at any moment, who can give it any direction, any speed he wishes. But let us keep in mind that the machine is moved by more than mechanical function. No, it is all animated by one feeling, an ancient legacy from our ancestors: allegiance, limitless confidence, and devotion to the Czar, their God on earth.

I ask: who can compare with us? Whom will we not force into submission? Is not the political fate of the world in our hands whenever we want to decide it one way or the other . . . ?

—Mikhail Petrovich Pobodin (Slavophil), 1837

The Bolsheviks held that there are two kinds of war:

(2) *Just* wars: wars that are not wars of conquest but wars of liberation, waged to defend the people from foreign attack and from attempts to enslave them, or to liberate the people from capitalist slavery, or, lastly, to liberate colonies and dependent countries from the yoke of imperialism; and

(b) *Unjust* wars, wars of conquest waged to conquer and enslave foreign countries and foreign nations.

—*Short History of the Communist Party of the Soviet Union,*
after Lenin. 1945 edition, Moscow, pp. 168–169

The Soviet Union is a brutal dictatorship that sways between boasting it is and professing it is not. The people are not overly unhappy, for they are physically vigorous by nature, of remarkable endurance, and have much laughter and innocence mixed with their morbidity and cultural primitiveness. They are, in the cities, rather better off than their Czarist forefathers and have been persuaded that much better days are yet to come—and soon. As *they never had political liberty, they do not seem to miss it.* Some even think there is something wrong with nations that change their Governments every four years or so! They have educational opportunities superior to those of their mothers and fathers and, to a large extent, careers open to their talents. Their standards of economic welfare are as yet miserable compared with what an American or English family expects, for only a few years ago they lived in millennial squalor and poverty. There is a little more for many more. What they have not got they are persuaded by propaganda that they have or will have; they believe the leaders are genuinely devoted to their welfare and so they live and work in ever-renewed hope of improvement.

There is, of course, much grousing and gibing at the government, meaning the officials and the Communist Party, for inefficiency, too high pay,

924

authoritarianism, usurpation of authority, favoritism, feathering their own nests. But there is everywhere a horrible fear to criticize Stalin, Malenkov, Khrushchev, and other leaders so high in the hierarchy, or to praise those condemned by the regime or to denigrate those lauded by it. They have been decreed to be robots; freedom for them would be rather less work discipline and more to eat and enjoy. Dead-pan and silence is their lot.

It appears that the Russian worker and peasant likes his recreation organized by authority, though he may grumble at specific incompetence or unequal treatment. There is widespread enjoyment in being irreligious, more so than being religious; but when was the Russian peasant ever a Christian since the year of Christianization, 1000?

A viciously false view of the world outside Russia has been inculcated in the intelligentsia as well as in the masses. They affect to believe the Western nations in particular to be poorer than they, slave-driven by capitalists, bestial to minorities, bent on destroying the Soviet Union by war in its most horrible forms, and to be users of germ warfare. Conversely, they parrot that their own rulers have only the noble intention of liberating all oppressed peoples everywhere whether from ordinary class exploitation or colonial rule, and to be the heroic and exclusive bearers of peace on earth, and to have no warlike intentions except defense. They are very solid with their government. As the Soviet people are illiterate peasantry not yet one generation removed, they are not capable of assessing their government's own infamy toward them. Moreover, they are almost entirely isolated from information about the rest of the world by their Government's own deliberate decision, for its own benefit. Yet they have to work in order to eat; human nature, even in prison camps, makes the best of this necessity.

The dictatorship is total. Yet the people's desires are not its aims by a considerable distance. Hence, much disobedience, loafing, nonfulfillment of work, poor quality attainment and passive resistance. Hence, the dictatorship is tempered by inefficiency and an astounding amount of corruption, which is connived in, because it is impossible to have one party or State controller over every worker and farmer, and even such an arrangement, where it

occurs, has broken down, by the formation of little mutual-protection confederacies of those who think the government Plans silly or impossible or undesirable. Hence, a low level of efficiency in the dictatorship. Educated people will not take factory jobs, it is complained (by whom? the intelligentsia already in command!) Youth, which has grown up entirely inside the Soviet system, gives the scandalous trouble, being delinquent, criminal, drunken, bestial, pleasure-loving, religious, and work-shy; and yet these have had no opportunity to learn such bad non-Communist, non-Soviet attitudes from the past or the foreign "bourgeoisie": it is all learned at home in the U.S.S.R.!

A high intelligentsia has made for itself the class privileges (similar, is meant) formerly possessed by the Russian bourgeoisie. It has a steady interest in exploiting the medium and unskilled laborers, especially poor women who are used as beasts of burden, while it enjoys the flesh-pots. The scientifically educated are critical of revealed religion, including that of the Communist Party. Even the cyclical erasure of the history that does not suit the current leaders' interests cannot stop the people's memory from drawing conclusions and breeding distrust. Tens of millions are being educated each year; it will be ultimately impossible to obstruct their asking disintegrative questions, subversive of work discipline.

Even Soviet novels have been allowed to express the bitterness of the educated Soviet society against the ice-binding character of Stalin's murderous rule.[1] Uncertainty seems already to have to some degree entered the mind of the Soviet top party command. Have they an interest in less dictatorship and less war by arms and infiltration outside their own territories? Can Leninist and Stalinist rancor, then, be perpetuated? Can the same intensity of malign persecution be expended when the new gains over those already made in the economy and society can only be of diminishing magnitude? The admission by the leaders, Khrushchev and Bulganin, in May 1955 that Tito of Yugoslavia had been abused by Stalin's government and that *his* form of communism had a right to exist as a descendant of Leninism must give food for doubts to Russian people. The technical and busi-

[1] See Ilya Ehrenberg, *The Thaw*, Chicago, 1955.

ness directors of Russian economic life—the cadres —want party policy to be shaped to *their* technical tasks and not *vice versa*. The Soviet press has even admitted an article (*Voprosy Ekonomiki*, No. 9, Moscow, 1954) arguing that "policy is a concentrated expression of economy, its generalization and fulfillment"; this goes back to Marx and clashes with the Stalinist doctrine that policy is the dominator of the economy, the political will over economic laws arising from the dispositions of the works. Khrushchev even declared (*Kommunist*, September 1953, reporting the current Supreme Soviet speeches) that he followed Lenin in believing that communism was to be obtained *in the long run* only via "personal interest, gain and economic considerations"; and from this was encouraged to seek greater farm output by the concessions we have noted (p. 919), in which "The principle of personal financial interest on the part of every enterprise and individual worker in the results of their labors is one of the basic principles of our socialist economy."

The return to Leninism, expunging Stalin, has also produced an unleashing of criticism of Stalinist brutality in various strata of the party membership. These are under a cloud. Also, a neo-Slavophil cliché that capitalist economies are decadent is being denounced in favor of propaganda that much must be learned from their scientific and technical and managerial attainments.

It used to be feared by some American governmental leaders that the U.S.S.R. would drain America dry economically by the "cold war." The judgment was always nonsense bred of ignorance, because the strain of the Soviet Union's much lower standard of living has been very much less supportable. Bad agricultural production; 3,000,-000 more mouths to feed each year; defense; the clamor for better living standards;[2] the loss of Stalin's *mystique;* disarray among Stalin's successors; the promises to industrialize China—these, for the moment, in July 1955, forced the Soviet leaders to a relaxation of international tensions, to

suing for disarmament, to fostering imports, and to spreading smiles all over the President of the United States in Geneva, even to exhibition of their canine teeth. It seems that the Stalin-Molotov aggressions since the end of World War II have at the least been stupid.

After the Hydrogen Bomb

America, not the Soviet Union, invented nuclear weapons, the "absolute" weapons as they have been called. Stalin resisted the United States' proposals to internationalize ownership of uranium deposits and manufacture of fissionable materials.[3] Faced with American superiority, and determined, as before and since, not to be at the mercy of another nation's power and ethics, he said in 1946 that atomic bombs would only "frighten the weak-nerved." He forced the Soviet Union, then, to rely on American ethics, which abhor "preventive" war, and meanwhile broke the American monopoly by September 1949. America was still far in advance with stockpiles and improved weapons, and went ahead to make the H-bomb in 1950. The Soviet Unions exploded an H-bomb by August 1953. In that interval, 1950–1953, in a ruder age, the stronger power would have destroyed the temporarily weaker one in its merciless stride, as the Soviet Union might well have done had she been the pioneer holder of substantial atomic supremacy.

By March 1954 Malenkov, then Prime Minister, declared that atomic war would cause "destruction of world civilization." This possibly humane view was bitterly resented by the sternest practitioner of brutal power in modern times, M. Molotov, the Soviet Foreign Minister. Malenkov's fall in February 1955 may well have been due to the more decent corollaries regarding international policy following from this premise. For in the speech made by Molotov directly after Malenkov's resignation, the old callous belligerence was resumed: "It is not 'world civilization' that will perish, however much it may suffer from new aggressions, but the decaying system of which bloodthirsty imperialism is the core." Here is Lenin's utter intransigence,

[2] In December, abortion, which had been legalized after 1917 and then outlawed in June 1936, was relegalized (to help keep down the population) by the reduction of penalties on duly qualified and equipped physicians. For the increase in population had been accelerated by taxes on bachelors and family allowances.

[3] *Cf.* Herman Finer, *America's Destiny*, New York, 1947, Chapter VI.

unremitting malevolence, coming out in the flesh again: rule or ruin. The party press loudly and often re-echoed this attitude.

Yet, by the beginning of 1955, their own tests and the American H-bomb test at Bikini in 1954, caused the Soviet dictations to change their strategy, not least after Mr. Churchill had pointed out the beneficent fact that radio-active dust could bring Russia to her knees, though her national area is so vast. He made this riposte to Molotov's atom-rattling speeches that suggested that atomic weapons were peculiarly dangerous to densely populated countries—like Britain.[4]

The Politbureau's problem now was, How can we avoid a surprise attack on ourselves, even avoid atomic warfare altogether, yet still retain our revolutionary *élan* throughout the world to mobilize the discontented peoples of the globe against (and so isolate) an America that has treaties with thirty-seven countries, that has created NATO and Western German democracy, and has built air bases all around us?

The top leaders agreed to a meeting of the heads of the Four Powers at Geneva in July 1955. Here, flattering the President of the United States in public and private and smiling violently, they concluded that the American declared policy of withdrawing forces from all the peripheries and relying on "massive retaliation" would operate only *in extremis,* and perhaps never, because of American good-naturedness and desire for peace and prosperity. At once Khrushchev and Molotov found their strategy. Under the shield of American withdrawal from smaller fights, lest any one of these force America into retaliation which would be "massive," the Soviet Union could win "competitive coexistence" by infiltration and disruption by such cruel strokes as arming Egypt, hotly embroiled with Israel, donating sovereign power over Berlin to the East German Government, and stirring up discontent among all peoples against the West and against each other, justified or not, tell the Russian people that the West was resuming the "cold war" while keeping out of the Soviet press the vile insults Khrushchev and Bulganin had pub-

[4] *Pravda,* March 4, 1955. "Who does not know, however, that this development [Britain as a U.S. atomic base] particularly threatens small countries with dense populations."

licly hurled at the Western nations during the tour of India, Burma, and Afghanistan in November–December 1955. The keynote was struck by Kaganovich in his Revolution Anniversary speech in November 1955:

> If the nineteenth century was a century of capitalism, the twentieth century is a century of the triumph of socialism and Communism.

The real issue, confused by this speaker, is democracy and dictatorship.

With consummate and unscrupulous skill, the Soviet dictators have made themselves strong where it is necessary for their survival and expansion in a world of national states: in science and technology (nuclear weapons, air power, missiles, etc.), in the supporting industries of war, in submarines, and in vast armies that can stand hard conditions, still massively deployed on all her borders, infiltrated among the satellite countries and spread throughout the homeland. (They are used for heavy industrial work while in uniform, the crassest form of "scab" labor.) The people of the Soviet lands are kept shockingly short in food and all other consumption goods for the sake of heavy and armament industries, the sweat of their brows being wrung from them more recently to give their leaders the diplomatic power of rivaling the American Point Four, the Marshall, and the Mutual Aid Plans, pioneered by the United States.

The Soviet dictators pursue the policy of overtaking the economic achievements of the United States in all respects, and, curiously enough, by being the showpiece to underdeveloped Asian and Middle Eastern nations because the U.S.S.R. has attained industrialization without political liberty! They play the strong propaganda hand of "peace" to gain friends, such as India, and foment rebellion everywhere, and so, by causing worry and confusion among the democratic countries, gain for themselves the maximum future time for the unmolested development of the industrial, agricultural, military, and political strength of their own country. Thus, they may be ever stronger and freer to dictate to the whole world the dominating terms upon which the Soviet Union is prepared alone to live with other countries, shown by the adamant vetoes in the United Nations and the brutally blunt refusal to allow East Germany to reunite with the West, and always the insistence that they cannot rely on Western guarantees but only on their own power and pawns. This they can do the more successfully, because they can wring, by force, and milk by guile, all the production and military sacrifice they need from their own people: today Russia, tomorrow, the world! They compel unpleasant choices in all other nations, above all the other Superpower, the United States.

Today the biggest imperialist and colonial power the world has or has ever known is Soviet Russia, enjoying the fruit of all Czarist seizures in Siberia, Central Asia, and Transcaucasia, and having engorged besides Lithuania, Latvia, Estonia, part of Poland, Bessarabia, Bukovina, Carpatho-Ukraine, East Prussia (in part), Petsamo, Karelo-Finland, Tannu Tova, South Sakhalin, and the Kuriles, and having subjugated Poland, Hungary, Czechoslovakia, Romania and Bulgaria, East Germany, Albania, and Outer Mongolia. Though since 1918 the Western Powers have freed 600,000,000 colonial peoples (who were taught liberalism, good government, and a rising standard of living, with emphasis on education), the Soviet Union, like its Czarist ancestor, has never yielded one square foot of land or one single soul that it has engorged. Hundreds of thousands of martyrs died to prevent the seizure of their native lands, hundreds of thousands still cherish the hope of liberation from the annihilating embrace of Great Russia.

This dictatorship cannot collapse, because its people have been subjugated and bound to it by welfare and security. The Army, which is divided, cannot overthrow it. It can only become different, more democratic, in one of two ways. The first is liberation from outside. The other is a serious split among the top leaders of such a kind as to leave two or more contending factions each with a substantial and revolutionary following of party members, police and Armed Forces. The more likely evolution is a declining ability, in the quite long run, of the party intelligentsia to make the masses do its bidding and therefore a relaxation of what it demands of them, ending in a kind of Thermidor (p. 300) of the general intelligentsia.

This is quite consistent with tactics useful in themselves, especially for men who may not have quite the vileness of Stalin. They may think: "Let us give our people some relaxation from force and police oppression, so that they may live in hope of easier times. This will encourage more self-criticism and exposition of the little Stalins who usurp our authority in the wards, blocks, and farms. Let us copy other nations' progressive ideas; this will give our people something to think about and more advanced examples, especially if we encourage cultural visits. We have everything to gain thereby and need never lose anything, because we can interpret events to the people as we choose and can change their opinion within twenty-four hours. Then they will be happier and more obedient. This could lead to a little decentralization, since we are so top-heavy, and it could mean more productiveness in goods and ideas and cut down our terribly high real cost of production. Thus we will look peaceful to the rest of the world, especially to the less informed peoples, and we can thus disarm such educated men as Nehru while undermining their authority. Also, we cannot live forever, so we had better not keep our people completely blind and in bonds." For the moment, the dictatorship of Stalin is without one dictator like Stalin. Is this why the rudder swings this way and that?

The End and the Means

As we observed in Lenin's writings (p. 754), and as the practice of Soviet dictatorship has so often demonstrated, following the counsel of Nechaev (p. 752), the Western rule (if not always observed) that the means ought to be ethical, even if it defeats the desired end, has been contemptuously discarded by the Soviet rulers. Western democracies have an ideal and distant end, even if vaguely conceived. Is it not Christian? (I am quite well aware of the fat and vulgar grossness of millions of common materialists—and yet?) But, what is the ultimate end of the Soviet Communists? They hardly go beyond the abolition of class exploitation. This, however, is negative. They are afraid of, and punish, philosophy, considered as free speculation on values. They persecute the freedom of mind this implies and forbid open discussion of the nature of man and his spirit outside Marxian materialism, and this denies or blinds itself to issues of the existence of the soul and such values as Charity and Mercy.

Their end is not ultimate, but proximate, chiefly a higher standard of material living, modified by the amassment of defensive weapons and vast armed forces. They have never sought to formulate, even with only tentative clarity, what Communism, which they profess to seek, concretely means in the private relations of man to man and the relationship of individual and community. They seem to fear to philosophize about such goals lest the resultant picture should condemn their present means. Their propagandist reasoning is always in a vicious circle: to fulfill production quotas in order to reach enough abundance to have a communistic society, but they give no indication of what features of such a society could justify the production quotas. Yet surely Communist society and production quotas require the continued operation of the Communist Party dictatorship and all its instruments as now deployed. The maximization of the power of the party becomes the concentrated and final end, so that it is free of any inhibitions of principle to do whatever it likes in the glamorous but cloudy name of Communism. Whatever the end proposed at any time, no one means is better or worse than any other or involves ethical principle: the only issue is which is the most useful, even if it means deserting already professed and previously enforced principles (by fire and sword) such as that the State will wither away.

Those who adhere to their own ethics in violation of such expedients are "egoists," and their "honor" and "scruples" are treated as "egoistic excesses." They are either stupid or imperfectly dedicated or too egoistically concerned whether they do or do not feel guilty.

There is a classic passage in Dostoevski's *The Brothers Karamazov,* echoed by so many of the Russian classic writers in the nineteenth century:

Imagine that you are creating a fabric of human destiny with the object of making men happy in the end, giving them peace and rest at last, but that it was essential and inevitable to torture to death only one tiny creature—that baby beating its breast with its fist, for instance—and to found that edifice on its unavenged tears, would you consent to be the architect on those conditions?

The classic writers—the true, because the magnanimous and charitable enemies of Czarist tyranny—rejected the immoral means, for they looked to a better morality. The Soviet Communists aver that to such architects as they are, nothing at all is holy except each step they feel they must take, even though they will not discuss where they are ultimately going. Bernard Shaw once said, "If the end does not justify the means, what does?" The answer is that the means justify the means, or nothing does.

Professions *versus* Achievements

Professions	Achieved	Reason Offered for Result	Real Reason
Total freedom	Total autocracy.	(1) People incompetent. (2) Encircled by foreign enemies. (3) Backward economy.	(1) People not tried. (2) Intransigence and revolution. (3) Backward economy. (4) Too speedy Plans. (5) Leaders' power lust. (6) Idolatry of social science.
Equality	Serious inequality.	(1) Differences of ability and effort. (2) Produce not abundant enough.	(1) True; but dictated valuation of values of ability and effort. Began too romantic about equal abilities. Equality, perhaps, was a deliberate deception to win over revolutionary power. (2) True: produce not abundant.

Professions *versus* Achievements

Professions	*Achieved*	*Reason Offered for Result*	*Real Reason*
Economic progress	Great, but less than expected.	(1) Belief in socialism and people's democracy. (2) "Class mentality" remnant. (3) Abilities lacking.	(1) Also massive *force*. (2) True; especially on the farms. (3) Ability small; also hostile to free consumers and private enterprise. (4) Fraudulent cries of imminent foreign aggression.
Self-government for labor	Labor enserfed.	Labor is free! No real differences of interest between classes and people *versus* government.	Utterly subjected to the Plans, willy-nilly.
The land to the Peasants	State property, almost totally.	(1) Petty bourgeois, if not. (2) Surplus labor on land. (3) Produce needed for workers. (4) Mechanization.	(1) This is private property instinct. (2) True. (3) True. (4) True.
Liquidate kulaks	Fulfilled, but M.T.S. is new class.	Party zeal corresponds to truth.	Yet—non-*kulak* peasantry find *kulakism* springs eternal in peasant breast.
Temperance	Besotted drunkenness.	Financial need of taxes.	(1) Consolation for Soviet hardships. (2) Revenues.
Justice to criminals	Severe; harsh; cruel; rehabilitation quite secondary to retribution.	"Class enemies," willful individual excesses; takes time to correct.	Crime is due not merely to "objective" social conditions as Communists earlier pretended. Need of social and economic discipline where Plan so exacting. Fear of opposition to Party.
Multinational State	Practically unitary.	(1) It *is* multinational! (2) Plan-Party-Revolution need unitary State against enemies domestic and foreign.	(1) Untrue! (2) True!
No bureaucracy; popularly conducted administration and judiciary	The most numerous and authoritarian-routinized and oppressive bureaucracy in the world. Neither popular nor independent justices.	Started with inferior material; long education of people needed, without time deadline stated.	Industrialization paramount to arrive at Communism and for national defense. Romantic error that people could speedily acquire official skills.
A noble society in freedom	A brutal, despotic, and degraded society.	"The most democratic free, equal, and wealthy society in the world."	The end—Communism—justifies the means, however ignoble and infamous: there are no such adjectives where the party is the sole means to the Golden Age of Communism.

Professions	Achieved	Reason Offered for Result	Real Reason
State withered away	The most authoritarian State in the modern world, perhaps in all history, in scope, depth, and coercion.	Needed to save this citadel of the Revolution and communism from capitalist aggressors; also to build communism.	To protect the dictators from retaliation by the victims of Communist imperialism. To enforce their personal lust of power, to compel others to live a good life as the dictator commands it. To fulfill by force their errors of judgment concerning human nature and destiny in Russia.
No classes	Abolition of landowners and private entrepreneurs, but strongly stratified intelligentsia, sweated labor, farmers, Army, militia, M.V.D., etc., only incipiently hereditary.	(1) Denial there are classes. (2) Concede slight difference between three. (3) Material primitive; it is early yet.	(1) Native inequalities of ability, etc., useful to economic progress. (2) Native unwillingness to work without corresponding rewards.
Peace-loving	War, hot and cold.	Fascist and capitalist aggression.	(1) Terrified of isolation by other-style ways of life. The craving for like-minded allies. (2) Imperialism, open and brutal.
No imperialism	Imperialism in satellites and occupied lands.	Freely joined by Soviet revolutions, for social "liberation."	Expansion for reasons ideological, strategic, economic.
Family freedom	As nucleated as respectable bourgeoisie.	None	Needed to teach industrial, educational, social discipline and morality. Easier to govern if father-image, then Stalin, and party.
Up-to-date education for all	Incomplete seriously; social differentiation; dogmatic.	Economic needs and time needed *versus* more pressing tasks and *versus* present poverty, plus supremacy of party truths.	Economic discipline and immediate productivity, plus social stratification by the intelligentsia for class reasons; differential rewards for economic and political service. Failure of romantic educational theories.
Citizen army	Old-fashioned, regular-style Army; highly officered, politically dominated and rewarded; primitive discipline.	(1) Technical necessities. (2) *versus* civil war; *versus* encircling capitalists.	(1) Technique—true. (2) Discipline—true.
Dissipate religion	Considerably achieved.	Not "really" against this "right."	Difficult to extirpate. Yielded for war, economic, social, and international expendiency.

Appendix

The Government of Great Britain

MAGNA CARTA, 1215

John, by the Grace of God, King of England, Lord of Ireland, Duke of Normandy and Acquitaine, and Earl of Anjou, to his Archbishops, Bishops, Abbots, Earls, Barons, Justiciaries, Foresters, Sheriffs, Governors, Officers, and to all Bailiffs, and his faithful subjects,—Greeting. Know ye, that We, in the presence of God, and for the salvation of our own soul, and of the souls of all our ancestors, and of our heirs, to the honour of God, and the exaltation of the Holy Church and amendment of our Kingdom, by the counsel of our venerable fathers . . . and others our liegemen; have in the first place granted to God, and by this our present Charter, have confirmed, for us and our heirs forever:—

1. That the English Church shall be free, and shall have her whole rights and her liberties inviolable; and we will this to be observed in such a manner, that it may appear from thence, that the freedom of elections, which was reputed most requisite to the English Church, which we granted, and by our Charter confirmed, and obtained the Confirmation of the same, from our Lord Pope Innocent the Third, before the rupture between us and our Barons, was of our own free will; which Charter we shall observe, and we will it to be observed with good faith, by our heirs forever.

We have also granted to all the freemen of our Kingdom, for us and our heirs forever, all the underwritten Liberties, to be enjoyed and held by them and by their heirs, from us and from our heirs.

. . .

12. No scutage nor aid shall be imposed on our kingdom, unless by the common council of our kingdom; excepting to redeem our person, to make our eldest son a knight, and once to marry our eldest daughter, and not for these, unless a reasonable aid shall be demanded.

13. In like manner let it be concerning the aids of the City of London. And the City of London shall have all it's ancient liberties and free customs.

14. And also to have the common council of the kingdom, to assess and aid, otherwise than in the three cases aforesaid: and for the assessing of scutages, we will cause to be summoned the Archbishops, Bishops, Abbots, Earls, and great Barons, individually by our letters. And besides, we will cause to be summoned in general by our Sheriffs and Bailiffs, all those who hold of us in chief, at a certain day, that is to say at the distance of forty days (before their meeting), at the least, and to a certain place; and in all the letters of summons, we will express the cause of the summons; and the summons being thus made, the business shall proceed on the day appointed, according to the counsel of those who shall be present, although all who have been summoned have not come.

. . .

17. Common Pleas shall not follow our Court, but shall be held in any certain place.

18. Trials upon the Writs of Novel Disseisin, of Mort d'Ancestre, and Darrien Presentment shall not be taken but in their proper counties, and in this manner:—We, or our Chief Justiciary, if we are out of the Kingdom, will send two Justiciaries into each county, four times in the year, who, with four Knights of each county, chosen by the county, shall hold the aforesaid assizes, within the county on the day, and at the place appointed.

19. And if the aforesaid assizes cannot be taken on the day of the county court, let as many knights and freeholders, of those who were present at the county court remain behind, as shall be sufficient to do justice, according to the great or less importance of the business.

. . .

27. If any freeman shall die intestate, his chattels shall be distributed by the hands of his nearest relations and friends, by the view of the Church, saving to every one the debts which the defunct owed.

28. No Constable nor other Bailiff of ours shall take the grain or other goods of any one without instantly paying money for them, unless he can obtain respite from the free-will of the seller.

. . .

38. No Bailiff, for the future, shall put any man to his law, upon his own simple affirmation, without credible witnesses produced for that purpose.

39. No freeman shall be seized, or imprisoned, or dispossessed, or outlawed, or in any way destroyed; nor will we condemn him, nor will we commit him to prison, excepting by the legal judgment of his peers, and by the laws of the land.

40. To none will we sell, to none will we deny, to none will we delay right or justice.

. . .

45. We will not make Justiciaries, Constables, Sheriffs, or Bailiffs, excepting of such as know the laws of the land, and are well disposed to observe them.

. . .

47. All Forests which have been made in our time shall be immediately disforested, and it shall be so done with water-banks, which have been taken or fenced in by us during our reign.

. . .

55. All fines that have been made by us unjustly, or contrary to the laws of the land, and all americia-ments that have been imposed unjustly, or contrary to the laws of the land, shall be wholly remitted, or or-dered by the verdict of the twenty-five Barons, of whom mention is made below, for the security of the peace, or by the verdict of the greater part of them, together with the aforesaid Stephen, Archbishop of Canterbury, if he can be present, and others whom he may think fit to bring with him; and if he cannot be present, the business shall proceed, notwithstanding, without him; but so that if any one or more of the aforesaid twenty-five Barons have a similar plea, let them be removed from that particular trial, and oth-ers elected and sworn by the residue of the same twenty-five, be substituted in their room, only for that trial.

. . .

60. Also all these customs and liberties aforesaid, which we have granted to be held in our Kingdom, for so much of it as belongs to us, all our subjects, as well clergy as laity, shall observe towards their ten-ants as far as concerns them.

61. But since we have granted all these aforesaid, for GOD and for the amendment of our kingdom, and for the better extinguishing the discord which has arisen between us and our Barons, we being desirous that these things should possess entire and unshaken stability forever, give and grant to them the security underwritten, namely, that the Barons may elect twenty-five Barons of the kingdom, whom they please, who shall with their whole power, observe, keep, and cause to be observed, the peace and liberties which we have granted to them, and have confirmed by this, our present charter, in this manner; that is to say, if we, or our Justiciary, or our bailiffs or any of our officers, shall have injured any one in anything, or shall have violated any article of the peace or se-curity, and the injury shall have been shown to four of the aforesaid twenty-five Barons, the said four Bar-ons shall come to us, or to our Justiciary if we be out of the kingdom, and making known to us the excess committed, petition that we cause that excess to be redressed without delay. And if we shall not have re-dressed the excess, or, if we have been out of the kingdom, our Justiciary shall not have redressed it within the term of forty days, computing from the time when it shall have been made known to us, or to our Justiciary, if we have been out of the kingdom, the aforesaid four Barons shall lay that cause before the residue of the twenty-five Barons; and they, the

twenty-five Barons, with the community of the whole land, shall distress and harass us by all the ways in which they are able; that is to say, by the taking of our castles, lands and possessions, and by any other means in their power, until the excess shall have been redressed, according to their verdict, saving our per-son and the persons of our Queen and children, and when it hath been redressed they shall behave to us as they have done before. And whoever of our land pleaseth may swear that he will obey the commands of the aforesaid twenty-five Barons in accomplishing all the things aforesaid, and that with them he will harass us to the utmost of his power; and we publicly and freely give leave to every one to swear who is willing to swear; and we will never forbid any to swear. But all those of our land, who, of themselves, and of their own accord, are unwilling to swear to the twenty-five Barons, to distress and harass us to-gether with them, we will compel them by our com-mand to swear as aforesaid. And if any one of the twenty-five Barons shall die, or remove out of the land, or in any other way shall be prevented from executing the things above said, they who remain of the twenty-five Barons shall elect another in his place, according to their own pleasure, who shall be sworn in the same manner as the rest. In all those things which are appointed to be done by these twenty-five Barons, if it happen that all the twenty-five have been present, and have differed in their opinions about anything, or if some of them who had been sum-moned would not or could not be present, that which the greater part of those who were present shall have provided and decreed, shall be held as firm and as valid as if all the twenty-five had agreed in it; and the aforesaid twenty-five shall swear that they will faithfully observe, and with all their power cause to be observed, all the things mentioned above. And we will obtain nothing from any one, by ourselves, nor by another, by which any of these concessions and liberties may be revoked or diminished. And if any such thing shall have been obtained, let it be void and null; and we will never use it, neither by ourselves nor by another.

62. And we have fully remitted and pardoned to all men all the ill-will, rancour and resentments which have arisen between us and our subjects, both clergy and laity, from the commencement of the dis-cord. . . .

63. Wherefore our will is, and we firmly command that the Church of England be free, and that the men in our kingdom have and hold the aforesaid liberties, rights and concessions, well and in peace, freely and quietly, fully and entirely, to them and their heirs, of us and our heirs, in all things and places for ever, as is aforesaid. It is also sworn, both on our part and on that of the Barons, that all the aforesaid shall be observed in good faith and without any evil intention.

Witnessed by the above and many others. Given by our hand in the Meadow which is called Running- mead, between Windsor and Staines, this 15th day of June, in the 17th year of our reign.

BILL OF RIGHTS, 1689

An Act Declaring the Rights and Liberties of the Subject and Settling the Succession of the Crown

I. Whereas the Lords Spiritual and Temporal, and Commons, assembled at Westminster, lawfully, fully, and freely representing all the Estates of the People of this Realm, did upon the Thirteenth day of February in the year of our Lord one thousand six hundred eighty-eight present unto their Majesties then called and known by the names and stile of William and Mary, Prince and Princess of Orange, being present in their proper persons, a certain Declaration in writing, made by the said Lords and Commons in the words following, viz.—

Whereas the late King James the Second, by the assistance of divers evil Councellors, Judges, and Ministers employed by him, did endeavour to subvert and extirpate the Protestant Religion, and the laws and liberties of this Kingdom;

1. By assuming and exercising a power of Dispensing with and Suspending of laws, and the execution of laws, without consent of Parliament;

2. By committing and prosecuting divers worthy Prelates, for humbly petitioning to be excused from concurring to the said assumed power;

3. By issuing and causing to be executed a Commission under the Great Seal for erecting a Court called the Court of Commissioners for Ecclesiastical Causes;

4. By levying Money for and to the use of the Crown, by pretence of Prerogative, for other time, and in other manner, than the same was granted by Parliament;

5. By raising and keeping a Standing Army within the Kingdom in time of Peace, without consent of Parliament, and quartering Soldiers contrary to law;

6. By causing several good subjects, being Protestants, to be disarmed, at the same time when Papists were both armed and employed contrary to law;

7. By violating the freedom of election of Members to serve in Parliament;

8. By Prosecutions in the Court of King's Bench, for matters and causes cognizable only in Parliament; and by divers other arbitrary and illegal courses;

9. And whereas of late years, partial, corrupt, and unqualified persons have been returned and served on Juries in trials, and particularly divers Jurors in trials for High Treason, which were not Freeholders;

10. And excessive Bail hath been required of persons committed in criminal cases, to elude the benefit of the laws made for the liberty of the subjects;

11. And excessive Fines have been imposed; and illegal and cruel punishments have been inflicted;

12. And several grants and promises made of Fines and Forfeitures, before any conviction or judgment against the persons, upon whom the same were to be levied.

All which are utterly and directly contrary to the known laws and statutes and freedom of this Realm.

And whereas the said late King James the Second having abdicated the Government and the Throne being thereby vacant, His Highness the Prince of Orange (whom it hath pleased Almighty God to make the glorious Instrument of Delivering this Kingdom from Popery and arbitrary power) did (by the advice of the Lords Spiritual and Temporal and divers principal Persons of the Commons) cause Letters to be written to the Lords Spiritual and Temporal, being Protestants; and other Letters to the several Counties, Cities, Universities, Boroughs, and Cinque-ports, for the choosing of such persons to represent them, as were of right to be sent to Parliament, to meet and sit at Westminster upon the two and twentieth day of January in this year one thousand six hundred eighty and eight, in order to such an Establishment as that their Religion, Laws, and Liberties might not again be in danger of being subverted: Upon which Letter Elections having been accordingly made,

And thereupon the said Lords Spiritual and Temporal, and Commons, pursuant to their respective Letters and Elections, being now assembled in a full and free Representative of the Nation, taking into their most serious consideration the best means for attaining the ends aforesaid; Do in the first place (as their Ancestors in like case have usually done) for the vindicating and asserting their ancient Rights and Liberties, Declare

1. That the pretended power of Suspending laws, or the execution of laws, by Regal authority, without consent of Parliament, is illegal.

2. That the pretended power of Dispensing with laws, or the execution of laws, by Regal authority, as it hath been assumed and exercised of late, is illegal.

3. That the Commission for erecting the late Court of Commissioners for Ecclesiastical Causes, and all other Commissions and Courts of like nature, are illegal and pernicious.

4. That levying of money for the use of the Crown, by pretence of Prerogative, without grant of Parliament, for longer time, or in other manner, than the same is or shall be granted, is illegal.

5. That it is the right of the subjects to Petition the King, and all Commitments and Prosecutions for such petitioning are illegal.

6. That the raising or keeping of a Standing Army within the Kingdom in time of peace, unless it be with the consent of Parliament, is against the law.

7. That the subjects which are Protestants, may have Arms for their defence suitable to their conditions, and as allowed by law.

8. That Election of Members of Parliament ought to be free.

9. That the Freedom of Speech, and Debates or Proceedings in Parliament, ought not to be impeached or questioned in any Court or place out of Parliament.

10. That excessive Bail ought not to be required, nor excessive Fines imposed, nor cruel and unusual punishments inflicted.

11. That Jurors ought to be duly impaneled and returned, and Jurors which pass upon men in trials for High Treason ought to be Freeholders.

12. That all Grants and Promises of Fines and Forfeitures of particular persons before conviction are illegal and void.

13. And that for redress of all grievances, and for the amending, strengthening, and preserving of the laws, Parliaments ought to be held frequently.

And They do claim, demand, and insist upon all and singular the premises, as their undoubted rights and liberties; And that no Declarations, Judgments, Doings, or Proceedings, to the Prejudice of the People in any of the said Premises, ought in any wise to be drawn hereafter into consequence or example.

To which demand of their rights they are particularly encouraged by the Declaration of His Highness the Prince of Orange, as being the only means for obtaining a full redress and remedy therein.

Having therefore an entire confidence, that His said Highness the Prince of Orange will perfect the deliverance so far advanced by Him, and will still preserve them from the violation of their rights, which they have here asserted, and from all other attempts upon their Religion, Rights, and Liberties.

II. The said Lords Spiritual and Temporal, and Commons, assembled at Westminster, do Resolve, that William and Mary Prince and Princess of Orange be, and be declared, King and Queen of England, France, and Ireland, and the Dominions thereunto belonging, to hold the Crown and Royal Dignity of the said Kingdoms and Dominions to them the said Prince and Princess during their lives, and the life of the Survivor of them; And that the sole and full exercise of the Regal Power be only in, and executed by, the said Prince of Orange, in the names of the said Prince and Princess, during their joint lives; And after their deceases, the said Crown and Royal Dignity of the said Kingdoms and Dominions to be to the Heirs of the Body of the said Princess, and for default of such Issue to the Princess Anne of Denmark, and the Heirs of the Body of the said Prince of Orange. And the Lords Spiritual and Temporal, and Commons, do pray the said Prince and Princess to accept the same accordingly.

III. And that the Oaths hereafter mentioned be taken by all persons of whom the Oaths of Allegiance and Supremacy might be required by law, instead of them; And that the said Oaths of Allegiance and Supremacy be abrogated.

"I, A. B., do sincerely promise and swear, That I will be faithful and bear true allegiance to their Majesties King William and Queen Mary. So help me God.

"I, A. B., do swear, That I do from my Heart abhor, detest, and abjure as impious and heretical, that damnable doctrine and position, That Princes excommunicated or deprived by the Pope, or any Authority of the See of Rome may be deposed, or murdered by their subjects, or any other whatsoever. And I do declare, that no Foreign Prince, Person, Prelate, State or Potentate, hath, or ought to have, any jurisdiction, power, superiority, preeminence, or authority ecclesiastical or spiritual, within this Realm. So help me God."

IV. Upon which their said Majesties did accept the Crown and Royal Dignity of the Kingdoms of England, France, and Ireland, and the Dominions thereunto belonging, according to the Resolution and Desire of the said Lords and Commons contained in the said Declaration.

V. And thereupon their Majesties were pleased, That the said Lords Spiritual and Temporal, and

Commons, being the two Houses of Parliament, should continue to sit, and with their Majesties' Royal concurrence make effectual provision for the settlement of the Religion, Laws and Liberties of the Kingdom, so that the same for the future might not be in danger of being subverted; To which the said Lords Spiritual and Temporal, and Commons, did agree and proceed to act accordingly.

VI. Now in pursuance of the premisses, the said Lords Spiritual and Temporal, and Commons, in Parliament assembled for the ratifying, confirming and establishing the said Declaration and the Articles, Clauses, Matters, and Things therein contained by the force of a law made in due form by authority of Parliament, do pray that it may be declared and enacted, That all and singular the Rights and Liberties of the people of this Kingdom, and so shall be esteemed, allowed, adjudged, deemed, and taken to be; and that all and every the particulars aforesaid shall be firmly and strictly holden and observed, as they are expressed in the said Declaration; And all Officers and Ministers whatsoever shall serve their Majesties and their Successors according to the same in all times to come.

VII. And the said Lords Spiritual and Temporal, and Commons, seriously considering how it hath pleased Almighty God, in his marvelous Providence, and merciful goodness to this Nation, to provide and preserve their said Majesties' Royal Persons most happily to reign over us upon the Throne of their Ancestors, for which they render unto him from the bottom of their hearts their humblest thanks and praises, do truly, firmly, assuredly, and in the sincerity of their hearts think, and do hereby recognize, acknowledge and declare, That King James the Second having abdicated the Government, and their Majesties having accepted the Crown and Royal Dignity as aforesaid, their said Majesties did become, were, are and of right ought to be, by the laws of this Realm, our Sovereign Liege Lord and Lady, King and Queen of England, France, and Ireland, and the Dominions thereunto belonging, in and to whose Princely Persons the Royal State, Crown and Dignity of the said Realms, with all Honours, Styles, Titles, Regalities, Prerogatives, Powers, Jurisdictions and Authorities to the same invested and incorporated, united and annexed.

MINISTERS OF THE CROWN ACT, 1937

Be it enacted by the King's most Excellent Majesty, by and with the advice and consent of the Lords Spiritual and Temporal, and Commons, in this present Parliament assembled, and by the authority of the same, as follows:—

PART I. SALARIES AND PENSION [1]

1. (1) The annual salaries payable—

(a) to each of the Ministers of the Crown named in Part I of the First Schedule to this Act, shall, subject to the provisions of this Act as to number, be five thousand pounds;

(b) to each of the Ministers of the Crown named in Part II of the said Schedule, shall be three thousand pounds;

(c) to the Minister of the Crown named in Part III of the said Schedule, shall be two thousand pounds.

(2) Subject to the provisions of this Act as to number, the annual salaries payable to the Parliamentary Undersecretaries to the Departments of State shall—

(a) in the case of the Parliamentary Secretary to the Treasury, be three thousand pounds, and in the case of the Financial Secretary to the Treasury, be two thousand pounds;

(b) in the case of the Secretary for Mines and of the Secretary of the Department of Overseas Trade, be two thousand pounds each;

(c) in the case of each of the Parliamentary Undersecretaries to the Departments of State specified in the Second Schedule to this Act, other than the Parliamentary Secretaries mentioned in the last foregoing paragraph, be fifteen hundred pounds;

(d) in the case of the Assistant Postmaster-General, be twelve hundred pounds;

Provided that, if and so long as there are two Parliamentary Undersecretaries to the Foreign Office, to the Admiralty, or to the War Office, the annual salary payable to each of the two Parliamentary Undersecretaries may be of such amount as may be determined by the Treasury, but so that the aggregate of the annual salaries payable to both of them does not exceed three thousand pounds.

(3) Subject to the provisions of this Act as to number, the annual salaries payable to each of the Junior Lords of the Treasury shall be one thousand pounds.

[1] The main provisions of the Act are still in force, but some changes in salaries were made in the Ministerial Salaries Act of 1946.

2. (1) The number of persons holding office as Secretary of State to whom salaries may be paid under this Act shall not exceed eight.

(2) The number of Parliamentary Undersecretaries to the Departments of State to whom salaries may be paid under this Act shall—

(a) in the case of the Treasury, not exceed two;

(b) in the case of the Board of Trade, not exceed three, including the Secretary for Mines and the Secretary of the Department of Overseas Trade;

(c) in the case of the Foreign Office, of the War Office, and of the Admiralty, not exceed two;

(d) in the case of any other Department of State mentioned in the Second Schedule to this Act, and in the case of the Post Office, not exceed one.

(3) The number of the Junior Lords of the Treasury to whom salaries may be paid under this Act shall not exceed five.

3. (1) If and so long as any Minister of the Crown to whom this section applies is a member of the Cabinet, there shall be paid to him an additional salary of such amount as together with the salary payable to him in respect of the office held by him will amount to five thousand pounds a year.

(2) The date upon which any Minister of the Crown to whom this section applies becomes or ceases to be a member of the Cabinet shall be published in the London Gazette, and any such notification shall be conclusive evidence for the purposes of this section. . . .

4. (1) There shall be paid to the person who is Prime Minister and First Lord of the Treasury an annual salary of ten thousand pounds.

(2) Any person who, whether before or after the passing of this Act, has been Prime Minister and has as First Lord of the Treasury taken the official oath prescribed by section five of the Promissory Oaths Act, 1868, shall be entitled to a pension of two thousand pounds a year:

Provided that no pension shall be payable under this subsection to any person so long as he is in receipt of any pension under the Political Offices Pension Act, 1869, or any salary payable out of moneys provided by Parliament, the revenues of the Duchy of Lancaster, or the Consolidated Fund of the United Kingdom.

5. There shall be paid to the Leader of the Opposition an annual salary of two thousand pounds:

Provided that, if the Leader of the Opposition is in receipt of a pension payable to him under this Act, no salary shall be payable to him under this section, and if he is in receipt of a pension under the Political Offices Pension Act, 1869, the salary payable to him under this section shall be reduced by an amount equal to the amount of that pension. . . .

6. (2) No person in receipt of a salary or pension under this Act shall be entitled to receive any sum out of moneys provided by Parliament by way of salary or allowance in respect of his membership of the House of Commons. . . .

PART II. CAPACITY TO SIT IN
THE HOUSE OF COMMONS

9. (1) Subject as hereinafter provided no person to whom a salary is payable under this Act shall by reason of his being the holder of the office or place in respect of which such a salary is payable, be rendered incapable of being elected, or of sitting and voting, as a member of the House of Commons:

Provided that—

(a) the number of persons entitled to sit and vote in that House while they are Ministers of the Crown named in Part I of the First Schedule to this Act shall not exceed fifteen;

(b) the number of persons entitled to sit and vote in that House while they are Ministers of the Crown named in Part II of the said Schedule shall not exceed three; and

(c) the number of persons entitled to sit and vote in that House while they are Parliamentary Undersecretaries shall not exceed twenty.

(2) If at any time the number of persons who are members of the House of Commons while they are Ministers of the Crown named in Part I or in Part II of the First Schedule to this Act, or while they are Parliamentary Undersecretaries, exceeds the number respectively entitled under this section to sit and vote in that House, the election of those members shall not be invalidated by reason of the excess, but of the number none except any who held his office and was a member of that House before the excess occurred, shall sit or vote therein until the number of Ministers of the Crown named in the said Part I or in the said Part II or of Parliamentary Undersecretaries, as the case may be, who are members of the House of Commons has been reduced, by death, resignation, or otherwise, to the number entitled under this section to sit and vote in that House.

(3) If any Minister of the Crown named in Part I or in Part II of the First Schedule to this Act or any Parliamentary Undersecretary sits or votes in the House of Commons at a time when he is not en-

titled to do so by virtue of this section he shall be liable to a penalty not exceeding five hundred pounds for each day on which he so sits or votes.

PART III. SUPPLEMENTARY

10. (1) In this Act unless the context otherwise requires the following expressions have the meanings hereby respectively assigned to them, that is to say:—

"Junior Lords of the Treasury" means the Lords Commissioners of the Treasury other than the First Lord and the Chancellor of the Exchequer;

"Leader of the Opposition" means that member of the House of Commons who is for the time being the Leader in that House of the party in opposition to His Majesty's Government having the greatest numerical strength in that House:

"Parliamentary Undersecretary" means the Parliamentary Secretary and the Financial Secretary to the Treasury, any Parliamentary Undersecretary of State, the Parliamentary and Financial Secretary to the Admiralty, the Financial Secretary of the War Office, the Civil Lord of the Admiralty, the Parliamentary Secretaries to the Departments of State specified in the Second Schedule to this Act, and the Assistant Postmaster-General; but does not include any Parliamentary Secretary to whom no salary is payable. . . .

(3) If any doubt arises as to which is or was at any material time the party in opposition to His Majesty's Government having the greatest numerical strength in the House of Commons, or as to who is or was at any material time the leader in that House of such a party, the question shall be decided for the purposes of this Act by the Speaker of the House of Commons, and his decision, certified in writing under his hand, shall be final and conclusive. . . .

The Government of France

DECLARATION OF THE RIGHTS OF MAN AND CITIZEN, AUGUST 26, 1789

The representatives of the French people, organized in National Assembly, considering that ignorance, forgetfulness or contempt of the rights of man, are the sole causes of the public miseries and of the corruption of governments, have resolved to set forth in a solemn declaration the natural, inalienable, and sacred rights of man, in order that this declaration, being ever present to all the members of the social body, may unceasingly remind them of their rights and their duties, in order that the acts of the legislative power and those of the executive power may be each moment compared with the aim of every political institution and thereby may be more respected; and in order that the demands of the citizens, grounded henceforth upon simple and incontestable principles, may always take the direction of maintaining the constitution and the welfare of all.

In consequence, the National Assembly recognizes and declares, in the presence and under the auspices of the Supreme Being, the following rights of man and citizen.

1. Men are born and remain free and equal in rights. Social distinctions can be based only upon public utility

2. The aim of every political association is the preservation of the natural and imprescriptible rights of man. These rights are liberty, property, security, and resistance to oppression.

3. The source of all sovereignty is essentially in the nation; no body, no individual can exercise authority that does not proceed from it in plain terms.

4. Liberty consists in the power to do anything that does not injure others; accordingly, the exercise of the natural rights of each man has no limits except those that secure to the other members of society the enjoyment of these same rights. These limits can be determined only by law.

5. The law has the right to forbid only such actions as are injurious to society. Nothing can be forbidden that is not interdicted by the law, and no one can be constrained to do that which it does not order.

6. Law is the expression of the general will. All citizens have the right to take part personally, or by their representatives, in its formation. It must be the same for all, whether it protects or punishes. All citizens being equal in its eyes, are equally eligible to all public dignities, places, and employments, according to their capacities, and without other distinc-

tion than that of their virtues and their talents.

7. No man can be accused, arrested, or detained, except in the cases determined by the law and according to the forms that it has prescribed. Those who procure, expedite, execute, or cause to be executed arbitrary orders ought to be punished: but every citizen summoned or seized in virtue of the law ought to render instant obedience; he makes himself guilty by resistance.

8. The law ought to establish only penalties that are strictly and obviously necessary, and no one can be punished except in virtue of a law established and promulgated prior to the offense and legally applied.

9. Every man being resumed innocent until he has been pronounced guilty, if it is thought indispensable to arrest him, all severity that may not be necessary to secure his person ought to be strictly suppressed by law.

10. No one should be disturbed on account of his opinions, even religious, provided their manifestation does not derange the public order established by law.

11. The free communication of ideas and opinions is one of the most precious of the rights of man; every citizen then can freely speak, write, and print, subject to responsibility for the abuse of this freedom in the cases determined by law.

12. The guarantee of the rights of man and citizen requires a public force; this force then is instituted for the advantage of all and not for the personal benefit of those to whom it is entrusted.

13. For the maintenance of the public force and for the expenses of administration a general tax is indispensable; it ought to be equally apportioned among all the citizens according to their means.

14. All the citizens have the right to ascertain, by themselves or by their representatives, the necessity of the public tax, to consent to it freely, to follow the employment of it, and to determine the quota, the assessment, the collection, and the duration of it.

15. Society has the right to call for an account of his administration from every public agent.

16. Any society in which the guarantee of the rights is not secured, or the separation of powers not determined, has no constitution at all.

17. Property being a sacred and inviolable right, no one can be deprived of it, unless a legally established public necessity evidently demands it, under the condition of a just and prior indemnity.

THE DRAFT CONSTITUTION OF 1946 *

DECLARATION OF THE RIGHTS OF MAN

Preamble:

On the day following the victory brought about by free peoples over the regimes which tried to enslave and debase man and which have just covered the world with blood, the French people, faithful to the principles of 1789—charter of its liberation—proclaims anew that each human being possesses inalienable and sacred rights, which no law may assail, and has decided, as in 1793, 1795, and 1848, to write them at the head of its Constitution.

The Republic guarantees to all men and all women living in the French Union the individual or collective exercise of the following liberties and rights.

I. LIBERTIES

ART. 1. All men are born and remain free and equal before the law.

The law guarantees women, in all domains, rights equal to those of men.

ART. 2. The origin of all sovereignty resides essentially in the people. No body of men, no individual can exercise any authority that does not emanate expressly from the people.

Law is the expression of the national will. It is the same for all, whether it protects, punishes, or obliges.

This will is expressed through the elected representatives of the people.

ART. 3. Freedom is the faculty of doing everything that does not infringe on the rights of others. The conditions of the exercise of freedom are defined by the law.

No one may be forced to do anything which the law does not command.

ART. 4. The law guarantees for all the equal exercise of the liberties and rights declared under this title; it cannot infringe upon them.

ART. 5. All men have the right to establish themselves anywhere and to move about freely.

ART. 6. All men persecuted in violation of the liberties and rights guaranteed by this declaration have the right of asylum in the territories of the Republic.

ART. 7. The home is inviolable. No search may take place except by virtue of the law, on written order emanating from judiciary authority.

ART. 8. The secrecy of all correspondence is inviolable. It cannot be infringed upon except by virtue of the law, under special decision emanating from judiciary authority.

ART. 9. No one can be pursued, arrested, or held except in cases determined by the law and according to forms prescribed by it.

* Rejected in the election of May 5, 1946 (see p. 326).

No one may be detained unless within forty-eight hours he has appeared before a judge called to rule upon the legality of the arrest and unless this judge confirms the detention each month by motivated decision.

All force or constraint not necessary for the apprehension or detention of a person, as well as all moral pressure or physical brutality, notably during interrogation, is forbidden.

Those who demand, edit, sign, execute, or cause acts to be executed in violation of these rules engage their personal responsibility. They will be punished.

ART. 10. The law can have no retroactive effect.

No one can be judged and punished except by virtue of a law promulgated and published prior to the punishable action.

Every accused person is deemed to be innocent until he has been declared guilty.

No one can be punished twice for the same act.

Penalties are personal and proportionate to the gravity of the infraction. Penalties of deprivation or restriction of liberty must tend toward the re-education of the guilty person. All treatment aggravating the penalty legally applicable entails the personal responsibility of its authors.

ART. 11. The law ensures to all men the right to have justice rendered them and lack of funds shall not hinder this.

ART. 12. In penal matters concurrent jurisdiction within the limits of the same territory is guaranteed to all inhabitants of the French Union.

ART. 13. No one shall be molested because of his origins, his opinions or beliefs in religious, philosophical, or political matters.

Freedom of conscience and religion is guaranteed by the neutrality of the State as regards all beliefs and all religions. It is guaranteed notably by the separation of the Churches from the State as well as by the fact that public powers and instruction are in the hands of lay authorities.

ART. 14. All men are free to speak, write, print, and publish. They may, either through the press or in any other manner, express, diffuse, and defend any opinion as long as they do not abuse this right notably in the violation of the liberties guaranteed by this declaration or in order unjustly to harm the reputation of another.

No manifestation of opinion may be imposed.

ART. 15. Everyone has the right to address a written petition to the public authorities in order to provoke an examination of problems of individual or collective interest.

ART. 16. The right of parading freely on public thoroughfares and the right of assembly are guaranteed to all.

ART. 17. All men have the right to associate unless this association infringes or may infringe on the liberties guaranteed in the present bill of rights.

No one can be forced to join an association.

ART. 18. Access to public functions is, without other conditions than those of capacity, aptitude, and talent, open to all subjects of the French Union enjoying the political rights given by this Constitution to the quality of citizen.

Access to all professions, positions, and private employment is open under the same conditions to all subjects of the French Union and, in the absence of special regulation fixed by law, to all people legally living in the French Union.

With equality of work, function, grade category, responsibilities, each person has the right to equality of material and moral situation.

ART. 19. The exercise of the rights guaranteed by this Declaration cannot be suspended.

However, when, under conditions determined by this Constitution, the Republic is declared to be in danger, the rights set forth in Articles 5, 8, 14 (first paragraph), and 16 may be suspended within the limits and forms determined by the law.

This measure may not be taken for a duration of more than six months; it may be renewed in the same manner.

Anyone who shall have abused this right to arbitrarily harm the material or moral rights of others will be held personally responsible.

During the period of suspension, anyone who shall consider himself arbitrarily wronged in his person or property may claim moral or material reparation before the courts.

ART. 20. The guarantee of the rights of men and of citizens necessitates a public force; this force, instituted for the advantage of all and not for the particular use of those in whom it is confided, must remain permanently in the service of the sovereign people.

ART. 21. When the government violates the liberties and rights guaranteed by the Constitution, resistance in all its forms is the most sacred of rights and the most imperious of duties.

II. SOCIAL AND ECONOMIC RIGHTS

ART. 22. Every human being possesses with regard to society rights that guarantee, in the integrity and dignity of his person, his full physical, intellectual, and moral development.

The law organizes the exercise of these rights.

ART. 23. The protection of health from the time of conception, the benefits of all measures of hygiene and of all the care which science permits, are guaranteed to all and ensured by the nation.

ART. 24. The nation guarantees to the family the necessary conditions for its free development.

It protects equally all mothers and all children by legislation and by appropriate social institutions.

It guarantees to woman the exercise of her functions of citizen and worker under conditions that permit her to fulfill her role of mother and her social mission.

ART. 25. The widest culture should be offered to all with no other limitation than the aptitudes of each. Each child has a right to instruction and education in respect of liberty.

The organization of public education on all levels is a duty of the State.

This education must be free and made accessible to all by material aid to those who, without it, would not be able to continue their studies.

ART. 26. It is the duty of every man to work and he has the right to obtain employment.

No one, in employment, may be discriminated against because of his origins, his opinions, or his beliefs.

ART. 27. The duration and conditions of work must not affect either the health, dignity, or family life of the worker.

Adolescents must not be forced to a work which hampers their physical, intellectual or moral development. They have a right to professional training.

ART. 28. Men and women have a right to a just remuneration according to the quality and quantity of their work, and in any case to those resources necessary to enable them and their families to live decently.

ART. 29. Everyone has a right to rest and leisure.

ART. 30. Every man has the right to defend his interests by trade-union activity.

Each shall belong to the union of his choice or to none.

ART. 31. Each worker has the right to participate through the intermediary of his delegates in the collective determination of conditions of work as well as in the management of enterprises.

ART. 32. The right to strike is recognized for all within the framework of the laws which regulate it.

ART. 33. Every human being who, by reason of his age, his physical or mental state of being, his economic situation, finds himself unable to work, has the right to obtain from the community proper means of subsistence.

The guarantee of this right is assured by the institution of public bodies of social security.

ART. 34. The losses caused by national calamities to persons or property are supported by the nation. The Republic proclaims the equality and solidarity of all in facing the burdens which result from them.

ART. 35. Property is the inviolable right to use, enjoy, and dispose of the goods guaranteed to each person by the law. Every man must be able to acquire property by work and thrift.

No one may be deprived of it unless it is for a

public purpose stated in law and on condition of a just indemnity fixed in conformity with the law.

ART. 36. The right of property may not be exercised in violation of social purposes or in such a way as to be detrimental to the security, liberty, existence, or property of others.

Every property or enterprise whose exploitation has or acquires the characteristics of a national public function or of a monopoly in fact must become the property of the community.

ART. 37. Participation of everyone in public expenses must be progressive and calculated with relation to the importance of the fortune and income of each, account being taken of family burdens.

ART. 38. No one can be placed in an inferior economic, social, or political position not in keeping with his qualifications and permitting his exploitation because of his sex, age, color, nationality, religion, opinions, ethnic origin, or for other reasons.

The exercise of the liberties and rights recognized as belonging to all subjects of the French Union implies condemnation of every practice of forced labor not in accord with the conditions of work established by law for metropolitan France.

Any propaganda contrary to the above dispositions will be punished by law.

ART. 39. The safeguarding of the rights inscribed in the present Declaration, the maintenance of democratic institutions, and social progress demand that all shall know and fill their duties: the citizens must serve the Republic, defend it at the price of their lives, participate in State expenses, contribute to the common good by their work and help each other fraternally.

INSTITUTIONS OF THE REPUBLIC

I. SOVEREIGNTY AND THE NATIONAL ASSEMBLY

ART. 40. France is a Republic, indivisible, democratic, and social.

ART. 41. France constitutes, with the overseas territories on one hand, and, with its associated States on the other, a union formed by free consent.

ART. 42. The national emblem is the tricolor flag, blue, white, and red, in three vertical bands.

The motto of the Republic is: "Liberty, Equality, Fraternity."

ART. 43. Sovereignty belongs to the people. It is exercised in conformity with the Constitution.

ART. 44. All subjects of the French Union enjoy the rights and liberties of man guaranteed by Articles 1 through 39 of the present Constitution.

All French nationals and subjects of the metropolitan and overseas territories enjoy the rights of citizenship.

ART. 45. Those whose place of origin is in overseas territories, and for whom the law recognizes a personal status, retain this status as long as they themselves have not renounced it.

This status may in no case constitute a reason for refusing or limiting the rights and liberties guaranteed by Articles 1 to 39 of the present Constitution.

ART. 46. The French Republic, faithful to its traditions, conforms to the rules of public international law. It will undertake no war with a view to conquest and will never employ its forces against the liberty of any people.

Under the reserve of reciprocity, France consents to the limitations of sovereignty necessary for the organization and defense of the peace.

ART. 47. The French people exercises its sovereignty through its Deputies in the National Assembly, elected by universal, equal, direct and secret suffrage.

The Constitution can only be modified by means of a referendum, in conformity with Article 119.

ART. 48. The overseas territories, under the conditions fixed by the electoral laws, elect Deputies to the National Assembly.

ART. 49. The electorate is composed of all French nationals and subjects of both sexes who have reached their majority and enjoy civil and political rights.

The age of majority is fixed at 20 years of age.

ART. 50. The Deputies of the National Assembly are elected for five years. The powers of an Assembly cease at the moment the new Assembly enters upon its functions.

Electors of both sexes at least 23 years of age are eligible to become Deputies. The causes of ineligibility and disqualification are fixed by law.

ART. 51. The National Assembly elects the President of the Council of Ministers in conformity with Articles 73 and 91 below.

ART. 52. War cannot be declared without the previous consent of the National Assembly and the previous advice of the Council of the French Union.

ART. 53. The National Assembly validates the election of its members. The procedure for the control of the regularity of electoral operations is determined by law.

ART. 54. The National Assembly meets by sole operation of law in annual session the second Tuesday in January.

The total duration of interruptions of the session cannot exceed four months. Adjournments of session for more than ten days are considered interruptions of the session.

ART. 55. The sessions of the National Assembly are public. Full reports of its debates are published in the Official Journal.

The Assembly may convene in secret committee.

It decides whether the subject debated in secret committee must again be taken up in a public session and whether the complete report of the debates held in secret committee must be published.

ART. 56. The National Assembly elects its officers each year at the beginning of its session on the principle of proportional representation of the various groups.

ART. 57. When the Assembly is not in session, its officers supervise the actions of the Cabinet. They may convene the Assembly; they must do so upon the request of one third of the Deputies or upon that of the Council of Ministers.

ART. 58. No Deputy may be prosecuted, called to account, arrested, detained, or tried because of opinions expressed or votes cast by him in the exercise of his duties.

ART. 59. No Deputy, during his term of office, can be prosecuted or arrested for felonies or misdemeanors, without authorization by the National Assembly except in cases of apprehension while committing the unlawful act. The detention or prosecution of a Deputy is to be suspended if the Assembly demands it.

ART. 60. The Deputies receive compensation guaranteeing both their independence and the dignity of their station.

The law fixes this compensation with reference to the salaries of a certain category of officials.

ART. 61. The members of the National Assembly cannot belong either to the Council of the French Union or to the Economic Council.

II. THE MAKING OF LAWS

ART. 62. The President of the Council of Ministers and the Deputies have the right to propose laws.

ART. 63. The National Assembly studies the drafts and proposals of laws brought before it by its commissions. It will fix the number, composition and jurisdiction of these commissions.

ART. 64. The Economic Council examines in an advisory capacity drafts and proposals of laws which come under its jurisdiction. The National Assembly submits these drafts to the Economic Council before deliberating upon them.

The opinion must be rendered within ten days, failing which it is dispensed with. This term may be reduced to two full days if the National Assembly so decides.

The Economic Council may furthermore be consulted by the Council of Ministers. Such consultation is mandatory for the establishment of a national economic plan whose object is full employment of men and the reasonable utilization of material resources.

ART. 65. The Economic Council is elected for a term of three years.

An organic law determines the composition and competence of the Economic Council.

III. THE DISCUSSION AND VOTING OF LAWS

ART. 66. The National Assembly alone has the right to legislate. It may not delegate this right to anyone in whole or in part.

Unless otherwise stipulated, the laws of the Re-public are applicable in the departments and overseas territories.

ART. 67. Diplomatic treaties regularly ratified and published have the force of law. Unless otherwise stipulated, they apply by sole operation of law to departments and overseas territories.

ART. 68. Treaties relative to international organization, peace treaties, treaties of commerce, treaties involving the finances of the State, and treaties concerning the status of persons and property rights of Frenchmen abroad, become definitive only after having been voted upon by the National Assembly. No cession, no exchange, no addition of territory may take place except by virtue of a law.

ART. 69. The National Assembly votes on the budget. Its members have the right to initiate appropriations.

ART. 70. Amnesty may only be granted by a law.

ART. 71. The Council of the French Union is made up of Councilors elected by the general councils of the departments of Metropolitan France and by the general councils or territorial assemblies of Overseas France.

ART. 72. The Council of the French Union is elected for a term of four years.

Its sessions are public and full reports are published in a special bulletin.

The Council of the French Union meets at the same time as the National Assembly. It cannot prolong its session beyond the time provided for the second reading of the texts it is studying.

ART. 72 *bis*. The Council of the French Union examines in an advisory capacity the drafts and proposals of laws sent to it either at its request, or by the Council of Ministers or the National Assembly. It renders its opinion within the month following transmittal by the National Assembly. When the National Assembly declares existence of a special need, the Council of the French Union will render its opinion within the same time limit as that provided for the debates of the National Assembly by the ruling of the latter.

If the Council of the French Union concurs or if its opinion is not rendered in the period provided for in the preceding paragraph, the law is promulgated in the text voted by the National Assembly.

If the Council does not concur, the National Assembly proceeds to a second reading. It decides definitively and sovereignly on the amendments proposed by the Council of the French Union.

ART. 72 *ter*. No legal action can be instituted on the basis of speeches made in the Council of the French Union, reports, or any other documents printed by order of the Council of the French Union.

Unless apprehended while committing the unlawful act, no Councilor, during his term of office, may be prosecuted or arrested for felonies or misdemeanors without the authorization of the National Assembly given upon the advice of the Council of the French Union. The detention or prosecution of a Councilor is to be suspended if the National Assembly demands it.

The Councilors of the French Union receive a compensation fixed by law.

ART. 72 *quater*. The members of the Council of the French Union cannot belong to the Economic Council.

IV. THE COUNCIL OF MINISTERS

ART. 73. The National Assembly elects the President of the Council of Ministers at the beginning of each legislative term by open ballot and an absolute majority of the Deputies.

The same procedure is followed during the legislative session to fill a vacancy caused by death, resignation, or any other cause, except that dealt with in Article 82 below.

ART. 74. Suppressed.

ART. 75. The President of the Council and the Ministers chosen by him are appointed by decree of the President of the Republic.

ART. 76. It is the duty of the President of the Council of Ministers to see to it that the laws are executed.

He makes all civil and military appointments except those provided for in Articles 75 and 93.

Instruments issued by the President of the Council of Ministers under the authority of this Article must be countersigned by the competent Ministers.

ART. 77. The structure, composition, and program of the Cabinet are submitted to the National Assembly, which gives or refuses a vote of confidence.

The Assembly must be summoned for this purpose the fourth day following the formation of the Cabinet at the latest.

ART. 78. The Ministers are collectively responsible to the National Assembly for the general policy of the Cabinet and individually responsible for their own acts.

ART. 79. The request for a vote of confidence may only be made after deliberation of the Council of Ministers; it may only be made by the President of the Council.

The actual vote can only come one full day after the request has been placed before the Assembly. It takes place by open ballot.

The vote of confidence may only be refused to the Cabinet by the absolute majority of the Deputies in the Assembly.

This refusal carries with it the collective resignation of the Cabinet.

ART. 80. If the National Assembly votes a motion of censure, the collective resignation of the Cabinet ensues.

This vote may only take place two full days after the motion has been made in the Assembly. It takes place by open ballot and roll call.

The motion of censure can only be adopted by the absolute majority of the Deputies in the Assembly.

ART. 81. The National Assembly has the right to declare itself dissolved by a resolution voted by a two-thirds majority of the Deputies.

ART. 81 *bis*. If, in the course of the same annual session, two ministerial crises occur under the conditions provided for in Articles 79 and 80, the dissolution of the National Assembly may be decided by the Council of Ministers upon the recommendation of the President of the Assembly. The dissolution will be pronounced in conformity with this decision by a decree of the President of the Republic.

This provision is not applicable during the first half of the legislative term.

ART. 82. The President of the Republic appoints the President of the National Assembly as new President of the Council of Ministers. The latter forms the Cabinet by assigning the different ministerial departments to the presidents of the corresponding parliamentary commissions.

Within forty days after the dissolution, the new Cabinet proceeds to general elections.

Except in the case mentioned in Article 102 below, the National Assembly meets by sole operation of law the fifteenth day after its election, to elect a new President of the Council of Ministers.

ART. 83. The Ministers may appear before the National Assembly, its commissions, and consultative bodies. They must be heard when they request it.

They may have the assistance of commissioners designated by decree.

ART. 84. The President of the Council of Ministers may delegate his powers to a Minister.

ART. 85. In case of vacancy because of death or any other reason, the Council of Ministers charges one of its members to carry out temporarily the duties of the President of the Council of Ministers.

V. THE CRIMINAL RESPONSIBILITY OF THE MINISTERS

ART. 86. Ministers are criminally responsible for felonies and misdemeanors committed in the exercise of their functions.

ART. 87. Ministers are indicted by the National Assembly only on a secret ballot and by an absolute majority of its members. Such indictments are tried by the High Court of Justice provided for in Article 88 below. Titular and deputy members of the High Court of Justice do not participate in the voting and are not counted in the determination of the majority.

ART. 88. The High Court of Justice is elected by the National Assembly at the beginning of each legislative term.

It is composed of thirty members: twenty elected

from among the members of the Assembly in proportion to the strength of the various groups, and ten elected from persons not members of the Assembly by absolute majority of the Assembly.

Thirty deputy members are elected under the same conditions.

Art. 89. The organization of the prosecutor's office of the High Court of Justice and the rules of procedure applied before it are determined by a special law.

VI. THE PRESIDENT OF THE REPUBLIC

Art. 90. The President of the Republic is elected by the National Assembly. This election takes place by open ballot, and roll call requires a two-thirds majority of the Deputies in the Assembly. If after three attempts this majority cannot be secured, the election is postponed until the next day. It takes place then in the same manner, a three-fifths majority being required.

The President of the Republic is elected for a term of seven years. He can only be re-elected once.

Art. 91. The President of the Republic, after the customary consultations, communicates to the National Assembly the names of the candidates for the presidency of the Council of Ministers.

Art. 92. He represents the permanent interest of the French Union and presides over national ceremonies.

Art. 93. In the Council of Ministers he appoints the Councilors of State, the Grand Chancellor of the Legion of Honor, Ambassadors and Envoys Extraordinary, Residents General, and the members of the Supreme Council of National Defense.

Art. 94. The President of the Republic is kept informed of the negotiation of treaties. He signs and ratifies them.

The President of the Republic accredits Ambassadors and Envoys Extraordinary are accredited to him.

Art. 95. The President of the Republic commands the Armed Forces.

Art. 96. The President of the Republic presides over the Council of Ministers. He provides for the recording and maintenance of minutes of the meetings.

Art. 97. He presides with the same functions over the High Council of National Defense.

Art. 98. The President of the Republic presides over the Superior Council of Magistracy.

Art. 99. He promulgates laws within the ten days following their transmission by the National Assembly. In order to provide for their execution, he signs implementing decrees.

The period foreseen in the preceding paragraph is reduced to two days when a special need has been declared.

If the President of the Republic does not promulgate laws within the stipulated period, the President of the National Assembly provides for their promulgation.

Art. 100. Each instrument of the President of the Republic must be countersigned by the President of the Council of Ministers and by one Minister.

Art. 101. Thirty days at the earliest, fifteen days at the latest before the expiration of the powers of the President of the Republic, the National Assembly proceeds to the election of the new President.

Art. 102. If, in the application of the preceding Article, the election must take place in a period when the National Assembly is dissolved in conformity with Articles 81 and 81 *bis,* the powers of the incumbent President of the Republic are extended until the election of the new President. The new Assembly proceeds to the election of this new President within ten days of its own election. In this case, the election of the new President of the Council of Ministers takes place within ten days after the election of the new President of the Republic.

Art. 103. In the event that the post becomes vacant because of death, resignation, or any other cause, the President of the National Assembly assumes *ad interim* the functions of the President of the Republic.

The new President of the Republic is elected within ten days except for the case indicated in the preceding article.

Art. 104. The President of the Republic is only responsible in a case of high treason.

He is indicted by the National Assembly and tried before the High Court of Justice under the conditions described in Article 87 above.

Art. 105. The President of the Republic communicates with the people by means of messages addressed to the National Assembly. These messages are read in the Assembly by its president after his approval and that of the President of the Council of Ministers have been secured.

Art. 106. The President of the Republic may hold no other public elective office.

Art. 107. Members of families which have ruled over France are ineligible for the presidency of the Republic.

VII. THE SUPERIOR COUNCIL OF MAGISTRACY

Art. 108. The Superior Council of Magistracy is made up of twelve members:

The President of the Republic, President;

The Keeper of Seals and Minister of Justice, Vice President;

Six persons elected for a six-year term by a two-thirds majority of the National Assembly, and chosen from outside of its own members, six Deputies being elected under the same conditions;

Four magistrates elected for a six-year term: one by the Presidents and Councilors at the Court of

Cassation, one by the Presidents and Councilors of the Courts of Appeal, one by the Presidents and Judges of the Tribunals of First Instance, one by the Justices of the Peace, four Deputies being elected under the same conditions.

The decisions of the Superior Council of Magistracy are taken by a majority of votes. In case the votes are equal that of the President decides.

ART. 109. The President of the Republic in the Superior Council of Magistracy appoints the magistrates with the exception of those on the prosecuting staff.

Under the same conditions and in accordance with the law the Superior Council of Magistracy provides for the rules and regulations of the magisterial office, the independence of the magistrates and the administration of the courts of law.

ART. 110. The Superior Council of Magistracy has the right of pardon.

VIII. LOCAL COMMUNITIES

ART. 111. The French Republic, one and indivisible, recognizes the existence of territorial communities.

These communities are the communes and departments, the overseas territories, and federations. They administer themselves freely, in conformity with national law.

ART. 112. The framework, scope, possible regrouping, and organization of the communes and departments, overseas territories, and federations are fixed by law.

ART. 113. The local communities are administered on the different levels by councils elected by universal suffrage and under the conditions established by the electoral laws. The execution of their decisions is provided for by their mayor or president.

ART. 114. The coordination of the activities of State officials, the representation of national interests, and the administrative control of local communities are provided for within the departmental framework by delegates of the government designated in the Council of Ministers.

ART. 114 *bis*. The law will determine the conditions under which the General Council will administer departmental affairs. The president of the General Council, assisted by his office, will provide, on a permanent basis, for the execution of decisions made by the General Council.

The law will furthermore so determine the conditions under which local branches of central departments will function as to bring them in close relation to the local administration.

ART. 115. The special interests of the overseas territories are administered and managed by local assemblies, elected by direct universal suffrage. Their electoral regime, composition, and jurisdiction are determined by special laws which assure freedom of voting.

These territories which form a group or a federation elect an assembly whose composition and jurisdiction are fixed by special laws.

ART. 116. In each federation or group of territories, the Minister in charge of all the problems of Overseas France is assisted by a resident Undersecretary of State.

The latter supervises the application of the laws. He coordinates the public services of the French Union and controls the functioning of the local administrations.

He is responsible for the maintenance of order and for the defense of the group or federation of territories.

IX. EXCEPTIONAL PROVISIONS

ART. 117. Any law which proclaims the Republic to be in danger must have been enacted by a two-thirds majority of the National Assembly.

The law will determine, if necessary, the conditions under which the terms of office of Deputies, Councilors of the French Union, Members of the Economic Council, and elected members of the Superior Council of Magistracy will be extended.

During the period in which the law mentioned in the first paragraph of the present Article is inoperative, Articles 81 and 81 *bis* cease to be operative.

ART. 118. During periods of hostilities, special laws determine, if necessary, the conditions under which the terms of office of Deputies, Councilors of the French Union, members of the Economic Council, and elected members of the Superior Council of Magistracy will be extended.

During the same periods, the operation of Articles 81 and 81 *bis* is suspended.

X. REVISION OF THE CONSTITUTION

ART. 119. The present Constitution, adopted by the French people, can only be revised by the people.

Revision takes place in the following manner:

The National Assembly, by a resolution taken by open ballot and roll call with the majority of Deputies assenting, declares that the Constitution should be revised.

The resolution will specify the object of the revision.

It is submitted to a second reading after a minimum period of three months. After this second reading, the National Assembly drafts a law revising the Constitution. This draft is passed by a majority and in the form prescribed for an ordinary law.

This draft is submitted to a referendum.

In case of adoption by the people, it is promulgated

as a constitutional law by the President of the Republic within the eight days following the date of the referendum.

ART. 119 *bis*. In case all or a part of the metropolitan territory is occupied by foreign forces, no procedure for revision can be instituted or continued.

ART. 120. The republican form of government cannot be the object of a proposed revision.

XI. TRANSITORY PROVISIONS

ART. 121. The office of the National Constituent Assembly has the duty of providing permanent national representation until the meeting of the Deputies in the new National Assembly.

ART. 122. In the case of exceptional circumstances, the Deputies now in office in the National Constituent Assembly may, until the date prescribed in the preceding Article, be called in session by the office of the Assembly, either on its own initiative, or at the request of the government.

ART. 122 *bis*. The President of the Provisional Government of the Republic will place his resignation in the hands of the President of the Republic upon the election of the latter by the National Assembly, in accordance with the terms of Article 90 above.

ART. 123. The office of the National Constituent Assembly is charged with preparing the meeting of the assemblies established by the present Constitution, and, especially, with providing, even before the meetings of their respective offices for the places and administrative means necessary to their functioning.

ART. 124. The Council of the French Union will meet by sole operation of law immediately after its election. Within a maximum period of three months after the meeting of the National Assembly, it may validly deliberate as soon as two thirds of its members have been declared elected.

ART. 124 *bis*. The election of the first Council of the French Union will proceed in the following manner:

A College of Delegates will be elected, in each department of metropolitan France, by direct universal suffrage and with proportional representation.

A law will determine the circumstances in which, in that case, the departmental Colleges of Delegates will be grouped in order to assure the election of the Council of the French Union on a basis of proportional representation.

ART. 125. Until the organization of the Economic Council and with a maximum delay of three months from the time of the first meeting of the National Assembly, the application of Article 64 of the present Constitution will be suspended.

ART. 126. The present Constitution will enter into force the day of the first meeting of the National Assembly.

The National Assembly will meet, by sole operation of law, the fourth Tuesday following the general elections.

ART. 127. The present Constitution will be promulgated by the President of the Provisory Government of the Republic within two days after the publication of the results of the referendum and in the following form:

"The National Constituent Assembly has adopted,
"The French people has approved,
"The President of the Provisional Government of the Republic promulgates the Constitution whose text follows":

THE CONSTITUTION OF THE FRENCH REPUBLIC, 1946 *

The National Constituent Assembly has adopted,
The French people has approved,
The President of the Provisional Government of the Republic promulgates the Constitution that follows:

PREAMBLE

On the morrow of the victory of the free peoples over the regimes that attempted to enslave and degrade the human person, the French people proclaims once more that every human being, without distinction of race, religion, or belief, possesses inalienable and sacred rights. It solemnly reaffirms the rights and freedoms of man and of the citizen consecrated by the Declaration of Rights of 1789 and the fundamental principles recognized by the laws of the Republic.

* Adopted in the election of October 13, 1946 (see p. 328).

It further proclaims as most vital in our time the following political, economic, and social principles:

The law guarantees to women equal rights with men in all domains.

Anyone persecuted because of his activities in the cause of freedom has the right of asylum within the territories of the Republic.

Everyone has the duty to work and the right to obtain employment. No one may suffer in his work or his employment because of his origin, his opinions, or his beliefs.

Everyone may defend his rights and interests by trade-union action and may join the union of his choice.

The right to strike may be exercised within the framework of the laws that govern it.

Every worker through his delegates may participate

in collective bargaining to determine working conditions, as well as in the management of business.

All property and all enterprises that now have or subsequently shall have the character of a national public service or a monopoly in fact must become the property of the community.

The nation ensures to the individual and the family the conditions necessary to their development.

It guarantees to all, and notably to the child, the mother, and the aged worker, protection of health, material security, rest, and leisure. Every human being who, because of his age, his physical or mental condition, or because of the economic situation, finds himself unable to work, has the right to obtain from the community the means to lead a decent existence.

The nation proclaims the solidarity and equality of all Frenchmen with regard to the burdens resulting from national disasters.

The nation guarantees equal access of children and adults to education, professional training, and culture. The establishment of free, secular, public education on all levels is a duty of the State.

The French Republic, faithful to its traditions, abides by the rules of international public law. It will not undertake wars of conquest and will never use its arms against the freedom of any people.

On condition of reciprocity, France accepts the limitations of sovereignty necessary to the organization and defense of peace.

France forms with the people of its overseas territories a Union based upon equality of rights and duties without distinction of race or religion.

The French Union is composed of nations and peoples who wish to place in common or coordinate their resources and their efforts in order to develop their civilization, increase their well-being, and ensure their security.

Faithful to her traditional mission, France proposes to guide the peoples for whom she has assumed responsibility toward freedom to govern themselves and democratically to manage their own affairs; putting aside any system of colonization based upon arbitrary power, she guarantees to all equal access to public office and the individual or collective exercise of the rights and liberties proclaimed or confirmed above.

THE INSTITUTIONS OF THE REPUBLIC

TITLE I. SOVEREIGNTY

ART. 1. France is a republic, indivisible, secular, democratic, and social.

ART. 2. The national emblem is the tricolor flag—blue, white, and red—in three vertical bands of equal dimensions.

The national anthem is the *Marseillaise.*

The motto of the Republic is—"Liberty, Equality, Fraternity."

Its principle is: government of the people, for the people, and by the people.

ART. 3. National sovereignty belongs to the French people.

No section of the people nor any individual may assume its exercise.

The people shall exercise it in constitutional matters by the vote of their representatives or by the referendum.

In all other matters they shall exercise it through their Deputies in the National Assembly, elected by universal, equal, direct, and secret suffrage.

ART. 4. All French citizens and nationals of both sexes, who are majors and enjoy civil and political rights, may vote under conditions determined by the law.

TITLE II. THE PARLIAMENT

ART. 5. The Parliament shall be composed of the National Assembly and the Council of the Republic.

ART. 6. The duration of the powers of each Assembly, its mode of election, the conditions of eligibility, and the bases of ineligibilities and incompatibilities shall be determined by the law.

However, the two Chambers shall be elected on a territorial basis, the National Assembly by universal, direct suffrage, the Council of the Republic by the communal and departmental bodies by universal, indirect suffrage. The Council of the Republic is renewable one-half at a time.

Nevertheless, the National Assembly may itself elect by proportional representation councilors whose numbers shall not exceed one sixth of the total number of members of the Council of the Republic.

The number of members of the Council of the Republic may not be less than 250 nor more than 320.

ART. 7.[1] War may not be declared without a vote of the National Assembly and the concurrent opinion of the Council of the Republic.

ART. 8. Each of the two Chambers shall pass upon the eligibility of its members and the regularity of their elections; it alone may receive their resignation.

ART. 9.[1] The National Assembly shall convene by right every year on the second Tuesday in January.

The total duration of the interruptions of each session may not exceed four months. Adjournments of more than ten days shall be considered as interruptions.

The Council of the Republic shall sit at the same time as the National Assembly.

ART. 10. The meetings of the two Chambers shall be public. Reports of the debates *in extenso,* as well as the parliamentary documents, shall be published in the *Journal Officiel.*

Each of the two Chambers may convene as a secret committee.

[1] See Amendments, p. *xxv.*

Art. 11.[2] Each of the two Chambers shall elect its secretariat every year, at the beginning of the session, by proportional representation of party groups.

When the two Chambers meet together to elect the President of the Republic, their secretariat shall be that of the National Assembly.

Art. 12.[2] When the National Assembly is not sitting, its secretariat, exercising control over the actions of the Council of Ministers, may convoke the Parliament; it must do this upon the request of one third of the Deputies or of the President of the Council of Ministers.

Art. 13. The National Assembly alone shall adopt the laws. It may not delegate this right.

Art. 14.[2] The President of the Council of Ministers and the members of the Parliament shall have the initiative in legislation.

Bills and proposed laws introduced by members of the National Assembly shall be filed with its secretariat.

Proposed laws introduced by members of the Council of the Republic shall be filed with its secretariat and sent without debate to the secretariat of the National Assembly. They may not be received if they would result in the reduction of revenues or the creation of new expenditures.

Art. 15. The National Assembly shall study the bills and proposed laws submitted to it in its committees, of which it shall determine the number, the composition and the jurisdiction.

Art. 16. The proposed budget shall be submitted to the National Assembly.

This bill may include only such provisions as are strictly financial.

An organic law shall regulate the method of presentation of the budget.

Art. 17. The Deputies of the National Assembly shall have the right to initiate appropriations.

However, no proposals which would tend to increase appropriations already decided upon or create new ones may be presented during the discussion of the budget and of prospective or supplementary appropriations.

Art. 18. The National Assembly shall regulate the accounts of the nation.

It shall be assisted in this task by the *Cour des Comptes*.

The National Assembly may entrust to the *Cour des Comptes* all investigations or studies concerning public revenues and expenditures or the administration of the Treasury.

Art. 19. Amnesty may not be granted except by a law.

Art. 20.[2] The Council of the Republic shall examine, in order to give its opinion thereon, the bills and proposed laws passed on first reading by the National Assembly.

It shall give its opinion not more than two months after a measure is sent to it by the National Assembly. When the budget law is under discussion, this time may be reduced, if need be, to such time as does not exceed that taken by the National Assembly for its consideration and vote. When the National Assembly has adopted a rule for emergency procedure, the Council of the Republic shall give its opinion within the same time as that provided for debate by the rule of the National Assembly. The time limit specified in the present Article shall be suspended during interruptions of the session. It may be extended by a decision of the National Assembly.

If the opinion of the Council of the Republic is in agreement with that of the National Assembly or if it has not been given within the time limit specified in the preceding paragraph, the law shall be promulgated as passed by the National Assembly.

If this opinion is not in agreement with that of the National Assembly, the latter body shall examine the bill or proposed law on second reading. It shall dispose definitively and absolutely of the amendments proposed by the Council of the Republic, accepting or rejecting them in whole or in part. When these amendments are completely or partially rejected, the vote on second reading of the law shall be by roll call and by an absolute majority of the members of the National Assembly, if the vote on the whole has been taken under the same conditions by the Council of the Republic.

Art. 21. No member of the Parliament may be prosecuted, sought by the police, arrested, detained, or tried because of opinions expressed or votes cast by him in the exercise of his function.

Art. 22.[3] No member of the Parliament may be prosecuted or arrested during his term of office for a criminal offense except with the authorization of the Chamber of which he is a member, or in the case of a major crime. The detention or prosecution of a member of the Parliament shall be suspended if the Chamber of which he is a member requests it.

Art. 23. Members of the Parliament shall receive compensation fixed in relation to that of a given grade of civil servants.

Art. 24. No one may be a member both of the National Assembly and of the Council of the Republic. Members of the Parliament may not be members of the Economic Council or of the Assembly of the French Union.

TITLE III. THE ECONOMIC COUNCIL

Art. 25. An Economic Council whose statutes shall be determined by law, shall examine the bills and proposed laws within its purview in order to give its

---

[2] See Amendments, p. *xxv*.

[3] See Amendments, p. *xxvi*.

opinion thereon. The National Assembly shall send such bills to this Council before considering them.

The Economic Council may also be consulted by the Council of Ministers. It must be consulted by that body concerning the establishment of a national economic plan for full employment and the rational utilization of our material resources.

TITLE IV. DIPLOMATIC TREATIES

ART. 26. Diplomatic treaties duly ratified and published shall have the force of law even when they are contrary to internal French legislation; they shall require for their application no legislative acts other than those necessary to ensure their ratification.

ART. 27. Treaties relative to international organization, peace treaties, commercial treaties, treaties that involve national finances, treaties relative to the personal status and property rights of French citizens abroad, and those that modify French internal legislation, as well as those that involve the cession, exchange, or addition of territories shall not become final until they have been ratified by a legislative act.

No cession, no exchange, and no addition of territory shall be valid without the consent of the populations concerned.

ART. 28. Since diplomatic treaties duly ratified and published have superior authority to that of French internal legislation, their provisions shall not be abrogated, modified, or suspended without previous formal denunciation through diplomatic channels. Whenever a treaty such as those mentioned in Article 27 is concerned, such denunciation must be approved by the National Assembly, except in the case of commercial treaties.

TITLE V. THE PRESIDENT OF THE REPUBLIC

ART. 29. The President of the Republic shall be elected by the Parliament.

He shall be elected for seven years. He shall be eligible for re-election only once.

ART. 30. The President of the Republic shall appoint in the Council of Ministers the Councilors of State, the Grand Chancellor of the Legion of Honor, the ambassadors and special envoys, the members of the Superior Council and the Committee for National Defense, the rectors of the universities, the prefects, the chiefs of the central administrative services, the general officers and the Government representatives in the overseas territories.

ART. 31. The President of the Republic shall be kept informed of the progress of international negotiations. He shall sign and ratify all treaties.

The President of the Republic shall accredit ambassadors and special envoys to foreign powers; foreign ambassadors and special envoys shall be accredited to him.

ART. 32. The President of the Republic shall preside over the Council of Ministers. He shall order the minutes of their meetings to be recorded and shall keep them in his possession.

ART. 33. The President of the Republic shall preside in the same capacity over the Superior Council and the Committee for National Defense, and shall have the title of Commander in Chief of the Armed Forces.

ART. 34. The President of the Republic shall preside over the Superior Council of the Judiciary.

ART. 35. The President of the Republic shall have the right of pardon in the Superior Council of the Judiciary.

ART. 36. The President of the Republic shall promulgate the laws within ten days after their text, as finally adopted, has been sent to the Government. This interval may be reduced to five days if the National Assembly declares an emergency.

Within the time limit fixed for promulgation of a law, the President of the Republic, in a message stating his reasons, may ask that it be reconsidered by both Chambers; this reconsideration may not be refused.

If the President of the Republic does not promulgate a law within the time limit fixed by the present Constitution, the President of the National Assembly shall promulgate it.

ART. 37. The President of the Republic shall communicate with the Parliament by means of messages addressed to the National Assembly.

ART. 38. Every act of the President of the Republic must be countersigned by the President of the Council of Ministers and by a Minister.

ART. 39. Not more than thirty and not less than fifteen days before the expiration of the term of office of the President of the Republic, the Parliament shall elect a new President.

ART. 40. If, in the application of the preceding article, the election must take place during the period when the National Assembly is dissolved in conformity with Article 51, the powers of the then President of the Republic shall be extended until such time as a new President is elected. The Parliament shall elect this new President within ten days after the election of the National Assembly.

In this case, the President of the Council of Ministers shall be designated within fifteen days after the election of the new President of the Republic.

ART. 41. If the President of the Republic is not able to exercise his office for reasons duly noted by a vote of the Parliament, or in the event of a vacancy caused by death, resignation, or any other circumstance, the President of the National Assembly shall assume the interim functions of the President of the Republic. He shall be replaced in his own duties by a Vice President.

The new President of the Republic shall be elected within ten days, except under the conditions specified in the preceding article.

ART. 42. The President of the Republic may not be tried except for high treason.

He may be indicted by the National Assembly and arraigned before the High Court of Justice under the conditions set forth in Article 57 below.

ART. 43. The office of President of the Republic is incompatible with any other public office.

ART. 44. Members of families that once reigned over France shall not be eligible for the presidency of the Republic.

TITLE VI. THE COUNCIL OF MINISTERS

ART. 45.[4] At the opening of each legislative session, the President of the Republic, after the customary consultations, shall designate the President of the Council.

The latter shall submit to the National Assembly the program and the policy of the Cabinet he intends to constitute.

The President of the Council and the Ministers may not be formally appointed until the President of the Council receives a vote of confidence from the National Assembly by a roll-call vote and by an absolute majority of the Deputies, except when *force majeure* prevents the National Assembly from meeting.

The same procedure shall be followed during a legislative session in the event of a vacancy caused by death, resignation, or any other circumstance, except in the case set forth in Article 52 below.

No ministerial crisis occurring within the fifteen-day period after the appointment of the Ministers shall require the application of Article 51.

ART. 46. The President of the Council and the Ministers chosen by him shall be formally appointed by a decree of the President of the Republic.

ART. 47. The President of the Council shall ensure the execution of the laws.

He shall appoint all civil and military officials except those specified in Articles 30, 46, and 84.

The President of the Council shall assume the direction of the Armed Forces and shall coordinate all measures necessary for national defense.

The acts of the President of the Council mentioned in the present article shall be countersigned by the Ministers concerned.

ART. 48. The Ministers shall be collectively responsible to the National Assembly for the general policy of the Cabinet and individually responsible for their personal actions.

They shall not be responsible to the Council of the Republic.

ART. 49.[4] A question of confidence may not be put except after discussion by the Council of Ministers; it can be put only by the President of the Council.

The vote on a question of confidence may not be taken until one full day after it has been put before the Assembly. It shall be taken by a roll call.

[4] See Amendments, p. *xxvi.*

The Cabinet may not be refused a vote of confidence except by an absolute majority of the Deputies in the Assembly.

Refusal to give such a vote shall automatically result in the collective resignation of the Cabinet.

ART. 50.[4] Passage of a motion of censure by the National Assembly shall automatically result in the collective resignation of the Cabinet.

The vote on such a motion cannot be taken until one full day after it has been made. It must be taken by a roll call.

A motion of censure may be adopted only by an absolute majority of the Deputies in the Assembly.

ART. 51. If in the course of an eighteen-month period two ministerial crises occur under the conditions set forth in Articles 49 and 50, the Council of Ministers, after obtaining the opinion of the President of the Assembly, may decide to dissolve the National Assembly. Its dissolution shall be proclaimed by a decree of the President of the Republic in accordance with such decision.

The provisions of the preceding paragraph may not be applied before the expiration of the first eighteen months of the legislature.

ART. 52.[4] In case of dissolution, the Cabinet, with the exception of the President of the Council and the Minister of the Interior, shall remain in office to carry on current business.

The President of the Republic shall appoint the President of the National Assembly as President of the Council. The latter shall appoint the new Minister of the Interior with the approval of the secretariat of the National Assembly. He shall appoint as Ministers of State members of party groups not represented in the Government.

General elections shall take place not less than twenty and not more than thirty days after the dissolution.

The National Assembly shall convene by right on the third Thursday after its election.

ART. 53. The Ministers shall have access to the two Chambers and to their Committees. They must be heard when they request it.

In discussion before the Chambers they may be assisted by representatives designated by decree.

ART. 54. The President of the Council of Ministers may delegate his powers to a Minister.

ART. 55. In the event of a vacancy caused by death or any other circumstance, the Council of Ministers shall call upon one of its members to exercise the functions of President of the Council of Ministers temporarily.

TITLE VII. THE LEGAL RESPONSIBILITY OF MINISTERS

ART. 56. The Ministers shall be legally responsible for crimes and misdemeanors committed in the exercise of their functions.

ART. 57. The Ministers may be indicted by the National Assembly and arraigned before the High Court of Justice.

The National Assembly shall vote upon this question by secret ballot and by an absolute majority of its members, with the exception of those who may be called upon to participate in the prosecution, investigation, or judgment of the case.

ART. 58. The High Court of Justice shall be elected by the National Assembly at the opening of each legislative session.

ART. 59. The organization of the High Court of Justice and the procedure to be followed before it shall be determined by a special law.

TITLE VIII. THE FRENCH UNION

Section I: Principles

ART. 60. The French Union shall be composed, on the one hand, of the French Republic which comprises Metropolitan France and the overseas departments and territories, and, on the other hand, of the Associated Territories and States.

ART. 61. The position of the Associated States within the French Union shall in each case depend upon the act which defines its relationship with France.

ART. 62. The members of the French Union shall place in common all their resources to guarantee the defense of the whole Union. The Government of the Republic shall coordinate these resources and direct such policies as will prepare and ensure this defense.

Section II: Organization

ART. 63. The central organs of the French Union shall be: the Presidency, the High Council, and the Assembly.

ART. 64. The President of the French Republic shall be the President of the French Union whose permanent interests he shall represent.

ART. 65. The High Council of the French Union, under the chairmanship of the President of the Union, shall be composed of a delegation of the French Government and of the representatives that each associated State is permitted to accredit to the President of the Union.

Its function shall be to assist the Government in the general conduct of the affairs of the Union.

ART. 66. The Assembly of the French Union shall be composed half of members representing Metropolitan France and half of members representing the overseas departments and territories and the Associated States.

An organic law shall determine the mode of representation of the different sections of the population.

ART. 67. The members of the Assembly of the Union shall be elected by the regional assemblies for the overseas departments and territories; for Metropolitan France, they shall be elected two thirds by the National Assembly representing the home country and one third by the Council of the Republic representing the home country.

ART. 68. The Associated States may appoint delegates to the Assembly of the Union within the limitations and conditions determined by a law and an internal legislative act of each State.

ART. 69. The President of the French Union shall convoke the Assembly of the French Union and shall close its sessions. He must convoke it upon the request of half of its members.

The Assembly of the French Union may not sit during interruptions of the session of the Parliament.

ART. 70. The rules set forth in Articles 8, 10, 21, 22, and 23 shall be applicable to the Assembly of the French Union under the same conditions as to the Council of the Republic.

ART. 71. The Assembly of the French Union shall examine the bills or proposals submitted to it by the National Assembly or the Government of the French Republic or the Governments of the Associated States in order that it may give its opinion thereon.

The Assembly shall have the power to express its opinion on resolutions submitted to it by one of its members and, if they meet with its approval, to instruct its secretariat to send them to the National Assembly. It may submit proposals to the French Government and to the High Council of the French Union.

In order to be admissible, the proposed resolutions referred to in the preceding paragraph must relate to legislation concerning the overseas territories.

ART. 72. Legislative power with regard to penal law, civil liberties and political and administrative organization in the overseas territories, shall rest with the Parliament.

In all other matters, French laws shall be applicable in the overseas territories only by an express provision to this effect or if they have been extended to the overseas territories by decree after consultation with the Assembly of the Union.

Moreover, as an exception to Article 13, special provisions for each territory may be enacted by the President of the Republic in the Council of Ministers after consultation with the Assembly of the Union.

Section III: The Overseas Departments and Territories

ART. 73. The legislative regime of the overseas departments shall be the same as that of the metropolitan departments save for exceptions determined by the law.

ART. 74. The overseas territories shall be given special status which takes into account their particular interests within the framework of the general interests of the Union.

This status and the internal organization of each overseas territory or group of territories shall be determined by law after the Assembly of the French Union has expressed its opinion thereon and after consultation with the Territorial Assemblies.

ART. 75. The respective status of the members of the French Republic and of the French Union shall be subject to modifications.

Modifications of status and passage from one category to another within the framework established in Article 60 may take place only as the result of a law passed by the Parliament after consultation with the Territorial Assemblies and the Assembly of the Union.

ART. 76. The representative of the Government in each territory or group of territories shall be the repository of the powers of the Republic. He shall be the Administrative head of the territory.

He shall be responsible to the Government for his acts.

ART. 77. An elective Assembly shall be instituted in each territory. The electoral regime, composition, and powers of this Assembly shall be determined by law.

ART. 78. In the groups of territories, the management of matters of common interest shall be entrusted to an Assembly composed of members elected by the Territorial Assemblies.

Its composition and its powers shall be determined by law.

ART. 79. The overseas territories shall elect representatives to the National Assembly and to the Council of the Republic under the conditions determined by the law.

ART. 80. All nationals of the overseas territories shall have the status of citizens, in the same capacity as French nationals of Metropolitan France or the overseas territories. Special laws shall determine the conditions under which they may exercise their rights as citizens.

ART. 81. All citizens and nationals of territories within the French Union shall have the status of citizens of the French Union, which ensures them the enjoyments of the rights and liberties guaranteed by the Preamble of the present Constitution.

ART. 82. Those citizens who do not have French civil status shall retain their personal status so long as they do not renounce it.

This status may in no case constitute a ground for refusing or restricting the rights and liberties pertaining to the status of French citizens.

TITLE IX. THE SUPERIOR COUNCIL OF THE JUDICIARY

ART. 83. The Superior Council of the Judiciary shall be composed of fourteen members:

The President of the Republic, President;
The Keeper of the Seals or Minister of Justice, Vice President;

Six persons elected for six years by the National Assembly, by a two-thirds majority and chosen outside its membership, and six alternates elected under the same conditions;

Six persons designated as follows:

Four judges elected for six years under the conditions determined by the law, and representing each category of the judiciary, and four alternates elected under the same conditions;

Two members appointed for six years by the President of the Republic and chosen outside the membership of the Parliament and the judiciary, but from among the members of the legal profession, two alternates being designated under the same conditions.

The decisions of the Superior Council of the Magistracy shall be taken by majority vote. In case of a tie the President shall cast the deciding vote.

ART. 84. The President of the Republic shall appoint the judges whose names are submitted to him by the Superior Council of the Judiciary with the exception of those in the office of the Public Prosecutor.

The Superior Council of the Judiciary, according to the law, shall ensure the discipline of these judges, their independence, and the administration of the courts.

The presiding judges shall not be removable.

TITLE X. LOCAL ADMINISTRATIVE UNITS

ART. 85. The French Republic, one and indivisible, recognizes the existence of local administrative units.

These units are the communes, the departments, and the overseas territories.

ART. 86. The framework, the scope, the eventual regrouping, and the organization of the communes, the departments, and the overseas territories shall be determined by law.

ART. 87. The local administrative units shall be governed freely by councils elected by universal suffrage.

The mayor or the president of these councils shall ensure the carrying out of their decisions.

ART. 88. The coordination of the activities of Government officials, the representation of the national interests, and the administrative control of these units shall be insured within the departmental framework by delegates of the Government appointed in the Council of Ministers.

ART. 89. Organic laws will further extend the liberties of the departments and municipalities; for certain large cities they may establish rules of operation and an administrative structure different from those of small towns, and include special provisions for certain departments; they will determine the conditions under which Articles 85 and 88 above are to be applied.

Laws will likewise determine the conditions under

which local agencies of central administrations are to function, in order to bring the central administration closer to the people.

TITLE XI. AMENDMENT OF THE CONSTITUTION

ART. 90. Amendment of the Constitution shall take place in the following manner:

Amendment must be decided upon by a resolution adopted by an absolute majority of the members of the National Assembly.

This resolution shall stipulate the purpose of the amendment.

Not less than three months later this resolution shall have a second reading under the same rules of procedure as the first, unless the Council of the Republic, to which the resolution has been referred by the National Assembly, has adopted the same resolution by an absolute majority.

After this second reading, the National Assembly shall draw up a bill to amend the Constitution. The bill shall be submitted to the Parliament and adopted by the same majority and according to the same rules established for any ordinary act of the legislature.

It shall be submitted to a referendum unless it has been adopted on second reading by a two-thirds majority of the National Assembly or by a three-fifths majority of each of the two assemblies.

The bill shall be promulgated as a constitutional law within eight days after its adoption.

No constitutional amendment relative to the existence of the Council of the Republic may be made without the concurrence of this Council or resort to a referendum.

ART. 91. The Constitutional Committee shall be presided over by the President of the Republic.

It shall include the President of the National Assembly, the President of the Council of the Republic, seven members elected by the National Assembly at the beginning of each annual session by proportional representation of party groups and chosen outside its own membership, and three members elected under the same conditions by the Council of the Republic.

The Constitutional Committee shall determine whether the laws passed by the National Assembly imply amendment of the Constitution.

ART. 92. Within the period allowed for the promulgation of the law, the Committee shall receive a joint request that it examine said law from the President of the Republic and the President of the Council of the Republic, the Council having decided the matter by an absolute majority of its members.

The Committee shall examine the law, shall strive to bring about agreement between the National Assembly and the Council of the Republic and, if it does not succeed in this, shall decide the matter within five days after it has received the request. This period may be reduced to two days in case of emergency.

The Committee shall be competent to decide on the possibility of amending only Titles I through X of the present Constitution.

ART. 93. A law which, in the opinion of the Committee, implies amendment of the Constitution shall be sent back to the National Assembly for reconsideration.

If the Parliament adheres to its original vote, the law may not be promulgated until the Constitution has been amended according to the procedure set forth in Article 90.

If the law is considered to be in conformity with Title I through X of the present Constitution, it shall be promulgated within the period specified in Article 36, said period being prolonged by the addition of the period specified in Article 92 above.

ART. 94. In the case of occupation of all or part of the metropolitan territory by foreign forces, no procedure of amendment may be undertaken or continued.

ART. 95. The republican form of government may not be the subject of any proposal to amend the Constitution.

TITLE XII. TEMPORARY PROVISIONS

ART. 96. The secretariat of the National Constituent Assembly shall be responsible for insuring the continuity of national representation until the meeting of the Deputies of the new National Assembly.

ART. 97. In case of exceptional circumstances, the Deputies of the National Constituent Assembly may, until the time specified in the preceding Article, be called together by the secretariat of the Assembly, either on its own initiative or upon the request of the Government.

ART. 98. The National Assembly will meet automatically on the third Thursday following the general elections.

The Council of the Republic will meet on the third Tuesday following its election. The present Constitution will take effect on that date.

Until the meeting of the Council of the Republic, the organization of public powers will be governed by the law of November 2, 1945, the National Assembly having the attributes conferred by that law on the National Constituent Assembly.

ART. 99. The Provisional Government constituted under the terms of Article 98, will hand its resignation to the President of the Republic as soon as the latter is elected by the Parliament under the conditions set forth in Article 29 above.

ART. 100. The secretariat of the National Constituent Assembly shall be responsible for preparing the meeting of the Assemblies created by the present Constitution and especially for providing, before the meeting of their respective secretariats, the meeting places and administrative facilities necessary to their functioning.

ART. 101. During a period of not more than one

year after the meeting of the National Assembly, the Council of the Republic may officially deliberate as soon as two thirds of its members shall have been proclaimed elected.

Art. 102. The first Council of the Republic will be renewed entirely within the year following the renewal of the municipal councils, which renewal will take place within one year after the promulgation of the Constitution.

Art. 103. Until the organization of the Economic Council and during a maximum period of three months dating from the meeting of the National Assembly the application of Article 25 of the present Constitution will be suspended.

Art. 104. Until the meeting of the Assembly of the French Union and during a maximum period of one year dating from the meeting of the National Assembly, the application of Articles 71 and 72 of the present Constitution will be suspended.

Art. 105. Until the promulgation of the laws provided for in Article 89 of the present Constitution, and without prejudice to the provisions fixing the status of the various departments and overseas territories, the departments and communes of the French Republic will be administered in accordance with the laws now in force, except for Paragraphs 2 and 3 of Article 97 of the law of April 5, 1884, for the enforcement of which the State police shall be placed at the disposal of the mayors.

However, the acts of the prefect in his capacity of representative of the department, will be carried out by him under the permanent supervision of the president of the departmental assembly.

The provisions of the preceding paragraph shall not be applicable to the Department of the Seine.

Art. 106. The present Constitution will be promulgated by the President of the Provisional Government of the Republic within two days after the date of the proclamation of the results of the referendum and in the following form:

> "The National Constituent Assembly has adopted,
> "The French people has approved,
> "The President of the Provisional Government of the Republic promulgates the Constitution that follows:

(Text of the Constitution)

The present Constitution, considered and adopted by the National Constituent Assembly and approved by the French people, shall become the law of the land.

Amended Articles of the French Constitution as Passed on November 30, 1954 *

Art. 7 [*State of Siege*]. War cannot be declared without a vote of the National Assembly and previous statement of view by the Council of the Republic.

The state of siege is declared according to conditions laid down in legislation.

Art. 9 [*Close of Sessions*]. The National Assembly meets by right in ordinary session the first Tuesday of October.

When this session has lasted at least seven months, the Prime Minister can pronounce its closure by a decree made in the Council of Ministers. In this period of seven months interruptions of sessions are not counted. Interruptions are defined as any adjournments of sittings for longer than eight days.

The Council of the Republic sits at the same time as the National Assembly.

Art. 11 [*Election of the Bureaus*]. Each of the two Chambers elects its bureau annually at the opening of the ordinary session and according to the conditions stipulated in its rules of procedure.

When the two Chambers meet in joint session to elect the President of the Republic, their bureau is that of the National Assembly.

Art. 12 [*Extraordinary Sessions*]. When the National Assembly is not sitting, its bureau can convoke Parliament in special session; the President of the National Assembly must do this upon demand by the President of the Council of Ministers or by the majority of members composing the National Assembly.

The President of the Council of Ministers pronounces the closure of the special session according to the forms laid down in Article 9.

When the special session takes place at the demand of the majority of the National Assembly or its bureau, the decree of closure cannot be made before Parliament has completed the limited agenda for which it was convoked.

Art. 14 [*Introduction of Bills*].[1] The President of the Council of Ministers and members of Parliament have the initiative in proposing laws.

Projets are deposited with the bureau of the National Assembly or the bureau of the Council of the Republic. Nevertheless, bills that are for authorizing the ratification of treaties as in Article 27, budgetary and financial bills, and bills proposing a diminution of receipts of the creation of expenditures must be deposited with the National Assembly.

Propositions formulated by members of Parliament are deposited with the bureau of the Chamber of which they are members and are transmitted after adoption to the other Chamber. *Propositions* of law formulated by members of the Council of the Republic are inacceptable if their consequence is to decrease receipts or create expenditures.

Art. 20 [*Powers of the Council of the Republic*]. All *projets* or *propositions* of law [bills] are exam-

* Translated from the official text by Herman Finer.

[1] *Projets* are Government-introduced bills; *propositions* are introduced by rank-and-file members.

ined successively in the two Chambers of Parliament with a view to arriving at the adoption of an identical text.

Unless either type of bill has been examined by it in first treatment,[2] the Council of the Republic must state its views thereon at the latest within the two months that follow the transmission of the text adopted in the first treatment of it in the National Assembly.

As regards budgetary texts and the law on finances, the time taken by the Council of the Republic may not exceed the time previously taken by the National Assembly in its deliberations and voting. In cases where the National Assembly has made a declaration of urgency, the period is double that allowed for the National Assembly's debates as allowed by its procedural rules.

If the Council of the Republic has not stated its opinion within the periods set down in the foregoing paragraphs, the law may be promulgated in the form of the text voted by the National Assembly.

If an agreement has not been reached, the consideration proceeds in each of the two Chambers. After two treatments by the Council of the Republic, each Chamber uses, for this purpose, the period used by the other Chamber since the preceding treatment, but this period cannot be less than seven days or one day for the texts mentioned in paragraph three.

If no agreement is reached within a period of 100 days counting from the transmission of the text to the Council of the Republic for its second treatment, reduced to one month for the laws of the budget and finances and to fifteen days in cases of procedure applicable to urgent affairs, the National Assembly can enact finally the text last voted by it or such modified by the adoption of one or more of the amendments proposed to that text by the Council of the Republic.

If the National Assembly goes outside or prolongs the periods of deliberation which it enjoys, the period allowed for agreement between the two Chambers is increased by as much.

The periods stipulated in the present article are suspended during interruptions of the session. They can be lengthened by decision of the National Assembly.

Art. 22 [*Prosecutions of Members of Parliament*]. No member of Parliament may be, during the period of the sessions, prosecuted or arrested for crimes or misdemeanors except with the authorization of the Chamber of which he is a member, except in the case of being caught in the act. Every parliamentarian arrested outside the sessions can vote by proxy so long as the Chamber of which he is a member has not voted the lifting of his parliamentary immunity. If it has so voted in the thirty days following the opening of the session, the member of Parliament arrested

[2] I translate *lecture* not as *reading*, but as *treatment*, because the latter consists of several readings and committee stage in Anglo-American terminology (p. 384ff.).

shall be freed unconditionally. Except when caught in the act, or of authorized prosecution or final sentence, no member can be, out of session, arrested except with the authorization of the bureau of the Chamber of which he is a member. Detention or prosecution of a member is suspended if the Chamber of which he is a member demands it.

Art. 45 [*Majority for Investiture*]. At the beginning of each legislature, the President of the Republic, after the customary consultations, designates the President of the Council.

The latter chooses the members of his Council of Ministers and makes the list known to the National Assembly, before which he presents himself in order to obtain its confidence on the program and policy he intends to pursue, except in the case where *force majeure* prevents the meeting of the National Assembly.

Voting takes place by roll call and simple majority.

The same process is carried out in the course of the legislature, in case of the vacating of the presidency of the Council, except for what appears in Article 52.

Ministerial crises arising within a period of 15 days from the nomination of ministers do not count in the application of article 51.

Art. 49 [*Vote of Confidence*]. The question of confidence cannot be raised except after deliberation in the Council of Ministers; it cannot be raised except by the President of the Council.

The vote on the question of confidence cannot be taken until twenty-four hours have elapsed since it was posed before the National Assembly. It is taken by roll call.

Confidence is refused to the Council of Ministers by an absolute majority of members of the Assembly.

This refusal produces the collective resignation of the Council.

Art. 50 [*Motion of Censure*]. The National Assembly's vote of a motion of censure brings about the collective resignation of the Council of Ministers.

The vote on the motion of censure takes place under the same conditions and the same procedure as that on the question of confidence.

The motion of censure can be adopted only by an absolute majority of the Deputies of the Assembly.

Art. 52 [*the Government at Dissolution*]. In case of dissolution, the Council of Ministers remains in office.

Nevertheless, if the dissolution is preceded by the adoption of a motion of censure, the President of the Republic names the President of the National Assembly President of the Council and Minister of the Interior.

The elections take place at least twenty and at most thirty days after the dissolution.

The National Assembly meets by unconditional right the third Thursday following its election.

The Government of Germany

BASIC LAW OF THE FEDERAL REPUBLIC OF GERMANY, 1949 *

PREAMBLE

Conscious of its responsibility before God and before man,

inspired by the resolve to preserve its national and political unity and to serve world peace as an equal partner in a united Europe, the German people,
in the Lander *Baden, Bavaria, Bremen, Hamburg, Hesse, Lower Saxony, North-Rhine-Wesphalia, Rhineland-Palatinate, Schleswig-Holstein, Württemberg-Baden und Wurttemberg-Hohenzollern,*

has, by virtue of its constituent power, enacted this Basic Law of the Federal Republic of Germany
to give a new order to political life for a transitional period.

It has also acted on behalf of those Germans to whom participation was denied.

The entire German people is called upon to achieve, by free self-determination, the unity and freedom of Germany.

I. BASIC RIGHTS

ART. 1. (1) The dignity of man is inviolable. To respect and protect it is the duty of all State authority.

(2) The German people therefore acknowledges inviolable and inalienable human rights as the basis of every human community, of peace, and of justice in the world.

(3) The following basic rights are binding on the legislature, on the executive, and on the judiciary as directly valid law.

ART. 2. (1) Everyone has the right to the free development of his personality, insofar as he does not infringe upon the rights of others or offend against the constitutional order or the moral code.

(2) Everyone has the right to life and to physical inviolability. The freedom of the individual is inviolable. These rights may be interfered with only on the basis of a law.

ART. 3. (1) All persons are equal before the law.

(2) Men and women have equal rights.

(3) No one may be prejudiced or privileged because of his sex, his descent, his race, his language, his homeland and origin, his faith, or his religious and political opinions.

ART. 4. (1) Freedom of faith and conscience and

* Adopted by the Parliamentary Council, May 8, 1949.

freedom of creed in religion and in philosophy of life (*weltanschaulich*) are inviolable.

(2) The practice of religion without interference is guaranteed.

(3) No one may be compelled against his conscience to perform military service as an armed combatant. Details are regulated by a federal law.

ART. 5. (1) Everyone has the right freely to express and to disseminate his opinion through speech, writing, and pictures and, without hindrance, to instruct himself from generally accessible sources. Freedom of the press and freedom of radio and motion-pictures reporting are guaranteed. There is no censorship.

(2) These rights are limited by the provisions of the general laws, the legal regulations for the protection of juveniles, and by the right to personal honor.

(3) Art and science, research, and teaching are free. Freedom of teaching does not absolve from loyalty to the Constitution.

ART. 6. (1) Marriage and family are under the special protection of the State.

(2) The care and upbringing of children are the natural right of parents and their duty, incumbent upon them primarily. The State watches over their performance.

(3) Children may be separated from the family against the will of those entitled to bring them up only on the basis of a law, if those so entitled fail to perform their duty, or if, on other grounds, the children are in danger of falling into neglect.

(4) Every mother has a claim to the protection and assistance of the community.

(5) For their physical and mental development and for their position in society, illegitimate children shall, by legislation, be given the same opportunities as legitimate children.

ART. 7. (1) The entire educational system is under the supervision of the State.

(2) Those entitled to bring up a child have the right to decide whether it shall receive religious instruction.

(3) Religious instruction shall form part of the curriculum in State and municipal schools, with the exception of nondenominational schools. Religious instruction shall, without prejudice to the State's right of supervision, be given according to the principles of the religious denominations. No teacher may against his will be placed under an obligation to give religious instruction.

(4) The right to establish private schools is guaranteed. Private schools as a substitute for State or municipal schools require the approval of the State and are subject to *Land* legislation. The approval must be given if the private schools, in their educational aims and facilities, as well as in the professional training of their teaching personnel, are not inferior to the State or municipal schools and if a segregation of the pupils in accordance with the [financial] means of the parents is not fostered. The approval must be withheld if the economic and legal status of the teaching personnel is not adequately ensured.

(5) A private elementary school is to be permitted only if the educational authority recognizes a specific pedagogic interest or if, at the request of those entitled to bring up children, it is to be established as an interdenominational school (*Gemeinschaftsschule*), as a denominational or an ideological school, and if a State or municipal elementary school of this type does not exist in the *Gemeinde*.

(6) Preparatory schools (*Vorschulen*) remain abolished.

ART. 8. (1) All Germans have the right, without prior notification or permission, to assemble peacefully and unarmed.

(2) In the case of open-air meetings this right may be restricted by legislation or on the basis of a law.

ART. 9. (1) All Germans have the right to form associations and societies.

(2) Associations, the objects or activities of which conflict with the criminal laws or which are directed against the constitutional order or the concept of international understanding, are prohibited.

(3) The right to form associations to safeguard and improve working and economic conditions is guaranteed to everyone and to all trades and professions. Agreements which restrict or seek to hinder this right are null and void; measures directed to this end are illegal.

ART. 10. Secrecy of the mail as well as secrecy of the postal services and of telecommunications is inviolable. Restrictions may be ordered only on the basis of a law.

ART. 11. (1) All Germans enjoy freedom of movement throughout the federal territory.

(2) This right may be restricted only by legislation and only for the cases in which an adequate basis of existence is absent, and, as a result, particular burdens would arise for the general public or in which it is necessary for the protection of juveniles from neglect, for combating danger of epidemics or in order to prevent criminal acts.

ART. 12. (1) All Germans have the right freely to choose their trade or profession, place of work and place of vocational training. The exercise of an occupation or profession may be regulated by legislation.

(2) No one may be compelled to perform a particular kind of work except within the scope of a customary general compulsory public service equally applicable to all.

(3) Forced labor is admissible only in the event of deprivation of freedom ordered by a court.

ART. 13. (1) The home is inviolable.

(2) Searches may be ordered only by a judge or, in the event of danger in delay, by other authorities provided by law, and may be carried out only in the form prescribed therein.

(3) In other cases interferences with, and restrictions of, this inviolability may be undertaken only to avert a common danger or mortal danger to individuals and, on the basis of a law, also to prevent imminent danger to public safety and order, especially for the relief of the housing and space shortage (*Raumnot*), for combating the danger of epidemics or for the protection of endangered juveniles.

ART. 14. (1) Property and the right of inheritance are safeguarded. [Their] scope and limitations are determined by legislation.

(2) Property commits to duties. Its use should at the same time serve the general welfare.

(3) Expropriation is admissible only for the welfare of the community at large. It may be effected only by legislation or on the basis of a law regulating the nature and extent of compensation. The compensation shall be determined after just consideration of the interests of the general public and the parties concerned. In case of dispute regarding the amount of compensation, there is recourse to the ordinary courts.

ART. 15. Land, natural resources, and means of production may, for the purpose of socialization, be transferred to public ownership or other forms of publicly controlled economy by means of a law regulating the nature and extent of compensation. For the compensation, Article 14, paragraph (3), sentences 3 and 4, applies correspondingly.

ART. 16. (1) No one may be deprived of his German citizenship. A person may be deprived of citizenship only on the basis of a law and, against his will, only if he is not thereby rendered stateless.

(2) No German may be extradited to a foreign country. The politically persecuted enjoy the right of asylum.

ART. 17. Everyone has the right, individually or jointly with others, to address written requests or complaints to the competent authorities and to the popular representative bodies.

ART. 18. Whoever abuses freedom of expression of opinion, in particular freedom of the press (Article 5, paragraph (1)), freedom of teaching (Article 5, paragraph (3)), freedom of assembly (Article 8), freedom of association (Article 9), the secrecy of the mail, of the postal services, and of telecommunications (Article 10), the [right of] property (Article 14), or the right of asylum (Article 16, paragraph (2)), in order to attack the libertarian democratic basic order, forfeits these basic rights. The forfeiture and its extent shall be pronounced by the Federal Constitutional Court.

ART. 19. (1) Insofar as, under this Basic Law, a basic right may be restricted by legislation or on the basis of a law, this law must be of general application and not applicable solely to an individual case. Furthermore, the law must specify the basic right and indicate the Article.

(2) In no case may a basic right be infringed upon in its essential content.

(3) The basic rights also apply to domestic juridical persons insofar as the former, according to their nature, are applicable to the latter.

(4) Should any person's rights be infringed by public authority, he shall have recourse to the courts. Insofar as there is no other jurisdiction, the recourse shall be to the ordinary courts.

II. The Federation and the Lander

ART. 20. (1) The Federal Republic of Germany is a democratic and social federal State.

(2) All State authority emanates from the people. It is exercised by the people by means of elections and plebiscites and through specific legislative, executive, and judicial agencies.

(3) Legislation is subject to the Constitution; the executive power and the administration of justice are subject to the law.

ART. 21. (1) The parties participate in the forming of the political will of the people. They can be freely formed. Their internal organization must conform to democratic principles. They must publicly account for the sources of their funds.

(2) Parties which, according to their aims and the conduct of their members, seek to impair or abolish the libertarian democratic basic order or to jeopardize the existence of the Federal Republic of Germany are unconstitutional. The Federal Constitutional Court decides on the question of unconstitutionality.

(3) Details are regulated by federal legislation.

ART. 22. The Federal flag is black, red, gold.

ART. 23. For the time being, this Basic Law applies in the territory of the *Lander* Baden, Bavaria, Bremen, Greater Berlin, Hamburg, Hesse, Lower-Saxony, North-Rhine-Westphalia, Rhineland-Palatinate, Schleswig-Holstein, Württemberg-Baden and Württemberg-Hohenzollern. It is to be put into force in other parts of Germany on their accession.

ART. 24. (1) The Federation may, by legislation, transfer sovereign powers to international institutions.

(2) For the maintenance of peace, the Federation may join a system of mutual collective security; in doing so it will consent to those limitations of its sovereign powers which will bring about and secure a peaceful and lasting order in Europe and among the nations of the world.

(3) For the settlement of disputes between nations, the Federation will accede to conventions concerning a general, comprehensive obligatory system of international arbitration.

ART. 25. The general rules of international law form part of Federal law. They take precedence over the laws and directly create rights and duties for the inhabitants of the federal territory.

ART. 26. (1) Activities tending to disturb, and undertaken with the intention of disturbing, the peaceful relations between nations, especially of preparing the conduct of an aggressive war, are unconstitutional. They are to be subject to punishment.

(2) Weapons designed for warfare may be manufactured, transported, or marketed only with the permission of the Federal Government. Details are regulated by a Federal law.

ART. 27. All German commercial vessels constitute a [federally] unified merchant fleet.

ART. 28. (1) The constitutional order in the *Lander* must conform to the principles of the republican, democratic, and social State based on the rule of law (*Rechtsstaat*) within the meaning of this Basic Law. In the *Lander, Kreise,* and *Gemeinden,* the people must be represented by a body created by universal, direct, free, equal, and secret elections. In *Gemeinden,* the assembly of the *Gemeinde* may take the place of an elected body.

(2) The *Gemeinden* must be safeguarded in their right to regulate, under their own responsibility, all the affairs of the local community within the limits of the laws. The *Gemeindeverbaende* also shall have the right of self-government within the legally established scope of their functions and in accordance with the laws.

(3) The Federation guarantees that the constitutional order of the *Lander* conforms to the basic rights and the provisions of paragraphs (1) and (2).

ART. 29. (1) The federal territory is to be reorganized by a federal law with due regard to regional ties, historical and cultural connections, economic expediency, and social structure. The reorganization should create *Lander* which, by their size and potentiality, are able to fulfill efficiently the functions incumbent upon them.

(2) In areas which, at the time of the reorganization of the *Lander* after May 8, 1945, became part, without plebiscite, of another *Land,* a specific change of the decision reached concerning this jurisdiction can be demanded by popular initiative within one year of the coming into force of this Basic Law. The

popular initiative requires the consent of one tenth of the population qualified to vote in *Landtag* elections. Should the popular initiative materialize, the Federal Government must, in the draft law regarding the reorganization, include a provision determining to which *Land* the area concerned shall belong.

(3) After adoption of the law, that part of the law which concerns an area which it is proposed to join to another *Land* must in each such area be submitted to a referendum. If, pursuant to paragraph (2), a popular initiative has materialized, a referendum must be held in any case in the area concerned.

(4) Insofar as the law is rejected in at least one area, it must then be reintroduced in the *Bundestag*. Insofar as it is then re-enacted, it shall to that extent require acceptance by referendum in the entire Federal territory.

(5) In a referendum, the majority of the votes cast is decisive.

(6) The procedure is regulated by a federal law. The reorganization should be concluded before the expiration of three years after promulgation of the Basic Law and, should it be necessary in consequence of the accession of another part of Germany, within two years after such accession.

(7) The procedure regarding any other change in the existing territory of the *Lander* is regulated by a federal law which shall require the approval of the *Bundesrat* and of the majority of the members of the *Bundestag*.

ART. 30. The exercise of the powers of the State and the discharge of State functions is the concern of the *Lander,* insofar as this Basic Law does not otherwise prescribe or permit.

ART. 31. Federal law overrides *Land* law.

ART. 32. (1) The maintenance of relations with foreign States shall be the concern of the Federation.

(2) Before the conclusion of a treaty affecting the special interests of a *Land*, this *Land* must be consulted in good time.

(3) Insofar as legislation falls within the competence of the *Lander,* these may, with the approval of the Federal Government, conclude treaties with foreign states.

ART. 33. (1) Every German has in every *Land* the same civic (*staatsbuergerliche*) rights and duties.

(2) Every German has equal access to any public office in accordance with his suitability, ability, and professional achievements.

(3) Enjoyment of civil and civic rights (*bürgerliche und staatsbuergerliche Rechte*) and access to public offices, as well as the rights acquired in the public service, are independent of religious denomination. No one may suffer prejudice on account of his adherence or nonadherence to a denomination or philosophy of life (*Weltanschauung*).

(4) The exercise of State authority (*hoheitsrecht-*

liche Befugnisse) as a permanent function shall, as a rule, be entrusted to members of the public service who are pledged to service and loyalty by public law.

(5) Law regarding the public service shall be regulated with due regard to the traditional principles concerning the status of professional civil servants (*Berufsbeamtentum*).

ART. 34. If any person, in exercising a public office entrusted to him, violates his official duty to a third party, responsibility rests in principle with the State or the public body which employs that person. In a case of willful intent or gross negligence, the [employing body's] right of recourse [against the civil servant or employee] is reserved. With respect to the claim for compensation of damage and to the right of recourse, the jurisdiction of the ordinary courts must not be excluded.

ART. 35. All Federal and *Land* authorities render each other mutual legal and administrative assistance.

ART. 36. Civil servants (*Beamte*) from all *Lander* shall be employed by the highest Federal authorities in appropriate ratio. Persons employed with the other Federal authorities should, as a rule, be taken from the *Land* in which they are employed.

ART. 37. (1) If a *Land* fails to fulfill its obligations towards the Federation under the Basic Law or any other federal law, the Federal Government may, with *Bundesrat* approval, take the necessary measures to force the *Land* by way of federal compulsion (*Bundeszwang*) to fulfill its duties.

(2) For the implementation of federal compulsion, the Federal Government or its commissioner has the right to give instruction to all *Lander* and their administrative agencies.

III. The Bundestag

ART. 38. (1) Representatives to the German *Bundestag* are elected by the people in universal, direct, free, equal, and secret elections. They are representatives of the whole people, not bound by orders and instructions, and subject only to their conscience.

(2) Any person who has reached the age of twenty-one years is entitled to vote, and any person who has reached the age of twenty-five years may stand for election.

(3) Details are determined by a Federal law.

ART. 39. (1) The *Bundestag* is elected for a four-year term. Its legislative term ends four years after its first convening, or with its dissolution. The new election takes place in the last three months of the legislative term or, in case of a dissolution, after sixty days at the latest.

(2) The *Bundestag* convenes not later than thirty days after the election, but in no case before the end of the legislative term of the previous *Bundestag*.

(3) The *Bundestag* determines the closure and re-

sumption of its meetings. The President of the *Bundestag* may convoke it at an earlier date. He is bound to do so if one third of the members, the Federal President or the Federal Chancellor so demand.

ART. 40. (1) The *Bundestag* elects its President, his deputies, and the secretaries. It draws up its Rules of Procedure.

(2) The President has charge of, and exercises police power in, the *Bundestag* building. No search or seizure may take place in the premises of the *Bundestag* without his permission.

ART. 41. (1) The scrutiny of elections is the responsibility of the *Bundestag*. It also decides whether a representative has lost his seat in the *Bundestag*.

(2) An appeal to the Federal Constitutional Court against the decision of the *Bundestag* is admissible.

(3) Details are regulated by a federal law.

ART. 42. (1) The deliberations of the *Bundestag* are public. Upon a motion of one tenth of its members, or upon a motion of the Federal Government, the public may, by a two-thirds majority, be excluded. The motion is decided in a closed meeting.

(2) Decisions of the *Bundestag* require the majority of votes cast insofar as this Basic Law does not otherwise provide. For the elections to be held by the *Bundestag,* exceptions in the Rules of Procedure are admissible.

(3) True records of the public meetings of the *Bundestag* and of its committees do not entail any responsibility.

ART. 43. (1) The *Bundestag* and its committees may demand the presence of any member of the Federal Government.

(2) The members of the *Bundestag* and of the Federal Government as well as persons commissioned by them have access to all meetings of the *Bundestag* and its committees. They must be heard at any time.

ART. 44. (1) The *Bundestag* has the right and, upon the motion of one fourth of its members, the obligation to set up an investigating committee which shall take the necessary evidence in public proceedings. The public may be excluded.

(2) The provisions relating to criminal procedure shall essentially apply to the taking of the evidence. Secrecy of the mail, postal services, and telecommunications remain unaffected.

(2) The courts and administrative authorities are bound to provide legal and administrative assistance.

(4) The decisions of the investigating committees are not subject to judicial review. The courts are free to appraise and judge the facts on which the investigation is based.

ART. 45. (1) The *Bundestag* appoints a Standing Committee which shall safeguard the rights of the *Bundestag* in relation to the Federal Government in the interval between two legislative terms. The Stand-

ing Committee has also the powers of an investigating committee.

(2) Any wider powers, in particular the right to legislate, to elect the Federal Chancellor, and to impeach the Federal President, are not vested in the Standing Committee.

ART. 46. (1) A Representative may at no time be proceeded against in the courts or be subjected to disciplinary action or otherwise called to account outside the *Bundestag* on account of a vote given or an utterance made by him in the *Bundestag* or one of its committees. This shall not apply in the case of defamatory insults.

(2) A Representative may be called to account or arrested for a punishable act only with the permission of the *Bundestag,* unless he be apprehended while committing the act or in the course of the following day.

(3) Furthermore, the permission of the *Bundestag* is required in respect of any other restriction of the personal freedom of a Representative or for the initiation of proceedings pursuant to Article 18 against a Representative.

(4) Any criminal proceedings and any proceedings pursuant to Article 18 against a Representative, any detention and any other restriction of his personal freedom, shall be suspended upon the demand of the *Bundestag.*

ART. 47. Representatives are entitled to refuse to give evidence concerning persons who have confided facts to them in their capacity as Representatives or to whom they have entrusted facts in this capacity, as well as concerning those facts themselves. Within the scope of this right to refuse to give evidence, the seizure of documents is inadmissible.

ART. 48. (1) Any person standing for election to the *Bundestag* is entitled to the leave necessary for the preparation of his election.

(2) No one may be prevented from accepting and exercising the office of representative. Notice of dismissal or dismissal [from employment] on these grounds are inadmissible.

(3) Representatives are entitled to a remuneration adequate to ensure their independence. They are entitled to free travel in all State-owned transport. Details are regulated by a federal law.

ART. 49. Articles 46, 47, and paragraphs (2) and (3) of Article 48 apply to the members of the Presidium and the Standing Committee, as well as to their chief deputies, also in the interval between two legislative terms.

IV. THE BUNDESRAT

ART. 50. By means of the *Bundesrat,* the *Lander* participate in the federal legislation and administration.

ART. 51. (1) The *Bundesrat* consists of members

of the *Lander* Governments which appoint and recall them. Other members of their Governments may represent them.

(2) Each *Land* has at least three votes; *Lander* with more than two million inhabitants have four, *Lander* with more than six million inhabitants, five votes.

(3) Each *Land* may delegate as many members as it has votes. The votes of each *Land* may be given only as a block vote and only by members present or their substitutes.

Art. 52. (1) The *Bundesrat* elects its President for one year.

(2) The President convokes the *Bundesrat*. He must convoke it if the members for at least two *Lander* or the Federal Government so demand.

(3) The decisions of the *Bundesrat* are taken by at least the majority of its votes. It draws up its Rules of Procedure. It deliberates in public. The public may be excluded.

(4) Other members of the *Lander* Governments or persons commissioned by *Lander* Governments may belong to the committees of the *Bundesrat*.

Art. 53. The members of the Federal Government have the right and, on demand, the duty to participate in the deliberations of the *Bundesrat* and its committees. They must be heard at any time. The *Bundesrat* must be kept currently informed, by the Federal Government, of the conduct of federal affairs.

V. The Federal President

Art. 54. (1) The Federal President is elected, without debate, by the Federal Convention (*Bundesversammlung*). Every German is eligible who is entitled to vote for the *Bundestag* and has reached the age of forty years.

(2) The term of office of the Federal President is five years. Re-election for consecutive term is admissible only once.

(3) The Federal Convention consists of the members of the *Bundestag* and an equal number of members elected by the popular representative bodies of the *Lander* according to the principle of proportional representation.

(4) The Federal Convention meets not later than thirty days before the expiration of the term of office of the Federal President and, in the case of premature termination, not later than thirty days after this date. It is convoked by the President of the *Bundestag*.

(5) Upon expiration of the legislative term, the time period provided for in paragraph (4), sentence 1, begins with the first convening of the *Bundestag*.

(6) The person receiving the votes of the majority of the members of the Federal Convention is elected. If such majority is not obtained by any candidate in two ballots, the candidate receiving most votes in a further ballot is elected.

(7) Details are regulated by a Federal law.

Art. 55. (1) The Federal President may not be a member of either the Government or a legislative body of the Federation or a *Land*.

(2) The Federal President may not hold any other salaried office or engage in a trade or practice a profession or belong to the management or the supervisory board (*Aufsichtsrat*) of a profit-making enterprise.

Art. 56. On assuming office, the Federal President takes the following oath in the presence of the assembled members of the *Bundestag* and the *Bundesrat:*

> "I swear that I shall dedicate my efforts to the well-being of the German people, enhance its prosperity, protect it from harm, uphold and defend the Basic Law and the laws of the Federation, fulfill my duties conscientiously and do justice to all. So help me God."

The oath may also be taken without the religious asseveration.

Art. 57. In the event of the Federal President's being prevented from exercising the authority of his office, or in the event of a premature vacancy in the office, this authority shall be exercised by the President of the *Bundesrat*.

Art. 58. Orders and decrees of the Federal President become valid only when countersigned by the Federal Chancellor or the competent Federal Minister. This does not apply in the case of the appointment and dismissal of the Federal Chancellor, of the dissolution of the *Bundestag* pursuant to Article 63, and of the request pursuant to Article 69, paragraph (3).

Art. 59. (1) The Federal President represents the Federation in matters concerning international law. He concludes treaties with foreign States on behalf of the Federation. He accredits and receives envoys.

(2) Treaties which regulate the political relations of the Federation or refer to matters of federal legislation require, in the form of a Federal law, the approval or the participation of the respective bodies competent for Federal legislation. For administrative agreements the provisions concerning the Federal administration apply correspondingly.

Art. 60. (1) Unless otherwise provided by law, the Federal President appoints and dismisses the Federal judges and the Federal civil servants.

(2) In individual cases, he exercises the right of pardon on behalf of the Federation.

(3) He may delegate these powers to other authorities.

(4) Paragraphs (2) to (4) of Article 46 apply to the Federal President correspondingly.

Art. 61. (1) The *Bundestag* or the *Bundesrat* may impeach the Federal President before the Federal

Constitutional Court for willful violation of the Basic Law or any other Federal law. The motion for impeachment must be introduced by at least one fourth of the members of the *Bundestag* or one fourth of the votes of the *Bundesrat*. The decision to impeach requires a majority of two thirds of the members of the *Bundestag* or of two thirds of the votes of the *Bundesrat*. The prosecution is conducted by a person commissioned by the impeaching body.

(2) If the Federal Constitutional Court finds the Federal President guilty of a willful violation of the Basic Law or of any other Federal law, it may declare him to have forfeited his office. Upon institution of impeachment proceedings, the Federal Constitutional Court may, by interim order, rule that the Federal President shall be debarred from exercising the authority of his office.

VI. THE FEDERAL GOVERNMENT

ART. 62. The Federal Government consists of the Federal Chancellor and the Federal Ministers.

ART. 63. (1) The Federal Chancellor is elected, without debate, by the *Bundestag* on the proposal of the Federal President.

(2) The person obtaining the majority of votes of the *Bundestag* members is elected. He is to be appointed by the Federal President.

(3) If the person proposed is not elected, the *Bundestag* may, within fourteen days of the ballot, elect a Federal Chancellor by more than one half of its members.

(4) If the Federal Chancellor is not elected within this time period, a new ballot shall take place without delay, in which the person receiving the greatest number of votes shall be elected. If the person elected obtains the votes of the majority of the *Bundestag* members, the Federal President must, within seven days of the election, appoint him. If the person elected does not obtain this majority, the Federal President must, within seven days, either appoint him or dissolve the *Bundestag*.

ART. 64. (1) The Federal Ministers are appointed and dismissed by the Federal President upon the proposal of the Federal Chancellor.

(2) The Federal Chancellor and the Federal Ministers, on assuming office, take before the *Bundestag* the oath provided in Article 56.

ART. 65. The Federal Chancellor determines, and assumes responsibility for, general policy. Within the limits of this general policy, each Federal Minister conducts the business of his department independently and on his own responsibility. The Federal Government decides on differences of opinion between the Federal Ministers. The Federal Chancellor conducts the business of the Federal Government in accordance with Rules of Procedure adopted by it and approved by the Federal President.

ART. 66. The Federal Chancellor and the Federal Ministers may not hold any other salaried office or engage in a trade or practice a profession or belong to the management or, without *Bundestag* approval, to the supervisory board (*Aufsichtsrat*) of a profit-making enterprise.

ART. 67. (1) The *Bundestag* may express its lack of confidence in the Federal Chancellor only by electing, by the majority of its members, a successor and by submitting a request to the Federal President for the dismissal of the Federal Chancellor. The Federal President must comply with the request and appoint the person elected.

(2) There must be an interval of forty-eight hours between the motion and the election.

ART. 68. (1) If a motion of the Federal Chancellor for a vote of confidence does not obtain the support of the majority of the members of the *Bundestag*, the Federal President may, upon the proposal of the Federal Chancellor, dissolve the *Bundestag* within twenty-one days. The right to dissolve lapses as soon as the *Bundestag*, with the majority of its members, elects another Federal Chancellor.

(2) There must be an interval of forty-eight hours between the introduction of the motion and the vote thereon.

ART. 69. (1) The Federal Chancellor appoints a Federal Minister as his deputy.

(2) The Federal Chancellor's or a Federal Minister's tenure of office ends in any case with the convening of a new *Bundestag;* a Federal Minister's tenure of office ends also with any other termination of the tenure of office of the Federal Chancellor.

(3) At the request of the Federal President, the Federal Chancellor or, at the request of the Federal Chancellor or of the Federal President, a Federal Minister, is bound to continue to transact the business of his office until the appointment of his successor.

VII. THE LEGISLATION OF THE FEDERATION

ART. 70. (1) The *Lander* have the power to legislate insofar as this Basic Law does vest legislative powers in the Federation.

(2) The delimitation of competence between the Federation and the *Lander* is determined in accordance with the provisions of this Basic Law concerning exclusive and concurrent legislation.

ART. 71. In the field of exclusive legislation of the Federation, the *Lander* have the power to legislate only if, and insofar as, they are expressly so empowered by a Federal law.

ART. 72. (1) In the field of concurrent legislation, the *Lander* have the power to legislate as long as, and insofar as, the Federation makes no use of its legislative power.

(2) The Federation has legislative power in this

field insofar as a need for regulation by Federal law exists because:

1. a matter cannot be effectively regulated by the legislation of individual *Lander,* or

2. the regulation of a matter by a *Land* law might prejudice the interests of other *Lander* or of the community at large, or

3. the preservation of legal or economic unity demands it, in particular the preservation of uniformity of living conditions beyond the territory of an individual *Land.*

ART. 73. The Federation has exclusive legislation on:

1. foreign affairs;

2. citizenship in the Federation;

3. freedom of movement, passports, immigration and emigration and extradition;

4. currency, money and coinage, weights and measures, and regulation of time and calendar;

5. the unity of the territory as regards customs and commercial purposes, commercial and navigation agreements, the freedom of traffic in goods, and the exchanges of goods and payments with foreign countries, including customs and border control;

6. Federal railroads, and air traffic;

7. postal services and telecommunications;

8. the legal status of persons in the service of the Federation and of public law corporations directly controlled by the Federal Government;

9. industrial property rights (including patents and trade marks), author's copyrights, and publisher's copyrights;

10. cooperation of the Federation and the *Lander* in the field of criminal police and in matters concerning the protection of the Constitution, the establishment of a Federal Office of Criminal Police, as well as international prevention and repression of crime;

11. statistics for Federal purposes.

ART. 74. Concurrent legislation extends over the following fields:

1. Civil law, criminal law, and execution of sentences, the constitution of courts and their procedure, the Bar, notaries, and legal advice (*Rechtsberatung*);

2. census and registry matters;

3. law pertaining to associations and assemblies;

4. the right of sojourn and of settlement of aliens;

5. the protection of German works of art and of cultural [historic] significance against removal abroad;

6. matters relating to refugees and expellees;

7. public welfare;

8. citizenship in the *Lander;*

9. war damage and compensation (*Wiedergutmachung*);

10. assistance to war-disabled persons and to surviving dependents, the care of former prisoners of war and the care of war graves;

11. law relating to the economy (mining, industry, power supply, crafts, trades, commerce, banking and stock exchange, insurance to which civil and not public law applies);

12. labor law, including the relationship between labor and management within an enterprise, the protection of workers and the conducting of employment agencies and exchanges, as well as social insurance, including unemployment insurance;

13. the furtherance of scientific research;

14. law regarding expropriation insofar as it is concerned with the matters enumerated in Articles 73 and 74;

15. transfer of land and real estate, natural resources and means of production to public ownership or to other forms of publicly controlled economy;

16. prevention of the abuse of economic power;

17. furtherance of agricultural and forestry production, safeguarding of food supply, import and export of agricultural and forestry products, deep-sea and coastal fishing, and the guarding and preservation of the coasts;

18. transactions in real estate, law concerning land and matters concerning agricultural leases, housing, settlements, and homesteads;

19. measures against epidemic and infectious diseases affecting human beings and animals, the admission to medical and other healing professions and healing practices and the traffic in drugs, medicines, narcotics, and poisons;

20. protection concerning traffic in food and stimulants as well as in necessities of life, in fodder, in agricultural and forestry seeds and seedlings, and protection of trees and plants against diseases and pests;

21. ocean and coastal shipping and aids to navigation, inland shipping, meteorological services, sea waterways, and inland waterways used for general traffic;

22. road traffic, motorized transport, and the construction and maintenance of highways used for long-distance traffic;

23. railroads other than Federal railroads, except mountain railroads.

ART. 75. Within the conditions set forth in Article 72, the Federation has the right to issue general provisions concerning:

1. The legal status of persons employed in the public service of the *Lander, Gemeinden,* and other public-law corporations;

2. the general law to govern the press and motion pictures;

3. hunting, the preservation of nature, and the care of the countryside;

4. land distribution, regional planning, and water conservation;

5. matters relating to registration and identity cards.

Art. 76. (1) Bills are introduced in the *Bundestag* by the Federal Government, by members of the *Bundestag* or by the *Bundesrat.*

(2) Bills of the Federal Government are to be submitted first to the *Bundesrat.* The *Bundesrat* is entitled to give its opinion on these bills within three weeks.

(3) Bills of the *Bundesrat* are to be submitted to the *Bundestag* by the Federal Government, which must add a statement of its own views.

Art. 77. (1) Federal laws are passed by the *Bundestag.* After their adoption, they shall, without delay, be submitted to the *Bundesrat* by the President of the *Bundestag.*

(2) The *Bundesrat* may, within two weeks of the receipt of the adopted bill, demand that a committee composed of members of the *Bundastag* and *Bundesrat* be convoked to consider the bill jointly. The composition and the procedure of this committee is regulated by Rules of Procedure which shall be agreed by the *Bundestag* and shall require the approval of the *Bundesrat.* The members of the *Bundesrat* delegated to this committee are not bound by instructions. If the approval of the *Bundesrat* is required for a law, both the *Bundestag* and the Federal Government may demand the convocation of the committee. Should the committee propose amendments to the adopted bill, a new vote must be taken by the *Bundestag.*

(3) Insofar as the approval of the *Bundesrat* is not required for a law, the *Bundesrat* may, if proceedings pursuant to paragraph (2) are completed, veto within one week a law passed by the *Bundestag.* The time period for a veto begins in the case of paragraph (2), last sentence, with the receipt of the bill as readopted by the *Bundestag;* in all other cases, with the conclusion of the proceedings before the committee provided for in paragraph (2).

(4) Should the veto be adopted by a majority of the *Bundesrat* votes, it may be rejected by the decision of a majority of the *Bundestag* members. If the *Bundesrat* has adopted the veto by at least a two-thirds majority of its votes, the rejection by the *Bundestag* shall require a majority of two thirds, and at least the majority of the members of the *Bundestag.*

Art. 78. A law adopted by the *Bundestag* is deemed to have been passed if the *Bundesrat* approves it, does not introduce a motion pursuant to Article 77, paragraph (2), does not impose a veto within the time period provided by Article 77, paragraph (3), or withdraws its veto; or, if the veto is overridden by the *Bundestag.*

Art. 79. (1) The Basic Law may be amended only by a law expressly amending or amplifying the text of the Basic Law.

(2) Such a law requires the approval of two thirds of the *Bundestag* members and two thirds of the *Bundesrat* votes.

(3) An amendment to this Basic Law affecting the organization of the Federation into *Lander,* the basic participation of the *Lander* in legislation, or the basic principles laid down in Articles 1 and 20 is inadmissible.

Art. 80. (1) The Federal Government, a Federal Minister, or the *Land* Governments may be empowered by a law to issue decrees having the force of law (*Rechtsverordnungen*). In such cases, the contents, purpose, and scope of such powers must be specified in the law. The legal basis must be cited in the decree. If a law provides that such power may be further delegated, such delegation shall require a decree having the force of law (*Rechtsverordnung*).

(2) *Bundesrat* approval is required, unless otherwise provided by Federal legislation, for decrees having the force of law (*Rechtsverordnungen*) issued by the Federal Government or a Federal Minister, concerning basic principles and charges for the use of facilities of the Federal railroads, of the postal services, and of telecommunications, concerning the construction and operation of railroads, as well as for decrees having the force of law (*Rechtsverordnungen*) issued on the basis of Federal laws which require *Bundesrat* approval or which are executed by the *Lander* on behalf of the Federation or as matters of their own concern.

Art. 81. (1) Should the *Bundestag* not be dissolved as provided for in Article 68, the Federal President may, at the request of the Federal Government and with *Bundesrat* approval, declare a state of legislative emergency with respect to a bill, if the *Bundestag* rejects the bill although the Federal Government has declared it to be urgent. The same applies if a bill has been rejected although the Federal Chancellor had combined with it the motion provided for in Article 68.

(2) If the *Bundestag,* after a state of legislative emergency has been declared, again rejects the bill or passes it in a version declared to be unacceptable to the Federal Government, the law shall be deemed passed provided that the *Bundesrat* approves it. The same applies if the bill has not been passed by the *Bundestag* within four weeks after its reintroduction.

(3) During the term of office of a Federal Chancellor, any other bill rejected by the *Bundestag* may be passed within a period of six months after the first declaration of a state of legislative emergency in accordance with paragraphs (1) and (2). After expiration of this period, a further declaration of a state of legislative emergency is inadmissible during the term of office of the same Federal Chancellor.

(4) The Basic Law may neither be amended nor wholly or partially repealed or suspended by a law enacted pursuant to paragraph (2).

ART. 82. (1) Laws enacted in accordance with the provisions of this Basic Law shall, after countersignature, be engrossed by the Federal President and promulgated in the *Federal Gazette*. Decrees having the force of law (*Rechtsverordnungen*) shall be signed by the issuing authority and, unless otherwise provided by law, promulgated in the *Federal Gazette*.

(2) Every law and every decree having the force of law (*Rechtsverordnungen*) should specify the date of its becoming effective. In the absence of such a provision, it shall become effective on the fourteenth day after the end of the day on which the *Federal Gazette* was issued.

VIII. THE EXECUTION OF FEDERAL LAWS AND THE FEDERAL ADMINISTRATION

ART. 83. The *Lander* execute the Federal laws as matters of their own concern insofar as this Basic Law does not otherwise provide or permit.

ART. 84. (1) If the *Lander* execute the Federal laws as matters of their own concern, they determine the establishment of authorities and administrative procedures insofar as Federal laws approved by the *Bundesrat* do not otherwise provide.

(2) The Federal Government may, with *Bundesrat* approval, issue general administrative provisions.

(3) The Federal Government exercises supervision to ensure that the *Lander* execute the Federal laws in accordance with the legislation in force. For this purpose the Federal Government may send commissioners to the highest *Land* authorities and, with their approval or, if this approval is refused, with *Bundesrat* approval, also to subordinate authorities.

(4) Should shortcomings in the execution of Federal laws which the Federal Government has found to exist in the *Lander* not be corrected, the *Bundesrat* shall decide, upon request of the Federal Government or of the *Land,* whether the *Land* has infringed the law. A decision of the *Bundesrat* may be challenged in the Federal Constitutional Court.

(5) For the execution of Federal laws the Federal Government may, by Federal legislation requiring *Bundesrat* approval, be granted the power to give individual instructions in special cases. They are, except if the Federal Government considers a case to be urgent, to be addressed to the highest *Land* authorities.

ART. 85. (1) Where the *Lander* execute the Federal laws on behalf of the Federation, the establishment of the administrative agencies remains a concern of the *Lander* insofar as Federal legislation approved by the *Bundesrat* does not otherwise provide.

(2) The Federal Government may issue, with *Bundesrat* approval, general administrative provisions. It may regulate the uniform training of civil servants and Government employees (*Angestellte*). The heads of the administrative agencies at intermediate level shall be appointed with its agreement.

(3) The *Land* authorities are subject to the instructions of the competent highest Federal authorities. Except if the Federal Government considers the matter urgent, the instructions are to be addressed to the highest *Land* authorities. Execution of the instructions is to be ensured by the highest *Land* authorities.

(4) Federal supervision extends to the legality and suitability of the manner of execution. The Federal Government may, for this purpose, require the submission of reports and documents and send commissioners to all authorities.

ART. 86. Where the Federation executes the laws by direct Federal administration or through public-law corporations or institutions directly under the Federation, the Federal Government issues, insofar as the law does not make any special provisions, general administrative provisions. It determines, insofar as it is not otherwise provided by the law, the establishment of the administrative agencies.

ART. 87. (1) The foreign service, the Federal finance administration, the Federal railroads, the Federal postal services, and, in accordance with the provisions of Article 89, the administration of the Federal waterways and shipping are conducted as integral parts of the Federal administration with their own subordinate administrative offices. Federal border control authorities and central offices for police information and communications, for the compilation of data for the purpose of protecting the Constitution, and for the criminal police may be established by Federal legislation.

(2) Social-insurance institutions, the sphere of competence of which extends beyond the territory of a *Land,* are conducted as public law corporations directly under the Federation.

(3) In addition, independent central Federal administrative agencies and new public law corporations and institutions directly under the Federation may be established by Federal legislation for matters on which the Federation has the power to legislate. Should new functions arise for the Federation in matters in respect to which it has legislative com-

petence, Federal administrative agencies at intermediate and lower levels may, in case of urgent need, be established with the approval of the *Bundesrat* and of the majority of the *Bundestag*.

ART. 88. The Federation establishes a bank of issue as a Federal bank.

ART. 89. (1) The Federation is the owner of the former Reich waterways.

(2) The Federation administers the Federal waterways through its own agencies. It exercises those State functions relating to inland shipping which extend beyond the territory of a *Land* and the functions relating to seagoing shipping which are conferred on it by legislation. Upon request, the Federation may delegate the administration of Federal waterways, insofar as they lie within the territory of a *Land,* to this *Land,* in administration by commission (*Auftragsverwaltung*). Should a waterway touch the territories of several *Lander,* the Federation may delegate the administration of it to the *Land* which is proposed in a request submitted by the *Lander* concerned.

(3) In the administration, development, and construction of waterways, the requirements of soil cultivation and of water conservation shall be safeguarded in agreement with the *Lander*.

ART. 90. (1) The Federation is the owner of the former Reich *Autobahnen* and Reich highways.

(2) The *Lander,* or such self-governing corporations as are competent under *Land* public law, administer on behalf of the Federation the Federal *Autobahnen* and other Federal highways used for long-distance traffic.

(3) At the request of a *Land,* the Federation may take under direct Federal administration Federal *Autobahnen* and other Federal highways used for long-distance traffic, insofar as they lie within the territory of the *Land.*

ART. 91. (1) In order to avert any imminent danger to the existence or the libertarian democratic basic order of the Federation or of a *Land,* a *Land* may appeal for the services of the police forces of other *Lander.*

(2) If the *Land* in which this danger is imminent is not itself prepared or in a position to combat the danger, the Federal Government may place the police in that *Land* and the police forces of other *Lander* under its own instructions. This order has to be rescinded after the elimination of the danger, or else at any time on the demand of the *Bundesrat*.

IX. THE ADMINISTRATION OF JUSTICE

ART. 92. Judicial authority is vested in the judges; it is exercised by the Federal Constitutional Court, by the Supreme Federal Court, by the federal courts provided for in this Basic Law and by the courts of the *Lander*.

ART. 93. (1) The Federal Constitutional Court decides:

1. on the interpretation of this Basic Law in the event of disputes concerning the extent of the rights and duties of any of the highest Federal agencies or of other parties granted independent rights by this Basic Law or by Rules of Procedure of the highest Federal agencies;

2. in case of differences of opinion or doubts as to the formal and material compatibility of Federal law or *Land* law with this Basic Law or on the compatibility of *Land* law with other Federal law, at the request of the Federal Government, of a *Land* Government or of one third of the *Bundestag* members;

3. in case of differences of opinion on the rights and duties of the Federation and the *Lander,* particularly in the execution of Federal law by the *Lander,* and in the exercise of Federal supervision;

4. on other public law disputes between the Federation and the *Lander,* between different *Lander* or within a *Land,* insofar as recourse to another court is not provided for;

5. in all other cases provided for in this Basic Law.

(2) Furthermore, the Federal Constitutional Court shall act in such cases as are otherwise assigned to it by Federal legislation.

ART. 94. (1) The Federal Constitutional Court consists of Federal judges and other members. Half of the members of the Federal Constitutional Court are elected by the *Bundestag* and half by the *Bundesrat*. They may not belong to the *Bundestag,* the *Bundesrat,* the Federal Government or corresponding agencies of a *Land.*

(2) A Federal law determines the constitution and procedure of the Federal Constitutional Court and specifies in what cases its decisions shall have the force of law.

ART. 95. (1) A Supreme Federal Court is established for the maintenance of the unity of Federal law.

(2) The Supreme Federal Court decides cases in which the decision is of fundamental importance for the uniformity of the administration of justice by the high Federal courts.

(3) The appointment of the judges of the Supreme Federal Court is decided jointly by the Federal Minister of Justice and a committee for the selection of judges consisting of the *Land* Ministers of Justice and an equal number of members elected by the *Bundestag*.

(4) In other respects, the constitution of the Supreme Federal Court and its procedure are regulated by Federal legislation.

ART. 96. (1) High Federal courts shall be established in the spheres of ordinary, administrative, finance, labor, and social jurisdiction.

(2) Article 95, paragraph (3), applies to the judges of the high Federal courts with the proviso that the Federal Minister of Justice and the *Land* Ministers of Justice shall be substituted by the Ministers competent in the particular matter. Their service status must be regulated by a special Federal law.

(3) The Federation may establish Federal disciplinary courts for disciplinary proceedings against Federal civil servants and Federal judges.

ART. 97. (1) Judges are independent and subject only to the law.

(2) Judges definitively appointed on a full-time basis to established court offices may, against their will, be dismissed before the expiration of their term of office, or permanently or temporarily suspended from office or transferred to another position or placed on the retired list, only by the decision of a court and only on grounds and according to the procedures provided for by law. Legislation may set age limits for the retirement of judges who have been appointed for life. In the case of changes in the structure of the courts or their area of jurisdiction, judges may be transferred to another court or suspended from office with the retention, however, of their full salary.

ART. 98. (1) The legal status of the Federal judges is to be regulated by a special Federal law.

(2) If a Federal judge, in his official capacity or unofficially, infringes on the principles of the Basic Law or the constitutional order of a *Land,* the Federal Constitutional Court may, upon request of the *Bundestag,* rule, with a two-thirds majority, that the judge be transferred to another office or placed on the retired list. In a case of willful infringement, dismissal may also be ordered.

(3) The legal status of the judges in the *Lander* is to be regulated by special *Land* legislation. The Federation may issue general provisions.

(4) The *Lander* may determine that the *Land* Minister of Justice shall, together with a committee for the selection of judges, decide on the appointment of judges in the *Lander.*

(5) The *Lander* may, in conformity with paragraph (2), provide a regulation for *Land* judges. *Land* constitutional law in force remains unaffected. The decision concerning a case of impeachment of a judge rests with the Federal Constitutional Court.

ART. 99. The decision on constitutional disputes within a *Land* may be assigned by *Land* legislation to the Federal Constitutional Court, and the decision of last instance, on such matters as involve the application of *Land* law, to the high Federal courts.

ART. 100. (1) If a court considers unconstitutional a law the validity of which is pertinent to its decision, proceedings must be stayed and, if a violation of a *Land* Constitution is at issue, the decision of the *Land* court competent for constitutional disputes shall be obtained and, if a violation of this Basic Law is at issue, the decision of the Federal Constitutional Court shall be obtained. This also applies if the violation of this Basic Law by *Land* law or the incompatibility of a *Land* law with a Federal law is at issue.

(2) If, in litigation, it is doubtful whether a rule of international law forms part of Federal law and whether it directly creates rights and duties for the individual (Article 25), the court has to obtain the decision of the Federal Constitutional Court.

(3) If the constitutional court of a *Land,* in interpreting the Basic Law, intends to deviate from a decision of the Federal Constitutional Court or of the constitutional court of another *Land,* the [said] constitutional court must obtain the decision of the Federal Constitutional Court. If, in interpreting other Federal law, it intends to deviate from the decision of the Supreme Federal Court or a high Federal court, it must obtain the decision of the Supreme Federal Court.

ART. 101. (1) Extraordinary courts are inadmissible. No one may be removed from the jurisdiction of his lawful judge.

(2) Courts dealing with matters in special fields may be established only by law.

ART. 102. The death sentence is abolished.

ART. 103. (1) Everyone is entitled to a proper hearing before the courts.

(2) An act may be punished only if the law defined it as punishable before it was committed.

(3) On the basis of the general criminal laws, no one may be punished for the same act more than once.

ART. 104. (1) The freedom of the individual may be restricted only on the basis of a formal law and only with due regard to the forms prescribed therein. Detained persons may be subjected neither to mental nor physical ill treatment.

(2) Only a judge is to decide on the admissibility and extension of a deprivation of liberty. In the case of every such deprivation which is not based on the order of a judge, a judicial decision must be obtained without delay. The police may, on its own authority, hold no one in its own custody beyond the end of the day following the arrest. Further details are to be regulated by law.

(3) Any person temporarily detained on suspicion of having committed a punishable act must, at the latest on the day following the detention, be brought before a judge who shall inform him of the reasons for the detention, interrogate him, and give him an opportunity to raise objections. The judge must, without delay, either issue a warrant of arrest, setting out the reasons thereof, or order the release.

(4) A relative of the person detained or a person

enjoying his confidence must be notified without delay of any judicial decision ordering or extending a deprivation of liberty.

X. Finance

Art. 105. (1) The Federation has exclusive legislation on customs and fiscal monopolies.

(2) The Federation has concurrent legislation on:

1. excise taxes and taxes on transactions, with the exception of taxes with localized application, in particular the taxes on real estate acquisition, incremental value, and fire protection;

2. the taxes on income, property, inheritance, and donations;

3. taxes on real estate and on business (*Realsteuern*), with the exception of the fixing of tax rates;

if it claims the taxes in their entirety or in part to cover Federal expenditures, or if the conditions set forth in Article 72, paragraph (2), exist.

(3) Federal legislation on taxes the yield of which accrues in their entirety or in part of the *Lander* or the *Gemeinden* (*Gemeindeverbaende*) require *Bundesrat* approval.

Art. 106. (1) Customs, the yield of monopolies, the excise taxes with the exception of the beer tax, the transportation tax, the turnover tax, and levies on property serving nonrecurrent purposes accrue to the Federation.

(2) The beer tax, the taxes on transactions with the exception of the transportation tax and turnover tax, the income and corporation taxes, the property tax, the inheritance tax, the taxes on real estate and on businesses (*Realsteuern*), and the taxes with localized application accrue to the *Lander* and, in accordance with provisions of *Land* legislation, to the *Gemeinden*.

(3) The Federation may, by means of a Federal law requiring *Bundesrat* approval, claim a part of the income and corporation taxes to cover its expenditures not covered by other revenues, in particular to cover grants which are to be made to *Lander* to meet expenditures in the fields of education, public health, and welfare.

(4) In order to ensure the working efficiency also of the *Lander* with low tax revenues and to equalize the differing burdens of expenditure of the *Lander,* the Federation may make grants and take the funds necessary for this purpose from specific taxes accruing to the *Lander*. A Federal law, requiring *Bundesrat* approval, shall determine which taxes shall be utilized for this purpose and in what amounts and on what basis the grants shall be distributed among the *Lander* entitled to equalization; the grants must be transferred directly to the *Lander*.

Art. 107. The final distribution, as between the Federation and the *Lander,* of the taxes subject to concurrent legislation shall be effected not later than December 31, 1952, and by means of a Federal law requiring *Bundesrat* approval. This does not apply to the taxes on real estate and on businesses, and the taxes with localized application. Thereby, each party should be assigned a legal claim to certain taxes or shares in taxes commensurate to their tasks.

Art. 108. (1) Customs, fiscal monopolies, the excise taxes subject to concurrent legislation, the transportation tax, the turnover tax, and the nonrecurrent levies on property are administered by Federal finance authorities. The organization of these authorities and the procedure to be applied by them are regulated by Federal legislation. The heads of the authorities at intermediate level shall be appointed in agreement with the *Land* Governments. The Federation may delegate the administration of the nonrecurrent levies on property to the *Land* finance authorities as administration by commission (*Auftragsverwaltung*).

(2) Where the Federation claims part of the income and corporation taxes it shall thus far administer them; it may, however, delegate the administration to the *Land* finance authorities as administration by commission (*Auftragsverwaltung*).

(3) The remaining taxes are administered by *Land* finance authorities. The Federation may, by Federal legislation requiring *Bundesrat* approval, regulate the organization of these authorities, the procedure to be applied by them, and the uniform training of the civil servants. The heads of the authorities at intermediate level must be appointed in agreement with the Federal Government. The administration of the taxes accruing to the *Gemeinden* may be delegated by the *Lander* in entirety or in part to the *Gemeinden*.

(4) Insofar as taxes accrue to the Federation, the *Land* finance authorities shall act on behalf of the Federation. The *Lander* are liable with their revenues for an orderly administration of these taxes; the Federal Minister of Finance may supervise the orderly administration through authorized Federal agents who have the right to give instructions to the authorities at intermediate and lower levels.

(5) The jurisdiction of Finance Courts shall be uniformly regulated by Federal legislation.

(6) The general administrative provisions shall be issued by the Federal Government and, insofar as the administration is incumbent upon the *Land* finance authorities, will require *Bundesrat* approval.

Art. 109. The Federation and the *Lander* are autonomous and mutually independent with regard to their respective budgets.

Art. 110. (1) All revenues and expenditures of the Federation must be estimated for each fiscal year and included in the budget.

(2) The budget shall be established by law before the beginning of the fiscal year. Revenue and expenditure must be balanced. Expenditures shall, as a rule, be approved for one year; in special cases, they may be approved for a longer period. Otherwise, the Fed-

eral budget law may contain no provisions which extend beyond the fiscal year or which do not concern the revenues and expenditures of the Federation or its administration.

(3) The assets and liabilities shall be set forth in an appendix to the budget.

(4) In the case of Federal enterprises commercially operated, only the final result, and not the detailed revenues and expenditures, need be included in the budget.

Art. 111. (1) If, by the end of a fiscal year, the budget for the following year has not been established by law, the Federal Government shall, until such a law comes into force, be empowered to effect such payments as are necessary:

(a) to maintain existing institutions established by law and to carry out measures adopted by law;

(b) to meet legal obligations of the Federation;

(c) to continue building projects, procurements, and other services or to grant further subsidies for these purposes, provided that funds have already been approved in the budget of a previous year.

(2) Insofar as revenues, provided by special legislation and derived from taxes, dues, and other sources, or working capital reserves do not cover the expenditures mentioned under paragraph (1), the Federal Government may, by way of credits, procure the funds, up to one fourth of the total amount of the previous budget, which are necessary to conduct current operations.

Art. 112. Expenditures exceeding the budget and any extraordinary expenditures require the approval of the Federal Minister of Finance. It may only be given in case of unforeseen and compelling necessity.

Art. 113. Decisions of the *Bundestag* and *Bundesrat* which increase the budget expenditure proposed by the Federal Government, or include or imply new expenditures for the future, require the approval of the Federal Government.

Art. 114. (1) The Federal Minister of Finance must submit to the *Bundestag* and the *Bundesrat* an annual account of all revenues and expenditures as well as of assets and liabilities.

(2) This account shall be audited by an Audit Office the members of which shall enjoy judicial independence. The general account and a survey of the assets and liabilities have to be submitted to the *Bundestag* and the *Bundesrat* in the course of the following fiscal year, together with the comments of the Audit Office, in order to secure a discharge for the Federal Government. The auditing of accounts shall be regulated by a Federal law.

Art. 115. Funds may be obtained by way of credits only in the case of extraordinary requirements and as a rule only for expenditure for productive purposes

and only on the basis of a Federal law. The granting of credits and providing of securities as a charge on the Federation, the effect of which extends beyond the fiscal year, may be undertaken only on the basis of a Federal law. The amount of the credits or the extent of the obligation for which the Federation assumes liability must be determined in the law.

XI. Transitional and Concluding Provisions

Art. 116. (1) Unless otherwise provided by law, a German within the meaning of this Basic Law is a person who possesses German citizenship or who has been accepted in the territory of the German Reich, as it existed on December 31, 1937, as a refugee or expellee of German ethnic stock (*Volkszugehoerigkeit*), or as the spouse or descendant of such person.

(2) Former German citizens, who, between January 30, 1933, and May 8, 1945, were deprived of their citizenship for political, racial, or religious reasons, and their descendants, shall be regranted German citizenship on application. They are considered as not having been deprived of their German citizenship if they have taken up residence in Germany after May 8, 1945, and have not expressed a desire to the contrary.

Art. 117. (1) Legislation which conflicts with Article 3, paragraph (2), remains in force pending harmonization with this provision of the Basic Law, but not beyond March 31, 1953.

(2) Laws restricting the right of freedom of movement, by reason of the present housing and space shortage, remain in force until repealed by Federal legislation.

Art. 118. The reorganization of the territory comprising the *Lander* Baden, Württemberg-Baden, and Württemberg-Hohenzollern may be effected, by agreement between the *Lander* concerned, in a manner deviating from the provisions of Article 29. Failing agreement, the reorganization shall be regulated by Federal legislation which must provide for a referendum.

Art. 119. In matters relating to refugees and expellees, in particular as regards their distribution among the *Lander*, the Federal Government may, with *Bundesrat* approval, issue decrees having the force of law, pending a settlement of the matter by Federal legislation. In special cases, the Federal Government may be empowered to issue individual instructions. Except in case of danger in delay the instructions are to be addressed to the highest *Land* authorities.

Art. 120. (1) In accordance with more detailed provisions of a Federal law, the Federation bears the expenses for occupation costs and the other internal and external burdens caused by war, and for the subsidies to [alleviate] the burdens of social insurance, including unemployment insurance, and public assistance for the unemployed.

(2) The revenues are transferred to the Federation at the same time as the Federation assumes responsibility for the expenditures.

ART. 121. Within the meaning of this Basic Law, a majority of the members of the *Bundestag* and of the Federal Convention (*Bundesversammlung*) is the majority of the statutory number of their members.

ART. 122. (1) As from the convening of the *Bundestag*, laws shall be passed exclusively by the legislative authorities recognized in this Basic Law.

(2) Where the competence of legislative bodies and of bodies participating in legislation in an advisory capacity ends in accordance with paragraph (1), such bodies shall be dissolved as of the same date.

ART. 123. (1) Law in existence prior to the [first] convening of the *Bundestag* remains in effect, insofar as it does not conflict with the Basic Law.

(2) The State treaties concluded by the German Reich concerning matters for which, under this Basic Law, *Land* legislation is competent, remain in force if they are valid and continue to be valid in accordance with general principles of law, subject to all rights and objections of the interested parties, pending the conclusion of new State treaties by the authorities competent under this Basic Law or until they are otherwise terminated pursuant to the provisions that they contain.

ART. 124. Legislation concerning matters within the exclusive legislative competence of the Federation shall become Federal law within the area of its application.

ART. 125. Legislation concerning matters of concurrent Federal legislation shall become Federal law within the area of its application

    1. insofar as it uniformly applies within one or more zones of occupation,

    2. insofar as it concerns legislation by which former Reich law has been amended since May 8, 1945.

ART. 126. Differences of opinion concerning the continuing validity of legislation as Federal law are settled by the Federal Constitutional Court.

ART. 127. Within one year of the promulgation of this Basic Law, the Federal Government may, with the approval of the Government of the *Lander* concerned, extend, to the *Lander* Baden, Greater Berlin, Rhineland-Palatinate, and Württemberg-Hohenzollern, legislation of the Bizonal Economic Administration insofar as it continues to be in force as Federal legislation under Articles 124 or 125.

ART. 128. Insofar as legislation continuing in force provides for powers to give instructions within the meaning of Article 84, paragraph (5), these powers remain in effect until otherwise provided by law.

ART. 129. (1) Insofar as legal provisions continuing in force as Federal law contain an authorization to issue decrees having the force of law or general ad-

ministrative provisions, and to perform administrative acts, this authorization passes to the [administrative] agencies henceforth competent in such matters. In cases of doubt, the Federal Government decides in agreement with the *Bundesrat;* the decision must be published.

(2) Insofar as legal provisions continuing in force as *Land* law contain such an authorization, it shall be exercised by the [administrative] agencies competent according to *Land* law.

(3) Insofar as legal provisions within the meaning of paragraphs (1) and (2) authorize their amendment or amplification or the issue of legal provisions in lieu of laws, these authorizations have expired.

(4) The provisions of paragraphs (1) and (2) apply correspondingly whenever legal provisions refer to regulations no longer valid or to institutions no longer in existence.

ART. 130. (1) Administrative agencies and other institutions which serve the public administration or the administration of justice and are not based on *Land* law or State treaties between *Lander*, as well as the amalgamated management of the South West German railroads and the Administrative Council for the postal services and telecommunications of the French Zone of Occupation, are placed under the Federal Government. The latter, with *Bundesrat* approval, regulates their transfer, dissolution, or liquidation.

(2) The highest disciplinary authority over the personnel of these administrations and establishments is the competent Federal Minister.

(3) Public Law corporations and institutions not directly under a *Land*, and not based on State treaties between *Lander*, are under the supervision of the competent highest Federal authority.

ART. 131. The legal status of persons, including refugees and expellees, who on May 8, 1945, were employed in the public service and who have left service for reasons other than those based on legal provisions concerning civil service or agreed employment regulations (*Tarif*), and who till now have not been employed or are not employed in a position corresponding to their former position, is to be regulated by Federal legislation. The same applies to persons, including refugees and expellees, who, on May 8, 1945, were entitled to a pension or other assistance and who no longer receive any assistance or any adequate assistance for reasons other than those based on legal provisions concerning civil service or agreed employment regulations (*Tarif*). Pending the coming into force of the Federal law, no legal claims may be made, unless otherwise provided by *Land* legislation.

ART. 132. (1) Civil servants and judges who, at the coming into force of this Basic Law, hold appointments for life may, within six months after the first convening of the *Bundestag,* be placed on the retired list or waiting list or be transferred to another office with lower remuneration, if they are personally or professionally unsuitable for their office. This provision applies correspondingly also to Government employees whose service cannot be terminated by notice of dismissal. In the case of Government employees whose service conditions provide for termination by notice of dismissal, the period of notice exceeding that required by agreed rules of employment may be canceled within the same period [of six months].

(2) These provisions do not apply to members of the public service who are not affected by the provisions regarding the "liberation from National Socialism, and militarism" or who are recognized victims of National Socialism, insofar as no serious grounds are to be found in their character.

(3) Persons affected [by the above] have recourse to the courts in accordance with Article 19, paragraph (4).

(4). Details are determined by a decree of the Federal Government, requiring *Bundesrat* approval.

ART. 133. The Federation succeeds to the rights and obligations of the Bizonal Economic Administration.

ART. 134. (1) Reich property becomes in principle Federal property.

(2) Insofar as such property was originally intended mainly for administrative functions which, under this Basic Law, are not administrative functions of the Federation, it is, without compensation, to be transferred to the authorities hereafter competent to carry out such functions, and to the *Lander* insofar as, according to its present, not merely provisional, use, it serves for administrative functions which, under this Basic Law, are hereafter to be fulfilled by the *Lander*. The Federation may also transfer other property to the *Lander*.

(3) Property which was placed at the disposal of the Reich by the *Lander* and *Gemeinden* without compensation shall again become the property of the *Lander* and *Gemeinden*, insofar as it is not required by the Federation for its own administrative functions.

(4) Details are regulated by a Federal law requiring *Bundesrat* approval.

ART. 135. (1) If, between May 8, 1945 and the coming into force of this Basic Law, a territory has passed from one *Land* to another, the property in this territory of the *Land* to which this territory had belonged devolves on the *Land* to which this territory now belongs.

(2) Property of no-longer-existing *Lander* or other public-law corporations and institutions, insofar as it was originally intended mainly for administrative functions, or in accordance with its present not merely provisional use serves mainly for administrative functions, devolves on the *Land* or public-law corporation or institution henceforth performing these functions.

(3) Insofar as it is not already included among

property within the meaning of paragraph (1), real estate of no longer existing *Lander*, including appurtenances, devolves on the *Land* in the territory of which it is located.

(4) Where an overriding interest of the Federation or the particular interest of a territory so requires, an arrangement deviating from paragraph (1) to (3) may be adopted by Federal legislation.

(5) Moreover, the legal succession and the settlement [of property], insofar as it has not been effected by January 1, 1952 by agreement between the *Lander* or public-law corporations or institutions concerned, shall be regulated by Federal legislation requiring *Bundesrat* approval.

(6) Participation of the former *Land* Prussia in civil-law enterprises devolves on the Federation. Details shall be regulated by a Federal law which may make deviating provisions.

(7) Insofar as, at the time of the coming into force of the Basic Law, property devolving on a *Land* or a public-law corporation or institution under paragraphs (1) and (3) has been disposed of by the party thereby authorized through a *Land* law, on the basis of a *Land* law, or in another way, the transfer of property is deemed to have taken place before the act of disposal.

ART. 136. (1) The *Bundesrat* convenes for the first time on the day of the first convening of the *Bundestag*.

(2) Pending the election of the first Federal President, his functions shall be exercised by the *Bundesrat* President. He does not have the right to dissolve the *Bundestag*.

ART. 137. (1) The right of civil servants, of employees of the public services and of judges of the Federation, of the *Lander*, and of the *Gemeinden* to stand for election may be restricted by legislation.

(2) The Electoral Law to be adopted by the Parliamentary Council applies for the election of the first *Bundestag*, of the first Federal Convention, and of the first Federal President of the Federal Republic.

(3) Pending its establishment, the function of the Federal Constitutional Court, pursuant to Article 41, paragraph (2), shall be exercised by the German High Court for the Combined Area, which shall decide in accordance with its Rules of Procedure.

ART. 138. Changes in the regulations of notaries, as they now exist in the *Lander* Baden, Bavaria, Württemberg-Baden, and Württemberg-Hohenzollern, require the approval of the Governments of these *Lander*.

ART. 139. The legal provisions enacted for the "liberation of the German people from National Socialism, and militarism" shall not be affected by the provisions of this Basic Law.

ART. 140. The provisions of Articles 136, 137, 138, 139, and 141 of the German Constitution of August 11, 1919, are an integral part of this Basic Law.

ART. 141. Article 7, paragraph (3), first sentence, finds no application in a *Land* where another regulation by *Land* law existed on January 1, 1949.

ART. 142. Notwithstanding the provision of Article 31, provisions of *Land* Constitutions remain in force also insofar as they guarantee basic rights in conformity with Articles 1 to 18 of this Basic Law.

ART. 143. (1) Whoever, by force or by threat of force, changes the constitutional order of the Federation or of a *Land,* deprives the Federal President of the powers accorded to him by this Basic Law, or, by force or by dangerous threats, compels him to exercise his powers or prevents him from exercising them altogether or in a specific manner, or separates from the Federation or from a *Land* a territory belonging to them, shall be sentenced to penal servitude for life or for not less than ten years.

(2) Whoever publicly incites to an action, within the meaning of paragraph (1), or plots it in connivance with another person, or otherwise prepares it, shall be sentenced to penal servitude up to ten years.

(3) In less serious cases, a sentence of not less than two years' penal servitude in the cases specified in paragraph (1), and of not less than one year's imprisonment in the cases specified in paragraph (2), may be imposed.

(4) Whoever of his own free will abandons an activity [of this sort] or, in case of participation of several persons, prevents the execution of a plot [of this sort], may not be punished in accordance with the provisions of paragraphs (1) to (3).

(5) Where such an action is directed exclusively against the constitutional order of a *Land,* the highest *Land* court competent for criminal cases shall, in the absence of any other provision in *Land* law, be competent to decide. In other cases, the regional superior court (*Oberlandesgericht*), in the district of which the first Federal Government has its seat, is competent.

(6) The aforementioned provisions apply pending other regulations by Federal law.

ART. 144. (1) This Basic Law requires adoption by the popular representative bodies in two thirds of the German *Lander* in which it shall for the time being apply.

(2) Insofar as restrictions are imposed on the application of the Basic Law in any of the *Lander* enumerated in Article 23, paragraph (1), or in a part of any of these *Lander,* that *Land* or that part of a *Land* has the right, in accordance with Article 38, to send delegates to the *Bundestag* and, in accordance with Article 50, to the *Bundesrat.*

ART. 145. (1) The Parliamentary Council, with the participation of the representatives of Greater Berlin, confirms in a public meeting the adoption of this Basic Law, engrosses, and promulgates it.

(2) This Basic Law becomes effective at the end of the day of its promulgation.

(3) It is to be published in the *Federal Gazette.*

ART. 146. This Basic Law becomes invalid on the day on which a Constitution adopted by the German people by means of a free decision becomes effective.

CONSTITUTION OF THE GERMAN DEMOCRATIC REPUBLIC, 1949 *

PREAMBLE

The German People, imbued with the desire to safeguard human liberty and rights, to reshape collective and economic life in accordance with the principles of social justice, to serve social progress, and to promote a secure peace and amity with all peoples, have adopted this Constitution.

A. FUNDAMENTALS OF STATE AUTHORITY

ART. 1. Germany is an indivisible democratic republic, the foundations of which are the German *Lander.*

The Republic decides on all issues which are essential to the existence and development of the German people as a whole, all other issues being decided upon by independent action of the *Lander.*

As a rule, decisions of the Republic are carried out by the *Lander.*

* Ratified by People's Congress, 2087 to 1, May 30, 1949.

There is only one German nationality.

ART. 2. The colors of the German Democratic Republic are black, red, and gold.

The capital of the Republic is Berlin.

ART. 3. All State authority emanates from the people.

Every citizen has the right and the duty to take part in the formation of the political life of his *Gemeinde, Kreis, Land,* and of the German Democratic Republic.

This right of codetermination takes the form of:

> voting in popular initiatives and referendums;
> exercising the right to vote and standing for election;
> entering upon public offices in general administration and in the administration of justice.

Every citizen has the right to submit petitions to the popular representative body.

State authority must serve the welfare of the people, liberty, peace, and the progress of democracy.

Those active in public service are servants of the community as a whole and not of any one party. Their activity is supervised by the popular representative body.

ART. 4. All measures taken by State authority must be compatible with the principles which the Constitution has declared to be contained in State authority. Pursuant to Article 66 of this Constitution, the popular representative body is to decide on the constitutionality of such measures. Everyone has the right and the duty to resist measures contradicting enactments of the popular representative body.

Every citizen is in duty bound to act in accordance with the Constitution and to defend it against its enemies.

ART. 5. The generally recognized rules of international law are binding upon State authority and every citizen.

It is the duty of State authority to maintain and cultivate amicable relations with all peoples.

No citizen may participate in belligerent actions designed to oppress any people.

B. Contents and Limits of State Authority

I. RIGHTS OF THE CITIZEN

ART. 6. All citizens have equal rights before the law.

Incitement to boycott of democratic institutions or organizations, incitement to attempts on the life of democratic politicians, the manifestation of religious and racial hatred and of hatred against other peoples, militaristic propaganda and warmongering as well as any other discriminatory acts are felonious crimes within the meaning of the Penal Code. The exercise of democratic rights within the meaning of the Constitution is not an incitement to boycott.

Whoever has been convicted of such a crime is disqualified from holding public office or a leading position in economic or cultural life. He also loses the right to vote and to stand for election.

ART. 7. Men and women have equal rights.

All laws and regulations which conflict with the equality of women are abolished.

ART. 8. Personal liberty, inviolability of the home, secrecy of the mail, and the right to take up residence at any place are guaranteed. State authority may restrict or revoke these freedoms only on the basis of a law applicable to all citizens.

ART. 9. All citizens have the right, within the limits of universally applicable laws, to express their opinion freely and publicly and to hold unarmed and peaceful assemblies for that purpose. This freedom shall not be restricted by any service or employment status, and no one may be discriminated against for exercising this right.

There is no press censorship.

ART. 10. No citizen may be turned over to a foreign power by extradition.

Allies shall neither be extradited nor expelled, if, outside this country, they are subject to persecution because of their struggle in support of the principles embodied in this Constitution.

Every citizen has the right to emigrate. This right may be restricted only by a law of the Republic.

ART. 11. Free ethnic development of foreign-language elements of the population of the Republic is to be promoted by legislative and administrative action. In particular, they must on no account be prevented from using their native language in matters of education, internal administration, and administration of justice.

ART. 12. All citizens have the right to form associations or societies for purposes not conflicting with criminal law.

ART. 13. Associations that, in accordance with their statutes, aim to bring about, on the basis of this Constitution, a democratic organization of public life and whose executive bodies are determined by their members, are entitled to submit nominations of candidates for election to membership in *Gemeinde*, *Kreis*, and *Land* popular representative bodies.

Nominations for the People's Chamber may be made only by those associations which, pursuant to their statutes, aim to bring about the democratic organization of public and social life in the entire Republic and which maintain an organization throughout the territory of the Republic.

ART. 14. Everyone is guaranteed the right to organize for the improvement of wages and working conditions. Any agreements and measures intended to restrict this right or impede it are unlawful and prohibited.

[Recognized] trade unions are vouchsafed the right to strike.

ART. 15. [The individual's] capacity for work is protected by State authority.

The right to work is guaranteed. By means of economic control the State ensures to each citizen work and a living. Whenever suitable work cannot be found for him, he shall be provided necessary sustenance.

ART. 16. Every worker is entitled to recreation, to an annual leave with pay, and to being provided for in illness and old age.

Sundays, holidays, and the first of May are days of rest and are protected by law.

On the principle of autonomous administration by the insured, a unitary and comprehensive social insurance system serves to maintain the health and strength of the working population, to protect motherhood, and to provide against the economic consequences of old age, disability, unemployment, and other vicissitudes of life.

ART. 17. Workers and employees shall play a decisive part in the regulation of industrial production, wages, and working conditions in enterprises.

Workers and employees shall exercise these rights through trade unions and Works Councils.

ART. 18. The Republic shall establish uniform labor legislation, a uniform system of labor courts, and uniform legislation for the protection of labor, in all of which the working population shall play a decisive part.

Working conditions must be such as to safeguard the health, cultural requirements, and family life of the workers.

Remuneration for work must correspond to performance and must provide a worthwhile existence for the worker and those dependents entitled to his support.

Men and women, adults and juveniles, are entitled to equal pay for equal work.

Women enjoy special protection in employment relations. The laws of the Republic shall provide for institutions enabling women to coordinate their tasks as citizens and workers with their duties as wives and mothers.

Juvenile workers shall be protected against exploitation and saved from falling into moral, physical, or mental neglect. Child labor is prohibited.

II. THE ECONOMIC ORDER

ART. 19. Organization of economic life must conform to the principles of social justice; it must guarantee to all an existence compatible with the dignity of man.

It is incumbent upon the economy to contribute to the benefit of the whole people and to the satisfaction of its wants and to insure that everybody will obtain, in accordance with his performance, a just share in the yield of production.

Freedom [of enterprise in the] economic [field] is guaranteed to the individual within the scope of the above tasks and aims.

ART. 20. Farmers, traders, and craftsmen are to be given support in the development of their private initiative. Mutual aid through cooperatives is to be expanded.

ART. 21. In order to secure the basic standard of living for its citizens and to promote their prosperity, the State, acting through its legislative bodies and with the direct participation of its citizens, establishes a public economic plan. It is the task of the popular representative bodies to supervise the implementation of the plan.

ART. 22. Private property is guaranteed by the Constitution. Its scope and its limitations are derived from law and from the obligations toward the welfare of the community at large.

The right of inheritance is guaranteed to the extent provided by civil law. The share of the Government in the estate is determined by law.

Intellectual work and the rights of authors, inventors, and artists enjoy protection, furtherance, and support by the Republic.

ART. 23. Restrictions on private property and expropriations may be imposed only for the benefit of the general public and on a legal basis. They shall take place against reasonable compensation unless the law provides otherwise. If the amount of compensation is in dispute, recourse to the ordinary courts shall be open insofar as a law does not provide otherwise.

ART. 24. Property commits to duties. Its use must not run counter to the public good.

Misuse of property with the intent of establishing an economic ascendancy to the detriment of the public good results in expropriation without compensation and transfer to the people's ownership.

Enterprises owned by war criminals and active National Socialists have been expropriated and will be transferred to the people's ownership [without compensation]. The same shall apply to private enterprises offering their services to a warlike policy.

All private monopolistic formations such as cartels, syndicates, combines, trusts, and similar private organizations aiming at an increase of profits through the control of production, prices, and markets have been abolished and are prohibited.

Privately owned large estates with an acreage of more than one hundred hectares are dissolved and shall be redistributed without compensation.

Following the accomplishment of the above agrarian reform, ownership of their land shall be guaranteed to the farmers.

ART. 25. All mineral resources, all economically exploitable natural power sources, as well as the mining, iron and steel, and electric power industries serving their exploitation, are to be transferred to the people's ownership.

Until such transfer, their use will be supervised by the *Lander* or by the Republic insofar as the interests of the whole of Germany are involved.

ART. 26. Distribution and utilization of the land shall be supervised, and each abuse thereof shall be prevented. Incremental value of landed property which has accrued without expenditure of labor or capital is to be made of use to the collectivity.

Every citizen and every family shall be assured of a healthy dwelling befitting their needs. Herein special consideration shall be given to victims of fascism, to seriously disabled persons, persons having incurred special war losses, and resettlers.

Maintenance and furtherance of assured returns from agriculture will be safeguarded also by means of land planning and conservation.

ART. 27. Private economic enterprises suitable for socialization may be transferred to collective ownership by law under the provisions dealing with expropriation.

The Republic, the *Lander,* the *Kreise,* and *Gemeinden* may be given by law a decisive voice in the management, or otherwise, of enterprises and associations.

Economic enterprises and associations may, by legislation, be combined into autonomous organizations in order to ensure the collaboration of all working elements of the nation, to give workers and employers a share in the management, and to regulate production, manufacture, distribution, utilization, prices, as well as import and export of commodities along the principles of collective economic interests.

Consumer and buying cooperatives, profit-making cooperatives, and agricultural cooperatives and their associations shall be integrated into the collective economy while preserving their statutes and characteristic features.

ART. 28. Any alienation or encumbrance of landed property, productive plants, or shares therein owned by the people must have the approval of the popular representative body exercising jurisdiction over the title-holding agency. Such approval requires at least a two-thirds majority of the statutory number of members.

ART. 29. Property and income shall be taxed according to progressively increasing rates on the basis of social viewpoints and with particular consideration of family obligations.

Taxation must give special consideration to earned property and income.

III. FAMILY AND MOTHERHOOD

ART. 30. Marriage and family are the foundations of collective life and are protected by the State.

All laws or statutory provisions by which the equal rights of men and women with the family are impaired are abrogated.

ART. 31. Parents have the natural right to bring up their children in a democratic spirit which will enable them mentally and physically to become responsible individuals, and this is their supreme duty toward society.

ART. 32. During maternity a woman has a rightful claim to particular protection and care by the State.

The Republic shall issue a law for the protection of mothers. Institutions are to be created to protect mother and child.

ART. 33. Extramarital birth is to be no ground for discrimination against either the child or the parents.

Any laws and statutory provisions to the contrary are abrogated.

IV. EDUCATION

ART. 34. Art, science, and their teaching are free.

The State participates in their cultivation and grants them protection, especially against their abuse for purposes which are contrary to the provisions or the spirit of the Constitution.

ART. 35. Every citizen has an equal right to education and to a free choice of his vocation.

Education of youth and adult education of the citizenry in intellectual or technical disciplines are provided by public institutions in all fields of national and social life.

ART. 36. The *Lander* are responsible for the establishment of a public school system and for the practical operation of school instruction. To this effect the Republic shall issue uniform legislative provisions of a basic character. The Republic may itself establish public educational institutions.

The Republic shall issue uniform provisions for the training of teachers. Such training shall take place in the universities or institutions of equal status.

ART. 37. The school educates the youth in the spirit of the Constitution to be independently thinking and responsibly acting individuals who will be able and willing to take their place in the life of the community at large.

As conveyor of culture, the school has the task of educating the youth to be truly humane in the spirit of peaceful and amicable cooperation in the life of nations and genuine democracy.

The parents shall participate in the school education of their children by councils of parents.

ART. 38. Attendance at school is compulsory for all until completion of the eighteenth year of life. After completion of a primary school course compulsory for all children, training is pursued in a vocational or technical school, in high school or in other public educational institutions. All juveniles under eighteen years of age must attend a vocational or training school unless they attend another [public] school. Private schools as substitutes for public schools [State or municipal] are inadmissible.

Vocational and technical schools afford general and vocational training.

High schools (*Oberschule*) pave the way for admission to a university. Such admission, however, does not require high school attendance; attendance at other public educational institutions, which shall be extended or created for that purpose, may take its place.

All citizens must be given the opportunity to prepare their admission to a university in special preparatory schools.

Members of all classes of the population shall be given an opportunity to acquire knowledge in colleges of the people without interruption of their occupational activities.

ART. 39. Every child must be given the opportunity fully to develop its physical, mental, and moral capacities. The school career of youth must on no account depend on the social or economic position of the parents. Indeed, children who are at a disadvantage because of social conditions are to be given special care. Attendance at vocational school, high school, and university must be open to gifted pupils from all classes of the population.

Tuition is free. Textbooks and instructional material used in compulsory schools are furnished without cost: in case of need, attendance at vocational school, high school, and university will be promoted through scholarships and other measures.

ART. 40. Religious instruction is a concern of the religious associations. The exercise of this right is guaranteed.

V. RELIGION AND RELIGIOUS ASSOCIATIONS

ART. 41. Every citizen enjoys complete freedom of faith and conscience. The practice of religion without interference enjoys the protection of the Republic.

Any abuse of establishments created by religious associations, of religious acts or religious instruction for purposes which are contrary to the principles of the Constitution or for purposes of party politics is prohibited. However, the right of religious associations to express an attitude in keeping with their own viewpoints toward issues vital for the people shall be uncontested.

ART. 42. Civil or civic rights and duties are neither conditioned nor restricted by the practice of religion.

Exercise of civil or civic rights or the admission to public service is independent of a religious creed.

No one is required to disclose his religious belief. Administrative agencies have the right to make inquiries about a person's membership in a religious association only insofar as rights and duties are connected therewith, or a statistical survey directed by law requires it.

No one may be forced to attend religious rites or celebrations, or to participate in religious exercises, or to use a religious form of oath.

ART. 43. There is no State church. Freedom of membership in religious associations is guaranteed.

Every religious association regulates and administers its affairs autonomously and in accordance with the laws applicable to all.

Religious associations remain public-law corporations insofar as they were such heretofore. Other religious associations are granted like rights upon their application, if through their organization and the number of their members they offer a guarantee of permanency. If several such public-law religious associations join in a union, this union is also a corporation of public law.

Religious associations having public-law status are entitled to levy taxes upon their members on the basis of the governmental tax list according to [the standards of] the general provisions.

Associations whose function is the common cultivation of a philosophy of life have the same status as religious associations.

ART. 44. The right of the church to give religious instruction on school premises is guaranteed. Religious instruction is given by personnel selected by the church. No one may be forced to give, or be prevented from giving, religious instruction. Those entitled to bring up a child shall determine whether the latter shall receive religious instruction.

ART. 45. Public contributions to religious associations, which rest upon law, contract, or special legal title, shall be abrogated by legislation.

Ownership and other rights of the religious associations and religious unions, in respect to their institutions, foundations, and other property devoted to purposes of worship, education, and charity, are guaranteed.

ART. 46. Insofar as there exists a need for religious service and spiritual guidance in hospitals, penal institutions, or other public institutions, the religious associations are to be given an opportunity for religious exercises. No person may be forced to participate.

ART. 47. Any person wishing to resign from a public-law religious association and to have such resignation become legally effective, shall declare his intention before a court, or submit it in form of a publicly attested individual declaration.

ART. 48. Decision as to whether children up to fourteen years of age shall belong to a religious association rests with the persons entitled to bring them up. Older children shall decide themselves whether or not they wish to be members of an association or organization professing a religious creed or a philosophy of life.

VI. EFFECTIVENESS OF BASIC RIGHTS

ART. 49. A basic right may not be violated in its essential content, not even where this Constitution authorizes its restriction by law or makes its further development subject to [specific] legislation.

C. ORGANIZATION OF STATE AUTHORITY

I. THE POPULAR REPRESENTATIVE BODY OF THE REPUBLIC

ART. 50. The supreme authority of the Republic is the People's Chamber.

ART. 51. The People's Chamber is composed of the Representatives of the German people.

Representatives are elected in universal, equal, direct, and secret ballot for a term of four years, according to the principles of proportional representation.

Representatives serve the people as a whole. They are bound only by their own conscience and are not bound by any instructions.

ART. 52. All citizens who have passed their eighteenth birthday have the right to vote.

All citizens who have passed their twenty-first birthday may stand for election.

The People's Chamber consists of four hundred representatives.

Details are determined by an Electoral Law.

ART. 53. Nominations for the People's Chamber may be submitted only by associations which satisfy the provisions of Article 13, paragraph 2.

Details are determined by a law of the Republic.

ART. 54. Elections are held on a Sunday or legal holiday. Freedom and secrecy of the ballot are guaranteed.

ART. 55. The People's Chamber convenes not later than thirty days after election, unless it is convoked by the previous Presidium for an earlier date.

The President must convoke the People's Chamber if the Government, or at least one fifth of the representatives in the People's Chamber, so request.

ART. 56. A new Chamber must be elected not later than sixty days after the end of a legislative term, or forty-five days after dissolution of the People's Chamber.

Before the completion of a legislative term, the People's Chamber may be dissolved only upon its own resolution or upon a referendum, except in the case described in Article 95, paragraph 6.

To dissolve the People's Chamber upon its own resolution, the consent of more than one half of the statutory number of representatives is necessary.

ART. 57. When first convening, the People's Chamber elects the Presidium and adopts Rules of Procedure.

Each parliamentary party is represented in the Presidium, provided that it has at least forty members.

The Presidium consists of the President, his deputies, and of associate members.

The President directs the business of the Presidium and presides over the deliberations of the People's Chamber. Maintenance of order on the premises of the Chamber is his prerogative.

ART. 58. Resolutions of the Presidium are adopted by majority vote.

A quorum exists when at least half the members of the Presidium are present.

Upon the resolution of the Presidium the acting President convokes the People's Chamber; he also fixes the date for new elections.

The Presidium continues in office until the convening of the new People's Chamber.

ART. 59. The People's Chamber examines the accreditation of its members and decides on the validity of elections.

ART. 60. For the periods when the People's Chamber is not in session, and after a legislative term has expired or the People's Chamber has been dissolved, the People's Chamber appoints three Standing Committees to carry on its functions, namely:

a Committee of General Affairs,
a Committee of Economic and Financial Affairs, and
a Committee of Foreign Affairs.

These Committees have the same rights as investigating committees.

ART. 61. The People's Chamber adopts laws and resolutions by majority vote, unless this Constitution provides otherwise.

A quorum exists when more than half of the members of the Chamber are present.

ART. 62. Deliberations of the People's Chamber and of its committees are open to the public. The public may be excluded from the People's Chamber if two thirds of the representatives present so request, and from the committees on the demand of the majority of the members of such committees.

True records of public meetings of the People's Chamber or its committees do not entail any responsibility.

ART. 63. The functions of the People's Chamber include:

the determination of the principles of governmental policy, and of its implementation;

the confirmation, supervision, and recall of the Government;

the determination of administrative policies and supervision over all governmental agencies;

the right to legislate, except when a [popular] referendum is held;

decisions on the national budget, on the Economic Plan, on loans and credits of the Republic, and the ratification of State treaties;

the granting of amnesties;

the election of the President of the Republic jointly with the *Lander* Chamber; and

the election and recall of the members of the Supreme Court of the Republic and of the Prosecutor General of the Republic.

ART. 64. For the purpose of obtaining information, the People's Chamber or any of its committees may request the presence of the Minister President or any other Minister, their permanent deputies, or the chiefs of administrative agencies of the Republic. The members of the Government and deputies designated by them are authorized to attend meetings of the People's Chamber and its committees at all times.

If they so request, members of the Government or their deputies must be given the floor during deliberations, regardless of the agenda.

They are subject to the disciplinary authority of the President.

ART. 65. For the purpose of supervising the activities of governmental agencies, the People's Chamber has the right, or, if at least one fifth of the statutory number of representatives so request, the duty, to appoint investigating committees. These committees take such evidence as they or the representatives having requested the investigation deem necessary. They may for this purpose be represented by persons commissioned by them.

Courts and administrations must comply with the request of these committees, or persons acting on their instructions, for the taking of evidence and, upon demand, present their files for inspection.

In the taking of evidence by the investigating committees the provisions of the Criminal Procedure are applied correspondingly.

ART. 66. For the duration of the legislative term the People's Chamber establishes a Constitutional Committee, in which all parliamentary parties are represented according to their [numerical] strength. To this Committee shall also belong three members of the Supreme Court of the Republic as well as three German professors of constitutional law who must on no account be members of the People's Chamber.

Members of the Constitutional Committee are elected by the People's Chamber.

[Only] the Constitutional Committee reviews laws of the Republic as to their constitutionality.

Constitutionality of laws of the Republic may be challenged by not less than one third of the members of the People's Chamber, by its Presidium, by the President of the Republic, by the Government of the Republic, and by the *Lander* Chamber.

Disputes on constitutional questions between the Republic and the *Lander,* and the compatibility of *Land* legislation and legislation of the Republic, are reviewed by the Constitutional Committee, with the assistance of three elected delegates of the *Lander* Chamber.

Final decision with respect to the report of the Constitutional Committee is reserved to the People's Chamber; the latter's decision is binding on everyone.

The People's Chamber also determines the execution of its decision.

The People's Chamber is, in the exercise of the administrative supervision delegated to it, responsible for determining whether an administrative measure is unconstitutional.

ART. 67. No proceedings, judicial or disciplinary, may at any time be instituted against any member of the People's Chamber for his vote or for any utterance made in the exercise of his parliamentary functions, nor may he be otherwise called to account outside the Chamber. This does not apply to defamation in the meaning of the Penal Code, if it has been established to be such by an investigating committee of the People's Chamber.

Restraint of personal freedom, house searches, seizures, or criminal prosecution may not be instituted against Representatives except with the consent of the People's Chamber.

Any criminal proceedings against a Representative in the People's Chamber, and any arrest or other restraint of his personal freedom, is suspended for the duration of the session upon demand of the Chamber of which the representative is a member.

Members of the People's Chamber have the right to refuse to give evidence concerning persons who confided facts to them in their capacity as Representatives, or to whom they have entrusted facts in this capacity, as well as concerning those facts themselves. In respect to seizure of documents, they enjoy the same privileges as persons who have the legal right to refuse testimony.

No search or seizure may be conducted in the premises of the People's Chamber without the consent of the Presidium.

ART. 68. Members of the People's Chamber do not require leave in order to perform their functions.

Persons standing as candidates for a seat in the People's Chamber must be granted such leave as is necessary to prepare for election.

Salaries and wages continue to be paid.

ART. 69. Members in the People's Chamber receive an allowance for expenses, which is tax exempt.

Renunciation of the allowance for expenses is inadmissible. The claim to the allowance for expenses cannot be transferred or garnished.

ART. 70. Members of the People's Chamber are entitled to free travel in all public transport.

II. REPRESENTATION OF THE LANDER

ART. 71. A *Lander* Chamber is established to represent the German *Lander.* In the *Lander* Chamber, each *Land* has one representative for every five hundred thousand inhabitants. Each *Land* has at least one representative.

ART. 72. The representatives in the *Lander* Chamber are elected by the *Landtage* in proportion to the numerical strength of the parliamentary parties represented therein. *Lander* Chamber representatives will serve for the duration of the legislative term of the respective *Landtag.* As a rule, *Lander* Chamber representatives should be *Landtag* members.

Each *Landtag* ascertains the wishes of its *Land* on matters to be deliberated in the *Lander* Chamber. This does not affect the rights of the representatives, as laid down in the *Land* Constitutions, to follow freely the dictates of their conscience.

ART. 73. The *Lander* Chamber elects its Presidium and adopts Rules of Procedure. The Presidium consists of the President, his deputies, and the associate members.

ART. 74. The *Lander* Chamber is convoked by its President whenever it is necessary for the transaction of its business.

The *Lander* Chamber is also convoked upon the demand of one fifth of its members.

ART. 75. Meetings of the *Lander* Chamber are open

to the public. As far as provided in the Rules of Procedure, the public may be excluded if certain items of the agenda are discussed.

ART. 76. The *Lander* Chamber makes its decisions by majority vote, unless this Constitution provides otherwise.

ART. 77. The *Lander* Chamber may set up all necessary committees as provided in the Rules of Procedure.

ART. 78. The *Lander* Chamber has the right to introduce bills in the People's Chamber. It has the right to reject legislation, as provided in Article 84 of this Constitution.

ART. 79. Members of the Government of the Republic and of that of a *Land* have the right to, and, upon the demand of the *Lander* Chamber, are required to, take part in the deliberations of the *Lander* Chamber and its committees. They must be given the floor on any matter under deliberation, if they so request.

The People's Chamber may, in special cases, delegate representatives from among their numbers to present the opinion of the People's Chamber to the *Lander* Chamber; the *Lander* Chamber has an equal right to present its opinion to the People's Chamber. The *Lander* Chamber may, if need be, instruct members of the *Land* Governments to present the attitude of their respective Governments to the People's Chamber.

ART. 80. Article 67 and subsequent articles of this Constitution concerning the rights of the members of the People's Chamber apply correspondingly to the members of the *Lander* Chamber.

III. LEGISLATION

ART. 81. Laws are enacted by the People's Chamber, or directly by the people by means of a referendum.

ART. 82. Bills are introduced by the Government, by the *Lander* Chamber, or by members of the People's Chamber. At least two readings will be held on any bill.

ART. 83. The Constitution may be amended by legislation.

The People's Chamber may enact legislation to amend the Constitution only if at least two thirds of the Representatives are present, and such enactments require a two-thirds majority of those present.

If an amendment to the Constitution is to be adopted by means of a [popular] referendum, the approval of the majority of those entitled to vote is required.

ART. 84. The *Lander* Chamber has the right to veto laws enacted by the People's Chamber. The veto must be lodged within two weeks after the final vote has been taken in the People's Chamber; reasons for the veto must be submitted within an additional two

weeks. Otherwise it is understood that the *Lander* Chamber will not exercise its right of veto.

The People's Chamber may override this veto by upholding its decision after renewed deliberations.

If a two-thirds majority of the *Lander* Chamber representatives casting their votes has decided to veto a measure, such veto can be overridden only if a two-thirds majority of the People's Chamber representatives casting their votes upholds the measure.

For the *Lander* Chamber to veto legislation enacted by the People's Chamber to amend the Constitution, at least two thirds of the members of the *Lander* Chamber must be present, and at least two thirds thereof must vote for the veto.

The People's Chamber may override the veto by upholding its amendment with the majority prescribed for amendments to the Constitution.

ART. 85. The President of the People's Chamber shall engross all constitutionally enacted laws within the period of one month.

They are promulgated without delay by the President of the Republic in the *Official Gazette* of the Republic.

A law cannot be engrossed or promulgated, if it has been declared unconstitutional within one month, as provided for in Article 66.

Unless otherwise provided, laws come into force on the fourteenth day after their promulgation.

ART. 86. Engrossment and promulgation of a law are to be suspended for two months, if one third of the representatives in the People's Chamber so request.

Upon expiration of this period, the law is to be engrossed and promulgated unless a popular initiative calls for a [popular] referendum against the enactment of the law.

Laws declared urgent by the majority of the Representatives in the People's Chamber must be engrossed and promulgated despite such [public] demand.

ART. 87. If the promulgation of a law has been suspended at the instance of at least one third of the Representatives in the People's Chamber, such law is to be submitted to a [popular] referendum upon the demand of one twentieth of those entitled to vote.

A [popular] referendum shall furthermore be held, if requested by one tenth of those entitled to vote or by recognized political parties or organized groups which can demonstrate satisfactorily that they represent one fifth of those entitled to vote [Constituting popular initiative].

A popular initiative must be based on a draft law, which law is to be submitted to the People's Chamber by the Government with a statement of the Government's position with respect to this law.

A [popular] referendum will take place only if the desired law has not been adopted by the People's Chamber in a version with which the petitioners or their representations are in agreement.

A [popular] referendum shall not be held on the budget, on tax legislation, or on salary schedules.

A law submitted to a [popular] referendum is considered as adopted if it has received the consent of a majority of the votes cast.

A specific law shall regulate the procedures for popular initiative and [popular] referendum.

ART. 88. The budget and the economic plan are adopted by law.

Amnesties require a [specific] law.

State treaties concerning matters of legislation are to be promulgated as laws.

ART. 89. Laws which have been duly promulgated cannot be reconsidered by the judiciary with respect to their constitutionality.

After the review proceedings provided for in Article 66 have been instituted, all pending court proceedings shall be suspended until the review proceedings have been completed.

ART. 90. General administrative regulations required for the implementation of the laws of the Republic will be issued by the Government of the Republic, unless the law provides otherwise.

IV. THE GOVERNMENT OF THE REPUBLIC

ART. 91. The Government of the Republic consists of the Minister President and the Ministers.

ART. 92. The Minister President is appointed by the party with the greatest strength in the People's Chamber; he forms the Government. All parties having at least forty Representatives [in the People's Chamber] are represented by Ministers or State Secretaries in proportion to their strength. State secretaries may attend meetings of the Government in an advisory capacity.

Should one parliamentary party refuse to be included, the Government will be formed without it.

Ministers should be members of the People's Chamber.

The People's Chamber approves the Government and the program submitted by it.

ART. 93. On taking office, members of the Government shall be sworn in by the President of the Republic and pledged to perform their duties impartially for the welfare of the people and in faithful observance of the Constitution and the laws.

ART. 94. The Government, and each of its members, require the confidence of the People's Chamber in order to perform their functions.

ART. 95. The functions of the Cabinet are terminated if and when the People's Chamber passes a motion of no confidence.

A motion of no confidence will be voted on only if at the same time a new Minister President and his program are proposed. The motion of no confidence and these proposals will be considered in one combined vote.

A vote of no confidence shall not be effective unless the motion is carried by at least one half of the statutory number of Representatives.

A motion of no confidence must be signed by at least one fourth of the members of the People's Chamber. A vote on such a motion may not be taken prior to the second day after it has been debated, and not later than one week after its presentation.

Unless the new Government takes office within twenty-one days after the motion of no confidence has been carried, that motion shall become void.

If the new Government receives a vote of no confidence, the People's Chamber shall be considered dissolved.

The former Government continues its functions until a new Government has taken office.

ART. 96. A member of the Government who receives a vote of no confidence from the People's Chamber must resign. Unless decided otherwise by the People's Chamber, he is to continue his functions until his successor takes office.

The provision of Article 95, paragraph (3), is applicable correspondingly.

Any member of the Government may resign at any time. Unless decided otherwise by the People's Chamber, his official functions shall be performed by his deputy until a successor has been appointed.

ART. 97. The Minister President presides over the Government and directs its business under Rules of Procedure to be decreed by the Government and communicated to the People's Chamber.

ART. 98. The Minister President determines governmental policy in accordance with the guiding principles laid down by the People's Chamber. For this, he is responsible to the latter.

Within the framework of these guiding principles, each Minister directs independently the department entrusted to him and is personally responsible to the People's Chamber.

ART. 99. Ministers shall refer to the Government, for deliberation and decision, all bills, any matters which must be referred to it under the Constitution or the law, as well as differences of opinion with respect to matters which fall within the competence of more than one Minister.

ART. 100. The Government makes decisions by majority vote. In case of a tie, the Minister President shall cast the deciding vote.

V. THE PRESIDENT OF THE REPUBLIC

ART. 101. The President of the Republic is elected for a term of four years by the People's Chamber and the *Lander* Chamber, meeting in joint session, which is convoked and presided over by the President of the People's Chamber.

Any citizen who has reached the age of thirty-five years may stand for election.

ART. 102. An assuming office, the President of the Republic takes the following oath before a joint session of the People's Chamber and the *Lander* Chamber:

"I swear that I will dedicate my strength to the welfare of the German people, that I will defend the Constitution and the laws of the Republic, that I will discharge my duties conscientiously and do justice to all."

ART. 103. The President of the Republic may be recalled before the expiration of his term by a joint resolution of the People's Chamber and the *Lander* Chamber. Such a resolution requires a two-thirds majority of the statutory number of representatives.

ART. 104. The President of the Republic promulgates the laws of the Republic.

He receives the oath of office from members of the Government upon their assumption of duties.

ART. 105. The President of the Republic represents the Republic in international relations.

He concludes and signs treaties with foreign countries on behalf of the Republic.

He accredits and receives ambassadors and ministers.

ART. 106. To become effective, all orders and decrees issued by the President of the Republic must be countersigned by the Minister President or the competent Minister.

ART. 107. The President exercises the right of pardon on behalf of the Republic. In this function he is advised by a committee of the People's Chamber.

ART. 108. Whenever the President of the Republic is unable to attend to his office, he is represented by the President of the People's Chamber. If such incapacity is expected to continue for a protracted period, a substitute will be appointed by [a specific] law.

Whenever the presidency is terminated prematurely, the same rule applies until the election of a new President.

VI. REPUBLIC AND LANDER

ART. 109. Each *Land* must have a constitution which conforms to the principles of the Constitution of the Republic and under which the *Landtag* is the supreme and sole popular representative body in the *Land*.

The popular representative body must be elected, by all citizens entitled to do so, in universal, equal, direct, and secret ballot held in accordance with the principles of proportional representation as laid down in the Electoral Law of the Republic.

ART. 110. Any change in the territory of a *Land* and the formation of a new *Land* within the Republic requires a law of the Republic amending the Constitution.

Only an ordinary law [of the Republic] is required if the *Lander* immediately affected concur.

An ordinary law will likewise suffice, even if one of the *Lander* affected does not concur, provided, however, that the territorial change or the formation of a new *Land* is demanded by a plebiscite held in the territories concerned.

ART. 111. The Republic may enact uniform legislation in any field. However, in so doing it should confine itself to laying down principles, provided this meets the need for uniform regulation.

To the extent that the Republic does not exercise its legislative power, the *Lander* shall have such power.

ART. 112. The Republic has the exclusive right to legislate on:

foreign relations;

foreign trade;

customs and the free movement of commodities within a unified customs and trade area;

citizenship; freedom of movement; immigration and emigration; extradition; passport regulations and laws affecting the status of aliens;

legislation on census and registry [marriage, divorce and status of children];

civil law; criminal law; the constitution of courts and their procedure;

labor law;

transport;

the fields of postal, telecommunication, and radio broadcasting services;

the fields of press and of film production, distribution and display;

currency and coinage, weights, measures, standards and gauging;

social insurance; and,

war damages, occupation costs and reparations.

ART. 113. Legislation in the field of finance and taxation must be of such nature as not to infringe upon the existence of the *Lander*, the *Kreise*, and *Gemeinden*.

ART. 114. Law of the whole of Germany overrides *Land* law.

ART. 115. As a rule, the laws of the Republic are carried out by the executive agencies of the *Lander*, unless otherwise provided for in this Constitution or by a law. The Republic, insofar as there is a necessity, establishes its own administrative agencies by law.

ART. 116. The Government of the Republic exercises supervision in those matters with respect to which the Republic has the right to legislate.

The Government of the Republic may issue general instructions where the laws of the Republic are not executed by its administrative authorities. For the supervision of the execution of these laws and instructions, it is authorized to delegate commissioners to the implementing agencies. As for the powers of these commissioners, Article 65 is correspondingly applicable.

Upon the request of the Republic, the *Lander* governments are bound to remedy deficiencies discovered in the execution of the laws of the Republic.

Any controversies arising therefrom are to be examined and settled in accordance with the procedure specified in Article 66, paragraph 5.

VII. ADMINISTRATION OF THE REPUBLIC

ART. 117. Maintenance of foreign relations is an exclusive concern of the Republic.

The *Lander* may conclude treaties with foreign states on matters within the competence of *Land* legislation; such treaties [before taking effect] are subject to the approval of the People's Chamber.

Treaties with foreign States concerning changes of national boundaries are concluded by the Republic, after the consent of the *Land* thereby affected has been obtained. Boundary changes may be effected only by a law of the Republic, unless a mere rectification of boundaries in uninhabited areas is involved.

ART. 118. Germany forms a single customs and trade area, bounded by a common customs frontier.

Territories of foreign States or parts of such territories may be included in the German customs area by treaty or convention. Parts of the German customs area may be excluded therefrom by law.

Any goods enjoying internal free trade within the German customs area may, within the area, freely be introduced into, or carried in transit across the boundaries of, German *Lander* and political subdivisions as well as, pursuant to paragraph 2, into, or across the boundaries of, the territories of foreign States or parts of such territories included.

ART. 119. Customs and such taxes as are regulated by laws of the Republic are administered by the Republic.

The power to levy taxes is, normally, vested in the Republic.

The Republic should levy taxes only to the extent required to cover its needs.

The Republic establishes its own agencies for the administration of taxes. In conjunction therewith, arrangements shall be made enabling the *Lander* to safeguard their special interests in the spheres of agriculture, commerce, handicrafts, trades or professions, manufacture, and industry.

To the extent required for the uniform and equitable enforcement of its tax laws, the Republic shall enact legislation on the organization of tax administrations in the *Lander*, the organization and powers of the authorities entrusted with the enforcement of the tax laws of the Republic, the settlement of ac-

counts with the *Lander*, and the reimbursement for the administrative costs incurred in the enforcement of the tax laws of the Republic.

ART. 120. Taxes and other levies may be assessed only as provided by law.

Property, income and excise tax legislation are to be kept in a suitable proportion to each other, and to be graduated according to social considerations.

Through sharply progressive tax rates on inheritance, the amassing of socially harmful fortunes should be prevented.

ART. 121. Revenues and expenditures of the Republic must be estimated for each fiscal year and provided for in the budget. The budget is to be enacted by legislation before the beginning of the fiscal year.

ART. 122. The Minister of Finance, in order to secure a discharge for the Government, gives an accounting to the People's Chamber of the revenues of the Republic and their use. The auditing of accounts is regulated by law of the Republic.

ART. 123. Funds may be procured by borrowing only for extraordinary needs. Borrowing of such funds and the guaranteeing of loans as a charge of the Republic may be effected only on the basis of a law of the Republic.

ART. 124. Postal, telecommunication, broadcasting, and railroad services are to be administered by the Republic.

The former Reich *Autobahnen* and Reich highways as well as all roads for long-distance traffic are under the control of the Republic. The same provisions apply to waterways.

ART. 125. Control of merchant shipping and the administration of maritime shipping, and of aids to navigation, are duties of the Republic.

VIII. ADMINISTRATION OF JUSTICE

ART. 126. The ordinary administration of justice is exercised by the Supreme Court of the Republic and by courts of the *Lander*.

ART. 127. In the exercise of their judicial function, the judges are independent and are bound only by the Constitution and the law.

ART. 128. Judges must be persons who, by their qualification and activity, offer the guarantee that they will exercise their office in accordance with the principles laid down in the Constitution.

ART. 129. Through the development of law schools, the Republic provides an opportunity for members of all classes of the population to become qualified for the profession of judge, attorney and public prosecutor.

ART. 130. Laymen are, as much as possible, to be used as judges.

Laymen are elected, on the proposal of democratic

parties and organizations, by the competent popular representative bodies.

ART. 131. Judges of the Supreme Court of the Republic, and the Prosecutor General of the Republic, are elected by the People's Chamber upon their nomination by the Government of the Republic.

Judges of the High Courts of the *Lander,* and the Prosecutors General of the *Lander,* are elected by the *Landtage* upon their nomination by the *Land* governments.

All other judges are appointed by the *Land* governments.

ART. 132. Judges of the Supreme Court, and the Prosecutor General of the Republic, may be recalled by the People's Chamber if they violate the Constitution, or the laws, or commit a serious breach of their duties as judge or public prosecutor.

This recall is effected after hearing the report of a Committee on Justice to be established in the People's Chamber.

The Committee on Justice is composed of the chairman of the Legal Committee of the People's Chamber, three members of the People's Chamber, two members of the Supreme Court and one member of the Prosecutor General's office. It is presided over by the Chairman of the Legal Committee. The other Committee members are elected by the People's Chamber for the legislative term. The members of the Supreme Court and the Prosecutor General's office serving on the Committee on Justice cannot be members of the People's Chamber.

Judges elected by a *Landtag,* or appointed by a *Land* government, may be recalled by the respective *Landtag.* Their recall will be effected after hearing the report of a Committee on Justice to be set up with the respective *Landtag.* The Committee on Justice is composed of the Chairman of the Legal Committee of the *Landtag,* three members of the *Landtag,* two members of the *Land* High Court, and one member of the Prosecutor General's office of the respective *Land.* It is presided over by the Chairman of the Legal Committee. The other Committee members are elected by the respective *Landtag* for the duration of the legislative term. The members of the [*Land*] High Court and of the Prosecutor General's office, and participating in the Committee on Justice, cannot be members of the *Landtag.*

Judges appointed by *Land* governments may, under the same conditions, be recalled by the respective *Land* government, provided that the consent of the *Landtag* Committee on Justice has been obtained.

ART. 133. All court proceedings are open to the public.

In all matters involving a threat to public safety and order, or to public morals, the court may order the public to be excluded.

ART. 134. No citizen should be deprived of his right to be tried before the judge having lawful jurisdiction in the matter. Extraordinary courts are inadmissible. The legislative authorities may set up courts for special matters only if their competence is to comprise categories of persons or issues defined beforehand and in a general way.

ART. 135. Only such penalties may be imposed as have been provided for by law at the time the punishable act was committed.

No penal law has retroactive force.

Exceptions to this rule are measures and the application of provisions which are adopted for the overcoming of Nazism, Fascism and militarism, or which are necessary for the prosecution of crimes against humanity.

ART. 136. In cases of temporary arrest, house searches, and seizures effected in the course of a preliminary investigation, the approval of a judge must be obtained without [undue] delay.

It rests with the judge alone to decide on the admissibility and continuance of an arrest. Persons arrested must be brought before a judge at the latest on the day after their apprehension. If pretrial confinement is ordered by the judge, he must make a periodic review as to whether continued detention is justified.

The reason for the detention is to be communicated to the arrested person at his first examination by a judge and, if he so desires, within an additional twenty-four hours to a person to be named by him.

ART. 137. Execution of sentences is founded on the concept of reforming persons capable of rehabilitation through common productive work.

ART. 138. Citizens are protected against unlawful administrative measures by the supervision exercised by the legislature and through recourse to administrative courts.

The structure and jurisdiction of administrative courts are regulated by law.

Principles applying to the election and recall of judges of ordinary courts apply correspondingly to the members of administrative courts.

IX. ADMINISTRATIVE AUTONOMY

ART. 139. *Gemeinden* and *Gemeindeverbaende* [communities and associated communities] enjoy administrative autonomy subject to the provisions of the laws of the Republic and the *Lander.*

Autonomy functions include determination and implementation of all policies concerning the economic, social and cultural life of the *Gemeinde* or *Gemeindeverband.* Each task is to be accomplished by the lowest [local] administrative unit qualified for this purpose.

ART. 140. *Gemeinden* and *Gemeindeverbaende* have representative bodies organized on democratic principles.

To assist them, committees are formed in which delegates of the democratic parties and organizations participate responsibly.

The right to vote and the procedure to be followed in [local] elections are governed by the provisions applying to elections to the People's Chamber and to the *Landtage*.

The right to vote may, however, by *Land* legislation be predicated on the length of residence in the [respective] locality for a period not to exceed half a year.

Art. 141. For the due exercise of their functions, the elected executive authorities of *Gemeinden* and *Gemeindeverbaende* require the confidence of the [local] representative bodies.

Art. 142. Supervision of the administrative autonomy practiced by *Gemeinden* and *Gemeindeverbaende* is limited to a review of the statutory compliance of administrative measures and of the observance of democratic administrative principles.

Art. 143. The Republic and the *Lander* may delegate functions, and the application of laws, to the *Gemeinden* and *Gemeindeverbaende*.

X. TRANSITIONAL AND CONCLUDING PROVISIONS

Art. 144. All provisions of this Constitution have direct force of law. Any provisions to the contrary are repealed herewith. Provisions superseding them and required to implement the Constitution are to take effect simultaneously with the Constitution. Existing laws are to be interpreted in the meaning of this Constitution.

Constitutional liberties and rights may not be used as arguments against past or future measures adopted for the overcoming of National Socialism and militarism, or to redress wrongs caused by them.

The Government of the U.S.S.R.

THE CONSTITUTION OF THE U.S.S.R., 1936 *

Chapter I. The Social Structure

Art. 1. The Union of Soviet Socialist Republics is a socialist state of workers and peasants.

Art. 2. The political foundation of the U.S.S.R. is the Soviets of Working People's Deputies, which grew and became strong as a result of the overthrow of the power of the landlords and capitalists and the conquest of the dictatorship of the proletariat.

Art. 3. All power in the U.S.S.R. belongs to the working people of town and country as represented by the Soviets of Working People's Deputies.

Art. 4. The economic foundation of the U.S.S.R. is the socialist system of economy and the socialist ownership of the instruments and means of production, firmly established as a result of the liquidation of the capitalist system of economy, the abolition of private ownership of the instruments and means of production, and the elimination of the exploitation of man by man.

Art. 5. Socialist property in the U.S.S.R. exists either in the form of State property (belonging to the whole people) or in the form of cooperative and collective-farm property (property of collective farms, property of cooperative societies).

Art. 6. The land, its mineral wealth, waters, forests, mills, factories, mines, rail, water and air transport, banks, communications, large State-organized agricultural enterprises (State farms, machine and tractor stations, and the like), as well as municipal enterprises and the bulk of the dwelling houses in the cities and industrial localities, are State property—that is, belong to the whole people.

Art. 7. The common enterprises of collective farms and cooperative organizations, with their livestock and implements, the products of the collective farms and cooperative organizations, as well as their common buildings, constitute the common, socialist property of the collective farms and cooperative organizations.

Every household in a collective farm, in addition to its basic income from the common, collective-farm enterprise, has for its personal use a small plot of household land and, as its personal property, a subsidiary husbandry on the plot, a dwelling house, livestock, poultry, and minor agricultural implements—in accordance with the rules of the agricultural artel.

Art. 8. The land occupied by collective farms is secured to them for their use free of charge and for an unlimited time—that is, in perpetuity.

Art. 9. Alongside the socialist system of economy, which is the predominant form of economy in the U.S.S.R., the law permits the small private economy of individual peasants and handicraftsmen based on their own labor and precluding the exploitation of the labor of others.

Art. 10. The personal property right of citizens in their incomes and savings from work, in their dwelling houses and subsidiary home enterprises, in articles of domestic economy and use and articles of personal use and convenience, as well as the right of citizens to inherit personal property, is protected by law.

Art. 11. The economic life of the U.S.S.R. is determined and directed by the State national-economic plan, with the aim of increasing the public wealth, of steadily raising the material and cultural standards of the working people, of consolidating the independence of the U.S.S.R., and strengthening its defensive capacity.

Art. 12. Work in the U.S.S.R. is a duty and a matter of honor for every able-bodied citizen, in accordance with the principle: "He who does not work, neither shall he eat."

The principle applied in the U.S.S.R. is that of socialism: "From each according to his ability, to each according to his work."

Chapter II. The State Structure

Art. 13. The Union of Soviet Socialist Republics is a federal State, formed on the basis of a voluntary union of equal Soviet Socialist Republics, namely:

The Russian Soviet Federative Socialist Republic
The Ukrainian Soviet Socialist Republic
The Byelorussian Soviet Socialist Republic
The Uzbek Soviet Socialist Republic
The Kazakh Soviet Socialist Republic

---

* As amended through June 17, 1950. Since publication of the original text in 1937, the Constitution was amended at the first (Jan. 12–19, 1938), second (Aug. 10–21, 1938), third (May 25–31, 1939), sixth (Mar. 29–Apr. 4, 1940), seventh (Aug. 1–7, 1940), and eighth (Feb. 25–Mar. 1, 1941) sessions of the Supreme Soviet, and at the third (February 1947) and sixth (March 1949) sessions of the second Supreme Soviet.

Law requiring amendments were adopted at the tenth (Jan. 28–Feb. 1, 1944) session of the first Supreme Soviet and at the first (spring 1946) session of the postwar Supreme Soviet and fall session of 1950.

The Georgian Soviet Socialist Republic
The Azerbaijan Soviet Socialist Republic
The Lithuanian Soviet Socialist Republic
The Moldavian Soviet Socialist Republic
The Latvian Soviet Socialist Republic
The Kirghiz Soviet Socialist Republic
The Tajik Soviet Socialist Republic
The Armenian Soviet Socialist Republic
The Turkmen Soviet Socialist Republic
The Estonian Soviet Socialist Republic
The Karelo-Finnish Soviet Socialist Republic

ART. 14. The jurisdiction of the Union of Soviet Socialist Republics, as represented by its higher organs of State power and organs of State administration, embraces:

(a) Representation of the U.S.S.R. in international relations, conclusion, ratification, and denunciation of treaties of the U.S.S.R. with other States, establishment of general procedure governing the relations of Union Republics with foreign States;

(b) Questions of war and peace;

(c) Admission of new republics into the U.S.S.R.;

(d) Control over the observance of the Constitution of the U.S.S.R. and ensuring conformity of the Constitutions of the Union Republics with the Constitution of the U.S.S.R.

(e) Confirmation of alterations of boundaries between Union Republics;

(f) Confirmation of the formation of new Territories and Regions and also of new Autonomous Republics and Autonomous Regions within Union Republics;

(g) Organization of the defense of the U.S.S.R., direction of all the Armed Forces of the U.S.S.R., determination of directing principles governing the organization of the military formations of the Union Republics;

(h) Foreign trade on the basis of State monopoly;

(i) Safeguarding the security of the State;

(j) Determination of the national-economic plans of the U.S.S.R.;

(k) Approval of the consolidated State budget of the U.S.S.R. and of the report on its fulfillment; determination of the taxes and revenues which go to the Union, the Republican and the local budgets;

(1) Administration of the banks, industrial and agricultural institutions and enterprises and trading enterprises of all-Union importance;

(m) Administration of transport and communications;

(n) Direction of the monetary and credit system;

(o) Organization of State insurance;

(p) Contracting and granting of loans;

(q) Determination of the basic principles of land tenure and of the use of mineral wealth, forests, and waters;

(r) Determination of the basic principles in the spheres of education and public health;

(s) Organization of a uniform system of national-economic statistics;

(t) Determination of the principles of labor legislation;

(u) Legislation concerning the judicial system and judicial procedure; criminal and civil codes;

(v) Legislation concerning Union citizenship; legislation concerning rights of foreigners;

(w) Determination of the principles of legislation concerning marriage and the family;

(x) Issuing of all-Union acts of amnesty.

ART. 15. The sovereignty of the Union Republics is limited only in the spheres defined in Article 14 of the Constitution of the U.S.S.R. Outside of these spheres each Union Republic exercises state authority independently. The U.S.S.R. protects the sovereign rights of the Union Republics.

ART. 16. Each Union Republic has its own Constitution, which takes account of the specific features of the Republic and is drawn up in full conformity with the Constitution of the U.S.S.R.

ART. 17. The right freely to secede from the U.S.S.R. is reserved to every Republic.

ART. 18. The territory of a Union Republic may not be altered without its consent.

ART. 18a. Each Union Republic has the right to enter into direct relations with foreign States and to conclude agreements and exchange representatives with them.

ART. 18b. Each Union Republic has its own Republican military formations.

ART. 19. The laws of the U.S.S.R. have the same force within the territory of every Union Republic.

ART. 20. In the event of divergence between a law of a Union Republic and a law of the Union, the Union law prevails.

ART. 21. Uniform Union citizenship is established for citizens of the U.S.S.R.

Every citizen of a Union Republic is a citizen of the U.S.S.R.

ART. 22.[1] The Russian Soviet Federative Socialist Republic consists of the Altai, Krasnodar, Krasnoyarsk, Primorye, Stavropol, and Khabarovsk Territories; the Amur, Archangelsk, Astrakhan, Bryanks, Velikiye-Luki, Vladimir, Vologda, Voronezh, Gorky, Grozny, Ivanovo, Irkutsk, Kaliningrad, Kalinin, Kaluga, Kemerovo, Kirov, Kostroma, Crimea, Kuibyshev, Kurgan, Kursk, Leningrad, Molotov, Moscow,

[1] Amended several times between January 1938 and March 1941 and several times since February 1947, to take care of several changes in territorial organization and terminology, and to assimilate the areas annexed from Poland, Romania, and Czechoslovakia during World War II and the wiping out of five national units for treason to Moscow during World War II.

Murmansk, Novgorod, Novosibirsk, Omsk, Orel, Penza, Pskov, Rostov, Ryazan, Saratov, Sakhalin, Sverdlovsk, Smolensk, Stalingrad, Tambov, Tomsk, Tula, Tyumen, Ulyanovsk, Chelyabinsk, Chita, Chkalov, and Yaroslavl Regions; the Tatar, Bashkir, Daghestan, Buryat-Mongolian, Kabardinian, Komi, Mari, Mordovian, North Ossetian, Udmurt, Chuvash, and Yakut Autonomous Soviet Socialist Republics; and the Adygei, Gorno-Altai, Jewish, Tuva, Khakass, and Cherkess Autonomous Regions.

ART. 23. The Ukrainian Soviet Socialist Republic consists of the Vinnitsa, Volhynia, Voroshilovgrad, Dnepropetrovsk, Drohobych, Zhitomir, Transcarpathian, Zaporozhye, Ismail, Kamenets-Podolsk, Kiev, Kirovograd, Lvov, Nikolayev, Odessa, Poltava, Rovno, Stalino, Stanislav, Sumi, Ternopol, Kharkov, Kherson, Chernigov and Chernovtsi Regions.

ART. 24. The Azerbaijan Soviet Socialist Republic includes the Nakhichevan Autonomous Soviet Socialist Republic and the Nagorno-Karabakh Autonomous Region.

ART. 25. The Georgian Soviet Socialist Republic includes the Abkhazian Autonomous Soviet Socialist Republic, the Adjar Autonomous Soviet Socialist Republic and the South Ossetian Autonomous Region.

ART. 26. The Uzbek Soviet Socialist Republic consists of the Andizhan, Bukhara, Kashka-Darya, Namangan, Samarkand, Surkhan-Darya, Tashkent, Ferghana and Khorezm Regions and the Kara-Kalpak Autonomous Soviet Socialist Republic.

ART. 27. The Tajik Soviet Socialist Republic consists of the Garm, Kulyab, Leninabad and Stalinabad Regions and the Gorno-Badakhshan Autonomous Region.

ART. 28. The Kazakh Soviet Socialist Republic consists of the Akmolinsk, Aktyubinsk, Alma-Ata, East Kazakhstan, Guriev, Jambul, West Kazakhstan, Karaganda, Kzyl-Orda, Kokchetav, Kustanai, Pavlodar, North Kazakhstan, Semipalatinsk, Taldy-Kurgan and South Kazakhstan Regions.

ART. 29. The Byelorussian Soviet Socialist Republic consists of the Baranovichi, Bobruisk, Brest, Vitebsk, Gomel, Grodno, Minsk, Moghilev, Molodechno, Pinsk, Polessye and Polotsk Regions.

ART. 29a. The Turkmen Soviet Socialist Republic consists of the Ashkhabad, Mari, Tashauz and Chardzhou Regions.

ART. 29b. The Kirghiz Soviet Socialist Republic consists of the Dzhalal-Abad, Issyk-Kul, Osh, Talas, Tien-Shan and Frunze Regions.

CHAPTER III. THE HIGHER ORGANS OF STATE POWER IN THE UNION OF SOVIET SOCIALIST REPUBLICS

ART. 30. The highest organ of State power in the U.S.S.R. is the Supreme Soviet of the U.S.S.R.

ART. 31.[2] The Supreme Soviet of the U.S.S.R. exer-

---

cises all rights vested in the Union of Soviet Socialist Republics in accordance with Article 14 of the Constitution, insofar as they do not, by virtue of the Constitution, come within the jurisdiction of organs of the U.S.S.R. that are accountable to the Supreme Soviet of the U.S.S.R.—that is, the Presidium of the Supreme Soviet of the U.S.S.R., the Council of Ministers of the U.S.S.R., and the Ministries of the U.S.S.R.

ART. 32. The legislative power of the U.S.S.R. is exercised exclusively by the Supreme Soviet of the U.S.S.R.

ART. 33. The Supreme Soviet of the U.S.S.R. consists of two Chambers: the Soviet of the Union and the Soviet of Nationalities.

ART. 34. The Soviet of the Union is elected by the citizens of the U.S.S.R. voting by election districts on the basis of one Deputy for every 300,000 of the population.

ART. 35. The Soviet of Nationalities is elected by the citizens of the U.S.S.R. voting by Union Republics, Autonomous Republics, Autonomous Regions, and National Areas on the basis of twenty-five Deputies from each Union Republic, eleven Deputies from each Autonomous Republic, five Deputies from each Autonomous Region and one Deputy from each National Area.

ART. 36. The Supreme Soviet of the U.S.S.R. is elected for a term of four years.

ART. 37. The two Chambers of the Supreme Soviet of the U.S.S.R., the Soviet of the Union and the Soviet of Nationalities, have equal rights.

ART. 38. The Soviet of the Union and the Soviet of Nationalities have equal powers to initiate legislation.

ART. 39. A law is considered adopted if passed by both Chambers of the Supreme Soviet of the U.S.S.R. by a simple majority vote in each.

ART. 40. Laws passed by the Supreme Soviet of the U.S.S.R. are published in the languages of the Union Republics over the signatures of the President and Secretary of the Presidium of the Supreme Soviet of the U.S.S.R.

ART. 41. Sessions of the Soviet of the Union and of the Soviet of Nationalities begin and terminate simultaneously.

ART. 42. The Soviet of the Union elects a Chairman of the Soviet of the Union and four Vice Chairmen.[3]

ART. 43. The Soviet of Nationalities elects a Chairman of the Soviet of Nationalities and four Vice Chairmen.[3]

---

[2] The original Revolutionary terms "Council of People's Commissars" and "People's Commissariats" were re-

placed throughout the Constitution (Arts. 31, 49, 56, 63–88, 93, 113) by the conventional appellations "Council of Ministers" and "Ministries of the U.S.S.R." The change was enacted by the second Supreme Soviet during its first postwar session, Mar. 15, 1946, and incorporated into the Constitution by amendment of February 1947.

[3] A decree changing the number of Vice Chairmen from two to four was adopted by the Supreme Soviet, June 17, 1950.

Art. 44. The Chairmen of the Soviet of the Union and the Soviet of Nationalities preside at the sittings of the respective Chambers and have charge of the conduct of their business and proceedings.

Art. 45. Joint sittings of the two Chambers of the Supreme Soviet of the U.S.S.R. are presided over alternately by the Chairman of the Soviet of the Union and the Chairman of the Soviet of Nationalities.

Art. 46. Sessions of the Supreme Soviet of the U.S.S.R. are convened by the Presidium of the Supreme Soviet of the U.S.S.R. twice a year.

Extraordinary sessions are convened by the Presidium of the Supreme Soviet of the U.S.S.R. at its discretion or on the demand of one of the Union Republics.

Art. 47. In the event of disagreement between the Soviet of the Union and the Soviet of Nationalities, the question is referred for settlement to a conciliation commission formed on a parity basis. If the conciliation commission fails to arrive at an agreement, or if its decision fails to satisfy one of the Chambers, the question is considered for a second time by the Chambers. Failing agreement between the two Chambers, the Presidium of the Supreme Soviet of the U.S.S.R. dissolves the Supreme Soviet of the U.S.S.R. and orders new elections.

Art. 48. The Supreme Soviet of the U.S.S.R. at a joint sitting of the two Chambers elects the Presidium of the Supreme Soviet of the U.S.S.R. consisting of a President of the Presidium of the Supreme Soviet of the U.S.S.R., sixteen Vice Presidents, a Secretary of the Presidium, and fifteen members of the Presidium of the Supreme Soviet of the U.S.S.R.

The Presidium of the Supreme Soviet of the U.S.S.R. is accountable to the Supreme Soviet of the U.S.S.R. for all its activities.

Art. 49. The Presidium of the Supreme Soviet of the U.S.S.R.:

(a) Convenes the sessions of the Supreme Soviet of the U.S.S.R.;

(b) Issues decrees;

(c) Gives interpretations of the laws of the U.S.S.R. in operation;

(d) Dissolves the Supreme Soviet of the U.S.S.R. in conformity with Article 47 of the Constitution of the U.S.S.R. and orders new elections;

(e) Conducts nationwide polls (referendums) on its own initiative or on the demand of one of the Union Republics;

(f) Annuls decisions and orders of the Council of Ministers of the U.S.S.R. and of the Council of Ministers of the Union Republics if they do not conform to law;

(g) In the intervals between sessions of the Supreme Soviet of the U.S.S.R. releases and appoints Ministers of the U.S.S.R. on the recommendation of the Chairman of the Council of Ministers of the

U.S.S.R., subject to subsequent confirmation by the Supreme Soviet of the U.S.S.R.;

(h) Institutes decorations (orders and medals) and titles of honor of the U.S.S.R.;

(i) Awards orders and medals and confers titles of honor of the U.S.S.R.;

(j) Exercises the right of pardon;

(k) Institutes military titles, diplomatic ranks, and other special titles;

(l) Appoints and removes the high command of the Armed Forces of the U.S.S.R.;

(m) In the intervals between sessions of the Supreme Soviet of the U.S.S.R., proclaims a state of war in the event of military attack on the U.S.S.R., or when necessary to fulfill international treaty obligations concerning mutual defense against aggression;

(n) Orders general or partial mobilization;

(o) Ratifies and denounces international treaties of the U.S.S.R.;

(p) Appoints and recalls plenipotentiary representatives of the U.S.S.R. to foreign States;

(q) Receives the letters of credence and recall of diplomatic representatives accredited to it by foreign states;

(r) Proclaims martial law in separate localities or throughout the U.S.S.R. in the interests of the defense of the U.S.S.R. or of the maintenance of public order and the security of the State.

Art. 50. The Soviet of the Union and the Soviet of Nationalities elect Credentials Committees to verify the credentials of the members of the respective Chambers.

On the report of the Credentials Committees, the Chambers decide whether to recognize the credentials of Deputies or to annul their election.

Art. 51. The Supreme Soviet of the U.S.S.R., when it deems necessary, appoints commissions of investigation and audit on any matter.

It is the duty of all institutions and officials to comply with the demands of such commissions and to submit to them all necessary materials and documents.

Art. 52. A member of the Supreme Soviet of the U.S.S.R. may not be prosecuted or arrested without the consent of the Supreme Soviet of the U.S.S.R., or, when the Supreme Soviet of the U.S.S.R. is not in session, without the consent of the Presidium of the Supreme Soviet of the U.S.S.R.

Art. 53. On the expiration of the term of office of the Supreme Soviet of the U.S.S.R., or on its dissolution prior to the expiration of its term of office, the Presidium of the Supreme Soviet of the U.S.S.R. retains its powers until the newly elected Supreme Soviet of the U.S.S.R. shall have formed a new Presidium of the Supreme Soviet of the U.S.S.R.

Art. 54. On the expiration of the term of office of the Supreme Soviet of the U.S.S.R., or in the event of its dissolution prior to the expiration of its term of office, the Presidium of the Supreme Soviet of the U.S.S.R. orders new elections to be held within a period not exceeding two months from the date of expiration of the term of office or dissolution of the Supreme Soviet of the U.S.S.R.

ART. 55. The newly elected Supreme Soviet of the U.S.S.R. is convened by the outgoing Presidium of the Supreme Soviet of the U.S.S.R. not later than three months after the elections.

ART. 56. The Supreme Soviet of the U.S.S.R., at a joint sitting of the two Chambers, appoints the Government of the U.S.S.R., namely, the Council of Ministers of the U.S.S.R.

Chapter IV. The Higher Organs of State Power in the Union Republics

ART. 57. The highest organ of state power in a Union Republic is the Supreme Soviet of the Union Republic.

ART. 58. The Supreme Soviet of a Union Republic is elected by the citizens of the Republic for a term of four years.

The basis of representation is established by the Constitution of the Union Republic.

ART. 59. The Supreme Soviet of a Union Republic is the sole legislative organ of the Republic.

ART. 60. The Supreme Soviet of a Union Republic:

(a) Adopts the Constitution of the Republic and amends it in conformity with Article 16 of the Constitution of the U.S.S.R.;

(b) Confirms the Constitutions of the Autonomous Republics forming part of it and defines the boundaries of their territories;

(c) Approves the national-economic plan and the budget of the Republic;

(d) Exercises the right of amnesty and pardon of citizens sentenced by the judicial organs of the Union Republic;

(e) Decides questions of representation of the Union Republic in its international relations;

(f) Determines the manner of organizing the Republic's military formations.

ART. 61. The Supreme Soviet of a Union Republic elects the Presidium of the Supreme Soviet of the Union Republic, consisting of a President of the Presidium of the Supreme Soviet of the Union Republic, Vice Presidents, a Secretary of the Presidium, and members of the Presidium of the Supreme Soviet of the Union Republic.

The powers of the Presidium of the Supreme Soviet of a Union Republic are defined by the Constitution of the Union Republic.

ART. 62. The Supreme Soviet of a Union Republic elects a Chairman and Vice Chairmen to conduct its sittings.

ART. 63. The Supreme Soviet of a Union Republic appoints the Government of the Union Republic, namely, the Council of Ministers of the Union Republic.

Chapter V. The Organs of State Administration of The Union of Soviet Socialist Republics

ART. 64. The highest executive and administrative organ of the state power of the Union of Soviet Socialist Republics is the Council of Ministers of the U.S.S.R.

ART. 65. The Council of Ministers of the U.S.S.R. is responsible and accountable to the Supreme Soviet of the U.S.S.R., or, in the intervals between sessions of the Supreme Soviet, to the Presidium of the Supreme Soviet of the U.S.S.R.

ART. 66. The Council of Ministers of the U.S.S.R. issues decisions and orders on the basis and in pursuance of the laws in operation, and verifies their execution.

ART. 67. Decisions and orders of the Council of Ministers of the U.S.S.R. are binding throughout the territory of the U.S.S.R.

ART. 68. The Council of Ministers of the U.S.S.R.:

(a) Coordinates and directs the work of the All-Union and Union-Republican Ministries of the U.S.S.R. and of other institutions [4] under its jurisdiction;

(b) Adopts measures to carry out the national economic plan and the state budget, and to strengthen the credit and monetary system;

(c) Adopts measures for the maintenance of public order, for the protection of the interests of the state, and for the safeguarding of the rights of citizens;

(d) Exercises general guidance in the sphere of relations with foreign states;

(e) Fixes the annual contingent of citizens to be called up for military service and directs the general organization of the Armed Forces of the country;

(f) Sets up, whenever necessary, special Committees and Central Administrations under the Council of Ministers of the U.S.S.R. for economic and cultural affairs and defense.

ART. 69. The Council of Ministers of the U.S.S.R. has the right, in respect of those branches of administration and economy which come within the jurisdiction of the U.S.S.R., to suspend decisions and orders of the Councils of Ministers of the Union Republics and to annul orders and instructions of Ministers of the U.S.S.R.

ART. 70. The Council of Ministers of the U.S.S.R. is appointed by the Supreme Soviet of the U.S.S.R. and consists of:

[4] The 1937 text listed explicitly "economic and cultural" institutions. The amendment of February 1947 assured the broadest possible scope of jurisdiction.

The Chairman of the U.S.S.R. Council of Ministers;

The Deputy Chairmen of the U.S.S.R. Council of Ministers;

The Chairman of the State Planning Committee of the U.S.S.R. Council of Ministers;

The Chairman of the State Committee of the U.S.S.R. Council of Ministers for the Material-Technical Supply of the National Economy;

The Chairman of the State Committee of the U.S.S.R. Council of Ministers for Introducing Advanced Techniques in the National Economy;

The Chairman of the State Committee of the U.S.S.R. Council of Ministers for Construction Affairs;

The U.S.S.R. Ministers;

The Chairman of the Committee on Art Affairs.

ART. 71. The Government of the U.S.S.R. or a Minister of the U.S.S.R. to whom a question of a member of the Supreme Soviet of the U.S.S.R. is addressed must give a verbal or written reply in the respective Chamber within a period not exceeding three days.

ART. 72. The Ministers of the U.S.S.R. direct the branches of State administration which come within the jurisdiction of the U.S.S.R.

ART. 73. The Ministers of the U.S.S.R., within the limits of the jurisdiction of their respective Ministries, issue orders and instructions on the basis and in pursuance of the laws in operation, and also of decisions and orders of the Council of Ministers of the U.S.S.R., and verify their execution.

ART. 74. The Ministries of the U.S.S.R. are either all-Union or Union-Republican Ministries.

ART. 75. Each all-Union Ministry directs the branch of State administration entrusted to it throughout the territory of the U.S.S.R. either directly or through bodies appointed by it.

ART. 76. The Union-Republic Ministries, as a rule, direct the branches of State administration entrusted to them through corresponding Ministries of the Union Republics; they administer directly only a definite and limited number of enterprises according to a list confirmed by the Presidium of the Supreme Soviet of the U.S.S.R.

ART. 77. The following Ministries are all-Union Ministries [5]:

The Ministry of the Aircraft Industry
The Ministry of the Automobile and Tractor Industry
The Ministry of Foreign Trade
The Ministry of the Navy
The Ministry of Munitions
The Ministry of Geological Survey
The Ministry of Town Development

The Ministry of State Food and Material Reserves
The Ministry of Agricultural Stocks [Procurements]
The Ministry of the Machine and Instrument-Making Industry
The Ministry of the Metallurgical [Iron and Steel] Industry
The Ministry of the Merchant Marine
The Ministry of the Oil Industry
The Ministry of the Communications Equipment Industry
The Ministry of Railways
The Ministry of Inland Water Transport [River Fleet]
The Ministry of Communications
The Ministry of the Agricultural Machinery Industry
The Ministry of the Machine-Tool Industry
The Ministry of the Building and Road-Building Machinery Industry
The Ministry of Construction of Machine-Building Works
The Ministry of Shipbuilding
The Ministry of the Transport Machinery Industry
The Ministry of Labor Reserves
The Ministry of Construction of Heavy Industry Works
The Ministry of the Heavy Machine-Building Industry
The Ministry of the Coal Mining Industry
The Ministry of the Chemical Industry
The Ministry of the Electrical Equipment Industry
The Ministry of Power Stations

ART. 78. The following Ministries are Union-Republican Ministries:

The Ministry of Internal Affairs
The Ministry of War
The Ministry of Higher Education
The Ministry of State Control
The Ministry of State Security
The Ministry of Public Health
The Ministry of Foreign Affairs
The Ministry of Cinematography
The Ministry of Light Industry
The Ministry of Forestry
The Ministry of the Timber and Paper Industry
The Ministry of the Meat and Dairy Industry
The Ministry of the Food Industry
The Ministry of the Building Materials Industry
The Ministry of the Fish Industry
The Ministry of Agriculture
The Ministry of State Farms
The Ministry of Trade
The Ministry of Finance
The Ministry of Cotton Growing
The Ministry of Justice [6]

[5] The departmental reconstructions have been so numerous and so detailed that they defeat a reasonable presentation. The subject of administrative reconstruction is touched on at p. 804.

[6] The Commissariat of Justice was removed from the exclusive jurisdiction of the constituent republics in 1936 and made a Union-Republican agency.

CHAPTER VI. THE ORGANS OF STATE ADMINISTRATION OF THE UNION REPUBLICS

ART. 79. The highest executive and administrative organ of the state power of a Union Republic is the Council of Ministers of the Union Republic.

ART. 80. The Council of Ministers of a Union Republic is responsible and accountable to the Supreme Soviet of the Union Republic, or in the intervals between sessions of the Supreme Soviet of the Union Republic, to the Presidium of the Supreme Soviet of the Union Republic.

ART. 81. The Council of Ministers of a Union Republic issues decisions and orders on the basis and in pursuance of the laws in operation of the U.S.S.R. and of the Union Republic, and of the decisions and orders of the Council of Ministers of the U.S.S.R., and verifies their execution.

ART. 82. The Council of Ministers of a Union Republic has the right to suspend decisions and orders of the Councils of Ministers of its Autonomous Republics, and to annul decisions and orders of the Executive Committees of the Soviets of Working People's Deputies of its Territories, Regions and Autonomous Regions.

ART. 83. The Council of Ministers of a Union Republic is appointed by the Supreme Soviet of the Union Republic and consists of: [7]

The Chairman of the Council of Ministers of the Union Republic;

The Vice Chairmen of the Council of Ministers;

The Chairman of the State Planning Commission;

The Ministers;

The Chief of the Arts Administration;

The Chairman of the Committee for Cultural and Educational Institutions.

ART. 84. The Ministers of a Union Republic direct the branches of state administration which come within the jurisdiction of the Union Republic.

ART. 85. The Ministers of a Union Republic, within the limits of the jurisdiction of their respective Ministries, issue orders and instructions on the basis and in pursuance of the laws of the U.S.S.R. and of the Union Republic, of the decisions and orders of the Council of Ministers of the U.S.S.R. and the Council of Ministers of the Union Republic, and of the orders and instructions of the Union-Republican Ministries of the U.S.S.R.

ART. 86. The Ministries of a Union-Republic are either Union-Republican or Republican Ministries.

[7] Up to 1947 the texts of the Constitution enumerated all the commissariats of the Union Republics, those corresponding to the Federal, Union-Republican agencies as well as non-Federal, exclusively republican departments; they also mentioned the "Delegates of All-Union People's Commissariats," the Federal inspectors. Since 1947 the texts leave only "The Ministers."

ART. 87. Each Union-Republican Ministry directs the branch of state administration entrusted to it, and is subordinate both to the Council of Ministers of the Union Republic and to the corresponding Union-Republican Ministry of the U.S.S.R.

ART. 88. Each Republican Ministry directs the branch of state administration entrusted to it and is directly subordinate to the Council of Ministers of the Union Republic.

CHAPTER VII. THE HIGHER ORGANS OF STATE POWER IN THE AUTONOMOUS SOVIET SOCIALIST REPUBLICS

ART. 89. The highest organ of state power in an Autonomous Soviet Socialist Republic is the Supreme Soviet of the Autonomous Republic.

ART. 90. The Supreme Soviet of an Autonomous Republic is elected by the citizens of the Republic for a term of four years on a basis of representation established by the Constitution of the Autonomous Republic.

ART. 91. The Supreme Soviet of an Autonomous Republic is the sole legislative organ of the Autonomous Republic.

ART. 92. Each Autonomous Republic has its own Constitution, which takes account of the specific features of the Autonomous Republic and is drawn up in full conformity with the Constitution of the Union Republic.

ART. 93. The Supreme Soviet of an Autonomous Republic elects the Presidium of the Supreme Soviet of the Autonomous Republic and appoints the Council of Ministers of the Autonomous Republic, in accordance with its Constitution.

CHAPTER VIII. THE LOCAL ORGANS OF STATE POWER

ART. 94. The organs of state power in territories, regions, autonomous regions, areas, districts, cities, and rural localities (*stanitsas,* villages, hamlets, *kishlaks, auls*) are the Soviets of Working People's Deputies.

ART. 95. The Soviets of Working People's Deputies of territories, regions, autonomous regions, areas, districts, cities, and rural localities (*stanitsas,* villages, hamlets, *kishlaks, auls*) are elected by the working people of the respective territories, regions, autonomous regions, areas, districts, cities, or rural localities for a term of two years.

ART. 96. The basis of representation for Soviets of Working People's Deputies is determined by the Constitutions of the Union Republics.

ART. 97. The Soviets of Working People's Deputies direct the work of the organs of administration subordinate to them, ensure the maintenance of public order, the observance of the laws and the protection of the rights of citizens, direct local economic and cultural affairs, and draw up the local budgets.

ART. 98. The Soviets of Working People's Deputies adopt decisions and issue orders within the limits of the powers vested in them by the laws of the U.S.S.R. and of the Union Republic.

ART. 99. The executive and administrative organ of the Soviet of Working People's Deputies of a territory, region, autonomous region, area, district, city, or rural locality is the Executive Committee elected by it, consisting of a Chairman, Vice Chairman, a Secretary, and members.

ART. 100. The executive and administrative organ of the Soviet of Working People's Deputies in a small locality, in accordance with the Constitution of the Union Republic, is the Chairman, the Vice Chairman,[8] and the Secretary elected by it.

ART. 101. The executive organs of the Soviets of Working People's Deputies are directly accountable both to the Soviets of Working People's Deputies which elected them and to the executive organ of the superior Soviet of Working People's Deputies.

CHAPTER IX. THE COURTS AND THE PROCURATOR'S OFFICE

ART. 102. In the U.S.S.R. justice is administered by the Supreme Court of the U.S.S.R., the Supreme Courts of the Union Republics, the Courts of the Territories, Regions, Autonomous Republics, Autonomous Regions and Areas, the Special Courts of the U.S.S.R. established by decision of the Supreme Soviet of the U.S.S.R., and the People's Courts.

ART. 103. In all courts cases are tried with the participation of people's assessors, except in cases specially provided for by law.

ART. 104. The Supreme Court of the U.S.S.R. is the highest judicial organ. The Supreme Court of the U.S.S.R. is charged with the supervision of the judicial activities of all the judicial organs of the U.S.S.R. and of the Union Republics.

ART. 105. The Supreme Court of the U.S.S.R. and the Special Courts of the U.S.S.R. are elected by the Supreme Soviet of the U.S.S.R. for a term of five years.

ART. 106. The Supreme Courts of the Union Republics are elected by the Supreme Soviets of the Union Republics for a term of five years.

ART. 107. The Supreme Courts of the Autonomous Republics are elected by the Supreme Soviets of the Autonomous Republics for a term of five years.

ART. 108. The Courts of Territories, Regions, Autonomous Regions, and Areas are elected by the Soviets of Working People's Deputies of the respective Territories, Regions, Autonomous Regions, or Areas for a term of five years.

ART. 109. People's Courts are elected by the citizens of the districts on the basis of universal, direct, and equal suffrage by secret ballot for a term of three years.

ART. 110. Judicial proceedings are conducted in the

language of the Union Republic, Autonomous Republic, or Autonomous Region, persons not knowing this language being guaranteed the opportunity of fully acquainting themselves with the material of the case through an interpreter and likewise the right to use their own language in court.

ART. 111. In all courts of the U.S.S.R. cases are heard in public, unless otherwise provided for by law, and the accused is guaranteed the right to defense.

ART. 112. Judges are independent and subject only to the law.

ART. 113. Supreme supervisory power to ensure the strict observance of the law by all Ministries and institutions subordinated to them, as well as by officials and citizens of the U.S.S.R. generally, is vested in the Procurator General of the U.S.S.R.

ART. 114. The Procurator General [9] of the U.S.S.R. is appointed by the Supreme Soviet of the U.S.S.R. for a term of seven years.

ART. 115. Procurators of Republics, Territories, Regions, Autonomous Republics, and Autonomous Regions are appointed by the Procurator General of the U.S.S.R. for a term of five years.

ART. 116. Area, district, and city procurators are appointed by the Procurators of the Union Republics, subject to the approval of the Procurator General of the U.S.S.R., for a term of five years.

ART. 117. The organs of the Procurator's Office perform their functions independently of any local organs whatsoever, being subordinate solely to the Procurator General of the U.S.S.R.

CHAPTER X. FUNDAMENTAL RIGHTS AND DUTIES OF CITIZENS [10]

ART. 118. Citizens of the U.S.S.R. have the right to work—that is, the right to guaranteed employment and payment for their work in accordance with its quantity and quality.

The right to work is insured by the socialist organization of the national economy, the steady growth of the productive forces of Soviet society, the elimination of the possibility of economic crises, and the abolition of unemployment.

ART. 119. Citizens of the U.S.S.R. have the right to rest and leisure.

The right to rest and leisure is insured by the establishment of an eight-hour day for factory and office workers, the reduction of the working day to seven or six hours for arduous trades and to four hours in shops where conditions of work are particularly arduous, by the institution of annual vacations with full pay for factory and office workers, and by the provision of a wide network of sanatoria, rest homes, and clubs for the accommodation of the working people.

[8] The 1937 text has "Vice Chairmen."

[9] This title replaced the earlier one of State Attorney (law of Mar. 19, 1946; amendment of February 1947).

[10] The 1924 Constitution had no comparable section.

Art. 120. Citizens of the U.S.S.R. have the right to maintenance in old age and also in case of sickness or disability.

This right is insured by the extensive development of social insurance of factory and office workers at State expense, free medical service for the working people, and the provision of a wide network of health resorts for the use of the working people.

Art. 121. Citizens of the U.S.S.R. have the right to education.

This right is insured by universal and compulsory elementary education; by free education [11] up to and including the seventh grade; by a system of State stipends for students of higher educational establishments who excel in their studies; by instruction in schools being conducted in the native language, and by the organization in the factories, State farms, machine and tractor stations, and collective farms of free vocational, technical, and agronomic training for the working people.

Art. 122. Women in the U.S.S.R. are accorded equal rights with men in all spheres of economic, government, cultural, political, and other public activity.

The possibility of exercising these rights is insured by women being accorded an equal right with men to work, payment for work, rest and leisure, social insurance and education, and by State protection of the interests of mother and child, State aid to mothers of large families and unmarried mothers,[12] maternity leave with full pay, and the provision of a wide network of maternity homes, nurseries, and kindergartens.

Art. 123. Equality of rights of citizens of the U.S.S.R., irrespective of their nationality or race, in all spheres of economic, government, cultural, political, and other public activity, is an indefeasible law.

Any direct or indirect restriction of the rights of, or conversely, the establishment of any direct or indirect privileges for, citizens on account of their race or nationality, as well as any advocacy of racial or national exclusiveness or hatred and contempt, is punishable by law.

Art. 124. In order to insure to citizens freedom of conscience, the church in the U.S.S.R. is separated

[11] Prior to the amendment of February 1947 the sentence read: "by education, including higher education, being free of charge; by the system of State stipends for the overwhelming majority of students in universities and colleges. . . ." Tuition fees for universities, colleges and upper high-school grades were introduced by decree of September 1, 1940.

[12] This clause was missing before the amendment of February 1947. A decree establishing aid to mothers of large families and to unmarried mothers was promulgated on July 18, 1944.

from the State, and the school from the church. Freedom of religious worship and freedom of antireligious propaganda is recognized for all citizens.

Art. 125. In conformity with the interests of the working people, and in order to strengthen the socialist system, the citizens of the U.S.S.R. are guaranteed by law:

(a) freedom of speech;

(b) freedom of the press;

(c) freedom of assembly, including the holding of mass meetings;

(d) freedom of street processions and demonstrations.

These civil rights are insured by placing at the disposal of the working people and their organizations printing presses, stocks of paper, public buildings, the streets, communications facilities, and other material requisites for the exercise of these rights.

Art. 126. In conformity with the interests of the working people, and in order to develop the organizational initiative and political activity of the masses of the people, citizens of the U.S.S.R. are guaranteed the right to unite in public organizations: trade unions, cooperative societies, youth organizations, sport and defense organizations, cultural, technical, and scientific societies; and the most active and politically conscious citizens in the ranks of the working class and other sections of the working people unite in the Communist Party of the Soviet Union (Bolsheviks), which is the vanguard of the working people in their struggle to strengthen and develop the socialist system and is the leading core of all organizations of the working people, both public and State.

Art. 127. Citizens of the U.S.S.R. are guaranteed inviolability of the person. No person may be placed under arrest except by decision of a court or with the sanction of a procurator.

Art. 128. The inviolability of the homes of citizens and privacy of correspondence are protected by law.

Art. 129. The U.S.S.R. affords the right of asylum to foreign citizens persecuted for defending the interests of the working people or for scientific activities or for struggling for national liberation.

Art. 130. It is the duty of every citizen of the U.S.S.R. to abide by the Constitution of the Union of Soviet Socialist Republics, to observe the laws, to maintain labor discipline, honestly to perform public duties, and to respect the rules of socialist intercourse.

Art. 131. It is the duty of every citizen of the U.S.S.R. to safeguard and fortify public, socialist property as the sacred and inviolable foundation of the Soviet system, as the source of the wealth and might of the country, as the source of the prosperity and culture of all the working people.

Persons committing offenses against public, socialist property are enemies of the People.

Art. 132. Universal military service is law.

Military service in the Armed Forces of the U.S.S.R.[13] is an honorable duty of the citizens of the U.S.S.R.

Art. 133. To defend the country is the sacred duty of every citizen of the U.S.S.R. Treason to the motherland—violation of the oath of allegiance, desertion to the enemy, impairing the military power of the State, espionage—is punishable with all the severity of the law as the most heinous of crimes.

Chapter XI. The Electoral System

Art. 134. Members of all Soviets of Working People's Deputies—of the Supreme Soviet of the U.S.S.R., the Supreme Soviets of the Union Republics, the Soviets of Working People's Deputies of the Territories and Regions, the Supreme Soviets of the Autonomous Republics, the Soviets of Working People's Deputies of the Autonomous Regions, and the area, district, city, and rural (*stanitsa,* village, hamlet, *kishlak, aul*) Soviets of Working People's Deputies—are chosen by the electors on the basis of universal, equal, and direct suffrage by secret ballot.

Art. 135. Elections of Deputies are universal: all citizens of the U.S.S.R. who have reached the age of eighteen, irrespective of race or nationality, sex, religion, education, domicile, social origin, property status, or past activities, have the right to vote in the election of Deputies, with the exception of insane persons and persons who have been convicted by a court of law and whose sentences include deprivation of electoral rights.

Every citizen of the U.S.S.R. who has reached the age of twenty-three [14] is eligible for election to the Supreme Soviet of the U.S.S.R., irrespective of race or nationality, sex, religion, education, domicile, social origin, property status, or past activities.

Art. 136. Elections of Deputies are equal: each citizen has one vote; all citizens participate in elections on an equal footing.

Art. 137. Women have the right to elect and be elected on equal terms with men.

Art. 138. Citizens serving in the Armed Forces of the U.S.S.R. have the right to elect and be elected on equal terms with all other citizens.

Art. 139. Elections of Deputies are direct: all Soviets of Working People's Deputies, from rural and city Soviets of Working People's Deputies to the Supreme Soviet of the U.S.S.R., are elected by the citizens by direct vote.

Art. 140. Voting at elections of Deputies is secret.

Art. 141. Candidates are nominated by election district.

The right to nominate candidates is secured to public organizations and societies of the working people: Communist Party organizations, trade unions, cooperatives, youth organizations, and cultural societies.

Art. 142. It is the duty of every Deputy to report to his electors on his work and on the work of his Soviet of Working People's Deputies, and he may be recalled at any time upon decision of a majority of the electors in the manner established by law.

Chapter XII. Arms, Flag, Capital

Art. 143. The arms of the Union of Soviet Socialist Republics are a sickle and hammer against a globe depicted in the rays of the sun and surrounded by ears of grain, with the inscription "Workers of All Countries, Unite!" in the languages of the Union Republics. At the top of the arms is a five-pointed star.

Art. 144. The State flag of the Union of Soviet Socialist Republics is of red cloth with the sickle and hammer depicted in gold in the upper corner near the staff and above them a five-pointed red star bordered in gold. The ratio of the width to the length is 1:2.

Art. 145. The Capital of the Union of Soviet Socialist Republics is the City of Moscow.

Chapter XIII. Procedure for Amending the Constitution

Art. 146. The Constitution of the U.S.S.R. may be amended only by decision of the Supreme Soviet of the U.S.S.R. adopted by a majority of not less than two thirds of the votes in each of its Chambers

[13] Amended in February 1947. Earlier texts read "Workers' and Peasants' Red Army." A decree of May 8, 1940, introduced military ranks and titles in the Soviet Army and Navy.

[14] This entire paragraph was added to Article 135 by amendment of February 1947. Soviet citizens had been eligible for election at the age of eighteen until a decree of October 10, 1945, raised the age limit for the 1946 elections to the second Supreme Soviet.

STATUTES OF THE COMMUNIST PARTY OF THE SOVIET UNION *

I. The Party. Party Members, Their Duties and Rights

1. The Communist Party of the Soviet Union is a voluntary militant union of Communists holding the same views, formed of people of the working class, the working peasantry, and the working intelligentsia.

Having organized the alliance of the working class and working peasantry, the Communist Party accomplished, through the *great* October *socialist* revolution of 1917, the overthrow of the rule of the capitalists and landowners, the organization of the dictatorship of the proletariat, the liquidation of capitalism and abolition of exploitation of man by man, and insured the construction of a socialist society.

The chief tasks of the Communist Party of the Soviet Union now are to build a communist society by gradual transition from socialism to communism, to bring about a constant rise in the living standards and cultural level of society, to educate the members of society in internationalism and establishment of fraternal bonds with the working people of all countries, and to strengthen in every respect the active defense of the Soviet country against aggressive actions of its enemies.

2. Any working person who is a Soviet citizen not exploiting anyone else's labor, accepting the Program and Statutes of the Party, taking active part in effecting them, working in one of the Party organizations, and carrying out all the decisions of the Party may become a member of the Communist Party of the Soviet Union.

Members of the Party pay the established membership dues.

3. It is the duty of a Party member:

(a) To guard the unity of the Party in every way, as the prime condition of the Party's strength and might.

(b) To be an active fighter for the fulfillment of Party decisions. Mere agreement with Party decisions does not suffice for a Party member; it is the Party member's duty to fight for the fulfillment of Party decisions. A passive and formal attitude on the part of Communists toward the decisions of the Party weakens the effectiveness of the Party and is therefore incompatible with membership.

(c) To set an example on the job and to master knowledge of it, constantly increasing his working skills; *in all ways to safeguard and strengthen public socialist property as the sacred and inviolable basis of the Soviet system.*

(d) Day in and day out to strengthen contact with the masses, to respond promptly to the desires and needs of the working people, and to explain to the non-Party masses the meaning of the Party policy and decisions, mindful that the strength and invincibility of our party lie in close, inseparable ties with the people.

(e) To work at increasing his political awareness, at mastering the principles of Marxism-Leninism.

(f) To observe Party and State discipline, obligatory for all Party members alike. There can be no two disciplines in the Party, one for the leaders and another for the rank and file. The Party has only one discipline, one law for all Communists, irrespective of their services and the offices they hold. Violation of Party and State discipline is a great evil, harming the Party and hence incompatible with membership.

(g) To develop self-criticism and criticism from below, to expose and seek to eliminate shortcomings in work, and to fight against a show of well-being and against being carried away by successes in work. Suppression of criticism is a great evil. He who silences criticism and substitutes ostentation and boastfulness in its place cannot remain in the ranks of the Party.

(h) To report to leading Party bodies, right up to the Party Central Committee, shortcomings in work, irrespective of the persons involved. A Party member has no right to conceal an unsatisfactory state of affairs or ignore wrongdoings which damage the interests of the Party and State. He who hinders a Party member from carrying out this duty must be severely punished as violating the will of the Party.

(i) To be truthful and honest before the Party and never permit concealment or distortion of truth. Untruthfulness of a Communist toward the Party and deception of the Party are grave misdeeds incompatible with Party membership.

(j) To keep Party and State secrets and to display political vigilance, keeping in mind that the vigilance of Communists is necessary on every sector and in all circumstances. Disclosing Party or State secrets is a crime before the Party and incompatible with Party membership.

(k) At any post entrusted to him by the Party, to carry out without fail the Party directives on correct

* From *Current Soviet Policies,* edited by Leo Gruliow, Frederick A. Praeger, Inc., New York, 1953. Copyright 1953 by the Joint Committee on Slavic Studies.

The "Draft of the Central Committee of the All-Union Communist Party: Revised Statutes of the Party," published in *Pravda,* August 20, 1952, pp. 3–4, is identical with the Statutes adopted by the Nineteenth Congress (below), except for additions indicated by italic type and deletions by square brackets.

selection of cadres with regard to political and working qualifications. Violating these directives—selecting cadres on the basis of friendship, personal loyalties, local allegiance, or kinship—is incompatible with Party membership.

4. The Party member has the right:

(a) To take part in free and businesslike discussion, at Party meetings and in the Party press, of matters of Party policy.

(b) To criticize any Party functionary at Party meetings.

(c) To elect or be elected to Party bodies.

(d) To insist on personal participation in all cases when decisions are adopted concerning his activities or behavior.

(e) To address any questions or statements to any Party body, at any level, right up to the Central Committee of the Communist Party of the Soviet Union.

5. Admission to membership in the Party is granted exclusively on an individual basis. New members of the Party are accepted from among candidates who have completed their period as candidates. Workers, peasants, and intelligentsia who are politically aware, active, and devoted to the Communist cause are accepted as Party members.

They must have attained the age of eighteen.

The method of admitting candidates into the Party is as follows:

(a) Persons to be admitted to the Party must be sponsored by three members of the Party of at least three years' standing who have been acquainted with the candidate in their joint work for a period of not less than one year.

(b) The question of admission to Party membership is discussed and decided by a general meeting of the primary Party organization; its decision comes into force upon ratification by the district Party committee, and, in cities where there is no district subdivision upon ratification by the city Party committee. When discussing admission to the Party, the presence of the persons recommending admission is not essential.

(c) Young people up to twenty years of age inclusive can join the Party only via the Young Communist League.

(d) Persons who have left other parties are admitted to the Party on the recommendation of five Party members—three having a membership of ten years and two who were Party members before the Revolution—and only through the primary Party organization with the approval of the Central Committee of the Communist Party of the Soviet Union.

6. The sponsors bear responsibility for their recommendations.

7. The Party membership of candidates admitted to the ranks of the Party dates from adoption, by the general meeting of the primary Party organization concerned, of a resolution confirming the given comrade's membership in the Party.

8. Each member of one Party organization, upon moving to a district under another organization's jurisdiction, is enrolled as a member of the latter organization.

9. Party members and candidates who have failed to pay their membership dues without valid reason for three months are considered to have automatically dropped out of the Party, and the primary Party organization adopts a resolution to that effect, which is ratified by the district or city Party committee.

10. The question of expelling a Communist from the Party is decided by the general meeting of the primary Party organization of which he is a member, and the resolution is confirmed by the district or city Party committee. The resolution of the district or city committee to expel a member from the Party comes into force only when it has been confirmed by the province Party committee, the territory Party committee, or the Central Committee of the Communist Party of a Union Republic.

Until the province Party committee, the territory Party committee or the Central Committee of the Communist Party of the Union Republic ratifies the resolution expelling the member from the Party, his Party membership card remains in his hands and he has the right to attend closed Party meetings.

11. The primary Party organization cannot adopt a resolution to exclude from the Party *or to return to candidate status* any Communist who is a member of the Central Committee of the Communist Party of the Soviet Union, the Central Committee of the Communist Party of a Union Republic or a territory, province, region, city, or district Party committee.

The question of expelling a member of the Central Committee of the Communist Party of a Union Republic or of a territory, province, region, city, or district Party committee from membership in the committee or the Party *or of returning the member to candidate status* is decided at a plenary session of the committee concerned by a two-thirds majority.

12. The question of expelling a member of the Central Committee of the Communist Party of the Soviet Union from the Central Committee or from membership in the Party *or of returning the member to candidate status* is decided by the Party Congress or, in the interval between Congresses, by a plenary session of the Central Committee of the Communist Party of the Soviet Union by a two-thirds majority. A person expelled from the Central Committee is automatically replaced by a candidate for membership in the Central Committee in the order established by the Congress in electing candidates to the Central Committee.

13. In cases where a Party member has committed an offense punishable by the courts, he is expelled

from the Party on receipt of the reports on his misdeeds from the administrative and judicial authorities.

14. When deciding the question of expulsion from the Party, the maximum care and comradely concern must be exercised, and a very careful examination must be made of whether the accusation leveled against the Party member is justified.

Minor misdeeds should be punished by Party educational measures and other means of influencing the individual (warning, reprimand, etc.) and not by expulsion from the Party, which is the severest form of Party punishment.

When it is necessary as a measure of Party discipline, a Party organization may transfer a member of the Party to the status of candidate for a period of up to one year. *The decision of a primary Party organization to return a Party member to candidate status is subject to ratification by the district or city Party committee. On expiration of the established period the person who has been returned to candidate status is admitted to Party membership on a regular basis and retains his former length of Party membership.*

15. Appeals by those expelled from the Party and the decisions of Party organizations to expel members from the Party must be reviewed by the Party bodies concerned within a period of twenty days from the day of receipt.

II. Candidates for Party Membership

16. All persons wishing to join the Party pass through a candidate stage, which is essential in order that the candidate may acquaint himself with the Program, Statutes, and tactics of the Party and that the Party organization may verify his personal qualifications.

17. The method of admitting candidates (individual admission, presentation of recommendations and their verification, the resolution of the primary organization on admission and its ratification) is identical with that of admission to Party membership.

18. The status of candidate lasts one year.

The Party organization is obliged to help candidates to prepare to become Party members. On the expiration of the candidature, the Party organization must take up the question of the candidate's Party membership at a Party meeting.

If the candidate has been unable to prove himself for reasons which the Party organization considers valid, the primary Party organization may prolong his candidature for a period not exceeding one year. In cases where it has become clear during the course of the candidature that in his personal qualifications the candidate is not worthy of admission to Party membership, the Party organization adopts a resolution to expel him from Party candidature. *Decisions of the primary Party organization prolonging candi-*

dature or expelling from candidature come into force after their ratification by the district or city Party committee.

19. Candidates for Party membership take part in meetings of the organization of which they are members, with the right to a consultative vote.

20. Candidates for Party membership pay the usual membership dues into the fund of the local Party committee.

III. Structure of the Party. Inner Party Democracy

21. The guiding principle of the organizational structure of the Party is democratic centralism, meaning:

(a) Election of all Party governing bodies from bottom to top.

(b) Periodic accountability of Party bodies to their Party organizations.

(c) Strict Party discipline and subordination of the minority to the majority.

(d) The decisions of higher bodies are unconditionally binding upon lower ones.

22. The Party structure rests on a territorial-production basis: the Party organization serving any given area is regarded as superior to all Party organizations serving parts of this area, and a Party organization serving an entire branch of production is regarded as superior to all Party organizations serving sections of this branch of production.

23. All Party organizations are autonomous in deciding local questions, provided that the decisions are not contrary to the Party's decisions.

24. The highest governing body of each Party organization is the general meeting (for primary organizations), the conference (for district and province organizations, for example), and the Congress (for the Communist Parties of Union Republics and the Communist Party of the Soviet Union).

25. The general meeting, conference, or Congress elects the bureau or committee which is the governing body and directs the entire current work of the organization.

26. In the election of Party bodies, voting by lists is forbidden. Voting must be on individual candidates. Moreover, all Party members are assured the unrestricted right to challenge candidates and to criticize them. Elections are held by closed (secret) balloting on candidates.

27. In cities and district centers the aktiv of city and district Party organizations is convened for discussion of the more important decisions of the Party and government. Moreover, the aktiv must be convened not for appearance's sake or for mere formal approval of these decisions, but for a genuine discussion of them.

28. The free and businesslike discussion of ques-

tions of Party policy in individual Party organizations or in the Party as a whole is the inalienable right of each Party member, a right which stems from inner Party democracy. Only on the basis of inner Party democracy can [Bolshevist] self-criticism be developed and Party discipline be strengthened. This must be conscious, not mechanical discipline.

However, broad discussion of questions of Party policy, especially discussion on an all-Union scale, must be organized in such a way as not to lead to attempts by an insignificant minority to impose its will on the Party majority, or to attempts to form fractional groupings destructive of Party unity, or to schismatic efforts which may shake the strength and stability of the socialist system.

Broad discussion on an all-Union scale can be considered essential only in the following cases:

(a) If it is considered essential by at least several local Party organizations on the province or republic level.

(b) If within the Central Committee of the Communist Party of the Soviet Union there does not exist a sufficiently firm majority on major questions of Party policy.

(c) If in spite of the fact that a firm majority in the Central Committee adheres to a definite view, the Central Committee nevertheless regards it as essential to verify the correctness of its policy by means of a discussion in the Party.

Only by meeting these conditions can the Party be safeguarded against misuse of inner Party democracy by anti-Party elements. Only under these conditions can one count on inner Party democracy to serve the cause and not be used to harm the Party and the working class.

IV. The Supreme Bodies of the Party

29. The highest body of the Communist Party of the Soviet Union is the Party Congress. Regular Congresses are convened not less often than once every four years. Extraordinary Congresses are convened by the Party Central Committee on its own initiative or on the demand of at least one third of the total number of members represented at the previous Party Congress.

Convocations of the Party Congress and its agenda are announced not later than one and one-half months before the Congress is to convene. Extraordinary Congresses are convened on two months' notice.

A Congress is considered valid if there is represented at it not less than one half of all members of the Party represented at the previous regular Congress. The norms of representation at the Party Congress are fixed by the Central Committee.

30. If no extraordinary Congress is convened by the Central Committee within the term indicated in Article 29, Party organizations demanding the convocation of an extraordinary Congress have the right to form an organizational committee possessing the right of the Central Committee to convene an extraordinary Congress.

31. The Congress:

(a) Hears and approves reports of the Party Central Committee, the Central Inspection Commission, and other central organizations.

(b) Reviews and amends the Program and Statutes of the Party.

(c) Determines the tactical line of the Party on fundamental questions of current policy.

(d) Elects the Central Committee of the Communist Party of the Soviet Union and the Central Inspection Commission.

32. The number of members of the Party Central Committee and Central Inspection Commission is determined and their members are elected by the Congress. In the event of loss of members of the Central Committee, its membership is replenished from among the candidates elected by the Congress.

33. The Central Committee of the Communist Party of the Soviet Union holds not less than one plenary session every six months. Candidates for membership in the Central Committee attend plenary sessions of the Central Committee with the right to a consultative vote.

34. The Central Committee of the Communist Party of the Soviet Union organizes a Presidium to direct the work of the Central Committee between plenary sessions and a Secretariat to direct current work, chiefly as concerns verification of the fulfillment of Party decisions and selection of cadres.

35. The Central Committee of the Communist Party of the Soviet Union organizes a Party Control Committee under the Central Committee. The Party Control Committee under the Party Central Committee:

(a) Verifies the observance of Party discipline by Party members and candidates; calls to account Communists guilty of violating the Party Program and Statutes or of breaches of Party and State discipline, as well as violators of Party ethics (those guilty of deception of the Party, dishonesty and insincerity in relation to the Party, slander, bureaucracy, moral turpitude, etc.).

(b) Examines appeals against decisions of the Central Committees of the Communist Parties of Union Republics and of territory and province Party committees concerning expulsions from the Party and Party disciplinary measures.

(c) Has its representatives, independent of local Party bodies, in the Republics, territories, and provinces.

36. In the intervals between Congresses the Central Committee of the Communist Party of the Soviet Union directs the whole work of the Party; represents the Party in its relations with other parties, organiza-

tions, and institutions; organizes various Party institutions and directs their activity; appoints editorial boards of central organs of the press, which function under its control and confirms the editorial boards of Party publications of large local organizations; organizes and directs undertakings of social significance; distributes the manpower and resources of the Party, and administers the central fund.

The Central Committee guides the work of the central Soviet and public organizations through the Party groups within them.

37. For purposes of strengthening administrative and political work, the Party Central Committee has the right to set up political sections and assign Party organizers of the Central Committee to individual sectors of socialist construction which may assume a special importance for the national economy of the country as a whole and, likewise, when these have fulfilled their tasks, to abolish them or turn them into ordinary Party bodies constituted on a territorial-production basis.

The political sections work on the basis of special instructions handed down by the Central Committee.

38. The Central Committee of the Communist Party of the Soviet Union keeps the Party organizations regularly informed about its work.

39. The Central Inspection Commission inspects: (a) the speed and correctness of the conduct of affairs in central bodies of the Party and the organizational condition of the apparatus of the Secretariat of the Central Committee; (b) the treasury and institutions of the Party Central Committee.

V. The Province, Territory, and Republic Organizations of the Party

40. The highest body of the province, territory, and Republic Party organizations is the province or territory Party conference or the Communist Party Congress in Union Republics, and, in the intervals between them, the province committee, territory committee, or the Union-Republic Central Committee of the Communist Party. These are guided in their work by the decisions of the Communist Party of the Soviet Union and its governing bodies.

41. A regular province or territory conference or Union-Republic Party Congress is convened by the province or territory committee or the Central Committee of the Communist Party of the Union Republic once every eighteen months, and extraordinary sessions by decision of the province committee, territory committee, or Central Committee of a Union Republic or on the demand of one third of the total membership of organizations subordinate to the province, territory, or Republic Party organizations.

The norms of representation at the province or ter-

ritory conference and the Union-Republic Party Congress are fixed by the province committee, territory committee, or Central Committee of the Communist Party of the Union Republic.

The province or territory conference or the Communist Party Congress of a Union Republic hears and approves the reports of the province or territory committee or the Central Committee of the Communist Party of the Union Republic, the Inspection Commission, and other province, territory, or Republic organizations; it discusses questions of Party, Soviet, economic and trade union work in the province, territory, or Republic, and elects the province committee, territory committee, or Central Committee of the Communist Party of the Union Republic, the Inspection Commission and delegates to the Congress of the Communist Party of the Soviet Union.

42. The province or territory committee or the Central Committee of the Communist Party of the Union Republic elects an executive body consisting of not more than eleven persons, including three secretaries whose election is ratified by the Party Central Committee. Party membership of not less than five years is compulsory for the secretaries.

In the province and territory and the Communist Party Central Committees of the Union Republics, Secretariats are formed to handle current questions and check on fulfillment. The Secretariat reports to the bureau of the province committee, territory committee, or Party Central Committee of the Union Republic on the decisions adopted.

43. The province committee, territory committee or Union Republic Party Central Committee organizes various offices of the Party within the province, territory, or Republic, and directs their activity; sees to undeviating fulfillment of the Party's directives and to developing criticism and self-criticism and educating the Communists in an uncompromising attitude toward shortcomings; directs the study of Marxism-Leninism by Party members and candidates; organizes the communist training of the working people; appoints the editorial boards of the province, territory, and Republic Party press organs, which function under its control; directs the activity of the province, territory, and Republic Soviet and public organizations through the Party groups in them; organizes and directs undertakings of general importance for the province, territory, or Republic; distributes within the jurisdiction of its organization the manpower and resources of the Party; administers the province, territory, or Republic Party funds; keeps the Party Central Committee regularly informed and, at specified times, submits to the Central Committee reports on its activity.

44. The plenary session of the province committee, territory committee or Central Committee of the Com-

munist Party of the Union Republic is convened not less than once in two months.

45. The Party organizations of the Autonomous Republics, as well as of national and other provinces within territories and Union Republics work under the direction of the territory committee or the Central Committee of the Communist Party of the Union Republic and, in their internal life, are guided by the regulations set forth in Section V of the Party Statutes concerning province, territory, and republic organizations.

VI. REGIONAL ORGANIZATIONS OF THE PARTY

46. In the provinces, territories, and Republics which have regions, regional Party organizations are formed in the latter.

The highest body of the regional Party organization is the regional Party conference, convened by the regional committee not less than once in eighteen months, and extraordinary conferences convened by decision of the regional committee or on the demand of one third of the total number of members of the organizations subordinate to the regional organization.

The regional conference hears and approves reports of the regional committee, the Inspection Commission and other regional Party organizations, and elects the regional committee of the Party, the Inspection Commission, and the delegates to the province or territory conference or the Party Congress of the Union Republic.

47. The regional committee elects a bureau consisting of not more than nine persons, including three secretaries of the regional committee. A three-year Party membership is compulsory for the secretaries. The secretaries of the regional committee are confirmed by the province committee, the territory committee, or, the Central Committee of the Communist Party of the Union Republic.

The plenary session of the regional committee is convened not less than once in one and one-half months.

48. The regional committee organizes various offices of the Party within the region and directs their activities; sees to undeviating fulfillment of Party directives, the development of criticism and self-criticism and the training of Communists in an uncompromising attitude toward shortcomings; directs the study of Marxism-Leninism by Party members and candidates; organizes the communist training of the working people; appoints the editorial boards of the regional Party press organ, which functions under its direction and control; directs the activity of regional Soviet and public organizations through the Party groups in them; organizes undertakings of regional importance; distributes within the region the man-power and the resources of the Party, and administers the regional Party funds.

VII. CITY AND DISTRICT (RURAL-DISTRICT; URBAN-BOROUGH) ORGANIZATIONS OF THE PARTY

49. The city and district Party conference is convened by the city or district committee not less than once a year, and extraordinary conferences by decision of the city or district committee or upon demand of one third of the total membership of the organizations subordinate to the city or district organization.

The city or district conference hears and approves reports of the city or district committee, the Inspection Commission, and other city or district organizations and elects the city or district committee, the Inspection Commission and the delegates to the territory or province conference or the Union-Republic Party Congress.

50. The city or district committee elects a bureau consisting of from seven to nine persons, including three secretaries of the city or district Party committee. Party membership of not less than three years is compulsory for the secretaries of the city or district committee. The secretaries of city and district committees are confirmed by the province committee, the territory committee or the Central Committee of the Communist Party of the Union Republic.

51. The city or district committee organizes and approves the primary Party organizations at enterprises, State farms, Machine and Tractor Stations, collective farms and offices, directs their activity and keeps the records of the Communists; sees to fulfillment of Party directives, the development of criticism and self-criticism and the training of Communists in an uncompromising attitude toward shortcomings; organizes the study of Marxism-Leninism by Party members and candidates; carries on the communist training of the working people; appoints the editorial boards of city or district Party press organs, which function under its direction and control; directs the activity of the city or district Soviet and public organizations through the Party groups in them; distributes within the city or district the manpower and resources of the Party, and administers the city or district Party funds.

The city or district committee submits reports on its activity to the province committee, the territory committee, or the Central Committee of the Communist Party of the Union Republic at the times and in the manner specified by the Party Central Committee.

52. Plenary sessions of city or district committees are convened not less than once a month.

53. With the permission of the Central Committee of the Communist Party of the Soviet Union, borough organizations subordinate to the city committee are established in large cities.

VIII. Primary Organizations of the Party

54. The primary Party organizations are the foundation of the Party.

The primary Party organizations are set up in factories, plants, State farms, Machine and Tractor Stations and other agricultural enterprises, collective farms, units of the Soviet Army and Navy, villages, offices, educational institutions, etc., wherever there are no less than three Party members.

Candidates' groups or Party-and-Young Communist League groups are formed at industrial enterprises, collective farms, institutions, etc., where there are fewer than three Party members; these groups are headed by a Party organizer assigned by the district or city Party committee or the political section.

The primary Party organizations are chartered by the district or city committees or the appropriate political departments.

The highest organ of the primary Party organization is the Party meeting, which is convened not less than once a month.

55. At industrial enterprises, institutions, and collective farms, etc., where there are more than 100 Party members and candidates within a single primary Party organization encompassing the entire enterprise or establishment, Party organizations may be established in shops, sectors, departments, etc., in each case with the sanction of the district or city Party committee or the appropriate political section.

Within the shop, department, etc., organizations, as well as within the primary Party organizations numbering fewer than 100 members and candidates, Party groups may be set up by brigades or sectors in the enterprise.

56. In large enterprises and establishments having more than 300 Party members and candidates, Party committees may be formed, but the shop Party organizations of these enterprises and establishments retain the rights of primary Party organizations; in each individual case the sanction of the Party Central Committee is required for this.

57. The primary Party organization links the mass of workers, peasants, and intelligentsia with the Party governing bodies. Its task consists of:

(a) Agitation and organizational work among the masses for carrying out the public appeals and decisions of the Party, and providing the leadership of the primary press (house organs, wall newspapers, etc.).

(b) Enlisting new members in the Party and organizing their political training.

(c) Organizing the political education of Party members and candidates and seeing that they acquire a certain minimum knowledge of Marxism-Leninism.

(d) Cooperation with the district Party committee, city Party committee, or political section in all their practical work.

(e) Mobilization of the masses in industrial enterprises, State farms, collective farms, etc., to fulfill the production plan, strengthen labor discipline, and develop socialist competition.

(f) Struggle against laxity and thriftlessness in management of enterprises, State farms, and collective farms, and constant concern for improving the cultural and living conditions of the workers, employees and collective farmers.

(g) Development of criticism and self-criticism and the training of Communists in an uncompromising attitude toward shortcomings.

(h) Active participation in the economic and political life of the country.

58. In order to increase the role played by the primary organizations of production and trade enterprises, including State farms, collective farms, and Machine and Tractor Stations, and their responsibility for the state of work in these establishments, these organizations are given the right to supervise the work of the managements of the enterprises.

Party organizations of Ministries, which, by virtue of the special conditions of work in Soviet establishments, cannot exercise supervisory functions, are obliged to signalize defects in the work of the establishment, report shortcomings in the work of the Ministry and its individual workers, and submit their data and views to the Central Committee and to the heads of the Ministries.

The secretaries of the primary Party organizations in Ministries are confirmed by the Central Committee of the Party.

All Communists working in the central apparatus of a Ministry form part of a single Party organization for the entire Ministry.

59. The primary Party organization elects a bureau to conduct current work, consisting of not more than eleven members and serving one year.

The bureaus of the primary Party organizations are set up in Party organizations numbering not less than fifteen members. In Party organizations numbering less than fifteen Party members, bureaus are not set up, but the primary Party organization elects a secretary instead.

With the aim of rapid development and education of Party members in the spirit of collective leadership, shop Party organizations numbering not less than fifteen and not more than 100 Party members have the right to elect a bureau of the shop Party organization consisting of from three to five persons, while those numbering more than 100 Party members have a bureau of from five to seven persons.

In primary Party organizations embracing not more than 100 Party members Party work is carried out, as a rule, by persons not excused from their jobs. Party membership of not less than one year is compulsory for secretaries of primary and shop Party organizations.

IX. The Party and the Young Communist League

60. The Young Communist League carries out its work under the guidance of the Communist Party of the Soviet Union. The Young Communist League Central Committee, which is the governing body of the Young Communist League, is subordinate to the Central Committee of the Communist Party of the Soviet Union. The work of local organizations of the Young Communist League is guided and controlled by the respective republic, territory, province, city, and district Party organizations.

61. Young Communist League members who become Party members or candidates leave the Young Communist League from the moment they join the Party, unless they occupy executive posts in Young Communist League organizations.

62. The Young Communist League is the active aide of the Party in all State and economic work. Young Communist League organizations must be channels for active application of Party directives in all fields of socialist construction, especially where there is no primary Party organization.

63. Young Communist League organizations have the right of broad initiative in discussing and submitting to the appropriate Party organizations all problems in the work of industrial enterprises, collective farms, State farms, and offices connected with the aim of eliminating shortcomings in their operations and rendering them help needed to improve work, organize socialist competition, carry out mass campaigns, etc.

X. Party Organizations in the Soviet Army, Navy, and Transportation

64. Party work in the Soviet Army and Navy is directed by the Chief Political Administrations of the Soviet Army and Navy of the U.S.S.R. and in transportation by the political administrations of the U.S.S.R. Ministries of Railroads, Merchant Marine, and Inland Shipping. The political administrations function with the powers of departments of the Central Committee of the Communist Party of the Soviet Union.

Party organizations in the Soviet Army and Navy and in transportation function on the basis of special instructions handed down by the Central Committee.

65. Party membership of five years is compulsory

for heads of the political administrations of regions, fleets, and armies, and heads of political sections of railroads; Party membership of three years is compulsory for heads of political administrations of divisions and brigades.

66. The political bodies [in the Army, Navy and transportation.—Trans.] must maintain close contact with local Party committees through constant participation in the local Party committees by the heads of the political bodies, as well as through regular hearing by Party committees of reports by the heads of the political bodies on political work in military units and in the political sections in transportation.

XI. Party Groups in Non-Party Organizations

67. At all congresses, conferences, and elections of governing bodies of Soviet, trade union, cooperative, and other mass organizations in which there are at least three Party members, Party groups are organized, the task of which is to intensify the Party's influence in every way, to carry out its policies among non-Party members, to strengthen Party and State discipline, to combat bureaucracy, and to check on fulfillment of Party and Soviet directives. For current work the group elects a secretary.

68. The Party groups are subordinate to the appropriate Party organizations (the Central Committee of the Communist Party of the Soviet Union, the Central Committee of the Communist Party of the Union republic, or the territory, province, region, city, or district Party committee).

In all matters the Party group must be strictly and undeviatingly guided by the decisions of the Party governing bodies.

XII. Party Finances

69. The financial resources of the Party and its organizations consist of membership dues, revenue from Party undertakings, and other revenue.

70. The monthly membership dues for Party members and candidates are established as follows (in percent of income):

Monthly Income	Percent
Below 500 rubles	½
Above 500 but not above 1000 rubles	1
From 1001 to 1500 rubles	1½
From 1501 to 2000 rubles	2
Above 2000 rubles	3

71. Initiation fees are assessed upon admission to the ranks of Party candidates in the sum of 2 percent of monthly income.

Bibliography

As I observed in the Preface, this is not intended to be a complete bibliography nor necessarily to include studies specially referred to already in the footnotes or the text. It is a beginner's working list of books, chosen, often, because they contain bibliographical leads to further study and research.

Those titles especially important for beginners are marked with an *.

General

There are several books that contain documents, some duplicating the contents of others. It is a pity that this very useful kind of work does not give a full critical bibliography.

L. H. Laing *et al.* (eds.), *Source Book in European Governments*, New York, 1950.

W. E. Rappard *et al.* (eds.), *Source Book of European Governments*, New York, 1950.

H. W. Stoke and N. Hill (eds.), *Background of European Governments*, 3d ed. New York, 1951.

On many topics, a further analysis is to be found in my *Theory and Practice of Modern Government*, 2 vols., London, 1932, and the one-volume revised edition, New York, 1949. Their indexes will facilitate discovery.

The Government of Great Britain

Historical and Cultural

*G. B. Adams and R. L. Schuyler, *Constitutional History of England*, New York, 1934. A good brief survey.

*W. Bagehot, *The English Constitution*, World's Classics, London and New York, 1928. A classic not to be omitted.

W. C. Costin and J. S. Watson, *Law and Working of the Constitution, Documents, 1660–1914*, 2 vols., London and New York, 1952. Most intelligent selection of instructive material.

*A. V. Dicey, *Introduction to the Study of the Law of the Constitution*, 9th ed. (E. C. S. Wade), London and New York, 1939. A classic that must be read.

*K. G. Feiling, *A History of England*, New York, 1951. This is superior to Trevelyan's but harder to read.

Sir Ivor Jennings, *The Law and the Constitution*, 2d ed. London, 1938. A commentary on Dicey.

Sir D. L. Keir, *The Constitutional History of Modern Britain, 1487–1937*, 5th ed. London, 1953.

Sir D. L. Keir and F. H. Lawson, *Cases in Constitutional Law*, 4th ed., Oxford, England, and New York, 1954. The contribution of the judicial decisions to the nature of the British Constitution. Necessary.

G. H. L. Le May (compiler), *British Government, 1914–1953*, London, 1955. Selections from official and political documents.

C. L. Mowat, *Britain Between the Wars*, Chicago, 1955.

K. B. Smellie, *The British Way of Life*, London, 1955.

K. B. Smellie, *A Hundred Years of English Government*, 2d ed., London, 1950; New York, 1951. Both very valuable.

C. Stephenson and F. G. Marcham (eds. and trans.), *Sources of English Constitutional History*, New York, 1937. The largest collection of documents.

G. M. Trevelyan, *History of England*, any inexpensive edition.

Institutions

C. K. Allen, *Law and Orders*, London, 1945. Expressing fear of bureaucracy.

*D. E. Butler, *British General Election*, London, 1955. Refers also to the series of such studies, 1945, 1950, and 1951. Excellent modern insight and statistical penetration.

C. T. Carr, *Concerning English Administrative Law*, New York, 1941. A wise commentary by a famous official.

H. E. Dale, *The Higher Civil Service*, London, 1939; New York, 1941.

*Herman Finer, *English Local Government*, London, 1950.

Alexander Fleck *et al.*, *Report on Organization*, National Coal Board, London, 1955.

George Gordon, Baron Hewart, *The New Despotism*, New York, 1920. The most notable of the attacks on "administrative law."

Quintin Hogg, *The Case for Conservatism*, London, 1947.

R. M. Jackson, *The Machinery of Justice in England*, 2d ed., Cambridge, England, and New York, 1953.

*Sir Ivor Jennings, *Cabinet Government*, 2d ed., Cambridge, England, and New York, 1951. The standard work on theory and practice. Valuable bibliography.

Jennings, *Parliament*, New York, 1948.

A. B. Keith, *The British Cabinet System, 1830–1938*, 2d ed., London, 1952. A very competent treatment, with good bibliography.

R. K. Kelsall, *The Higher Civil Service of Britain*, London, 1955. A study in social mobility.

J. D. Kingsley, *Representative Bureaucracy*, Yellow Springs, Ohio, 1944. History of development, a little marred by a "class" thesis.

*R. T. McKenzie, *British Political Parties*, London and New York, 1955. Comprehensive and analytical. The bibliography lists earlier and other works, and also the principal political biographies.

Sir J. P. R. Maud and S. E. Finer, *Local Government in England and Wales*, 2d ed., Oxford, England, and New York, 1953. An excellent brief account, with bibliography.

Herbert S. Morrison, *Government and Parliament*, Oxford, England, and New York, 1954. First-hand account by a notable participant.

*W. A. Robson, *Justice and Administrative Law*, London, 1947.

W. A. Robson (ed.), *Political Quarterly*, number devoted to the Civil Service, October 1954.

W. A. Robson (ed.), *Problems of Nationalized Industry*, London, 1952. Has bibliography.

B. Schwartz, *Law and the Executive in Britain*, New York, 1949.

Political Theory

Sir Ernest Barker, *Political Thought in England, 1848 to 1914*, 2d ed., New York, 1947. This and the following titles contain bibliographies.

G. P. Gooch, *From Bacon to Halifax*, London, 1937.

Elie Halévy, *The Growth of Philosophic Radicalism*, London and New York, 1949.

H. J. Laski, *Political Thought in England: Locke to Bentham*, New York, 1950.

*Basil Willey, *The Eighteenth Century Background*, New York, 1941.

The Dominions

* Alexander Brady, *Democracy in the Dominions*, Toronto, 2d ed., 1952.

Periodicals

The student can keep himself *au fait* with developing events and ideas by relying in the first place on the weeklies: *The Economist, The New Statesman and Nation*, and the weekly editions of the *Manchester Guardian* and *The Times*. A remarkably inexpensive and valuable journal is *The Listener*, published weekly by the BBC, since it contains verbatim the principal broadcasts. The journals, *Political Studies, Public Administration, The Sociological Review*, and the *Political Quarterly*, are published at longer intervals.

The Government of France

Historical and Cultural

F. M. Anderson, *Constitutions and Other Select Documents Illustrative of the History of France, 1789–1907*, Minneapolis, 1908.

J. E. C. Bodley, *France*, London, 1898. A classic interpretation.

*D. W. Brogan, *France under the Republic; the Development of Modern France*, New York, 1940. An indispensable study, as Bodley was in his day, of the years 1870 to 1939, showing the political institutions in their development and operation.

Georges Burdeau, *Manuel de droit constitutional*, 5th ed., Paris, 1947.

*J. P. T. Bury, *France, 1814 to 1940*, Philadelphia and London, 1949. Brief, lucid, perspicuous.

J. Deslandres, *Histoire Constitutionel 1815–1914*, 2 vols., Paris, 1931. This reference is given in order to say that there is not available a French constitutional history in English.

*G. Lowes Dickinson, *Revolution and Reaction in Modern France*, London, 1892. A brilliant short survey from 1789 to the end of the nineteenth century.

*E. M. Earle (ed.), *Modern France: Problems of the Third and Fourth Republics*, Princeton, 1951. A valuable work.

C. H. Hayes, *France: A Nation of Patriots*, New York, 1930.

Hans Kohn, *Making of the Modern French Mind*, New York, 1955. Readings with notes, 185 pp.

Philippe Maillaud, *France*, 2d ed., Oxford, 1945. A brilliant evocation of culture.

Kingsley Martin, *French Liberal Thought in the Eighteenth Century*, London, 1929.

*R. H. Soltau, *French Political Thought in the Nineteenth Century*, London, 1931. Particularly intelligent and comprehensive.

David Thomson, *The Democratic Ideal in France and England*, Cambridge, England, and New York, 1941.

*Alexis de Tocqueville, *The Old Regime and the French Revolution*, Anchor Books edition, New York, 1955. Indispensable.

Institutions

*H. W. Ehrmann, *French Labor from Popular Front to Liberation of Vichy*, Oxford, England, and Ithaca, N.Y., 1947. Essential.

*F. Goguel, *La Politique des Partis sous la Troisième Republique*, Paris, 1946. Masterly.

A. Guérard, *The France of Tomorrow*, Cambridge, Mass., 1942. A cultural appreciation.

J. H. Jackson, *Clemenceau and the Third Republic*, London, 1946; New York, 1948.

W. L. Middleton, *French Political System*, London, 1932.

*Pertinax (pseudonym of André Géraud of *Le Temps*), *The Gravediggers of France*. [of the Third Republic], New York, 1944. An excellent and mordant famous insideviewer's explanation of French politics bearing on the defeat of 1940.

*A. Rossi (pseudonym of A. Tasca) *A Communist Party in Action*, New Haven, Conn., 1949. Finest study of this party during 1939–1941.

W. R. Sharp, *Government of the French Republic*, New York, 1938. Solid and comprehensive.

W. R. Sharp, *The French Civil Service*, New York, 1938.

André Siegfried, *France: A Study in Nationality*, New Haven, Conn., 1930.

*D. Thomson, *Democracy in France*, 2d ed., Oxford, England, and New York, 1952. This is a superb introduction, learned, cogent, luminous, and has a valuable bibliography. It covers the Third Republic and the origins of the Fourth.

P. Tissier, *Pierre Laval*, London, 1942.

Fourth Republic

Bruce Chapman, *French Local Government*, London, 1953. An excellent introduction; aware of the problems and instructive.

*M. Duverger, *Political Parties*, New York, 1955. An interesting attempt at a general comparative theory of political parties, in which much prominence is given to French experience.

Charles de Gaulle, *Call to Honor*, New York, 1955. First volume of memoirs; beautiful and sapient writing. Important.

F. Goguel, *France under the Fourth Republic*, Ithaca, N.Y., 1952. Valuable.

*Roger Grégoire, *La Fonction Publique*, Paris, 1954.

*Herbert Luethy, *France against Herself*, New York, 1955. A gifted politico-sociological study by a Swiss journalist of long years of observation of French politics. Indispensable.

D. M. Pickles, *French Politics*, London, 1953. A helpful narrative of economic, social, and constitutional currents since the Liberation.

Paul Reynaud, *In the Thick of the Fight*, New York, 1955.

M. Waline, *Traité Elementaire de Droit Administratif*, 5th ed., Paris, 1951.

*Philip Williams, *Politics in Post-War France*, London, 1954. The best by far of academic works on the political parties and constitution in operation. An excellent bibliography.

Gordon Wright, *Reshaping of French Democracy*, London, 1950. France from the Liberation to the making of the Fourth Republic. Valuable.

The novelists Balzac, Anatole France, Jules Romains, and Roger Martin du Garde will be read with profit for an understanding of France. Anatole France's *Penguin Island* might be a starting point.

Periodicals

The weekly editions of *Le Monde* and *Figaro* are helpful for news and editorials. The periodical *Esprit*, Paris, is published monthly and has some very important political science symposia. The articles in the following reviews are important: *Revue du Droit Publique, Revue Politique et Parlementaire*, and *Revue Française de Science Politique* (French Political Science Association). The *Année Politique* is an excellent annual political and economic record of domestic, international and colonial affairs, edited by André Siegfried and others, Paris. See also UNESCO's periodical publication, *International Abstracts of Social Sciences*.

The Government of Germany

Historical and Cultural

G. Barraclough, *Factors in German History*, London, 1946.

W. H. Bruford, *Germany in the Eighteenth Century*, New York, 1935.

J. Bryce, *The Holy Roman Empire*, London, 1919.

*Rohan Butler, *The Roots of National Socialism*, New York, 1942. Penetrating account of German totalitarian political philosophy.

F. L. Carsten, *The Origins of Prussia*, Oxford, England, and New York, 1954. Fundamental.

W. H. Dawson, *The German Empire, 1867–1914*, 2 vols., London, 1919. A well-founded survey.

R. A. Dorwart, *The Administrative Reforms of Frederick William I of Prussia*, Cambridge, Mass., 1953.

*Koppel S. Pinson, *Modern Germany*, New York, 1954. Excellent; up-to-date; sound perspective; comprehensive bibliography in notes.

*Karl Popper, *The Open Society and Its Enemies*, Princeton, N.J., 1950. Plato, Hegel, Marx and Toynbee—for Russia also. Indispensable.

A. Rosenberg, *Birth of the German Republic, 1871–1918*, London, 1931. Talented.

A. J. P. Taylor, *Bismarck*, London, 1955. Gifted.

*A. J. P. Taylor, *The Course of German History*, New York, 1946. Brilliant and indispensable.

A. W. Ward, *Germany, 1815–1890*, 3 vols., Cambridge, 1916–1918.

W. F. Wright, *Constitutions of the States at War, 1914–1918*, Washington, 1919. For the text of the 1871 Constitution.

The Weimar Period

*J. Wheeler Bennett, *The Nemesis of Power*, New York, 1954. A most talented view of the relations (1918–1945) of the *Reichswehr* to the politicians of the Republic. Essential.

F. Blachly and M. Oatman, *Government and Administration of Germany*, Baltimore, 1928. A static snapshot of governmental institutions at that moment; contains text of Weimar Constitution.

*S. W. Halperin, *Germany Tried Democracy*, New York, 1946. A most illuminating history, with comprehensive bibliography. Essential.

*Paul Kosok, *Modern Germany*, Chicago, 1933. An excellent analysis of the public mind.

Karl Loewenstein, *Government and Politics of Germany*, in J. T. Shotwell (ed.), *Governments of Continental Europe*, New York, edition of 1940. Excellent.

G. Scheele, *The Weimar Republic*, London, 1946.

*G. A. Craig, *Politics of the Prussian Army, 1640–1945*, Oxford, 1955. A scholarly study of the rise and influence of the German Army. Essential.

The Third Reich

Hannah Arendt, *Origins of Totalitarianism*, New York, 1951. A wise contribution to totalitarian governments and their psychological origins.

Norman H. Baynes (ed.), *Hitler's Speeches, 1922–1939*, Oxford, England, and New York, 1943.

*Alan Bullock, *Hitler*, London, 1952. Important.

William Ebenstein, *The Nazi State*, New York, 1943.

Adolf Hitler, *Mein Kampf*, Munich, 1925–1926; translated by Ralph Manheim, Boston, 1943.

Adolf Hitler (H. Picker, ed.), *Secret Conversations*, New York, 1953. Translation of his *Tischgespräche*, with introduction by H. Trevor Roper.

Daniel Lerner *et al.*, *The Nazi Élite*, Stanford, 1951. Clever sociological analysis.

Karl Loewenstein, *op. cit.*

*M. S. Mayer, *They Thought They Were Free*, Chicago, 1955. A most important close psychological study of ten Germans who were Nazis. Perhaps the most thoughtful and imaginative study of all; yet debatable.

*Friedrich Meinecke, *The German Catastrophe*, Cambridge, Mass., 1950. (It is a pity that there are no English translations of this author's *Die Idee der Staatsräson* and *Weltbürgertum und Nationalstaat*, both classics of history.)

*F. L. Neumann, *Behemoth*, New York, 1944 edition.

Nürnberg Tribunal, *Nazi Conspiracy and Aggression*, 8 vols., Washington, D.C., 1946.

Hermann Rauschning, *The Voice of Destruction*, New York, 1940.

*H. R. Trevor-Roper, *The Last Days of Hitler*, London and New York, 1947. Perfect characterization, consummately written. Essential.

*Ernst von Salomon, *Fragebogen*, New York, 1955. This is essential as a defense of Nazism and German chauvinism by a high-placed scoundrel.

B. H. Schaffner, *Father Land*, New York, 1948. A study of the German family and its relationship to political authority.

*Paul Seabury, *The Wilhelmstrasse*, Berkeley, Calif., 1954.

*UNESCO (J. H. Fried, ed.), *The Third Reich*, published by Praeger, New York, 1955. Indispensable.

United States Military Tribunals, Nurnberg, *Trials of War Criminals*, 16 vols., Washington, D.C., 1946–1951. Invaluable testimony from documents and participants in the highest levels of Nazi Government.

After 1945

No comprehensive book has yet appeared on postwar German institutions in the West or East. There are two general surveys, both important.

*E. H. Litchfield et al., *Governing Post-war Germany*, Ithaca, 1953. Excellent articles by interested and participating experts in the rebuilding of Germany.

*Karl Loewenstein, "Governments and Politics of Germany," in J. T. Shotwell (ed.), *Governments of Continental Europe*, New York, 1952 edition. Scholarly account, able judgment, comprehensive bibliography.

Then special studies follow.

Gabriel Almond et al., *The Struggle for Democracy in Germany*, Chapel Hill, N.C., 1949. Symposium and bibliography.

Lucius D. Clay, *Decision in Germany*, New York, 1950.

H. Morgenthau (ed.), *Germany and the Future of Europe*, Chicago, 1951.

For the Bonn Constitution the material lies in articles in the learned journals; in German commentaries; and in current German periodicals.

A. J. Abraham, *et al.*, *Kommentar zum Bonner Grundgesetz*, published by Joachim Heitmann, Hamburg. Indispensable; currently maintained to date.

Arnold Brecht, "The New German Constitution," *Social Research*, 1949, pp. 425ff. As usual, magnificent. This author's *Prelude to Silence*, New York, 1944, on events leading to Hitler's Reich, should be read.

O. G. Fischbach, *Bundes Beamtengesetz*, Berlin, 1954.

O. F. Flechteim, *Die Deutsche Politische Parteien Seit 1945*, Berlin, 1955. Documents.

C. J. Friedrich, "Rebuilding the German Constitution," *American Political Science Review*, 1949, pp. 461ff. and 704ff.

F. A. Heydte and K. Sacherl, *Soziologie der Deutschen Parteien*. Munich, 1955. A modern analysis of the German postwar parties; well informed, apt methodology, statistically illustrated. References give rich bibliography.

Hermann von Mangoldt, *Das Bonner Grundgesetz*, Berlin, 1950 and later revision.

Periodicals

Periodical literature from the West German Government: *The Bulletin* (weekly); Social Democratic Party's *News from Germany* (monthly); the Government's occasional *Germany Reports* (gratuitous from consulates); *Zeitschrift fur die Gesammte Staatswissenschaft; Archiv des Öffentlichen Recht; Deutsche Verwaltung; Die Öffentliche Verwaltung; Die Gegenwart; Der Monat* (especially interesting articles by many, among others, Fritz Alemann).

Government of the U.S.S.R.

Historical and Cultural

*N. Berdyaev, *The Origin of Russian Communism*, London, 1948. An insight into the Russian "soul," indispensable.

*Isaiah Berlin, *Karl Marx*, 2d ed., Oxford, England, and New York, 1948.

E. Crankshaw, *Russia and the Russians*, New York, 1948. A study by a wise observer.

*Marquis de Custine, *Journey for Our Time* (translated by P. P. Kohler) New York, 1951. Journals of the 1830's in Russia.

M. T. Florinsky, *Russia*, 2 vols., New York, 1953. A sound history from the origins to 1917. Has bibliography.

*R. Hare, *Pioneers of Russian Social Thought*, New York, 1951. The non-Marxist political writers.

Chauncey Harris (ed.), *Economic Geography of the U.S.S.R.*, New York, 1949.

Hans Kohn, *The Mind of Modern Russia*, New Brunswick, N.J., 1955. Readings, with commentary.

J. Maynard, *Russia in Flux*, New York, 1948.

J. Maynard, *The Russian Peasant and Other Studies*, London, 1942. Unusual insight into the Russian economy, history and character.

*E. J. Simmons (ed.), *Continuity and Change in Russian and Soviet Thought*, Cambridge, Mass., 1955. A series of excellent essays.

*B. H. Sumner, *Short History of Russia*, rev. ed., New York, 1949. Acute history, by topics, and going backward from our own day.

The Revolution

*Emile Burns (comp.), *A Handbook of Marxism*, New York, 1935. Extensive readings from Marx, Engels, Lenin, and Stalin.

E. H. Carr, *The Bolshevik Revolution, 1917–1923*, 4 vols., New York, 1950–1954. Party, State, nationalities, the economy, and foreign relations; fine scholarship and writing. Willful.

W. H. Chamberlin, *The Russian Revolution*, 2 vols., New York, 1952. A sound appreciation of the causes and course of the Revolution.

Leon Trotsky, *History of the Russian Revolution*, 3 vols. in 1, New York, 1936. The story from the inside by a participant as important as Lenin and more important than Stalin. He can write!

*B. D. Wolfe, *Three Who Made a Revolution*, New York, 1948. Now available in pocket edition. Indispensable for its narration of the rise of Lenin, Trotsky, and Stalin; deeply learned and not born yesterday!

The Dictatorship

*R. A. Bauer and E. Wasiolek, *Nine Soviet Portraits*, Cambridge, Mass., 1955. Soviet people and life fashioned from refugee data.

*F. Beck and W. Godin, *Russian Purge and the Extraction of Confession*, New York, 1951.

*Max Beloff, *The Foreign Policy of Soviet Russia*, 2 vols., Oxford, England, and New York, 1947–1949. Scope is 1929 to 1941. Fundamental.

H. J. Berman, *Justice in Russia*, Cambridge, Mass., 1950.

J. R. Deane, *The Strange Alliance*, New York, 1947. A very important account of Soviet relations with foreign powers.

R. Dennett and J. E. Johnson (eds.), *Negotiating with the Russians*, Boston, 1951. Personal accounts by ten negotiators.

*Merle Fainsod, *How Russia Is Ruled*, Cambridge, Mass., 1953. *The* book.

*Herman Finer, *America's Destiny*, New York, 1947. Virtually, the war between the United States and the U.S.S.R.

George Fischer, *Soviet Opposition to Stalin*, Cambridge, Mass., 1952. The defections during World War II.

*Jerzy Gliksman, *Tell the West*, New York, 1948. One of the firsthand accounts of Russian brutality.

*L. Gruliow, *Current Soviet Policies*, New York, 1953. A full verbatim account of the Nineteenth Party Congress and proceedings after the death of Stalin.

Vladimir Gsovski, *Soviet Civil Law*, 2 vols., Ann Arbor, Mich., 1948–1949.

*J. N. Hazard, *Law and Social Change in the U.S.S.R.*, London, 1953.

*A. Inkeles, *Public Opinion in Soviet Russia*, Cambridge, Mass., 1950.

W. W. Kulski, *The Soviet Regime*, Syracuse, 1954. Encyclopedic in topics and comprehension.

Marshal MacDuffie, *The Red Carpet*, New York, 1955. 10,000 miles through Russia. Alert.

*J. S. Reshetar, *Problems of Analyzing and Predicting Soviet Behavior*, New York, 1955. An extremely thoughtful discussion, with abundant bibliography, not least on psychoanalytic anthropology of the Russians. Only 69 pp.

W. W. Rostow, *The Dynamics of Soviet Society*, New York, 1953 (Mentor Books, 1954). A brief but pregnant interpretation. Bibliography.

H. E. Salisbury, *American in Russia*, New York, 1955. An experienced journalist's estimate after many years' residence.

U.S. Congress, 81st Cong., 2d Sess., House Doc. No. 3135, *Background Information on the Soviet Union in International Relations*, 1950.

*U.S. Congress, 80th Cong., 2d Sess., House Doc. No. 619, *Strategy and Tactics of World Communism*, 1948. This and the following document contain invaluable documents and narratives.

U.S. Congress, 84th Cong., 2d Sess., House Documents, Committee on Communist Aggression, 1954 and 1955; numerous reports on "Communists Take Over in ——," various countries; see especially *Hearings* on Non-Russian Nations of the U.S.S.R., House Doc. No. 54938.

A. Weissberg, *The Accused*, New York, 1951.

A. Weissberg, *Spy Network*, New York, 1955. To be used with some caution—and yet!

Economic and Social Systems

A.M. Baykov, *Development of the Soviet Economic System*, New York, 1947. Best general description. Indispensable.

A Bergson (ed.), *Soviet Economic Growth*, Evanston, Ill., 1953. Indispensable articles, with countercomments of the authors. Incidental bibliography.

G. S. Counts and N. P. Lodge, *The Country of the Blind: The Soviet System of Mind Control*, Boston, 1949.

Isaac Deutscher, *Russia, What Next?* New York, 1953.

Isaac Deutscher, *Soviet Trade Unions*, London, 1950.

*Isaac Deutscher, *Prophet Armed: Trotsky, 1879–1921*, New York, 1954.

*Isaac Deutscher, *Stalin, a Political Biography*, New York, 1949.

David Granik, *Management of the Soviet Firm*, New York, 1954.

Walter Kolarz, *Russia and Her Colonies*, New York, 1953.

N. C. Leites, *The Operational Code of the Politburo*, New York, 1951.

N. C. Leites, *A Study of Bolshevism*, Glencoe, Ill., 1953. The Bolshevik spirit in Russian literature and psychoanalytical speculation.

Nikolai Lenin (J. Fineberg, ed.), *Selected Works*, New York, 1935–1938.

*J. H. Meisel and E. S. Kozera, *Materials for the Study of the Soviet Unions*, rev. ed., Ann Arbor, Mich., 1953. Indispensable documents.

Barrington Moore, *Soviet Politics—the Dilemma of Power*, Cambridge, Mass., 1950. Subtle account of development.

*Barrington Moore, *Terror and Progress*, U.S.S.R., Cambridge, Mass., 1954. An instructive inquiry into the clash of the dictatorial with the freedom of mind required by progress.

*Harry Schwartz, *Russia's Soviet Economy*, New York, 1954. Valuable survey by an authority.

Joseph Stalin, *Leninism, Selected Writings*, New York, 1942.

*Julian Towster, *Political Power in the U.S.S.R., 1917–1947*, New York, 1948. The constitutional evolution from original sources. Essential.

*A. S. Vucinich, *Soviet Economic Institutions*, Stanford, 1952.

*A. Y. Vyshinsky (H. W. Babb, trans.), *The Law of the Soviet State*, New York, 1948. What the Soviet leaders and scholars affect to believe about their own Constitution and "bourgeois" States. Most instructive, especially when unintended.

D. F. White, *The Growth of the Red Army*, Princeton, N.J., 1944.

Novels and Memoirs

Among the many published, the following are especially interesting:

Ilya Ehrenburg, *The Thaw*, Chicago, 1955. The novelist-apologist for the U.S.S.R. hopes that the ice age of Stalin is over.

Igor Gouzenko, *The Iron Curtain*, New York, 1948.

Igor Gouzenko, *The Titan*, New York, 1955.

Arthur Koestler, *Darkness at Noon*, New York, 1941. (Modern Library edition available.)

V. A. Kravchenko, *I Chose Freedom*, New York, 1946.

V. A. Kravchenko, *I Chose Justice*, New York, 1950.

G. A. Tokaev, *Betrayal of an Ideal*, London, 1954. Most interesting account of an air force officer escapee from Russia.

Victor Serge, *The Case of Comrade Tulayev*, New York, 1950. A remarkable inside view of the Kremlin during the 1930's and the Great Purge; even Stalin is interviewed.

Periodicals

The Current Digest of the Soviet Press, a weekly translation of Soviet daily press and periodicals by the Joint Committee on Slavic Studies, New York, N.Y. An indispensable instrument for understanding Soviet policy and occurrences. The monthly *Bulletin* of the Institute for Study of the History and Culture of the U.S.S.R., Munich, Germany (a Soviet refugee corporation of scientists and people of letters).

Index